Vietnam

written and researched by

Jan Dodd and Mark Lewis

with additional research by

Ron Emmons

**ROUGH
GUIDES**

NEW YORK • LONDON • DELHI

www.roughguides.com

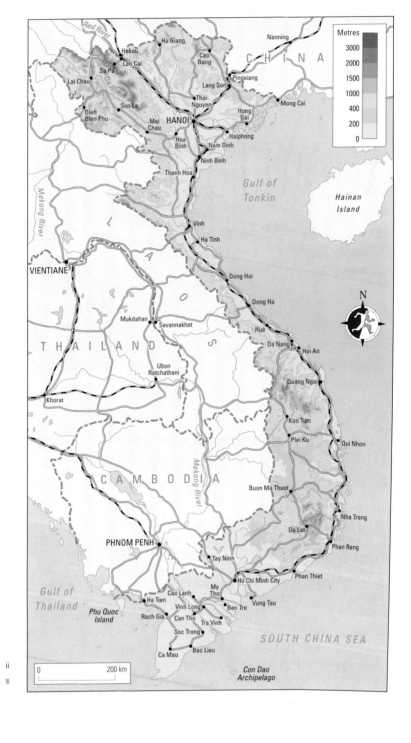

Introduction to

Vietnam

History weighs heavily on Vietnam. For more than a decade, reportage of the war that racked this slender country portrayed it as a netherworld of savagery and slaughter; and even after the American War ended it was further pigeon-holed by Hollywood's seamless chain of combat movies. Yet, only twenty-odd years after the war's end, this resilient nation is fast emerging from the shadows: access is now easier than ever, and the country has reinvented its old-style communist system as a socialist market economy that, by and large, encourages contact. As the number of tourists finding their way here soars, the word is out that this is a land not of bomb craters and army ordnance but of

shimmering paddy fields and sugar-white beaches, full-tilt cities and venerable pagodas – often overwhelming in its sheer beauty.

The speed with which Vietnam's population has been able to put the bitter events of its recent past behind it, and focus its gaze so steadfastly on the future, comes as a surprise to visitors expecting to encounter shell-shocked resentment of the West and war fatigue. It wasn't always like this, however. The reunification of North and South Vietnam that ended twenty years of bloody civil war, in 1975, was followed by a decade or so of hardline centralist economic rule from which only the shake-up of **doi moi**, Vietnam's equivalent of *perestroika*, could awaken the

Fact file

- The Socialist Republic of Vietnam, the **capital** of which is Hanoi, shares land borders with China, Laos and Cambodia. It is a long, thin country comprising over 330,000 square kilometres, with more than 3000km of coastline. At its narrowest point it measures a mere 50km wide.

- Vietnam has a **population** of 80 million, of which 77 percent live in the countryside, giving Vietnam some of the highest rural population densities in Southeast Asia. Over half the people are under 25 years old and 10 percent belong to a mosaic of **ethnic minority groups**.

- One of the world's last surviving one-party **communist states**, Vietnam is also one of the poorest countries in Asia. Two-thirds of the population earn their living from **agriculture**. The average per capita **income** is just $365 per year, though many people survive on less than $0.50 a day.

- During the last decade the **economy** has grown at over 7 percent per year. Vietnam has also transformed itself from being a rice-importer prior to 1986 to now being the world's third largest exporter of **rice** after India and Thailand.

- Vietnam is home to a tremendous diversity of **plant and animal life**, including some of the world's rarest species, a number of which have only been discovered in the last few years. The Javan rhino, Asiatic black bear, Sarus crane and Golden-headed langur are just some of the endangered species maintaining a toehold in the forests and wetlands of Vietnam.

country. By lifting the lid off private enterprise, *doi moi* has, since its conception in 1986, signalled a renaissance for Vietnam, and today a high fever of commerce grips the nation. Needless to say, the shift to a market economy would have been only notional without accompanying shifts in international relations – in particular 1994's ending of the US trade embargo, which released the log jam of foreign investment; and the diplomatic rehabilitation that ensued once Vietnamese forces were pulled out of Cambodia in 1989, culminating in the restoration of US–Vietnamese diplomatic relations in July 1995. From a tourist's point of view, it's a great time to come – thanks to an intoxicating sense of vitality and optimism, not to mention the chance to witness a country in profound flux.

Inevitably, that's not the whole story. *Doi moi* is an economic policy, not a magic spell, and life, for most of the population, remains hard. Indeed, *doi moi* has introduced its own problems, with the adoption of a market economy predictably polar-

izing the gap between rich and poor. Despite the numerous Japanese, Taiwanese and Korean assembly plants springing up, average monthly incomes for city dwellers remain at around US$50, while in the poorest provinces workers may scrape by on as little as US$15 a month – a difference that amply illustrates the growing gulf between urban and rural Vietnam.

The long-standing antipathy and deep psychological divide between the **north and south** endures. This was around long before the American War, and is engrained in the bedrock of Vietnamese culture. Northerners are typically considered reticent, dour, law-abiding, and lacking the dynamism and entrepreneurial know-how of their more worldly-wise southern compatriots. A cartoonist's caricature of a southerner would most likely depict a flashy wheeler-dealer, shades on, barking into a mobile phone as he weaves his Honda Dream through the busy streets; while his northern counterpart would appear in green army tunic and helmet, tootling along on his duck-laden bicycle.

Many visitors find more than enough to amuse them in Hanoi, Ho Chi Minh City and the other major centres; but despite the cities' allure, it's the country's striking **landscape** that most impresses. Vietnam occupies a narrow strip of land that hugs the eastern borders of Cambodia and Laos, hemmed in by rugged mountains to the west, and by the South China Sea to the east. To the north and south of its narrow waist, it dovetails out into the splendid deltas of the Red River and the Mekong, and it's in these regions that you'll encounter the paddy fields, dragonflies, buffaloes and conical-hatted farmers that constitute the classic image of Vietnam. In stark contrast to the pancake-flat riceland of the deltas, Ha Long Bay's labyrinthine network of **limestone outcrops** loom dramatically out of the Gulf of Tonkin – a magical spectacle in the early morning mist. None of Vietnam's mountains reach particularly

Dong or dollars?

Both the local currency, dong, and US dollars are used in Vietnam and are generally interchangeable. Despite government efforts to promote the dong, prices are frequently quoted in US$. For this reason, and because dong amounts tend to be unwieldy and more volatile, we've largely given prices in US$ throughout the Guide.

impressive heights, so any trip to the remote upland regions of central and northern Vietnam is far likelier to focus upon the **ethnic minorities** who reside there. Elaborate tribal costumes, age-old customs and communal long-houses await those visitors game enough to trek into the sticks – though if you're fortunate enough to sample the legendary hilltribe hospitality, you may find that the knockout rice wine they brew leaves memories hazy. As for **wildlife** the discovery, in the last decade of several previously unknown species of plants, birds and animals speaks volumes for the wealth of Vietnam's biodiversity – that, despite the decade-long pasting the country received from American bombers – and makes the improving access to the country's several **national parks** all the more gratifying.

Where to go

The "Hanoi or bust" attitude, whereby new arrivals doggedly labour between the country's two major cities, no matter how limited their time, blights many a trip to Vietnam. If you want to travel the length of the country at some leisure, see something of the highlands and the deltas and allow for a few rest days, you'll really need to be in-country for a month. With only two weeks at your disposal, the choice is either to hop-scotch up the coast calling at only the most mainstream destinations; or, per-haps better, to concentrate on one region and enjoy it at your own pace. However, if you *do* want to see both north and south in a fortnight, internal flights can speed up an itinerary sub-stantially, and aren't so expensive that they should be rejected out of hand.

For the majority of visitors, **Ho Chi Minh City** provides a head-spinning introduction to Vietnam. Set beside the broad swell of the Saigon River, the

southern capital is rapidly being transformed into a Southeast Asian mover and shaker to compete with the best of them. In Ho Chi Minh, the absurd becomes commonplace. The city's breakneck pace of life translates into a stew of bizarre characters and unlikely sights and sounds, and ensures that almost all who come here quickly fall for its singular charm. Furious commerce carries on cheek-by-jowl with age-old traditions; grandly indulgent colonial edifices peek out from under the shadows of looming office blocks and hotels; and cyclo drivers battle it out with late-model Japanese taxis in the chaotic boulevards. The city's unrelenting thrum of life is best soaked up over a roadside coffee and croissant. Few tourists pass up the opportunity to take a day-trip out of the city to **Tay Ninh**, the nerve centre of the indigenous Cao Dai religion.

Tet

The biggest bash in Vietnam's festive calendar is the lunar New Year holiday known as **Tet Nguyen Dan**, or simply Tet. The date of the festival, which lasts for several days, varies from one year to the next, but falls somewhere between late January and the middle of February. Tet is the Vietnamese equivalent of thanksgiving, New Year and a nationwide birthday celebration rolled into one – everyone becomes a year older at New Year. It is a time of forgiveness and fresh starts, when the trials and tribulations of the old year are left behind, to be replaced by renewed optimism for the year ahead. As the festival approaches, the streets fill with people buying new clothes, having their hair cut and stocking up on seasonal delicacies such as candied lotus seeds and sweetmeats made of sticky rice. Flower markets add to the colour with the first shy blossoms of peach, plum or apricot alongside miniature kumquat trees laden with their brash, golden fruit – the traditional symbols of Tet. The excitement culminates with municipal fireworks displays on New Year's eve, after which the first few days of the year are traditionally devoted to renewing family ties – both with the living and with the ancestral spirits who come back to share in the feasting.

The jury is still out on whether the ostentatious Cao Dai Holy See constitutes high art or dog's dinner, but either way it's one of Vietnam's most arresting sights, and is normally twinned wih a stop-off at the Cu Chi Tunnels, where Vietnamese villagers dug themselves a warren stretching over two hundred kilometres, out of reach of US bombing. With Ho Chi Minh City seen off, most tourists next venture southwest to explore some or all of the **Mekong Delta**, where one of the world's truly mighty rivers finally offloads into the South China Sea; its skein of brim-full tributaries and waterways has endowed the delta with a lush quilt of rice-rich flats and abundant orchards. You won't want to depart the delta without having

Water puppets

Vietnam's unique contribution to the world of marionettes, **water puppetry** is a delightful quirky form of theatre in which the action takes place on a stage of water. It was probably spawned in the murky rice paddies of the northern Red River Delta where performances still take place after the spring planting. Obscured by a split-bamboo screen, puppeteers standing chest-deep in water manipulate the wooden puppets, some weighing over 10kg, which are attached to the end of long poles concealed beneath the surface. Dragons, ducks, lions, unicorns, phoenixes and frogs spout smoke, throw balls and generally cavort on the watery stage – miraculously avoiding tangled poles. Brief scenes of rural life, such as water-buffalo fights, fishing or rice planting, take place alongside the legendary exploits of Vietnam's military heroes or perhaps a promenade of fairy-like immortals. In the more sophisticated productions staged for tourists in Hanoi and Ho Chi Minh City, even fireworks emerge to dance upon the water, which itself takes on different characters, from calm and placid to seething and furious during naval battles.

enjoyed a day's messing about on the water, typically arranged through the boat operators of **My Tho**, **Vinh Long** or the delta's largest settlement, **Can Tho**. At these last two places you'll be able to incorporate a trip to a floating market into your waterborne idling. Far removed from the stereotype of the Asian city, **Da Lat**, the "capital" of the southern and central highlands, is chalk to Ho Chi Minh City's cheese. Life passes by at a rather more dignified pace at this altitude, and the raw breezes that fan this oddly quaint hillside settlement provide the best air-conditioning in Vietnam. **Minority peoples** inhabit the countryside around Da Lat, but to visit some really full-on *montagnard* villages you'll need to push north to the modest towns of **Buon Ma Thuot**, **Plei Ku** and **Kon Tum**, which are surrounded by Ede, Jarai and Bahnar communities. Opt for Kon Tum, and you'll be able to visit minority villages independently or join treks that include river rafting.

Vietnam's ethnic minorities

The population of Vietnam is made up of an estimated 54 **ethnic groups**. By far the largest of these is the lowland Viet, or Kinh, people who comprise nearly 90 per cent (72 million) of the population, with the one million or so largely urban ethnic Chinese (Hoa) a distant second. The remaining six or seven million people belong to some 52 minority groups divided into dozens of subgroups, giving Vietnam the richest and most complex ethnic make-up in Southeast Asia. Most of these minority people scrape a living from Vietnam's marginal mountainous regions, where some of the more isolated groups have managed to preserve their time-honoured ways of life, from the characteristic wooden stilthouse to a dazzling array of traditional costumes.

Northeast of Ho Chi Minh City, Highway 1, the country's jugular, girds its loins for the arduous journey up to Hanoi and the north. For many people, first stop is at the delightful beach and sand dunes of **Mui Ne**, which is fast becoming one of the country's top coastal resorts. Another popular spot is **Phan Rang** – a sloppy little place, but blessed with some of the most splendid examples of the **Cham towers** that punctuate Vietnam's south-central coast. **Nha Trang** has grown into a crucial stepping stone on the Ho Chi Minh–Hanoi run, and the tirelessly touted boat trips around the city's outlying islands are a must. North of Nha Trang, **Son My** village attained global notoriety when a company of American soldiers massacred some 500 Vietnamese, including many women and children; unspeakable horrors continue to haunt the village's unnervingly idyllic rural setting.

Once a bustling seaport, the diminutive town of **Hoi An** perches beside an indolent backwater, its narrow streets of wooden-fronted shophouses and weathered roofs making it an enticing destination. Inland, the war-battered ruins of **My Son**, the greatest of the Cham temple sites, lie mouldering in a steamy forest-filled valley. **Da Nang**, just up the coast, lacks Hoi An's charm but good transport links make it a convenient base for the area, while echoes of the American War still resound across the sands of China Beach. From Da Nang a corkscrew ride over clifftop Hai Van Pass brings you to the aristocratic city of **Hué**, where the Nguyen emperors established their capital in the nineteenth century on the banks of the languid Perfume River. The temples and palaces of this highly cultured city still testify to past splendours, while its imperial mausoleums are masterpieces of architectural refinement, slumbering among pine-shrouded hills. Only a hundred kilometres north of Hué, the tone changes as war-sites litter the Demilitarized Zone (**DMZ**), which cleaved the country in two from 1954 to 1975. More than two decades of peace have done much to heal the scars, but these windswept, wasted hills bear eloquent witness to a generation that lost their lives in the tragic struggle between South and North. The DMZ is most easily tackled as a day-trip from Hué, after which most people hop straight up to Hanoi. And there's little to detain you on the northward trek, save the glittering limestone caverns of **Phong Nha**, the entrance to a massive underground river system tunnelling under the Truong Son Mountains. Then, on the very fringes of the northern Red River Delta, lie the ancient incense-steeped temples of **Hoa Lu** and, nearby, the mystical landscapes of **Tam Coc** and **Van Long**, where paddy fields lap at the feet of limestone hummocks.

Anchored firmly in the Red River Delta, **Hanoi** has served as Vietnam's capital for close on a thousand years. It's a relatively small, decidedly proud city, a place of pagodas and dynastic temples, tamarisk-edged lakes and elegant boulevards of French-era villas, of national monuments and stately government edifices. But Hanoi is also being swept along on a tide of change as Vietnam forges its own shiny high-rise capital. Though life proceeds at a slightly gentler pace than in Ho Chi Minh, Hanoi is still an all-absorbing place, a city on the move, throwing up new office blocks, hotels and restaurants as it jostles to attract its share of international investment and the swell of

tourists. From Hanoi the majority of visitors strike out east to where northern Vietnam's premier natural attraction, **Ha Long Bay**, provides the perfect antidote to such urban exuberance, rewarding the traveller with a leisurely day or two drifting among the thousands of whimsically sculpted islands anchored in its aquamarine waters. Bai Chay, a resort town on the northern coast, is the usual embarkation point for Ha Long Bay, but a more appealing gateway is mountainous **Cat Ba Island**, which defines the bay's southwestern limits and is inhabited mostly by fisherfolk. The route to Cat Ba passes via the north's major port city, **Haiphong**, an unspectacular but genial place with an attractive core of faded colonial facades.

To the north and west of Hanoi mountain ranges rear up out of the Red River Delta. Vietnam's northern provinces aren't the easiest to get around, but these wild uplands are home to a patchwork of ethnic minorities and the country's most dramatic mountain landscapes. The bustling market-town of **Sa Pa**, set in a spectacular location close to the Chinese border in the far northwest, makes a good base for exploring nearby minority villages, though a building boom is fast destroying its laid-back vibe. Farther south, the stilthouse-filled valley of **Mai Chau** offers another opportunity to stay in a minority village. Though few people venture further inland, rough backroads heading upcountry link isolated outposts and give access to the northwest's only specific sight, where the French colonial dream expired in the dead-end valley of **Dien Bien Phu**. East of the Red River Valley lies an even less-frequented region, whose prime attraction is its var-

xii

ied scenery, from the vertigo-inducing valleys of **Ha Giang** to the limestone crags and multi-layered rainforest of **Ba Be National Park**, then
east over immense, empty hill country to the remote valleys of **Cao Bang**,
farmed by communities still practising their traditional ways of life.

When to go

Vietnam has a tropical monsoon **climate**, dominated by the south
or southwesterly monsoon from May to September and the northeast monsoon from October to April. The southern summer monsoon brings rain to the two deltas and west-facing slopes, while the
cold winter monsoon picks up moisture over the Gulf of Tonkin and
dumps it along the central coast and the eastern edge of the central highlands. Within this basic pattern there are marked differences according to
altitude and latitude; temperatures in the south remain equable all year
round, while the north experiences distinct seasonal variations.

In **southern Vietnam** the dry season lasts from December to late April or
May, and the rains from May through to November. Since most rain falls in
brief afternoon downpours, this need not be off-putting, though flooding at
this time of year can cause problems in the Mekong Delta. Daytime temperatures in the region rarely drop below 20°C, occasionally hitting 40°C during the hottest months (March, April and May). The climate of the central
highlands generally follows the same pattern, though temperatures are cooler, especially at night. Again, the monsoon
rains of May to October can make transport
more complicated, sometimes washing out
roads and cutting off remoter villages.

Along the **central coast** the rainfall pattern reverses under the influence of the
northeast monsoon. Around Nha Trang the
wet season starts with a flourish in November and continues to December. Further
north, around Hué and Da Nang, the rains
last a bit longer, lasting from September to
February, though even the dry season
(March to August) brings a fair quantity of
intermittent rain. If possible it pays to visit
these two cities in the spring (February to
May), just before the rains break in Septem-

ber or as they begin to fizzle out in November. Temperatures reach their maximum (often in the upper 30s) from June to August, when it's pleasant to escape into the hills. The northern stretches of this coastal region experience a more extreme climate, with a shorter rainy season (peaking in September and October) and a hot dry summer. The coast of central Vietnam is the zone most likely to be hit by **typhoons**, bringing torrential rain and hurricane-force winds. Though notoriously difficult to predict, in general the typhoon season lasts from August to November.

Northern Vietnam is generally warm and sunny from October to December, after which cold winter weather sets in, accompanied by fine persistent mists which can last for several days. Temperatures begin to rise again in March, building to summer maximums that occasionally reach 40°C between May and August, though average temperatures in Hanoi hover around a more reasonable 30°C. However, summer is also the rainy season, when heavy downpours render the low-lying delta area almost unbearably hot and sticky, and flooding is a regular hazard. The northern mountains share the same basic regime, though temperatures are considerably cooler and higher regions see ground frosts, or even a rare snowfall, during the winter (December to February).

With such a complicated weather picture, there's no one particular season to recommend as the **best time** for visiting Vietnam. Overall, autumn (September to December) and spring (March and April) are probably the most favourable seasons if you're covering the whole country.

Vietnam's climate

	J	F	M	A	M	J	J	A	S	O	N	D
Ho Chi Minh City												
Av daily temp°C	27	28	29	30	29	29	28	28	27	27	27	27
Av monthly rainfall mm	15	3	13	43	221	330	315	269	335	269	114	56
Relative humidity (pm)	61	56	58	60	71	78	80	78	80	80	75	68
Da Nang												
Av daily temp°C	22	23	24	27	29	30	30	30	28	26	25	23
Av monthly rainfall mm	102	31	12	18	47	42	99	117	447	530	221	209
Rel. humidity (all hours)	86	86	86	85	81	77	78	77	84	85	86	86
Hanoi												
Av daily temp°C	17	18	20	24	28	30	30	29	28	26	22	19
Av monthly rainfall mm	18	28	38	81	196	239	323	343	254	99	43	20
Relative humidity (pm)	68	70	76	75	69	71	72	75	73	69	68	67

32

things not to miss

It's not possible to see everything Vietnam has to offer in one trip – and we don't suggest you try. What follows is a selective taste of the country's highlights; outstanding architecture, classic landscapes and great things to eat and drink. Arranged in five colour-coded categories, you can browse through to find the very best things to see, do and experience. All highlights have a page reference to take you straight into the guide, where you can find out more.

01 Browse the markets Page **102** • Markets such as Binh Tay are good grazing grounds for snacks such as soups, spring rolls and sticky rice cakes. Try a banana-leaf filled with pâte to keep you going while you shop.

02

Traditional music Page **535** • Music is the most important of all Vietnam's performing arts and a traditional performance should feature on every itinerary.

03 Trekking around Sa Pa

Page **448** • Go trekking in the northern mountains around Sa Pa – a small market town perched on a high plateau facing Fan Si Pan, Vietnam's highest peak.

04 Express silk tailoring

Page **283** • Pick up a bargain at Hoi An market from one of the many tailors who can rustle up a made-to-measure silk dress, suit or even shoes for you in just a few hours.

05 Nha Trang Page **246** • Take a snorkelling trip in the emerald waters of the outlying islands around Nha Trang, followed by a seafood feast on board your boat.

06 The Mekong Delta Page **133** • Putter through this fertile farming region, surrounded by classic Vietnamese scenery.

07 Cao Dai Cathedral Page **131** • Vietnam's most charismatic indigenous religion has goes in for exuberant architecture, with its supreme being symbolized by the all-seeing Eye.

08 Dak Lake Page **188** • Paddle around the serene waters of Dak Lake in a dug-out canoe, take a guided trek into the surrounding forests and then feast at sunset whilst overlooking the sparkling water.

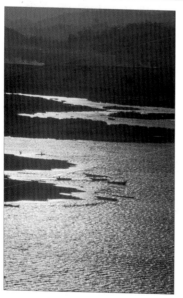

09 The Red River Delta Page **405** • Slow the pace down with a trip to the countryside and experience a lifestyle little changed in centuries.

10 **The citadel, Hue** Page **311** • The former capital's historic citadel, mausoleums and gardens are idiosyncratic enough to impress even the most jaded traveller.

11 **Snake wine** Page **50** • Partake in a glass of "snake wine", a snake-laced liquor that's supposedly imbued with all sorts of health-giving properties.

12 **Hon Chong peninsula** Page **179** • Enjoy the Mekong Delta's most attractive palm-fringed beaches and calm waters.

13 **Take a cyclo ride** Page **41** • The quintessential Vietnamese mode of transport gives you a up-close view of street life.

14 **Ride the Reunification Express** Page **35** • Sit back and relax as the train slowly chugs its way between Ho Chi Minh City and Hanoi, with no shortage of picnic breaks.

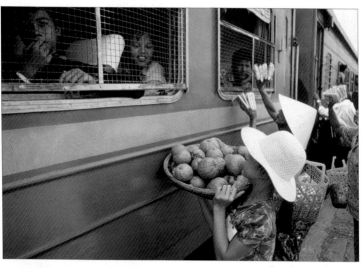

16 **Chill out on Phu Quoc** Page **183** • Unspoilt beaches lined with coconut trees circle the island. Feel the sand of Bai Sao between your toes or sail south to the unspoilt An Thoi islands for fine swimming in crystal-clear waters.

15 **Street food** Page **45** • Soak up the atmosphere at a street kitchen and have your plate piled as high as you like with a selection of fresh food for next to nothing – but get there early for the best choice.

17 Shopping Page **357** • Browse the streets in Hanoi to pick up some unusual souvenirs, such as these traditional prayer flags.

18 Ethnic markets Pages **455** & **457** • Spectacular traditional dress and a lively atmosphere make the ethnic minority markets a must – especially those in Bac Ha and Can Cau.

19 Cu Chi tunnels Page **127** • Go underground for a glimpse of tunnel life as experienced by the Viet Cong during the American War.

20 Hon Ong (Whale Island) Page **260** • Take it easy with a stay on this relaxed island that has fabulous views of fine golden sand, aquamarine water and, in season, glimpses of Humpback whales and whale sharks swimming in the bay.

24

Colonial architecture

Page **374** • The legacy of French rule can be seen in the Vietnamese fondness for baguettes and, more impressively, the instances of colonial architecture, such as Hanoi's Opera House.

25 Bia hoi
Page **396** •

Bia hoi bars are fun, friendly, cheap and a great way to mingle with the locals. Order a refreshing glass of *bia hoi* (lager-like beer) in any of the back lanes in The Old Quarter of Hanoi.

26 Water puppets
Page **532** • Enjoy a performance of *mua roi nuoc* (puppets that dance on the water), an art-form developed in the Red River Delta around Hanoi.

27 **Coffee** Page **211** •
Vietnam's best coffee grows around the hills of Buon Me Thuot. Drink it the Vietnamese way – strong and short, with a dollop of condensed milk – at one of the quirky cafés scattered all over town.

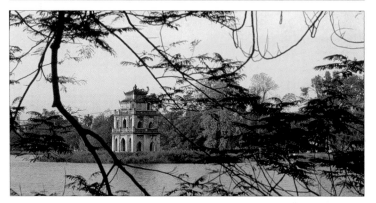

28 **Temples and pagodas** Page **370** • The Vietnamese architectural style is best represented by its temples and pagodas, which reflect the country's diverse range of religions. Ngoc Son on Hoan Kiem Lake is a particularly good example.

29
Hoi An
Page **274** •
With its rich cultural heritage and slow pace of life, Hoi An is a captivating place to spend a few days.

31 **The northern mountains** Page **439** • Vietnam's most impressive mountainscapes offer not just scenic rewards but also the chance to visit an ethnic minority village.

30 **Bahnar villages** Page **220** • Spend the night in a communal house (*rong*) where timeless village ceremonies are performed and important decisions are made.

32 **Tet** Page **56** • The most important festival in the Vietnamese calendar, Tet sees the New Year ushered in with colourful flower markets, spectacular fireworks and exuberant dragon dances.

Contents

Using this Rough Guide

We've tried to make this Rough Guide a good read and easy to use. The book is divided into six main sections, and you should be able to find whatever you want in one of them.

Colour section

The front colour section offers a quick tour of Vietnam. The **introduction** aims to give you a feel for the place, with suggestions on where to go. We also tell you what the weather is like and include a basic country fact file. Next, our authors round up their favourite aspects of Vietnam in the **things not to miss** section – whether it's great food, amazing sights or a special activity. Right after this comes a full **contents** list.

Basics

The Basics section covers all the **pre-departure** nitty-gritty to help you plan your trip. This is where to find out which airlines fly to your destination, what paperwork you'll need, what to do about money and insurance, about internet access, food, security, public transport, car rental – in fact just about every piece of **general practical information** you might need.

Guide

This is the heart of the Rough Guide, divided into user-friendly chapters, each of which covers a specific region. Every chapter starts with a list of **highlights** and an **introduction** that helps you to decide where to go, depending on your time and budget. Likewise, introductions to the various towns and smaller regions within each chapter should help you plan your itinerary. We start most town accounts with information on arrival and accommodation, followed by a tour of the sights, and finally reviews of places to eat and drink, and details of nightlife. Longer accounts also have a directory of practical listings. Each chapter concludes with **public transport** details for that region.

Contexts

Read Contexts to get a deeper understanding of what makes Vietnam tick. We include brief **history**, articles about **music**, **film** and the **environment**, and a detailed further reading section that reviews dozens of **books** relating to the country.

Language

The **language** section gives useful guidance for speaking Vietnamese and pulls together all the vocabulary you might need on your trip, including a comprehensive menu reader. Here you'll also find a glossary of words and terms peculiar to the country.

Index + small print

Apart from a **full index**, which includes maps as well as places, this section covers publishing information, credits and acknowledgements, and also has our contact details in case you want to send in updates and corrections to the book – or suggestions as to how we might improve it.

Map and chapter list

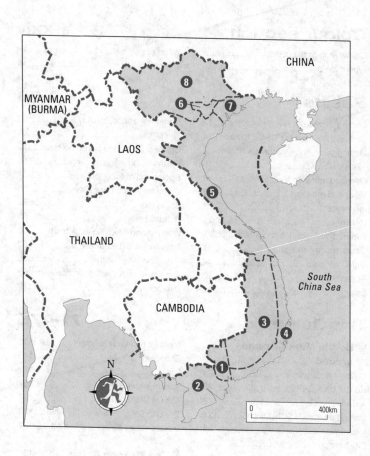

Contents

Contexts

481

Language and glossaries   **567**

Index + small print   **579**

Map symbols

maps are listed in the full index using coloured text

—·—·—	International boundary	♠	Pagoda
—— ··	Provincial boundary	⚑	Mosque
— — —	Chapter division boundary	⚐	Golf course
═══	Main road	⚑	Lighthouse
═══	Minor road	♟	Museum
- - - -	Path	♁	Gardens
▬▬▬	Railway	⚓	Swimming a
— —	Ferry route	⚑	Snorkelling
——	River	✈	Airport
▪▪▪▪▪▪	City wall/battlement	★	Bus stop
♦	Point of interest	⊠	Post office
✝	Boarder crossing	(i)	Tourist offic(
⋏	Mountain range	@	Internet acc
▲	Mountain peak	⊞	Hospital
⨅	Pass	◉	Accommod:
⚶	Viewpoint	▪	Restaurant
⌂	Cave	▬	Building
⌇	Waterfall	⊞	Church
⛩	Hindu temple	▨	Park
◬	Cao Dai temple	⚏	Beach

7

Basics

Basics

Getting there

While the number of airlines offering non-stop services to Vietnam is gradually increasing, the majority of visitors take the cheaper option of an indirect flight routed through a carrier's domestic hub to one of Vietnam's three international airports: Hanoi, Ho Chi Minh City and Da Nang. With time in hand, you can generally build a stopover in Bangkok, Singapore or Hong Kong, for example, into your schedule, usually at no extra cost. Some regional airlines, such as Thai Airways, also offer "tour fares", including a minimum number of nights' accommodation in their home city, which may work out cheaper than a standard return flight. It's also worth investigating the cost of buying a bargain-basement flight to Bangkok and a separate ticket through Thai Airways or Vietnam Airlines for the Vietnam leg.

Airlines that fly in and out of both Hanoi and Ho Chi Minh will normally be able to sell you an **open-jaw ticket**, which allows you to fly into one city and out of the other, leaving you to travel up or down the country under your own steam.

Airfares always depend on the **season**, with the highest generally being July to August and during the Christmas and New Year holidays; fares drop during the "shoulder" season – September to mid-December – and you'll get the best prices during the low season, January to June. Note also that flying at weekends is generally more expensive; price ranges quoted below assume midweek travel.

You can often cut costs by going through a **specialist flight agent** – either a consolidator, who buys up blocks of tickets from the airlines and sells them at a discount, or a **discount agent**, who in addition to dealing with discounted flights may also offer special student and youth fares and a range of other travel-related services such as travel insurance, rail passes, car rentals, tours and the like. Some agents specialize in **charter flights**, which may be cheaper than any available scheduled flight, but departure dates are fixed and withdrawal penalties are high. For Vietnam, you may even find it cheaper to pick up a bargain **package deal** from one of the tour operators listed below and then find your own accommodation when you get there.

If Vietnam is only one stop on a longer journey, you might want to consider buying a **round-the-world** (RTW) ticket. Some travel agents can sell you an "off-the-shelf" RTW ticket that will have you touching down in about half a dozen cities; others will have to assemble one for you, which can be tailored to your needs but is apt to be more expensive. Although few off-the-shelf tickets take in Ho Chi Minh or Hanoi, several offer a stop in Bangkok, Singapore or Hong Kong, from where you can make a side-trip to Vietnam. The most comprehensive and flexible deals are offered by Star Alliance, One World and Sky Team, all of which allow you to take in a huge number of destinations around the globe. Prices are either mileage-based or calculated according to how many continents you cover.

Booking flights online

Many airlines and discount travel websites offer you the opportunity to book your tickets online, cutting out the costs of agents and middlemen. Good deals can often be found through discount or auction sites, as well as through the airlines' own websites.

Online booking agents and general travel sites

ⓦ **travel.yahoo.com** Incorporates a lot of Rough Guide material in its coverage of destination countries and cities across the world, with information about places to eat, sleep and so on.
ⓦ **www.cheapflights.com** Bookings from the UK and Ireland only (for US, ⓦ www.cheapflight.com; for Canada, ⓦ www.cheapflights.ca; for Australia,

Ⓦ www.cheapflights.com.au). Flight deals, travel agents, plus links to other travel sites.

Ⓦ **www.cheaptickets.com** Discount flight specialists (US only).

Ⓦ **www.etn.nl/discount.htm** A hub of consolidator and discount agent Web links, maintained by the non-profit European Travel Network.

Ⓦ **www.expedia.com** Discount airfares, all-airline search engine and daily deals (US only; for the UK, Ⓦ www.expedia.co.uk; for Canada, Ⓦ www.expedia.ca).

Ⓦ **www.flyaow.com** Online air travel info and reservations site.

Ⓦ **www.gaytravel.com** Gay online travel agent, offering accommodation, cruises, tours and more.

Ⓦ **www.geocities.com/thavery2000** Has an extensive list of airline toll-free numbers (from the US) and websites.

Ⓦ **www.hotwire.com** Bookings from the US only. Last-minute savings of up to forty percent on regular published fares. Travellers must be at least 18 and there are no refunds, transfers or changes allowed. Log-in required.

Ⓦ **www.lastminute.com** Offers good last-minute holiday package and flight-only deals (UK only; for Australia, Ⓦ www.lastminute.com.au).

Ⓦ **www.opodo.co.uk** User-friendly, UK-only booking site – owned by major airlines such as BA and Air France – with good deals on flights and packages.

Ⓦ **www.priceline.com** Name-your-own-price website that has deals at around forty percent off standard fares. You cannot specify flight times (although you do specify dates) and the tickets are non-refundable, non-transferable and non-changeable (US only; for the UK, Ⓦ www.priceline.co.uk).

Ⓦ **www.skyauction.com** Bookings from the US only. Auctions tickets and travel packages using a "second bid" scheme. The best strategy is to bid the maximum you're willing to pay, since if you win you'll pay just enough to beat the runner-up regardless of your maximum bid.

Ⓦ **www.smilinjack.com/airlines.htm** Lists an up-to-date compilation of airline website addresses.

Ⓦ **www.travelocity.com** Destination guides, hot Web fares and best deals for car rental, accommodation and lodging as well as fares. Provides access to the travel agent system SABRE, the most comprehensive central reservations system in the US.

Ⓦ **www.travelshop.com.au** Australian website offering discounted flights, packages, insurance and online bookings.

From the UK and Ireland

There are as yet no non-stop flights to Vietnam from the UK or Ireland. Instead, most people fly with a Southeast Asian carrier such as Singapore Airlines, Thai Airways, Malaysia Airlines or Cathay Pacific via their home city, or with Air France via Paris. The latter has connecting flights to Paris from regional airports such as Dublin, Edinburgh and Manchester, whereas all the Southeast Asian airlines operate out of London. Standard low-season fares start at around £550, rising to £800 or so at peak periods.

A good place to look for **discount fares** is the travel sections of papers such as the *Guardian*, *Independent* and *Daily Telegraph* (Saturday editions), and the *Observer*, *Sunday Times* and *Independent on Sunday*, where agents advertise special deals. In London, check the back pages of the listings magazine *Time Out*, the *Evening Standard* or the free travel mag *TNT*, found outside main-line train stations. Independent travel specialists such as STA Travel do deals for students and anyone under 26, or can simply sell a scheduled ticket at a discount price.

As far as **round-the-world** tickets are concerned, deals offered by Star Alliance are of greatest interest since both Thai Airways and Singapore Airlines are partner airlines, allowing you to include Vietnam as one of your stops. Tickets cost between £1250 and £1750 excluding taxes. Sky Team's Air France and Korean Air also cover Vietnam, while One World includes Bangkok and a number of other regional hubs, from where you could buy a cheap return ticket to Vietnam.

If you want to cover a lot of ground in a short time in Vietnam or have a specific interest, an organized tour might be worth considering. **Specialist tour operators** (see pp.13–14) offer packages that typically include flights, accommodation, day excursions and internal travel by plane, train or road. These work out to be expensive compared to what you'd pay if you arranged everything independently, but the more intrepid tours often feature activities it would be difficult to set up yourself. Alternatively, you can make arrangements through **local tour operators** in Ho Chi Minh, Hanoi and other tourist centres either before you arrive or on the ground: we've given details of recommended agents throughout the Guide. Check carefully before booking to make sure you know exactly what's included in the price.

There are also a number of research outfits that allow paying **volunteers** to participate in their projects on a short-term basis; see pp.66–67 for details.

Airlines

Aeroflot UK ☏020/7355 2233, ⓦwww.aeroflot.co.uk.
Air France UK ☏0845/0845 111, ⓦwww.airfrance.co.uk; Republic of Ireland ☏01/605 0383, ⓦwww.airfrance.com/ie.
Alitalia UK ☏0870/544 8259, Republic of Ireland ☏01/677 5171; ⓦwww.alitalia.co.uk.
British Airways UK ☏0845/77 333 77, Republic of Ireland ☏1800/626 747; ⓦwww.ba.com.
Cathay Pacific UK ☏020/8834 8888, ⓦwww.cathaypacific.com/uk.
China Airlines UK ☏020/7436 9001, ⓦwww.china-airlines.com.
EVA Airways UK ☏020/7380 8300, ⓦwww.evaair.com.
Finnair UK ☏0870/241 4411, Republic of Ireland ☏01/844 6565; ⓦwww.finnair.com.
KLM UK ☏0870/507 4074, ⓦwww.klmuk.com.
Korean Air UK ☏0800/0656 2001, Republic of Ireland ☏01/799 7990; ⓦwww.koreanair.eu.com.
Lauda Air UK ☏0845/601 0948, ⓦwww.aua.com.
Lufthansa UK ☏0845/7737 747, Republic of Ireland ☏01/844 5544; ⓦwww.lufthansa.co.uk.
Malaysia Airlines (MAS) UK ☏0870/607 9090, Republic of Ireland ☏01/676 1561 or 676 2131; ⓦwww.malaysiaairlineseurope.com.
Qantas UK ☏0845/774 7767, ⓦwww.qantas.com.
SAS Scandinavian Airlines UK ☏0845/607 2772, Republic of Ireland ☏01/844 5440; ⓦwww.scandinavian.net.
Singapore Airlines UK ☏0870/608 8886, Republic of Ireland ☏01/671 0722; ⓦwww.singaporeair.com.
Swiss UK ☏0845/601 0956, ⓦwww.swiss.com.
Tarom Romanian Air Transport UK ☏020/7224 3693, ⓦwww.tarom.ro.
Thai Airways International UK ☏0870/606 0911, ⓦwww.thaiair.com.
Vietnam Airlines UK representative West-East Travel ☏020/8749 0292 ⓦwww.vietnamairlines.com.

Flight and travel agents

Bridge the World UK ☏0870/444 7474, ⓦwww.bridgetheworld.com. Everything from discounted flights to tailor-made tours.
Flightbookers UK ☏0870/010 7000, ⓦwww.ebookers.com. Low fares on an extensive selection of scheduled flights.
Flynow UK ☏0870/444 0045, ⓦwww.flynow.com. Large range of discounted tickets.
McCarthy's Travel Republic of Ireland ☏021/427 0127, ⓦwww.mccarthystravel.ie. General flight agent.
North South Travel UK ☏ & ⒻF01245/608 291, ⓦwww.northsouthtravel.co.uk. Friendly, competitive travel agency, offering discounted fares worldwide – profits are used to support projects in the developing world, especially the promotion of sustainable tourism.
Quest Travel UK ☏0870/442 3542, ⓦwww.questtravel.com. Specialists in round-the-world discount fares.
STA Travel UK ☏0870/1600 599, ⓦwww.statravel.co.uk. Worldwide specialists in low-cost flights and tours for students and under-26s, though other customers welcome.
Top Deck UK ☏020/7244 8000, ⓦwww.topdecktravel.co.uk. Long-established agent dealing in discount flights.
Trailfinders UK ☏020/7628 7628, ⓦwww.trailfinders.co.uk; Republic of Ireland ☏01/677 7888, ⓦwww.trailfinders.ie. One of the best-informed and most efficient agents for independent travellers; they produce a very useful quarterly magazine worth scrutinizing for round-the-world routes.
Travel Bag UK ☏0870/890 1456, ⓦwww.travelbag.co.uk. Large range of discounted flights; official Qantas agent.
usit NOW Republic of Ireland ☏01/602 1600, Northern Ireland ☏028/9032 7111, ⓦwww.usitnow.ie. Student and youth specialists for flights and trains.

Tour operators

Abercrombie & Kent ☏020/7730 9600, ⓦwww.abercrombiekent.co.uk. Specialist in luxury tours.
Audley Travel ☏01869/276 200, ⓦwww.audleytravel.com. Upmarket tailor-made and escorted small-group tours, including "Classic Vietnam" and "Classic Indochina".
Bales Worldwide ☏0870/241 3208, ⓦwww.balesworldwide.com. Family-owned company offering high-quality escorted tours to Southeast Asia, as well as tailor-made itineraries.

Destinations Worldwide Holidays Dublin ℡ 01/855 6641, ⓦ www.destinations.ie. Specialists in Far Eastern and exotic destinations.

Explore Worldwide ℡ 01252/760 000, ⓦ www .explore.co.uk. Big range of small-group tours, treks and expeditions, staying mostly in small local hotels.

Guerba ℡ 01373/858956, ⓦwww.guerba.com. Adventure travel specialist with a few Vietnamese options.

Imaginative Traveller ℡ 020/8742 8612, ⓦ www.imaginative-traveller.com. Wide range of itineraries, either exclusively in Vietnam or as part of a wider programme.

Kuoni Travel ℡ 01306/742 888, ⓦ www.kuoni.co.uk. Flexible package holidays to long-haul destinations; good family offers.

Live Limited ℡ 020/8894 6104, ⓦ www .live-travel.com. Run by Phil Haines – "youngest person to visit every country in the world" – this company organizes group and tailor-made tours to Vietnam amongst other exotic locations.

Magic of the Orient ℡ 01293/537 700, ⓦ www.magic-of-the-orient.com. Tailor-made holidays, rather than packages; very well-informed consultants can lead you off the beaten track.

Mountain Travel Sobek ℡ 01494/448901, ⓔ sales@mtsobekeu.com. The UK arm of a US adventure travel company, offering a hiking and cycling trip combined with sea-kayaking on Ha Long Bay, plus customized itineraries.

Regent Holidays ℡ 0117/921 1711, ⓦ www.regent-holidays.co.uk. Well-established Indochina specialist with a reputation for good-value, tailor-made travel arrangements.

Silk Steps ℡ 01454/888850, ⓦ www.silksteps .co.uk. Tailor-made and group travel to Vietnam and Indochina, including a Mekong World Heritage Tour.

Silverbird Travel ℡ 020/8875 9090, ⓦ www.silverbird.co.uk. Specialist in Far East tailor-made tours.

Symbiosis Expedition Planning ℡ 0845/123 2844 ⓦ www.symbiosis-travel.com. Highly rated tailor-made and small-group adventure tours.

Tennyson Travel ℡ 020/7736 4347, ⓦ www.visitvietnam.co.uk. Vietnam specialists offering tours ranging from stopovers in Ho Chi Minh and Hanoi to full-length excursions.

Thomas Cook ℡ 0870/5666 222, ⓦ www .thomascook.co.uk. Long-established, one-stop 24-hour travel agency offering discount flights.

Williames ℡ 028/9023 0714, ⓕ 9043 9637. Belfast-based long-haul specialists.

World Expeditions UK ℡ 020/8870 2600, ⓦ www.worldexpeditions.co.uk. Australian-owned adventure company with a programme ranging from sea-kayaking on Ha Long Bay to climbing Mount Fansipan. All expeditions are graded by difficulty; brochure available for hardcore adventurers, and over-50s adventurers are well catered for with a separate brochure.

World Travel Centre ℡ 01/671 7155. Dublin specialists in long-haul flights and packages.

From the US and Canada

As yet, no American or Canadian carriers offer direct services to Vietnam, which means you'll have to catch one of the many flights to a regional hub, such as Bangkok, Singapore or Hong Kong, and continue on from there. Local discount agents can't usually offer a better price than the airlines, so you may as well book this leg from home.

Prices quoted below assume low-season, midweek travel (weekends are usually slightly pricier), exclude taxes and are subject to change. Scheduled flights start at around $1500 from New York, $1300 from Los Angeles, CAN$1850 from Vancouver and CAN$2300 from Toronto. However, since discounts are offered at different times by different airlines, it's worth checking with more than one carrier, or indeed more than one travel agent, to find the best fare.

As always, fares vary depending on the time of year, but **discount tickets** are now widely available for Vietnam. However, don't automatically assume that tickets purchased through a flight specialist will be the cheapest available – once you get a quote, check with the individual airlines and you may be able to turn up an even better deal.

Note that some routings require an overnight stay in another city such as Bangkok, Taipei, Hong Kong or Seoul, and often a hotel room will be included in your fare – ask the airline and shop around since travel agents' policies on this vary. Even when an overnight stay is not required, going to Vietnam can be a great excuse for a **stopover**. Most airlines will allow you one free stopover in either direction.

Another option is a **round-the-world** (RTW) ticket. Some travel agents can sell you "off-the-shelf" RTW tickets that will have you touching down in about half a dozen cities; others will have to tailor-make one for you, which is apt to be more expensive, but these are still worth investigating. The most comprehensive and flexible deals are those offered by the three big airline alliances, of which Star Alliance and Sky Team include Vietnam as a destination. Prices are based either on the mileage or on the number of continents you cover, but you should figure on between $3600 and $4800, excluding taxes and surcharges, from the US and CAN$4300 to CAN$5700 from Canada. The One World alliance has flights to Bangkok, Singapore and Hong Kong, from where you can buy a separate airline ticket for the Vietnam leg.

Some airlines also offer **air passes**, which are good for extended tours of the region. The ASEAN Air Pass, for example, covers air travel within the ASEAN federation (Brunei, Indonesia, Malaysia, Philippines, Singapore, Thailand, Vietnam, Laos and Myanmar). Your international flight must be with one of these country's national airlines. The pass allows you to purchase between three and six contiguous internal flights, at $120 per segment. Malaysia Airlines' Access Asia Pass is somewhat broader and offers excellent value. The flat-rate fare, starting at around $900 excluding taxes, includes a return flight from Los Angeles or Newark and allows travel to 24 destinations in Southeast Asia (including Hanoi and Ho Chi Minh City) during a thirty-day period. The ticket can be extended to Australia, Europe, South America or Africa for a supplement.

The cost of a **Circle Pacific** ticket may work out about the same as that of an air pass. They tend to be for longer periods, but are less flexible since there are usually restrictions on backtracking.

Some agents specialize in **charter flights**, which may be cheaper than a scheduled flight, but departure dates are fixed and withdrawal penalties are high (check the refund policy). If you travel a lot, discount travel clubs are another option – the annual membership fee may be worth it for benefits such as cut-price air tickets.

There's a wide variety of all-inclusive **packages** available, as well as **organized tours** that cover everything from hilltribe visits to trekking and biking. Tours range in length from a few days to several weeks, and you can choose to explore Vietnam only, or combine a tour with Laos and Cambodia. On p.16 we list a selection of specialist agents offering tours to Vietnam. Note, however, that you can also make arrangements with a local tour operator in Ho Chi Minh, Hanoi or other major tourist centre; details of recommended agents are listed in the Guide. Whichever you opt for, always check exactly what is included in the price before booking.

Finally, be advised that the pool of travel companies is swimming with sharks – *never* deal with a company that demands cash upfront or refuses to accept payment by credit card.

Airlines

Air Canada ☎1-888/247-2262, ⓦwww.aircanada.ca.
Air China East Coast ☎1-800/982-8802, West Coast ☎1-800/986-1985, Canada ☎416/581-8833; ⓦwww.airchina.com.cn/index_en.html.
Air France US ☎1-800/237-2747, ⓦwww.airfrance.com; Canada ☎1-800/667-2747; ⓦwww.airfrance.ca.
American Airlines ☎1-800/433-7300, ⓦwww.aa.com.
Asiana Airlines ☎1-800/227-4262, ⓦwww.flyasiana.com.
Cathay Pacific ☎1-800/233-2742, ⓦwww.cathay-usa.com.
China Airlines ☎917/368-2000, ⓦwww.china-airlines.com.
Continental Airlines ☎1-800/231-0856, ⓦwww.continental.com.
Delta Air Lines ☎1-800/241-4141, ⓦwww.delta.com.
EVA Airways ☎1-800/695-1188, ⓦwww.evaair.com.
Japan Air Lines ☎1-800/525-3663, ⓦwww.japanair.com.
Korean Air ☎1-800/438-5000, ⓦwww.koreanair.com.
Malaysia Airlines ☎1-800/552-9264, ⓦwww.mas.com.my.
Northwest/KLM Airlines ☎1-800/447-4747, ⓦwww.nwa.com, ⓦww.klm.com.
Qantas ☎1-800/227-4500, ⓦwww.qantas.com.
Singapore Airlines ☎1-800/742-3333, ⓦwww.singaporeair.com.
Swiss ☎1-877/359-7947, ⓦwww.swiss.com.
Thai Airways International ☎1-800/426-5204, ⓦwww.thaiair.com.
United Airlines ☎1-800/538-2929, ⓦwww.ual.com.
Virgin Atlantic Airways ☎1-800/862-8621, ⓦwww.virgin-atlantic.com.

Discount travel companies

Air Brokers International ☎1-800/883-3273, ⓦwww.airbrokers.com. Consolidator and specialist in RTW and Circle Pacific tickets.

Air Courier Association ☎1-800/282-1202, ⓦwww.aircourier.org. Courier flight broker with membership fees starting at $16 for three months.

Airtreks.com ☎1-877/AIRTREKS or 415/912-5600, ⓦwww.airtreks.com. Round-the-world and Circle Pacific tickets. The website features an interactive database that lets you build and price your own round-the-world itinerary.

Council Travel ☎1-800/2COUNCIL, ⓦwww.counciltravel.com. Nationwide organization that mostly specializes in student/budget travel. Flights from the US only.

International Association of Air Travel Couriers ☎308/632-3273, ⓦwww.courier.org. Courier flight broker with membership fee of $45 per year.

STA Travel US ☎1-800/781-4040, Canada 1-888/427-5639; ⓦwww.sta-travel.com. Worldwide specialists in independent travel; also student IDs, travel insurance, car rental, rail passes, etc.

Travel Cuts Canada ☎1-800/667-2887, US ☎1-866/246-9762; ⓦwww.travelcuts.com. Canadian student-travel organization.

Worldtek Travel ☎1-800/243-1723, ⓦwww.worldtek.com. Discount travel agency for worldwide travel.

Tour operators

Abercrombie & Kent ☎1-800/323-7308 or 630/954-2944, ⓦwww.abercrombiekent.com. Specialist in luxury tours.

Absolute Asia ☎1-800/736-8187, ⓦwww.absoluteasia.com. De luxe customized tours.

Adventure Center ☎1-800/228-8747 or 510/654-1879, ⓦwww.adventurecenter.com. Hiking and "soft adventure" specialists.

Adventures Abroad ☎1-800/665-3998 or 360/775-9926, ⓦwww.adventures-abroad.com. Adventure specialists.

Asia Transpacific Journeys ☎1-800/642-2742, ⓦwww.southeastasia.com. Tailor-made itineraries.

Asian Pacific Adventures ☎1-800/825-1680 or 818/886-5190, ⓦwww.asianpacificadventures.com. Off-the-beaten-track cycling and trekking tours.

Backroads ☎1-800/GO-ACTIVE or 510/527-1555, ⓦwww.backroads.com. Cycling, hiking and multi-sport tours.

Common Ground Journeys ☎1-503/307-7524, ⓦwww.commongroundjourney.com. Specialist Vietnamese cycle-tour company.

Cox & Kings ☎1-800/999-1758, ⓦwww.coxandkingsusa.com. Luxury escorted and tailor-made tours.

Elderhostel ☎1-877/426-8056, ⓦwww.elderhostel.org. Not-for-profit organization providing educational adventures for people 55 and over.

Geographic Expeditions ☎1-800/777-8183 or 415/922-0448, ⓦwww.geoex.com. Adventure travel and cultural tours.

Global Exchange ☎1-800/497-1994 or 415/255-7296, ⓦwww.globalexchange.org. Operate educational "reality" tours.

Global Volunteers ☎1-800/487-1074, ⓦwww.globalvolunteers.org. Charity taking paying volunteers to work on English-language teaching programmes in the Mekong Delta.

Globus ☎1-866/755-8581, ⓦwww.globusjourneys.com. Planned vacation packages.

Goway Travel Experiences ☎1-800/387-8850 or 416/322-1034, ⓦwww.goway.com. Long-haul destination specialist.

Himalayan Travel ☎1-800/225-2380 or 203/743-2349, ⓦwww.himalayantravelinc.com. Cycling, trekking and other adventure tours.

Journeys International ☎1-800/255-8735 or 734/665-4407, ⓦwww.journeys-intl.com. Culture and adventure tours.

Mountain Travel Sobek ☎1-888/687-6235 or 510/527-8100, ⓦwww.mtsobek.com. Group and customized adventure travel.

Nature Expeditions International ☎1-800/869-0639, ⓦwww.naturexp.com. Educational adventure travel.

Pacific Delight Tours ☎1-800/221-7179 or 212/818-1781, ⓦwww.pacificdelighttours.com. Upscale tours at affordable prices.

REI Adventures ☎1-800/622-2236, ⓦwww.rei.com/travel. Two-week Vietnam cycle tour.

Velo Asia ☎1-415/731-3360, ⓦwww.veloasia.com. Organized and tailor-made cycling adventure tours.

Wilderness Travel ☎1-800/368-2794 or 510/558-2488, ⓦwww.wildernesstravel.com. Specialists in worldwide hiking, cultural and wildlife adventures.

Worldwide Adventures ☎1-800/387-1483 or 416/633-5666, ⓦwww.100adventures.com. Adventure specialist.

From Australia and New Zealand

A reasonable range of flights connect Australia and New Zealand with Vietnam. The main carriers with direct services are Qantas and

Vietnam Airlines. Alternatively you could fly to another Asian gateway, such as Bangkok, Kuala Lumpur, Singapore or Hong Kong, and then either get connecting flights or travel overland to Hanoi or Ho Chi Minh City.

From Australia, direct flights to Ho Chi Minh City go from Melbourne with Qantas and from Sydney and Melbourne with Vietnam Airlines; fares start at around A\$1500. If you want to stop off on the way, there are good deals to Hanoi and Ho Chi Minh with Malaysia Airlines via Kuala Lumpur, Singapore Airlines via Singapore and Thai Airways via Bangkok, all starting at around A\$1300.

From New Zealand, Malaysia Airlines fly to Ho Chi Minh and Hanoi via Kuala Lumpur for a low-season fare in the region of NZ\$1300. Fares with Thai, Qantas and Singapore Airlines all start at around NZ\$1650, with a change of plane in the carrier's home airport.

If you want to take in Vietnam as part of a longer trip, another option is a **round-the-world** ticket. Both Star Alliance (whose members include Thai Airways and Singapore Airlines) and Sky Team (Air France and Korean Air) include Vietnam as a destination, while One World offer a stop in Bangkok and other regional hubs, from where you can take a side-trip to Vietnam. Prices range between A\$2900/NZ\$3500 and A\$4000/NZ\$4500, excluding taxes, and are either mileage-based or calculated according to how many continents you cover.

Various **Circle Pacific** tickets are also available through consolidators or regional airlines. Vietnam Airlines, for example, has a Circle Asia fare from Australia via Bangkok, Singapore or Hong Kong to Hanoi or Ho Chi Minh, starting at around A\$1200 excluding taxes. From New Zealand, Star Alliance's Circle Pacific fares start at roughly NZ\$3000 excluding taxes. The ticket allows you to travel up to 35,000km during a six-month period.

An **organized tour** is worth considering if you have ambitious sightseeing plans and only a short time to accomplish them. Some of the adventure-oriented tours can also help you to get to more remote areas and organize activities that may be difficult to arrange yourself, such as trekking and cycling. You can also arrange tours in advance through a local operator (details of reliable agents are given throughout the Guide), often at a cheaper price, but it's important to check exactly what you're paying for before confirming.

Airlines

Air China Australia ☎02/9232 7277, New Zealand ☎09/379 7696; ⓦwww.airchina.com.cn.
Air New Zealand Australia ☎13 24 76, ⓦwww.airnz.com.au; New Zealand ☎0800/737 000, ⓦwww.airnz.co.nz.
Air Pacific Australia ☎1800/230 150, New Zealand ☎0800/800 178; ⓦwww.airpacific.com.
Cathay Pacific Australia ☎13 17 47, ⓦwww.cathaypacific.com/au; New Zealand ☎09/379 0861 or 0508/800 454, ⓦwww.cathaypacific.com/nz.
China Airlines Australia ☎02/9244 2121, New Zealand ☎09/308 3364; ⓦwww.china-airlines.com.
China Eastern Airlines Australia ☎02/9290 1148, ⓦwww.ce-air.com/cea/en_US/homepage.
EVA Air Australia ☎02/9221 7055, New Zealand ☎09/358 8300; ⓦwww.evaair.com.
Japan Air Lines Australia ☎02/9272 1111, New Zealand ☎09/379 9906; ⓦwww.japanair.com.
Korean Air Australia ☎02/9262 6000, New Zealand ☎09/914 2000; ⓦwww.koreanair.com.au.
Malaysia Airlines Australia ☎13 26 27, New Zealand ☎0800/777 747; ⓦwww.malaysiaairlines.com.my.
Qantas Australia ☎13 13 13, ⓦwww.qantas.com.au; New Zealand ☎0800/808 767, ⓦwww.qantas.co.nz.
Singapore Airlines Australia ☎13 10 11, New Zealand ☎0800/808 909; ⓦwww.singaporeair.com.
Thai Airways International Australia ☎1300/651 960, New Zealand ☎09/377 0268; ⓦwww.thaiair.com.
Vietnam Airlines Australia ☎02/9283 1355, ⓦwww.vietnamairlines.com.vn.

Travel agents

Flight Centre Australia ☎13 31 33 or 02/9235 3522, ⓦwww.flightcentre.com.au; New Zealand ☎0800/243 544 or 09/358 4310, ⓦwww.flightcentre.co.nz.
STA Travel Australia ☎1300/733 035, ⓦwww.statravel.com.au; New Zealand ☎0508/782 872, ⓦwww.statravel.co.nz.
Student Uni Travel Australia ☎02/9232 8444, ⓦwww.sut.com.au; New Zealand ☎09/379 4224, ⓦwww.sut.co.nz.
Trailfinders Australia ☎02/9247 7666, ⓦwww.trailfinders.com.au.

Specialist agents

Birding Worldwide Australia ☎03/9899 9303, ⓦwww.birdingworldwide.com.au. Organizes group trips around the globe for those wanting to glimpse typical, unique and rare species.

Kumuka Expeditions Australia ☎1800/804 277 or 02/9279 0491, ⓦwww.kumuka.com.au. Independent tour operator specializing in overland expeditions, as well as local and private transport tours.

Plan It Holidays Australia ☎03/9245 0747, ⓦwww.planit.com.au. Discounted airfares and accommodation packages.

San Michele Travel Australia ☎02/9299 1111 or 1800/22 22 44, ⓦwww.asiatravel.com.au. Long-running Southeast Asia specialist.

Silke's Travel Australia ☎1800/807 860 or 02/8347 2000, ⓦwww.silkes.com.au. Gay and lesbian specialist travel agent.

travel.com.au and **travel.co.nz** Australia ☎1300/130 482 or 02/9249 5444, ⓦwww.travel.com.au; New Zealand ☎0800/468 332, ⓦwww.travel.co.nz. Comprehensive online travel company.

Travel Indochina Australia ☎1300/365 355, ⓦwww.travelindochina.com.au. Goes beyond the obvious sights and can arrange cross-border visas for Thailand, Laos, Vietnam, China and Cambodia.

Tour operators

Abercrombie & Kent Australia ☎03/9536 1800 or 1300/851 800, New Zealand ☎0800/441 638; ⓦwww.abercrombiekent.com.au. Upmarket tour specialist.

Active Travel Australia ☎02/6249 6122, ⓦwww.activetravel.com.au. Broad range of culture and adventure tours, plus customized itineraries.

Asian Explorer Holidays Australia ☎1300/737 838, ⓦwww.i-xplore.com.au. Flight, accommodation and tour packages.

Community Aid Abroad Tours ⓦwww .caa.org.au/travel. Small-group, low-impact tours with a development focus under the auspices of Oxfam. Online only.

Griswalds Vietnamese Vacations Australia ☎02/9564 5040, ⓦwww.vietnamvacations .com.au. Vietnam specialist offering tours and tailor-made packages.

Intrepid Travel Australia ☎03/9473 2626, ⓦwww.intrepidtravel.com.au. Small-group tours with the emphasis on cross-cultural contact and low-impact tourism.

Peregrine Adventures Australia ☎02/9290 2770, New Zealand ☎03/9663 8611; ⓦwww.peregrine.net.au. Trekking, cycling and explorer tours.

From neighbouring countries

It's now possible to enter Vietnam overland from China, Laos or Cambodia, an option that means you can see more of the region than you would if you simply jetted in.

From China there are three possibilities. The Beijing–Hanoi train enters Vietnam at Dong Dang, north of Lang Son, where there's also a road crossing known as Huu Nghi Quan (see p.476). The border is also open to foot traffic at Lao Cai (see p.447) in the northwest and Mong Cai in the far northeast (see pp.435–436).

From Laos, two border crossings are currently open to foreigners: Lao Bao (see p.333), the easiest and most popular, some 80km west of Dong Ha; and Cau Treo (see p.333), 105km southwest of Vinh. In the summer of 2003 a further crossing opened at Nam Can, 230km northwest of Vinh, although it's not yet known when, or if, foreigners will be permitted to use it. While it's perfectly possible – and cheaper – to use local buses, international bus services also run from Savannakhet and Vientiane to Dong Ha, Vinh, Da Nang and other destinations in Vietnam.

From Cambodia you can travel by bus from Phnom Penh straight through to Ho Chi Minh City via Moc Bai (about 60km northwest of Ho Chi Minh; see p.124–125), or take a local bus to the border and continue by share taxi. The other option is to cross at Vinh Xuong or Tinh Bien (respectively 30km north and 25km west of Chau Doc in the Mekong Delta). Vinh Xuong is the most popular crossing, as it entails a cheap boat ride (around $10) from Chau Doc to Phnom Penh, organized through Ho Chi Minh City's budget tour operators or through hotels in Chau Doc.

As long as you have a valid visa, crossing these borders is generally not a problem. Note that most border gates are open from around 7am to 5–6pm and may also close for an hour over lunch. As yet none of the crossings offers official exchange facilities, but you'll usually find someone willing to change money on the black market, albeit at a bad rate. Alternatively, you can always pay for things in dollars until you reach a bank.

Red tape and visas

All foreign nationals need a visa to enter Vietnam, with the exception of Thai, Malaysian and Philippine passport-holders travelling to Vietnam for less than a month. Tourist visas are generally valid for thirty days and for a single entry, though some embassies issue visas for three months or longer and may also issue multiple-entry visas. A standard thirty-day visa costs the local equivalent of US$40–100, depending on how quickly you want it processed.

The majority of visitors apply for a visa in their country of residence, either from the embassy direct (see p.20), or through a specialist visa agent or tour agent. Processing normally takes around a week, though many embassies now also offer a more expensive "express" service. To be on the safe side, it's best to allow several weeks as delays and mistakes can occur (check the details carefully on receipt). For people travelling via neighbouring Asian countries, Bangkok is still the most popular place to apply for a Vietnamese visa, since it's relatively straightforward (1–5 working days; around US$55–80), though the embassy in Phnom Penh, Cambodia, has a reputation for being quick, helpful and cheap.

To apply for a tourist visa, you have to submit two **application forms** with two passport-sized photographs and the fee. The visa shows specific start and end **dates** indicating the period of validity within which you can enter and leave the country.

Business visas are valid for one month upwards and can be issued for multiple entry, though you'll need a sponsoring office in Vietnam to underwrite your application.

One-year **student visas** are relatively easy to get hold of if you enrol, for example, on a Vietnamese language course at one of the universities; you'll be required to attend a minimum number of classes per week to qualify. It's easiest to arrange it in advance, but you can enter Vietnam on a tourist visa and apply for student status later – the only downside is that you may have to leave the country in order to get the visa stamp.

Special circumstances affect **overseas Vietnamese** holding a foreign passport. Questions should be directed to the Vietnamese embassy in your country of residence.

Certain local tour agents are now authorized to issue **visas on arrival** at Hanoi, Ho Chi Minh and Da Nang international airports. At the time of writing these include Ann's Tourist in Hanoi (see p.405) and Ho Chi Minh City (see p.126), Danatours and the *Furama Resort* in Da Nang (see p.298 & p.300 respectively); note that the *Furama* only handles applications for those staying at the hotel. Getting a visa on arrival need not be any more expensive (prices range from US$30 to US$90 for a one-month tourist visa), but check carefully to make sure you're quoted a price including the visa and not just the handling fee. There's also an element of risk since you are reliant on the agency completing the paperwork in time and meeting you at the airport. However, it can be handy if there is no Vietnamese embassy in your home country. The agency will need a photocopy of your passport, your full name, date of birth, date and time of arrival in Vietnam, flight details and a fax number to which they will send an "invitation letter" saying you have approval to enter the country. You need to show this letter to the immigration authorities on arrival. Some agencies ask for payment in advance (by credit card or bank transfer), while in other cases you pay at the airport – make sure you bring enough dollars with you. While some agencies are able to process the application in two days, allow at least one week to be on the safe side.

On **arrival** at the airport or border immigration desk you'll need to fill in an Arrival and Departure Card. The yellow copy of this form, which will be returned to you, is often required when registering at hotels and has to be submitted when you eventually leave the country. As there's a risk of leaving it at a hotel, having a photocopy's not a bad idea – it won't be accepted in lieu of the original, but may help streamline things in case of loss.

If you should lose your passport, on the other hand, first go to your embassy in Hanoi (or consulate in Ho Chi Minh City) for a replacement. Then you need to get a new visa from the Immigration Department (see "Listings", p.404 & p.122 respectively).

Visa extensions

In recent years the possibility of getting a **visa extension** has swung back and forth from relatively easy to impossible, so it's best to check the latest situation with the embassy or a specialist tour agent before arriving in Vietnam. At the time of writing, thirty-day extensions were being issued fairly readily in Hanoi, Ho Chi Minh, Nha Trang, Da Nang, Hué and Hoi An. Some people have managed to obtain second and third extensions, usually in Hanoi and Ho Chi Minh City. Applications have to be made via a tour agent. In general they take two or three days to process and it costs US$25 for the first one-month extension.

Holders of **business visas** can apply for an extension only through the office that sponsored their original visa, backed up with reasons as to why an extension is necessary.

Incidentally, **overstaying** your visa will result in fines of between US$10 and US$50, depending how long you overstay and the mood of the immigration official, and is not recommended.

Vietnamese embassies and consulates

A full list of Vietnamese embassies and consulates is available on the Ministry of Foreign Affairs website: ⓦ www.mofa.gov.vn.

Australia Embassy: 6 Timbarra Crescent, O'Malley, Canberra, ACT 2606 ☏ 02/6286 6059,

ⓦ www.au.vnembassy.org; Consulate: 489 New South Head Rd, Double Bay, NSW 2028 ☏ 02/9327 1912, ⓔ vnconsul@ihug.com.au.
Cambodia Embassy: 436 Blvd Preach, Monivong, Phnom Penh ☏ 023/362 741, ⓔ embvnpp @camnet.com.kh. Consulates: Sihanoukville ☏ 034/1534 5361, ⓔ consul@camintel.com; Road No.3, Batambang ☏ 053/952 894, ⓔ lsqvnbat@camintel.com.
Canada 470 Wilbrod St, Ottawa K1N 6M8 ☏ 613/236-0772, ⓦ www.vietnamembassy -canada.ca.
China Embassy: 32 Guang Hua Lu, Jian Guo Men Wai, Beijing 100600 ☏ 10/6532 1155, ⓔ vinaemba@mailhost.cinet.com.cn. Consulates: 2F Hotel Landmark B Building North, Qiaoguang Rd (Haizhu Square), Guang Zhou ☏ 20/8330 5916, ⓔ tlsqvn@mx2.gd.cei.gov.cn; 15F Great Smart Tower, 230 Wanchai Rd, Hong Kong ☏ 022/591 4510, ⓔ vnconsul@netvigator.com.
Ireland Contact UK office (see below).
Lao PDR Embassy: 1 That Luang Rd, Vientiane ☏ 021/413400, ⓔ dsqvn@laotel.net. Consulates: 31 Ban Pha Bat, Pakxe ☏ 031/212 058, ⓔ ksvnps@laotel.com; 118 Sisavang Rd, Savannakhet ☏ 041/212418, ⓔ tlsxavan@laotel.com.
Malaysia 4 Persiaran Stonor, 50450 Kuala Lumpur ☏ 03/2148 4534, ⓔ daisevn@putra.net.my.
New Zealand Contact embassy in Canberra, Australia (see above).
Singapore 10 Leedon Park, Singapore 267887 ☏ 462 5938, ⓔ vnemb@singnet.com.sg.
Thailand Embassy: 83/1 Wireless Rd, Bangkok 10330 ☏ 02/251 5836, ⓔ vnembassy@bkk .a-net.net.th. Consulate: 65/6 Chatapadung, Khonkaen 40000 ☏ 043/242190.
UK 12–14 Victoria Rd, London W8 5RD ☏ 020/7937 1912, ⓔ vp@dsqvnlondon.demon.co.uk.
US Embassy: 1233 20th St NW, Suite 400, Washington DC 20036 ☏ 202/861-0737, ⓦ www.vietnamembassy-usa.org. Consulate: 1700 California St, Suite 430, San Francisco, CA 94109 ☏ 415/922-1707, ⓦ www.vietnamconsulate-sf .org.

Information, websites and maps

Tourist information on Vietnam is at a premium. The Vietnamese government maintains a handful of tourist promotion offices and a smattering of accredited travel agencies around the globe, most of which can supply you with only the most general information. A better source of information, much of it based on firsthand experiences, is the Internet, with numerous sites around to help you plan your visit. Maps of Vietnam are widely available, although regular name-changing means that country maps tend to give different names for the same settlement – especially for smaller villages.

Information

In Vietnam itself there's a frustrating dearth of free and impartial advice. The state-run **tourist offices** – under the auspices of either the Vietnam National Administration of Tourism (Ⓦwww.vietnamtourism.com) or the local provincial organization – are thinly disguised tour agents, profit-making concerns which don't take kindly to being treated as information bureaux. In any case, Western concepts of information don't necessarily apply here – bus timetables, for example, simply don't exist. The most you're likely to get is a glossy brochure detailing their tours and affiliated hotels.

You'll generally have more luck approaching one of the many **private tour agencies**, including the so-called "travellers' cafés", operating in all the major tourist spots (see "Listings" for individual cities in the Guide), where staff have become accustomed to Westerners' demands for advice.

Another useful source of information, including restaurant and hotel listings as well as feature articles, is the growing number of **English-language magazines**, such as *Vietnam Discovery*, *Time Out*, *The Guide* and *Vietnam Pathfinder* (see p.55).

There's also now a government-run **telephone information service** with some English-speaking staff who will answer all manner of questions – if you can get through, since the lines are often busy. Call ☎1080 in Hanoi, Ho Chi Minh City, Haiphong and Da Nang, and ☎108 elsewhere. There is a minimal charge for this service.

Vietnamese government tourist offices abroad

The number of tourist offices abroad is limited but includes:

Singapore 101 Upper Cross St #02-44, Peoples Park Center, Singapore 0105 ☎532 3130.
US 2974 Monticello Drive, Falls Church, VA 22042 ☎703/641-7738, Ⓔdreese@erols.com.

Websites

There's ever more Vietnam coverage on the **Internet** as local hotels, tour agents and other businesses gradually go online. Most include a smattering of background information, but on the whole you're better off browsing sites generated by the overseas Vietnamese community, academics, foreign tour companies and returning travellers. Bear in mind that there's no guarantee the information is either accurate or up to date. However, persistent combing of links pages and use of search engines (among the best are Ⓦwww.google.com and Ⓦwww.dogpile.com) may turn up the information you're looking for. Another option is to post a message on the rec.travel.asia **newsgroup**.

Web or email addresses are given where available throughout the Guide, while a few of the more useful and well-established general sites are detailed below.

Travel resources

Ⓦ**www.thingsasian.com** Informative and entertaining site with an emphasis on culture, history and travel.
Ⓦ**www.vietnamadventures.com** Another nicely

designed site looking at Vietnamese customs and culture, as well as having features on tourist destinations around the country.

Ⓦ**www.vietnamtourism.com** The site of the Vietnam National Administration of Tourism contains plenty of potentially useful background and tourist information, though it's not as up to date as it should be.

Ⓦ**weather.yahoo.com** Current weather information and five-day forecasts for over thirty Vietnamese cities.

General resources

Ⓦ**coombs.anu.edu.au** The Vietnam Virtual Library is a large, well-organized site with over 1000 Vietnam links – still useful even though it's in need of updating.

Ⓦ**www.ibiblio.org/vietnam** To whet your appetite, this huge picture gallery covers art, people, history, monuments and scenery.

Ⓦ**www.mofa.gov.vn** The Ministry of Foreign Affairs site is good for news and its list of Vietnamese embassies and consulates. Other information is not always updated regularly.

Ⓦ**www.vietnamembassy-usa.org** Vietnam's US Embassy posts general background and business information plus a list of embassies and consulates and a selection of links.

Ⓦ**www.vietgate.net** Selective, searchable listing of links, but best for its online dictionary.

Media resources

Ⓦ**vietnamnews.vnagency.com.vn** A round-up of the daily news from the online edition of *Vietnam News*.

Ⓦ**www.vir.com.vn** Catch up with what's going on in the business world in the weekly *Vietnam Investment Review*.

Ⓦ**www.vneconomy.com.vn** Monthly overview of the major business stories from the *Vietnam Economic Times* online.

Environmental resources

Ⓦ**www.birdlifevietnam.com** Good background information and links to related sites from Birdlife International's Vietnam office.

Ⓦ**www.wcmc.org.uk/infoserv/countryp /vietnam** The World Conservation Monitoring Centre runs a huge site with everything you might want to know about the environment and conservation in Vietnam.

Travel advice

Australian Department of Foreign Affairs
Ⓦwww.dfat.gov.au. Advice and reports on unstable countries and regions.
British Foreign & Commonwealth Office
Ⓦwww.fco.gov.uk. Constantly updated advice for travellers on circumstances affecting safety in over 130 countries.
Canadian Department of Foreign Affairs
Ⓦwww.dfait-maeci.gc.ca/menu-e.asp. Country-by-country travel advice.
US State Department Travel Advisories
Ⓦtravel.state.gov/travel_warnings.html. Website providing "consular information sheets" detailing the dangers of travelling in most countries of the world.

Maps

The best general maps are either the "International Travel Map of Vietnam" (1:1,000,000) or Nelles 1:1,500,000 map of Vietnam, Laos and Cambodia. The 1:2,000,000 "Vietnam, Cambodia & Laos World Travel Map" from Bartholomew isn't too bad either, though it lacks any details of tourist attractions, or pick up a copy of Saigontourist's "Vietnam Tourist Map" (1:1,500,000), updated annually, from one of their branches in Vietnam. All but the Nelles map feature plans of Ho Chi Minh City and Hanoi. If you need larger-scale **city maps** than the ones we provide in this book (which also show our recommended hotels and restaurants), reasonable ones are available from street vendors and newsstands in Hanoi, Ho Chi Minh, Hué and other major cities or tourist destinations.

Map outlets

In the US and Canada

Adventurous Traveler.com US ☎1-800/282-3963, Ⓦwww.adventuroustraveler.com.
Book Passage 51 Tamal Vista Blvd, Corte Madera, CA 94925 ☎1-800/999-7909, Ⓦwww.bookpassage.com.
Distant Lands 56 S Raymond Ave, Pasadena, CA 91105 ☎1-800/310-3220, Ⓦwww.distantlands.com.
Elliot Bay Book Company 101 S Main St, Seattle, WA 98104 ☎1-800/962-5311, Ⓦwww.elliotbaybook.com.

Globe Corner Bookstore 28 Church St, Cambridge, MA 02138 ☎1-800/358-6013, ⓦwww.globercorner.com.

Map Link 30 S La Patera Lane, Unit 5, Santa Barbara, CA 93117 ☎1-800/962-1394, ⓦwww.maplink.com.

Rand McNally US ☎1-800/333-0136, ⓦwww.randmcnally.com. Around thirty stores across the US; dial ext 2111 or check the website for the nearest location.

The Travel Bug Bookstore 2667 W Broadway, Vancouver V6K 2G2 ☎604/737-1122, ⓦwww.swifty.com/tbug.

World of Maps 1235 Wellington St, Ottawa, Ontario K1Y 3A3 ☎1-800/214-8524, ⓦwww.worldofmaps.com.

In the UK and Ireland

Blackwell's Map and Travel Shop 50 Broad St, Oxford OX1 3BQ ☎01865/793 550, ⓦwww.maps.blackwell.co.uk.

Easons Bookshop 40 O'Connell St, Dublin 1 ☎01/858 3881, ⓦwww.eason.ie.

Heffers Map and Travel 20 Trinity St, Cambridge CB2 1TJ ☎01865/333 536, ⓦwww.heffers.co.uk.

Hodges Figgis Bookshop 56–58 Dawson St, Dublin 2 ☎01/677 4754.

The Map Shop 30a Belvoir St, Leicester LE1 6QH ☎0116/247 1400, ⓦwww.mapshopleicester.co.uk.

National Map Centre 22–24 Caxton St, London SW1H 0QU ☎020/7222 2466, ⓦwww.mapsnmc.co.uk.

Newcastle Map Centre 55 Grey St, Newcastle-upon-Tyne NE1 6EF ☎0191/261 5622.

Ordnance Survey Ireland Phoenix Park, Dublin 8 ☎01/802 5300, ⓦwww.osi.ie.

Ordnance Survey of Northern Ireland Colby House, Stranmillis Ct, Belfast BT9 5BJ ☎028/9025 5755, ⓦwww.osni.gov.uk.

Stanfords 12–14 Long Acre, London WC2E 9LP ☎020/7836 1321, ⓦwww.stanfords.co.uk, Ⓔsales@stanfords.co.uk.

The Travel Bookshop 13–15 Blenheim Crescent, London W11 2EE ☎020/7229 5260, ⓦwww.thetravelbookshop.co.uk.

In Australia and New Zealand

Mapland 372 Little Bourke St, Melbourne, Victoria 3000 ☎03/9670 4383, ⓦwww.mapland.com.au.

The Map Shop 6–10 Peel St, Adelaide, SA 5000 ☎08/8231 2033, ⓦwww.mapshop.net.au.

MapWorld 173 Gloucester St, Christchurch ☎0800/627 967 or 03/374 5399, ⓦwww.mapworld.co.nz.

Perth Map Centre 900 Hay St, Perth, WA 6000 ☎08/9322 5733, ⓦwww.perthmap.com.au.

Specialty Maps 46 Albert St, Auckland 1001 ☎09/307 2217, ⓦwww.specialtymaps.co.nz.

Insurance

Most people find it essential to take out a good travel insurance policy before travelling to cover against theft, loss and illness or injury. Before paying for a new policy, however, it's worth checking whether you are already covered: some all-risks home insurance policies may cover your possessions when overseas, and many private medical schemes include cover when abroad. In Canada, provincial health plans usually provide partial cover for medical mishaps overseas, while holders of official student/teacher/youth cards in Canada and the US are entitled to meagre accident coverage and hospital in-patient benefits. Students will often find that their student health coverage extends over the vacations and for one term beyond the date of last enrolment.

After exhausting the possibilities above, you might want to contact a specialist travel insurance company, or consider the travel insurance deal we offer (see box overleaf). A typical travel insurance policy usually provides cover for the loss of baggage, tickets and – up to a certain limit – cash or cheques, as well as cancellation or curtailment of your journey. Most of them exclude so-called dangerous sports unless an extra premium is paid: in

Rough Guides travel insurance

Rough Guide offers its own low-cost travel insurance, especially customized for our statistically low-risk readers by a leading British broker, provided by the American International Group (AIG) and registered with the British regulatory body, GISC (the General Insurance Standards Council).

There are five main Rough Guides insurance plans: **No Frills** for the bare minimum for secure travel; **Essential**, which provides decent all-round cover; **Premier** for comprehensive cover with a wide range of benefits; **Extended Stay** for cover lasting two months to a year; and **Annual Multi-Trip**, a cost-effective way of getting Premier cover if you travel more than once a year. Premier, Annual Multi-Trip and Extended Stay policies can be supplemented by a "Hazardous Pursuits Extension" if you plan to indulge in sports considered dangerous, such as scuba-diving or trekking.

For a policy quote, call the Rough Guide Insurance Line: toll-free in the UK ☎0800/015 0906 or ☎+44 1392 314 665 from elsewhere. Alternatively, get an online quote at ⓦ**www.roughguides.com/insurance**.

Vietnam this can mean scuba-diving, whitewater rafting, windsurfing and trekking. Many policies can be chopped and changed to exclude coverage you don't need – for example, sickness and accident benefits can often be excluded or included at will. If you do take medical coverage, ascertain whether benefits will be paid as treatment proceeds or only after return home, and whether there is a 24-hour medical emergency number. When securing baggage cover, make sure that the per-article limit – typically under £500/US$750 – will cover your most valuable possession. If you need to make a claim, you should keep receipts for medicines and medical treatment, and in the event that you have anything stolen, you must obtain an official statement from the police.

Health

Vietnam's health problems read like a dictionary of tropical medicine. Diseases that are under control elsewhere in Southeast Asia have been sustained here by poverty, dietary deficiencies, poor healthcare and the disruption caused by half a century of war. However, by coming prepared and taking a few simple precautions while in the country, you're unlikely to come down with anything worse than a cold or a dose of travellers' diarrhoea.

If you do get ill in Vietnam, international clinics in Hanoi and Ho Chi Minh City can provide diagnosis and treatment or sound advice. While you shouldn't run to a doctor with every headache or bout of diarrhoea, in general it's far better to seek medical advice at an early stage rather than attempt to treat yourself with potentially dangerous drugs or leave it too late.

Before you go

When planning your trip it's wise to visit a **doctor** as early as possible, preferably at least two months before you leave, to allow time to complete any recommended courses of **vaccinations**. If you have any long-standing medical conditions or particular health concerns or are travelling with young children, consult your doctor and take any required medications with you. It's also advisable to have a trouble-shooting **dental check-up** – and remember that you generally need to start taking **anti-malarial tablets** at least one week before your departure.

For up-to-the-minute information, it may be worth visiting a specialized **travel clinic** (see overleaf); most clinics also sell travel-associated accessories, including mosquito nets and first-aid kits.

Vaccinations

No **vaccinations** are required for Vietnam (except yellow fever if you're coming directly from an area where the disease is endemic), but typhoid and hepatitis A jabs are recommended; it's also worth ensuring you're up to date with boosters such as tetanus and polio. Additional injections to consider, depending on the season and risk of exposure, are hepatitis B, Japanese encephalitis, meningitis and rabies. All these immunizations can be obtained at international clinics in Ho Chi Minh City and Hanoi, but it's less hassle and usually cheaper to get them done at home. Get all your shots recorded on an **International Certificate of Vaccination** and carry this with your passport when travelling abroad.

Typhoid vaccine is reasonably effective and can be administered either by injection or orally. Most medical authorities no longer recommend the **cholera** vaccine for tourists since it has proved only fifty percent effective and can provoke a severe reaction.

Hepatitis is an inflammation of the liver in which the most distinctive characteristic is yellowing of the eyes and skin, usually preceded by tiredness, high fever, and pain in the upper right abdomen. There are many different strains but the most common are hepatitis A and B, both of which can be prevented to a large extent by vaccination. For protection against **hepatitis A**, which is spread by contaminated food and water, the vaccine is expensive but extremely effective – an initial injection followed by a booster after six to twelve months provides immunity for up to ten years. If only gammaglobulin is available, leave the injection as late as possible before departure as it wears off after three to six months, depending on the dosage. **Hepatitis B**, like the HIV virus, can be passed on through unprotected sexual contact, blood transfusions and dirty needles. The very effective vaccine (three injections over six months) is recommended for anyone in a high-risk category, including those travelling extensively in rural areas for prolonged periods, with access to only basic medical care. It's also now possible – and cheaper – to have a combined vaccination against both hepatitis A and B: the course comprises three injections over six months.

The risks of contracting **Japanese encephalitis** are extremely small, but, as the disease is untreatable, those travelling for a month or more in the countryside, especially in the north during and soon after the summer rainy season (June–Nov), should consider immunization. The course consists of two injections at two-week intervals plus a booster for longer protection, but is not recommended for those with liver, heart or kidney disorders, or for multiple-allergy sufferers. If your plans include long stays in remote areas your doctor may also recommend vaccination against **meningitis** (a single shot) and **rabies**. The pre-exposure vaccine for rabies consists of two injections over a month with a booster a year later if further protection is required; if bitten, you still need to have shots, but fewer than otherwise – and it gives you a little more time (5–7 days) to reach medical help.

Medical resources for travellers

Websites

Ⓦ **health.yahoo.com** Information on specific diseases and conditions, drugs and herbal remedies, as well as advice from health experts.

Ⓦ **www.fitfortravel.scot.nhs.uk** UK NHS website carrying information about travel-related diseases and how to avoid them.

Ⓦ **www.istm.org** The website of the International Society for Travel Medicine, with a full list of clinics specializing in international travel health.

Ⓦ **www.tmvc.com.au** Contains a list of all Travellers Medical and Vaccination Centres in Australia, New Zealand and Southeast Asia, plus general information on travel health.

Ⓦwww.tripprep.com Travel Health Online provides an online-only database of vaccinations and medical service-provider information.

Travel clinics in the UK and Ireland

British Airways Travel Clinics 213 Piccadilly, London W1 (Mon–Fri 9.30am–6pm, Sat 10am–5pm, no appointment necessary); 101 Cheapside, London EC2 (hours as above Mon–Fri only, appointment required) ⓉT 0845/600 2236; Ⓦwww.britishairways.com/travel/healthclinintro. Vaccinations, tailored advice from an online database and a complete range of travel healthcare products.
Communicable Diseases Unit Brownlee Centre, Glasgow G12 0YN ⓉT 0141/211 1062. Travel vaccinations including yellow fever.
Dun Laoghaire Medical Centre 5 Northumberland Ave, Dun Laoghaire, County Dublin ⓉT 01/280 4996, ⒻF 280 5603. Advice on medical matters abroad.
Hospital for Tropical Diseases Travel Clinic 2nd floor, Mortimer Market Centre, off Capper St, London WC1E 6AU Mon–Fri 9am–5pm by appointment only; ⓉTn 020/7388 9600, Ⓦwww.masta.org. A consultation costs £15, which is waived if you have your injections here. A recorded Health Line (ⓉT 0906/133 7733, 50p per min) gives hints on hygiene and illness prevention as well as listing appropriate immunizations.
Liverpool School of Tropical Medicine Pembroke Place, Liverpool L3 5QA ⓉT 0151/708 9393. Walk-in clinic Mon–Fri 1–4pm; appointment required for yellow fever, but not for other jabs.
MASTA (Medical Advisory Service for Travellers Abroad) 40 regional clinics (call ⓉT 0870/606 2782 for the nearest). Also operates a pre-recorded 24-hour Travellers' Health Line (UK t0906/822 4100, 60p per min), giving written information tailored to your journey by return of post.
Nomad Pharmacy surgeries 40 Bernard St, London WC1N 1LE; and 3–4 Wellington Terrace, Turnpike Lane, London N8 0PX (Mon–Fri 9.30am–6pm, ⓉT 020/7833 4114 to book vaccination appointment). They give advice free if you go in person, or their telephone helpline is t0906/863 3414 (60p per minute). They can give information tailored to your travel needs.
Trailfinders Immunization clinics (no appointments necessary) at 194 Kensington High St, London W8 7RG (Mon–Fri 9am–5pm except Thurs to 6pm, Sat 9.30am–4pm; ⓉT 020/7938 3999).
Travel Health Centre Department of International Health and Tropical Medicine, Royal College of Surgeons in Ireland, Mercers Medical Centre, Stephen's St Lower, Dublin 2 ⓉT 01/402 2337. Expert pre-trip advice and inoculations.

Travel Medicine Services PO Box 254, 16 College St, Belfast BT1 6BT ⓉT 028/9031 5220. Offers medical advice before a trip and help afterwards in the event of a tropical disease.
Tropical Medical Bureau Grafton Buildings, 34 Grafton St, Dublin 2 ⓉT 01/671 9200, Ⓦtmb.exodus.ie.

Travel clinics in the US and Canada

Canadian Society for International Health 1 Nicholas St, Suite 1105, Ottawa, Ontario K1N 7B7 ⓉT 613/241-5785, Ⓦwww.csih.org. Distributes a free pamphlet, *Health Information for Canadian Travellers*, containing an extensive list of travel health centres in Canada.
Centers for Disease Control 1600 Clifton Rd NE, Atlanta, GA 30333 ⓉT 1-800/311-3435 or 404/639-3534, Ⓦwww.cdc.gov. Publishes outbreak warnings, suggested inoculations, precautions and other background information. Useful website plus International Travelers Hotline on t1-877/FYI-TRIP.
International Association for Medical Assistance to Travellers (IAMAT) 417 Center St, Lewiston, NY 14092 ⓉT 716/754-4883, Ⓦwww.iamat.org, and 40 Regal Rd, Guelph, Ontario N1K 1B5 ⓉT 519/836-0102. A non-profit organization supported by donations, it can provide a list of English-speaking doctors in Vietnam, climate charts and leaflets on various diseases and inoculations.
International SOS Assistance Eight Neshaminy Interplex Suite 207, Trevose, USA 19053-6956 ⓉT 1-800/523-8930, Ⓦwww.intsos.com. Members receive pre-trip medical referral info, as well as overseas emergency services designed to complement travel insurance coverage.
MEDJET Assistance ⓉT 1-800/9MEDJET, Ⓦwww .medjetassistance.com. Annual membership program for travellers ($175 for individuals, $275 for families) that, in the event of illness or injury, will fly members home or to the hospital of their choice in a medically equipped and staffed jet.
Travel Medicine ⓉT 1-800/TRAVMED, Ⓦwww .travmed.com. Sells first-aid kits, mosquito netting, water filters, reference books and other health-related travel products.
Travelers Medical Center 31 Washington Square West, New York, NY 10011 ⓉT 212/982-1600. Consultation service on immunizations and treatment of diseases for people going to developing countries.

Travel clinics in Australia and New Zealand

Travellers' Medical and Vaccination Centres 27–29 Gilbert Place, Adelaide, SA 5000 ⓉT 08/8212 7522, ⒺⒺ adelaide@traveldoctor.com.au; 1/170

Queen St, Auckland ℡ 09/373 3531, ℮ auckland
@traveldoctor.co.nz; 5/247 Adelaide St, Brisbane,
Qld 4000 ℡ 07/3221 9066, ℮ brisbane
@traveldoctor.com.au; 5/8–10 Hobart Place,
Canberra, ACT 2600 ℡ 02/6257 7156, ℮ canberra
@traveldoctor.com.au; Moorhouse Medical Centre,
9 Washington Way, Christchurch ℡ 03/379 4000,
℮ christchurch@traveldoctor.co.nz; 270 Sandy Bay
Rd, Sandy Bay, Hobart, Tas 7005 ℡ 03/6223 7577,
℮ hobart@traveldoctor.com.au; 2/393 Little
Bourke St, Melbourne, Vic 3000 ℡ 03/9602 5788,
℮ melbourne@traveldoctor.com.au; Level 7,
Dymocks Bldg, 428 George St, Sydney, NSW 2000
℡ 02/9221 7133, ℮ sydney@traveldoctor.com.au;
Shop 15, Grand Arcade, 14–16 Willis St, Wellington
℡ 04/473 0991, ℮ wellington@traveldoctor.co.nz.

General precautions

There's no point in getting paranoid about
your health while travelling in Vietnam, but
it's worth being aware of the dangers and
taking several common-sense **precautions**.
The most important measures are to keep
your resistance high and allow adequate
time to acclimatize to the heat, humidity and
an unfamiliar diet. Ensure you eat sufficient
quantities and maintain a balanced diet in
order to keep up mineral and vitamin
intakes; eating lots of peeled fresh fruit
helps, though you may also want to bring
some multi-vitamin and mineral tablets to
make up for any shortfalls. If you tend to
sweat a lot, add a little extra salt to your food
and drink plenty of bottled water or hot tea.
In tropical climates it's easy to get run-down
and become more susceptible to whatever's
around, especially if you're doing a lot of
travelling.

Personal hygiene is one area you can
control and it pays to be vigilant in a climate
where bacteria thrive. Wash your hands frequently, especially before eating, and avoid
sharing drinks, cigarettes or toothbrushes.
Infections take hold easily, so treat even the
smallest cuts, scratches and bites with care:
clean thoroughly with boiled water, apply
iodine or antiseptic (a spray is useful) and
then keep them dry and covered. Change
dressings frequently and repeat the process
after washing as the water may be contaminated. It's advisable to wear shoes at all
times, and don't slosh around in lakes and
irrigation canals, since they often harbour
snails which carry bilharzia (river blindness).

Bottled **water** is plentiful in Vietnam and
there should be no difficulty finding it, even in
the remoter regions (for more on water, see
the box overleaf). As regards **food**, the two
most important precautions are to eat at
places that are busy and look clean, and to
stick to fresh, thoroughly cooked foods. Just
because a restaurant is expensive doesn't
mean it's necessarily safe, and outside the
main tourist centres, you're generally better
off sticking to Vietnamese dishes. Ingredients
tend to be ultra-fresh, but if a dish seems
tired or looks as if it might have been reheat-
ed give it a miss, and send back anything
undercooked or lukewarm. Food that is
boiled or fried in front of you – such as bowls
of steaming-hot *pho* (soup) – is a good bet.
Seafood is such a feature of Vietnamese cuisine that it's a shame to miss out, but it pays
to be extra wary of shellfish. Fresh fruit
you've peeled yourself is safe; other
uncooked foods such as salads and raw
vegetables can be risky, but as they're often
an integral part of Vietnamese dishes it's difficult to avoid them entirely. Ice creams and
yoghurts from reputable outlets in the main
cities shouldn't cause problems.

If it becomes essential for you to have an
injection or a transfusion in Vietnam, try to
make sure that new, sterile equipment is
used; blood for transfusions should come
from a known donor rather than a blood
bank. Don't undergo acupuncture, tattooing
or the like unless you're certain the equipment is absolutely sterile.

Following these precautions will greatly
increase your chances of staying healthy.
However, if you do fall ill and are concerned
by the symptoms, get yourself to Hanoi or
Ho Chi Minh City for diagnosis.

Finally, remember that some of the illnesses you can pick up in Vietnam may not show
themselves immediately. If you become ill
within a year of returning home, tell whoever
treats you where you have been.

Intestinal troubles

As P.J. O'Rourke helpfully pointed out, travel
in developing countries "entails an extraordinary amount of having to go to the bathroom". **Diarrhoea** is the most common ail-
ment to afflict travellers, often in a mild form
while your stomach adapts to an unfamiliar

diet. If there are no other major symptoms, then it will probably all be over in two or three days and shouldn't require any treatment. The sudden onset of diarrhoea accompanied by severe stomach cramps and vomiting could indicate food poisoning, which should also run its course within a couple of days. In either case, it's essential to drink lots of water and in severe cases replace lost salts by taking oral rehydration solution (commonly known as ORS); this is especially important with young children. Sachets are widely available, or you can make your own ORS by adding half a level teaspoon of salt and at least three of sugar to a litre of cool, bottled or previously boiled water. At the same time avoid milk, greasy or spicy foods, coffee and most fruit, in favour of bland foodstuffs such as eggs, bread, rice, noodles, banana, papaya and soup. Anti-diarrhoea medication tends to undermine the body's own efforts to fight off the infection and masks the symptoms, though tablets such as Lomotil and Imodium can be a useful stop-gap measure if you need to travel. If diarrhoea persists beyond two or three days, is very painful, or if you notice blood or mucus in your stools,

then it could be something more serious and you should seek medical advice.

Dysentery is an intestinal inflammation, indicated by diarrhoea with blood and mucus plus abdominal pain. There are two main types to be wary of: bacillary and amoebic. **Bacillary dysentery** has an acute onset with fever, discomfort and vomiting, as well as serious abdominal pains with watery, bloody diarrhoea. In mild cases spontaneous recovery occurs within a week, but severe illness may require antibiotics. **Amoebic dysentery** is the more serious as bouts last for several weeks and usually recur. Symptoms appear gradually and are marked by bloody faeces accompanied by cramps in the lower abdomen, but no fever or vomiting. If left untreated, amoebic cysts enter the bloodstream and may cause long-term problems, but a prompt course of antibiotics should be completely effective.

Two symptoms distinguish **giardia**: highly sulphuric belches and farts, plus discoloured stools but with no sign of blood or pus. Another strong indication is urgent but inconsistent diarrhoea, which may lay you low one day and leave you feeling fine the

What about the water?

The simple rule is don't drink river **water** in Vietnam, nor the tap water, with the exception of one or two top hotels which now offer filtered tap water. It's wise also to resist the temptation to have **ice** in your drinks except, again, in top hotels and other trustworthy places. Contaminated water is a major cause of sickness due to the presence of pathogenic organisms: bacteria, viruses and cysts. These microorganisms cause ailments and diseases such as diarrhoea, gastroenteritis, typhoid, cholera, dysentery, poliomyelitis, hepatitis A and giardia – and can be present even when water looks clean and safe to drink.

Fortunately there are plenty of alternative drinks around: hot tea is always on offer, while cheap, **bottled water** and carbonated drinks are widely available. When buying bottled water check the seal is unbroken and the water is clear, as bottles are occasionally refilled from the tap. Tap water in Hanoi and Ho Chi Minh City is chlorinated and most travellers use it for brushing their teeth without problem, but this is not recommended in rural areas, where water is often untreated. Particular care should be taken anywhere where there is flooding as raw sewage may be washed into the water system. The only time you're likely to be out of reach of bottled water is trekking into remote areas, when you'll be relying on **boiled water**. Boiling for ten minutes gets rid of most bacteria in water but at least twenty minutes is needed to kill amoebic cysts, a cause of dysentery. To be safe you may wish to use some kind of **chemical sterilization**. Iodine purification tablets or solutions are more effective than chlorine compounds, though still leave a nasty aftertaste – using a filter afterwards makes the water slightly more palatable. Note that iodine products are unsuitable for pregnant women, babies and people with thyroid problems.

next. Again the disease is treatable with antibiotics under medical supervision.

Typhoid and cholera are also spread via contaminated food and water, generally in localized epidemics. **Typhoid** symptoms are varied but usually include high fever, headaches, constipation and then diarrhoea in the later stages. The disease is highly infectious and needs immediate medical treatment but it's also difficult to diagnose. The first sign of **cholera** is the abrupt but painless onset of watery, copious and unpredictable diarrhoea, combined later with nausea, vomiting and muscle cramps. It's the rapid dehydration caused by diarrhoea that's the main danger rather than the intestinal infection itself. However bad the diarrhoea and vomiting, you can treat cholera well with plenty of oral rehydration solutions, but if you can't take enough fluids seek medical help.

Finally, bear in mind that if you are suffering from diarrhoea, oral drugs, such as anti-malaria or contraceptive pills, pass through your system too quickly to be absorbed effectively.

Mosquito-borne diseases

Both the Red River and Mekong deltas (including Hanoi and Ho Chi Minh City) have few incidences of malaria. The coastal plain north of Nha Trang is also considered relatively safe. Malaria occurs frequently in the highlands and rural areas, where the majority of cases involve the most dangerous strain, *Plasmodium falciparum*, which can be fatal if not treated promptly.

The key preventive measure is to avoid getting bitten by mosquitoes (which carry the disease), but if you're travelling in high-risk areas it's advisable to take **preventive tablets**. The weekly drug mefloquine (Lariam) is the most effective of these, since in Vietnam the parasite is now largely resistant to chloroquine and fansidar. However, mefloquine has some nasty side-effects, including dizzy spells, nausea and neuropsychiatric disturbances, which can persist even after you've stopped taking the drug; ensure you discuss any concerns you might have with your prescribing physician. Women in the first trimester of pregnancy or while breast-feeding should avoid mefloquine, and it's also important not to get pregnant for three months after taking the drug. Note that you need to start taking tablets at least a week before exposure to gauge any adverse side-effects, and continue for at least three weeks after leaving a malarial region.

A slightly less effective alternative to mefloquin is Doxycycline – essentially an antibiotic – which is taken daily after food. Note that it is only effective against the *Plasmodium falciparum* parasite (see above), so you still need to take other precautions. The side-effects are increased sensitivity to sun – so you need to use a good sunblock – and vaginal candidiasis (thrush). It's also not advised for children under 12 and women who are pregnant or breast-feeding. Tablets should be taken two days before entering the malarial region and continued for four weeks afterwards.

A relatively new drug now on the market is Malarone. It appears to be as effective as mefloquine and Doxycycline against the *falciparum* strain of malaria, with the benefit of few side-effects. The tablets are taken daily at meal times, starting two days before entering a malarial zone and continuing for a week after leaving. Again, the drug should not be taken by pregnant women or nursing mothers.

None of these antimalarials is infallible and it's still possible, though rare if the regime is followed correctly, to contract malaria while taking preventive drugs. If you develop regularly recurring fevers with flu-like **symptoms** of shivering and headaches, you should seek medical advice. A blood test will confirm the diagnosis; if the disease is caught early, treatment can be quick and effective.

Mosquitoes are also responsible for transmitting dengue fever and Japanese encephalitis. The symptoms of **dengue fever** (also known as breakbone fever) are similar to malaria but with more pronounced and severe headaches, together with aching muscles and sometimes with a rash spreading from the trunk onto the limbs and face. It is carried by a variety of mosquitoes active in the daytime (particularly two hours after sunrise and several hours before sunset) and occurs mostly in the south, including Ho Chi Minh City, although the chances of catching it are small. There's no specific cure but most people recover completely after a week of rest, paracetamol and plenty of fluids; aspirin should be avoided as it provokes internal bleeding. However, there is a more dangerous version called dengue haemorrhage fever, which primarily affects children but is extremely rare among foreign visitors to Vietnam. If you notice an unusual tendency to bleed or bruise, seek medical advice immediately.

Japanese encephalitis produces symptoms ranging from mild, non-specific fevers, vomiting and weight loss to severe headaches, delirium and loss of consciousness; in a tiny minority of cases, the disease can prove fatal. It is a seasonal disease, normally occurring from June to September, and is confined to rural areas where pig-farming and rice-growing coexist.

The most important means of combating all mosquito-borne diseases is simply not to get bitten in the first place. Though most mosquitoes lurk all day in dark, steamy forests, humid bathrooms and so on, they tend to be most rampant at dawn and dusk. At these times wear long sleeves, trousers and socks, avoid dark colours and perfumes, which attract mosquitoes, and put **repellent** on all exposed skin. Sprays and lotions containing around thirty to forty percent DEET (diethyltoluamide) are effective and can also be used to treat clothes, but the chemical is toxic: keep it away from eyes and open wounds – and follow the manufacturer's recommendations carefully, particularly with young children. DEET sometimes causes bad dreams, nausea and dizziness, in which case try Mosi-Guard Natural, X-Gnat or Gurkha repellents.

Most hotels and guesthouses provide **sleeping nets**, but you may want to bring your own if you intend to do much trekking in remote areas; a net that hangs from a single point is the most practical. Many nets are already impregnated with pyrethroids (repellant), but need re-treating every six months; all the gear is available from travel clinics (see p.26) and good travel shops. Tuck the edges in well at night, sleep away from the sides and make sure there are no tears in the mesh. Air-conditioning and fans help keep mosquitoes at bay, as do mosquito coils and knockdown insecticide sprays (available locally), though none of these measures is as effective as a decent net.

Bites and creepy-crawlies

Unfortunately, mosquitoes aren't the only things that **bite**. Bed bugs, fleas, lice or scabies can be picked up from dirty bedclothes, though this is relatively unusual in Vietnam. Try not to scratch bites, which easily become septic. Ticks picked up walking through scrub may carry a strain of typhus; carry out regular body inspections and remove ticks promptly.

Rabies is contracted by being bitten, or even licked on broken skin or the eyes, by an infected animal. The best strategy is to give all animals, especially dogs, cats and monkeys, a wide berth. If bitten, wash the wound immediately but gently with soap or detergent and apply alcohol or iodine if possible. Find out as much as you can about the animal, and if there's any chance it might be infected get to a clinic for a course of injections.

Vietnam has several poisonous **snakes** but in general snakes steer clear of humans and it's very rare to get bitten. Avoid walking through long grass or undergrowth, and wear boots when walking off-road. If bitten, immobilize the limb (most snake bites occur on the lower leg) to slow down absorption of the venom and remove any tight-fitting socks or other clothing from around the wound. It's important to seek medical assistance as quickly as possible. It helps if you can take the (dead) snake to be identified, or at least remember what it looked like.

Leeches are more common and, though harmless, can be unpleasant. Long trousers, shirtsleeves and socks help prevent them getting a grip. The best way to get rid of leeches is to burn them off with a lighted match or cigarette; alternatively rub alcohol or salt onto them.

Worms enter the body either via contaminated food, or through the skin, especially the soles of the feet. You may notice worms in your stools, or experience other indications such as mild abdominal pain leading, very rarely, to acute intestinal blockage (roundworm, the most common), an itchy anus (threadworm) or anaemia (hookworm). An infestation is easily treated with worming tablets from a pharmacy.

Heat trouble

If you're not used to travelling in tropical areas it can take a couple of weeks to acclimatize to the high temperatures and humidity, during which time you may feel listless and tire easily. And don't underestimate the strength of the tropical sun: **sunburn** can be avoided by restricting your exposure to the midday sun and liberal use of high-factor sunscreens. Sunglasses help to protect your eyes from damaging rays, while a wide-brimmed hat reduces the risk of sunstroke. Drinking plenty of water will prevent **dehydration**, but if you do become dehydrated – signs are infrequent or irregular urination – drink a salt and sugar solution (see "Intestinal troubles", p.27).

Heat stroke is more serious and may require hospital treatment. Indications are a high temperature, lack of sweating, a fast pulse and red skin. Reducing your body temperature with a lukewarm shower will provide initial relief.

High humidity often causes **heat rashes, prickly heat** and **fungal infections**. Prevention and cure are the same: wear loose clothes made of natural fibres, wash frequently and dry off thoroughly afterwards. Talcum powder helps, particularly zinc oxide-based products (prickly heat powder), as does the use of mild antiseptic soap.

Sexually transmitted diseases

As yet Vietnam carries out very little screening for sex workers or other high-risk groups and, as a result, **sexually transmitted diseases** such as gonorrhoea and syphilis, both easily treated with antibiotics, and AIDS (known locally as **SIDA**) are flourishing. It is, therefore, extremely unwise to contemplate casual unprotected sex, and bear in mind that Vietnamese condoms (*bao cao su*) are often poor-quality (more reliable imported varieties are available in major cities).

Getting medical help

Pharmacies can generally help with minor injuries or ailments and in major towns you may well find a pharmacist who speaks French or even English. The selection of reliable Asian and Western products on the market is improving rapidly and both Ho Chi Minh City and Hanoi now have reasonably well-stocked pharmacies. That said, drugs past their shelf life and even counterfeit medicines are rife, so inspect packaging carefully, check use-by dates – and bring anything you know you're likely to need from home.

Local **hospitals** can also treat minor problems, but in a real emergency your best bet is to head for Hanoi or Ho Chi Minh City. Hospitals in both these cities can handle most eventualities and you also have the option of one of the excellent international medical centres. Addresses of clinics and hospitals can be found in our "Listings" sections for major towns throughout the book. Note that doctors and hospitals expect immediate cash payment for health services rendered; you will then have to seek reimbursement from your insurance company (hang on to receipts for any payments you make).

Costs, money and banks

Despite what you might have heard, travelling in Vietnam needn't be much more expensive than in its Southeast Asian neighbours. With the average annual income hovering around US$300–400, daily expenses are low, and if you come prepared to do as the locals do, then food, drink and transport can all be incredibly cheap – and even accommodation needn't be too great an expense.

Pricing policy

Because dong amounts tend to be unwieldy and slightly more volatile, we've largely given **prices in US$** throughout the Guide. Note, however, that you always have the option of paying for things in dong.

Incidentally, don't be alarmed if you notice that Vietnamese pay less than you for plane tickets, at some hotels and at certain sights: Vietnam maintains a **two-tier pricing system**, with foreigners sometimes paying many times more than locals. The good news is that the system is being phased out, with prices for foreigners being adjusted downwards while those for Vietnamese rise to meet them. A single price system now applies on the trains, for example, while the gap has gradually been narrowing for air travel. It will take several more years before the practice disappears completely, however, and for the moment it remains something of a grey area, particularly as regards hotels and bus tickets, where the amount you pay may well depend on the person you happen to be dealing with.

Bargaining is very much a part of everyday life. Almost everything is negotiable, from fruit in the market to a room for the night – with the notable exception of meals. A few tricks of the trade are given on p.63, but don't get too carried away; a few thousand extra dong won't do irreparable damage to your budget, and will probably mean much more to the recipient than it does to you.

Average costs

By eating at simple *com* (rice) and *pho* (noodle soup) stalls, picking up local buses and opting for the simplest accommodation there's no reason why you shouldn't be able to adhere to a daily budget in the region of around US$12–15. Upgrading to more salubrious lodgings with a few mod cons, eating good food followed by a couple of beers in a bar, and signing up for the odd minibus tour and visiting a few sights (see below) could bounce your expenditure up to a more realistic US$25–35. And if you stay at the ritziest city hotels, dine at the swankiest restaurants and rent cars with drivers wherever you go, then the sky's the limit. It's worth noting that, as competition increases, costs of hotel accommodation and tours have been dropping. While we have made every effort to ensure that the information in the Guide is correct at the time of going to press, prices will undoubtedly change, particularly in somewhere as fast-moving as Vietnam.

Admission charges

There's usually an **admission charge** levied at museums, historic sights, national parks and any place that attracts tourists – sometimes even beaches. Charges at some **major sights** range from a dollar or two up to US$3–4 each for the Cham ruins at My Son or Hué's citadel and royal mausoleums. Elsewhere, however, the amount is usually minimal and is only given in the Guide if the fee is over $1. Note that there's often a hefty additional fee for **cameras** and **videos** at major sights.

Apart from those with some historical significance, **pagodas and temples** are usually free, though it's customary to leave a donation of a thousand dong or so in the collecting box or on one of the altar plates.

Currency

Vietnam's unit of currency is the **dong**, which you'll see abbreviated as "d" or "VND" after an amount – as in 1000d, 10,000VND and so on. **Notes** come in denominations of 200d, 500d, 1000d, 2000d, 5000d, 10,000d, 20,000d, 50,000d and 100,000d; there are no coins in circulation. In addition, the **American dollar** operates in parallel to the dong as unofficial tender and most travellers carry some dollars as a back-up for when banks won't change travellers' cheques. On the whole, though, it's more convenient to operate in dong. Indeed, you'll often find dong prices are slightly lower than the equivalent in dollars.

If you have some dong left over at the end of your trip you can change them back into dollars at a bank or, failing that, at the airport; you'll be required to produce an exchange certificate or ATM receipts to prove that you obtained the currency legally in the first place. You may also be asked for your air ticket and passport. A fee of one percent (minimum US$2) is the norm, though some banks waive this if you produce an exchange certificate issued by one of their branches.

At the time of writing, the **exchange rate** was around 25,000d to £1 and 15,000d to US$1; current rates are posted at all banks with exchange facilities. Though the country saw massive inflation during the late 1980s – one-dong notes were still being printed as recently as 1985 – Vietnam's currency is now relatively stable, with inflation down to around five percent per annum. For the latest exchange rates go to ⓦ www.xe.com.

Cash and travellers' cheques

Dong are not available outside Vietnam at present. If you take in some small-denomination American **dollars**, however, you'll have no problems getting by until you reach a bank.

Otherwise, **travellers' cheques** are easily the safest method of carrying money around in Vietnam. Cheques denominated in sterling, the euro and other major currencies are accepted in Hanoi and Ho Chi Minh, but American dollars are still far and away the best currency in which to buy them. Those issued by Visa, MasterCard and American Express are the most widely recognized. It's also worth noting that not all banks – especially in smaller towns – will change travellers' cheques, so get into the habit of carrying some dollars with you to allow for unforeseen circumstances.

The usual fee for travellers' cheques sales is one or two percent, though this fee may be waived if you buy the cheques through a bank where you have an account. It pays to get a selection of denominations. Make sure to keep the purchase agreement and a record of cheque serial numbers safe and separate from the cheques themselves. In the event that cheques are lost or stolen, the issuing company will expect you to report the loss immediately; most companies claim to replace lost or stolen cheques within 24 hours.

Cheques can be cashed at major banks (you need your passport as ID), for a commission of up to four percent depending on the bank. Vietcombank, the country's largest, usually charges the lowest rates, with slightly lower commission for changing travellers' cheques into dong rather than dollars.

Credit and debit cards

Major **credit cards** – Visa, MasterCard and, to a lesser extent, American Express – are becoming more acceptable in Vietnam, particularly in the main cities and major tourist spots. All top-level and many mid-level hotels will accept them, as will a growing number of restaurants, though note that some places levy surcharges of as much as five percent.

Better news for travellers is Vietcombank's rapidly expanding network of **ATMs**, some of which are open 24 hours. At present these machines only accept Visa and MasterCard, though other cards may be added in future. The maximum withdrawal is two million dong at a time, up to ten million per day, with a flat-rate charge of 20,000d per transaction (in addition to whatever surcharges your own bank levies). Note that, unless your card already uses a four-digit PIN number, you'll need to ask your bank to issue one before you leave home.

In Hanoi and Ho Chi Minh City you'll also find ATMs operated by ANZ and HSBC. These accept a wider range of cards, including those in the Cirrus and Plus networks. Details of ATMs are given in the Guide where relevant. Vietcombank also produces a reasonably up-to-date list of their machines – ask for it at main branches in Hanoi and Ho Chi Minh City.

Where there are no ATMs, banks (usually the main branch in each city) and some travellers' cafés and tour agents can now make **cash advances** against credit and debit cards (generally Visa and MasterCard), for which you'll be charged a minimum of three percent commission. You'll need your passport but no PIN number – you just sign the docket.

A compromise between travellers' cheques and plastic is Visa TravelMoney, a disposable pre-paid debit card with a PIN which works in all ATMs that take Visa cards. You load up your account with funds before leaving home, and when they run out, you simply throw the card away. You can buy up to nine cards to access the same funds – useful for couples or families travelling together – and it's a good idea to buy at least one extra as a back-up in case of loss or theft. There is also a 24-hour toll-free customer assistance number (make a collect call to ☎410/581-9994 in the US). The card is available in most countries from branches of Thomas Cook and Citicorp. For more information, check the Visa TravelMoney website at ⓦusa.visa.com/personal/cards /visa_travel_money.html.

Wiring money

Having money wired from home using one of the companies listed below is never convenient or cheap, and should be considered a last resort. It's also possible to have money wired directly from a bank in your home country to a bank in Vietnam, although this is somewhat less reliable as it involves two separate institutions. If you go this route, your home bank will need the address of the branch bank where you want to pick up the money and the address and telex number of the head office, which will act as the clearing house; money wired this way normally takes two working days to arrive, and costs around £25/$40 per transaction.

Money-wiring companies

Thomas Cook Canada ☎1-888/823-4732, Great Britain ☎01733/318 922, Northern Ireland

☎028/9055 0030, Republic of Ireland ☎01/677 1721, US ☎1-800/287-7362, ⓦwww .thomascook.com.
Travelers Express MoneyGram Australia ☎1800/230 100, Canada ☎1-800/933-3278, New Zealand ☎0800/262 263, Republic of Ireland ☎1850/205 800, US ☎1-800/955-7777, UK ☎0800/018 0104, ⓦwww.moneygram.com.
Western Union Australia ☎1800/501 500, New Zealand ☎0800/270 000, Republic of Ireland ☎1800/395 395, UK ☎0800/833 833, US and Canada ☎1-800/325-6000, ⓦwww.westernunion.com.

Banks and exchange

Banking hours are generally Monday to Friday 8–11.30am and 1–4pm, though in major tourist spots some branches stay open over lunch and may even open on Saturdays and Sundays. At other times you can change cash at registered exchange counters, often located in jewellery shops, and at some travellers' cafés and hotels.

When changing money, ask for a mix of denominations (in some places, especially backwaters, bigger bills can be hard to split), and refuse really tatty banknotes, as you'll have difficulty getting anyone else to accept them.

A **black market** of sorts exists in Vietnam, and marketeers will sometimes approach you offering to change your cash. Since they generally quote below the official rate, it certainly doesn't justify the risks.

Getting around

Bombed almost into oblivion during successive wars, Vietnam's transport network has improved markedly in recent years. Massive infrastructure projects have seen the country's main thoroughfare, Highway 1 – which runs from Hanoi to Ho Chi Minh, passing through Hué, Da Nang and Nha Trang en route – widened and resurfaced for much of its length, while the nation's first stretch of motorway was inaugurated early in the new millennium. State-run bus services are slowly being upgraded and there's an increasing number of relatively comfortable, privately owned minibuses in operation, especially in the south, while the introduction of new rolling stock, complete with air-conditioned carriages and restaurant cars, has transformed train travel.

That said, there's plenty of room for improvement, particularly as regards road transport: local bus timetables are for the most part redundant; clapped-out buses are sometimes packed to the gunnels; and passengers – not just foreigners - are sometimes overcharged or forced to change buses and pay a second time. It's therefore not surprising that an increasing number of tourists are opting for internal flights, privately operated "open-tour" buses or organized tours. Doing as the locals do shouldn't be rejected out of hand, though: many visitors have their warmest encounters with the Vietnamese within the chaos of a bus or train.

Security is an important consideration. Never fall asleep with your bag by your side, and never leave belongings unattended. On trains, be especially vigilant when the train stops at stations and ensure your money belt is safely tucked under your clothes before going to sleep and that your luggage is safely stowed (preferably padlocked to an immovable object).

By plane

Flying comes into its own on longer hauls, and can shave precious hours or even days off journeys – the two-hour journey between Hanoi and Ho Chi Minh City, for instance, compares favourably with the thirty to forty hours you might spend on the train.

The Vietnamese national carrier, **Vietnam Airlines** (Ⓦwww.vietnamairlines.com), operates a reasonably cheap, efficient and comprehensive network of domestic flights. The company maintains **booking offices** in all towns and cities with an airport; addresses and phone numbers are listed throughout the Guide. If you're booking international flights with Vietnam Airlines, it's worth checking their domestic fares at the same time as they sometimes offer good discounts as part of a package; otherwise, it's generally cheaper to buy tickets in Vietnam.

The only other airline operating internal flights is **Pacific Airlines** (Ⓦwww.pacificairlines.com.vn), currently flying a very limited range of routes linking Hanoi, Ho Chi Minh and Da Nang.

Ticketing on both airlines is still at a fairly basic stage, with options limited to standard single or return trips. Book as far ahead as you can. You'll need to have your **passport** with you.

There's a **departure tax**, known as a "passenger service charge", ranging between 10,000d (US$0.70) and 25,000d (US$1.60) on domestic flights depending on the airport. Increasingly, however, this tax is included in the ticket price.

The shuttle **between Hanoi and Ho Chi Minh City** is the route most frequently used by tourists. Vietnam Airlines flies at least ten times daily each way, taking two hours, for a standard one-way fare of around US$110. Pacific Airlines also flies four times a day in each direction for roughly the same price. Other useful services from Hanoi and Ho Chi Minh fly to **Hué**, **Da Nang** and **Nha Trang**. Ho Chi Minh City also has flights to **Phu Quoc Island**.

By train

Vietnam's single-track **train** network comprises more than 2500km of track, stretching from Ho Chi Minh City to the Chinese border. Much of it dates back to the colonial period, though it's gradually being upgraded. Most of the services are still relatively slow, but travelling by train can be a pleasant experience – often far preferable to going by road – especially if you splash out on a soft-class berth or seat. Scrimp on your ticket, on the other hand, and you'll probably regret it.

The most **popular routes** with tourists are the shuttle from Da Nang to Hué (2–3hr), a picturesque sampler of Vietnamese rail travel, and the overnighters from Hué to Hanoi (13–16hr) and from Hanoi up to Lao Cai, for Sa Pa (8–9hr).

Services

The country's **main line** shadows Highway 1 on its way from Ho Chi Minh City to Hanoi (1729km), passing through Nha Trang, Da Nang and Hué en route. From Hanoi, three branch lines strike out towards the northern coast and into its hinterland. One line traces the Red River northwest to **Lao Cai**, site of a border crossing into **China**'s Yunnan Province. Another runs north to **Dong Dang**, and is the route taken by the trains from Hanoi **to Beijing**. The third branch, a shorter spur, links the capital with **Haiphong**. All that remains of the **Phan Rang–Da Lat** branch line that once linked the central highlands with the southern coast is a truncated tourist excursion service that runs, on request, from Da Lat to Trai Met, a few kilometres down the line.

Five **Reunification Express** services depart daily from Hanoi to Ho Chi Minh and vice versa, a journey that takes somewhere between 30 and 41 hours: these trains are labelled E1, E2 and S1 to S8; odd-numbered trains travel south, even ones north, hence the E2 (30hr), S2 (32hr), S4, S6 and S8 (all 41hr) depart daily from Ho Chi Minh City, while the E1 and S1 to S7 (same times) make the trip in the opposite direction.

On the **northern lines**, at least two trains per day make the run from Hanoi to Haiphong (2–3hr), while there are also two trains a day to Dong Dang (5hr), and a daytime service to Lao Cai (8hr).

Note that **departure times** change regularly – current times are displayed in stations and on the tickets themselves – and that trains generally leave pretty much on schedule. You'll also find timetables on the Vietnam Railway's website (Ⓦwww.vr.com.vn), though it's always wise to double-check at the station.

When it comes to choosing which **class** to travel in, it's essential to aim high. At the bottom of the scale is a **hard seat**, which is just as it sounds, though bearable for shorter journeys; **soft seats** offer slightly more comfort, but are still fairly grim for long hauls. On overnight journeys, you'd be well advised to invest in a berth of some description. **Hard-berth** compartments have six bunks, three either side – with the cramped top ones being the cheapest, and the bottom ones (under which there's handy storage space) the priciest. Roomier **soft-berth** compartments, containing only four bunks, offer more sleeping space.

The fastest Reunification Express services (E1/2 and S1/2) are equipped with air-conditioning throughout. They also boast double-decker carriages with reclining soft seats and even a restaurant car. The remaining services (S3–S8) have air-conditioning in their soft-sleeper compartments and it's gradually being installed in soft-seat carriages. Similarly, the overnight Lao Cai trains are also being upgraded, with soft-sleeper berths and air-con in some carriages. All trains are non-smoking.

Simple **meals** are included in the price of the ticket, but you might want to stock up with goodies of your own; you'll also have plenty of opportunities to buy snacks when the train pulls into stations – and from carts that ply the aisles.

Tickets

Booking ahead is essential, and the further ahead the better, especially if you intend travelling at the weekend or over a holiday period; sleeping compartments should be booked at least three days before departure. Note that it's not possible to buy through tickets and break your journey en route; each journey requires you to buy a separate ticket from the point of departure.

Fares vary according to the class of travel and the train you take; as a rule of thumb, the faster the train, the more expensive it is. Prices (which are always quoted in dong) change regularly, but the following figures give a rough indication of what you can expect to pay on the slowest service from Ho Chi Minh to Hanoi (S4–S8). A hard seat from Ho Chi Minh to Nha Trang costs around US$9, and a soft berth $15; going as far as Da Nang, the same classes cost $21 and $34, respectively; for the entire journey to Hanoi they cost $36 and $59.

By bus

Vietnam's national **bus** network offers daily services between all major towns. The government is slowly upgrading state buses, but for now many remain unbearably cramped, with hard seats designed for the diminutive Southeast Asian frame. Once the roof is laden, luggage (which could be anything from live pigs in baskets to scores of sacks of rice) is piled into the vehicle itself. Breakdowns are fairly common and can sometimes necessitate a roadside wait of several hours while driver, fare collector and mechanic roll up their sleeves and improvise a repair. Even relatively healthy buses make agonizingly slow progress as they stop frequently along the road to pick up passengers or for meal breaks.

Bus stations can be found in most towns, and larger communities have both a local and a long-distance station. Though there are occasional early evening departures, most buses depart early, from 5am through to mid-morning, waiting only as long as it takes to muster a decent quota of passengers, so it pays to set your alarm if you want to be sure of a seat. That said, all is not lost if you oversleep or miss your connection: with so many buses plying the highways, it's often possible to wave down a bus that's headed your way, if you can get yourself to the nearest main road. The majority of buses have a sign on the front indicating their destination, though it's always wise to double-check with the driver or conductor.

For longer journeys, tickets are best bought a day in advance since many routes are heavily oversubscribed. Prices are difficult to predict, since how much you pay depends very much upon where you are: at certain tourist hot spots, especially in the south, you'll often be charged over the odds; elsewhere, you might pay the going price. Station staff will sometimes tell you to buy a ticket on the bus; if this happens, try to ascertain the correct price before boarding as fare collectors will often take advantage of your captive position.

Privately owned minibuses compete with public buses on most routes; they sometimes share the local bus station, or simply congregate on the roadside in the centre of a town. You can also flag them down on the road. If anything, they squeeze in even more people per square foot than ordinary buses, and often drive interminably around town, touting for passengers. On the other hand, they do at least run throughout the day and serve routes not covered by public services. Again, you should always agree a fare before boarding. Even so, be prepared to find the price has suddenly increased once you've got going. You may also find yourself dumped at the side of the road before reaching your destination and having to cram onto the next passing service.

There are also an increasing number of privately owned "luxury" air-con minibuses, particularly in the south. These tend to be slightly more reliable: they usually stick to a timetable, have limited seating and don't pick up passengers en route. In general, they operate from their own offices as opposed to bus stations; details of the more useful services are given in the Guide.

Special "open-tour" buses shuttling between the major tourist destinations are an increasingly popular way for tourists – and a few wealthier locals – to travel around Vietnam. Though some operators are more reliable than others, on the whole these buses are reasonably comfortable and tend to run on time. They are, of course, vastly more expensive than local services, but competition is fierce and prices have been drifting down.

The downside of these open-tour buses is that you'll be encouraged to book into the company's own or affiliated hotels, though there's nothing to stop you staying elsewhere. You'll also have less choice when it comes to meal stops, which tend to be at rather mediocre and overpriced restaurants; it's worth taking a picnic. Finally, bear in mind that the buses between Hué and Hanoi (and vice versa) run overnight. You save on a night's accommodation, but don't expect to get much sleep.

Most people buy a one-way through ticket, for example from Ho Chi Minh to Hué (US$18–20/$14) or Hanoi (US$27–29/$20), or vice versa, which enables you to stop off at specified destinations en route: heading south to north, the main stops are Da Lat, Mui Ne, Nha Trang, Hoi An, Da Nang, Hué and Ninh Binh. On the way buses also call at the occasional tourist sight, such as the Marble Mountains and Lang Co, and at a number of minor towns. You can either make firm bookings at the outset or opt for an open-dated ticket for greater flexibility, in which case you'll need to book your onward travel at least a day in advance to be sure of a seat. Alternatively, you can buy separate tickets as you go along, though this works out slightly more expensive. Each main town on the itinerary has an agent (one for each tour company) where you can buy tickets and make onward reservations. To avoid being sold a fake ticket, it's best to buy direct from the relevant agent rather than from hotels, restaurants or unrelated tour companies.

By ferry and boat

Ferries sail year-round – weather permitting – to the major islands off Vietnam's coastline, including Phu Quoc, Cat Ba and Con Dao. In addition, ferry and hydrofoil services run from Haiphong to Ha Long City (Hong Gai) and to Cat Ba, and hydrofoils from Ho Chi Minh City to Vung Tau, Da Nang to Hué and from both Haiphong and Ha Long City (Bai Chay) to Mong Cai. Tickets can be bought on the boats, but it's better to get them in advance (details are given in the relevant chapters of the Guide). Though they are gradually being replaced by bridges, a few river ferries still haul themselves from bank to bank of the various strands of the Mekong from morning until night. Numerous aged (and often less than seaworthy) cargo vessels also dawdle between towns, and some ply the route to Ho Chi Minh City, but they tend to be slow and basic; we've outlined a handful of the more do-able ones in the text.

By car and jeep

Self-drive in Vietnam is not yet an option for tourists and other short-term visitors. However, it's easy to rent a **car**, **jeep** or **minibus** with driver from the same companies, agencies and tourist offices that arrange tours (see p.40). This can be quite an economical means of transport if you are travelling in a group. Moreover, it means you can plan a trip to your own tastes, rather than having to follow a tour company's itinerary.

Prices are in the region of US$25–45 per day for a car, and $30–60 per day for a jeep or other 4WD, depending on the vehicle's size, age and level of comfort. Rates vary wildly so it pays to shop around. When negotiating on the price, it's important to clarify exactly who is liable for what. Things to check include who pays for the driver's accommodation and meals, fuel, road and ferry tolls, parking fees, repairs and what happens in the case of a major breakdown. There should then be some sort of contract to sign showing all the details, including an agreed itinerary, especially if you are renting for more than a day; make sure the driver is given a copy in Vietnamese. In some cases you'll have to settle up in advance, though, if possible, it's best if you can arrange to pay roughly half before and the balance at the end.

Hitching

Although not really comparable to **hitching** in the Western sense, there is a tradition of drivers (especially truck drivers) picking up passengers from the roadside, in exchange for a small payment – and this system has been used to great effect by some travellers. However, in addition to the **risks** associated with hitching anywhere, you're also quite likely to be overcharged, due to the prevailing (and not unreasonable) assumption that all foreigners are wealthy. Set against the relatively low cost of other forms of transport, hitching is an ill-advised and unattractive proposition.

By motorbike

Motorbike rental is possible in most towns and cities regularly frequented by tourists, and pottering around on one can be a most enjoyable and time-efficient method of sightseeing. Lured by the prospect of independent travel at relatively low cost, some tourists cruise the countryside on motorbikes, but inexperienced bikers would do well to think very hard before undertaking any **long-distance biking** since Vietnam's roads can be distinctly dangerous (see "Rules of the road" on p.40).

The appalling road discipline of most Vietnamese drivers and the number of badly maintained vehicles on the road mean that the risk of an accident is very real – with potentially dire consequences should it happen in a remote area. Well-equipped hospitals are few and far between outside the major centres, and there'll probably be no ambulance service to help you out.

On the other hand, many people ride around with no problems and thoroughly recommend it for both day-trips and touring. The best biking is to be found in the northern mountains, the central highlands and around the Mekong Delta. Many people also do the long haul up Highway 1 from Ho Chi Minh to Hanoi (or vice versa), a journey of around two weeks, averaging 150km per day, though you can do it in a week if you really push it.

There's no shortage of motorbikes **for rent** (generally 100–125cc) in Vietnam's major tourist centres, and we give details of outlets throughout the Guide. The average rate is around US$5–7 per day, cheaper in the main tourist destinations, with discounts for longer periods. You'll sometimes be asked to pay in advance, sign a rental contract and/or leave some form of ID (a photocopy of your passport should suffice). If you're renting for a week or so, you may be asked to leave a deposit, often the bike's value in dollars though it might also be your air ticket or departure card. In the vast majority of cases, this shouldn't be a problem.

Although it's technically illegal for non-residents to own a vehicle, there's a small trade in **secondhand motorbikes** in the two main cities – look at the noticeboards in hotels, travellers' cafés and tour agents for adverts. So far the police have ignored the practice, but check the latest situation before committing yourself.

In peak season (Sept–Dec) you should be able to find a foreign buyer in either Ho Chi Minh City or Hanoi, in which case you should be able to get a reasonable price. Otherwise, a Vietnamese will probably take your bike to sell on, though they know you're generally in a hurry to leave and won't offer much.

The bike of choice is usually a **Minsk 125cc**, particularly for the mountains; it's sturdy, not too expensive (US$300–400 secondhand), and is the easiest to get repaired outside the main cities. It's also fairly comfortable, though you might want to add some extra padding to the seat.

Whether you're renting or buying, remember to check everything over carefully, especially brakes, lights and horn. Wearing a **helmet** is now a legal requirement on all major highways as well as an essential safety precaution. Rental outlets usually have helmets you can borrow, sometimes for a small charge, though they may not be top-quality. If you plan on doing a lot of biking you're probably best off either bringing your own or buying locally; a decent Korean or Japanese made helmet will set you back about US$40. Other equipment to consider, especially if you're going off the beaten track, are gloves and a good sturdy pair of boots.

You should get an **international driving licence** before leaving home; for information on how to obtain one, contact your insurance company or the national licensing authority. It's also a good idea to check the small print on your **insurance** policy and, if necessary, take out full medical evacuation cover. In theory you're supposed to have local accident insurance as well. However, for this you need a Vietnamese driving licence which isn't available to anyone on a tourist visa, so you're in a catch-22.

Though **road conditions** have improved remarkably in recent years, off the main highways they can still be highly erratic, with pristine asphalt followed by stretches of spine-jarring potholes, and plenty of loose gravel on the sides of the road. It's inevitable that you'll need one or two simple repairs sooner or later. **Repair shops** are fairly ubiquitous – look for a Honda sign or ask for *sua chua xe may* (motorbike repairs) – but you should still carry at least a puncture-repair kit, pump and spare spark plug. Fuel (*xang*) is cheap (around 6000d, less than US$0.40 per litre) and widely available, though it's best to fill up at town pumps as petrol sold in bottles beside the road is likely to be more expensive and of inferior quality.

Vietnamese road **maps** tend to be unreliable, so ask at junctions and check if the route ahead is driveable, especially in the mountains where summer rains regularly take out roads and bridges.

Finally, try to travel in the company of one or more other bikes in case one of you gets into trouble. And if you want to get off the main highways, it really pays to take a guide.

By bicycle

Cycling is an excellent way of sightseeing around towns, and you shouldn't have to pay more than US$1 per day for the privilege, even outside the main tourist centres.

While you can now buy decent Japanese-made bikes in Vietnam for around $100, if you decide on a **long-distance cycling** holiday, you should really bring your own bike – not forgetting the necessary spares and tools – with you. Hardy **mountain bikes** cope best with the country's variable surfaces, though tourers and hybrids are fine on the main roads. Bring your own helmet and a good loud bell; a rear-view mirror also comes in handy.

When it all gets too much, or you want to skip between towns, you can always put

Rules of the road

There's no discernible method to the madness that passes as a **traffic** system in Vietnam so it's extremely important that you don't stray out onto the roads unless you feel a hundred percent confident about doing so. The theory is that you **drive on the right**, though in practice motorists and cyclists swoop, swerve and dodge wherever they want, using their **horn** as a surrogate indicator and brake. Unless otherwise stated, the **speed limit** is 100kph on motorways, 60kph on highways and 40kph in towns.

Right of way invariably goes to the biggest vehicle on the road, which means that motorbikes and bicycles are regularly forced off the highway by thundering trucks or buses; note that overtaking vehicles assume you'll pull over onto the hard shoulder to avoid them. It's wise to use your horn to its maximum and also to avoid being on the road after dark, since many vehicles either don't have functioning headlights or simply don't bother to turn them on.

On the whole the **police** seem to leave foreign riders well alone, and the best policy at roadside checkpoints is just to drive by slowly. However, if you are involved in an **accident** and it was deemed to be your fault, the penalties can involve fairly major fines.

When **parking** your bike, it's advisable to leave it in a parking compound (*gui xe*) – the going rate is 1000d for a motorbike and 500d for a bicycle – or paying someone to keep an eye on it. If not, you run the risk of it being tampered with.

---

your bike on the train (but not the E1/2 and S1/2 express services) for a small fee; take it to the station well ahead of time, where it will be packed and placed in the luggage van. Some open-tour buses will also take bikes – you simply have to pay for an extra seat.

If you want to see Vietnam from the saddle, there are several companies that offer specialist **cycling tours** – see details of specialist tour operators on p.13–14, p.16 and p.18.

Organized tours

Ever-increasing numbers of tourists are seeing Vietnam through the window of a minibus, on **organized tours**. Ranging from one-day jaunts to two- or three-week trawls upcountry, tours are ideal if you want to acquaint yourself speedily with the highlights of Vietnam; they can also work out much cheaper than car rental. On the other hand, by relying upon tours you'll have little chance to really get to grips with the country and its people, or to enjoy things at your leisure.

If you're really pressed for time but are still determined to cover a lot of ground, think about arranging a package tour to suit your interests before you leave home, though this tends to be expensive (see p.13–14, p.16 and p.18).

Hordes of state-owned and private **tour**

companies compete for business in Hanoi, Ho Chi Minh City and other major destinations. While a few companies are getting more innovative, the vast majority offer similar ranges of tours. However, it pays to shop around since **prices** vary wildly depending, for example, on how many people there are in a group, the standard of transport, meals and accommodation, whether entry fees are included and so forth. Generally speaking, a day-trip, say, from Ho Chi Minh to the Cu Chi tunnels and Tay Ninh, starts at around US$4 a head excluding entry fees; a two-day trip into the Mekong Delta costs from $15 a head; while an extended ten-day journey up the coast to Hué would be around $60 a head. All these prices are for a seat on a full minibus: you will sometimes pay more if there are fewer takers.

It's important to check exactly what is included in the price before handing over any cash. It's also a good idea to ask about the maximum number of people on the trip and whether your group will be amalgamated with others if you don't want to be travelling round in a great horde. Bear in mind, as well, that you're far better off dealing directly with the company organizing the tour, rather than going through a hotel or other intermediary. Not only are you more likely to get accurate information about the details of the tour, but you'll also be in a much stronger position should you have cause for complaint.

The other alternative is to set up your own **custom-made tour** by gathering together a group and renting a car, jeep or minibus plus driver (see "By car and jeep", p.38).

Local transport

In a country with a population so adept at making do with limited resources, it isn't surprising to see the diverse types of **local transport** dreamt up. While taxis are increasingly common and a number of cities now boast reasonable **bus services**, elsewhere you'll be reliant on a host of two- and three-wheeled vehicles for getting around.

Cheap, ubiquitous and fun, **cyclos** – three-wheeled rickshaws comprising a "bucket" seat attached to the front of a bicycle – are the quintessential Vietnamese mode of transport. They can carry one person, or two people at a push, with a corresponding reduction in comfort. A **fair price** for a five- or ten-minute hop is 8000–10,000d, though if you hire one for a few hours' touring you should budget on a figure of at least 15,000d per hour.

Recently, however, there have been reports of cyclo drivers in tourist centres charging outrageous sums for their services. To avoid getting badly ripped off, find out first what a reasonable fare might be – from your hotel or the like – and, if the first driver won't agree to your offer, simply walk on and try another. When haggling, ensure you know which currency you are dealing in (five fingers held up, for instance, could mean 5000d or US$5), and whether you're negotiating for a single or return trip, and for one passenger or two; it's always best to write

the figures down. Should a difference of opinion emerge at the end of a ride, having the exact fare ready to press into an argumentative driver's hand can sometimes resolve matters.

It's worth noting that cyclo drivers in Ho Chi Minh have a particularly bad reputation, not only for overcharging: there have been instances of tourists being taken down dark alleys and robbed. You're advised not to travel by cyclo at night in the city, and people on their own – especially women – should avoid using cyclos after dark anywhere in Vietnam.

Throughout Vietnam cyclos are rapidly being replaced by motorbike taxis, known as **Honda om** in the south and **xe om** in the north (*om* translates as "embrace"). They are invaluable in highland regions, where pedal power is not an option. In the cities, you'll often find going by Honda om a shade cheaper than a cyclo, generally around 5000–8000d for a good five- or ten-minute ride.

Taxis are becoming an increasingly common sight on the streets of big cities. The vast majority are metered (with prices in dong) and fares are not expensive; a short ride within central Hanoi, for example, should cost around 12,000d (under a dollar). However, the number of complaints about dodgy taxis has been increasing over the last couple of years. When arriving in a town, beware of drivers who insist the hotel you ask for is closed and want to take you elsewhere; this is usually a commission scam – be firm with your directions. Some drivers need persuading to use their meters, others dawdle along while the meter spins suspiciously fast, or take you on an unnecessarily long route. In general, smarter-looking taxis and those waiting outside big hotels tend to be more reliable.

Accommodation

Compared to other Southeast Asian countries, accommodation in Vietnam can be poor-quality and expensive. However, tourists have not flocked to Vietnam in the huge droves that were anticipated a few years back, and this fact, coupled with the ever-increasing number of hotels opening up, is keeping competition hot. The result is that prices are dropping and standards improving in the major tourist spots, though in remoter areas, where competition is less intense, change is coming more slowly.

Another consequence of the number of new hotels springing up in recent years is that getting **a reservation** is no longer the nightmare it once was, and even among international-class hotels there are some bargains to be had, particularly at weekends. However, if you're keen to stay in a specific hotel, especially the more central or popular addresses, it pays to book ahead. Around the **Tet** festival (early spring) booking in advance is a must.

Getting help in **finding a room** isn't easy. There's a booth at Ho Chi Minh airport that will phone to reserve a room for you, though not at budget hotels, while in Hanoi the airport information desk simply hands out brochures. A more likely source of help is cyclo or taxi drivers looking for a commission (usually ten percent or more of the first night's charge). The room may well turn out to be fine – often they know the newest places – but bear in mind that you'll be paying that much extra. Similarly, if they tell you that the hotel of your choice has closed, politely insist on taking a look anyway.

Once you've found a hotel, look at a range of rooms before opting for one, as standards can vary hugely within the same establishment. You'll also need to check the bed arrangement, since there are many permutations in Vietnam. A "**single**" room could have a single or twin beds in it, while a "**double**" room could have two, three or four single beds, a single and a double, and so on. Incidentally, not all places are permitted to take foreigners: if you walk into a place and the staff merely smile and shake their heads, chances are this is the case.

When you **check in** at a Vietnamese hotel or guesthouse, you are required to complete a simple registration form and hand in your **passport** and often your **departure card** as well for presentation to the local police. Depending on the establishment, your passport will be either returned to you the same night, or kept as security until you check out. If you're going to lose sleep over being separated from your passport, say you need it for the bank. It's normally possible to pay your bill when you leave, although a few budget places ask for payment in advance.

Room **rates** fluctuate according to demand, so it's always worth bargaining – making sure, of course, that it's clear whether both parties are talking per person or per room. Your case will be that much stronger if you are staying several nights.

All hotels charge ten percent **government tax**, while top-class establishments also add a five percent **service charge**. These taxes may or may not be included in the room rate, so check to be sure. (Our price codes – see box on p.43 – include all applicable taxes.) Increasingly, **breakfast** is included in the price of all but the cheapest rooms, though in budget places it will consist of little more than bread with jam or cheese and a cup of tea or coffee.

Hotel **security** can be a big problem. Never leave valuables lying about in your room and keep documents, travellers' cheques and so forth with you at all times, in a money pouch. While upmarket hotels provide safety deposit boxes, elsewhere you can sometimes leave things in a safe or locked drawer at reception; put everything in a sealed envelope and ask for a receipt. In the real cheapies, where the door is often secured with a padlock, you can increase security by using your own lock.

In some budget hotels, rooms are cleaned irregularly and badly, and **hygiene** can be a problem, with cockroaches and even rats roaming free; you can at least minimize health risks by not bringing foodstuffs or sugary drinks into your room. Finally, **prostitution** is rife in Vietnam, and in less reputable budget hotels it's not unknown for Western men to be called upon, or even phoned from other rooms, during the night.

Types of accommodation

Grading accommodation isn't a simple matter in Vietnam. The names used (guesthouse, rooms for rent, mini-hotel, hotel and so on) can rarely be relied upon to indicate what's on offer, and there are broad overlaps in standards. Some of Vietnam's largest hotels are austere, state-owned edifices styled upon unlovely Eastern European models, while even the tiniest rooms-for-rent operations often make a real effort. Some hotels cover all bases by having a range of rooms, from simple fan-cooled rooms with cold water, right up to cheerful air-conditioned accommodation with satellite TV, fridge and mini-bar. As a rule of thumb, the newer a place is, the better value it's likely to represent in terms of comfort, hygiene and all-round appeal.

Throughout the Guide we've given comprehensive listings of the options available and allocated price codes (see box below).

Budget accommodation

The very cheapest form of accommodation in Vietnam is a bed in a **dormitory**; there are no youth hostels as yet. Dormitories are not a new concept in Vietnam: many bus and train stations have on-site dorms known as *nha tro*, but these practically never take for-

eigners – which is no loss, since they generally have appalling standards of cleanliness and little security.

However, there are now a few "backpackers" dorms in Ho Chi Minh and, to a lesser extent, Hanoi, where you can expect to pay US$3–4 (❶) for a bed or a mattress on the floor, sharing common facilities. Dorms are generally located in the budget **guesthouses** (*nha khach*) and **rooms-for-rent** set-ups (private homes with a handful of rooms to let) that proliferate around Ho Chi Minh's Pham Ngu Lao enclave. In Hanoi, a couple of travellers' cafés in the Old Quarter offer dormitory accommodation. Details are given in the Guide.

Otherwise, you'll need to upgrade to a simple fan room with shared washing facilities, in either a guesthouse or **hotel** (*khach san*), which will set you back anywhere between US$4 and 7 (❶). Don't expect much panache, though. Rooms at this level are generally plain boxes, often with no windows, where furnishings typically consist of a rickety chair, desk and wardrobe – if you're lucky.

In the main tourist destinations you should be able to find fairly decent rooms with fan and en-suite bathroom for around US$6–10 (❶) in privately owned establishments – although you might not get hot water for this price in the warmer south. Add air-conditioning, satellite TV and slightly better furnishings, maybe even a window, and you'll be paying between $10 and $15 (❷). Upgrading to $15–30 (❸) will get you a larger room with better-standard fittings, usually including a fridge and bathtub, and possibly a balcony. Note that while many hotels advertise satellite TV, which channels you actually get varies wildly, so check first if it matters to you.

Accommodation price codes

All accommodation listed in this guide has been categorized according to the following scale:

❶ under US$10 ❸ US$15–30 ❺ US$75–150
❷ US$10–15 ❹ US$30–75 ❻ over US$150

Rates are for the cheapest available **double** or twin **room**. During holiday periods, rates are liable to rise, and proprietors may be less amenable to bargaining. Although the law requires prices to be quoted in dong, most hotels also give their rates in US$; payment can be made in either currency.

In remoter regions, you'll probably be stuck with the local state-run hotel. These tend to be fairly uninspiring places which charge over the going rate for aged facilities.

Mid- and upper-range accommodation

For upwards of US$30 per room per night, accommodation can begin to get quite rosy. Rooms at this level will be comfortable, reasonably spacious and well appointed with decent furniture, air-conditioning, hot water, fridge, phone and satellite TV in all but the most remote areas.

Paying US$30–75 (**4**) will get you a room in a **mid-range hotel** of some repute, with in-house restaurant and bar, booking office, room service and so on. At the **top of the range** (**5**–**6**) the sky's the limit – if you want the last word in splendour, you could easily spend up to US$200 a night. International-class hotels are for the most part confined to the two major cities, which also have some reasonably charismatic places to stay, such as the *Metropole* in Hanoi and Ho Chi Minh's *Continental*. However, in recent years developers have targeted Nha Trang, Da Nang and Ha Long City, all of which now boast upmarket resort hotels.

Village accommodation and camping

As Vietnam's minority communities have become more exposed to tourism, staying in stilthouses or other **village accommodation** has become more feasible.

In the north of the country, notably around Sa Pa and in the Mai Chau Valley, you can either take one of the tours out of Hanoi which includes overnighting in one of the **minority villages** (see p.363), or make your own arrangements when you get there (see p.450–451 for details). In the central highlands, rangers at Yok Don National Park can arrange a stay in surrounding village stilt-houses (see p.215); while at Ban Don Village (p.215) there is the choice of village accommodation or the tourist centre guest stilt-house. The Plei Ku and Kon Tum tourist offices can also arrange a stilthouse overnighter for you.

Accommodation usually consists of a mattress on the floor in a communal room. Those villages more used to tourists normally provide a blanket and mosquito net, but it's advisable to take your own net and sleeping bag to be on the safe side, particularly as nights get pretty cold in the mountains.

Prices in the villages vary from US$3 to $15 per person per night, depending on the area and whether meals are included. Unless you're arriving before midday, it's generally a good idea to take food for your first night. As a sign of appreciation, your hosts will welcome **gifts** – fresh fruit is always appreciated in the mountain areas.

Where boat trips operate in the Mekong Delta, notably around Vinh Long, the local tourist board can arrange for visitors to stay with owners of **fruit orchards**, allowing a close-up view of rural life.

Virutually no provisions exist in Vietnam for foreign tourists to try **camping** at the present time. The exceptions are at Nha Trang and Mui Ne, where you'll pay around $3.30 per tent for basic facilities.

Eating and drinking

At its best, Vietnamese food is light, subtle in flavour and astonishing in its variety. Though its cuisine is related to that of China, Vietnam has its own distinct culinary tradition, using herbs and seasoning rather than sauces, and favouring boiled or steamed dishes over stir-fries.

In the south, **Indian** and **Thai** influences add curries and spices to the menu, while other regions have evolved their own array of specialities, most notably the foods of Hué and Hoi An. Buddhism introduced a **vegetarian** tradition to Vietnam, while much later the **French** brought with them bread, dairy products, pastries and the whole café culture. Hanoi, Ho Chi Minh City and the major tourist centres are now well provided, with everything from hawker stalls to hotel and Western-style restaurants, and even ice-cream parlours.

The quality and variety of food is generally better in the main towns than off the beaten track, where restaurants of any sort are few and far between. That said, you'll never go hungry; even in the back of beyond, there's always some stall selling a noodle soup or rice platter and plenty of fruit to fill up on.

Vietnam's national **drink** is green tea, which is the accompaniment to every social gathering or business meeting and is frequently drunk after meals. At the harder end of the spectrum, there's also **rice wine**, though some local **beer** is also excellent, and an increasingly wide range of imported **wines** and **spirits**.

For a glossary of **food and drink terms**, see "Language", p.573.

Where to eat

Broadly speaking, there are three types of eating establishment to choose from. One step up from **hawkers** peddling their dish of the day from shoulder poles or handcarts are **street kitchens**, inexpensive joints aimed at locals. More formal, Western-style **restaurants** come in many shapes and sizes, from simple places serving unpretentious Vietnamese meals to top-class establishments offering high-quality Vietnamese specialities and international cuisine. Finally, there are the **travellers' cafés** which, among other things, lay on inexpensive if rather banal meals, along the lines of burgers and banana pancakes alongside spring rolls, noodles and other Vietnamese standards.

Throughout the Guide we've given phone numbers for those restaurants where it's advisable to make **reservations**. While most eating establishments stay open throughout the year, note that some close over Tet (see "Festivals and religious events", p.56 for more on Tet). Though places stay open later in the south, especially in Ho Chi Minh, the Vietnamese **eat early**: outside the major cities and tourist areas, food stalls and street kitchens rarely stay open beyond 8pm and may close even earlier. You'll need to brush up your **chopstick**-handling skills, too, although other utensils are always available in places frequented by tourists – and in French restaurants you won't be expected to tackle your *steak-frites* with chopsticks.

When it comes to **paying**, the normal sign language will be readily understood in most restaurants. In street kitchens you pay as you leave – either proffer a few thousand dong to signal your intentions, or ask *bao nhieu tien?* ("how much is it?").

Street kitchens

Street kitchens range from makeshift food stalls, set up on the street round a cluster of pint-size stools, to eating houses where, as often as not, the cooking is still done on the street but you either sit in an open-fronted dining area or join the overspill outside. Like the food stall, these streetside restaurants offer few concessions to comfort, but they are permanent, with an address if not a name, and serve basic meals for next to nothing. Some places stay open all day (7am–8pm), while many close once they've run out of ingredients and others only open at lunchtime (10.30am–2pm). To be sure of the widest choice and freshest food, it pays to get there early (as early as 11.30am at lunchtime, and by 7pm in the evening), and note that the best places will be packed around noon.

Most specialize in one type of food, generally indicated on a signboard, or offer the ubiquitous *com* and *pho* rice dishes and noodle soups; what's available is usually displayed in a glass cabinet or on a buffet table. *Com binh dan*, "people's meals", are also popular. Here you select from an array of prepared dishes, piling your plate with such things as stuffed tomatoes, fried fish, tofu, pickles or eggs, plus a helping of rice; expect to pay from around US$1 for a good plateful. Though it's not a major problem at these prices, some street kitchens overcharge, so double-check when ordering.

While regular restaurants in Vietnam are definitely improving, the food served at many street kitchens is often superior in quality and much cheaper; they're also a lot more fun. All you need is a bit of judicious selection – look for clean places with a fast turnover, where the ingredients are obviously fresh – plus a smattering of basic vocabulary (see p.51).

In a smiliar vein to street kitchens are **bia hoi outlets**. Though these are primarily drinking establishments, many provide good-value snacks or even main meals (see p.51 for more on *bia hoi*).

Restaurants

If you're after more relaxed dining, where people aren't queuing for your seat, then head for a Western-style **Vietnamese restaurant** (*nha hang*), which will have chairs rather than stools, a name, a menu and often be closed to the street. In general these places serve a more varied selection of Vietnamese dishes than the street kitchens.

Menus at these places don't always show prices and overcharging is a regular problem, making for tedious ordering as you check the cost of each dish or risk an astronomical bill at the end. Another thing to watch out for are the extras: peanuts, hot towels and packs of tissues on the table may be added to the bill even if untouched; ask for them to be taken away if you don't want them, and check the bill carefully. A modest meal for two should cost roughly US$8–10.

Opening hours are usually during lunch, from 10.30am to 2pm, and in the evening from 5pm to no later than 9pm, or 8pm in the north.

The more **expensive restaurants** (including the smarter hotel dining rooms) tend to stay open later in the evening, perhaps until 9.30pm or 10.30pm, have menus priced in dollars and, in some cases, accept credit cards. Usually their menus indicate if there's a service charge, but watch out for an additional four to five percent on credit card payments. These restaurants can be relatively fancy places, with at least a nod towards decor and ambience, and correspondingly higher prices (a meal for two is likely to cost at least US$10–15 and often much more).

The most popular **foreign cuisine** on offer is French, though both Hanoi and Ho Chi Minh City boast some pretty good international restaurants, including Thai, Chinese, Tex Mex, Indian and Italian. As yet, high-class restaurants are scarce in the rest of Vietnam, though Hué, Da Nang, Hoi An and Nha Trang are beginning to get in on the act.

Travellers' cafés

Catering primarily to budget travellers, what have become known as **travellers' cafés** tend to serve fairly mediocre Western and Vietnamese dishes – from pancakes to steak and chips – and have the advantage of **all-day opening**, usually from 7am to 11pm or midnight. If you crave a reasonably priced Western-style breakfast, fresh fruit salad or a mango-shake, these are the places to go. Such cafés naturally flourish in the popular tourist towns, notably Hanoi, Ho Chi Minh, Hoi An, Hué, Nha Trang and Da Lat.

Vietnamese food

The staple of Vietnamese meals is **rice**, with noodles a popular alternative at breakfast or as a snack. Typically, rice will be accompanied by a fish or meat dish, a vegetable dish and soup, followed by a green tea digestive.

Breakfast

Vietnamese traditionally breakfast on *pho* or some other **noodle soup**. Alternatively, you might find early-morning hawkers peddling *xoi*, a wholesome mix of steamed **sticky rice** with soya bean, sweet corn or peanuts. Simple **Western breakfasts** (such as bread with jam, cheese or eggs, and coffee) are usually available in the travellers' cafés or hotels. More upmarket places increasingly stretch to cereals and fresh milk, while some top-class hotels lay on the full works in their breakfast buffets. In towns, you could always buy jam and bread or croissants for a **do-it-yourself** breakfast; however, things get more difficult out in the sticks, where you may even develop a taste for starting the day on a *pho*.

Seafood and fish – from rivers, lakes, canals and paddy fields as well as the sea – are favoured throughout the country, either fresh or dried. The most commonly used **flavourings** are shallots, coriander and lemon grass, though ginger, saffron, mint, anise and a basil-type herb also feature strongly, and coconut milk gives some southern dishes a distinctive richness.

Even in the south, Vietnamese food tends not to be over-spicy; instead chilli sauces or fresh chillies are served separately. Vietnam's most famous seasoning is the ubiquitous **nuoc mam**, a nutrient-packed sauce which either is added during cooking or forms the base for various dipping sauces. *Nuoc mam* is made by fermenting huge quantities of fish in vats of salt for between six months and a year, after which the dark brown liquid is strained and graded according to its age and flavour. Phu Quoc Island is widely held to produce the finest quality, though both Phan Thiet and Phan Rang also turn out a mean *nuoc mam*. Foreigners usually find the smell of the sauce pretty rank, but most soon acquire a taste for its distinctive salty-sweetness.

The use of **monosodium glutamate** (MSG) can be excessive, especially in northern cooking, and some people are known to react badly to the seasoning. A few restaurants in the main cities have cottoned on to the foibles of foreigners and advertise MSG-free food; elsewhere, try saying *khong co my chinh* (without MSG), and keep your fingers crossed. Note that what looks like salt on the table is sometimes MSG, so taste it first.

The most famous Vietnamese dish has to be **spring rolls**, variously known as *cha gio*, *cha nem*, *nem ran* or just plain *nem*. Various combinations of minced pork, shrimp or crab, rice vermicelli, onions, bean sprouts and an edible fungus are rolled in rice-paper wrappers, and then eaten fresh or deep-fried. In some places they're served with a bowl of lettuce or mint, in which case you're supposed to wrap some leaves around each roll – using deft chopstick manoeuvres – before dipping it in the accompanying sauce. In addition, a southern variation has barbecued strips of pork wrapped in semi-transparent rice wrappers, along with raw ingredients such as green banana and star fruit, and then dunked in a rich peanut sauce.

Soups and noodles

Though it originated in the north, another dish you'll find throughout Vietnam is *pho* (pronounced "fur"), a noodle **soup** eaten at any time of day but primarily at breakfast. The basic bowl of *pho* consists of a light beef broth, flavoured with ginger, coriander and sometimes cinnamon, to which are added broad, flat rice-noodles, spring onions and slivers of chicken, pork or beef. At the table you add a squeeze of lime and a sprinkling of chilli flakes or a spoonful of chilli sauce. There are numerous variations on the theme, such as adding a raw egg to make a more substantial meal. If you stray far off the beaten track, you're likely to become quite a connoisseur of *pho*.

Countless other types of soup are dished up at street restaurants. *Bun bo* is another substantial beef and noodle soup eaten countrywide, though most famous in Hué, while in the south, *hu tieu*, a soup of vermicelli, pork and seafood noodles, is best taken in My Tho. *Chao* (or *xhao*), on the other hand, is a thick rice gruel served piping hot, usually with shredded chicken or filleted fish, flavoured with dill and with perhaps a raw egg cooking at the bottom; it's often served with fried breadsticks (*quay*). Sour soups are a popular accompaniment for fish, while *lau*, a standard of most restaurant menus, is more of a main meal than a soup, where the vegetable broth arrives at the table in a steamboat (a ring-shaped metal dish on live coals or, nowadays, often electrically heated). You cook slivers of beef, prawns or similar in the simmering soup, and then drink the flavourful liquid that's left in the cooking pot.

Fish and meat

Among the highlights of Vietnamese cuisine are its succulent **seafood** and freshwater **fish**. *Cha ca* is a famous fish dish (sautéed in butter at the table with dill and spring onions, then served with rice noodles and a sprinkling of peanuts) invented in Hanoi but now found in most upmarket restaurants, while *ca kho to*, fish stew cooked in a clay pot, is a southern speciality. Another dish found in more expensive restaurants is *chao* *tom* (or *tom bao mia*), consisting of savoury shrimp pâté wrapped round sweet sugar cane and fried.

Every conceivable type of meat and part of the animal anatomy finds itself on the Vietnamese dining table, though the staples are straightforward beef, chicken and pork. **Ground meat**, especially pork, is a common constituent of stuffings, for example in spring rolls or the similar *banh cuon*, a steamed, rice-flour "ravioli" filled with minced pork, black mushrooms and bean sprouts; a popular variation uses prawns instead of meat. Pork is also used, with plenty of herbs, to make Hanoi's *bun cha*, small **hamburgers** barbecued on an open charcoal brazier and served on a bed of cold rice-noodles with greens and a slightly sweetish sauce. One famous southern dish is *bo bay mon* (often written *bo 7 mon*), meaning literally **beef** seven ways, consisting of a platter of beef cooked in different styles.

Roving gourmets may want to try some of the more unusual meats on offer. **Dog** meat (*thit cay* or *thit cho*) is a particular delicacy in the north, where "yellow dog" (sandy-haired varieties) is considered the tastiest. Winter is the season to eat dog meat – it's said to give extra body heat, and is also supposed to remove bad luck if consumed at the end of the lunar month. **Snake** (*thit con ran*), like dog, is supposed to improve male virility. Dining on snake is surrounded by a ritual, which, if you're guest of honour, requires you to swallow the still-beating heart. Another one strictly for the strong of stomach is *trung vit lon*, embryo-containing **duck eggs** boiled and eaten only five days before hatching – bill, webbed feet, feathers and all.

Vegetables – and vegetarian food

If all this has put you off meat for ever, it is possible to eat **vegetarian** food in Vietnam, though not always easy. The widest selection of vegetables is to be found in Da Lat where a staggering variety of tropical and temperate crops thrive. Elsewhere, most restaurants offer a smattering of meat-free dishes, ranging from stewed spinach or similar greens, to a more appetizing mix of onion, tomato, bean sprouts, various mushrooms, peppers and so on; places used to

foreigners may be able to oblige with vegetarian spring rolls (*nem an chay*, or *nem khong co thit*). At street kitchens you're likely to find tofu and one or two dishes of pickled vegetables, such as cabbage or cucumber, while occasionally they may also have aubergine, bamboo shoots or avocado, depending on the season.

However, unless you go to a **specialist** vegetarian outlet – of which there are some excellent examples in Ho Chi Minh City, Hanoi and Hué – it can be a problem finding genuine veggie food: soups are usually made with beef stock, morsels of pork fat sneak into otherwise innocuous-looking dishes and animal fat tends to be used for frying.

The phrase to remember is *an chay* (vegetarian), or seek out a vegetarian rice shop (*tiem com chay*). Otherwise, make the most of the 1st and 15th days of the lunar month when many Vietnamese Buddhists spurn meat and you're more likely to find vegetarian dishes on offer.

Snacks

Vietnam has a wide range of snacks and nibbles to fill any yawning gaps, from huge rice-flour **crackers** sprinkled with sesame seeds to all sorts of dried fish, nuts and seeds. The white steamed **dumpling** called *banh bao* is a Chinese import, filled with tasty titbits, such as pork, onions and tangy mushrooms or strands of sweet coconut. *Banh xeo*, meaning sizzling **pancake**, combines shrimp, pork, bean sprouts and egg, all fried and then wrapped in rice paper with a selection of greens before being dunked in a spicy sauce. A similar dish, originating from Hué – a city with a vast repertoire of snack foods – is *banh khoai*, in which the flat pancake is accompanied by a plate of star fruit, green banana and aromatic herbs, plus a rich peanut sauce.

Markets are often good snacking grounds, with stalls churning out soups and spring rolls or selling intriguing banana-leaf parcels of pâté (a favourite accompaniment for *bia hoi*), pickled pork sausage or perhaps a cake of sticky rice.

A relative newcomer on the culinary scene is French **bread**, made with wheat flour in the north and rice flour in the south. Baguettes – sometimes sold warm from streetside stoves – are sliced open and stuffed with pâté, soft cheese, or ham and pickled vegetables.

Fruit and sweet things

Vietnam is not strong on desserts, and restaurants usually stick to ice cream and fruit, although fancy international places might venture into *crêpe suzette* territory. Those with a sweet tooth are better off browsing around street stalls where there are usually candied fruits and other Vietnamese **sweetmeats** on offer, as well as sugary displays of French-inspired cakes and pastries in the main tourist centres.

Green-coloured *banh com* is an eye-catching local delicacy made by wrapping pounded glutinous rice around sugary, green-bean paste. A similar confection, found only during the mid-autumn festival, is the "earth cake", *banh deo*, which melds the contrasting flavours of candied fruits, sesame and lotus seeds with a dice of savoury pork fat. **Fritters** are popular among children and you'll find opportunistic hawkers outside schools, selling banana fritters, *banh chuoi*, or mixed slices of banana and sweet potato, *banh chuoi khoai*.

Most cities now have **ice-cream** parlours selling tubs or sticks of the local, hard ices in chocolate, vanilla or green-tea flavours, though for health reasons it's safest to buy only from the larger, busier outlets and not from street hawkers. More exotic tastes can be satisfied at the European- and American-style ice-cream parlours of Hanoi and Ho Chi Minh City, while excellent yoghurts are also increasingly available at ice-cream parlours and some cafés.

With its diverse climate, Vietnam is blessed with both tropical and temperate **fruits**, including dozens of banana species. The richest orchards are in the south, where pineapple, coconut, papaya, mango, longan and mangosteen flourish. Da Lat is famous for its strawberries, while the region around Nha Trang produces the peculiar "dragon fruit" (*thanh long*). The size and shape of a small pineapple, the dragon fruit has a mauvish-pink skin, studded with small protuberances,

and smooth, white flesh speckled with tiny black seeds. The slightly sweet, watery flesh is thirst-quenching, and hence is often served as a drink, crushed with ice.

A fruit that is definitely an acquired taste is the durian, a spiky, yellow-green football-sized fruit with an unmistakably pungent odour reminiscent of mature cheese and caramel, but tasting like an onion-laced custard. Jackfruit looks worryingly similar to durian but is generally larger and has smaller spikes. Its yellow segments of flesh are deliciously sweet.

Drinks

Giai khat means "quench your thirst" and you'll see the signs everywhere, on stands selling fresh juices, bottled cold drinks or outside cafés and *bia hoi* (draught beer) outlets. Many drinks are served with ice: tempting though it may be, the only really safe policy is to avoid **ice** altogether – *dung bo da, cam on* ("no ice, thanks") should do the trick. That said, ice in the top hotels, bars and restaurants is generally reliable, and some people take the risk in far dodgier establishments with apparent impunity.

Water and soft drinks

Bottled **water** is widely available at around US$0.50 per litre; avoid any other water, and even drinks that may have been diluted with suspect water (see p.28 for more on this).

Locally made **soft drinks** are tooth-numbingly sweet, but are cheap and safe – as long as the bottle or carton appears well sealed – and on sale just about everywhere. The Coke, Sprite and Fanta hegemony also means you can find fizzy drinks in surprisingly remote areas. Oddly, canned drinks are usually more expensive than the equivalent-sized bottle, whether it's a soft drink or beer – apparently it's less chic to drink from the old-fashioned bottle.

A more effective thirst-quencher is fresh coconut juice, though this is more difficult to find in the north. Fresh juices such as orange and lime are also delicious – just make sure they haven't been mixed with tap water – or try sugar-cane juice (*mia da*) with a dash of lime. Pasteurized milk, produced by Vinamilk, is now sold in the main towns and cities.

Somewhere between a drink and a snack, **ché** is made from taro flour and green bean, and served over ice with chunks of fruit, coloured jellies and even sweet corn or potato. In hot weather it provides a refreshing sugar-fix.

Tea and coffee

Tea drinking is part of the social ritual in Vietnam. Small cups of refreshing, strong, green tea are presented to all guests or visitors: the well-boiled water is safe to drink, as long as the cup itself is clean, and it's considered rude not to take at least a sip. Although your cup will be continually replenished to show hospitality, you don't have to carry on drinking; the polite way to decline a refill is to place your hand over the cup when your host is about to replenish it. Green tea is also served at the end of every meal, particularly in the south, and is usually provided free in restaurants and at food stalls.

There's a current fad for teashops, of which the Dilmah Tea House chain is the most widespread. They serve an extensive range of teas and herbal infusions – including such exotica as English-style black tea with fresh milk – as well as beer, juices and basic snacks.

Vietnam's best tea is said to grow around Bao Loc, southwest of Da Lat in the central highlands, and the best **coffee** a few kilometres further north among the hills of Buon Me Thuot. The Vietnamese drink coffee very strong and in small quantities, with a large dollop of condensed milk at the bottom of the cup. Traditionally, coffee is filtered at the table by means of a small dripper balanced over the cup or glass, which sometimes sits in a bowl of hot water to keep it warm. However, places accustomed to tourists increasingly run to fresh (pasteurized) milk, while in the main cities you'll now find fancy Western-style cafés turning out quite decent lattes and cappuccinos. Out in the sticks, look out for the Trung Nguyen chain of coffee houses – they're cheap and cheerful and the coffee isn't bad either.

Alcoholic drinks

Canned and **bottled beers** brewed under licence in Vietnam include Tiger, Heineken, Carlsberg and San Miguel, but there are also plenty of very drinkable – and cheaper – local beers around, such as Halida, 333 (Ba Ba Ba) and Bivina. Some connoisseurs rate Saigon Export tops, though Hanoi Beer, BGI and Bière la Rue from Da Nang are also fine brews. Many other towns boast their own local beers, such as Hué (where the brand is Huda) and Thanh Hoa (where it's simply Thanh Hoa) – all worth a try.

Roughly forty years ago technology for making **bia hoi** (draught beer) was introduced from Czechoslovakia and is now quaffed in vast quantities, particularly in the north. *Bia hoi* may taste fairly weak, but it measures in at up to four percent alcohol. It's also cheap – between 1500d and 4000d a glass – and supposedly unadulterated with chemicals, so in theory you're less likely to get a hangover. *Bia hoi* has a 24-hour shelf life, which means the better places sell out by early evening and you're unlikely to be drinking it into the wee hours. In the south, you're more likely to be drinking **bia tuoi** ("fresh" beer), a close relation of *bia hoi* but served from pressurized barrels.

There are countless *bia hoi* outlets in most major cities, ranging from a few ankle-high stools gathered round a barrel on the pavement to beer gardens. Quality tends to be more consistent at the larger outlets supplied by major breweries such as Hanoi Beer and Halida (under the name Viet Ha), rather than the smaller places which usually buy their beer from microbreweries. On the whole, the more expensive – and colder – the beer, the better it is.

Bia hoi culture is about enjoying a few beers with a group of friends – usually all male, though in the cities you see a few women these days. People almost never drink alone and rarely drink without eating and many places serve a range of snacks and more extensive dishes; see box opposite for a list of classic *bia hoi* dishes. Outlets are usually open at lunchtime and then again in the evening from 5pm to 9pm.

Almost anything edible in Vietnam is turned into **wine** or **spirit** (*ruou*), or steeped

Bia hoi know-how

To help you order food in a *bia hoi* outlet, we've listed a few classic dishes below. Menus, if they exist, will be in Vietnamese. They normally give a price range for each dish (meat dishes typically range between $1 and $2), so you order a small, medium or large amount, for example, depending on the size of your group. To maximize the variety, it makes sense to order small quantities of several dishes and share. If no prices are indicated on the menu, be sure to ask when ordering. Usually a note with the running total is left on the table, so you can keep track of how much you're spending.

bo luc lac	cubed spicy beef and green pepper stir-fry	*khoai tay ran lac*	chips/French fries peanuts
ca ba lo	oven-cooked fish	*muc chien bo*	squid fried in butter
dau chien ron	fried tofu	*muc kho*	dried squid
dau tu xuyen	tofu in a Chinese pork and tomato sauce	*muc tam bot*	battered squid
		nem chua	minced spicy cured pork wrapped in banana leaf
dua chuot che	sliced cucumber	*nom du du*	papaya salad
de tai chanh	lightly-cooked goat with green banana, pineapple and lemon	*nom hoa chuoi*	banana-flower salad
		nom ngo sen	lotus-stem salad
ech chien bo	deep-fried battered frogs legs	*oc xao xa ot*	stir-fried snail, lemongrass and chilli
ech xao mang	frogs legs with bamboo shoots	*rau bi xaoi bo/toi*	beef/pumpkin-leaf fried with garlic
ga xe phay	shredded chicken salad with bean sprouts, carrot, peanuts and basil	*tho quay*	roast rabbit
		tom hap bia	shrimps steamed in beer
		tom nuong	grilled shrimps

in it – including rice, strawberries, mulberries, snakes and assorted herbs. As often as not, these drinks are medicinal tonics rather than alcoholic beverages, and there's a lively export trade in sending such efficacious brews up to China. The most common local wine is **rice alcohol**, which features heavily at festivals and for making toasts at official receptions. The ethnic minorities of the northwest (Thai and Muong) concoct their own version, called stem alcohol (*ruou can*), which is drunk from a communal jar using thin, bamboo straws. The recipe for *ruou can* is a closely guarded secret, but its basic constituents are sticky rice, herbs and spices, which are heated together and then buried in the ground for a month or more to ferment. You can indulge in some of the best *ruou can* in Son La or Mai Chau.

Wine made from grapes is becoming increasingly popular in Vietnam. Local production – dating from the French era and centred around Da Lat – has been ramped up in recent years and even in fairly small towns you'll find the odd bottle of imported wine for sale. Many bars and restaurants in the major tourist destinations now serve wine, though some of it is pretty disgusting. For a decent bottle that's been properly stored you'll be paying premium prices at one of the top restaurants or specialist shops in Hanoi and Ho Chi Minh City.

Communications

Vietnam has been investing heavily in its communications networks. International phone connections are among the most expensive in the world, but on the whole it's easy to phone or fax abroad, even from the smaller towns. International mail services also seem to work fairly efficiently and are reasonably reliable to or from any of the major cities. However, a quicker and relatively reliable way of keeping in touch is by email, with new outlets opening all the time.

Domestic telephone calls are less reliable, plagued by poor-quality lines and bad connections, while in-country post usually gets there eventually.

Mail

Mail can take anything from four days to four weeks in or out of Vietnam, depending largely where you are. Services are quickest and most reliable from the major towns, where eight to ten days is the norm. **Overseas postal rates** are reasonable: a postcard costs around 8000d, while the price of a letter is in the region of 12,000d for the minimum weight. **Express Mail Service** (EMS) operates to most countries and certain destinations within Vietnam; the service cuts down delivery times substantially and the letter or parcel is automatically registered.

Main **post offices** are open seven days a week, normally 6.30am–9.30pm; smaller offices may close for an hour at lunch and at weekends. Rates for phone and fax services are posted up in the main halls.

Poste restante services are available at all main post offices. You'll need to show your passport to collect mail and will be charged a small amount per item. Mail is held for two months before being returned. To avoid misfiling, your name should be printed clearly, with the surname in capitals and underlined, and it's still worth checking under your first name, just in case. Have letters addressed to you c/o Poste Restante, GPO, town or city, province.

When **sending parcels** out of Vietnam, take everything to the post office unwrapped since it will be inspected by customs officials. Novels and other material about Vietnam printed abroad can cause problems, and you may also be charged customs duty on items

such as CDs. After inspection, and a good deal of form-filling, the parcel will be wrapped for you; there's a small charge for both the wrapping and the customs inspection. Surface mail is the cheapest option, with parcels taking between one and four months. Note that some parcel counters are only open in the morning.

Receiving parcels is not such a good idea. Some parcels simply go astray; those that do make it are subject to thorough customs inspections, import duty and even confiscation of suspicious items – particularly printed matter, videos or cassettes. However, if you do need to collect a parcel, remember to take your passport.

Telephones

One benefit of Vietnam's late entry into modern telecommunications has been the opportunity to leapfrog straight in with the latest technology: where the system does work, it works well. The massive amount of capital investment required is how the government justifies its high tariffs on **international calls**, though charges have been falling. The cheapest method of calling abroad is to use the **171 call service** which routes calls over the Internet; to use this service, simply dial 171 before the international access code (see box opposite for details of dialling codes). There's a flat rate of US$1.20 per minute during peak hours and US$0.95 off-peak (cheap rates apply Mon–Sat 11pm–7am, all day Sun and on public holidays). By contrast, the per-minute charge for regular calls, not using the 171 prefix, stands at just over US$1.50 and US$1.30 respectively. It's worth noting that the 171 service doesn't cover operator-assisted calls, mobile phones, cardphones or faxes, and that post offices may charge a small fee for using it.

That said, the best place to call abroad is from a post office, nearly all of which have IDD (international direct dialling) facilities. In addition you can call from IDD phone kiosks along Ho Chi Minh City's Pham Ngu Lao and De Tham streets. Most hotels now offer IDD from your room, but you'll usually be charged at least ten percent above the norm and a minimum charge of one minute even if the call goes unanswered.

If you're running short of funds, you can almost always get a "call-back" at post offices. Ask to make a minimum (one-minute) call abroad and remember to get the phone number of the booth you're calling from. You can then be called back directly, at a total cost to you of a one-minute international call plus a small charge for the service. It's also possible to make **collect calls** to certain countries; ask at the post office or call the international operator on ☎110.

Long-distance domestic calls are far more reasonably priced, of course, but again the cheapest option is to dial direct using the 171 prefix from a phone box or post office. There's a one-minute minimum charge for this too and the same off-peak periods apply. The minimum charge for **local calls** made from a post office or phone box within the city or town limits is three minutes, though in theory calls are free from private phones (including hotels and restaurants). Note that you always have to pay when making a call *to* a mobile phone.

Finding a phone number is not so easy. The better hotels should have up-to-date directories and their reception staff will usually help; otherwise, try asking in the post office, or calling **directory enquiries** (☎116) and speaking to one of their English-speak-

ing staff, for which you pay a small charge.

Public phones (all cardphones) are becoming more widespread, though most cabins offer little protection from street noise. Phonecards can be purchased at the post office: to phone abroad you'll need to buy one of the more expensive cards (approximately US$6 and $10), while the cheapest card (roughly US$3) is good for domestic calls. Instructions are displayed on the phone in a variety of languages, including English.

International and domestic **fax** is widely available at many hotels, but cheaper at post offices, which charge per page rather than per minute. Both hotels and post offices charge a small fee for receiving faxes on your behalf; post offices will deliver them to your hotel (if specified on the fax) for no extra charge.

Mobile/cell phones

If you want to use your own **mobile/cell phone** in Vietnam, the simplest – and cheapest – thing to do is to buy a SIM card and a prepaid phonecard locally. Both the big phone companies, Mobiphone and Vinaphone, offer similar prices, geographical coverage (which extends pretty much nationwide) and English-language support. At the time of writing, for example, a package including a SIM card and roughly US$20 worth of calls costs around US$30, with further prepaid cards available in various sizes between approximately US$6 and $30. Calls cost slightly more than from a land line and, as usual, you'll be docked a small amount for incoming calls.

The other, far more expensive, option is to stick with your home service-provider – though you'll need to check whether they offer coverage in Vietnam.

Dialling codes

Every province in Vietnam has an **area code** that must be used when phoning from outside that province. Area codes are included in telephone numbers throughout the Guide – omit them if dialling within the province.

To **call Vietnam from abroad**, dial your international access code, then ☎84 + area code minus first 0 + number.

To **call abroad from Vietnam**, dial either ☎171 00 or just ☎00 followed by the country code (see below) + area code minus first 0 + number.

Australia ☎61	Ireland ☎353	UK ☎44
Canada ☎1	New Zealand ☎64	USA ☎1

In the **UK**, for all but the very top-of-the-range packages, you'll have to contact your phone-provider to get international access switched on, for which there may be a charge. If you want to retrieve messages while you're away, you'll have to ask your provider for a new access code. For further information about using your phone abroad, check out ⓦwww.telecomsadvice.org.uk /features/using_your_mobile_abroad.htm.

Unless you have a tri-band phone, it's unlikely that a cell phone bought for use in the **US** will work outside the States. For details of which phones will work outside the US, contact your service-provider.

Most mobiles in **Australia and New Zealand** use GSM, which works well in Southeast Asia – check with your provider.

Email and the Internet

Linking to the **Internet** from Vietnam has become a great deal easier, though direct access is still tightly controlled by a government fearful of this potentially subversive means of communication. The best option, particularly if you're travelling for several months, is to sign up for a free Web-based **email** addres with a company such as Hotmail (ⓦwww.hotmail.com) or YahooMail (ⓦwww.yahoo.com) before leaving home. Once you've set up an account, you can use these sites to pick up and send mail from anywhere with Internet access.

There's no problem about logging on in the major cities and tourist centres in Vietnam, where you'll find dozens of **cybercafés,** while many hotels and travellers' cafés also offer Internet access. Once you get into the remoter regions, however, the opportunities are few and far between, though the situation is improving.

Current rates vary wildly from 100d to 400d per minute, with some places charging by the hour or half-hour. Outside the big cities connections can be frustratingly slow, though after 9pm things generally speed up a bit.

If you're **travelling with a lap-top** and wanting to use your home-based email account, your best option is to check if your service-provider has links with a Vietnamese ISP through an organization such as GRIC (ⓦwww.gric.com), the largest of the informal networks of ISPs. Alternatively, you can buy a prepaid Internet access card through FPT (ⓦcardvn.net; Hanoi ☎04/822 3100; Ho Chi Minh ☎08/821 4160) which gives you password-protected local access. The cards are available in five denominations, from the fifteen-day Family Net Card (around US$3) up to a Business Card lasting one year (US$20).

ⓦwww.kropla.com is a useful website giving details of how to plug your lap-top in when abroad and other general information about such things as plugs and electrical systems.

The media

Vietnam has several English-language newspapers and magazines, of which the daily *Vietnam News* has the widest distribution. It provides a brief – and very select – rundown of local, regional and international news, as well as snippets on art and culture. Though short on general news, both the weekly *Vietnam Investment Review* and the monthly *Vietnam Economic Times* cover issues in greater depth and are worth looking at for an insight into what makes the Vietnamese economy tick. Both also publish useful supplements (respectively, *Time Out* and *The Guide*) with selective but up-to-date restaurant and nightlife listings mainly covering Hanoi and Ho Chi Minh, plus feature articles on culture and tourist destinations.

The Vietnam Department of Tourism also puts out the excellent free monthly, *Vietnam Discovery*. In addition to travel articles and restaurant and shop reviews, the magazine includes a handy pull-out listings supplement covering the main tourist destinations. Lastly, *Vietnam Pathfinder*, also published monthly, is usually worth a look for its travel features.

Foreign publications, such as the *International Herald Tribune*, *Time*, *The Economist*, *The Financial Times* and the Bangkok papers are available at some of the larger bookshops and in the newsstands of more upmarket hotels in Ho Chi Minh City and Hanoi (see "Listings", p.121 and p.401 respectively).

The government **radio** station, Voice of Vietnam (Ⓦwww.vov.org.vn), began life in 1945 during the August Revolution. It became famous during the American War when "Hanoi Hannah" broadcast propaganda programmes to American GIs. Nowadays it maintains six channels, of which VOV5 (105.5MHz) broadcasts English-language programmes several times a day covering a whole range of subjects: news, weather, sport, entertainment and culture, even market prices.

To keep in touch with the full spectrum of international news, however, you'll need a short-wave radio to pick up one of the world service channels, such as **BBC** World Service (Ⓦwww.bbc.co.uk/worldservice), **Radio Canada** (Ⓦwww.rcinet.ca), and **Voice of America** (Ⓦwww.voa.gov); local frequencies are listed on the relevant website.

Vietnamese **television** (VTV, Ⓦwww.vtv.org.vn) is also government-run and airs a mix of films, music shows, news programmes, soaps and foreign (mostly American, Korean and Japanese) imports. VTV1, the main domestic channel, presents the news in English twice a day, usually at 2pm and 6pm. However, hotels increasingly provide satellite TV, and even budget places in the main cities now offer CNN and MTV as standard.

Opening hours

Basic hours of business are 7.30–11.30am and 1.30–4.30pm, though after lunch nothing really gets going again before 2pm. The standard closing day for offices is Sunday, and many now also close on Saturdays, including most state-run banks and government offices.

At the time of writing, most **banks** tend to work Monday to Friday 8–11.30am and 1–4pm, though some stay open later in the afternoon or may forego a lunch break. In tourist centres you'll even find branches open evenings and weekends. **Post offices** keep much longer hours, in general staying open from 6.30am through to 9.30pm with no closing day. Some sub-post offices work shorter hours and close at weekends.

Shops and **markets** open seven days a week and in theory keep going all day, though in practice most stallholders and many private shopkeepers will take a siesta. Shops mostly stay open late into the evenings, perhaps until 8pm or beyond in the big cities.

Museums tend to close one day a week, generally on Mondays, and their core opening hours are 8–11am and 2–4pm. **Temples** and **pagodas** occasionally close for lunch but are otherwise open all week and don't close until late evening.

Festivals and religious events

The Vietnamese year follows a rhythm of festivals and religious observances ranging from solemn family gatherings at the ancestral altar to national celebrations culminating in Tet, the Vietnamese New Year. In between are countless local festivals, most notably in the Red River Delta, honouring the tutelary spirit of the village or community temple.

The majority of festivals take place in spring, with a second flurry in the autumn months. One festival you might want to make a note of, however, is **Tet**: not only does most of Vietnam close down for the week, but either side of the holiday local transport services are stretched to the limit and international flights are filled by returning overseas Vietnamese.

Many Vietnamese festivals are **Chinese** in origin, imbued with a distinctive flavour over the centuries, but minority groups also hold their own specific celebrations. The ethnic **minorities** continue to punctuate the year with rituals that govern sowing, harvest or hunting, as well as elaborate rites of passage surrounding birth and death. The **Cao Dai** religion has its own array of festivals,

Vietnam's major festivals

Spring festivals (Jan–April)
Tet The most important date in the Vietnamese festival calendar is New Year (*Tet Nguyen Dan*). After an initial jamboree, Tet is largely a family occasion when offices are shut, and many shops and restaurants may close for the seven-day festival. Officially only the first three days are public holidays, though many people take the whole week. First to seventh days of first lunar month; late Jan to mid-Feb.
Tay Son Festival Martial arts demonstrations in Tay Son District, plus garlanded elephants on parade. Fifth day of first lunar month; late Jan to mid-Feb.
Water Puppet Festival As part of the Tet celebrations a festival of puppetry is held at Thay Pagoda, west of Hanoi. Fifth to seventh days of first lunar month; Feb.
Lim Singing Festival Two weeks after Tet, Lim village near Bac Ninh, in the Red River Delta, resounds to the harmonies of "alternate singing" (*quan ho*) as men and women fling improvised lyrics back and forth. Thirteenth to fifteenth days of the first lunar month; Feb–March.
Hai Ba Trung Festival The two Trung sisters are honoured with a parade and dancing at Hanoi's Hai Ba Trung temple. Sixth day of the second lunar month; March.
Perfume Pagoda Vietnam's most famous pilgrimage site is Chua Huong, west of Hanoi. Thousands of Buddhist pilgrims flock to the pagoda for the festival, which climaxes on the full moon (fourteenth or fifteenth day) of the second month, though the pilgrimage continues for a month either side. March–April.
Den Ba Chua Kho The full moon of the second month sees Hanoians congregating at this temple near Bac Ninh, to petition the goddess for success in business. March–April.
Thanh Minh Ancestral graves are cleaned and offerings of food, flowers and paper votive objects made at the beginning of the third lunar month. April.

Summer festivals (May–Aug)
Phat Dan Lanterns are hung outside the pagodas and Buddhist homes to commemorate Buddha's birth, enlightenment and the attainment of Nirvana. Eighth day of the fourth moon; May.

while **Christian** communities throughout Vietnam observe the major ceremonies. Christmas is marked as a religious event only by the faithful, but Christmas Day is now a public holiday in Vietnam and city-dwellers, particularly in Ho Chi Minh City, increasingly enter into the spirit of the occasion with parties and family gatherings.

Some festivities have seen a revival since *doi moi* (see p.507) but on the whole the number of such celebrations is in decline, not least because of the expense involved. You may be lucky enough to happen on a local festival, but the ceremonies you're most likely to see are **weddings** and **funerals**. The tenth lunar month is the most auspicious time for weddings, though at other times you'll also encounter plenty of wedding cavalcades on the road, their hired buses decked out with red-paper stencils of the Chinese ideograph for "happiness".

Funeral processions are recognizable from the white headbands worn by mourners, while close family members dress completely in white. It's considered lucky to meet a funeral procession: the deceased will soon ascend to heaven and might see fit to put in a favourable word with the gods on your behalf.

Most festivals take place according to the **lunar calendar**, which is also closely linked to the Chinese system with a zodiac of twelve animal signs. The most important times during the lunar month (which lasts 29 or 30 days) are the full moon (day one) and the new moon (day fourteen or fifteen). Festivals are often held at these times, which also hold a special significance for Buddhists, who are supposed to pray at the pagoda and avoid eating meat during the two days. On the eve of each full moon, Hoi An now celebrates a **Full-Moon Festival**: traffic is barred from the town centre, where

Chua Xu Festival The stone statue of Chua Xu at Sam Mountain, Chau Doc, is bathed, and thousands flock to honour her. Twenty-third to twenty-fifth day of fourth lunar month; May.

Tet Doan Ngo The summer solstice (fifth day of the fifth moon) is marked by festivities aimed at warding off epidemics brought on by the summer heat. This is also the time of dragon-boat races. Late May to early June.

Trang Nguyen (or *Vu Lan*) The day of wandering souls is the second most important festival after Tet. Offerings of food and clothes are made to comfort and nourish the unfortunate souls without a home, and all graves are cleaned. This is also time for the forgiveness of faults, when the King of Hell judges everyone's spirits and metes out reward or punishment as appropriate. Until the fifteenth century prisoners were allowed to go home on this day. Fourteenth or fifteenth day of the seventh lunar month; Aug.

Autumn festivals (Sept–Dec)

Do Son buffalo fighting festival Held in Do Son village, near Haiphong. Ninth and tenth days of the eighth lunar month.

Kate Festival The Cham New Year is celebrated in high style at Po Klong Garai and Po Re Me, both near Phan Rang. Sept–Oct.

Trung Thu The mid-autumn festival, also known as Children's Day, is when dragon dances take place and children are given lanterns in the shape of stars, carp or dragons. Special cakes, *banh trung thu*, are eaten at this time of year. These are sticky rice cakes filled with lotus seeds, nuts and candied fruits and are either square like the earth (*banh deo*), or round like the moon (*banh nuong*) and containing the yolk of an egg. Fourteenth or fifteenth day of the eighth lunar month; Sept–Oct.

Whale Festival Lang Ca Ong, Vung Tau. Crowds gather to make offerings to the whales. Sixteenth day of the eighth lunar month; Sept–Oct.

Ghe Ngo Festival Boat-racing festival in Soc Trang. Tenth day of tenth lunar month; Nov–Dec.

Christmas Midnight services at the cathedrals in Hanoi and Ho Chi Minh and much revelry in the streets. December 24.

traditional games, dance and music performances take place under the light of silk lanterns.

All Vietnamese calendars show both the lunar and solar (Gregorian) months and dates, but to be sure of a festival date it's best to check locally.

Tet: the Vietnamese New Year

"Tet", simply meaning festival, is the accepted name for Vietnam's most important annual event, properly known as **Tet Nguyen Dan**, or festival of the first day. Tet lasts for seven days and falls sometime between the last week of January and the third week of February, on the night of the new moon. This is a time when families get together to celebrate renewal and hope for the new year, when ancestral spirits are welcomed back to the household, and when everyone in Vietnam becomes a year older – age is reckoned by the new year and not by individual birthdays.

There's an almost tangible sense of excitement leading up to midnight on the eve of Tet, though the welcoming of the New Year is now a much more subdued – and less dangerous – affair since firecrackers were banned in 1995. Instead, all the major cities hold fireworks displays.

Tet kicks off seven days before the new moon with the **festival of Ong Tau**, the god of the hearth (23rd day of the twelfth month). Ong Tau keeps watch over the household throughout the year, wards off evil spirits and makes an annual report of family events, good or bad, to the Jade Emperor. In order to send Ong Tau off to heaven in a benevolent mood, the family cleans its house from top to bottom, and makes offerings to him, including pocket money and a new set of clothes. Ong Tau returns home at midnight on the first chime of the new year and it's this, together with welcoming the ancestral spirits back to share in the party, that warrants such a massive celebration.

Tet is all about **starting the year afresh**, with a clean slate and good intentions. Not only is the house scrubbed, but all debts are paid off and those who can afford it have a haircut and buy new clothes. To attract favourable spirits, good-luck charms are put in the house, most commonly cockerels or the trinity of male figures representing prosperity, happiness and longevity. The crucial moments are the first minutes and hours of the new year as these set the pattern for the whole of the following year. People strive to avoid arguments, swearing or breaking anything – at least during the first three days when a single ill word could tempt bad luck into the house for the whole year ahead. The first visitor on the morning of Tet is also vitally significant: the ideal is someone respected, wealthy and happily married who will bring good fortune to the family; the bereaved, unemployed, accident-prone and even pregnant women, on the other hand, are considered ill-favoured. This honour carries with it an onerous responsibility, however: if the family has a bad year, it will be the first-footer's fault.

The week-long festival is marked by **feasting**: special foods are eaten at Tet, such as pickled vegetables, candied lotus seeds and sugared fruits, all of which are first offered at the family altar. The most famous delicacy is *banh chung* (*banh tet* in the south), a thick square or cylinder of sweet, sticky rice that is prepared only for Tet. The rice is wrapped round a mixture of green-bean paste, pork fat and meat marinated in *nuoc mam*, and then boiled in banana leaves, which impart a pale green colour. Good-quality cakes can go for as much as US$1 apiece. According to legend, an impoverished prince of the Hung dynasty invented the cakes over two thousand years ago; his father was so impressed by the simplicity of his son's gift that he named the prince as his heir.

Public holidays

January 1: New Year's Day
Late January/mid-February (dates vary each year): Tet, Vietnamese New Year (three days, though increasingly offices tend to close down for a full week)
February 3: Founding of the Vietnamese Communist Party
April 30: Liberation of Saigon, 1975
May 1: International Labour Day
May 19: Birthday of Ho Chi Minh
June: Birthday of Buddha (eighth day of the fourth moon)
September 2: National Day
December 25: Christmas Day

Tet is an expensive time for Vietnamese families, many of whom save for months to get the new year off to a good start. Apart from special foods and new clothes, it's traditional to give children red envelopes containing *li xi*, or lucky money, and to decorate homes with spring blossoms. In the week before Tet, flower markets grace the larger cities: peach blossoms in the north, apricot in Hué and mandarin in the south. Plum and kumquat (symbolizing gold coins) are also popular, alongside the more showy, modern blooms of rose, dahlia or gladioli.

Sports and outdoor pursuits

Vietnam has been slow to develop its huge potential as an outdoor adventure destination. Things are starting to take off, however, as previously remote areas become more accessible and specialist tour agencies begin to offer activities ranging from trekking to kayaking and white-water rafting.

Trekking

While **trekking** in Vietnam remains fairly low-key, at least compared to the likes of Thailand and Nepal, there are still plenty of opportunities for one-day hikes and longer treks with overnight stops in minority villages.

The easiest and most popular area for trekking is in the northwest mountains around Sa Pa (see p.448) and, to a lesser extent, Mai Chau. In both cases there's plenty of interest in the immediate vicinity, although you'll have to trek for at least a day or so to reach unspoilt minority villages. Sa Pa is also the starting point for ascents of the country's highest peak, Fan Si Pan, a challenge to be undertaken only by experienced hikers. Other options include hiking around Kon Tum or Da Lat in the central highlands or in one of Vietnam's many national parks, including Cat Ba, Cuc Phuong, Bach Ma, Cat Thien and Yok Don. In Yok Don you can even go elephant trekking, though prices are rather steep. Also, a couple of new adventure sports companies in Da Lat have recently started incorporating rock climbing, abseiling and canyoning into their itineraries.

There's no problem about striking out on your own for a day's hiking. However, for anything more adventurous, particularly if you want to overnight in the villages, you'll need to make arrangements in advance. This is easily done either before you arrive in Vietnam or through local tour agents, most of which offer organized tours and tailor-made packages. In most cases you can also make arrangements through guesthouses and guides on the spot. Note that it's essential to take a guide if you are keen to get off the beaten track: many areas are still sensitive about the presence of foreigners.

Water sports

With its 3000-kilometre-long coastline, Vietnam should be a paradise for **water sports**, but the options remain fairly limited at present, for a variety of reasons. One is simply a matter of access: the infrastructure is not yet in place. More crucial is the presence of potentially dangerous undercurrents along much of the coast accompanied by strong winds at certain times of year. Many of the big beach resorts have guards or put out flags in season indicating where it's safe to swim. Elsewhere, check carefully before taking the plunge.

Whilst many of the beaches along the central and south-central coast are great for **swimming**, the best are those around Mui Ne, with Nha Trang, Hoi An and Da Nang close behind. Phu Quoc Island, off Vietnam's southern coast, is rapidly becoming known not only for its excellent beaches but also as the country's top spot for **snorkelling** and **scuba-diving**. Nha Trang is another popular place to don a snorkel or wet suit, but wherever

Messing about on the water

If your interest in water extends no further than wanting to gently float along it, then it's possible to **charter** a vessel in any seaside or riverside town simply by asking around at the water's edge – some places are better geared up to tourists than others.

In the **Mekong Delta**, the main centres for excursions are **My Tho** (p.138), **Vinh Long** (p.147), **Can Tho** (p.156) and **Chau Doc** (p.168), while up the coast **Nha Trang**'s tour companies do a roaring trade in boat trips to the nearby islands (p.259). You can take boat trips from **Hoi An** (p.274), putter up the Perfume River to visit **Hué**'s royal mausoleums (p.326) and be rowed through the caves of Tam Coc, near **Ninh Binh** (see p.349). But perhaps the quintessential waterborne experience is to glide across island-strewn, magical **Ha Long Bay** (p.429).

you dive, it's worth noting that standards of maintenance aren't always great, so check equipment carefully and only go out with a properly qualified and registered operator that you trust.

Both Non Nuoc beach near Da Nang and Mui Ne have a good reputation for **wind-surfing**. Mui Ne even hosts an international surfboard and **kite-surfing** competition each spring (usually February).

In north Vietnam Ha Long Bay is the centre of water-borne activity. Most boat tours of the bay allow time for swimming – weather permitting – while there are decent beaches on Cat Ba and better still on remote Quan Lan Island. For those in search of more strenuous exercise, a few holiday companies and Hanoi tour agents now offer **sea-kayaking** trips on the bay – not recommended in the heat of summer. Heading inland, the first **river kayaking** and **white-water rafting** expeditions are just starting in the northwest mountains.

Other activities

Vietnam has over 770 species of bird, including several which have only been identified in the last few years. The best places for **birdwatching** are the national parks, including Cuc Phuong (famous also for its springtime butterfly displays), Bach Ma and Cat Thien. The rare Sarus crane, amongst many other species, overwinters in the Tam Nong Bird Sanctuary, on the edge of the Plain of Reeds.

At the other extreme, north Vietnam is becoming increasingly popular among the **motorbiking** fraternity, with several outfits in Hanoi offering to take you way off the beaten track. There are also possibilities for **mountain biking** here and in the central highlands.

Finally, there are now **golf** courses and driving ranges near Hanoi, Ho Chi Minh and Da Lat, with more on the drawing board.

Crime and personal safety

Vietnam is a relatively safe country for travellers, including women travelling alone. In fact, given the country's recent history, many visitors, particularly Americans, are pleasantly surprised at the warm reception that foreign travellers receive. That said, petty crime is on the rise – though it's still relatively small-scale and shouldn't be a problem if you take common-sense precautions. Generally, the hassles you'll encounter will be the milder sort of coping with over-enthusiastic hawkers, touts and beggars.

Petty crime

As a tourist, you're an obvious target for thieves (who may include your fellow travellers): carry your passport, travellers' cheques and other valuables in a concealed **money belt**. Don't leave anything important lying about in your room, and if your hotel has a safe, use it. A cable lock, or **padlock** and chain, comes in handy for doors and windows in cheap hotels, and is useful for securing your pack on trains and buses. It's not a bad idea to keep US$100 or so separately from the rest of your cash, along with your travellers' cheques receipts, insurance policy details, and photocopies of important documents such as the relevant pages of your passport, departure card and baggage declaration form.

At street level it's best not to be ostentatious: forego eye-catching jewellery and flashy watches, try to be discreet when taking out your cash, and be particularly wary in **crowds** and on **public transport**. If your pack is on the top of the bus, make sure it's attached securely (usually everything is tied down with ropes) and keep an eye on it during the most vulnerable times – before departure and on arrival at your destination. On trains, either cable-lock your pack or put it under the bottom bench-seat, out of public view. The odd case has been reported of travellers being drugged and then robbed, so it's best not to accept food or drink from anyone you don't know and trust. Bear in mind that when walking or travelling on a cyclo you are vulnerable to moped-borne **snatch-thieves**; don't wear cameras or expensive sunglasses hanging round your neck and keep a firm grip on your bags. If you do become a target, however, it's best to let go rather than risk being pulled into the traffic and suffering serious injury.

Though petty crime is on the increase in Hanoi, on the whole, it is more of a problem in the south. Ho Chi Minh City now has a fairly bad reputation for bag-snatchers, pickpockets and con artists. Be wary of innocent-looking kids and grannies who may be acting as decoys for thieves – especially on or around Dong Khoi, in the bar districts and other popular tourist hangouts. It's best to avoid taking cyclos at night, while you'd be unwise to walk alone at any time in District 4 (below the Ho Chi Minh Museum), and Thu Duc District, across the far side of the Saigon River.

Petty crime, much of it drug- and prostitution-related, is also a problem in Nha Trang, where you should watch your belongings at all times on the beach. Again, be wary of taking cyclos after dark and women should avoid walking alone at night. Single males, on the other hand, are a particular target for "taxi girls", many of whom also double as thieves. That said, the authorities are trying to clamp down. There is now a special brigade of tourist police and some beachfront cafés have set up seating areas where hawkers are banned.

It's important not to get paranoid, however: crime levels in Vietnam are still a long way behind those of Western countries, and violent crime against tourists is extremely rare.

If you do have anything stolen, you'll need to go to the nearest **police** station for a report in order to claim on your insurance. Try to recruit an English-speaker to come along with you – someone at your hotel should be able to help.

Corruption among police and other officials is fairly widespread. Very occasionally, trumped-up fines are imposed on bus, cyclo or other drivers seen carrying a Westerner – fines *you'll* often be expected to pay. But with patience, plus a few cigarettes to hand round, you should be able to bargain fines down considerably. In general, however, the police steer clear of foreigners – partly under instructions from the government not to upset the lucrative tourist business.

"Social evils" and serious crime

Since liberalization and *doi moi*, Vietnamese society has seen an increase in prostitution, drugs – including hard drugs – and more serious crimes. These so-called "**social evils**" are viewed as a direct consequence of reduced controls on society and ensuing westernization. Such undesirable trends have prompted the government to instigate measures such as seizing pornographic videos and literature, censoring song lyrics and raiding gambling dens. From time to time, they also try to impose midnight closing on bars and clubs, mainly because of drugs, but also to curb general rowdiness. In the past, these curfews have tended to fizzle out after a few months, although the current crackdown seems to be more protracted. That apart, the campaign against social evils should have little effect on most foreign tourists, although it's as well to be aware of it and sensitive to the issues involved.

Single Western males tend to get solicited by **prostitutes**, occasionally in cheap provincial hotels, though more commonly from women cruising on motorbikes. Quite apart from any higher moral considerations, bear in mind that AIDS is on the increase in Vietnam.

Finally, having anything to do with **drugs** in Vietnam is extremely unwise. At night there's a fair amount of drug selling on the streets of Ho Chi Minh City, Hanoi, Nha Trang and even Sa Pa, and it's not unknown for dealers to turn you in to the police. A substantial bribe might persuade them to drop the matter; otherwise, you're looking at fines and jail sentences for lesser offences, while the death penalty is regularly imposed for possessing, trading or smuggling larger quantities.

Military and political hazards

Not surprisingly, the Vietnamese authorities are sensitive about **military installations** and strategic areas – including border regions, military camps (of which there are many), bridges, airports and train stations. Anyone taking photographs in the vicinity of such sites risks having the film removed from their camera or being fined.

Unexploded ordnance from past conflicts still poses a threat in some areas: the problem is most acute in the Demilitarized Zone, where each year a few local farmers or scrap-metal scavengers are killed or injured. Wherever you are, stick to well-trodden paths and never touch any shells or half-buried chunks of metal.

Needless to say, **political activists** aren't exactly welcome in Vietnam and anyone

carrying political literature or in contact with known activists will be treated with suspicion, possibly tailed and even deported. Their Vietnamese contacts will be treated less leniently.

Beggars, children and overcharging

Given the number of disabled, war-wounded and unemployed in Vietnam, there are surprisingly few **beggars** around. Most people are actually trying hard to earn a living somehow, and in the circumstances it doesn't seem unreasonable to have your shoes cleaned more times than they might need, or buy a couple of extra postcards.

At many tourist spots, you may well be swamped by a gaggle of **children** or teenagers selling cold drinks, fruit and chewing gum. Although they can sometimes be a bit overwhelming, as often as not they're just out to practise their English and be entertained for a while. They may even turn out to be excellent guides, in which case it's only fair that you buy something from them in return.

Many visitors complain about the constant need to double-check prices and to guard against **overcharging**. It helps to know the going rate before entering into any transaction, and writing the agreed price down is always a good idea, but even then it's not uncommon for the amount to increase suddenly when it's time to pay. In general, cyclo drivers, taxis, and honda om and bus conductors are the worst offenders.

Women travellers

Vietnam is generally a safe country for women to travel around alone. Most Vietnamese will simply be curious as to why you are on your own and the chances of encountering any threatening behaviour are extremely rare. That said, it pays to take the normal precautions, especially **late at night** when there are few people on the streets and you should avoid taking a cyclo by yourself; use a taxi instead. There are certain areas of Ho Chi Minh which are best avoided altogether (see above).

Most Vietnamese women **dress** modestly, keeping covered from top to toe. It helps to

Emergency phone numbers

The following numbers apply throughout Vietnam. If possible, get a Vietnamese-speaker to phone on your behalf.
Police ☏113
Fire ☏114
Ambulance ☏115

do the same and to avoid skimpy shorts and vests, which are considered offensive. Topless sunbathing, even beside a hotel pool, is a complete no-no. On rare occasions Asian women travelling with a white man have reported cases of harassment, from verbal abuse to rock throwing – attributed to the tendency of some Vietnamese men to automatically label all such women as prostitutes.

Shopping

Souvenir-hunters will find rich pickings in Vietnam, whose eye-catching handicrafts and mementos range from colonial currency and stamps to fabrics and basketware crafted by the country's ethnic minorities, and from limpet-like conical hats to replica US Army-issue Zippo lighters.

Throughout the Guide, we've highlighted places to shop, but in general you'll find the best quality, choice and prices in Ho Chi Minh, Hanoi and Hoi An. Remember that **prices** in Vietnam are almost always open to negotiation (see the box below for some tips on successful bargaining).

Clothing, arts and crafts

Few Western tourists leave Vietnam without the obligatory **conical hat**, or *non la*, sewn from rain- and sun-proof palm fronds; at under US$1 for a basic version, they're definitely an affordable keepsake. From the city of Hué comes a special version, the **poem hat** or *non bai tho*, in whose brim are inlays which, when held up to the light, reveal lines of poetry or scenes from Vietnamese legend. Vietnamese women traditionally wear the **ao dai** – baggy silk trousers under a knee-length silk tunic slit up both sides. Extraordinarily elegant, *ao dai* can be bought off the peg anywhere in the country for around US$10; or, if you can spare a few days for fitting, you can have one tailor-made for US$20 or so, depending on the material.

Local **silk** is sold by the metre in Vietnam's more sizeable markets and in countless outlets in Hoi An, along Dong Khoi in Ho Chi Minh City and on Hanoi's Hang Gai. These same

The art of bargaining

The Vietnamese, not unreasonably, see tourists as wildly rich – how else could they afford to stop working and travel the world – and a **first quoted price** is usually pitched accordingly. It makes sense, therefore, to be prepared.

First of all, do your homework. Find out the approximate going rate, either from your hotel or fellow tourists, or from one of the increasing number of fixed-price shops – remembering to take into account the difference in quality, for example, between mass-produced and hand-crafted goods.

The trick then is to remain **friendly** and amused, but also to be realistic: traders will quickly lose interest in a sale if they think you aren't playing the game fairly. Any show of aggression, and you've lost it in more ways than one.

If you feel you're on the verge of agreement, **moving away** often pays dividends – it's amazing how often you'll be called back.

Keep a sense of **perspective**. If a session of bargaining is becoming very protracted, step back and remind yourself that you're often arguing the toss over mere pennies – nothing to you, but a lot to the average Vietnamese.

shops also sell ready-made clothes and accessories, including embroidered silk handbags and shoes. Embroidered **cotton**, in the form of pyjamas, sheets and pillowcases, also makes a popular souvenir. Meanwhile, the sartorial needs of backpackers are well catered for in major tourist destinations, where **T-shirt** sellers do brisk business. Predictably popular designs include a portrait of Uncle Ho, and the yellow communist star on a red background.

Traditional handicrafts

Of the many types of traditional handicrafts on offer in Vietnam, **lacquerware** (son mai) is among the most beautiful. Made by applying multiple layers of resin onto an article and then polishing vigorously to achieve a deep, lustrous sheen, lacquer is used to decorate furniture, boxes, chopsticks and bangles and is sometimes embellished with eggshell or inlays of **mother-of-pearl** (which is also used in its own right, on screens and pictures) – common motifs are animals, fish and elaborate scrolling. More recently, the lacquerware tradition has been hijacked by more contemporary icons, and it's now possible to buy colourful lacquerware paintings of Mickey Mouse, Tin Tin and Batman. Imported synthetic lacquer has also made an appearance. These brightly coloured, almost metallic, finishes may not be for the purist, but they make for eye-catching bowls, vases and all sorts of household items.

Bronze, **brass** and **jade** are also put to good use, appearing in various forms such as carvings, figurines and jewellery. In Hué, brass and copper **teapots** are popular. Of the earthenware, porcelain and ceramics available across the country, thigh-high **ceramic elephants** and other animal figurines are the quirkiest buys – though decidedly tricky to carry home. Look out, too, for boxes and other knick-knacks made from wonderfully aromatic **cinnamon** and **camphor wood**. For something a little more culturally elevated, you could invest in a **water puppet** or a traditional **musical instrument** (for more on both of these, see "Music and theatre", p.582).

Vietnam's **ethnic minorities**, or montagnards as the colonial French designated them, are cashing in on the possibilities of selling crafts to the tourist market. Fabrics – sometimes shot through with shimmering gold braid – are their main asset, sold in lengths and also made into **purses**, **shoulder bags** and other accoutrements. Some cloths woven in the central highlands feature intriguing designs that incorporate the helicopters and guns which strafed the region during wartime. The southern minorities are also adept at **basketwork**, fashioning backpacks, baskets and mats, and **bamboo pipes**. Hanoi and Ho Chi Minh now each boast a number of excellent hilltribe shops. In the far north, Sa Pa is a popular place to buy Hmong clothes, bags and **skull-caps**, and you'll find lengths of woven fabrics or embroidery in markets throughout the northern mountains.

Paintings

A healthy fine arts scene exists in Vietnam, and **painting** in particular is thriving. In the galleries of Hanoi, Ho Chi Minh and Hoi An you'll find exquisite works in oil, watercolour, lacquer and charcoal by the country's leading artists. Where many once looked – inevitably – to the war with America for subject matter, they are nowadays more likely to produce abstract works or find inspiration in contemporary life.

For these top names you can expect to pay hundreds or even thousands of dollars. Buyer beware, however: many artists find it lucrative to knock out multiple copies of their own or other people's work. You'll need to know what you're doing, or to buy from a reputable gallery.

Many commercial galleries and souvenir shops peddle hackneyed works featuring willowy women in ao dai walking or cycling through the streets of Hoi An, and conical-hatted workers tending paddy fields. This is a shame, as more original works are going unpainted as a consequence.

Watercolours that are anything but hackneyed are churned out nineteen to the dozen by **Vien Thuc**, the prolific "mad monk" of Da Lat (see p.206); his prices are negotiable, but US$2–3 apiece isn't untypical. If you can't even stretch to this, you could always snap up some of the charming hand-painted silk **greetings cards** sold in most tourist centres.

Books, stamps and coins

You can buy photocopied editions of almost all the **books** ever published on Vietnam from

Export restrictions

Bear in mind, especially when buying older artefacts, that **export restrictions** apply on all items deemed to be of "cultural or historical significance". This includes objects made of bronze, porcelain, ivory or precious stones, works of art and anything over fifty years old. That said, the regulations seem to be applied in a fairly piecemeal fashion.

To be sure, it's best to buy through a reputable shop or gallery, which will be able to advise whether an export licence is necessary and handle the paperwork for you. Some shops now specialize in producing excellent reproductions to get round the problem; in which case, make sure this is stated clearly on the invoice.

hawkers and street stalls in Hanoi and Ho Chi Minh. There are also an increasing number of locally published coffee-table books, histories and guides available from bona-fide bookshops and the more upmarket hotels. However, if all you want is some general reading matter, both Hanoi and Ho Chi Minh now have secondhand bookshops where you can exchange or buy used books.

Philatelists meanwhile will enjoy browsing through the old Indochinese **stamps** sold in the souvenir shops of Hanoi and Ho Chi Minh. Similarly, old **notes** and **coins**, including French-issue piastres and US Army credits, are available.

Memorabilia, trinkets and food

Army surplus gear is still a money-spinner, though fatigues, belts, canteens and dog tags purportedly stolen from a dead or wounded GI aren't the most tasteful of souvenirs – and most are fakes now anyway. The khaki **pith helmets** with a red star on the front, worn first by the NVA during the American War and

now by the regular Vietnamese Army, find more takers. Other items that sell like hot cakes are **Zippo lighters** bearing such pithy adages as "When I die bury me face down, so the whole damn army can kiss my ass" and "We are the unwilling, led by the unqualified, doin' the unnecessary for the ungrateful", though again they're unlikely to be authentic GI issue.

In the streets of Ho Chi Minh, nimble-fingered children hawk **model helicopters**, **planes** and **cars** recycled from discarded soft drinks cans, and beside the *Continental* extravagant wooden model ships go for US$15–30.

Finally, **foodstuffs** that may tempt you include coffee from the central highlands, candied strawberries and artichoke tea from Da Lat, coconut candies from the Mekong Delta, preserved miniature tangerines from Hoi An and packets of tea and dried herbs and spices from the northern highlands. As for **drinks**, most of the concoctions itemized on p.49–50, including rice wine, are securely bottled.

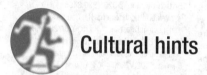

Cultural hints

With its blend of Confucianism and Buddhism, Vietnamese society tends to be both conservative and, at the same time, fairly tolerant. This means you will rarely be remonstrated with for your dress or behaviour. Furthermore, by following a few simple rules, you can minimize the risk of causing offence. This is particularly important in rural areas and small towns where people are less used to the eccentric habits of foreigners.

As a visitor, it's recommended that you err on the side of caution. Shorts and sleeveless shirts are fine for the beach, but are not welcome in pagodas, temples and other religious sites. When dealing with officialdom, it also pays to look as neat and tidy as possible. Anything else may be taken as a mark of disrespect.

Women in particular should dress modestly, especially in the countryside and ethnic minority areas, where revealing too much flesh – no shorts or sleeveless shirts – is regarded as offensive.

It's also worth noting that **nudity**, either male or female, on the beach is absolutely beyond the pale.

When entering a Cao Dai temple, the main building of a pagoda or a private home it's the custom to remove your **shoes**. In some pagodas nowadays this may only be required when stepping onto the prayer mats – ask or watch what other people do. In a pagoda or temple you are also expected to leave a small donation.

As in most Asian countries, it's not done to get angry, and it certainly won't get things moving any quicker. Passing round cigarettes (to men only) is always appreciated and is widely used as a social gambit aimed at progressing tricky negotiations, bargaining and so forth.

Other social conventions worth noting are that you shouldn't touch **children** on the head and, unlike in the West, it's best to ignore a young baby rather than praise it, since it's believed that this attracts the attention of jealous spirits who will cause the baby to fall ill.

Working and studying in Vietnam

Without a prearranged job and work permit, don't bank on finding work in Vietnam. With specific skills to offer, you could try approaching some of the Western companies now operating in Hanoi and Ho Chi Minh. Otherwise, English-language teaching is probably the easiest job to land. There are also opportunities for volunteer work.

English-language teaching

Finding work as an English teacher in Vietnam isn't difficult, especially if you come armed with a **TEFL** (Teaching English as a Foreign Language) qualification. Universities are worth approaching, though pay is better at private schools, where qualified teachers earn around $15 an hour. In either case, your employer should be able to sort out a work visa for you. Private tutoring is an unwieldy way of earning a crust, as you'll have to pop out of the country every few months to procure a new visa.

Study and work programmes

From the UK and Ireland

British Council ☎020/7930 8466, ⓦwww.britishcouncil.org. The Council's Central Management Direct Teaching (☎020/7389 4931) recruits TEFL teachers for posts worldwide, and its Central Bureau for International Education and Training (☎020/7389 4004, ⓦwww.centralbureau .org.uk) enables those who already work as educators to find out about teacher development programmes abroad.
Earthwatch Institute ☎01865/318 838, ⓦwww.uk.earthwatch.org. Long-established international charity with environmental and archeological research projects worldwide,

including Vietnam. Participation mainly as a paying volunteer (pricey) but fellowships for teachers and students available.

Frontier ☎020/7613 2422, ⓦwww.frontierprojects.ac.uk. Environmental conservation and research organization which combines biodiversity surveys with socio-economic work and practical conservation projects in partnership with local communities.

i to i International Projects ☎0870/333 2332, ⓦwww.i-to-i.com. TEFL-training provider operating voluntary teaching, conservation, business and medical schemes.

VSO (Voluntary Service Overseas) ☎020/8780 7200, ⓦwww.vso.org.uk. Highly respected charity that sends qualified professionals (in the fields of education, health, community and social work, engineering, information technology, law and media) to spend two years or more working for local wages on projects beneficial to developing countries.

From the US and Canada

Association for Bernan Associates ☎1-800/274-4888, ⓦwww.bernan.com. Distributes UNESCO's encyclopedic *Study Abroad.*

Council on International Educational Exchange (CIEE) ☎1-800/2COUNCIL, ⓦwww.ciee.org. The non-profit parent organization of Council Travel, CIEE runs semester and academic-year programmes in Vietnam.

Earthwatch Institute ☎1-800/776-0188 or 978/461-0081, ⓦwww.earthwatch.org. International non-profit organization with supporters spread across the US, Europe, Africa, Asia and Australia who volunteer to work with 120 research scientists each year on Earthwatch field research projects in over fifty countries including Vietnam.

Global Exchange ☎415/255-7296, ⓦwww.globalexchange.org. A not-for-profit organization that leads "reality tours" to Vietnam, among other countries, giving participants the chance to learn about the country while seeing it.

Global Volunteers ☎1-800/487-1074, ⓦwww.globalvolunteers.org. Offers three-week volunteer service projects, mostly teaching English, in Vietnam. Participants pay programme and travel costs and donate their services.

Harper Collins Perseus Division ☎1-800/242-7737, ⓦwww.harpercollins.com. Publishes *International Jobs: Where They Are, How to Get Them.*

Volunteers for Peace ☎802/259-2759, ⓦwww.vfp.org. Non-profit organization with links to a huge international network of "workcamps", two-to four-week programmes that bring volunteers together from many countries to carry out needed community projects. Most workcamps are in summer, with registration in April–May. Annual membership including directory costs $20.

From Australia and New Zealand

Australian Volunteers International Melbourne ☎03/9279 1788, ⓦwww.ozvol.org.au. Postings for up to two years, from language training to community forest projects.

Travellers with disabilities

Despite the fact that Vietnam is home to so many war-wounded, few provisions are made for the disabled, so you'll have to be pretty self-reliant. It's important to contact airlines, hotels and tour companies as far in advance as possible to make sure they can accommodate your requirements.

Getting about can be made a little easier if you can afford to take internal flights, or to rent a private car or minibus with a driver. Taxis are widely available in Hanoi, Ho Chi Minh and other major cities. Even so, trying to cross roads with speeding traffic and negotiating the cluttered and uneven pavements – where pavements exist – pose real problems. Furthermore, few buildings are equipped with ramps and lifts.

When it comes to **accommodation**, Vietnam's new luxury hotels usually offer one or two specially adapted rooms. Elsewhere, the best you can hope for is a ground-floor room, or a hotel with a lift.

Contacts for travellers with disabilities

In the UK and Ireland

Holiday Care 2nd floor, Imperial Building, Victoria Rd, Horley, Surrey RH6 7PZ ☏0845/124 9971, minicom ☏0845/124 9976, ⓦwww.holidaycare .org.uk. Provides information on all aspects of travel, including financial aid for holidays, although nothing specific on Vietnam.
Irish Wheelchair Association Blackheath Drive, Clontarf, Dublin 3 ☏01/818 6400, ⓦwww.iwa.ie. Useful information provided about travelling abroad with a wheelchair.
Tripscope Alexandra House, Albany Rd, Brentford, Middlesex TW8 0NE ☏0845/7585 641, ⓦwww.tripscope.org.uk. This registered charity provides a national telephone information service offering free advice on transport for those with a mobility problem.

In the US and Canada

Access-Able ⓦwww.access-able.com. Online resource for travellers with disabilities.
Directions Unlimited 123 Green Lane, Bedford Hills, NY 10507 ☏1-800/533-5343 or 914/241-1700. Travel agency specializing in bookings for people with disabilities.

Global Access ⓦwww.geocities.com/paris/1502. Online information service, with general tips, links and a useful bulletin board.
Mobility International USA 451 Broadway, Eugene, OR 97401 ☏541/343-1284, ⓦwww.miusa .org. Information and referral services, access guides, tours and exchange programmes. Annual membership $35 (includes quarterly newsletter).
Society for the Advancement of Travelers with Handicaps (SATH) 347 5th Ave, New York, NY 10016 ☏212/447-7284, ⓦwww.sath.org. Non-profit educational organization that has actively represented travellers with disabilities since 1976.
Wheels Up! ☏1-888/38-WHEELS, ⓦwww.wheelsup.com. Provides discounted airfares, tour and cruise prices for disabled travellers; also publishes a free monthly newsletter and has a comprehensive website.

In Australia and New Zealand

ACROD (Australian Council for Rehabilitation of the Disabled) PO Box 60, Curtin, ACT 2605; Suite 103, 1st floor, 1–5 Commercial Rd, Kings Grove NSW 2208; ☏02/6282 4333, TTY ☏02/6282 4333, ⓦwww.acrod.org.au. Provides lists of travel agencies and tour operators for people with disabilities.
Disabled Persons Assembly 4/173–175 Victoria St, Wellington, New Zealand ☏04/801 9100 (also TTY), ⓦwww.dpa.org.nz. Resource centre with lists of travel agencies and tour operators for people with disabilities.

Travelling with children

Travelling through Vietnam with children can be challenging and fun. The Vietnamese adore kids and make a huge fuss of them. However, it's worth giving some thought as to whether your children – and you – can cope with all the attention; fair-haired kids come in for even more manhandling. You'll also need to take account of Vietnam's poor sanitation and demanding roads.

The main concern for those travelling with children will probably be **hygiene**. Vietnam can be distinctly unsanitary, and children's stomachs tend to be more sensitive to bacteria. Avoiding spicy foods will help while their stomachs adjust, but if children do become sick it's crucial to keep up their fluid intake, so as to avoid dehydration. Bear in mind, too, that **healthcare facilities** are fairly basic outside Hanoi and Ho Chi Minh. Make sure your travel insurance includes full medical evacuation.

When planning your trip, don't make your itinerary too ambitious. Long bus journeys are tough on young children. Wherever possible, take the train – at least the kids can get up and move about in safety. Domestic flights and open-tour bus tickets are half-price for children and free for under-2s, while tours are usually either free or half-price.

Many budget **hotels** have rooms with three or even four single beds in them. At more expensive hotels under-12s can normally stay free of charge in their parents' rooms and baby cots are becoming more widely available.

For more **advice** on taking children to developing countries, consult Maureen Wheeler's *Travel with Children* (Lonely Planet). You should also talk to your doctor about your children's specific health concerns, or consult one of the travellers' medical services listed on p.26. In the US, Travel with Your Children (☎1-888/822-4388 or 212/477-5524) publishes a regular newsletter, *Family Travel Times* (⊛www.familytraveltimes.com), as well as a series of books on travel with children including *Great Adventure Vacations With Your Kids*.

The environment and ethical tourism

Tourism can play an important part in maintaining indigenous cultures, and also provides an invaluable source of foreign currency for many developing countries. Although there are many benefits, there are also some irreversible and detrimental consequences that need to be considered when organizing a trip.

The expansion of tourism in Vietnam has been spectacular, growing from just ten thousand foreign visitors in 1993 to 2.6 million in 2002. In addition, some 13 million Vietnamese now take holidays in Vietnam each year.

While this has undoubtedly been a boon for the economy, tourism has brought with it serious and potentially disruptive effects environmentally, socially, culturally, and economically. Some of the most distressing examples are to be found in Vietnam's ethnic minority areas. Sa Pa's famous "love market" attracted so much tourist attention it eventually relocated to a more remote location. Many families in the area have sold off their antique jewellery, while Hmong children beg for sweets, pens and money. Some have even started peddling drugs.

These and other local issues have been covered throughout this book, while environmental concerns are dealt with on p.543.

If you're concerned about the impact of tourism and environmental matters, get in touch with the organizations mentioned in the text, or the ones listed below.

Contacts

Campaign for Environmentally Responsible Tourism (CERT) ⊛www.c-e-r-t.org. Lobbies to educate tour operators and tourists in a sensitive approach to travel, focusing on immediate practical ways in which the environment can be protected.

EarthWise Journeys ⊛www.teleport.com/~earthwyz. American organization promoting environmentally responsible travel.

OneWorld ⊛www.oneworld.net. Global network of organizations working for sustainable development and human rights. It includes a daily news service, as well as details of voluntary work, job vacancies and campaigns.

Partners in Responsible Tourism (PIRT) ⊛www.pirt.org, ⓔinfo@pirt.org. An organization of individuals and travel companies promoting responsible tourism to minimize harm to the environment and local cultures. Their website features a "Traveler's Code for Traveling Responsibly".

Tourism Concern ☏020/7753 3330, ⓦ www.tourismconcern.org.uk. Campaigns for the rights of local people to be consulted in tourism developments affecting their lives, and produces a quarterly magazine of news and articles. Also publishes the *Good Alternative Travel Guide*.

World Travel and Tourism Council ☏020/7481 8007, ⓦ www.wttc.org. Though aimed mainly at the travel industry and other professionals, this huge website is packed with information and has useful links to related sites.

Directory

Addresses Locating an address is rarely a problem in Vietnam, but there are a couple of conventions it helps to know about. Where two numbers are separated by a slash, such as 110/5, you simply make for no. 110, where an alley will lead off to a further batch of buildings – you want the fifth one. Where a number is followed by a letter, as in 117a, you're looking for a single block encompassing several addresses, of which one will be 117a. Vietnamese cite addresses without the words for street, avenue and so on; we've followed this practice throughout the Guide except where ambiguity would result.

Contraceptives Medicines in Vietnamese pharmacies are limited and sometimes way beyond their sell-by date, so if you're following a course of oral contraceptives, stock up before arrival. Reliable, imported brands of condoms (*bao cao su*) are sold in Hanoi and Ho Chi Minh, but don't count on getting them easily elsewhere.

Departure tax Passengers on international flights have to pay a departure tax of US$14 when leaving Hanoi, and US$12 from Ho Chi Minh (payable in dong, dollars and other major currencies).

Electricity 220 volts. Plugs generally have two round pins, though you may come across sockets requiring two flat pins and even some requring three pins. Power supplies are erratic, so be prepared for cuts and surges.

Gay and lesbian Vietnam The gay scene in Vietnam is extremely low-key, and non-existent for lesbians.

Laundry It's possible to get clothes washed at pretty much any guesthouse or hotel, and Western-style laundry and dry-cleaning services are widely available in Hanoi, Ho Chi Minh and other major cities. Washing is often given a rigorous scrubbing by hand, so don't submit anything delicate.

Left luggage Ho Chi Minh airport now has a left-luggage service inside the arrival hall (US$2–3 per day). Otherwise, most hotels will have a room or cupboard earmarked for luggage, though this system may not be one hundred percent secure.

Tampons Available in supermarkets in Hanoi and Ho Chi Minh City only.

Time differences Vietnam is seven hours ahead of London, twelve hours ahead of New York, fifteen hours ahead of Los Angeles, one hour behind Perth and three hours behind Sydney – give or take an hour or two when summer time is in operation.

Tipping Smart restaurants and hotels normally add a service charge. Elsewhere, while not expected, a tip is always appreciated – around ten percent in a restaurant, while the amount in a hotel will depend on the grade of hotel and what services they've provided. In general, a few thousand dong should suffice.

Guide

Guide

Ho Chi Minh City
and around

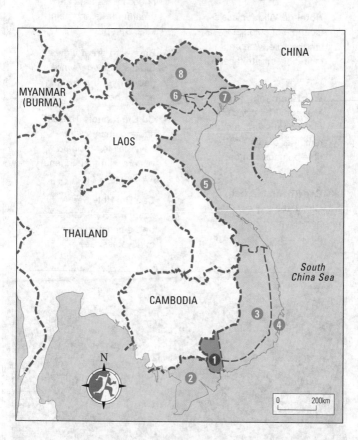

CHAPTER 1 # Highlights

* **Jade Emperor Pagoda**
Beautiful carved wood-work, an eclectic collection of deities and a constant fog of incense make this place well worth a visit. See p.100

* **Hotel de Ville** A classic example of colonial architecture, with an incredibly ornate facade. See p.93

* **War Remnants Museum** The city's most moving museum, a stark reminder of just how terrible humans can be. See p.98–99

* **Ben Thanh Market** Check the city's pulse here on an early-morning stroll. See p.95

* **Saigon's restaurants** The city's restaurants are the place to savour the delights of Vietnamese cuisine. See p.108

* **Dong Khoi** The boutiques in this area are great for silks and paintings. See p.91

* **Bars with great views** Sip a sundowner while gazing over the bustling activity below. See p.116

* **Cu Chi tunnels** These subterranean shelters never fail to fascinate visitors with their ingenuity. See p.127

* **Cao Dai Holy See** A riotous decor is tempered by the haunting chanting of devotees. See p.127

1

Ho Chi Minh City
and around

Twenty years after its humiliating defeat, [Ho Chi Minh] looks and feels much as it
did before. The southern metropolis has cast off the dour sackcloth the victor
forced it to wear. That it has been able to do so with such aplomb is not really surprising. The hair shirt never fit.

Henry Kamm, 1996

Washed ashore above the Mekong Delta, some 40km north of the
South China Sea, **HO CHI MINH CITY** is a boom town where
the rule of the dollar is absolute. Fuelled by the sweeping economic
changes wrought by *doi moi* in 1986, this effervescent city, perched
on the west bank of the Saigon River, is in the throes of a programme of re-
invention shaking it to its French-built foundations. Years of rubbing shoulders
with the consumer-oriented Americans made the Saigonese wise to how to
coin a profit. Now they are pressing old, near-forgotten skills back into service, as the market economy shifts into gear again, challenging Singapore, Kuala
Lumpur and the other traditional Southeast Asian powerhouses. All the accoutrements of economic revival – fine restaurants, flash hotels, glitzy bars and
clubs, and shops selling imported luxury goods – are here, adding a glossy
veneer to the city's hotch-potch landscape of French stones of empire, venerable pagodas and austere, Soviet-style housing blocks. And, sadly, Ho Chi Minh
City is still full to bursting with people for whom economic progress has not
yet translated into food, housing and jobs. Street children range through tourist
enclaves hawking T-shirts, postcards and cigarette lighters; limbless mendicants
haul themselves about on crude trolleys; and watchful pickpockets prowl Dong
Khoi on the lookout for unguarded wallets. Indeed, begging is now of such
epidemic proportions in Ho Chi Minh City that tourists must quickly come
to accept it as a hassle that goes with the territory. In addition, the arrival, en
masse, of wealthy Westerners has lured many women into prostitution, for
which the go-go bars of Dong Khoi became famous during the American War.

If Hanoi is a city of romance and mellow charms, then Ho Chi Minh – locals
prefer its pre-1975 name of Saigon – is its antithesis, a fury of sights and sounds,
and the crucible in which Vietnam's rallying fortunes are boiling. Few corners
of the city afford respite from the cacophony of **construction work** casting up
new office blocks and hotels with logic-defying speed. An increasing number of

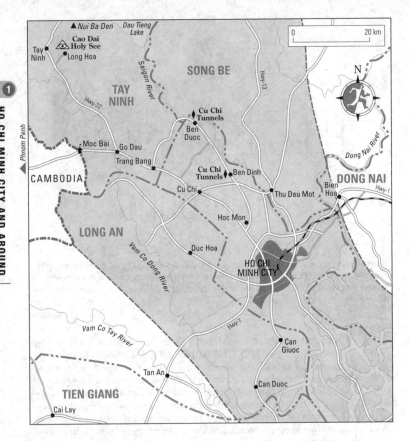

cars and minibuses jostle with an organic mass of state-of-the-art jeeps, land-cruisers, Hondas and cyclos, so that tree-lined streets and boulevards will soon need to be resculpted to cope. And amid this melee of change, a population of around six million goes about its daily life: schoolgirls clad in the traditional silk *ao dai* glide past streetside baguette-sellers; moneyed teenagers in designer jeans chirrup into mobile phones; and Buddhist monks walk with measured pace from shopfront to shopfront in search of alms. Adding a **cosmopolitan** dash to the mix is the influx of Western tourists and expats in the last decade or so, many of them French and American. Much of the fun of being in Ho Chi Minh City derives from the simple pleasure of absorbing its flurry of activity – something best done from the safety of a roadside café. To blink is to miss some new and singular sight, be it a cyclo piled high with wicker baskets of fruit, or a boy rapping out a staccato tattoo on pieces of bamboo to advertise noodles for sale.

It's one of Ho Chi Minh City's many charms that once you've exhausted, or been exhausted by, all it has to offer, paddy fields, beaches and wide-open countryside are not far away. If you take only one trip **out of the city**, make it to the **Cu Chi tunnels**, where villagers dug themselves out of the range of American shelling. The tunnels are normally twinned with a tour around the fanciful Great Temple of the indigenous Cao Dai religion at **Tay Ninh**. A brief taster of the Mekong Delta at **My Tho** or a dip in the South China Sea at **Mui Ne** are also eminently possible in a long day's excursion, but we've covered these last two places, together with the regions to which they belong, on p.138 and p.231 respectively.

The **best time to visit** tropical Ho Chi Minh City is in the dry season, which runs from December through to April. During the wet season, May to November, there's a short downpour every afternoon, though this won't disrupt your travels. Average temperatures, year-round, hover between 26 and 29°C; March, April and May are the hottest months.

Ho Chi Minh City

Knowledge of Ho Chi Minh City's early history is sketchy, at best. Between the first and sixth centuries, the territory on which it lies fell under the nominal rule of the **Funan Empire** to the west. Funan was subsequently absorbed by the Kambuja peoples of the pre-Angkor **Chen La Empire**, but it is unlikely that these imperial machinations had much bearing upon the sleepy fishing backwater that would later develop into Ho Chi Minh City.

The Khmer fishermen who eked out a living here would recognize little today beyond the city's web of waterways. So besieged by forest and swampland were their homes, that they named their settlement **Prei Nokor**, "settlement in the forest". Set on stable ground just north of the delta wetlands, though, and surrounded on three sides by navigable waterways, the settlement was destined for greater things. In time, Chen La was absorbed into the Khmer empire of **Angkor**, which ruled the roost until the fifteenth century, and Prei Nokor flourished as an entrepôt for Cambodian boats pushing down the Mekong River. By the seventeenth century it boasted a garrison and a mercantile community that embraced Malay, Indian and Chinese traders.

Such a dynamic settlement was bound to draw attention from the north. By the seventeenth century's close, the **Viets** had trampled over the kingdom of Champa on their march south, and the following century saw this area swallowed up by Hué's **Nguyen Dynasty**. With new ownership came a new name, **Saigon**, thought to be derived from the Vietnamese word for the kapok tree. Upon the outbreak of the **Tay Son Rebellion**, in 1772, Nguyen Anh of the Nguyen dynasty hastened south to Saigon which he named as his interim capital and bricked the whole settlement into a walled fortress, the eight-sided **Gia Dinh Citadel**, built, on the advice of his geomancers, to resemble a lotus flower in bloom. Having quelled the rebellion, in 1802, Nguyen Anh returned to Hué as Emperor Gia Long; but Saigon remained his regional administrative centre in the south.

The army that put down the Tay Son brothers included an assisting **French** military force. From this early foothold the French grappled for seven decades to undermine Vietnamese control in the region and develop a trading post in Asia. Finally, in 1861, they seized Saigon, using Emperor Tu Duc's persecution of French missionaries as a pretext. The 1862 **Treaty of Saigon** declared the city the capital of French Cochinchina.

Ho Chi Minh City owes its form and character to the French colonists. As part of a broad **public works** programme, channels were filled in, marshlands drained, and steam tramways set to work along its regimental grid of tamarind-shaded boulevards, which by the 1930s sported such wildly incongruous names as Boulevard de la Somme and Rue Rousseau. Flashy examples of European architecture were erected, cafés and boutiques sprang up to cater for its new, Vermouth-sipping, baguette-munching citizens, and the city was imbued with such an all-round Gallic air that Somerset Maugham, visiting in the 1930s, found it reminiscent of "a little provincial town in the south of France... a blithe and smiling little place". The French *colons* (colonials) bankrolled improvements to Saigon with the vast profits they were able to cream from exporting Vietnam's **rubber** and **rice** out of the city's rapidly expanding seaport.

On a human level, however, French rule was invariably harsh; dissent crystallized in the form of strikes through the 1920s and 1930s, but the nationalist movement hadn't gathered any real head of steam before **World War II**'s tendrils spread to Southeast Asia. At its close, the **Potsdam Conference** of 1945 set the British Army the task of disarming Japanese troops in southern Vietnam. Arriving in Saigon two months later, they promptly returned power to the French, and so began thirty years of war (see p.495). Saigon saw little action during the anti-French war, which was fought mostly in the countryside and resulted in the French capitulation at Dien Bien Phu.

Designated the capital of the **Republic of South Vietnam** by President Diem in 1955, Saigon was soon both the nerve centre of the American war effort, and its R&R capital, with a slough of sleazy bars along Dong Khoi (known then as Tu Do) catering to GIs on leave from duty. Despite the communist bomb attacks and demonstrations by students and monks that periodically disturbed the peace, these were good times for Saigon, whose entrepreneurs prospered on the back of the tens of thousands of Americans posted here. The gravy train ran out of steam with the withdrawal of American troops in 1973, and two years later the **Ho Chi Minh Campaign** rolled into the city and through the gates of the presidential palace and the communists were in control. Within a year, Saigon had been renamed **Ho Chi Minh City**.

The **war years** extracted a heavy toll: American carpet-bombing of the Vietnamese countryside forced millions of refugees into the relative safety of the city, and ill-advised, post-reunification policies triggered a social and economic stagnation whose ramifications are still plain for all to see. To make matters worse, persecution of southerners with links to the Americans saw many thousands sent to re-education camps, and millions more flee the country by boat.

Only in 1986, when the **economic liberalization** of *doi moi* was established, and a market economy reintroduced, did the fortunes of the city show signs of taking an upturn. Now this slumbering giant has its eye on the future once more.

Arrival

With the lion's share of new **arrivals** to Vietnam flying into Ho Chi Minh City, Tan Son Nhat Airport is likely to provide you with your first glimpse of the country; it's also the terminus for all internal flights. Arriving overland from other regions of Vietnam, you'll end up either at the train station, a short distance north of the downtown area, or at one of a handful of bus terminals scattered across the city.

By plane

Tan Son Nhat Airport is 7km northwest of the city centre, on Truong Son. Facilities at the airport include duty-free, foreign exchange (daily 10am–11pm), and a post office with telephone service (daily 7.30am–10pm). Just beyond the baggage claim area, a Saigontourist desk sells city maps and books rooms in upmarket hotels, but you're better turning right as you leave the arrivals hall to the SASCO (Southern Airports Services Company) desk, where they can give you a free map and advice. There are also left-luggage facilities here (daily 7.30am–9pm; $2 per bag per day, $3 for larger items). There are a couple of small restaurants within the terminal and a larger one located in the car park outside.

The best way to get into the city centre is to take a **taxi**. Hordes of drivers will greet you as you emerge into the car park, along with touts brandishing hotel brochures. Metered taxicabs make the run downtown for $3-4, though if you have a large group you could consider renting a minibus for about $2 a head. Some drivers will recommend hotels from which they get a commission, but if you know where you want to go, just be firm. With any taxi ride, make sure that the meter is set before you start your journey, to ensure that there is no doubt about the correct fare for the trip. If you don't have much baggage, a motorbike will run you into town for about $2. If you don't see one handy, walk outside the airport gates (only a few hundred metres) where you can hail either a motorbike or a cyclo (see "City transport", p.82).

By train

Trains from the north pull in at the **train station**, or Ga Saigon (☎08/823 0105), 3km northwest of town, on Nguyen Thong. The ticket office is open 7.30–11am and 1–3pm, though you can also book tickets with agents around Pham Ngu Lao. There's bound to be a cluster of cyclo drivers on the lookout for fares in the forecourt, but given the distance into the centre you're better off taking a taxi (about $4) – even if it means ordering one (☎08/842 4242 or 811 1111).

By bus

Buses stop at a clutch of different terminals. Arrivals **from Phnom Penh** in Cambodia terminate in two places: Sinh Café buses drop you off at their offices in De Tham, right in the heart of Pham Ngu Lao's budget accommodation area; other buses drop you outside the garages at 145 Nguyen Du, west of Notre Dame Cathedral, from where you'll have to take a cyclo or motorbike.

Buses **from the north** arrive at sprawling **Mien Dong bus station**, 5km northeast of the city on Xo Viet Nghe Tinh; local buses shuttle between here and **Ben Thanh bus station**, which is a five-minute walk from Pham Ngu Lao. Buses **from the southwest** terminate at **Mien Tay bus station**, 10km west of the city centre in An Lac District; local buses shuttle into town from here, passing along Pham Ngu Lao en route. Again, there are exceptions, with buses out of My Tho and some out of My Thuan stopping instead at **Cholon bus station**. Well-signposted **shuttle buses** between Mien Tay and Mien Dong terminals make it possible to bypass central Ho Chi Minh altogether in the event that you want to travel direct from the Mekong Delta to the north, or vice versa.

Finally, most buses from Tay Ninh pull in at the **Tay Ninh bus station**, west of the centre in Tan Binh District, which is linked by bus with Ben Thanh and the other bus stations; others arrive at Mien Dong. Most arrivals **from Cu Chi town** also end their journeys at Tay Ninh, though some continue to Ben Thanh.

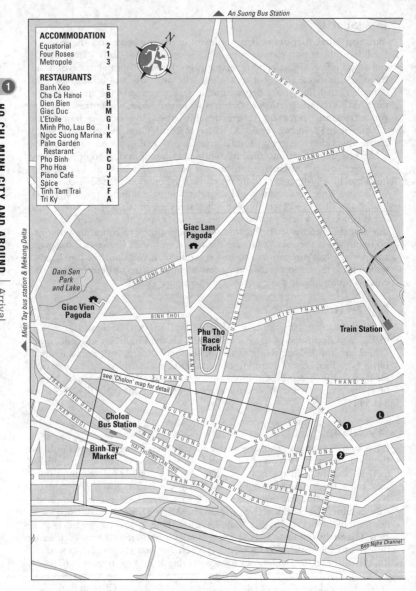

ACCOMMODATION
Equatorial	2
Four Roses	1
Metropole	3

RESTAURANTS
Banh Xeo	E
Cha Ca Hanoi	B
Dien Bien	H
Giac Duc	M
L'Etoile	G
Minh Pho, Lau Bo	I
Ngoc Suong Marina	K
Palm Garden	
Restarant	N
Pho Binh	C
Pho Hoa	D
Piano Café	J
Spice	L
Tinh Tam Trai	F
Tri Ky	A

▲ Mien Tay bus station & Mekong Delta

Giac Lam
Pagoda

Dam Sen
Park
and Lake

Giac Vien
Pagoda

BINH THOI

Phu Tho
Race
Track

Train Station

see 'Cholon' map for detail

3 THANG 2

3 THANG 2

Cholon
Bus Station

Binh Tay
Market

Ben Nghe Channel

By boat

The only regular waterborne arrivals in Ho Chi Minh City are the **hydrofoils from Vung Tau**, which dock at the **Bach Dang jetty**, on Ton Duc Thang. Otherwise, boats from the Mekong Delta float up to several places: most services from My Tho and Ben Tre moor about 1.5km south of the Ho Chi Minh Museum on Ton That Thuyet, while others arrive near Ham Nghi at Cau

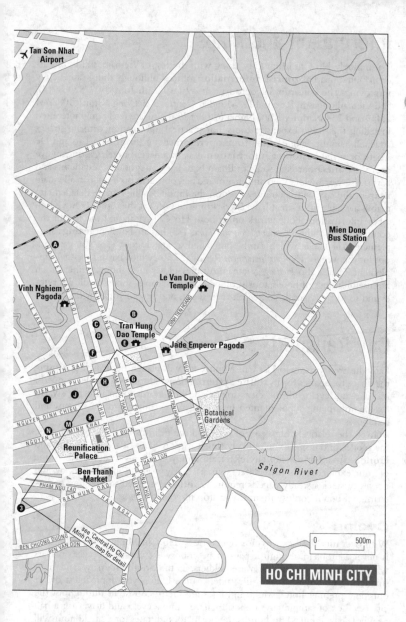

Tan Son Nhat Airport

NGUYEN VAN TROI

HOANG VAN THU

NGUYEN KIEM

NGUYEN THAI SON

PHAN VAN TRI

Mien Dong Bus Station

DINH TIEN HOANG

VO NGHE TINH

Le Van Duyet Temple

A

Vinh Nghiem Pagoda

LE VAN SY

PHAN DINH PHUNG

B

Tran Hung Dao Temple

C

D

E

F

Jade Emperor Pagoda

NGUYEN

VO THI SAU

HAI BA TRUNG

PHAM NGOC THANH

G

DIEN BIEN PHU

H

NAM KY

KHOI NGHIA

DINH TIEN HOANG

BINH KHIEM

Botanical Gardens

I

J

NGUYEN DINH CHIEU

LE DUAN

Saigon River

K

LE THANH TON

NGUYEN THI MINH KHAI

N

M

Reunification Palace

Ben Thanh Market

NGUYEN THI

DONG KHOI

LE LOI

TON DUC THANG

PHAM NGU LAO

TRAN HUNG DAO

HAM NGHI

3

BEN CHUONG DUONG

BEN VAN DON

see 'Central Ho Chi Minh City' map for detail

0   500m

HO CHI MINH CITY

Khanh Hoi and Cau Calmette. Boats from further afield terminate either just behind Cholon's Binh Tay Market, or a little below the market at the junction of Chu Van An and Tran Van Kieu.

Information and maps

Frustratingly, Ho Chi Minh City, along with the rest of Vietnam, still lacks efficient and impartial **tourist information** offices, although things are slowly improving. The state-run Saigontourist, at 49 Le Thanh Ton (℡08/829 8914), and Vietnamtourism, Room 101, Mondial Centre, 203 Dong Khoi (℡08/824 2000) and 234 Nam Ky Khoi Nghia (℡08/829 0776), are really only interested in selling their own expensive tours. For practical information with no strings attached, enquire at one of the **tour operators** along Pham Ngu Lao and De Tham or at the **customer information** desk in a decent hotel. Casting an eye over the **noticeboards** in some of Pham Ngu Lao's guesthouses, restaurants and bars is also worthwhile. Vietnamtourism and Saigontourist both offer an adequate **map** of the city with a country map on the flipside, while a more detailed city map is available from street hawkers or from the GPO at the top of Dong Khoi.

For information about what's on in both Ho Chi Minh and the rest of the country, the monthly *Vietnam Economic Times* ($5) has an excellent **listings** supplement, *The Guide*, which can be purchased separately for $1; or you can fork out for the weekly *Vietnam Investment Review* ($2.50), which has a *Time Out* supplement. There's also *Heritage*, Vietnam Airlines' glossy in-flight magazine, which has useful listings of hotels, tourist offices, cinemas, banks, shops, medical services and so forth; it's available free on their flights and at some of their offices.

City transport

Faint-hearted visitors to Ho Chi Minh City will blanch upon first glimpsing the chaos that passes for its **traffic system**. Thousands of motorcycles, mopeds, bicycles and cyclos fill the city's streets and boulevards in an insectile swarm that is now being supplemented by a burgeoning number of cars, jeeps and minibuses.

Given the relatively high cost of taxis and the dearth of reliable bus services, the modes of transport you're likely to get most use out of are the **cyclos** and **Honda oms**. For the full city effect, though, you'll want to do at least some of your exploring **on foot**. There's an art to jay-walking in Vietnam: besides nerves of steel, a steady pace is required – drivers are used to dodging pedestrians, but you'll confuse them if you stop in your tracks.

Cyclos

With over fifty thousand **cyclos** operating in Ho Chi Minh City, hailing one is never a problem, though it pays to be choosy – some of the cyclo drivers who congregate downtown were soldiers in the Southern Army, and their smattering of English makes life much easier. Unless you approach a driver outside a premier hotel, you'll find rates are pretty consistent throughout the city (see box of sample fares opposite); if you hire a cyclo and driver for a half or whole day, about $1 an hour is the norm, though rates for a single hour will generally be higher. Though it's feasible to ride two (very small) passengers to a cyclo, the corresponding rise in cost and lessening of comfort make this a false economy.

Finally, bear in mind that many roads around the centre of the city are off limits to cyclos, so if your driver follows a circuitous course, or drops you short of your destination, it's probably because he can't get any closer.

Sample fares around town

Costs of local transport, excluding taxis, are extremely low and are usually paid in dong. Though drivers will gladly take dollars, it works out more expensive, so it's good to carry a fistful of dong for such occasions. For example, you can expect to pay a minimum of 5000d per kilometre for a **cyclo** or **Honda om** ride within central Ho Chi Minh, while the standard fare for such **bus services** as exist is 2000–3000d. Fares for cyclos and Honda oms are negotiable, though the list below provides a guideline. Note that cyclo drivers charge more for extra passengers or luggage, and that by "centre" we mean Dong Khoi.

Pham Ngu Lao to GPO: 8000–10,000d

Train station to centre: 8000–10,000d

Pham Ngu Lao to Cholon: 10,000–15,000d

Centre to Jade Emperor Pagoda: 8000–10,000d

Mien Dong bus station to centre: 20,000d

Taxis and Honda oms

Taxis have become a much more common sight on the streets of Ho Chi Minh City of late, with several companies now offering metered services in air-conditioned vehicles, and their prices are generally affordable. You'll often spot Airport Taxis and Vinataxis (see "Listings", p.126 for contact numbers) on the street, but if time is of the essence it's safer to book a car over the phone; expect a trip within the city centre to cost $1–2.

The two-wheeled taxi or **Honda om** is a faster alternative to the cyclo. Translated, it means "Honda embrace": passengers ride pillion on a motorbike, hanging on for dear life. Honda oms are even more prevalent than cyclos, so you'll probably find yourself using them at some stage, but beware of riders who double up as pimps and drug dealers, of which there are many. If you find a reliable driver, take his phone number so you can call him again. Prices are about the same as cyclos.

Buses

So undeveloped is Ho Chi Minh City's public transport network that the only time you're likely to resort to a **bus** – apart from getting to one of the city's outlying long-distance bus terminals (see p.79) – is if you visit **Cholon**. The air-conditioned Saigon Star Co service (daily 5am–10pm) loops between the south side of Mei Linh Square, and Huynh Thoai Yen, below Binh Tay Market. From Pham Ngu Lao, head down to the eastern end of Bui Vien to pick up the service en route to Cholon; on the return journey, you'll be dropped off at the far side of Tran Hung Dao. When leaving the city, **Ben Thanh bus station** is a useful point of departure, linking other long-distance bus stations in Ho Chi Minh City, as well as offering direct services to Vung Tau and other places.

Motorbikes, bicycles and car rental

Motorbike rental in Vietnam peaked in popularity a few years ago, when biking up- or down-country was all the rage. With the tourist minibus network growing ever more comprehensive, this trend seems to be fading, though motorbiking is still an efficient and romantic means of viewing the city. You need to be wary, though, of the scams pulled by less reputable companies, as well as the dangers of Vietnamese roads (see Basics, p.40). The same goes for **bicycle rental** – a charming way to see the city but fraught with danger if you aren't road-aware. Many hotels, guesthouses and cafés advertise bicycles for rent, especially around Pham Ngu Lao (see p.122 for outlets).

Self-drive isn't an option yet in Ho Chi Minh City, but pretty much every one of the city's tour operators can arrange **car rental** plus driver for you; tour agencies are listed on p.126. Drivers rarely speak much English, so if you want a guided tour you'll have to pay extra for the guide. Given Ho Chi Minh City's one-way systems and traffic flow, travelling by car doesn't represent the most efficient way of city sightseeing. However, car rental comes into its own if you want to take a day-trip out of the city – to Tay Ninh or My Tho, for example – but don't relish being shoehorned into a tour bus all day; prices average $40–50 per day.

Boats

Pass by the Passengers Quay of Ho Chi Minh City, opposite the end of Ham Nghi on Ton Duc Thang, and you're bound to be harangued by people offering **trips along the Saigon River** and its canals, at $4–5 an hour. These touts seem particularly keen to take you up Ben Nghe Channel to Cholon, though the trip – along a truly filthy and squalid stretch of water – is harder to recommend than the journey up the Thi Nghe Channel and past the back of the zoo. Kim Travel (see p.126) organizes full-day tour cruises ($12 including lunch) on its own boats to Lai Thieu and Binh Duong; you'll travel about 30km upstream on the Saigon River – a more picturesque stretch of water – stopping off at various villages en route. Another more wholesome option is to board one of the floating restaurants moored in the evenings along Ton Duc Thang, and take a **dinner cruise** along the Saigon River (see pp.108–110).

Accommodation

Hotels have been spreading like wildfire across Ho Chi Minh City ever since *doi moi* paved the way for foreign investors and local entrepreneurs to chance their arm in the tourist sector, so finding **accommodation** should cause you no headaches: unfussy places at the bottom end of the scale are easily affordable, while a room in an accredited hotel can be an excellent bargain. There shouldn't be any need to **book in advance** unless you're hitting town during Tet (usually late Jan/mid-Feb), or you want to be sure of staying at one of the city's finer addresses.

Generally the most pleasant and convenient area in which to stay is the region around **Dong Khoi**, which is home to several of Vietnam's most venerable hotels as well as a host of intermediate options, including some smart mini-hotels on **Mac Thi Buoi**. Ho Chi Minh's budget enclave centres around **Pham Ngu Lao**, **De Tham** and **Bui Vien**, 1km west of the city centre. The area, of which De Tham is the axis, has been dubbed "Western Street" by locals, and it's easy to see why: besides having over a hundred accommodation choices, there are also travel agencies, restaurants, bars and shops catering for travellers. It's worth bearing in mind that by staying in this area, you'll save not only on accommodation, but on food and drinks as well, since the restaurants round here are significantly cheaper than those downtown. **Hotels**, **mini-hotels**, **guesthouses** and **rooms for rent** are ten-a-penny here, and stiff competition means there's little point in going for a grim and tiny room with shared facilities at $4–5, when for just a few dollars more you can stay in an air-conditioned room with en-suite bathroom. Having said that, there are some well-maintained dormitory rooms available at around $3 per bed. Also worth considering are the

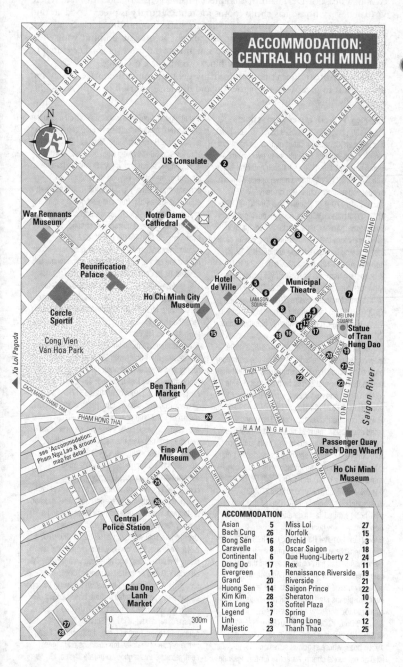

ACCOMMODATION: CENTRAL HO CHI MINH

War Remnants Museum

Reunification Palace

Cercle Sportif

Cong Vien Van Hoa Park

Xa Loi Pagoda

US Consulate ❷

Notre Dame Cathedral

Hotel de Ville

Ho Chi Minh City Museum

Municipal Theatre

LAM SON SQUARE

MEI LINH SQUARE

Statue of Tran Hung Dao

Ben Thanh Market

Fine Art Museum

Central Police Station

Cau Ong Lanh Market

Passenger Quay (Bach Dang Wharf)

Ho Chi Minh Museum

Saigon River

see 'Accommodation: Pham Ngu Lao & around' map for detail

0   300m

ACCOMMODATION

Asian	5	Miss Loi	27
Bach Cung	26	Norfolk	15
Bong Sen	16	Orchid	3
Caravelle	8	Oscar Saigon	18
Continental	6	Que Huong-Liberty 2	24
Dong Do	17	Rex	11
Evergreen	1	Renaissance Riverside	19
Grand	20	Riverside	21
Huong Sen	14	Saigon Prince	22
Kim Kim	28	Sheraton	10
Kim Long	13	Sofitel Plaza	2
Legend	7	Spring	4
Linh	9	Thang Long	12
Majestic	23	Thanh Thao	25

two alleys east of De Tham that connect Pham Ngu Lao and Bui Vien, where virtually every house has cheap rooms for rent. **Security** is pretty good around Pham Ngu Lao, as all guesthouse lobbies are staffed round the clock. Even so, it pays to ensure that a room locks up adequately before you commit yourself to it. If the Pham Ngu Lao region is too much for you, there's a smaller clutch of budget hotels in a quiet alley a few blocks south off Co Giang.

Finally, **Cholon** doesn't jump into many people's minds as a place to stay, but if you want to give Westerners the slip and immerse yourself in authentic sights and smells, this is your spot.

Dong Khoi and around

Asian 150 Dong Khoi ☎08/829 6979, @asianhotel @hcm.fpt.vn. Centrally located mid-range hotel, but compact and intimate enough not to overwhelm. All rooms have satellite TV, IDD, bathtub and mini-bar with complimentary fruit and newspapers; $5 more will get you a larger room with balcony. ➍

Bach Cung 170–172 Nguyen Thai Binh ☎08/821 2777, ⓕ821 2983. With its gaudy wedding-cake exterior, the "White Castle" certainly lives up to its name; the room rates are reasonable given its facilities, including bathtubs, fridge and satellite TV. ➌

Bong Sen 117–123 Dong Khoi ☎08/829 1516, @bongsen@hcm.vnn.vn. Stylish yet personable upmarket hotel right at the heart of Dong Khoi with an in-house business centre. The *Bong Sen II* (☎08/823 5818), around the corner at 61 Hai Ba Trung, has newer rooms at slightly cheaper rates. ➍–➎

Caravelle 19 Lam Son Square ☎08/823 4999, ⓦwww.caravellehotel.com. A grandiose entrance leads to the city's most prestigious hotel, featuring luxurious rooms and suites with all conceivable comforts and dizzying views across the city. ➏

Continental 132–134 Dong Khoi ☎08/829 9203, ⓦwww.continentalvietnam.com. The grandly carpeted staircases, marbled floors and dark-wood doors of this venerable address's halls and corridors convey a colonial splendour that doesn't quite extend to its rooms, though some do boast commanding views down Dong Khoi. ➎–➏

Dong Do 35 Mac Thi Buoi ☎08/827 3637, @dongdohotel@hcm.vnn.vn. Nicely furnished mini-hotel with all facilities and a restaurant with a view on the sixth floor. ➌–➍

Evergreen 261 Hai Ba Trung ☎08/829 8875, @bichlien@hcm.vnn.vn. One of several monolith-like hotels in this part of town. Ignore the sickly, pale green exterior and you'll find pleasing, competitively priced en-suite rooms and friendly, eager-to-please staff. The hotel also boasts a small rooftop pool and restaurant. ➌

Grand 8 Dong Khoi ☎08/823 0163, ⓕ823 5781, ⓦwww.grandsaigon.com. Painstakingly restored 1930s hotel, whose spacious suites and friendly staff lend an old-world charm. Attractive furnishings, orig-inal fittings and polished wooden floors all add to the effect, while modern facilities include swimming pool and Jacuzzi. Breakfast is included. ➎–➏

Huong Sen 66–70 Dong Khoi ☎08/829 9400, @huongsen@hcm.vnn.vn. An Oriental influence is evident in the lobby; beyond its lacquerwork screens and chairs, you'll find the rooms are well equipped. Breakfast, fruit and use of the sauna are included, and other facilities include an airline booking service and currency exchange. ➍–➎

Kim Long 58 Mac Thi Buoi ☎08/822 8558, @annamtour@hcm.fpt.vn. Another good mini-hotel right in the centre, with bathtubs in some rooms and satellite TV. Discounts available off-season. ➌

Legend 2a–4a Ton Duc Thang ☎08/823 3333, ⓦwww.legendhotelsaigon.com. Recently completed concrete monolith with all facilities. Most rooms face the river. ➎–➏

Linh 16 Mac Thi Buoi ☎08/824 3954, @annamtour@hcm.fpt.vn. Friendly and family-run, this central mini-hotel with ten well-appointed rooms and attractive bamboo furnishings is a fair proposition. Breakfast included. ➌–➍

Majestic 1 Dong Khoi ☎08/829 5517, ⓦwww.majestic-saigon.com. Historic 1920s-built riverfront hotel, still oozing character. All the rooms are charming (especially those with a river view) and the staff fall over themselves to be helpful; buffet breakfast included. ➎–➏

Norfolk 117 Le Thanh Ton ☎08/829 5368, @norfolk@bdvn.vnd.net. Unfussy yet pleasantly coordinated rooms with access to all the usual facilities, and efficiently run by friendly staff. The attached restaurant, where complimentary breakfast and a Sunday carvery are served, is recommended. ➎

Orchid 29a Thai Van Lung ☎08/823 1809, ⓕ829 2245. Rooms at this low-key, mid-range hotel are clean, if a little dated, and fitted out with satellite TV, air-con, IDD and en-suite bathrooms. Cheaper rooms don't have a lot of space, so it's worth paying $5 extra to upgrade; rates include breakfast. ➌–➍

Oscar Saigon 68a Nguyen Hué ☎08/829 2959, @rsvn.oscar@bdvn.vnd.net. Soulless but well-appointed rooms behind a grand colonnaded facade in the centre of the city; the business and fitness centres make this a good corporate choice. ➍–➎

Que Huong-Liberty 2 129–133 Ham Nghi ☎08/822 4922, ✉qhuong2@quehuonghotel.vnn .vn. Recently renovated and incorporated into the *Que Huong-Liberty* hotel empire; some of the spacious, tasteful rooms command good city views at no extra cost, or you can settle for gazing across the city from the tenth-floor restaurant. Competitive business rates. ➍

Renaissance Riverside 8–15 Ton Duc Thang ☎08/822 0033, ☏823 5666. A new addition down by the river offering a challenge to other top-line hotels with its immaculate rooms and personalized, friendly service. ➎–➏

Rex 141 Nguyen Hué ☎08/829 2185, ⓦwww.rexhotelvietnam.com. The *Rex* shamelessly milks its fame, but its rooms are extremely comfortable and the grand lobby area is breathtaking; one of the stronger personalities on the Ho Chi Minh hotel scene. ➍–➏

Riverside 18–20 Ton Duc Thang ☎08/822 4038, ✉hotelriversidesg@hcm.vnn.vn. Grand colonial pile recently modernized, proudly eyeing the river from the base of Dong Khoi, but remarkably tranquil given its location. The good-value upgraded rooms are stylish but functional, and breakfast is included; $20 more buys you a river view. ➍–➎

Saigon Prince 63 Nguyen Hué ☎08/822 2999, ✉saigon-princehtl@hcm.vnn.vn. Within a lurid pink toytown exterior, this classy boutique hotel in the heart of the city boasts over two hundred elegant rooms and suites. ➍–➏

Sheraton 88 Dong Khoi ☎08/827 2828, ⓦwww.sheraton.com/saigon. New monolith on Dong Khoi, ideally located for shopping and sights. Sumptuous rooms, but prices are sky-high. ➏

Sofitel Plaza 17 Le Duan ☎08/824 1555, ✉sofsgn-resa@hcmc.netnam.vn. One of the jewels in Ho Chi Minh's crown, firmly established as a favourite with business travellers. The hi-tech open-plan lobby is a masterpiece and the rooftop pool is simply stunning. Both the rooms and facilities boast luxurious elegance with the most modern trimmings. ➏

Spring 44–46 Le Thanh Ton ☎08/829 7362, ✉springhotel@hcm.vnn.vn. An excellent mid-range hotel with top-quality services, conveniently located just north of the centre. ➌–➍

Thang Long 48 Mac Thi Buoi ☎08/822 2595, ✉thanglonghotel@hcm.fpt.vn. Same facilities as *Dong Do* and *Kim Long*, offering a reasonably priced base in the centre. ➌–➍

Thanh Thao 71 Le Thi Hong Gam ☎08/822 5664, ☏825 1836. Sparkling, minty-fresh rooms with air-con, fridge, telephone and hot water – good rates, but with six floors and no lift it's a long haul to the top. ➋

Pham Ngu Lao and around

An An 40 Bui Vien ☎08/837 8087, ⓦwww .ananhotel.com. This new mini-hotel has twenty bright and airy rooms, all with air-con and bathtubs, some with computers and Internet connections. It also has an eleventh-floor restaurant and a $1 buffet breakfast. ➌

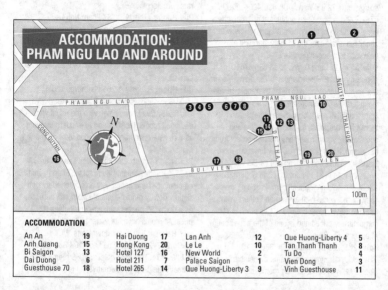

ACCOMMODATION: PHAM NGU LAO AND AROUND

ACCOMMODATION

An An	19	Hai Duong	17	Lan Anh	12	Que Huong-Liberty 4	5
Anh Quang	15	Hong Kong	20	Le Le	10	Tan Thanh Thanh	8
Bi Saigon	13	Hotel 127	16	New World	2	Tu Do	4
Dai Duong	6	Hotel 211	7	Palace Saigon	1	Vien Dong	3
Guesthouse 70	18	Hotel 265	14	Que Huong-Liberty 3	9	Vinh Guesthouse	11

Anh Quang 217/12 De Tham ☎08/836 9906. One of several private homes offering bargain lodgings down the Dickensian alleyway between 217 and 219 De Tham. Others include the *Ngoc Yen*, 217/29 (☎08/836 0200) directly opposite. ❶

Bi Saigon 185/16 and 185/26 Pham Ngu Lao ☎08/836 0678, ✉bisaigon@saigonnet.vn. Gloomy corridors, but clean and comfortable, if rather chintzy, rooms with hot water and satellite TV, as well as four expensive suites with balconies; free airport transfers provided. Both locations have more than adequate restaurants. ❸

Dai Duong 217 Pham Ngu Lao ☎08/836 8231. Also known as *Ocean Hotel*, this mini-hotel has 22 clean but smallish rooms, all with hot water and a choice of air-con and fan, plus a lift to all six floors. A good-value budget option. ❶–❷

Guesthouse 70 70 Bui Vien ☎ & ⓕ08/836 9569, ✉phanlan36@yahoo.com. Hugely popular, friendly and almost legendary place, offering free tea, coffee and fruit as well as breakfast and evening vegetarian meal. Of the eleven rooms, most are fairly small, but bright and pleasant; there's also one large dorm room with five beds. If rooms are full here, the same people run guesthouses at 100/23 Tran Hung Dao and 35/2 Tran Hung Dao, a short walk away. ❶–❸

Hai Duong 82 Bui Vien ☎08/836 9080, ✉phuongpham@hcm.fpt.vn. This friendly and modern place has seventeen clean rooms all boasting TV, hot water and tasteful pine furnishings; facilities also run to rooftop terrace, restaurant and bar. ❷

Hong Kong 22 Bui Vien ☎08/836 4904, ⓕ836 8757. Long-running and popular mini-hotel, offering a selection of clean, comfortable rooms with either fan or air-con; the friendly staff will also help with tour bookings. ❶–❷

Hotel 127 127 Cong Quynh ☎08/836 8761, ✉guesthouse127@bdvn.vnd.net. The genial Madam Cuc pays more attention to detail than most, resulting in a range of wholesome rooms, some sleeping up to four. Staff are informative and helpful and there's free breakfast, fruit, tea and coffee and, occasionally, spring rolls. They will also collect from the airport. If this place is full, they have two more branches at 184 Cong Quynh and 64 Bui Vien. ❸

Hotel 211 211–213 Pham Ngu Lao ☎08/836 7353, ✉hotelduy@hotmail.com. Providing over sixty rooms, some with air-con and others with fan, and all with free breakfast, this place is very competitively priced and is one of the better budget options. ❶–❸

Hotel 265 265 De Tham ☎08/836 7512, ✉hotelduy@hotmail.com. Same ownership as *Hotel 211*, with some air-con rooms, others with fan, and $3 dorm up top. ❶–❷

Kim Kim 178/13 Co Giang ☎08/837 4693; see map, p.87. Not as attractive as *Miss Loi*, but another budget option a bit away from backpackersville. ❶

Lan Anh 252 De Tham ☎08/836 5197, ✉lan-anh-hotel@hcm.vnn.vn. In a prime location, this friendly, family-run mini-hotel in the heart of De Tham has 22 bright, clean rooms with a choice of air-con or fan; the rooms at the front with balconies are good value, but the six floors mean a bit of a hike for some guests (a lift is promised soon). Breakfast included. ❶–❷

Le Le 171 Pham Ngu Lao ☎08/836 8686, ✉lelehotel@hcm.fpt.vn. Comfortable and popular mini-hotel that appeals to tourists and business people alike. Rooms all have hot water, satellite TV and IDD, and breakfast is included in the price. ❷–❹

Miss Loi 178/20 Co Giang ☎08/837 9589, ✉missloi@hcm.fpt.vn; see map, p.87. Located out of sight of the Pham Ngu Lao activity, this cosy guesthouse has a range of rooms in a quiet back-street community. ❶–❷

New World 76 Le Lai ☎08/822 8888, ⓦwww.newworldvietnam.com. A benchmark on the Ho Chi Minh hotel scene since its opening in 1993 – over 500 luxurious rooms complemented by impressive sports and leisure facilities and a business centre. ❺

Palace Saigon (Hoang Thanh) 82 Le Lai ☎08/832 2803. Rooms are cheery and capacious and include air-con, TV and breakfast; four sleep for the same price as two in the double rooms and rates are negotiable. ❷

Que Huong-Liberty 3 187 Pham Ngu Lao ☎08/836 9522, ✉qhuong3@libertyhotel.vnn.vn. The hotel formerly known as *Prince* is now part of the *Que Huong* chain, and offers smart, well-equipped rooms right in the heart of Pham Ngu Lao. ❹

Que Huong-Liberty 4 265 Pham Ngu Lao ☎08/836 4556, ✉qhuong4@libertyhotel.vnn.vn. The fourth *Que Huong* hotel, with the usual well-equipped rooms, facilities and all-modern interiors as well as a restaurant with a good view on the ninth floor. ❹

Tan Thanh Thanh 205 Pham Ngu Lao ☎08/837 3595, ✉tanthanhthanh@hcm.fpt.vn. Friendly and efficient staff and generously proportioned though slightly dowdy rooms – one of which can be used as a dorm ($3 per person); air-con doubles the price. All rooms have hot water and include breakfast. Resident tour agent downstairs. ❶

Tu Do 267–269 Pham Ngu Lao ☎08/836 7345, ✉836 8171. This mini-hotel with 45 rooms is an attractive mid-range alternative; all rooms have air-con, bathtubs and satellite TV, and breakfast is included. ③–④

Vien Dong 275a Pham Ngu Lao ☎08/836 8941, Ⓔviendonghotel@hcm.fpt.vn. Dependable first-night mid-range option, but don't get put near the karaoke rooms or night club; all rooms have air-con, fridge, satellite TV and complimentary breakfast. Discounts are negotiable during quieter periods. ③–④

Vinh Guesthouse 269 De Tham ☎08/836 8585, Ⓕ836 8787. More intimate sister hotel of the *Le Le*, with similar facilities in its nine lower-priced rooms. ②–③

West of Pham Ngu Lao

Equatorial 242 Tran Binh Trong ☎08/839 7777, Ⓔinfo@hcm.equatorial.com. Mustard-hued monolith – the latest in a respected Asian chain – offering very comfortable rooms with the full gamut of facilities, although it's lacking a bit in atmosphere. Two recommended restaurants, *Golden Phoenix* and *Kampachi*, are on site too (see p.114). ⑥

Four Roses 790/5 Nguyen Dinh Chieu ☎ & Ⓕ08/832 5895, Ⓔroseminne@hcm.vnn.vn. It may be located in no-man's-land between Cholon and the city centre, but the *Four Roses* is an unexpected delight. Set in a tranquil bougainvillea garden, there are ten immaculately clean, pleasantly furnished rooms each with balconies. Family-run with a distinctly French flavour, it offers the perfect antidote to hectic Ho Chi Minh; there's a beauty salon in the basement (the owner is a beautician) and meals can also be rustled up on request. ②–③

Metropole 148 Tran Hung Dao ☎08/920 1943, Ⓔmetropole-sgn@hcm.vnn.vn. Known as the *Binh Minh* in Vietnamese, a sedate and friendly 74-room hotel, set west of the city centre, but still worth considering for its business facilities, modest pool and well-turned-out rooms enjoying 24-hour room service and free breakfast. Prices are negotiable. ③–④

Cholon

Arc en Ciel 52–56 Tan Da ☎08/855 2550, Ⓔthienhong@hcm.vnn.vn. Standard mid-range hotel, though looking a little jaded. The 91 rooms include satellite TV, IDD phone and complimentary breakfast, and there are the usual in-house services. ③–④

Hanh Long 2 1115 Tran Hung Dao ☎08/838 1173, Ⓕ923 5941. The cheap, functional rooms appear far more inviting than the run-down exterior, and are perhaps the only possible attraction at this noisy hotel, patronized mainly by Chinese, Taiwanese and Vietnamese; pricier rooms have air-con. ①–②

Phuong Huang 411 Tran Hung Dao ☎08/855 1888, Ⓕ855 2288. An aesthetic nightmare, and somewhat overpriced, but worth considering if you want to soak up the atmosphere of central Cholon. ①–③

Tan Da 22–24 Tan Da ☎08/855 5711. Mini-hotel with 24 reasonably well-appointed rooms on four floors, the lowest prices found on the upper level. Its sidestreet location gives some respite from the noise. Staff can be surly, however. ①–②

The City

Ho Chi Minh City – or Thanh Pho Ho Chi Minh, to give it its Vietnamese name – is divided into eighteen districts, though tourists rarely travel beyond districts One, Three and Five, unless it's to visit the outlying districts of Cu Chi (see p.127) or Thu Duc (see p.127). The city proper hugs the west bank of the **Saigon River**, and its central area, District One, nestles in the hinge formed by the confluence of the river with the silty ooze of the **Ben Nghe Channel**; traditionally the French Quarter of the city, this area is still widely known as Saigon. **Dong Khoi** is its delicate backbone, and around the T-shape it forms with **Le Duan Boulevard** are scattered most of the city's museums and colonial remnants.

Excepting the commercial fever of **Cholon**, its frenetic Chinatown, the city refuses to carve up into homogeneous, tourist-friendly districts, so visitors have to effect a dot-to-dot of the sights that appeal most. These invariably include one or more of the museums that pander to the West's fixation with the American War, the pick of the bunch being the **War Remnants Museum** and **Ho Chi Minh City Museum**. For some visitors, the war is their primary frame of reference, and such historical hot spots as the **Presidential Palace** (now the Reunification

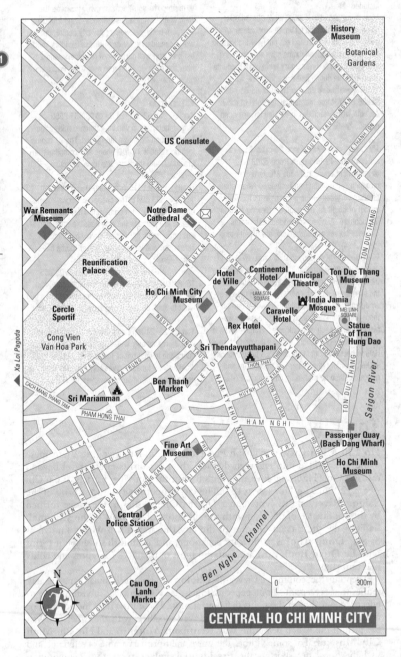

▲ Xa Loi Pagoda

CENTRAL HO CHI MINH CITY

History Museum

Botanical Gardens

US Consulate

War Remnants Museum

Notre Dame Cathedral

Reunification Palace

Hotel de Ville

Continental Hotel

Municipal Theatre

Ton Duc Thang Museum

Ho Chi Minh City Museum

LAM SON SQUARE

India Jamia Mosque

Cercle Sportif

Caravelle Hotel

MEI LINH SQUARE

Rex Hotel

Statue of Tran Hung Dao

Cong Vien Van Hoa Park

Sri Thendayyutthapani

Saigon River

Sri Mariamman

Ben Thanh Market

Passenger Quay (Bach Dang Wharf)

Fine Art Museum

Ho Chi Minh Museum

Central Police Station

Ben Nghe Channel

N

0   300m

Cau Ong Lanh Market

Palace) rank highly on their itineraries; but the city predates American involvement by several centuries, and not all of its sights revolve around planes, tanks and rusting ordnance. Ostentatious reminders of French rule abound, among them such memorable buildings as **Notre Dame Cathedral** and the grandiose **Hotel de Ville** – but even these look spanking-new when compared to gloriously musty edifices like **Giac Lam Pagoda** and the **Jade Emperor Pagoda**, only a taster of the many captivating places of worship across the city. And if the chaos becomes too much, you can escape to the relative calm of the **Botanical Gardens** – also home to the city's **History Museum** and **zoo**.

Dong Khoi

Slender **Dong Khoi**, running for just over 1km from Le Duan to the Saigon River, has long mirrored Ho Chi Minh's changing fortunes. The French knew the road as Rue Catinat, a tamarind-shaded thoroughfare that constituted the heart of French colonial life. Here the *colons* would promenade, stopping at chic boutiques and perfumeries, and gathering at noon and dusk at cafés such as the *Rotonde* and the *Taverne Alsacienne* for a Vermouth or Dubonnet, before hailing a *pousse-pousse* (a hand-pulled variation on the cyclo) to run them home. With the departure of the French in 1954, President Diem saw fit to change the street's name to Tu Do, "Freedom"; and it was under this guise that a generation of young American GIs came to know it, as they toured the glut of bars – *Wild West, Uncle Sam's, Playboy* – that sprang up to pander to their more lascivious needs. After Saigon fell in 1975, the more politically correct monicker of Dong Khoi, or "Uprising", was adopted, but the street quickly went to seed in the dark, pre-*doi moi* years, and by the Seventies had gone, in the words of Le Ly Hayslip, from "bejewelled, jaded dowager to shabby, grasping bag lady".

Ever receptive to the needs of Saigon's latest foreign invaders, Dong Khoi is today enjoying a renaissance. Its eclectic melange of buildings – from grand colonial facades and slender shophouses to unlovely concrete-slab buildings – is fast topping up with **souvenir shops** and **designer boutiques** catering for the current wave of tourism. Each Sunday evening, the city's trendsetting teenage boys converge on Dong Khoi and parallel Nguyen Hué on their Hondas, to circle round and round, girlfriends riding pillion, in a kind of mating ritual. Inevitably, the street has also become a site frequented by those who've fared less well in the economic resurgence – **beggars**, with their battered plastic cups.

Notre Dame Cathedral

Straddling the northern reach of Dong Khoi is the pleasing redbrick bulk of the late nineteenth-century **Notre Dame Cathedral**, whose twin spires the novelist Anthony Grey memorably compared to "the ears of a hidden jackrabbit". Aside from the few stained-glass windows above and behind its altar, and its marble relief *Stations of the Cross*, the interior boasts only scanty decoration, but there's plenty of scope for people-watching, as a steady trickle of women pass through in their best silk tunics and black pants, fingering rosary beads, their whispered prayers merging with the insistent murmur of the traffic outside. Towards dusk, the neon-lit halo and blue neon words, *Ave Maria*, that shine above the figure of Christ at the head of the nave are disconcertingly reminiscent of a nightclub entrance. A statue of the Virgin Mary provides the centrepiece to the small **park** fronting the cathedral, where cyclo drivers loiter and kids hawk postcards and maps.

The cathedral's twin compass-point spires were, for decades, one of Saigon's handiest landmarks, but they're now dwarfed by the glass facade of **Diamond Plaza**, one of the city's gleaming **shopping malls**, and by the telecom tower above the **General Post Office**, east of the park. A classic colonial edifice unchanged since its completion in the 1880s, the GPO is worth a peek inside for its nave-like foyer, lent character by two huge map-murals, one charting Saigon and its environs in 1892, the other the telegraphic lines of southern Vietnam and Cambodia in 1936. Further in, a huge portrait of Uncle Ho sporting a healthy tan and warm smile gazes down at the aged wooden benches and tables of the cavernous main hall.

Lam Son Square

Dong Khoi briefly widens a couple of hundred metres south of the cathedral, where the smart, white walls, revolving globe and clay-coloured roof of the **Hotel Continental** (see p.86 for review) announce your arrival in **Lam Son Square**. Once a bastion of French high society, and still one of the city's premier addresses, the hotel's front terrace was *the* place to see and be seen earlier last century. Little wonder, then, that Somerset Maugham's nose for a story led him here in the mid-Twenties: "Outside the hotels are terraces," he recounted, "and at the hour of the aperitif, they are crowded with bearded, gesticulating Frenchmen drinking the sweet and sickly beverages ... which they drink in France and they talk nineteen to the dozen in the rolling accent of the Midi... It is very agreeable to sit under the awning on the terrace of the *Hotel Continental*, with an innocent drink before you, [and] read in the local newspaper heated controversies upon the affairs of the colony." Sadly the terrace no longer exists, so if you want to tap into the history of the place, the best you can do is to ensconce yourself in the hotel's café.

Standing grandly on the eastern side of Lam Son Square, its cyclopean, domed entrance peering southwestwards down Le Loi, is the century-old **Municipal Theatre**. The National Assembly was temporarily housed here in 1955, but today, lovingly restored to its former glory, it once again embraces programmes that include fashion shows, drama and dance. The ground in front of the broad sweep of its staircase once featured a statue of a group of South Vietnamese marines, but its days were numbered after Saigon fell in 1975. Just below the theatre, the 1958-built and now grandiosely revamped **Caravelle Hotel** (see p.86 for review) gazes down across the square at the more diminutive *Continental*. In its former incarnation, the *Caravelle* found favour with those Western journalists assigned to cover the war, and its terrace bar saw many a report drafted over a stiff drink. From Lam Son, it's only a couple of minutes' walk down Le Loi to Nguyen Hué and the Hotel de Ville.

Down towards the riverbank

Though souvenir shops are in the ascendancy below the *Caravelle*, they haven't yet managed entirely to eradicate the past, and it's still possible to winkle out relics of old Saigon. Wander south of Lam Son and you'll soon meet Dong Du, where a left turn reveals the white and blue-washed walls of the 1930s **Indian Jamia Muslim Mosque**. There's really nothing to see here, and the empty, red-carpeted hall belies the drama of the four minarets sprouting from it; however, there's a reassuring sense of peace that's enhanced by the slumbering worshippers lazing around the complex. The mosque's low-key dining room, situated around the back of the building, does a roaring trade at lunchtimes. Continuing down Dong Khoi to the river takes you past two of the city's more venerable hotels, the lovingly restored *Grand* (see p.86) on the left, followed 30m later on the right by the lavish but architecturally less interesting *Majestic* (see p.86).

Around Nguyen Hué

When Saigon's French administrators laid the 750-metre sweep of Charner Boulevard over a filled-in canal and down to the Saigon River, their brief was to replicate the elegance of a tree-lined Parisian boulevard, and in its day this broad avenue was known as the *Champs Elysées* of the East. Since then, a swarm of Hondas has laid siege to the thoroughfare – now known as **Nguyen Hué** – and any romance has been dispelled. Recent renovations have attempted to spruce it up, but though the paving may have been redone, and the slummy booths that spined it demolished, the facelift has failed to revive the street's glamour. Only at Tet does Nguyen Hué spring to life, when it hosts a vast, riotously colourful flower market which draws Vietnamese belles in their thousands to pose in their best *ao dai*s among the roses, sunflowers, chrysanthemums and conical orange trees.

The stately edifice that deigns to stand at Nguyen Hué's northern extent is the former **Hotel de Ville**, an ostentatious reminder of colonial Europe's stubborn resolve to stamp its imprint on the countries it subjugated, no matter how incongruous. Built in 1908 as the city's administrative hub, this yellow and white striped hatbox of a building today houses the People's Committee behind its showy jumble of Corinthian columns, classical figures and shuttered windows. While not to everyone's taste, it at least adds a sense of age to Nguyen Hué. A statue of Uncle Ho cradling a small child in his lap mounts watch over the tiny **park** fronting the building, where roving photographers loll around touting polaroid snaps to passing pedestrians; while on the pavements around the park, hawkers brandish postcards, balloons, maps, toys crafted from beer cans and photocopied versions of Graham Greene's *The Quiet American*.

Though the **Rex Hotel** (see p.87), a few paces below the park at the junction of Nguyen Hué and Le Loi, may give the impression of being venerable, in fact it has only operated as a hotel since 1976. Having started out as a garage for the Renaults and Peugeots of the city's French expat community, during the Sixties it billeted American officers, and hosted regular press briefing sessions that came to be known by jaded members of the press as the "Five O'Clock Follies". From its fifth-floor *Rooftop Garden*, the hotel yields a superb view of the whirl of life on the street below, best enjoyed over a cool glass of 333 beer. At night, the hotel's emblem, a giant **crown**, lights up on the terrace, providing the city with one of its best-known landmarks.

The southern face of the block south of the *Rex* hides peaceful **Sri Thendayyutthapani Temple**, whose *gopuram* (sculpted gate tower) stands at 66 Ton That Thiep. The place manages a certain rag-tag charisma, the lavish murals normally associated with Hindu temples replaced by faded paintings of Jawaharlal Nehru, Mahatma Gandhi, and various deities from the Hindu pantheon, plus a ceiling gaily studded with coloured baubles and lamps. Steps beyond the topiary to the right of the main sanctuary lead to a roof terrace that's dominated by a weather-beaten tower of deities, whose ranks have been infiltrated by two incongruous characters dressed like public schoolboys in braces, shorts and striped ties, and waving merrily.

The Ho Chi Minh City Museum

Of all the stones of empire thrown up in Vietnam by the French, few are more eye-catching than the former **Gia Long Palace**, a block west of the Hotel de Ville at 65 Ly Tu Trong, built in 1886 as a splendid residence for the governor of Cochinchina. Homeless after the air attack that smashed his own palace, Diem decamped here in 1962, and it was in the tunnels under the building that he spent his last hours of office, before fleeing to the church in Cholon where he finally surrendered (see p.104). Ironically, it now houses the **Ho Chi Minh City Museum** (daily 8am–4pm; small admission fee), which makes use of photographs, documents and artefacts to trace the struggle of the Vietnamese people against France and America. Even if you're not desperate to learn more about the country's war-torn past, you're likely to be enchanted by the grandeur of the building, and you might even witness couples posing for wedding photographs, as the regal structure and well-tended gardens are a favourite backdrop for photographers.

The downstairs area is a hotchpotch of ancient artefacts and antique collections, along with a section on nature and another featuring ethnic clothing and implements. The museum shifts into higher gear upstairs, where the focus turns to the war with America. The best exhibits are those showcasing the ingenuity of the Vietnamese – bicycle parts made into mortars, a Suzuki motorbike in whose inner tubes documents were smuggled into Saigon, a false-floored boat in which guns were secreted, and so on. Look out, too, for sweaters knitted by female prisoners on Con Dao Island, and bearing the Vietnamese words for "peace" and "freedom". Elsewhere, there's a cross-sectional model of the Cu Chi tunnels, and a rewarding gallery of photographs of the Ho Chi Minh Campaign and the fall of Saigon.

As with many of Vietnam's museums, the hardware of war is on display in the **gardens**. Tucked away behind the frangipanis and well-groomed hedges out back are a Soviet tank, an American helicopter and an anti-aircraft gun, while out front are two sleek but idle jets.

Along the waterfront

For decades, the **quay** hugging the confluence of the Saigon River and Ben Nghe Channel provided new arrivals with their first real glimpse of Indochina – scores of coolie-hatted dock-workers lugging sacks of rice off ships, shrimp farmers dredging the oozy shallows, and junks and sampans bobbing on the tide under the vigilant gaze of *colons* imbibing at nearby cafés. Arriving by steamer in 1910, Gabrielle Vassal felt as if "all Saigon had turned out...Some expected friends, others came in the hope of meeting acquaintances or as mere spectators. One was reminded of a fashionable garden party, for the dresses and equipages were worthy of Paris itself." These days there's no such activity and many of the boats docked here are floating restaurants (see pp.108–110), but a stroll along riverside Ton Duc Thang still unearths the odd heavily laden boat just in from the Mekong Delta. At night the river reflects the blue, green and red of the monumental advertising signs on the far bank.

Take a left onto Ton Duc Thang at the base of Dong Khoi, and it's only a short skip to **Mei Linh Square**, long a popular haunt for early-morning practisers of *tai chi*, and radiating out from a statue of Tran Hung Dao, who points across the river. Ton Duc Thang draws its name from a former president of the Democratic Republic of Vietnam, whose life is celebrated at the nearby **Ton Duc Thang Museum** (Tues–Fri, 7.30–11.30am & 1.30–5pm; small admission fee). Don't expect any fireworks here: besides some grim photographs highlighting the many years he spent de-husking rice on the prison island of Poulo Condore (now known as Con Dao, see p.237), a few evocative photos of old Saigon and some of the bric-a-brac of the man's life comprise the museum's principal highlights.

The Ben Nghe Channel

Back at the foot of Dong Khoi, a right turn whisks you to the mouth of the **Ben**

Nghe Channel, where a signal mast marks the position of the **Pointe des Blagueurs** (Jokers' Point), once the epicentre of the colonial promenading circuit. With the bells of the evening Mass still ringing in their ears, French strollers would have hastened here to catch up on the latest gossip. The impressive Oriental roof of the mansion across the mouth of the channel broke onto the Saigon skyline in the 1860s. Known as the *Nha Rong*, or Dragon House, this former headquarters of a French shipping company is now home to the **Ho Chi Minh Museum** (1 Nguyen Tat Thanh, ☎08/940 2060; daily 7.30–11.30am & 1.30–4.30pm; small admission fee) – an apposite venue, given that it was from the abutting wharf that Ho left for Europe in 1911. Sadly, the collection within fails to capture the spirit of this man whose life was dedicated to liberating his homeland from colonialism. If you decide to visit, you'll need to wring all the interest you can out of personal effects such as Ho's walking stick, rattan suitcase, sandals made from tyres and watering can, a map of his itinerant wanderings, and a few blurred photographs of him at official receptions. If all the Ho Chi Minh museums in Vietnam are to be believed, Ho was evidently a compulsive hoarder.

The days when Ben Nghe was choked with sampans are long gone, and now its pitch-black waters are eerily calm, but there's still a pocket of interest on its north bank, where a brace of austere buildings signals the city's **financial district**, home to the State Bank and the mausoleum-like hulk of the Government Bank of Vietnam next door. An alternative to wading back into the downtown area is to push on southwest along the bank of the channel towards the base of Nguyen Thai Hoc, the focus of Cau Ong Lanh **street market**, a vast, rambling affair which operates virtually around the clock. In the small hours, traders can be seen negotiating bulk purchases of vegetables, fruit and other commodities for resale in the city's smaller markets later in the day.

Ben Thanh Market and around

There's much more beneath the pillbox-style clock tower of **Ben Thanh Market** than just the cattle and seafood pictured on its front wall. The city's busiest market for almost a century, and known to the French as the *Halles Centrales*, Ben Thanh's dense knot of trade has caused it to burst at the seams, disgorging stalls onto the surrounding pavements. Inside the main body of the market, a tight grid of aisles, demarcated according to produce, teems with shoppers, and, if it's souvenirs you're after, a reconnaissance here will reveal conical hats, basketware bags, shoes, Da Lat coffee and Vietnam T-shirts. All this, though, is tame stuff compared with the wet market along the back of the complex, where you'll find buckets of eels, clutches of live frogs tied together at the legs, heaps of pigs' ears and snouts, and baskets wedged full of hens, among other gruesome sights. If you can countenance the thought of eating after seeing – and smelling – this patch of the market, *com*, *pho* and baguette stalls proliferate towards the back of the main hall.

The aroma of jasmine and incense replaces the stench of butchery a block northwest of Ben Thanh, at Truong Dinh's **Sri Mariamman Hindu Temple**. Less engaging than Sri Thendayyutthapani (see p.93), Sri Mariamman's imposing yellow walls are sometimes besieged by vendors selling oil, incense and jasmine petals, and are topped by a colourful *gopuram*, or bank of sculpted gods. Inside, the gods Mariamman, Maduraiveeran and Pechiamman reside in stone sanctuaries reminiscent of the Cham towers upcountry, and there are more deities seated around the courtyard.

South of Ben Thanh

A short stroll from Ben Thanh Market down Pho Duc Chinh, in a grand colonial mansion, Ho Chi Minh City's **Fine Art Museum** (Tues–Sun, 9am–4.45pm; small admission fee) is worth a visit to view some of the country's best Cham and Oc Eo relics on the third floor. The first floor is given over to commerce in the form of art works on sale by various city galleries, and there are more in the basement. If you're in the market for a piece of Vietnamese art, it's worth checking these places out as standards are high and some prices are affordable. Revolutionary art dominates the second floor, relying heavily on hackneyed images of soldiers, war zones and Uncle Ho, though a few offerings capture the anguish and turmoil of the conflicts. Things get better on the third floor where there's an impressive collection of Oc Eo and Cham statues, gilt Buddhas and other antiquities.

Across the road from the museum, **Le Cong Kieu** is stuffed with antique shops selling Oriental and colonial bric-a-brac. Memorabilia reflecting Vietnam's more recent history are available at the army surplus stalls at the back of **Dan Sinh Market**, the entrance found between 336 and 338 Nguyen Cong Tru; here you can pick up khaki gear, VC pith helmets, old compasses and Zippo lighters embossed with saucy pearls of wisdom coined by GIs.

Along Le Duan Boulevard to the Botanical Gardens

Above Notre Dame, **Le Duan Boulevard** runs between the Botanical Gardens and the grounds of the presidential palace. Known as Norodom Boulevard to the French, who lined it with tamarind trees to effect a Gallic thoroughfare, it soon became a residential and diplomatic enclave with a crop of fine pastel-hued colonial villas to boot. Its present name doffs a cap to Le Duan, the secretary-general of the *Lao Dong*, or Workers Party, from 1959. Turn northeast from the top of Dong Khoi and the sense of harmony created by Le Duan's graceful colonial piles ends abruptly with a number of brand-new edifices. One of these, the nondescript building that is the new US Consulate, was built right on top of the site of the infamous former **American Embassy**, where a commemorative plaque is now the only reminder of its existence and significance in the American War.

Two events immortalized the former building on this site, in operation from 1967 to 1975 and left standing half-derelict until 1999 as a sobering legacy. The first came in the pre-dawn hours of January 31, 1968, when a small band of VC commandos breached the embassy compound during the nationwide **Tet Offensive**. That the North could mount such an effective attack on the hub of US power in Vietnam was shocking to the American public. In the six hours of close-range fire that followed, five US guards died, and with them the popular misconception that the US Army had the Vietnam conflict under control.

Worse followed seven years later, during "Operation Frequent Wind", the chaotic **helicopter evacuation** that marked the United States' final undignified withdrawal from Vietnam. The embassy building was one of thirteen designated landing zones where all foreigners were to gather upon hearing the words, "It is 112 degrees and rising" on the radio followed by Bing Crosby singing *White Christmas*. At noon on April 29, 1975, the signal was broadcast, and for the next eighteen hours scores of helicopters shuttled passengers out to the US Navy's Seventh Fleet off Vung Tau. Around two thousand evacuees were lifted from the roof of the embassy alone, before Ambassador Graham Martin finally left with the Stars and Stripes in the early hours of the following morning. In a tragic postscript to US involvement, as the last helicopter lifted off, many of the Vietnamese civilians who for hours had been clamouring at the gates were left to suffer the communists' reprisals.

The breaching of the presidential palace

If the frantic airlift from the roof of the US Embassy symbolized the American capitulation in Vietnam, then the **breaching of the presidential palace** grounds by a tank belonging to the Northern Army, on April 30, 1975, was the defining moment of the fall of Saigon and the South.

Of the many Western journalists on hand to witness the spectacle, none was better placed than English journalist and poet James Fenton, who conspired to hitch a ride on the tank that first crashed through the gates: "The tank speeded up, and rammed the left side of the palace gate. Wrought iron flew into the air, but the whole structure refused to give. I nearly fell off. The tank backed again, and I observed a man with a nervous smile opening the centre portion of the gate. We drove into the grounds of the palace, and fired a salute. An NLF soldier took the flag and, waving it above his head, ran into the palace. A few moments later, he emerged on the terrace, waving the flag round and round. Later still, there he was on the roof. The red and yellow stripes of the Saigon regime were lowered at last."

Inside the palace, Duong Van Minh ("Big Minh"), sworn in as president only two days before, readied to perform his last presidential duty. "I have been waiting since early this morning to transfer power to you," he said to General Bui Tin, to which the general replied: "Your power has crumbled. You cannot give up what you do not have."

The Botanical Gardens and zoo

The pace of life slows down considerably – and the odours of cut grass and frangipani blooms replace the smell of exhaust fumes – when you duck into the city's **Botanical Gardens** (daily 7am–10pm; small admission fee), accessed by a gate at the far eastern end of Le Duan, and bounded to the east by the Thi Nghe Channel. Established in 1864 by the Frenchmen Germain and Pierre (respectively a vet and a botanist), the gardens' social function has remained unchanged in decades, and their tree-shaded paths still attract as many courting couples and promenaders as when Norman Lewis followed the "clusters of Vietnamese beauties on bicycles" and headed there one Sunday morning in 1950 to find the gardens "full of these ethereal creatures, gliding in decorous groups…sometimes accompanied by gallants". In its day, the gardens harboured an impressive collection of tropical flora, including many species of orchid. Post-liberation, the place went to seed but nowadays a bevy of gardeners keep it reasonably well tended again, and portrait photographers are once again lurking to take snaps of you framed by flowers.

Stray right inside and you'll soon reach the **zoo**, home to camels, elephants, crocodiles and big cats, and komodo dragons – a gift from the government of Indonesia. It's not a cheerful sight: cages are ancient and dingy and the stench is sometimes overpowering. The small walk-through aquarium is more appealing, should you be lucky enough to find it open. With kids in tow, keep your fingers crossed that the motley rides of the **amusement park** are open – if not, you can appease them with an ice cream or a coconut from one of the several **cafés** sprinkled around the grounds.

The History Museum

A pleasing, pagoda-style roof crowns the city's **History Museum** (Mon–Sat 8–11am & 1.30–4pm; Sun 8.30am–4pm; small admission fee). It houses a train of galleries illuminating Vietnam's past from primitive times to the end of French rule by means of a decent if unastonishing array of artefacts and pictures. Dioramas of defining moments in Vietnamese military history lend the collection some cohesion – included are Ngo Quyen's 938 AD victory at Bach Dang (see p.484), and the sinking of the *Esperance*. Should you tire of Vietnamese history, you might explore halls focusing on such disparate subjects as Buddha images from around Asia; seventh- and eighth-century Champa art; and the customs and crafts of the ethnic minorities of Vietnam. There's also a room jam-packed with exquisite ceramics from Japan, Thailand and Vietnam, and you could round off your visit at the **water puppetry theatre** (shows are performed on the hour from 9am to 4pm, though not at 1pm; small admission fee).

The Reunification Palace and around

Five minutes' stroll through the leafy parkland northwest of the cathedral, a red flag billows proudly above the **Reunification Palace** (daily 7.30–11.30am & 1.30–4.30pm; $1 including guided tour; entrances on Nam Ky Khoi Nghia and Nguyen Du), a whitewashed concrete edifice with all the charm of a municipal library, which occupies the site of the Norodom Palace, a colonial mansion erected in 1871 to house the governor-general of Indochina. With the French departure in 1954, Ngo Dinh Diem commandeered this extravagent monument as his presidential palace, but after sustaining extensive damage in a February 1962 assassination attempt by two disaffected Southern pilots, the place was condemned and pulled down. The present building was labelled the Independence Palace upon completion in 1966, only to be retitled the Reunification Hall when the South fell in 1975 (see box on p.97). The reversion to the label "Palace" was doubtless made for tourist appeal.

Spookily unchanged from its working days, much of the building's **interior** is a time capsule of Sixties and Seventies kitsch: pacing its airy banqueting rooms, conference halls and reception areas, it's hard not to think you've strayed into the arch-criminal's lair in a James Bond movie. Guides usher you through the hall's many chambers, proudly pointing out every piece of porcelain, lacquerwork, rosewood and silk on display. Most interesting is the **third floor**, where, as well as the presidential library (with works by Laurens van der Post and Graham Greene alongside heavyweight political tomes), there's a sassily curtained projection room, and an entertainment lounge complete with tacky circular sofa and barrel-shaped bar. Nearby, two stuffed tigers (a gift from a highland tribe) mark the way to the **movie room**, where a potted account of the war is screened half-hourly. Once the credits roll, move on to the atmospheric **basement** and former command centre, where wood-panelled combat staff quarters yield archaic radio equipment and vast wall maps.

Adjoining the western edge of the Reunification Palace's grounds is **Cong Vien Van Hoa Park**, a municipal park whose tree-shaded lawns heave with life each Sunday. During the colonial era, the park's northernmost corner was home to one of the linchpins of French expat society, the **Cercle Sportif**, a Westerners-only sports club where the *colons* gathered to swim and play tennis before sinking an aperitif and discussing the day's events. Surveying the grandiose swimming pool with its Grecian pillars, a leftover from those days, and the dilapidated clubhouse, it's easy to conjure up the tennis whites and parasols of Saigon high society. In time, American names replaced French on the members' list; and today the place is called the Workers' Sports Club – though the many men who gather to play *boules* provide a quaint link with their country's colonial past.

The War Remnants Museum

A block above the park, at 28 Vo Van Tan, lies the **War Remnants Museum** (daily 7.30–11.45am & 1.30–5.15pm; small admission fee), the city's most popular attraction. Formerly known as the "War Crimes Museum", it has now lost the one-sided and accusatory tone that once marred it. Its exhibits for the most part speak for themselves, a distressing compendium of the horrors of modern warfare. Some of the instruments of destruction are on display in the courtyard outside, including a 28-tonne howitzer and a ghoulish collection of bomb parts. There's also a guillotine that harvested heads at the Central Prison on Ly Tu Trong, first for the French and later for Diem. The centrepiece of the yard, though, is a renovated Douglas Skyraider plane, known to combatants as a "squad". Inside, a series of halls present a grisly portfolio of **photographs** of mutilation, napalm burns and torture. Most shocking is the gallery detailing the effects of the 75 million litres of defoliant sprays dumped across the country: beside the expected images of bald terrain, hideously malformed foetuses are preserved in pickling jars. A gallery that looks at international opposition to the war as well as the American peace movement adds a sense of balance, reflecting the museum's shifting attitude. It also contains accounts of servicemen – such as veteran B52 pilot Michael Heck – who attempted to discharge themselves from the war on ethical grounds. Artefacts donated to the museum by returned US servicemen add to the reconciliatory tone.

The museum rounds off with a grisly mock-up of the **tiger cages**, the godless prison cells of Con Son Island (see p.237), which could have been borrowed from the movie set of *Papillon*. The **souvenir shop** outside vends US Army-issue fungicidal foot powder and dog tags, and models crafted from spent bullets. There's also a **water puppetry theatre** opposite, which at the time of writing was under reconstruction.

Xa Loi Pagoda

Vapid **Xa Loi Pagoda** (daily 7–11am & 2–5pm), a five-minute walk west of the museum at 89 Ba Huyen Thanh Quan, became a hotbed of Buddhist opposition to Diem in 1963. The austere, 1956-built complex is unspectacular, its most striking component a tall **tower** whose unlovely beige blocks lend it a drabness even six tiers of Oriental roofs can't quite dispel. The main **sanctuary**, accessed by a dual staircase (men scale the left-hand flight, women the right), is similarly dull: beyond a vast joss-stick urn inventively decorated with marbles and shards of broken china, it's a lofty hall featuring a huge gilt Buddha and fourteen murals that narrate his life. Turn left and around the back of the Buddha, and you'll come across a shrine commemorating Thich Quang Duc and the other monks who set fire to themselves in Saigon in 1963 (see box below). Quang Duc's is the ghostly figure holding a set of beads, to the left of the shrine.

The self-immolation of Thich Quang Duc

In the early morning of June 11, 1963, a column of Buddhist monks left the **Xa Loi Pagoda** and processed to the intersection of Cach Mang Thang Tam and Nguyen Dinh Chieu. There, **Thich Quang Duc**, a 66-year-old monk from Hué, sat down in the lotus position and meditated as fellow monks doused him in petrol, and then set light to him in protest at the repression of Buddhists by President Diem, who was a Catholic. As flames engulfed the impassive monk and passers-by prostrated themselves before him, the cameras of the Western press corps rolled, and by the next morning the grisly event had grabbed the world's headlines. More self-immolations followed, and Diem's heavy-handed responses at Xa Loi – some four hundred monks and nuns were arrested and others cast from the top of the tower – led to massed popular demonstrations against the government. Diem, it was clear, had become a liability. On November 2, he and his brother were assassinated after taking refuge in Cholon's Cha Tam Church (see p.104), the victims of a military coup.

North of Dien Bien Phu

Take a stroll northwest from the Botanical Gardens up Nguyen Binh Khiem, and ten minutes later you'll reach the broad boulevard of **Dien Bien Phu**. Once over Dien Bien Phu, Nguyen Binh Khiem peters out beside the banks of the Thi Nghe Channel; but Mai Thi Luu, one block to the west, yields up the spectacular **Jade Emperor Pagoda** (daily 6am–6pm), built by the city's Cantonese community around 1900, and still its most captivating pagoda. If you visit just one temple in town, make it this one, with its exquisite panels of carved gilt woodwork, and its panoply of weird and wonderful deities, both Taoist and Buddhist, beneath a roof that groans under the weight of dragons, birds and animals.

Within the tree-lined **courtyard** out front is a grubby pond whose occupants have earned the temple its alternative moniker of Tortoise Pagoda. Once over the threshold, look up and you'll see Chinese characters announcing: "the only enlightenment is in Heaven" – though only after your eyes have adjusted to the fug of joss-stick smoke. A statue of the **Jade Emperor** lords it over the main hall's central altar, sporting an impressive moustache. It's the Jade Emperor who monitors entry into Heaven, and his two keepers of Heaven – one holding a lamp to light the way for the virtuous, the other wielding an ominous-looking axe – are on hand to aid him.

A rickety flight of steps in the chamber to the right of the main hall runs up to a **balcony** looking out over the pagoda's elaborate **roof**. Set behind the balcony, a neon-haloed statue of Quan Am (see p.512) stands on an altar banked high with offerings of lotus flowers and fruit. Left out of the main hall, meanwhile, you're confronted by Kim Hua, to whom women pray for fertility; judging by the number of babies weighing down the female statues around her, her success rate is high. The Chief of Hell resides in the larger chamber behind Kim Hua's niche. Given his job description, he doesn't look particularly demonic, though his attendants, in sinister black garb, are certainly equipped to administer the sorts of punishments depicted in the ten dark-wood reliefs on the walls before them.

Less impressive, but still worthy of a flying visit if you're in the vicinity, **Tran Hung Dao Temple** (daily 7–11am & 2–5pm) is a few hundred metres west of the Jade Emperor Pagoda, at 36 Vo Thi Sau. Built in 1932, and reconstructed in 1973, the temple is dedicated to legendary military tactician Tran Hung Dao, who in 1287 won a resounding victory against Kublai Khan's 300,000-strong invading Mongol hordes, by luring their fleet onto bamboo stakes driven into the banks of the Bach Dang River (see p.484). Tran Hung Dao confirmed his nationalistic credentials when he had the words *sat dat*, "death to the enemy", tattooed on the arms of his soldiers. A statue of the great man dominates the temple's modest courtyard, fittingly warlike except for its pair of curly-toed pixie boots. Beyond it, a couple of gaudy tigers stand guard in front of the unprepossessing exterior of the temple, their gaping maws occasionally filled with raw meat by worshippers and janitors, but more usually burning incense. In a pavilion to the right of the temple is a small exhibition of the Tran Dynasty (thirteenth to fourteenth centuries). Opposite the temple, **Le Van Tam Park** stands on the site of an early French colonial graveyard, the Massiges Cemetery, but nothing remains of the tombs of the pioneering soldiers, sailors, traders and settlers once laid to rest here.

Further north: Le Van Duyet Temple and Vinh Nghiem Pagoda

Another national hero is commemorated at the **Temple of Marshal Le Van**

Duyet (daily 6am–5pm), known locally as Lang Ong and sited at the top of Dinh Tien Hoang, in the region of the city where the **Gia Dinh Citadel** once stood. A military mandarin and eunuch who lived around the turn of the nineteenth century, Le Van Duyet succeeded in putting down the Tay Son Rebellion, and later became military governor of Gia Dinh. Sadly, his endorsements of French expansionism haven't endeared him to today's government, a fact that explains the temple's down-at-heel appearance. Strolling around the grounds reveals the two unmarked oval mounds under which the marshal and his wife are buried. The temple itself, which stretches through three halls behind a facade decorated with unicorns assembled from shards of chinaware, manages only to be shabby, rather than atmospheric. In the first hall, two portraits of the marshal stand on an altar teeming with dragons, unicorns and phoenixes, and beyond these lies a jumbled collection of artefacts – cut glass, chinaware, weaponry and gowns – that either belonged to the marshal or were left by devotees. Look out, too, for a tablet recording the names of donors to the renovations of 1937, on which the *colons* are predictably flattered with top billing. On the first day of the eighth lunar month, to coincide with the marshal's birthday, a **theatre** troupe dramatizes his life; and there's more activity around Tet, when crowds of pilgrims gather to ask for safekeeping in the forthcoming year. At other times you're likely to see worshippers rattling fortune sticks or consulting the numerous fortune-tellers who ply their trade here.

From here, you'll need to take a cyclo to reach swish but missable **Vinh Nghiem Pagoda** (daily 7–11am & 1.30–5pm), whose spacious sanctuary and soaring tower face an austere-looking war memorial across Nam Ky Khoi Nghia. There's a decidedly well-to-do air about this place, and its janitor obviously plans to keep it that way, with guests required to remove shoes, and joss-sticks confined to a lotus-shaped urn out front. Inside, a huge golden Buddha perched on a lotus gazes serenely over proceedings, flanked by two of his students, but more striking is the intricate gilt woodwork through which your view of him is framed. A mass of wooden funerary tablets are crammed into the **memorial room** behind the altar. Each one bears the picture, name and death date of a deceased worshipper, and monks bustle around setting offerings of rice and tea before them.

A terrace runs from the hall round to the seven-storey **tower** – you can climb the tower, though there's nothing to see other than a statue of Quan Am on each level. Below the terrace and in the school behind, monks apply themselves diligently to their studies, while a copse of bamboo behind the main sanctuary reveals an ugly and angular **repository**, stacked to the rafters with thousands of decorous funerary urns. Immediately behind, a foul-smelling and litter-strewn canal assaults the senses after the pagoda's orderly calm.

Cholon

The dense cluster of streets comprising the Chinese ghetto of **CHOLON** was once distinct from Saigon, though linked to it by the five-kilometre-long umbilical cord of Tran Hung Dao. The distinction was already somewhat blurred by 1950, when Norman Lewis found the city's Chinatown "swollen so enormously as to become its grotesque Siamese twin"; and the steady influx of refugees into the city during the war years saw to it that the two districts eventually became joined by a swathe of urban development. Even so, a short stroll around Cholon, whose name, meaning "**big market**", couldn't be more apposite, will make clear that, even by Ho Chi Minh's standards, the mercantile mania here is breathtaking. The largest of Cholon's many covered markets are Tran Phu's five-storey An Dong, built in 1991, and the more recent but equally vast An Dong II. If you're looking to sightsee rather than shop, then historic Binh Tay (see below) is of far more interest. You'll get most out of Cholon simply by losing yourself in its amorphous mass of life: amid the melee, streetside barbers clip away briskly, bird-sellers squat outside tumbledown **pagodas and temples**, heaving markets ring to fishwives' chatter, and stores display mushrooms, dried shrimps and rice paper.

The **ethnic Chinese**, or **Hoa**, first began to settle here around 1900; many came from existing enclaves in My Tho and Bien Hoa. The area soon became the largest Hoa community in the country, a title it still holds, with a population of over half a million. Residents gravitated towards others from their region of China, with each congregation commissioning its own places of worship and clawing out its own commercial niche – thus the Cantonese handled retailing and groceries, the Teochew dealt in tea and fish, the Fukien were in charge of rice, and so on.

The great wealth that Cholon generated had to be spent somewhere. By the early twentieth century, sassy restaurants, casinos and brothels existed to facilitate this. Also prevalent were **fumeries**, where nuggets of opium were quietly smoked from the cool comfort of a wooden opium bed. Among the expats and wealthy Asians who frequented them was Graham Greene, and he recorded his experiences in *Ways of Escape*. By the 1950s, Cholon was a potentially dangerous place to be, its vice industries controlled by the **Binh Xuyen** gang. First the French and then the Americans trod carefully here, while Viet Minh and Viet Cong **activists** hid out in its cramped backstreets – as Frank Palmos found to his cost, when the jeep he and four other correspondents were riding in was ambushed in 1968 (see p.555).

Post-reunification, Cholon saw hard times. As Hanoi aligned itself increasingly with the Soviet Union, Sino-Vietnamese tensions became strained. Economic **persecution** of the Hoa made matters worse, and, when Vietnam invaded Chinese-backed Cambodia, Beijing launched a punitive **border war**. Hundreds of thousands of ethnic Chinese, many of them from Cholon, fled the country in unseaworthy vessels, fearing recriminations. Today, the business acumen of the Chinese is valued by the local authorities, and the distemper that gripped Cholon for over a decade is a memory. Tran Hung Dao remains the jugular of the enclave. You'll reach Cholon's hub if you travel southwest along Tran Hung Dao from Ben Thanh Market, but the best and cheapest means of getting here is to take a bus to the west side of Cholon and then wander.

Binh Tay Market and around

Buses disgorge their passengers at the Cholon bus station on Cholon's western border, from where seething **Binh Tay Market** is a stone's throw away, on Thap Muoi. First impressions of the market, with its multi-tiered, mustard-coloured roofs stalked by serpentine dragons, are of a huge temple complex. Once inside, however, it quickly becomes obvious that only mammon is deified here. If any one place epitomizes Cholon's vibrant commercialism, it's Binh Tay, its well-regimented corridors abuzz with stalls offering products of all kinds, from dried fish, pickled vegetables and chilli paste pounded before your eyes, to pottery piled up to the rafters, and the colourful bonnets crafted from knotted lengths of twine that Vietnamese women so favour. A pair of marvellously dilapidated blocks of shophouses, each capped by four Moorish domes, hems in the market; while a veritable army of cyclo drivers lays siege to its front entrance. Beyond Binh Tay's south side, a shantytown of makeshift stalls provides cheap snacks for the shoppers and traders.

Walk north from Cholon bus station and you'll soon reach **Tran Chanh Chieu**, a street clogged by a **poultry market** full of chickens, geese and ducks

CHOLON

ACCOMMODATION

Arc en Ciel	2
Hanh Long 2	4
Phuong Huang	1
Tan Da	3

▲ Phu Tho Race Track, Giac Vien Pagoda & Giac Lam Pagoda

An Dong Market

Jade shops

Phuoc An Hoi Quan Temple

Nghia An Hoi Quan Temple

Cholon Mosque

Shark Waterland

Thien Hau Temple

Tam Son Hoi Quan Temple

Street fruit market

Quan Am Pagoda

Dried fish market

Cha Tam Church

Cholon Bus Station

Binh Tay Market

Ben Nghe Channel

SU VAN HANH

NGUYEN DUY DUONG

HUNG GIANG

AN DUONG VUONG

TRAN PHU

TRAN HUNG DAO

HAM TU

HUNG PHU

NGO QUYEN

NGUYEN CHI THANH

NGUYEN KIM

LY THUONG KIET

KY NAM DE

LA DAI HANH

PHO CO DIEU

CHAU VAN LIEM

NGUYEN CHI THANH

HUNG VUONG

TA UYEN

HA TON QUYEN

3 THANG 2

NGUYEN TRAI

TRAN HUNG DAO

PHUNG HUNG

HOC LAC

HAI THUONG LAN ONG

NGUYEN KIEU

TRAN VAN KIEU

HAI THUONG LAN ONG

BEN BINH DONG

LUNG THIEN VUONG

BEN BA DINH

HUNG PHU

BEN PHAN VAN KHOE

BEN BAI SAY

THAP MUOI

E QUANG SUNG

TRAN CHANH CHIEU

TRANG TU

HAI YEN

HUNG VUONG

N

0   500m

tied together in bundles. **Cereals and pulses** are the speciality at the street's east end, with weighty sacks of rice, lentils and beans forming a sort of obstacle course for the cyclos that try to negotiate the narrow strip of roadway still visible.

The slender pink spire of **Cha Tam Church** peers down from above the eastern end of cramped Tran Chanh Chieu, but you'll have to walk either left or right, and round onto Hoc Lac, to find the entrance. It was in this unprepossessing little church, with its Oriental outer gate and cheery yellow walls, that President Ngo Dinh Diem and his brother Ngo Dinh Nhu holed up on November 1, 1963, during the coup that saw them chased out of the Gia Long Palace (see p.94). Early the next morning, Diem phoned the leaders of the coup and surrendered. An M-113 armoured car duly picked them up, but they were shot dead by ARVN soldiers before the vehicle reached central Saigon.

With clearance from the janitor (who's always somewhere around hoping for a tip) you can clamber up into the **belfry** and under the bells, Quasimodo-style, to join the statue of St Francis Xavier for the fine views he enjoys of Cholon. The janitor can also point out the pew where Diem and his brother sat praying as they awaited their fate.

Exiting Cha Tam Church along Tran Hung Dao, you're almost immediately swallowed up by Cholon's vast and colourful cloth market, while a further five minutes' walk towards the river brings you to the eastern end of **Hai Thuong Lan Ong**. Shops specializing in Chinese and Vietnamese traditional medicine have long proliferated here, identifiable by the sickly-sweet aroma that hangs over them. Named after a famous herbalist who practised and studied in Hanoi two centuries ago, the street is lined by dingy shophouses banked with cabinets whose wooden drawers are crammed full of herbs. Step over the sliced roots laid out to dry along the pavement and peer inside any one of the shops, and you'll see rheumy men and women weighing out prescriptions on ancient balances. Steepled around them are boxes, jars and paper bags containing anything from dried bark to antler fur and tortoise glue. Predictably popular is **ginseng**, the Oriental cure-all said to combat everything from heart disease to acne. Also available are monkey-, tiger- and rhino-based medicines – despite a government ban on these products. Stuffed animals serve as none-too-discreet advertisements.

Down to the waterfront

Hai Thuong Lan Ong peels off southwards to meet waterfront Tran Van Kieu. Shops on the south side of Tran Van Kieu shield the **Ben Nghe Channel** from view, but if you turn right, past the pungent **dried fish market** and over the bridge, you'll be able to study the godowns, stilthouses and boat-houses on its oily waters. Old men crouch arthritically along the bridge trying to make a few dong from the motley arrays of bric-a-brac – odd shoes, spanners and spoons – laid out before them. Head east instead from the foot of Hai Thuong Lan Ong, and soon you'll delve into Ben Ham Tu, where dozens of stores pander to the Chinese predilection for **jade**.

Nguyen Trai and around

Cholon's greatest architectural treasures are its temples and pagodas, many of which stand on or around **Nguyen Trai**, whose four-kilometre sweep northeast to Pham Ngu Lao starts just beyond the row of streetside **barbers** above Cha Tam Church. Past the street's junction with Phung Hung (where a riotous street **fruit market** stands to your left, and a glut of shops selling scarlet Chinese roast pork, sausages and chickens to your right) is its intersection with Chau Van Liem. From here you can thread your way up to **Quan Am Pagoda**, set back from the bustle of Cholon on tiny Lao Tu, its existence betrayed by a cluster of stallholders selling incense and caged birds. An almost tangible air of antiquity broods over the place, enhanced by the film of dust left by the spiral incense sticks hanging from its rafters. Don't be too quick to dive inside, though: the pagoda's ridged roofs are impressive enough from the outside, their colourful crust of "glove-puppet" figurines, teetering houses and temples from a distance creating the illusion of a gingerbread house; while framing the two door gods and the pair of stone lions assigned to keeping out evil spirits are gilt panels depicting petrified scenes from traditional Chinese court life – dancers, musicians, noblemen in sedan chairs, a game of chequers being played.

When Cholon's Fukien congregation established this pagoda well over a century ago, they dedicated it to the Goddess of Mercy, but it's **A Pho**, the Queen of Heaven, who stands in the centre of the main hall, beyond an altar tiled like a mortuary slab. A pantheon of deities throngs the open courtyard behind her, attracting a steady traffic of worshippers; most dominant are the two statues of **Quan Am** – one with its back to A Pho, the other a dignified burnt-gold colour. Keep an eye out too for the calligrapher who sets up shop in the corridor to the right of the main chamber: for around $1 he'll daub your name on a prayer paper. The turtles in the tiny pond beside him also come under his jurisdiction, and you'll sometimes catch him slipping them bananas between scribbling prayers. Twin ovens, flanking the main chamber, burn a steady supply of fake money offerings and incense sticks.

Phuoc An Hoi Quan Temple, three minutes' walk north, is a disarming place, seemingly erected bang in the middle of an old Chinese merchant's residence. Beyond the menacing dragons and sea monsters patrolling its roof, and the superb wood carving depicting a king being entertained by jousters and minstrels hanging over the entrance, is the temple's **sanctuary**, in which stately Quan Cong sits, instantly recognizable by his blood-red face, and fronted by two storks standing on top of turtles fashioned from countless plectrum-shaped ceramic shards. It's the **chambers** that lie either side of him, however, crammed with rosewood furniture, grand old clocks and framed mirrors, liver-spotted photographs, and mounted stags' heads, that really stoke the imagination.

Along Nguyen Trai, at **Thien Hau Temple** local women come in numbers to make offerings to Me Sanh, Goddess of Fertility, and to Long Mau, Goddess of Mothers and Newborn Babies. When Cantonese immigrants established the temple towards the middle of the nineteenth century, they named it after Thien Hau, Goddess of Seafarers. New arrivals from China would have hastened here to express their gratitude for a safe passage across the South China Sea. Three statues of her stand on the altar, one behind the other, while an eye-catching mural on the inside of the front wall depicts her guiding wildly pitching ships across a storm-tossed sea. The temple's most attractive aspect is its **roof**, bristling with so many figurines you wonder how those at the edge can keep their balance.

Two more religious sites – both of them missable, if you're suffering from pagoda fatigue – face one another 100m further down Nguyen Trai. Beyond its impressively whiskered door gods, **Nghia An Hoi Quan Temple** has a quiet, shabby air, disturbed only by the occasional rattle of fortune sticks at its altar or playground noise from the school next door. Ruddy Quan Cong again holds sway, sporting a lurid green robe; beside him are his aides-de-camp, goggle-eyed General Chau Xuong and the mandarin Quan Binh. If you can bear to examine any more roof decorations, the peacocks, fish and frolicking lambs on the temple's eaves are pretty enough. Across the street, but accessed by an entrance on Trieu Quang Phuc, **Tam Son Hoi Quan Temple** looks similarly sorry for itself. Quan Cong turns up yet again, as do Thien Hau and, to her left, Me Sanh, sitting with her daughters as if for a portrait photographer. Look out for the dragon-dance costume in the chamber to the left of the main hall. Across Nguyen Trai's intersection with Ly Thuong Kiet, **Cholon Mosque** strikes an oddly un-Chinese chord. White and duck-egg blue, with green railings, its unfussy architecture and slender minarets are in stark contrast to the pagodas nearby.

North of Cholon

Two of Ho Chi Minh City's more engaging places of worship, Giac Lam Pagoda and Giac Vien Pagoda, are kept under wraps out in the hinterland to the north of Cholon – as is the thriving Phu Tho Racecourse, if you fancy a flutter. Given their similarities, there's little to be gained by seeing both pagodas; whichever one you choose is sure to be known to downtown cyclo drivers. Giac Vien borders Dam Sen, a sprawling leisure park that's chock-full of tacky but enjoyable diversions.

Giac Lam Pagoda

You'll see the gate leading up to **Giac Lam Pagoda** on Lac Long Quan, a couple of hundred metres northeast of its intersection with Le Dai Hanh. From there, a short track passes a new tower (its six levels are scaleable and afford good city views) and a cluster of monks' tombs on its way to the actual pagoda. Built in 1744 – and looking every bit its age – rambling Giac Lam is draped over 98 hardwood pillars, each inscribed with traditional *chu nom* characters (Vietnamese script, based on Chinese ideograms). From its terracotta floor-tiles and extravagant chandeliers to the antique tables at which monks sit to take tea, Giac Lam is characterized by a clutter that imbues it with an appealingly fusty feel, and a reassuring sense of age. Access is through an **entrance** at the rear of the right-hand wall, which leads into a cobwebbed **funerary chamber** flanked by row upon row of gilt tablets above photos of the deceased. The many-armed goddess that stands in the centre of the chamber, illuminated by shafts of light that slice through windows punched into the roof, is Chuan De, a manifestation of Quan Am. A right turn leads to a **courtyard-garden**, around which runs a roof studded with blue and white porcelain saucers. A quaint mini-mountain, complete with model bridges, pagodas and greenery,

---

Phu Tho Racecourse

There's no more potent symbol of the regeneration of capitalism in Ho Chi Minh City than Cholon's **Phu Tho Racecourse** (☎08/855 1205). Upon the liberation of the South in 1975, gambling was declared an example of bourgeois decadence and outlawed, and it's only since 1989 that the country's political climate has become sufficiently liberal for the course to re-open. **Meetings**, which take place on Saturday and Sunday afternoons (noon–4.30pm), attract punters in their thousands. Collectively, they've been known to spend over $30,000 in a day. Ringing the course's dusty track is a wire fence intended, it's said, to thwart spectators wanting to influence a race by throwing stones at the horses. Such tricks aren't confined to the grandstand, a dilapidated hangover from the colonial era: horse-drugging is not unheard of, and jockeys (many of whom are as young as 14) have been known to accept bribes to throw a race. Hundreds of racehorses are now bred in Ho Chi Minh. Their numbers are boosted periodically by imports from Europe and Hong Kong, which are then put to stud in order to improve the bloodstock. Foreigners are not barred from betting. **To win**, you have to select correctly both the first- and second-place horse; all gambling is on-course, and the maximum bet is around $2. Pickpocketing is rife in the stands, so the extra $1 for entry to the terrace above is a wise investment. Phu Tho Racecourse is just north of Cholon, at 2 Le Dai Hanh.

provides the garden with a centrepiece. Monks would once have sat studying on the huge wooden benches in the peaceful old **classroom** at the back of the complex, still in use as a study centre today. The cloth panels in this chamber depict the ten Buddhist hells; study them carefully, and you'll see sinners being variously minced, fed to dogs, dismembered and disembowelled by toothsome demons.

To the left of the funerary chamber as you enter the pagoda is the **main sanctuary**, whose multi-tiered altar dais groans under the weight of the many Buddhist and Taoist statues it supports (remember to take off your shoes before entering). Elsewhere in this chamber you'll spot an ensemble of oil lamps balanced on a Christmas-tree-shaped wooden frame. Worshippers pen prayers on pieces of paper, which they affix to the tree and then feed the lamps with an offering of oil. A similar ritual is attached to the bell across the chamber, though in this case people believe that their prayers are hastened to the gods by the ringing of the bell.

Giac Vien Pagoda

From Giac Lam, you'll need to head southwest along Lac Long Quan to reach **Giac Vien Pagoda**; take the right turn between nos. 247 and 249 – if you see Binh Thoi to your left you've gone too far – then turn left and then right. The track to the pagoda is lined by shanty houses that have encroached up to and over the monks' tombs outside. Founded in the eighteenth century, and said to have been frequented by Emperor Gia Long, the pagoda has much in common with Giac Lam. Here, too, there's a dark lived-in atmosphere – so dark, indeed, that bats hang in its smokey rafters, squeaking intermittently. Upon entering through the pagoda's red doors daubed with yellow *chu nom* characters, visitors are confronted by banks of old photos and funerary tablets flanking long refectory-style tables. The two rows of black pillars lend an arresting sense of depth to this first chamber, which is dominated by a panel depicting a ferocious-looking red lion, and a statue of a slouching Ameda, grinning and fiddling with a set of beads. Go on around the sky-blue-washed stone walls (crafted, incongruously, in classical Greek style) and into the **main sanctuary**, and you'll find a sizeable congregation of deities, as well as a tree of lamps similar to the one at Giac Lam. The monks residing in Giac Vien are hospitable to a fault, and you'll quite probably be sat down for a cup of tea poured from beneath a varnished coconut-husk cosy.

While you're out here, you might want to dip into **Dam Sen leisure park** at 3 Hoa Binh (daily 8am–6pm; ☎08/865 3453; $3), whose sprawling grounds edge onto the pagoda. Its kitsch diversions – fountains, themed gardens, fairground rides and a water park – won't appeal to everyone, but it's a welcome retreat from the frenetic pace of the city.

Eating

If Hanoi is Vietnam's first city, then Ho Chi Minh is without doubt its culinary capital. Such is the size of the expat community here that the majority of new ventures opening up specialize in **non-Vietnamese foods**: whatever your craving – Tex Mex or tandoori, shish kebab or sushi – it's bound to be catered for, though **French** restaurants predictably comprise the most formidable foreign contingent in town. The French legacy is also evident in the city's abundance of **cafés**, which are currently enjoying a resurgence. Confronted by such a global restaurant scene, it's easy to ignore indigenous cuisine, but **Vietnamese food** comes no better than in Ho Chi Minh, whether taken in a sophisticated **restaurant** or at a **streetside stall**. Owing to the transitory nature of foodstalls, it's impossible to make specific recommendations, but there are plenty to choose from (see p.46 for more on how to spot a good one).

Most of Ho Chi Minh City's eating establishments stay **open** throughout the year, but remember that some will close down over Tet. Increasingly the demands of travellers are leading to more flexible hours. Given this variability, we've specified exact times wherever possible.

Restaurants

One step up from street stalls are the **eating houses**, where good, filling *com* and *pho* meals are served from buffet-style tin trays and vast soup urns. **Travellers' cafés**, concentrated around De Tham and Pham Ngu Lao, and catering exclusively for the banana-pancake brigade, are fine if you want an inexpensive steak and chips or some fried noodles, but hardly in the league of the city's heavyweights, its **specialist restaurants**. Of course, by Vietnamese standards, these restaurants are incredibly expensive – eat at one and you'll probably spend enough to feed a Vietnamese family for a month – but by Western standards they are low-priced, and the quality of cooking is consistently high. What's more, ingredients are fresh, with vegetables transported from Da Lat, and meat often flown in from Australia. Many of the upmarket hotels now run weekend buffets and carveries, which at around $10 for as much as you can eat are excellent value. Certain swankier restaurants have taken to laying on inexpensive **set lunch menus** and also live **traditional music** in order to lure diners – we've mentioned a few such places in our listings.

Upper Dong Khoi and around

Chu 158 Dong Khoi. American-style café, popular with well-off locals who enjoy the eclectic menu including Cajun chicken wings, pasta, Asian dishes and sundaes (see "Cafés, ice cream and desserts" p.115) as well as the nightly live music. 8am–midnight.

Cung Dinh *Rex Hotel*, 146–148 Nguyen Hué ☎08/829 2185. Some may find the lavish Oriental decor oppressive but there's no knocking the food: try the steamed chicken with lemon leaves or one of the reasonable set meals (from $5 per head for lunch). There are traditional nightly music performances; you'll probably need to book ahead. 11am–2.30pm & 5.30–10.30pm.

Daruma 75 Pasteur. Hole-in-the-wall Japanese restaurant specializing in sashimi and tempura. Eat either canteen-style downstairs or at a table in the restaurant or the private rooms above; proximity to the *Rex* keeps prices relatively high. 11.30am–2pm & 5.30–10pm.

Givral 169 Dong Khoi. A Ho Chi Minh institution, with an extensive light Western and Asian menu, plus an adjoining patisserie. It boasts a prime position facing the *Continental* on Lam Son Square. 6am–10pm.

Manhattan's 94 Hai Ba Trung (in Saigon Square). American-style burger bar knocking out Ho Chi Minh's best burgers and fries as well as flavoursome fried chicken and pizzas. 7.30am–11.30pm.

Miss Saigon 86 Le Thanh Ton. This establishment offers reasonably priced Vietnamese and seafood specialities in a pleasant garden restaurant backing onto the grounds of the Revolutionary Museum. 10am–late.

Ngon 138 Nam Ky Khoi Nghia ☎08/825 7179. An experience not to be missed – delicious regional specialities served in and around a delightful colonial building at very reasonable prices. Extremely popular, so be prepared to book or wait for a table at peak eating times. They also have a more upmarket branch at 88 Nguyen Du ☎08/827 7896. 7am–late.

Quan An 39 39 Nguyen Trung Truc. Hectic streetside operation, a 10 min walk west of Dong Khoi, dishing up tasty and remarkably good-value set lunches – grilled pork on rice, veggies, soup and iced tea – all around $1. Lunchtime only, 11am–1pm.

Qucina 7 Cong Truong ☎08/824 6325. Recently opened by the owners of *Q Bar*, this place has minimalist decor and some of the best Italian food in town. Entrance on the north side of the Municipal Theatre. 11.30am–2.30pm & 4.30–11pm.

Lower Dong Khoi and the waterfront

Amigo 55 Nguyen Hué. Recommended for its T-bone steaks and seafood prepared on an open

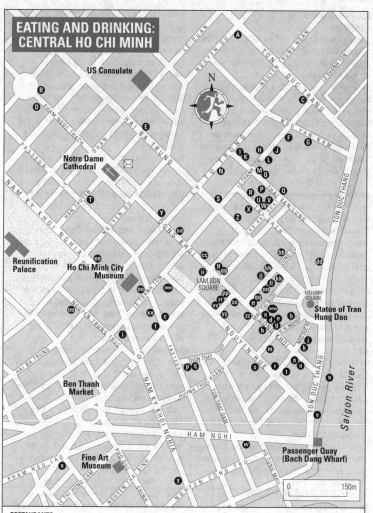

EATING AND DRINKING: CENTRAL HO CHI MINH

US Consulate

Notre Dame Cathedral

Reunification Palace

Ho Chi Minh City Museum

LAM SON SQUARE

MEI LINH SQUARE

Statue of Tran Hung Dao

Ben Thanh Market

Saigon River

Fine Art Museum

Passenger Quay (Bach Dang Wharf)

0   150m

RESTAURANTS

Amigo	s	Lemongrass	pp	Tan Nam	jj
Annie's Pizza	ww	Liberty	tt	Temple Club	p
Ashoka	O	Mali Thai	nn	Tex Mex	H
Augustin's	vv	Manderine	G	Tin Nghia	x
Bi Bi	Q	Manhattan's	E	Underground	h
Blue Ginger	y	Marine Club	J	Vietnam House	zz
Camargue	W	Maxim's Dinner Theatre	o	Why Not	I
Cay Xoai	X	Miss Saigon	oo		
Chao Thai	K	Nam An	m	**CAFÉS**	
Chu	Y	Nam Phan	S	Au Parc	T
Continental Palace		Ngon	ee	Bo Gia	b
Cung Dinh	mm	Phuoc Loi	w	Brodard Restaurant	ss
Daruma	xx	Quan An 39	uu	Chi Lang Café	aa
Dong Du	qq	Qucina	ff	Ciao Café	yy
Gartenstadt	d	Restaurant 13	k	Dong Du Café	nn
Givral	ii	Saigon Floating Restaurant	u	Fanny's Ice Cream	q
Globo Café	rr	Saigontourist Cruise	v	Java Coffee Bar	hh
Hoi An	F	Santa Lucia	r	Kem Bach Dang	c, f
La Fourchette	j	Seoul House	t	Kem Cong Truong	B
La Villa	P	Shunka	L	La Fenetre Soleil	i
Le Mekong	qq	Sushi Bar	C	Napoli Café	D

Paloma Café	g
Paris Deli	n

BARS/ PUBS

Bia Hoi – Bia Chai	bb
Blue Gekko	N
Bodega	n
Café Latin	ll
Cati Club	e
Ice Blue	a
La Fenêtre Soleil	i
Maya	V
Mogambo	U
O'Briens Factory	Z
Old Saigon	R
Panorama	A
Q Bar	gg
Sheridan's Irish House	M
Vasco's	W
Wild West	kk

grill, plus good salad bar. 11.30am–2pm & 5.30–10pm.

Annie's Pizza 45 Mac Thi Buoi ☎08/839 2577. A Saigon institution with an extensive, good-value range of pizzas, recognized for its efficient delivery service. 11am–late.

Augustin's 10 Nguyen Thiep. Secreted down a narrow lane linking Dong Khoi and Nguyen Hué, an intimate bistro serving well-cooked but pricey French dishes. 11.30am–2pm & 6–10.30pm.

Dong Du 57 Dong Du. Sharing an entrance with *Le Mekong*, as well as a reputation for high-quality Vietnamese dishes. Same management as *Blue Ginger*. 11am–2pm & 5–10pm.

Gartenstadt 34 Dong Khoi. High-quality German bar/restaurant; generous portions, imported sausages and a good selection of German beers, some on draught. 10.30am–midnight.

Globo Café 6 Nguyen Thiep. The tasteful Mediterranean decor reflects the authentic Italian cuisine. Wood-fired pizzas go for around $5, and other delicacies include wild boar pâté or wild mushroom panzerotti. 8am–11pm.

La Fourchette 9 Ngo Duc Ke. Varnished light-wood panelling, dark-wood floor and murals of rural France; the compact menu features melt-in-your-mouth imported steaks ($9) and a well-stocked cheeseboard. Noon–2.30pm & 6.30–10pm.

Le Mekong 57 Dong Du. This established French favourite still draws the crowds with tempting French cuisine such as roasted duck with orange and pepper sauce and hot chocolate soufflé with Grand Marnier; set menus from around $9. Serenading guitarists meander between the tables. 11am–2pm & 5–10pm.

Lemongrass 4 Nguyen Thiep. Traditional upmarket establishment, whose highly rated Vietnamese food is eaten to the strains of serenading players. 11am–2pm & 5–10pm.

Liberty 80 Dong Khoi. Popular place, with musicians playing romantic tunes 7–9.30pm, and serving well-prepared Vietnamese dishes. 11am–midnight.

Maxim's Dinner Theatre 15–17 Dong Khoi ☎08/823 0644. Choose from the extensive French and Asian menus, sit back and enjoy the traditional live entertainment as you dine, and then move upstairs for a dance if you aren't too full. Book ahead for weekend dining. 6–10pm.

Nam An 57–69 Dong Khoi. Just off Dong Khoi, with outdoor dining in a traditional Asian setting, surrounded by lotus ponds. Two can eat for around $10 from the Vietnamese menu; the freshwater fish in pineapple sour soup comes recommended. 6.30–11pm.

Restaurant 13 15 Ngo Duc Ke. Simple but clean spot which serves some of the cheapest food downtown – a seafood or meat and rice dish will set you back less than $2, and the beers are relatively cheap too. 6.30am–11.30pm.

Saigon Floating Restaurant Ton Duc Thang, between Dong Khoi and Nguyen Hué. One of four boats offering two-hour evening dinner cruises on the Saigon River, though these tend to be overrun with tour groups. Choose between set meals ($10 a head) or the pricey à la carte menu. Departures 7.30–8pm.

Saigontourist Cruise Ton Duc Thang, bottom of Nguyen Hué ☎08/829 8914. Tickets ($20) for the dinner cruise include a show upriver at Binh Quoi Cultural Village (see p.116); return journey is by bus. Departs Tues, Thurs & Sat at 5.30pm, but ring ahead to confirm.

Santa Lucia 14 Nguyen Hué. Classic and stylish Italian venue, serving traditional pizzas and pasta; two dine for around $20 including wine. 9.30am–11pm.

Seoul House 37 Ngo Duc Ke. *Bulgogi* (marinated beef, barbecued at table), pork with *kimchi* (vegetables in chilli sauce), and other good-value, authentic Korean dishes, eaten sitting on the floor or, if you prefer, Western-style in utilitarian but friendly surroundings. 7am–10pm.

Temple Club 29 Ton That Thiep. Wonderful relaxed atmosphere with tasteful decor and excellent Vietnamese food at around $5 a dish. Live piano Wed–Sat, 8.30–10.30pm. Also has a comfy lounge bar out back. 11am–midnight.

Underground basement of Lucky Plaza, 69 Dong Khoi. Better known as a night spot (see "Bars and pubs"), but also turns out some of the tastiest and most imaginative Western food in town. Try the succulent New Zealand grilled steaks, as thick as your fist, for around $8.

Vietnam House 93–95 Dong Khoi. Occupying a splendid louvred colonial building, this is a cracking introduction to Vietnamese food, featuring staff in traditional garb. There's a pianist on the ground floor and traditional folk music upstairs; set lunches from $4. 11am–2pm & 5–10pm.

Thi Sach and around

Ashoka 17a/10 Le Thanh Ton. Smart Indian restaurant offering authentic Moghul Indian dishes – some, such as *cho cho tikka* (chicken marinated in yoghurt), cooked in the tandoor – and a satisfying range of veggie dishes. 11.30am–2pm & 5–10pm.

Bi Bi 8a/8d2 Thai Van Lung. Cosy French restaurant serving Mediterranean specialities, popular with expats. Set lunch $10. 11.30am–2pm & 6.30–10pm.

Camargue 16 Cao Ba Quat. Expensive French restaurant set in colonial-style modern villa, overlooking a leafy courtyard. Rattan furniture and old wooden ceiling fans set the scene of a bygone era. 6–11pm.

Cay Xoai 15a Thi Sach. Thi Sach has a growing number of intriguing eateries, and *Cay Xoai* is one of several restaurants along this strip; excellent seafood is guaranteed. A second outlet is located further along at no. 15c/8 called *Xoai Quan*. 10am–11pm.

Chao Thai 16 Thai Van Lung ☎08/824 1457. Probably the best Thai food in town; certainly the most Thai-style decor. Try the *yam tua plu* (winged bean salad) or the *hor mok talay* (seafood curry in banana leaves). Most dishes around $3–4; delivery service too. 11am–2pm & 6–10.30pm.

Hoi An 11 Le Thanh Ton ☎08/823 7694. Refined eating of traditional Vietnamese food in a sumptuous wooden house, run by the owners of *Mandarine*. Set menus start at $17. Book ahead to reserve a table. 5.30–10.45pm.

La Villa 11 Thai Van Lung. A short but tempting menu of French and Thai food, served up in a stylish French villa. Main dishes around $10. Closed for lunch Sat & Sun. 11am–2pm & 6pm–late.

Mali Thai 37 Dong Du. Most central of the few Thai restaurants in town, with spicy curries and *tom yam* soup that are sure to bring tears to your eyes. Set lunches under $3. 11am–10pm.

Manderine 11a Ngo Van Nam ☎08/822 9783. Established upmarket restaurant, beautifully decorated in traditional Vietnamese style, serving well-prepared Vietnamese standards. Prices aren't cheap, though a range of set menus starts from $15. Live traditional music in evenings; reservations essential. 11.30am–2pm & 6–11.30pm.

Marine Club 17a4 Le Thanh Ton. Set amongst tasteful nautical themes, the *Marine Club* describes itself as a "pizza-grill-piano bar" with background music occasionally provided by a pianist. A traditional pizza oven ensures a good-quality pizza. Mon–Sat noon–2pm & 6.30–11pm, Sun 6.30–11pm.

Nam Phan 64 Le Thanh Ton ☎08/829 2757. Good place for a splurge – attractively presented and delicious Vietnamese fare served up in a colonial villa among landscaped gardens. 11am–2.30pm & 6–11pm.

Shunka 17a/9 Le Thanh Ton. Serene, two-floor Japanese restaurant with minimalist decor and enticing food. 11.30am–2pm & 6–11pm.

Sushi Bar 2 Le Thanh Ton. Highly rated sushi or sashimi mix for around $10, plus Japanese beer and sake. Delivery service too. 11.30am–2pm & 5.30–11.30pm.

Tan Nam 60–62 Dong Du. Top-notch Vietnamese meat and fish dishes, served in modern surroundings opening onto the street with traditional touches to the decor. One or two veggie alternatives also available. 8am–10.30pm.

Tex Mex 24 Le Thanh Ton. Fair approximations of tacos, chilli and guacamole amid a typical melange of stuffed lizards, Mexican wall-hangings and sombreros. The set meal is good value at $6 – though chucking down litres of San Miguel and margarita ($18 a litre) seems to be the priority for most regulars. Pool, darts and sports TV. Noon–late.

Why Not 24 Thai Van Lung. Popular French restaurant with daily specials and set menu for around $10. Closed Sun. 10am–late.

From Tran Hung Dao to the Ben Nghe Channel

Blue Ginger 37 Nam Ky Khoi Nghia. Refined, low-ceilinged dining room with eye-catching artwork on the walls and traditional live evening music as you tuck into quality Vietnamese dishes (main courses around $4, excellent suggested menus at $10–15). Popular with tour groups but still worth checking out for its agreeable ambience and great food. 7am–2.30pm & 4–10pm.

Phuoc Loi 75 Ham Nghi. You won't find cheaper Chinese food anywhere in the city – though basic surroundings are the trade-off. 11am–2pm & 4–9pm.

Tin Nghia 9 Tran Hung Dao. Mushrooms and tofu provide the backbone to the inventive menu in this friendly "pure vegetarian" restaurant, now into its eighth decade. You could do far worse than the potato curry or mushroom roasted with lettuce. 7am–2pm & 4–8.30pm.

Pham Ngu Lao and around

Allez Boo 187 Pham Ngu Lao. It may be better known as a watering hole (see "Bars and pubs"), but this place also turns out very acceptable Vietnamese, Thai and Western dishes at about $2 each. 7am–late.

Asian Kitchen 185/22 Pham Ngu Lao. Tucked away down the alley east of De Tham, this laid-back place features well-priced Vietnamese, Japanese and vegetarian dishes. 7am–midnight.

Bao 132 Nguyen Thai Hoc. One of a rowdy gaggle of functional restaurants along Nguyen Thai Hoc. Try barbecued beef wrapped in rice paper with mint leaves and noodles – fiddly but full of flavour – or the terrific *lau* (steamboat). 11am–1am.

Bodhi Tree 175/4 Pham Ngu Lao. The original *Bodhi Tree* vegetarian restaurant, lying next door to another with the same name. Larger, friendlier and

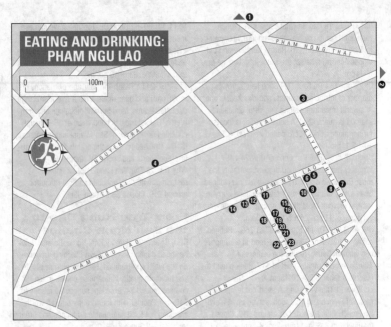

EATING AND DRINKING: PHAM NGU LAO

0 ─ 100m

N

RESTAURANTS AND BARS

Allez Boo	11	Café Sinh To	18	Kim Café	17	Margherita	9	Sinh Café	20
Asian Kitchen	15	Cappuccino	19	Long Phi	5	My Vi	14	Thu Thuy	1
Bao	7	Cay Dua	4	Lost in Saigon	6	Pho 2000	2	Zen	16
Bia Hoi 181	8	Dynasty	3	Lotus Café	13	Saigon Café	12		
Bodhi Tree	10	Good Morning Vietnam	22	Lucky Café	23	Sasa Café	21		

cheap, its menu still doesn't quite match the variety of *Zen*'s (see below). 7am–midnight.

Cappuccino 258 De Tham. Serves up good pizzas at around $3 as well as reasonable Vietnamese fare. Delivery service too. 8.30am–midnight.

Cay Dua 154 Le Lai. Also known as the *Coconut Tree* (two trees stand, sentry-style, out front), handily placed if you feel the need to duck out of Pham Ngu Lao. Braised rice with chicken in an earthenware pot is a speciality. Two eat handsomely for $6. 10am–10pm.

Dynasty *New World Hotel*, 76 Le Lai. Overlooking the lobby of the hotel, the noise may irritate but there's no faulting the elegant decor (porcelain and bonsai), nor the splendid food, created by a Chinese chef who knocks out delicious *dim sum* every lunchtime. Set menus start at around $10 and two can dine well for $20, but the sky's the limit if you plump for delicacies like bird's-nest soup or shark's fin. 11am–2.30pm & 6–10pm.

Good Morning Vietnam 197 De Tham. Part of an Italian-run chain of restaurants that serves

dependably good pizza and pasta in a cosy environment. 8am–10pm.

Kim Café 268 De Tham. Smaller and slightly more intimate than *Sinh Café*, which may explain why its terrace is heaving at night. Besides breakfasts and veggie meals galore, there's guacamole, garlic bread, mashed potatoes, and a fantastic chicken curry ($2). 7am–late.

Lotus Café 197 Pham Ngu Lao. Better than average Vietnamese and Western dishes in friendly surroundings. The mountainous "big breakfast" is worth trying, as are the chicken in spicy peanut sauce and delicious fruit shakes. 7.30am–midnight.

Lucky Café 224 De Tham. Food and drink is pricier here than at some of its neighbours, but the quality is generally high. Rice soups come recommended, as do the set meals ($3–4). Sports on satellite TV too. 7am–late.

Margherita 175/1 Pham Ngu Lao. Some of the cheapest and tastiest pizzas and pasta dishes in town ($2–3) served in low-key surroundings with just the faintest whiff of Italy. They also do home deliveries. 7am–1pm & 3pm–midnight.

My Vi 223 Pham Ngu Lao. Unpretentious place providing cheap and tasty Vietnamese and Western dishes. 7am–11pm.

Pho 2000 1–3 Phan Chu Trinh ☎08/822 2788. *Pho* taken into the 21st century, located next to Ben Thanh Market. Clean surroundings and big bowls of delicious noodle soup and other Vietnamese staples for around $1. 6am–2am.

Saigon Café 195 Pham Ngu Lao. Often busy all through the day due to its dirt-cheap prices, such as eggs with pork chop for around $1, and beer as cheap as you can find it. 7am–late.

Sasa Café 242 De Tham. Not exactly gourmet food, but it has a huge menu of international dishes at cheap prices, and Internet access upstairs. 7am–late.

Sinh Café 246 De Tham ☎08/836 7338. The big daddy of the traveller scene, doling out average but affordable meals in its busy, kitchen-like dining room; the fresh squid over hot charcoal ($2) is highly recommended. Bike rental, bookshop and money exchange at the tour agency next door, and Sinh Café tours depart from outside. 6am–midnight.

Zen 175/18 Pham Ngu Lao. One of the few really authentic eating options around Pham Ngu Lao. Decor couldn't be simpler, but what you're here for are bargain-priced, imaginative veggie dishes including filled Mexican pancakes, wild red rice and Chinese mushrooms, and a coconut and pumpkin soup to die for; don't miss their divine fruit shakes either. 7am–11.30pm.

From Nguyen Thi Minh Khai to Dien Bien Phu

Dien Bien 165 Dien Bien Phu ☎08/829 0286; see map, p.80. Cheap and cheerful soup kitchen and *com* shop, one of several along this stretch of Dien Bien Phu, dishing out flavoursome *pho* and rice dishes in workaday surroundings. 6am–11pm.

Giac Duc 492 Nguyen Dinh Chieu. Hole-in-the-wall eating house, specializing in Vietnamese and Taiwanese vegetarian foods, and favoured by local monks; soups, rice and a tempting spread of cakes, in addition to delicious spring rolls and *banh bao*. 6am–10pm.

L'Etoile 180b Hai Ba Trung ☎08/829 7939; see map, p.80. High-class French cuisine that has won numerous awards, complemented by guitar music and an expansive wine cellar, housed in a charismatic villa. Expect to pay $15 a head for a set menu and more for à la carte. 11am–2pm & 5–10pm.

Minh Pho, Lau Bo 107/12 Truong Dinh ☎08/829 5861. *Lau* (steamboat) and *pho* are the staple

---

Buying your own food: markets and supermarkets

With baguettes, cheese and fruit in such abundant supply in Vietnam, making up a picnic is easy. All the basics can be found at any of the city's **markets**, though if you're homesick for peanut butter, Vegemite or other such exotica, you'll need to head for a specialist **supermarket** or **provisions store**.

Markets

The handiest market for Pham Ngu Lao is **Thai Binh Market**, down at the street's southwestern end. Hardly less close, and larger, **Ben Thanh Market** (see p.95), the central market in the city centre, is at the far eastern end of Tran Hung Dao. Cholon is served by **Binh Tay Market** (see p.102) on its southwestern border and by **An Dong Market**, northeast of it at the junction of Tran Phu and An Duong Vuong. **Cau Ong Lanh Market**, centred around the foot of Nguyen Thai Hoc, is one of the cheapest, but geared more towards wholesale.

Supermarkets and provisions stores

Annam Gourmet Shop 50 Ho Tung Mau. Huge deli located downtown, pandering to the whims of expats and visitors alike.

Citimart 21–23 Nguyen Thi Minh Khai. Compact supermarket selling Western foods such as cheese, cream, ketchup and chocolates.

Co-op Mart 189c Cong Quynh. Huge Western-style supermarket within easy walking distance of Pham Ngu Lao, selling clothes, toys, household goods, cosmetics and a good selection of Western foods. There's a large branch at 168 Nguyen Dinh Chieu.

Kim Thanh 62 Ham Nghi. One of numerous stores between nos. 54 and 74 selling Branston pickle, Hershey's syrup, Russian caviar, imported biscuits, baked beans and other canned foods, as well as wines and spirits.

products at this streetside, no-frills restaurant. Optional extras include oxtails and plates of bone marrow. 6am–10pm.

Ngoc Suong Marina 19c Le Quy Don ☎08/930 5234; see map, p.80 The newest branch of one of the most popular seafood restaurants in town, drawing big crowds every evening. 10am–11pm.

Palm Garden Restaurant *Saigon Star Hotel*, 204 Nguyen Thi Minh Khai ☎08/930 6290. Well-loved Singaporean classics such as *bak kut teh* (pork ribs in soy sauce), Hainanese chicken rice and fried noodles, all prepared to a dependable standard in this rooftop open-terraced restaurant with great views. 3–11pm.

Pho Hoa 260c Pasteur. High-quality *pho* shops proliferate along Pasteur, none better than *Pho Hoa*. On offer are huge bowlfuls of soup complemented with chunks of chicken or beef and plenty of fresh greens on the tables to add yourself. You'll pay more than the usual price but it's well worth it. 6am–midnight.

Spice 100a Nguyen Thi Minh Khai ☎08/829/4020; see map, p.80. Stylishly furnished Thai restaurant with menu that looks like a newspaper, featuring classics like *tom yam* and *som tam*, but also some unusual dishes like "volcano chicken". 11am–2pm & 5.30pm–late.

Thu Thuy 26 Cach Mang Thanh Tam. Grilled meat on skewers is the speciality at this no-frills roadside stall. 5am–10pm.

North of Dien Bien Phu

Banh Xeo 46a Dinh Cong Trang ☎08/824 1110. Vietnamese pancakes, stuffed with a mixture of shrimps, pork, beans, bean sprouts and egg are the speciality at this streetside eatery off Hai Ba Trung. At around $1 a throw, they'll fill you up for most of the day, and there's an English menu. 10am–10pm.

Cha Ca Hanoi 5a Tran Nhat Duat ☎08/848 4240. Very smart café-style restaurant serving three types of tasty Hanoi specialities, including grilled, marinated fish served with noodles. 11am–2pm & 4–10pm.

Pho Binh 7 Ly Chinh Thang ☎08/848 3775. A must-see for all war buffs: a wartime safe house for communists, it was from here that the command was given to kick off the 1968 Tet Offensive. Don't make the trip for the soup alone, though.

Rooms for rent upstairs. 6am–11pm.

Tinh Tam Trai 170a Vo Thi Sau ☎08/820 2230. No-frills veggie restaurant where you choose your meal from the window or take your pick from the English menu. Popular with locals, a mural of Quan Am looks serenely down upon diners from the back wall. 6am–1pm & 3–9pm.

Tri Ky 82 Tran Huy Lieu ☎08/844 0968. Located some way up towards the airport, this smart restaurant offers "jungle cuisine" – cobra, bat, fox, venison, turtle and even armadillo – for those who can stomach it. 11am–2pm & 6–10pm.

Cholon and the outskirts

Golden Phoenix *Hotel Equatorial*, 242 Tran Binh Trong ☎08/839 7777. A rising star in the Ho Chi Minh restaurant firmament, though its Szechuan and Cantonese treats don't come cheap; expect to pay upwards of $15 per head for a decent feed. 11.30am–2.30pm & 6.30–10.30pm.

Kampachi *Hotel Equatorial*, 242 Tran Binh Trong ☎08/839 7777. Japanese chefs ensure that sushi, *teppanyaki* and other standards are up to scratch for the mostly Japanese diners who frequent this stylish and reputable joint. Sake provides the perfect liquid accompaniment. 11.30am–2.30pm & 6.30–10.30pm.

Maxi-Mart 3c Ba Thang Hai. Huge city supermarket with a food hall, plus household and electrical goods, clothes and cosmetics.

Nhat Nam Mini-Mart 54–56 Nguyen Trai. The sixth-floor supermarket in this shopping complex sells wines, tinned goods, plus cheeses, milk and yoghurts.

Nhu Lan Bakery 66–68 Ham Nghi. Famed bakery selling bread, croissants and cakes. Nearby no. 62 has a mouthwatering deli with ham, pâtés and sausages.

Sama 35 Dong Du. Classy deli-cum-restaurant specializing in French and Italian produce. Also mouthwatering sandwiches you can devour in a small café area.

Thong Xa Mini-Mart 135 Nguyen Hué. Inside the centrally located tax shopping plaza, this large supermarket sells, amongst other things, Western tinned and dairy products.

Cafés, ice cream and desserts

Café culture, introduced by the French, is still very much alive in Ho Chi Minh, and there are numerous places at which to round dinner off with an ice cream, crêpe or sundae. Earlier in the day, the same venues offer the chance to linger over a coffee and watch things tick along.

All the following are on the map on p.109 except where indicated.

Au Parc 23 Han Thuyen. Stylish, two-floored sandwich and salad bar serving smoothies and

shakes just near the cathedral. 7.30am–9.30pm.

Bo Gia 20 Ho Huan Nghiep. Bookshop converted

into a tiny pavement café, popular with locals. Drinks plus a mouthwatering selection of ice creams (the plum and lime juice is excellent) and some books still for sale. 7am–late.

Brodard Restaurant 131 Dong Khoi. Really more of a café, smartly refurbished but still maintaining a traditional feel. Prices aren't cheap: sandwiches start at around $2.50, but it's still very popular with expats and tourists alike. 6.30am–11pm.

Café Sinh To 231 De Tham (see map, p.112). A no-frills but remarkably good-value juice bar bang in the centre of De Tham. Serves sandwiches too. 8am–11pm.

Chi Lang Café Chi Lang Park, Dong Khoi. The *Chi Lang*'s commanding position, set back from and above Dong Khoi, makes it a prime site for people-watching. 8am–11pm.

Chu 158 Dong Khoi. Coco Chanel, Kenzo, Versace and other fashion-house-inspired ice cream sundaes, alongside international dishes (see "Restaurants", p.108). 8am–midnight.

Ciao Café 72 Nguyen Hué. Conveniently central, bright and breezy, this café-cum-restaurant serves up a wide range of Western and Asian dishes, but its forte is Italian ice creams and sundaes. 7am–11.30pm.

Dong Du Café 31 Dong Du. Modern-style chic Italian café serving traditional Italian ice cream, coffee and light pasta dishes. 7am–10pm.

Fanny's Ice Cream 29-31 Ton Thap Thiep. With its mustard-coloured walls, wrought-iron chairs, bookshelves and magazines to read, this is an ideal spot to enjoy a peach melba or maybe even a cocktail. 9am–11pm.

Java Coffee Bar 38–42 Dong Du. Pick up your "caffeine withdrawal card" and get treatment for around $2 a cup. Also a varied menu of Western food, with set meals at around $7 in a large, relaxing lounge. Good antidote to shopping in the nearby boutiques. 7.30am–11.30pm.

Kem Bach Dang 26 & 28 Le Loi. Twin open-front-ed ice-cream parlours, revered for extravagant creations, some of which feature fruits from Da Lat; unfortunately, it's a magnet for beggars who periodically stray inside. 8am–11pm.

Kem Cong Truong 10 Pham Ngoc Thach. Locals swear by this roadside café, close to Dong Khoi's cathedral and serving inexpensive ice creams, fresh coconuts and beers. 6am–11pm.

La Dolce Vita Bar *Hotel Continental*, 132–134 Dong Khoi. Café, restaurant, bar and *gelateria* rolled into one, set in the refined courtyard surroundings of this Saigon institution. 6am–10pm.

La Fenetre Soleil 1st floor, 135 Le Thanh Ton (entrance at 125 Nam Ky Khoi Nghia). Don't be put off by the dingy stairwell that leads up to this quirky café. An odd collection of chairs and tables, sofas and even a four-poster bed give the place a wonderfully offbeat feel. Order up coffee or tea, a juice or a shake, a pudding or a jelly, and kick back. Functions as a bar (see "Bars and pubs", p.117) in the evening. 11.30am–midnight.

Napoli Café 5 Pham Ngoc Thach. Fresh-cut flowers, terracotta tiles and al fresco tables breathe a rustic sigh through the *Napoli*, a short stroll above the cathedral; choose from a modest selection of cakes, pastries and sundaes or indulge in the *mangia e bevi* – a sensational blend of ice cream, orange juice and fresh fruit. 7.30am–11pm.

Paloma Café 26 Dong Khoi. Immensely popular café – candlelit and romantic at night – at the lower end of Dong Khoi. Ice creams start at $2 on a menu that also has filling breakfasts. Live music every night. 7.30am–midnight.

Paris Deli 31 Dong Khoi. Parisian-style café serving croissants, sandwiches and patisserie delights; also does office and home deliveries. 7am–10pm.

Piano Café 33 Le Quy Don; see map, p.80. Couples canoodle over glasses of iced coffee in a darkened courtyard under the porch of an old French villa, while every evening musicians play classicized versions of old pop songs. 6am–11pm.

Drinking, nightlife and entertainment

Ho Chi Minh boasts a range of nightlife that's expanding in direct proportion to the number of foreigners hitting town, so there's no need to head back to your hotel once dinner is through. **Bars** and **pubs** abound, and an increasing number of them now feature live music to pull the crowds – normally either Filippino or local covers bands, who play safe pop-rock sets that lean heavily on Creedence Clearwater and the Eagles. Home-grown talent is on display in **Cong Vien Van Hoa Park**, on Cach Mang Thang Tam, and **Son Tra Park**, on Nguyen Thai Hoc, where Vietnamese crooners in chintzy cocktail dresses and cockatoo hairstyles belt out Western and Vietnamese pop tunes to largely local audiences. It isn't unheard-

...biz names from the West to make appearances, either: Bryan Adams
...e years ago, and if another eminent visitor is coming the local press
...ou know about it. Later at night, a growing number of **clubs** and
...bing, enabling you to continue drinking and have a boogie.
...ly *The Guide* and weekly *Time Out* supplements boast the most
...inute listings of the city's latest bars, plus the hottest new clubs and
...ghbrow entertainment on offer (see p.55 for more details).

Traditional entertainment

Few places cater for Westerners wanting an insight into Vietnamese culture. For
Western and Vietnamese **classical music**, the best thing you can do is drop by the
Conservatory of Music (☎08/822 5841) at 112 Nguyen Du, and ask about HCM
City Youth Chamber Music Club's performances, which can be scheduled on
demand. There are regular performances of **modern** and **traditional Vietnamese
music**, too, at 3 Thang 2's Hoa Binh Theatre (☎08/865 5199), as well as traditional
theatre and dance, fashion shows, concerts (sometimes featuring Western acts) and
dubbed movies. The Youth Cultural House at 4 Pham Ngoc Thach (☎08/829
4345) is another venue for **cultural events** and **movies**; while Lam Son Square's
Municipal Theatre hosts fashion shows, traditional **drama** and **dance**. The only
real tourist-oriented venue in the city is presently the **Binh Quoi Village**, whose
regular programmes ($5) of folk music, traditional dancing and **water puppetry**,
organized by Saigontourist, can be coupled with a Saigon River dinner-cruise (see
p.110). The village is at 1147 Xo Viet Nghe Tinh (☎08/899 1831) – or contact
Saigontourist (☎08/829 8914). Water puppetry isn't as big in Ho Chi Minh City
as it is in Hanoi, though if you aren't going to the north you might attend one of
the shows laid on at the History Museum, Le Duan (on the hour; $1).

Bars and pubs

Bars and pubs have taken the city by storm. Dong Khoi is predictably well
endowed, while another boozy enclave has developed around Le Thanh Ton,
Hai Ba Trung and Thi Sach, where a glut of places ranging from slick yuppie
haunts to watering holes which hark back to the raunchy GI bars of the Sixties
has developed to cater for expats renting apartments nearby. At the other end
of the scale, all Pham Ngu Lao's travellers' cafés turn their hand to drink at
night – fine if you're willing to forego atmosphere in order to save a dollar or
two on a beer, and great for meeting like-minded tourists. For more of a bar
atmosphere, head for somewhere like **Allez-Boo** or **Lost in Saigon**.

Bars open either late in the morning, to catch the lunchtime trade, or early
in the evening. At the time of writing, a police crackdown had the city strangely silent after midnight, with the notable exception of several bars around
Pham Ngu Lao, which seemed to be spared the blitz. In general, bar owners
want to stay open as long as they have punters, so expect the situation to loosen
up in time. **Prices** vary wildly: a big BGI beer at a streetside café in Pham Ngu
Lao will cost you less than $1, but you can multiply that by four or five in a
more upmarket bar on Dong Khoi; wines and spirits are only available at the
top end of the market, and prices are slightly steeper. One way to economize
while downtown is to take advantage of early-evening **happy hours**, or check
out the surprisingly cheap and tasty **bia hoi** (see box on p.119). Several of the
pricier bars, such as *Saigon-Saigon*, *Le Caprice* and *Panorama*, offer sweeping
views across the city, best enjoyed as the sun sets.

With competition hotting up, landlords are increasingly looking to attract
customers, offering diversions such as live music, darts, pool and karaoke.

Allez-Boo 187 Pham Ngu Lao, ⓦwww.allezboo.com; see map, p.112. Bamboo and thatch decor complete with loud music, great food (see p.111) and a good selection of cocktails make this hugely popular with the backpacker crowd and it's heaving most nights; currently Pham Ngu Lao's largest bar. 7am–late.

Blue Gekko 31 Ly Tu Trong. Expat hangout offering pub atmosphere with pool, darts and sports TV. Happy hour is 5.30–7.30pm, but at other times drinks are pricey. 4.30pm–late.

Bodega 27 Ngo Duc Ke. Live music every night in this large bar located above the *Paris Deli*. Beers around $2, cocktails $3, and an extensive menu with dishes at $2–3. 6pm–late.

Café Latin 25 Dong Du. Trendy (and pricey) bar-restaurant with stylish metallic decor and designer furniture. Its international menu and screenings of worldwide sports and films in the upper Sports Bar makes this an expats' favourite. Latin music on Fri nights. 10am–midnight.

Cati Club 46–50 Dong Khoi. A few tables on a terrace for people-watching on Dong Khoi, and a large, smart interior with stage where bands play 9–11pm. 10am–late.

Ice Blue 54 Dong Khoi. Supposedly modelled on a traditional English pub, though apart from the dartboard there's little to suggest Blighty. However, it has a friendly atmosphere and a range of international beers; 4–8pm is happy hour. 4pm–late.

La Fenetre Soleil 1st floor, 135 Le Thanh Ton (entrance at 125 Nam Ky Khoi Nghia). Once you've solved the puzzle of how to enter this place, it's happily worth discovering. Functioning as a chill-out café (see p.115) during the day, this little gem turns its hand to mixing cocktails in the evenings. 11.30am–midnight.

Le Caprice 15th floor, Landmark Building, 5b Ton Duc Thang. A pricey and stylish restaurant, but it's worth splashing out on an expensive cocktail to enjoy the view along the river. 10am–late.

Long Phi 163 Pham Ngu Lao; see map, p.112. Decor is more stylish than in most of its competitors and the drinks slightly more expensive, but this is a relaxing, popular bar with a small French restaurant. 11.30am–late.

Lost in Saigon 169 Pham Ngu Lao; see map, p.112. Long-established faithful, with a dark bar, pool table and good mix of contemporary and classic rock music. 6pm–late.

Maya 6 Cao Ba Quat. A touch of Latin America in Saigon, in the form of a cosy bar serving a good range of beers and cocktails as well as South American food and tapas. Classes in salsa dancing too. 5pm–late.

Mogambo 20 Thi Sach. Fish and chips, steaks, pies and Mexican food, and a good stock of movies on video. Pelts on the walls give the place a faintly sassy feel. 7am–late.

O'Briens Factory 74 A2 Hai Ba Trung. *O'Briens Factory* isn't a world away from a smart London pub, and is popular with expats for its good atmosphere, well-stocked bar and comforting Western menu. Happy hour 4.30–7pm (except Sun). 4.30pm–late.

Old Saigon 20 Thi Sach. Waitresses in *ao dai*, black and white photos of the city in former days, plus antique fans create a theme of nostalgia in this two-storeyed bar, which serves beer, cocktails and snacks at reasonable prices. 2pm–late.

Panorama Level 32–33, Saigon Trade Centre, 37 Ton Duc Thang. An aptly named bar worth visiting for the view alone. Look down on the tiny Notre Dame Cathedral and *Caravelle Hotel*, and a sweeping bend in the Saigon River while enjoying a predictably high-priced drink. 11am–midnight.

Q Bar 7 Cong Tuong, Lam Son Square. Located under the Municipal Theatre, facing the *Caravelle Hotel*, this leading bar attracts the city's fashion-conscious to its stylish bars and alcoves. Cocktails around $4, beers around $2. 5pm–late.

Rooftop Garden *Rex Hotel*, 141 Nguyen Hué. Sky-high prices, but a drink amidst the fairy-lit topiary and clumsy model animals of the *Rex* terrace is still *de rigueur* on a trip to the city. Green tea ($1) is the cheapest tipple on the menu. 7am–late.

Saigon-Saigon Rooftop Bar *Caravelle Hotel*, 19 Lam Son Square. Romantic views of the city and nightly live music in a stylish ambience more than compensate for the pricey drinks list in this lofty (11th floor) hotel bar. Popular with local expats. 4.30pm–1am.

Sheridan's Irish House 17/13 Le Thanh Ton. Live music every night, but different styles and performers, in this cosy bar which also has an extensive menu. 8am–late.

Underground basement of Lucky Plaza, 69 Dong Khoi. The ideal location, along with $1 happy-hour beers (4–7pm) and a good range of Western food on the menu, make this place perpetually busy. Pool table too. 10am–late.

Vascos 16 Cao Ba Quat. Live bands on Fridays and Saturdays when it positively heaves with an expat crowd, spilling out into the palm-shaded courtyard of the adjoining *Camargue* restaurant. Films shown thrice weekly and tapas served. Closed Sun & Mon. 6pm–late.

Wild West 33 Hai Ba Trung. Fairly large saloon-style dark interior with high stools and pool table. Happy hour 6–8pm. Often deserted, though more popular at the weekends. 6pm–late.

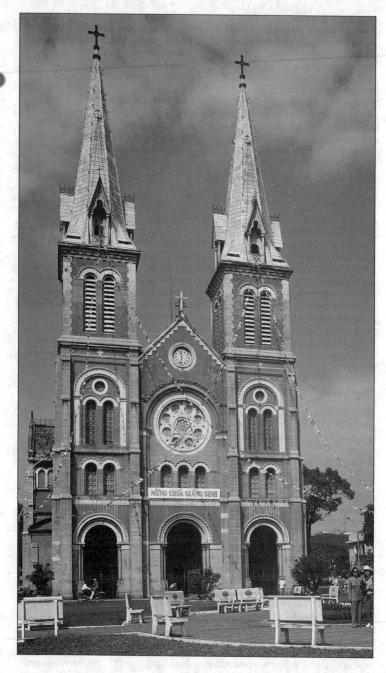

Bia hoi bars

If you can't afford the price of a bottle of BGI, you might try a **bia hoi bar**, where locals glug cheap local draught beer over ice by the jug-full; you might want to pass on the ice if you're wary of catching something. These spit-and-sawdust bars tend to open in the morning and close early in the evening. They crop up all over the city, but the two listed below are convenient for Dong Khoi and Pham Ngu Lao.

Bia Hoi – Bia Chai 20 Dong Du; see map, p.109. If the restaurants and bars around Dong Khoi seem too expensive, duck in here and drown your sorrows in a jug of the local special.

Bia Hoi 181 181–183 Nguyen Thai Hoc; see map, p.112. Located just to the east of Pham Ngu Lao's epicentre, this streetside bar is crowded in the afternoon and evening. They also serve *lao de*, or goat hotpot, a local speciality.

Discos and clubs

Ho Chi Minh's **disco and club scene** is picking up rapidly, and Vietnam's increased contact with the West is reflected in the improving standards of dance music on the city's turntables. That said, some clubs are still extremely naive (refreshingly so, if you're used to the studied posturing of clubbers in London or New York), and the practice of employing hostesses in slit gowns is still prevalent. In addition, some establishments continue to cater for the locals' love of **ballroom dancing** – a tradition which is sadly fading out, as MTV turns local youngsters on to the latest Western sounds. Most clubs and discos levy a **cover charge** (normally $3–5) entitling you to your first drink free, though some just charge higher prices for drinks. Again, see local listings magazines for the hottest new clubs.

Apocalypse Now 2c Thi Sach. A pioneer of the city's resurgent nightlife, always rowdy and sweaty at weekends with an eclectic crowd, though can be rather dull during the week. Dark and cavernous, with two dance floors and a compact garden. 7pm–late.

Canto Lounge and KTV *Vien Dong Hotel*, 275a Pham Ngu Lao. Nightclub with Cantonese flavour and music, popular with Ho Chi Minh's young and trendy. Dance the night away in the disco or make your own music in private karaoke rooms. 8pm–late.

Catwalk *New World Hotel*, 76 Le Lai. Slick but unatmospheric club, with $7 entrance fee; 8pm–late.

Club 777 5 Cong Truong Me Linh. The city's newest disco, located in a cavernous hall just off Dong Khoi. $4 entrance. 8pm–late.

Liberty 80 Dong Khoi. A largely Vietnamese crowd waltzes along to the smoochy live music in this dark upstairs club; disco music takes over later. 8.30pm–late.

Liquid 104 Hai Ba Trung. House and local pop both feature at this venue that draws a lively local crowd. 8pm–late.

Maxim's 15–17 Dong Khoi. Sedate dancing upstairs after a meal in the restaurant (see p.110). 8.30pm–midnight.

Mecca 129a Nguyen Hué. No-nonsense house with hip-hop, as well as hormone-awakening dance performances. 8pm–late.

Mua Rung ("Rain forest") 5–15 Ho Huan Nghiep. Nightclub with state-of-the-art light show and sound system; contemporary dance music attracts the very young Viets; entrance is free before 8pm. 7.30pm–late.

Planet Europa Saigon Superbowl, A43 Truong Son. Draws a young and moneyed crowd, with mostly Western sounds. 8pm–late.

Markets and shopping

Ho Chi Minh City may be no mecca for **shopping**, but it has a growing number of souvenir shops, allowing you to stock up with gifts before departure. Paintings on rice paper, silk *ao dais*, lacquerware, embroidered cloth, musical instruments and ethnic garments are all popular, as are **curios** such as opium pipes, antique watches, French colonial stamps and banknotes, and US Army-issue cigarette lighters, while the cheapest items are the ubiquitous T-shirts and conical hats. Visitors interested in Vietnam's history will find a wealth of copied **books** on the subject, mostly sold by wandering vendors, though few bookshops have a wide range of English-language books. For cheap and cheerful souvenirs, head for Le Loi or De Tham; for something precious and pricey, browse the upmarket boutiques along Dong Khoi and its tentacles, such as Dong Du and Ngo Duc Ke. **Bargaining** is an essential skill to cultivate if you're going to be doing much shopping – see Basics, p.63, for some tips.

Shopping malls are a new feature of the city, attracting curious crowds with their glitz and glamour; some offer distractions other than shopping in the form of cinemas and bowling alleys. The local **markets** are also well worth checking out, both as a source of bargains and as a window on Vietnamese culture. The biggest is **Ben Thanh Market** (p.95), at the junction of Tran Hung Dao, Le Loi and Ham Nghi, which has a huge variety of cheap clothes (*ao dai* under $20) and all kinds of souvenirs like chopstick sets and carved seals. Cholon's equivalent is **Binh Tay Market** (p.102), below Thap Muoi on its southwestern edge. **Thai Binh Market**, at Pham Ngu Lao's western end, is modestly proportioned, but a mere stone's throw from the travellers' enclave up the street, while **Dan Sinh Market**, 336 Nguyen Cong Tru (p.96), has a section specializing in army surplus, both American and Vietnamese. For other smaller souvenirs, check out the booths inside the GPO on Dong Khoi (and on the street itself) for old **coins**, **stamps**, notes, and **greetings cards** featuring typical Vietnamese scenes hand-painted onto silk. **Antiques and curios** are available in several stores along Le Cong Kieu (see p.96), while intriguing **model ships** are sold on Cao Ba Quat, north of the Municipal Theatre, at the eastern flank of the *Continental*.

Generally speaking, shops **open** daily 10am to dusk, although some shopkeepers take an extended afternoon break, while larger stores often stay open beyond 8pm.

Department stores and shopping malls

Diamond Plaza 34 Le Duan. Currently the city's favourite mall, featuring department store, supermarket, fitness centre, hospital, swimming pool, bowling alley, cinemas and serviced apartments.

Nhat Nam Plaza 54–56 Nguyen Trai. Black and white eight-storey shopping complex, packed with cosmetics, toys, electrical and household goods, video games, and a cafeteria on the top floor with stunning views of the city.

Saigon Centre 65 Le Loi. Cafés, souvenir shops, boutiques, small department store and supermarket in convenient location between downtown and budgetsville.

Saigon Square corner of Hai Ba Trung and Nguyen Du. Ground-level shopping arcade covering an entire block, with supermarket, hundreds of boutiques and souvenir shops, burger bars and ice-cream parlours.

Saigon Superbowl A43 Truong Son – beside the airport. Vietnam's first shopping and leisure mall could have been lifted straight out of Singapore, chock-full of familiar names such as Lego, Swatch and KFC.

Saigontourist Department Store 41 Le Thanh Ton. Upmarket department store in the heart of the hotel district, selling overpriced handicrafts, jewellery and cosmetics among other things.

Savico-Kihn-Do Shopping Mall between Dong Khoi and Nguyen Hué. Pedestrianized ground-level open-air mall, containing boutiques, bakeries, fast food, and gift shops, but mostly notable for its convenient public toilets.

Thong Xa Tax Shopping 135 Nguyen Hué. Known locally as the Russian Market and located opposite the *Rex*, this is a sprawling mass of stores selling electronic goods, cameras, watches, pirate cassettes and videos, jewellery, leather goods and lacquerware.

Books, newspapers and magazines

Bookazine 28 Dong Khoi. Stocks a range of newspapers and magazines, as well as detailed maps of Vietnamese provinces and an intriguing hotchpotch of secondhand books, some of which look like collectors' items.

Con Meo 243 De Tham and **Nhan Binh** 251 De Tham. Both of these places have small selections of new and secondhand books and maps, plus dirt-cheap pirate CDs.

Lao Dong 104 Nguyen Hué. Opposite the entrance to the *Rex*, stocking a wide range of magazines and newspapers.

Phuong Nam 2a Le Duan. A good range of fiction and non-fiction, as well as magazines and CDs. Open until 9.30pm.

Thu Van 179 Pham Ngu Lao. Of the many places selling secondhand and photocopied books in backpackerland, this has one of the widest selections.

Xuan Thu Foreign Language Bookshop 185 Dong Khoi. Large store selling a few English and French publications, though most are grammar and business books; some newspapers too.

Handicrafts, fabrics and antiques

A.M. Lacquerware 185 Pham Ngu Lao. Lacquerware, ceramic, stone, bamboo, shell and horn products at affordable prices.

Art Arcade 151 Dong Khoi. Paintings, lacquerware and ceramics, plus Buddha statues, old watches and trinkets.

Authentique Interiors 6 Dong Khoi. Massive display area with a huge range of clothes and other textiles, ceramics, lacquerware and other gifts.

Bich Lien 125 Dong Khoi. General souvenirs-cum-handicrafts, plus a good range of Tin Tin and Disney paintings on lacquer.

Butterfly 26b Le Thanh Ton. Three floors of good-quality crafts and home decor.

Celadon Green 51 Ton That Thiep. Specializing in celadon tableware, but also has many attractive items of home decor.

For You 59 Dong Du. Bright, modern lacquerware bowls and food sets, plus eye-catching decorative items.

Kim Phuong 77 Le Thanh Ton. Good array of tablecloths, napkins, hand-embroidered pictures and pyjamas.

Lac Viet 40 Ngo Duc Ke. All kinds of souvenirs such as ceramics, paintings and bags, as well as videos, greetings cards, newspapers and magazines.

Minh Huong 85 Mac Thi Buoi. Hand-embroidered cotton wares.

Phuong Tam 153 Dong Khoi. Tin Tin lacquerware,

copies of old French advertisements, antique watches and handicrafts.

Precious Qui 29a Dong Khoi. Exquisite, high-quality bamboo and lacquerware objects and gifts.

Sapa 222 De Tham and 64 Dong Du. Attractive garments and artefacts from Vietnamese ethnic minority groups.

Tay Son 198 Vo Thi Sau. Frequented by tourist groups, since you can watch processes such as making lacquerware as well as browse their large warehouse of furniture, wooden carvings and lacquered art.

Xa Saigon 259 De Tham. Stocks a smattering of traditional handicrafts such as *montagnard* bags, ready-to-wear hilltribe hemp clothing and Vietnamese musical instruments.

Paintings

Apricot Gallery 50–52 Mac Thi Buoi. One of the city's most exclusive galleries, with intriguing, original oils by local artists from $650 upwards.

Esprit d'Ami 31 Ngo Duc Ke. Striking work on Vietnamese themes by French artists Tara Guillermin and Christian DePlante. Be prepared to dig deep to buy.

Gallery Lotus 55 Dong Khoi. Classy oils and drawings with an authentic, traditional Vietnamese flavour.

Nam Phuong 105 Bui Vien. One of many artists making a living by reproducing classic images in the travellers' quarter; good work and reasonable prices.

Van Gogh Art Gallery 114b Nguyen Hué. Reproductions of classic paintings.

Workshop Hai 241 De Tham. Specializes in inexpensive rice-paper and silk paintings.

World Art Gallery 59 Bui Vien. Painstaking copies of the world's classic works.

Tailors

Chuong 270 Hai Ba Trung. A long-established and reliable tailor located a few blocks north of downtown.

Sy Than 221 De Tham. Recommended tailor; a sister shop at 107a Bui Vien is geared towards men's tailoring.

Zakka 134 Pasteur. High-quality tailor, also sells divine ready-to-wear silk creations.

Listings

Airlines Air France, 130 Dong Khoi ☎ 08/829 0981; British Airways, 1st Floor, 114a Nguyen Hué ☎ 08/822 4141; Cathay Pacific, Jardine House, 58 Dong Khoi ☎ 08/822 3203; China Airlines, 132–134 Dong Khoi ☎ 08/825 1388; China

Southern Airlines, Somerset Chancellor House, 1st Floor, 21–23 Nguyen Thi Minh Khai ☎ 08/823 5588; Emirates, 1st Floor, 114a Nguyen Hué ☎ 08/825 6576; Garuda, 132–134 Dong Khoi ☎ 08/829 3644; Japan Air Lines, 17th Floor, Sun

Wah Tower, 115 Nguyen Hué ☎08/821 9098; KLM, Saigon Riverside, 2a–4a Ton Duc Thang ☎08/823 1990; Lao Aviation, 181 Hai Ba Trung ☎08/822 6990; Lufthansa, 132–134 Dong Khoi ☎08/829 8529; Malaysia Airlines, 132–134 Dong Khoi ☎08/829 2529; Pacific Airlines, 177 Vo Thi Sau ☎08/932 5979; Philippine Airlines, 229 Dong Khoi ☎08/827 2105; Qantas, 1st Floor, 114a Nguyen Hué ☎08/823 8844; Royal Cambodia Airlines, 343 Le Van Sy ☎08/844 0126; Siem Reap Airways, 132–134 Dong Khoi ☎08/823 9288; Singapore Airlines, Saigon Tower, 29 Le Duan ☎08/823 1588; Thai Airways, 65 Nguyen Du ☎08/829 2809; United Airlines, 7th Floor, Jardine House, 58 Dong Khoi ☎08/823 4755; Vietnam Airlines, 116 Nguyen Hué ☎08/829 2118 and 265 De Tham ☎08/836 9630.

Banks and exchange Most banks and foreign exchange bureaux can arrange cash advances on Visa and MasterCard, some on JCB (usual fee is 3–4 percent), and also electronic money transfers from abroad. 24-hour cash dispensers (ATMs) can be found at HSBC and ANZ; both accept Cirrus, Plus, Visa and MasterCard, and dispense in dong and US dollars. HSBC, 235 Dong Khoi, will only change cash and travellers' cheques for HSBC members, but there's an adjoining ATM annexe and service desk, which can arrange Visa and MasterCard cash advances (daily 8.30am–noon & 1–4.30pm). Vietcombank's main branch at 29 Chuong Duong (for Visa and MasterCard cash advances) and a second branch at 17 Chuong Duong (for telegraphic transfers) offer good rates for travellers' cheques and cash (Mon–Fri 7.30–11.30am & 1–4pm), as does Vietincombank, 1st Floor, 79a Ham Nghi (Mon–Fri 7.30–11.30am & 1–4.30pm). ANZ, 11 Me Linh Square (Mon–Fri 8.30am–4pm), charges slightly higher rates for travellers' cheques and cash advance, as does Tacombank, 51 Bui Vien (Mon–Sat 7.30–11.30am & 1.30–4pm). For exchange outside normal banking hours, try the Vietcombank bureau within Fiditourist, 195 Pham Ngu Lao (Mon–Sat 7.30–11am & 1.30–9pm), the airport exchange (daily 10am–11pm), or Sacombank's foreign exchange annexe on the corner of Pham Ngu Lao at 211 Nguyen Thai Hoc (Mon–Fri 7.30–11.30am & 1–7pm, Sat 7.30am–noon, closed Sun). Otherwise, foreign exchange kiosks on Nguyen Hué and Le Loi have extended daily opening times.

Bike and motorbike rental Most rental operations are in Pham Ngu Lao and De Tham; average daily costs are $1 for a bicycle and $5–7 for a medium-sized motorbike. Example outlets are *Hotel 265*, 265 De Tham, and *Hotel 211*, 211 Pham Ngu Lao, with 100cc bikes at $5 per day,

and *Thanh Thanh Guesthouse*, 205 Pham Ngu Lao, with 175cc bikes at $8 a day; all outlets offer long-term rental discounts. *Sinh Café*, 246–248 De Tham, has mountain bikes at $2 per day and 100cc motorbikes at around $7 per day. In the centre, Getrantours, 24 Hai Ba Trung, rents 250cc motorbikes at $10 per day and 125cc bikes at $7 per day. If you want to buy a new bike, check out the shops along the western end of Le Thanh Ton and the scores of motorbike shops along the western end of Ly Tu Trong. To buy secondhand bikes, you're better off buying tourist cast-offs which are advertised in cafés around Pham Ngu Lao and De Tham.

Car and minibus rental Car and minibus rental with driver can be arranged through tour agencies (see p.126), Getrantours at 24 Hai Ba Trung and also at 21 Ngo Duc Ke. Self-drive is still not an option, as yet.

Cinema The only place in town showing English-soundtrack films on a regular basis is the Diamond Cinema complex on the 13th floor of Diamond Plaza (see "Department stores and shopping malls", p.120); tickets $2–3. Phone ☎08/825 7751 to find out what's showing and when. Tan Son Nhat Cinema, 186 Nguyen Van Troi (☎08/842 1613), runs an "English-speaking film club". Also check local press for details.

Consulates Australia, Landmark Building, 5b Ton Duc Thanh ☎08/829 6035; Cambodia, 41 Phung Khac Khoan ☎08/829 2751; Canada, 235 Dong Khoi ☎08/824 5025; China, 39 Nguyen Thi Minh Khai ☎08/829 2457; Indonesia, 18 Phung Khac Khoan ☎08/825 18880; Laos, 93 Pasteur ☎08/829 7667; Malaysia, 2 Ngo Duc Ke ☎08/829 9023; New Zealand, 41 Nguyen Thi Minh Khai ☎08/822 6907; Singapore, Saigon Centre, 65 Le Loi ☎08/822 5173; Thailand, 77 Tran Quoc Tuan ☎08/932 7637; UK (& British Council), 25 Le Duan ☎08/823 2604; US, 4 Le Duan ☎08/822 9433.

Courier services DHL head office is near the airport at 4 Phan Thuc Duyen (☎08/844 6203), and there's also a branch at the GPO. Airborne Express is just below the GPO at 80c Nguyen Du (☎08/829 4310). FedEx is at 146 Pasteur (☎08/829 0995), close to the *Rex Hotel*.

Dentists Grand Dentistry, Ground Floor, Sun Wah Tower, 115 Nguyen Hué (☎08/821 9446) is an international-standard dental clinic; basic check-ups start at around $30. The Faculty of Dentistry, Office 9, 652 Nguyen Trai (☎08/855 9225), has a consultation fee of $1; the Orthodontology Centre, opposite the *Metropole Hotel*, 263–265 Tran Hung Dao ☎08/836 0191, specializes in jaw, facial and teeth problems, consultation fee $1; or the

International SOS Clinic (see below) has a flat rate of $50 per consultation. Viet Phap at 153 Nguyen Van Tho ☎ 08/825 0939 also comes recommended and charges around $3 per consultation.

Email and Internet access Many hotels have business centres, and there are countless Internet outlets around De Tham and Pham Ngu Lao; rates are currently 100–300d per minute. Try Dai Ly Internet at 220 & 276 De Tham, or FPT Internet, 239 Pham Ngu Lao; both have email rates of around 200d per minute and hourly computer rates of 6000–9000d including use of scanner and printer. Downtown, try CyberCafe, 48 Dong Du, an air-con business centre; email rates are 300d per minute, hourly computer rates are around 9000d. You can even rent a mobile phone here for around $1 a day.

Emergencies Dial ☎ 113 for the police, ☎ 114 in case of fire or ☎ 115 for an ambulance; if possible, get a Vietnamese speaker to call on your behalf.

Hospitals and clinics International SOS Clinic, 65 Nguyen Du (☎ 08/829 8424), has international doctors with consultation fees starting at $80; they also have a dental clinic, can arrange emergency evacuation and have a 24hr emergency service (☎ 08/829 8520). Columbia Saigon, 8 Alexandra De Rhodes (☎ 08/823 8455), and Columbia Gia Dinh at 1 No Trang Long, Binh Thanh (☎ 08/803 0678), have multinational doctors with 24hr emergency cover and evacuation, charging from $43 for consultations. HCM City Family Medical Practice, Diamond Plaza, 34 Le Duan (☎ 08/822 7848), is an international clinic with multinational doctors, a dental surgery and specialist knowledge in vaccinations, as well as 24hr emergency cover and evacuation; consultations start at $50. International Medical Centre, 1 Han Thuyen (☎ 08/827 2366), is a French-run, non-profit, 24hr hospitalization centre with in-patient wards, intensive care and emergency surgery; general consultations start at $40. Cholon's Cho Ray Hospital, at 201 Nguyen Chi Thanh (☎ 08/855 4137), has an outpatients' room for foreigners ($4 per consultation) and a foreigners' ward ($27 per night); St Paul Hospital, 280 Dien Bien Phu (☎ 08/829 8732), is an eye specialist, charging around $6 per consultation. The Hospital of Traditional Medecine, 187 Nam Ky Khoi Nghia (☎ 08/932 6579), has acupuncture treatment. At the Blind Massage Centre, Municipal Association for the Blind, 185 Cong Quynh (daily 9am–8.30pm; ☎ 08/839 6697), massages at around $2 an hour are delivered by trained, blind masseurs, which also help raise money for the blind school next door.

Immigration Department For extension visas: Immigration of HCMC, 161 Nguyen Du. Visa extensions must be organized through an agent or tour operator; process takes about 4 days for a 30-day extension and costs $25. For re-entry visas: the Ministry of the Interior, 254 Nguyen Trai, at the junction with Nguyen Cu Trinh (Mon–Fri 8–11am & 1.30–4.30pm).

Laundry Most hotels and guesthouses will wash clothes for you, but rates vary wildly so check first; upmarket hotels can do dry-cleaning; there are also a number of laundry and dry-clean operators around Pham Ngu Lao such as at 107/1 Bui Vien.

Pharmacies There are several pharmacies in and around the De Tham area, such as 214 De Tham and 81 Bui Vien. Downtown is the large pharmacy at 197–199 Dong Khoi, plus at 199 and 205 Hai Ba Trung and 14a Nguyen Dinh Chieu, or make for the couple of pharmacies at 60 Nguyen Du. A bit further afield, the pharmacy at 389 Hai Ba Trung is reputed to be the best-stocked in the city.

Police Main police station is at 73 Yersin ☎ 08/829 7073. You must first go to the police station in the ward where the crime took place to obtain an initial report before coming here; try to avoid lunchtime visits, as there's likely to be nobody on duty.

Post offices The GPO (daily 6am–10pm) is beside the cathedral at the head of Dong Khoi. Poste restante is kept here, but incoming faxes (☎ 08/829 8540) are held nearby at 230 Hai Ba Trung, and there's a small pick-up fee. International parcel dispatch is located behind the main post office at 117 Hai Ba Trung; parcels are received next door at no. 119 – bring your passport and a small fee for customs (Mon–Fri 7.30am–noon & 1–4pm). There are also post offices at 303 Pham Ngu Lao, at 200 Cong Quynh (with poste restante), and at Ga Saigon train station.

Spas If you need to pamper yourself, head for Spa Tropic, 187b Hai Ba Trung ☎ 08/822 8895 and choose from aromatherapy and various other treatments at around $30 a go.

Sports Many upmarket hotels have excellent sport and leisure facilities which non-residents can generally use – at a price – but it's wise to check ahead first. The International Club, 285b Cach Mang Thang (☎ 08/865 1709), has bowling and a gym; further up, Lan Anh Country Club, 291 Cach Mang Thang (☎ 08/862 7420), has international-standard tennis courts, squash courts and also a gym. There are tennis courts at the *Rex Hotel*, and (cheaper) Workers' Club, in the northern corner of the Cong Vien Van Hoa Park, on Nguyen Thi Minh Khai. Badminton courts are at Cau Lac Bo Bong Ban, 143 Nguyen Du ☎ 08/823 7928. The World Gym is at 26 Le Thanh Ton, and the Hash House

For addresses and telephone numbers of airlines and foreign consulates in Ho Chi Minh City, see "Listings", p.121–122.

By plane

The easiest way to get to Tan Son Nhat is by taxi ($3–4; see p.79). If you're desperate to economize, contact Sinh Café or one of the other Pham Ngu Lao operations advertising airport shuttles ($1–2, depending on passenger numbers). If you take a cyclo, they drop you outside the gates, a few hundred metres from the departure terminal, though this doesn't apply to Honda oms. Note, also, that there's a **departure tax** of $12 levied on international flights. **Flight enquiries** should be made at the office of the relevant carrier (see "Airlines", p.121).

By train

Vietnamese trains are oversubscribed, so book as far ahead as possible – particularly for a sleeping berth (see p.35 for details). Some tour operators, travel cafés, travel agents and hotels can reserve tickets for a small fee. The official agent for the railways is Saigon Railways Tourist Service Company (275c Pham Ngu Lao ☎08/836 7640), which has computerized reservations and doesn't charge any extra commission. Otherwise, go along in person to the main station, Ga Saigon, which is a fifteen-minute cyclo ride from the city centre. Ignore the bank of counters on the right as you enter the station concourse and continue to the **foreigners' and overseas Viets enquiries counter** (daily 7.30–11.30am & 1.30–4.30pm; ☎08/843 6527 or 844 0218), where you can get reservations and timetables. On the opposite wall, a massive board details arrivals, departures, fares and regulations in English.

By bus and taxi

To the Mekong Delta: apart from a tour, the easiest way of starting a journey round the Mekong Delta is to take a bus (p.83) to **Cholon bus station**, from where there are frequent departures throughout the day to My Tho (p.138), My Thuan and a few other minor Mekong places. For all other destinations, go to distant **Mien Tay bus station** (daily 3.30am–4.30pm), where several buses a day leave for all the delta's major towns. Take either a Honda om ($3) to Mien Tay, or a bus from Ben Thanh, Cholon, An Suong and Mien Dong stations.

To Vung Tau, **central highlands, Nha Trang and the north**: buses to **points north** depart from Xo Viet Nghe Tinh's **Mien Dong bus station**. Some distant towns and cities are only served by one or two buses a day, and as these tend to leave before dawn it's wise to buy a ticket in advance at the ticket booth (daily 5am–5pm) opposite the blue one-storey building marked "Phong Ve Toc Hanh", to your left as you enter the terminal. Shuttle buses run up to Mien Dong from the other bus stations. For Vung Tau, there are fast, air-conditioned buses departing every half-hour, but you can also pick up a Vung Tau bus in town at Ben Thanh bus station.

Finally, buses bound for **Cu Chi** and **Tay Ninh** run from **An Suong bus station**, along Highway 22; buses to the station depart regularly from Ben Thanh bus station, from where there are also some direct services to Cu Chi Town. Some departures to Tay Ninh also run from Mien Dong station. However, this is one trip that's much easier and cheaper by **open-tour buses** run by Sinh Café and Kim Travel (see p.126), which set down outside their offices in De Tham, just off Pham Ngu Lao.

To Cambodia: direct buses to Phnom Penh ($20) leave daily around 5.30am, arriving 2.30pm, from outside the garage at 145 Nguyen Du; buy tickets on board the bus. Note that this service is withdrawn periodically, so make enquiries beforehand (☎08/822 2496). A better option may be the travellers' cafés: Sinh Café organizes daily air-conditioned buses direct to Phnom Penh ($6) leaving at

8.45am from outside their offices and arriving at 5pm. You can also sign up for a shared **taxi** in Pham Ngu Lao ($20–25 for a full car) taking you as far as the **Moc Bai border crossing**, from where you can walk over the border and connect with waiting air-conditioned local buses ($5) to Phnom Penh. A cheaper alternative is either to buy an open-tour ticket (see below) from the travellers' cafés for the Cao Dai Temple at Tay Ninh ($4), or catch a public bus to Tay Ninh Province and en route alight at Go Dau, about 12km from the border, where a Honda om ($1–2) can take you to the Moc Bai border crossing. You can obtain the necessary **Cambodian visa** ($30) from the consulate (see p.122); allow up to three days for processing. Some travel agents and tour operators will organize the visa for you for a small fee.

Note that while the **political situation in Cambodia** seems fairly stable at present, it can be unpredictable, with tourists occasionally targeted by guerrilla groups; be aware of the latest news, and comply with any travel security advice issued by your own government.

By open-tour bus

Many of the travellers' cafés concentrated around Pham Ngu Lao and De Tham sell tickets for **open-tour buses** that criss-cross the country; for names and contact details see "Listings", p.126. One-way tickets from Ho Chi Minh to Hanoi (around $20) or Hué (about $15) allow you to break your journey at various points along the way, including Da Lat and Nha Trang. Tickets for shorter, in-between trips are also available, such as Ho Chi Minh to: Nha Trang ($7); Da Lat ($5); Ca Na ($6); Hoi An ($15); and Cu Chi/Tay Ninh ($4). You can purchase tickets in advance, or from the various branch offices across the country (see Basics, p.36, for more information). In Ho Chi Minh, tickets, information, and departing buses, which leave daily in the early morning or evening, can be found at the various companies' offices around De Tham and Pham Ngu Lao.

By boat

Hydrofoils to Vung Tau depart from the **Passenger Quay of Ho Chi Minh City** (Bach Dang Wharf), opposite the end of Ham Nghi at 2 Ton Duc Thang. For Vung Tau ($10) there are currently six departures on weekdays, seven at the weekend. For tickets and further information, contact the Vina Express booth at the jetty (daily 6.30–11am & 1.30–4.30pm; ☏08/829 7892).

Now the Cambodian border near Chau Doc has re-opened to foreigners, many travellers combine a glimpse of the delta with their journey to Cambodia. Outfits around Pham Ngu Lao offer trips for around $10.

By organized tour

Tour agencies abound in Ho Chi Minh and offer a range of itineraries, from one-day whistle-stop tours around the region, to lengthy trips upcountry including accommodation. Tours can be arranged either through a private tour operator such as Sinh Café or (more expensive) through a state-run agent. Operators on De Tham and Pham Ngu Lao generally offer the most competitive prices. Popular jaunts include a one-day trip to Tay Ninh and the Cu Chi tunnels for around $4; one- to five-day tours of the Mekong Delta; the ten-day trawl up to Hué, taking in the central highlands and the south-central coast en route; and even all the way to Hanoi – though the overnight train from Hué to the capital is a better option. Tours travel by **bus** or **minibus**, depending upon passenger numbers; tour operators can also lay on **tailor-made itineraries**, **private cars**, and personal **guides** for you. Recommended tour operators are listed on p.126. See Basics, p.40, for provisos and tips on signing up for a tour in Vietnam.

Harriers meet every Sun afternoon; check the local press for details. For golf, the Vietnam Golf and Country Club, Thu Duc (⚏08/065 825 2951), has two high-quality courses and a driving range.

Swimming There are inexpensive but extremely busy pools at the Workers' Club, Cong Vien Van Hoa Park, and at Lam Son, 242 Tran Binh Trong. For a little more peace and quiet, try the relatively cheap pools favoured by expats at the International Club and the Lan Anh Country Club, or the more luxurious hotel pools at the *Rex, Metropole, Sofitel, Majestic* and *Grand* for a daily fee of between $2 and $10 (some include use of sauna and steam bath). Some shopping malls like Diamond Plaza also have pools.

Tampons are sold at Kim Thanh, 64 Ham Nghi; Minimart, 101 Nam Ky Khoi Nghia; Maxi-Mart, 3c Ba Thang Hai; Hong Hoa shop, 250 De Tham; and the pharmacy at 214 De Tham.

Taxis These gather outside the *Rex* in the city centre; otherwise, phone Airport Taxis (⚏08/844 6666) or Vinataxis (⚏08/811 1111); a short trip across the city centre costs $1–2, while the trip out to the airport is around $3–4.

Telephone services There are IDD, fax and telex facilities at the GPO (see above) and numerous IDD telephone kiosks around De Tham and Pham Ngu Lao; otherwise, IDD calls can be made (more expensively) from most hotels.

Tour agencies Ann Tours, 58 Ton That Tung (⚏08/833 2564, ✉anntours@yahoo.com), comes highly recommended; it offers good-value, tailor-made tours including trekking and cycling. Atlas Tours, 30 Thai Van Lung (⚏08/822 4122, ✉atlasviet@hcm.fpt.vn), organizes tailor-made tours for niche groups such as gourmets or divorcees. Cam On Tours, Unit 63, 6th Floor, 7 Phung Khac Khoan (⚏08/825 6074, ✉camoncom@hcm.vnn .vn), is another friendly outfit worth trying for travel advice, visa services, car rental and tours. Diethelm Travel, International Business Centre, 1a Me Linh Square (⚏08/829 4932, ✉dtvlsgn@hcm.vnn.vn), offers well-crafted tours, but at a price. Exotissimo

Travel, Saigon Trade Centre, 37 Ton Duc Thang (⚏08/825 1723, ✉info@exotissimo.com), has an extensive tour programme that includes special interest, Laos and Cambodia add-ons, and also arranges tailor-made tours and transportation. Though not as slick as Kim Travel and Sinh Café, Fiditourist is very helpful, offering the usual services; their office at 195 Pham Ngu Lao (⚏ & ⚏08/836 1922) is geared towards budget tours, while their head office at 127–129 Nguyen Hué (⚏08/914 0440, ✉Fiditour@hcm.vnn.vn) is more upmarket. Kim Travel, 270 De Tham (⚏ & ⚏08/836 9859, ✉cafékim@hcm.vnn.vn), is a veteran of the independent travel scene, with popular and cut-price Mekong Delta trips and other tours, open-tour buses, airplane and train bookings, car and minibus rental, and guides. Sinh Café, 246–248 De Tham (⚏08/836 7338, ✉sinhcafévietnam@hcm.vnn.vn), is a travellers' café-cum-tour agency, offering cut-price organized tours of Vietnam, open-bus tours, guides, visa services, buses and boats to Cambodia and vehicle rental. Sinhbalo Adventures, 283/20 Pham Ngu Lao (⚏08/837 6766, ⓦwww.sinhbalo.com), arranges private trips such as bicycle tours of the Mekong Delta (see also ⓦwww.cyclingvietnam.net) or motorbike tours in the central highlands, and has a wealth of reliable travel info. TM Brothers, 269 De Tham (⚏08/837 8394, ✉nguyenvantuan@yahoo .com), offers a range of budget tours along the lines of Sinh Café and Kim Travel. Tours offered by the state-run agencies, Saigontourist, 49 Le Thanh Ton (⚏08/829 8914, ⓦwww.saigontourist.net) and 187a Pham Ngu Lao (⚏08/836 8542), plus Vietnamtourism, Room 101, Mondial Center, 203 Dong Khoi (⚏08/824 2000, ⚏823 1534), and 234 Nam Ky Khoi Nghia (⚏08/829 0776, ✉vnthcm @hcm.vnn.vn), tend to be rather mediocre and over-priced. Vietnam-Europe, 40 Truong Quyen (⚏08/820 2563, ⓦwww.vietnameurope.com), has a range of cultural tours or can custom-build for individual requirements.

Around Ho Chi Minh City

When Ho Chi Minh's chaotic streets become too much for you, you'll find you can get quite a long way **out of the city** in a day. With public transport

Ho Chi Minh City's water parks

If the dust and heat of Ho Chi Minh begin to get oppressive, head out to one of the city's water parks and cool down. There are two large ones a short drive out of town, and a third, smaller option in Cholon, if you're too lazy to travel far. Most tour agents can help obtain tickets. Longest-established is the **Saigon Water Park** (weekdays 9am–5pm, weekends 8.30am–6.30pm, closed Tues; adults $5, kids under 1.4m $3; ☎08/897 0456), which boasts some impressive slides, a wave pool and – for less energetic souls – a meandering stream to float in. It also has a restaurant with good river views, and is located in Thu Duc District, about 8km east of the city centre. A shuttle bus service operates from Ben Thanh bus station. Further out (about 20km) and even bigger is the **Vietnam Water World** (8.30am–5pm, closed Monday; adults $4, kids $2.50; ☎08/897 7977), which has even more facilities, and includes free use of tents on the camp-ground. A shuttle bus leaves from 55b Nguyen Thi Minh Khai, behind the Reunification Palace. Finally, **Shark Waterland** (10am–9pm; adults $3, kids $2; ☎08/853 7867) is much smaller but has pools and slides and is conveniently located in Cholon.

slow and erratic, day-trips are best arranged through a tour agency (see "Listings", p.126), though public buses also ply the routes. The single most popular trip out of the city takes in two of Vietnam's most memorable sights: the **Cu Chi tunnels**, for twenty years a bolt hole, first for Viet Minh agents, and later for Viet Cong cadres; and the weird and wonderful **Cao Dai Holy See** at Tay Ninh, the fulcrum of the country's most charismatic indigenous religion. Another enjoyable day (or half-day) out can be had at one of the **water parks** that are located on the fringe of the city (see box). Southwest of the city Highway 1 runs down to **My Tho** (see p.138), where you can catch a glimpse of the Mekong River; while to the northeast, it breezes up to the dreary orbital city of **Bien Hoa**, from where Highway 51 drops down to the beaches of **Vung Tau** (see p.231).

The Cu Chi tunnels

During the American War, the villages around the district of **Cu Chi** support-ed a substantial **Viet Cong** (VC) presence. Faced with American attempts to neutralize them, they quite literally dug themselves out of harm's way, and the legendary **Cu Chi tunnels** were the result. Today, tourists can visit a short stretch of the tunnels, drop to their hands and knees and squeeze underground for an insight into life as a tunnel-dwelling resistance fighter. The tunnels have been widened to allow passage for the fuller frame of Westerners but it's still a dark, sweaty, claustrophobic experience, and not one you should rush into unless you're confident you won't suffer a subterranean freak-out.

There are two sites where the tunnels can be seen – **Ben Dinh** and, 15km beyond, **Ben Duoc** (both daily 7.30am–5pm; about $5 entrance, not general-ly included in tour price), though most foreigners get taken to Ben Dinh. Ben Duoc has the dubious additional attraction of a grounded helicopter. If you don't want to squeeze into a minibus (around $4 per person), four people will pay around $40 for a **taxi** following the same itinerary. **Buses** covering the 40km to **CU CHI** town depart from **Ben Thanh** and **An Suong** stations in Ho Chi Minh (see p.83), but from the town you'll need to take a **motorbike** (about $5) for the final 20km to the site; turn right off the highway when you reach Cu Chi post office.

A history of the tunnels

When the first spades sank into the earth around Cu Chi, the region was covered by a rubber plantation tied to a French tyre company. Anti-colonial **Viet Minh** dug the first tunnels here in the late 1940s; intended primarily for storing arms, they soon became valuable hiding places for the resistance fighters themselves. Over a decade later, VC activists controlling this staunchly anti-government area, many of them local villagers, followed suit and went to ground. By 1965, 250km of tunnels criss-crossed Cu Chi and surrounding areas – just across the Saigon River was the notorious guerrilla power base known as the **Iron Triangle** – making it possible for the VC guerrilla cells in the area to link up with each other and to infiltrate Saigon at will. One section daringly ran underneath the Americans' Cu Chi Army Base.

Though the region's compacted red clay was perfectly suited to tunnelling, and lay above the water level of the Saigon River, the **digging parties** faced a multitude of problems. Quite apart from the snakes and scorpions they encountered as they laboured with their hoes and crowbars, there was the problem of inconspicuously disposing of the soil by spreading it in bomb craters or scattering it in the river under cover of darkness. With a tunnel dug, ceilings had to be shored up, and as American bombing made timber scarce the tunnellers had to resort to stealing iron fence posts from enemy bases. Tunnels could be as small as 80cm wide and 80cm high, and were sometimes four levels deep; **vent shafts** (to disperse smoke and aromas from underground ovens) were camouflaged by thick grass and termites' nests. In order to throw the Americans' dogs off the scent, pepper was sprinkled around vents, and sometimes the VC even washed with the same scented soap used by GIs.

Tunnel life

Living conditions below ground were appalling for these "human moles". Tunnels were foul-smelling, and became so hot by the afternoon that inhabitants had to lie on the floor in order to get enough oxygen to breathe. The darkness was absolute, and some long-term dwellers suffered temporary blindness when they emerged into the light. At times it was necessary to stay below ground for weeks on end, alongside bats, rats, snakes, scorpions, centipedes and fire ants. Some of these unwelcome guests were co-opted to the cause: boxes full of scorpions and hollow bamboo sticks containing vipers were secreted in tunnels, where GIs might unwittingly knock them over.

Within the multi-level tunnel complexes, there were latrines, wells, meeting rooms and dorms. Rudimentary **hospitals** were also scratched out of the soil. Operations were carried out by torchlight using instruments fashioned from shards of ordnance, and a patient's own blood was caught in bottles and then pumped straight back using a bicycle pump and a length of rubber hosing. Such medical supplies as existed were secured by bribing ARVN soldiers in Saigon. Doctors also administered herbs and acupuncture – even honey was used for its antiseptic properties.

The **guided tour** of Ben Dinh kicks off in a **classroom**, where a wall chart, a cross-section of the tunnels and a black and white movie bristling with national pride fill you in on the background. From there, you head out into the bush, where your guide will point out lethal booby-traps, concealed trap doors and an abandoned tank, but it's the **tunnels** themselves that are most thought-provoking. While negotiating them, bear in mind that people lived below ground here for weeks on end. There are several models showing how unexploded ordnance was ingeniously converted into lethal mines and traps, and a demonstration of how smoke from underground fires was cleverly dispersed far from its source. If the temptation to play at being a guerrilla gets too strong, you can shoulder an AK47 and shoot off a few rounds ($1 per bullet) at the shooting range. The tour is usually rounded off with much-needed

Kitchens cooked whatever the tunnellers could get their hands on. With rice and fruit crops destroyed, the diet consisted largely of tapioca, leaves and roots, at least until enough bomb fragments could be transported to Saigon and sold as scrap to buy food. Morale was maintained in part by **performing troupes** that toured the tunnels, though songs like "He who comes to Cu Chi, the Bronze Fortress in the Land of Iron, will count the crimes accumulated by the Enemy" were not quite up to the standard set by Bob Hope as he entertained the US troops.

The end of the line

American attempts to **flush out** the tunnels proved ineffective. Operating out of huge bases erected around Saigon in the mid-Sixties, they evacuated villagers into strategic hamlets and then used defoliant sprays and bulldozers to rob the VC of cover, in "scorched earth" operations such as January 1967's **Cedar Falls**. Even then, tunnels were rarely effectively destroyed – one soldier at the time compared the task to "fill[ing] the Grand Canyon with a pitchfork". GIs would lob down gas or grenades or else go down themselves, armed only with a torch, a knife and a pistol. Die-hard soldiers who specialized in these underground raids came to be known as **tunnel rats**, their unofficial insignia *Insigni Non Gratum Anus Rodentum*, meaning "not worth a rat's arse". Booby-traps made of sharpened bamboo stakes awaited them in the dark, as well as "bombs" made from Coke cans and dud bullets found on the surface. Tunnels were low and narrow, and entrances so small that GIs often couldn't get down them, even if they could locate them. Maverick war correspondent Wilfred Burchett, travelling with the NLF in 1964, found his Western girth a distinct impediment: "On another occasion I got stuck passing from one tunnel section to another. In what seemed a dead end, a rectangular plug was pulled out from the other side, and, with some ahead pulling my arms and some pushing my buttocks from behind, I managed to get through...I was transferred to another tunnel entrance built especially to accommodate a bulky unit cook."

Another American tactic aimed at weakening the resolve of the VC guerrillas involved dropping leaflets and broadcasting bulletins that played on the fighters' fears and loneliness. Although this prompted numerous desertions, the tunnellers were still able to mastermind the **Tet Offensive** of 1968. Ultimately, the Americans resorted to more strong-arm tactics to neutralize the tunnels, sending in the B52s freed by the cessation of bombing of the North in 1968 to level the district with **carpet bombing**. The VC's infrastructure was decimated by Tet, and further weakened by the **Phoenix Programme** (see p.502). By this time, though, the tunnels had played their part in proving to America that the war was unwinnable. At least 12,000 Vietnamese guerrillas and sympathizers are thought to have perished here during the American War, and the terrain was laid waste – pockmarked by bomb craters, devoid of vegetation, the air poisoned by lingering fumes.

refreshments of tea and boiled roots, often the only food source available to tunnel-dwellers.

The Cao Dai Holy See at Tay Ninh

Above Cu Chi, Highway 22 pushes on northwestward through idyllic paddy flatlands. After several kilometres the highway runs through **TRANG BANG**, where the photographer Nick Ut captured one of the war's most horrific and enduring images – that of a naked girl with her back in flames running along the highway, fleeing a napalm attack. The girl, Phan Thi Kim Phuc, now married and living in Canada, was named in 1997 as a goodwill ambassador for UNESCO.

Cao Daism

The basic tenets of **Cao Daism** were first revealed to **Ngo Van Chieu**, a civil servant working in the criminal investigation department of the French administration on Phu Quoc Island, at the beginning of the 1920s. A spiritualist, Ngo was contacted during a seance by a superior spirit calling itself Cao Dai, or "high place". This spirit communicated to him the basics of the Cao Daist creed, and instructed him to adopt the Divine Eye as a tangible representation of its existence. Posted back to Saigon soon afterwards, Ngo set about evangelizing, though according to French convert and chronicler Gabriel Gobron the religion didn't gather steam until late in 1925, when Ngo was contacted by a group of mediums sent his way by the Cao Dai.

At this stage, **revelations** from the Cao Dai began to add further meat to the bones of the religion. Twice already, it informed its mediums, it had revealed itself to mankind, using such vehicles as Lao-tzu, Christ, Mohammed, Moses, Sakyamuni and Confucius to propagate systems of belief tailored to suit localized cultures. Such religious intolerance had resulted from this multiplicity, that for the **third alliance** it would do away with earthly messengers, and convey a universal religion via spirit intermediaries, including Louis Pasteur, William Shakespeare, Joan of Arc, Sir Winston Churchill and Napoleon Bonaparte. The revelations of these "saints" were received using a *planchette* (a pencil secured to a wooden board on castors, on which the medium rests his hand, sometimes known as a *corbeille à bec*).

Though a fusion of Oriental and occidental religions, propounding the concept of a **universal god**, Cao Daism is primarily entrenched in Buddhism, Taoism and Confucianism, to which cause-and-effect creeds, elements of Christianity, Islam and spirituality are added. By following its five commandments – Cao Daists must avoid killing living beings, high living, covetousness, verbal deceit and the temptations of the flesh – adherents look to hasten the evolution of the soul through reincarnation.

The religion was effectively **founded** in October 1926, when it was also officially recognized by the French colonial administration. Borrowing the structure and terminology of the Catholic Church, Cao Daism began to grow rapidly, its emphasis upon simplicity appealing to disaffected peasants, and by 1930 there were 500,000 followers. In 1927, Tay Ninh became the Cao Daists' Holy See; Ngo opted out of the papacy, and the first pope was **Le Van Trung**, a decadent mandarin from Cholon who saw the error of his ways after being visited by the Cao Dai during a seance.

Inevitably in such uncertain times, Cao Daism developed a **political agenda**. Strongly anti-French during World War II, subsequently the Cao Daist militia turned against the Viet Minh, with whom they fought, using French arms, in the French War. By the mid-Fifties, the area around Tay Ninh was a virtual Cao Daist fiefdom. In *The Quiet American*, Graham Greene describes the Cao Dai militia as a "private army of 25,000 men, armed with mortars made out of the exhaust-pipes of old cars, allies of the French who turned neutral at the moment of danger". Even then, however, they were feuding with the rival Hoa Hao sect, and in a few years their power had waned.

Post-liberation, the communist government confiscated all Cao Daist land, though it was returned ten years later. Today, the religion continues to thrive in its twin power bases of Tay Ninh District and the Mekong Delta.

Despite third-degree burns covering half of her body, she remains remarkably unembittered, stating "I am happy because I am living without hatred." A sign marked "Tay Ninh 10km, Long Hoa 4km" signals the turning off the highway to **LONG HOA**, the site of the enigmatic **Cao Dai Cathedral**, or Great Temple, of the Holy See of Tay Ninh District. **Joss-stick factories** line the road into Long Hoa, their produce bundled into mini-haystacks by the roadside to dry. Around 4km later you reach Long Hoa's **market**, from where the cathedral itself is another 2km. Most go on a **tour** (see p.125), but if you'd rather go it alone, **buses** to Tay Ninh depart from Ho Chi Minh City's An Suong station; ask the driver to drop you off at the front gates of the temple.

The Cathedral

A grand gateway marks the entrance to the grounds of the 1927-built Cao Dai Cathedral. Beyond it, a wide boulevard escorts you past a swathe of grassland used on ceremonial occasions, to the wildly exotic cathedral itself, over whose left shoulder rises distant **Nui Ba Den**, Black Lady Mountain.

On first sighting, the **Cathedral** seems to be subsiding, an optical illusion created by the rising steps inside it, but your first impressions are more likely to be dominated by what Graham Greene described as a "Walt Disney fantasia of the East, dragons and snakes in Technicolor". Despite its Day-Glo hues and rococo clutter, this gaudy construction somehow manages to bypass tackiness. Two square, pagoda-style **towers** bookend the front facade, whose central portico is topped by a bowed, first-floor balcony and a **Divine Eye**. The most recurrent motif in the cathedral, the eye, is surrounded by a triangle, as it is on the American one-dollar bill. A figure in semi-relief emerges from each tower: on the left is Cao Daism's first female cardinal, Lam Huong Thanh, and on the right, Le Van Trung, its first pope.

The eclectic ideology of Cao Daism is mirrored in the **interior**. Part cathedral and part pagoda, it draws together a potpourri of icons and elements under a vaulted ceiling, and daubs them all with the primary colours of a Hindu temple, to create Norman Lewis's vision of "fun-fair architecture in extreme form … one expected continually to hear bellowing laughter relayed from some nearby Tunnel of Love". Men enter the cathedral through an entrance in the right wall, women by a door to the left, and all must take off their shoes. Inside the lobby, a **mural** shows the three "signatories of the 3rd Alliance between God and Mankind": French poet Victor Hugo and the fifteenth-century Vietnamese poet, Nguyen Binh Khiem, are writing the Cao Dai principles of "God and humanity, love and justice" in French and Chinese onto a shining celestial tablet. Beside them, the Chinese nationalist leader Sun Yat Sen holds an inkstone, a symbol of "Chinese civilization allied to Christian civilization giving birth to Cao Daist doctrine", according to a nearby sign.

Tourists are welcome to wander through the **nave** of the cathedral, as long as they remain in the aisles, and don't stray between the rows of **pink pillars**, entwined by green dragons, that march up the chamber. Cut-away windows punctuate the outer walls, their grillework consisting of the Cao Daist Divine Eye, surrounded by bright pink lotus blooms. Walk up the shallow steps that lend the nave its litheness, and you'll reach an **altar** that groans under the weight of assorted vases, fruit, paintings and slender statues of storks. The **papal chair** stands at the head of the chamber, its arms carved into dragons. Below it are six more chairs, three with eagle arms, and three with lion arms, for the cardinals. Dominating the chamber, though, and guarded by eight scary silver dragons, a vast, duck-egg-blue **sphere**, speckled with stars, rests on a polished, eight-sided dais. The ubiquitous Divine Eye peers through clouds painted on the front. You'll see more spangly stars and fluffy clouds if you look up at the sky-blue **ceiling**, in whose mouldings of lions and turtles swallows have nested.

Services

Services are held daily at 6am, noon, 6pm and midnight. Tours usually arrange their visit to coincide with the midday one. Though other times are inconvenient, they do offer the opportunity to concentrate on what's happening without the accompanying roadshow of hundreds of clicking and flashing cameras. Visitors are shepherded past the traditional **band** that plays behind the front balcony, and on into the gods, from where they can look down on proceedings and take photographs. Most worshippers dress in white robes, though some dress in yellow, blue and red, to signify the Buddhist, Taoist and Confucian elements of Cao Daism. Priests don square hats emblazoned with the Divine Eye. At the start of a service, worshippers' heads nod, like a field of corn in the breeze, in time to the clanging of a gong. Then a haunting, measured chanting begins, against the insect whine of the string band playing its own time. As prayers and hymns continue, incense, flowers, alcohol and tea are offered up to the Supreme Being.

Travel details

Trains

Ho Chi Minh City to: Da Nang (4 daily; 16–19hr); Dieu Tri (4 daily; 11–13hr); Hanoi (5 daily; 30–41hr); Hué (4 daily; 21–23hr); Muong Man (3 daily; 4–5hr); Nam Dinh (3 daily; 36–39hr); Nha Trang (5 daily; 9–10hr); Ninh Binh (3 daily; 38–40hr); Quang Ngai (3 daily; 13–16hr); Thap Cham (3 daily; 7–9hr); Vinh (4 daily; 33–35hr).

Hydrofoils

Ho Chi Minh City to: Vung Tau (Mon–Fri 6 daily, Sat & Sun 7 daily; 1hr 15min).

Flights

Ho Chi Minh City to: Buon Ma Thuot (5 weekly; 55min); Da Lat (1 daily; 50min); Da Nang (2–3 daily; 1hr 10min); Haiphong (5 weekly; 2hr); Hanoi (6–8 daily; 2hr); Hué (1–2 daily; 1hr 40min); Nha Trang (2–3 daily; 1hr 10min); Phu Quoc (6 weekly; 1hr); Plei Ku (3 weekly; 1hr 15min); Qui Nhon (4 weekly; 1hr 10min).

Buses

It's almost impossible to give the frequency with which buses run, and long-distance public buses, although scheduled, won't depart if empty. Moreover, private services, often minibuses or pick-ups, ply more popular routes such as the one to Vung Tau, and depart only when they have enough passengers to make the journey worthwhile. It's advisable to start your journey early – most long-distance departures leave between 5am and 9am, and few run after midday. Journey times can also vary. Figures below show the normal length of time you can expect the journey to take.

Ho Chi Minh City to: Buon Ma Thuot (7hr); Ca Mau (8hr 30min); Can Tho (4hr); Chau Doc (6hr); Da Lat (7hr); Da Nang (21hr); Hanoi (41hr); Ha Tien (9hr); Hué (25hr); My Tho (1hr 50min); Nha Trang (10hr); Phan Thiet (4hr); Qui Nhon (13hr); Vung Tau (2hr).

The Mekong Delta

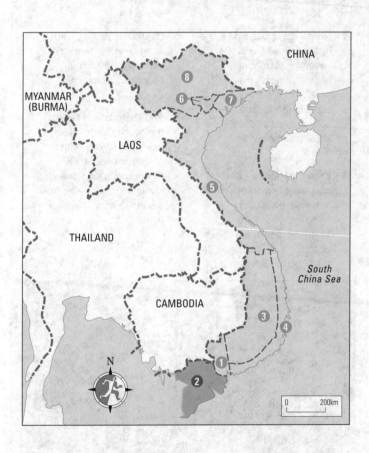

CHAPTER 2 # Highlights

∗ **Boat trips** Travel along narrow canals, visiting floating markets and fruit orchards. One of the best places to explore is around Vinh Long. See p.150

∗ **Home-stays** Staying in rural communities is becoming increasingly popular, offering the chance to observe daily aspects of Vietnamese culture, and to get to know your hosts. See p.151

∗ **Khmer pagodas** Often painted in bright colours, these are particularly common around Tra Vinh. The monks are often keen to practise their English. See p.152

∗ **Bird sanctuaries** Flocks of migrating cranes and other birds can be observed in the appropriate season at Tam Nong near Cao Lanh. See p.146

∗ **Chau Doc** Visit a Cham village and fish farms on the river, and explore nearby Sam Mountain. See p.168

∗ **Phu Quoc Island** One of the country's hottest new destinations, with gorgeous beaches, a mountainous interior and diving and snorkelling around its coastline. See p.183

2

The Mekong Delta

Touring the orchards, paddy fields and swamplands of the **Mekong Delta**, you could be forgiven for thinking you've stepped into the pages of a geography textbook. A comma-shaped flatland stretching from Ho Chi Minh's city limits southwest to the Gulf of Thailand, the delta is Vietnam's **rice bowl**, an agricultural miracle that pumps out 38 percent of the country's annual food crop from just ten percent of its total land mass. Rice may be the delta's staple crop, but coconut palms, fruit orchards and sugar-cane groves also thrive in its nutrient-rich soil, and the sight of conical-hatted farmers tending their land is one of Vietnam's most enduring images. To the Vietnamese, the region is known as *Cuu Long*, "Nine Dragons", a reference to the nine tributaries of the **Mekong River** which dovetail across plains fashioned by millennia of flood-borne alluvial sediment. By the time it reaches Vietnam, the Mekong has already covered more than four thousand kilometres from its source high on the Tibetan Plateau; en route it traverses southern China, skirts Burma (Myanmar), then hugs the Laos–Thailand border before cutting down through Cambodia and into Vietnam – a journey that ranks it as Asia's third-longest river, after the Yangtse and Yellow rivers. **Flooding** has always blighted the delta; ever since Indian traders imported their advanced methods of irrigation more than eighteen centuries ago, networks of canals have been used to channel the excess water, but the rainy season still claims lives from time to time.

Surprisingly, agriculture gripped the delta only relatively recently. Under **Cambodian** sway until the close of the seventeenth century, the region was sparsely inhabited by the *Khmer krom*, or "downstream Khmers", whose settlements were framed by swathes of marshland. The eighteenth century saw the Viet **Nguyen** lords steadily broaden their sphere of influence to encompass the delta, though by the 1860s **France** had taken over the reins of government. Sensing the huge profits to be gleaned from such fertile land, French *colons* spurred Vietnamese peasants to tame and till tracts of the boggy delta; the peasants, realizing their colonial governors would pay well for rice harvests, were quick to comply. Ironically, the same landscape that had served the French so well also provided valuable cover for the Viet Minh resistance fighters who sought to overthrow them; later it did the same for the Viet Cong, who had well-hidden cells here – inciting the Americans to strafe the area with bombs and defoliants.

One of the most attractive aspects of the Mekong Delta is its **diversity**. Some visitors would single out its sweeping panoramas of paddy, fruit orchards and Khmer pagodas, others the friendliness of its people, but for most it's the delta's skein of waterways, canals and tributaries that makes the region so special. It's difficult to overstate the influence of the river: the lifeblood of the rice and fruit crops grown here, it's also a crucial means of transportation, teeming with craft

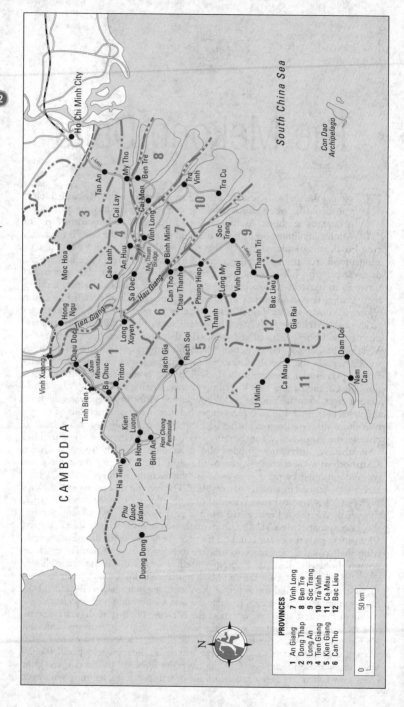

PROVINCES
1 An Giang
2 Dong Thap
3 Long An
4 Tien Giang
5 Kien Giang
6 Can Tho
7 Vinh Long
8 Ben Tre
9 Soc Trang
10 Tra Vinh
11 Ca Mau
12 Bac Lieu

0   50 km

that range in size from delicate rowing boats to hulking sampans, and it forms a backdrop to everyday activities – some of the region's biggest markets are waterborne. One of the most enjoyable ways to experience riverine life is on a **boat trip**, and trips are organized at My Tho, Vinh Long, Can Tho and Chau Doc. Since they all follow a similar itinerary (a visit to a floating market and stops at cottage industries on the shore), you'll probably want to choose just one. Though Can Tho is most popular for its good range of hotels and restaurants, you're likely to see more tourists than locals in the nearby floating markets. A good alternative is Vinh Long, from where boats head out in many different directions through the canals of An Binh Island to the floating market at Cai Be.

There are over a dozen towns in the delta with facilities for tourists, though some are rarely visited as they are not on the way to anywhere. **My Tho** has traditionally been a first stop, and with good reason: near enough to Ho Chi Minh to be seen on a day-trip, the town affords an appetizing glimpse of the delta's northernmost tributary, the Tien Giang, and is well geared up for boat trips. From My Tho, laidback **Ben Tre** and the bounteous fruit orchards besieging it are only a hop and a skip away. **Cao Lanh** is strictly for bird enthusiasts, but **Sa Dec**, with its timeless river scenes and riotously colourful flower

Getting around the delta

Most visitors hurtle around on a **tour bus** out of Ho Chi Minh City, denying themselves the chance to sink into the languid life of the delta. With time in hand, it's far more satisfying to take **local transport** – not nearly as daunting a prospect as it is up the coast, since the number of settlements with hotels means journeys can be kept relatively short. Buses have to stop occasionally at the **ferries** that make road travel in the delta possible, though construction of some long-awaited bridges is speeding up travel times. The enforced halts at the ferries are at least enlivened by strolling hawkers. Locals do some of their travelling on the **passenger and cargo boats** that crawl around the delta's waterways, and some tourists have a wild time doing likewise. However, these vessels tend to be poorly maintained, and there have also been reports of travellers agreeing on a price, only to get ripped off out on the water. For the determined, we've mentioned a few of the more accessible stopping points in this chapter, though remember that these boats run to the sketchiest of schedules.

Travelling by road, you'll encounter a complicated mesh of roads and ferry crossings as you progress through the delta. From Ho Chi Minh City, **Highway 1** bears southwest towards My Tho, from where a ferry crosses the uppermost strand of the **Tien Giang** to Ben Tre. An enormous bridge currently under construction to the west of My Tho will bring big changes to the region, but for now probing deeper into the delta from Ben Tre means hacking cross-country, so it's easier to return, via My Tho, to the highway, which pushes on west. Most tourists cross the Tien Giang via the impressive **My Thuan Bridge**. This is convenient for visting Sa Dec, Vinh Long or Tra Vinh, though there's also a small ferry at **Cao Lanh**, if you want to make a beeline for Long Xuyen and on towards the Cambodian border.

Another bridge is under construction here, which, when it's completed, will make the journey to Can Tho a little easier. At **Can Tho**, Highway 1 runs south to the remote mangrove swamps of Ca Mau, from where, until the proposed upgrade of road northwards up to Rach Gia is completed, the best way out is to retrace your steps. A second road runs northwest from Can Tho to Long Xuyen, the eastern corner of the square of settlements it forms in the delta's northwestern extremities with Chau Doc, Rach Gia and Ha Tien. From Chau Doc there are two ways to reach the delta's northwestern coastline: Ha Tien is accessible by boat or road along the border-hugging **Vinh Te Canal**, though most people backtrack through Long Xuyen and then forge across to Rach Gia.

markets, has a more universal appeal, while just down the road, **Vinh Long** is another jumping-off point for boat trips.

Most visitors spend a day or two in **Can Tho**, taking advantage of its decent hotels and restaurants to recharge batteries, before venturing out to the fascinating **floating markets** nearby. From Can Tho, there's something to be said for dropping down to the foot of the delta, where the swampland that surrounds **Ca Mau** can be explored by boat. Pulling up, en route, at the Khmer stronghold of **Soc Trang** is especially rewarding if your trip coincides with the colourful Ghe Ngo Festival, during which the local Khmer community takes to the river to stage spectacular longboat races. Northwest of Can Tho meanwhile, and a stone's throw from the Cambodian border, is **Chau Doc**, an ebullient town below which **Sam Mountain** provides a welcome undulation to the surrounding plains. The recent opening of the border here has opened up the possibility of travelling on to **Phnom Penh** by boat, which has quickly become a popular route. A bustling fishing port due south of Chau Doc on the Gulf of Thailand, **Rach Gia** is the place to catch a boat to remote **Phu Quoc Island**, whose splendid beaches are a big draw for tourists. North of Rach Gia, **Ha Tien**, a delightful border town surrounded by Khmer villages, represents the end of the line – though before you get up this far you might want to investigate the beach at **Hon Chong**, accessed via a pagoda hewn into a rockface.

Given its seasonal flooding, **the best time to visit** the delta is, predictably enough, in the dry season, which runs from December to May.

My Tho and around

Southwest of Ho Chi Minh City, buses plying Highway 1 soon emerge from the city's unkempt urban sprawl and into the pastoral surrounds of the Mekong Delta's upper plains. The delta is too modest to flaunt its full beauty so soon, but rice fields stretching beyond the scruffy settlements draped along the highway hint at things to come, their burnished golds and brilliant greens broken only by the occasional white ancestral grave. Seventy kilometres out of Ho Chi Minh City, a left fork marks the turning to **MY THO**, an amiable market town that nestles on the north bank of the Mekong River's northernmost strand, the Tien Giang, or Upper River. My Tho's proximity to Ho Chi Minh City means that it soaks up much of the volume of tourism headed for the delta, resulting in a central jumble of hotels, restaurants and cafés that won't be to everyone's taste. Nevertheless, the town comes as a great relief after the onslaught of Ho Chi Minh City, its uncrowded boulevards belying a population of around 200,000, and you can easily escape the central melee by hopping onto a boat.

My Tho's recent influx of visitors seems appropriate, given its **history**. Chinese immigrants fleeing Formosa (modern-day Taiwan) after the collapse of the Ming dynasty established the town in the late seventeenth century, along with a Vietnamese population keen to make inroads into this traditionally Khmer-dominated region. Two centuries later the French, wooed by the district's abundant rice and fruit crops, rated it highly enough to post a garrison here, and to lay a (now-defunct) rail line to Saigon; while the American War saw a consistent military presence in town. Today My Tho's commercial importance is as pronounced as ever, something a walk through the busy town market amply illustrates.

Moving on from My Tho

Bus departures are from Tien Giang station (see below); there are numerous express buses to and from Ho Chi Minh City plying the route. **Ferries** for Ben Tre depart from the Ben Tre Ferry Terminal (see below). A three-kilometre-long bridge is currently under construction to the west of My Tho, which will render this ferry obsolete when complete. **Cargo/passenger boats** heading deeper into the delta use the jetty below Vong Nho Market, 200m west of the foot of Tran Hung Dao. There are daily departures around noon to Vinh Long (3hr) and Chau Doc (17hr), though it's best to enquire at the jetty beforehand as prices and departure times tend to change.

Arrival, information and accommodation

Buses terminate at Tien Giang station, 3km northwest of town, from where cyclos shuttle into the centre. **Ferries** from Ben Tre arrive at the Ben Tre Ferry Terminal, about a kilometre west of My Tho's centre.

Cyclos are in plentiful supply around town, and a gaggle of Honda oms await custom at the junction of Trung Trac and Thu Khoa Huan, though for more flexibility you may consider renting a bicycle from Tieng Giang Tourist or Ben Tre Tourist along the river, who can also arrange car rental plus driver (see p.142).

Most people planning to take a **boat tour** will have already made arrangements in Ho Chi Minh City, but boat owners are always on the prowl for customers. Some may offer cheap rates but no guarantee that you'll actually enjoy the trip. The two state-run companies (Tien Giang and Ben Tre Tourist, see p.142) are the best organized, but their services don't come cheap.

The State Bank, two blocks north of here at Thu Khoa Huan's western end, is at present the only place in town that will **exchange** travellers' cheques or arrange cash advances for Visa and MasterCard. The Agribank at the opposite end of Thu Khoa Huan on the corner of Le Loi will change dollars for dong. The **post office** is conveniently located opposite the boat jetty on 30 Thang 4, and Internet and email services can be found along Nam Ky Khoi Nghia.

Accommodation

The *Cong Doan* (☎073/874324; ❶–❷), beside the GPO on 30 Thang 4, has spartan but light double rooms, some with river views, which can accommodate up to four people. The *Rang Dong* (☎073/874400; ❶–❷), 300m west along the street, has slightly smarter rooms, all boasting air-conditioning. The murky and grimy *Huong Duong* (☎073/872011; ❶), on a sidestreet off Trung Trac, will appeal only to the most budget-conscious, while its neighbour on Trung Trac, the six-storey *Song Tien* (☎073/872009; ❶–❷), has large, clean rooms behind its unappealing exterior. The impressive *Chuong Duong* (☎073/870875; ❸), opposite the GPO on 30 Thang 4 with prime views of the river, is the town's smartest place to stay; its sparkling rooms all have air-conditioning, hot water and TV, and those upstairs have riverfront balconies. If you're looking for a relaxing spot in the countryside, take the public ferry to Ben Tre and make for the *Thao Nhi Guest House* (see p.144).

The Town

The abiding reason for a trip to My Tho is to explore its surrounding waterways by boat (see p.141), but landlubbers will get a working impression of the majestic Tien Giang by strolling along waterfront **30 Thang 4**. The river's relentless traffic – which ranges from elegant sampans to vast, lumbering junks, unpainted and crude – is best viewed from the small park, at the street's east-

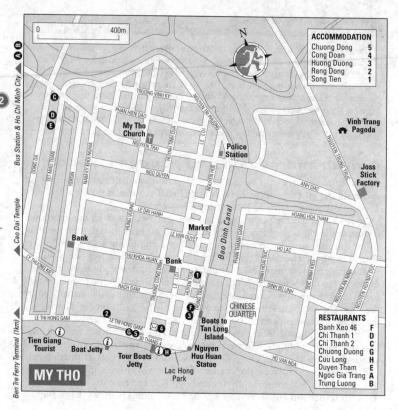

MY THO

ACCOMMODATION

Chuong Dong	5
Cong Doan	4
Huong Duong	3
Rang Dong	2
Song Tien	1

RESTAURANTS

Banh Xeo 46	F
Chi Thanh 1	D
Chi Thanh 2	C
Chuong Duong	G
Cuu Long	H
Duyen Tham	E
Ngoc Gia Trang	A
Trung Luong	B

ern end. Also visible from here is the clot of cheery blue fishing vessels that moor at the mouth of the Bao Dinh Canal, while cargos are humped up and down precariously bowed gangplanks; feline eyes painted on their prows continue an ancient tradition and were originally intended to scare off "river monsters", probably crocodiles. In the evenings, especially at weekends this corner of town is packed as families stroll up and down, interspersed with sellers of balloons, popcorn and even tropical fish. At night, the park's pine trees provide cover for young lovers, while men play shuttlecock football on the street above, under the intent gaze of a statue of nineteenth-century anti-French hero Nguyen Huu Huan, who studied in My Tho.

Follow the direction of the canal up past Trung Trac and you'll soon be gobbled up by My Tho's vast daily **market**, which is at its busiest early in the morning. As well as the usual piles of fruit, cereals and tobacco, several stalls sell ships' chandlery, their heaped fishing nets almost indistinguishable from the fresh noodles on sale nearby. Practising Christians may want to stroll north of the market, to low-key **My Tho Church**, but others needn't bother; shaded by rose apple trees, the church harbours no stained glass and only the simplest of altars.

East of the canal

The most southern of the two bridges spanning the canal deposits you at the start of waterfront Phan Thanh Gian, home to My Tho's modest **Chinese**

Quarter, though there's little to betray its existence other than a feverish sense of commerce. Shopfronts here are piled to the rafters with sugar-cane poles, watermelons and fish awaiting transportation to Ho Chi Minh, as well as half-hatched eggs (containing chick embryos), prized as the perfect complement to a *bia hoi*.

A cyclo journey east of Phan Thanh Gian to Nguyen Trung Truc's attractive **Vinh Trang Pagoda** (daily 7.30am–noon & 2–5pm), with its rajah's palace-style front facade, is a worthwhile side-trip. It was built in 1849, since when it has been renovated three times, most recently in 1990. It's said that VC soldiers hid here in the Sixties, but today it's home only to monks. The entrance, round to the right, leads into the heart of the temple, where a tiny courtyard is flanked by the cubicles where the monks sleep. The main chamber, beyond the miniature mountain to your left, is characterized by dark-wood pillars and tons of gilt woodwork, but of more interest are the eclectic influences at play in the pagoda's decor – classical pillars, Grecian-style mouldings of urns and bowls of fruit, and glazed tiles similar to Portuguese *azulejos*. Outside, the tombs of several monks stand near a pond patrolled by huge elephant-ear fish, while the path outside and to the right of the ornate front gates wends its way through fruit gardens.

On your return to town, it's worth keeping an eye open for the small **joss-stick factory** at the corner of Anh Giac and Nguyen Trung Truc, where sticks are made by rolling splinters of bamboo, first in a composite of scented sawdust and glue, and then in a yellow dye. Sacks of sawdust and bundles of drying sticks outside make the factory easy to spot.

Eating

My Tho's main clutch of **restaurants** is located at the north end of Tet Mau Than in the northwest corner of town, overlooking a park. The *Chi Thanh 1* and *2*, the second of which is around the corner on Nguyen Trai, are probably the best, with well-prepared Vietnamese food drawing nightly crowds. The *Duyen Tham*, just south of the *Chi Thanh 1*, serves ice cream, cake and fresh coconut. Further out to the northwest of town are two large establishments that cater predominantly to tourist groups but welcome independent travellers and have lush garden environments along with a good range of food. The first, the *Ngoc Gia Trang*, is a little further beyond the *Chi Thanh 2* from the town centre, on the north side of Nguyen Trai, while the *Trung Luong* is a couple of kilometres further still, to the right just past the city sign that straddles the road. Unfortunately, most of My Tho's restaurants are a bit far from the hotels on the front, so it's best to take a cyclo. Of the smattering of riverside restaurants along 30 Thang 4, a couple are worth checking out. The *Cuu Long*, opposite the *Cong Doan* hotel, has a passable menu, and the *Chuong Duong* hotel restaurant, which boasts a waterfront terrace, specializes in seafood; the large portions are reasonably priced and it's a great place to catch a Mekong sunset. Round the corner on Trung Trac, the *Banh Xeo 46* serves up tasty shrimp pancakes. If money is tight, you'd do well to make for the daytime **food stalls** at the top end of Nguyen Hue.

Around My Tho: boat trips on the delta

Taking a boat trip on the Mekong is the undoubted highlight of a stay in My Tho, and most people come straight in and out on organized day-trips from Ho Chi Minh City. If you plan to charter a boat by yourself (see p.142), it's important to know first what your priorities are. There are four nearby islands: Tan Long Island, Thoi Son Island, Phung Island and Qui Island. All are regularly

Ong Dao Dua, the Coconut Monk

Ong Dao Dua, the **Coconut Monk**, was born Nguyen Thanh Nam in the Mekong Delta, in 1909. Aged 19, he travelled to France where he studied chemistry until 1935, when he returned home, married and fathered a child. During a lengthy period of meditation at Chau Doc's Sam Mountain (see p.172) he devised a new religion, a fusion of Buddhism and Christianity known as **Tinh Do Cu Si**. By the Sixties, this new sect had established a community on Phung Island, where the monk lorded it over his followers from a throne set into a man-made grotto modelled on Sam Mountain. The monk became as famous for his idiosyncrasies as for his doctrine: his name, for instance, was coined after it was alleged he spent three years meditating and eating nothing but coconuts.

Unfortunately, the Coconut Monk never got to enjoy his "kingdom" for long: his belief in a peaceful reunification of North and South Vietnam (symbolized by the map of the country behind his grotto, on which pillars representing Hanoi and Saigon are joined by a bridge) landed him in the jails of successive South Vietnamese governments, and the communists were no more sympathetic to his beliefs after 1975. Ong Dao Dua died in 1990.

visited by boats, though you'll get more time on the water if you ask to explore the north coastline of Ben Tre Province, or just idle along the river.

The cheapest way of getting onto the water is to travel by public ferry to one of the islands: those to Tan Long leave from opposite the Huong Duong hotel; Thoi Son ferries leave from either Vong Nho or Binh Duc markets; boats to Phung Island use the Ben Tre Ferry Terminal, so you first need to take a public ferry from My Tho across to Ben Tre.

For a full-on tropical river experience, though, you'll want to **charter a boat** with a guide. Two state-run companies offer such boat trips to the islands: Tien Giang Tourist Company has three offices along 30 Thang 4, with their main branch located next to the Tourist Jetty at no.8 (☎073/873184, ⓔdulichtg@bdvn.vnn.net); Ben Tre Tourist Company is at 4/1 Le Thi Hong Gam (☎073/879103, ⓔmekongtourbentre@hcm.vnn.vn). Both charge $20–50 depending on how long you want to hire for. Touts plying for trade along Trung Trac and 30 Thang 4 undercut their prices substantially, and $10 should get you a three-hour trip in a privately owned boat – time enough to explore the waterways along the coast of Ben Tre Province, and to land on an island in the river. However, bear in mind that these unofficial boat owners are not insured and that communication is likely to be a problem. Local police intermittently crack down on them, so if you're planning to hire one, ask about the situation in Ho Chi Minh before you set out.

The islands

Beyond its chaotic shoreline of stilthouses and boatyards, **Tan Long** ("Dragon Island") boasts bounteous sapodilla, coconut and banana plantations, as well as highly regarded longan orchards. The white glare you'll see as you approach is the reflection of sun-bleached seashells spread to bolster the shoreline. **Thoi Son** ("Unicorn Island") is the largest of the four islands and most of the organized tours out of Ho Chi Minh stop here for lunch and fruit sampling. Slender canals, their banks shaded by water palms, allow boats to weave through its interior. Both these islands lie within Tien Giang Province, so are the domain of the Tien Giang Tourist Company.

The two other, smaller islands lie in Ben Tre Province and are served by the Ben Tre Tourist Company. **Qui** ("Turtle") **Island** is the newest of the group, having been formed by sediment in the river, then stabilized by planting mangroves, and is overflowing with longans, dragon fruit, mango, papaya, pineapple and jackfruit. A small, family-run coconut candy factory is located just opposite on the Ben Tre coastline. Here you can watch the coconut being pressed, and the extracted juice being mixed with sugar and heated, then dried and cut into bite-size pieces. **Phung** ("Phoenix") **Island** is famed as the home of an offbeat religious sect set up three decades ago by the eccentric **Coconut Monk**, Ong Dao Dua (see box on p.142), although there's not much left to see from his era, and only the skeleton of the open-air **complex** he established remains. Among its mesh of rusting staircases and platforms, you'll spot the rocket-shaped elevator the monk had built to whisk him up to his private meditation platform. Elsewhere are nine dragon-entwined pillars, said to symbolize the Mekong's nine tributaries and betraying a Cao Daist influence. The Coconut Monk's story is told (in Vietnamese) on a magnificent **urn** which he is said to have crafted himself out of shards of porcelain from France, Japan and China. Beyond the urn stretch acres of **orchards**, whose fruits can be sampled at the several cafés dotted around the island – as can the acrid sticky-rice wine brewed locally. The tourist companies are now able to arrange home-stays on these islands for around $15 a night.

The Ben Tre coastline

For more of an adventure, push on to the coastline of **Ben Tre Province**, south of My Tho (see below for more on this area), whose labyrinthine creeks afford marvellous scope for exploring. Gliding along these slender waterways, overhung by handsome water-palm fronds which interlock to form a cathedral-like roof, it's easy to feel you're charting new territory. Swooping, electric-blue kingfishers and sumptuously coloured butterflies add to the romance. Boatmen usually incorporate stops at apiaries, rice wine and sugar-processing workshops into your trip. If the laidback feel of this side of the river appeals, you might want to spend some time at the *Thao Nhi Guest House* (see overleaf), located near the Ben Tre Ferry Terminal, where they can arrange cheap boat trips to watch a sunrise or sunset over the Mekong River.

South of My Tho: Ben Tre and around

The few travellers who push on beyond My Tho into riverlocked **Ben Tre Province** are rewarded with some of the Mekong Delta's most breathtaking scenery. Famed for its fruit orchards and coconut groves (Vietnamese call it the "coconut island"), the province has proved just as fertile a breeding ground for revolutionaries, first plotting against the French, and later against the Americans, and was one of the areas seized by the Viet Cong during the Tet Offensive of 1968. Of the US bombing campaign on the provincial capital of **BEN TRE**, a US major was quoted as saying, "It became necessary to destroy the town in order to save it." Today, Ben Tre is a pleasant and industrious town displaying none of the wounds of its past, and is a world away from the tourist menus and boat-trip touts of nearby My Tho. Though rather short on sights, it's still a relaxing and friendly place to hole up for a couple of days, and a springboard for exploring the surrounding districts.

Once you've scanned the buzzing **town market**, you'll want to pass over the quaint bridge leading to the Ben Tre River's more rustic south bank, where scores of cross-eyed boats moor in front of a jumble of thatch houses. With a

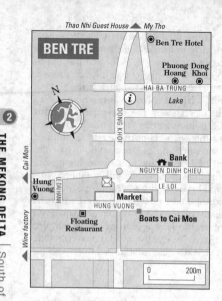

Thao Nhi Guest House ▲ My Tho

BEN TRE

Ben Tre Hotel

Phuong Dong
Hoang Khoi

HAI BA TRUNG

Lake

Bank

NGUYEN DINH CHIEU

LE LOI

Hung
Vuong

Market

HUNG VUONG

Floating
Restaurant

Boats to Cai Mon

0   200m

▲ Cai Mon

◀ Wine factory

bicycle or motorbike (bring one from My Tho, or ask at your hotel reception), you can explore the maze of dirt tracks on this side of the river. Before striking off, though, duck into the riverside **wine factory**, 450m west of the bridge, where fermenting *ruou trang* (Vietnamese rice wine) fizzes away in vast earthenware jars. A mountain of rice husks indicates the factory's location, though you'll find it easily if you follow your nose.

Practicalities

Ferries from My Tho disgorge their passengers 11km north of Ben Tre, from where you can take the bus that alights from the ferry to town. The ferry crossing is about forty minutes and the bus ride about half an hour. The bus terminates either at the **Phu Khuong bus station**, 2km short of the town centre, or nearer to town by Truc Giang Lake, around Hai Ba Trung. As you run down Dong Khoi to the centre of town, look out for Ben Tre Tourist Company (☎075/829618) on your left, which organizes car rental, bicycles and some tours. The State **Bank** on Nguyen Dinh Chieu can change dollars.

The riverside *Hung Vuong Hotel* (☎075/822408; ❸) has easily the best location of Ben Tre's hotels. Its large, well-equipped rooms all have air-conditioning and TV, and some have bathtubs and river views. The pokier *Ben Tre Hotel* (☎075/825332; ❷–❸) has cheaper rooms, which are clean enough, but it is located a bit far from the river and market, opposite a small park. Another option on Hai Ba Trung is the *Dong Khoi Hotel* (☎075/822240; ❸), which faces a small lake. The rooms here are a bit overpriced and the wailing from the karaoke lounge could be a problem.

The only good budget option is the *Thao Nhi Guest House* (☎075/860009; ❶), set in the grounds of a longan orchard, near the ferry and about 11km from Ben Tre town. There is a range of rooms here, including small ones with fan and larger ones with air-conditioning, and the staff are very friendly and helpful. The atmosphere is very relaxing and it's the kind of place to settle in for a few days. To get there, take the first left after leaving the Ben Tre ferry and look for a sign after a few hundred metres pointing down a dirt road to the right. From here it's another 150m.

There's not a great deal of choice for **places to eat** in Ben Tre; if you don't fancy the restaurants at the *Hung Vuong* or *Dong Khoi* hotels, the hulking boat that holds the *Ben Tre Floating Restaurant* has seen better days, but remains a fine venue for a sunset drink or dinner; main courses cost around $2. Failing that, there are plenty of **food stalls** around the market. The *Thao Nhi Guest House* also has a good menu that features elephant-ear fish and huge prawns, and the hammocks slung in the shade tempt diners (including non-guests) to linger for a siesta.

It's not unprecedented for travellers with their own transport to brave the knot of dirt tracks west of the town, and find their way to Vinh Long (see p.147), but it is currently possible only by motorbike; by far the easiest means of **moving on** is to backtrack to My Tho.

Cai Mon and Ba Vat

Honda oms congregate outside the GPO in the centre of Ben Tre, and for a few dollars they'll whisk you off on a three-hour round trip to the celebrated fruit orchards of **CAI MON**, to the southwest. Ten minutes' ride west of town a modest river is negotiated by the **Ham Luong Ferry**, after which a further five minutes reveals a right turn onto a red dirt track. Now the countryside unfurls grandly – waxy green paddy fields stretch away to the horizon, tufted with "islands" of coconut trees, while along the road stand groves of bamboo, eucalyptus, and the grassy mop-tops of sugar-cane plants.

Twenty minutes beyond the ferry station, you'll reach the village of **BA VAT**, enveloped in the intoxicating aroma of coconuts being processed. Fringing this small town is a narrow river shaded by bowed water palms. Twenty-five minutes and a succession of rickety bridges later, the road reaches Cai Mon, a sleepy community whose extremely friendly residents make a living by cultivating fruit.

Hasten across the steep bridge ahead of you to the far bank of the tiny river threading the town, and you'll confront a vast plain of bounteous **orchards**, veined by kilometre after kilometre of narrow, duck-patrolled canals, and maze-like paths, along which kids run with homemade paper kites. March to May is high season for the huge variety of tropical fruits grown here, but whenever you go you're guaranteed a lush vista. As you walk, you'll likely be invited by local farmers into their thatched huts to sample their produce.

West and north of My Tho

The hour-long bus journey along Highway 1 from My Tho to the **My Thuan Bridge** across to **Vinh Long** is a sporadically beautiful one that takes in expanses of longan orchards and picturesque river-hugging settlements. From one of these, **CAI LAY**, a minor track strikes northwards, skirting the eastern edge of **Dong Thap Muoi**, or the **Plain of Reeds** (for more on which see "Cao Lanh and around", overleaf). Today, the cajeput trees and waist-high grasses carpeting this large tract of marshland are home only to storks, cranes and herons, but formerly they harboured cells of guerrillas fighting successively against France and America – the latter despite US bombing sorties out of nearby **MOC HOA**.

It was in the rice fields northeast of Cai Lay that the **Battle of Ap Bac** was fought in January 1963. A heavily outnumbered group of 350 Viet Cong soldiers registered a victory over the forces of the South Vietnamese Army (ARVN), at least 150 of whom were left either wounded or dead. Ill-led and badly organized, ARVN troops even fired on each other at one stage, while the communist guerrillas were able to down five helicopters with only the most rudimentary weapons. Before this, it had been assumed that South Vietnam could fight its own battles; the debacle at Ap Bac was instrumental in persuading US military observers that heightened American involvement was necessary in order to stamp out the communist threat.

A turning to the northwest 4km before the bridge leads to Cao Lanh (see below), from where it's possible to connect with Long Xuyen and beyond. The more usual route, though, is to cross the impressive bridge across the river, after which you can head west to the charismatic town of Sa Dec (p.155), or east to Vinh Long (p.147) and Tra Vinh (p.152).

Cao Lanh and around

Highway 30 peels off north from Highway 1 at An Huu, rolling into modest **CAO LANH** 34km later. The town is no oil painting, and offers little unless you're charmed by **wading birds**; its location beside the western edge of the **Plain of Reeds** makes Cao Lanh an ideal launching pad for trips out to the herons and cranes that nest in the nearby swamplands. Coming from Ho Chi Minh, you'll pass the two great concrete tusks (intended to resemble lotus petals) of the **war memorial** as you veer onto the main drag, Nguyen Hue. One tusk bears a hammer and sickle, the other a Vietnamese red star. Way across on the southwestern outskirts of town, another concrete edifice, shaped like an open clam, marks the burial place of Ho Chi Minh's father, **Nguyen Sinh Sac**.

And that's about it, unless you're here for the birds. Of the 130 species nesting 45km northwest of Cao Lanh at the **Tam Nong Bird Sanctuary**, it's the cranes, with their distinctive red heads, that most visitors come to see. In flight above the marshland of the sanctuary, the slender grey birds reveal spectacular black-tipped wings. Cranes feed not from the water but from the land, so when the spate season (Aug–Nov) waterlogs the delta, they migrate to Cambodia. You can learn more about them and the terrain they favour at the sanctuary's Center for Environment Education and Crane Protection. To get the best view of the birds themselves, plan to be around either at dawn when they fly off in search of food, or at dusk when they return to roost. It's possible to reach Tam Nong by Honda om, though a boat trip (around $50 per boat) arranged through the tourist office is more of a special experience.

You'll also need to approach the tourist office if you want to take a trip out to the **Xeo Quit Tourist Jungle**, deep in the cajeput forest 20km southeast of Cao Lanh. The district's dense cover provided the perfect bolt hole for Viet Cong guerrillas during the American War, and from 1960 to 1975 the struggle

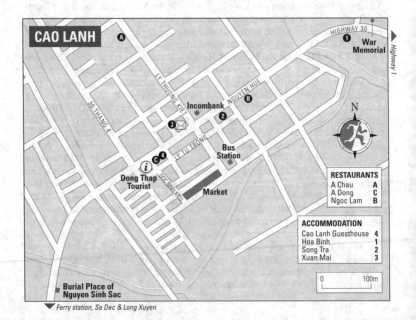

▼ Ferry station, Sa Dec & Long Xuyen

against America and the ARVN was masterminded from here. The boggy nature of the terrain made a tunnel system similar to Cu Chi's (see p.127) unfeasible, so they made do with six submerged metal chambers sealed with tar and resin. Suspecting the base's existence, Americans bombed the area regularly, and even broadcast propaganda from the air to demoralize its occupants; but by developing a policy of "going without trace, cooking without smoke, speaking without noise", the cadres residing here escaped discovery throughout the war. The **boat trip** ($20–30 per boat) from Long Hiep bridge to Xeo Quit is a charming glide along eucalyptus-shaded canals teeming with freshwater fish and shrimps. Xeo Quit is often combined with a trip up to **Vuon Co Thap Muoi**, a bird garden 44km northeast of Cao Lanh whose bamboo and eucalyptus groves harbour herons, white storks and black ibises. Tens of thousands of wading birds nest here around hatching season, and at dawn you'll see them taking to the sky in their thousands to search for food. Prices for the combined trip are around the $50–60 mark per boat.

Practicalities

Buses to and from Cao Lanh halt at the bus station, a few paces below the town centre; express buses from Ho Chi Minh City will drop you just north of the war memorial as they continue along Highway 1. From Long Xuyen or beyond, buses cross the Tien Giang via the Cao Lanh ferry, around 4km southwest of town, necessitating a short Honda ride to the town centre. The Incombank on Ly Thuong Kiet **exchanges** dollars and travellers' cheques. Dong Thap Tourist, whose office (☎067/855637, ✉dothatour@hcm.vnn.vn) is at 2 Doc Binh Kieu, just off the main road, Nguyen Hue, is in its infancy when it comes to providing **tourist information**, so you may find this a wasted journey; tour programmes are available for the surrounding area (see p.146), but you may be better off arranging these at one of the tour agents in Ho Chi Minh City.

The tourist board-accredited *Song Tra* (☎067/852504; ❸) is Cao Lanh's poshest **place to stay**, a smart building with thirty or so rooms, all equipped with air-conditioning, hot water and satellite TV. Alternatively, there are cheery doubles with similar facilities at the *Hoa Binh* or *"Peace" Hotel* (☎067/851218; ❸) – symbolically situated across from the war memorial, east of the town centre on Highway 30. Another option is the *Xuan Mai* (☎067/852852; ❸), just west of the post office at 2 Le Quy Don, where the larger rooms have bathtubs and breakfast is included in the price, although the place is rather dingy. Budget travellers will have to make do with the *Cao Lanh Guest House* (☎067/851061; ❶), at 72 Nguyen Hue, where you might spot the odd cockroach scuttling about but otherwise its basic rooms are just about acceptable.

As for **eating**, the in-house restaurant at the *Song Tra* is a rather uncharismatic affair but there are a couple of decent places along Nguyen Hue: the *A Dong*, a tidy *com* shop offering cheap and cheerful meals served over rice as well as fried eggs for breakfast; and the *Ngoc Lam*, just east of the *Song Tra* hotel, which is very popular with locals. The *A Chau*, at 105b Ly Thuong Kiet, also has a good range of dishes such as chicken fried rice for around $1.

Vinh Long

Ringed by water and besieged by boats and tumbledown stilthouses, the island that forms the heart of **VINH LONG** has the feel of a medieval fortress. However, if you find yourself yearning for a peaceful backwater, first impressions

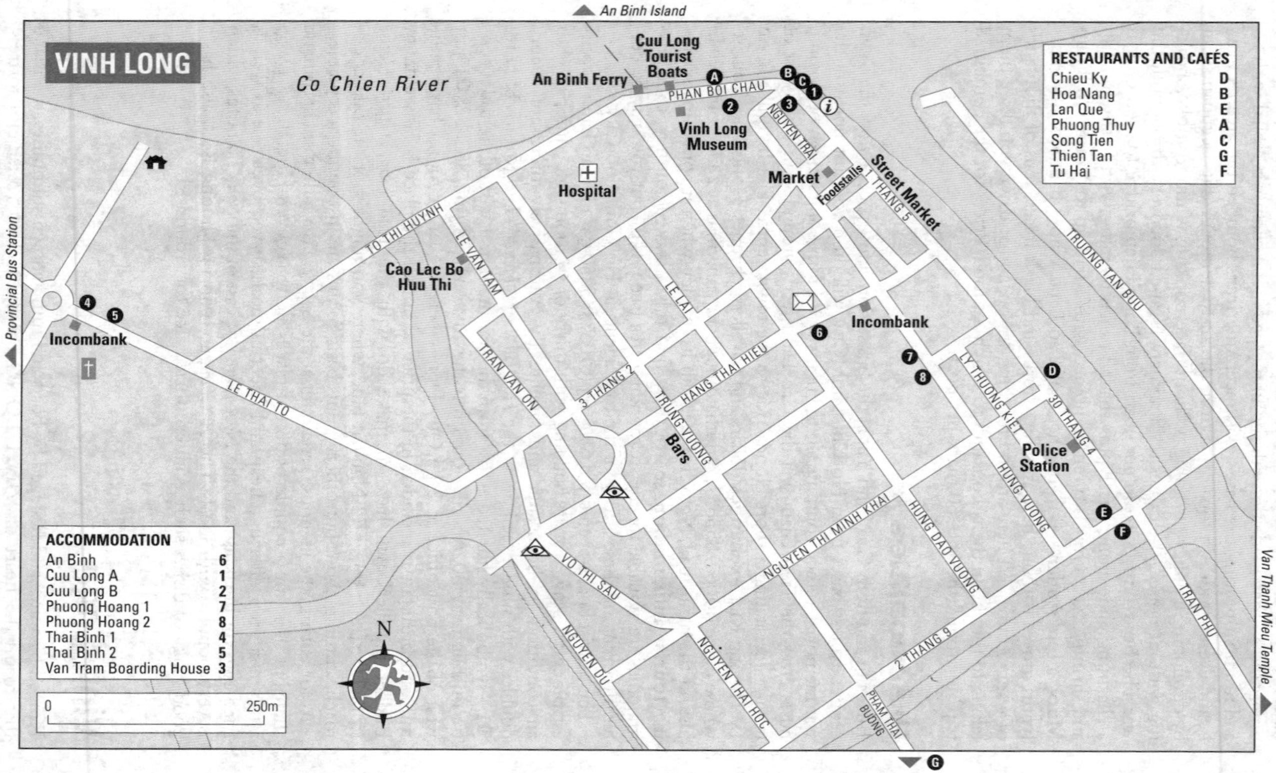

VINH LONG
Co Chien River
An Binh Island
An Binh Ferry
Cuu Long Tourist Boats
Phan Boi Chau
Vinh Long Museum
Nguyen Trai
Market
Foodstalls
Street Market
1 Thang 5
Hospital
To Thi Huynh
Le Van Tam
Cao Lac Bo Huu Thi
Le Lai
Incombank
Provincial Bus Station
Le Thai To
Tran Van On
3 Thang 2
Hang Thai Hieu
Trung Vuong
Bars
Ly Thuong Kiet
30 Thang 4
Police Station
Hung Vuong
Truong Tan Buu
Tran Phu
Hung Dao Vuong
Nguyen Thi Minh Khai
Vo Thi Sau
Nguyen Du
Nguyen Thai Hoc
2 Thang 9
Pham Thai Buong
Van Thanh Mieu Temple
G
N
0
250m
RESTAURANTS AND CAFÉS
Chieu Ky D
Hoa Nang B
Lan Que E
Phuong Thuy A
Song Tien C
Thien Tan G
Tu Hai F
ACCOMMODATION
An Binh 6
Cuu Long A 1
Cuu Long B 2
Phuong Hoang 1 7
Phuong Hoang 2 8
Thai Binh 1 4
Thai Binh 2 5
Van Tram Boarding House 3

will be a let-down; central Vinh Long is hectic and noisy, its streets a blur of buses and motorbikes. Make for the waterfront, though, and it's a different story. Here, hotels, restaurants and cafés conjure a riviera atmosphere far quainter and more genuine than My Tho's. From here you can watch the **Co Chien River** roll by, dotted with sampans, houseboats, and the odd raft of river-weed.

Arrival, information and accommodation

Long-distance **buses** pull into the provincial bus station, a couple of kilometres southwest of town on Nguyen Hue; from here take a xe om into the centre of town. If you're coming from Can Tho, buses can drop you off at the three-way roundabout at the northern end of Nguyen Hue, about 800m west of the centre, as they pass through here en route. Buses from Sa Dec and Long Xuyen bypass Vinh Long completely, crossing over the My Thuan Bridge, 7km west of Vinh Long, so you'll need to arrange with your driver a convenient point where xe oms can take you into town. If you've battled across from Ben Tre, you'll need to take a **ferry** from An Binh Island (see p.150), which will drop you either at the main jetty in town or at another 3km east of central Vinh Long.

Cuu Long Tourist at the top of 1 Thang 5 will arrange leisurely **boat trips** on the Co Chien River – though at a price. You might consider speaking to the unofficial boat-owners who approach you along the waterfront, even though they're not supposed to take tourists; their boats usually set off from the back of the market on 1 Thang 5. Incombank, at the three-way roundabout west of town, **exchanges** travellers' cheques and can arrange cash advances for Visa and MasterCard, though for straight US currency transactions its Hoang Thai Hieu branch is more central. If you're heading for Tra Vinh, note that you can't change travellers' cheques there.

The **post office** is located in the middle of town on Hoang Thai Hieu, and **Internet access** is available at the *Cuu Long 'B' Hotel*, or more cheaply just north of the *Phuong Hoang* hotels on Hung Vuong.

Accommodation

Most of Vinh Long's **accommodation** options are along 1 Thang 5. Where boat trips operate in the Mekong Delta, notably around Vinh Long, the local tourist board can also arrange for visitors to stay with the owners of fruit orchards, allowing a close-up view of rural life. The cost is in the region of $12–15 per night, including meals.

An Binh 3 Hoang Thai Hieu ☎070/823190. Situated away from the river, with a range of rather gloomy overpriced quarters, some at the back suffering from karaoke fallout. ❷

Cuu Long 'A' ☎070/822494. This ageing edifice offers great views of the river, and has air-con, satellite TV and the like, but its grimy rooms are uninspiring. ❷–❸

Cuu Long 'B' ☎070/823656. Much newer and better maintained than its older sister, with higher prices to match. Some rooms have fine views of the Vinh Long riviera and all include satellite TV, air-con, hot water and breakfast. ❹

Phuong Hoang 1 and **Phuong Hoang 2** 2 Hung Vuong ☎070/825185. This pair of mini-hotels represents some of the best value in town. Each has a dozen or so rooms with varying sizes and facilities, all with chintzy furnishings, and the staff are very friendly. ❶–❸

Thai Binh I and **Thai Binh II** Le Thai To ☎070/827161. Located out near the bus station, and street noise could be a problem here, but they are the cheapest rooms in town. ❶

Van Tram Boarding House 4, 1 Thang 5 ☎070/823820. Just five rooms here, but all are a good size and well equipped with TV, fridge and hot water, and a choice of air-con or fan. Add in its prime location and cheap prices, and the result is great value. ❶

The Town

The main reason for a trip to Vinh Long is to get a taste of river life in the delta – other than An Binh Island (see below), Vinh Long isn't spoilt for attractions. The doors and shutters of **Vinh Long Museum**, facing the waterfront, were padlocked long ago, but war enthusiasts can still amble past the tank, flame-thrower, helicopter, planes and artillery left to rust under the unsightly plastic hangar in its open gardens. From here, you might walk west along colourful To Thi Huynh. There's a cache of impressive French colonial buildings on this side of town, none more eye-catching than Le Van Tam's **Cau Lac Bo Huu Thi**. Scanning this oddly shaped mansion, with its red-tiled roof and shuttered windows topped by mouldings of garlands, it's easy to picture the ghosts of French *colons* and rice merchants in your mind's eye.

Thereafter, you'll have to journey 2km down the bumpy road that runs parallel to the Rach Long Canal and southeast of town, to the **Van Thanh Mieu Temple**, in search of diversion. If you wander into the tiny lanes that back onto the river along the way, you can watch tiles and coffins being made in the simplest of surroundings, and you might even be invited to take a tea with the friendly locals. The temple itself is dedicated to Confucius – unusually for southern Vietnam – and a heavily bearded portrait of him watches over proceedings. The splendid blue robes he wears contrast starkly with the mildewed and moth-eaten old canopies above him. Another temple in the compound honours local mandarin Phan Thanh Gian (see box opposite), who is pictured in red robes, flanked by slender storks. Fronting the temple are two cannons that rained fire on the French in 1860. Unfortunately, both temples are usually kept locked.

Boat trips from Vinh Long

A five-minute ferry ride across the Co Chien River from the top of town accesses a patch of the delta's most breathtaking scenery. Known by locals as **AN BINH ISLAND**, in fact it's a jigsaw of bite-sized pockets of land, skeined by a fine web of channels and gullies, eventually merging, to the east, with the province of Ben Tre. This idyllic landscape is criss-crossed by a network of dirt paths, making it ideal for a morning's rambling.

A grove of longan trees a few paces north of the jetty shades sandy, century-old **Tien Chau Pagoda**. Inside its harmonious rear chamber, monks sup tea against the ghoulish backdrop of a mural depicting sinners being variously trampled by horses, trumpeted at by elephants and devoured by snakes in the ten Buddhist hells. One hundred metres east of the jetty, meanwhile, a hellish stink betrays the location of a **fish sauce factory**. Fish too small to be sold off are chopped up at the water's edge, before being fermented in huge barrels to produce *nuoc mam*, or fish sauce. Keep an eye out, too, for the self-satisfied factory cat, which makes a luxurious living foraging for scraps.

Moving on from Vinh Long

Moving on, you'll need to head for the bus station (see p.149), or you can flag down buses bound for Can Tho or Ho Chi Minh City at the three-way roundabout. Alternatively, express minibuses run to Ho Chi Minh City from either 166a Nguyen Hue, near the bus station (☏070/824634) or 15 Pham Hung, just north of the roundabout (☏070/831980); both can arrange hotel pick-ups. If you're heading for My Tho, take a Ho Chi Minh-bound bus and ask the driver to drop you off at the Nga Ba Trung Luong roundabout, a few kilometres out of My Tho.

Phan Thanh Gian

Born in Vinh Long Province in 1796, the mandarin diplomat **Phan Thanh Gian** was destined to be involved in a chain of events that was to shape over a century of Vietnamese history.

On August 31, 1858, French naval forces attacked Da Nang, citing persecution of Catholic missionaries as their justification: the French colonial land-grabbing that would culminate, in 1885, in the total conquest of Vietnam, had begun. By 1861, the three eastern provinces of Cochinchina had been conquered by the **French Expeditionary Corps**, and although there were popular anti-French uprisings Emperor Tu Duc sold out the following year, when the three provinces were formally ceded to the French by the **Treaty of Saigon**, which was signed by Phan Thanh Gian. A year later he had the opportunity to redress the situation, when he journeyed to Paris as ambassador to Emperor Napoleon III, to thrash out a long-term peace – the first Vietnamese ambassador ever to be despatched to Europe.

However, efforts to reclaim territory given up under the terms of the treaty failed, and by 1867 France moved to take over the rest of Cochinchina. Unable to persuade the spineless Tu Duc to sanction popular uprisings, Phan Thanh Gian embarked on a hunger strike in protest at French incursions and Hué's ineffectuality. When, after fifteen days, he had still not died, he swallowed **poison**, and his place among the massed ranks of Vietnamese heroes was assured.

Next, simply strike off in any direction to explore the verdant beauty of An Binh's orchards and gardens. As an alternative to following the island's narrow tracks and single-log bridges, you could rent a **boat** out of Vinh Long, or join one of the many tours leaving every day. Few visitors will want to take river trips in all delta locations (My Tho, Vinh Long, Can Tho, Chau Doc) for the simple reason that all offer pretty much the same schedule – chugging along canals watching the passing boats, a visit to a fruit orchard and a floating market, plus a stop at a local cottage industry, like peanut brittle or coconut candy workshops. If you have to choose one, a morning spent on a boat around An Binh Island is highly recommended. It's possible, with an early start, to head upriver to the floating market at **CAI BE** (5–11am); three hours is sufficient time for a round trip to the market, four hours if you combine it with An Binh Island; some tours also stop for a fish lunch at a rural outpost. Watching the river traffic, from the tiny rowing boats to huge sampans loaded with rice husks (fuel for the nearby brick kilns), is fascinating, and stepping ashore from time to time reveals insights into the lifestyles of the locals. Another activity which is becoming increasingly popular is a **home-stay** with one of a dozen or so families living in remote corners of the island; ask at Cuu Long Tourist (see p.149) or at tour operators in Ho Chi Minh City (see p.126) for details.

Eating and drinking

For **restaurants**, the Cuu Long Tourist-owned *Phuong Thuy*, built out over the river, boasts the prime spot in town, but the food (a mix of Vietnamese and Western) is only average and you'll become invisible to the staff as soon as a tour bus arrives. The *Hoa Nang Café*, next to the *Cuu Long 'A'*, is a perfect place to sip a cool drink watching the sun sink into the Mekong, and the *Song Tien*, accessed through the *Hoa Nang* and located above *Cuu Long 'A'*, has a reasonably extensive menu and good river views. Further down on 30 Thang 4, the hole-in-the-wall *Chieu Ky Restaurant* provides basic rice and soup meals. For a touch more class, though, you'll want to make for either the *Lan Que*, where locals flock for the fish dishes and delicacies such as snake and turtle, or the simpler but more upbeat *Tù Hai*: the two restaurants face each other on 2 Thang 9. There are basic **food stalls** beside the covered market, on Bach Dang, and a batch of equally basic **bars** along the central section of Trung Vuong. There is little to do after dark in Vinh Long, but there is a **club**, *Mekong Queen*, located in the *Cuu Long 'B' Hotel*, which serves expensive cocktails.

Tra Vinh and around

It's only another 65km southeast through some classic delta scenery – vivid green rice paddies, backed by coconut and water palms – to **TRA VINH**, an outback market town whose broad, tree-lined streets and smattering of colonial piles have yet to see tourists in any numbers. Even if you don't plan to stay here, it makes an interesting day out from Vinh Long. This region of the delta is Khmer country; as you get nearer to Tra Vinh, distinctive pagodas begin to appear beside the road, painted in rich pastel shades of lilac, orange and turquoise, their steep horned roofs puncturing the sky.

Most visitors come here to visit the storks at nearby Chua Hang (see p.155), although the town's low-key charm makes it an intriguing place to spend a day or two. Unusually, Tra Vinh isn't ostensibly dominated by a branch of the Mekong – you'll have to journey a couple of hundred metres east of the 800-metre-square grid forming the town centre to find the river. A hike through the **market** to riverside Bach Dang (stopping en route to dip into the colourful, Chinese Ong Pagoda) makes the most engaging approach. The bridge 100m north of the fish market commands great views of the **Tra Vinh River**, whose eddying waters run canal-straight to the north. In places the river is almost corked by boats moored seven or eight deep, while boat-builders occupy several of the thatched stilthouses spilling off its east bank. Walk north of the town centre up Le Loi to the golden-roofed **Ong Met Pagoda**, and you're assured of a friendly reception from the monks studying at its English school. Beyond, on the left, is pretty **Tra Vinh Church**, a cream-coloured buttressed construction, fronted by a statue of Christ taking refuge from the tropical sun in a niche above the front entrance, while waves of stonework ripple up its salmon-pink spire.

Practicalities

Buses from Vinh Long and beyond hit the southwest corner of Tra Vinh, terminating about 800m from the centre of town at the bus station on Nguyen Dang, off Dien Bien Phu. The Agribank, one block west of the market at 70–72 Le Loi, will change cash (US$ only). Cargo/passenger **boats** to Ho Chi Minh (three times weekly) and Ben Tre (daily) depart from the pier near Ly Tu Trong, just up from the bridge over the Tra Vinh River – contact the helpful Tra Vinh Tourist Company at 64–66 Le Loi (☎074/858556, ⓕ858768) for the current schedule or other local **information**.

The *Cuu Long Hotel* (☎074/862615, ⓕ866027; ❸), on the main road just before entering town, is the plushest **place to stay** around, and brings an aura of prosperity to the small town with its surprisingly well-equipped rooms that have a touch of elegance. Conversely, the smart exterior of the *Thanh Tra Hotel* (☎074/853626; ❶–❷) at the top of Pham Thai Buong, disappoints inside; many rooms are windowless and the place is devoid of character. There are a few budget alternatives on Le Thanh Ton, of which the *Thanh Binh* (☎074/858170, ⓕ858906; ❶) and the *Phuong Dong* (☎074/865486; ❶), just round the corner

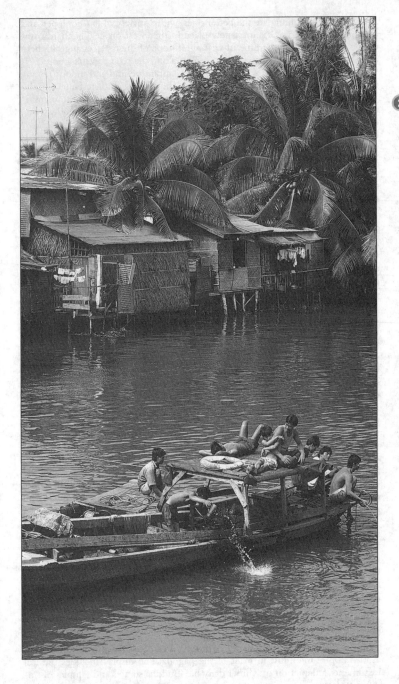

at 1a Phan Dinh Phung are the better ones, with a variety of fan-equipped and air-conditioned rooms. A smart new place further west on Le Thanh Ton was under construction at the time of writing. If none of these places appeals, there are a couple of smartish mini-hotels 2–3km along the road to Vinh Long.

Eating options include a thatched bar/restaurant behind and indoor restaurant at the *Cuu Long Hotel*, just out of town, the ground-floor restaurant in the *Thanh Tra Hotel*, which serves decent enough meals, or, for a little more ambience, try the *Tuy Huong*, opposite the front of the market, whose friendly owners offer a range of Chinese and Vietnamese dishes, as well as a fine *pho* at breakfast. Otherwise, there's Tran Phu's smart *Viet Hoa*, specializing in seafood; to get there walk 120m south of the front of the market along Dien Bien Phu and turn right. Finally, **stalls** towards the eastern edge of the market hawk *pho* and *com* until the early evening.

Ba Om Pond

A few kilometres out of town, off the road to Vinh Long, **Ba Om Pond** and its environs make for an interesting outing. Five kilometres southwest of town, a road on the left after the second of two Khmer pagodas runs down to **Ba Om Pond**, beloved of Tra Vinh picnickers and courting couples. Along the trackway, a gaggle of cottage industries churn out **rice papers** for making spring rolls – go to any house fronted by thatch drying-frames and you'll see puddles of rice gruel being steamed over a rice-husk fire, then dried and trimmed.

Around the pond, deck chairs are lined up and drinks and snack vendors lie in wait for visitors. Though it can get crowded at weekends, on weekdays it is usually restful. Bordered by grassy banks, and shaded by towering, aged trees whose roots clutch at the ground, Ba Om is seasonally cloaked by lotus blossoms that attract flocks of blackbirds in the late afternoon. The origin of Ba Om is clouded by time, but one version of events is enshrined in a quaint legend. Many centuries ago, the men and women of a village in the area were embroiled in an argument over which sex should shoulder marriage expenses. A race was decided upon to settle the dispute: women were to build a square pond, and men a round one, with the team managing the biggest pond by morning escaping marital expenses henceforth. Both teams dug all day and into the night, by which time it was clear that the men were winning. Ba Om, leader of the women, resorted to desperate measures. Setting up a lantern, she duped the opposing team into thinking the morning star had risen. While the men stopped digging and went to bed, the women continued, and the competition was won. To this day, the pond is square – and locals say that the town's male contingent has managed, on the whole, to keep its side of the bargain.

The area across the far side of the pond has been a Khmer place of worship since the eleventh century, and today it's occupied by **Ang Vuong Pagoda**. Steep-roofed, stained with age, and ringed by frangipani trees, the pagoda makes an affecting sight, especially when it echoes with the chants of its resident monks. Fronting it is a nest of stupas guarded by stone lions, while colourful murals inside depict scenes from the Buddha's life. In season, rice from the pagoda's paddy fields is heaped next to the altar, where it's guarded by an impressive golden Sakyamuni image and a host of smaller ones. Several Cambodian monks are resident here, who are thrilled at the chance of practising their English with visitors from afar.

Also worth a look is the **Khmer Minority People's Museum** (7.30–11am; 1.30–4.30pm; free), just in front of the pagoda. The display includes musical instuments, a depiction of Khmer daily life, Buddha statues and samples of traditional dress.

Chua Hang and Giong Lon

The sight of the hundred or so **storks** that nest in the grounds of **Hang Pagoda**, a Khmer pagoda around 6km south of town along Dien Bien Phu, is one which will linger in the memory. Timing, however, is all-important, and you should aim to catch these magnificent creatures – ideally in the rainy season when there are greater numbers – before dusk, when they wheel and hover over the treetops, their snowy wings catching the evening's sunlight. It's a stirring sight, though one you'll appreciate more fully if you can shake off the saffron-robed monks who clamour to practise their English with you. Arrive in the midday heat, when the birds are nesting, and you're unlikely to catch anything more than an eyeful of droppings. Chua Hang itself – an arched stone gate to the left of the main road betrays the entrance to the compound – is nothing to write home about. Dominating it is a **Sakyamuni statue**, hooped by a halo of fairy lights and flanked by murals depicting scenes from his life. There's no public transport to the pagoda, so you'll have to take a Honda om: about $2 for the return trip.

For a real storkfest, **Giong Lon Pagoda**, 43km southeast of Tra Vinh, takes some beating. The number of storks in residence here is in the thousands, but sadly the logistics of a trip out this far aren't in your favour, unless you take a Honda om all the way, which will cost $5–10 (round trip); alternatively, Tra Vinh Tourist (see p.152) include this as part of a two-day tour from Ho Chi Minh City.

Sa Dec

A cluster of brick and tile kilns announces your arrival in the charming town of **SA DEC**, a little over 20km upriver of Vinh Long. French novelist Marguerite Duras lived here as a child, and decades later the town's stuccoed shophouse terraces, riverside mansions and remarkably busy stretch of the rumbling Mekong provided the backdrop for the movie adaptation of her novel *The Lover*.

As you come in from the bus station, the town's three main arteries – Nguyen Hue, Tran Hung Dao and Hung Vuong – branch off to your right. Duck straight down into Nguyen Hue, whose umbrella-choked ways hide Sa Dec's extensive riverside market. Further along the street, waterfront comings and goings are observed by rheumy old men playing chequers, and women squat on their haunches, selling fruit from wicker baskets. From about halfway down Nguyen Hue, ferries cross to the childhood **home of Marguerite Duras** – hers is the nearest of the two villas that stand beside the place where boats drop you, and is now a police station. A crumbling old colonial villa that's been harshly treated by the tropical climate, its green shutters and red-tiled roof are tired and faded, though the glazed bricks arching over its windows still glint defiantly in the sun.

Once you've explored the town, negotiate the narrow bridge that runs over the top of Nguyen Hue and across the river. At the far bank, climb down the steps to your left and follow the river road west and past Sa Dec's **Cao Dai temple**: after 25 minutes, a gaggle of cafés tells you that you've hit **Qui Dong**, Sa Dec's famed flower village, where over a hundred farms cultivate a host of ferns, fruit trees, shrubs and flowers. Villagers are used to people strolling through their regimented rows of blooms, which grow on raised bamboo platforms, tended by conical-hatted workers who wade through the mud ponds below. The 6000 hectares of **Tu Ton Rose Garden** get the lion's share of tourists visiting the village. In addition to the varieties of roses cultivated here (among them the *Brigitte Bardot*, the *Jolie Madame* and the *Marseille*), over 580 species of plants are grown, ranging from orchids, carnations and chrysanthemums, through to medicinal herbs and pines grown for export around Asia. Bear in mind that Qui Dong is overrun on Sundays by tourists from Ho Chi Minh City, who come to pose for photos among the blooms; and that things get particularly busy and colourful in the run-up to Tet, as farms prepare to transport their stocks to the city's flower markets.

Practicalities

Buses terminate 300m southeast of the town centre: turn left out of the station and continue straight across the bridge. For onward connections, you're better off heading for Vinh Long and picking up a bus to Ho Chi Minh City or Can Tho.

The only tourist **hotel** in town at present is Hung Vuong's reasonably appealing but jaded *Sa Dec* (T067/861430; ●—●); choices, however, will soon run to two after the rebuilding of the *Bong Hong Hotel* on Quoc Lo 80. Sa Dec has no tourist office as such, and you'll have to make do with the one at Cao Lanh for **information**, though the friendly staff at the *Sa Dec* might be able to assist.

Two **restaurants** on the main road just down from the *Sa Dec Hotel* serve up reasonable dishes. The *Quan Com Cay Sung* is a pleasant enough *com* shop offering the normal pork, fish and chicken on rice dishes and is popular with locals, while next door the *Com Thuy* has a few offerings on display and an English menu. The *Sa Dec Hotel* also has its own, rather glum, attached restaurant. On Quoc Lo 80, the family-run *Chanh Ky* doles out Chinese noodles and rice dishes for under $1 that you can wash down with cold beer.

Can Tho

A population of nearly half a million makes **CAN THO** the delta's biggest city, and losing yourself in its commercial thrum for a few days is the perfect antidote to time spent in quiet backwaters of the delta. Approaching from the ferry terminal northeast of the city, first impressions are rather less than encouraging: Can Tho is a hefty settlement but, with the oppressive urban sprawl encasing the top of town negotiated, its breezy waterfront comes as a pleasant surprise.

At the confluence of the Can Tho and Hau Giang rivers, the city is a major mercantile centre and transport interchange. But Can Tho is no mere staging post. Some of the best restaurants in the delta are located here; what's more, the abundant rice fields of Can Tho Province are never far away, and at the intersections of the canals and rivers that thread between them you'll find some interesting floating markets. Can Tho was the last city to succumb to the North Vietnamese Army, a day after the fall of Saigon, on May 1, 1975 – the date that has come to represent the reunification of the country.

Arrival, information and transport

Long-distance buses whisk you across the Hau Giang estuary and into the Mekong's transportational hub, Can Tho's **bus station**, 1200m northwest of town at the junction of Cach Mang Thang Tam and Hung Vuong. Most buses will terminate here, though local services from Vinh Long dump you on the north bank of the Hau Giang River at **Binh Minh**, from where you'll have to take a short **ferry** ride. The much-touted **bridge** across the Hau Giang River to Can Tho has been due for completion for a considerable time – cautious current statements suggest 2005. A central shuttle bus service aimed at both tourists and locals runs continuously along the main streets in the city; look for the thirty-seater buses with "Xe Buyt" on the front. For onward travel, see "Listings", p.160.

For **information** about boat trips and other local attractions, drop in at Can Tho Tourist at 20 Hai Ba Trung (☎071/821852, ✉canthotour@hcm.vnn.vn). Some Can Tho Tourist tour **boats** depart from the tourist jetty ("Ben Tau Du Lich"), as do hour-long evening river **cruises** (6.30pm & 8.15pm; $2), which feature traditional music. Free shuttle boats to the *Victoria Can Tho Hotel* (see overleaf) across the river also depart from here (daily 6am–10pm). There's a passenger/cargo boat to Ca Mau (see p.163), which departs from the jetty at the top of the market daily at 5pm; journey time is approximately ten hours and it costs just a few dollars. Can Tho Tourist can also arrange boat tours along

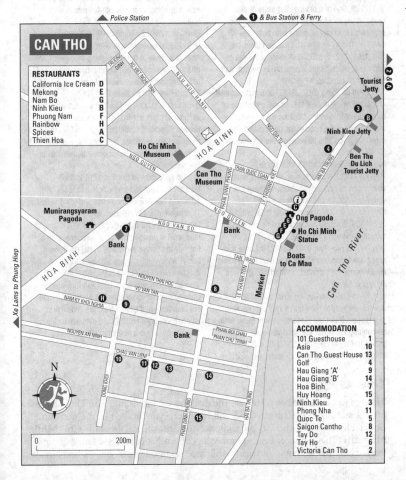

CAN THO

RESTAURANTS
California Ice Cream	D
Mekong	E
Nam Bo	G
Ninh Kieu	B
Phuong Nam	F
Rainbow	H
Spices	A
Thien Hoa	C

▲ Police Station   ▲ ❶ & Bus Station & Ferry

Tourist Jetty

Ninh Kieu Jetty

Ben Thu Du Lich Tourist Jetty

Ho Chi Minh Museum

Can Tho Museum

Munirangsyaram Pagoda

Bank

Ong Pagoda

Ho Chi Minh Statue

Bank

Boats to Ca Mau

Market

Bank

Bank

Can Tho River

◄ Xe Lams to Phung Hiep

N

0   200m

ACCOMMODATION
101 Guesthouse	1
Asia	10
Can Tho Guest House	13
Golf	4
Hau Giang 'A'	9
Hau Giang 'B'	14
Hoa Binh	7
Huy Hoang	15
Ninh Kieu	3
Phong Nha	11
Quoc Te	5
Saigon Cantho	8
Tay Do	12
Tay Ho	6
Victoria Can Tho	2

the river and to the markets. As usual, for lower prices you can go with an unofficial boat through one of the many touts prowling Hai Ba Trung; $2–3 per hour is the going rate, depending on the kind of boat you choose, but be on the lookout for scams.

Accommodation

Hai Ba Trung and Chau Van Liem together form the axis of Can Tho's healthy **hotel** scene. Cyclo drivers from either the bus or ferry station will take you from one hotel to another until you make your choice, in return for a modest commission from the reception desk.

101 Guesthouse 101 Nguyen Trai ☏071/825074. On the road out towards the bus station, this place is a bit far from the action but has good-value basic rooms. Those out back are a bit quieter. ❶

Asia 91 Chau Van Liem ☏071/812800, ℻812779. One of a bewildering array of mid-range hotels on Chau Van Liem, this one offers spacious, clean rooms, some with bathtubs. ❸

Can Tho Guest House 41 Chau Van Liem ☏071/811772, ℻820356. A reasonable-value, mid-range place. Some rooms are large with bath-tubs and all facilities. ❸

Golf 2 Hai Ba Trung ☏071/812210, ℮golfcanthohtl @hcm.vnn.vn. With over 100 rooms, a pool and all facilities, not to mention fabulous river views, this place stands at the head of the pack in Can Tho, even though it's all a bit soulless and international. ❹–❻

Hau Giang 'A' 34 Nam Ky Khoi Nghia ☏071/821139. A selection of 35 clean, comfortable rooms suiting most pockets; all have hot water, satellite TV and breakfast. ❷–❸

Hau Giang 'B' 27 Chau Van Liem ☏071/821636, ℻821806. Smallish and basic rooms but clean, though some are a bit dingy. ❶–❷

Hoa Binh 5 Hoa Binh ☏071/810218. Large mid-range hotel, conveniently located next to the bank. Its 50 rooms are carpeted, comfortable and well equipped. ❸–❹

Huy Hoang 35 Ngo Duc Ke ☏071/825833. Well-maintained budget hotel that's very popular with tour groups. Basic but pleasant rooms; those with air-con and hot water are good value. ❶

Ninh Kieu 2 Hai Ba Trung ☏071/824583. Attractive place offering good-value, well-appoint-ed rooms off coolly tiled halls; all rates include breakfast. Some more expensive rooms enjoy great river views, and a riverside extension is being built. ❸–❹

Phong Nha 75 Chau Van Liem ☏071/821615. Showing its age, this spot is for those who seek economy above character; its fan rooms with bathroom are tiny but adequate. ❶

Quoc Te 12 Hai Ba Trung ☏071/822080, ℻821039. Some of the well-equipped rooms here have fine views of the river, giving those with attached balcony something of a honeymoon feel at a reasonable price; breakfast included. ❸–❹

Saigon Can Tho 55 Phan Dinh Phung ☏071/825831. One of Can Tho's smarter address-es, geared more towards the business than tourist market. Spacious, carpeted rooms, with 24-hour room service; breakfast, newspapers, fruit and coffee are complimentary; discounts available in low season. ❹

Tay Do 61 Chau Van Liem ☏071/821009. Possibly the best mid-range option in town, with 40 rooms boasting all mod cons, including satellite TV, and breakfast is included. ❸–❹.

Tay Ho 36 Hai Ba Trung ☏071/823392. Cramped little hotel in an aged row of shophouses, with a balcony to observe the bustle in Hai Ba Trung below. Basic rooms, a few with air-con. ❶

Victoria Can Tho Cai Ke Ward ☏071/810111, ℮victoriact@hcm.vnn.vn. Built and furnished in classic French colonial style but with all the mod-ern facilities you'd expect from the delta's first international-style hotel. Grand riverside location opposite town and a free shuttle boat service. ❺–❻

The City

Though its boat trips (see p.160) are the main reason for visiting Can Tho, a hand-ful of lesser diversions on dry land will help keep you amused in the meantime. Broad Hoa Binh is the city's backbone, and the site of the **Ho Chi Minh Museum** (Tues, Thurs & Fri 8–11am & 2–4.30pm, Sat & Sun 8–11am & 7–9pm; free), where photographs and army ordnance (look out for a vicious homemade crossbow strung with hundreds of elastic bands) pertaining to the war have been dredged up and mounted or framed, above signs written solely in Vietnamese. If you've seen any of the museums in Hanoi or Ho Chi Minh, you'll know the plot by now; outside in the museum's grounds it's a familiar tale of burnt-out helicopters and rusting planes. The recently opened, impressive **Can Tho Museum**, 1 Hoa Binh (Tues, Wed & Thurs 8–11am & 2–5pm, Sat & Sun 8–11am & 6.30–9pm; free), presents "the history of the resistance against foreign aggression of Can Tho people", as well as local economic and social achievements.

The 1946-built **Munirangsyaram Pagoda**, 250m south of the museum, warrants examination only if the more impressive Khmer pagodas around Tra Vinh or Soc Trang aren't on your itinerary. Entrance into the pagoda compound is through a top-heavy stone gate weighed down with masonry reminiscent of Angkor Wat. Don't be fooled by the false promise of the faded, three-headed snake bannisters that slither lithely up the steep steps fronting the pagoda – its upper hall is empty but for two statues of Sakyamuni, one seated and the other reclining. Only fractionally more arresting is the main hall below, though the colourful rattan mats on the floor do at least testify to the continuing activity of its few remaining monks.

The waterfront

Walking east of Munirangsyaram Pagoda for five minutes, along Nguyen Thai Hoc, deposits you bang in the middle of the city's **central market**, which swallows up the central segment of Hai Ba Trung. Fans of frenetic Asian markets will find much to enjoy here, with hundreds of makeshift stalls chock-a-block with exotic produce.

Once you've squeezed out of the top of the market, and past the troop of very vocal baguette sellers at the junction of Hai Ba Trung and Ngo Quyen, an imposing silver statue of a waving Uncle Ho announces the start of Can Tho's modest riviera. Your next stop, however, should be **Ong Pagoda**, a prosperous place built in the late nineteenth century by wealthy Chinese townsman Huynh An Thai. Inside, a ruddy-faced Quan Cong presides, flaunting Rio Carnival-style headgear, and separated from proceedings by a tin-topped altar supporting several intricately painted incense urns. On his right is Than Tai, to whom a string of families come on the first day of every month, asking for money and good fortune. There's a small chamber dedicated to Quan Am to the left of the main hall. Look out, too, for the counter selling incense sticks, where a calligrapher blithely daubs Chinese characters onto red prayer scrolls.

Waterfront **cafés** will rustle up a fresh coconut or a pot of green tea to clear the incense smoke out of your lungs, and from your seat you can watch the relentless sampan traffic of the Can Tho River.

Eating

Can Tho is well endowed with good, affordable **restaurants**, most of them serving Vietnamese food. Those along Hai Ba Trung target a primarily foreign market, while locals tend to patronize places around the market and along Nam Ky Khoi Nghia. An uninspiring selection of snacks are sold at the daytime **food stalls** at the upper end of the market, along Hai Ba Trung. For **ice cream**, try Kem My California Ice Cream at 16a Hoa Binh, a tiny parlour that will satisfy even the sweetest tooth.

Hoang Cung Restaurant 55 Phan Dinh Phung. Located on the ground floor of the *Saigon Can Tho Hotel*, this place serves decent Western and

Vietnamese dishes in a stylish environment at reasonable prices. 6am–10pm.
Mekong Restaurant 38 Hai Ba Trung. Into its fifth

decade and still hard to top for cheap, flavoursome Vietnamese and Chinese meals – fried fish in sour sauce ($1.50) comes highly recommended and there is a good vegetarian selection; still lively into the early hours. 24hr.

Nambo Café-Restaurant 50 Hai Ba Trung ☎071/812024. French-café-inspired place with a colonial ambience of polished floors, rattan furnishings and wooden ceiling fans; dining on the first floor balcony gives a bird's-eye view of waterfront activities. Tempting salads, sandwiches and desserts at $2–3. Gets crowded in the evening when it's a good idea to reserve a table. 9am–11pm.

Ninh Kieu 2 Hai Ba Trung. Stylish riverside venue with a terrace that takes full advantage of its location. Steamboat for two comes to around $6 and the grilled shrimps are tasty. 6am–10pm.

Phuong Nam 48 Hai Ba Trung. A good range of cheap and tasty Western and Vietnamese dishes. 7am–11pm.

Quoc Te *International Hotel*, 12 Hai Ba Trung. Characterless first-floor hotel restaurant specializing in the less appealing (to Western tastes) side – tortoise, snake and frog – of Vietnamese cuisine. 6am–10pm.

Rainbow 54 Nam Ky Khoi Nghia. Civilized, pleasing restaurant, where Chinese and Western dishes rub shoulders with American, Belgian and even Italian steaks; two people can eat for around $7. 9am–2pm & 4–9.30pm.

Spices *Victoria Can Tho Hotel*, Cai Ke Ward. Fine dining in a tasteful ethnic interior, or outside on the romantic riverside terrace; this and the extensive menu with Vietnamese, Asian and Western dishes such as shrimp mousse on sugar cane and beef hotpot with peanut sauce (about $5 each) make the detour to this hotel restaurant worth the effort. Barbecue buffets are sometimes held at weekends. 6am–10pm.

Thien Hoa 26 Hai Ba Trung. Yield to the hard sell of the proprietress and you'll enjoy big portions of sour soups and other Vietnamese food, either in the simple dining room or at a streetside table. 9am–2pm & 5pm–midnight.

Listings

Airlines Vietnam Airlines has a branch at Can Tho Tourist, 20 Hai Ba Trung.
Bakery Duc Phat, 91a Nguyen Trai. Large outlet selling bread, croissants and pastries.
Banks Vietcombank, 7 Hoa Binh (Mon–Fri 7.30–10.30am & 1.30–4.30pm), changes cash and travellers' cheques and can arrange cash advances for Visa and MasterCard. It also has an ATM machine open 7.30am–11pm. Vietincombank at 9 Phan Dinh Phung (Mon–Fri 7–11am & 1–5pm), and the Maritime Bank, 40 Phan Dinh Phung (Mon–Fri 7–11am & 1–5pm), both change travellers' cheques and cash for similar rates.
Bicycles Enquire at the tourist office or at the nearby *Quoc Te Hotel*.
Email and Internet access Several hotels offer Internet access, and there are independent operators on Vo Van Tan and Chau Van Liem. The one at 29 Chau Van Liem, next to the *Hau Giang 'B' Hotel*, has two floors of terminals.
Hospital The general hospital is located on the corner of Chau Van Liem and Hoa Binh.
Mini-market Ngo Quyen, 1 Ngo Quyen, next to the covered market. Stocks a range of Western products, including alcohol, toiletries and tinned goods.
Pharmacy 88–90 Ly Tu Trong and 34 Ngo Quyen.
Police 67–69 Hung Vuong, just down from the bus station.
Post office 2 Hoa Binh (daily 6am–8pm). IDD, poste restante, fax and express mail service.
Sports Non-residents can use the tennis courts at *Victoria Can Tho Hotel* (floodlit in the evening), or the riverside pool for a few dollars.
Tour operators and onward travel Can Tho Tourist travel service centre, 20 Hai Ba Trung (☎071/821852, ☞ 822719, ✉canthotourist@hcm.vnn.vn), is extremely helpful and can arrange car and boat rental, tours, train tickets and guides; My Khanh Tours, 3 Ngo Gia Tu (☎&☞071/825280, ⌨www.mykhanh.com), is a small, private operation offering very competitive prices for tours to floating markets, temples and basketry villages. Onward routes from Can Tho either veer up to Long Xuyen, Chau Doc and the Cambodian border, or follow Highway 1 to Soc Trang and on to Ca Mau.

Around Can Tho: boat trips and floating markets

Every morning an armada of boats takes to the web of waterways spun across Can Tho Province and makes for one of its **floating markets**. Lacking the almost staged beauty and charm of Bangkok's riverine markets, as snapshots of

Mekong life these tableaux are still worth a look, though if you have already been on a boat tour in My Tho or Vinh Long you'll find it rather repetitive. Everything your average villager could ever need is on sale, from haircuts to coffins, though predictably fruit and vegetables make up most of what's on offer. Each boat's produce is identifiable by a sample hanging off a bamboo mast in its bow, but it's difficult to get colourful pictures as the produce is stored below. Among the flotilla of craft are ancient luggers piled so high they seem sure to sink, and sampans whose oarsmen and women stand up to strain against their scissor-oars. Few boats are painted, so photographers will have to rely on the glimpses of fruit for splashes of colour.

Of the three major markets in the province, two are west of the city. The most commonly visited, 7km out of Can Tho, is **Cai Rang**, but you'll have to be prepared to queue up with all the other tourist boats before you can weave among the fervent waterborne activity, with drinks vendors clamouring to make a sale. This market is particularly active on Sundays. Another 10km west and you're at modest **Phong Dien**. The appeal of this one is that it sees relatively few tourists and so the locals are correspondingly friendly. If you're lucky, you'll be tossed fruits to sample from passing launches.

Phung Hiep market, 32km south of Can Tho, on the road to Soc Trang, was once the largest market in the area; it's now somewhat reduced in size, but still warrants a visit. It's better to go by car or motorbike to arrive early and take a walk through the narrow lanes of the colourful street market, where you'll see mounds of longans and custard apples, squid and crab, paper flowers, baguettes and chillies, before making your way to the river. Here, dozens of boats jostle and bump along the water's edge, their owners shouting out to advertise their wares. There is a good view of the maelstrom from Phung Hiep Bridge, which carries the main road across the river. This was once a main centre for buying and selling snakes, but dwindling numbers have forced the government to ban this trade.

Practicalities

It's possible to visit all three markets **by boat**, but with the round trip to Phong Dien (passing Cai Rang) taking around five hours, and getting to Phung Hiep and back taking more like eight, you'd be wiser to go **by road**, and rent a sampan (approximately $2–3 an hour) on arrival if you want to join the melee. A Honda om (about $4 return) is the safer bet for Phong Dien, while Phung Hiep is served by xe lams from Ly Tu Trong. You can also ask to be dropped off at the local orchards on the return journey, and for a small donation you can sample their produce and be shown around. However you travel, you'll need a really **early start**, since the markets are at their best around 7–9am. Any boat-owner who tells you the spectacle is just as impressive throughout the day is lying. Most organized tours take in one of the above markets and make a leisurely return to Can Tho via the maze of picturesque canals and orchards that surround it, usually stopping to sample star fruit and sapodilla, longan and rambutan along the way.

Soc Trang

Straddled across an oily branch of the Mekong, **SOC TRANG** lacks the panache of other delta towns. Scruffy and down-at-heel, the area is not without its offbeat attractions. On the tenth day of the tenth lunar month (Nov–Dec) the town springs to life as thousands converge to see traditional Khmer boats (*thuyen dua*) racing each other during the Ghe Ngo **festival**.

Khmer pagodas are ten-a-penny in this region of the delta; the distinctive feature of **Matoc Pagoda**, 2km south of town along Le Hong Phong, and then 800m down a track on the right, is that the trees surrounding it carry a vast community of golden-bodied fruit bats, which spectacularly take to the skies at dusk. Plan to get here around 5.30pm and as the drop in temperature wakes them you'll see the bats spinning, preening and flapping their matt-black wings – some have a span of 1.5m. Khmer monks have worshipped at this site for four hundred years. The present pagoda is a hundred years old, and inside, bright murals bearing the names of the Khmer communities around the world that financed them recount the life of the Buddha.

If Matoc Pagoda fires an interest in all things Khmer, you might venture into the **Khmer Museum** (Mon–Sat 7–11am & 1–5pm; free), whose low-key exhibits include stringed instruments made of snakeskin and coconut husks, and some wonderfully colourful food covers, shaped like conical hats, but with a stippled surface. From the museum, cross the street to **Kleang Pagoda**, a fine Khmer pagoda surrounded by a two-tiered terrace. The doors and windows are adorned with traditional Khmer motifs in greens, reds and golds, while inside is a wonderfully reposeful golden Sakyamuni statue, with a wheel of fairy lights spinning around his head. Unfortunately, the doors are often locked. Both the museum and Kleang Pagoda are at the eastern end of Nguyen Chi Thanh, at the top of town. Head south from here along Mau Than 68 and after a few minutes you'll pass a Chinese cemetery, set back from the road on your left. From here it's only another hundred metres or so to **Dat Set Pagoda** (daily 7.30am–5pm). Its tiny entrance is on the right. Constructed almost entirely from clay, with a smart sheet-metal roof to keep the rain off, Dat Set makes a welcome change from the more numerous Khmer pagodas in this region of the delta. Chinese visitors flock here to see the pagoda's impressive and highly colourful collection of statues; many are life-size, with animals and figures from Chinese mythology being the most popular subjects. The pagoda is also home to some truly gargantuan candles, the largest of which weighs around 200kg and is said to last seventy years of continuous burning.

Practicalities

The waterway running roughly west to east splits Soc Trang in two, with most of the town nestling on its south bank. The town's spine is Hai Ba Trung, which runs across the water, before becoming Tran Hung Dao on the southern outskirts. The **bus station** is north of the river, on Nguyen Chi Thanh. Long-distance buses leave in the early hours, so unless you're up with the lark ask your cyclo driver to carry on a few hundred metres west of here, to where Hung Vuong hits Highway 1, and wave down a passing bus. Soc Trang Tourist is across the road from the bus station at 131 Nguyen Chi Thanh (☎079/822024), though it's easier to find the entrance at 68 Le Loi; its staff are keen to help with local **information** but not always able.

The best **place to stay** in town is the *Khanh Hung Hotel* (☎079/821026; ❶–❹), located at 15 Tran Hung Dao on the south side of town. Its 55 rooms range from basic and cheap to carpeted suites with all facilities. The *Phong Lan II Hotel* (☎079/821757; ❷–❸), opposite the bus station, has seen better days, but the *Phong Lan I* (☎079/824229; ❸) on the south bank of the river at 124 Dong Khoi is fine; some rooms have a balcony over the river and the management sometimes agrees to a discount. Breakfast is included.

Eating options include *Quan Com Hung*, north of the river on Mau Than 68, which serves generous portions of *com*, although its speciality is steamboat and it has a fuller menu in Vietnamese. If tables are full, which they often are, the *Hang Ky*, just around the corner on Le Lai, off Le Loi, is equally good. The *Alo! Quan*, at 2/1 Mau Than 68, enjoys a breezy, riverside location just north of the bridge and offers such oddities as snake's head, turtle, swamp eel and goat's testicles, though they also turn out good soups and stir-fries. For a snack you could try the local speciality *banh bia*, a round cake with a filling made from sweetened beans or durian – something of an acquired taste.

Bac Lieu

Beyond Soc Trang the landscape becomes progressively more waterlogged and water palms hug the banks of the waterways that criss-cross it. A little over 40km southwest of Soc Trang, Highway 1 dips south towards the crown of **BAC LIEU**, before veering off west to Ca Mau. An unremarkable town centred around shrimp farming, oyster gathering and salt production, Bac Lieu may not be able to boast sights to set the pulse racing, but with the only places to stay between Soc Trang and Ca Mau it's worth keeping in mind as a staging post.

The **bus station** is 1.5km north of town, and cyclos shuttle back and forth to the centre. Moving on, it's best to get back on Highway 1 and flag down express buses passing through. The town's main **hotel**, *Bac Lieu* (☎0781/822437; ❶–❸), located on central Hoang Van Thu, caters for all pockets, from their dreary budget quarters in the old wing to bright, modern, well-equipped rooms, complete with satellite TV and hot water, in the renovated section. You could also try the friendly *Hoang Cung* mini-hotel (☎0781/823362; ❶–❸) at 1b/5 Tran Phu, which has nineteen clean and comfortable rooms all with en-suite bathrooms, though you'll find upgrading secures a larger-size room with balcony. The newly created Bac Lieu Tourist Company (☎0781/824272) is conveniently situated next to the *Bac Lieu*, though their **information** services seem to be fairly limited at the moment.

There is a **restaurant** on the ground floor of the *Bac Lieu* where the food isn't bad; alternatively, head down the road leading to the bus station, where *banh bao* and baguette stalls and *com* shops proliferate.

Ca Mau and around

With its left shoulder braced against the Bac Lieu Canal, the main road now trundles westwards towards the **Ca Mau Peninsula**, the area which briefly hit the headlines in 1997 when it was devastated by "Typhoon Linda". Thousands were killed during the storm and an estimated 200,000 homes destroyed, along with a large proportion of the region's fishing fleet.

Few travellers make it this far south, but those who do will find that waterways are the most efficient means of travel – a point pressed home by the slender ferries moored in all the villages the road passes. Much of this pancake-flat region of the delta is composed of silt deposited by the Mekong, and the swamplands covering portions of it are home to a variety of wading birds. In addition to rice cultivation, shrimp farming is a major local concern – along the way you're sure to spot shrimp ponds, demarcated by mud banks that have been baked and cracked crazily by the sun.

CA MAU itself, Vietnam's southernmost town of any size, has few redeeming features, and has changed little since 1989 when travel writer Justin Wintle described it as a "scrappy clutter … a backyard town in a backyard province".

Sadly, the typhoon also robbed Ca Mau of one of its main tourist draws, as much of the nearby Minh Hai mangrove forest has been wiped out. The Vietnamese regard Ca Mau as something of a frontier town and in this perhaps lies its only remaining appeal. If you take an improvised wander around the streets of the town looking for something interesting, you will quickly find that *you* are the main attraction for the local people, and thus the constant centre of attention. This sensation can irritate some travellers, but it's best to make the most of it, and revel in having got off the beaten track.

The town centre is banked against the narrow Ca Mau River, which snakes through it as though trying to wriggle free before the encroaching stilthouses squeeze the life from it. Lurking along its north bank is the rag-tag squall of the **market**, a shantytown of canvas and sacking. To the west of town, the Cultural Park (small charge) is an interesting place to go late in the afternoon to see some of the sixty species of birds that nest here returning at day's end.

Practicalities

Central Ca Mau lies north of the river, along the stretch of Ly Bon running southwest to northeast between Ngo Quyen and Phan Ngoc Hien. On arrival at the **bus** station 2km southeast of town, ask a xe dap loi driver to take you to the junction of Phan Ngoc Hien and Ly Bon. Minh Hai Tourist is here at 1 Ly Bon (☎0780/831828, ℻837022), where the staff are very helpful with local **information** and can arrange a **tour** of the region. Most of Ca Mau's hotels are located nearby. To **exchange** travellers' cheques and arrange cash advances on credit cards, you'll need to cross over the river to the Vietcombank at 4 Lac Long Quan, although the more convenient branch at 53 De Tham will exchange dollars; Vietincombank at 94 Ly Thuong Kiet can also change travellers' cheques. The GPO (daily 6am–10pm) on Luu Tan Tai offers **email** and **Internet** services. Internet access is also available at 66 Ly Bon.

With limited serviceable roads around Ca Mau, locals rely on **ferries** to get around. From Boat Station A ("Ben Tau A"), a kilometre west of the centre, boats generally leave for points north, while vessels heading south and for Rach Gia depart from Boat Station B, 2km over the river and south of town, off Cao Thang. Apart from the regular ferry to Rach Gia, which costs just over $1 and takes ten hours, there is an expensive ($80) speedboat that covers the journey in under three hours. Ferries on the peninsula can be flagged down in the same way as buses. There are also water taxis that depart from behind Ca Mau market. If you need to get to Ho Chi Minh City in a hurry, there is an express bus (7hr) that leaves from opposite the *Supermarket Hotel*. There is a small airport near town which may even have planes landing and taking off at some stage in the future.

Accommodation

Ca Mau's **hotels** aren't up to much. The *Ca Mau Hotel*, 20 Phan Ngoc Hien (☎0780/831165; ❶–❷), has large, reasonably equipped rooms, although you should avoid those backing onto the karaoke lounge; its near-neighbour, the *Sao Mai Hotel* (☎0780/831035; ❶) is a budget option, where some rooms share bathrooms, though the best rooms have hot water and air-conditioning. Squeezed between these two is the *Song Hung* (☎0780/822822; ❷), a newish mini-hotel with nine well-equipped rooms and staff who are eager to help out. A little further up the road at 91 Phan Dinh Phung there's the ageing *Phuong Nam* (☎0780/831752; ❸), which has comfortable rooms with air-conditioning and breakfast included – though rates are significantly higher for foreigners than for Vietnamese. There's a budget option round the corner at 11 Ly Bon, where the *Tan Hung Guesthouse* (☎0780/831622; ❶), has very basic partitioned rooms with shared bathroom. On the other side of the river, the oddly named *Supermarket Hotel* (T0780/832789, F836880; ②–④) was probably once an impressive sight, with some truly enormous rooms, but has now become a bit run-down and grubby. Although it's convenient for shopping at the adjacent supermarket, it's a bit far from the centre of town.

Eating

While all of the big hotels have their own **restaurants**, most of them are of the "hostess" variety, and it's difficult to enjoy your food if that's all you've come for. There are several other eateries around the town centre, though none has an English menu. The *Thieu Phat* is conveniently located next to the *Ca Mau Hotel*, and serves basic rice and noodle dishes. Further north and round the corner at 257 Ly Thai Ton, the *257* is extremely popular among locals, especially for fish dishes. For a bit of ambience, the *Van Thuy* is located on an island in the middle of Dieu Hoa Lake in the southeast corner of town and accessed by an attrtactive wooden bridge, though the food is only average. If you're looking for a snack in town, head for *Huong Nam*, at 21 De Tham, where you can get a sandwich to take away. If you then need somewhere to eat it, drop into the nearby coffee shop at 17 De Tham and wash it down with a strong coffee or soft drink.

Around Ca Mau

The **marshes** circling Ca Mau form one of the largest areas of swampland in the world, covering about 150,000 hectares. The Ca Mau Peninsula was a stronghold of resistance against France and America, and for this it paid a heavy price, as US planes dumped millions of gallons of Agent Orange over it to rob guerrilas of jungle cover. Further damage has been done by the shrimp-farm industry, but pockets of mangrove and cajeput forests remain, inhabited by sea birds, wading birds, waterfowl and also honey bees, attracted by the mangrove's blossoms.

Unless you can afford a private vessel chartered through the local tourist office, the only way to access Ca Mau's swamps is to take a **public ferry** to an outlying settlement, and **rent a boat** there. However, you will need some language skills to negotiate this alone. In any case, check with Minh Hai Tourist (see opposite) before setting out, as access to the forests is subject to change. At the time of writing, the mangrove forests near **Nam Can**, the bird sanctuaries at **Dam Doi** and the cajeput forest at **Vo Doi** were all closed to allow for regeneration after typhoon damage. The best place to see a mangrove forest is at **Lam Truong 184**, a reserve about 60km south of Ca Mau. Minh Hai Tourist can arrange a trip there, or to take a look at the Ca Mau Cape, where the accumulation of silt causes the country to grow by about 100m each year.

It is also possible to head for the cajeput forests at **U Minh.** In fact the ferry ride here makes a cheap and interesting river trip even if you can't run to the extra expense of chartering a boat at the other end. Lining the ferry route are water palms, modest groves of cajeput, and fish traps consisting of triangles of bamboo sticks driven into the riverbed. You'll need to catch a ferry at Boat Station A in Ca Mau, then from U Minh's jetty you need to go at least 5km further to reach the forest. Ask a boatman to take you to "Rung U Minh Ha" or tell them you want to see the cajeput forest, "rung tram"; about three hours touring should be sufficient. The slender white trunks of the cajeput thrive in U Minh's shallow, marshy waters, and gliding through them in a boat is a truly tranquil experience. Along the way, you will likely spot apiarists collecting honeycombs from the trees, which attract bees in huge numbers.

Long Xuyen

The road northwest of Can Tho runs into **LONG XUYEN**, some 60km later. There is little of interest in the town itself, but its location at the junction of the two main routes to the delta's northwestern corner means you may find yourself passing through. Dominating the town is the spire of the ugly concrete **Cathedral**, shaped like two upstretched arms whose hands clasp a cross. Numerous tiny portals shed light on the anaemic interior, illuminating gilt stations of the cross and another giant pair of hands over the altar, clutching a globe.

Of passing interest is the **An Giang Museum** (Tues & Thurs 7.30–10.30am, Sat & Sun 7.30–10.30am & 2–4.30pm; free), currently at 77 Thoai Ngoc Hau, though there are plans to move it to Ly Thuong Kiet, opposite the People's Committee Building in the north part of town in the near future. In the first room are clothing and household implements of the Chams and musical instruments of the Khmers, which are rather ordinary, but the second gallery out back is a treasure-trove of remnants of Oc Eo culture (see box on p.175 for more on the ancient port of Oc Eo). Among the exhibits are a large lingam and an elegant wooden Buddha, so decayed it now resembles the running flesh of a golem; and a stone cairn, in which the ashes of the dead would have been deposited.

There is little to detain you in Long Xuyen's untidy **market**, but if you head on up to the western ends of Le Minh Nguon and Le Thi Nhieu, you'll find cyclos whizzing by and a real hotbed of commerce. En route, you'll pass the dragon-stalked roofs of the grandest building in town, **My Phuoc Communal Hall**.

Long Xuyen makes much of being the birthplace of Ton Duc Thang, successor to Ho Chi Minh as president of the Democratic Republic of Vietnam; a visit to his birthplace and childhood home on **My Hoa Hung Island** leads you to the **Ton Duc Thang Exhibition House** (daily 7–11am & 1–5pm; free), which displays well-presented photos and memorabilia such as the leg irons he wore in Con Dao Prison and the prime ministerial bicycle. The island is very tranquil and unspoiled, and makes a good place to explore by bicycle. Home-stays on the island can also be arranged through An Giang Tourist (see "Practicalities", below).

Practicalities

Buses from Can Tho and Chau Doc stop a few hundred metres south of town, opposite 96 Tran Hung Dao – if you are arriving from Chau Doc, yell for the driver to stop as you pass the cathedral. Some local buses from Chau Doc and Rach Gia terminate at a second bus station, Binh Khanh, to the north of town, also on Tran Hung Dao. Travelling to and from Cao Lanh by **ferry**, you'll come via Choi Moi Isle – to the east – and the An Hoa Ferry terminal, at the end of Ly Thai To in the centre of town. Transportation services from Ho Chi Minh City come either through Can Tho, to the south, or via Sa Dec, across Choi Moi and the An Hoa Ferry. The main and largest ferry terminal, Van Long, 7km south of the city, links back up with the main highway to Ho Chi Minh City, via Sa Dec. If you are heading for Ho Chi Minh City or Sa Dec, you can take one of the high-quality minibuses that operate from 58 Nguyen Trai (☎076/840950); alternatively, you can catch onward buses at the intersection of Tran Hung Dao and Hung Vuong – express buses to Chau Doc also pass through here – or at the Van Long and An Hoa ferry terminals. **Passenger/cargo boats** for Tan Chau (for Chau Doc) and Rach Gia depart from Long Xuyen's local ferry terminal in the centre of town, at the corner of Pham Hong Thai and Le Thi Nhieu – enquire locally for times and costs. Smaller craft make the trip over to My Hoa Hung Island from the jetty at the end of Nguyen Hue.

The main office of An Giang Tourist is at 80e Tran Hung Dao (☎076/841036, ✆angiangtour@hcm.vnn.vn), and the staff are helpful with local **information**. Vietnam Airlines' office is located in the *Dong Xuyen Hotel*, while Vietcombank, at 1 Hung Vuong, can arrange cash advances against Visa and MasterCard and **exchange** travellers' cheques – something none of Chau Doc's banks does yet, so plan ahead if that's your next destination. There is **Internet access** at Lan Vy Internet, 48 Nguyen Thi Minh Khai.

Accommodation

The fanciest **place to stay** is the glitzy *Dong Xuyen* (☎076/942260, ✆dongxuyen@hcm.vnn.vn; ❸), at 9a Luong Van Cu. This place occupies almost an entire block and boasts sauna, Jacuzzi, Internet access and swish carpeted rooms that represent good value. A close competitor, located at 5–9 Thi Sach, is the *Kim Anh Hotel* (☎076/942551, ✆kimanh-hotel @hcm.vnn.vn; ❸–❹), an eight-storey block with comfy rooms and a palatial suite on the top floor. There are cheaper, well-maintained rooms in the ageing *Long Xuyen* (☎076/841927, ✆longxuyenhotel@hcm.vnn.vn; ❶–❸) at

19 Nguyen Van Cung, and even cheaper ones still at the *An Giang* (076/841297, 846716; **①–②**) at 40 Hai Ba Trung, where the rooms are smallish but clean. A couple of central budget options are the *Thai Binh 2* (076/846453, 846451; **①–②**) at 4–8 Nguyen Hue, and the *Xuan Phuong* (076/841041, 846716; **①–②**), both with uninspiring but acceptable rooms. There are several hotels on Tran Hung Dao, leading south out of town, of which the *An Long* at no. 279 (076/843298; **①–②**), and the *Thoai Chau 2* at 283a (076/843882; **①–②**), both have reasonably priced rooms, but make sure you don't get put near the karaoke rooms. Across the river to the north, at 130 Tran Hung Dao, the *Hoa Binh* (076/857225, 853035; **②–③**) is a mini-hotel with cosily furnished rooms and all facilities.

Eating

All the big hotels in Long Xuyen have their own **restaurant**s, and the one at the *Kim Anh* offers good views of town from the fifth floor as well as a good range of inexpensive Vietnamese food. The *Hoa Binh* restaurant, located a couple of doors up from the hotel, has a pleasant outdoor dining area with resident giant storks standing by the fountain, plus an extensive, reasonably priced range of Asian dishes. The *Long Xuyen's* restaurant serves specialities such as snake, turtle, pigeon and eel. On Nguyen Trai, *Tiem Com Huynh Loi* at no. 252/1 has delicious, cheap *pho*, *com* and *bun bo Hué* served in clean surroundings. Round the corner, at 242/4 Luong Van Cu, the smart *Hong Phat* has tasty Chinese and Vietnamese fish and meat dishes.

Chau Doc and around

The road northwest from Long Xuyen splices huge expanses of paddy en route to **CHAU DOC**. Snuggled against the west bank of the Hau Giang River, Chau Doc these days falls on the Vietnamese side of the Cambodian border, though until it was awarded to the Nguyen lords in the mid-eighteenth century for their help in putting down a localized rebellion, it came under Cambodian rule. The area sustains a large Khmer community, which combines with local Chams and Chinese to form a diverse social melting pot. Just as diverse is Chau Doc's religious make-up: as well as Buddhists, Catholics and Muslims, the region supports an estimated 1.5 million devotees of the indigenous Hoa Hao religion (see box on p.169). Forays by Pol Pot's genocidal Khmer Rouge into this corner of the delta led to the Vietnamese invasion of Cambodia in 1978. Today Chau Doc is a bustling, friendly town, deserving of a prominent place on any Mekong Delta itinerary.

Rather than retracing your steps from Chau Doc, a more exciting alternative is to head east, following the road through Triton and Kien Luong, or by boat along the Vinh Te Canal that defines the border with Cambodia, to Ha Tien, from where you can loop back via Rach Gia. There are several daily bus departures to Triton (see p.174), from where you can catch another bus out to the coast, although the latter has a limited service. With your own motorbike or the services of a Honda om driver you can follow the same route, taking in Ba Chuc and Tap Duc, or negotiate the Chau Doc–Ha Tien road, running more or less parallel to the Vinh Te Canal. It's a rough and tiring ride, but the stunning **scenery** more than compensates.

The Hoa Hao religion

Sited 20km east of Chau Doc, the diminutive village of Hoa Hao lent its name to a unique religious movement at the end of the 1930s. The **Hoa Hao Buddhist sect** was founded by the village's most famous son, Huynh Phu So. A sickly child, Huynh was placed in the care of a hermitic monk under whom he explored both conventional Buddhism and more arcane spiritual disciplines. In 1939, at the age of 20, a new brand of Buddhism was revealed to him in a trance. Upon waking, Huynh found he was cured of his congenital illness, and began publicly to expound his breakaway theories, which advocated purging worship of all the clutter of votives, priests and pagodas, and paring it down to simple unmediated communication betwen the individual and the Supreme Being. The faith has a fairly strong **ascetic** element, with alcohol, drugs and gambling all discouraged. Peasants were drawn to the simplicity of the sect, and by rumours that Huynh was a faith healer in possession of prophetic powers.

Almost immediately, the Hoa Hao developed a **political agenda**, and established a **militia** to uphold its fervently nationalist, anti-French and anti-communist beliefs. The Japanese army of occupation, happy to keep the puppet French administration it had allowed to remain nominally in charge of Vietnam on its toes, provided the sect with arms. For themselves, the French regarded the Hoa Hao with suspicion: Huynh they labelled the "Mad Monk", imprisoning him in 1941 and subsequently confining him to a psychiatric hospital – where he promptly converted his doctor. By the time of his eventual release in 1945, the sect's uneasy alliance with the Viet Minh, which had been forged during World War II in recognition of their common anti-colonial objectives, was souring, and two years later Viet Minh agents assassinated him. The sect battled on until the mid-Fifties when **Diem's purge** of dissident groups took hold; its guerrilla commander, Ba Cut, was captured and beheaded in 1956, and by the end of the decade most members had been driven underground. Though in the early Sixties some of these resurfaced in the Viet Cong, the Hoa Hao never regained its early dynamism, and any lingering military or political presence was erased by the communists after 1975.

Today there are thought to be somewhere approaching 1.5 million Hoa Hao worshippers in Vietnam, concentrated mostly around Chau Doc. Some male devotees still sport the distinctive long beards and hair tied in a bun that traditionally distinguished a Hoa Hao adherent.

Arrival, information and getting around

Buses offload 2km southeast of town at the bus station on Le Loi, from where xe dap lois run into town; some minibuses terminate in the centre on Nguyen Van Thoai or at the open-ground area found at the intersection of Thu Khoa Nghia and Thuong Dang Le. Chau Giang is reached by ferry from the jetty opposite the GPO, or from the jetty about 100m past the *Victoria Chau Doc* hotel. Boats **to Con Tien Island** depart from the jetty at the end of Thuong Dang Le, near to the *Thuan Loi* hotel. A new bridge being built to the north of town will shortly render this ferry obsolete. Smaller passenger boats make the trip **to Phu Hiep** from the Phu Hiep ferry terminal, a few kilometres south of town along Le Loi.

The state-run An Giang Tourist does not have an office in Chau Doc, but most hotel and guesthouse owners are aware of travellers' needs and can help out with local **information**, as well as arrange **local excursions** and **onward travel**.

If you're carrying travellers' cheques, make sure you **exchange** sufficient money in Long Xuyen, since the Incombank in Chau Doc at 68–70 Nguyen

Moving on from Chau Doc

Moving on, tickets for onward express minibuses **to Ho Chi Minh City** ($4) can be purchased at the kiosk at 62 Nguyen Huu Canh. Boat services now also operate directly **to and from Phnom Penh**, and can be booked in all hotels here, though most travellers make their arrangements in Ho Chi Minh City. Around 400m up Tran Hung Dao from the Con Tien jetty, at no. 86a, a narrow concrete path marked "Ben Tau Ha Tien" signals the departure point for the passenger/cargo boats along the Vinh Te Canal **to Ha Tien.** They usually leave daily very early (cost around $5), though check with your hotel as the service is sometimes erratic.

Huu Canh changes US cash only – something to bear in mind also if you're cutting across to Ha Tien, where there are very limited exchange facilities.

Accommodation

As one of the Delta's most popular destinations, Chau Doc's range of **accommodation** runs from windowless hovels up to luxury quarters with river views, air-conditioning and TV. Most establishments are near the town centre, though there are several alternatives around Sam Mountain, about 5km southwest of town.

Ben Da Nui Sam 91 Nui Sam ☎076/861746, ⓔbendanuisam@hcm.vnn.vn. A large, low-rise resort geared towards families, out near Sam Mountain and with comfortably equipped rooms. ❷–❸

Hang Chau II 10 Nguyen Van Thoai ☎076/868891. Excellent mini-hotel, with a tiled, cool interior and fourteen rooms all with hot water, air-con, satellite TV and fridge; a few extra dollars buys better views. The largest room sleeps six. ❶–❸

Mekong Guesthouse Duong Len Vuon Tao Ngo ☎076/861870, ⓔmekongguesthouse@yahoo .com. A budget traveller's dream tucked away on the slopes of Sam Mountain (follow the road up a couple of hundred metres and it's on the right); very good-value rooms, some with fan others with air-con, plus a dorm, friendly staff, free bicycle use and acres of grounds to explore. ❶

My Loc 51 Nguyen Van Thoai ☎076/866455. A lick of paint wouldn't go amiss here but still, this friendly place is geared to tourists and the atmosphere is pleasant. $3 extra gets you air-con. ❶–❷

Ngoc Phu 17 Doc Phu Thu ☎076/866484. Formerly the *Chau Doc*, the lobby looks a bit desolate but this no-frills establishment is perfectly habitable, and even the cheapest rooms boast toilet and shower. ❶–❷

Nui Sam Nui Sam ☎076/861999, ⓔksnhnsag@hcm.vnn.vn. Comfy rooms, some geared to families, located on the left at the base of Sam Mountain. For some reason the lobby contains a post office too. ❸

Song Sao 12–13 Nguyen Huu Canh ☎076/561777. Smart rooms, all fully equipped with hot water, air-con and so on. Smaller rooms are a bit cheaper. ❷–❸

Tai Ngan 11 Nguyen Huu Canh ☎076/866435, ⓔhoteltaingan@yahoo.com. Friendly mini-hotel with a choice of fan or air-con rooms that represent good value. ❶

Thanh Tra 77 Thu Khoa Nghia ☎076/866788. Patronage by Sinh Café means this place is often full, but you're not missing much as the cell-like rooms are rather cramped. ❶

Thuan Loi 18 Tran Hung Dao ☎076/866134. This delightful riverside mini-hotel near the market offers some of the best value in town. The stilted wooden restaurant and upper balconies afford a great front-seat view of the Mekong, and the rooms are clean and comfortable. ❶–❷

Trung Nguyen 86 Bach Dang ☎076/868674, ⓔtrunghotel@yahoo.com. Very smart mini-hotel, right in the town centre, with fifteen smallish but well-furnished rooms. ❷

Victoria Chau Doc 32 Le Loi ☎076/865010, ⓔvictoriachaudoc@hcm.vnn.vn. Just 300m east of the town centre, this colonial-style hotel lords it over the three river crossings and Chau Doc; rooms are tastefully furnished with *Indochine* elegance and some have glorious river views; for spectacular sunsets the bar located on the fourth floor should not be missed. There is another *Victoria* on the western slopes of Sam Mountain, which was about to open at the time of writing. ❺

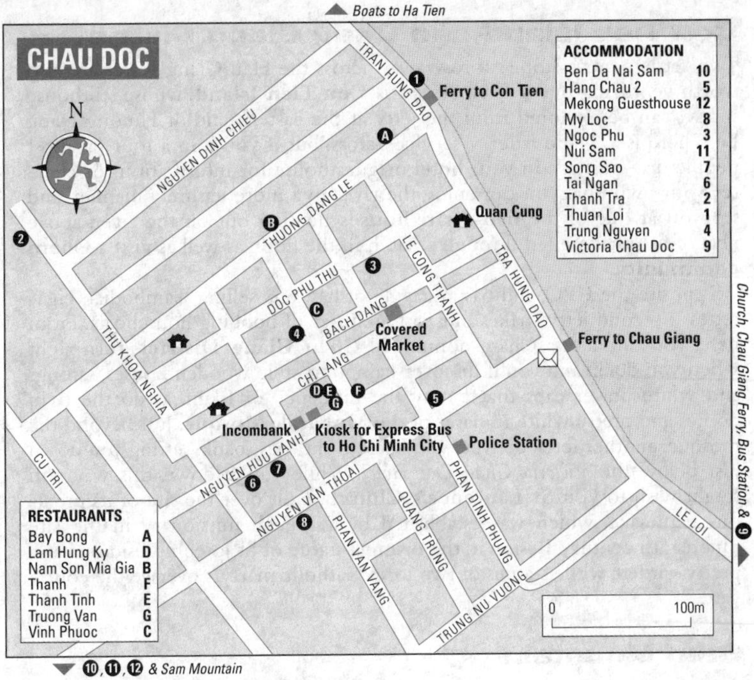
Boats to Ha Tien
CHAU DOC
N
ACCOMMODATION
Ben Da Nai Sam 10
Hang Chau 2 5
Mekong Guesthouse 12
My Loc 8
Ngoc Phu 3
Nui Sam 11
Song Sao 7
Tai Ngan 6
Thanh Tra 2
Thuan Loi 1
Trung Nguyen 4
Victoria Chau Doc 9
RESTAURANTS
Bay Bong A
Lam Hung Ky D
Nam Son Mia Gia B
Thanh F
Thanh Tinh E
Truong Van G
Vinh Phuoc C
Ferry to Con Tien
Quan Cung
Covered Market
Ferry to Chau Giang
Incombank
Kiosk for Express Bus to Ho Chi Minh City
Police Station
TRAN HUNG DAO
NGUYEN DINH CHIEU
THUONG DANG LE
DOC PHU THU
BACH DANG
LE CONG THANH
TRA HUNG DAO
CHI LANG
THU KHOA NGHIA
NGUYEN HUU CANH
NGUYEN VAN THOAI
PHAN VAN VANG
QUANG TRUNG
PHAN DINH PHUNG
TRUNG NU VUONG
LE LOI
CU TRI
0 100m
Church, Chau Giang Ferry, Bus Station & 9
10, 11, 12 & Sam Mountain

The Town

First stop should be the town's **covered market**, located roughly between Quang Trung, Doc Phu Thu, Tran Hung Dao and Nguyen Van Thoai, although, sadly, the old colonial structure has now been replaced with a metal monstrosity, complete with red plastic tiles for the roof. On nearby Doc Phu Thu, colonial relics are still evident, but their grand shophouse terraces, flaunting arched upper-floor windows and awnings propped up by decorous wrought-iron struts, are interspersed with characterless new edifices. Nevertheless, this doesn't detract from the frenetic commercial activities in the surrounding streets, and it's well worth picking your way through the rows of neatly stacked stalls of fresh produce, household goods, fish and flowers. Further down, the market stalls blur into narrow alleyways which run towards the river, where you're greeted by a multitude of bobbing boats and waterside activities.

A grand, four-tiered gateway deep in the belly of the open market announces **Quan Cong Temple**. Beyond the courtyard, two rooftop dragons oversee its entrance and the outer walls' vivid murals, their baubled whiskers bouncing in the wind. Tread carefully inside: two roving tortoises have been granted the freedom of the pagoda, at whose head is the familiar red visage of Quan Cong, sporting green robe and bejewelled crown, and surrounded by a rhinestone-studded red velvet canopy. In comparison, the lofty chambers of nearby **Chau Phu Temple** seem devoid of character; fans of gilt woodwork will find much to divert them, but others should head northwest up Tran Hung Dao, where long boardwalks lead to sizeable **stilthouse communities**.

Con Tien Island and Chau Giang District

Two settlements a stone's throw away across the Hau Giang River are also worth venturing out to. The closest is **Con Tien Island**, whose stilthouse sprawl can be explored from the jetty at the eastern end of Thuong Dang Le. There is a 24-hour ferry service across, but if you join a tour (as most people do – just ask in your hotel or guesthouse for information) or charter your own boat you can enjoy the river in a more leisurely manner, and stop off at one of the **fish-farm houses** floating out on the river, above nets of fish that are fed through a hatch in the floor, as well as visit a **Cham community**.

Opposite the GPO, and past a gaggle of hawkers selling Cambodian cigarettes, a second jetty strikes out past a cluster of bobbing houseboats. From here, you can access Cham-dominated **Chau Giang District**. Turn right when you dock, and you'll discover kampung-style wooden houses, sarongs and white prayer caps that betray the influence of Islam, as do the twin domes and pretty white minaret of the **Mubarak Mosque**. Just beyond the mosque, another ferry delivers you back to the west bank, setting you down just below the *Victoria Chau Doc Hotel*. While you're down this way you might wish to visit **St Laurence's Church**, built over the site of its previous namesake, which was established by a French missionary in the late nineteenth century. Beside it, the original statue of St Joseph presides over a pretty garden, while statues of two local Catholic martyrs oversee the courtyard.

Sam Mountain

Arid, brooding **Sam Mountain** rises dramatically from an ocean of paddy fields 5km southwest of Chau Doc. More hill than mountain, it's known as *Nui Sam* to Vietnamese tourists, who flock here in their thousands to worship at its clutch of pagodas and shrines. A trip to the mountain has become *de rigueur* for visitors to town, but it's a distinctly tacky experience. From town, a road runs bowling-alley-straight to the foot of the mountain, hemmed in on the left by a canal lined with eucalyptus and *vo* (retractable fishing nets), while to the right is an expanse of rice paddies. An arm of karaoke-belching cafés reaches out to greet you as you near the foot of the mountain.

Sam doesn't believe in saving the best until last: ahead, as you approach from town, is kitsch, 1847-built **Tay An Pagoda**, the pick of the bunch, its frontage awash with portrait photographers, beggars, joss-stick vendors and bird-sellers (liberating a caged bird is believed to bring good fortune). Tourist blurb describes its style as "Hindu-Islamic", and certainly the central tower is reminiscent of a minaret. Guarding the pagoda are two elephants, one black, one white, and a shaven-headed Quan Am Thi Kinh. The number of gaudy statues inside exceeds two hundred: most are of deities and Buddhas, but an alarmingly lifelike rendering of an honoured monk sits at one of the highly varnished tables in the rear chamber. To the right of this room an annexe houses a goddess with a thousand eyes and a thousand hands, on whose mound of heads teeters a tiny Quan Am.

Ba Chua Xu Temple, 50m to the right beyond Tay An, honours Her Holiness Lady of the Country, a stone statue said to have been found on Sam's slopes in the early nineteenth century. The present building, with its four-tiered, glazed green-tile roof, dates only from 1972. Inside, the Lady sits in state in a marbled chamber, resplendent in red gown and peacock feathers. Glass cases in corridors either side of her are crammed to bursting with splendid garb and other offerings from worshippers, who flood here between the 23rd and 25th of the fourth lunar month, to see her ceremonially bathed and dressed. Multi-storey **Chua Hang** (Cave Pagoda), a few hundred metres further along, is a popular stopping-off point for local tourists, although the tiny grotto after which the pagoda is named is rather a let-down after the sweaty ascent.

Having toured its religious sites, it'd be a shame not to head **up the mountain** itself – take the road to the left by the *Nui Sam Hotel* and then take the first right after about about 300m. It's a long, steep walk to the top, so the route is better tackled with a rented motorbike or xe om. Plans are also afoot to build a cable car up the mountain. After a short ascent, you will come to a superb **viewpoint**, next to the new *Victoria Nui Sam*, with patchwork fields below, best visited around sunset. To the right is a looming tyrannosaurus rex (one of several plastic creatures inhabiting a tacky park, among them rhinos, elephants and zebras) and an observatory that also affords good views. There's a marked contrast between the lush paddy fields – scored by hundreds of waterways, like scratches on a school desk – and the barren mountain, on whose slopes scrub and massive boulders are strewn around.

It's another twenty minutes' clamber to the top if you're walking, where signs prohibit photography of a tiny military outpost. Vietnamese soldiers keep a sharp eye on the Cambodian border, their barracks and the hilltop café making unlikely bedfellows. As well as enjoying the magical view to the west, you can also look back over Chau Doc from here.

Eating

Chau Doc has more **places to eat** than most Mekong Delta towns: it's mostly Vietnamese food that's available, though if you're crying out for a steak, or eggs for breakfast you'll find somewhere that can oblige. Most of the recommendations below are in the town centre – there's a further glut of places at the base of Sam Mountain (see opposite), though none is particularly outstanding and their prices are over the odds. A snack at one of the **food stalls** around the market, particularly on Tran Hung Dao, Chi Lang and Le Cong Thanh, is the go if you're strapped for cash.

Bassac *Victoria Chau Doc Hotel*, 32 Le Loi. Imaginative Western and Asian dishes, such as duck breast with five spices in apple and almond sauce, served in a romantic riverside dining terrace overlooking the Mekong; with dishes averaging around $4, this is an affordable treat.

Bay Bong 22 Thuong Dang Le. Delicious pork cooked in a clay pot and sweet-and-sour fish at very cheap prices.

Lam Hung Ky 71 Chi Lang. Friendly family-run eatery opposite the market, whose imaginative Chinese-influenced menu features beef with bitter melon and black beans; a full meal, including a beer, will come to around $3.50.

Mekong Guesthouse On the slopes of Sam Mountain. If you get hungry while visiting Sam Mountain, the guesthouse has a good range of cheap Western and Vietnamese dishes and a spa-

cious garden in which to enjoy them.

Nam Son Mia Gia 100 Thuong Dang Le. Small but clean roadside eating house serving tasty *hu tieu*; a little pricier than normal, but worth it.

Thanh 40–42 Quang Trung. Justifiably popular with locals and tourists alike for its extensive good-value menu and well-presented Vietnamese dishes.

Thanh Tinh 13 Quang Trung. Reliable vegetarian outlet next door to the *Truong Van*, serving cheap and cheerful dishes.

Truong Van 15 Quang Trung. Above average *com* shop, a stone's throw from the market and usually busy, serving Chinese and Vietnamese staples.

Vinh Phuoc 14 Quan Trung. Smart place with appealing dishes such as chicken with chilli and lemon grass for just over $1.

Southwest to Ba Chuc and Tup Duc

With your own transport, or the services of a Honda om driver, it's possible to explore the sweep of staggeringly beautiful countryside southwest of Chau Doc. Refugees fleeing Pol Pot's Cambodia boosted the Khmer population here in the late Seventies, and pursuit by the Khmer Rouge ended in numerous indiscriminate massacres; a grisly memorial to one of these, at the village of Ba Chuc (see below), lends a tragic focus to a trip through the region. It's about 40km from Chau Doc to Triton and another 10km or so to Ba Chuc.

With Sam Mountain rounded, the road is marshalled ahead by lush paddy fields etched by an intricate canal system. Beyond a left fork at **NHA BANG**, the variable road chicanes through gently sloping hills, some dark and littered with scree, others green and wooded. There's a timeless grandeur to the scenery here: distant waterways are lined by spiky *thot not* (sugar palm) trees, whose fronds are clustered like firework flashes, and whose fruits, reminiscent of coconuts roasted in a fire, yield a handful of transparent, edible seeds; and you're likely to see cattle- and pony-drawn carts as well as cars or trucks. On the right is a turning for Cam Mountain, the highest peak in the region at 716m, where a new resort, the *Lam Vien Cam Mountain Resort* (☎076/760229, ✉lamvientbagg@hcm.vnn.vn; ➌), offers a countryside retreat, along with entertainment such as "dinghy hitting, batttery vehicles, flying fortress and highspeed trainway". In this area, darker skins, red-and-white checked turbans and horned temples indicate you're in Khmer territory. As you hit **TRITON**, a road to your right just past the bus station signals the way to Ba Chuc.

You'll know you're upon **BA CHUC** when you notice graceful glades of bamboo flanking the road. The return trip by Honda om from Chau Doc should cost around $10. Scoot through the town's tatty main drag and bear right, and you'll quickly spot the **memorial** to the thousands massacred in twelve days in April 1977, standing peacefully in a field. An unattractive pink concrete canopy fails to lessen the impact of the eight-sided memorial: behind its glass enclosure, the bleached skulls of the dead of Vietnam's own "killing fields" are piled in ghoulish heaps, grouped according to age to highlight the youth and innocence of many of the dead. The wooden table that serves as a shrine bristles with joss-stick stems. Beside the memorial is a small room, where a horrific set of black and white photos taken just after the massacre shows buckled, abused corpses scattered around the countryside. Some of the images on display are extremely disturbing and you should only enter if you are not a sensitive type. There are also several food stalls set up to cater to the steady stream of visitors to the site.

Another possible side-trip from Triton is to visit the former Viet Cong base at **TUP DUC** (daily 7am–5pm; small admission charge), half an hour's drive from Triton – take the right turn at the end of town. During the American war, Tup Duc gained the rather ignominious moniker "Two Million Dollar Hill", a reference to the amount the US military is said to have spent trying to dislodge the enemy from its slopes. Now the Vietnamese government has ploughed in money of its own in an attempt to turn it into a tourist resort, by installing pedal boats on a lake, an ostrich-breeding farm, a flower garden, a shooting range ("national defence entertainment"), a restaurant and refreshment kiosks at the foot of the hill. There is also a small museum here, an electronic mock-up of the battle (both closed 11am–1pm) and dummies in a cave on the hill, re-creating a Viet Cong briefing scene. Kids will probably latch on to you and lead you up a stairway past the massive boulders that provided such effective cover to the Viet Cong. Reminders of the American failure to capture the hill greet you as you approach; ARVN and US insignia daubed onto the rocks are symbolically crossed out in black, serving to make the point that the base never effectively fell under American control. US forces usually abandoned the position shortly after it had been "neutralized", only for Viet Cong cadres to move in and re-establish themselves weeks or even days later. Squeezing through the narrow passageways formed by the jumble of boulders, it is easy to see how it made such a perfect hide-out.

It is possible to head on from here to the coast, by taking a turn to the left just before re-entering Triton. The road follows a canal for about 30km with views of rice paddies and eucalyptus plantations. After crossing a small ferry at Vam Ray, the route joins Highway 80, the main coast road, from where it is 47km northwest to Ha Tien, or 57km southeast to Rach Gia.

Rach Gia and around

Roughly 11km below Long Xuyen the main road that connects **Kien Giang Province** with the rest of Vietnam shoots off southwest towards the coast, chased all the way by the Cai San Canal.

A couple of hours after leaving Long Xuyen you'll reach the thriving port of **RACH GIA**, which teeters precariously over the Gulf of Thailand. Rach Gia is home to a community of around 150,000 people, who eke out a living through rice cultivation in the surrounding fields, or by tapping the gulf's rich vein of seafood. A small islet in the mouth of the Cai Lon River forms the hub of the town, but the urban sprawl spills over bridges to the north and south of it and onto the mainland. At first sight, Rach Gia is a noisy, claustrophobic and not immediately likeable place, its central area shoehorned tightly between Le Loi and Tran Phu. Given time, though, its nautical charm can work quite a spell on visitors.

Oc Eo and the Funan Empire

Between the first and sixth centuries AD, the western side of the Mekong Delta, southern Cambodia and much of the Gulf of Siam's seaboard came under the sway of the Indianized **Funan Empire**, an early forerunner of the great Angkor civilization. The heavily romanticized annals of contemporary Chinese diplomats describe how the Funan Empire was forged when an Indian Brahmin visiting the region married the daughter of a local serpent-god, and how the serpent rendered the region suitable for cultivation by drinking down the waters of the flood plains. Such fables are grounded in truth: Indian traders would have halted here to pick up victuals en route from India to China, and would have disseminated not only their Hindu beliefs, but also their advanced irrigation and wet-rice cultivation methods.

One of Funan's major trading ports, **Oc Eo**, was located east of Rach Gia. In common with other Funan cities, Oc Eo was ringed by a moat and consisted of wooden dwellings raised off the ground on piles. Given the discovery of Persian, Egyptian, Indian and Chinese artefacts (and even a gold coin depicting the Roman Emperor Marcus Aurelius) at Oc Eo sites, the port must have played host to a fair number of traders from around the world.

The Funan Empire finally disappeared in the seventh century, when it was absorbed into the adjacent **Chen La** Empire (see p.77).

Arrival and information

Buses from points north pull up 500m above town, at Rach Gia's local bus station on Dong Khoi. Arrivals from Long Xuyen and beyond hit the coast at Rach Soi, 7km southeast of Rach Gia. Some continue into town, dropping you outside the *Palace Hotel*; others terminate at Rach Soi bus station, from where a shuttle bus will get you to the centre. Arriving at the **airport** (flights from Ho Chi Minh or Phu Quoc), you can also take a shuttle bus into town. If you need a taxi from the airport, call ☎077/878787 or 912912. Arriving boats dock at the same jetties used for departures (see 'Moving on' box below).

You can **exchange** travellers' cheques and cash at Vietcombank, just over the river on Mac Cuu, as well as get cash advances against Visa and MasterCard – a priority if you're pushing on to Ha Tien or the Hon Chong Peninsula. Kien Giang Tourist at 12 Ly Tu Trong (☎077/862081) can also arrange **car rental** and **tours** around Rach Gia.

Accommodation

As far as **accommodation** goes, the cheery *Palace Hotel* (☎077/863049; ❶–❸) has some big, smart rooms as well as a handful of cheaper, smaller rooms near the top. Round the corner, the riverside *Hoa Binh* (☎077/861523; ❷) offers clean doubles with all facilities. Otherwise, the central *To Chau* (☎077/863718; ❶–❷) has a selection of prices to suit most pockets, and all rooms have air-condition-ing, though some don't have windows and noise could be a problem at the front. Smallish rooms characterize the *1.5* (May 1) *Hotel* (☎077/862103; ❶–❷) on Nguyen Hung Son, though its top-grade rooms are a fair size and offer good value. To the west of the town centre, a couple of mini-hotels have plushly-equipped rooms at competitive rates. The nearer one to town is the *Nam Nho* (☎077/866644; ❶–❷) at 21 Tran Phu, though the *Tuyet Mai* (☎077/873048; ❶–❷) at 33b Dien Bien Phu is only a few steps further. The *Hoa Binh 1* and *2* (☎077/863053 and ☎077/861921 respectively; both ❶) are both pretty grubby places with tiny fan rooms and shared toilets, but offer the cheapest beds in town. The first is at 11 Ly Tu Trong and the second is at 37 Hung Vuong.

Moving on from Rach Gia

When you're ready to move on, shuttle **buses** heading back to Rach Soi can be picked up on Tran Phu, but if you're heading for Ha Tien or Hon Chong you'll depart from the bus station on Dong Khoi. If you're taking one of the hourly express buses to Ho Chi Minh, which depart between 6pm and midnight, you'll board in town; buy tickets in advance from the booths marked "Toc Hanh" either in front of the Vietcombank or just across from the Kien Long Bank.

Boats out of Rach Gia depart from one of two sites. Ferries bound for Phu Quoc Island (see p.183) depart daily at 8am (speedboat; 3hr; $8) and 9am (regular boat; 6–7hr; $4) from Ben Tau Khach Bien quay 200m west of the Nguyen Trung Truc Temple (see p.178). It's better to buy a ticket for the speedboat in advance at 14 Tu Dao (☎077/877742, ⓕ877741), just round the corner from the pier. From Ben Tau Rach Meo quay, 5km south of town on Ngo Quyen, passenger/cargo boats leave for Ca Mau and other destinations in the delta.

If you're doing a circuit that includes Phu Quoc Island, check out the regular **flights** from Ho Chi Minh City that call first at Phu Quoc Island before reaching Rach Gia. For tickets or information, contact either the airport (☎077/861848) or Kien Giang Tourist (see above), who can arrange car rentals and **tours** around Rach Gia.

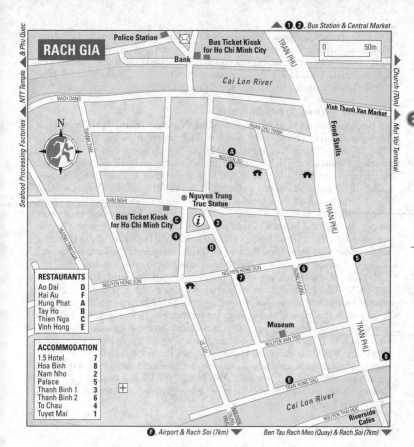

The Town

Once you've seen the wartime souvenirs and Oc Eo relics – shards of pottery, coins and bones – of the pedestrian **museum** at 21 Nguyen Van Troi (Mon–Fri 7–11am & 1.30–5pm; free), and toured the lively **markets**, you've pretty much seen the sights. Walk west along **Bach Dang** for a few hundred metres, though, and the town springs spectacularly to life. To your right is the upper channel of the Cai Lon River, choked by an armada of blue fishing boats, on each of whose red-painted decks sits a "lifeboat" coracle. Boats are often decked out as for a parade, their masts and rigging traced with bunting and colourful flags, under which cooks squat, preparing food for their crews. The **shoreline** is a hive of activity: men and women darn and fold nets, charcoal-sellers hawk their wares to ships' captains and roadside cafés heave with fishermen – many of whom have seen the bottoms of a few BGI bottles – awaiting the next tide.

Turn onto the dirt track to your right, 50m after Bach Dang veers left onto Hoang Dieu: past the boats laid up for repainting, and the chicken-wire frames pegged with drying fish, you'll reach Rach Gia's **seafood processing factories**. In corrugated iron sheds around here, conical-hatted women squat over buckets of octopus and squid, which they scrape clean for export to other Asian countries, receiving less than $2 a day for their trouble.

There's another flotilla of fishing boats one block south, beyond the *Vinh Hong Restaurant*. Rowing-boat **ferries** thread these waters, taking fishermen back to their boats – take one yourself, and you may be invited onto a ship. Sunsets over distant **Turtle Island** (so called because its dual humps look like a turtle's head and shell) are breathtaking viewed from the makeshift cafés around here.

Nguyen Trung Truc Temple

Of Rach Gia's handful of pagodas, only the **Nguyen Trung Truc Temple**, at 18 Nguyen Cong Tru, is really worth making an effort to see. From 1861 to 1868, Nguyen Trung Truc spearheaded anti-French guerrilla activities in the western region of the delta: a statue in the centre of Rach Gia depicts him preparing to unsheathe his sword and harvest a French head. In 1861, Nguyen masterminded the attack that culminated in the firing of the French warship *Esperance*; as a wanted man, he was forced to retreat to Phu Quoc, from where he continued to oversee the campaign. Only after the French took his mother hostage in 1868 did he turn himself in, and in October of the same year he was executed by a firing squad in the centre of Rach Gia. Defiant to the last, his final words could have been lifted from a Ho Chi Minh speech: "So long as grass still grows on the soil of this land, people will continue to resist the invaders."

The riotous colour scheme of the temple roof, with its lurid pink tiles rising to powder-blue crests that are stalked by dragons made of porcelain shards, is plainly visible from a distance. Inside, a portrait of Nguyen in black robe and hat provides the main chamber with its centrepiece. Before it stands a framed poster of other nineteenth-century anti-colonialists – Ky Con, Ham Nghi, Duy Tan and Phan Chu Trinh among them – which reads like a Vietnamese street directory. Two darkened paintings above the front doors, one of which depicts the *Esperance* in flames, continue the anti-colonial theme. Up at the main altar, the brass urn labelled "Anh hung N.T.T." and flanked by slender storks standing on two cheeky-looking yellow turtles, is said to hold the ashes of Nguyen Trung Truc himself.

Eating

When it's time to **eat**, seafood is the obvious choice in this bustling port. However, there are no outstanding restaurants. The best of the bunch is probably the *Hai Au*, which serves steamboat and fish specialities in a prime open-terraced riverside location, just across the bridge to the southeast of town on Nguyen Trung Truc. Also facing the river on Tran Hung Dao is the *Vinh Hong*, where the staples of its seafood dishes eye you warily from tanks mounted on the walls. In the town centre on Nguyen Du, a couple of reasonable places, the *Tay Ho* and the *Hung Phat*, stand opposite each other. Both have English menus and are quite popular with locals, though the surroundings are none too inspiring. The *Ao Dai* at 26 Ly Tu Trong is recommended for good breakfasts, though if you are heading off early to Phu Quoc, you will find *pho* and sandwich vendors lined up along the quayside.

Oc Eo

The ancient ruins of **Oc Eo**, 20km east of Rach Gia, are definitely not worth a visit. Time and museum curators have conspired to strip this former outpost of the Funan Empire (see box on p.175) down to its pilings, and there's now so little to see that even the provincial tourist office advises against the excursion. If you are still tempted but don't want to shell out the dollars for a boat at the tourist office in Rach Gia (see p.176), take the boat from the Ben Tau

Rach Meo jetty as far as Tan Hoi village ($1 round trip), then walk to Vong The village. It is also possible to go by car or motorbike, but the route is tricky to follow, so it's best to go with a guide, or at least a driver.

Hon Chong Peninsula

After a little over two hours the road running northwest of Rach Gia to Ha Tien hits **BA HON**, a once pretty settlement now scarred by industrial development; your only reason for stopping here is if you are taking the boat across to Phu Quoc Island (contact Kien Giang Tourist in Rach Gia for departure times, prices and booking; see p.176). Onwards, a left turn leads, after around 10km, to the **Hon Chong Peninsula**. A string of offshore isles has earned this region the moniker "mini-Ha Long", but it's as a coastal resort that it draws tourists. At present, these are vastly outnumbered by scores of foreign engineers and consultants employed by the cement factories nearby. While Hon Chong has yet to suffer any significant environmental degradation as a result of these factories, their ugly presence looms over the area and certainly detracts from its appeal. For the moment, Hon Chong's calm waters and beaches fringed with palms and casuarinas remain among the most attractive in the delta, though they cannot compare with the beaches on Phu Quoc.

Though described as being in the peninsula's main settlement of **BINH AN**, the bulk of the area's accommodation lies a couple of kilometres south of the village's core, though all bus and Honda om drivers will know where to drop you. The sweep of **beach** in front of most resorts is fine for sunbathing and enjoys a decidedly unspoilt feel with few signs of tourist trappings, but is too shallow and spongy for swimming. Things are better nearer the *Hon Trem* (see overleaf), but the most picturesque beach – for which there is a small admission charge – lies 1.5km further south. After passing pandanus, tamarind and sugar palm trees, the coastal track ends at a towering cliff, into which **Sea and Mountain Pagoda** ("Hai Son Tu") has been hewn: a low doorway leads from its outer chamber to a grotto in the cliff's belly, where statues of Quan Am and several Buddhas are lit by gas lamps. The cramped stone corridor that runs on from here makes as romantic an approach to a beach as you could imagine. As you hit the sand, the twin peaks of **Father and Son Isle** ("Hon Phu Thu") rear up in front of you; if they look familiar it's because they feature on the logo of Kien Giang Tourist. The beach itself is reasonably attractive, though sadly overrun with cafés and restaurants whose plastic chairs and patchwork parasols considerably dent its appeal. For a small fee, kids armed with torches will take you round nearby **Diamond Cave** and point out stalactites supposed to resemble monkeys, eagles and Buddhas.

Boat men and women will offer to take you to the surrounding islands, which will set you back at least $40–60 for a whole day depending on the type of boat. If you're still keen, your best bet is to head for the caves and monkey-infested forests of **Nghe Island**, an hour and a half away. Best of the area's handful of grottoes is **Hang Tien Grotto**, known locally as Ca Sau Grotto, and reached by sampan from the centre of Binh An. Nguyen Anh (later to become Gia Long) hid here while on the run after the Tay Son Rebellion, and locals have dubbed its stone plateaux as his throne, sofa, bed and so on.

Binh An practicalities

Irregular **buses** ply the route between Binh An and Rach Gia. Check with Kien Giang Tourist (see p.176) for times. If these times are inconvenient on leaving, take a Honda om (about $2) to Ba Hon and the main Rach Gia–Ha Tien road and wave down a bus there.

All of the **accommodation** places south of Binh An are a few steps from the beach, though the shallow bays make them unsuitable for swimming. Perched on the hillside at the top end of the strip, the friendly *Green Hill Guesthouse* (☎077/854369; ❷–❸) lives up to its billing, its handful of beautifully furnished rooms all commanding sea views and probably representing the best deal around here. Next up is the *Phuong Thao Guesthouse* (☎077/854357; ❶), which has dingy chalets with wobbly floors; there's little to recommend it except cheap prices. Two new and well-managed places follow, the *An Hai Son* (☎077/759226; ❷) and the *My Lan* (☎077/759044; ❷). Both have smart rooms with air-conditioning, TV and fridge, as well as a decent restaurant. The *Binh An Guesthouse* (☎077/854332; ❶–❷) has dingy fan rooms in billet-style quarters, and much smarter air-conditioned doubles in a newer wing. The *Hon Trem Hotel* (☎077/854331; ❶) was about to undergo a face-lift at the time of writing. Its big wooden villas will be replaced by a major holiday complex, including swimming pool, tennis courts, karaoke, massage and smart, new rooms – expect higher prices too.

Food couldn't be fresher at the beachfront **restaurants**, where fruits of the sea are bought off fishermen on the beach right in front of you. Each displays its produce in bowls in the shade, and gives the chance to settle down and grill your own prawns – but you'll miss the sunset from here.

Ha Tien

Past the turning to the Hon Chong Peninsula, buses whizz over a bridge spanning an estuary crammed with blue fishing boats, (worth stopping for a picture if you have your own transport) and continue up to the far northwestern corner of the delta. Beyond Ba Hon, the road is funnelled by the coastline to the left and vast tracts of water palm to the right, towards endearing Ha Tien, 93km northwest of Rach Gia. As you near Ha Tien, keep an eye out for the Khmer pagoda at **Hon Heo**, some 15km away; bordered by a glistening lake and green paddy fields, it's an arresting sight viewed from the vantage point of the road. Lapped by the waters of the Gulf of Thailand, and only a few kilometres from the Cambodian border, **HA TIEN** has a real end-of-the-line feel, despite its population of around 100,000. This impression of remoteness is accentuated by the aged pontoon bridge you may need to cross to reach the town proper. However, a large new road bridge to the west of town shows that development in Vietnam has now reached all corners of the country.

Many visitors find Ha Tien, with its shuttered terraces, crumbling colonial buildings and mats of seafood drying in the sun, the quaintest and most beautiful town in the delta. It's also one of the few with a substantial recorded history. Founded with the permission of the local Cambodian lords by Chinese immigrant **Mac Cuu** in 1674, the town thrived, thanks to its position astride the trade route between India and China. By the close of that century, Siam (later Thailand) had begun to eye the settlement covetously, and Mac Cuu was forced to petition Hué for support. The resulting alliance, forged with Emperor Minh Vuong in 1708, ensured Vietnamese military back-up, and the town continued to prosper. Mac Cuu died in 1735, but the familial fiefdom continued for seven generations, until the French took over in 1867. Subsequently, the town became a resistance flash point, with Viet Minh holing up in the surrounding hills, and even sniping at French troops from the **To Chau Mountain**, to the south.

Once you've seen Ben Tran Hau's lively waterfront **market** and the fishing boats unloading below the common land to the west of it, you've pretty much exhausted the sights of Ha Tien. You might take a walk up Mac Thien Tich and west along Mac Cuu, to where a temple dedicated to Mac Cuu stands at the foot of the hill where he and his relatives lie buried in semicircular Chinese graves. Beyond courtyard walls as fiery red as the dragons on its roof, three electric "incense" sticks glow constantly before Mac Cuu's funerary tablet, keeping the memory of Ha Tien's founding father alive. Mac Cuu's actual **grave** is uppermost on the hill, daubed with a yin and yang symbol, and guarded by two swordsmen, a white tiger and a blue dragon. From this vantage point, there are good views from the hill over the mop-tops of the coconut trees below and down to the river.

Biking around Ha Tien

A full day can be spent **biking** through the countryside around Ha Tien, with a convenient circular route northwest of town meaning you won't need to backtrack; bikes can be rented through hotels like the *Dong Ho* and *To Chau* for a little over a dollar a day (see "Practicalities", p.182).

Strike off west along Lam Son, and you'll soon be touring through picturesque countryside, peopled by ducks, pigs, and children riding their pet buffaloes. Endless rice fields, coconut groves and swathes of water palm border the road as it kinks gently around low-lying hills towards the Cambodian border. A **war cemetery** serves as a landmark 2.5km from town, and from here it's another 1.5km to the first of two marked turnings to **Mui Nai** – "Stag's Head Peninsula" (small entrance fee), though you'd be hard-pressed to see the silhouette of a stag's head in of any of the surrounding hills. The turning leads past a picturesque village to a peaceful, dark-sand cove.

If you hadn't already guessed this was Khmer country, **Mui Nai Pagoda**, just beyond the turning, leaves you in no doubt. Given its unremarkable fittings, though, sneaking past the aggressive geese that patrol the pagoda's yard represents an unnecessary risk. Several hundred metres further is the second Mui Nai turning, from which a track marked by a toll gate (small fee) leads to the best stretch of beach in the area. A pleasant – if not idyllic – 400-metre curve of sand, shaded by coconut palms and backed by lush green hills, the beach offers reasonable swimming in clean, shallow waters, and a bunch of plastic inflatables in a roped-off area for kids to fool around on. There's nowhere to stay, but a handful of beachside cafés means you can kick back and crack open a few crabs while enjoying a fresh coconut juice or a refreshing slice of watermelon. There is even a proper restaurant, the *Hai Dang*, with an extensive menu. Follow the track around the southern promontory and you'll find an almost identical but more secluded beach.

Continue up the coast and you'll see the 48-metre-high granite outcrop housing **Thach Dong**, or Stone Cave, long before you reach it; 3–4km past Mui Nai the road reaches a junction, and a right turn (a sign reading "Frontier Area" makes a left turn impossible) deposits you at its base. A **monument** shaped like a defiant clenched fist and commemorating the 130 people killed by Khmer Rouge forces near here in 1978 marks the entrance (daily 7am–6pm) to Thach Dong, beyond which steps lead up to a **cave-pagoda** that's home to a colony of bats. Its shrines to Quan Am, Buddha et al are unremarkable, but balconies hewn from the side of the rock afford great views over the hills, paddy fields and sea below. Look to your right and you're peering into Cambodia. From here, continue along the circular road which brings you after a few kilometres back into Ha Tien.

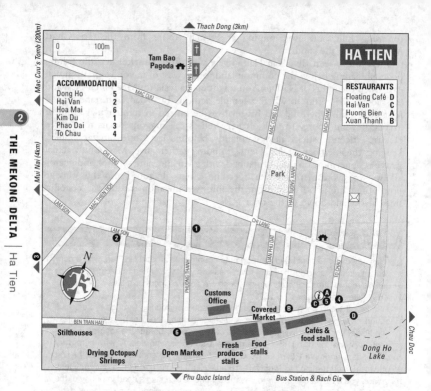

Further up Mac Thien Tich, meanwhile, is mellow **Tam Bao Pagoda**, set in tree-lined grounds dominated by an attractive lotus pond and a huge statue of Quan Am. Out the back of this gaudy yellow pagoda, said to have been founded by Mac Cuu himself, is a pretty garden tended by the resident nuns, its colourful flowers interspersed with tombs. In the rear chamber of the pagoda, a statue of the goddess with a thousand hands and a thousand eyes sits on a lurid pink lotus. Behind her are photos and funerary tablets remembering the local dead, while rudimentary drawings of the ten Buddhist hells hang on her left.

Practicalities

Buses terminate at the bus station below the southern end of the pontoon bridge, from where it's a short, swaying walk into town; onward buses to Chau Doc, Rach Gia and Ho Chi Minh City also depart from here. Street names count for more than numbers, the most important being waterfront Ben Tran Hau, where **passenger boats** arrive from and depart for Chau Doc and Phu Quoc Island daily (check locally for times). Note that foreigners are currently forbidden to use the Ha Tien–Phu Quoc ferry, though several have done so without major recrimination. In any case, it's much easier to get to Phu Quoc Island from Rach Gia or Ba Hon.

Kien Giang Tourist sometimes operates from the reception of the *Dong Ho Hotel*, where staff should be able to organize **guides** as well as **motorbike** and **bicycle rental**; more importantly, they can also **exchange** most cash currencies into dong, the only place in town that does so.

Accommodation

Directly ahead from the pontoon bridge at the bus station, two of Ha Tien's more venerable **hotels** square up to each other at the southern end of To Chau. The *To Chau* (☎077/852148; ❶) has a variety of fan and air-conditioned rooms – ask for the ones at the front for views with balcony; while nearby, the *Dong Ho* (☎077/852141; ❶–❷) is a real colonial relic, with some grand rooms out front and some cramped quarters out back. Unfortunately the metalled-over shutters cut out the view. The smartest option in town is the *Kim Du* (☎077/851929; ❸), at 14 Phuong Thanh, offering air-conditioning, satellite TV and fridge, with breakfast included. The convivial *Hai Van* (☎077/852872; ❶) at 646a Lam Son seems more geared up to taking foreigners than most, and its larger, air-conditioned rooms are a good deal. Along the waterfront, at 1–3 Duong Tran Hau, the friendly *Hoa Mai* (☎077/852670; ❶–❷) has clean and comfortable air-conditioned and fan rooms with en-suite bathrooms, the most expensive with river views. You won't be able to miss the imposing *Phao Dai* (☎077/851849; ❶), which sits majestically over Ha Tien, beside the new bridge over the river. Appearing more expensive than it really is, the rooms are clean and functional with en-suite facilities, and the fan rooms upstairs are a bargain; all have use of communal balconies affording stunning views across the To Chau River or, if you're round the back, Mui Nai bay.

Eating

The waterfront *Xuan Thanh* is a good choice for **eating**. Serving cheap Vietnamese and a few Western dishes from an English menu in clean sur-roundings, it's no wonder they're usually busy; try the stir-fried squid with pineapple or the popular steamboat. Also along the front, the *Hai Van*, operated by the hotel of the same name in town, serves up good breakfasts and has an extensive menu of Vietnamese dishes. The modest *Huong Bien* round the corner on To Chau also has a good range of reliable staples averaging around $1.50. Conveniently located for people-watching, a floating café right by the boat jetty offers coffee, soft drinks and snacks. Finally, there's a gaggle of cafés and **food stalls** on the waterfront, some of which keep a few simple *com* dishes on the go.

Phu Quoc Island

It's a little under 120km from Rach Gia and about 60km from Ba Hon to **PHU QUOC ISLAND**, which rises from its slender southern tip like a genie released from a bottle. Stranded just off the southern coast of Cambodia in the Gulf of Thailand, the island – which spans 46km from north to south – is Vietnam's largest offshore island (593 square kilometres) and classed as a dis-trict of Kien Giang Province, though it's also claimed by Cambodia, which calls it Kho Tral.

The geology and vegetation are quite different to the rest of the delta, and give the place a totally different feel. Phu Quoc's isolation made it an attractive hiding place for two of the more famous figures from Vietnam's past. **Nguyen Anh** holed up here while on the run from the Tay Son Brothers in the late eighteenth century (see p.220), and so too, in the 1860s, did **Nguyen Trung Truc** (see p.178). Today, over 75,000 people and a sizeable population of indigenous dogs (recognizable by a line of hair running up the spine instead of down) dwell on the island, famous throughout Vietnam for its black pepper and its fish sauce (*nuoc mam*), which is graded like olive oil.

Until recently, Phu Quoc cropped up only rarely on tourists' agendas, but now that developers have started to move in on its lush forests and fine beaches this is changing rapidly. If this boom is carefully controlled, the island could become one of Southeast Asia's most beautiful spots, though the signs are that the growth will be chaotic. The island is already a favourite bolt hole for expats working in Ho Chi Minh City, who arrive on the frequently full, regular flights. With the recent lengthening of the airport runway to accommodate jets rather than the sixty-seater propeller planes that currently ply the route, and plans to make it an international airport with flights arriving from places like Thailand and Singapore, Phu Quoc's future looks rosy. Yet while resorts and bars are springing up fast, for the moment Phu Quoc retains a pioneer outpost feel: electricity cuts are frequent, many places can only be reached via dirt tracks and the unspoiled beaches are thankfully free of vendors. In the rainy season, May to October, Phu Quoc is relatively quiet, and room rates become more easily negotiable.

Arrival

Flights from Ho Chi Minh via Rach Gia (see box on p.176; 3 daily in high season; 1hr) land at Phu Quoc Airport, on the edge of Duong Dong town; motorbikes and taxis waiting there can whisk you to most resorts for under a dollar, though most resorts will pick you up at the airport or boat jetty if you prearrange it.

A hardy few brave the arduous journey by regular **boat** from Rach Gia – about seven hours in a ropey vessel on often choppy seas, but there is a daily speedboat service to and from Rach Gia, which cuts the journey time down to three hours (though the crossing can still be rough and the crew hand out seasickness tablets as the boat leaves the harbour). If you do arrive by boat from Rach Gia, you'll disembark at An Thoi Quay, a small settlement in the south of the island. From here, an infrequent minibus service ($1) shuttles back and forth to Duong Dong – look for buses marked "Huong Toan"; if you negotiate with the driver, he may drop you off at your hotel before the bus terminates in town. The alternative is to hire a Honda om (about $1); there should be plenty on hand as you disembark.

If you've arrived from Ba Hon, however, your boat will arrive at Ham Ninh Quay about halfway up the east coast. With no buses standing by, your best bet is to jump on a waiting motorbike ($1–2) to Duong Dong.

Information, tours and trips

Most resorts or guesthouses can provide local **information**, **guides** for hiking and **tours**, one of the most experienced being *Thang Loi Resort* (see p.187). There is a branch of the state-run Kien Giang Tourist in the *Huong Bien Hotel* (see opposite), but the staff are often out on lunch breaks. You might get more joy at the tourist office at the *Saigon-Phu Quoc Resort* (☏077/846510), which organizes a range of upmarket tours. These include visits to the local pearl farm on Bai Truong or joining a fishing boat for an evening of cuttlefish fishing, using coloured plastic shrimps as bait. If you need the services of an **independent tour guide**, contact Huynh Van Anh, also known as Tony, who has an encyclopedic knowledge of the island, on ☏091/319 7334. Just about all resorts rent out **motorbikes** at $5–7 a day, with reductions for longer periods. Check the bike over carefully if you're riding yourself, as many of these machines are falling apart.

The Kien Long Bank (Western Union) on 30 Thang 4 in Duong Dong will **exchange** US dollars and Thai baht (cash) for dong, and also cashes travellers' cheques and gives advances against Visa and MasterCard. Some hotels such as

Moving on from Phu Quoc

Moving on, **boats** bound for Rach Gia leave from An Thoi Quay (speedboat $8, 3hr; regular boat $4, 7hr), while boats bound for Ba Hon leave from Ham Ninh Quay ($4; 5hr); regular boat services depart daily at 10am subject to weather conditions. To book in advance (certainly advisable for the speedboat), contact the office at 1 Tran Hung Dao (☏077/980111). The speedboat to Rach Gia leaves at midday, and a new speedboat service is planned for Ba Hon too. However, schedules do change so it's best to check the up-to-date situation. There are boats that leave for Ha Tien from the north of the island, but at the time of writing these were strictly off limits to foreigners.

Flights to Ho Chi Minh via Rach Gia (3 daily in high season; 1hr) leave from Phu Quoc Airport (see opposite).

the *Tropicana* and *Saigon-Phu Quoc Resort* will exchange US dollars and travellers' cheques; however, rates are not favourable. The **post office** is also on 30 Thang 4, and **Internet** access is available about 100m down Bach Dang Street, to the right just before crossing the bridge to the market from the south. There is also very expensive Internet access at the *Tropicana* and *Saigon-Phu Quoc Resort* (see p.187 and p.185 respectively).

Most resorts run **snorkelling trips** to the offshore islands (see p.188), charging around $10 per person, which include snorkelling, fishing and lunch. The well-organized Rainbow Divers (☏091/340 0964, ⓦwww.divevietnam.com) also operate **diving** outings that leave from the *Saigon-Phu Quoc Resort* (see below) at about 8am on most days during the diving season, charging $30 for snorkelling, $50 for one dive or $100 for three dives, and include all equipment and a tasty lunch. They also offer PADI courses in open-sea and advanced diving.

Accommodation

Apart from the options mentioned below, there are many **private houses** tucked back behind Long Beach that rent out rooms at cheap prices, and a clutch of them located on the main road near the *Huong Bien Hotel*. They offer reduced rates for long stays, which may interest you if you want to settle in for a while.

Duy Khoa By the jetty at An Thoi Quay ☏077/844832. This is a reasonable option if you need to sleep in An Thoi to catch a ferry. It's down an alley to the right as you approach the jetty, and has clean twins and doubles, some with fan, others with air, and good views from the upstairs balcony. ➊

Hong Hanh Mini-Hotel Immediately opposite the entrance to the airport ☏077/847708. Very basic rooms and complaints of pungent plumbing. Only of interest if you want to stay in Duong Dong for some reason. ➊–➋

Huong Bien Hotel ☏077/846113. Government-run hotel with well-appointed rooms, enjoying a central beachfront position, but it's a rather soulless place and the beach here is a bit unsavoury. Major expansion is planned for the near future, so beware of construction noise. ➋–➌

Kim Hoa Guesthouse Off Tran Hung Dao ☏077/847039. A choice of pleasant wooden bungalows and rooms in a block set back from the beach, all comfortably furnished. The service leaves something to be desired, though. ➋–➌

Mango Bay Guesthouse Ong Lang Beach, about 7km north of Duong Dong ☏091/391 7369. Located just south of the *Thang Loi Resort*, this place, approached through a delightful cashew orchard, enjoys a lovely tranquil location and offers spacious, stylish rooms and bungalows with fan and large verandah. The coast is rocky in front but there are deserted sandy bays on each side. ➋–➍

Nam Phuong Resort Off Tran Hung Dao ☏077/846319. Best budget deal on Long Beach, for the moment at least. Smallish but clean fan rooms, a few of which have beach views. Independent tour guides hang out here, too. ➊–➋

Saigon-Phu Quoc Resort Off Tran Hung Dao ☏077/846510. Well-equipped but overpriced villa-style rooms set across landscaped gardens overlooking the beach; facilities include free shuttle bus and a swimming pool. A cheaper extension is currently under construction. ➍–➐

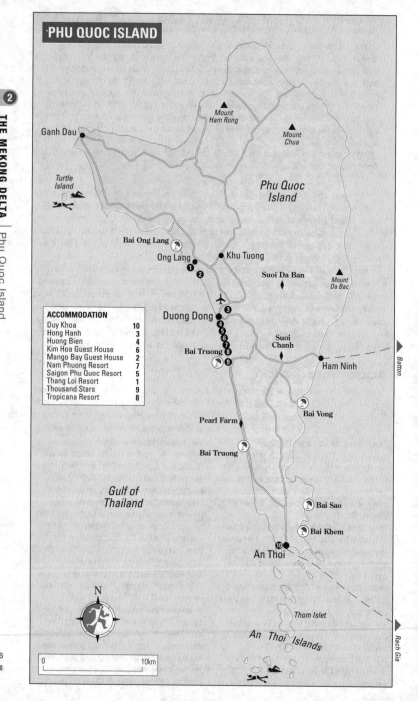

PHU QUOC ISLAND

Ganh Dau

Turtle
Island

Bai Ong Lang

Ong Lang

1
2

Khu Tuong

Mount
Ham Rong

Mount
Chua

Phu Quoc
Island

Suoi Da Ban

Mount
Da Bac

Duong Dong

3
4
5
6
7

Bai Truong

8
9

Suoi
Chanh

Ham Ninh

Bai Vong

Pearl Farm

Bai Truong

Gulf of
Thailand

Bai Sao

Bai Khem

10

An Thoi

Batton

Rach Gia

N

Thom Islet

An Thoi Islands

0   10km

ACCOMMODATION	
Duy Khoa	10
Hong Hanh	3
Huong Bien	4
Kim Hoa Guest House	6
Mango Bay Guest House	2
Nam Phuong Resort	7
Saigon Phu Quoc Resort	5
Thang Loi Resort	1
Thousand Stars	9
Tropicana Resort	8

Thang Loi Resort Ong Lang Beach, about 7km north of Duong Dong ☎091/8073494. A remote setting, with twelve simple bamboo and wood huts overlooking a pristine stretch of beach. Facilities are basic, with no hot water or fans and electricity in the evening only, but the resort is gaining popularity with those who want to get away from it all; the snorkelling is excellent too. ❷–❸

Thousand Stars 3km south of Duong Dong on Long Beach ☎077/848203. A quirky resort with statues of a mermaid and dolphins on the beach and other oddities in the grounds. Popular with overseas Vietnamese for its large, comfortable and well-equipped rooms and bungalows. The cheapest rooms, set back from the beach, are some of the best value on Long Beach. ❸–❹

Tropicana Resort Off Tran Hung Dao ☎077/847127. Popular place with somewhat overpriced bamboo bungalows and semi-detached low-level rooms with porches, though its setting of manicured tropical gardens plus attractive bar-restaurant might make it worth the extra dollars. ❸–❹

Duong Dong

Though you'll probably want at some time to go into the main town of **Duong Dong**, the island's only settlement of any size, for the post office, Internet or to buy supplies in the **market**, there's not a lot else to see. There is a small **lighthouse** and **temple** (Dinh Cau) situated on a promontory at the entrance to the harbour, which is if no great consequence but does provide good **views** up and down the coast. When you've explored one of the town's **nuoc mam factories** and strolled its **waterfront** (at its busiest and most colourful during the squid and cuttlefish season, normally between January and May), you'll probably want to rent a motorbike or xe om and explore further afield.

The west and north coasts

The main attraction of Phu Quoc is its fabulous beaches. The majority of resorts and guesthouses are strung out on the **west coast**, to the south of Duong Dong. This is **Bai Truong (Long Beach)**, an appropriate name, as it stretches almost to the southern tip of the island some 20km away. Most resorts have fine stretches of soft yellow sand right in front, which are ideal for sunbathing, sunset-watching and swimming, though at times tiny creatures in the water can cause an itching or mild stinging sensation. Beyond the first few kilometres south of town the beach is completely deserted, and the road which runs behind the palm trees provides some classic tropical beach views. For travellers arriving by boat from Rach Gia, this is one of the first sights of the island on the way to the resorts.

The west coast north of town is a bit more rugged, but the beautiful bays tucked along **Ong Lang Beach** are certainly worth visiting, and a couple of cosy resorts offer the chance to really get away from it all. Even here, the tentacles of development are already probing, and a golf course will open shortly at the north end of this beach. Over seventy percent of the island is forested at present, and the hills of the north are particularly verdant, but there are fewer beaches up here and nothing in the way of accommodation.

The east coast

The **east coast** is, so far, largely undeveloped, and best experienced during the dry season, November to April. It does, however, have a good sealed road that makes a pleasant change from the constant dust kicked up off the dirt roads around the rest of the island. The most impressive beach here is **Bai Sao** (Star Beach), which is signposted just north of the T-junction where the road from Duong Dong meets the road up the east coast. Its dazzling white sand and pale blue water are a great attraction for local people at weekends, and a couple of beach restaurants do a healthy trade. The one towards the north of the beach has better prices and particularly tasty seafood. A little south of Bai Sao, **Bai Kem** (Ice Cream Beach) is also of a blinding white colour, but there is no shade, the beach is full of rubbish washed in by the tide, and in any case, the military generally prohibit entry to foreigners. North of Bai Sao, **Bai Vong** (Vong Beach) is worth a look, though it is very shallow for swimming and there is little available in the way of refreshment.

Inland Phu Quoc

Inland Phu Quoc is the kind of island that is ideal for exploration, though until the roads are sealed, you are likely to return at the end of day covered in a film of red dust. All over the island, and particularly in the north, you will pass by **pepper plantations**, the plants easily identifiable as climbers on three-metre-high poles – at places like **Khu Tuong**, they welcome visitors to look around. There are also two cleansing **springs** in the centre of Phu Quoc, which thankfully have yet to be commercialized – ask for **Suoi Da Ban** or **Suoi Chanh**. They tend to dry up in the dry season, when the trip is not worth it, and are sometimes unsightly with rubbish.

This mountainous area – which is typical of the surrounding forested region – makes for excellent **hiking**. There are no marked trails or signposts, so it's vital you go with a guide – it's also likely to be more enjoyable early in the dry season (Nov–Dec). Most resorts or guesthouses can provide guides for such a trip; see p.185 for details. Note also that the three northernmost peaks on the island are off limits, due to their proximity to Cambodia.

The An Thoi and Turtle islands

The **coral reefs** around Phu Quoc are teeming with tropical fish, and most visitors like to spend at least a day or so snorkelling or diving. There are a few corals just off Ong Lang Beach, but the best locations are around the **An Thoi Islands** to the south or **Turtle Island** off the northwest coast, both of which entail a boat trip. At these reefs – the former of which is rated by some as the best dive site in Vietnam – you can float above brain and fan corals, watching parrot fish, scorpion fish, butterfly fish, huge sea urchins and a host of other marine life. See p.185 for details of diving- and snorkelling-trip operators.

Eating

Eating options are improving all the time, which is at least one benefit of the development boom. Not surprisingly, every beach resort has its own restaurant; most have reasonable menus and some have sea views, but the quality is erratic and prices are often inflated. One of the best is undoubtedly the *Tropicana Resort* (see p.187), with its bamboo-and-thatch restaurant and bar overlooking the beach, a decent menu of Western and Asian dishes and laidback atmosphere. The *Thousand Stars* (see p.187), about a kilometre further south on Long Beach, also has excellent food – try the stir-fried noodles with seafood and one of their delicious custard-apple shakes.

Cheaper than both of these and set right on the beach just south of the *Tropicana* is the *Hieu Family Restaurant*. Consisting of little more than a few poles holding up a corrugated roof, the place is often packed – not for its ambience (though sunsets are great) but for its down-home cooking at very reasonable prices. At the time of writing, two other beach restaurant/bars were about to open, the *Boat House,* just down from *Hieu Family Restaurant,* and the

Beach Club, just south of the *Thousand Stars*. Up on Ong Lang Beach, both the *Mango Bay Guesthouse* (see p.185) and the *Thang Loi Resort* (see p.187) have pleasant terraced restaurants with sea views and excellent food. In Duong Dong, the cheap and cheerful *Gop Gio* is popular with the locals, but also provides an extensive menu in English; no doubt as tourists arrive in greater numbers, other restaurants, coffee bars and food stalls in town will follow suit.

Travel details

Buses

It's almost impossible to give the frequency with which buses run. Long-distance public buses, though scheduled, won't depart if empty. It's advisable to start your journey early – most long-distance departures leave between 5am and 7am, and few run after midday. Journey times can also vary; figures below show the normal length of time you can expect the journey to take.

Ca Mau to: Bac Lieu (1hr); Can Tho (4hr); Ho Chi Minh City (7hr); Long Xuyen (5hr); Soc Trang (2hr).

Can Tho to: Bac Lieu (3hr); Ca Mau (4hr); Chau Doc (2hr 30min); Ha Tien (5hr); Ho Chi Minh City (4hr); Long Xuyen (1hr 30min) ; My Tho (2hr 30min).

Chau Doc to: Ca Mau (7hr); Can Tho (2hr 30min); Ha Tien (4hr); Ho Chi Minh City (5hr); Long Xuyen (1hr).

Ha Tien to: Can Tho (5hr); Chau Doc (4hr); Ho Chi Minh City (8hr); Long Xuyen (5hr); Rach Gia (2hr 30min).

Long Xuyen to: Ca Mau (5hr); Chau Doc (1hr); Ha Tien (5hr); Ho Chi Minh City (5hr).

My Tho to: Can Tho (2hr 30min); Cao Lanh (2hr); Cholon, Ho Chi Minh City (1hr 50min).

Vinh Long to: Sa Dec (50min); Tra Vinh (1hr 30min).

Boats

See "Getting around the delta," p.137, for more on the various craft that ply the delta's waterways.

Ba Hon to: Phu Quoc (speedboat daily, 2hr; regular boat daily, 4hr).

Chau Doc to: Ha Tien (usually daily; 7–8hr); Phnom Penh (daily; 4hr).

Ha Tien to: Chau Doc (usually daily; 7–8hr).

Phu Quoc to: Ba Hon (speedboat daily, 2hr; regular boat daily, 4hr); Rach Gia (speedboat daily, 3hr; regular boat daily, 6–7hr).

Rach Gia to: Phu Quoc (speedboat daily, 3hr; regular boat daily, 6–7hr).

Flights

Phu Quoc to: Ho Chi Minh City (daily; 1hr); Rach Gia (3 daily; 40min).

Rach Gia to: Ho Chi Minh City (5 weekly; 1hr); Phu Quoc (3 daily; 40min).

The southern and central highlands

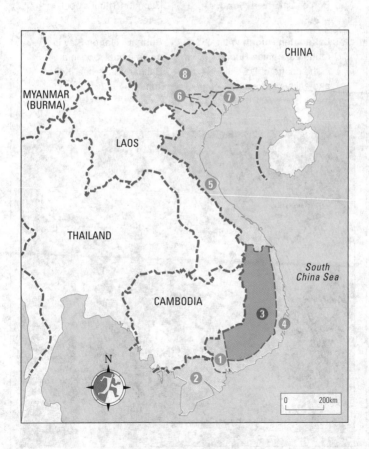

CHAPTER 3 # Highlights

* **Dambri Waterfalls** Feel the spray from Dambri Waterfalls on your face as you stand right below them. See p.197

* **Trekking** Go trekking in a national park at Yok Don or Cat Thien. See p.215

* **Lake Xuan Huong** Walk round Lake Xuan Huong in the centre of Da Lat and enjoy the fresh climate. See p.202

* **Lak Lake** Paddle around Lak Lake in a dug-out canoe at dawn. See p.216

* **Coffee in Buon Me Thuot** Enjoy a cup of fresh coffee in one of Buon Ma Thuot's cool cafés. See p.214

* **Bahnar villages** Stay in a communal *rong* in a Bahnar village near Kon Tum. See p.221

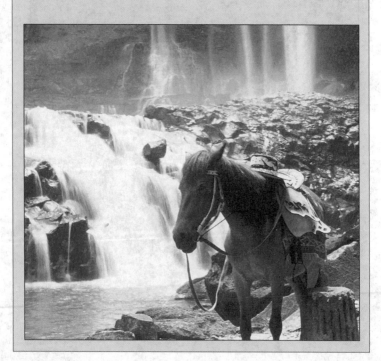

3

The southern and central highlands

Vietnam's mountainous midriff isn't the first region of the country that most tourists think to visit. And yet, after a hot and sticky stint labouring across the coastal plains, these southern and central highlands, with their host of ethnic minorities, mist-laden mountains and thundering waterfalls, can provide an enjoyable contrast to the Tropics. Pinpointing the appeal of the area isn't easily done: travel can be a headache, and roads at times impassable; local tourist authorities have been known to raise a fuss about tourists travelling independently; and there are no really heart-stopping sights. But the highlands' allure lies in such simple pleasures as inhaling their invigoratingly chill airs, and walking or cycling with a spray of mist on your face. And, cocooned in woolly jumpers, scarves and bobble hats, the highlanders exude a warmth unsurpassed elsewhere in the country, making a trip here doubly appealing.

Bounded to the west by the Cambodian border, and spreading out over the lofty peaks and broad plateaux of the **Truong Son Mountains**, the southern and central highlands stretch from the base of Highway 1 right up to the bottleneck of land that squeezes past Da Nang towards Hanoi and the north. The slash-and-burn approach that once characterized the region's agriculture is being gradually phased out, and today its fertile red soils yield considerable **natural resources**, among them coffee, tea, rubber, silk and hardwood. Not all of the highlands, though, have been sacrificed to plantation-style economies of scale – or to the napalm that US planes emptied over swathes of the region. Tracts of primeval forest still thrive, where **wildlife** including elephants, bears and gibbons somehow survived the days when the region was a hunting ground for Saigon's idle rich and Hué's idle royal.

Of the highlands' 2.5 million inhabitants, many belong to the **ethnic minorities** that live on its plateaux, struggling to maintain their identities in the face of persistent pressure from Hanoi to assimilate. The French knew them as **montagnards** (or *Moï*, meaning "savages", if they were feeling less charitable), and the name, meaning "mountain folk", has stuck – though *montagnards* themselves would reject the suggestion of unity implicit in this generic term. The peoples of the central highlands – the Bahnar, E De, Jarai, Sedang, Koho and Mnong are the largest – belong to one of two ethno-linguistic groups, Mon-Khmer or Malayo-Polynesian. Perhaps because of the substantial number

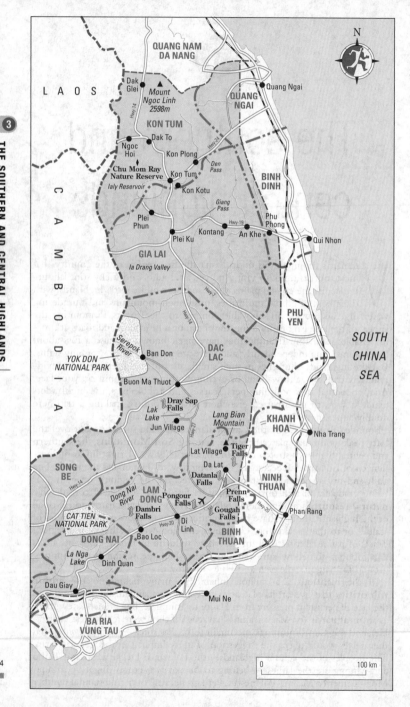

of *montagnards* forced into labour on French plantations in colonial days, Viet Minh agents mined a rich vein of anti-colonial feeling. Years later the highlands were of sufficient strategic importance for several American army bases to be established here, and *montagnard* conscripts put their knowledge of the upper plateaux to work for the forces of the South. For their pains, the minorities' villages were parcelled into strategic hamlets, and their land was devastated by carpet bombing.

Postwar, the communists proved unsympathetic to the *montagnards'* wish to retain their cultural identity. The rebel organization, **FULRO** (United Front for the Liberation of Oppressed Races; see p.522), which had emerged in the Sixties to uphold tribal rights, was weakened and ultimately extinguished by the government. Hanoi, for over a decade, followed a policy of **forced assimilation**, drawing together numerous villages into new settlements where they could be more easily monitored. Recently, the **liberalization** of *doi moi* has led to a positive shift in attitudes towards the minorities, and moves to preserve their unique cultures have gained further impetus due to their appeal to tourists. Ironically, most of the minorities themselves now aspire to a more modern lifestyle: it's becoming increasingly difficult for tourists to find villages of stilthouses, and traditional dress is worn only for festive occasions or tourist shows.

Visiting one or other of the highlands' many minority villages independently can be difficult (see box on p.444 for some tips on village etiquette): in most cases you'll need to go through a local tourist office (and pay handsomely for the privilege), but in each area it's best to double-check the current regulations, especially concerning overnight stays in villages.

For most of the tourists who ascend to these altitudes, the main target is **Da Lat**, an erstwhile French mountain retreat that appears more or less romantic in direct proportion to the density of the mists draped across it. Visitors are often disappointed by Da Lat, however. The only settlement of any size in the region, it falls short of the idyll promised by many guidebooks, thanks to some dreary architecture and drearier tourist trappings. That said, the city is not without its charms, among them some beguiling colonial buildings, picturesque bike rides and a market overflowing with delectable fruits and vegetables. Above Da Lat, the **central highlands** harbour a series of gritty towns whose reputations rest less on tourist sights than on the villages and open terrain that ring them. Sensitive to the minority rights issue, the Vietnamese authorities opened this region to foreigners only in 1993, and the majority of tourists remain too intent on the beckoning charms of Highway 1 to drop by its main towns, **Buon Ma Thuot** and **Kon Tum**, and the city of **Plei Ku**.

At present, the favoured way of seeing the highlands is on a minibus **tour** out of Hanoi or Ho Chi Minh City, but if the pace of a tour isn't to your taste it's certainly possible to swing through these regions independently, by motorbike or local bus. It's an easy journey **to reach Da Lat**: perfectly good roads shoot up from the east side of Ho Chi Minh and from Phan Rang on the coast. When **pushing on from Da Lat**, it's possible to drop down to the coast at Phan Rang, or head south from Da Lat on Highway 20 for about 20km before turning right onto **Highway 27**, which snakes its way northwards over the hills, passing pretty **Lak Lake** on the way to **Buon Ma Thuot.** Though parts of this road have recently been upgraded, if travelling during the wet season, check on its condition before leaving Da Lat. Another option is to head directly to Buon Ma Thuot from Ho Chi Minh City on **Highway 14**, which has recently been widened and improved, and will eventually provide an alternative route to Hanoi. North of Buon Ma Thuot, Highway 14 makes a beeline across the Dac Lac Plateau to **Plei Ku**, and then continues to **Kon Tum**, a journey of less than an hour. From Kon Tum you can head straight for the coast, along the attractive **Highway 24** to **Quang Ngai**, or even follow **Highway 14** north along the route of the **Ho Chi Minh trail**, later branching off on **Highway 14B** to **Da Nang**. Since restrictions on independent travel are less stringent in Kon Tum than around Plei Ku or Buon Ma Thuot, and given the fact that there are several nearby minority villages where home-stays are possible, Kon Tum is likely to grow in popularity.

Unless you have your own transport, or travel with expensive tourist office tours, once up in the central highlands you've no option other than to get around by Honda om. Finding a driver who speaks English isn't always easy outside of Da Lat (where the Easy Riders are a very knowledgeable crowd), but it's worth persisting, especially if you plan to head out into remoter areas. Your highland experience will also vary enormously depending upon **when you visit**. The dry season runs from November through to April. To see the region at its atmospheric best, though, you're better going in the wet season, May to October, although the rain can cause problems: some less polished roads will be awash and you could have trouble getting out to some less accessible villages.

Da Lat and the southern highlands

The conical-hatted tappers who work the regimented avenues of the rubber plantations around **Dau Giay**, 67km east of Ho Chi Minh, have long since ceased to bat an eyelid at the scores of minibuses that hurtle past them to **Da Lat and the southern highlands**. As the road – **Highway 20** – starts its ascent, the rubber trees corralling its traffic occasionally peel away to permit tantalizing views of the valleys below. Tourist buses out of Ho Chi Minh invariably screech to a brief halt on the causeway traversing **La Nga Lake**, from where the wood and thatch **houseboats** cast adrift on its waters are only a zoom lens away. Locals use curious foot-powered rowing boats to access their homes, under which lie fish farms similar to those at Chau Doc (see p.72). East of La Nga, Highway 20 drags its heels through wooded slopes, whose peaks are almost invariably draped with tousled clouds. The slopes' verdant greens are flecked only occasionally by the red-tiled roofs of farmsteads and the roving figures of grazing cattle. Keep an eye out for unusual rock formations, which signal your arrival at the diminutive town of **Dinh Quan**, 180km south of Da Lat. Once an area of intense volcanic activity, the landscape around here retains an almost otherworldly aspect.

In time the hills yield to the tea, coffee and mulberry plantations of the **Bao Loc Plateau**. If you want to make a pit stop between Ho Chi Minh and Da Lat, your best bet is the plantation town of **Bao Loc**, as more diminutive **Di Linh**, 35km further on, is bereft of hotels. Unless you're effecting a very round-about route to Phan Rang, **Da Lat** signposts journey's end.

Bao Loc and around

The terrain around the mid-sized settlement of **BAO LOC** resembles a sheet of paper that's been first crumpled, and then flattened out again. The plains pinched between the low ridges of the Bao Loc Plateau provide rich agricultural pickings. As well as **tea** and **coffee**, locals cultivate the mulberry bushes off whose leaves **silkworms** feed.

The area's outstanding attraction is **Cat Tien National Park** (T & F 061/791227-8, E cattien_nationalpark@fptnet.com.vn; $1.30 per day for first two days, $0.70 for subsequent days), a protected area situated 150km north of Ho Chi Minh City along Highway 20, and about 50km south of Bao Loc, covering the largest lowland tropical rainforest in south Vietnam. The park hosts nearly 350 species of birds, over 450 species of butterfly, and over 100 mammals, including wild cats, elephants, monkeys, and the rare Javan rhinoceros. Don't bank on seeing a rhino, though, as the few residing here are said to be in a secluded reserve closed to visitors. If you're coming by public transport, take a bus for Da Lat from Mien Dong station in Ho Chi Minh; tell the driver you want "Vuon Quoc Gia Cat Tien" (Cat Tien National Park), and he will drop you at the "km125" junction at Tan Phu town. From here, motorbikes ($2) cover the final 25km to the park along a narrow sealed road. If you're arriving from the north, a signposted road (also sealed) to the park branches right just south of Madagui. You need to pay the entrance fee at a park office on stilts about 100m before the ferry across the Dong Nai River to park headquarters. As the park can only accommodate about seventy visitors at a time, it's important to phone ahead for reservations. **Accommodation** here (①) consists of simple rooms with with fan or air-conditioning, and a campsite but no tents, though there are plans to upgrade (and bump up costs) in 2004. You can also hire vehicles and boats for travel to the park's more remote areas, but there are few English-speaking guides. Though a dozen walking trails exist, the catch is that you need to hire a jeep or pick-up to get to the start of most of them, plus a guide to go with you, so a day out can easily cost $15-20. You might be better off signing up for the "night safari" ($10) where there could be a chance of seeing one of the 18 mammals or 12 reptiles reputed to be in the park that are on the endangered species list. Some tour operators in Ho Chi Minh and Da Lat do organize tours, but few have much knowledge of the park itself.

Another interesting attraction of the area is the impressive drop (about 50m) of **Dambri Waterfalls** (daily 7am–5pm; small entrance fee), some 18km northwest of Bao Loc. The falls feature on many a Ho Chi Minh City tour agenda, but a Honda om from Bao Loc will also get you there. If you've reached Bao Loc under your own steam, follow the road that strikes north from beside the post office, veer left at the first two forks and then follow the signs. The road to the falls bisects rolling countryside carpeted by coffee, tea and mulberry plantations. Once you arrive, there are two paths leading to the falls. The main one to the right leads to the top of the falls, where some ugly spider's-web fencing stands between you and a precipice over which a torrent tumbles in the rainy season. From here, you can descend to the base of the falls by steep steps, or if you're feeling lazy, there's a lift available for 5000d. Another path to the left by a restaurant leads down a steep stairway among towering trees to a superb view of the falls from in front. The two paths are linked by a bridge over the river, where you're likely to get drenched in spray even during the dry season. The path continues downstream to a smaller cascade, Dasara Falls, but the trail can be slippery after rain. Surrounded as they are by dense forest, Dambri Falls are much more attractive than any of those in the vicinity of Da Lat, and the only ones worth visiting in the dry season. There's even a hotel here, the *Dambri* (☎063/751517, ℱ751566; ❶–❷), with smart rooms that could make a good place to rest up in the countryside for a few days.

Accommodation in Bao Loc itself is rather limited. The smartest place in town, but somewhat overpriced, is the *Seri Bank* (☎063/864150; ❸–❹), set back from the main highway behind a small lake. It's a sizeable but friendly place with satellite TV, IDD and exchange facilities. The other alternatives are on the main road (Highway 20) heading south out of town. Rooms at the *Bao Loc* (☎063/864107; ❶–❷) are good value, and those out back have nice views over the countryside, but it's better known among locals for its massage service. The smaller rooms at the *Hong Hoang* (☎063/863117; ❶–❷), a few hundred metres south along the highway, are a less appealing but passable alternative. When it's time to eat, three decent **restaurants** operate on the main road south of the town centre. Best bet is the *Lien Do*, the furthest south of the three, which is well set up for tour groups, though the *Na Hue* and the *Hung Phat*, located near the *Bao Loc Hotel*, are also reliable.

More hummocky tea plantations abound along the road around quaint **DI LINH**. Aged shuttered terraces mingle with more faceless buildings here, to create the feel of a provincial French hamlet. The pretty old **church** puts the icing on the cake. Around 25km beyond Di Linh, pine trees begin to feature in the landscape. At this point you'll see signs for two more of the region's most impressive waterfalls, **Pongour** to the left, and **Gougah** to the right. The former are about 7km to the left off the main road, but the latter are just 100m to the right of the road, and are worth stopping for a look in the wet season. From here it's about 40km to Da Lat, of which the final ten-kilometre stretch cuts through heavily wooded slopes.

Da Lat and around

Hinged by the Cam Ly River, and nestled at an elevation of around 1500m among the pitching hills of the **Lang Bian Plateau**, the city of **DA LAT** is Vietnam's premier hill station, a beguiling amalgam of mazy streets, picturesque churches, bounteous vegetable gardens and crashing waterfalls, all suffused with the intoxicating scents of pine trees and wood-smoke. The city's more fanciful historians swear its name as an acronym of the Latin, *dat aliis laetitiam aliis temperiem*, "offering pleasure to one and freshness to another", though a far likelier derivation renders it as the stream ("da") of a local hilltribe, the Lat.

It was Dr Alexander Yersin who first divined the therapeutic properties of Da Lat's temperate climate on an exploratory mission into Vietnam's southern highlands, in 1893. His subsequent report on the area must have struck a chord, for four years later Governor-General Paul Doumer of Indochina ordered the founding of a convalescent hill station, where Saigon's hot-under-the-collar *colons* could recharge their batteries, and perhaps even partake in a day's game-hunting. The city's Gallic contingent had to pack up their winter coats after 1954's Treaty of Geneva, but by then the cathedral, train station, villas and hotels had been erected, and the French connection well and truly forged. By tacit agreement during the American War, both Hanoi and Saigon refrained from bombing the city and it remains much as it was half a century ago.

It's important to come to Da Lat with no illusions, though. With a population of 135,000, the town is anything but an idyllic backwater: sighting its for-

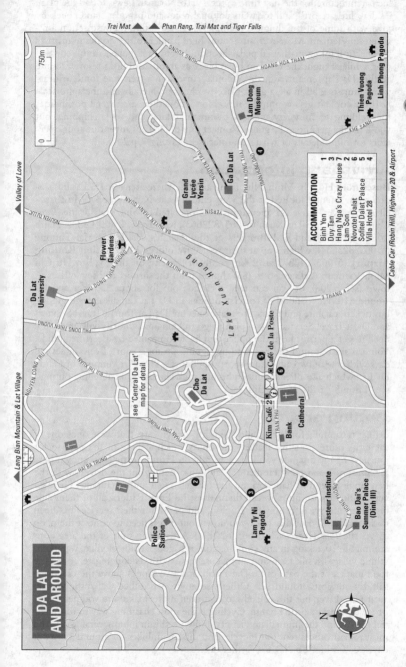

3

DA LAT AND AROUND

Trai Mat ▲ ▲ Phan Rang, Trai Mat and Tiger Falls

▲ Valley of Love

▲ Lang Bian Mountain & Lat Village

► Cable Car (Robin Hill), Highway 20 & Airport

ACCOMMODATION

Binh Yen	1
Duy Tan	3
Hang Nga's Crazy House	7
Lam Son	2
Novotel Dalat	6
Sofitel Dalat Palace	5
Villa Hotel 28	4

Linh Phong Pagoda

Thien Vuong Pagoda

Khe Sanh

Lam Dong Museum

Hoang Hoa Tham

Hung Vuong

Nguyen Trai

Ga Da Lat

Pham Hong Thai

Tran Hung Dao

Grand Lycée Yersin

Yersin

Ba Huyen Thanh Quan

Nguyen Tu Luc

Flower Gardens

Phu Dong Thien Vuong — Thanh Quan

Da Lat University

Ba Huyen Thanh Quan

Lake Xuan Huong

Phu Dong Thien Vuong

Nguyen Cong Tru

Bui Thi Xuan

3 Thang 4

Café de la Poste

see 'Central Da Lat' map for detail

Cho Da Lat

Phan Dinh Phung

Kim Café 2

Tran Phu

Bank

Cathedral

Hai Ba Trung

Police Station

Lam Ty Ni Pagoda

Pasteur Institute

Le Hong Phong

Bao Dai's Summer Palace (Dinh III)

N

750m

0

lorn architecture for the first time in the 1950s, Norman Lewis found the place "a drab little resort", and today its colonial relics and pagodas stand cheek by jowl with some of the dingiest examples of East European construction anywhere in Vietnam. Moreover, attractions here pander to the domestic tourist's predilection for swan-shaped pedal-boats and pony-trek guides in full cowboy gear, while at night the city can be as bleak as an off-season ski resort. Despite all this, Da Lat remains a quaint colonial curio, and a welcome tonic to heat-worn tourists – all in all, a great place to chill out, literally and metaphorically. If the cool air gets you in the mood there are several possibilities for trekking to minority villages, mountain biking and rock climbing, but you'll need a permit and a guide. Contact one of Da Lat's adventure tour operators for more details of what's on offer (see "Listings", p.207).

Arrival and information

Buses from Ho Chi Minh, Nha Trang and elsewhere arrive at Da Lat bus station, conveniently located at the west end of Lake Xuan Huong. Most travellers, however, arrive on open-tour buses operated by Sinh Café at the *Trung Cang Hotel*, 4a Bui Thi Xuan (☎063/822663), Kim Travel 2 at 9 Le Dai Hanh (☎063/822479) and TM Brothers at the *Binh Yen Hotel*, 7/2 Hai Thuong (☎063/823631), which stop at their respective offices. Modest **Lien Khuong Airport** (☎063/843373) is 29km south of the city, off the road to Ho Chi Minh: Vietnam Airlines buses ($3) shuttle from the airport to their offices in town (see p.208), or you can take a Honda om for about $3, or a taxi for around $10. The handful of **tourist offices** in Da Lat can all arrange guides, bus tickets, car hire and tours; the main ones are Da Lat Tourist Travel Services and Dalat Travel Service. If you plan to go trekking to minority villages, you'll need to get a permit from the police and be accompanied by a certified guide. You can skirt around the red tape by signing up for a tour of one or several days with one of two adventure sports operators – Phat Tire Ventures or Hardy Da Lat, which also offer mountain biking, rock climbing and abseiling outings; see "Listings", p.207, for details.

Getting around

Da Lat is too hilly for cyclos, and the horse-drawn carts that were once one of the city's more attractive features are pretty much a thing of the past, so for journeys of any distance you'll have to rely on **Honda oms** (also known here as "Simsons") and taxis. Honda oms are ten-a-penny, but the drivers with the best English tend to hang around the budget hotels and restaurants. There's a very distinctive group who call themselves the **Easy Riders**; all of them ride big bikes and speak reasonable English, and praise for their services has been gushing. They'll probably track you down, but if you need to contact them, do so via the *Phu Hoa Hotel* (☎063/822194). A day-long tour of the area costs around $8–10, taking in any combination of pagodas, colonial villas, waterfalls, ethnic villages, a silk farm and an incense factory. **Taxis** congregate beside the food market at the base of Le Dai Hanh, and two blocks above the cinema; a full day out costs around $20. Otherwise, any tourist office will rustle you up a car plus driver, but this is likely to cost even more; make sure you get someone who speaks a little English. Cycling is the most charming way to tour central Da Lat and the immediate vicinity, and with this in mind several hotels and most tourist offices rent out bicycles and mountain bikes for around $2–3 per day; see "Listings", p.208, for further details.

Accommodation

Enduringly popular with both Western and domestic tourists, Da Lat has a wide range of places to stay, from cheap, grimy billets, to luxury, international-standard hotels. However, if your visit coincides with a **public holiday**, especially Tet, either arrive early or book ahead.

The densest concentrations of **budget hotels** lie on the web of roads around the cinema and along Phan Dinh Phung; check that prices include hot water – a luxury in much of southern Vietnam, but a necessity in Da Lat, and on Phan Dinh Phung ask for a room out back, as the main road can be noisy. There also some good-value places along Nguyen Chi Thanh, some of which have partial views over the lake. A couple of classier hotels operate downtown, but there are many more out in the open spaces south and west of the city centre. If you feel ready to splurge, it's sometimes possible to rent one of the colonial villas along Tran Phu and Tran Hung Dao – enquire at one of the tourist offices for further details.

Binh Yen 7/2 Hai Thuong ☎063/823631. Tucked away at the top of Hai Thuong and overlooking parts of the city, there's much to like about the *Binh Yen*'s location and helpful staff. Rooms are nothing special, but all have hot water and TV, and the larger ones sleeping three are a good deal. Also serves as a base for TM Brothers tours. ❶–❷

Chau Au-Europa 76 Nguyen Chi Thanh ☎063/822870, ✆europa@hcm.vnn.vn. Professionally run place with a range of rooms. All are dazzlingly clean with homely touches – an extra $5 secures a front room with view; staff are extremely helpful and breakfast is included with some rooms. ❶–❸

Dreams 151 Phan Dinh Phung ☎063/833748, ✆dreams@hcm.vnn.vn. Sparkling new mini-hotel; rooms are well equipped and spotlessly clean, with modern bathrooms. Free Internet access 7–10pm, generous free breakfasts and helpful staff. ❶–❷

Duy Tan 83, 3 Thang 2 ☎063/823564. Mid-range friendly motel-style place, ten minutes' walk from the city centre, featuring smart but rather characterless rooms; insist on one on the upper floor to avoid facing the car park. Breakfast is included. ❸

Empress 5 Nguyen Thai Hoc ☎063/833888. Small but attractive, colonial-style building overlooking the lake with tastefully furnished rooms and all facilities. ❹–❻

Golf 3 4 Nguyen Thi Minh Khai ☎063/826042, ✆golf3hot@hcm.vnn.vn. Part of the *Golf* empire, an upmarket tower-block hotel situated slap-bang in the centre of town. Choose from a selection of comfortable suites or cheaper standard rooms. ❹–❺

Hang Nga's Crazy House 3 Huynh Thuc Khang ☎063/822070, ☏831480. Childhood-fantasy construction resembling the knotted trunks of huge trees. Rooms have entertaining *Alice in Wonderland*-style interiors and follow different themes, though some are short on space. The main problem, however, is over-commercialization. With a constant stream of tourists paying 5000d to look around, guests end up feeling like animals in a zoo. ❸–❺

Hoa Binh I 64 Truong Cong Dinh ☎063/822787. Budget hotel that's reliably popular with backpackers. All rooms have hot water and private bathrooms, and some have balconies with good views of the busy square below – or opt for quieter rooms with a terrace at the back. There's also a café downstairs. ❶

Hoa Binh II 67 Truong Cong Dinh ☎063/822787. Small, cosy auberge-style hotel just around the corner from its sister hotel, with the same good-value rooms, all with hot water and generous-sized bathrooms and, as before, friendly staff. ❶

Hoang Hau Villa 8a Ho Tung Mau ☎063/821431. Just below the GPO, an appealing mini-hotel with an art gallery and café in the lobby, and well-appointed rooms, some with balconies; breakfast is included. ❷–❸

Lam Son 5 Hai Thuong ☎ & ☏063/822362. A homely place on a hill just outside the centre, with some spacious rooms in the old wing and discounts possible out of season. ❶–❷

Lyla 5 Nam Ky Khoi Nghia ☎063/820051, ✆lylahotel@hcm.vnn.vn. Small mini-hotel with smartly furnished rooms, some with lake views, well maintained by a friendly family who run an equally smart restaurant downstairs. ❷–❸

Ngoc Lan 42 Nguyen Chi Thanh ☎063/822136. Soccer-pitch-sized rooms in this central hotel offer "every modern comfort" plus bird's-eye views of Lake Xuan Huong. ❷–❹

Novotel Dalat 7 Tran Phu ☎063/825777, ✆novotel@bdvn.vnd.net. A sympathetically restored colonial edifice that plays second fiddle to the more expensive *Sofitel Dalat Palace* nearby. Pleasing, well-ventilated rooms with elegant interiors and polished wooden floors; rates are sometimes reduced in low season. **4**

Phu Hoa 8 Tang Bat Ho ☎063/822194. The 34 rooms in this aged hotel are not particularly attractive and the staff are not always friendly, but the cheapest rates are as low as $4, the bedrooms presentable, and the location couldn't be more central; taking one of several rooms with three double beds makes sense if you're in a group. **1–2**

Sofitel Dalat Palace 12 Tran Phu ☎063/825444, ⓔsofitel@bdvn.vnd.net. Extensive renovations to Da Lat's most magnificent colonial pile have restored it to something like its 1930s splendour. All rooms are lavishly appointed, especially the presidential suite. Drinks on the garden terrace

aren't extortionate given the setting, and there's a rooftop bar as well. **5–6**

Thanh The 118 Phan Dinh Phung ☎063/822180. Under renovation at the time of writing but likely to re-open with competitively priced rooms in the budget quarter. **1–2**

Thuy Tien 7, 3 Thang 2 ☎063/822125. If you can ignore the sickly hues of the decor, rooms are comfortable and welcoming, with satellite TV and modern bathrooms; the tourist office is in the reception area. **1**

Villa Hotel 28 28 Tran Hung Dao ☎063/822764. Spurn the modern annexe, and opt for a room with a view over the surrounding countryside in the quaint auberge-style house. All thirteen rooms have hot water and include breakfast in the price, and guests have access to a cosy sitting room with open fire. **3**

The City

Central Da Lat forms a rough crescent around the western side of man-made **Lake Xuan Huong**, created in 1919 when the Cam Ly River was dammed by the French, who named it the "Grand Lac". The city escaped bomb damage, and a French influence is still evident when meandering its central area, whose twisting streets and steps, lined with stone buildings rising to red-tiled roofs, cover a hillock defined by the streets of Le Dai Hanh and Phan Dinh Phung. Your first stop, though, should be at the market, **Cho Da Lat**, a charmless reinforced-concrete structure housing a staggering range of fruit and vegetables. Strawberries, beetroot, fennel, avocados, blackberries and cherries grown in the market gardens surrounding the city are all sold here, along with a riot of flowers. Artichoke teabags, with their "propitious functions for liver, bile" and their "diuretic" properties, make quirky **souvenirs**, and candied Da Lat strawberries are also sold at many stalls. The market's upper level, linked by a raised walkway to the top of Le Dai Hanh, is pale and pasty by comparison, though a dig through its household goods unearths such buyables as watergourds, lacquerware, and hilltribe bags and fabrics. **Montagnards** carrying their chattels in decorated backpacks are a fairly common sight at the market, especially early in the morning when they come to trade with stallholders.

Around Lake Xuan Huong

It's possible to make a pleasant cycling or walking tour around the 7km perimeter of glassy **Lake Xuan Huong**. Start from the western end of the lake and head eastwards around the north side of the lake along **Nguyen Thai Hoc**. Soon you leave the bustle of the city behind as you pass between the lake and the extensive grounds of Da Lat's **golf club**. A small island in the lake and (usually) a cluster of minivans signals that you have reached Da Lat's **flower gardens** (daily 6am–6pm; small entrance fee) on the left. Inside, paths lead you past hydrangeas, roses, orchids, poinsettia, topiary and a nursery. There's nothing outstanding on display here, but at the weekend the place is packed with Vietnamese taking photos of each other standing in front of the flowerbeds. Besides bobble hats and some extremely tacky souvenirs on sale in the gardens, **stalls** outside the entrance sell knotted lumps of a golden fern fibre called *cu ly*, whose properties are used to staunch bleeding.

CENTRAL DA LAT

N

▓▓▓▓ Steps

ACCOMMODATION

Chau Au-Europa	11
Dreams	2
Empress	9
Golf 3	7
Hoa Binh I	3
Hoa Binh II	5
Hoang Hau Villa	12
Lyla	8
Ngoc Lan	10
Phu Hoa	4
Sofitel Dalat Palace	13
Thanh The	1
Thuy Tien	6

Cho
Da Lat

Cinema

Bank

Food stalls

Lake Xuan Huong

Bus
Station

Taxis

**RESTAURANTS,
CAFÉS & BARS**

Art Café	G
Café Artista	O
Café Gia Nguyen	L
Café Tung	F
Dong A	E
Hoang Lan	B
Huong Tra	P
Long Hoa	K
Nhat Ly	C
Pho Ngoc Hiep	J
Saigon Nite Bar	H
Stop and Go Café	D
Thanh Thuy	N
Trong Dong	A
V Café	I
Viet Hung	M

0   200m

Continue along **Ba Huyen Thanh Quan**, and trace its broad arc past cows and horses and around the lake. As you double back, you'll see the slate belfry of the **Grand Lycée Yersin** peeping out from the trees above and to your left. Where Ba Huyen Thanh Quan turns into Yersin, you can head one of two ways: west, and back into the city centre; or east up Nguyen Trai to **Ga Da Lat**, the city's train station, built in 1938 and a real time capsule of the period. Below its gently contoured red-tiled roof and behind the multicoloured Art Deco windows striping its front facade, its marble and glass ticket booths (one still advertises trips to Hanoi) are reminiscent of a provincial French station. Outside, the rail yard is in a charming state of dilapidation, with cattle grazing on the grass and flowers that grow among its tracks and ancient locomotives. Trains ran on the rack railway linking Da Lat to Thap Cham (see p.243) and beyond from 1933 until the mid-Sixties, when Viet Cong attacks became too persistent a threat for them to continue. Nowadays two trains are kept operational, and enthusiasts may enjoy the **shuttle service** (about $5; trains leave on demand with a minimum of two foreign passengers) across horticultural land and market gardens to the village of **Trai Mat**, a few kilometres away; the train idles for thirty minutes – time enough to take a look at **Linh Phuoc Pagoda** (see p.210) before returning to Da Lat.

Tran Hung Dao and beyond

By retracing your steps down Nguyen Trai and ascending Pham Hong Thai you reach **Tran Hung Dao**, the central segment of Da Lat's southern rim, from where two slender roads wiggling south offer cyclists pleasant detours out into the countryside. One of these, **Hoang Hoa Tham**, targets colourful **Linh Phong Pagoda**, which is fronted by a gateway bearing a fierce, panting dragon face with protruding eyes. Behind its gaudy yellow doors, blue ceramic roof dragons and pillbox-red pillars etched with Chinese inscriptions, the pagoda itself is something of a disappointment. However, its resident nuns are very friendly and the tranquil location affords peerless views of the cultivated and wooded valley below, from where threads of smoke rise from wood fires.

Much the same is true of **Khe Sanh**, almost immediately opposite you as you access Tran Hung Dao. This time, the focus of the detour is **Thien Vuong Pagoda**, remarkable for its trio of four-metre-tall, caramel-coloured sandalwood statues (Sakyamuni, in the centre, rubs shoulders with the Goddess of Mercy and the God of Power) imported from Hong Kong in 1958; and for the huge **statue of Buddha** seated on a lotus, 100m up the hill above the pagoda. Stalls near Thien Vuong hawk the usual candied strawberries, artichoke tea and *cu ly* to the Vietnamese tourists who flock here, many of whom are young girls who come from all over Vietnam to pray for good fortune and a successful marriage.

The movers and shakers who once maintained **villas** in Da Lat preferred to site their homes along the city's bottom lip, rather than in the maws of its central area; the villas survive today and their timberwork, slated roofs and pastel hues lend an air of distinction to Tran Hung Dao, though some of them are in a sad state of disrepair. You'll pass below one of the less impressive examples, **Dinh II**, now used as a guesthouse for government employees and closed to the public, though it was once the residence of the French governor-general of Indonesia, at the street's western end. Set on a hill near the beginning of Hung Vuong, the **Lam Dong Museum**, 4 Hung Vuong (Tues–Sat 7.30–11.30am & 1.30–4.30pm; small admission fee; ☎063/823704), is well worth visiting. Located in a lovely colonial building that once belonged to Emperor Bao Dai's wife, the Empress Nam Phuong, the displays are thoughtfully laid out and give a tantalizing taste of the region's rich history. Beginning with some Cham artefacts from recent archeological digs, the exhibits also include a collection of rice jars, ceramics and jewellery found in tombs, and some vicious-looking spears. The second floor gives a thorough introduction to the lifestyles of the local minority groups such as the Ma, Koho and Churu, along with a map showing their distribution in the province and many of their handicrafts and household implements. This is probably the best museum in the highlands, though the third-floor display covering the French and American Wars is little different to similar displays around the rest of the country.

Continuing east along Hung Vuong, a small lane to the right leads to **Dinh I**, 1 Tran Quang Dieu (daily, 7.30–11.30am & 1.30–4.30pm; small admission fee; ☎063/823704), one of Bao Dai's many palaces in the region. If you visit **Dinh III**, which features strongly on many tours of the town, you might want to give this a miss, as the layout and furnishings are rather similar, though Dinh I enjoys better views over the town and is in a more peaceful setting. It also receives fewer visitors, so you can wander round without hordes of other tourists to disturb you. This building was used as Bao Dai's workplace, and the conference room upstairs, with its large map of the country, has a business-like air to it. There are several interesting photos on the walls of the other rooms, including one of Bao Dai in a racing car, and another of his concubines. As at Dinh III, the furnishings are classic 1930s; other points of interest are a doorway to a secret tunnel and an archaic phone switchboard at the entrance to the building.

Tran Phu and around

West of Dinh II, Tran Hung Dao segues into **Tran Phu**, which cradles two of the city's most memorable French-era buildings. First up is the splendidly restored **Palace Hotel**, now part of the *Sofitel* hotel empire. The social heart of colonial-era Da Lat following its construction in the 1920s, the *Sofitel Dalat Palace* is blessed with wonderful prospects of Lake Xuan Huong below, and enjoying a long, cool drink overlooking its manicured lawns is a luxury that's well worth the expense.

Across the road, Da Lat's dusty pink **Cathedral**, consecrated in 1931 and completed eleven years later, is dedicated to St Nicholas, protector of the poor; a statue of him stands at the opposite end of the nave to the simple altar, with three tiny children loitering at his feet. Light streaming in from the cathedral's seventy stained-glass windows, mostly crafted in Grenoble, teases a warm, sunny glow from the mellow pink of the interior walls, and picks out the flamboyant colours of the fresh-cut flowers adorning the nave. Of the cathedral's unspectacular fittings, the **collage** beside the altar is perhaps the most interesting. Depicting Vietnam's Catholic martyrs, it was made using waste paper to reflect the renewal of the Catholic Church in Vietnam; bones of some of these martyrs are kept under the altar itself. A tiny metal cockerel perched almost invisibly at the top of the steeple has earned the cathedral its rather unglamorous moniker, "Chicken Church".

Bao Dai's Summer Palace

The nautical portholes punched into its walls, and the mast-like pole sprouting from its roof, give **Dinh III** (daily 7.30–11.30am & 1.30-4.30pm; small admission fee), erstwhile summer palace of Emperor Bao Dai, the distinct look of a ship's bridge. Reached by bearing left onto Le Hong Phong 500m west of the cathedral, and then left again when you see the wide mansion housing the **Pasteur Institute** to your right, the building is indeed palatial – but don't expect Buckingham Palace. The palace was erected between 1933 and 1938 to provide Bao Dai with a bolt hole between elephant-slaughtering sessions, and its mustard-coloured bulk, etched with stark white grouting, is set amid rose and pine **gardens**. Past the two large blue metal lanterns flanking the front entrance, the first room to your right is Bao Dai's **working room**, dominated by a bust of the man himself, and home both to the imperial motorbike helmet, and to a small book collection that includes Bibles, a Shakespeare edition and even Charlotte Brontë's *Shirley*. Buffalo horns in the **reception room** come from animals bagged by Bao Dai himself on one of his hunting forays into the forests around Da Lat. His queen preferred more sedate pastimes, and would have tinkled on the piano here. The palace's most elegant common room is its **festivities room** or dining room, though catching a whiff of furniture polish in this dark, echoing chamber, it's hard to imagine the royal revelries that once went on here.

Royal ghosts are far easier to summon upstairs, where the musty **imperial bedrooms** seem just to have had the dustsheets whipped back for another royal season. Princes and princesses all had their quarters, as did the queen, whose chamber features a chaise longue that looks unnervingly like a dentist's chair. But the finest room, predictably enough, went to Bao Dai, who enjoyed the luxury of a balcony for his "breeze-getting and his moon-watching". Out on the landing, look out for a bizarre mini-sauna, labelled a *Rouathermique*. The place is surrounded by the usual attractions – pony rides and dressing up in minority costume, and the exit forces you to pass through a gauntlet of souvenir stalls.

On your return to town, you can't fail to spot the fairy-tale construction, **Hang Nga's Crazy House** (small admission fee), rising up on your left. Perennially popular with tourists, the citizens of Da Lat are more divided over the merits of this unusual building, shaped to resemble the knotted trunks of huge trees. It functions as a guesthouse (see "Accommodation", p.201), but day visitors are welcome to look around any unoccupied rooms, most of which have entertaining *Alice in Wonderland*-style interiors with mirrors and mushrooms in abundance. There's also a café and small courtyard garden to while away time over a drink. In the café, a selection of old photographs on the walls provide clues as to how such a bizarre construction got planning permission. As the daughter of former president Truong Chinh, its owner, Hang Nga, is above the usual planning constraints.

Lam Ty Ni Pagoda

Dropping in at **Lam Ty Ni Pagoda**, north of Le Hong Phong on Thien My, represents one of the oddest attractions of a stay in Da Lat. The focus of interest here is not the pagoda itself but its sole occupant. It is home to Vien Thuc, the so-called "mad monk" of Da Lat, who lives there alone and whose dogs alert him to guests' arrival at the front gate, which you may find locked. Poet, gardener, builder and artist, Vien Thuc is a monk of all trades, but his proudest achievement is his painting – which started out as finger-daubing on the walls of the pagoda he entered at the age of 10. His normal outfit, a dark-brown monk's habit with a pointed cowl, is usually spattered with paint. His studio, a warren of lean-tos behind the pagoda, is stacked to the rafters with over 100,000 paintings, some in watercolour and others in oil; the paint of the latter is spread so thick on the canvas they look almost three-dimensional. The paintings have names like "Golden Dragon Swimming in the River Milky Way" and "Blue Music in the Bosom of a Human World", though the great majority are self-portraits – a strange circumstance given the Buddha's exhortation for his followers to subdue the ego. Vien Thuc has gained fame for something else that Buddhism discourages – his commercial instinct. All his work is for sale, and he closes deals with what the *New York Times* called "the skill of a car dealer". The man is not at all mad, just a little eccentric, and like most people his moods vary from friendly to indifferent to aggressive, so be prepared for any kind of reception when you arrive.

Eating, drinking and nightlife

Da Lat has a broad range of **restaurants** serving Vietnamese, Chinese and French cuisines. The majority are situated either along Phan Dinh Phung, or near to the cinema in the city centre. **Food stalls** are also abundant. *Pho, com* and the like are dished out at the covered food market at the base of Le Dai Hanh. There are also one or two vegetarian stalls here, signposted as *com chay*. But the stalls pitched on the steps running down from the cinema and across to the market offer the most **exotic dishes**: snails, quail's eggs and shellfish in huge, steaming cauldrons. Finally, if you're taking a bike out for the day you could stop by at the central market and make up a **picnic** of bread, cheese and cake, complemented by fresh local berries.

For most locals, **nightlife** means a cup of coffee in one of the city's atmospheric **cafés**. For visitors, there's not much more unless you fancy shaking your stuff at one of the hotel discos.

Restaurants

Art Café 70 Truong Cong Dinh. Located in the heart of the budget hotel district, this place has stylish, bamboo-themed decor, and appealing dishes like capsicum stuffed with pork and minced beef wrapped in a herbal leaf for just over $1. Burgers, spaghetti and vegetarian dishes too, plus cheap cocktails. 10am–late.

Café Artista 9 Nguyen Chi Thanh. Cosy café-restaurant with violins on the walls and nightly piano music, plus a choice of Western dishes such as spaghetti, toasted sandwiches and tzatsiki bread. 7am–midnight.

Dong A 82 Phan Dinh Phung. Not much to look at, but offers a wide-ranging menu, including a limited vegetarian selection. 8am–10pm.

Hoang Lan 118 Phan Dinh Phung. Next door to the *Thanh The* hotel, a bare but reputable restaurant where Vietnamese and Chinese cuisines share top billing; the Vietnamese meat and vegetable soup, *ta pin lu*, is worth investigating. 8am–10pm.

Huong Tra 1 Nguyen Thai Hoc. The lakeside setting makes this a popular choice. Rice dishes cooked in a clay pot are a speciality here, though the menu also runs to rabbit and frog. 6am–9pm.

Long Hoa 3 Thang 2. French-café ambience with attentive staff, serving decent and filling Vietnamese food and steaks – kick off with a strawberry wine aperitif, while for dessert, the homemade yoghurt takes some beating. Two can dine for around $7. The room out back is a bit quieter. 11am–9pm.

Lyla 18 Nguyen Chi Thanh. Starched tablecloths and smart decor in this small, family-run restaurant beneath the hotel of the same name, serving Vietnamese and Western food such as burgers and spaghetti for around $2 a dish. 6.30am–late.

Nhat Ly 88 Phan Dinh Phung. A hugely popular place with Vietnamese and foreigners alike for its wide menu of dishes, including several vegetarian options, at very reasonable prices. 9am–9pm.

Pho Ngoc Hiep 58 Tang Bat Ho. The speciality here is steamy bowls of tasty *pho* that fill a gap. 7am–10pm.

Thanh Thuy 2 Nguyen Thai Hoc. Lake-view address with a reasonable menu and plenty of ambience. Sometimes busy with tour groups. 7am–late.

Trong Dong 220 Phan Dinh Phung. Impressive service and menu, with tasty sugar-cane prawns and a Vietnamese special salad (shrimps, peanuts, lotus gourd, pork and herbs, eaten with prawn crackers) in a refined setting. 9.30am–11pm.

V Cafe 1/1 Bui Thi Xuan. A bit removed from the hotel district, but worth tracking down for its cosy atmosphere and good cooking, including some great pies and cakes, at very affordable prices. 8.30am–10.30pm.

Viet Hung 7 Nguyen Chi Thanh. One of a clutch of cafés offering partial views across the lake. Vietnamese and fast food, catering to Western tastes (fruit shakes, soups, pizzas and pancakes), with free 30min Internet use if you order breakfast. 6.30am–midnight.

Cafés, bars and discos

Café De La Poste Tran Phu. Modern, French-style café opposite the post office on Tran Phu; part of the *Sofitel* empire, so smart but also pricey (set menu $7.50). The pool table seems incongruous in such refined surroundings. 10am–10.30pm.

Café Gia Nguyen 1 Nguyen Chi Thanh. Elevated over Le Dai Hanh, this popular, gaily decorated terraced café is an ideal place to watch the world go by; and if it gets too chilly there's the candlelit interior. Fair range of ice creams and coffees. 6.30am–11pm.

Café Tung 6 Khu Hoa Binh. Leather upholstery, dark varnished wood and covers of old 45s by Nancy Sinatra and Jacques Brel on the walls: truly a café lost in time. 6am–10pm.

Golf 3 Disco 4 Nguyen Thi Minh Khai. Situated beneath the hotel, this is one of the only places in town where you can party. $2 entrance. 7pm–midnight.

Larry's Bar *Sofitel Dalat Palace Hotel*. Wood-panelled bar in the hotel basement that tries a little too hard for a rustic European look; its casual ambience belies the relatively high prices. 4pm–midnight.

Saigon Nite Bar 11a/1 Hai Ba Trung. Da Lat's only independent Western-style bar, with friendly, welcoming staff, pool table, darts and a reasonable selection of CDs. The guest books chronicle a stream of drunk but contented customers. 3pm–late.

Skyview Café *Golf 3 Hotel*. Perched on the hotel's top floor, this is a fine venue for relaxing over a beer and watching the city unfurl below. 1–11pm.

Stop and Go Café 2a Ly Tu Trong. Intriguing café in the rambling home and gardens of celebrated local poet and artist Duy Viet; you can view his paintings and be serenaded with guitar strumming and poetry readings by the man himself as you enjoy a coffee or beer. Browse through the visitors' book to see photos and signatures of famous people like the late John F Kennedy Jr. 7am–8.30pm.

Listings

Adventure tours Phat Tire Ventures, 73 Truong Cong Dinh (T & F063/829422, W www.phattireventures .com), and Hardy Da Lat, 66 Phan Dinh Phung (T063/836840, E hardydl@hcm.vnn.vn), are located almost opposite each other in the budget district. Both offer treks of one or several days, beginning at around $15 per day including permit, guide and food, as well as mountain biking, rock climbing, abseiling and canyoning trips.

Airlines Vietnam Airlines Booking Office, 40 Ho Tung Mau (daily 7.30–11.30am & 1–4.30pm; ☎063/822895).

Banks Both Vietincombank, 46–48 Khu Hoa Binh, and Agribank, 216 Tran Phu, can change travellers' cheques and cash, and arrange Visa and MasterCard advances.

Bike hire Mountain bikes can be hired from the *Novotel* and *Sofitel Dalat Palace*; *Duy Tan, Hoa Binh* and *Binh Yen* hotels can also arrange motor-bike hire, and tourist offices can assist too.

Email and Internet access Many hotels and guesthouses provide Internet access, sometimes free to guests, and the *Viet Hung Café* at 7 Nguyen Chi Thanh has rates of 4000d per hour.

Hospital Lam Dong Hospital is at 4 Pham Ngoc Thach ☎063/822154.

Police 9 Tran Binh Trong ☎063/822032.

Post office 14 Tran Phu (daily 6.30am–9pm), with poste restante, IDD, fax and DHL courier services.

Sports There's an eighteen-hole golf course at Da Lat Palace Golf Club, Phu Dong Thien Vuong, ☎063/821201; the *Sofitel Dalat Palace* and *Novotel* have tennis courts.

Tourist office Da Lat Travel Service, 7, 3 Thang 2 ☎063/822125, ⓔttdhhd@hcm.vnn.vn; Da Lat Tourist Travel Service, 2 Nguyen Thai Hoc ☎063/822520, ⓦwww.dalattourist.com; Da Lat Tourism Service Company (Kim Café 2), 9 Le Dai Hanh ☎063/822479, ⓔdltoseco@hcm.vnn.vn.

Around Da Lat

While there is some spectacular scenery in the vicinity of Da Lat which lends itself to challenging **treks**, **bike rides** and other **adventure activities**, don't expect too much of the local attractions, which pander to the Vietnamese taste for pony rides, dressing up in minority costumes for photographs, and tacky souvenir stalls. None of the local waterfalls is worth visiting in the dry season (Dec–May), with the possible exception of **Tiger Falls**, though you might enjoy a **boat ride** on one of the local lakes or a **cable car ride** from Robin Hill to Lake Tuyen Lam. Another popular jaunt is by **train** to **Trai Mat**, taking time out to admire the adornments on the **Linh Phuoc Pagoda**. It's rather difficult to visit a **genuine minority village**, as most places now have electricity and most groups have been assimilated into mainstream Vietnamese culture. If you want to visit one of the few remaining traditional communities, contact one of the adventure tour operators (see "Listings", p.207), and be prepared for some tough trekking.

North of Da Lat

Thung Lung Tinh Yeu, or the **Valley of Love** (daily 6am–5pm), located 5km north of town, offers typical kitsch diversions. The valley's still waters and wooded hills are actually quite enticing and, were it not for the music blasting from souvenir stalls at the entrance, and the buzzing of rented motorboats, Lam Dong Tourist's brave assertion that the valley "makes sense for you, poetically and romantically" might actually hold water. It's said that Bao Dai and his courtiers used to hunt here in the 1950s, though a damming project in 1972 flooded part of the valley and created **Lake Da Thien**.

If you bother to travel up to the Valley of Love, you'll be aware of the twin peaks of 2160-metre-high **Lang Bian Mountain** looming above you to the north. Inevitably, a schmaltzy legend has been concocted to explain the mountain's formation. The story tells of two ill-starred lovers, a Lat man called Lang and a Chill girl named Bian, who were unable to marry because of tribal enmity. Broken-hearted, Bian passed away, and the peaks of Lang Bian are said to represent her breast heaving its dying breath. Bian's death seems not to have been wholly in vain: so racked with guilt was her father, that he called a halt to tribal unrest by unifying all of the local factions into the Koho.

It's possible to **climb** or **drive** up to the canopy of pines at the top of Lang Bian Mountain from where, it's said, you can see the coast on a clear day. There's now a resort and restaurant near the top of the mountain, *Thung Lung Tram Nam* (☎063/839088; ❸), with smart rooms and great views. Though a new road has been cut up to the resort, some may enjoy the challenge of climbing the mountain. The four-hour ascent on foot begins at the nine hamlets that are collectively known as **Lat Village**, 12km north of Da Lat along Xo Viet Nghe Tinh. The village's thatch-roofed bamboo stilthouses are occupied by Chill and Ma, but mostly Lat, groups of Koho peoples eking out a living growing rice, pulses and vegetables. Tourist offices such as Da Lat Travel Service are still insisting that you buy a **permit** (about $5) to visit either the village or mountain, though the total amount you end up paying depends on the mood of the tourist office. At best, you may only have to pay for the permit, and can then either hire a Honda driver, or cycle; at worst, you'll have to fork out $10 a day for an official guide ($15 if you plan to climb Lang Bian), and $15–20 for a car. Regulations, though, are in a state of flux, and it's best to seek current advice from tour operators in town. If you've hired a motorbike or Honda om for the day, you could combine a visit to Lat Village with a jaunt out to **Ankroet lakes and falls**, signposted 8km along the road to Lat. The falls are more secluded and attractive than most in the area but the road can be in bad condition during the wet season.

South of Da Lat

As you leave town to the south on Highway 20, a slip road to the right leads to the top of **Robin Hill**, crowned by a huge **cable car** terminus. Cable car rides (daily, 7.30–11.30am & 1.30–5pm; $3 return) are available here, and offer fantastic views over the pine-clad slopes around the city. The trip takes about twelve minutes to cover the 2km down to **Lake Tuyen Lam** (7am–5pm), a placid and attractive expanse of water. There are a few **refreshment kiosks** on the shore of the lake, and **boat trips** ($15–20 per boat) round the lake are also possible. Just beside the cable car terminal at the lake is **Truc Lam Pagoda**, a modern, Chinese-style temple that houses a meditation centre. The lake can also be approached by road; look for a turning to the right off Highway 20 about 5km from the centre of Da Lat as you go down the hill. (At the time of writing, a new road was being cut just east of Highway 20, with a view to making both entry to and exit from Da Lat one-way. However, it was not clear which road would take traffic in which direction, so be prepared for a possible detour to these attractions.) Just a couple of hundred metres further south is a turning for **Datanla Falls** (7am–5pm; small entrance fee), signposted on the right of the road as "Thac Datanla". In Koho, *datanla* means "water under leaves", and that pretty much sums up the place: from the car park, it's a steep fifteen-minute clamber down to the falls, probing some splendidly lush forest. The falls themselves are unthrilling, their muddy waters cascading onto a plateau spanned by a wooden footbridge that provides a hackneyed photo opportunity. In the dry season, this and most of Da Lat's waterfalls, are a great disappointment and not worth the effort of visiting.

The **Prenn Waterfall** (7am–5pm; small entrance fee) is about another 6km down Highway 20 on the left. A major attraction for Vietnamese tourists, the fall sees a convoy of buses roll into its car park, harried by a stampede of cigarette and chewing-gum vendors. Unlike Datanla, the attraction here is the waterfall itself, which thunders (or trickles, depending on the season) over a wide overhang and into a broad pool below. By following the path that circles the pool, you can walk right behind the fall. Surrounding Prenn Waterfall are a host of tacky diversions: mock-up rope bridges and tree houses, souvenir shops and a pond with a few lethargic crocodiles. If you're too lazy to walk down the few steps to the base of the falls, you can hop in a cable car for

5000d. Back up at the car park, the *Prenn Restaurant* is on hand to cater for hungry visitors, overlooked by a modern, octagonal pagoda.

Formerly billed as a good place to visit a minority village, **Chicken Village** (ask for Lang Con Ga), 18km south of Da Lat and just west of Highway 20, is now just like any other Vietnamese village, apart from the bizarre, five-metre-high cement cockerel that stands proudly on a plinth in the centre, its mouth open in mid-squawk. The local Koho women pounce on any visitors who turn up in a desperate effort to sell their textiles, on display in many makeshift stalls around. Whether you're a potential buyer or not, it's interesting to take a look at the rudimentary looms that the women need to strap themselves into to operate. It's also possible to go rambling through the nearby fields and foothills without a permit.

East of Da Lat

Seven kilometres east of Da Lat and accessible by road or by rail (see p.203), the orbital village of **TRAI MAT** is ideally placed for a short excursion. The journey there takes you past a sweep of some of the region's most splendid countryside. Terraced fields crammed full of crops and immaculately tended market gardens escort you for most of the way, and the elevated road provides an excellent vantage point.

The village appears rather shabby by comparison but it's well worth stopping to take a look at **Linh Phuoc Pagoda** (6am–6pm), an incredibly ornate building which showcases the art of tessellation, whereby small pieces of broken china or glass are painstakingly arranged in cement. The first thing to catch the eye is the huge dragon in the courtyard to the right of the main building, constructed from over 12,000 carefully broken beer bottles. Art work inside the pagoda is more intricate, with mosaic dragons entwined around the main hall's pillars, while stairs lead up on the left to colourfully inlaid galleries, shrines and good views. The main hall is very atmospheric, with the deep sound of bells rung by devotees resonating around.

About 4km beyond Trai Mat, a left turn points the way to **Tiger Falls** (7.30am–5pm; small entrance fee), though you still need to descend a few more kilometres on a precarious switchback road to reach them. If travelling by minibus, you'll have to park halfway down and pay a jeep or motorbike to take you the rest of the way. Above the falls are a couple of restaurants, as well as a statue of a primitive hunter and another of a huge hollow tiger, into which you can climb to take a photo while sitting in its mouth. A steep concrete stairway leads down to the base of the falls, which tumble from a great height and offer good photo opportunities. The falls are a very popular destination for Vietnamese, so you're unlikely to be able to enjoy the place alone. Pools and boulders around the base of the falls make ideal spots for a picnic.

The central highlands

North of Da Lat, the yawning plateaux of the **central highlands** are worth visiting for their scenery and minority peoples. First stop is usually **Lak Lake**, an attractive body of water surrounded by minority villages, on Highway 27 about

60km south of **Buon Ma Thuot**. The town of Buon Ma Thuot itself is an unlovely place, but it is the gateway to E De longhouses, elephant-back rides and treks into **Yok Don National Park**. From Buon Ma Thuot, Highway 14 probes further north to **Plei Ku**, where it's possible (with a guide) to visit Jarai villages. From Plei Ku it's little over an hour's journey straight north on Highway 14 to the likeable town of **Kon Tum**, where you don't need a permit to visit villages of minority groups like the Bahnar, with their towering tribal **rong**, or communal halls. From Kon Tum you can follow Highway 24 eastwards over a high pass to the coast at Quang Ngai, or get into high-adventure gear and continue north through the highlands along Highway 14, on the route of the Ho Chi Minh trail, branching off on Highway 14B to hit the coast at Da Nang.

Buon Ma Thuot and around

Without the added incentive of its nearby minority villages and waterfalls, **BUON MA THUOT** would have little to offer. Of those who do make the journey up from the coast's well-trodden tourist trail, or direct from Ho Chi Minh City, many expect a quaint longhouse community, and for them the town's central sprawl of buildings splayed across a grid of streets can only disappoint. Seeing **longhouses** and traditional **minority communities** – of which most around these parts comprise E De people – is possible at **Ako Dhong**, on the northern outskirts of town, and in the surrounding countryside at **Ban Don** near **Yok Don National Park**, or some other outlying *montagnard* village. Enough E Des have by now been assimilated into Buon Ma Thuot's population of around 150,000 for a public-address system to relay the news across the town in E De, daily at dusk. Although Dak Lak Province is fairly relaxed about visits to these villages, some, particularly those near the Cambodian border, are still theoretically off limits to travellers, while others are not permitted to take foreign overnight guests. Check with the Dak Lak Tourist Office (☎050/852108, ✉daklaktour@dng.vnn.vn), located in the middle of town at 3 Phan Chu Trinh, before heading out.

Sited 160km west of Ninh Hoa, Buon Ma Thuot is both administrative centre to Dak Lak Province, and the western highlands' unofficial capital. During French colonial times, the town developed on the back of the coffee, tea, rubber and hardwood crops that grew in its fertile red soil, and was the focal point for the **plantations** that smothered the surrounding countryside. Plantation-owners and other *colons* would amuse themselves by picking off the **elephants**, **leopards and tigers** once prevalent in the area, and Bao Dai himself enjoyed bagging game so much that he had a house built some way south of the town on **Lak Lake** connected by a private track to his summer palace in Da Lat. In later years Americans superseded the French, but they were long gone by the time the North Vietnamese Army (NVA) swept through in March 1975, making Buon Ma Thuot the first "domino" to fall in the Ho Chi Minh Campaign. More recently, natural resources and coffee in particular have made the town a comparatively affluent community, as evidenced by the number of Hondas and jeeps buzzing its streets, and the glut of restaurants and cafés.

The Town

Central Buon Ma Thuot can't throw up much of interest for tourists, though the **Khai Doan Pagoda**, built in 1951, is an interesting fusion of E De longhouse and Hue imperial architecture. Located west of the centre on Phan Boi

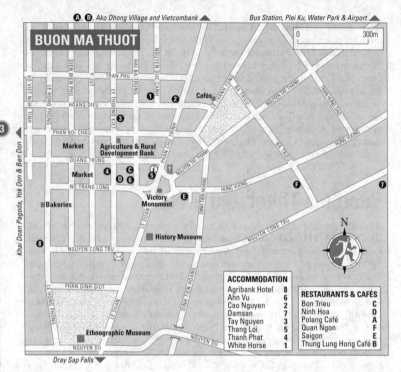

Khai Doan Pagoda, Yok Don & Ban Don

BUON MA THUOT

Ako Dhong Village and Vietcombank ▲

Bus Station, Plei Ku, Water Park & Airport ▲

0   300m

Cafés

Market

Agriculture & Rural
Development Bank

Market

Bakeries

Victory
Monument

History Museum

Ethnographic Museum

Dray Sap Falls ▼

N

ACCOMMODATION
Agribank Hotel	8
Ahn Vu	6
Cao Nguyen	2
Damsan	7
Tay Nguyen	3
Thang Loi	5
Thanh Phat	4
White Horse	1

RESTAURANTS & CAFÉS
Bon Trieu	C
Ninh Hoa	D
Polang Café	A
Quan Ngon	F
Saigon	E
Thung Lung Hong Café	B

Chau, it stands on a slope beside a large bo tree, underneath which sits a Buddha image in meditation posture. The front of the building, approached by steps, is made of huge slabs of glossy, painted wood, with the approximate dimensions of a longhouse, but the ornate, double-layered roof is classic Hue architecture. Just below the roof at the front runs a frieze of gold-painted panels depicting scenes from the life of the Buddha. A more recent extension of brick and cement at the back houses the altar with several more Buddha images, while the bright pillars have dragons leaping off them. The pagoda was built to honour Emperor Khai Dhin's wife, Hoang Thi Cuc, who was also mother of the last emperor, Bao Dai.

The only other real sight in town is south of **Victory Monument** on Le Duan, in the form of the **Dak Lak Museum** (daily 7.30–10.30am & 2–4.30pm), which is divided into two parts. Both the **History Museum** and **Ethnographic Museum** ($5 for each museum for a group of 1–5 people) are missable if you've seen any other war museums in the country or the excellent Lam Dong Museum in Da Lat. If you didn't visit the latter, you might want to fork out for the Ethnographic Museum (entrance on Nguyen Du), with exhibits pertaining to local minority peoples. Among them are a waistcoat made of bark, some unusual stone gongs, funerary statues of peacocks and tusks, and instruments for taming elephants, like vicious mahouts' spikes and two thorny harnesses.

If you want to actually visit a minority group, then the tidy E De weaving village of **Ako Dhong** is well worth a look; it is located on the northern fringes of town, and easily accessible by walking or Honda om. Follow Phan Chu Trinh towards the northeast, then turn left on Tran Nhat Duat, which leads you into the community. The sturdy longhouses on stilts with their tiled roofs spaced out evenly down the road, and the clean-swept yards and trim hedges give the feel of an affluent suburb. The tantalizing aroma of roasting coffee beans often fills the air, and the gentle clack-clack emanating from the buildings signals the weavers at work. The locals are very welcoming and are likely to invite you in to watch the process and perhaps to buy a sample of their work. It's a good idea to take the chance, as the work is of a high standard and prices very appealing. A colourfully embroidered shoulder bag, for example, sells for less than $2.

Finally, if you're in need of cooling down, you can head for the recently opened **Dak Lak Water Park** (T050/950381; $2), which is situated 4km northeast of town on Nguyen Chi Thanh.

Practicalities

Buon Ma Thuot's **bus station** (T050/952603) is 2km above town on Nguyen Tat Thanh; from here, there are four air-conditioned express buses daily to Nha Trang ($3-4) and three express buses to Ho Chi Minh ($6–7). The **airport** is a few kilometres back off the road towards Da Lat; Vietnam Airlines (T050/955055), at 67 Nguyen Tat Thanh, has an airport shuttle to and from the city ($1.50). Dak Lak Tourist (T050/852108, E daklaktour@dng.vnn.vn), just up from the *Thang Loi Hotel* at 3 Phan Chu Trinh, is very helpful and can arrange car hire, guides, visa extensions and tours. Dam San Tourist is a small, private tour operator based at the *Dam San Hotel* (see below). Vietcombank at 5 Tran Hung Dao, can change travellers' cheques, foreign currency and advance cash on Visa, MasterCard and JCB credit cards. It also has an ATM machine. If you just want to change foreign cash, the Agriculture & Rural Development Bank at 37 Phan Boi Chau is more central. The **post office** (7am–8.30pm) is on Le Duan just south of Victory Monument, and also has **Internet** access. Another cheap place to go online is a small Internet shop opposite the *White Horse Hotel*, at the south end of Nguyen Duc Canh.

There's a healthy range of **accommodation** in Buon Ma Thuot. Pick of the crop is the restful *Dam San Hotel* at 212–214 Nguyen Cong Tru (T050/851234, E damsanhotel@dng.vnn.vn; ❸). Its smart rooms are tastefully furnished using local textiles and most have lovely views south across fields of coffee. There's also a pool and tennis courts, but its one drawback is that it's quite a way from the centre. All options in the centre, both mid-range and budget, tend to be rather characterless, though there are plenty to choose from. The smart *Thang Loi* (T050/857615, F857622; ❹), at 1 Phan Chu Trinh across from the Victory Monument, boasts all mod cons, including satellite TV, as do the *Cao Nguyen*, a little further north at 65 Phan Chu Trinh (T050/855962, F851912; ❹), and the sparkling new *White Horse* (T050/815656, F815588; ❸–❹), tucked away at 9–11 Nguyen Duc Canh, which provides the best value of the trio. A cheaper mid-range option can be found at the *Tay Nguyen* (T050/851009, F852250; ❸) at 110 Ly Thuong Kiet near the town centre, which has large functional rooms, some with three beds. Ly Thuong Kiet has the greatest concentration of hotels in town, including some good budget options. One clean place is the *Thanh Phat* (T050/854857, F813366; ❶–❷), a mini-hotel at 41 Ly Thuong Kiet with a choice of fan or air-conditioned rooms. Other reasonable budget hotels are the *Agribank* at 111 Le Hong Phong (T050/857828, F851338; ❶), where all rooms have hot water as well as air-conditioning, and the *Ahn Vu* at 7 Hai Ba Trung (T & F050/814045; ❶–❷), a centrally-located place run by a friendly family.

When it's time to **eat**, most hotels have attached restaurants, of which the *Dam San* is probably the best. *Saigon*, a no-frills eating house on a sidestreet off Hung Vuong near Victory Monument, serves stuffed tofu and prawns as well as flavoursome *com suon* and excellent *thit kho tau* (slow-boiled pork and eggs). The *Ninh Hoa* on Ly Thuong Kiet is famed locally for its fine *nem* (spring rolls) and now has copycat restaurants on either side. Hai Ba Trung's *Bon Trieu* cooks up tasty beef dishes that are perennially popular. If you're looking for a bit of ambience and adventurous eating, head out to the *Quan Ngon* at 72–74 Ba Trieu, where you'll be greeted by a veritable zoo of animals floating in huge jars of exotic wine. Java mouse deer, weasel, porcupine and conger eel all feature in various preparations, and if you're having trouble deciding, try the grilled porcupine and pigeon rice soup, washed down with a big BGI. Back in the centre of town, a string of bakeries lining the bottom end of Le Hong Phong rustle up fresh sandwiches all day.

It would be a crime to visit the heart of Vietnam's coffee industry without tasting the product itself, and there are plenty of opportunities in Buon Ma Thuot's **cafés**. They're scattered all over town, so you need never suffer from caffeine withdrawal, but there's a particular concentration along the south end of Le Thanh Tong, facing a small park. These are packed in the evenings and surrounded by a sea of motorbikes, whose owners sip their drinks in the dim-lit interiors. The most atmospheric places, however, are situated north of town, but well worth the effort of hunting down. Most intriguing is the *Thung Lung Hong Café*, Hem 153 Phan Chu Trinh, which is snuggled at the base of a steep valley at the end of a sidestreet off Phan Chu Trinh. It's hugely popular among locals and, given the dearth of nightlife in Buon Ma Thuot, a godsend for visitors too. Over on Tran Khanh Du, the *Polang Café* has a striking facade which resembles a longhouse entrance, and inside the decor utilizes minority patterns and motifs, while the bases of some tables and chairs are made of the gnarled stumps of coffee bushes – an inspired use of the plant. The menu includes coffee, tea, cocktails, rice wine and fast food at very reasonable prices.

Around Buon Ma Thuot

Once you've exhausted Buon Ma Thuot's urban attractions, which doesn't take too long, it's time to get out and explore the highlands. There are some impressive **waterfalls** southwest of town, while the northwest route out of town leads to **Yok Don National Park** and the touristy village of **Ban Don**. Around 60km south of Buon Ma Thuot, just off Highway 27 on the way to Da Lat, lies peaceful **Lak Lake**, a good place to stay overnight or even rest up a few days.

The waterfalls

About 30km southwest of Buon Ma Thuot are several waterfalls (small admission and parking fee at each one) that are worth visiting, especially in the wet season, though unless you're a real waterfall fan, there's no real point in seeing them all. **Dray Sap** and **Dray Nur**, situated side by side, are the most impressive and most popular. There's also some simple but comfortable **accommodation** at **Trinh Nhu Falls**, in case you're in the mood for a countryside idyll.

To get to the falls, follow Highway 14 for 20km southwest of town, then turn left at the village of **Ea Ting**. Just a kilometre down this road, a left turn leads to **Trinh Nhu Falls**, a narrow chute of water approached by a steep path. At the top of the falls is a **restaurant** with small, inviting pavilions overlooking the river – a good spot to rest up for refreshment or lunch. There are a few concrete and thatch **bungalows** for rent here (☎050/882587, ⑤882167; ❷), as well as floor space in a couple of longhouses for $5 a night (mattress, sheet, pillow and mosquito net provided). Guests get free use of a fishing rod to try their luck in the pond behind the restaurant.

The crescent-shaped **Dray Sap** and neighbouring **Dray Nur Falls** are about 10km down the road from Ea Ting. After a short descent down steps from the car park, a wooden **suspension bridge** to the left leads to Dray Nur Falls, which, though not as wide as Dray Sap, carry more water in the dry season. On the other hand, at the end of the wet season, in September, water levels are usually too high for the short walk to the falls to be accessible. Almost 15m high and over 100m wide, Dray Sap doesn't mean "waterfall of smoke" for nothing: a fug of invigorating spray sags the air, though to feel it on your face you'll need to clamber through bamboo groves and over rocks to the right of the pool formed by the falls. The area round the falls can get very crowded at weekends and on public holidays, but midweek a trip here makes a pleasant outing for a half or full day. Just after passing the ticket office at the approach to Dray Sap Falls, a road branching to the right leads another 7km to **Gia Lo Falls**, yet another waterfall in the region, where there's also the chance of **camping**.

Yok Don National Park and Ban Don

Exit west out of Buon Ma Thuot along Phan Boi Chau, and 45km later you'll arrive at the entrance to Vietnam's largest wildlife preserve, the **Yok Don National Park**, whose 115,000 hectares lie nestled into the hinge of the Cambodian border and the **Serepok River**. The sealed road to the park makes a pleasant journey, and if you start off early in the morning you'll be able to see the minority peoples leaving their split-bamboo thatch houses lined along the route for work in the fields, carrying their tools in raffia backpacks.

Over 60 species of animals, including tigers, leopards and bears, and more than 450 types of birds, from peacocks to hornbills, populate Yok Don Park. Most of them, however, reside in the 90,000-hectare "strictly protected area" – off limits to everyone except park staff – which stretches from a short distance inside the park to the Cambodian border. Of all its exotic animals, **elephants** are what the park is best known for. Elephant-hunters found rich pickings in the region's lush forest for centuries, and today an elephant-back ride is the park's main attraction, though the prices are a bit steep. For $30 for an hour and a half (maybe less if you haggle), two can lumber around the park's eastern edge by elephant – ask early on to reserve some elephants if there's a group of you – while $200 buys a two-day, one-night safari for two ($180 for one person) deeper into the forest, a trip best saved for the dry season, when the park's wildlife makes for **Yok Don Mountain** in search of food and water, and your chances of seeing something interesting improve. Longer safaris can be arranged by the park HQ. If you're only here for the day, the park can arrange elephant trekking tours (around $50) or one-day walking tours (around $20) into the forest. There's a handful of twin-bedded cabin-style rooms with attached bathrooms ($10), should you wish to overnight; for **bookings**, prices and enquiries, contact the park HQ (T050/793049, F783156) and ask for Hung.

The three sub-hamlets that comprise **BAN DON** lie a few kilometres beyond Yok Don's park HQ on the bank of the crocodile-infested Serepok. Khmer, Thai, Lao, Jarai and Mnong live in the vicinity, though it's the **E De** who are again in the majority. They adhere to a matriarchal social system, whereby a groom takes his bride's name, lives with her family and, should his wife die subsequently, marries one of her sisters so that her family retains a male workforce. Houses around the village, a few of which are longhouses, are built on stilts, and some are decorated with ornate woodwork.

Village life in Ban Don has become somewhat commercial with the Ban Don Tourist Centre (☎050/783019) organizing its residents into a tourist-welcoming taskforce. Though constantly visited by busloads of Vietnamese, the rampant commercialism and fees charged for low-grade attractions will make most Westerners want to turn round and get out straight away. If you linger, you can pay a small fee to walk on a rickety bamboo suspension bridge through a tangle of banyan roots, or to look around the village's oldest house, which seems to be under constant repair. The village's other attractions include expensive elephant rides and a glut of souvenir stalls.

Ban Don village has a long and distinguished tradition of elephant-taming; indeed, elephants were still caught and trained until recently, though dwindling numbers of wild elephants make it a vanishing art. (If you're lucky you may get a chance to see the annual elephant races held here some time after the Tet Festival.) Beyond its final sub-hamlet stands an elephant trainers' graveyard, which includes the tomb of the legendary Y Thu Knu (1850–1924), the greatest elephant-catcher of them all. His lifetime tally of 244 included an auspicious white elephant which he presented to the King of Siam, from whom he received the honorary title **khusunop**, meaning something like "great elephant catcher". Y Thu Knu's is the square tomb, and the pointed one in front is his nephew's, also a prodigious elephant-hunter. Other tombs nearby are adorned with paintings of elephants and wooden carvings of peacocks standing on tusks – the latter being considered expensive items to take into the next life.

There are no public buses going to either the national park or the village, so you'll have to join a group tour, or hire a car or Honda om. The latter should cost around $10 for the round trip.

Lak Lake

Some 60km south of Buon Ma Thuot, Highway 27 passes serene **Lak Lake**, a charming spot that has become very popular with tourists, aided by the recent upgrading of the highway between Buon Ma Thuot and Da Lat. Emperor Bao Dai grabbed some of the best sites in southern Vietnam for his many palaces, so it comes as no surprise to find the ruins of one here, in a prime spot on a small hill overlooking the lake. At present the shell of the building is an ugly sight, smothered with graffiti, but Dak Lak Tourist plans to build a small museum dedicated to Bao Dai here, as well as a mini-hotel and, predictably, a souvenir stall. A new road spirals to the top, and another runs round the base of the hill; both afford spectacular views, particularly at sunset, of the lake. Snuggled into a protected bay east of the hill, a **tourist resort** (☎050/586184; ❶) has been fashioned from a former military barracks, with simple but adequate twin bedrooms with fan, some with attached bathroom, as well as two longhouses ($5) beneath a grove of tall, shady trees. There's also a floating **restaurant** where the food is reasonable and Mnong staff wear traditional dress. If you're intent on getting the whole minority village experience, complete with grunting pigs and squawking chickens waking you in the morning, head on round to **Jun Village**, a thriving Mnong community on the west side of the hill, whose longhouses crowd together near the shore. Dak Lak Tourist has a branch office here (☎050/586268), and a longhouse where it's possible to overnight ($5); mosquito nets and mattresses are provided, and there are outside toilet facilities. They can also organize rice-wine feasts ($60 per group) and elephant rides around the lake ($30 for two for an hour and a half). You can take a dug-out canoe with one of the locals ($10 per hour for two through Dak Lak Tourist, cheaper if you bargain with a local boatman) on the wonderfully calm lake, a great experience early in the morning, and the tourist office can even organize guided treks into the surrounding forested hills.

Although Lak Lake is mostly geared towards organized tour groups, it's entirely possible to arrive here independently, either by Honda om, or by the local bus from Buon Ma Thuot, with two departures leaving early in the morning. For bookings and enquiries, contact Dak Lak Tourist Office (☎050/852108).

Plei Ku and around

North of Buon Ma Thuot, Highway 14 rocks and rolls over the hills and plains of the **Dak Lak Plateau**, passing rubber plantations, hardwood forests and the corrugated leaves of coffee plants on its way to **PLEI KU**. The band of peaks to the west of the highway, and the rugged terrain buttressing them, constituted one of the American War's major combat theatres. It was an NVA (North Vietnamese Army) attack on Plei Ku, in February 1965, that elicited the "Rolling Thunder" campaign (see p.499); the war's first conventional battle of any size was fought in the **Ia Drang Valley**, southwest of Plei Ku, eight months later. Hundreds of Americans died at Ia Drang, but many times more communists perished, spurring America to claim victory by dint of a higher body count. A decade later, in March 1975, Plei Ku was abandoned when NVA troops overran Buon Ma Thuot. As the South's commanding officers flew by helicopter to safety, 200,000 Southern soldiers and civilians were left to make their own way down to the coast, hounded at every step by NVA shells.

So little of Plei Ku was left standing by these last days of the war, that a near-total reconstruction was required. The 1990s reincarnation that you'll see, stacked up the side of a gentle slope, lacks any charm. Indeed, you'd be hard-pushed to find any real reason for spending time here, as you need a permit and guide to visit the few minority villages that are open to foreigners, and there's little to see in any case. If you're keen to explore minority villages without a government chaperone, it makes sense to push on 50km north, just an hour's journey, to Kon Tum, where there are fewer restrictions.

Barring an early morning stroll along central, east–west **Tran Phu**, where hawkers sell eggplants, shallots, parsnips and garlic, and into the adjacent town market, there's little to do in Plei Ku. Should you get stalled by the weather, you could check out the two museums in town. The **Ho Chi Minh Museum** (Mon–Sat 7–11am & 1.30–4pm) across from the *Plei Ku Hotel* is well laid out but throws up few surprises. The **Gia Lai Museum** (7.30–11am & 1.30–4pm; $1; book at tourist office in advance), at 28 Quang Trung, fares little better, but there is an impressive gong and rice-wine jar collection in the first gallery and, in the fourth, replicas of a Bahnar grave and longhouse are displayed.

This far north in the highlands, the **Jarai** and, to a lesser extent, the **Bahnar** outnumber the E De, though many of them have been assimilated into mainstream Vietnamese culture. Also, Plei Ku's tourist board, Gia Lai Tourist, is notoriously defensive of the region's few remaining traditional settlements and doesn't approve of individuals making forays into the wilds, insisting that you should always be with a licensed guide when visiting villages. If you try to bypass this regulation and just turn up in villages, you'll get little co-operation from the locals, who receive a cut from the fees for "official" visitors.

Practicalities

Plei Ku's **airport** (☎059/823058) lies 7km northeast of the city, from where taxis and Honda oms make the journey to the centre; Vietnam Airlines, at 55 Quang Trung (☎059/824680; closed Sun), can arrange onward flight reservations. Plei Ku's long-distance **bus station** sits above the three-way crossroads 600m southeast of the centre. From here, it's a short Honda om trip into the city along Hung Vuong, Plei Ku's southern limit, from which its main roads shoot north. When you see a broad flight of steps cut into the middle of the road you'll know you've reached northbound Le Loi, to all intents and purposes the town's eastern extent. **Buses to Kon Tum** (gateway to Bahnar villages) terminate and originate east of the market, on open ground near the intersection of Le Lai and Tran Phu; but your best bet when moving on is to flag down a passing minibus heading north along Le Loi. If you're travelling to **Qui Nhon**, minibuses prowl along Le Loi and eastern Hung Vuong looking for passengers before pushing onwards.

The **bank** at 12 Tran Hung Dao can change travellers' cheques and arrange cash advances for Visa and MasterCard – important if you're moving on to Kon Tum, which as yet does not have these facilities. Gia Lai Tourist (☎059/874571, ✉gialaitourist@fptnet.com.vn) has its offices at 215 Hung Vuong, right next door to the *Hung Vuong Hotel* (see below), and can provide **information** as well as arrange expensive, tailor-made trekking and battlefield tours and overnight stays in minority villages. **Internet access** is available at many places in town, such as 10 Nguyen Dinh Chieu, just north of the centre.

Accommodation in Plei Ku is decidedly uninspiring. Most people make do with the *Plei Ku* (☎059/824628, ☎822151; ❷–❸) at 124 Le Loi, where the top-end rooms are spacious and comfortable. The *Hung Vuong* (☎059/824270; ❷–❸), at the junction of Hung Vuong and Le Loi, has a wing at the back that's preferable to the front rooms to escape traffic noise. Another reasonable choice is the *Ialy* (☎059/824843; ❸), opposite the GPO at the junction of Hung Vuong and Tran Hung Dao, where the better rooms are carpeted and have bathtubs. There are a few budget rooms with shared bathroom at the *Vinh Hoi* (☎059/824644; ❶–❷) at 39 Tran Phu, as well as some smarter rooms with air-conditioning and attached bathrooms. The most popular budget option in town, however, is the *Thanh Lich* (☎059/824674; ❶–❷) at 86 Nguyen Van Troi, which has a range of dingy but cheap rooms.

There are no outstanding places to **eat** in Plei Ku, though the basic *My Tam* at 3 Quang Trung produces tasty staple rice dishes. Also on Quang Trung, the hole-in-the-wall *Nem Ninh Hoa* churns out delicious *nem*. Around the corner on Trang Hung Dao, the *Hung Long* has tasty rice dishes, and their chicken cooked with lotus root is recommended. North of town, at 127 Phan Dinh Phung, the *Ngoc Lam* draws crowds of locals with its forest food, including deer and frog. If you're looking for somewhere with a bit of ambience, head north on Le Loi beyond the *Plei Ku Hotel* and look for a sign to the right leading down a steep lane to *Thien Thanh*. This attractive place has a landscaped garden with small ponds and sweeping views over rice fields, as well as a good range of Vietnamese food. For a decent coffee, the *Café Tennis* at 61 Quang Trang is a reasonable spot.

The Jarai and Bahnar villages

Once past the *Plei Ku Hotel* and out of town, Le Loi probes the coffee, tea and rice crops that hem the road to Kon Tum. A right turning 7km north of town will take you after just 500m to **Bien Ho**, a volcanic lake which is also the town's reservoir; it's pretty enough viewed from the observation point, but doesn't warrant much more than a five-minute stop. About 16km north of Plei Ku, a left turn leads through some pretty countryside and some **Jarai** villages and continues 23km to the hydroelectric dam recently created at **Ialy**. To visit the Jarai village of

PLEI PHUN, you'll need to be with an official guide from Gia Lai Tourist (about $16), who will show you around the headman's house, the local graveyard and village spring. The only real interest is in the graveyard, where roughly-hewn **hardwood statues** depicting figures in a range of moods are placed around each family grave. In the past the Jarai would stick bamboo poles through the earth and into a fresh grave, through which to "feed" the dead, though now they tend to leave fruit and bowls of rice on top of the grave. If you're interested in the workings of the hydroelectric dam, it's possible to take a tour, lasting an hour and a half, for a small fee at the **Ialy Hydro Electric Plant**, which marks the end of the road. The reservoir created by the dam covers 650 hectares and produces 720 megawatts of electricity, making this the second-largest plant in the country (after Hoa Binh). It took nine years to build and was completed in 2001.

There's also a group of four secluded but easily accessible **Bahnar** settlements, lying 38km east of Plei Ku, en route to Qui Nhon. The villages of **DEK TU**, **DE COP**, **DE DOA** and **DEK ROL** all rub shoulders with one another across a small area of forests and streams. Small split-bamboo and straw houses on stilts proliferate through these orderly communities and each one boasts an impressive, steeply thatched *rong* or communal house, where ceremonies are performed, local disputes are resolved and decisions taken. The villages are slowly heading towards modernity, with aluminium roofs more and more common and the odd battery-powered TV. At Dek Tu, there's a good example of a Bahnar cemetery where the practice of feeding the dead is prevalent. Curiously, unlike the Jarai, each of the deceased has his own individual grave complete with a small sloping roof. Ladders made out of bamboo poles leaning against the graves will aid the journey to a new life. As at Plei Phun, you need to be accompanied by a guide, and it is also possible to arrange a **home-stay** in the largest village of the four, De Cop. Gia Lai Tourist have commandeered a house on stilts here, from where you can visit each village on a one-day hike. A two-day programme works out about $12 a head for a group of five people. Further afield, to the southeast of Plei Ku, there are even more remote settlements, such as **AN KHE** and **AYUNPA**, which can be incorporated into a longer trek.

Downhill to Qui Nhon

As recently as four decades ago, tigers stalked the upper reaches of **Highway 19** from Plei Ku down to Qui Nhon, known as the **Giang Pass**. Norman Lewis, travelling here in the 1950s, found a French military outpost commanded by "a slap-happy sergeant from Perpignan, a cabaret-Provençal, who roared with laughter at the thought of his isolation, and poured us out half-tumblers of Chartreuse". The fort may have gone, but scores of **Bahnar settlements** speckle the route, as it snakes its way through a majestic blister of hills and down to the coast.

For the most spectacular panoramas, you'll need to wait until you're 65km out of Plei Ku, when the countryside slowly begins to level out. Shortly after scruffy An Khe, a kink in the highway leads you round onto the **An Khe Pass**, from where you can see the coastal plain yawning magnificently below you, embroidered by the Ha Giao River. By the time you've passed through **VINH SON**, and traversed the bridge that crosses to more sizeable **PHU PHONG**, 50km from Qui Nhon, you're down in the paddy of the coastal plain. Phu Phong lies under the jurisdiction of **Tay Son District** whose most famous sons, the Tay Son brothers, engineered a popular uprising that succeeded in unifying Vietnam for the first time, in the 1770s. Sickened by the land-grabbing and hunger afflicting their countrymen, Nguyen Nhac, Nguyen Lu and

Nguyen Hue in 1771 mustered a peasant army, in order more volubly to express their anger. The army exceeded all expectations: by 1788 it had defeated the Trinh dynasty to the north and the Nguyen dynasty to the south, and Nguyen Hue had proclaimed himself Emperor Quang Trung of Vietnam – a situation he buttressed further a year later when he booted the Chinese out of northern Vietnam at the battle of Dong Da. Quang Trung's death in 1792 deprived the Tay Son dynasty of his charismatic leadership, and ten years later French-backed Nguyen Anh of the Nguyen dynasty snatched power once more. Despite its brevity, the Tay Son period is recalled as a prosperous one, when economic reforms were established and education encouraged. The brothers' escapades are celebrated at the **Quang Trung Museum** (Tues–Sun 7–11am & 2–4.30pm; small admission fee), a three-kilometre Honda om ride from Phu Phong, whose mediocre ensemble of weapons, clothes and armour is really only worth a visit if you're around for the Dong Da Festival, at which demonstrations are staged of the **martial arts** taught here throughout the year.

Beyond Phu Phong, countless brick kilns pepper the landscape, their rippling roofs seeming to melt in the heat. Qui Nhon itself is covered in Chapter Four, on p.261.

Kon Tum and the minority villages

Some 49km north of Plei Ku, northbound Highway 14 crosses the Dakbla River and runs into the southern limits of **KON TUM**, a sleepy, friendly town which serves as a springboard for jaunts to its outlying villages of the **Bahnar** and other minority groups such as the **Sedang**, **Gieh Trieng** and **Rongao**. There are about 650 minority villages in the province, of which only about 30 have been visited by foreigners, so the scope for adventure here is broad indeed. Unlike other provinces in the central highlands, local authorities in Kon Tum do not insist on the need for visitors to obtain permits and guides to visit minority villages, so you are more or less free to explore as you like. However, you're strongly advised to discuss your travel plans with the local tourist office to check on their feasibility.

Under the guise of Phan Dinh Phung, Highway 14 forms the western edge of Kon Tum; running east above the river is Nguyen Hue, and between these two axes lies the town centre. In common with Buon Ma Thuot and Plei Ku, Kon Tum had a hard time of it during the American War, and yet a stroll along Nguyen Hue still reveals a handful of red-tile terraces of shophouses left over from the French era, their low, bowed roofs blackened with age, as well as two churches. At the base of Tran Phu stands the grand, whitewashed bulk of **Tan Huong Church**. Further east is the so-called **Wooden Church**, built by the French in 1913, and lovingly restored to its highly varnished prime in the mid-1990s. A statue of Christ stands behind glass over the front entrance; below him, a stained-glass window neatly fuses the classic Christian symbol of the dove with images of local resonance – a Bahnar village and an elephant. In the grounds, a statue of the nineteenth-century French bishop who established the diocese of Kon Tum stands before a scale model of a *rong*, or communal house.

Behind the church, a Bahnar orphanage looks after children of all ages in spartan but well-cared-for surroundings. Visitors are welcome to look around, and are usually offered homemade wine and croissants; a donation is expected. There is another branch of the orphanage tucked away down by the river off Ly Thai To, which receives fewer visitors, so you're likely to get a warm welcome. At 56

Tran Hung Dao is a **Catholic seminary** and **minorities museum** (7.30–10.30am & 2–4pm) that is worth a look for its impressive architecture alone. The museum contains examples of minority handicrafts, work implements and clothes, as well as a history of Christianity in the hills of Vietnam. It doesn't stick rigidly to its opening hours, so if you can't find anyone around, contact one of the local branches of Kon Tum Tourist to arrange a visit.

One good thing about Kon Tum is that you don't have to go far to get a feel of a minority village, as there are a couple of Bahnar villages on the eastern fringe of town. Following Nguyen Hue to its eastern end brings you to **Kon Tum Konam**, while following Tran Hung Dao to the east takes you directly to **Kon Tum Kopong**, where there is a wonderful example of a *rong*, or communal house, which is such a striking feature of Bahnar villages. Built on sturdy stilts with a platform and entrance at either end (or in the middle, as is the case here); the interior is generally made of split bamboo and protected by a towering thatched roof, usually about 15m high. The *rong* is used as a venue for festivals and village meetings, and as a village court at which anyone found guilty of a tribal offence has to ritually kill a pig and a chicken, and must apologize in front of the village.

Practicalities

Kon Tum's **bus station** is to the northwest of town on Phan Dinh Phung. From here, it's best to take a Honda om to the town centre, which is about 2km away. **Currency exchange** is possible at the Investment and Development Bank on Nguyen Hue near the junction with Tran Phu. The **post office** is at 205 Le Hong Phong. There are several places offering **Internet access**, including the centrally located shop at 183 Tran Hung Dao.

There are not yet many **hotels** in Kon Tum. Most popular is the *Dakbla* (T060/863333; ❸), at 2 Phan Dinh Phung (don't confuse it with the dingy *Dakbla 2* nearby), a large, modern place with functional rooms, all with satellite TV, bathtub and hot water, and some with balconies and views of the Dakbla River. Meanwhile, north of the centre, the endearing *Quang Trung* (T060/862249; ❸–❹), at 168 Ba Trieu, has cheaper air-conditioned and fan rooms complete with hot water, and is a good deal cosier than the austere reception would suggest. The best budget alternative is the *Family Guest House* (T & F060/865748; ❶–❷), which has two places, at 55 and 61 Tran Hung Dao. Rooms are clean and the owners are very friendly and helpful. Most hotels rent **bicycles** and **motorbikes**.

Kon Tum Tourist (T060/861626, ⓔkontumtourist@dng.vnn.vn) is on the ground floor of the *Dakbla Hotel*, with another branch at the *Quang Trung Hotel*. They can organize a wide range of tailor-made **tours**, which include trekking, river trips and traditional dance performances, with prices to suit all types, and offer **information** on new areas opening up in the surrounding region. Even if you don't plan to book a tour through them, they're very happy to give independent advice. Ask for Mr Huynh, who is a mine of information on the local area and minority culture in particular.

When it's time to **eat**, there are several options along Nguyen Hue. The *Dakbla*, at no. 168, serves surprisingly sophisticated Vietnamese and Western dishes from English and French menus and also has a selection of ethnic souvenirs for sale. Other options along here are the *Hiep Thanh* at no. 129, a reliable place for unfussy Vietnamese food, and the *90 Restaurant,* a smart place not surprisingly located at no. 90. The *Dakbla Hotel* restaurant enjoys an idyllic setting and panoramic views across the river from its wooden stilt terrace; its extensive menu, which includes vegetarian dishes, is reasonably priced, and this is probably the best spot for a cool drink around sunset. The place to savour the excellent local coffee is *Café Eva*, 1 Phan Chu Trinh, run by a local sculptor, whose work is also displayed here; the three-storey café has been built to resemble a stilthouse, and its surrounding garden yields fountains, wooden sculptures of distorted faces and a waterfall trickling down the back wall. There isn't much **nightlife** in Kon Tum, though a couple of bars on Phan Chu Trinh, the *Ngoc Lan* and the *Paradise*, have been known to get their customers dancing at the weekend.

Around Kon Tum

There are dozens of Bahnar villages encircling Kon Tum. As they seem to be free of the official restrictions that hang over Plei Ku, you're very much at liberty to explore this area at will, although for overnight stays it's best to check first with the local tourist office. At some villages, such as **KON ROBANG**, 2km west of Phan Dinh Phung along Ba Trieu, the village *rong*, or communal house, has been robbed of much of its drama by an aluminium roof. A couple of kilometres further west, however, is **KON HONGO**, which is inhabited by members of the Rongao, one of the smaller minority groups in the region. Women are often busy weaving in the shade of their simple, wooden huts, ox carts trundle along the dusty road, and children splash about in the Dakbla River.

About 5km to the east of town is the most frequently visited of Bahnar villages, **KON KOTU**. Though now linked to Kon Tum by a sealed road, it makes a pleasant walk to go there by country paths (contact the local tourist office for details) and it's possible to overnight in the village *rong*. To get there by road, follow Tran Hung Dao east out of town, passing stilt villages, cassava and sugarcane plantations as you move into the Bahnar heartland. Eventually, you'll cross over a bridge at **KON KLOR**, beside which on the right is a very impressive *rong* with attractive patterning along the peak of the roof. A couple of hundred metres beyond the bridge, turn left and follow the road to Kon Kotu. Most of the dwellings here are made of bamboo and secured with rattan string, although some houses now are made of timber and sport tiled or aluminium roofs, and the newly constructed schoolhouse has been built from brick. However, it's the village's immaculate *rong* that commands the most attention. It also doubles as an occasional overnight stop for local trekking tours organized by Kon Tum Tourist. No nails were used in the construction of the bamboo walls, floor, and the impossibly tall thatch roof of this lofty communal hall.

There are plenty of other villages of interest on the road east to **KON PLONG**, the only town of any size between Kon Tum and the coast at Quang Ngai. About 36km from Kon Tum, there's a **Sodra** village on the left, while a kilometre further on the right is a **Jolong** village with a very different type of *rong*, without the towering roof favoured by other groups. To reach this village, you need to negotiate a hanging bridge, which sways precariously above the Dakbla River. Beyond Kon Plong, Highway 24 climbs up to a pass at 1200m called **Den Pass**, where there is a lovely stand of pine trees. This is also the beginning point for one of the many treks organized by Kon Tum Tourist in the area.

Heading 30km west of Kon Tum takes you along a sealed route towards the village of **Sa Thay**, after which the road continues to **Chu Mom Ray Nature Reserve**. Covering about 50,000 hectares running towards the Cambodian border, Chu Mom Ray is a rugged mountainous region covered by virgin forest. At the time of writing, a guide and permit were necessary to enter this area, but there are plans to upgrade it to a national park, which will probably lead to easier access. Once fully operational, Chu Mom Ray will afford unique opportunities to view the rare monkeys and other endangered species that live here. For latest information, make enquiries at Kon Tum Tourist.

Surrounding the outskirts of the reserve and at the base of Chu Mom Ray are also a number of Jarai villages that are worth visiting, their traditions very much in evidence, with stilt longhouses made from split bamboo and straw housing numerous families, hand-weaving on giant looms, and graveyards yielding wondrously eerie wooden statues.

On from Kon Tum

Until recently it was necessary to backtrack from Kon Tum in order to get down to the coast or head northwards, but as a result of improved roads, travellers now have the choice of heading down to the coast at **Quang Ngai** on Highway 24, or continuing north on Highway 14, the famed **Ho Chi Minh trail**, then branching off on Highway 14B to reach **Da Nang**. Many sections of this road have recently been upgraded, making it a pleasure to travel on. There are also plans to open the **border** to **southern Laos** at **Ngoc Hoi**, 30km west of Dak To, by 2005, which will open up intriguing travel possibilities in the region.

Around 42km north of Kon Tum is the district of **DAK TO**, which witnessed some of the most sustained fighting of the American War; to the west of the road to Dak To is Rocket Ridge, a brow of hills that earned its name from the heavy bombing – napalm and conventional – it received during this

Vietnam's real-life Kurtz

The Sedang played their part in one of colonial Vietnam's oddest interludes and one which mirrored events in Joseph Conrad's novella, *Heart of Darkness*, in which a mysterious voyager named Kurtz proclaims himself king, deep in the Belgian Congo – a story later borrowed by Francis Ford Coppola for his film *Apocalypse Now*.

The career of French rogue **Marie-David de Mayréna** was a chequered one to say the least. After a stint with the French Army in Cochinchina in the mid-1860s, he made his way back to Paris, only to return to the East after having failed as a banker. Back in Vietnam by the 1880s, he established himself as a planter around Ba Ria, until 1888 when the governor sent him to explore the highlands. Of the hundred or so porters and soldiers who accompanied him, only one, a Frenchman named Alphonse Mercurol, remained by the time he reached Kon Tum. Through the contacts of the French missionaries based there, Mayréna was able to arrange meetings with local tribal chiefs; soon the leaders fell under the spell of his "blue eyes" and "bold, confident stare", and he conspired to proclaim himself **King Marie I of Sedang**, while Mercurol adopted the title "Marquis of Hanoi". For three months, Mayréna ruled from a straw hut flying the national flag (a white cross on a blue background, with a red star in the centre), legislating, creating an army and even declaring war on the neighbouring Jarai people.

But Mayréna was more interested in money than sovereignty, and within months he had decamped, setting off in the hope of getting some mileage from his "title". In his book, *Dragon Ascending*, Henry Kamm quotes an erstwhile manager of Saigon's *Continental*, where Mayréna boarded on credit with assorted courtiers: "Alas, when, several days later, Mayréna moved out of the hotel, nothing was left to Laval [the then hotel manager] as payment for his services, except for a decoration, that of the National Order of the Kingdom of the Sedangs, which the king gave him before departure." Returning to Europe, Mayréna took to selling fictitious titles and mining concessions to raise cash but, inevitably, cracks began to appear in his story, and he fled back to Southeast Asia in 1890 where he died in penury on Malaya's Tioman Island, supposedly of a snake bite.

time. There's a *rong* right in the middle of Dak To, where the inhabitants are mostly Sedang, and with a little exploration you should be able to find more Sedang longhouses in the settlements surrounding Dak To.

Heading north along the route from Dak To, the road passes through **DAK GLEI**, where there's another spectacular *rong*. Directly east is virgin jungle surrounding Mount Ngoc Linh (2598m), the highest peak in the central highlands, though unfortunately at the time of writing this was off limits to foreigners. Beyond here, the route takes you through wonderfully verdant and unpopulated countryside before Highway 14B branches off to the right at **Nam Giang**, taking you down to the coast at Hoi An or Da Nang.

Travel details

Trains

Da Lat to: Trai Mat (on demand; 40min).

Flights

Buon Ma Thuot to: Da Nang (5 weekly; 1hr 10min); Hanoi (5 weekly; 3hr 25min); Ho Chi Minh City (daily; 1hr).
Da Lat to: Hanoi (daily; 3hr 30min); Ho Chi Minh City (daily; 50min).
Plei Ku to: Da Nang (6 weekly; 50min); Hanoi (6 weekly; 3hr 10min); Ho Chi Minh City (6 weekly; 1hr).

Buses

It's almost impossible to give the **frequency** with which buses run. Long-distance public buses, though scheduled, won't depart if empty. Moreover, private services, often minibuses or pick-ups, ply more popular routes, and depart only when they have enough passengers to make the journey worthwhile. It's advisable to start your journey early – most long-distance departures are between 5am and 9am, and few run after midday. **Journey times** can also vary; figures below show the normal length of time you can expect the journey to take.
Buon Ma Thuot to: Da Nang (12hr); Ho Chi Minh City (7hr); Nha Trang (4hr); Plei Ku (4hr).
Da Lat to: Buon Ma Thuot (4–6hr); Da Nang (16hr); Ho Chi Minh City (6hr); Nha Trang (5hr); Phan Rang (3hr).
Plei Ku to: Buon Ma Thuot (4hr); Da Nang (10hr); Kon Tum (1hr); Qui Nhon (4hr).

The south-central coast

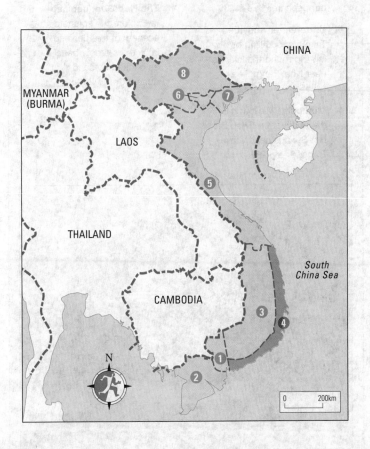

CHAPTER 4

Highlights

✳ **Lazing on the beach**
Sprawl on a deserted
beach at Ho Coc or Ca
Na. See p.236

✳ **Mui Ne** Stay in a fancy
resort at Mui Ne and
soak up its laidback
atmosphere. See p.239

✳ **Underwater activities**
Take a snorkelling or diving trip round the islands
near Nha Trang. See
p.255

✳ **Mud baths** Wallow in a
mud bath at the Thap Ba
Hot Springs near Nha
Trang. See p.253

✳ **Cham monuments** Visit
the impressive Po Klong
Garai towers, just out-
side Phan Rang, one of
the country's best-pre-
served Cham monu-
ments. See p.252

✳ **The Hon Gom peninsu-
la** Explore the splendid
scenery of this peninsu-
la, with its empty beach-
es backed by sand
dunes. See p.253

The south-central coast

O nce you've dusted off the grime of Ho Chi Minh City, you're ready to head up the elongated flatlands that comprise Vietnam's south-central coast. Extending from the wetlands of the Mekong Delta right up to the central provinces (see p.269), and bounded by the South China Sea to the east and the Truong Son mountain range to the west, the south-central coast is braced by the twin backbones of Highway 1 and the pan-Vietnam rail line. In some places, the mountains' rugged crests stoop right down to peer into the turquoise shallows of the sea; at these points along the coast, both highway and rail line scythe through the heights, across precipitous passes that afford bewitching views of the countryside below.

Sea-fishing provides a living for a considerable percentage of the region's population. Fleets of fishing boats jostle for space in the cramped ports and estuaries of the coastal towns, awaiting the turn of the tide; and fish and seafood drying along the road are a common sight. The farmers who till the region's soils tend to leave rice-growing to the people of the Mekong Delta, and the crops you're likeliest to see here are coconut and rubber **plantations**, shrimp farms, wintry salt flats and fruit **orchards**.

Historically, this region of Vietnam was the domain of the Indianized trading empire of **Champa**. Courted in its prime by seafaring merchants from around the globe, Champa was steadily marginalized from the tenth century onwards by the march south of the Vietnamese. These days a few enclaves around Phan Thiet and Phan Rang are all that remain of the Cham people; but the gnarled remnants of the towers which once punctuated the countryside – most in evidence within the bowl of hills cupping the impressive My Son ruins (covered in Chapter Five, see p.288) – recall Champa's former magnificence. The power struggles of the Chams and Vietnamese were still fairly recent history when the French took advantage of factional strife in Hué's royal court, following the passing of the Emperor Tu Duc in 1883, to sidle into the region, seize it and declare it as the French Protectorate of Annam. Many a Vietnamese peasant was consigned to a life of forced labour in the plantations that the French subsequently established. The American War brought still further social dislocation. Hundreds of thousands of villagers were uprooted from their homes and boxed up in strategic hamlets. Their lands were rendered "free-fire zones" and bombed pancake-flat by planes making sorties out of the US army bases that peppered the region.

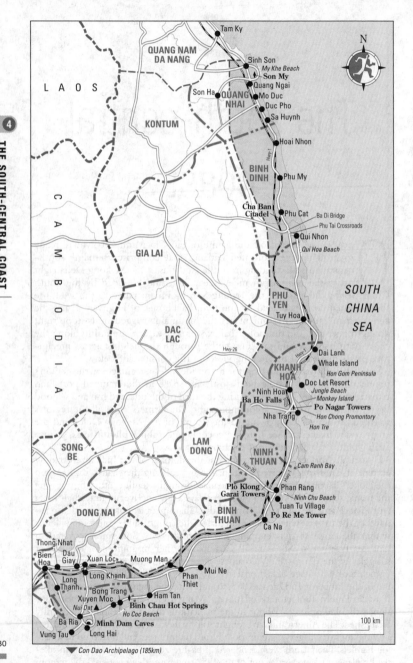

Strung out between raucous Ho Chi Minh and the cultural showpieces of Hué and Hoi An, and serving as a springboard for travel in the central highlands, this section of the coastline is largely perceived as a somewhat dull interlude between more rewarding destinations. While sites of considerable interest and beauty do exist along this portion of coast, most tourists are merely **passing through**. Nonetheless, all but the hardiest of travellers will need to work at least one pit stop into their itinerary. For this, you'll have to juggle tranquil beaches – and there are some real gems on offer – with more cultural pursuits.

Coming from Ho Chi Minh, there's an early choice to be made. Highway 1 has to wait until it reaches Phan Thiet to see the South China Sea, but you needn't: from Bien Hoa, a road drops down to **Vung Tau**, once a French seaside resort, and now a smart, oil-rich coastal town with average beaches. Much better beaches can be found further up the coast at places like **Ho Coc**, while to the south, the former French prison island of **Con Dao** can be reached either by boat or by helicopter. With tourism still largely in its infancy across Vietnam, few beaches along the south-central coast have been developed as yet, so with your own transport and an adventurous spirit, you'll find somewhere to pace out a solitary set of footprints in the pristine sand. It won't be at **Mui Ne**, however, which is perhaps a sign of things to come for Vietnamese tourism – slick resorts rubbing shoulders along a fine sweep of soft sand, looking out over aquamarine waters. This tourist enclave attracts a steady stream of overseas visitors as well as expats from Ho Chi Minh City on a short break. Those for whom a day sunbathing is a day wasted will prefer to make a little more headway, and rest up around **Phan Rang**, site of the most impressive of the many **tower complexes** erected by the once mighty empire of **Champa** (see box on p.245). The nearby beach at **Ca Na** isn't in the same league as Mui Ne, but its location just beyond the hard shoulder of the highway makes it a convenient short-term staging post. If you press on to **Nha Trang**, however, you have the best of both worlds: arresting Cham towers, attractive municipal beach and a brisk trade in diving and snorkelling trips. Other, more secluded, beaches that warrant an expedition include **Doc Let** and **Sa Huynh**, while for a little more civilization, **Qui Nhon** makes a useful halt above Nha Trang. The scars of war tend not to intrude too much along this stretch of the country, though many visitors make time to visit **Quang Ngai**, where Vietnam's south-central arc of coastline culminates, and view the sombre site of the notorious **My Lai** massacre perpetrated by US forces in 1968.

Vung Tau and around

From **Bien Hoa**, just outside Ho Chi Minh, Highway 51 drops southward via modest **Long Thanh** (famed locally for its impressive **fruit market**) to **Ba Ria**. From there, a dog-legged road ventures out across the swampland and shrimp farms of the **Vung Tau Peninsula** to Vung Tau itself, home of the most southerly beaches on the eastern Vietnamese coast.

With every passing day, a little more of the charm ebbs from **VUNG TAU**, "The Bay of Boats", located some 125km southeast of Ho Chi Minh City on a hammerheaded spit of land jutting out into the mouth of the Saigon River. Once a thriving riviera-style beach resort, the city is now a shadow of its former self, its several strips of sand looping out from a city centre that lacks any real finesse. As Vung Tau's **offshore oil** industry and steadily growing port have bloated the city into a more business-oriented conurbation, tourism has been given a lower profile, and despite a recent effort to clean them up, the town's **beaches** – **Bai Dau**, **Bai Truoc**, **Bai Dua** and **Bai Sau** – are all second-rate.

Portuguese ships are thought to have exploited the city's deep anchorage as early as the fifteenth century. By the turn of the twentieth, French expats, who knew the place as "Cap Saint-Jacques", had adopted it as a retreat from the daily rigmarole of Saigon, and set to work carving colonial villas into the sides of **Nui Lon** and **Nui Nho**, two low hills near the coast. Shifts in Vietnam's political sands duly replaced French visitors with American GIs. With them gone, and the communist government in power, the city became a favoured launch pad for the vessels that spirited away the **boat people** (see p.504) in the late 1970s. These days, it's become a weekend bolt hole for the stressed-out inhabitants of Ho Chi Minh City.

Arrival, information and getting around

Minibuses pull up in the square below the cathedral on Tran Hung Dao, while other **buses** terminate at the bus station at 192 Nam Ky Khoi Nghia; either way, cyclo drivers will be on hand to ferry you to a hotel. **Hydrofoils** from Ho Chi Minh usually dock at the south end of Bai Truoc ("Front Beach"), though in bad weather they are forced to use a more sheltered location 12km away, from where free shuttle buses are provided. Once in Vung Tau, you can **get around** by cyclo, Honda om or taxi, though for more independence, rent a bicycle or motorbike, either at *Dai Loc* (see "Accommodation", below) or at any of the major hotels. For local **information**, go to Vung Tau Tourist (☎064/857527, ✆vungtautour@hcm.vnn.vn) at 29 Tran Hung Dao, which is next door to the Vietnam Airlines office (☎064/856099), where you can book domestic or international flights, as well as helicopters to Con Dao Island ($150 return; 3 flights per week). The **post office** (7am–8.30pm; closed Sun) is at 408 Le Hong Phong, and several hotels have **Internet access**, though for cheaper rates, try the shops on Bacu . If you need a **bank**, Vietcombank, 27 Tran Hung Dao (Mon–Fri 7–11.30am & 1.30–4pm) can change travellers' cheques and make advances on Visa and MasterCard.

Accommodation

Most of Vung Tau's **hotels** and **guesthouses** are located on Bai Sau, which boasts the most varied lodgings, from comfortable hotels to cheap dives, while the classier (and more expensive) places tend to be clustered around the town centre. Two of the swankier places downtown are the *Petro House*, 63 Tran Hung Dao (☎064/852014, ✆petro.htl@hcm.vnn.vn; ❹–❺) and the *Royal*, 36 Quang Trung (☎064/859852, ℗859851; ❹–❺), both of which have smart, attractive rooms, attentive staff and good facilities for business travellers. The *Royal* is right on the front and many of its rooms boast delightful sea views. Among the mid-range options on Bai Sau, the *Thang Muoi*, 151 Thuy Van (☎064/852665, ℗859876; ❸), has ageing but smart rooms set in a quiet compound opposite the beach, while the *Nha Rong Bimexco*, at the northern end of Thuy Van (☎064/859916, ℗853470; ❶–❸), has a range of wooden beach chalets, some of which sleep four people. One of the best budget hotels is the *Phong Tro 27*, at 170a Hoang Hoa Tham (☎064/858124; ❶), which has about sixty reasonably clean rooms just a few steps from the beach. For a friendly family feel, head for *Dai Loc*, 87 Thuy Van (☎064/852933; ❶). The well-kept rooms hidden behind the restaurant of the same name are good value, and besides turning out good food, the owner Mr Si rents out bicycles and motorbikes, and is a helpful source of travel information.

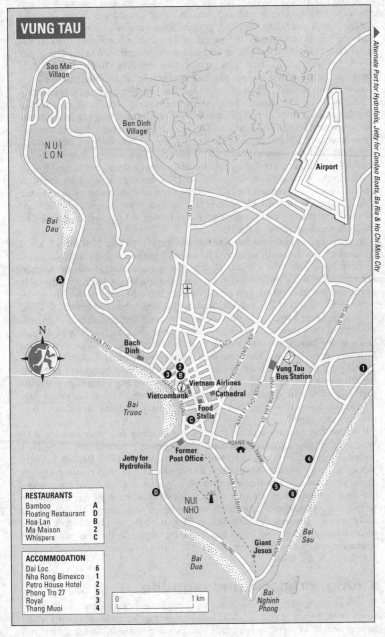

VUNG TAU

Alternate Port for Hydrofoils, Jetty for Condao Boats, Ba Ria & Ho Chi Minh City

Sao Mai Village

Ben Dinh Village

N U I L O N

Bai Dau

Airport

Bai Truoc

TRAN PHU

Bach Dinh

QUANG TRUNG

BACU

TRUONG CONG DINH

NAM KY KHOI NGHIA

LE LOI

Vung Tau Bus Station

Vietnam Airlines

Vietcombank

Cathedral

Food Stalls

KO VIET NGHE TINH

30 THI SAU

Jetty for Hydrofoils

Former Post Office

HOANG HOA THAM

PHAN CHU TRINH

NUI NHO

Giant Jesus

HALONG

THUY VAN

Bai Sau

Bai Dua

Bai Nghinh Phong

N

RESTAURANTS

Bamboo	A
Floating Restaurant	D
Hoa Lan	B
Ma Maison	2
Whispers	C

ACCOMMODATION

Dai Loc	6
Nha Rong Bimexco	1
Petro House Hotel	2
Phong Tro 27	5
Royal	3
Thang Muoi	4

0   1 km

The City

Scouting around central Vung Tau unearths precious little to see or do, though its clean, tree-lined boulevards are pleasant enough to wander along. Take care on the streets after dark, however, as there have been several reports of "grab and run" thefts perpetrated by youngsters. There are a handful of colonial villas at Tran Hung Dao's northern end and along waterfront Quang Trung. Just north of here, at 12 Tran Phu, stands the imposing **Bach Dinh** (daily 7am–5pm; small admission fee), peeping out from behind a vanguard of frangipani and bougainvillea. Built at the end of the nineteenth century, it served as a holiday home to Vietnam's political players, hosting such luminaries as Paul Doumer, Governor-General of Indochina (for whom it was originally erected), emperors Thanh Thai and Bao Dai, and President Thieu. Recent renovations have done little to atone for decades of neglect, but the front facade's classical busts and the mosaics under the eaves still catch the eye. Inside you can thrill to the building's collection of "valuable antique items", excavated from a seventeenth-century shipwreck off Con Dao; among the exhibits are such unmissables as "dry burned fruits", "beard-tweezers" and "pieces of stone in the ship". Snakeskin-patterned bannisters lead up to the first floor's tiled chambers, whose Cambodian Buddhist statuary and shards of old pottery are eclipsed by the commanding views of the bay.

To see Vung Tau's other sights of marginal interest, head for **Nui Nho** ("Small Mountain"), to the south of town. The town's **lighthouse**, built in 1910, seems to have been based on a child's sketch of a space-rocket. It can be reached either on foot or by motorbike, by turning up a small lane, Hem 150, from Ha Long, just past the former post office, or from the other end of the lane at the extreme south end of Bai Sau. Off limits in the days when the French retained a strong military presence in the city, it's now accessible and affords panoramic views of the peninsula. This walk or ride is best done early or late in the day to avoid the blazing sun, and can be combined with a visit to Vung Tau's own little touch of Rio, its 33-metre-high **Giant Jesus** (daily 7.30–11.30am & 1.30–5pm), further south on the hill. Cherubs wielding harps and trumpets herald your approach to the outstretched arms of the city's most famous landmark. Climb the steps inside the wind-buffeted statue and you can perch, parrot-like, on Jesus's shoulder, from where you'll enjoy giddying views of the surrounding seascape.

If swimming and sun-seeking brought you to Vung Tau, your best bet is to head for the yellow sands of **Bai Sau** ("Back Beach"), far and away Vung Tau's widest, longest (5km) and best, which is not saying much. Backed by ugly block-buildings, and a little unkempt, it's not exactly a tropical paradise, though on Sundays, when it's cluttered with deckchairs and umbrellas, and the pineapple- and banana-sellers are out in force, it's pleasant enough. At the time of writing, however, cheap food stalls on the beach were being cleared out to make way for modern facilities such as **Ocean Park**, which occupies a 700-metre beach frontage and offers beach games, lifeguards, showers and a smart restaurant; it remains to be seen what effect these changes will have on the popularity of the beach.

Eating, drinking and nightlife

With a large number of resident expats, Vung Tau supports a marginally more cosmopolitan span of **restaurants** than your average Vietnamese town; French cuisine weighs in particularly heavily, but it's also possible to find spaghetti and burgers. Menus are far more traditional once you leave the central area. In addition, there are a number of **bars** in the town centre catering to the expat community, while some upmarket hotels have their own nightclub or dance floor.

For a fancy meal, try *Ma Maison*, 63 Tran Hung Dao, attached to the *Petro House Hotel*. Adorned with crisp white tablecloths and terracotta floor tiles, this stylish restaurant boasts a surprisingly affordable menu of international cuisine. Specializing in seafood prepared in Vietnamese or Chinese style, the *Floating Restaurant*, 150 Ha Long, is housed in a custom-built circular building set over the sea, with the *Hai Ly Club* downstairs, should you want to dance away the calories after dinner. Another beachfront restaurant north of town at 7 Tran Phu is *Bamboo*, a garden restaurant that could have been lifted straight from the South of France; the extensive menu ranges from grilled kangaroo to red clam salad. Back in town, *Whispers*, 15 Nguyen Trai, is one of the most popular haunts for resident expats, with its traditional roasts and good-quality Western fare.

If your culinary requirements are cheap and cheerful, the *Hoa Lan*, 27 Trung Nhi, is a large, no-frills place serving up stir-fries, salads and rice dishes at around $1 each. There's also a clutch of food stalls along the south end of Tran Hung Dao, where you can point at whatever takes your fancy and be charged next to nothing for it.

Several bars along Nguyen Trai, the lower part of Quang Trung and nearby Truong Cong Dinh, provide the epicentre of what **nightlife** exists in Vung Tao.

Around Vung Tau

Apart from its pretty, yellow-washed and twin-towered church, **Ba Ria** has nothing worth seeing, but with buses leaving for points east of Vung Tau from the station beside the market, on the western outskirts of town, you may still have cause to linger here. As you move up the coast northeast of Vung Tau, the beaches gradually get more enticing, but as the region is near to Ho Chi Minh City, you have to go quite a way before you escape the hordes of domestic tourists who head for the area at weekends and on public holidays.

The right turn at a forked road a couple of kilometres east of Ba Ria gives, 12km later, onto the frontage of the resort of **LONG HAI**, located 20km around the coast from Vung Tau below a wall of impressive mountains. Once a lure for French holidaymakers, it's now popular with Vietnamese, who find its wide beach and fishing-village atmosphere more appealing than Vung Tau. Dunes fringe the town's eastern extreme; while to the west stands a fishing village, complete with stilthouses, a huge flotilla of fishing boats, and assorted coracles sporting brightly coloured flags. Long Hai is served by **buses** from Ho Chi Minh's Mien Dong station; coming from Vung Tau, you'll need to take a bus to Ba Ria and then change, or take one of the many waiting Honda oms. Few foreigners stay here, though there are a few **hotels**, of which the best is probably the *Military Guest House* (☎064/868316; ❶–❷), located at the end of the road that runs into the village. It has basic rooms with a choice of fan or air-conditioned rooms, and looks out over a wide expanse of beach shaded by casuarinas. There are a few **food stalls** by the road leading up to the guesthouse.

Many visitors now bypass the town altogether and head straight along to the **resort area** east of town, where the aptly named *Anoasis Beach Resort* (☎064/868227, ⓦwww.anoasisresort.com.vn; ❺–❻) is a lovingly restored former residence of Emperor Bao Dai overlooking a deserted coastline. The thatched-roofed individual bungalows discreetly set amongst pine-studded hills are something very special, with gorgeous bamboo furnishings and fittings and huge bathtubs. Facilities also run to a business centre, swimming pool and charming open-air terraced restaurant. The resort recently won the much coveted award from *The Guide* magazine for "best resort in Vietnam". Non-residents can enjoy the facilities for $10 a day at weekends or $6 a day on weekdays. At the time of writing, another large resort was under construction just east of here. A little further along, the *Thuy Duong Resort* (☎064/886215, ✉tranchauld@hcm.vnn.vn; ❸–❺) is also appropriately named, since "thuy duong" means casuarina, and the fine strip of beach in front is lined with these graceful trees. It offers a good mid-range alternative to the grubby rooms in Long Hai and the opulence at *Anoasis*; accommodation ranges from pleasant and relatively inexpensive beach huts to luxurious suites in the main hotel.

Trace the road hugging the east coast and just beyond *Thuy Duong Resort* you'll find a signposted left turn that runs up to the elevated **Minh Dam caves**, a communist bolt hole from 1948, from where you can enjoy prodigious views of the rice fields that quilt the coastal plain stretching to the horizon to the northeast, and of the boulder-strewn coastline below. Reached via steps hewn into the rock and rickety bamboo ladders, the caves are really more like gaps between piled boulders; yet with a little imagination it's still possible to picture Viet Minh and Viet Cong soldiers lounging, cooking and sleeping here. Regular skirmishes took place on the mountainside – bullets have left pock-marks on some of the rocks, and joss sticks are still lodged in crevices in memory of those who fell here. Since there are many forks in the path, however, you really need a guide to find your way around.

The road linking this stretch of coast to Ba Ria loops up to the marketplace in little **Dat Do**, a genial one-horse town 25km east of Ba Ria. East of Dat Do, the road from Ba Ria pushes past groves of bamboo, eucalyptus and coconut and through **XUYEN MOC**, before reaching diminutive **BONG TRANG**, from where a road leads to **Ho Coc Beach**. Ho Coc is a spell-binding, five-kilometre stretch of wonderfully golden sand, dotted with cora-cles and deckchairs, lapped by clear waters and backed by fine dunes. As with most places around here, it gets crowded with day-trippers at the weekend but is practically deserted during the week. There are two beachside accommoda-tion choices here: the best is the *Khu Du Lich Bien* (☎064/878175; ❷–❸), located to your left as you arrive at the beach. It has three types of room, rang-ing from modest bamboo beach huts with fan and attached bathrooms to com-fortably furnished rooms with fridge and TV, set on concrete "tree stumps" that give them expansive views. To the right is the *Hang Duong Ho Coc* (☎064/878145; ❶–❸), which is very sleazy by comparison, though it has some large rooms that can sleep up to seven people if you're in a group. All rooms are set back from the beach, so none have good views. Both places have **restaurants** with limited menus. **Buses** from Ho Chi Minh, Vung Tau and Ba Ria trundle as far as Xuyen Moc, from where you'll need to take a Honda om.

Binh Chau Hot Springs ($1 entry; ☎064/871131, ✉saigonbinhchau @hcm.vnn.vn) are 10km further east, and at the time of writing the site was being totally revamped to add a golf-driving range, tennis courts, sand volley-ball court, billiards and ox-cart rides to the basic hot springs. The sulphurous waters bubbling hellishly in the streams and wells here vary greatly in temper-ature. Old people soothe their aching limbs in the foot-soaking stream, while elsewhere visitors boil eggs sold on site to make up ad hoc picnics. For just over $1, you can bathe in the mineral waters of the "Dreaming Lake", a communal **swimming pool**, but renting your own **mini-pool** (about $2 per person per hour) is a more tempting option. There's also a sauna, massage and mud baths in the main complex, which features five small hotels (❶–❸) offering com-fortable, bungalow-style accommodation, with names like Sunrise, Peace and Cherry. The complex also features a large **restaurant**. There's no public transport to Binh Chau Hot Springs, but if you fancy spending a night or two there, call their Ho Chi Minh City office (☎08/997 0677), and they will arrange a pick-up.

If you have your own transport (either rented motorbike or car with driver), you can explore the stretch of **Highway 55** along the coast between Binh Chau and **Ham Tan**, passing through cashew orchards with glimpses of huge sand dunes to your right. This route is so far off the beaten track that ox carts outnumber motorized vehicles. Occasional dirt tracks lead down to some fantastic stretches of deserted beach, where a few coracles pulled up beyond the tide level hint at human habitation. Once you arrive in Ham Tan District, a right turn leads down to the fishing village of **Lagi**, which is not really geared up for tourism as yet. However, there are one or two places to stay, of which the *Nhat Anh* (☎062/844199; ❶), with a choice of simple air-conditioned and fan rooms, is the best. From Ham Tan, Highway 55 heads north to link up with

The Con Dao Archipelago

Cast adrift in the South China Sea some 185km south of Vung Tau, the dozen or so islands of the **Con Dao Archipelago** are actually far closer to the base of the Mekong Delta, yet the helicopters and ships linking them with the mainland leave from Vung Tau. Had the **fortified outpost** established here by the British East India Company in 1703 flourished, **CON SON**, by far the largest of the islands, could by now have been a more diminutive Hong Kong or Singapore, given its strategic position on the route to China. But within three years, the Bugis mercenaries (from Sulawesi) drafted in to construct and garrison the base had murdered their British commanders, putting paid to this early experiment in colonization. Known then as Poulo Condore, Con Son was still treading water when the American sailor John White spied its "lofty summits" a little over a century later, in 1819. White deemed it a decent natural harbour, though blighted by "noxious reptiles, and affording no good fresh water".

The island finally found its calling when decades later the French chose it as the site of a **penal colony** for anti-colonial activists. Con Son's savage regime soon earned it the nickname "Devil's Island". Prisoners languished in squalid pits called "tiger cages", which featured metal grilles instead of roofs, allowing guards to tower above and intimidate them. As the twentieth century progressed the colony developed into a sort of unofficial "revolutionary university". Older hands instructed their greener cell-mates in the finer points of Marxist-Leninist theory, while the dire conditions they endured helped reinforce the lessons. Should you decide to trek out to Con Son, you'll find a **museum** that sketches out the struggle against the French, as well as the prison itself, but anyone simply interested in prison life on the island would do better to settle for the mocked-up tiger cages at Ho Chi Minh's War Remnants Museum (see p.98).

Modern-day inhabitants live by fishing, growing cashews, peanuts and teak, and the more exotic pursuits of diving for pearls and collecting swallows' nests. Con Son is ringed by coral, and boasts dense patches of forest and fine beaches where turtles lay their eggs, but at present **getting there** is either too time-consuming or too costly a business for most tourists. There are rumours of a hydrofoil service starting up; for the latest information, contact Greenlines' head office in Ho Chi Minh City (☎08/940 6083). Until then, Southern Service Flight Company lays on thrice-weekly helicopter trips ($150 return), and Con Dao Transportation (☎064/859089), based at 35 Truong Cong Dinh in Vung Tau, runs one or two overnight ferryboats a week, subject to weather conditions, that cost about $30 per person. There are currently only a few mid-range government-run **hotels** on the island, catering mostly for the tour groups that find their way here.

Highway 1, but with your own transport you could continue along a narrow, sealed road, unmarked on most maps, that hugs the coast heading northeast for a further 20km or so before heading inland. The landscape here is beautiful, with remote fishing villages sheltered by coconut palms, and dragon-fruit orchards lining the road, which eventually veers away from the coast to join the unrelenting traffic of Highway 1 about 30km before Phan Thiet.

The coastal road to Nha Trang

Highway 1 marches east from Bien Hoa, passing through **Thong Nhat**, **Dau Giay** (from where Highway 20 shoots up to Da Lat) and untold acres of rubber plantations before reaching **Xuan Loc**, 78km from Ho Chi Minh. It's 100km from Xuan Loc's orbital town of **Long Khanh** to the seaside fishing community of **Phan Thiet**; for the last fifty, the horizon is blistered by the foot of the Truong Son mountain range, which escorts the highway on its laborious ascent to Hanoi. The first of the scores of weathered towers left by the ancient kingdom of **Champa** stand just outside Phan Thiet, but the town's fishing fleet and the fine sands of nearby Mui Ne are far more beguiling. There's another chance to take a dip in the South China Sea a little further north at **Ca Na**, but, if you are keen to see some superb Cham towers, beat a path straight to **Phan Rang**, an undistinguished town salvaged by the impressive **Po Klong Garai complex** nearby. From Phan Rang, Highway 1 ploughs through sugar-cane plantations, salt flats and shrimp farms on its way into **Nha Trang**.

Phan Thiet

Bunched around the Ca Ty River, and home to a sizeable fishing armada, **PHAN THIET** is the unassuming capital of Bin Thuan Province. Apart from a few minor sights, there's little to see or do here, though just a short drive up the coast, secreted away from Highway 1, lies Vietnam's fastest-growing beach resort – **MUI NE**. Phan Thiet has a reasonably attractive beach of its own, which is very popular with Vietnamese, but foreigners in Phan Thiet tend to be "just passing through".

Tran Hung Dao Bridge, over which Phan Thiet's main drag vaults the river, yields one of the town's few interesting sights – a fleet of fishing boats straight off a Hans Kemp postcard. Turn left off the bridge's southwestern end and stroll along Trung Trac, and you'll soon plunge into the thick of things at the wharfside **fish market**. Be prepared for a major sensory assault: the market is enveloped by a stench as heady as any produced at the *nuoc mam* factories that proliferate around this region of Vietnam. Packed close with hoary fishermen, fishwives and shoppers clustered around great, fly-blown wicker baskets of seafood, there's a jamboree atmosphere every morning, though especially between June and October, when daily catches reach a peak. North of the bridge, fishermen in coracles and with miners' lamps strapped to their heads try their luck after dusk.

In the other direction, Trung Trac skirts the city centre en route to the sedate riverside position occupied by the **Ho Chi Minh Museum** (Tues–Sun 7.30–11.30am & 1.30–4.30pm; small admission fee). Wending its way through Ho's life from his early days abroad up to his death in 1969, it's rather a flat museum, though it's leavened somewhat by memorabilia such as his white tunic, walking stick, sandals and metal helmet, and an offbeat action shot of him playing volleyball. The rows of varnished wooden desks and tables in the charismatic **Duc Thanh School** (same hours) next door have remained unchanged since Ho's brief spell as a teacher here, and effortlessly conjure up another age.

Over Tran Hung Dao Bridge, Vo Thi Sau strikes off to the right and to the city **beach**. The scruffy patch of sand it hits first doesn't look too promising, but 700m northeast it opens out into a more wholesome pine-shaded spot, backed up by a couple of smart hotels. You can walk back up Nguyen Tat Thanh to get back into Phan Thiet – turn left when you reach the **Victory Monument**, which depicts machine-gun-toting patriots gazing expectantly into the future, sheltered by an arrow-headed concrete umbrella.

Practicalities

Buses terminate at the **bus station** a couple of kilometres north of the centre. There are a few passable but characterless hotels nearby, or a Honda om or cyclo will run you to the centre. If you want to explore the region around Phan Thiet, try to catch the staff when they're in at Binh Thuan Tourist, 82 Trung Truc (℡062/816821, ✆binhthuantourist@hcm.vnn.vn). The office is just southwest of the Tran Hung Dao Bridge on Trung Truc. You can **exchange** US dollars at the Incombank on Tran Hung Dao, but for travellers' cheques and cash advances on Visa, MasterCard and JCB you'll need to go to the larger branch on Nguyen Tat Thanh, just off Victory Monument. The **post office** is also on Nguyen Tat Thanh, and there are several places offering **Internet access** along Tran Hung Dao.

There are plenty of **places to stay** in Phan Thiet, though there's nothing exciting about any of them. The best place near to the bus station is *Hotel 19–4* (℡062/821794; ❶–❸), a modern block with an older, motel-style wing on Tu Van Tu; in the centre of town, the spacious rooms at the *Phan Thiet*, 276 Tran Hung Dao (℡062/819907; ❷–❸) are reasonable value and include breakfast. Down on the beach are a few fancier places, including the *Doi Duong* (℡062/822108, ✆825858; ❹), a smart high-rise that has over seventy well-equipped rooms, a swimming pool, tennis courts and two restaurants. Bigger still is the mammoth *Novotel Ocean Dunes Resort* (℡062/822393, ✆novpht @hcm.vnn.vn; ❺–❻), a little further along, which has an eighteen-hole golf course, two swimming pools and free use of bicycles; $20 extra gets you a room with sea view.

There are few appealing **eating** options in town, though on the southwestern side of the square below the city's central bridge, the *Nam Thanh Lau* has great seafood and the generous portions are good value. Upmarket dining can be found at the *Sea Horse*, at the *Novotel Ocean Dunes Resort*, where dishes such as pan-fried swordfish with Provençal sauce or pumpkin ravioli with basil will cost you around $5.50.

Mui Ne

From being a snoozy backwater ignored by domestic and international tourist alike, **MUI NE** has become one the country's hottest beach destinations, thanks largely to an eclipse of the sun in the mid-1990s that had its optimum viewing spot at this pretty beach and attracted people who recognized a prime location when they saw it. Now it's popular as a weekend retreat for resident expats as well as a favourite with upmarket visitors happy to pay $50 a day to lounge around in a luxurious **resort**. Budget **accommodation** options are available but few, squeezing like squatters between the ample acreage of the big resorts.

Mui Ne lies just 22km east along the coast road from Phan Thiet. After about 8km on the right is the **Po Shanu** tower, which dates from the eighth century, but lacks the high definition and sandstone ornamentation of others upcountry. Much of the route is barren and arid in the dry season, but as it approaches Mui Ne, coconut palms form a shady avenue that passes behind the resorts and gives occasional glimpses of golden sands lapped by clear waters. After several kilometres of shoulder-to-shoulder resorts, the road reaches the small village and harbour of Mui Ne, where small fishing boats cluster together. On the left (north) side of the road just before the village are several small **fish sauce** plants, where you might like to nose around the pungent vats. A left turn at the village leads after a few kilometres to Mui Ne's most famous attraction – its **sand dunes,** Sahara-style red drifts creating dramatic perspectives. The softness of the sand makes the dunes difficult to climb, but the resulting views are ample reward. The sand can also get very hot, so it makes sense to go early or late in the day.

Though the number one activity at Mui Ne is **relaxing on the beach**, the place also attracts **surfers** when the wind is up between August and April, and Mui Ne even hosts an event in the Asian Windsurf Tour each February. If you'd like a crack at **windsurfing** or **kitesurfing**, head on down to *Jibes*, more or less at the centre of the bay, where an hour's instruction costs $12–15.

There's no doubt that its laidback atmosphere is one of its best features, but Mui Ne is fast becoming a tourist enclave, separated as it is from any Vietnamese community. If you're just here to chill out on the beach, that probably won't bother you, but if you crave interaction with locals or dancing at night, you'd be better off heading on up to Nha Trang.

Arrival and information

Daily **open-tour buses** arrive in Mui Ne from Nha Trang and Ho Chi Minh City. Kim Travel buses stop at *Hanh Café 2*, km14, Ham Tien (call the café on ☎062/847347 for details of buses), just up from the *Full Moon Beach Guesthouse*. As well as selling onward tickets to Ho Chi Minh City and Nha Trang (both $6), *Hanh Café 2* can arrange local tours, car and motorbike hire, train tickets and bicycle rental. TN Brothers buses arrive and depart from the *Coco Café* (☎062/847195), a few metres further along the main drag; onward tickets can be purchased here and they can also arrange local transportation. *Blue Ocean Resort* (☎062/847322) runs an **express minibus** service most days to central Ho Chi Minh City; it's more expensive than the others ($9 one way, $16 return), but it's a faster service and their timetable (with a departure at 4pm on Sun) makes weekend jaunts possible for city residents. If you're coming from Phan Thiet, a Honda om should cost around $1.50, a taxi $5.

There are no shuttle buses along the main drag, so your best option for **getting around** is to use local Honda oms, or rent a bicycle ($1–2 a day) or motorbike ($5–7 a day) from one of the resorts or guesthouses, or from *Coco Café*. **Internet access** is available at many resorts, though rates can be high and connections frustratingly slow. The *Coco Café* currently charges 250d per minute. There's a **bank** (Mon–Fri 7.30am–noon & 1–4.30pm) next door to the *Swiss Village Resort*, where you can exchange cash or change travellers' cheques, or get an advance against Visa or MasterCard. Most resorts will also change money, but at less favourable rates.

Accommodation

Since the main activity in Mui Ne is lazing on the beach, choosing where to stay is the biggest decision to make while here. Ideally, you should have a peek in several places in your price range, but since the properties are spread out over a stretch of more than 10km, this is impractical if you don't have your own transport. Bear in mind that with new resorts opening all the time, and discounts offered by many places during low season or for long stays, it's sometimes worth haggling about the price. There are some very attractive resorts here (our current pick for best design is the *Mui Ne Sailing Club*) and a few budget options, though it's very much a matter of getting what you pay for. None of the cheaper options in Mui Ne can compare with the great budget hotels in Nha Trang. There are no street numbers along the beach; instead places are identified by kilometre distances along the road from Phan Thiet.

Bamboo Village Seaside Resort km11.8 ☏062/847007, ✉bamboo_village@hcm.vnn.vn. Set in exquisite gardens, the 37 attractive bamboo bungalows surrounding the pool and restaurant area offer a choice of air-con or fan. ❹–❺

Blue Ocean Resort km12 ☏062/847322, ⓦwww.blueoceanresort.com. Compact but smart rooms around a trim garden and pool, with a branch of *Sheridan's Irish Bar and Restaurant* opposite reception. ❹

Coco Beach km12.5 ☏062/847111, ✉paradise@cocobeach.net. This French-run resort has 34 tasteful, thatched wooden bungalows and some family-size villas, complete with verandahs, Cham-style fabrics, air-con and all modern comforts, set among tropical gardens off the beach. The relaxed style and friendly staff have made this an established favourite. ❺–❻

Full Moon Beach Guesthouse km13 ☏062/847008, ✉fullmoon@windsurf-vietnam .net. Thatched bamboo huts with verandahs or spacious rooms, all on stilts and with attached bathrooms; rates are negotiable. ❸–❹

Hiep Hoa km13.3 ☏062/847262, ✉hiephoatourism@yahoo.com. Just eight basic but smart rooms, some with fan and others air-con, in this tiny, friendly compound facing a fine stretch of beach. ❶–❷

Mui Ne Sailing Club km11 ☏062/847440, ✉info@sailingclubvietnam.com. Delightfully landscaped resort, featuring rooms and bungalows topped with Mexican-style thatched roofs and mustard-coloured walls, plus imaginative interiors with good use of local textiles. Swimming pool, popular bar and restaurant too. ❹–❺

Nhan Hoa km16 ☏062/847371. Cheaper rooms have fan and shared toilet; more expensive rooms have well-appointed balconies; all are clean and good value. ❶–❸

Palmira Resort km11 ☏062/847383, ✉cocogarden@palmiraresort.com. The Art Deco style and sickly pastel shades of this resort – run by a Vietnamese-Russian couple – are reminiscent of Miami Beach, but the well-equipped rooms are reasonably priced and $5 extra secures you a sea view; there's also a stunning pool area. ❹

Phu Hai Resort km8 ☏062/812799, ✉info@phuhairesort.com. Currently the biggest resort at Mui Ne, with over eighty villas snuggled away behind lush tropical growth. Large pool with waterfall, tennis courts, fitness club and stylish restaurant. ❺–❻

Rang Dong km19 ☏062/848645. A reasonable budget option with good-sized, adequate rooms, some with fan, others with air-con, TV and hot water. ❶–❸

Red Sun km13 ☏062/847387. Small, shady compound with eight rooms, some with fan and shared bathrooms, others with air-con and attached bathrooms; simple but clean and good value. ❷–❸

Sea Breeze Resort km13.7 ☏062/847373, ⓦwww.muineseabreeze.com. Some attractive, A-frame bungalows with beach views, and other smart, cosy rooms at competitive prices, make this a tempting mid-range option. ❸–❹

Small Garden km11 ☏062/847012, ✉smallgarden@hcm.vnn.vn. Appropriate name for this place run by a Swiss-Vietnamese couple. Rooms range from thinly partitioned closets in the house to bungalows with balcony and beach view. Free use of kitchen for guests gives it a communal feel. ❶–❸

Swiss Village Resort km12 ☏062/847399, ✉swissvill@hcm.vnn.vn. Sixty smart rooms with tasteful furnishings, surrounded by lush greenery. Discounts available in low season. ❺–❻

Victoria Phan Thiet Resort km9 ☏062/813000, ✉victoriapt@hcm.vnn.vn. Fifty sea-view bungalow cottages set amongst tropical gardens; spacious interiors with tasteful European decor and all modern comforts. Excursions arranged and free use of mountain bikes for guests. ❺–❻

Vietnam-Austria House km13.5 ☏062/847047. A charming Austro-Vietnamese couple welcome guests into their aptly named guesthouse; sparkling clean and adorned with chintzy trimmings, there are immaculate fan rooms with shared bathroom and two good-value bungalows near the beach with private facilities. ❷–❸

Eating and drinking

Your host will hope you find the food so good at your base that you won't wander far at night, but if you want a change of scene or a bit of exercise, there are several **restaurants** worth checking out, and some that might save you some bucks. All the resorts offer fine dining with fine prices to match, but these are not the only options. Several savvy shopkeepers with properties on the opposite (and cheaper) side of the road to the resorts, have set up small but smart restaurants with a good range of Vietnamese and Western food at very reasonable prices. There's a cluster opposite the *Blue Ocean Resort*, among which the *Hoang Vu* is recommended. Try the fried chicken with peanut sauce ($2). There are also a couple of reliable Italian places on this side of the road, the *Good Morning Vietnam*, which also has branches in Hanoi and Ho Chi Minh City, and the swisher *Luna d'Autunno*, with tasteful bamboo decor, a range of wines and wood-fired pizzas at about $5 each.

Nightlife in Mui Ne is decidedly low-key, with most folks turning in early, but there's often a crowd at *Jibes*, near the centre of the beach at km13.5, where spontaneous parties have been known to happen. The beers here are lower-priced than at most seafront locations, and there's an interesting range of food on offer too. It's also a useful place to exchange travellers' tales and find out about places worth visiting locally.

Ca Na

Highway 1 ducks inland above Phan Thiet, which is how Mui Ne remained a secret so long. Hemmed in by paddy fields and eucalyptus trees, it's also strung with stalls doing a roaring trade in the dragon fruits (see p.49) that grow in this neck of the woods. You'll see orchards of the cactus that bears them set back from the road, their fronds hanging like dreadlocks from the levelled tree stumps on which they bloom. By the time you coast down into **CA NA**, a little over 100km northeast of Phan Thiet as the crow flies, you're tightly sandwiched between hills and the choppy, turquoise waters of the South China Sea. Just 3km before reaching town, *Vietnam Scuba* (T062/853917, F853918; ●) on the right offers **accommodation** and **dive trips**. Smart and well-equipped bungalows with balconies look out over an azure sea and sun-bleached jetty, from where dive trips head out. It costs $75 to join a day's dive, with all equipment provided, or you can opt for room, diving and all meals at $130 per day. They also organize night diving trips according to demand.

Hardly more than a wide spot in the road, Ca Na is nevertheless reasonably well equipped for feeding and watering passing tourists and, with time in hand, you might consider an overnight stay in this area. Given its proximity to the highway, Ca Na is a more relaxing place than it has any right to be. Beyond the coracles parked along the beach the water is relatively clean, and snorkelling is a possibility, though you'd be wise to ask locals where to wade in as the coral here is razor sharp. If you crave a little more solitude, a spine of decent dunes back up another good stretch of sand a couple of kilometres south; while a fifteen-minute walk north of the resort area is Ca Na Village itself, characterized by the blue fishing boats typical of coastal Vietnam. A set of steps leading up to a tiny pagoda carved into the hillside behind Ca Na demand to be climbed, although there's very little to see once you're up there, other than the splendid view out to sea.

There are only two **places to stay** at Ca Na. The *Hai Son* (T068/861339, E haison_hotel@hcm.vnn.vn; ●) is showing signs of age, but has clean and simple fan rooms, some with back doors onto the beach. Otherwise the *Ca Na* (T068/861320; ●–●), 150m up the beach, has some newly built rooms with air-conditioning and hot water set back from the beach, or several smart rooms in bungalows out on the sand. Both the *Ca Na* and *Hai Son* have their own **restaurants** – prices at the *Ca Na* are usually a little cheaper – or else there's the *Ca Na Quan*, tucked between them, which has a booth selling biscuits, nibbles and drinks, though as you'd expect, fresh seafood is the order of the day here.

Phan Rang and around

The numerous vine trellises that abut the highway are the biggest surprise of the journey between Ca Na and Phan Rang. Grapes are a speciality of **Ninh Thuan Province** (of which Phan Rang is the capital) and the vineyards in which they grow lend the area a faintly Mediterranean tang. **PHAN RANG** itself is an unsettling and unlovely place, with the main thoroughfare, Thong Nhat, dissecting the centre of town. Its western limits have fused with the neighbouring town of **THAP CHAM**, whose name, meaning "Cham Towers", gives a clue to the real reason for stopping here. This region of Vietnam once comprised the Cham kingdom of Panduranga, and of the nearby Cham remnants none is better preserved than those at **Po Klong Garai**. If ancient ruins aren't your thing, you might like to check out the qualities of nearby **Ninh Chu Beach**, a glorious sweep of wide sand that is sometimes deliciously quiet on weekdays, and often overrun with Vietnamese at weekends. There are a few striking resorts along the beach, which make much better **accommodation** alternatives than staying in Phan Rang's drab hotels. Even if beaches and Cham ruins aren't on your agenda, you may have to overnight in the area if you're heading into the hills around **Da Lat** (see p.198).

Arrival, information and accommodation

Arriving in Phan Rang by **bus** you'll be dropped at the bus station 300m north of the *Thong Nhat* hotel; **trains** pull in 7km northwest of town at Ga Thap Cham. The **tourist office**, situated above a motorbike showroom on the corner of Nguyen Trai, at 505 Thong Nhat (☎068/836405), can arrange trips out to the surrounding countryside, but at a price, so you may prefer to use Honda oms. As for changing **money**, the Agribank at the southern end of Thong Nhat accepts dollars but not travellers' cheques.

Places to stay in **Phan Rang** itself are not inspiring, though there are a few interesting options on the nearby beach of **Ninh Chu**. The *Thong Nhat* (☎068/827201; ❸–❹), at 343 Thong Nhat, has some carpeted rooms with bathtubs that make it marginally cosier than the town's only other option, *Ninh Thuan* (☎068/827100; ❸–❹) on Le Hong Phong; both have satellite TV and hot water. A better bet is to avoid the town completely and run for the beach, where a few unusual establishments offer a range of environments. At the far (north) end of the bay, which is often quieter than the centre of the bay, the *Ninh Chu* (☎068/873900; ❸–❹) is the most like a regular hotel; it has polished rooms in the tidy main block, and some ugly concrete "bungalows" (❷) on the beach. Back in the centre of the beach, the *Den Gion Resort* (☎068/874223, ⓦwww.dengionninhchu.com; ❺–❻) is a clever mix of modern and Cham styles, the rust-coloured pottery set off well by the clean wooden room fittings. There's a swimming pool, tennis courts, two restaurants and 600m of beach frontage. Right next door, with its own mini water park, is the bizarre *Hoang Cau* (☎068/890077, ⓕ890252; ❷). Rooms here are made to look like old tree stumps by some very shoddy cement work, and though they're ugly and cramped together, the rooms inside are spacious and good value, and very popular among Vietnamese. Another popular haunt for Vietnamese is the *Phong Lan* (☎068/890027, ⓕ890216; ❷–❸), set back from the beach opposite the *Den Gion Resort*, which charges higher fees for foreigners in its old and new blocks, where all rooms have air-conditioning and hot water.

The Town

Though their kingdom may have fractured long ago, many thousands of Chams still live in the province, and an introduction to their way of life may be gleaned from Phan Rang's pink and grey **Cham Collectives Display Museum** (Mon–Fri 8–11am & 2.30–5pm; small admission fee). To reach the museum, walk east off Thong Nhat at the tourist office and then left along the track beside 17 Nguyen Trai. The collection is a rag-tag one which has shards of pottery and items of jewellery alongside a Cham typewriter and a copy of a statue of Shiva; a helpful English-speaking guide is usually on hand to offer extra information. Not far from the museum is Phan Rang's 1900-built **church**, whose impressive spire you're sure to have spotted if you approached the town across the bridge to the south. Up close, there's very little else to be impressed by, though the building does have a certain dilapidated charm.

Otherwise, forays into the town centre are limited to peeking into Thong Nhat's impressive 150-year-old **Quan Cong Temple**. Its faded, pink-wash walls rise to three consecutive roofs, each draped upon huge red wooden piles imported from China, and laden with fanciful figurines and dragons. Quan Cong is at the head of the third and final chamber, framed by ornate gilt woodwork and rows of pikes. Chams sometimes come to shop at the **market** immediately below the pagoda, but for closer encounters you'll need to venture out to Tuan Tu (see p.246).

Chams and Cham towers

Elevated with fitting grandeur on a granite mound known as Trau Hill, the **Po Klong Garai Cham towers** (daily 7am–6pm; small admission fee) are far worthier of your time than anything in the town centre. Dating back to around 1400 and the rule of King Jaya Simharvarman III, the complex comprises a *kalan*, or sanctuary, a smaller gate tower and a repository, under whose boat-shaped roof offerings would have been placed. It's the 25-metre-high *kalan*, though, that's of most interest. From a distance its stippled body impresses; up close, you see a bas-relief of six-armed Shiva cavorting above doorposts etched with Cham inscriptions and ringed by arches crackling with stonework flames, while other gods sit cross-legged in niches elsewhere around the exterior walls. In days gone by, the statue of Shiva's bull (Nandi) that stands in the vestibule would have been "fed" by farmers wishing for good harvests; nowadays it only gets a feed at the annual **Kate Festival** (the Cham New Year), a great spectacle if you're here around October. Push deeper into the *kalan*'s belly and there's a *mukha* lingam fashioned in a likeness of the Cham king, Po Klong Garai, after whom the complex is named. On the eve of the festival, there's traditional Cham music and dance at the complex, followed, the next morning, by a lively procession bearing the king's raiment to the tower.

To reach the complex, take the road to Da Lat for 7km, then veer north for a further 500m ($2–3 return by Honda om from Phan Rang). On your way back down Trau Hill, look above the arched stone gateway below the complex and you'll spot **pill-box defences**, established by the French to protect trains pulling out of the station below from Viet Minh attack.

If Po Klong Garai inspires further interest in Cham towers, you could make the trickier journey out to **Po Re Me Tower**, the sole survivor of three towers built at the turn of the sixteenth century during the final phase of Cham tower architecture. Like its near-neighbour, the tower (which draws its name from the last Cham king) enjoys a fine hilltop location, though its four storeys tapering to a lingam are sturdier and less finished than Po Klong Garai. Its high point is the splendid bas-relief in the *kalan*'s entrance, depicting Shiva manifest

The kingdom of Champa

The weathered but beguiling **towers** that punctuate the scenery upcountry from Phan Thiet to Da Nang are the only remaining legacy of **Champa**, an Indianized kingdom that ruled parts of central and southern Vietnam for over fourteen centuries. In 192 AD, Chinese annals reported that a man named Khu Lien (later to be titled King Sri Mara) had gathered a chain of coastal chiefdoms in the region around Quang Tri in defiance of the expansionism of the Han Chinese to the north, and established an independent state which the Chinese referred to as **Lin Yi**. Subsequently, Champa unified an elongated strip from Phan Thiet to Dong Hoi, and by the end of the fourth century Champa comprised four provinces: **Amaravati**, around Hué and Da Nang; **Vijaya**, centred around Qui Nhon; **Kauthara**, in the Nha Trang region; and **Panduranga**, which corresponds to present-day Phan Thiet and up to Phan Rang. The unified kingdom's first capital, established in the fourth century in Amaravati, was **Simhapura** ("Lion City"); nearby, just outside present-day Hoi An, **My Son**, Champa's holiest site, was established (see p.288).

Concertinaed between the Khmers to the south and the clans of the Vietnamese (initially under Chinese rule) to the north, Champa's history was characterized by consistent **feuding with the neighbours**. Between the third and fifth centuries, relations with the **Chinese** followed a cyclical pattern of antagonism and tribute, culminating in the 446 AD sacking of Simhapura when the Chinese made off with a fifty-tonne, solid-gold Buddha statue. Wars raged with the **Khmers** in the twelfth and thirteenth centuries, one fateful retaliatory Cham offensive culminating in the destruction of Angkor. With the installation on Champa's throne of warmongering **Binasuor** in 1361, three decades of Cham expansionism ensued; upon his death in 1390, though, the Viets regained all lost ground, and soon secured the region around Indrapura. In a decisive push south, the Viets, led by **Le Thanh Tong**, overran Vijaya in 1471; Champa shifted its capital south again, but by now it was becoming profoundly marginalized. For a few centuries more, the Cham kings still claimed nominal rule of the area around Phan Rang and Phan Thiet, but in 1697 the last independent Cham king died, and what little remained of the kingdom became a Vietnamese vassal state. **Minh Mang** dissolved even this in the 1820s, and the last Cham king fled to Cambodia. Most of the estimated 100,000 **descendants** of the Cham Empire reside around Phan Rang and Phan Thiet, though there are also tiny pockets in Tay Ninh and Chau Doc.

Champa's **economy** hinged around agriculture, wet-rice cultivation, fishing and maritime trade, which it carried out with Indians, Chinese, Japanese and Arabs through **ports** at Hoi An and Qui Nhon. Exposure to Indian traders in the fourth century had a particularly strong influence upon the kingdom's culture, agriculture and religion. Though Buddhism flourished for a time in the ninth century, **Hinduism** was the dominant religion in Champa, until Islam started to make inroads in the second half of the fourteenth century. Orthodox Hindu gods, and in particular Shiva, were fused with past kings, in accordance with the belief that kings were *devaraja* – reincarnations of deities.

To honour their gods, Cham kings sponsored the construction of the **religious edifices** that still stand today. The typical Cham **temple complex** is centred around the **kalan**, or sanctuary, normally pyramidal inside, and containing a lingam, or phallic representation of Shiva, set on a dais that was grooved to channel off water used in purification rituals. Having first cleansed themselves and prayed in the **mandapa**, or meditation hall, worshippers would then have proceeded under a **gate tower** and below the *kalan*'s (normally) east-facing vestibule into the sanctuary. Any ritual objects pertaining to worship were kept in a nearby repository room, which normally sported a boat-shaped roof.

Cham towers crop up at regular intervals, all the way up the coast from Phan Thiet to Da Nang, but many of them are inaccessible, and many more so weathered as to be of only fleeting interest. A handful of sites representing the **highlights** of what remains of Champa civilization would include: Po Klong Garai towers (opposite); Thap Doi towers (p.263); Po Re Me Tower (opposite); My Son (p.288); Po Nagar towers (p.246).

in the image of mustachioed King Po Re Me waggling his arms, and watched over by two Nandins. Po Re Me is also a focus of Cham festivities during the Kate Festival. To reach the tower, follow Highway 1 south for 8km and then bear west at Hau Sanh; the track is hard to find, so a Honda om is a wise option.

There's still a Cham presence around Phan Rang. **Tuan Tu Village** is home to more than a thousand Chams, whom you'll recognize by the headcloths that they favour over conical hats. Largely Muslim, they maintain an unpretentious, 1966-built mosque free of any trappings, not even a minaret. More enjoyable than the village itself is the trip out, though, which leads you through cacti, rice paddies and vineyards along a track that's often congested by bullock carts. Tuan Tu is 3–4km along a track that veers east after the BP service station, 350m below the bridge at the bottom of town; a Honda om shouldn't be more than $1–2 for the round trip.

Ninh Chu Beach

A more indolent alternative to trekking around Phan Rang's Cham towers is to visit **Ninh Chu Beach**, a reasonably clean and wide crescent of sand that's at least soft, if not exactly golden. Ninh Chu doesn't have the same pulling power for foreigners as Mui Ne or Nha Trang, but its beach is good for swimming, sunbathing, beach games and jogging too. With comfortable resorts opening up here, it's worth considering as a place to rest up, particularly midweek, when it can be very quiet. If you're here at a weekend, be prepared for crowds of noisy teenagers. To reach Ninh Chu, turn onto Nguyen Van Troi just above the bus station and immediately to the right of the post office, and carry on for 5km.

Eating and drinking

Eating out in Phan Rang is a decidedly low-key experience. The *Thong Nhat* and *Ninh Thuan* hotels have uncharismatic restaurants, and the *Ninh Chu* boasts both restaurant and beach-view coffee shop. The restaurants at the *Den Gion Resort* out on Ninh Chu Beach are not cheap, but the food is good and staff very attentive. Back in town, budget *com* and *pho* is on hand at the *Nam Thanh*, immediately above Quan Cong Temple on Thong Nhat.

Nha Trang and around

From Phan Rang, the highway pushes on against a consistent backdrop of first sugar-cane plantations, then toothpaste-white salt flats and shrimp farms, on its way to the city of **NHA TRANG**. Nestled below the bottom lip of the Cai River, some 260km north of Phan Thiet, Nha Trang has earned its place on Vietnam's tourist mainline partly on merit and partly due to its location. Much has changed here since the days when the Chams knew the area as *Eatrang*, the "river of reeds", and the city now supports a population of over 300,000. By the time the Nguyen lords wrested this patch of the country from Champa in the mid-seventeenth century, the intriguing **Po Nagar Cham towers** had already stood, stacked impressively on a hillside above the Cai, for over 700 years. They remain Nha Trang's most famous image, yet it's the **coastline** that brings tourists flocking: boasting the finest municipal beach in Vietnam, Nha Trang offers splendid scope for mellowing out on the sand, with hawkers on hand to supply paperbacks, fresh pineapple and massages. **Scuba-diving** classes are available here, and several local companies offer popular day-trips to Nha Trang's outlying **islands** that combine island visits and **snorkelling** with an onboard feast of seafood. Other water sports, like **jet-skiing** and **parasailing**, are available on Nha Trang Beach too. Bear in mind that there is a rainy season in Nha Trang, around November–December, when the sea gets choppy and the beach loses its appeal.

Nha Trang is much more than a pretty strip of sand, however. The southern streets around **Biet Thu** are packed with great-value budget hotels and restaurants, plus some stylish boutiques and bars that are actually worth hanging out in. The **downtown** area, which swirls aound **Cho Dam** ("central market"), its colourful epicentre, heaves with life; while the route up to the Po Nagar towers escorts you past the city's huge and photogenic fishing fleet. Should none of this appeal, Nha Trang is still a convenient staging post on the long haul between Hanoi and Ho Chi Minh.

Arrival and getting around

Nha Trang's **long-distance bus station** (daily 4am–10pm; ☎058/820227) sits a kilometre west of the city centre at 58, 23 Thang 10; the **train station** (☎058/822113; ticket office daily 7.30–11am & 1.30–9pm) is a few hundred metres east along Thai Nguyen, a continuation of the same road; both are a short cyclo journey from central Nha Trang. Flights into the city land at the **airport** (☎058/823797) just below town; again, hop into a taxi or cyclo to get to a hotel.

Nha Trang isn't a very large city, so **walking** may well be your means of covering ground – especially if a daily pilgrimage to the municipal beach marks the extent of your peregrinations. Should you plan to stray a little further afield, **bicycle rental** is the most efficient and enjoyable way to go. Bicycles are available for around $1 per day at most of the city's hotels, though less active souls will always find **cyclos** and **Honda oms** aplenty. Fully fledged **car** tours of the region can be arranged through the provincial tourist board, such as Khanh Hoa Tourism (see Listings, p.259), while a number of operators offer day-trips to the islands off Nha Trang and minibus tours of the central highlands.

Accommodation

The fact that Nha Trang is chock-full of hotels doesn't seem to be discouraging developers, and the city's already wide choice of **accommodation** seems to just keep on growing. Even so, it's worth bearing in mind that the city draws Vietnamese as well as foreign tourists, and that you could have difficulties finding a room over public holidays, when prices take a hike. Equally, remember that in many hotels, opting for a cheaper room consigns you to a dingy annexe far from the main building, and you may well judge the extra few dollars' upgrading cost as money well spent. That said, Nha Trang offers some of the best budget accommodation outside of Ho Chi Minh City or Hanoi, with great deals hidden away in the backstreets.

52 Tran Phu 52 Tran Phu ☎058/524228, ✉ctthanhdat@dng.vnn.vn. Brand-new beachfront property offering very reasonably priced rooms, all with air-con and hot water. ②–③
Ana Mandara Resort Beachside Tran Phu ☎058/829829, ✉resvana@dng.vnn.vn. Nha Trang's most luxurious resort, located to the south of the main drag; attractive bungalow villas and

suites with all mod cons and some traditional touches, including ethnic minority tapestries and wooden buckets and pails for outdoor ablutions. Facilities include two pools, tennis courts, a new spa and beach restaurant. Prices lower off-season. ⑥
Bao Dai's Villas Tran Phu ☎058/590147, ✉baodai@dng.vnn.vn. Once holiday homes to the emperor of Vietnam, these five villas divided into

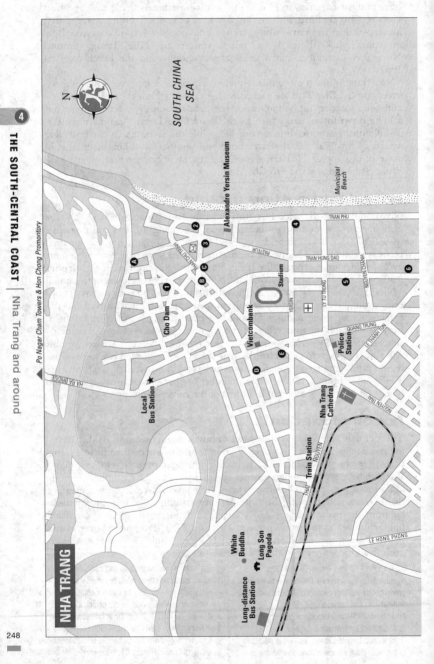

NHA TRANG

Po Nagar Cham Towers & Hon Chong Promontory

SOUTH CHINA SEA

Municipal Beach

Alexandre Yersin Museum

TRAN PHU

PASTEUR

TRAN HUNG DAO

NGUYEN CHANH

LY TU TRONG

QUANG TRUNG

LE THANH TON

NGUYEN TRAI

LE HONG PHONG

YERSIN

PHAN CHU TRINH

HA BA BRIDGE

Cho Dam

Vietcombank

Stadium

Local
Bus Station

Police
Station

Nha Trang
Cathedral

Train Station

NGUYEN THAT

White Buddha

Long Son
Pagoda

Long-distance
Bus Station

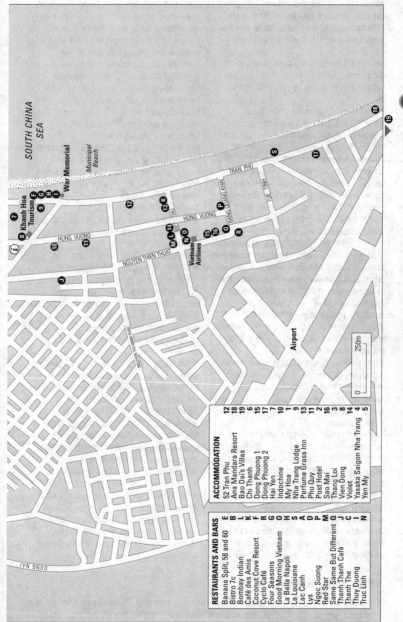

SOUTH CHINA SEA

War Memorial

Municipal Beach

Khanh Hoa Tourism

HUNG VUONG

HUNG VUONG

NGUYEN THIEN THUAT

Vietnam Airlines

TRAN PHU

TRANG QUANG KHAI

TUE TINH

THU

BICH

NGUYEN THI MINH KHAI

DONG NAI

Airport

0   250m

RESTAURANTS AND BARS

Banana Split, 58 and 60	E
Bistro 7c	B
Bombay Indian	L
Café des Amis	F
Coconut Cove Resort	R
Cyclo Café	G
Four Seasons	O
Good Morning Vietnam	H
La Bella Napoli	S
La Louisiane	A
Lac Canh	D
Lys	P
Ngoc Suong	M
Red Star	Q
Same Same But Different	J
Thanh Thanh Café	C
Thanh The	I
Thuy Duong	T
Truc Linh	N

ACCOMMODATION

52 Tran Phu	12
Ana Mandara Resort	18
Bao Dai's Villas	19
Chi Thanh	6
Dong Phuong 1	15
Dong Phuong 2	17
Hai Yen	7
Indochine	10
My Hoa	1
Nha Trang Lodge	9
Perfume Grass Inn	13
Phu Quy	11
Post Hotel	2
Sao Mai	16
Thang Loi	3
Vien Dong	8
Violet	14
Yasaka Saigon Nha Trang	4
Yen My	5

rooms and suites are set in extensive and well-kept gardens – the swish bedchambers of Bao Dai are good for a splurge – but inconveniently placed way down the beach from the city. Some quarters boast commanding views out to sea, as does the hotel's terrace restaurant, which is well worth a visit. ③–⑤

Chi Thanh 17b Hoang Hoa Tham ☎ 058/822092, ✉ chi_thanh_Hotel@yahoo.com. Mini-hotel with budget rooms – big with air-con, small with fan. ①

Dong Phuong 1 103 Nguyen Thien Thuat ☎ 058/825896, ✉ dongphuongnt@dng.vnn.vn. Hugely popular family-run hotel, and one of many budget options clustered around this area. Functional but spacious rooms, ranging from small fan rooms to the enormous, air-con penthouse. Discounts negotiable, free shuttle service and staff falling over themselves to be helpful. The same owners run *Dong Phuong 2*, facing the beach at 96a6/1 Tran Phu, which has sea views (kind of) and a rooftop restaurant. ①–③

Hai Yen 40 Tran Phu ☎ 058/822828, ✉ haiyenhotel @dng.vnn.vn. Plays second fiddle to the nearby *Vien Dong* (see below), but rooms are still well fitted and comfortable. Hairdresser, souvenir shop and currency exchange downstairs. Shares swimming pool with *Vien Dong*. ③–④

Indochine 14 Hung Vuong ☎ 058/815333, ✉ indochinehotel@yahoo.com. Smart, competitively priced mid-range hotel with fifty rooms, all with air-con and hot water. ②–③

My Hoa 7 Hang Ca ☎ 058/810111, ✉ myhoahotel @dng.vnn.vn. This smart, family-run mini-hotel with a central location is an excellent budget option. Tidy rooms all with satellite TV, hot water and attached shower; free fruit, tea and coffee are a welcome bonus. ①–③

Nha Trang Lodge 42 Tran Phu ☎ 058/810500, ✉ nt-lodge@dng.vnn.vn. With over 120 rooms on its thirteen floors, some with fantastic views of the beach, this is currently Nha Trang's flashiest and trendiest hotel. ④–⑤

Perfume Grass Inn 4a Biet Thu ☎ 058/826345, ✉ huanaz@dng.vnn.vn. A reasonably priced place with lots of character. Some rooms with wood-panelled floors, others with reclining chairs and bathtubs; all are tastefully furnished. There's also an attractive, cheap café downstairs. ①–③

Phu Quy 54 Hung Vuong ☎ 058/810609, ✉ phuquyhotel@dng.vnn.vn. Welcoming, reasonably priced family-run mini-hotel. Air-con and fan rooms are small and middle ones don't have outside windows, but all are spotlessly clean and have en-suite bathrooms; there's also a small rooftop terrace with sun-loungers. ①–③

Post Hotel 2 Le Loi ☎ 058/821252, ✉ posthotel@dng.vnn.vn. Slightly oppressive rooms peeling off utilitarian corridors belie this hotel's posh white facade, but have all mod cons. Sea views cost more, while two top-floor air-con rooms with shared bathroom are a bargain. Discounts are negotiable. ①–③

Sao Mai 99 Nguyen Thien Thuat ☎ 058/827412, ✉ saomaiht@dng.vnn.vn. Yet another reliable budget option, this one with a $3 dorm. A second branch at 96b Tran Phu, near the beach, is slightly more expensive. ①–②

Thang Loi 4 Pasteur ☎ 058/822523, ✉ 4pasteur@dng.vnn.vn. Light, spacious, cheerily painted en-suite rooms handily placed just east of the city centre. ①–③

Vien Dong 1 Tran Hung Dao ☎ 058/821606, ✉ viendonghtl@dng.vnn.vn. Professionally run operation counting swimming pool, tennis courts, satellite TV, currency exchange and a decent restaurant among its amenities. Rooms in the main building are scrupulously clean, but those in the poolside annexe are less polished. Live music and traditional dance enliven the restaurant at night. ③–④

Violet 12a Biet Thu ☎ 058/814314, ✉ ctminhhoang @dng.vnn.vn. Well-maintained mini-hotel on trendy Biet Thu with helpful staff. Good-sized air-con rooms and smaller fan rooms available. ①–②

Yasaka Saigon Nha Trang 18 Tran Phu ☎ 058/820090, ✉ sg-nthotel@dng.vnn.vn. One of Nha Trang's most impressive high-rise hotels, in a prime location along Tran Phu. Facilities include a fitness and conference centre, swimming pool, disco and tennis courts. All rooms face the sea, the higher ones with fabulous views, and are well appointed and chintzy; price includes free airport transfer and breakfast. ⑤–⑥

Yen My 22 Hoang Hoa Tham ☎ 058/829064, ✉ yenmyhotel@hotmail.com. Mini-hotel run by friendly family with very cheap fan-only rooms. Good-value budget option. ①–②

The city centre

The disorienting knot of roads constituting **central Nha Trang** hugs the southern lip of the Cai River. Its beating heart is the hectic central market, semicircular **Cho Dam**, which stands on land reclaimed from the Cai; the market positively churns with life from morning to night. Most new arrivals in the city, however, make a beeline for its **municipal beach**, a grand six-kilometre scythe of soft yellow sand lapped by rolling waves, whose upper extent lies five minutes' stroll east of the market. The tourists who descend on the beach every day are promptly besieged by traders hawking massages, tropical fruits, T-shirts and paperbacks, though it's possible to escape their clutches by taking a boat trip (see p.259); alternatively you can sunbathe undisturbed at the southern end of the beach past the *Ana Mandara Resort*, where a couple of beachfront restaurants provide free sun-loungers, or at the pool in the *Vien Dong Hotel* ($1.50 per day for non-residents). There's even a small but well-organized **water park** ($1.30) at the south end of Tran Phu, just north of the *Ana Mandara*. To avoid the midday sun, locals wait until the hour before dusk to do their bathing, at which time the surf is peppered with squealing, splashing kids. (The beach at night is notorious for thieves, so don't leave anything lying around if you do go in for a post-dusk swim.) The Americans sought wartime R&R on the beach, and contemporary accounts describe the cyclo races they held along the palm-lined **corniche**, Tran Phu.

Over recent years the centre of activity for budget travellers has drifted south, and currently finds its epicentre around **Biet Thu**, just a couple of minutes' walk away from a good stretch of the beach, where every property seems to be a budget hotel, cheap restaurant, bar, convenience store or stylish boutique.

The Alexandre Yersin Museum

There are oodles of waterfront cafés to duck into along Tran Phu when the sun gets strong. Alternatively, you could dart up to the top of Tran Phu and into the Pasteur Institute, where the **Alexandre Yersin Museum** (Mon–Fri 7–11.15am & 2–4.30pm, Sat 2–4.30pm; $2) profiles the life of the Swiss-French scientist who transformed Da Lat, and who settled in Nha Trang in 1893 after travelling to Southeast Asia as a ship's doctor. By the time of his death in 1943, Yersin had become a local hero, thanks not to his greatest achievement – the discovery of a plague bacillus in Hong Kong in 1894 – but rather to his educational work in sanitation and agriculture, and to his ability to predict typhoons and thus save the lives of fishermen. Yersin's desk is here, with his own French translations of Horace still slotted under its glass top; so too, are the barometers and telescope he used to forecast the weather, and a model boat presented to him by grateful fishermen. But it's the doctor's library, where French, English, Latin and Vietnamese tomes cover subjects from medicine to horticulture, astrology to bacteriology, that conveys most strongly Yersin's thirst for knowledge. Guided tours are given regularly, and a short video on Yersin's life is also available for viewing. The institute (which Yersin himself set up in 1895) is still active today, and you'll see white-coated technicians buzzing about.

Along Thai Nguyen

Thread your way southwest from the Pasteur Institute, and after a few minutes you'll hit Thai Nguyen, home to two of Nha Trang's lesser sights. Presiding over the street's eastern end, stolid, grey-brick **Nha Trang Cathedral** casts its shadow over the head of a sloping cobbled track that peels up and round to its front doors from Nguyen Trai. Under the lofty, vaulted ceilings within the cathedral's dowdy exterior, vivid stained-glass windows depict Christ, Mary, Joseph, Joan of Arc and St Theresa. If you feel as if you're being watched as you climb up to the cathedral, it's probably the disconcerting effect of the huge white Buddha image seated on a hillside above **Long Son Pagoda**, 800m west along Thai Nguyen. Stone gateposts topped by white orchids mark the entrance to the

1930s-built pagoda, which replaced a simpler thatched-roof construction that stood nearby. An impressive, 700-kilogram bronze Buddha stands at the head of the altar, and there are the usual capering dragons on the eaves, but it's the huge **White Buddha**, 152 steps up the hillside behind, that's the pagoda's greatest asset – and Nha Trang's most recognizable landmark. Crafted in 1963 to symbolize the Buddhist struggle against the repressive Diem regime, around its lotus-shaped pedestal are carved images of the monks and nuns who set fire to themselves in protest, among them Thich Quang Duc (see box on p.99)

North to the Po Nagar Cham towers

North of the city centre along 2 Thang 4, two bridges whisk you safely over the **Cai River**, affording wonderful views en route of Nha Trang's immense fishing fleet. Massed palm trees riot to the west of Ha Ra Bridge, while to the east, tumbledown stilthouses teeter over the estuary. The lion's share of the city's flotilla of cheery blue-and-red fishing boats harbour east of Xom Bong Bridge; from this vantage point you'll spy fishermen scrubbing down decks and getting things shipshape before the next tide. Scissor-boats and coracles glide between this congregation of vessels, and balanced precariously on a boulder in the water is a small joss-house where fishermen make offerings prior to setting sail. Behind the boats to the east, the sleek lines of Nha Trang's newest bridge, connecting Tran Phu with the coast further north, testify to the city's continuing development.

Xom Bong Bridge deposits you right in front of the entrance to Nha Trang's most gripping attraction, the **Po Nagar Cham towers** (daily 6am–6pm; small admission fee) just 1.5km north of the city centre. Of the estimated ten towers, or *kalan*, constructed by the Hindu Chams (see box p.245 for more on the Cham civilization) on Cu Lao Hill between the seventh and twelfth centuries, only four remain, their baked red bricks weathered so badly through the centuries that recent restoration work on the towers has been necessary. Despite the restoration, this complex of age-old towers manages to produce an evocative atmosphere, and represents big business for the gaggles of young postcard-sellers who counter rebuffs with a plaintive "Maybe later?" Visitors to the complex approach the towers via a curling flight of steps swarming with beggars, but Cham worshippers would have entered the *mandapa*, or meditation and offerings hall, whose stone pillars are still visible on the hillside; and from there they would have mounted a set of steps directly up to the main tower.

The complex's largest and most impressive tower is the 23-metre-high **northern tower**, built in 817 by Harivarman I and dedicated to Yang Ino Po Nagar, tutelary Goddess Mother of the Kingdom and a manifestation of Uma, Shiva's consort. Restored sections stand out for their lighter hue, but the lotus-petal and spearhead motifs that embellish the tower are original, as is the lintel over the outer door, on which a lithe four-armed Shiva dances, flanked by musicians, on the back of an ox. The two sandstone pillars supporting this lintel bear spidery Cham inscriptions. Inside, a vestibule tapering to a pyramidal ceiling leads to the main chamber, whose sooty darkness takes a little getting used to. The golden statue that originally stood in here was pilfered by the Khmers in the tenth century and replaced by the black stone statue of Uma still here today – albeit minus its head, which was plundered by the French, and now resides in a Parisian museum. The ten arms of cross-legged Uma are nowadays obscured by a gaudy yellow robe, and a doll-like face has been added. Yang Ino Po Nagar is still worshipped as the protectress of the city, and the statue bathed during the **Merian Festival** each March.

Possessing neither the height nor the intricacy of the main *kalan*, the **central tower**, dating back to the seventh century, is dedicated to the god Cri Cambhu, and sees a steady flow of childless couples pass through to pray for fertility at its lingam. The main chamber contains candlesticks, incense urns and flower vases, and its weighty stone altar has been given a glass top and draped with cloth. The **southern tower** is the smallest of the four; viewed from the west it has a certain crumbling beauty, its sloping trunk vaguely recalling the Sphinx.

Beneath its boat-shaped roof, half-formed statues in relief are still visible at the **northwest tower**, and the frontal view of an elephant is just about discernible on the western facade, its serpentine trunk and tusks now blackened with age. Climb the **granite boulders** behind this tower, and there are great views back over the Cai River to Nha Trang and the endless coconut palms west of it – a more interesting alternative to nosing through the dreary on-site **museum** (daily 7.30am–5pm), whose handful of modest stone statues and grainy old photographs can't hold a light to those on show in Da Nang's (see p.296).

Thap Ba Hot Springs

A road heading west just to the north of the Po Nagar Cham towers takes you through distant suburbs of Nha Trang to **Thap Ba Hot Springs** (daily 8.30am–5.30pm; ☎ 058/835335, ⓕ 835287; prices vary according to treatment chosen). There are many different options for pampering your body but if you believe, as the brochure claims, that "soaking in mineral mud is very interesting", you can ooze down into a tub of the messy stuff for half an hour ($2) and see what wonders it does for your skin. After allowing the mud to dry on the skin, take an invigorating shower, then a swim in the mineral-water pool or stand under a mineral-water fall. Finally, finish off with a water massage from a high pressure spray. The waters here are rich in sodium silicate chloride, which has beneficial effects on stress, arthritis and rheumatism. The place is well known by most hotels, who can arrange transport.

Hon Chong Promontory and Beach

Crossing the new bridge at the north end of Tran Phu leads to the **Hon Chong Promontory** (daily 6.30am–6pm; small admission fee), a finger of granite boulders dashed by the sea. It's quite possible to clamber down to the rocks, the largest of which is said to bear a handprint, left, if you believe the local folklore, by a clumsy giant who slipped and fell while ogling a bathing fairy. The headland above the rocks makes a refreshingly blustery venue for a fresh coconut bought at one of the stalls in the shantytown of cafés and souvenir stalls here. Looking northwest you'll spot **Nui Co Tien**, or the Heavenly Maid Mountains, so called because their three ridges resemble the head, breasts and legs of a woman. Immediately up the coast from the promontory is **Hon Chong Beach**, scruffier and shinglier than the city beach and not so clean, but more secluded. Cheap seafood restaurants proliferate at its far end. Though this area of town still has a very natural feel to it, a new road being cut round the coast to the north will probably lead to hotel and resort development in the near future. At night, the views from this new road across the bay to the central beach zone are very impressive.

South to Cau Da Wharf

Six kilometres south of Nha Trang, the **National Oceanographic Institute** (daily 7.30–11.30am & 1.30–4.30pm; $1), housed in a colonial mansion established in 1923 (under renovation at the time of writing), is a veritable

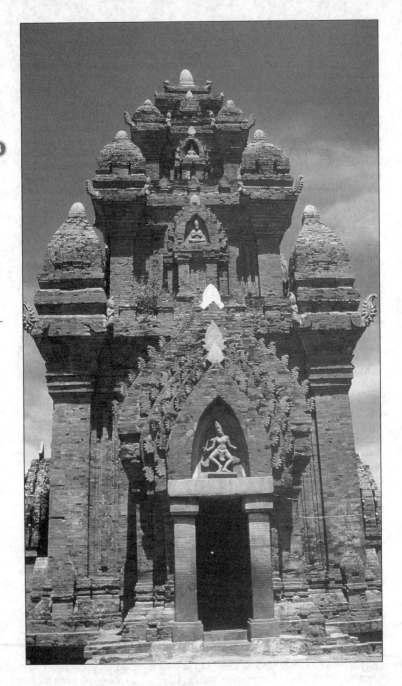

Frankenstein's lab of pickling jars and glass cases yielding crustaceans, fish, seaweed and coral. In one room an eighteen-metre-long humpback whale skeleton is displayed, plus a hammerhead shark and bow-mouth guitarfish. If you've been out snorkelling you might spot some recent acquaintances in the aquarium's twenty or so tanks of primary-coloured live fishes and sea horses. There are three large open ponds in the forecourt, home to horseshoe crabs, green turtles and various local species of fish. Just beyond the museum is **Cau Da Wharf**, the jumping-off point for the mini-archipelago off Nha Trang.

Scuba-diving and water sports

Nha Trang is the **dive centre of Vietnam**, as is well evidenced by the number of dive companies that operate here. It's best avoided between October and December, when the waters can get stirred up and murky, but during the dry season (Jan–May) there are dive boats kitting out and casting off every day to one of over twenty dive sites in the region. A typical day out, including a couple of dives and lunch, costs around $50 for an experienced diver, more if you need instruction. Two reliable companies are Rainbow Divers (℡058/829946, ⓦwww.divevietnam.com), which has a base at the Nha Trang Sailing Club, and Octopus Diving Club (℡058/810629) with its office at 62 Tran Phu. Both these setups offer PADI courses, including a $70 Discover Scuba Diving course for beginners.

If you'd rather get your kicks above water, head on down to Wave Killer, an agent renting out water-sports equipment in *La Louisiane* (see "Eating and drinking", p.257). For a mere $10 you can scare the wits out of swimmers on the beach by zapping them with a **jet-ski** spray for fifteen minutes, but keep in mind that you will be held responsible for any injuries or damages. Less environmentally disastrous is the sport of **parasailing**, which also costs $10 for a ride suspended from a parachute over the bay that lasts about seven minutes.

The islands

Perhaps the single greatest pleasure of a stay in Nha Trang, whether or not you're a diver, is a **day-trip to the islands** that speckle the adjoining waters. Some are just a stone's throw away, others several hours by boat. Independent sea travel is expensive, as you'll have to charter your own boat from **Cau Da Wharf** (prices start at $50 per boat per day); Khanh Hoa Tourism (see p.259) or *Bao Dai's Villas* (see p.247) can also organize chartered boats, or at the other end of the scale there are dirt-cheap local ferries to some of the islands (see below). Fortunately, several companies in Nha Trang (see "Listings" on p.259 for details) offer day-trips to a selection of islands, including a stop for **snorkelling** and a **seafood lunch** on board – all for around $6 per person or less. There are currently five main island boat tours, all of whose tickets are sold at countless outlets across Nha Trang. It's worth noting that each boat trip will tend to cater to a specific crowd: if you're after a peaceful, relaxing time you won't want to be stuck with a group of party-animals and loud music, as tends to be the case on Mama Hanh's trips. Mama Linh's trips are the current recommendation of the tourist board.

The closest of the islands to Cau Da, **HON MIEU**, is actually served by a local ferry (15min; $1 return), which docks at **Tri Nguyen**, a colourful if not particularly picturesque fishing village. From Tri Nguyen, a walk of only a few minutes brings you to **Tri Nguyen Aquarium**, which comprises a series of saltwater ponds constructed for breeding and research purposes and a small indoor aquarium. If the sight of all the fishes, crabs, turtles and baby sharks on display makes you come over a little peckish, you might consider a seafood feast at the restaurant built over the ponds. Pedal and rowing boats are available for rent, but if that doesn't take your fancy you could always check out the shingly beach southeast of the aquarium at the small fishing village of **Bai Soi**. There are a couple of thatched bamboo bungalows on the island, complete with hot water and attached bathroom (❶) for overnight stays; for more information, contact Khanh Hoa Tourism (see "Listings", p.259).

The shallows that ring **HON TAM**, 2km southeast of Mieu and plainly visible from Bai Soi, presently afford a decent beach and good snorkelling, although, with boat anchors daily damaging the coral and increasing numbers of visitors, this may not be the case for long. The low-key *Hon Tam Resort* (☏058/829100; ❷–❹), to the west of the jetty, offers jet skiing, volleyball and diving tours, as well as a pricey seafood restaurant and passable air-conditioned and fan rooms with attached bathrooms. Over to the east of the jetty, a new clutch of luxury bungalows offer a quieter retreat.

Meaning "Bamboo Island", **HON TRE** has been compared to a crocodile crawling in a vast lake. Its cliffs lend a welcome dash of drama to this, the largest of Nha Trang's islands, and offset the fine white sand of its beach, **Bai Tru** (accessible only at certain times of the year). The island belongs mostly to the military, but there are also a few villages, plus the resort of **Con Tre** (see below). If you plan to travel here by public ferry, boats depart from the jetty at **Chua village** (above Cau Da Wharf) for the village of **Vung Me** in the far northwest of the island; or from Cau Da for **Dam Bay** in the southeast part of the island, though the ferries mostly run to erratic timetables.

Two smaller isles hover off Hon Tre's southern coast. The first, **HON MOT** (One Island), has a stony beach but good snorkelling; the other is **HON MUN**, or Black Island, named after the dark cliffs that rear up from it. Caves within these cliffs harbour salangenes, whose **nests**, made from saliva, are harvested and then sold on – at thousands of dollars per kilo – for use in soups, aphrodisiacs and tonics. There's no beach to speak of on Mun, but the island boasts one of the best places for snorkelling in the area, with some great coral. Hon Mun is now part of a marine conservation area, but that hasn't halted the numerous boat tours that make this their first stop.

A slightly pricier boat excursion (about $10) takes in some of the above islands before finishing up at the resort area of **Con Se Tre**, fifteen minutes by boat from Nha Trang beach, on Hon Tre. Currently undergoing massive expansion, this is a cross between a standard beach resort and a living history museum, attempting to "recreate the atmosphere of a Vietnamese countryside village". Not surprisingly, it doesn't quite succeed, but its cluster of thatched huts, bamboo bridges, and amusements such as traditional Vietnamese games and wicker-boat excursions, are all reasonably engaging – there are even the ubiquitous souvenir shops with local crafts. A seafood lunch served at the resort restaurant is included in the price, before an afternoon of snorkelling. Facilities include a variety of rooms for overnight stays, and there's also sometimes an evening excursion to the resort, which includes a beach barbecue and traditional dancing with music; tickets and further information are available from the Con Se Tre office (see "Listings", p.259).

Eating and drinking

Finding a decent place to **eat** presents no problem in Nha Trang. Beachfront Tran Phu is awash with breezy café-restaurants where parched and hungry sunbathers can adjourn for a bite to eat. Nha Trang's heavyweight restaurants are inland in the city centre and on Phan Chu Trinh, where a cluster of seafood operations grapple nightly for the passing tourist trade. You can also dine along the beachfront, listening to the waves lap on the beach, or nose out the cheapest eateries, which tend to be concentrated along and around Biet Thu.

Banana Split, 58 and 60 58–60 Quang Trung. Enter Nha Trang's own version of the ice-cream wars and a prime example of copycat business practice common to Vietnam: two cafés next door to each other competing under the same name, both laying claims to originality. Both offer exactly the same format, tasty ice creams and cheap but uninspiring food. 7am–11pm.

Bistro 7C 7c Le Loi. German-run place, offering good breakfasts ($1–2). Bratwurst, spaghetti or goulash will set you back around $2; San Miguel draught for less than $1 and there's a happy hour 6–10pm. 9am–late.

Bombay Indian 15 Biet Thu. This popular restaurant should soothe your craving for Indian fare with authentic dishes such as squid masala, chicken korma or vegetarian biryani, washed down with a lassi, or a free pina colada while you wait. 3–10pm.

Café des Amis 2d Biet Thu. Perennial favourite and heaving most nights, this café run by two former academics from Hué serves well-prepared Vietnamese and Western dishes with a good vegetarian selection; the steamed fish with ginger is particularly recommended. 7.30am–late.

Coconut Cove Resort opposite *Hai Yen Hotel*, Tran Phu. More laidback, less windswept than most of its beach front competition, and a fair stab at desert-island decor; the eclectic (and a little pricey) menu spans Vietnamese dishes, sandwiches, salads and even pizzas. Afterwards you can retire to the *Log Bar*, attractively carved from a single tree trunk. 7am–midnight (food); 5pm–late (bar).

Cyclo Café 5a Tran Quang Khai. Delightful decor and friendly ambience, along with a solid menu of Vietnamese, Italian and vegetarian food, make this place worth checking out. 7am–late.

Four Seasons Tran Phu. Snuggled between *La Bella Napoli* and *Coconut Cove Resort*, this smart beachfront restaurant serves seafood specials at around $2 plus a good range of shakes and ice creams. 6am–11pm.

Good Morning Vietnam 19b Biet Thu. Yet another branch of the nationwide chain, offering reliable pasta and pizza at around $3–4 per dish. Chill-out terrace upstairs with soft cushions and satellite TV. 10am–11pm.

La Bella Napoli Tran Phu. Just north of the *Thuy Duong*, La Bella Napoli produces some of the city's best homemade pizza and pasta, as well as Italian-style seafood. Good coffee and ice creams too. 8.30am–11pm.

La Louisiane Tran Phu Beach. Ideal for a snack while on the beach (great cakes and pastries), and perhaps a free dip in its pool. You might even get tempted to sign up for one of the water sports on offer at Wave Killer, attached to the bar/restaurant. 7.30am–late.

Lac Canh 44 Nguyen Binh Kiem. A table-side grill hugely popular among locals; some might bridle at its brusque staff, and at the eye-watering smoke off the cooked-at-table barbecues, but the food compensates for these discomforts. 9am–9.30pm.

Lys 117a Hoang Van Thu. Enormously popular family-run restaurant, thanks to specialities like venison, wild pig, and duck cooked in wine. The uninspiring street-level dining area does a tasty line in breakfast *pho* and *bun bo Hué*. 9am–9.30pm.

Ngoc Suong 16 Tran Quang Khai. Smart seafood restaurant tucked away near the budget district, with prices according to weight. 11am–10.30pm.

Red Star 14 Biet Thu. Occupying a double shop front in the heart of the budget district, this place is well set up for travellers and gets plenty stopping by for its breakfasts, shakes or curries. 8am–late.

Same Same But Different 111b Nguyen Thien Thuat. One of many places in the budget district offering a wide range of Vietnamese and Western dishes, including good muesli and hash browns, at very reasonable prices. 7am–10pm.

Thanh Thanh Café 10 Nguyen Thien Thuat ☎058/824413. Extensive menu of reasonably priced Vietnamese, Western and vegetarian dishes, but it's the wood-fire range of pizzas which is their forte; also offers city deliveries. 8am–10pm.

Thanh The 3 Phan Chu Trinh. A bright, open-fronted seafood restaurant on Phan Chu Trinh; the shrimps grilled with garlic ($4) won't disappoint. 7.30am–late.

Thuy Duong junction of Le Thanh Ton and Tran Phu. With beachfront dining on candlelit terraces, tasteful surroundings and fresh seafood you can choose from the aquarium tank, this restaurant is a hit with tourists and locals alike; prices average $2.50. 6am–11pm.

Truc Linh 21 and 11 Biet Thu. Two very different locations, both with great food. The first, at no. 21 (5–11pm), a smart restaurant fronted by brick and bamboo with a good seafood selection, is part of the *Villa Hotel*. The second, at no. 11 (6am–10pm) is a no-frills, street-corner setup that serves up some great soups and stir-fries. Try the street corner for lunch and the smart place for dinner.

Nightlife

One aspect of Nha Trang which swings it over Mui Ne when it comes to choosing a beach haunt is its buzzing **nightlife**. There are plenty of places to check out and several hotels have discos, but you'll need to ask locally to find which are currently worth visiting. Nightspots along the beachfront tend to be a bit pricier than ones located inland, but all of them have generous **happy hours**, guaranteed to bring you back for more. Occasional crackdowns have the bars closing at midnight, but left to their own devices, most bar-owners will stay open till the wee hours.

Crazy Kims Bar 19 Biet Thu. Two-foot-tall cocktails, happy hour that runs 10am–10pm, great selection of CDs, hedonistic party atmosphere and hangover breakfasts make this place very popular with expats, tourists and brave locals, who rave till late. Proceeds from their T-shirts go towards helping Nha Trang's street children. 10am–late.

Jack's Bar 96a/8 Tran Phu. Down at the south end of the beach, *Jack's* is nothing to look at outside, but inside it has the whiff of a welcoming bar, with pool tables both downstairs and upstairs. The terrace has good views and fresh breezes, and the extensive menu appeals to most tastes. 8am–late.

Jungle Pub 90a Hung Vuong. On the edge of the budget district, this well-lit bar has pool table,

movies on TV, a range of Western food and plenty of beers, wines and cocktails. 3pm–late.

Nha Trang Sailing Club 72–74 Tran Phu. For some years this has been a favourite spot for an eclectic group of party animals to get their kicks. It draws a well-heeled expat crowd and hordes of tourists to its refined beachfront bar which gets progressively less refined as the night wears on. 7am–late.

Shorty's 1 Biet Thu. Just a few steps from the beach, this friendly bar has free use of pool table, movies and sport on TV upstairs, a good book exchange and a wide range of Vietnamese and Western food. Good place to chill. 8am–late.

Listings

Airlines Vietnam Airlines, 91 Nguyen Thien Thuat (daily 7.30–11am & 2–4.30pm), and at Khanh Hoa Tourism, 1 Tran Hung Dao (Mon–Fri, same hours).

Bank Vietcombank, 17 Quang Trung, changes cash and travellers' cheques, and can also advance cash against Visa, MasterCard and JCB cards; Agribank at 2 Hung Vuong will change cash and advance cash against Visa and MasterCard.

Bicycles and motorbikes Just about everybody and their grandmother, including most hotels, wants to rent you a bike or motorbike in Nha Trang, so you shouldn't have difficulty finding one; $1 for bicycles, $3–5 for a motorbike per day; just check that it's roadworthy.

Book exchange You can't beat *Shorty's*, at 1 Biet Thu, if you need to replace your book for the beach. Good selection of fiction and non-fiction, salvaged from the ghosts of travellers past.

Car rental Most tour operators, plus *Vien Dong Hotel*, can arrange car rental for $30–35 per day; Mama Linh's rents minibuses for around $50 per day locally, $70 for further afield.

Hospital Nha Trang's hospital is below the city stadium, at 19 Yersin ☏058/822168.

Internet access There are hundreds of places offering Internet access in Nha Trang, so you shouldn't have difficulty getting online. If you do, head for 8c Biet Thu, on the corner with Hung Vuong,

where rates are a standard 100d per minute.

Mini-markets Mini-Mart, 66 Quang Trung; Thien Hoa Bakery, 76a Ly Thanh Ton.

Pharmacy 23d Biet Thu.

Police 5 Ly Tu Trong ☏058/822400.

Post office Nha Trang's GPO, 4 Le Loi (daily 6.30am–10pm), has fax, IDD facilities, poste restante and DHL courier desk (closed Sun); there's also the smaller Post & Telecommunications Service Centre opposite the *Vien Dong*, at 50 Le Thanh Ton (6.30am–midnight), and another branch at 23c Biet Thu (daily 6.30am–9.30pm).

Souvenirs Cua Hang Luu Niem Gift Shop, 8 Phan Boi Chau, has paintings, ceramics, traditional handicrafts and antiques; Vietnam Pure Silk, 19 Le Thanh Ton, ready-to-wear silk garments and tailor shop plus embroidery, artwork and ethnic souvenirs. Bambou, 15 Biet Thu, offers original-design T-shirts at $7 each, plus other bright and colourful souvenirs.

Sports Olympia Gymnasium, 47a/1 Nguyen Thien Thuat (Mon–Sat 5.30–10am & 2–8pm), has a fully equipped body-building gym; *Yasaka Saigon Nha Trang Hotel* has a fitness centre, as does *Nha Trang Lodge*. Nha Trang Sailing Club rents windsurfers and jet skis, and there's a water-sports club at *La Louisiane* called Wave Killer. There's also the water park on Tran Phu just north of the

Ana Mandara Resort. *Vien Dong* and *Bao Dai's Villas* hotels have tennis courts; *Hai Yen* and *Vien Dong* have badminton courts.

Swimming pool *Vien Dong Hotel* offers use of its pool to non-residents at around $1.50 per day.

Tour operators Most of the following operators can book tickets for trips round the islands or book open-tour tickets to anywhere in the country. Some are open all day long; others close for a long lunch break between 11.30am and 1.30pm. Con Se Tre Tourist, 100/16 Tran Phu ☎058/811163; Hanh Café, 26 Tran Hung Dao ☎058/814227,

Ⓔhanhcafe@dng.vnn.vn; Khanh Hoa Tourism, 1 Tran Hung Dao (☎058/823709, Ⓔkhtourism.dng .vnn.vn), is the official government office, so the best place to go for visa extensions; Mama Linh, 2a Hung Vuong ☎058/826693; My A Tours, 10 Hung Vuong ☎058/826195, Ⓔmyaco.nt@dng .vnn.vn; Nam Long Tours, 52 Tran Phu ☎058/824494 for Mama Hanh's boat trips and Rainbow Divers scuba-diving; Sinh Café, 10 Biet Thu ☎058/811981, Ⓔsinhcafent@dng.vnn.vn; TM Brothers Café, 22 Tran Hung Dao ☎058/814556, Ⓔhuuhanhnguyen@hotmail.com.

Around Nha Trang

Above Nha Trang, Highway 1 marches northward, scattering several noteworthy attractions in its wake. The most practical means of exploring this area is to rent a motorbike out of Nha Trang; alternatively, you could catch a service from the local bus station in Nha Trang and return on one of the numerous buses plying the highway at your day's end.

Following the main road running north from the Cham towers and over the **Ru Ri Pass**, after 14km at Da Chung village you'll see a track to your right signposted "Dao Khi" that terminates after a few hundred metres at the jetty for departures to Hon Lao or **Monkey Island** (7.30am–5pm). Predictably enough, the island plays host to a colony of inquisitive monkeys, and a boat trip to see them is great fun – especially if you've got kids with you. The return boat trip costs $3 per person and takes an hour or so; boats depart every fifteen minutes or when there are six takers, and the price includes a guide on the island. Nearby **Thi Island** has a decent beach with good swimming, and at **Orchid Stream**, further east on Hon Heo Peninsula, there are picturesque waterfalls among dramatic cliffs and forests; boats run from either Monkey Island or the mainland jetty.

Therapeutic properties are attributed to the waters of the three pools at **Ba Ho Falls**, the turning for which is signposted on a stone gateway to the left several kilometres further up the highway. The falls can be tricky to find – branch right after passing through a village and follow the road to the parking area. From here it's a walk of about 3km, sometimes clambering over large boulders (so wear sturdy footwear), to the lowest of the falls. The water is beautifully clear, ideal for a refreshing dip. From there, pick your way up the steep track through lush forest to the second pool (described somewhat poetically in the tourist literature as a mirror "by sheer negligence left behind by a certain fairy") and the third. To get there by public transport, take a bus headed for Ninh Hoa District from Nha Trang's local station, and tell the driver your destination; a Honda om from the turn-off should cost around 5000d.

With the left turn to Buon Ma Thuot behind you, next up is splendid **Doc Let Beach**, 12km down a road peeling off east along Hon Khoi Peninsula and signposted on the highway, 38km north of Nha Trang. You'll be keen to linger at Doc Let: its casuarinas and toothpaste-white sands are perfect for a day's beach-bumming, although you do have to pay a small entrance fee for the privilege. If you want to stay overnight, *Doc Let Beach Resort* (☎058/849663, Ⓕ849506; ❷–❸) has beach huts with air-conditioning or fan, or standard fan rooms set back from the beach in a single concrete block; all have attached bathroom and some have satellite TV. The resort also has a large restaurant, souvenir shop and tour booking service to the islands, including its own fishing boat.

If the dazzling sands and empty spaces of the Hon Khoi Peninsula get you in the mood for adventure, consider a visit to *Jungle Beach Resort* (☎091/342 9144, ✆syl@dng.vnn.vn; ❷–❸), one of the most secluded places to stay on the entire Vietnamese coast. Run by a Canadian-Vietnamese couple, *Jungle Beach* has basic rooms for rent in the house, plus a few bungalows in the garden, though most visitors end up sleeping under the stars. All meals are included with room price, and the food is excellent. There's a glorious, deserted beach here and trails on the hillside behind are ripe for exploring. The enthusiastic owner, Sylvio, can arrange treks as well as kayaking (April–Sept) and fishing outings, and several guests have spent a week or two in the region. Finding the place is difficult – it's at the far end of the road on the northeast coast of the peninsula, past the shipyards and shrimp-farming village of Ninh Phuoc. Phone before going, and staff there will guide you or your driver in. A taxi from Nha Trang costs about $13.

North to Son My

Most tourists leapfrog the 400-plus kilometres of coastline between Nha Trang and Hoi An on a tour bus, and it's hard to fault their decision. Though swathes of splendid coastline do exist along this stretch of the country, none has been exploited to any extent as yet. That may change soon, with a new road cut down the **Hon Gom Peninsula** that suddenly makes the endless beaches on both sides of this swan's neck of land accessible. Look out for resorts to spring up here in the future, but in the meantime if you have your own transport, take a drive down the peninsula just to look at its wild sand dunes and islands sitting in the bay. The peninsula is 30km long, but as yet the road only goes about halfway. Fortunately, it's far enough to make access to *Whale Island Resort* (☎058/840501, Ⓦwww.whaleislandresort.com; ❹), located on **Hon Ong** (Whale Island), just a five-minute hop by speedboat from **Dammon jetty**, compared with what used to be a two-hour boat journey from Van Gia, back on Highway 1. As with *Jungle Beach*, rates at *Whale Island Resort* include all meals, and cheaper rates are available for longer stays, though they're still rather steep for budget travellers. The place has a wonderfully relaxing feel; simple but tasteful bungalows peek out over dense vegetation at a fabulous view of the bay where humpback whales and whale sharks are often seen from May to August. Rainbow Divers (see p.259) run frequent dives from here, and the resort has catamarans, canoes, coracles and snorkelling equipment available for guests' use for a nominal fee. The easiest way to book a stay is through their website, but if you're coming from Nha Trang, call first to co-ordinate a pick-up at the jetty.

Back on Highway 1, the main road also passes some impressive but empty beaches. You can get a taster 83km from Nha Trang, just beyond the Hon Gom Peninsula at the tiny fishing village of **DAI LANH**, whose appeal lies in the fact that there's absolutely nothing to do. With its patchwork of clay-tile roofs and modest fleet of blue fishing boats, the village dots the "i" of the kilometre-long beach curving around Vung Ro Bay, a beach whose casuarinas and searing white sands are hemmed between the clear, turquoise waters of the South China Sea and a mantle of green mountains. Open-tour buses usually make a brief stop here en route to Hoi An; but sadly, although there are several eating options in the village, there's presently nowhere decent to stay.

Beyond Dai Lanh, you'll have to wait until just before **Qui Nhon** to get more glimpses of idyllic beaches. A new road branches off from Highway 1 about

30km south of town, and passes some sheltered pristine bays as it squiggles up the coast. About 15km south of town on this new road, the *Baidai Resort* (T & F056/893310, Ebaidairesort@dng.vnn.vn; ④–⑤) has sixty luxurious rooms and suites on a tranquil beach, offering several water sports for guests. **Qui Nhon** itself has little to recommend it, though if you're heading **up Highway 19 to Plei Ku** (see p.218) you might be glad of a night here to break up the journey; the most memorable of the many **Cham sites** scattered around the city are probably too remote for any but the most serious aficionados.

About 100km north of Qui Nhon, shortly before reaching Quang Ngai, Highway 1 passes through **Sa Huynh**, which has a long, inviting beach that is often empty. The final "attraction" of the south-central coast is near **Quang Ngai**, at the eerily quiet **Son My Village**, site of one of the American War's most horrific incidents, the My Lai massacre.

Qui Nhon and around

With the attractions of Hoi An to the north and Nha Trang to the south, **QUI NHON**, a mid-sized seaport set on a narrow stake of land harpooning the South China Sea, attracts few foreign visitors, though for a certain type of traveller this only adds to its intrigue. Whichever way you look at it, the beach just isn't as appealing as many others along this coast, though there are lovely bays not far south. Qui Nhon's origins lie in the Cham migration south, at the start of the eleventh century, under pressure from the Vietnamese to the north. They named the empire they established in the area Vijaya ("Victory"); its epicentre was the citadel of Cha Ban (see p.264), and Qui Nhon – then known as Sri Bonai – developed into its thriving commercial centre. Centuries later, the Tay Son Rebellion boiled over in this neck of the woods; and during the American War the city served as a US port and supply centre, and was engorged by refugees from the vicious bombing meted out to the surrounding countryside. Yet for all its historical resonance, there's nothing here to set pulses racing and, unless you've developed an inordinate interest in **Cham towers**, you'll only be here to refuel and sleep.

Arrival and information

There are half a dozen weekly **flights** between Ho Chi Minh City and Qui Nhon, touching down at Phu Cat Airport, 35km north of town. A Vietnam Airlines minibus shuttles passengers into and out of town ($2), and the company has an office at the top of An Duong Vuong, which used to be the town's airstrip. **Open-tour buses** pull up at *Barbara's On The Beach* (see "Accommodation", overleaf), located towards the southwest end of the beach. It's a good place to rent a bicycle or motorbike, or just to get information on exploring the area and onward travel possibilities, if you can rouse Barbara from her siesta. Qui Nhon's **long-distance bus station** is a several-kilometre Honda om ride west of the city centre, at the corner of Tay Son and Nguyen Thai Hoc. The easiest way of moving on to Plei Ku is to head for Quang Trung Park, where minibuses circle on the lookout for passengers. As always, negotiate the fare before boarding. **Train** tickets can be booked at Qui Nhon's branch-line station beside Quang Trung Park (the main Ho Chi Minh City–Hanoi line passes by west of here, with a station at Dieu Tri). Binh Dinh Tourist Travel Centre (T056/822329) has a small office beside the *Seaview Café* on Nguyen Hue, but it's often unoccupied. The Vietcombank, 152 Le Loi, will **exchange** dollars and travellers' cheques and advance cash against credit cards.

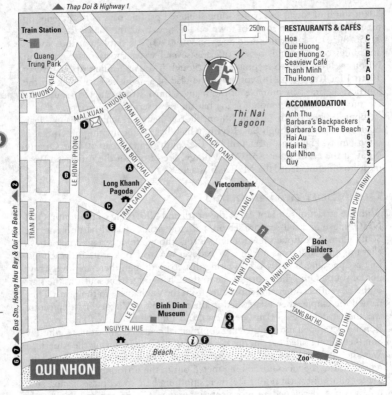

▲ Thap Doi & Highway 1

Train Station

Quang
Trung Park

LY THUONG

MAI XUAN THUONG

Long Khanh
Pagoda

Thi Nai
Lagoon

Vietcombank

Boat
Builders

Binh Dinh
Museum

NGUYEN HUE

Beach

Zoo

QUI NHON

RESTAURANTS & CAFÉS

Hoa	C
Que Huong	E
Que Huong 2	B
Seaview Café	F
Thanh Minh	A
Thu Hong	D

ACCOMMODATION

Anh Thu	1
Barbara's Backpackers	4
Barbara's On The Beach	7
Hai Au	6
Hai Ha	3
Qui Nhon	5
Quy	2

Accommodation

Of the many **places to stay** in Qui Nhon most are, to say the least, under-whelming, although several new places under construction at the time of writing may change that. At present, the city's two brightest and possibly largest hotels are the modern but somewhat isolated *Hai Au* (☎056/846473, ⓔks.haiau@dng.vnn.vn; ③–④) at 489 An Duong Vuong, whose facilities run to tennis courts and a business centre with Internet; and the *Qui Nhon*, 8 Nguyen Hue (☎056/892401; ③–④), which is similar in quality, with the dubious pleasure of being plumb in the centre of the town's best strip of beach. A little further west from the *Hai Au*, the all-new *Barbara's On The Beach* (☎056/846992, ⓔnzbarb@yahoo.com; ①) is sure to become a backpackers' favourite with its well-designed doubles or twins and dorms ($3 per bunk) in a renovated colonial villa on a nice stretch of beach. Back in town, *Barbara's Backpackers* at 18 Nguyen Hue (☎056/892921; ①) offers a much drearier budget option. There are also a few inexpensive mini-hotels that are worth considering. The *Hai Ha* at 5 Tran Binh Trong (☎056/891295, ⓕ892300; ③), down a quiet sidestreet by *Barbara's Backpackers*, has sixteen reasonably smart rooms, all with air-conditioning, though some are rather dim. Another alternative is up in town by the post office, where the *Anh Thu* (☎ & ⓕ056/823043; ②–③) has small but clean rooms run by a friendly family. Finally, the *Quy* at 9 Chu Van An (☎056/813567, ⓕ812188; ①–③) has rooms of a similar standard to the *Hai Ha* but at slightly cheaper prices.

The city and beaches

Central Qui Nhon is almost bereft of interest, though at a push you could drop by well-maintained **Long Khanh Pagoda** at 141 Tran Cao Van. The present sanctuary was built on the site of an eighteenth-century pagoda founded by a Chinese trader, and stands amid grounds dominated by a tall, white Buddha and two turrets – one containing a drum, the other a giant bell. On the back wall of the main sanctuary, and below its varnished wooden roof, a Bodhi Tree mural provides an appropriate backdrop for the large copper Buddha sitting in meditative pose on the altar; below him is a portrait of many-armed Chuan De. The room behind the pagoda's courtyard contains an intriguing statue of a fabulous thousand-eyed and thousand-handed Buddha, with the white figure of Avalokitesvara perched on its head. Otherwise, there's the rather thrown-together collection of artefacts at Nguyen Hue's **Binh Dinh Museum** (Mon–Fri 7–11am & 2–4.30pm; free). Highlights include some nice examples of Cham masonry and one or two reproductions of anti-colonial art from the French era.

The most accessible of all the Cham monuments around Qui Nhon are the **Thap Doi** or "Double Towers" (daily 7–11am & 1.30–5pm), 2km west of town. The shabby backstreet setting does nothing to enhance the towers, so it's a testament to their grandeur that your first sight of them still stops you in your tracks. Square-trunked, and recently restored with a pretty garden around them, both date from around the end of the twelfth century. Embellishments such as sandstone pilasters, spearhead-shaped arches and the sandstone statues of winged Garuda, the vehicle of Vishnu, give the buildings a spiritual aura. To reach Thap Doi, head west out of town along Tran Hung Dao, and turn right into the street called Thap Doi, where the towers are 100m on the right.

The strand of **beach** in front of the *Qui Nhon Hotel* is the most popular in town: fairly wide, and passably clean, it still doesn't see many tourists, so you can expect your presence to draw a crowd. At low tide you may witness the eerie spectacle of a **rusted jeep** appearing on the sand, a sad remnant of the almost forgotten American War. The square nets of numerous **fish traps** are draped over the water just offshore; watching over them from the distant tip of the promontory that shelters the city is a huge statue of Quang Trung. Monkeys, snakes, bears, pelicans and tortoises are kept in truly rancid conditions at the waterfront **zoo**, a short walk east of the *Qui Nhon*.

From the central area, coastal Nguyen Hue slopes away southwest, passing first the fishing village, which can get photogenic when the catch comes in during the afternoon. Nguyen Hue blends into An Duong Vuong, where there are agreeable stretches of beach behind the hotels before the road reaches the pebbly inlet of **Hoang Hau Bay** (daily 7am–7pm), a five-kilometre Honda om or cyclo ride later. Its name translates as "Queen's Bay", and it was said to be a favourite spot of Bao Dai's consort, but if you're looking for some peace and quiet press on for a further 3–4km to one of the region's cleanest and most attractive stretches of sand, three-kilometre-long **Qui Hoa**, accessed, rather oddly, through the grounds of a leper hospital: both beaches require a small entrance fee at the barrier posts. With the opening of the new road south along the coast, previously inaccessible beaches will likely be opened up for tourism – keep track of the latest situation at *Barbara's On The Beach* (see "Accommodation", above).

Eating and drinking

When it comes to **eating**, you could do far worse than Tang Bat Ho's *Thu Hong*, a bright and breezy, open-fronted joint with a menu of standard Vietnamese dishes. Indeed, there are several congenial venues along Tang Bat Ho: *nem* lovers should make for the *Hoa* at no. 124; while the three-storey *Que*

Huong, on the corner at no. 125, has a formidable local reputation and is regularly full to bursting in the early evenings; a similar two-storey outlet is found at its sister branch, *Que Huong 2*, at 185 Le Hong Phong. If the "browned rolling froggy" is not quite to your liking, you may want to sample the hole-in-the-wall vegetarian restaurant *Thanh Minh* at 151 Phan Boi Chau, where dirt-cheap, simple vegetarian fare is continuously doled out. There are not too many places on the central seafront, but the *Seaview Café* on Nguyen Hue has a reasonable menu, and the nearby *Kiwi Café* in *Barbara's Backpackers* turns out cheap and cheerful backpacker staples. The other branch of *Barbara's*, a few kilometres west of the town centre, claims to have the best Western food in town, so check it out and let them know.

North to Sa Huynh

Ten kilometres northwest along Qui Nhon's feeder road, the throng of cafés and restaurants operating around **Phu Tai Crossroads** heralds your arrival at the junction with Highway 1. From here it's another 9km north to **Ba Di Bridge** (Cau Ba Di), where highways 1 and 19 meet, and buses await fares to Plei Ku. Clearly visible from Ba Di Bridge, the **Banh It** Cham towers, known locally as *Thap Bac*, cut a dash on a hilltop over the river, and can be accessed by a road off to the right above the bridge. Their site yields tremendous views of the surrounding countryside, enhanced by the giant white statue of a seated Buddha below. The towers are currently undergoing a much needed restoration.

North of Ba Di, Highway 1 rushes on towards Sa Huynh. If you are travelling under your own steam you could visit the last vestiges of **Cha Ban Citadel**, the erstwhile capital of Vijaya, a kilometre west of the highway and around 27km north of Qui Nhon. This site constituted the epicentre of Champa from the early eleventh century until 1471, when Le Thanh Ton finally seized it, killing 50,000 Chams in the process. The Tay Son brothers renamed the site Hoang De and made it their base in the mid-1770s (see p.220) but it's been neglected since then, and now all that remains, apart from its several-kilometre-long square protective wall, is **Canh Tien Tower**, a rectangular brick and sandstone edifice framed by sandstone pilasters below a crenellated roof.

After racing across terrain whose fertile soil supports huge coconut plantations and through **Phu Cat**, **Phu My** and **Hoai Nhon**, small towns that saw great suffering in the war, the highway nears the coast at **SA HUYNH**, a pleasing fishing backwater perched on a broad curve of palm-fringed, golden sand. Speckled with scores of blue fishing boats, sleepy Sa Huynh makes a convenient and relaxing staging post en route from Nha Trang to Hoi An, and the roaring of its excitable surf masks the noise of traffic from the road; open-tour buses usually make a brief stop here. The best way to enjoy the town's deserted beach is to make for its sole **place to stay**, the laidback *Sa Huynh* (☎055/860311; ❶–❷), 2km below town, whose sixteen simple fan rooms and eleven smarter air-conditioned ones are set in billet-style blocks above the fringe of the beach. There's a **restaurant** at the hotel, though you'd be better off at *Thuy*, which has a tiny sign but serves up excellent seafood at give-away prices, just a little further along the highway on the right.

Shrimp farms, salt flats and vast expanses of paddy characterize the countryside above Sa Huynh. Once past **Duc Pho**, an R&R base for the Viet Minh in the late 1940s, and the tobacco plantations of **Mo Duc**, you quickly hit Quang Ngai.

Quang Ngai and around

Slender **QUANG NGAI**, clinging to the south bank of the Tra Khuc River some 130km south of Da Nang, is about as pleasant as you could expect of a town skewered until recently by Vietnam's main highway. Highway 1, which once ripped through town, now skirts it to the east, leaving the town in a state of shocked silence. The area's long tradition of resistance against the French found further focus during American involvement, for which the reward was some of the most extensive bombing meted out during the war: by 1967, American journalist Jonathan Schell was able to report that seventy percent of villages in the town's surrounding area had been destroyed. A year later, the Americans turned their focus upon **Son My Village**, site of the My Lai massacre (see box overleaf), whose moving memorial garden and museum are the only justifications for a stopover in this workaday settlement.

Son My Village

From the stele immediately to your right over the bridge at the top of Quang Ngai, it's 12km east to **SON MY**, the site of an infamous massacre of civilians by American soldiers in early 1968 that's remembered at the **Son My Memorial Park** (daily 7am–6pm; about $3) in the village's sub-hamlet of Tu Cung. Pacing through this peaceful and dignified place, set within a low perimeter wall surrounded by rice fields, you'll be accompanied by a feeling of blanched horror, and a palpable sense of the dead all around you. Wandering the garden, visitors effect a ghoulish dot-to-dot of the visible scars left by the atrocities that took place here – bullet holes in trees; foundations of homes burnt down, each with a stone tablet recording its family's losses; and blown-out bomb shelters. After skirting three haunting statues of bodies on the brink of death, the path through the centre of the garden ends at a large, Soviet-style statue of a woman cradling a baby amid the fallen, raising her right fist in defiance. Once you've seen the garden, step inside the second of two buildings on its western flank. Here, beyond a plaque recording the names of the dead, family by family, and a montage of rusting hardware, a grisly **photograph gallery** documents the events of March 16, 1968, from snaps of American helicopters disgorging GIs in the paddy outside the hamlet, to spine-chilling intrusions into the villagers' last moments of life. Perhaps more affecting, though, are simpler relics – the teapot top of Mr Nguyen Gap, and a plate broken by a bullet as Mrs Nguyen Thi Doc and her family were breakfasting. **Buses** for Son My leave occasionally from the bus station in Quang Ngai, but the most efficient means of reaching the village is by Honda om.

In stark contrast, secluded **My Khe Beach**, 3km east of My Lai, is several kilometres long and very good for swimming. Hamlets stand along the back of the beach, while fishing boats are moored off it. A large new **hotel**, the *My Tra 3*, was under construction at the time of writing, as was a new bridge to access it; expect rooms with all facilities at around $35. On your return to town you could ascend the area's last attraction of note, **An Mountain**. At the top it's easy to see why the American military sited an observation post here; views out over the surrounding flatlands are spectacular. Seventeenth-century Thien An pagoda provides an additional focus.

Practicalities

The junction of Quang Trung with westward-pointing Hung Vuong effectively forms central Quang Ngai. **Trains** arrive 3km west of town along Hung Vuong, while the **bus** station is a little over 500m south of the centre, and 50m east of Quang Trung on Le Thanh Ton. For what it's worth, you'll find Quang

The My Lai massacre

The massacre of civilians in the hamlets of **Son My Village**, the single most shameful chapter of America's involvement in Vietnam, began at dawn on March 16, 1968. US Intelligence suggested that the 48th Local Forces Battalion of the NVA, which had taken part in the Tet Offensive on Quang Ngai a month earlier, was holed up in Son My. Within the task force assembled to flush them out was **Charlie Company**, whose First Platoon, led by Lieutenant William Calley, was assigned to sweep through **My Lai 4** (known to locals as **Tu Cung Hamlet**). Recent arrivals in Vietnam, Charlie Company had suffered casualties and losses in the hunt for the elusive 48th, but always inflicted by snipers and booby-traps. Unable to contact the enemy face to face in any numbers, or even to distinguish civilians from Viet Cong guerrillas, they had come to feel frustrated and impotent. Son My offered the chance to settle some old scores.

At a briefing on the eve of the offensive, GIs were told that all civilians would be at market by 7am and that anyone remaining was bound to be an active VC sympathizer. Some GIs later remembered being told not to kill women and children, but most simply registered that there were to be no prisoners. Whatever the truth, a massacre ensued, whose brutal course Neil Sheehan describes with chilling understatement in *A Bright Shining Lie*:

The American soldiers and junior officers shot old men, women, boys, girls, and babies. One soldier missed a baby lying on the ground twice with a .45 pistol as his comrades laughed at his marksmanship. He stood over the child and fired a third time. The soldiers beat women with rifle butts and raped some and sodomised others before shooting them. They shot the water buffalos, the pigs, and the chickens. They threw the dead animals into the wells to poison the water. They tossed satchel charges into the bomb shelters under the houses. A lot of the inhabitants had fled into the shelters. Those who leaped out to escape the explosives were gunned down. All of the houses were put to the torch.

In all, the Son My body count reached 500, 347 of whom fell in Tu Cung alone. Not one shot was fired at a GI in response, and the only US casualty was thought to have deliberately shot himself in the foot to avoid the carnage. The 48th battalion never materialized. The military chain of command was able temporarily to suppress reports of the massacre, with the army newspaper, *Stars and Stripes*, and even the *New York Times* branding the mission a success. But the awful truth surfaced in November 1969, through the efforts of former GI Ronald Ridenhour and investigative journalist Seymour Hersh, and the incontrovertible evidence of the grisly colour slides of army photographer Ron Haeberle. When the massacre did finally make the cover of *Newsweek* it was under the headline "An American Tragedy" – which, as John Pilger pointed out, "deflected from the truth that the atrocities were, above all, a *Vietnamese* tragedy".

Of 25 men eventually charged with murder over the massacre, or for its subsequent suppression, only Lieutenant William Calley was found guilty, though he had served just three days of a life sentence of hard labour when Nixon intervened and commuted it to house arrest. Three years later he was paroled.

It's all too easy to dismiss Charlie Company as a freak unit operating beyond the pale. A more realistic view may be that the very nature of the US war effort, with its resort to unselective napalm and rocket attacks, and its use of body counts as barometers of success, created a climate in which Vietnamese life was cheapened to such an extent that a My Lai became almost inevitable. If indiscriminate killing from the air was justifiable, then random killing at close quarters was only taking this methodology to its logical conclusion.

Michael Bilton and Kevin Sim, whose *Four Hours in My Lai* remains the most complete account of the massacre, conclude that "My Lai's exposure late in 1969 poisoned the idea that the war was a moral enterprise." The mother of one GI put it more simply: "I gave them a good boy, and they made him a murderer."

Ngai Tourist 150m north of Hung Vuong at 310 Quang Trung (☎055/822836); the **post office** is about 100m west of the highway, at the junction of Hung Vuong and Phan Dinh Phung. **Internet access** is available at 102 Phan Dinh Phung, though there are several other outlets scattered round town. At the western end of Hung Vuong, you'll find the Vietcombank, which can **exchange** travellers' cheques, dollars and can arrange cash advances for Visa, MasterCard and JCB cards, though the more central Vietincombank at 89 Hung Vuong also changes travellers' cheques and dollars.

One of the most convenient **places to stay** in town is the aptly named *Central* at 784 Quang Trung (☎055/829999, ⓔcentral@dng.vnn.vn; ❸–❹), near the bus station, which has large, comfortable rooms, and friendly, helpful staff. Other big hotels in town are the *Petro-Song Tra* (☎055/822665, ⓔpvstc@dng.vnn.vn; ❸–❹), and the *My Tra 1* (☎055/842986, ⓔks-mytra @dng.vnn.vn; ❹–❺), which face each other across the broad Tra Khuc River at the north end of Quang Trung. All three of these have a swimming pool and restaurant. If you're looking for something less impersonal, try one of the 23 rooms, some with balcony, in the clean and friendly *Kim Thanh* (☎055/823471; ❶–❸) at 19 Hung Vuong. Finally, *Hung Ha* (☎055/815772; ❶–❷), a family-run mini-hotel at 495 Quang Trung, has air-conditioned rooms with hot water at budget prices.

There are no great **places to eat** in Quang Ngai, though the *My Tra Hotel's* open-air terrace restaurant looking out across the river makes a nice enough setting. Food is rather ordinary in all the hotels, but you could head for one of two good-value and tidy enough *com* shops – the *Mimosa* and the *Bac Son* – next door to the *Kim Thanh Hotel* in town; or for the *Long Hue*, secreted around the corner from the post office – turn left at the sign for the *Long Hue*, at 93 Phan Ding Phung. At 7 and 9 Hung Vuong, you'll find **stalls** selling *ram*, barbecued shrimp or meat folded in rice paper and then dipped in a tasty peanut sauce.

Travel details

Trains

Dieu Tri to: Da Nang (3 daily; 4hr 30min–5hr 30min); Ho Chi Minh City (3 daily; 12hr 30min–15hr 30min); Hué (3 daily; 8–10hr); Nha Trang (3 daily; 4–5hr).
Muong Man to: Da Nang (3 daily; 12–17hr); Ho Chi Minh City (3 daily; 4hr 10min–4hr 50min); Hué (3 daily; 12–15hr); Nha Trang (3 daily; 5hr–5hr 40min).
Nha Trang to: Da Nang (4 daily; 9hr–12hr 30min); Hanoi (3 daily; 24–32hr); Ho Chi Minh City (5 daily; 7hr 10min–11hr 15min); Hué (4 daily; 12hr–16hr 10min).
Thap Cham to: Da Nang (3 daily; 12hr 25min–13hr 30min); Ho Chi Minh City (3 daily; 6hr 40min–7hr 30min); Hué (3 daily; 16–17hr); Nha Trang (3 daily; 1hr 30 min– 2hr 10min).

Boats

Vung Tau to: Con Son (1–2 weekly; 15hr).

Hydrofoils

Vung Tau to: Ho Chi Minh City (Mon–Fri 6 daily, Sat & Sun 7 daily; 1hr 15min).

Flights

Nha Trang to: Da Nang (daily; 1hr 20min); Hanoi (daily; 1hr 50min); Ho Chi Minh City (3 daily; 1hr 10min).
Qui Nhon to: Hanoi (daily; 5hr 40min); Ho Chi Minh City (daily; 1hr 30min).

Buses

It's almost impossible to give the **frequency** with which buses run. Long-distance public buses, though scheduled, won't depart if empty.

5

The central provinces

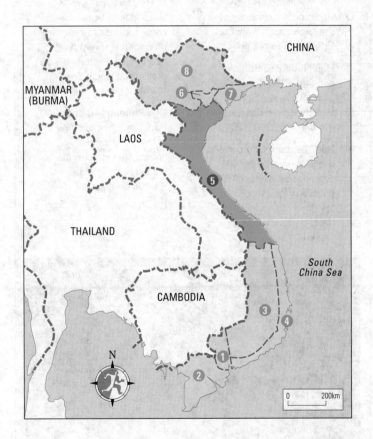

CHAPTER 5 # Highlights

✳ **Hoi An's Full-Moon Festival** Step back in time as this beguiling town celebrates its rich heritage. **See p.275**

✳ **My Son** These mouldering, mystical ruins provide a potent reminder of the once vibrant Champa kingdom. **See p.288**

✳ **Non Nuoc Beach** Kick back for a few days on sugar-white sands stretching as far as the eye can see. **See p.301**

✳ **Hué** The erstwhile imperial capital is home to the evocative temples and palaces of the citadel and the Royal Mausoleums' lyrical pleasure gardens. **See p.304**

✳ **Phong Nha Cave** Take a boat trip into the mouth of one of Asia's most extensive cave systems. **See p.340**

✳ **Cycling from Tam Coc to Hoa Lu** A fantasy landscape of limestone crags provides the backdrop for a leisurely cycle ride through Ninh Binh's prolific rice lands. **See p.349**

✳ **Cuc Phuong National Park** Get close to some of the world's most endangered species at the excellent Primate Rescue Center. **See p.351**

5

The central provinces

Vietnam's narrow waist comprises a string of provinces squeezed between the long, sandy coastline and the formidable barrier of the Truong Son Mountains, which mark the border between Vietnam and Laos. Ragged spurs sheer off the Truong Son range towards the South China Sea, cutting the coastal plain into isolated pockets of fertile rice land. For much of Vietnam's early history, one of these spurs, the thousand-metre-high Hoanh Son Mountains north of Dong Hoi, formed the cultural and political divide between the northern, Chinese-dominated sphere and the Indianized Champa kingdom to the south. As independent Vietnam grew in power in the eleventh century, so its armies pushed southwards to the next natural frontier, the Hai Van Pass near Hué. Here again, the Cham resisted further invasion until the fifteenth century, when their great temple complex at My Son was seized and their kingdom shattered.

Since then other contenders have battled back and forth over this same ground, among them the Nguyen and Trinh lords, whose simmering rivalry ended in victory for the southern Nguyen and the emergence of **Hué** as the nation's capital in the nineteenth century. The Nguyen dynasty transformed Hué into a stately imperial city, whose palaces, temples and grand mausoleums now constitute one of the highlights of a visit to Vietnam, despite the ravages they suffered during successive wars. In 1954, Vietnam was divided at the Seventeenth Parallel, only 100km north of Hué, where the Ben Hai River and the **Demilitarized Zone** (**DMZ**) marked the border between North and South Vietnam until reunification in 1975. Though there's little to see on the ground these days, the desolate battlefields of the DMZ are a poignant memorial to those who fought here on both sides, and to the civilians who lost their lives in the bitter conflict.

Da Nang and nearby **China Beach** are other evocative names from the American War, but the region has more to offer. The compact, riverside town of **Hoi An**, with its core of traditional, wood-built merchants' houses and jaunty Chinese Assembly Halls, is a particularly captivating place. Inland from Hoi An, the Cham spiritual core, **My Son**, survives as a haunting array of overgrown ruins in a hidden valley, while the coast here presents a succession of empty, white-sand beaches that are among the finest in Vietnam.

All these highlights lie in the southernmost of the central provinces. In stark contrast, the more northerly provinces suffer a particularly hostile climate, and were also the hardest-hit by bombing raids during the American War. Without exception, the towns here are postwar reconstructions with little to recommend them other than as overnight stops on the long haul north. In fact, from Hué most people skip straight up to Hanoi, but if you're travelling overland,

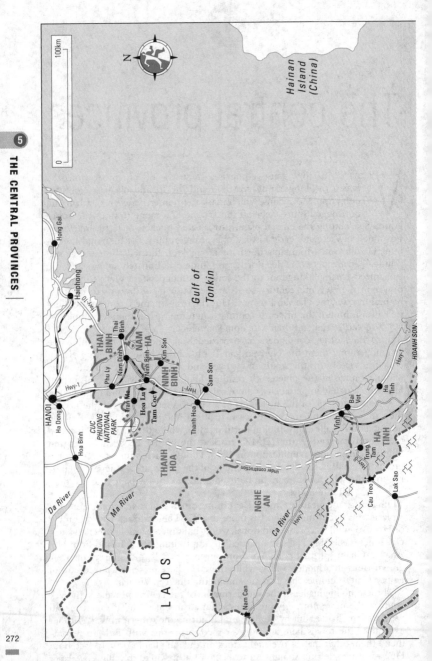

SOUTH
CHINA
SEA

*Cham
Islands*

Hai Van
Pass

Lang Co

Da Nang

Hoi An

Hwy 1

Cau Hai

QUANG NAM

Hue

BACH MA
NATIONAL
PARK

Tra Kieu

My Son

BA NA
NATURE
RESERVE

Hwy 1

THUA
THIEN-HUE

A Luoi

A Shau

Hwy 14

The DMZ

Dong Ha

Quang Tri

*Ben Hai
River*

QUANG TRI

Khe
Sanh

Ngang
Pass

Bo Trach

Dong Hoi

QUANG
BINH

Gianh River

MOUNTAINS

Phong
Nha
Cave

Lao Bao

TRUONG SON MOUNTAINS

Hwy 9

LAOS

Savannakhet

Mukdahan

Mekong River

THAILAND

there are a couple of places en route that warrant a stop. First of these is the **Phong Nha Cave**, near Dong Hoi, where boats take you into the mouth of an extensive underground river system. Then right up in the north, and within easy striking distance of Hanoi, **Ninh Binh** is the base for a number of attractions, from engaging river trips to ancient temples and reserves of primary rainforest. For those travelling by car or minibus, the usual place to break the journey between Hué and Hanoi is **Vinh**, though if you stop off at Dong Hoi for the caves you should be able to press on to Ninh Binh in a long day.

Finally, if you're heading **overland to Laos**, the only two functioning border gates for foreigners are at **Lao Bao**, along Highway 9 from Dong Ha, and at **Cau Treo**, on Highway 8 from Vinh. However, there's a rumour that the new crossing at **Nam Can**, 230km northwest of Vinh, will eventually be open to foreigners; ask locally for the latest information.

When to go

This region has a particularly complicated climate as it forms a transitional zone between the north and south of Vietnam. In general, **around Da Nang and Hué** the rainy season lasts from September to February, with most rain falling between late September and December; during this season it's not unusual for road and rail links to be cut. Hué suffers particularly badly and, even during the "dry season" from March to August, it's possible to have several days of torrential rain, giving the city an annual average of three metres. Overall, the best time to visit this southern region is in spring, from February to late May, before both temperatures and humidity reach their summer maximum (averaging around 30°C), or just at the end of the summer before the rains break. The region **north of the Hoanh Son Mountains** experiences a drier climate and a more marked rainy season, with September and October again the wettest months. Summers are hot and dry, though from August to November **typhoons** can bring periods of heavy rain and severe flooding.

Hoi An

The approach to **HOI AN** across sandy scrubland and through straggling modern outskirts may be disappointing, but its ancient core is a rich architectural fusion of Chinese, Japanese, Vietnamese and European influences dating back to the sixteenth century. In its heyday the now drowsy channel of the Thu Bon River was a jostling crowd of merchant vessels representing the world's great trading nations, and there's still a compelling sense of history in the mellow streets of this small, amiable town. Hoi An's most noteworthy monuments are the 200-year-old homes of prosperous Chinese merchants whose descendants, surrounded by astonishing collections of antiques and family memorabilia, continue to inhabit the cool, dark houses. Between their sober wooden facades, riotous confections of glazed roof tiles and writhing dragons mark the entrances to **Chinese Assembly Halls**, which form the focal point of civic and spiritual life for an ethnic Chinese community that constitutes one quarter of the population.

Hoi An was inscribed on UNESCO's World Heritage list in 1999 and is now firmly on the tourist agenda. For some it's already too much of a trap with its profusion of tailors' shops and art galleries and its rapidly proliferating hotels, and the majority of visitors pause only briefly, but it takes time to tune in to the town's subtle charms, which are as much about human encounters as ancient vestiges. At least a day is needed to cover the central sights and sample some of Hoi An's mouthwatering speciality dishes, and by then most people are hooked. It's easy to spend longer, taking day-trips to the atmospheric Cham ruins of **My Son** or some of the other sights closer to town (see "Around Hoi An", pp.286–290), biking out into the surrounding country or opting for a leisurely sampan ride on the Thu Bon River. If possible, try to time your visit to coincide with the recently inaugurated **Full-Moon Festival**, on the fourteenth day of the lunar calendar, when the town centre is closed to traffic and traditional arts performances take place in the lantern-lit streets.

Some history

For centuries Hoi An played an important role in the **maritime trade** of Southeast Asia, going back to perhaps the second century BC, when people of the so-called Sa Huynh culture exchanged goods with China and India. But things really took off in the mid-sixteenth century when Chinese, Japanese and European vessels ran with the trade winds to congregate at a port then called Fai Fo. Its annual spring fair grew into an exotic showcase of world produce: from Southeast Asia came silks and brocades, ivory, fragrant oils, fine porcelain and a cornucopia of medicinal ingredients; while the Europeans brought their textiles, weaponry, sulphur, lead – and the first Christian missionaries in 1614. During the four-month fair, merchants would rent lodgings and warehouses; many went on to establish a more permanent presence through marriage to Vietnamese women, renowned for their business acumen. Tax collectors arrived to fill the imperial coffers, and the town swelled with artisans, moneylenders and bureaucrats as trade reached a peak in the seventeenth century.

Commercial activity was dominated by Japanese and Chinese merchants, many of whom settled in Fai Fo, where each community maintained it's own governor, legal code and strong cultural identity. But in 1639 the Japanese Shogun prohibited foreign travel and the "Japanese street" dwindled to a handful of families, then to a scattering of monuments and a distinctive architectural style. Unchallenged, the Chinese community prospered, and its numbers grew as every new political upheaval in China prompted another wave of immigrants to join one of the town's self-governing "congregations", organized around a meeting hall and place of worship.

In the late eighteenth century, silt began to clog the Thu Bon River just as markets were forced open in China, and from then on the port's days were numbered. Although the French established an administrative centre in Fai Fo, and even built a rail link from Tourane (Da Nang), they failed to resuscitate the economy, and when a storm washed away the tracks in 1916 no one repaired them. The town, renamed Hoi An in 1954, somehow escaped damage during both the French and American wars and retains a distinctly antiquated air, its narrow streets comprising wooden-fronted shophouses topped with moss-covered tiles.

Arrival, information and getting around

People generally **arrive** in Hoi An by taxi or Honda om from Da Nang (30km), which serves as Hoi An's nearest airport and train station, or on an open-tour bus, which usually drops you at the relevant booking office or their affiliated hotel. Local buses terminate at the bus station 500m north of the town centre. For local **information**, ask in your hotel or try one of the dozens of private tour agencies (see "Listings", p.286): most offer similar services – tours, transport, rail and air tickets – but prices and itineraries vary so it's worth shopping around.

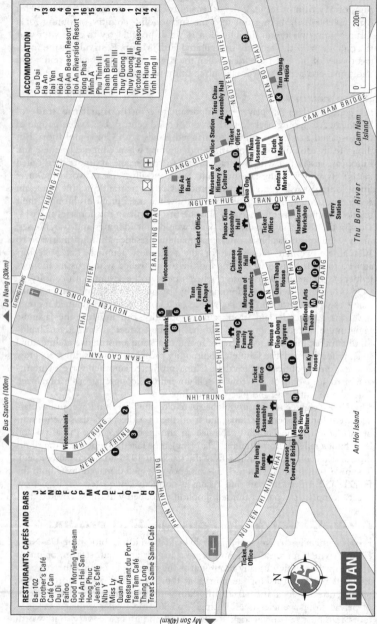

▲ **7**, **8**, **9**, **10**, **11**, **12** & *Cua Dai Beach (4km)*

ACCOMMODATION

Cua Dai	7
Ha An	13
Hai Yen	8
Hoi An	4
Hoi An Beach Resort	10
Hoi An Riverside Resort	11
Hong Phat	16
Minh A	15
Phu Thinh II	9
Thanh Binh I	5
Thanh Binh III	3
Thuy Duong I	6
Thuy Duong III	1
Victoria Hoi An Resort	12
Vinh Hung I	14
Vinh Hung II	2

RESTAURANTS, CAFÉS AND BARS

Bar 102	J
Brother's Café	K
Café Can	N
Du Di	B
Faifoo	F
Good Morning Vietnam	C
Hoi An Hai San	P
Hong Phuc	M
Jean's Café	A
Miss Ly	D
Nhu Y	E
Quan An	L
Restaurant du Port	O
Tam Tam Café	I
Thang Long	H
Treat's Same Same Café	G

HOI AN

▲ *Da Nang (30km)*

▲ *Bus Station (100m)*

▲ *My Son (40km)*

Moving on from Hoi An

When it comes to onward transport, the most popular option is to hop on one of the **open-tour buses** heading north to Da Nang ($2–3) and Hué ($2–4) – with some services stopping briefly at the Marble Mountains, Hai Van Pass and Lang Co – or south to Nha Trang ($5–8) with stops at Sa Huynh, Song Cau and Dai Lanh. Each of the open-tour operators has an office in Hoi An where you can purchase tickets and make reservations (see "Listings", p.286). While you can buy tickets almost anywhere, it's best to go to the company direct to ensure it's valid.

If you're headed **to Da Nang**, however, and want to spend longer at the various stops en route – the Marble Mountains, Non Nuoc Beach and the Cham Museum – a better alternative is to take a **hired car** ($8–10) or **Honda om** ($3–5). Afterwards you can get the driver to drop you at your hotel or at the train station or airport. Hotels and tour agencies in Hoi An will help with the arrangements. Local **buses** plying between Hoi An and Da Nang are very much a last resort: ancient vehicles, often stuffed to the gunnels, leave Hoi An bus station every half-hour or so, taking up to two hours to cover the 30km (under $1; services stop 5pm).

Almost every hotel and many shops and tour agents have well-priced **bicycles** for rent (less than $0.50 per day), or can arrange **motorbikes** at around $2–4 per day – a popular way to visit My Son (see p.286); for motorbikes, try Mr My who hangs out opposite 6 Le Loi. While bikes are recommended for touring the outlying districts, Hoi An's central sights are all best approached **on foot**, especially since **traffic restrictions** apply in the town centre. The regulations are part of a much needed effort to save the old town from the worst effects of fame: cars are prohibited from the core streets south of Phan Chu Trinh and west of Hoang Dieu; and all vehicles are banned in the vicinity of the market and on the Japanese bridge, though you can push pedal bikes across.

Accommodation

The number of **hotels** in Hoi An continues to grow at an astonishing rate. The local authorities did put a block on developments in the centre – too late to prevent some eyesores in the old streets – but a whole new enclave has sprung up to the north of the centre along Nhi Trung, with ornate, mock-Chinese facades and tiny pools. New hotels are also spreading east along Cua Dai towards the beach, while a couple of swanky resort hotels have opened on the beach itself. Although there's still a lack of decent budget accommodation, the good news is that in general prices have come down and standards have risen, most places will bargain and there's no longer a shortage of beds in peak season. If you do have difficulty, just head for the hotels further from the centre.

Cua Dai 18a Cua Dai ☎0510/862231, @cuadaihotel@dng.vnn.vn. Airy communal areas and rattan sofas give this small hotel on the eastern outskirts of Hoi An a slightly colonial feel. The rooms are simple but well appointed, some with balcony; those in the new extension at the back are slightly smarter. There's no pool, but they provide free tea and coffee. ③

Ha An 6 Phan Boi Chau ☎0510/863126, @tohuong@fpt.vn. Welcoming, family-run hotel, set back from the street in a quiet residential area. Its ten rooms are arranged around a spacious lobby and, though not huge, are beautifully deco-

rated in a mix of traditional and contemporary styles, all with en-suite bathrooms, air-con, phone and TV. ③

Hai Yen 22a Cua Dai ☎0510/862445, @kshaiyen@dng.vnn.vn. Once past the saccharine-pink staircase, this quiet hotel with a small pool and garden is a good choice on the road to the beach. Decent-sized, comfortable rooms come with a bathtub, and other facilities include a restaurant, Internet access, bike rental and all the usual tours and ticketing services. ③

Hoi An 6 Tran Hung Dao ☎0510/861373,

Ⓦ www.hoiantourist.com. A state-run, colonial-style hotel and former billet for US Marines, the Hoi An has now been upgraded to three-star and boasts 160 rooms in three low-rise blocks set among gardens. The rooms are unusually spacious and well equipped, while the hotel also boasts a restaurant, bar, money exchange, tour agent and tennis courts. Its pool is another big plus, especially as it's open to non-residents ($2). ④–⑤

Hoi An Beach Resort Cua Dai Beach ☎ 0510/927011, Ⓦ www.hoiantourist.com. Separated from the beach by a quiet road, this is the slightly cheaper of Cua Dai's two new resort hotels. Rooms are elegant in cool, sand colours and bathrooms are generously proportioned; best are the river-view rooms. Other attractions include two pools, a private beach and a restaurant recommended for its well-priced local dishes. Free shuttle bus to Hoi An. ⑤

Hoi An Riverside Resort Cua Dai Road ☎ 0510/864800, Ⓔ hoianriver@dng.vnn.vn. Romantic riverside resort 3km from Hoi An (shuttle buses run to the town and beach) comprising two-unit villas in a lush garden setting. The rooms come in four categories, with a choice of river or garden views and of Vietnamese or Japanese decor, the latter with rice-paper wall-coverings, futon and such-like. The hotel also has a pool and restaurant. ⑤

Hong Phat 41 Nguyen Thai Hoc ☎ 0510/910100, Ⓔ quanghuy.ha@dng.vnn.vn. Book ahead to sample the delights of this atmospheric 350-year-old house. The four rooms – all on the ground floor and therefore lacking exterior windows – are decked out in traditional style although creature comforts such as air-con and modern bathrooms have been added. ③

Minh A 2 Nguyen Thai Hoc ☎ 0510/861368. This little guesthouse right by Hoi An market offers just five rooms in an ancient shophouse. Facilities are basic – there's no air-con and access to the shared bathroom and toilet is through the kitchen – but it's a good opportunity to stay in a traditional family home. ①–②

Phu Thinh II 144 Cua Dai ☎ 0510/923923, Ⓦ www.phuthinhhotels.com. With its grand lobby, pool and garden restaurant, this new hotel just outside town offers surprisingly good value. Ground-floor rooms are cheapest, while those at the top of the range boast balconies overlooking the garden and rice fields beyond. ②–③

Thanh Binh I 1 Le Loi ☎ 0510/861740, Ⓔ vothihong@dng.vnn.vn. A central location plus cheap and cheerful but unremarkable rooms with

fridge, bathtub, satellite TV and air-con make this a popular budget option, not least because you can use the pool at their sister hotel, the *Thanh Binh III*, below. ②

Thanh Binh III (New) Nhi Trung ☎ 0510/916777, Ⓔ vothihong@dng.vnn.vn. There's not a lot to choose between the hotels along (New) Nhi Trung, but the *Thanh Binh III* offers a range of rooms around a courtyard pool – downstairs rooms can be a bit noisy, though. ②

Thuy Duong I 11 Le Loi ☎ 0510/861574, Ⓔ thuyduongco@dng.vnn.vn. This friendly little hotel is a mainstay of the budget scene. There's a choice between fan-only rooms and slightly larger ones with air-con. You can use the pool at the *Thuy Duong III*. ①–②

Thuy Duong III (New) Nhi Trung ☎ 0510/916565, Ⓔ thuyduongco@dng.vnn.vn. Don't be put off by the fact that Sinh open-tour buses drop you here. The rooms are comfortable, well maintained and reasonably priced, though those on the ground floor around the courtyard pool can be noisy. ③

Victoria Hoi An Resort Cua Dai Beach ☎ 0510/927040, Ⓦ www.victoriahotels-asia.com. At Hoi An's ritziest hotel the top-rated bungalows open right onto a lovely stretch of beach, while the cheapest rooms occupy two-storey villas. The *Victoria* has all the amenities you'd expect of an international-class resort, including a restaurant serving good but expensive meals, a free shuttle bus to Hoi An and a whole range of activities (for which you pay extra). ⑤–⑥

Vinh Hung I 143 Tran Phu ☎ 0510/861621, Ⓔ quanghuy.ha@dng.vnn.vn. Apart from an unbeatable location and excellent service, the highlights of this lovely old Chinese shophouse are the two superbly restored rooms upstairs complete with balcony, wood panelling, antique furniture and four-poster beds as well as tiny bathrooms; they're in great demand, so book ahead. The other rooms, in a modern extension at the back, are decorated in traditional style but dark and rather expensive for what you get. ②–③

Vinh Hung II (New) Nhi Trung ☎ 0510/863717, Ⓔ quanghuy@dng.vnn.vn. The latest addition to the *Vinh Hung* empire maintains similarly high standards of service and continues the traditional Chinese theme in its more expensive rooms, while those at the bottom of the price range are adequate if unexciting. Facilities include a small courtyard pool, restaurant and Internet access. ③

The Town

The **historic core** of Hoi An consists of just three short streets running parallel to the river. Tran Phu is the oldest and is still the principal commercial street, running from Hoi An's most famous monument, the Japanese Covered Bridge, in the west, to the market in the east. One block south is Nguyen Thai Hoc, with a fine array of wooden townhouses, traditional pharmacists and an overspill of galleries, tailors and antique shops. Finally comes riverfront Bach Dang, site of the ferry station and a line of attractive, waterside café-restaurants. Just north of this central core is a scattering of sights, including two of the less visited merchants' houses, that shouldn't be overlooked.

Japanese Covered Bridge

The western extremity of Tran Phu is marked by a small arched bridge of red-painted wood, popularly known as the **Japanese Covered Bridge**, which has been adopted as Hoi An's emblem. It was known to exist in the mid-sixteenth century, and has subsequently been reconstructed several times to the same simple design. According to local folklore, the bridge was erected after Japan suffered a series of violent earthquakes which geomancers attributed to a restless monster lying with its head in India, tail in Japan and heart in Hoi An. The only remedy was to build a bridge whose stone piles would drive a metaphorical sword through the beast's heart, and fortuitously provide a handy passage across the muddy creek. Inside the bridge's narrow span are a collection of stelae and four statues, two dogs and two monkeys, which suggest that work began in the year of the monkey and ended in that of the dog. The small **temple** suspended above the water is a later addition dedicated to the Taoist god Tran Vo Bac De ("Emperor of the North"), a favourite of sailors as he controls wind, rain and other "evil influences".

The Chinese Assembly Halls

Historically, Hoi An's ethnic Chinese population organized themselves according to their place of origin (Fujian, Guangdong, Chaozhou or Hainan). Each group maintained its own assembly hall as both community centre and house of worship, while a fifth hall also provided assistance to all the local groups and to visiting Chinese merchants. The most populous group hailed from Fujian, or Phuoc

Visiting Hoi An's sights

Hoi An has a **ticket scheme** covering the majority of its most famous sights, the proceeds of which contribute to the preservation of the old centre. A ticket, costing in the order of $3.50, allows access to five places: either the temple on the Japanese Covered Bridge or Chua Ong; one of the museums (the Museum of History and Culture, the Museum of Trade Ceramics and the Museum of Sa Huynh Culture); one of the participating Chinese Assembly Halls (the Phuoc Kien, Trieu Chau and Cantonese halls); one of the participating merchants' houses or family chapels (the houses of Tan Ky, Phung Hung and Quan Thang and the Tran Family Chapel); and the Hoi An Handicraft Workshop at 9 Nguyen Thai Hoc. If you want to visit more sights in the scheme, you have to fork out for another ticket.

Tickets are on sale at six **outlets**: 52 Nguyen Thi Minh Khai, 19 Nhi Trung, 5 Hoang Dieu, 12 Phan Chu Trinh, 37 Tran Phu and 78 Le Loi (all marked on the map on p.276). Groups of more than eight people are entitled to a guide for the day; otherwise, you can hire a guide for around $3.50. The ticket outlets are **open** from 6.30am to 6pm, as are the sights included in the scheme. For sights not in the ticket scheme, we've given details of opening hours in the accounts.

Kien, and their **Phuoc Kien Assembly Hall**, at 46 Tran Phu, is a suitably imposing edifice with an ostentatious, triple-arched gateway added in the early 1970s. The hall started life as a pagoda built in the late seventeenth century when, so it's said, a Buddhist statue containing a lump of gold washed up on the river bank. Almost a century later, the Chinese took over the decaying structure and rededicated it as a temple to Thien Hau, Goddess of the Sea and protector of sailors. She stands, fashioned in 200-year-old papier-mâché, on the principal altar flanked by her two assistants, green-faced Thien Ly Nhan and red-faced Thuan Phong Nhi, who between them can see or hear any boat in distress over a range of a thousand miles. A second sanctuary room behind and to the right of the main altar shelters a deity favoured by couples and pregnant women: the awesome Van Thien and her aides, the "twelve heavenly midwives", who decide the fundamentals of a child's life from conception onwards, including the fateful matter of gender. On the way out of the main building, take a look at the entrance porch decorated with colourful wooden friezes and delicate stone motifs.

It's worth strolling out to the **Trieu Chau Assembly Hall**, on the far eastern edge of town at 157 Nguyen Duy Hieu. Built in the late eighteenth century by Chinese from Chaozhou, or Trieu Chau, it's renowned for its remarkable display of woodcarving. In the altar-niche sits the gilded Ong Bon, a general in the Chinese navy believed to hold sway over the wind and waves, surrounded by a frieze teeming with bird, animal and insect life so lifelike you can almost hear it buzz. The altar table itself depicts life on land and in the depths of the ocean, while panels on either side show two decorative ladies of the Chinese court modelling the latest Japanese hair fashions. On the way to Trieu Chau hall, you'll pass **Hai Nam Assembly Hall**, at 10 Tran Phu (not covered by ticket scheme; 7–11.30am & 2–5pm), founded by the Chinese community from Hainan, or Hai Nam, and also noted for its ornately carved, gilded altar table – though its unusual history is more intriguing. In 1851 a Vietnamese general plundered three merchant ships, killing 107 passengers, after which the vessels were painted black to imply they were pirate ships. A lone survivor revealed

---

Unravelling the architectural features of Hoi An

You can't walk far in Hoi An without confronting a **mythical beast** with fish's body and dragon's head; though they're found all over northern Vietnam they seem to have struck a particular chord with Hoi An's architects. One of the most prominent examples tops a weather vane in the Phuoc Kien Assembly Hall, but there are plenty of more traditional representations about, carved into lantern brackets and beam ends, or forming the beams themselves. The **carp** symbolizes prosperity, success and, here, metamorphosing into a **dragon**, serves as a reminder that nothing in life comes easily. To become a dragon, and thereby attain immortality, a fish must pass through three gates – just as a scholar has to pass three exams to become a mandarin, requiring much patience and hard work.

Another typical feature of Hoi An's architecture are "**eyes**" watching over the entrance to a house or religious building. Two thick wooden nails about 20cm in diameter are driven into the lintel as protection against evil forces, following a practice that originated in the pagodas of northern Vietnam. Assembly halls offer the most highly ornamented examples: that of Phuoc Kien consists of a yin and yang with two dragons in obeisance to the sun, while the Cantonese version is a fearsome tiger. The **yin and yang** symbol became fashionable in the nineteenth century and is the most commonly used image on houses, sometimes set in a chrysanthemum flower, such as at the Tan Ky House, or as the octagonal talisman representing eight charms.

the crime to King Tu Duc, who promptly condemned the general to death and ordered that the booty be returned to the victims' families. When the hall was built later in the century, it was dedicated to the unlucky passengers.

Just east of the Japanese bridge you can't miss the **Cantonese Assembly Hall**, its gaudy entrance arch a recent embellishment to the original late eighteenth-century hall built by immigrants from Guangdong. Though there's nothing of particular merit here, it's an appealing place, mostly because of its plant-filled courtyard, ornamented with dragon and carp carvings (see box above). The main altar is dedicated to the red-faced Quan Cong, a Chinese general of the Han dynasty revered for his loyalty, honesty and exemplary behaviour. Lastly, plum in the centre of town is the **Chinese Assembly Hall**, or Chua Ba (not covered by ticket scheme; 7–11.30am & 2–5pm), built in 1740 as an umbrella organization for all Hoi An's ethnic Chinese population. Thien Hau graces the altar but the hall is nowadays used mainly as a language school where local ethnic Chinese children and adults come to learn their mother tongue. The school was closed in 1975 and only permitted to re-open in 1990.

The merchants' houses

The majority of Hoi An's original wooden buildings are found along Tran Phu and south towards the river, which is where you'll find the most well-known merchant's house, at 101 Nguyen Thai Hoc. The **Tan Ky House** is a beautifully preserved example of a two-storey, late eighteenth-century shophouse, amalgamating Vietnamese, Japanese and Chinese influences in an architectural style typical of Hoi An. The present house was built by a second-generation member of the Tan Ky family, who fled China as political refugees in the late sixteenth century, and took eight years to complete. The long, narrow building has shop space at the front, a tiny central courtyard and direct access to the river at the back, from where merchandise would be hauled upstairs to storerooms safe above the floods. The house, wonderfully cluttered with the accumulated property of seven generations grown wealthy from trading silk, tea and rice, is constructed of dark hardwoods, including termite-resistant jackfruit for its main columns. The skill of local woodcarvers is evident throughout, but most stunning is the inlay work: look out for two hanging poem-boards on which mother-of-pearl brush-strokes form exquisitely delicate birds in flight. Guides, speaking French and English, are on hand to answer questions, but at times the house is completely overwhelmed with visitors – far better to come, if you can, at a quieter time (early or late in the day) to appreciate the weight of history here. Diagonally across the street, at 80 Nguyen Thai Hoc, poke your nose in at the **house of Diep Dong Nguyen**. Built at the end of the nineteenth century for a Chinese merchant and later converted into a pharmacy, nowadays the glass medicine cases are stuffed full of dusty family heirlooms.

Just up from the covered bridge at 4 Nguyen Thi Minh Khai, **Phung Hung House** has been home to the same family for eight generations since they moved from Hué in about 1780 to trade cinnamon and hardwoods from the central highlands, as well as silk and glass. The large two-storey house is Vietnamese in style although its eighty ironwood columns and small glass skylights denote Japanese influence, while the gallery and window shutters are in Chinese style. An upstairs living area features a shrine to the ancestors as well as a large shrine to the protector deity Thien Hau, suspended from the ceiling. Prayers were said here for the safe return of family members away on trading trips. A set of seven dice in a bowl on a table in front of the altar used to be thrown to determine the auspicious time to set out on a journey, although a plastic set has since replaced the bone or marble originals.

More modest is **Quan Thang House** at 77 Tran Phu. This single-storey shophouse was founded in the early eighteenth century by a captain from Fujian in China, and was home to a medicine-trading business. It features a courtyard and carved teak partitions in the front room.

On the face of it, Phan Chu Trinh, one block north of Tran Phu, is an unspectacular road but it hides two "family chapels", again houses built by wealthy Chinese merchants, but to a design reflecting their spiritual rather than predominantly commercial focus. Here the central element is an imposing sanctuary room in which stands the ancestral altar, under the guardianship of the family head. On Phan Chu Trinh itself is the 200-year-old **Tran Family Chapel** within a walled compound on the junction with Le Loi. Over homemade lotus-flower tea and sugared coconut you learn about the building and family traditions, going back thirteen generations (300 years) to when the first ancestor settled in Hanoi. The move to Hoi An came, so the story goes, when one son married a Vietnamese woman. Such was the parental disapproval that he fled south to make his fortune trading silk, pepper and ivory in Hoi An, but, miraculously, all was forgiven and the whole family turned up on the doorstep. Succeeding generations continued to shine, with one mandarin to their credit – his portrait and ceremonial sword, bearing the imperial insignia, are displayed in the reception room. On the altar itself, oblong wooden funerary boxes contain a name-tablet and biographical details of deceased family leaders and their wives – carved lotus blossoms indicate adherents of Buddhism. Each year the entire family, in the Tran case more than eighty people, gather round the altar to venerate their ancestors and discuss family affairs.

The smaller, more elaborate **Truong Family Chapel** (not covered by ticket scheme; 7.30am–noon & 2–5pm; small donation expected) is hidden down an alley beside 69 Phan Chu Trinh. The Truong ancestors, like many ethnic Chinese now in Hoi An, fled China in the early eighteenth century following the collapse of the Ming dynasty. The ground-breaking ceremony took place in 1840 at the auspicious moment of 5am on the fifth day of the eleventh lunar month – that is, on the hour of the cat and day of the cat, in the month and year of the mouse. In the late nineteenth century, family members made their first pilgrimage back to Fujian, returning to Hoi An with an unwieldy souvenir of four finely carved wooden partitions for their sanctuary room. This family also embraces mandarin forefathers and cherishes gifts from the Hué court, but more intriguing is an inscribed panel bestowed by Emperor Bao Dai on the wife of the fifth generation who, widowed at 25 and with three children, nevertheless remained faithful to her dead husband.

Museums

Hoi An has a clutch of fairly modest historical museums, the most rewarding of which is the **Museum of Trade Ceramics** at 80 Tran Phu, housed in a traditional timber residence-cum-warehouse. It showcases the history of Hoi An's ceramics trade, which peaked in the fifteenth and sixteenth centuries. Most of the exhibits are sixteenth- or seventeenth-century pieces from Vietnam, China and Japan, although a few Islamic fragments – found on the Cham islands – date from the ninth or tenth centuries. The rear room on the ground floor houses a small display about the architecture of Hoi An.

The **Museum of Sa Huynh Culture**, occupying a two-storey French-era house at 149 Tran Phu, focuses on a distinct culture which flourished along the coast of central Vietnam between the second century BC and the second century AD; the name comes from the town 130km south of Hoi An where evidence was first discovered in 1902 (see p.264). The two-room display comprises a number of metre-high clay funeral urns in which the ashes of the dead were interred, along with a variety of grave goods. Of these, ceramic fragments show trade links to Han-dynasty China, while agate jewellery suggests contact with southern India. Upstairs is an incongruous and predictable display about the French and American wars.

Further east along Tran Phu, the north side of the market square is dominated by the colourful frontage of **Chua Ong**, a seventeenth-century pagoda-temple conversion dedicated to General Quan Cong. Behind the temple lies Hoi An's **Museum of History and Culture**, attractively housed in another former pagoda. Apart from the copies of ancient maps of Fai Fo, the primary appeal of this small, informative museum is its quiet courtyard and carved, wooden door panels, depicting the four sacred animals: crane, dragon, turtle and the mythical kylin.

The market and around

Hoi An **market** retains the atmosphere of a typical, traditional country market, despite the number of tourists. Like most, it's best in the early morning, especially among the riverfront fresh-food stalls. Look out for jars of tiny preserved tangerines, a regional speciality, amid neat stacks of basketware, bowl-shaped lumps of unrefined cane-sugar, liniments, medicinal herbs and every variety of rice. Wandering down through the market square brings you out by the ferry docks and Bach Dang, which regularly disappears each autumn under the swollen **Thu Bon River**. The floods are bad news for Hoi An's ancient buildings, occasionally precipitating the collapse of weakened roofs and walls, and the deterioration of the fabric as pollution levels increase. The worst flood in recent years was in 1999 when the water rose over two metres, causing enormous damage to the nearby restaurants and houses, but for the most part you can go dry-shod along Bach Dang and watch the river scene from beneath the cheery awning of a waterside café. It's a spectacle best captured between 6 and 7am when the fishing boats are unloading their catch.

From the market, walk east along the river and you come to Phan Boi Chau, where the town takes on a distinctly European flavour – louvred shutters, balconies and stucco – in what was the beginnings of a **French quarter**. The interiors of these late nineteenth-century townhouses are characterized by vast, high-ceilinged rooms and enormous roof-spaces, markedly different from the Chinese abodes. You can take a brief tour round **Tran Duong House**, at no. 25, the home of an enterprising man who owns a smattering of period furniture (small donation expected).

Eating and drinking

Hoi An has a fine choice of **restaurants** at which you can sample an array of local speciality dishes (see box overleaf) or opt for some fairly upmarket international cuisine. In the evenings, tables and chairs line Bach Dang, looking more Mediterranean than Vietnamese, while Tran Phu has no shortage of popular outlets, spreading up Nguyen Hue near the market. There's also a growing number of restaurants on Le Loi and round the corner on Phan Dinh Phung, which is now something of a backpacker centre. Hoi An even boasts a few **bars** nowadays, the best of which occupy restored merchants' houses.

Bar 102 102 Nguyen Thai Hoc. The latest addition to Hoi An's burgeoning bar scene occupies a UNESCO-listed building. French-run, it serves a wide range of local and imported beers, cocktails with and without alcohol, tapas and meze.

Brother's Café 27 Phan Boi Chau. The food's a bit on the expensive side, but the garden of this beautiful colonial villa on the banks of the Thu Bon River is perfect for a quiet drink. You'll want to linger, especially as the cheapest coffee costs

Hoi An specialities

Hoi An has excellent food of all kinds, including a number of tasty specialities. Most famous is *cao lau*, a mouthwatering bowlful of thick rice-flour **noodles**, bean sprouts and pork-rind croutons in a light soup flavoured with mint and star anise, topped with thin slices of pork and served with grilled rice-flour crackers or sprinkled with crispy rice paper. Legend has it that the genuine article is cooked using water drawn from one particular local well. Lovers of **seafood** should try the delicately flavoured steamed manioc-flour parcels of finely diced crab or shrimp called *banh bao*, translated as "white rose". Lemon, sugar and *nuoc mam*, complemented by a crunchy onion-flake topping, add extra flavour. A local variation of *hoanh thanh chien* (fried wonton), using shrimp and crab meat instead of pork, is also popular. To fill any remaining gaps, there's even a special Hoi An *cake*, *banh it*, made by steaming green-bean paste and strands of sweetened coconut in banana leaves – you'll see these triangular parcels on sale in the market and at various outlets around town, of which the most famous is 22 Tran Phu.

almost $2 and beers around $3 a pop.

Café Can 74 Bach Dang. A welcoming restaurant offering Hoi An specialities and a good-value three-course set menu for $3. As with all these waterside places, you're a target for kids hawking postcards and tiger balm.

Du Di 12 Le Loi. A simple, clean and welcoming backpacker haunt serving above-average traveller-friendly fare – everything from muesli, banana pancakes and hamburger and chips to local dishes.

Faifoo 104 Tran Phu. Locals rate the *banh bao* at this well-established and attractive restaurant to be the best in town. Or for $5 you can tuck into a five-course sampler of Hoi An specialities.

Good Morning Vietnam 34 Le Loi. The popular Ho Chi Minh-based chain has brought its winning formula – authentic pasta and pizza dishes at moderate prices (around $3), plus a bit of ambience – north to Hoi An. There are good, fresh salads for starters and luscious homemade desserts including a chocolate mousse that hits the spot. You can even wash it down with a bottle of Chianti or Valpolicella.

Hoi An Hai San 64 Bach Dang. This seafood restaurant featuring a bizarre blend of Vietnamese, Turkish and Scandinavian dishes (with music to match) is one of the smarter options along the river. There's a choice of three set menus, the most expensive being Turkish meze at $8, or à la carte for around the same price. Portions aren't huge, but the quality is good and the food is well presented.

Hong Phuc 86 Bach Dang. A friendly, good-value and deservedly popular place – get here early for a table on the balcony – in a great waterside location, run by two multilingual female cousins. The signature dish is fish grilled in banana leaf, though the squid with lemon and garlic, or squid with chilli, gar-

lic and sesame, are equally scrumptious. If you want to know the secret, you can sign up for an afternoon cookery class ($10) during which you learn how to make four dishes. Happy hour 5–7.45pm.

Jean's Café 48 Phan Dinh Phung. Cheap prices and a jovial patron have earned this little café a place on the backpacker circuit. It serves all the old favourites – pizza, pasta, sandwiches and omelettes – as well as Vietnamese dishes.

Miss Ly (Cafeteria 22) 22 Nguyen Hue. *Miss Ly's* is a pretty little place with a well-deserved reputation for serving up some of the best *cao lau* and *banh bao* in Hoi An. Try the Vietnamese set menu ($3) to sample a bit of everything. They also offer a good range of vegetarian dishes, plus Vegemite on toast for homesick Aussies.

Nhu Y 2 Tran Phu. Run by the owner of the *Cua Dai* hotel, the restaurant shares the hotel's strong reputation for service and value. Their speciality is grills, such as snapper on banana leaf with ginger or tuna with turmeric, or try the set dinner – a starter, choice of two main courses plus dessert for under $4.

Quan An 18 Hoang Van Thu. On a quiet street near the river, this simple restaurant serves mouthwatering local cuisine at very reasonable prices. The duck dishes are particularly recommended, and they also rustle up a mean fried wonton. While you're waiting, slake your thirst on a glass of chilled *bia tuoi* (local draught beer).

Restaurant du Port 70 Bach Dang. An unpretentious and friendly restaurant on the river offering well-cooked Vietnamese dishes. The four-course menu represents good value at under $4.

Tam Tam Café 2f/110 Nguyen Thai Hoc ☎0510/862212. Stylish French-run bar (serving bar meals such as sandwiches, salads, apple pie and the like) that's open late, with music, pool and happy-hour beers (4–9pm). Head for the comfy sofas at the back if you want to chill out. There's also a separate upscale international restaurant (reservations recommended) ideal for those needing a hearty steak/wine fix on the road. Not cheap, but worth it.

Thang Long 136 Nguyen Thai Hoc. Generous portions of good, fresh food at the quieter end of the waterfront. Kick back and watch the river life drift by – or step inside and surf the Internet.

Treat's Same Same Café 158 Tran Phu. Upbeat bar-restaurant with good music, a shady interior courtyard, pool and cheap happy-hour deals (4–9pm). A second, less popular outlet at 31 Phan Dinh Phung enigmatically promises to be "same same but different".

Arts, handicrafts and shopping

With the influx of tourists, Hoi An is becoming a centre for the **arts**. A delightful hour-long medley of **traditional music and dance** is performed most evenings in a cramped room rather grandly known as the Traditional Arts Theatre, 75 Nguyen Thai Hoc (Mon–Sat 9pm; $3). Folk musicians also play short concerts at the Hoi An Handicraft Workshop, 9 Nguyen Thai Hoc (Mon–Sat 10.15am & 3.15pm; included in ticket scheme, see p.279). Then once a month, vehicles are banned from the town centre, coloured silk lanterns replace electric lights and shopkeepers don traditional costume to celebrate the **Full-Moon Festival** (fourteenth day of the lunar calendar). It's a tourist event, but a great occasion nonetheless: there are traditional music performances, people play Chinese chess and there are the inevitable food stalls set up by the Japanese bridge and on the waterfront, peddling local specialities. During the **Mid-Autumn Festival**, a much bigger affair celebrated nationwide on the fourteenth day of the eighth lunar month, people also float lanterns on the river. In recent years – usually in spring but dates vary – Quang Nam province has also staged a week-long "**cultural heritage**" festival in Hoi An and My Son, including Cham dances and folk songs.

Tourism has also led to a revival in local **crafts**, though there are plenty of second-rate **souvenirs** as well. Dedicated browsers can occupy several hours in the shops and galleries along Tran Phu, Nguyen Thai Hoc and Le Loi, while just over the Japanese bridge a cluster of old houses double as showrooms. Scattered here and there are **workshops** where you can see a range of local crafts, from embroidery, woodcarving and pottery to silk being made by traditional methods; visits are free, though afterwards you'll be directed to the souvenir shop-cum-showroom, not that there's any obligation to buy. The most interesting are the Hoi An Handicraft Workshop at 9 Nguyen Thai Hoc, where they also give folk concerts (see above) and the House of Traditional Handicrafts, 41 Le Loi. The Kim Bong traditional carpentry studio is also worth a look at 108 Nguyen Thai Hoc and look out, too, for a tiny stall at 49 Le Loi where the same family has been making silk lanterns for generations.

Hoi An is now well known for its **silk** and **tailoring**, with prices generally cheaper than those in Hanoi or Ho Chi Minh City. You'll find shops all over town but the original outlet was the market, where even now rows of tailors sit at sewing machines next to rainbow-coloured stacks, and for a few dollars will knock up beautiful garments in a matter of hours. It's worth shopping around and ask to see some finished articles before placing an order. If you have time, it's a good idea to have one item made first to check the quality and fit. A few places with a reputation for reliability include Bi Bi Silk, 13 Phan Chu Trinh, with a good range of linen, wool and silk; the irrepressible Mr Xe at 71 Nguyen Thai Hoc; Thoi Trang, 4 Tran Phu, specializing in men's suits; and the more upmarket Yaly at 47 Nguyen Thai Hoc (Ⓔyalyshop@dng.vnn.vn). To complete the outfit you can have **shoes** made to match. Most shops can do this for you, or there are dozens of outlets towards the bridge on Hoang Dieu.

Listings

Banks and exchange There's an ATM (daily 7am–11pm; Visa and MasterCard only) at Vietcombank's exchange bureau at 37 Tran Hung Dao, where you can also exchange cash and travellers' cheques and get over-the-counter cash advances on credit cards. Other banks with exchange facilities include the main Vietcombank, 21 Nhi Trung; Hoi An Bank, 4 Hoang Dieu; and Vietincombank, 9 Le Loi. Both Sinh Café and An Phu Tourist (see "Tour agencies", below) also handle money exchange and cash advances.

Books If you're looking for new reading matter, browse the secondhand bookshops along Le Loi (nos. 52 and 48 have a wide selection), and Anh Khoa at 18a Phan Dinh Phung; they all take books in exchange.

Email and Internet access While the going rate for Internet access is just 100d per minute in Hoi An, connections can be excruciatingly slow. The main centre of activity is along Phan Dinh Phung and (New) Nhi Trung. Sinh Café, 2 Phan Dinh Phung, and the *Thang Long* restaurant (see "Eating and drinking", above) are among the few places with a printer.

Ferries From the market end of Bach Dang, small ferryboats depart for villages along the Thu Bon River.

Hospital 4 Tran Hung Dao ☎0510/861218.

Laundry Places along Tran Hung Dao offer laundry services at around $0.50 per kilo.

Open-tour buses For tickets and onward reservations contact Sinh Café, 2 Phan Dinh Phung (☎0510/863948, ⓦwww.sinhcafevn.com), or An Phu Tourist, 29 Phan Dinh Phung (☎0510/862643, ⓔanphutourist@hotmail.com). Local operator

Seventeen's, 17 Tran Hung Dao (☎0510/861947, ⓔseventeentours@yahoo.com), also runs minibuses to Da Nang, Hue, Nha Trang and so forth, with stops en route.

Pharmacies In addition to small pharmacies near the hospital, Bac Ai, at 68 Nguyen Thai Hoc, is well stocked.

Police 8 Hoang Dieu ☎0510/861204.

Post office The unusually fancy and well-organized GPO is at 4b Tran Hung Dao (6am–1pm & 2–9pm). There's a sub-post office at 19 Phan Dinh Phung.

River trips Along Bach Dang, sampan owners will take you out on the river for about $1 an hour, or you can take a boat out to the craft villages and downstream as far as the Cua Dai estuary (see below and opposite). Starting prices vary from $3 to $5 per hour for an eight-person boat, but it's worth bargaining.

Tour agencies Hotel booking desks and tour agents along Tran Hung Dao, Phan Dinh Phung and Nhi Trung offer outings to My Son and craft villages around Hoi An. Sinh Café, 2 Phan Dinh Phung (☎0510/863948, ⓦwww.sinhcafevn.com), and An Phu Tourist, 29 Phan Dinh Phung (☎0510/862643, ⓔanphutourist@hotmail.com), are the two biggest operators, but Seventeen's (☎0510/861947, ⓔseventeentours@yahoo.com or laochamsailing@hotmail.com) has some interesting variations, including canoeing on the Thu Bon River and trips out to the Cham Islands (see opposite). All these agents can buy onward train and plane tickets from Da Nang and handle applications for visa extensions for you for a small commission.

Around Hoi An

From Hoi An you can bike out along meandering paths to the white expanse of **Cua Dai Beach**, or hop on a sampan to one of the islands of the Thu Bon River, just for the ride. River tours take you to low-lying, estuarine islands and the craft villages along their banks, while it's also now possible to visit the distant **Cham Islands**, renowned for their sea swallows' nests. Turning inland, Hoi An makes a good base from which to visit the sacred heartland of the ancient Champa kingdom, **My Son**. Despite extensive war damage and the rough ride out there, the sanctuary is well worth devoting a half-day to, a mystical place that still bears witness to the once vibrant Cham civilization. Finally, heading north, both China Beach and the Marble Mountains (see p.299) are convenient stops on the road to Da Nang, or can be covered on an easy day's outing from Hoi An.

Beaches and islands

A popular bike ride takes you 4km east of Hoi An to the clean, white sands of **Cua Dai Beach**. The inevitable hawkers patrol the area, but you can minimize the hassle by walking away from the main centre, or by taking an umbrella and deck chair for the day at one of the many beachfront café-restaurants; in return you'll be expected to buy at least a drink, though many also serve excellent seafood – just be sure to check the prices before ordering. Be prepared, too, for the strict parking regulations, which require you to leave your bicycle or motorbike at the car park a few hundred metres from the beach for a handful of dong; these regulations don't apply if you're heading to one of the resort hotels (see "Accommodation", p.277) south along the beach road. You can also get out to Cua Dai by Honda om ($2 return) or car ($5) – just tell the driver when to come and pick you up.

Even closer at hand, you can take a bike over either Cam Nam or An Hoi bridge and cycle round **Cam Nam Island**. Sandy tracks lead off in all directions between smallholdings and private houses, but the first lane right over Cam Nam Bridge brings you to a great viewpoint with Hoi An across the other side of the river. You can then work your way round to the south side of the island (or simply follow the metalled road from Cam Nam Bridge) and you'll reach a row of waterside restaurants serving *banh dap* (a sandwich of crispy and fresh rice-crackers served with a shellfish dipping sauce) and *hen tron* (fried clams). Even if you aren't tempted, it's a nice breezy place for a drink.

Specialist **craft villages**, inhabited by skilled artisans, developed around Hoi An during the sixteenth and seventeenth centuries. The work of one famous community of woodcarvers, from Kim Bong Village, can be seen throughout Hoi An. Most carpenters have moved out of the village but a handful remain on **Cam Kim Island**, building fishing boats or crafting furniture for export. This large island is a ten-minute ride from the Hoi An ferry station (see "Listings", opposite) heading west up the river. You'll find one of the few surviving boatyards right beside the island's jetty, but it's worth taking a bike over and exploring the rest of the island. Cam Kim is also a stop on the boat trip back from My Son (see overleaf).

A group of mountainous islands lying 10km offshore are clearly visible from the coast near Hoi An. Cu Lao Cham, or the **Cham Islands**, are inhabited by fishermen, the navy and collectors of highly prized birds' nests. Cham islanders have been harvesting sea swallows' nests since the late sixteenth century and today the government-controlled trade contributes greatly to the local economy, with prices up to $2500 per kilo for the culinary delicacy, to which extraordinary medicinal virtues are also attributed. Each spring, when thousands of the tiny, grey-and-black birds nest among the islands' caves and crevices, villagers build bamboo scaffolding or climb up ropes to prise the diminutive structures, about the size of a hen's egg, off the rock. Three thousand people live on the main island, where there's no electricity, but until 1995 even Vietnamese people weren't allowed to visit because of the naval base. Now you can take a boat trip out to the main island (2hr each way) to swim at unspoiled beaches, snorkel over coral reefs and wander around a fishing village – though during the breeding season the smaller islands on which the sea swallows nest are, not surprisingly, off limits.

Although the development of a beach resort is rumoured, as yet there are no hotels on the islands. Hoi An tour agencies (see "Listings", opposite) offer day-trips at around $15–20 per head (with a minimum of 4 people), and Seventeen's can also arrange longer trips with the option of sleeping on board or camping. The best time to visit the islands is in spring (March to June) when the seas are more likely to be calm and the weather is beginning to warm up.

My Son

Vietnam's most evocative Cham site, **MY SON** (daily 6.30am–4.30pm; $3.50, includes jeep transport 3km from the ticket office to the start of the ruins), lies 40km southwest of Hoi An, in a bowl of lushly wooded hills towered over by aptly named Cat's Tooth Mountain. My Son may be no Vietnamese Angkor Wat, but it is now inscribed on UNESCO's World Heritage list, and richly deserves its place on the tourist map. The riot of vegetation that until recently enveloped the site has now largely been cleared away, but the near-tangible sense of faded majesty still hangs over the mouldering ruins, enhanced by the assorted lingam and Sanskrit stelae strewn around and by the isolated rural setting, whose peace is broken only by the wood-gatherers who trace the paths around the surrounding coffee and eucalyptus glades.

Most people visit on a **guided tour** from Hoi An ($2 per person plus entrance; see p.286 for agencies); a popular variation is to return part of the way by boat, stopping at a couple of craft villages along the way ($4 plus entrance). Now that the road to the site, which strikes west from Highway 1 at Duy Xuyen, has been metalled, it's also possible to rent a **motorbike** in Hoi An and travel to My Son independently. If so, it pays to get there early (around 7am) to avoid the worst of the crowds and also the heat.

Excavations at My Son have revealed that Cham kings were buried here as early as the fourth century, indicating that the site was established by the rulers of the early Champa capital of **Simhapura**, sited some 30km back towards the highway, at present-day Tra Kieu. (See box on p.245 for more on the **Kingdom of Champa**.) The stone towers and sanctuaries whose remnants you see today were erected between the seventh and thirteenth centuries, with successive dynasties adding more temples to this holy place, until in its prime it comprised some seventy buildings. The area was considered the domain of gods and god-kings, and living on site would have been an attendant population of priests, dancers and servants.

The inventory of My Son's elegant assembly of ruins, compiled by the French archeologists who discovered them in the late nineteenth century, gathered all its buildings into distinct groups, prosaically labelled A, B, C, and so forth. Within these groups, each monument was given its own number. The Chams' fine **masonry** skills – instead of mortar, they used a resin mixed with ground mollusc shells and crushed bricks, which left only hairline cracks between brick courses – ensured that the passing of the centuries left much for the French to admire. But after the Viet Cong based themselves here in the Sixties, many unique buildings were pounded to oblivion by American B52s, most notably the once magnificent A1 tower. Craters around the site and masonry pocked with shell and bullet holes testify to this tragic period in My Son's history.

While we've outlined a handful of the site's particularly noteworthy edifices below, you'll get most out of My Son simply by wandering at your leisure – but don't stray far from the towers and marked paths, as **unexploded mines** may still be in the ground.

Groups B, C and D

Of all the groupings of ruins at My Son, those labelled B, C and D most warrant your attention: viewing these, it's possible, with a little stirring of the imagination, to visualize how a functioning temple complex would have appeared in My Son's heyday.

Archeologists regard **Group B** as the spiritual epicentre of My Son. Of the central **kalan**, **B1**, only the base remains, along with a lingam discovered under the foundations a few years ago; but stone epitaphs found nearby reveal that it

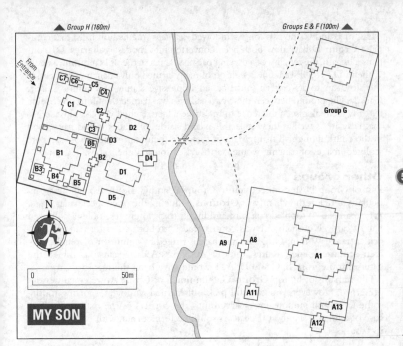

From Entrance ▼

C7 C6 C5 C4
C1 C2
C3 D2
B6 D3
B1 B2 D4
B3 D1
B4 B5
D5

N

Group G

A9 A8
A1
A11
A13
A12

0   50m

MY SON

was dedicated to the god-king Bhadresvara, a hybrid of Shiva and fourth-century King Bhadravarman, and erected in the eleventh century, under King Harivarman IV, on the site of an earlier, wooden temple. Fortunately, other elements of Group B have fared rather better, particularly **B5**, the impressive **repository room**, boasting a bowed, boat-shaped roof still in reasonably good condition. Votive offerings and other ritual paraphernalia would have been stored in B5's chimney-shaped interior, while its outer walls support ornate columns and statues of deities. The carving on the southern facade is particularly well preserved; on the west look out for a fine bas-relief depicting two elephants with their trunks entwined around a coconut tree. The carving of Vishnu sitting below the thirteen heads of the snake-god Naga that adorned the roof of **B6** was an early casualty of war, but the oval receptacle for the holy water used in purification rituals and statue-washing ceremonies is still intact inside. The two smaller temples flanking B1's south side, **B3** and **B4**, would have been dedicated to Skanda and Ganesha, the children of Shiva, while posted around the complex are the remains of seven tiny shrines honouring the gods of the elements and of the points of the compass.

East of the foundations of B1, and precisely aligned with it, is D1 (see overleaf), the **mandapa**, where the priests would meditate prior to proceeding through the (now ruined) gate **B2** to worship.

A similar pattern is at work next door in **Group C**, a complex quite distinct from B and originally separated from it by a wall. This time the central *kalan*, **C1**, is standing and fairly well preserved, though the statue of Shiva that it was built to house long since went to Da Nang's museum, leaving only its base in place. The statues of standing gods around the walls have been allowed to stay, though, as has the carved lintel that runs across the entrance.

East of B and C, the two long, windowed *mandapa* (meditation halls) that comprise **Group D** have now both been converted into modest **galleries**. D1 contains a lingam, the remains of a carving of Shiva, and a statue of Nandi, Shiva's bull; while in **D2** you'll see a fine rendition of many-armed Shiva dancing, and, beside the steps up to its eastern entrance, an impressive statue of Vishnu's vehicle, Garuda. The ground between these two galleries was named the **Court of Stelae** by early archeologists, a reference to the stone tablets, etched with Sanskrit script, that litter it. As well as these stelae, altars and statues of deities would have stood in the court, though all that remain of these are their plinths, on whose sides are sculpted images of dancing women, arms raised to carry their gods.

Other groups

East of Group D, signs direct you to Groups A and G. Bomb damage was particularly cruel in the vicinity of **Group A**, reducing the once spectacular *kalan*, **A1**, to a heap of toppled columns and lintels that closely resembles a collapsed hall of cards. Unusually, A1 was constructed with both an eastern and a western entrance. Within, a huge lingam base is ringed by a number of detailed, fifteen-centimetre-high figures at prayer. You'll pass **A9**, the *mandapa*, and **A8**, the gate, en route from B, C and D; **A11** would have been the repository room.

The remains of hilltop **Group G**, 60m north of Group A, are equally badly preserved. However, you can still pick out horned gargoyles, sporting toothsome fangs and bulbous eyes, carved into the corners of the main *kalan*. The base of a lingam stands at the *kalan*'s southwestern corner, with breasts around its base.

Da Nang

Sitting on the southerly curve of a vast, well-protected bay, **DA NANG** has developed into central Vietnam's dominant port and its third largest city. The real spur to this growth came in the American War when the neighbouring air base spawned the greatest concentration of US military personnel in South Vietnam. But walking around central Da Nang today, it's the earlier, French presence which is more apparent, in the leafy boulevards and colonial edifices along the riverfront promenade. Considering its size (it has a population of around 700,000), its history and the fact that this is a major transport hub offering air connections as well as road and rail links, Da Nang is an unexpectedly amiable place.

Though Da Nang harbours few specific sights of its own beyond the **Cham Museum** with its unique collection of Cham sculpture, the city makes a reasonable base for exploring this stretch of coast. Some of Vietnam's best **beaches** are to be found only a few kilometres from the city (see "Around Da Nang", p.298), while, further afield, My Son (see p.288) and Hoi An itself can be covered on day-trips.

Some history

During the sixteenth and seventeenth centuries trading vessels waiting to unload at Fai Fo (Hoi An) often sheltered in nearby Da Nang Bay, until Hoi An's harbour began silting up and Da Nang developed into a major **port** in its own right. After 1802, when Hué became capital of Vietnam, Da Nang naturally served as the principal point of arrival for foreign delegations to the royal court. The new emperor, Gia Long, had earlier promised France a concession at Da Nang (which the French called **Tourane**) in return for their help in gaining the throne, but it didn't become a reality until 1888 after the French had repeatedly attacked the port.

In 1954 Vietnam was effectively partitioned at the Seventeenth Parallel only 200km north of Da Nang, from where bombing sorties could easily reach into communist-held territory or strike westwards to the Ho Chi Minh Trail. The city grew rapidly around the South Vietnamese air base and then mushroomed after 1965 when America entered the war in earnest, heralded by the arrival of the first American combat troops on March 8, 1965. An advance guard of two battalions of Marines waded ashore at Red Beach in Da Nang Bay, providing the press with a photo opportunity that included amphibious landing craft, helicopters and young Vietnamese women handing out garlands – not quite as the generals had envisaged. The Marines had come to defend Da Nang's massive **US Air Force base**; as the troops flew in so the base sprawled. Eventually Da Nang became "a small American city", as journalist John Pilger remembers it, "with its own generators, water purification plants, hospitals, cinemas, bowling alleys, ball parks, tennis courts, jogging tracks, supermarkets and bars, lots of bars". For most US troops the approach to Da Nang airfield formed their first impression of Vietnam, and it was here they came to take a break from the war at the famous **China Beach**.

At the same time the city swelled with thousands of **refugees**, mostly villagers cleared from "free-fire zones" but also people in search of work – labourers, cooks, laundry staff, pimps, prostitutes and drug pushers, all inhabiting a shantytown called Dogpatch on the base perimeter. Da Nang's population rose inexorably: 20,000 in the 1940s, 50,000 in 1955 and, some estimate, a peak of one million during the American years. North Vietnamese mortar shells periodically fell in and around the base, but the city's most violent scenes occurred when two South Vietnamese generals engaged in a little power struggle. In March 1966 Vice Air Marshal Ky, then prime minister of South Vietnam, ousted a popular Hué overlord, General Thi, following his open support of Buddhist dissidents. Demonstrations spread from Hué to Da Nang where troops loyal to Thi seized the airfield in what amounted to a **mini civil war**. After much posturing Ky crushed the revolt two months later, killing hundreds of rebel troops and many civilians. In the preceding chaos, the beleaguered rebels held forty Western journalists hostage for a brief period in Da Nang's largest pagoda, Chua Tinh Hoi, while streets around filled with Buddhist protesters.

When the North Vietnamese Army finally arrived to **liberate** Da Nang on March 29, 1975, they had less of a struggle. Communist units had already cut the road south and panic-stricken South Vietnamese soldiers battled for space on any plane or boat leaving the city, firing on unarmed civilians. Many drowned in the struggle to reach fishing boats, while planes and tanks were abandoned to the enemy. Da Nang had been all but deserted by South Vietnamese forces, leaving the mighty base to be "taken by a dozen NLF cadres waving white handkerchiefs from the back of a truck", according to John Pilger. After 1975 thousands of refugees living in Da Nang were sent back to their native villages or packed off to reclaim agricultural land. Da Nang's army faction still wields considerable power but their grip is beginning to weaken, as evidenced by a more liberal outlook, less suspicion of foreigners, and an upbeat local economy.

In 1997, Da Nang's administration was separated from that of Quang Nam Province and placed in the hands of the central government, joining Hanoi, Ho Chi Minh City and Haiphong. The move reflected plans to develop the city as a regional hub for tourism and trade, both nationally and internationally. Da Nang is also hoping to benefit from the much touted "trans-Asia link"

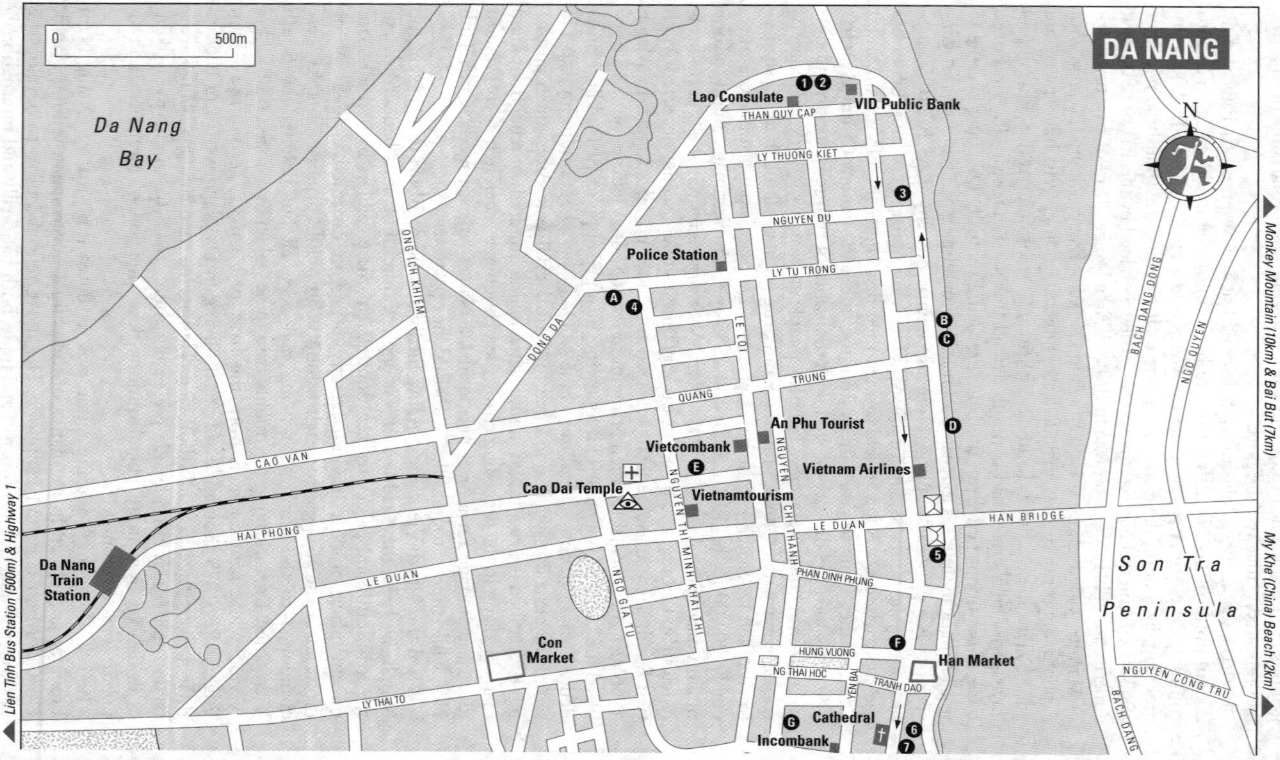

DA NANG

Monkey Mountain (10km) & Bai But (7km)

My Khe (China) Beach (2km)

Son Tra Peninsula

NGO QUYEN

BACH DANG DONG

NGUYEN CONG TRU

BACH DANG

HAN BRIDGE

Han Market

TRAN HAO

VID Public Bank

Lao Consulate

THAN QUY CAP

LY THUONG KIET

NGUYEN DU

LY TU TRONG

TRUNG

Vietnam Airlines

LE DUAN

An Phu Tourist

NGUYEN CHI THANH

PHAN DINH PHUNG

HUNG VUONG

YEN BAI

NG THAI HOC

Cathedral

Incombank

Police Station

LE LOI

QUANG

Vietcombank

Vietnamtourism

NGUYEN THI MINH KHAI THI

DONG DA

Cao Dai Temple

NGO GIA TU

Con Market

ONG ICH KHIEM

LE DUAN

LY THAI TO

Da Nang Bay

CAO VAN

HAI PHONG

Da Nang Train Station

500m

0

Lien Tinh Bus Station (500m) & Highway 1

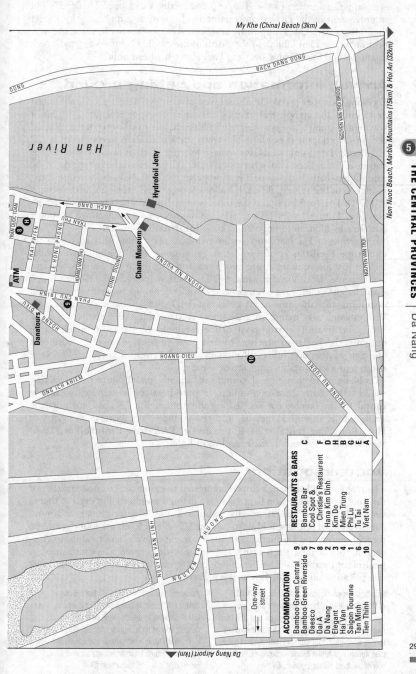

My Khe (China) Beach (3km) ▲

Non Nuoc Beach, Marble Mountains (15km) & Hoi An (32km) ►

BACH DANG DONG

DONG

Han River

Hydrofoil Jetty

NGUYEN VAN TROI BRIDGE

BACH DANG

TRAN QUOC TOAN

THAI PHIEN

TRAN PHU

LE HONG PHONG

HOANG VAN THU

Cham Museum

TRUONG ON VUONG

ATM

Danatours

THU

PHAN CHU TRINH

LE DINH DUONG

HOANG DIEU

NGUYEN VAN TROI

ONG ICH KHIEM

HOANG DIEU

TRUONG ON VUONG

NGUYEN VAN LINH

NGUYEN TRI PHUONG

▲ Da Nang Airport (1km)

One-way
street

ACCOMMODATION

Bamboo Green Central	9
Bamboo Green Riverside	5
Daesco	7
Dai A	8
Da Nang	2
Elegant	3
Hai Van	4
Saigon Tourane	1
Tan Minh	6
Tien Thinh	10

RESTAURANTS & BARS

Bamboo Bar	C
Cool Spot &	F
Christie's Restaurant	
Hana Kim Dinh	D
Kim Do	H
Mien Trung	B
Phi Lu	G
Tu Tai	E
Viet Nam	A

– a planned upgrade of Laos's Route 9 connecting Vietnam to Thailand – and improvement of the city's infrastructure has been made a high priority. Direct flights from Bangkok, Hong Kong and Siam Reap are already in place, the new port facility at Lien Chieu, to the north of the city, has been completed, and a much needed road bridge over the Han River has been built.

Arrival, information and getting around

Da Nang's **airport** is only 3km southwest of the city. There are a couple of taxi desks inside the arrivals hall offering reasonable rates for Hoi An ($10), but if you're only going to the city centre, it's a little cheaper to take one of the metered taxis waiting outside ($2 or less). The **train station** lies 2km west of town at 122 Hai Phong. Long-distance **buses** arrive a kilometre further out at Lien Tinh bus station, 33 Dien Bien Phu, where local buses also gather on the other side of the road. **Open-tour buses** generally drop passengers at the Cham Museum, at the south end of Bach Dang, although An Phu Tourist's buses stop outside their office at 147 Le Loi. An Phu is also the most switched-on of Da Nang's **tour agencies** (see "Listings", p.298). They offer various day-trips, mostly aimed at budget travellers, in addition to providing a basic **information** service.

If arriving in Da Nang on an international flight, note that there are no **exchange facilities** at the airport, so bring some small-denomination dollar bills to pay for your transport into town, and then head for one of the city-centre banks. Both Vietcombank, 140 Le Loi, and Incombank, 36 Tran Quoc Toan, handle credit card advances and travellers' cheques, with a more limited operation for the northern hotels at VID Public Bank, 2 Tran Phu. Vietcombank also maintains a 24-hour ATM outside the *Orient Hotel* at 97 Phan Chu Trinh. The main **post office** overlooks the river at 60 Bach Dang, but cross the Le Duan junction to find poste restante at no. 66, announcing "foreign services post office". Bookstalls along the riverfront here sell Da Nang **maps** and local English-language newspapers.

Da Nang is big enough and its sights sufficiently spread out to make walking round town fairly time-consuming. If your hotel can't help with **bicycle rental**, try the *Bamboo Bar* (see "Eating and drinking", p.297) or Danatours; the going rate is around $1 per day. Otherwise, there's no shortage of cyclos or Honda om. **Car rental** ($20–40 per day) and self-drive **motorbikes** ($5–8) are available from tour agencies and most hotels.

Accommodation

The majority of Da Nang's **hotels** are geared to either the business traveller or the tour group. Off-season bargaining is a definite possibility, but even so there's very little for the budget traveller, who will find a better choice and more attractive set of options in Hoi An (see pp.277–278). Hotels are found scattered throughout central Da Nang, with the more expensive places tending to concentrate on or near Bach Dang. If you fancy the seaside, accommodation is available at nearby My Khe Beach (see p.300), and the luxurious Furama resort (see p.300) is also within easy striking distance.

Bamboo Green Central 158 Phan Chu Trinh ☎ 0511/822996, ✉ bamboogreen1@dng.vnn.vn. Upmarket hotel popular with tour groups and business people. A good range of facilities, including money exchange, tour desk, restaurant and bar, plus decent – if rather bland – rooms make this one of the best hotels in town. ❹

Bamboo Green Riverside 68 Bach Dang ☎ 0511/832591, ✉ riversidets@dng.vnn.vn. The latest addition to the *Bamboo* chain makes up for smaller rooms with slightly cheaper prices and river views from most rooms, some with balcony. Facilities include Internet access as well as a restaurant, bar and tour desk. ❹

Heading on **up the coast to Hué** it's a difficult choice between road and rail over the dramatic Hai Van Pass. If you plump for **train**, the early-afternoon E2 service is fastest; ask for seats on the right, looking east, for the best views as the train hugs the cliff. Highway 1 winds much higher but keeps more inland and clouds often shroud the top. **Local buses** for Hué leave from the main Lien Tinh bus station, and **open-tour buses** ($3) pick up passengers outside the Cham Museum or from An Phu Tourist at 147 Le Loi; open-tour services stop briefly at the Hai Van Pass and Lang Co Beach. Alternatively, hire a car and driver ($25–45) for the three-hour trip so you can enjoy the scenery at your leisure.

Though you miss out on the panoramic views, it's also now possible to travel between Da Nang and Hué by hydrofoil. Services depart once a day from in front of Da Nang's Cham Museum. The journey takes two hours and costs around $4.

Travelling south from Da Nang, Honda om compete to whisk you off to **Non Nuoc** (for the Marble Mountains and beach) for $2, and to **Hoi An**. A one-way ride to Hoi An (45min) should cost $3 including waiting time at the Marble Mountains; the same journey by taxi or hire car will come in at around $10–15. Local buses run out to Hoi An from Lien Tinh bus station but are way too overcrowded to be a comfortable, or safe, proposition. A more popular option is one of the open-tour buses ($3), with a choice of morning services via the Marble Mountains or direct afternoon services. Open-tour buses also leave daily for Nha Trang ($8–10), Da Lat ($13–15) and other destinations en route to Ho Chi Minh ($16–17). You can get tickets for An Phu Tourist buses from their office. For other services, tour agents and hotels should be able to help.

The most popular land crossing **into Laos** open to foreigners is Lao Bao border gate, west of Dong Ha (see p.333 for details). Tourist visas for Laos are obtainable at the Lao Consulate in Da Nang, located at 16 Tran Quy Cap (☎0511/821208; Mon–Fri 8–11.30am & 2–4.30pm). A thirty-day tourist visa will cost around $50 to $60 and a seven-day transit visa around $25 to $40, depending on your nationality. In either case you need two passport photos, and visas are issued on the spot. **International bus** services run from Da Nang's Lien Tinh bus station direct to Savannakhet four times a week (Mon, Wed, Thurs & Sun at 6.30pm; 24hr; $17). There's often a delay at the border while you wait for the 7am opening. Tickets are available through tour agents and hotels.

From Da Nang airport Vietnam Airlines operates at least three **flights** a day to Ho Chi Minh City. There are also now direct international services to Bangkok, Hong Kong and Siam Reap.

Da Nang 1–3 Dong Da ☎0511/821986, @dananghotel@dng.vnn.vn. Rooms in the reno-vated western block of this sprawling complex, once the US Army officers' billets, are comfortable enough with phone, satellite TV and air-con. The eastern block, where you'll find the cheapest rooms, is grubby and run-down, and only for the desperate. ❶–❸

Daesco 155 Tran Phu ☎0511/892807, @daescohotel@dng.vnn.vn. Another business hotel with reasonably well equipped rooms, all with balcony, though it's worth paying a little more for better-quality furnishings in the "Superior" rooms. Internet access, fitness centre, and top-floor restaurant complete the picture. ❹

Dai A 51 Yen Bai ☎0511/827532, @daiahotel@dng.vnn.vn. A central location,

friendly welcome and simple but well-maintained rooms, all with bathroom, air-con and satellite TV, make this a popular option at the cheaper end of the market. ❸

Elegant 22a Bach Dang ☎0511/892893, @ele-gant@dng.vnn.vn. Efficient business hotel on the riverfront which lives up to its name. Both the decor and standard of furnishings are a cut above the competition at this price range. There's a restaurant, bar, small business centre and money-exchange facilities. ❹

Hai Van 2 Nguyen Thi Minh Khai ☎0511/821300, ⓕ821300. It could do with a lick of paint, but oth-erwise this budget hotel offers reasonable value for money. Big, basic rooms have bathroom, hot water, TV, phone and air-con, or pay extra for a few more creature comforts. ❷–❸

Saigon Tourane 5 Dong Da ☎0511/821021, ⓦwww.saigontourane.com.vn. The most upmarket hotel in town boasts a restaurant serving international cuisine, piano-bar, health club and business centre. The 82 rooms are very comfortable, equipped to three-star standards, albeit slightly soulless. It's also a little out of the way. ❹

Tan Minh 142 Bach Dang ☎0511/827456, ⓔtanminhhotel@dng.vnn.vn. Popular hotel at the south end of Bach Dang, handy for the Cham Museum, with basic but adequate rooms with air-con, phone and fridge. Those at the rear are quieter and slightly cheaper. ❷

Tien Thinh 448 Hoang Dieu ☎0511/834566, ⓔtthotel@dng.vnn.vn. Small, welcoming hotel providing good service and excellent value for money. Bright and absolutely immaculate rooms come with satellite TV, bathroom with tub and IDD phone as standard. The only drawback is its out-of-centre location. ❷

The City

The elongated oval of Da Nang occupies a small headland protruding into the southern curve of Da Nang Bay. The city faces east, fronting onto Bach Dang and the Han River, across which the narrow Son Tra Peninsula shelters it from the South China Sea. Its streets follow a rough grid plan, dissected by two main thoroughfares, Le Duan and Le Loi/Phan Chu Trinh. Hung Vuong and streets around form the commercial heart of Da Nang, running between the two central **markets**: sprawling, oppressive Cho Con in the west and orderly Cho Han by the river. Two blocks south of Han market, past the soft, salmon-mousse cathedral, colonial Da Nang is represented by a few wooden and stucco houses at the eastern end of Tran Quoc Toan. From here turn right along riverfront **Bach Dang** for 750m to reach the **Cham Museum**, the city's only real tourist attraction, or left to stroll north past a collection of well-restored French-era administrative buildings, some of them now occupied by People's Committees and hotels.

The Cham Museum

Even if you're just passing through Da Nang, try to spare an hour for the small **Cham Museum** at 2 Duong 2 Thang 9 (daily 7am–5pm; $1.30), particularly if you plan to visit the Cham ruins at My Son (see p.288). Note that the duplicated booklet, "Cham Sculpture Museum" ($1.30), on sale at the kiosk, is an academic work, outlining the historical background and Cham artistic development, rather than a guide to the exhibits.

The museum sits in a garden of frangipani trees at the south end of Bach Dang, and its display of graceful, sometimes severe, terracotta and sandstone figures gives a tantalizing glimpse of an artistically inspired culture that ruled most of southern Vietnam for a thousand years (see box on p.245 for more on the Kingdom of Champa). In the late nineteenth century French archeologists started collecting statues, friezes and altars from once magnificent Cham cities and sanctuaries dotted around the hinterland of Da Nang. In 1916 they opened the museum in an attractive, open-sided building whose design incorporates Cham motifs. Though this is undoubtedly the most comprehensive display of Cham art in the world, it's said many of the best statues were carried off into European private collections.

A long-overdue extension at the rear of the museum is due to open in 2004, but for the moment exhibits are grouped according to their place of origin in four rooms starting from the left as you enter: sculpture from My Son (fourth to eleventh centuries) in the left wing; Tra Kieu (Simhapura; fourth to tenth centuries) in the connecting building, with the Dong Duong pieces (Indrapura; eighth to tenth centuries) in a room behind; and finally, sculpture from Binh Dinh Province (eleventh to fifteenth centuries) occupies the right wing. Recurring images in Cham art are lions, elephants and Hindu deities, predominantly Shiva (founder and defender of Champa) expressed either as a vigorous, full-lipped man or as a lingam, but Vishnu, Garuda, Ganesha and Nandi the bull are also portrayed. Buddhas feature strongly in the ninth-century art of Indrapura, a period when Khmer and Indonesian influences were gradually assimilated. But the most distinctive icon is Uroja, a breast and nipple that represents the universal "mother" of Cham kings.

The first two rooms demonstrate Cham art at its height. A massive, square altar pedestal (late seventh century) from the religious centre of My Son is considered a masterpiece of early Cham craftsmanship, particularly its frieze depicting jaunty dancing-girls, and a soulful flute player. However, experts and amateurs alike usually nominate two lithe dancers with Mona Lisa smiles, their soft, round bodies seemingly clad in nothing but strings of pearls, as the zenith of Cham artistry. The piece, displayed in the second room, also features two musicians on a fragment of capital produced by Tra Kieu sculptors in the late tenth century, just before Cham art, and the Champa kingdom, started to decline. A monumental, seventh-century altar dominates the Tra Kieu exhibits; scenes of Princess Sita's wedding from the Hindu epic *Ramayana* decorate the pedestal frieze.

As the Viets pushed south during the eleventh century, so the Chams retreated, and their sculptures evolved a bold, cubic style. Though less refined than earlier works, the chunky mythical animals from this period retain a distinctive, playful charm and a pleasing solidity.

Cao Dai Temple

Da Nang's **Cao Dai Temple** at 63 Hai Phong opposite the hospital, built in 1956, is Vietnam's second most important after Tay Ninh (see p.129), where an elderly archbishop, assisted by fifteen priests, ministers to a congregation said to number 50,000. The temple, which sees few tourists, is a smaller, simpler version of Tay Ninh, dominated inside by the all-seeing eye of the Supreme Being and paintings of Cao Dai's principal saints, Lao-tzu, Confucius, Jesus Christ and Buddha (see box on p.130 for more on these tenets). Services were banned between 1975 and 1986 and the building locked up, but now adherents gather to worship four times a day (6am, noon, 6pm & midnight). The occasional tourists who do turn up find it has more erratic opening times than its larger sister temple outside Ho Chi Minh City; you may find the gate locked when there is no service on.

Eating and drinking

Da Nang has no shortage of places to eat, ranging from food stalls to full-blown, top-notch restaurants. Fruitful hunting grounds for local restaurants and **food stalls** are the west end of Hai Phong and streets to the south of Hung Vuong, particularly Nguyen Chi Thanh. For a mid-morning snack, browse the little **bakeries** at the north end of Phan Chu Trinh. There are also a couple of decent **bars** where, amongst other things, you can quaff the local beers – Da Nang Export and Bière la Rue.

Bamboo Bar 11 Bach Dang. Cosy riverside bar-cum-restaurant with cheap beers, good music, free pool and a breezy terrace. They also serve tasty Western and Vietnamese home cooking along the lines of mashed potatoes, baked tuna with veg and spring rolls – at reasonable prices. Bicycle and motorbike rental available.

Cool Spot & Christie's Restaurant 112 Tran Phu. This Japanese/Australian-owned bar and restaurant doesn't pack the atmosphere of the *Bamboo Bar*, but if you suddenly have a craving for *yakitori* or lemon pie, this is the place for you. You can eat at the bar or in the upstairs restaurant, where there's also a small book exchange.

Hana Kim Dinh 15 Bach Dang. Da Nang's attempt at plush dining, a floating restaurant to the north of the Han Bridge, in air-con rooms or outside terraces. It's not as expensive as it looks and the quality is good, a mix of Western and Asian foods, with fish specialities. Alternatively, settle back into one of the comfy cane chairs for a quiet coffee or early-evening drink.

Kim Do 180 Tran Phu. Da Nang's best-known restaurant serves a broad range of Chinese cuisine. Comfortable, air-con dining to soothing music with attentive service, though a bit touristy for some. The portions can be on the small side, but with a bit of care you can eat reasonably well for around $10 per head – or splash out on the *salangane* (sea swallow) nest at $16 a pop.

Mien Trung 9 Bach Dang. Big, open-fronted riverside restaurant catering mostly to a local crowd.

Minimal decor is offset by an extensive choice of reasonably priced Vietnamese dishes. You won't leave hungry.

Phi Lu 225 Nguyen Chi Thanh. Bustling Chinese place popular with the locals. It's less slick than the *Kim Do*, and lacking in ambience, but it's also less expensive; main dishes cost around $2–3, or plump for a filling noodle or fried-rice dish at just over $1.

Tu Tai 62 Hai Phong. Cheap and cheerful street kitchen serving a mean *com ga* (chicken rice) and other rice dishes. If they're full, try the noodles at *Mi Quang* across the street.

Viet Nam 53–55 Ly Tu Trong. It's worth the walk to this excellent popular eatery where well-prepared and well-priced dishes come in small, medium or large sizes. The fresh trout is highly recommended.

Listings

Airlines Pacific Airlines, 35 Nguyen Van Linh ☏0511/583538; PB Air, Da Nang Airport ☏0511/656060, ⓦpbair.com; Siam Reap Airways, 84 Nguyen Van Linh ☏0511/582361;Vietnam Airlines, 35 Tran Phu ☏0511/821130.

Banks and exchange Vietcombank, 140 Le Loi; Incombank, 36 Tran Quoc Toan; VID Public Bank, 2 Tran Phu. Da Nang's first 24hr ATM is at 97 Phan Chu Trinh.

Hospital Benh Vien C, 74 Hai Phong, opposite the Cao Dai Temple ☏0511/821480.

Immigration police 78 Le Loi. The place to go if you've lost your passport or have similar difficulties.

Internet access Club Internet at 90 Hai Phong has plenty of machines, or there are a couple of places at 51 and 64 Tran Quoc Toan.

Post office Main office at 60 Bach Dang, poste restante at no. 66; other branches at 80 Hung

Vuong, 41 Tran Quoc Toan and 20 Dong Da.

Silks and tailoring Outlets line the north end of Phan Chu Trinh (try Hanh Silk Shop at no. 91), although the best quality and prices are to be found in Hoi An.

Taxi Dana Taxi ☏0511/815815; Airport Taxi ☏0511/615615.

Tour agents and open-tour buses An Phu Tourist, 147 Le Loi ☏0511/818366, ⓔanphuc-ndn@yahoo.com; Danatours, 25 Hoang Dieu ☏0511/825653, ⓔdanamarle@dng.vnn.vn; Vietnamtourism, 83 Nguyen Thi Minh Khai ☏0511/823660, ⓔvitoursdad@dng.vnn.vn. An Phu Tourist's open-tour buses stop outside their office, while other operators drop off and pick up passengers outside the Cham Museum; local tour agents will be able to help with tickets and reservations.

Around Da Nang

Beaches are mostly what's around Da Nang, from Red Beach (Nam O) in the north where the first US Marines came ashore, down the broad, bleached-white fringe of **China Beach** (My Khe), and continuing all the way south through **Non Nuoc** to Hoi An. Of all the beaches in Vietnam, these are the most coveted by international developers, though only one resort has been completed so far along this empty, attractive coastline. A note of warning, however: there's a powerful undertow off this coast and when the northeast, winter monsoon blows up, riptides become particularly dangerous. Guards patrol the main swimming beaches during the day, where flags also indicate safe spots. Best months on the beach are April to August, with the peak season for local holidaymakers in July and August.

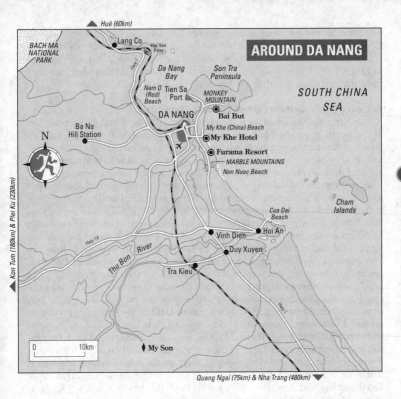

Heading south down the coast, past old US installations occupied these days by the People's Army, you come to a group of abrupt hills constituting the coast's other main tourist attraction, usually a stop on the trip to or from Hoi An: the **Marble Mountains**. The five limestone and marble knobbles are peppered with sacred caves, wrapped in legend – and liberally sprinkled with souvenir stands. For generations Non Nuoc Village at the mountains' base has resonated with the chink of stone masons chiselling away at religious statues, memorials and imitation Cham figures. Further south still, both Hoi An (p.274) and My Son (pp.288–290) can also be visited on day-trips from Da Nang. Another possible excursion is to **Ba Na**, west of Da Nang, where an old French hill station has been developed as a summer retreat.

Up the coast from Da Nang, Highway 1 zigzags over the **Hai Van Pass**, affording sweeping views of the bay and north to the brilliant white sands of **Lang Co** beach. From here you can head into the mountains to explore the walking trails of **Bach Ma National Park**, where the remains of another French-era hill station are swamped by some of the most lush vegetation in the whole of Vietnam. All three places can be visited on a long day's excursion from Da Nang, or covered on the road to Hué.

South of Da Nang

Long, lumpy Son Tra Peninsula, tipped by **Monkey Mountain**, shelters Da Nang and its port from the worst winter monsoons. The peninsula's seaward side provides the city with its nearest unpolluted beach, My Khe, the original **China Beach**. Its rival to the south, the quieter **Non Nuoc Beach**, also claims the same sobriquet. If you're heading for Non Nuoc, or down the coast to Hoi An, the honeycomb cave-shrines of the **Marble Mountains**, just back from the beach, are worth a quick trot round in passing.

Monkey Mountain and China Beach

A low-lying neck of land forms the Han River's east bank and then rises 700m in the north to rolling Nui Tien Sa. The name means "descending angels", a reference to heavenly creatures who apparently would often alight on the summit for a game of chess, but most people know it as **Monkey Mountain** on account of its wildlife population. Monkeys still inhabit the promontory, which is mostly a restricted military area. At present you can follow the busy road out to Tien Sa docks, 15km from central Da Nang, past an Export Processing Zone and nineteenth-century European graves. A few people with their own transport have made it past the military for a panorama from Tien Sa's first cluster of observatories, but otherwise, skirt round the northern tip where you can scramble down to coves and beaches in several places. A new road along the promontory's south coast provides easier access to a sandy cove called **Bai But**, about 8km from the city centre. At weekends Da Nang day-trippers fill the beach, but at other times it's a good place to escape the noise and bustle of the city. Refreshments and reasonably priced seafood are on offer at a simple bar-restaurant behind the beach. A return trip to Bai But by Honda om will cost around $5 including a couple of hours' waiting time.

Da Nang's nearest beach resort, My Khe, lies at the southern end of the peninsula and less than 3km southeast of the centre, close enough to fill with Da Nang townspeople at dawn and dusk though largely empty during the day. My Khe is better known as **China Beach** where US servicemen were helicoptered in for R&R during the American War. Just behind the beach the *My Khe Hotel* (T0511/836125, F836123; ❸–❹) offers slightly pricey **accommodation** – it's worth paying the extra for a room in the new block, but even so the hotel's best asset is its location. As for eating, stalls along the seafront sell ultra-fresh seafood. A Honda om should cost under $1 for the ride from Da Nang.

Three kilometres south again, on the road to Hoi An and the Marble Mountains, you come to a turning for Bac My An Beach, which is home to the five-star *Furama Resort* (T0511/847888, Wwww.furamavietnam.com; ❻). This $40-million development set in lush gardens stands out as Vietnam's top beach resort. It offers luxuriously appointed rooms, international cuisine, two swimming pools plus a guarded beach and a range of recreational activities from tennis and golf to scuba-diving, ocean kayaking and windsurfing. Prices reflect the high standards of service and accommodation.

The Marble Mountains

As you continue down the road to Hoi An, an unattractive stretch of storage tanks and scrubby, postwar wasteland eventually gives way to Vietnam's most southerly limestone outcrops, known as the **Marble Mountains**. Despite all the fuss, only one of the mountains' caves rates above ordinary, but it's a good place to stretch your legs and admire the views. A torch is useful for exploring the caves and, although everything is well signposted, it's still worth picking up a sketch map (small charge) at the ticket desk.

The simplest way of covering the 12km to the Marble Mountains and Non Nuoc **from Da Nang** is by **car**, **Honda om** ($2) or **bicycle**. Just past the first mountain, turn left at a T-junction down a road called Huyen Tran Cong Chua and find the main entrance on your left after a few hundred metres. Da Nang city **buses** run infrequently out to Non Nuoc (7am–5pm), heading down Phan Chu Trinh and terminating at the Non Nuoc T-junction. Finally, if you can face the scrum, Hoi An-bound **pick-ups** will drop you off at Non Nuoc. If you're pressing on from here, Hoi An is another 20km down the coast from Non Nuoc – take a Honda om ($2) or squeeze onto a passing local bus.

Local **mythology** tells of the Turtle God hatching a divine egg on the shore from which emerged a nymph as the shell cracked into five pieces, represented by the five small mountains. Historically, Cham people came here to worship their Hindu gods and then erected Buddhist altars in the caves, which became places of pilgrimage, drawing even the Nguyen kings to the sacred site. When Ho Chi Minh died, marble from these mountains was used for his mausoleum in Hanoi, but quarrying has since been banned. In Vietnamese the mountains are named Ngu Hanh Son, meaning the five ritual elements: Thuy Son (water mountain) and Moc Son (wood) to the east of the road; Tho Son (earth), Kim Son (gold or metal) and Hoa Son (fire) to the west.

The highest, at 107m, and most important mountain is **Thuy Son** (5am–5pm). Two staircases, built for the visit of Emperor Minh Mang, lead up its southern flank. The main, westernmost entrance, the first you reach coming from the main road, brings you to the hollow summit surrounded by jagged rocks with grottoes in every direction. In the middle the Tam Thai Pagoda sits beside a crossroads. Turn left here, pass through a narrow defile, under a natural rock arch and you enter the antechamber to the most impressive of Thuy Son's warren of **cave pagodas**; follow the path to the left of the sandstone Quan Am statue, down steep, dark steps into the eerie half-light and swirling incense of **Huyen Khong Cave**. Straight ahead across the thirty-metre-high cavern is a large, seated Buddha, while small altars and temples around venerate Hindu, Buddhist, Taoist and Confucian deities. Locals will point out stalactites resembling wrinkled faces and so on, but the cave's best feature is its roof through which midday sunlight streams like spotlights. A wall plaque commemorates a deadly accurate women's Viet Cong guerrilla unit, based here during the American War, which destroyed 19 planes with just 22 rockets.

Backtracking to Tam Thai Pagoda, the path heading east under a couple more rock arches climbs slightly before starting to descend towards the eastern exit, affording expansive views over Non Nuoc Beach, the Cham Islands and north to Monkey Mountain. About halfway down you pass Linh Ung Pagoda behind which lurks **Tang Chon Cave**, in this case occupied by tenth-century Cham Hindu altars and two Buddhas, one sitting and one standing.

You emerge again at the foot of the mountain in **NON NUOC** Village. Since the fifteenth century, Non Nuoc has been inhabited by stone-carvers, who coax life out of the local white, grey and rose marble. Nowadays workshops generally churn out mass-produced souvenirs using marble imported from Thanh Hoa Province, but it's fascinating to watch the masons at work – just follow your ears.

Non Nuoc Beach

Follow the paved road east from Non Nuoc Village for about 500m, round a dogleg, and you reach **Non Nuoc Beach**, promoted locally as "new China Beach". Huge, empty, and consisting of clean, fine white sand, it's far enough from Da Nang to leave you unpestered. There's a cluster of cafés, restaurants and souvenir stalls beside the car park and **hotel** complex of *Non Nuoc Seaside Resort* (T0511/836216, F836335; ❸–❹), a 1970s development currently undergoing an upgrade to four-star status. Instead, head back to the dogleg and turn down towards the beach to find a warm welcome at *Hoa's Place* (☎0511/969216, ⓔhoasplace@hotmail.com; ➊), a delightfully laidback **guesthouse** offering clean, good-value accommodation. They also lay on very reasonably priced and convivial meals and can arrange motorbike rental ($3) or a Honda om to Hoi An or Da Nang; count on $2–3 in either direction for a one-way journey.

West of Da Nang

Perched 1500m up a mountain 48km west of Da Nang, **Ba Na Hill Station** provides a welcome change from the coast. The site was first developed by the French in the 1920s, who escaped the summer heat for its cool, mountain air. After a brief heyday in the 1930s the resort was abandoned and soon fell victim to the ravages of war and the encroaching jungle. Thanks to a high annual rainfall together with temperatures at a constant 17–20°C, dense forest growth cloaks the mountain, which is home to over 500 species of flora and 250 fauna. In the last few years the local authorities have poured money into Ba Na, converting some of the old French villas into guesthouses and restaurants, laying forest trails and a new access road and even putting in a cable car – a great hit with the locals, who come up here at night to admire the lights of Da Nang twinkling far below. Not that the daytime **views** are to be scoffed at, taking in the Hai Van Pass, Son Tra Peninsula and Marble Mountains if you're lucky. Given the weather, you may have to content yourself with a more atmospheric scene of mountains wreathed in mist, but one peculiar feature of Ba Na is that, while it's raining on the lower slopes, the summit may be above the clouds, enjoying brilliant sunshine.

Views apart, the main attraction is exploring the **forest paths** and wandering among the ruined villas, for which half a day will suffice. You may want to avoid summer weekends when the place can be packed out. A return trip by **Honda om** from Da Nang will cost around $10 including waiting time, or you can expect to pay in the region of $20 for a **car** and driver. Da Nang tour agents (see p.308) also offer various **organized bus tours**, mostly in summer: a one-day tour costs $15 per person.

North of Da Nang

Thirty kilometres **north of Da Nang**, beyond a region of grave-pocked, sandy desolation, the first and most dramatic of three mountain spurs off the Truong Son range cuts across Vietnam's pinched central waist. This thousand-metre-high barrier forms a climatic frontier blocking the southward penetration of cold, damp winter airstreams which often bury the tops under thick cloud banks and earn it the title **Hai Van**, or "Pass of the Ocean Clouds". These mountains once formed a national frontier between Dai Viet and Champa, and Hai Van's continuing strategic importance is marked by a succession of forts, pillboxes and ridge-line defensive walls erected by Nguyen-dynasty Vietnamese, French, Japanese, and American forces. Now, in these more peaceful times, a massive construction project is under way, blasting a new road tunnel through the mountains to carry Highway 1. Tourist traffic, however, will continue to grind over the col at nearly 500m above sea level. From the top there are superb views, weather permitting, south over the sweeping curve of Da Nang Bay, with glimpses of the rail lines looping and tunnelling along the cliff.

Lang Co

Descending again into warmer air, a white-tipped spit of land comes into view round a hairpin bend, jutting into an aquamarine lagoon strung with fishing nets. Sadly, this much photographed scene is now marred by the new road bridge marching across it. The original bridge spanning the lagoon has the dubious distinction of being the Viet Minh bomb squads' first target in 1947 and its ruined piles are still visible. **LANG CO** Village hides among coconut palms on the sandy peninsula, its presence revealed only by a white-spired church. It makes a popular lunch stop on the road between Da Nang and Hué, followed by a quick swim from the narrow beach, spoilt by a string of electricity pylons. There's also a good deal of rubbish. If you want to swim, head north away from the fishing village to find cleaner sand.

Nevertheless, Lang Co is earmarked for tourist development and already there's one beach resort here, in addition to a few more modest guesthouses. If you decide to **stay**, the best all-round option is *Thanh Tam* (☎054/874456; ❷), on the highway about 1500m north of the village; ask for a sea view. On the opposite side of the highway, *Anh Nguyen* (☎054/874448; ❶) has spotless ensuite rooms, all with hot water, while nearby *Chi Na* (☎054/874597; ❶) is another friendly place with a handful of simple but clean rooms at slightly cheaper rates. The government-owned *Lang Co Beach Resort* (☎054/873555, ✉langco@dng.vnv.vn; ❹), opposite *Chi Na*, stands out a bit with its complex of green-roofed, Hué-style villas, landscaped pool and replica covered bridge. The rooms are big, light and well equipped and the beach here is kept scrupulously clean. All these places have restaurants, or will at least rustle up a meal, but for simple home cooking the best place to **eat** is *Chi Na*. Don't miss out on the fresh seafood for which Lang Co is famous.

Lang Co lies about 40km north of Da Nang and 65km from Hué. The train station is on the lagoon's western side, or public buses will drop you off anywhere on the highway. Sinh Café open-tour buses stop at *Thanh Tam*, while An Phu Tourist uses the very run-down *Tourist Hotel* towards the southern end of the strip.

Bach Ma National Park

Well off the beaten track, **Bach Ma National Park** is being developed as an eco-tourism destination, and dedicated ornithologists and botanists may want to make the effort to get here for the chance of seeing some of the region's 230 bird species and more than 1400 species of flora. Bach Ma is also home to 83 mammal species, including the Asiatic black bear, leopard and the recently discovered saola and giant muntjac (see "Environmental issues", p.542), as well as more visible deer and macaque monkeys. It was to preserve this exceptional biodiversity that a national park was established here in 1991, covering 22,000 hectares of evergreen forests and surrounded by a buffer zone almost equal in extent. The highlands were previously the location of a French summer resort, where Emperor Bao Dai also kept several luxury villas. The majority of buildings, tennis courts and rose-beds are now in ruins, but a number of villas have been restored to provide tourist accommodation. One word of warning before you set off: Bach Ma is one of the wettest places in Vietnam, with a staggering 8m of rainfall a year at the summit. The best time to visit is from May to early September, but even then be prepared to get wet. And remember to take warm clothes since it can get pretty chilly at the top.

At the entrance to the park, stop first at the **Visitors' Centre** (daily: March–Sept 7am–5pm, Oct–Feb 7.30am–4.30pm; ☎054/871330, ⓦwww.bachma.vnn.vn) to buy your tickets and arrange transport and accommodation (see overleaf). Make sure you pick up a map of the trails, and it's also well worth investing in the excellent English-language booklet (small fee). While you're here, take a quick look round the exhibition; it's aimed at kids but is still very informative. Although it's not a requirement, it's definitely a good idea to take a **guide** (around $6 per day, $10 for an English-speaker) when you're walking in the park, principally for your own safety – it's easy to get lost. Note that it's normal "forest etiquette" to share drinks, meals and carrying the loads. If you want to make a positive contribution to the onerous task of **reforestation**, the park has a programme whereby you can buy a sapling and help plant it in one of the denuded areas of the park.

Six short **nature trails** branch off the steep, tarmacked road which leads 16km from the gate almost to the summit of Hai Vong Dai Mountain (1450m). The first, **Pheasant Trail** (2.5km), starts at the kilometre 7 marker (note that all distances refer to the distance from Highway 1 rather than from the park entrance) to reach a series of waterfalls and pools, where you can swim. On the way you may hear the calls of black gibbons or some of the seven types of pheasant that inhabit the park, or see the fifty-centimetre-long earthworms which the locals cook and eat as a treatment for malaria. The short but very steep **Parashorea Trail** (300m), at kilometre 14, is named after this area's towering trees, while 2km further on **Rhododendron Trail** (1.5km), takes you to the top of a waterfall, with views over primary forest. **Five Lakes Trail** (2km), at kilometre 17.5, ends at a series of five pools fed by a waterfall, where you can also swim. **Summit Trail** leads 500m from the end of the road to the crest of Hai Vong Dai with good views over Cau Hai lagoon and surrounding mountains. From here, instead of retracing your steps, you can walk back down the **Nature Exploration Trail** (2.5km) past ruined villas to rejoin the road at kilometre 17 beside the **Orchid House** where nearly a hundred species from Bach Ma and elsewhere in Vietnam are carefully nurtured.

By far the easiest way to get to Bach Ma is with your own **transport**: 26km north of Lang Co (40km south of Hué), look for a sign pointing west off Highway 1 in Cau Hai Village (Phu Loc District), then drive for another 3km to the park gate. Alternatively, both public and open-tour buses will drop you at the turning in Cau Hai, from where you can pick up a Honda om ($1.30) for the final stretch. A Honda om from Lang Co will cost a minimum of $10 for the return trip. Note that, while cars are allowed inside the park, motorbikes and bicycles are not. Instead, you'll have to rent one of the park's jeeps which will take you to the summit and back again ($16), but can't drop off or pick up passengers en route.

Should you wish to stay in the park, you can opt for the **campsite** (❶), at kilometre 18, or simple **guesthouse** accommodation (❶) either near the summit or beside the entrance. In peak season (June–Aug) it's advisable to book in advance; contact the Visitors' Centre for reservations. There's a small **restaurant** at the park entrance, where you can also buy biscuits, water and snacks, whereas meals have to be ordered in advance if you're staying at the summit. Alternatively, you can bring your own food from Cau Hai market.

Hué and around

Unlike Hanoi, Ho Chi Minh and most other Vietnamese cities, **HUÉ** somehow seems to have stood aside from the current economic frenzy and, despite its calamitous history, has retained a unique cultural identity. It's a small, peaceful city, full of lakes, canals and lush vegetation, all celebrated in countless romantic outpourings by its much esteemed poetic fraternity. Since the early nineteenth century, when Hué became the capital of Vietnam, it has also been a city of scholars, and today boasts no fewer than five universities. Though it's considered too highbrow by the rest of the country, there's a discernible touch of refinement in the Hué air and an easy-going tolerance that stems from a long tradition of popular Buddhism. More recently, French culture has left a strong impression on Hué, perhaps the most Francophile of all Vietnamese cities.

Hué repays exploration at a leisurely pace, and contains enough in the way of historical interest to swallow up a few days with no trouble at all. The city divides into three clearly defined urban areas, each with its own distinct character. The nineteenth-century walled **citadel**, on the north bank of the Perfume River, contains the once magnificent **Imperial City** as well as an extensive grid of attractive residential streets and prolific gardens. Across Dong Ba Canal to the east lies **Phu Cat**, the original merchants' quarter of Hué where ships once pulled in, now a crowded district of shophouses, Chinese Assembly Halls and pagodas. What used to be called the **European city**, a triangle of land caught between the Perfume River's south bank and the Phu Cam Canal, is now Hué's modern administrative centre, where you'll also find most hotels and tourist services. Pine-covered hills, scattered with tombs and secluded pagodas, form the city's southern bounds, where the Nguyen emperors built their palatial **Royal Mausoleums**. And through it all meanders the **Perfume River**, named somewhat fancifully from the tree resin and blossoms it carries, passing on its way the celebrated, seven-storey tower of **Thien Mu Pagoda**. If you can afford the time, cycling out to **Thuan An Beach** makes an enjoyable excursion, or head inland to soak in the pools of **Thanh Tan Hot-Spring Resort**. Hué is also the main jumping-off point for day-tours of the DMZ (see p.334).

With all this to offer, Hué is inevitably one of Vietnam's pre-eminent tourist destinations. The choice and standard of accommodation are generally above average, as are its restaurants serving the city's justly famous speciality foods. Nevertheless, the majority of people pass through Hué fairly quickly, partly because high entrance fees make visiting more than a couple of the major sights beyond many budgets, and partly because of its troublesome **weather**. Hué suffers from the highest rainfall in the country, mostly falling over just three months from October to December when the city regularly floods for a few days, causing damage to the historic architecture, though heavy downpours are possible at any time of year.

Some history

The land on which Hué now stands belonged to the Kingdom of Champa until 1306 when territory north of Da Nang was exchanged for the hand of a Vietnamese princess under the terms of a peace treaty. The first Vietnamese to settle in the region established their administrative centre near present-day Hué at a place called Hoa Chan, and then in 1558 Lord Nguyen Hoang arrived from Hanoi as governor of the district, at the same time establishing the rule of the Nguyen lords over southern Vietnam which was to last for the next two hundred years. In the late seventeenth century the lords moved the citadel to its present location where it developed into a major town and cultural centre, **Phu Xuan**, which briefly became the capital under the Tay Son emperor, Quang Trung (1788–1801). But it was the next ruler of Vietnam, Emperor Gia Long, founder of the Nguyen dynasty, who literally put Hué on the map after 1802 when he sought to unify the country by moving the capital, lock, stock and dynastic altars, from Thang Long (Hanoi) to the renamed city of **Hué**. Gia Long owed his throne to French military support but his Imperial City was very much a Chinese concept, centred on a Forbidden City reserved for the sovereign, with separate administrative and civilian quarters.

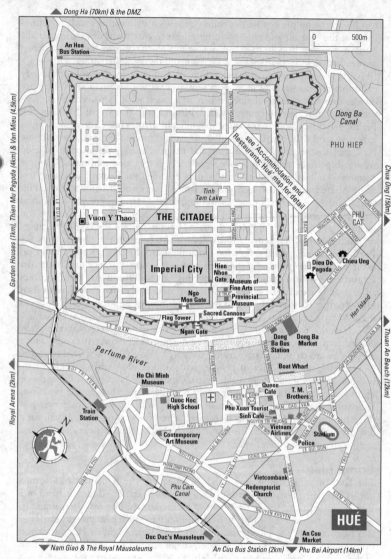

The map shows:

▲ *Dong Ha (70km) & the DMZ*

0 500m

An Hoa
Bus Station

Dong Ba Canal

PHU HIEP

Chua Ong (150m) ▶

Tinh
Tam Lake

THE CITADEL

PHU CAT

Vuon Y Thao

Dieu De
Pagoda   Chieu Ung

Imperial City

Hien
Nhon
Gate

Museum of
Fine Arts

Ngo
Mon Gate

Provincial
Museum

Flag Tower

Sacred Cannons

Han Island

Ngan Gate

Thuan An Beach (12km) ▶

Dong
Ba Bus
Station

Dong Ba
Market

Perfume River

Boat Wharf

Ho Chi Minh
Museum

Queen
Café

T. M.
Brothers

Quoc Hoc
High School

Phu Xuan Tourist

Sinh Café

Train
Station

Vietnam
Airlines

Stadium

Contemporary
Art Museum

Police

Phu Cam
Canal

Vietcombank

Redemptorist
Church

HUÉ

Duc Duc's Mausoleum

An Cuu
Market

▼ *Nam Giao & The Royal Mausoleums*   *An Cuu Bus Station (2km)* ▼ *Phu Bai Airport (14km)*

Garden Houses (1km), Thien Mu Pagoda (4km) & Van Mieu (4.5km) ◀

Royal Arena (2km) ◀

see 'Accommodation and
Restaurants: Hué' map for detail

The Nguyen emperors (see box, p.308) were Confucian, conservative rulers, generally suspicious of all Westerners, who were nevertheless unable to withstand the power of France. In 1884 the French were granted land northwest of Hué citadel, and they then seized the city entirely in 1885, leaving the emperors as nominal rulers. Under the Nguyens, Hué became a famous centre of the arts, scholarship and Buddhist learning, but their extravagant building projects and luxurious lifestyle demanded crippling taxes.

Hué ceased to be the capital of Vietnam when Emperor Bao Dai abdicated in 1945; two years later a huge fire destroyed many of the city's wooden temples and palaces. From the early twentieth century the city was engulfed in social and political unrest led by an anti-colonial educated elite, which simmered away until the 1960s. Tensions finally boiled over in May 1963 when troops fired on thousands of Buddhist nationalists demonstrating against the strongly Catholic regime of President Ngo Dinh Diem (see p.498). The protests escalated into a wave of self-immolations by monks and nuns until government forces moved against the pagodas at the end of the year, rounding up the Buddhist clergy and supposed activists in the face of massive public demonstrations.

During the 1968 **Tet Offensive** Hué was torn apart again when the North Vietnamese Army (NVA) held the city for 25 days. Communist forces entered Hué in the early hours of January 31, hoisted their flag above the citadel and found themselves in control of the whole city bar two small military compounds. Armed with lists of names, they began searching out government personnel, sympathizers of the Southern regime, intellectuals, priests, Americans and foreign aid workers. Nearly 3000 bodies were later discovered in mass graves around the city – the victims were mostly civilians who had been shot, beaten to death or buried alive. But the killing hadn't finished: during the ensuing counter-assault as many as 5000 North Vietnamese and Viet Cong, 384 Southern troops and 142 American soldiers died, plus at least another thousand civilians. Hué was all but levelled in the massive fire power unleashed on NVA forces holed up in the citadel but it took a further ten days of agonizing, house-to-house combat to drive the communists out, in what Stanley Karnow described as "the most bitter battle" of the entire war. Seven years later, on March 26, 1975, the NVA were back to liberate Hué in its pivotal position as the first major town south of the Seventeenth Parallel.

The mammoth task of **rebuilding** Hué has been going on now for twenty years but received a boost in 1993 when UNESCO listed Hué as a World Heritage Site, which served to mobilize international funding for a whole range of projects, from renovating palaces to the revival of traditional arts and technical skills. Then in 1995 the Vietnamese government recognized Hué's growing economic importance by granting it independent city status, almost on a par with Hanoi and Ho Chi Minh City.

Arrival, information and getting around

Flights arriving at Hué's **Phu Bai Airport**, 15km southeast of the city, are met by a bus ($1.60) which takes you to central hotels, and by metered taxis (around $7). The **train station** lies about 1.5km from the centre of town at the far western end of Le Loi, a boulevard running along the south bank of the Perfume River. Note that trains out of Hué get booked up, especially sleepers to Ho Chi Minh City and Hanoi, so make onward travel arrangements as early as possible (ticket office open daily 7–11.30am & 1.30–6pm). Hydrofoils from Da Nang dock at the **wharf** beside the *Huong Giang Hotel*.

Hué has two long-distance **bus stations**: services from the south pull into An Cuu station, 3km southeast of the centre on Highway 1. A Honda om or cyclo into town should cost around $1. Buses from Hanoi and the north dump you at An Hoa station, 4km northwest on Highway 1, from where a Honda om or cyclo to the centre costs $1.50. Sinh Café and TM Brothers (An Phu Tourist) **open-tour buses** set down at their town-centre offices at 7 Nguyen Tri Phuong and 11 Nguyen Tri Phuong respectively. Note that some streets in Hué, including Nguyen Tri Phuong and Ben Nghe, are being allocated new numbers. The situation is confused, but we use the new numbers wherever possible in the account below.

The Nguyen dynasty

In 1802 Prince Nguyen Anh, one of the southern Nguyen lords, defeated the Tay Son dynasty with the help of a French bishop, Pigneau de Behaine. When Nguyen Anh assumed the throne under the title Emperor Gia Long he thus founded the **Nguyen dynasty**, which ruled Vietnam from Hué until the abdication of Emperor Bao Dai in 1945. Eleven of the Nguyen emperors are buried in Hué, the exceptions being Ham Nghi, and Bao Dai, who died in Paris in 1997 after four decades in exile.

Gia Long	1802–1820	
Minh Mang	1820–1841	(fourth son of Gia Long)
Thieu Tri	1841–1847	(eldest son of Minh Mang)
Tu Duc	1847–1883	(second son of Thieu Tri)
Duc Duc	1883	(eldest adopted son of Tu Duc, reigned three days; dethroned)
Hiep Hoa	1883	(brother of Tu Duc, reigned four months; died from suspected poisoning)
Kien Phuc	1883–1884	(adopted son of Tu Duc, reigned eight months)
Ham Nghi	1884–1885	(younger brother of Kien Phuc; exiled to Algeria, where he is buried)
Dong Khanh	1885–1889	(elder brother of Ham Nghi and Kien Phuc)
Thanh Thai	1889–1907	(son of Duc Duc; exiled to Réunion)
Duy Tan	1907–1916	(son of Thanh Thai; exiled to Réunion)
Khai Dinh	1916–1925	(son of Dong Khanh)
Bao Dai	1926–1945	(son of Khai Dinh)

The best bet for **tourist information** is either your hotel or one of the tour agents. Staff at the *Mandarin Café*, 12 Hung Vuong, are particularly helpful. Every hotel and tour agent hands out photocopied **maps**, but for a detailed city plan try the big hotels and bookstalls on Le Loi. The main **post office** is at 8 Hoang Hoa Tham and offers Internet connections in addition to the usual facilities; handy sub-post offices are located at 38 Le Loi and in the train station complex. Vietcombank, 78 Hung Vuong, has an **exchange** desk for cash and travellers' cheque transactions and an ATM (open during banking hours only). However, its exchange bureau on Hung Vuong outside the *Saigon Morin Hotel* is not only more convenient, but is also open longer hours (Mon–Sat 7am–10pm) and offers a 24-hour ATM.

Even Hué's wide avenues become crowded during rush hour (7–9am & 4–6pm), but generally the most enjoyable way of **getting around** the city's scattered sights – and especially of touring the Royal Mausoleums – is by **bicycle**. Most hotels and guesthouses, plus a few cafés, offer bike rental (at less than $1 per day) and **motorbikes** ($4–5 a day). A popular option is to take a guided **motorbike tour** of Hué and its environs ($5–6) offered by a number of tour agents (see "Listings", p.320); you either ride pillion or take your own bike. All the above places can usually help with **car rental** ($20–30 per day). Hué has no shortage of cyclos or Honda om and also boasts metered **taxi** services (see "Listings", p.320).

Accommodation

The majority of accommodation in Hué is located south of the Perfume River, where the **top-class** establishments overlook the river, while **budget hotels** and **guesthouses** are scattered in the streets behind, particularly the backpacker enclave of Hung Vuong and Nguyen Tri Phuong, and along Pham Ngu Lao. A few hotels have opened up within the citadel, though as yet you'll

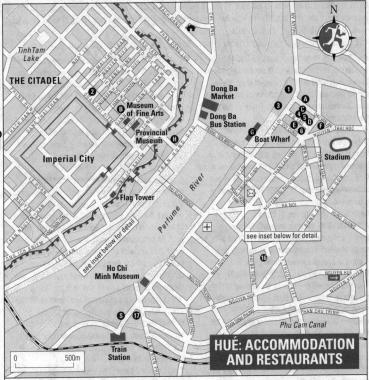

HUÉ: ACCOMMODATION AND RESTAURANTS

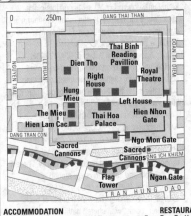

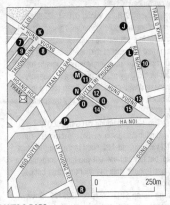

ACCOMMODATION

An Phuoc	6
Binh Duong II	16
Binh Minh I	12
Binh Minh II	10
Century Riverside Inn	3
Dong Duong	8
Duy Tan	11
Huong Giang	1
Le Loi	17

Mimosa	5
Saigon Morin	7
Thai Binh I	14
Thai Binh II	9
Thang Long	15
Thanh Noi	2
Thanh Thuy	4
Vong Canh	13

RESTAURANTS & BARS

Bun Bo Hué	R
Banh Khoai Hanh	P
Café 3	S
Café on Thu Wheels	Q
Club Garden	F
Co Do	L
Dong Tam	C
Hang Me	E
La Carambole	D
Lac Thien	H

Mandarin Café	M
Minh & Coco	K
Omar Khayyam's	O
Quoc Huy	B
Song Huong Floating Restaurant	G
Stop & Go Café	J
Tropical Garden	A
Vuon Y Thao	I
Xuan Trang Café	N

find better value south of the river. Thanks to a dramatic increase in the number of private hotels, there's now an oversupply of rooms most of the year and you should be able to bargain.

The following accommodation places are marked on the map on p.309.

An Phuoc 26 Pham Ngu Lao ☎054/824925, ⓕ826090. Located on a quiet backstreet, this An Phu-owned hotel offers a range of good, clean rooms prettied up with the odd bit of plasterwork and Chinese-style ink painting. Those at the top of the scale get a balcony. ②

Binh Duong II 8 Ngo Gia Tu ☎054/846466, ⓔbinhduong1@dng.vnn.vn. Though a bit off the main drag, it's worth seeking out this hotel in an interesting residential area for its unusually bright, well-maintained rooms. They're good value, too, with air-con, satellite TV, fridge and stylish bathrooms, but no phone. ①–②

Binh Minh I 36 Nguyen Tri Phuong ☎054/825526, ⓔbinhminhhue@dng.vnn.vn. Bright, welcoming hotel in a great location with a range of clean, homely rooms, some with balcony. A popular and good-value option. ②

Binh Minh II 45 Ben Nghe ☎054/849007, ⓔbinhminhhue@dng.vnn.vn. Bigger and slightly smarter rooms than the *Binh Minh I*, but still the same friendly atmosphere. ②

Century Riverside Inn 49 Le Loi ☎054/823390, ⓦwww.centuryhotels.com. International hotel on the banks of the Perfume River with swimming pool, bar, post office and souvenir shops. The comfortable but characterless rooms, some very small, are overpriced. ④–⑤

Dong Duong 2 Hung Vuong ☎054/823866, ⓔindochine-hotel@dng.vnn.vn. This smart-looking hotel in a central location set back off the main road is a decent mid-level choice as long as you stick to the more expensive rooms in the new, main block. They're not huge, but reasonably spruce and well appointed. Cheap rooms in the old block at the rear are seriously overpriced. ②–③

Duy Tan 12 Hung Vuong ☎054/825001, ⓔnkduytan@dng.vnn.vn. Big, government-run hotel with big, old-fashioned rooms on the main drag, but not bad-value if you fancy something a bit less frenetic than many of the other budget options. ②

Huong Giang 51 Le Loi ☎054/822122, ⓦwww.huonggiangtourist.com. One of Hué's top three hotels, originally built in 1962 but well renovated, with a pool, gardens, tennis court and other four-star facilities. It's a more homely establishment than the next door *Century Riverside*, but can't match the *Saigon Morin* for service and room size. Larger rooms overlooking the river offer better value for money. ④–⑤

Le Loi 2 2 Le Loi ☎054/824668, ⓦwww.leloihue-hotel.com. A labyrinthine hotel of unattractive concrete blocks, but close to the train station, and its renovated rooms are OK if you're stuck. Avoid the overpriced rooms in the old block, however. ②–③

Mimosa 46/6 Le Loi ☎054/828068. One of several small guesthouses on an alley leading off Le Loi, this attractive, family-run place has clean, air-con and fan rooms with communal terraces. ①–②

Saigon Morin 30 Le Loi ☎054/823526, ⓦwww.morinhotel.com.vn. Hué's most famous, French-era hotel has been painted pink, renovated to four-star standards and there are plans to add an extra floor, but nevertheless, it still retains some of its colonial charm, not least in the garden courtyard. The rooms are a good size, if a little bland, and kitted out with all the equipment you'd expect, including mini-bar, bathtub and hairdryer. There's a rooftop bar, two restaurants, small pool ($3 to non-residents), Internet access and so forth. Prices reflect the standard of service and location. ⑤–⑥

Thai Binh I 10/9 Nguyen Tri Phuong ☎054/828058, ⓔksthaibin@dng.vnn.vn. Spotlessly clean, friendly and popular hotel with a good range of well-equipped rooms, down a quiet alley beside *Binh Minh I*. ②

Thai Binh II 2 Luong The Vinh ☎054/828058, ⓔksthaibin@dng.vnn.vn. At six floors, this place sticks out a bit, but inside, the rooms are immaculate, light and airy, all with good bathrooms, pine furniture and balconies. ③–④

Thang Long 16 Hung Vuong ☎054/826462, ⓔdinhxuanglong@dng.vnn.vn. A range of well-equipped rooms, slightly old now but more than adequate, make this hotel a good option. There's no lift, so rates get lower the higher you climb. ①–②

Thanh Noi 3 Dang Dung ☎054/522478, ⓔthanhnoi@dng.vnn.vn. One of the few hotels north of the river, near the citadel, offering a touch of character in its imperial-style decor. Ask to see a range of rooms since some are a bit musty. There's a small pool and some greenery around. ③

Thanh Thuy 46/6 Le Loi ☎054/824585, ⓔthanhthuy66@dng.vnn.vn. A handful of basic but clean rooms, with shared bathroom, on the same quiet alley off riverside Le Loi as the *Mimosa* (see above). ①–②

Vong Canh 25 Huong Vuong. This friendly, family-run hotel has recently added a new block at the rear, offering a broad range of stylish, spacious rooms with excellent bathrooms. Internet access available. ①–③

The citadel

Hué's days of glory kicked off in the early nineteenth century when Emperor Gia Long laid out a vast **citadel**, comprising three concentric enclosures, ranged behind the prominent flag tower. Within the citadel's outer wall lies the **Imperial City**, containing administrative offices, parks and dynastic temples, with the royal palaces of the **Forbidden Purple City** at its epicentre. Though wars, fires, typhoons, floods and termites have all taken their toll, it's these imperial edifices, some now restored to their former magnificence, that constitute Hué's prime tourist attraction. Apart from one museum, there are no specific sights in the outer citadel, but it's a pleasant area to cycle round, especially the northern sector where you'll find many lakes and the prolific **gardens** for which Hué is famed.

In accordance with ancient tradition the citadel was built in an **auspicious location** chosen to preserve the all-important harmony between the emperor and his subjects, heaven and earth, man and nature. Thus the complex is oriented southeast towards the low hummock of Nui Ngu Binh ("Royal Screen Mountain"), which blocks out harmful influences, while to either side two small islands in the Perfume River represent the Blue Dragon's benevolent spirit in balance with the aggressive White Tiger. Just in case that wasn't protection enough, the whole 520 hectares are enclosed within seven-metre-high, twenty-metre-thick brick and earth walls built with the help of French engineers, and encircled by a moat and canal. Eight villages had to be relocated when construction began in 1805, and over the next thirty years tens of thousands of workmen laboured to complete more than three hundred palaces, temples, tombs and other royal buildings, some using materials brought down from the former Imperial City in Hanoi.

The flag tower and the sacred cannons

The citadel's massive, ten-kilometre-long perimeter wall has survived intact, as has its most prominent feature, the **flag tower**, or *Cot Co* (also known as *Ky Dai*, "the King's Knight"), which dominates the southern battlements. The tower is in fact three squat, brick terraces topped with a flagpole first erected in 1807, where the yellow-starred Viet Cong flag flew briefly during the 1968 Tet Offensive. Ten gates pierce the citadel wall: enter through Ngan Gate, east of the flag tower, to find a parade ground flanked by the nine **sacred cannons**, which were cast in the early nineteenth century of bronze seized from the Tay Son army. The cannons represent the four seasons and five ritual elements (earth, fire, metal, wood and water); originally they stood in front of Ngo Mon Gate, symbolizing the citadel's guardian spirits.

The Imperial City

A second moat and defensive wall inside the citadel guard the **Imperial City** (daily 7am–5pm; $3, an optional guide costs $3), which follows the same symmetrical layout about a north–south axis as Beijing's Forbidden City. The city, popularly known as *Dai Noi* ("the Great Enclosure"), has four gates – one in each wall – though by far the most impressive is south-facing **Ngo Mon**, the Imperial City's principal entrance. In its heyday the complex must have been truly awe-inspiring, a place of glazed yellow and green roof tiles, pavilions of rich red and gilded lacquer, and lotus-filled ponds – all surveyed by the emperor with his entourage of haughty mandarins. However, many of its buildings were badly neglected even before the battle for Hué raged through the Imperial City during Tet 1968, and by 1975 a mere twenty out of the original 148 were left standing among the vegetable plots. Some are in the midst of

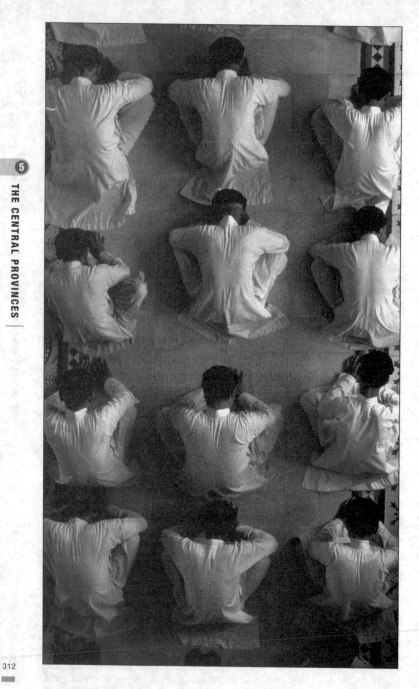

extensive restorations, and those which have been completed, notably **Thai Hoa Palace** and the **The Mieu** complex, are stunning. Among the others, the charming Royal Reading Pavilion and a pair of octagonal music pavilions are less formal mementos of the dynasty. The rest of the Imperial City, especially its northern sector, is a grassed-over expanse full of birds and butterflies where you can still make out foundations and find bullet pockmarks in the plaster-work of ruined walls.

Ngo Mon Gate

In 1833 Emperor Minh Mang replaced an earlier, much less formidable gate with the present dramatic entrance way to the Imperial City, **Ngo Mon**, con-sidered a masterpiece of Nguyen architecture. Ngo Mon (the "Noon" or "Southwest" Gate) has five entrances: the emperor alone used the central entrance paved with stone; two smaller doorways on either side were for the civil and military mandarins, who only rated brick paving, while another pair of giant openings in the wings allowed access to the royal elephants. The bulk of Ngo Mon is constructed of massive stone slabs, but perched on top is an ele-gant pavilion called the **Five Phoenix Watchtower** as its nine roofs are said to resemble five birds in flight when viewed from above. Note that the central roof, under which the emperor passed, is covered with yellow-glazed tiles, a fea-ture of nearly all Hué's royal roofs. Emperors used the watchtower for two major ceremonies each year: the declaration of the lunar New Year; and the announce-ment of the civil service exam results, depicted here in a lacquer painting. It was also in this pavilion that the last Nguyen emperor, Bao Dai, abdicated in 1945 when he handed over to the new government his symbols of power – a solid gold seal weighing ten kilos and a sheathed sword encrusted with jade.

Thai Hoa Palace

Walking north from Ngo Mon along the city's symmetrical axis, you pass between two square lakes and a pair of *kylin*, mythical dew-drinking animals that are harbingers of peace, to reach **Thai Hoa Palace** ("the Palace of Supreme Harmony"). Not only is this the most spectacular of Hué's palaces, its interior glowing with sumptuous red and gold lacquers, but it's also the most important since this was the throne palace, where major ceremonies such as coronations or royal birthdays took place and foreign ambassadors were received. On these occasions the emperor sat on the raised dais, wearing a gold-en tunic and a crown decorated with nine dragons, under a spectacular gilded canopy. He faced south across the **Esplanade of Great Salutations**, a stone-paved courtyard where the mandarins stood, civil mandarins to the left and military on the right, lined up in their appointed place beside eighteen stelae denoting the nine subdivided ranks. A French traveller in the 1920s witnessed the colourful spectacle, with "perfume-bearers in royal-blue, fan-bearers in sky-blue waving enormous yellow feather fans, musicians and guardsmen and ranks of mandarins in their curious hats and gorgeous, purple-embroidered dragons, kow-towing down, down on their noses amidst clouds of incense – and all in a setting of blood-red lacquer scrawled with gold".

The palace was first constructed in 1805, though the present building dates from 1833 when the French floor tiles and glass door panels were added, and was the only major building in the Imperial City to escape bomb damage. Nevertheless, the throne room's eighty ironwood pillars, swirling with dragons and clouds, had been eaten away by termites and humidity and were on the point of collapse when rescue work began in 1991. During the restoration every column, weighing two tonnes apiece, had to be replaced manually and then painted with twelve coats of lacquer, each coat taking one month to dry. Behind the throne room a souvenir shop now sells books and tapes of Hué folk songs where once the emperor prepared for his grand entrance. It also contains two large dioramas depicting the Imperial City and flag tower in their heyday.

The Forbidden Purple City

From Thai Hoa Palace the emperor would have walked north through the Great Golden Gate into the third and last enclosure, the **Forbidden Purple City**. This area, enclosed by a low wall, was reserved for residential palaces, living quarters of the state physician and nine ranks of royal concubines, plus kitchens and pleasure pavilions. Many of these buildings were destroyed in the 1947 fire, leaving most of the Forbidden Purple City as open ground, a "mood piece", haunted by fragments of wall and overgrown terraces.

However, a handful of buildings remain, including the restored **Left House** and **Right House** facing each other across a courtyard immediately behind Thai Hoa Palace. Civil and military mandarins would spruce themselves up here before proceeding to an audience with the monarch. Of the two, the Right House (actually to your left – the names refer to the emperor's viewpoint) is the more complete with its ornate murals and gargantuan mirror in a gilded frame, a gift from the French to Emperor Dong Khanh. It also contains an exhibition of old photos of Hué and of imperial robes, including a few originals, such as a lovely summer gown of silk gauze embroidered with nine five-clawed dragons. Walking northeast from here you pass behind the Royal Theatre, built in 1826 and now belonging to the University of Fine Arts, to find the **Thai Binh Reading Pavilion**, an appealing, two-tier structure surrounded by bonsai gardens. The pavilion was built by Thieu Tri and then restored by Khai Dinh, who added the kitsch mosaics. The only other buildings left standing near here are a pair of octagonal pavilions, where the emperor came to listen to music and commune with nature.

The Ancestral Altars

The other main cluster of sights lies a short walk away in the southwest corner of the Imperial City. Again, they are all aligned on a south–north axis, kicking off with **Hien Lam Cac** ("Pavilion of Everlasting Clarity"), a graceful, three-storey structure with some notable woodwork, followed by the **Nine Dynastic Urns**. Considered the epitome of Hué craftsmanship, the bronze urns were cast during the reign of Minh Mang and are ornamented with scenes of mountains, rivers, rain clouds and wildlife, plus one or two stray bullet marks. Each urn is dedicated to an emperor: the middle urn, which is also the largest at 2600 kilos, honours Gia Long. They stand across the courtyard from the long, low building of **The Mieu**, the Nguyens' dynastic temple erected in 1822 by Minh Mang to worship his father. Since then altars have been added for each emperor in turn, except Duc Duc and Hiep Hoa, who reigned only briefly, and Bao Dai who died in exile in 1997; those of the three anti-French sovereigns – Ham Nghi, Thanh Thai, and Duy Tan – had to wait until after Independence in 1954 for theirs. Take a look inside to see the line of altar tables, most sporting a portrait or photo of the monarch. Behind each is a bed equipped with a sleeping mat, pillows and other accoutrements and, finally, a shrine holding funeral tablets for the emperor and his wife or wives. Anniversaries of the emperors' deaths are still commemorated at The Mieu, attended by members of the royal family in all their finery.

Exit The Mieu by its west door, beside a 170-year-old pine tree trained in the shape of a flying dragon, and follow the path north into the next compound to find **Hung Mieu**. This temple is dedicated to the Nguyen ancestors and specifically to the parents of Gia Long, and is distinguished by its fine carving. North again, **Dien Tho**, the Queen Mother's residence, is still undergoing restoration but worth a quick look. Built in a mix of Vietnamese and French architectural styles, the palace later served as Bao Dai's private residence, and the downstairs reception rooms are now set out with period furniture, echoing the photos of the palace in use in the 1930s.

The museums

Instead of leaving the Imperial City via Ngo Mon Gate, cut east to exit via the well-preserved *Cua Hien Nhon* ("Gate of Humanity"). From here it's a short walk to the **Museum of Fine Arts**, at 3 Le Truc (7am–7pm; $1.50), which boasts an interesting display of former royal paraphernalia. Its most valuable exhibits are the lively paintings on glass which adorn the ironwood columns, and a series of stone gongs. But the museum's greatest asset is the building it's housed in, **Long An Palace**, built in 1845 inside the Imperial City and then moved to its present location in 1909 to become the National University Library before Khai Dinh turned it into a dynastic museum in 1923. The palace was renovated in 1995 and decorated with rich browns, highlighting the wealth of furniture decorated with mother-of-pearl inlay.

Directly across Le Truc, the **Provincial Museum** (Bao Tang Thuan Thien–Hué) was closed at the time of writing. If it re-opens, it's worth visiting for its well-presented coverage of Hué during the American War. Photos, documents and original film clips cover both the Buddhist demonstrations in 1963 and the 1968 battle, including footage of the National Liberation Front flag being hoisted above the citadel.

Phu Cat

Hué's civilian and merchant quarter grew up alongside the citadel on a triangular island now divided into **Phu Cat**, Phu Hiep and Phu Hau districts. This part of town has a completely different atmosphere: it's a lively, crowded, dilapidated area centred on Chi Lang, in Phu Cat District, which still boasts some single-storey, wood and red-tiled houses as well as more ornate, colonial-era shophouses. The area was once home to the Chinese community, and five **Assembly Halls** still stand along Chi Lang. Old trees shade the Dong Ba Canal on the island's southwestern side, where Bach Dang was the site of anti-government demonstrations in the 1960s, centred around **Dieu De Pagoda**. There's nothing compelling to draw you onto the island, particularly if you've already seen the Chinese temples of Hoi An and Ho Chi Minh City, but the area provides a bustling contrast to the otherwise sedate streets of Hué.

The Chinese Assembly Halls

Chinese immigrants to Hué settled in five congregations around their separate **Assembly Halls**, of which the most interesting is **Chua Ong**, 319 Chi Lang. Founded by the Phuoc Kien (Fujian) community in the mid-1800s and rebuilt on several occasions, including after Viet Cong mortars hit a US munitions boat on the river nearby in 1968 and destroyed the pagoda plus surrounding houses. Surprisingly, there's no Buddha on the main altar but instead several doctors of medicine, along with General Quan Cong to the right and Thien Hau to the left, both protectors of sailors. The story goes that Quan Cong sat on the main altar until a devastating cholera epidemic in 1918 when he was displaced by the doctors, and the outbreak ended soon after. Of the other halls, **Chieu Ung**, at no. 223, is worth dropping in to. The gilded altar displays some skilled carpentry. This pagoda was also founded in the nineteenth century by ethnic Chinese from Hai Nam, and has been rebuilt at least twice since.

Dong Ba Market

En route to or from Phu Cat you pass **Dong Ba Market**, the epicentre of Hué commercial life, a rambling covered market at the southeast corner of the citadel. Fruit, fish and vegetable vendors overflow into the surrounding spaces, while in the downstairs hall you'll find Hué's contribution to the world of fashion, the *non bai tho* or **poem hat**. These look just like the normal conical hat but have a stencil, traditionally of a romantic poem, inserted between the palm fronds – and only visible when held up to the light. The market is within walking distance of the centre, but a more enjoyable way to get there is to hop on one of the sampans that shuttle back and forth from beside the Dap Da causeway.

The European city

Although the French became the de facto rulers of Vietnam after 1884, they left the emperors in the citadel and built their administrative city across the Perfume River on the south bank. The main artery of the **European city** was riverside Le Loi where the French Resident's office stood, together with other important buildings such as **Quoc Hoc High School** and the *Frères Morin* hotel (now the *Saigon Morin*). Residential streets spread out south of the river as far as the Phu Cam Canal, and were linked to the citadel by Clemenceau Bridge, renamed Trang Tien Bridge after 1954. Apart from the high school, the only major sight is the **Ho Chi Minh Museum**, not just the obligatory gesture in this case as Ho actually did spend much of his childhood in Hué. The extraordinary, tiered spire of the **Redemptorist Church** dominates the southern horizon with its improbable blend of Gothic and Cubism created by a local architect in the late 1950s. The church caters to some of Hué's 20,000 Catholics and is interesting to view in passing, though the interior is less striking. Admirers of modern Vietnamese art should call in at the **Museum of Contemporary Art**, 1 Pham Boi Chau (daily 7.30–11am & 2–5pm) – in fact an exhibition of the works of Diem Phung Thi, who was born in Hué in 1920. The old villa provides the perfect setting for her chunky "modules" developed from Chinese calligraphy.

The Ho Chi Minh Museum

Ho Chi Minh was born near Vinh in Nghe An Province (see p.341), but spent ten years at school in Hué (1895–1901 and 1906–1909) where his father worked as a civil mandarin. The modern **Ho Chi Minh Museum** at 7 Le Loi (Tues–Sun 7.30–11am & 1.30–4.30pm; small entrance fee) presents these years in the context of the anti-French struggle and then takes the story on to 1960s' peace protests in Hué and reunification. The most interesting material consists of family photos and rare glimpses of early twentieth-century Hué. You can still see the house where Ho lived for a time with his father in Duong No Village on the way to Thuan An Beach (see p.330), but the primary school he attended near Dong Ba Market no longer exists.

Quoc Hoc High School

Ho Chi Minh was the most famous student to attend **Quoc Hoc High School**, which stands almost opposite his museum on Le Loi. The school was founded in 1896 as the National College, dedicated to the education of royal princes and future administrators who learnt about the history of their

One good argument for staying in Hué an extra couple of days is its many speciality foods, best sampled at local stalls and street kitchens. The most famous Hué dish is **banh khoai**, a small, crispy yellow **pancake** made of egg and rice flour, fried up with shrimp, pork and bean sprouts and eaten with a special peanut and sesame sauce (*nuoc leo*), plus a vegetable accompaniment of star fruit, green banana, lettuce and mint. Hué is also well known for its **noodles** and has its own spicy version of the rice-noodle soups, called *bun bo*, *bun ga* or *bun bo gio heo* depending on the meat used – beef, chicken or beef and pork – and flavoured with citronella, shrimp and basil.

There are even special **snacks**, usually eaten around four or five o'clock in the afternoon. Order *banh beo* and you get a whole trayful of individual dishes containing a small amount of steamed rice-flour dough topped with spices, shrimp flakes and a morsel of pork crackling; add a little sweetened *nuoc mam* sauce to each dish and tuck in with a teaspoon. *Banh nam*, or *banh lam*, is a similar idea but spread thinly in an oblong, steamed in a banana leaf and eaten with rich *nuoc mam* sauce. Manioc flour is used instead of rice for *banh loc*, making a translucent parcel of whole shrimps, sliced pork and spices steamed in a banana leaf, but this time the *nuoc mam* is pepped up with a dash of chilli. Finally, *ram it* consists of two small dollops of sticky rice-flour dough, one fried and one steamed, to dip in a spicy sauce.

One Hué dish that most people steer clear of, for fear of health repercussions, is *com hen* whose main ingredient is a small **shellfish** of the mussel family (*hen*) dredged up from around the Perfume River's Hen Island and further down the estuary. It's a popular and very tasty breakfast dish in summer, the main *hen* season, but can occasionally be found at other times of year in restaurants at the west end of Truong Dinh. *Com hen* is complicated to prepare, but its main constituents are *hen*, rice vermicelli noodles, shrimp sauce and chilli.

European "motherland" – all in French until 1945. Ho studied here for at least a year before being expelled for taking part in anti-government demonstrations. Other revolutionary names that appear on the roster are Prime Minister Pham Van Dong, General Giap and Party Secretary Le Duan, while former president of South Vietnam Ngo Dinh Diem was also a student. Even during the 1960s Quoc Hoc had a justly earned reputation for breeding dissident intellectuals, and after reunification in 1975 some staff were sent for "re-education".

Eating

It's not only Hué people who say their cuisine is the best in Vietnam, combining as it does special dishes originating from the imperial kitchens, vegetarian meals prepared with exquisite care in the pagodas, and simple but delicious "frugal meals" which are the essence of Hué home cooking; see the box above for more on Hué's **speciality foods**.

Much of the local cuisine originated from **imperial meals**, which involved many elaborate dishes presented like works of art before the royal family. Some of the large hotels, such as the *Saigon Morin* and *Huong Giang*, now stage "royal meals" for tourists, including traditional music and the opportunity to embarrass yourself in imperial togs. All this frivolity doesn't come cheap, though – the food is rich and plentiful, but at more than $80 for two it's really aimed at tour groups and business entertaining. If you fancy something sweet, the *Mai Huong* **patisserie** at 44 Nguyen Tri Phuong, next to the *Binh Minh I* hotel, is a good spot for coffee and pastries. Or you could try Hué's most famous *chè* outlet down the alley beside 29 Hung Vuong, where for next to nothing you can have a refreshing **drink** made from green bean and coconut (*chè xanh dua*), fruit (*chè trai cay*) or, if you're lucky, lotus seed (*chè hat sen*).

Most of the places listed below (and marked on the map, p.309) are found **south of the Perfume River**, near the hotels and guesthouses, but a few restaurants now opening up **in the citadel** make convenient lunch stops or are worth an excursion in their own right. Several of the smaller hotels serve decent food, usually all day, and there's no shortage of cafés or cheap and cheerful local hostelries scattered throughout the city.

Banh Khoai Hanh 4 Nguyen Tri Phuong. This tiny place tucked under an ancient banyan tree opposite the entrance to Le Loi school cooks up the best *banh khoai* in town.

Bun Bo Hué 11b Ly Thuong Kiet. Join breakfasting locals for spicy *bun bo* at this big, popular and scrupulously clean outlet.

Café 3 3 Le Loi. A cheap and cheerful streetside café opposite the *Le Loi 2 Hotel*, serving the standard range of Western and Vietnamese dishes, from spring rolls to fruit shakes. They also have an interesting range of tours on offer.

Café on Thu Wheels 10/2 Nguyen Tri Phuong. This tiny café-bar owned by the high-octane Ms Thu is a favourite among backpackers for its good food, loud music and friendly staff that run excellent motorbike tours around Hué. If you can come up with a new pun on "Thu", add it to the graffiti-covered walls and ceiling.

Club Garden 8 Vo Thi Sau ☏054/826327. One of several upscale garden restaurants along this street serving classic Vietnamese cuisine, with reasonably priced set menus ($8–15). Try and reserve a table outside.

Co Do 22 Ben Nghe. Small and inexpensive no-frills restaurant offering a limited menu of local dishes. Lemongrass and chilli are the predominant flavours, accompanying squid, chicken or shrimps. Some may find the seasoning on the heavy side, but the food is all very fresh and well prepared.

Dong Tam 48/7 Le Loi. This vegetarian restaurant run by a Buddhist family is an oasis of calm. The short menu includes vegetarian *banh khoai* and good-value combination plates, as well as a decent set menu for under $2. It's best at lunchtime when the food's freshest and you can sit in the garden courtyard.

Hang Me 20 Pham Ngu Lao. A locally famous establishment where you can sample *banh beo*, *banh loc* and *banh nam*. Look for a blue house set back from the road.

La Carambole 19 Pham Ngu Lao ☏054/810491. Innovative and attractive French/Vietnamese-owned restaurant serving good-quality international dishes, such as quiche, sandwiches, banana flambé and the like, as well as local foods. Other plus points are the range of set menus (from

around $4) and the attentive service. Reservations recommended.

Lac Thien 6 Dinh Tien Hoang. Probably Hué's friendliest and most interesting restaurant, located on the citadel side, *Lac Thien* is run by a deaf-mute family who communicate by sign language. The food is excellent, taking in the Hué staples, and prices remain reasonable, despite its fame. Not to be confused with other similarly named places along this street.

Mandarin Café 12 Hung Vuong. A leading light of Hué's backpacker business, this unassuming café off the main road rustles up cheap but very tasty Vietnamese and Western fare. Owner-photographer Mr Cu and his staff are also excellent sources of information and can assist with boat trips, bike/car rental and tours.

Minh & Coco 1 Hung Vuong. These two sisters pack them in with their cheery welcome and huge platefuls of food at rock-bottom prices. Next-door *Thuy Tien*, which shares the same awning, is equally good. Indeed, it's hard to tell them apart, though they are fierce rivals – even down to using the same party trick for opening the beer bottles.

Omar Khayyam's 34 Nguyen Tri Phuong. Good-value Indian restaurant, deservedly popular for its authentic North Indian fare, which includes a good vegetarian and *thali* selection.

Quoc Huy 43 Dinh Cong Trang. A useful pit stop in a quiet courtyard just east of the Imperial City. It's clean and friendly and offers some slightly unusual dishes, such as beef or chicken cooked in beer, all freshly prepared.

Saigon Morin 30 Le Loi. In addition to its swish European restaurant (set meals from around $10), the four-star hotel also runs a surprisingly cheap café with a good range of Vietnamese and international dishes at $1 (plus taxes), though drinks can bump it up. The food is well prepared and plentiful.

Song Huong Floating Restaurant Le Loi, just east of Trang Tien Bridge. If you can get one of the few outdoor tables, this makes a peaceful, breezy spot for a coffee or early-evening drink. The food's not bad either, with a set menu at around $3.

Stop & Go Café 10 Ben Nghe. Delightfully cluttered café-cum-beer garden run by the genial, silver-haired Mr Do. He offers the standard range of

Western comfort foods and local dishes, which you can wash down with a glass of rice wine, and also runs motorbike tours around Hué and up to the DMZ.
Tropical Garden 5 Chu Van An. Sister restaurant to the *Club Garden* above, offering similar deals but with a bigger garden and traditional music performances every night (7–9pm).
Vuon Y Thao 3 Thach Han ☎054/523018. It's worth splashing out to eat at this restaurant on the western edge of the citadel, where you feast on

beautifully presented imperial foods ($7 for a set meal) in the garden of a colonial villa. Reservations are required and traditional music can be arranged on request.
Xuan Trang Café 5 Nguyen Tri Phuong. Above-average backpackers' place with an extensive and reasonably priced menu (set meals start at $1.30); its ice creams and Hué speciality dishes are recommended. There's another branch nearby at 14 Hung Vuong.

Festivals and entertainment

Under the Nguyen emperors Hué was the cultural and artistic as well as political capital of Vietnam. A rich tradition of dance and music evolved from popular culture, from the complex rituals of the court and from religious ceremonies. Though much of this legacy has been lost over the last fifty years, considerable effort has gone into reviving Hué folk songs, *Ca Hué*, which you can now sample, drifting down the Perfume River on a balmy Hué evening. The city authorities have also instigated a **biennial arts festival** featuring not only folk songs, kite-flying, water-puppetry and other local traditions, but also international groups.

Historically the Perfume River was a place of pleasure where prostitutes cruised in their sampans and artists entertained the gentry with poetry and music. While the former officially no longer exist, today's **folk song performances** are based on the old traditions, eulogizing the city's beautiful scenery or the ten charms of a Hué woman – including long hair, dreamy eyes, flowing *ao dai*, and a conical hat – while she waits for her lover beside the river. Another popular strain is an improvised courtship song between a boy and girl, and occasionally you'll hear hypnotic, blues-like music, *Chau Van*, which accompanies the dance-trances at Hon Chen Temple, or the rhythmic chants of sampan rowers. The instruments themselves are intriguing, particularly the percussion section of four bone-china coffee cups and a wooden instrument garnished with old coins. Tickets ($3–4) can be arranged through hotels and tour agents. Alternatively, you can catch free performances at the *Tropical Garden* restaurant and in the courtyard of the *Saigon Morin* (both detailed under "Eating", above).

If you like your nightlife a bit more upbeat, then try one of Hué's two most popular **bars**, the *DMZ Bar* at 44 Le Loi for beers, pool and dancing, and the friendly *Café on Thu Wheels* (see "Eating", above) with cheap beer and loud music. Other, more laidback options for a drink include the *Saigon Morin's* rooftop bar (6.30–11pm), the *Song Huong Floating Restaurant* and the *Stop & Go Café* (all listed under "Eating").

Listings

Airlines Vietnam Airlines, in the *Thuan Hoa Hotel* at 7 Nguyen Tri Phuong ☎054/824709.
Airport bus A privately run bus service shuttles to and from the airport ($1.60). Organize a hotel pickup via your reception.
Bank and exchange Vietcombank, 78 Hung Vuong, exchanges cash and travellers' cheques and also has an ATM (open banking hours only). More convenient is the exchange bureau outside

the *Saigon Morin Hotel*. It's also open longer hours (Mon–Sat 7am–10pm) and boasts a 24hr ATM.
Email and Internet access Cybercafés can be found in the backpacker enclave of Hung Vuong and Nguyen Tri Phuong.
Hospital Hué Central Hospital is at 16 Le Loi ☎054/822325.
Immigration police 77 Ben Nghe. If you lose your passport, this is the place to head for.

Pharmacies You'll find well-stocked pharmacies at 9 Hoang Hoa Tham (actually round the corner on Tran Cao Van) and 37 Ben Nghe.

Post office The GPO occupies a grand new building at 8 Hoang Hoa Tham. Sub-branches are located at 38 Le Loi and in the station complex.

Taxi For a metered taxi call Mai Linh Taxi (ML; ☎054/898989), Hué Taxi (☎054/818181) or Gili Taxi (☎054/828282).

Tours and onward transport Mandarin Café (12 Hung Vuong, ☎054/534485, ✉mandarin@dng.vnn.vn), Sinh Café (7 Nguyen Tri Phuong; ☎054/845022, ✉sinh5hue@dng.vnn.vn), Queen Café (8 Hung Vuong; ☎054/849643, ✉phigreentravel@yahoo.com) and Phu Xuan Tourist (12 Hung Vuong; ☎054/848686) all offer reliable tours of Hué and the surrounding sights, including Perfume River boat trips, the DMZ and Bach Ma

National Park. For motorbike tours, contact Café on Thu Wheels (10/2 Nguyen Tri Phuong; ☎054/832241, ✉minhthu1970@hotmail.com), Stop & Go Café (10 Ben Nghe; ☎054/827051, ✉stop-and-go-cafe@yahoo.com) or Mandarin Café. Most of these places can also help arrange hire cars and other onward transport. Open-tour bus operators with offices in Hué include Sinh Café, Queen Café and TM Brothers (An Phu Tourist; 11 Nguyen Tri Phuong; ☎054/833897). If you're heading into Laos, your best option is to take the 6am DMZ tour bus as far as Dong Ha, then change to the 9am tourist bus bound for Savannakhet (odd days only). The total trip takes about 10hr and costs $16 to $17. A daily hydrofoil service departs from the wharf beside the Huong Giang Hotel for the 2hr journey south to Da Nang.

Around Hué

For the most part the Nguyen emperors lived their lives within Hué's citadel walls, but on certain occasions they emerged to participate in important rituals at symbolic locations around the city. Today these places are of interest more for their history than anything much to see on the ground, though the mouldering **Royal Arena** still hints at past spectacles.

A visit to at least a couple of the **Royal Mausoleums**, however, is not to be missed. It's in these eclectic architectural confections in the hills to the south of Hué that the spirit of the Ngueyn emperors lives on. Taking a boat along the **Perfume River** to get to the best mausoleums also offers the chance to stop off at the **Thien Mu Pagoda** and **Hon Chen Temple** on the way.

With time and energy, **Thuan An Beach** is a bike ride away, making for an attractive journey across the estuary with views of fish farms to either side, though the beach itself is nothing spectacular. Heading inland, you can kick back in **Thanh Tan Hot Spring Resort**, while further afield, one of the most popular excursions from Hué is a whirlwind day-trip round the **DMZ** (see p.334). **Bach Ma National Park** (see p.303) is also within striking distance.

Nam Giao

First and foremost in the ceremonial and religious life of the nation was **Nam Giao** ("Altar of Heaven"), where the emperor reaffirmed the legitimacy of his rule in sacred rituals, held here roughly every three years from 1807 to 1945. The ceremonies were performed on a series of hilltop terraces, two square-shaped and one round, symbolizing heaven, earth and man. Before each occasion the monarch purified himself, keeping to a strict regime of vegetarian food and no concubines for several days. He then carried out the sacrifices, with the assistance of some 5000 attendants, to ensure the stability of both the country and the dynasty. Nam Giao is 3km south of central Hué at the end of Dien Bien Phu.

Van Mieu

Confucianism had been the principal state religion in Vietnam since the eleventh century and the Nguyens were a particularly traditional dynasty. Early in his reign, in 1808, Gia Long dedicated a national temple to Confucius, known as **Van Mieu** or Van Thanh (the "Temple of Literature"), to replace that in Hanoi. Nothing much remains of the complex, beyond a collection of 32 stone stelae listing the names of 297 recipients of doctorates from exams held between 1822 and 1919. Two other stelae, under small shelters, record edicts from Minh Mang and Thieu Tri banning the "abuse of eunuchs and royal maternal relatives". You get a fine view of the royal landing stage and temple gate passing by on a Perfume River boat trip (see box overleaf). Alternatively, Van Mieu is only 500m by road west of Thien Mu Pagoda (see p.323).

AROUND HUÉ

Dong Ha (60km), Thanh Tan Hot Spring Resort (30km) & the DMZ

SOUTH CHINA SEA

Thuan An Beach

Perfume River

Duong No Village

Hwy-1

Hué

Hué Citadel

Van Mieu

Thien Mu

Train Station

Royal Arena

Tu Hieu

Duc Duc's Mausoleum

Phu Cam Canal

Ngu Binh Mountain

Nam Giao

Tu Duc's Mausoleum

Dong Khanh's Mausoleum

Hon Chen

Ferry

Thieu Tri's Mausoleum

Khai Dinh's Mausoleum

under construction

Ferry

Minh Mang's Mausoleum

Gia Long's Mausoleum

Phu Bai Airport

Bach Ma National Park (30km) & Da Nang (90km)

0   5km

The Royal Arena

On the opposite bank of the Perfume River stands the **Royal Arena**, or *Ho Quyen*, where the emperors amused themselves with fights between elephants and tigers. Not that this was entirely sport: elephants symbolized the unequalled might of the sovereign while tigers represented rebel forces, and the arena was built on the site of an old Cham fort just to underline the message of imperial power. It was, apparently, a pretty one-sided fight which the elephant was never allowed to lose, and contemporary accounts suggest that in later years the tigers were tied to a stake and had their claws removed. Originally the contests were held on open ground in front of the citadel, but after a tiger attacked Minh Mang they were staged in the arena from 1830 until the last fight in 1904.

The Royal Arena still exists almost in its original state, though the royal pavilion has rotted away. For the best view, climb up the staircase on the north wall to where the emperor would have sat facing south over the small arena only 44m across. After they died, the elephants were worshipped nearby in a small temple, **Long Chau Dien**, which stands to the west of the arena, although almost completely hidden by undergrowth and with only a couple of elephant statues to see: follow the path round the arena's south side to find the temple, overlooking a small lake.

The Royal Arena is 4km from central Hué, taking Bui Thi Xuan along the Perfume River's south bank through Phuong Duc, a famous metal-casting village. At 198 Bui Thi Xuan, turn left up a dirt track and take the left fork after 20m to see the arena's brick steps in front of you. If you want to combine the arena with the Royal Mausoleums (see p.325), you can use a rough backroad from Phuong Duc Village, though this takes you up steeper inclines than the main route to the mausoleums, via Dien Bien Phu.

Along the Perfume River

A boat trip on the **Perfume River** is one of the city's highlights (see box below), puttering in front of the citadel on a misty Hué morning, watching the slow bustle of river life. A sizeable number of people still live in boats on the Perfume River and the waterways of Hué, such as the Dong Ba and Phu Cam canals, despite government efforts to settle them elsewhere. Leaving the city behind, the first distinctive feature as you head upstream is the tower of **Thien Mu Pagoda**, which played a prominent role in the founding of Hué and in Vietnam's more recent history, but which is also famous for the natural beauty of its setting. Then, where the river loops south among low pine-clad hills, **Hon Chen Temple** harks back to the earlier Cham rulers of this region.

Boat trips on the Perfume River

A day's boating on the Perfume River is a good way to soak up some of the atmosphere of Hué and do a little gentle sightseeing off the roads. The standard **boat trip** takes you to Thien Mu Pagoda, Hon Chen Temple and the most rewarding mausoleums, usually those of Tu Duc, Khai Dinh and Minh Mang. However, if you want to visit some of the others or spend more time exploring, it's usually possible to take a bicycle on the boat and cycle back to Hué, though double-check this when you book the trip. Most tour agents (see "Listings", p.320) and hotels offer river tours starting at $1.50 per person, including a very meagre lunch but no guide. However, note that all the entrance fees are extra. If you'd rather do it independently, the same agents can arrange charter boats at $20–30 for the day, or go direct to the boat wharf beside the Trang Tien Bridge, where the going rate should be around $2–3 per hour.

As an alternative to going by boat, you can also cycle to Thien Mu along the north bank of the river. On the way, it's worth exploring the quiet lanes of Kim Long Village, where a number of traditional "**garden houses**" are open to the public.

Thien Mu Pagoda

Two closely related legends recount the history of **Thien Mu Pagoda**, also known as *Linh Mu* ("Pagoda of the Celestial Lady"), which stands on the site of an ancient Cham temple. In 1601 Lord Nguyen Hoang left Hanoi to govern the southern territories. Upon arriving at the Perfume River he met an elderly woman who told him to walk east along the river carrying a smouldering incense stick and to build his city where the incense stopped burning. Later Lord Hoang erected a pagoda in gratitude to the lady, whom he believed to be a messenger from the gods, on the site where they met. Another version has the white-haired lady, dressed in a red tunic with green trousers, appearing on a small hill shaped like a dragon's head and resting on a dragon's vein, and predicting that a lord would build a pagoda on the site and bring everlasting prosperity to the country. In either case Nguyen Hoang is credited with founding the pagoda in 1601, making it the oldest in Hué.

During the 1930s and 1940s Thien Mu was already renowned as a centre of Buddhist opposition to colonialism, and then in 1963 it became instantly famous when one of its monks, the Venerable Thich Quang Duc, burned himself to death in Saigon, in protest at the excesses of President Diem's regime (see box on p.99). The monk drove down from Thien Mu in his powder-blue Austin car, which is now on display just behind the main building with a copy of the famous photograph that shocked the world. Thien Mu has continued to be a focus for Buddhist protest against repression and a sore spot for the government.

Despite its turbulent history, the pagoda is a peaceful place where the breezy, pine-shaded terrace affords wide views over the Perfume River. Approaching by either road or river you can't miss the octagonal, seven-tier brick **stupa**, built by Emperor Thieu Tri in the 1840s, in which each tier represents one of Buddha's incarnations on earth. Two **pavilions**, one on each side respectively shelter a huge bell, cast in 1710, weighing over 2000 kilos and said to be audible in the city, and a large stele erected in 1715 to record the history of Buddhism in Hué. Walk inland to find the main sanctuary, fronted by a gilded Maitreya Buddha.

While most people arrive at Thien Mu Pagoda by tour boat, it's also within cycling distance of Hué (6km; 30min). Follow Le Duan (Highway 1) south from the citadel as far as the train tracks and then just keep heading west along the river where the road eventually gets quieter. If you've got time there's a pleasant **cycle ride** on from Thien Mu, past Van Mieu (see p.320) along an empty country lane beside the river, or you could explore the "garden houses" of Kim Long Village (see overleaf).

Hon Chen Temple

From Thien Mu boats continue westwards for a while, passing Van Mieu on the right, and then head south to stop at the rocky promontory of **Hon Chen Temple** ($1.60), named "Temple of the Jade Bowl" after the concave hill under which it sits. Again it's the scenery of russet temple roofs among towering trees that is memorable, though the site has been sacred since the Cham people came here to worship their divine protectress Po Nagar, whom the Vietnamese adopted as Y A Na, the Mother Goddess. Emperor Minh Mang restored Hon Chen Temple in the 1830s, but it was Dong Khanh who had a particular soft spot for the goddess after she predicted he would be emperor. He enlarged the temple in 1886, declared himself Y A Na's younger brother and is now worshipped alongside his favourite goddess in the main sanctuary, **Hue Nam**, up from the landing stage and to the right. Of several shrines and temples that populate the hillside, Hue Nam is the most interesting, particularly for its unique nine-tier altar table and a small, upper sanctuary room accessible via two steep staircases.

Festivals at Hon Chen were banned between Independence and 1986 but have now resumed, taking place twice yearly in the middle of the third and seventh lunar months. The celebrations, harking back to ancient rituals, include trance-dances performed by mediums, usually females dressed in brightly coloured costumes, who are transported by a pulsating musical accompaniment.

Hon Chen Temple is 9km from Hué and is only accessible from the river. If you don't want to take a **tour**, hire a sampan either from the **ferry** station directly opposite the temple (accessible from the riverside road), or from Minh Mang pier. Either way, expect to pay a couple of dollars per person for the return ride.

The Garden Houses

Travelling by road to Thien Mu along the north bank of the river you pass through **Kim Long** Village, a peaceful area of quiet lanes and canals where in the late nineteenth century mandarins and other imperial officials built their houses, surrounded by lush gardens. The seven most interesting of these "**garden houses**" have now been preserved and are open to the public. They're still lived in and, although there's no entry fee, a donation is expected (up to $1 would be appropriate). Note that it's best to avoid meal times and to dress conservatively.

The houses are strung along Phu Mong lane, which heads north from the riverbank between 68 and 70 Kim Long. The turning is a good kilometre west of the train tracks; keep your eyes peeled for a sign announcing "Tourism Centre Garden House" beside the turning. The first of the houses you come to, on the right behind an entrance arch at no. 20, was built by one of Emperor Gia Long's most senior generals. It's nevertheless a simple structure, consisting of a temple dedicated to the general and the house where his descendants now live. Continuing along Phu Mong lane, take the first turning right to find the next house second on the left behind a wire-mesh fence at 2 Diem Tham Quan. This house originally belonged to a Minister of Foreign Affairs under Emperor Tu Duc and is one of the few which still retains the original connecting passage between the house and temple. In front of the temple, a water basin backed by a stone screen represents the lake and mountain required by geomantic principles to defend the family from evil influences. The mangosteen tree, a rarity in Hué, growing behind the screen is said to have sprouted from a seed given to the mandarin by Tu Duc.

Perhaps the most interesting of the garden houses is the last, **An Lac Vien**, 1c Phu Mong. To reach it, head east for another 500m or so along Phu Mong, take a right fork and then follow the lane round to the end. It was built in 1888 by a junior mandarin under Thanh Thai. His grandson can give you an English-language leaflet and proudly show you round the house, full of family heirlooms, and – his pride and joy – the garden. Here he grows all manner of fruits (banana, sapodilla, persimmon, plum and papaya, to name but a few) for the family altar, vegetables and a number of medicinal plants, while the canal at the bottom of the garden doubles as a fish farm.

The Royal Mausoleums

These wise kings of Annam, who make death smile.

Charles Patris, late 1800s

Unlike previous Vietnamese dynasties, which buried their kings in the ancestral village, the Nguyen built themselves magnificent **Royal Mausoleums** in the valley of the Perfume River among low, forested hills to the south of Hué. For historical reasons only seven mausoleums were built, but each one is a unique expression of the monarch's personality, usually planned in detail during his lifetime to serve as his palace in death. It's here more than anywhere else in Hué that the Nguyen emperors excelled in achieving a harmony between the works of man and his natural surroundings and, along with the Imperial City, these are Hué's most rewarding sights.

It often took years to find a site with the right aesthetic requirements that would also satisfy the court cosmologists charged with interpreting the underlying supernatural forces. Artificial lakes, waterfalls and hills were added to improve the geomantic qualities of the location, at the same time creating picturesque, almost romantic, **garden settings** for the mausoleums, of which the finest examples are those of Tu Duc and Minh Mang. Though the details vary, all the mausoleums consist of three elements: a **temple** dedicated to the worship of the deceased emperor and his queen; a large, stone **stele** recording his biographical details and a history of his reign, usually written by his successor; and the royal **tomb** itself. The main temple houses the funerary tablets and possessions of the royal couple, many of which have been stolen, while nearby stand ancillary buildings where the emperor's concubines lived out their years. In front of each stele-house is a paved courtyard, echoing the Imperial City's Esplanade of Great Salutations, where officials and soldiers lined up to honour their emperor, but in this case the mandarins, horses and elephants are fashioned in stone; military mandarins are easily distinguished by their swords, whereas the civil variety clutch sceptres. Obelisks nearby symbolize the power of the monarch, and lastly, at the highest spot, there's the royal tomb enclosed within a wall and a heavy, securely fastened door. Traditionally the burial place was kept secret as a measure against grave-robbers and enemies of the state, and in extreme cases all those who had been involved in the burial were killed immediately afterwards.

Visiting the mausoleums

The mausoleums are intoxicating places, occasionally grandiose but more often achieving an elegant simplicity, where it's easy to lose yourself wandering in the quiet gardens. Of the seven, the contrasting mausoleums of Tu Duc, Khai Dinh and Minh Mang are the most attractive and well-preserved, as well as being easily accessible. These are also the three covered by the boat trips, so they can get crowded; don't let this put you off – but if you do want something more off the beaten track then those of Gia Long, Dong Khanh and Thieu Tri are worth calling in on. Finally, Duc Duc's temple and mausoleum is very modest but is the closest to Hué, and is still tended by members of the royal family. Even if time allows, however, you probably won't want to visit all the mausoleums at a **ticket price** of $3.50 a pop for the first three and $1.30 for the rest. The mausoleums are **open** from 7am to 5pm every day, but note that it's best to avoid weekends if possible when they're at their busiest.

To get to the mausoleums you can either rent a **bicycle** or **motorbike** for the day (see "Arrival, information and getting around", p.307), or take a **motorbike tour**, which normally includes at least one mausoleum, with one of the tour agents listed on p.320. The most popular option, however, is a Perfume River boat trip (see box on p.322). On a **boat tour**, you'll face a couple of longish walks, while with your own wheels you'll have to negotiate your own ferry crossings, but will have more time to explore, and won't be restricted to the three main mausoleums. A good compromise is to take a bike on board a tour boat and cycle back to Hué from the last stop.

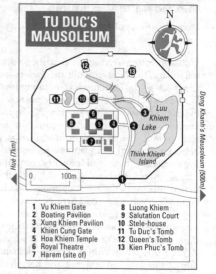

1 Vu Khiem Gate
2 Boating Pavilion
3 Xung Khiem Pavilion
4 Khien Cung Gate
5 Hoa Khiem Temple
6 Royal Theatre
7 Harem (site of)
8 Luong Khiem
9 Salutation Court
10 Stele-house
11 Tu Duc's Tomb
12 Queen's Tomb
13 Kien Phuc's Tomb

The Mausoleum of Tu Duc

Emperor Tu Duc was a romantic poet trying to rule Vietnam at a time when the Western world was challenging the country's independence. Although he was the longest-reigning of the Nguyen monarchs, he was a weak ruler who preferred to hide from the world in the lyrical pleasure gardens he created. The **Mausoleum of Tu Duc** is the most harmonious of all the mausoleums, with elegant pavilions and pines reflected in serene lakes. The walled, twelve-hectare park took only three years to complete (1864–67), allowing Tu Duc a full sixteen years for boating and fishing, meditation, drinking tea made from dew collected in lotus blossoms, and composing some of the 4000 poems he is said to have written, besides several important philosophical and historical works. Somehow he also found time for fifty-course meals, plus 104 wives and a whole village of concubines living in the park, though – possibly due to a bout of smallpox – he fathered no children. Perhaps it's not surprising that Tu Duc was also a tyrant who pushed the 3000 workmen building his mausoleum so hard that they rebelled in 1866, and were savagely dealt with.

Entering by the southern gate, **Vu Khiem**, brick paths lead beside a lake covered in water lilies and lotus to a small three-tiered **boating pavilion** which looks across to larger **Xung Khiem Pavilion**, where Tu Duc drank wine and wrote poetry; *khiem*, meaning "modest", appears in the name of every building. From the lake, steps head up through a triple-arched gateway, the middle door painted yellow for the emperor, into a second enclosure containing the main temple, **Hoa Khiem**, which Tu Duc used as an office before his death. The royal funerary tablets here are unusual in that Tu Duc's, bearing a dragon, is smaller than the phoenix-decorated tablet of the queen. Beyond is a second temple, **Luong Khiem**, which served as the royal residence, and the elegant **royal theatre**, while behind the storerooms opposite once stood the quarters for Tu Duc's numerous concubines.

The second group of buildings, to the north, is centred on the emperor's tomb, preceded by the salutation court and stele-house. Tu Duc's stele, weighing twenty tonnes, is by far the largest; unusually, Tu Duc wrote his own eulogy, running to over 4000 characters to elucidate all his difficulties. Behind the stele is a kidney-shaped pond, representing the crescent moon, and then a bronze door leading into a square enclosure where the unadorned tomb shelters behind a screen adorned with the characters for longevity. Emperor Kien Phuc, one of Tu Duc's adopted sons, is also buried here, just north of the lake.

Tu Duc's Mausoleum is 7km from central Hué **by road**. From the **boat** jetty, it's a walk of 2km from the river on a dirt track, or take one of the **Honda om** waiting on the river bank (around $1.50–2 return). On the way you pass incense sticks out to dry and people making – and selling – Hué's famous conical hats.

The Mausoleum of Khai Dinh

By way of a complete contrast the **Mausoleum of Khai Dinh** is a monumental confection of European baroque, highly ornamental Sino-Vietnamese style, and even incorporates elements of Cham architecture. Its most attractive feature is the setting, high up on a wooded hill, but it's worth climbing the 130-odd steps to take a look inside the sanctuary itself, still in its original state. Khai Dinh was the penultimate Nguyen emperor and his mausoleum is a radical departure from its predecessors, with neither gardens nor living quarters and only one main structure. Khai Dinh was also a vain man, a puppet of the French very much taken with French style and architecture, and though he only reigned for nine years it took eleven (1920–31) to complete his mausoleum, and it cost so much he had to levy additional taxes for the project.

The approach is via a series of grandiose, dragon-ornamented stairways leading first to the salutation courtyard, with an unusually complete honour guard of mandarins, and on to the stele-house. Climbing up a further four terraces brings you to the **principal temple**, built of reinforced concrete with slate roofing imported from France, whose extravagant halls are a startling contrast to the blackened exterior. Walls, ceiling, furniture, everything is decorated to the hilt, writhing with dragons and peppered with symbolic references and classic imagery such as the Four Seasons panels in the antechamber. Most of this lavish display, not as garish as it might sound, is worked in glass and porcelain mosaic – even the central canopy, which looks like fabric though it's actually made of cement. A life-size gilded bronze statue of the emperor holding his royal sceptre sits under the canopy, while his altar table and funerary tablet are up on the mezzanine floor behind. His portrait stands on the incense table in the antechamber. Khai Dinh was a particularly flamboyant dresser and it's rumoured that he brought back a string of fairy lights from France and proceeded to wear them around the palace, twinkling, until the batteries ran out.

Khai Dinh's Mausoleum is 10km from Hué **by road**. Arriving **by boat**, it's a 1.5-kilometre walk, heading eastwards up a valley with a giant Quan Am statue on your right until you see the mausoleum on the opposite hillside.

The Mausoleum of Minh Mang

Court officials took fourteen years to find the location for the **Mausoleum of Minh Mang** – for which the mandarin responsible was awarded two promotions – and then only three years to build (1841–43), using 10,000 workmen. Minh Mang, the second Nguyen emperor, was a capable, authoritarian monarch who was selected for his serious nature and distrust of Western religious infiltration. He was also passionate about architecture – it was Minh Mang who completed Hué citadel after Gia Long's death – and designed his mausoleum along traditional Chinese lines, with all the principal buildings symmetrical about an east–west axis. But the mausoleum's stately grandeur is softened by fifteen hectares of superb landscaped gardens, almost a third of which is taken up by lakes reflecting the handsome, red-roofed pavilions.

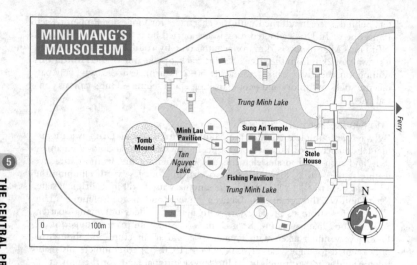

MINH MANG'S MAUSOLEUM

Trung Minh Lake

Minh Lau Pavilion

Sung An Temple

Tomb Mound

Tan Nguyet Lake

Stele House

Fishing Pavilion

Trung Minh Lake

Ferry

N

0   100m

Inside the mausoleum a processional way links the series of low mounds bearing all the main buildings. After the salutation courtyard and stele-house comes the **principal temple** (*Sung An*), where Minh Mang and his queen, who died at the age of 17, are worshipped. Despite this early loss, Minh Mang managed to father 142 children with his 33 wives and 107 concubines. Though beautifully restored, the only point of interest about the temple itself is that local Christians vandalized it in 1885 to protest against Minh Mang's virulent anti-Catholicism. Continuing west you reach **Minh Lau**, the elegant, two-storey "Pavilion of Pure Light" standing among clouds of frangipani trees, symbols of longevity, while beyond two stone gardens trace the Chinese character for long life. From here the ceremonial pathway crosses a crescent lake and ends at the circular burial mound.

Until the new road bridge is completed, getting to Minh Mang's Mausoleum by road is a little complicated: from Khai Dinh's tomb, follow the **road** west until you hit the Perfume River (1.5km) and turn left along the bank, looking out on your left for the village post office, opposite which you'll find **sampans** to take you across the river (under a dollar return per person). The entrance is then a couple of hundred metres' walk through a barrage of souvenir-sellers. Note that this is also where you'll pick up sampans for Gia Long's Mausoleum and the Hon Chen Temple (see p.323).

The Mausoleum of Gia Long

As the first Nguyen ruler, Gia Long had his pick of the sites, and he chose an immense natural park 16km from Hué on the left bank of the Perfume River. Unfortunately the **Mausoleum of Gia Long** was badly damaged during the American War and there's not a great deal to see beyond some fine carving and a double tomb with pitched roofs housing Gia Long and his wife. However, this is the least-visited of Hué's mausoleums and is recommended for the boat trip and the peaceful stroll through sandy pine forest – though some visitors complain of attracting a convoy of persistent soft-drink sellers for the duration of the two-kilometre walk. You approach the complex from the north to find the main temple, tomb and stele-house all aligned on a horizontal axis, looking south across a lake towards Thien Tho Mountain. The mausoleum was begun in 1814 and completed shortly after the emperor's death in 1820.

The easiest way to reach Gia Long's Mausoleum is **by road** as far as the Minh Mang boat station, from where a **sampan** (20min each way) costs around $6, including waiting time.

The Mausoleum of Dong Khanh

Dong Khanh died suddenly at the age of 25 after only three years on the throne, and so never got round to planning his final resting place but was buried near the temple he dedicated to his father. As a result the **Mausoleum of Dong Khanh** is a modest affair built in open countryside, but it has a rustic charm and is particularly well preserved. Dong Khanh was put on the throne by the French in 1885 as titular head of their new protectorate. He was a pliant ruler with a fondness for French wine, perfume and alarm clocks.

The mausoleum consists of two parts: the main temple, and then the tomb and stele in a separate, walled enclosure on a slight rise 100m to the northwest. The complex was built mostly by Dong Khanh's son, Khai Dinh, after 1889, though has been added to since. The **main temple** holds most of interest: the first thing you notice are the coloured-glass doors and windows, but the faded murals on each side wall showing scenes of daily life are far more attractive. Twenty-four glass-paintings, illustrated poems of Confucian love, hang on the temple's ironwood columns and, at either end of the first row, are two engravings of Napoleon and the Battle of Waterloo. The three principal altars honour Dong Khanh with his two queens to either side, while his seven concubines have a separate altar in the back room. Finally, don't miss the altar to Y A Na in a small side-chamber, off to the right as you enter: Dong Khanh often consulted the goddess at Hon Chen Temple (see p.323) and dedicated an altar to her after she appeared in a dream and foretold that he would be emperor.

Dong Khanh's Mausoleum is only 500m from Tu Duc's. Follow the **road** round to the southeast or take a **short cut** over the hill by the **footpath** from between the refreshment stalls, forking left twice before you see Dong Khanh's tomb on your right and the temple straight ahead behind some trees.

The Mausoleum of Thieu Tri

Emperor Thieu Tri was the son of Minh Mang and shared his father's aversion to foreign influences – it's said he destroyed anything Western he found in the imperial palaces – and his taste in architecture. The **Mausoleum of Thieu Tri** follows the same basic pattern as Minh Mang's though without the attractive walled gardens, and is split into two sections placed side by side. As it's also smaller it took less than a year to build (1847–48), but its most distinctive feature is that it faces northwest, a traditionally inauspicious direction, and many people believed that this was the reason the country fell under the French yoke a few years later. Although the salutation courtyard, stele-house and tomb are suffering from serious neglect, the temple itself is in reasonable shape. It contains numerous poems, in mother-of-pearl or painted on glass, since Thieu Tri was a prolific poet who would pen a stanza or two at a moment's notice.

To get here from Hué follow the **road** towards Khai Dinh's Mausoleum, but after Cau Lim Bridge branch right beside a faded sign saying "Lang Thieu Tri" opposite the Social Welfare School. The mausoleum is 6km from the centre of Hué.

The Mausoleum of Duc Duc

Three emperors are buried at the **Mausoleum of Duc Duc** which, although it's the closest to Hué, is rarely visited. Duc Duc and his wife are buried in a walled compound, while emperors Thanh Thai and Duy Tan are interred in a separate row of graves behind the main temple, built in 1899. Duc Duc was forced to resign by his senior courtiers after a mere three days as emperor in 1883 and died a year later in prison, while his son, Thanh Thai, was also removed in 1907 after a suspected anti-French conspiracy. The French then put Thanh Thai's 8-year-old son, Duy Tan, on the throne, but he fled the palace nine years later amid another revolutionary plot, and was eventually exiled with his father to the French territory of Réunion in the Indian Ocean. Duy Tan died in a World War II plane crash in 1945, fighting on the side of the Allies, but Thanh Thai was allowed back to Vietnam in 1947 and died in Saigon in the 1950s. Descendants of the imperial family, two French-speaking nephews of Bao Dai, still live in the temple buildings and possess a historic collection of family photos including some of the funeral of Thanh Thai.

Find the mausoleum down **Duong Duy Tan** (opposite 74 Tran Phu), 100m along on the right; someone will show you around for a small donation.

Tu Hieu Pagoda

While you're out exploring the mausoleums it's worth making a short detour to visit **Tu Hieu Pagoda**, buried in the pine forests northeast of Tu Duc's Mausoleum. Although it's not the most famous pagoda in Hué, Tu Hieu is one of the most attractive, and it does have an imperial link since this is where royal eunuchs retired to and were worshipped after their deaths. The pagoda was founded in 1843 and still houses an active community of forty monks who extend a warm welcome to their occasional visitors. The main altar is dedicated to Sakyamuni, with the Buddhist trinity sitting up above, while a secondary shrine room behind contains altars to several famous mandarins and the eunuchs. Between the two buildings is a small courtyard festooned with orchids and a 100-year-old star-fruit vine. To find the pagoda, take the road towards Tu Duc's Mausoleum from the Nam Giao T-junction and near the top of the hill look out for two tall columns announcing "Tu Hieu". Turn right here down a dirt road and then fork left to reach the pagoda's triple-arched gate behind which lies a peaceful, crescent-moon lake. There is no charge to visit the Tu Hieu Pagoda.

Thuan An Beach

Northeast of Hué, the Perfume River ends in a vast estuary lagoon, sheltered by a long sandy spit with **Thuan An Beach** at its northern end. It was here that Rear Admiral Courbet landed a thousand members of the French Expeditionary Force in August 1883, which ultimately persuaded the Vietnamese monarchs to recognize the French Protectorate. Nowadays Thuan An is a quiet place where residents of Hué come to escape the summer heat. The beach itself is inferior to Hoi An's Cua Dai or Da Nang's China Beach (see p.287 and p.300 respectively), but nice enough once you get away from the litter and the pestering, sometimes aggressive, deck-chair attendants – head south down the beach for the quieter, cleaner sands. You'll also find a number of small seafood restaurants along here; remember to check the prices before ordering.

Thuan An is 14km from Hué by road, through flat rice country and via a causeway which floods easily in the monsoon season (late Sept to early March), when the sea here also gets very rough. On the way you pass through Duong No Village, 8km outside Hué, where Ho Chi Minh once lived with his father. It's a pleasant **cycle** ride or, alternatively, you can take a local **bus** from Hué's Dong Ba bus station, beside Dong Ba Market on the river's north bank, for the thirty-minute ride, but note that the last bus back leaves around 4pm. If you have your own transport, you'll have to pay a nominal **parking fee** at the beach.

Thanh Tan Hot Spring Resort

If you have a half-day to spare in Hué and want to experience something different, you could soak in the soothing waters of **Thanh Tan Hot Spring Resort** ($1; ☎054/553192, ⓦwww.thanhtan.com), 33km northwest of the city. It's an attractive setting, located on the edge of the hills in extensive landscaped gardens. The water, which is channelled to a series of pools and private baths, comes out of the ground at a hot 60°C – it's best appreciated on chilly winter days. Note, too, that weekends get crowded at any time of year. Local women tend to bathe in shorts and a T-shirt rather than a swimming costume, while men wear trunks. Don't forget to bring a towel, and you might also like to bring a picnic, though there's a reasonable restaurant on site. If you get thirsty, you can buy bottles of Thanh Tan mineral water to sup while you soak.

If you've got your own **transport**, head north up Highway 1 to An Lo Town, then look out for the turning signed to the left just after you've crossed the Song Bo River. Some Hué tour agents offer **tours** to Thanh Tan, priced at around $5 including entry, or you could rent a car and driver for around $15 to $20 for a half-day excursion.

Dong Ha and the DMZ

Quang Tri and Quang Binh, the two provinces either side of the **DMZ** (Demilitarized Zone), were the most heavily bombed and saw the highest casualties, civilian and military, American and Vietnamese, during the American War. Names made infamous in 1960s' and 1970s' America have been perpetuated in countless films and memoirs: Con Thien, the Rockpile, Hamburger Hill and Khe Sanh. For some people the DMZ will be what draws them to Vietnam, the end of a long and difficult pilgrimage; for others it will be a bleak, sometimes beautiful, place where there's nothing particular to see but where it's hard not to respond to the sense of enormous desolation. Most visitors take an organized trip out of Hué (see "Listings", p.319 for recommended operators). It's also possible to use **Dong Ha** as a base or cover a more limited selection of sights on the drive north. From Dong Ha the old French road, Highway 9, runs parallel to the DMZ on its way west to the **Lao Bao** border gate, the main land crossing into Laos from Vietnam.

Quang Tri

American troops weren't the first to suffer heavy losses in this region: during the 1950s French soldiers dubbed the stretch of Highway 1 north of Hué as *la rue sans joie*, or "street without joy", after they came under constant attack from elusive Viet Minh units operating out of heavily fortified villages along the coast. Later, in the 1972 Easter Offensive, communist forces overran the whole area, capturing **QUANG TRI** Town, some 60km from Hué, from the South Vietnamese Army (ARVN) and holding it for four months while American B-52s pounded the township and surrounding countryside, before it was retaken at huge cost to both sides as well as to hapless civilians caught up in the battle. Quang Tri was simply wiped off the map, and though a town of sorts has risen in its stead, known officially as **Trieu Hai**, you could be forgiven for missing it. Keep your eyes peeled for one of its few identifying features, the small, pockmarked shell of **Long Hung Church** to the east of the road, 55km from Hué, kept as a memorial to victims of 1972. Soon after, a track on the opposite side of the highway leads 4km south to the more impressive ruin of **La Vang**

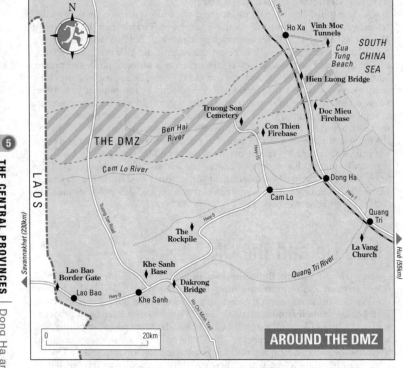

Church, beside which stands an extraordinary monument of *Alice in Wonderland* mushrooms supposedly representing the apparition of the Virgin Mary to persecuted Catholics on this spot in 1798.

The town itself lies off to the right of the highway down Tran Hung Dao, the last sealed road before you reach the Quang Tri River. There's not a lot to see, but if you've got your own transport the remains of **Quang Tri Citadel** ($1) are worth a look. The square, walled structure, resembling a smaller version of the citadel in Hué, was originally built from earth in 1806 by the Nguyen dynasty, fortified with bricks in 1827, and served in turn as a base for the French and the ARVN before being overrun and destroyed in 1972. Parts of the wall and moat remain, and the south gate, through which visitors enter, has been rebuilt. Inside is a war memorial, the remains of a nineteenth-century French prison consisting of fourteen tiny cells measuring 1m by 2m, and a small war **museum** ($1). Though there are no captions in English, the museum houses some excellent photos of the fierce hand-to-hand fighting that took place towards the end of 1972 as ARVN troops eventually retook the city after 81 days. Stick to established paths, as unexploded ordnance may still lurk. To find the citadel, continue on Tran Hung Dao for 2km, passing a market on your left, then turn down a dirt road, Ly Thai To, which leads to the entrance. Back on the highway, the road and rail line share a bridge over the Quang Tri River from where it's only another 13km to the town of Dong Ha, which took over as provincial capital when Quang Tri ceased to exist.

Dong Ha

As a former US Marine Command Post and then ARVN base, **DONG HA** was also obliterated in 1972, but unlike Quang Tri it has bounced back, thanks largely to its administrative status and location at the eastern end of Highway 9 which leads through Laos to Savannakhet on the Mekong River (see below for details of cross-border travel). The future looks rosy as well: a new deep-water port has been built to serve landlocked Laos, a number of special economic zones are under construction along the border, and there are plans to upgrade Highway 9 as part of the massive Trans-Asian Highway project. As the closest town to the DMZ, Dong Ha also attracts a lot of tourist traffic, though few people choose to stay here, preferring the comfort and facilities of Hué.

Dong Ha is essentially a two-street town: Highway 1, known here as Le Duan, forms the main artery as it passes through on its route north, while Highway 9 takes off inland at a central T-junction. The town's **bus station** is located immediately north of this junction, while its **train station** lies a kilometre south towards Hué and just west of the highway. The market and bridge over the Cua Viet River, a kilometre beyond the bus station, mark Dong Ha's northern extremity, where Tran Hung Dao branches left to the **post office** (spot the telltale radio mast) and the remains of three US tanks rotting beside the junction. **Information**, car rental and **guides** can be found at the Thuong Mai Travel Agency (☎053/855289, ✆tmqttour@dng.vnn.vn), based in the *Thuong Mai Hotel* (see overleaf), and at the *Trung Tam Quan Guesthouse* (see overleaf). Both places sell tickets for **open-tour buses** and for DMZ tours ($10–11), on

Across the border into Laos

Though there are now two **border crossings** open to foreigners between Vietnam and Laos, the most popular is still **Lao Bao**, 80km west of Dong Ha along Highway 9. It's an attractive ride, through misty mountains on a reasonable road, and the crossing is hassle-free beyond having to walk a kilometre between inspection posts. Frequent local **buses** and **minibuses** run from Dong Ha to the border and back (2hr; $2–3), though some stop at Lao Bao Village, in which case you'll have to pick up a **Honda om** for the final 3km. On the Laotian side, buses leave for Savannakhet, from where there are connections north to Vientiane by road, river (both unpredictable during the rains) and air, or you can head straight over the Mekong River to Mukdahan in Thailand. A quicker and more comfortable alternative is to take the morning air-conditioned **tourist bus** direct from Dong Ha to Savannakhet (8hr; $13). At the time of writing these left Dong Ha for Savannakhet around 9am on odd days and returned on even days, though there's talk of starting a daily service. Alternatively, there's an **overnight bus** all the way from Da Nang to Savannakhet; see p.295 for details.

It's also possible to cross into Laos at **Cau Treo**, 105km southwest of Vinh (see p.342) on Highway 8. Early-morning **public buses** (5–9am) depart from Vinh's provincial bus station (Ben Xe Cho Vinh) as far as Trung Tam, the last settlement of any size before the border. From there you'll have to pick up a minibus or xe om (under $2) for the last 25km to Cau Treo or, better still, **hitch** a ride on a truck heading all the way to Lak Sao, 20km across the border in Laos. There's also a **tourist bus** all the way to Vientiane from Hanoi (22hr; $22–25) via Vinh (12–14hr; $20); it leaves Hanoi at 7pm and reaches Vinh around midnight. Crossing **into Vietnam** at Cau Treo, if there are no Trung Tam minibuses waiting, a car to Vinh should cost around $30 with a bit of bargaining.

You can obtain Lao **visas** at either the Lao Consulate in Da Nang or their Hanoi embassy; see p.295 and p.402 respectively.

which you join the coach originating in Hué, while the latter also offers guided motorbike tours ($15) as well as motorbike rental ($7 per day) and **Internet** access. The town's **bank** at 1 Le Quy Don – the first main road on the left heading north on Highway 1 from the bus station – can exchange US dollars and handle advances on Visa and MasterCard, but can't change travellers' cheques.

Accommodation and eating

The **accommodation** market in Dong Ha is dominated by a string of dreary, damp, state-run guesthouses. There are a few exceptions, however, of which by far the best is the clean and comfortable *Phung Hoang II* at 146 Le Duan (℡053/854567, ©victoryqt@dng.vnn.vn; ❷), with a range of en-suite rooms, on Highway 1 about 500m south of the bus station. Otherwise, there's the shabbier *Thuong Mai* at 1 Phan Boi Chau (℡053/856489, ℱ858337; ❶–❷), signed off Tran Hung Dao between the market and the post office, where cheaper rooms come with cold-water showers, and the *Trung Tan Quan Guesthouse* at 201 Le Duan (℡053/852972, ©ttquan@dng.vnn.vn; ❶), about a 100m south of the bus station on the opposite side of the highway. It has just two fan rooms with reasonably clean shared toilets and hot-water shower.

Both the *Thuong Mai Hotel* and *Trung Tan Quan Guesthouse* serve cheap and acceptable meals, but Dong Ha's best **restaurants** are first and foremost the *Tan Chau II* at 222 Le Duan, near the *Phung Hoang II Hotel*, followed by the *Hiep Loi*, at the intersection of highways 1 and 9. Otherwise, there's no shortage of no-nonsense places serving *com* and *pho* all along Highway 1.

The DMZ and around

Under the terms of the 1954 Geneva Accords, Vietnam was split in two along the Seventeenth Parallel, pending elections intended to reunite the country in 1956. The demarcation line ran along the Ben Hai River and was sealed by a strip of no-man's-land 5km wide on each side known as the **Demilitarized Zone**, or DMZ. All communist troops and supporters were supposed to regroup north in the Democratic Republic of Vietnam, leaving the southern Republic of Vietnam to non-communists and various shades of opposition. When the elections failed to take place, the Ben Hai River became the de facto border until 1975.

In reality both sides of the DMZ were anything but demilitarized after 1965, and anyway the border was easily circumvented – by the Ho Chi Minh Trail to the west (see box on p.336) and sea routes to the east – enabling the North Vietnamese to bypass a string of American fire bases overlooking the river. One of the more fantastical efforts to prevent communist infiltration southwards was US Secretary of Defense Robert McNamara's proposal for an electronic fence from the Vietnamese coast to the Mekong River, made up of seismic and acoustic sensors that would detect troop movements and pinpoint targets for bombing raids. Though trials in 1967 met with some initial success, the "McNamara Line" was soon abandoned: sensors were confused by animals, especially elephants, and could be triggered deliberately by the tape-recorded sound of vehicle engines or troops on the march.

Nor could massive, conventional bombing by artillery and aircraft contain the North Vietnamese, who finally stormed the DMZ in 1972 and pushed the border 20km further south. Exceptionally bitter fighting in the territory south of the Ben Hai River (I Corps Military Region) claimed more American lives in the five years leading up to 1972 than any other battle zone in Vietnam.

Figures for North Vietnamese losses during that period are not known, but it's estimated that up to thirty percent of ordnance dropped in the DMZ failed to detonate on impact and that these have, since 1975, been responsible for up to 10,000 deaths and injuries. So much fire power was unleashed over this area, including napalm and herbicides, that for years nothing would grow in the impacted, chemical-laden soil, but the region's low, rolling hills are now almost entirely reforested with a green sea of pine, eucalyptus, coffee and acacia.

Some civilians north of the DMZ managed to escape the onslaught by relocating their villages into tunnels deep underground, of which the most famous are those of Vinh Moc. Unlike the Cu Chi tunnels, near Ho Chi Minh City (see p.127), these ones were built primarily for civilian use and have been preserved in their original form. Apart from Vinh Moc, the area's main sights lie south of the Ben Hai River. Even in a long day it's not possible to cover everything, but the most interesting of the places described below are included on organized tours from Hué. If you have limited time then the Vinh Moc tunnels should be high on your list, along with a drive up Highway 9 to Khe Sanh, both for the scenery en route and the sobering battleground itself. Note that, although you can now visit the DMZ without a local guide, this is not recommended as most sites are unmarked and, more importantly, the guides know which paths are safe – local farmers are still occasionally killed or injured by unexploded ordnance in this area. Guides can be arranged in Dong Ha (see p.333).

North to the Vinh Moc tunnels

The American front line comprised a string of fire bases set up on a long, low ridge of hills looking north across the DMZ and the featureless plain of the Ben Hai River. Although there's nothing much to see now, you pass the site of one of these, **Doc Mieu Fire Base**, to the east of Highway 1 about 14km north of Dong Ha. Before the NVA overran Doc Mieu in 1972, the base played a pivotal role in the South's defence. From here American guns shelled seaborne infiltration routes and, for a while, this was the command post for the "McNamara Line", calling in airstrikes from Da Nang to pound targets – both real and faked – along the Ho Chi Minh Trail.

Just beyond Doc Mieu, Highway 1 drops down into the DMZ, running between paddy fields to **Hien Luong Bridge** and the Ben Hai River, which lies virtually on the Seventeenth Parallel. Until it was destroyed in 1967, the original bridge was painted half red and half yellow as a vivid reminder that this was a physical and ideological boundary separating the two Vietnams. The present iron-girder bridge was reconstructed in 1973 and officially re-opened in 1975 as a symbol of reunification, though it still represents an important psychological barrier between north and south.

In Ho Xa township, 7km north of the Ben Hai River and 28km from Dong Ha, a signpost indicates a right turn which takes you 15km to an amazing complex of tunnels where over a thousand people sheltered, sometimes for weeks on end, during the worst American bombardments. A section of the **Vinh Moc tunnels** has been restored and opened to visitors as a powerful tribute to the villagers' courage and tenacity, with a small museum at the entrance providing background information (daily 7am–5pm; $1.60 including English-speaking guide and flashlight). Although not recommended for the claustrophobic, the tour only takes around fifteen minutes and these tunnels were built bigger (the ceiling is almost 2m high in places) than those of Cu Chi.

When American bombing raids north of the DMZ intensified in 1966 the inhabitants of Vinh Linh District began digging down into the red laterite soils, excavating more than fifty tunnels over the next two years. Although they were also used by North Vietnamese soldiers, the tunnels were primarily built to shelter a largely civilian population who worked the supply route from the Con Co Islands lying 28km offshore. Five tunnels belonged to Vinh Moc, a village located right on the coast where for two years 250 people dug more than

The Ho Chi Minh Trail

At the end of its "working" life, the Ho Chi Minh Trail had grown from a rough assemblage of animal tracks and **jungle paths** to become a highly effective **logistical network** stretching from near Vinh, north of the Seventeenth Parallel, to Tay Ninh Province on the edge of the Mekong Delta. Initially it took up to six months to walk the trail from north to south, most of the time travelling at night while carrying rations of rice and salt, medicines and equipment; in four years one man, Nguyen Viet Sinh, is reputed to have carried more than fifty tonnes and covered 40,000km, equivalent to walking round the world. By 1975, however, the trail – comprising at least three main arteries plus several feeder roads leading to various battlefronts and totalling over **15,000km** – was wide enough to take tanks and heavy trucks, and could be driven in just one week. It was protected by sophisticated anti-aircraft emplacements and supported by regular service stations (fuel and maintenance depots, ammunition dumps, food stores and hospitals), often located underground or in caves and all connected by field telephone. Eventually there was even an oil pipeline constructed alongside the trail to take fuel south from Vinh to a depot at Loc Ninh. All this absorbed thousands of men and women in maintenance work, as engineers, gunners and medical staff, while as many as 50,000 Youth Volunteers repaired bridges and filled in bomb craters under cover of darkness.

The trail was conceived in early 1959 when **General Giap** ordered the newly created Logistical Group 559 to reconnoitre a safe route by which to direct men and equipment down the length of Vietnam in support of communist groups in the south. Political cadres blazed the trail, followed in 1964 by the first deployment of 10,000 regular troops, and culminating in the trek south of 150,000 men in preparation for the **1968 Tet Offensive**. It was a logistical feat that rivalled Dien Bien Phu (see p.459) in both scale and determination: this time it was sustained over fifteen years and became a symbol to the Vietnamese of both their victory and their sacrifice. For much of its southerly route the trail ran through **Laos** and **Cambodia**, sometimes on paths forged during the war against the French, sometimes along riverbeds, and always through the most difficult, mountainous terrain plagued with leeches, snakes, malaria and dysentery.

On top of all this, people on the trail had to contend with almost constant bombing. By early 1965, **aerial bombardment** had begun in earnest, using napalm and defoliants as well as conventional bombs, to be joined later by carpet-bombing B-52s. Every day in the spring of 1965 the US Air Force flew an estimated three hundred bombing raids over the trail and in eight years dropped over two million tonnes of bombs, mostly over Laos, in an effort to cut the flow. Later they experimented with seismic and acoustic sensors to eavesdrop on troop movements and pinpoint targets, but the trail was never completely severed and supplies continued to roll south in sufficient quantities to sustain the war.

Now the sons of Vietnamese soldiers who forged the Ho Chi Minh Trail are busy resurrecting sections of it as part of a controversial government scheme to construct a two-lane highway from Hanoi to Ho Chi Minh City down the west side of the country. The 1690-kilometre-long **Truong Son Road** (also known as the Ho Chi Minh Road) is designed to provide an alternative to Highway 1, which is vulnerable to flooding, and to promote economic development in some of the country's poorest regions. Opponents argue that the road, which is due for completion in 2010, will threaten a number of crucial wildlife reserves.

2km of tunnel, which housed all 600 villagers over varying periods from early 1967 until 1969, when half decamped north to the relative safety of Nghe An Province. The tunnels were constructed on three levels at 10, 15 and 20–23m deep (though nowadays you can't visit the lowest level) with good ventilation, freshwater wells and, eventually, a generator and lights. The underground village was also equipped with a school, clinics, and a maternity room where seventeen children were born. Each family was allocated a tiny cavern, the four-person space being barely larger than a single bed. They were only able to emerge at night and lack of fresh air and sunlight was a major problem, especially for young children who would sit in the tunnel mouths whenever possible. In 1972, the villagers of Vinh Moc were finally able to abandon their underground existence and rebuild their homes, rejoined by relatives from Nghe An a year later.

The Truong Son Cemetery and Con Thien Fire Base

Thirty-odd kilometres northwest of Dong Ha along highways 9 and 15, **Truong Son War Martyr Cemetery** is dedicated to the estimated 25,000 men and women who died on the Truong Son Trail, better known in the west as the Ho Chi Minh Trail (see box opposite). Many bodies were never recovered, but a total of 10,036 graves lie in the fourteen-hectare cemetery among whispering glades of evergreen trees. Arranged in five geographical regions, the graves are subdivided according to native province, and centred round memorial houses listing every name and grave number in the sector. Each headstone announces *liet si* ("martyr"), together with as many details as are known: name, date and place of birth, date of enrolment, rank, and the date they died.

To reach the cemetery, drive west on Highway 9 as far as Cam Lo Town (12km) and then turn north for 22km following signs along Highway 15. On the way, roughly 12km out of Cam Lo, you pass the site of **Con Thien Fire Base**. Again, there's precious little left to see, beyond a view north to what were once NVA positions, chillingly close on the opposite bank of the Ben Hai River. The largest American installation along the DMZ, Con Thien Fire Base was first established by the Special Forces (Green Berets) and then handed over to the Marines in 1966, whose big guns could reach from here far into North Vietnam. In the lead-up to the 1968 Tet Offensive, as part of the NVA's diversionary attacks, the base became the target of prolonged shelling, followed by an infantry assault during which it was briefly surrounded. The Americans replied with everything in their arsenal, including long-range strafing from gunships in the South China Sea and carpet-bombing by B-52s. The North Vietnamese were forced to withdraw temporarily, but then completely overran the base in the summer of 1972.

Khe Sanh

Continuing west on Highway 9, you begin to climb into the foothills of the Truong Son range. Where the highway veers south, a sheer-sided isolated stump 230m high dominates the valley: the **Rockpile**. For a while American troops, delivered by helicopter, used the peak for directing artillery to targets across the DMZ and into Laos, but the post was abandoned after 1968. The highway continues over a low pass and then follows a picturesque valley past the **Dakrong Bridge**, which carries a spur of the Ho Chi Minh Trail, before climbing among ever-more forested mountains to emerge at **KHE SANH** (now officially rechristened **Huang Hoa**), 63km from Dong Ha. This bleak, one-street settlement, its frontier atmosphere reinforced by the smugglers' trail across the border to Laos only 19km away (see p.333 for more on crossing the border), sits on the edge of a windswept plateau that was the site of a pivotal battle in the American War.

The **battle of Khe Sanh** was important not because of its immediate outcome, but because it attracted worldwide media attention and, along with the simultaneous Tet Offensive, demonstrated the futility of America's efforts to contain their enemy. In 1962 an American Special Forces team arrived in Khe Sanh Town to train local Bru minority people in counter insurgency, and then four years later the first batch of Marines was sent in to establish a forward base near Laos, to secure Highway 9 and to harass troops on the Ho Chi Minh Trail. Skirmishes around Khe Sanh increased as intelligence reports indicated a massive build-up of North Vietnamese Army (NVA) troops in late 1967, possibly as many as 40,000, facing 6000 Marines together with a few hundred South Vietnamese and Bru. Both the Western media and American generals were soon presenting the confrontation as a crucial test of America's credibility in South Vietnam and drawing parallels with Dien Bien Phu (see p.459). As US President Johnson famously remarked, he didn't want "any damn Dinbinfoo".

The NVA attack came in the early hours of January 21, 1968 when rockets raining in on the base added to the terror and confusion by striking an ammunition dump, gasoline tanks and stores of tear gas. There followed a seemingly endless, nerve-grinding NVA artillery barrage, when hundreds of shells fell on the base each day, interspersed with costly US infantry assaults into the surrounding hills. In an operation code-named "Niagara", General Westmoreland called in the air battalions to silence the enemy guns and break the siege by unleashing the most intense bombing raids of the war: in nine weeks nearly 100,000 tonnes of bombs pounded the area round the clock, averaging one airstrike every five minutes, backed up by napalm and defoliants. Unbelievably the NVA were so well dug in and camouflaged that they not only withstood the onslaught but continued to return fire, despite horrendous casualties, estimated at 10,000. On the US side around 500 troops died at Khe Sanh (although official figures record only 248 American deaths, of which 43 occurred in a single helicopter accident), before a relief column broke through in early April, seventy-odd days after the siege had begun. Meanwhile NVA forces gradually pulled back and by the middle of March had all but gone, having successfully diverted American resources away from Southern cities prior to the Tet Offensive. Three months later the Americans also quietly withdrew, leaving a plateau that resembled a lunar landscape, contaminated for years to come with chemicals and explosives; even the trees left standing were worthless because so much shrapnel was lodged in the timber.

It's only in the last few years that the soil around Khe Sanh has been able to support vegetation again, and the hills are now green with coffee plantations. A few optimistic teenagers still peddle "genuine" dog-tags, and guides point out the red gash of the airstrip, but nothing else remains: when American troops were ordered to abandon Khe Sanh, everything was blown up and bulldozed flat. The only memorial is a small **museum** (daily 7am–5pm; $1.60), 2km north of Khe Sanh Town, commemorating the siege – made even more poignant by the hauntingly beautiful mountains all around.

Dong Hoi to Ninh Binh

North of the DMZ, Vietnam shrinks to a mere 50km wide and is edged with sand dunes up to 80m high, marching inland at a rate of 10m per year despite efforts to stabilize them with screw-pine and cactus. The narrow coastal plain is walled in by the jagged Truong Son Mountains and drained by short, flood-prone rivers. But one of these rivers, the Son, has created an extensive underground drainage system that constitutes one of the few sights of any note in the region. **Phong Nha Cave**, where the river emerges, attracts a steady stream of visitors, mostly on excursions from Hué or the nearby town of **Dong Hoi**. There's little else to tempt the tourist on the route north and most people push straight through to Ninh Binh or even Hanoi. Those travelling by road usually overnight in **Vinh**, where there's the opportunity to visit **Ho Chi Minh's birthplace** in the nearby village of Kim Lien. For motorcyclists and others in need of accommodation en route, both **Ha Tinh** and **Thanh Hoa** furnish the basic requirements, but hold no particular interest otherwise.

Dong Hoi and Phong Nha Cave

The first town of any size north of the Seventeenth Parallel is **DONG HOI** and, as such, it was flattened in the American War's bombing raids. The town has risen from its ashes to become a prosperous provincial capital of over 60,000 people, built on a grand scale with well-ordered streets, massive theatre hall and an attractive riverfront boulevard – though bereft of any particular sights. Those tourists who do stop in Dong Hoi are usually heading for the **Phong Nha Cave**, a genuinely impressive cave system.

The Town
Tourism is becoming big business in Dong Hoi as Phong Nha attracts ever more visitors and developers eye up the region's beaches. The town's southern extremity is marked by the broad expanse of the Nhat Le River and a **monument**, said to be a gateway of the eighteenth-century citadel, a couple of hundred metres further on. Continuing north you reach the landmark **post office** radio mast on a crossroads which constitutes the town centre: south of this junction Highway 1 is named Quang Trung, becoming Ly Thuong Kiet to the north; Tran Hung Dao leads west to the **train station**, 3km out of town, while east takes you 50m to riverfront Quach Xuan Ky, where a new bridge is being built across the Nhat Le Estuary. There's no long-distance **bus station** in Dong Hoi – just stand on the highway and flag a bus down. The provincial **tourist office**, Quang Binh Tourism (☎052/828228), is located on the riverfront beside the *Phuong Dong Hotel* at 20 Quach Xuan Ky; they offer car rental and English-speaking guides, though you can easily organize transport to Phong Nha through your hotel. **Vietcombank** at 54 Nguyen Huu Canh handles foreign exchange (cash and travellers' cheques) as well as credit card advances; to find it take the road (Le Loi) leading west from the monument and turn right onto Nguyen Huu Can after about 100m. Heading east from the monument, Me Suot leads down to a lively, riverside **market** and an area of covered stalls where in summer vendors sell ice-cold glasses of sweet-bean *chè*.

Accommodation and eating
The accommodation scene in Dong Hoi has improved dramatically with a rash of privately owned **hotels** all along Highway 1. Unless you're a heavy sleeper, however, you'll be better off opting for somewhere off the road, such as the clean, friendly and well-equipped *Kim Lien* at 4 Le Van Huu (☎052/822154; ②) or the next-door *Thanh Binh* (☎052/822181, ⓕ823132; ②); they're tucked down a backstreet immediately northwest of the monument. The *Dong Hoi*, round the corner at 50 Quang Trung (☎052/822289, ⓕ828117; ③) is an old-fashioned government-owned place on the highway, but the rooms are set back a bit and it's not too bad if you're stuck. Until the new luxury hotel opens

across the river on My Canh Beach (scheduled for 2004 at the earliest), the *Phong Nha* at 5 Truong Phap (☎052/824971, ☏824973; ❸–❹) is what passes for Dong Hoi's top hotel. Though not very central, it's in a pleasant location beside the mouth of the estuary about 500m north of town – ask for a sea-view room. There's also a couple of riverfront places further south along Quach Xuan Ky near the junction with Tran Hung Dao. Both look pretty dire, but the new block being added to the *Huu Nghi* at 22 Quach Xuan Ky (☎052/822567, ☏822763; ❷–❸) might be worth investigating. Rooms at the *Phuong Dong*, one block south at no. 20 (☎052/822276, ☏822404; ❸), are uninspiring and overpriced.

Dong Hoi's most popular **restaurant** – where all the tour buses stop – is the *Anh Dao*, run by a Hué emigré and serving reasonably priced Vietnamese and international foods. It's just west of Highway 1 beside the bridge at the southern end of town. Hué specialities, such as *banh beo* and *banh khoai*, as well as the standard rice and noodle dishes, are also available at a strip of small restaurants on Co Tam, one block north of the market. As usual, the market itself is home to a number of cheap and cheerful foodstalls. And look out for signs announcing the **local speciality** of *chao luon*, a thick eel soup sold at roadside restaurants.

Phong Nha Cave

Since time immemorial the underground river emerging at **Phong Nha Cave** has held a mystical fascination for the local population. The earliest-known devotees were ninth- and tenth-century Cham people, followed by Vietnamese who petitioned the **guardian spirits** during periods of drought, with great success by all accounts. When Europeans started exploring the caves early in the twentieth century it's said the rainmaker took everlasting umbrage. However, the explorers were undeterred and by the 1950s, tunnels 2km long had been surveyed and the number of visitors warranted a small hotel. Owing to the intervening wars, when Phong Nha provided safe warehousing – you can see evidence of an American rocket attack on the cliff above the cave entrance – nothing further happened until a British expedition was allowed to investigate in 1990 and began pushing upriver, eventually penetrating deep into the limestone massif. What they discovered is a spelunker's delight: 8km of underground waterway, vast chambers full of magical rock formations and intriguing side-channels waiting to be explored. For the less intrepid, tour boats take you on an attractive, thirty-minute trip meandering up the peaceful Son River. You only go into the first 600m of the cave, between rippling walls of limestone, but certainly far enough to be awed by the scale of Phong Nha and its immense stalactites and stalagmites, lit by multicoloured spotlights. The boats drop you at the far end to see a Cham inscription and then again to walk through a dry cave back to the entrance. Afterwards, you can climb steps leading up the cliff face to another dry cave for views back across the valley. Note, however, that the boats may not operate **after heavy rain** if the water level is too high.

To **get to the cave**, Dong Hoi's hotels and Quang Binh Tourism can help with car rental (from $25–30 for a half-day), or alternatively it's a long xe om ride ($8–10 return, including waiting time). Some Hué tour agents already offer Phong Nha excursions, but at five hours on the road each way it's too far for a comfortable day-trip and most overnight in Dong Hoi anyway. Once you've got transport sorted out, finding the cave isn't difficult: take Highway 1 north for 15km to Bo Trach Village where a signpost indicates a left to Phong Nha, heading west until you reach Son Trach Village 30km later (1hr); for the last bit you join the new Truong Son Road. The whole village is devoted to servicing boat-trippers: there's a Visitors' Centre where you can buy **tickets** (6am–6pm;

$1.60 entry plus $4 per boat), a couple of **guesthouses** (T & F 052/675016; ❶), offering fan and cold-water rooms, and the inevitable **restaurants**. Of these, a good option is *Phong Nha Quan*, across from the gate to the Visitors' Centre; there's no menu, but you can easily see what's on offer in the open kitchen.

Over the Ngang Pass to Vinh

A few kilometres north of Dong Hoi, Highway 1 grinds to a halt at a ferry across the turbulent Gianh River which formed the boundary between the southern Nguyen and the northern Trinh lords during the seventeenth and eighteenth centuries. The region around the **Ngang Pass** is empty, wild country which heralds Vietnam's poorest provinces, Ha Tinh and Nghe An. Summer droughts and winter flooding, exacerbated by typhoons from August to November, cause frequent crop failures and high levels of malnutrition.

The region's few bright spots are areas of exceptionally dense highland forests on the border with Laos, harbouring **rare species** such as the Asian elephant and tiger. Since 1992 scientists have identified two new species of mammal (previously known only to local hunters) in these hills: the elusive **saola ox** and the more numerous **giant muntjac** deer. The government has enlarged the area of local nature reserves to almost 160,000 hectares and is implementing a programme to protect the highly vulnerable mammals. Breeding more commonplace species of deer is big business in Nghe An as young antlers fetch high prices for their medicinal properties.

Highway 1 rumbles into the large-featureless city of **HA TINH**, 150km north of Dong Hoi. The rail tracks, forced inland by the Hoanh Son Mountains, bypass Ha Tinh to rejoin the coast at Vinh, but train travellers need not feel left out – there's nothing to stop for in Ha Tinh and most tourists head straight on to Vinh's greater choice of hotels. If you do need **accommodation**, the most central choice is *Binh Minh Hotel* (T 039/856825; ❸), located on the main highway opposite the post office radio mast; take a room at the back if possible. As there's no handy bus station, just flag down **buses** going your way on the main street which, in typical fashion, is lined with cheap **eating** houses.

Vinh and around

Just 48km further north, **VINH** is a sprawling grey city with a sad past, sitting astride Highway 1 – which throws up dust and a steady trickle of tourists breaking their journey between Hué and Hanoi or heading to (or from) Laos. Soviet-style apartment blocks and socialist town planning on a grand scale may hold a certain historical interest, but there's nothing attractive about the town and for most people its saving grace is a selection of reasonable-standard hotels. Nevertheless, the province of Nghe An savours its proud history, having spawned a wealth of revolutionary figures, many of them enshrined in street names: Le Hong Phong, Nguyen Thi Minh Khai, Phan Boi Chau and, top of the list, Ho Chi Minh. **Ho's birthplace** and childhood home are found in **Kim Lien** Village, 14km from Vinh, a place of pilgrimage for Vietnamese, though rather sterile for most foreign visitors. **Cua Lo** beach resort lies 19km north of the city, comprising a straggle of overpriced hotels beside a long, unspoilt beach with good white sand but too much rubbish to make you want to linger.

Arrival and information

Vinh's main axis is Highway 1, renamed in the centre as Quang Trung and then Le Loi streets. Heading up Quang Trung, after about 500m you'll find the *Saigon Kim Lien Hotel*, good for **information**, followed by the long-distance

bus station (Ben Xe Vinh) a kilometre further on; public buses from Trung Tam (and the border with Laos; see p.333) terminate at the provincial bus station (Ben Xe Cho Vinh) at the south end of Quang Trung behind Vinh market. **Open-tour buses** can set down passengers in Vinh en route; however, make sure you confirm onward travel with the relevant company beforehand. Two kilometres north of the market the nine-storey *Huu Nghi Hotel* dominates a major crossroads: turn left here for Vinh **train station**, a kilometre west at the end of Phan Boi Chau (ticket office hours 7.30–10.30am, 2–4.30pm & 8–9.30pm); right brings you to an **Internet** café at 2 Nguyen Si Sach and **Vietcombank** at no. 9, with a 24-hour ATM. Vinh **airport**, with connections to Ho Chi Minh only, lies a short taxi ride ($1.50–2) north of the city. The main **post office** is nearly a kilometre east of the *Sagion Kim Lien* beside the unmissable radio tower, but there are more convenient sub-branches outside the train station and at 73 Le Loi. Car and motorbike rental in Vinh is available through most hotels, and you can pick up xe om anywhere in town.

For details of **heading to Laos** via the Cau Treo border gate (105km south-west of Vinh), see the box on p.333.

The City

Vinh has fared particularly badly in the twentieth century. As an industrial port-city dominating major land routes, whose population was known for rebellious tendencies, the town became a natural target during both French

The life of Ho Chi Minh

So inextricably is the life of **Ho Chi Minh** intertwined with Vietnam's emergence from colonial rule that his biography is largely an account of the country's struggle for independence in the twentieth century. As Ho adopted dozens of pseudonyms and never kept diaries, uncertainty clouds his public life and almost nothing is known about the private man beneath the cultivated persona of a celibate and aesthete, totally dedicated to his family – a concept that embraced all the Vietnamese people. Ho's **origins** were humble enough – he was born in 1890 Nguyen Sinh Cung, the youngest child of a minor mandarin who was dismissed from the imperial court in Hué for anti-colonialist sympathies. For a while Ho attended Hué's Quoc Hoc High School until he was expelled for taking part in a student protest and left Vietnam in 1911 on a steamship bound for France. Then began several years of wandering the world, including spells in the dockyards of Brooklyn and as pastry chef under Escoffier in London's *Carlton Hotel*, before returning to France in the aftermath of World War I, to earn his living retouching photographs. In Paris, Ho became an increasingly active **nationalist**, going by the name Nguyen Ai Quoc ("Nguyen the Patriot"), and caused quite a stir during the Versailles Peace Conference when he published a petition demanding democratic constitutional government for Indochina. For a while Ho joined the French Socialists, but when they split in 1920 he defected to become one of the founder members of the French Communist Party, inspired by Lenin's total opposition to imperialism.

Ho's energetic role in French communism was rewarded when he was called to Moscow in 1923 to begin a career in **international revolution**, and a year later he found himself posted to southern China as a Comintern agent. Within a few months he had set up Vietnam's first Marxist-Leninist organization, the Revolutionary Youth League, which attracted a band of impassioned young Vietnamese eager to hear about the new ideology. But in 1927, Chiang Kai-shek, leader of the Chinese nationalists, turned against the communists and Ho was forced to flee. For a while he lived in Thailand, disguised as a Buddhist monk, before turning up in Hong Kong in 1930 where he was instrumental in founding the **Vietnamese Communist Party**. By now and American wars. In the 1950s French bombs destroyed large swathes of Vinh, after which the Viet Minh burnt down what remained rather than let it fall into the hands of their enemy. Then the rebuilt town was flattened once again in American air raids of the 1960s and 1970s. Reconstruction proceeded slowly after 1975, mostly financed by East Germany; the decrepit hulks of these barrack-like apartment blocks, totally unsuited to the Vietnamese climate, still dominate the city centre. But things are beginning to improve as trade with Laos brings more money into the region: Vinh's streets are being repaved and pavements laid; smart new villas and hotels in garish colours are being built; and there's even a multistorey supermarket stocked with all manner of goodies. Vinh's only sight, the **Nghe Tinh Soviet Museum**, has also been given a face-lift, but was still closed at the time of writing. It celebrates a mass uprising against French rule in the 1930s (see Contexts, p.492), relating the causes, development and aftermath of the uprising, but is really only for the specialist.

Kim Lien: Ho Chi Minh's birthplace

Ho Chi Minh was born in 1890 in Hoang Tru Village, **KIM LIEN** commune, 14km west of Vinh. The two simple houses made of bamboo wattle and palm-leaf thatch are 1959 reconstructions, now surrounded by fields of sweet potatoes. Ho's birthplace is said to be the hut by itself on the left as you approach, while behind stands the brick-built family altar. At the age of 6 Ho moved 2km west, to what is now called Lang Sen (Lotus Village), to live with his father

the French authorities had placed a death sentence on Ho's head, for insurrection, and while in Hong Kong he was arrested on trumped-up charges, released and then re-arrested before finally escaping with the help of prison hospital staff, who managed to persuade everyone, including the French police, that Ho had died of tuberculosis.

Ho disappeared again for a few years while the fuss died down, before reappearing on China's southern border in the late 1930s. From here he re-entered Vietnam for the first time in thirty years, in early 1941, wearing Chinese-style tunic, rubber-tyre sandals and carrying just a small rattan trunk plus his precious typewriter. He was aged 51, had dysentery, malaria and tuberculosis, and was about to embark on the most momentous task of his life. In the mountains of northern Vietnam, Ho, now finally known as Ho Chi Minh (meaning "He Who Enlightens"), was joined by Vo Nguyen Giap, Pham Van Dong and other young militants. Together they laid the groundwork for the anticipated national uprising, establishing a united patriotic front, the League for the Independence of Vietnam – better known by its abbreviated name, the **Viet Minh** – and training the guerrilla units that would eventually evolve into the Vietnamese People's Army. But events conspired against Ho: in 1942 he was arrested as a Franco-Japanese spy when he crossed back into China to raise support for the nationalist cause, and languished for more than a year in various prisons, writing a collection of poetry later published as the "Prison Diary".

Meanwhile, however, events were hotting up, and when the Japanese occupation of Vietnam ended in August 1945, the Viet Minh were ready to seize control. Ho Chi Minh, by this time seriously ill, led them to a brief period in power following the August Revolution, and then ultimately to Independence in 1954. For the next fifteen years, as **President of the Democratic Republic of Vietnam**, Uncle Ho took his country along a sometimes rocky socialist path, continually seeking reunification through negotiation and then war. But he didn't live to see a united Vietnam: early in 1969 his heart began to fail and on September 2, Vietnam's National Day, he died. Since then, myth and fact have converged in a cult placing Ho Chi Minh at the top of Vietnam's pantheon of heroes, true to Confucian tradition – though against Ho's express wishes.

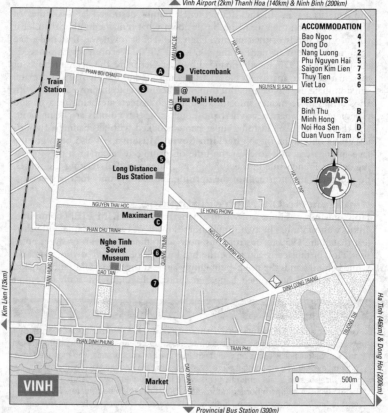

ACCOMMODATION

Bao Ngoc	4
Dong Do	1
Nang Luong	2
Phu Nguyen Hai	5
Saigon Kim Lien	7
Thuy Tien	3
Viet Lao	6

RESTAURANTS

Binh Thu	B
Minh Hong	A
Noi Hoa Sen	D
Quan Vuon Tram	C

Train Station

PHAN BOI CHAU

Vietcombank

NGUYEN SI SACH

Huu Nghi Hotel

Long Distance Bus Station

NGUYEN THAI HOC

LE HONG PHONG

Maximart

PHAN CHU TRINH

Nghe Tinh Soviet Museum

DAO TAN

PHAN DINH PHUNG

TRAN PHU

VINH

Market

0   500m

MAI HAC DE

HA HUY TAP

LE LOI

QUANG TRUNG

NGUYEN THI MINH KHAI

DINH CONG TRANG

TRUONG THI

THANH HUNG DAO

LE DAI HANH

CAO XUAN HUY

◄ Kim Lien (13km)

Ha Tinh (46km) & Dong Hoi (200km) ►

in very similar surroundings. The two Sen houses are also replicas, built in 1955, with nothing much to see inside, but the complex is peaceful and alive with dancing butterflies. A **museum** nearby (daily: April–Sept 7.30–11am & 2.30–5pm; Oct–March 8.30–11.30am & 2–5pm) illustrates Ho's world travels with memorabilia and many photos you've probably seen before.

To reach Kim Lien by **car or motorbike**, take Phan Dinh Phung in front of Vinh market and follow signs along a smooth new highway until you reach the turning for Lang Sen and Kim Lien. The signed route takes you first to Ho's birthplace and then looping round to find the museum beside a car park and Ho's father's house a little further back, down a path beside a small lotus pond. A **xe om** from Vinh should set you back around $3 including waiting time, but make sure you visit both sites.

Accommodation and eating

Because it's such a transport hub, Vinh has a large number of **hotels**, which means places are willing to bargain. The main drawback is that many hotels sit right on the highway, so wherever possible go for a room at the back. Ignoring several grotty, socialist-style places, there's still a reasonable choice among those listed below.

There's less of a choice when it comes to **places to eat**. The smartest option is the restaurant at the *Saigon Kim Lien Hotel* which serves well-priced Asian and European dishes, including a good buffet breakfast ($1.30). On a fine day, *Noi Hoa Sen*, in the middle of a lake at the west end of Phan Dinh Phung, makes a pleasant and inexpensive place to eat, while *Quan Vuon Tram* at 49b Le Loi is a popular choice for the evening. This beer garden serves jugs of *bia hoi* accompanied by chicken curry, spicy beef, pork skewers and the like – ask for their English-language menu. Otherwise, there's a whole host of street kitchens on Le Loi, with a group outside the bus station and another towards the *Huu Nghi Hotel* and spreading down Phan Boi Chau: *Minh Hong* at 3 Phan Boi Chau and *Binh Thu* at 72 Le Loi are decent choices.

Hotels

Bao Ngoc 99 Le Loi ☎038/569999, ⓕ585097. A friendly place just north of Vinh bus station, the violent-green "Ruby Hotel" was financed by the gem mines of Nghe An. The well-scrubbed en-suite rooms represent good value with air-con, satellite TV, phone and fridge. ❶

Dong Do 14 Mai Hac De ☎038/846989, ⓕ531646. One of the better budget options within easy reach of the train station. It's a touch jaded but reasonably well maintained, offering simple en-suite, air-con rooms. ❷

Nang Luong 2 Mai Hac De ☎038/844788, ⓕ848873. If you're after a few more creature comforts near the train station, this place has old-fashioned but decent-size rooms. Other plus points are the small pool and friendly welcome. ❸

Phu Nguyen Hai 79 Le Loi ☎038/848429, ⓔctpnh@hn.vnn.vn. Unmissable, cerise-coloured hotel (which also doubles as a jewellers) right next to Vinh bus station – double glazing helps keep the noise levels bearable. Ask to see several rooms since some are showing signs of age. ❸

Saigon Kim Lien 25 Quang Trung ☎038/838899, ⓦwww.saigon-tourist.com/saigon-kimlien. Vinh's top hotel opened in 1990 to commemorate the hundredth anniversary of Ho Chi Minh's birth. Prices are surprisingly affordable for comfortable and well-proportioned rooms. Facilities include a recommended restaurant, bar, pool, business centre and money exchange (cash only). Staff can assist with transport arrangements and general information. ❹

Thuy Tien 36 Phan Boi Chau ☎038/853814. These fan and hot-water rooms (from $7) are acceptable if you need somewhere cheap to crash near the train station. ❶

Viet Lao 37a Quang Trung ☎038/564911, ⓕ565004. One of the better maintained Soviet-style hotels, which is also a popular place to book bus tickets for Laos. $8 will get you a three-bed room with hot water and fan, while $12 buys you such luxuries as air-con, TV and phone.

Thanh Hoa

North of Vinh the narrow waist of Vietnam begins to open out towards the northern delta, entering the region known to the French as Tonkin. It's only a short haul to the town of **THANH HOA** which produces good beer, though there's not a lot else to the place. The province was home to an impressive number of Vietnamese kings, of whom the most illustrious was **Le Loi**, born here in 1385. Delving further back, the Ma River Valley has yielded rich archeological evidence of Neolithic settlement, notably some of the glorious Bronze Age drums found at **Dong Son Village**, northwest of Thanh Hoa, but there's precious little to see nowadays. The only other notable site is **Ham Rong Bridge**, or "Dragon's Jaw", which spans the Ma River 3km north of town, and gained almost mythical status during the American War. US bombers tried for three years to destroy the heavily defended, 160-metre-long road and rail link. Around seventy aircraft were lost, more than against any other single target in the North, and the land around was bombed into a moonscape. Eventually, a laser-guided bomb found its target in May 1972, but the victory was short-lived as the NVA immediately rigged up a pontoon bridge and had a permanent structure in place soon after. The name Dragon's Jaw refers to a sinuous, nine-peaked ridge of hills – the dragon – to the west of the river, which holds in its mouth an isolated hump on the east bank called Nui Ngoc, or "Ruby Mountain".

Most people either press on to Hanoi, only 150km to the north, or make Ninh Binh their next stop. If you do need to overnight, Thanh Hoa has one or two decent hotels (see below), or you can get a sea-view room in **Sam Son**, a passably spruce resort with a wide sandy beach, 16km to the southeast.

Practicalities

Thanh Hoa is a sprawling town with no focal point and almost no landmarks apart from a huge **post office** where Highway 1 crosses Le Loi. About 400m north of this is another major junction where Phan Chu Trinh leads west past several **banks** to Thanh Hoa's **train station**. Or continue on Highway 1 to find the northern **bus station** 300m further on. Inconveniently, buses heading south depart from Nga Ba Voi bus station, 3km down the highway. English-speaking staff in the hotels and guesthouses are the best source of **information**.

The range of **accommodation** in Thanh Hoa will be much improved when the new three-star hotel, the *Sao Mai*, halfway along Phan Boi Chau, opens towards the end of 2004. Until then, the big, state-run *Thanh Hoa* (T037/852517, E dulichth@hn.vnn.vn; ❶–❸) is where most people end up staying since it's easy to find and offers comfortable if expensive accommodation in the new block, as well as a garden of sorts and a restaurant. However, the cheapest rooms in the old block are not good value. A much better option is the *68 Han Thuyen Guesthouse* round the corner at 68 Han Thuyen (T037/850359; ❷); take a left turn about 300m north along Highway 1 from the *Thanh Hoa*. This welcome newcomer boasts a range of tidy, well-priced rooms. Continuing north up Highway 1, look out on the left for the distinctive blue and purple facade of the simple, clean and friendly *Loi Linh Guesthouse* at 22 Tran Phu (T037/853309; ❷), where you'll find some of Thanh Hoa's cheapest rooms.

Another possibility is to stay at Sam Son beach resort, where there are now some more appealing privately run hotels in among the concrete blocks. One of the nicest along the seafront is the *Song Ma* (T037/822293, F856648; ❶), followed by the slightly cheaper *Hoa Hong I* (T037/821505, F822479; ❶). One hundred metres back from the beach on the road to Thanh Hoa, the *Huong Ly* at 21 Le Loi (T & F037/821079; ❶) has simple fan and hot-water rooms for around $5. Unless you've got your own transport, add a dollar each way for the xe om ride out to Sam Son.

As for **eating**, the restaurant at the *Thanh Hoa Hotel* is okay if a bit soulless. The street kitchens across the road boast a bit more atmosphere; try the *Tuan Dung*, 31 Tran Phu. There's another batch around the junction with Phan Chu Trinh, which is where you'll also find the upmarket *Da Lan* at 630 Quang Trung, serving expensive seafood.

Ninh Binh and around

The provincial capital **NINH BINH** is another dusty town straddling Highway 1, no more attractive than those to the south but slightly smaller and with sugar-loaf hillocks encroaching on the western horizon. While the town itself has little to detain you, the surrounding hills shelter **Tam Coc**, where sampans slither through the limestone tunnels of "Ha Long Bay on land", and one of Vietnam's ancient capitals, **Hoa Lu**, represented by two darkly atmospheric dynastic temples. Both places can be tackled in one day by car or motorbike, or

ACCOMMODATION		RESTAURANTS	
New Guesthouse	7	Café Be	A
Queen	6	Huong Hai	C
Quoc Binh	3	Thao Son Tuu Quan	B
Star	5		
Thanh Binh	2		
Thanh Thuy	1		
Thuy Anh	4		

0   250m

Nam Dinh (29km)

Duc Thuy

& Haiphong (135km)

TRAN HUNG DAO

Van River

LE HONG PHONG

Incombank

Market

LE DAI HANH

TRUONG

VAN GIANG

HAN SIEU

Police

Train Station

TRAN PHU

N

Phat Diem Cathedral (30km)

LIM BRIDGE   Bus Station

NINH BINH

Tam Coc (8km) & Bich Dong (10km)

by bicycle via the back lanes. To the east, the stone mass of **Phat Diem Cathedral** wallows in the rice fields, an extraordinary amalgam of Western and Oriental architecture that still shepherds an active Catholic community. Further afield, **Cuc Phuong** is one of Vietnam's more accessible national parks and contains some magnificent, centuries-old trees. More boat trips are in store at **Kenh Ga**, to visit a limestone cave, and at **Van Long** nature reserve, both on the Cuc Phuong road. These last sights are more distant: the cathedral requires a half-day outing, while Cuc Phuong and either Kenh Ga or Van Long can be combined in a long day-trip.

Hanoi is only 90km (2hr) away and the Hoa Lu/Tam Coc–Bich Dong circuit makes a popular and inexpensive day tour out of the capital. However, with more time, it's far better to take advantage of Ninh Binh's hotels and services to explore the area at a more leisurely pace.

The Town

Two radio masts provide convenient landmarks in **Ninh Binh**: the taller stands over the post office in the south, while the shorter signals the northern extremity 2km away up Highway 1 (Tran Hung Dao). Exactly halfway between the two, Le Hong Phong shoots off east at a major junction, taking traffic to join the Haiphong road. The town claims just one sight of its own: a kilometre to the north a picturesque little pagoda nestles at the base of **Non Nuoc Mountain**, also known as Duc Thuy. This knobbly outcrop – no more than 60m high – is noted for an eminently missable collection of ancient poetic inscriptions and views east over a power station to the graphically named "sleeping lady mountain".

Ninh Binh's pint-sized **train station** and the refreshingly well-organized **bus station** both lie on the east side of town, a short walk across the Van River from the post office. **Open-tour buses** drop you at their affiliated hotels and guesthouses, all of which can help with **information,** tours and transport; staff at the *Thuy Anh*, *Thanh Thuy* and *Queen* hotels are particularly knowledgeable about the area. The going rate for motorbike rental is around $5 or $6 per day and $1 or less for a bicycle. You can get credit card advances and **exchange** cash (dollars and euros only) and travellers' cheques at the Incombank located on the main strip, Tran Hung Dao. If where you're staying doesn't provide **Internet access**, try *Olympia Internet Café*, 55 Luong Van Tuy.

Accommodation and eating

The standard and range of **hotels** in Ninh Binh continues to improve as ever-greater numbers of tourists are discovering this accessible province, and the

5

THE CENTRAL PROVINCES | Ninh Binh and around

increased competition means it's usually possible to bargain. Don't be put off by places along the main roads, some of which are now installing double and even triple glazing.

Ninh Binh has a more limited choice of **eating** places. Among the hotels, best for both value and quality is the *Thuy Anh*, while the *Thanh Thuy* provides cheap and cheerful backpacker fare. There are also a couple of good-value independent restaurants to head for: the *Huong Hai*, just down from the *Thuy Anh* at 36 Truong Han Sieu, serves an excellent fish steamboat (*lau ca*) amongst other things; and you'll also find generous portions and friendly service at *Thao Son Tuu Quan*, 144 Le Hong Phong. Otherwise, check out the roadside braziers around the market and the **cafés** in streets west of Tran Hung Dao, where the little courtyard behind *Café Be*, 142 Cu Chinh Lan, is a decent place for a coffee or beer. The rooftop **bar** of the *Thuy Anh Hotel* provides a scenic spot to unwind at the end of a heavy day's sightseeing.

Hotels

New Guesthouse 3 Hoang Hoa Tham ☎030/872137. Six cheerful rooms with fan and hot water, right beside the train station. ❶
Queen 21 Hoang Hoa Tham ☎030/871874, ✉luongvn2001@yahoo.com. A few doors along from the train station on a pleasant tree-lined street, this small, friendly hotel is basic but clean and sports a pleasant rooftop eating area. ❶
Quoc Binh 9 An Thanh ☎030/881605. A spick-and-span guesthouse tucked down a back alley on the west side of town. Rooms with air-con, TV, fridge and a fair-sized bathroom are good value. ❷
Star 267 Tran Hung Dao ☎030/871522, ✉starhotel@hn.vnn.vn. Rooms are small and a bit noisy, but they come with bathrooms, TV and air-con as standard. ❶
Thanh Binh Luong Van Tuy ☎030/872439. Spruce, well-equipped rooms off the highway make this a good alternative if the *Thuy Anh* and *Thanh Thuy* are full. The meals here are also recommended. ❶–❷

Thanh Thuy 128 Le Hong Phong ☎030/871811, ✉tuc@hn.vnn.vn. This friendly, family-run guesthouse has ten rooms, with plans to add another twelve. The cheapest room has a fan and shared bathroom while the most expensive is en suite with air-con. There's a small but decent restaurant offering a limited range of tasty, fresh food. It's also a good place to come for local information and their guided motorbike tours are highly recommended. ❶–❷
Thuy Anh 55a Truong Han Sieu ☎030/871602, ✉thuyanhhotel@hn.vnn.vn. Ninh Binh's smartest hotel offers efficient service and a range of immaculately kept rooms, from a couple with fan and shared bathroom up to huge rooms furnished and equipped to a high standard. The food in the downstairs restaurant is prepared with the same attention to detail, and there's also a bar (evenings only) on the sixth floor with views over Ninh Binh. The full range of tours and transport, including good-quality bicycles and motorbikes for rent, completes the picture. ❷–❹

Tam Coc and Bich Dong

The film *Indochine* put the **Tam Coc "three caves" region**, 7km southwest of Ninh Binh, firmly on the tourist map and the government is now pouring money into developing Tam Coc: the access road has been upgraded, a grand Visitors' Centre is under way and concrete lines the canal banks – but fortunately only as far as the first bridge. They're even trying to clamp down on the overzealous – occassionally aggressive – peddling of embroideries and soft drinks by the sampan-rowers. Despite all this, it's hard not to be won over by the mystical, watery beauty of the area, which is a miniature landlocked version of Ha Long Bay. The two-hour sampan-ride is a definite highlight, meandering among dumpling-shaped, karst hills in a flooded landscape where river and rice paddy merge serenely into one; keep an eye open for mountain goats high on the cliffs, and bright, darting kingfishers. Journey's end is **Tam Coc**, three long, dark tunnel-caves (Hang Ca, Hang Giua and Hang Cuoi) eroded through the limestone hills with barely sufficient clearance for the sampan after heavy rains. On the way back, you can ask to stop at **Thai Vi Temple**, a short walk from the river. Dating from the thirteenth century and dedicated to the founder of the Tran dynasty, it's a peaceful, atmospheric spot.

If you have time after the boat trip, follow the road leading southwest from the boat dock (see below) for about 2km to visit the cave-pagoda of **Bich Dong**, or "Jade Grotto". Stone-cut steps, entangled by the thick roots of banyan trees, lead up a cliff face peppered with shrines to the cave entrance, believed to have been discovered by two monks in the early fifteenth century. On the rock face above, two giant characters declare "Bich Dong". The story goes that they were engraved in the eighteenth century by the father of Nguyen Du (author of the classic *Tale of Kieu*), who was entrusted with construction of the complex. The cave walls are now scrawled with graffiti but the three Buddhas sit unperturbed on their lotus thrones beside a head-shaped rock which bestows longevity if touched. Walk through the cave to emerge higher up the cliff, from where steps continue to the third and final temple and viewpoint over the waterlogged scene.

Practicalities

The easiest and most enjoyable way to reach Tam Coc is to rent a **bicycle** or **motorbike** from hotels and guesthouses in Ninh Binh; the turning, signed to "Bich Dong", is 4km south on Highway 1, before the cement factory. Hiring a **xe om** for the excursion will cost about $3 including waiting time. If your next stop is Hoa Lu (see below), you could take a partly unpaved back road for a delightful ten-kilometre **cycle ride** through rice fields and limestone karst scenery. To pick up the road, heading back from Tam Coc towards the highway, look out on the left for a pond and a big old banyan tree, from behind which a paved road leads north through a small village. It's signed to Hang Mua ($1.30), a rather gaudy pleasure park 2km from the turning, where you can walk through a dry tunnel-cave and climb steep steps for views back over the Tam Coc valley. After that the route basically heads north, but meanders a bit towards the end, so keep asking "*di Hoa Lu*" at junctions.

To avoid the worst of the crowds at Tam Coc, it's best to set off either very **early** in the morning or in the **late** afternoon (boats run between 6.30am and 5pm). **Tickets** ($3.60), which include the boat trip and entry to Bich Dong, are currently on sale at a kiosk beside the boat dock in Van Lam village, although this may change when the Visitors' Centre – on the right as you come into the village – opens. **Restaurants** and **cafés** catering to tour groups line the approach to Van Lam, and some of the smaller places aren't too bad. There's also a clutch of cheap noodle and rice stalls beside the entrance to Bich Dong.

Hoa Lu

Twelve kilometres northwest of Ninh Binh, **Hoa Lu**, site of the tenth-century capital of an early, independent Vietnamese kingdom called Dai Co Viet, makes another rewarding excursion. The fortified royal palaces of the Dinh and Le kings are now reduced to archeological remains, but their dynastic temples, seventeenth-century copies of eleventh-century originals, still rest quietly in a narrow valley surrounded by wooded, limestone hills. Though the temple buildings and attractive walled courtyards are unspectacular, the inner sanctuaries are compelling – mysterious, dark caverns where statues of the kings, wrapped in veils of pungent incense, are worshipped by the light of candles.

First stop at the site should be the more imposing **Den Dinh Tien Hoang**, on the left as you approach from the car park and ticket office, dedicated to

King Dinh Tien Hoang (also known as Dinh Bo Linh) who seized power in 968 AD and moved the capital south from Co Loa in the Red River Delta to this secure valley far from the threat of Chinese intervention. Dinh Tien Hoang's gilded effigy can be seen in the temple's second sanctuary room, flanked by his three sons. Dinh Tien Hoang was born near Hoa Lu. He was the illegitimate son of a provincial governor and was known as a reforming monarch who ruled with a firm hand; he is reputed to have placed a bronze urn and caged tiger in front of his palace and decreed that "those who violate the laws will be boiled and gnawed". However, in 979 an assassin, variously rumoured to be a mad monk or a palace hitman, killed the king and his two eldest sons as they lay in a drunken sleep.

In the anarchy that followed, Le Hoan, commander of Dinh Tien Hoang's army and supposed lover of his queen (whom Le Hoan later married), wrested power and declared himself King Le Dai Hanh in 980. The second temple, **Den Le Dai Hanh**, is dedicated to the earlier of the two Le dynasties which itself spiralled into chaos 25 years later while the king's three sons squabbled over the succession. Le Dai Hanh is enshrined in the temple's rear sanctuary with his eldest son and Queen Duong Van Nga. On the way out, signs direct you to an adjacent archeological dig where some tenth-century foundations have been unearthed, along with tiles and pottery shards.

After visiting the two temples, energetic types could climb the steps of neighbouring "Saddle Mountain" (*Nui Ma Yen*) for a panoramic view of Hoa Lu and its surroundings.

Practicalities

The quickest way out to Hoa Lu is to rent a motorbike for the day or take a xe om ($4–5 for the round trip), but if time allows this is definitely one to do by **bicycle** in combination with Tam Coc (see above for directions); allow at least one hour for the journey. To get back to Ninh Binh you can either wind your way through the back lanes (you'll need to ask for directions) or cut east to brave the last 6km among the lorries and buses on Highway 1. Hoa Lu is just as popular as Tam Coc and the temples can be swamped, particularly mid-morning and early afternoon when tour groups arrive from Hanoi. The hawkers can also be just as enthusiastic, though fortunately they aren't allowed to pursue you into the temples. **Admission** to both temples costs $2.

Phat Diem

Strike southeast from Ninh Binh and there's no mistaking that you've stumbled on a Christian enclave, where church spires sprout out of the flat paddy land on all sides and it's said that 95 percent of the district's population attend church on a regular basis. These coastal communities of northern Vietnam were among the first to be targeted by Portuguese missionaries in the sixteenth century. This area owes its particular zeal to the Jesuit Alexandre de Rhodes who preached here in 1627. The greatest monument to all this religious fervour is the century-old stone cathedral, **Phat Diem**, situated 30km from Ninh Binh in **Kim Son Village**. Note that opening times vary, so check in Ninh Binh before setting off.

The first surprise is the cathedral's monumental **bell pavilion**, whose curved roofs and triple gateway could easily be the entrance to a Vietnamese temple save for a few telltale crosses and a host of angels. The structure is built entirely of dressed stone, as is the equally impressive cathedral facade sheltering in its wake; both edifices rest on hundreds of bamboo poles embedded in the marshy ground. Behind, the tiled double roof of the **nave** extends for 74m, supported by 52 immense ironwood pillars and sheltering a cool, dark and peaceful sanctuary. The **altar** table is chiselled from a single block of marble, decorated with elegant sprays of bamboo, while the altarpiece above glows with red and gold lacquers in an otherwise sober interior. Twelve priests conduct daily services here for a diocese that musters 140,000 Catholics.

The cathedral was conceived and designed by Father Tran Luc (also known as Father Sau), whose tomb lies behind the bell tower, and was more than ten years in the preparation, as stone and wood were transported from the provinces of Thanh Hoa and Nghe An, though it apparently took a mere three months to build in 1891. During the French War, the Catholic Church formed a powerful political group in Vietnam, virtually independent of the French administration but also opposed to the communists. The then bishop of Phat Diem, Monseigneur Le Huu Tu, was outspokenly anti-French and an avowed nationalist, but, as his diocese lay on the edge of government-held territory, the French supplied him with sufficient arms to maintain a militia of 2000 men in return for containing Viet Minh infiltration. However, in December 1951 the Viet Minh launched a major assault on the village and took it – with suspicious ease for French tastes, who felt the Catholics were withholding information on enemy activities in the area, if not actually assisting them. When paratroops came in to regain control, the Viet Minh withdrew, taking with them a valuable supply of weapons. The author Graham Greene was in Phat Diem at the time, on an assignment for *Life Magazine*, and watched the battle from the bell tower of the cathedral – later using the scene in *The Quiet American*.

Practicalities

Frequent public **buses** depart from Ninh Binh bus station for the hour's journey **to Kim Son**, though note the last bus back leaves around 3.30pm. Otherwise, it's near enough to reach by rented **motorbike**, or the return trip by **xe om** will cost around $4. If you're riding here yourself, take the road heading straight east from Ninh Binh's Lim Bridge and, when you get to Kim Son Village, 100m after passing an elegant covered bridge, take a right turn to the cathedral; follow the compound wall anticlockwise to reach the entrance.

Cuc Phuong National Park

In 1962 Vietnam's first national park was established around a narrow valley between forested limestone hills on the borders of Ninh Binh, Thanh Hoa and Hoa Binh provinces, containing over 200 square kilometres of tropical evergreen rainforest. **Cuc Phuong** is well set up for tourism and sees a steady stream of visitors, attracted principally by the excellent primate rescue centre, but also by the easy access to impressively ancient trees. With more time you can walk into the park interior, to overnight in a Muong village and experience the multi-layered forest. The most enjoyable time for walking in these hills is October to January, when mosquitoes and leeches take a break and temperatures are relatively cool – but this is also peak season. Flowers are at their best during February and March, while April to May are the months when lepidopterists can enjoy the "butterfly festival" as thousands of butterflies colour the forest.

Even now the park has not been fully surveyed but is estimated to contain approximately three hundred **bird species** and ninety **mammal species**, some of which were first discovered in Cuc Phuong, such as red-bellied squirrels and a fish that lives in underground rivers. Several species of bat and monkey, including the critically endangered Delacour's langur, inhabit the park, while bears and leopards roam its upper reaches. Hunting has taken its toll, though, and you're really only likely to see butterflies, birds and perhaps a civet cat or a tree squirrel, rather than the more exotic fauna. What you can't miss, though, is the luxuriant **vegetation** including 1000-year-old trees (living fossils up to 70m high), tree ferns and kilometre-long corkscrewing lianas, as well as a treasure-trove of medicinal plants.

Some of the luckier victims of illegal hunting are now to be seen in the **Endangered Primate Rescue Center** (daily 9–11am & 1.30–4pm; ⓦ www.primatecenter.org) located near the park gate. Opened in 1993, the centre not only cares for rescued animals, but also tries to rehabilitate them by releasing them into an adjacent semi-wild area. In addition, they run crucial research, conservation and breeding programmes. At any one time there may be between sixty and a hundred animals here, including Delacour's langur, with its distinctive black body and white "shorts", the Cat Ba or Golden-headed langur and the Grey-shanked douc langur, as well as various lorises and gibbons. It's a unique opportunity to see these incredibly rare species at close quarters.

Of several **walks** in the park, one of the most popular starts at Car Park A, 18km from the park gate. For seven steamy kilometres (roughly 2hr) a well-trodden path winds through typical rainforest to reach the magnificent **cho xanh tree**, a 45-metre-high, 1000-year-old specimen of *Terminalia myriocarpa* – its dignity only slightly marred by a viewing platform. Dropping back down to the flat, take a left turn at the unmarked T-junction to bring you back to the road higher up at Car Park B. This second car park is also the start of the "Adventurous Trail", an eighteen-kilometre hike through the park to Muong villages, noted for their gigantic wooden water wheels, for which you'll need a guide ($15) plus a night's accommodation at the top ($5, excluding food).

Much is made of Cuc Phuong's **prehistoric caves**, the most accessible of which is Dong Nguoi Xua, only 300m from the road, 7km from the park gate. Joss sticks burn in the cave mouth near three tombs estimated to be over 7000 years old but there's nothing to see that justifies the steep climb.

Practicalities

Cuc Phuong **park gate**, just beyond which you'll find the Primate Centre and then the **Visitors' Centre** (☎030/848006, ⓔ dulichcucphuong@hn.vnn .vn), lies 45km north and west of Ninh Binh; head north on Highway 1 for 10km to find the sign indicating "Cuc Phuong" to the left. From the gate it's a further 18km to the heart of the forest. There are no public buses so you'll either have to rent a **car** or **motorbike** in Ninh Binh, or haul out there with a **xe om** (around $8 for the round trip). Visiting the park is also feasible as a day-trip out of Hanoi – an option offered by several tour agencies (see p.363).

Entry **tickets** are on sale at the Visitors' Centre ($2.60, including Primate Center), where you can also arrange **accommodation** (❶–❸), ranging from unexpectedly comfortable, if somewhat expensive, bungalows and bamboo chalets to a basic hostel, located either at the headquarters or in the interior. You can also organize **guided treks**, including overnighting in a Muong village, through the Visitors' Centre or through hotels in Ninh Binh, such as *Thuy Anh* and *Thanh Thuy* (see p.348). Be aware that Cuc Phuong is some way above the plains and winter nights can get chilly.

Van Long and Kenh Ga

TRAN ME, a town 23km from Ninh Binh on the road to Cuc Phuong, is the departure point for a couple of very different but worthwhile boattrips. It's possible to do them both in a day, or either one can be combined with a visit to Cuc Phuong or Hoa Lu.

The more beguiling of the two takes you round the shallow, reed-filled lagoons of **Van Long Nature Reserve**, signed to the right about 2km to the east of Tran Me. The road ends beside the ticket office, where you pay $1.60 per person for a ninety-minute trip, being poled across the wetlands and among the limestone outcrops in a low-slung bamboo sampan. Take your binoculars: the crags are home to a small, isolated population of Delacour's langur, and the reed beds provide refuge for migratory waterfowl. At present there's a good chance you'll have the place to yourself, with only the eerie cries of monkeys and birds to break the silence, but this is unlikely to last. Hawkers are banned from using boats, but already they gather round the ticket office whenever a tour bus hovers in sight and there is even talk about opening restaurants along the dyke.

The second boat trip departs from a canal bank about 7km away on the south side of Tran Me; take the lane immediately after the post office with its landmark radio tower. In this case a skinny motor launch takes you on a 45-minute ride ($3–5 per person depending on the size of the group; allow at least two hours for the round trip) through scenery which is certainly attractive but doesn't quite stand up beside that of Tam Coc or Van Long. However, the main purpose is to visit **Kenh Ga**, a village accessible only by water. The village boasts houses and even an ornate church, but many families live on boats and the whole place seems to be engaged in watery pursuits: boat yards turn out concrete-hulled barges to take gravel and quarried stone downstream; there are fish farms and great flocks of ducks, and sampans bustle about, often propelled by people rowing with their feet. Kenh Ga (Chicken Canal) supposedly gets its name from a hot spring where chickens were soaked in the near-boiling water to make them easier to pluck. The water is also said to be good for digestion, skin ailments and general recuperation and the site was developed for bathing, but the facilities are very run-down now. Better to press on to the final destination, **Van Trinh grotto**, a little-visited cave system where the guide will point out gnarled rocky outcrops which conjure up images of turtles, dragons, elephants and wizened faces. The local tourist authority has now installed lighting and concrete pathways, but you'll still need stout shoes, especially during the dry season when boats can't pull up outside the cave and you may have to walk the final kilometre.

Practicalities

Van Long and Kenh Ga can be reached independently by **car** or **motorbike**; count on at least $6 for a **xe om** for the return trip from Ninh Binh. Hotels in Ninh Binh and a few Hanoi tour agencies also offer **organized tours** combining both places, with prices starting at around $15 per person for a one-day excursion.

There are cheap food stalls in Tran Me, but the best place to eat is the small **restaurant** next to the Kenh Ga ticket office. You'll need a phrasebook since nobody speaks English and there's no menu – a good choice would be local fish and a dish of their excellent spring rolls. If you order before you set off on the boat trip, the meal will be ready on your return.

Travel details

Trains

Da Nang to: Hanoi (5 daily; 15–20hr); Ho Chi Minh City (5 daily; 16–21hr); Hué (5 daily; 2hr 30min–3hr); Nha Trang (5 daily; 9–12hr).
Dong Ha to: Dong Hoi (4 daily; 1hr 20min–2hr 10min); Hanoi (4 daily; 12–15hr); Hué (4 daily; 1hr 20min).
Dong Hoi to: Dong Ha (4 daily; 1hr 40min–2hr 35min); Hanoi (5 daily; 10–12hr); Hué (5 daily; 2hr 35min–4hr); Ninh Binh (2 daily; 9–10hr); Vinh (5 daily; 3hr 30min–5hr).
Hué to: Da Nang (5 daily; 2hr 20min–3hr); Dong Ha (4 daily; 1hr–1hr 20min); Dong Hoi (5 daily; 2hr 40min–3hr 30min); Hanoi (5 daily; 13–16hr); Ho Chi Minh City (5 daily; 19–24hr); Nha Trang (5 daily; 11hr 20min–15hr); Ninh Binh (2 daily; 14hr).
Ninh Binh to: Dong Hoi (2 daily; 10hr); Hanoi (2 daily; 2hr 30min); Hué (2 daily; 13–14hr); Vinh (2 daily; 4hr).
Thanh Hoa to: Hanoi (4 daily; 3hr 30min); Ninh Binh (2 daily; 1hr 20min); Vinh (3 daily; 2hr 30min).
Vinh to: Dong Ha (4 daily; 5hr–7hr 30min); Dong Hoi (5 daily; 4–5hr); Hanoi (5 daily; 6hr–6hr 30min); Hué (5 daily; 6–9hr); Ninh Binh (2 daily; 4hr).

Flights

Da Nang to: Bangkok (3 weekly; 2hr 40min); Buon Ma Thuot (5 weekly; 1hr 10min); Hanoi (3–5 daily; 1hr 10min–1hr 45min); Ho Chi Minh City (3–6 daily; 1hr 10min–1hr 50min); Hong Kong (2 weekly; 2hr 40min); Nha Trang (1–2 daily; 1hr 20min); Plei Ku (6 weekly; 50min); Siam Reap (3 weekly; 1hr 40min).
Hué to: Hanoi (2–3 daily; 1hr 10min); Ho Chi Minh City (2 daily; 1hr 20min).
Vinh to: Ho Chi Minh City (5 weekly; 2hr 40min).

Ferries

Da Nang to: Hué (1 daily; 2hr).

Buses

It's almost impossible to give the **frequency** with which buses run. Scheduled, long-distance public buses won't depart if empty and private services, often minibuses or pick-ups, ply more popular routes, and depart only when they have enough passengers to make the journey worthwhile. Highway 1 sees a near-constant stream of buses passing through to various destinations, and it's possible to flag something down at virtually any time of the day. Off the highway, to be sure of a bus it's advisable to start your journey early – most long-distance departures are between 5 and 9am, and very few run after midday. **Journey times** can also vary; figures below show the normal length of time you can expect the journey to take.

Da Nang to: Dong Ha (5hr); Hoi An (1hr 30min–2hr); Hué (3–4hr); Quang Ngai (5hr); Qui Nhon (11hr) Savannakhet (4 weekly; 24hr).
Dong Ha to: Dong Hoi (2hr); Hué (2hr 30min); Lao Bao (2hr); Savannakhet (alternate days; 8hr).
Dong Hoi to: Dong Ha (2hr); Hué (4–5hr); Vinh (4hr).
Hoi An to: Da Nang (1hr 30min–2hr); Quang Ngai (4hr).
Hué to: Da Nang (3–4hr); Dong Ha (2hr 30min); Dong Hoi (5hr).
Ninh Binh to: Haiphong (3hr); Hanoi (2hr); Kim Son (Phat Diem) (1hr); Son La (8hr); Thanh Hoa (1hr 30min); Vinh (5hr).
Thanh Hoa to: Hanoi (3hr 30min); Ninh Binh (1hr 30min); Vinh (4hr).
Vinh to: Dong Ha (6–7hr); Dong Hoi (4hr); Hué (8–10hr); Ninh Binh (5hr); Thanh Hoa (4hr); Trung Tam (2hr); Vientiane (daily; 12–14hr).

Hanoi and around

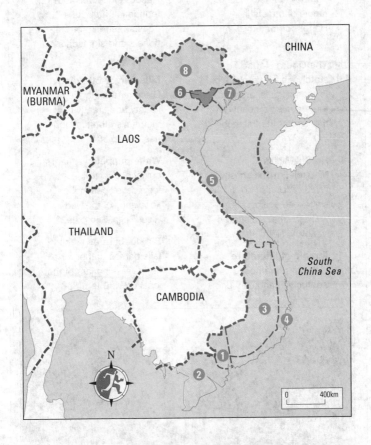

CHAPTER 6

Highlights

✳ **Pho** Join the locals at street kitchens to slurp on Hanoi's traditional beef-and-noodle breakfast soup. See p.386

✳ **The Old Quarter** Wander the intoxicating tangle of streets in Hanoi's commercial heart. See p.372

✳ **The Opera House** This stately signature-piece of French colonial architecture flaunts its beauty by the light of the full moon. See p.374

✳ **Ho Chi Minh's Mausoleum** The ghostly figure of "Uncle Ho", embalmed against his wishes, remains a strangely moving sight. See p.377

✳ **Temple of Literature** Vietnam's foremost Confucian sanctuary and centre of learning, the temple complex provides a haven of green lawns amidst the chaotic streets. See p.381

✳ **Tran Quoc Pagoda** Hanoi's oldest religious foundation attracts a constant stream of petitioners and sightseers. See p.383

✳ **Museum of Ethnology** Discover the staggering variety and creativity of Vietnam's ethnic minorities. See p.384

✳ **Water puppets** Vietnam's quirky but charming art form developed in the floodlands of the Red River Delta. See p.397

✳ **Bia hoi bars** As night falls parties gather for a few refreshing jars of the local brew. See p.396

Hanoi and around

The Vietnamese nation was born among the lagoons and marshes of the Red River Delta around 4000 years ago, and for most of its independent existence has been ruled from Hanoi, Vietnam's comparatively small, elegant capital lying in the heart of the northern delta. The region is steeped in the past and, while it lacks the bustling river life and rich physical beauty of the Mekong Delta, there's a wealth of historical and spiritual sights to explore – despite innumerable wars and a sometimes hostile natural environment that's only partly been tamed by an elaborate, centuries-old network of canals and embankments.

Given the political and historical importance of Hanoi and its burgeoning population of three million, it's a surprisingly low-key city with a more intimate appeal than brash, young Ho Chi Minh City. At its centre lies a tree-fringed lake and shaded avenues of classy French villas dressed up in jaded stucco, but, despite first impressions, Hanoi is bursting at the seams and nowhere is this more evident than in the teeming traffic and the vibrant, intoxicating tangle of streets known as the **Old Quarter**, the city's commercial heart since the fifteenth century. Delving back even further, a handful of Hanoi's more than six hundred temples and pagodas hail from the original, eleventh-century city, most notably the **Temple of Literature**, which encompasses both Vietnam's foremost Confucian sanctuary and its first university. Many visitors, however, are drawn to Hanoi by more recent events, seeking answers among the exhibits of the **Museum of Military History** and in **Ho Chi Minh's Mausoleum** to the extraordinary Vietnamese tenacity displayed during the wars of the twentieth century.

Modern Hanoi has an increasingly confident, "can do" air about it. In general, there's far more money about and the wealthier Hanoians are prepared to spend it in the ever-more sophisticated restaurants, cafés and boutiques that have exploded all over the city. The city now boasts glitzy shopping malls and supermarkets selling expensive imports, cybercafés open and close on street corners with dizzying regularity and almost everyone zips around on motorbikes rather than the deeply untrendy bicycle. The authorities are trying to temper the anarchy with laws to curb traffic and regulate unsympathetic building projects in the Old Quarter, amongst other things, coupled with an ambitious twenty-year development plan which aims to ease congestion by creating satellite towns. Nevertheless, the city has not completely lost its old-world charm nor its distinctive character. Hanoians are well known for being reserved, but they are also said to be less corrupt and more hospitable than southerners. Cut off from the non-communist world for two decades, the city may still be catching up with other Asian hubs in terms of high-standard services, but the signs are it won't take long.

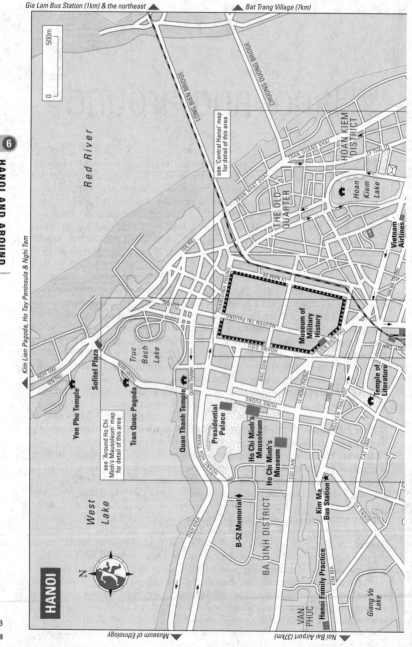

HANOI

N

500m
0

Gia Lam Bus Station (1km) & the northeast

Bat Trang Village (7km)

Red River

LONG BIEN BRIDGE

CHUONG DUONG BRIDGE

HOAN KIEM
DISTRICT

TRAN QUANG KHAI

LY THAI TO

see 'Central Hanoi' map
for detail of this area

TRAN NHAT DUAT

THE OLD
QUARTER

Hoan
Kiem
Lake

Vietnam
Airlines

Kim Lien Pagoda, Ho Tay Peninsula & Nghi Tam

YEN PHU

NGHI TAM

Yen Phu Temple

Sofitel Plaza

Truc
Bach
Lake

Tran Quoc Pagoda

Quan Thanh Temple

QUAN THANH

YEN PHU

PHAN DINH PHUNG

LY NAM DE

NGUYEN TRI PHUONG

Museum of
Military
History

Museum of History

HOANG DIEU

DIEN BIEN PHU

THAI BA TRUNG

QUY DAP

see 'Around Ho Chi
Minh's Mausoleum' map
for detail of this area

HOANG HOA THAM

HUNG VUONG

LE HONG PHONG

NGUYEN THAI HOC

BAC SON

Temple of
Literature

CAT LINH

GIANG VO

Presidential
Palace

Ho Chi Minh's
Mausoleum

Ho Chi Minh's
Museum

DOI CAN

West
Lake

B-52 Memorial

BA DINH DISTRICT

THUY KHUE

Kim Ma
Bus Station

VAN
PHUC

KIM MA

Hanoi Family Practice

Giang Vo
Lake

Museum of Ethnology

Noi Bai Airport (37km)

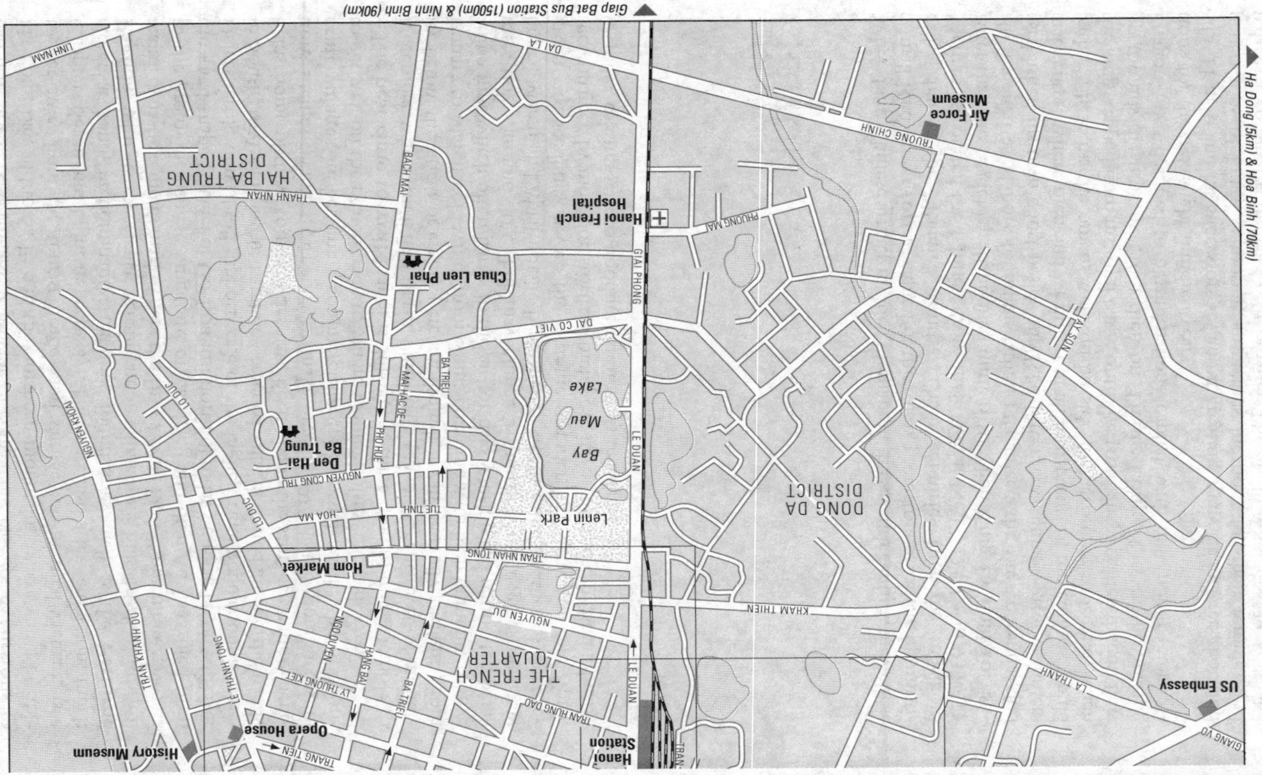

History Museum

TRAN KHANH DU

NGUYEN KHOAI

TRANG TIEN

Opera House

LE THANH TONG

LO DUC

HAI BA TRUNG
DISTRICT

Hom Market

HANG BAI

LY THUONG KIET

NGO QUYEN

BA TRIEU

HO MA

HOA MA

NGUYEN CONG TRU

Den Hai
Ba Trung

THANH NHAN

LO DUC

PHO HUE

MAI HAC DE

BACH MAI

THE FRENCH
QUARTER

NGUYEN DU

TRAN NHAN TONG

LE VAN

LE DAI

BA TRIEU

Chua Lien Phai

Hanoi/
Station

TRAN HUNG DAO

Lenin Park

Bay
Mau
Lake

DAI CO VIET

DAI LA

LE DUAN

LE DUAN

GIAI PHONG

TRAN

Hanoi French
Hospital

Giap Bat Bus Station (1500m) & Ninh Binh (90km)

KHAM THIEN

DONG DA
DISTRICT

PHUONG MAI

TRUONG CHINH

LA THANH

TAY SON

Air Force
Museum

US Embassy

GIANG VO

Ha Dong (5km) & Hoa Binh (70km)

Hanoi, somewhat unjustly, remains less popular than Ho Chi Minh City as a jumping-off point for touring Vietnam, with many making the journey from south to north. Nevertheless, it provides a convenient base for **excursions** to Ha Long Bay, and to Sa Pa and the northern mountains, where you'll be able to get away from the tourist hordes and sample life in rural Vietnam (see Chapters Seven and Eight respectively). There are also a few attractions much closer at hand, predominantly religious foundations such as the **Perfume Pagoda**, with its spectacular setting among limestone hills. In the historical realm, dynastic temples mark where the Bronze Age Dong Son culture gave rise to the proto-Vietnamese kingdoms of Van Lang and then Au Lac, ruled from the spiral-shaped citadel of **Co Loa** just north of today's capital. The Red River Delta's fertile alluvial soil supports one of the highest rural population densities in Southeast Asia, living in bamboo-screened villages dotted among the paddy fields. Some of these communities have been plying the same trade for generations, such as ceramics, carpentry or snake breeding. While the more successful **craft villages** are becoming commercialized, it's possible, with a bit of effort, to get well off the beaten track to where Confucianism still holds sway.

The **best time to visit** Hanoi is during the three months from October to December, when you'll find warm, sunny days (25–30°C) and levels of humidity below the norm of eighty percent, though it can be chilly at night. From January to March, cold winds from China combine with high humidity to give a fine mist which often hangs in the air for days. During this period temperatures hover around 20°C but may plunge as much as ten degrees in a few hours. March and April usually bring better weather and swathes of electric-green rice seedlings, before the extreme summer heat arrives in late April, accompanied by monsoon storms which peak in August and can last until early October, causing serious flooding throughout the delta.

Hanoi

When Tang Chinese armies invaded Vietnam in the seventh century, they chose a small **Red River fort** as capital of their new protectorate, named, optimistically, *Annam*, the "Pacified South". Three centuries later the rebellious Vietnamese ousted the Chinese from their "Great Nest", *Dai La*, in 939 AD. After that, the citadel lay abandoned until 1010 when **King Ly Thai To**, usually credited as Hanoi's founding father, recognized the site's potential and established his own court beside the Red River, envisaging a great commercial centre "where men and wealth from all four points of the compass could gather". It seems the omens were on his side for, according to legend, when the king stepped from his royal barge onto the riverbank a golden dragon flew up towards the heavens. From then on **Thang Long**, "City of the Soaring Dragon", was destined to be the nation's capital, with only minor interruptions, for the next eight hundred years.

Ly Thai To and his successors set about creating a city fit for "ten thousand generations of kings", choosing auspicious locations for their temples and palaces according to the laws of geomancy. They built protective dykes, established a town of artisans and merchants alongside the **Imperial City**'s eastern wall, and set up the nation's first university, in the process laying the foundations of modern Hanoi. From 1407, the country was again under Chinese occupation, but this time only briefly before the great hero **Le Loi** retook the capital in 1428. The Le dynasty kings drained lakes and marshes to accommodate their new palaces as well as a growing civilian population, and towards the end of the fifteenth century Thang Long was enjoying a **golden era** under the great reformer, King Le Thanh Thong. Shortly after his death in 1497, however, the country dissolved into anarchy, while the city slowly declined until finally Emperor Gia Long moved the royal court to Hué in 1802.

By the 1830s Thang Long had been relegated to a provincial capital, known merely as *Ha Noi* or "City within the River's Bend", and in 1882 its reduced defences offered little resistance to **attacking French forces**, led by Captain Rivière. Initially capital of the French Protectorate of Tonkin, a name derived from *Dong Kinh* meaning "Eastern Capital", after 1887 Hanoi became the centre of government for the entire Union of Indochina. Royal palaces and ancient monuments made way for grand residences, administrative offices, tree-lined boulevards and all the trappings of a **colonial city**, more European than Asian. It seems to have been a congenial place in its heyday: Joleaud-Barral, a French geographer visiting Hanoi in the 1890s, enthused "at Singapore, at Saigon, one exists; at Hanoi, one lives". However, while the French erected fine buildings and a modern infrastructure, the Vietnamese community lived a largely separate, often impoverished existence, creating a seedbed of insurrection.

During the 1945 August Revolution, thousands of local nationalist sympathizers spilled onto the streets of Hanoi and later took part in its defence against returning French troops, though they had to wait until 1954 for their city finally to become the **capital of an independent Vietnam**. Hanoi sustained more serious damage during the air raids of the American War, particularly the infamous Christmas Bombing campaign of 1972 (see box on p.385). The subsequent political isolation together with lack of resources preserved what was essentially the city of the 1950s, somewhat faded, a bit battered and very overcrowded. These characteristics are still in evidence today, even as Hanoi is reinventing itself as a dynamic international capital. New market freedoms combined with an influx of tourists since the early 1990s have led to a huge growth in privately run hotels and restaurants, several of international standard, and boutiques, craft shops and tour agencies. Indeed, the area around Hang Bac and Ma May, two of the Old Quarter's main drags which are home to a large number of travellers' hangouts, is starting to resemble Ho Chi Minh's Pham Ngu Lao. As ancient – and antiquated – buildings give way to glittering high-rises, and as traffic congestion increases, the big question is how much of this historic and charming city will survive the onslaught of modernization.

Arrival and information

Hanoi's smart new international **Noi Bai Airport** (℡04/886 6527), 35km north of the city, is equipped with two **exchange** bureaux (daily 7am–10pm), a 24-hour ATM and a tourist information desk (daily 8am–7pm). By far the cheapest option for getting into town is the #7 **city bus** (2hr; under \$0.20), which departs from outside the arrivals hall every fifteen to twenty minutes from 5am to 9pm, with stops around Hoan Kiem Lake, convenient for most central hotels and guesthouses. Quicker is the shuttle service run by **Noi Bai Minibus** (5am–5.30pm; 45min–1hr; $2), which also leaves from outside the terminal and drops you near the Vietnam Airlines office just south of Hoan Kiem Lake. **Taxis** cost a fixed-rate $10 for the 45-minute ride into town; always insist on being taken to your chosen hotel, as some drivers will try to direct you elsewhere in order to gain a commission.

Hanoi's **train station** is roughly a kilometre west of centre, on Le Duan. Arriving from Ho Chi Minh City and all points south or from China, you exit the main station onto Le Duan. However, trains from the east and north (Haiphong, Lang Son and Lao Cai) pull into platforms at the rear of the main station, bringing you out among market stalls on a narrow street called Tran Quy Cap. There are a few places to stay within a short walk of the station that are useful if you arrive late or have an early start; otherwise, pick up a cyclo or xe om to the centre of town.

Hanoi's three long-distance **bus stations** are all located several kilometres from the centre, and you'll need to catch a city bus or hop on a cyclo or xe om. Buses **from the south** terminate at Giap Bat station (℡04/864 1467), 6km south of town on Giai Phong. Most services **from the northeast** (Lang Son and Cao Bang) arrive at Gia Lam station (℡04/827 1529), 4km away on the east bank of the Red River, while express buses from Haiphong and Ha Long and all those **from the northwest** (Son La, Mai Chau and Lao Cai) use Kim Ma station (℡04/845 2846), located at the junction of Giang Vo and Kim Ma, 2km west of the centre. However, some **private services** drop passengers at more convenient, though unofficial and unpredictable, spots in the centre. Open-tour buses, for example, terminate on Tran Nhat Duat, to the east of the Old Quarter. Note that buses **from Mai Chau and Hoa Binh** sometimes dump you in Ha Dong, a suburb of Hanoi 10km from the centre; jump on one of the waiting city buses for the forty-minute ride into town.

For details of **moving on** from Hanoi, see p.402.

Information

The big state-run tour agencies, such as Vietnamtourism at 30a Ly Thuong Kiet (℡04/826 4089, ⓦwww.vn-tourism.com) or Vinatour, 54 Nguyen Du (℡04/942 2986, ⓦwww.vinatour.com.vn), will be more interested in signing you up for a tour than dishing out **information**. A far better option is to try one of the well-established and reliable private **tour agencies** and travellers' cafés (see box opposite), which can provide information on visas, tours, transport and so forth. Most also arrange day tours of the city ($12–20 including entrance fees and lunch).

Standard Hanoi **maps** are available from hawkers and from bookshops and stalls on Trang Tien: those with a street index and inset of the Old Quarter are the most useful. Four publications carry **listings** information: the monthly tourist magazine, *Vietnam Discovery* (in theory $1, though available free at tourist-oriented cafés, restaurants, bars and so forth at the time of writing); *The Guide*, a supplement of the monthly *Vietnam Economic Times*; *Time Out*, produced weekly with the *Vietnam Investment Review*; and the free, monthly *Vietnam Pathfinder*. Anyone moving to Hanoi, or planning to stay more than a few weeks, should invest in a copy of the *Hanoi Guide* (around $10) published annually by the Hanoi International Women's Group.

Tour agents and travellers' cafés

In the last few years, Hanoi's tourist-service industry has become increasingly sophisticated as companies begin to specialize rather than offering a one-stop café, bar, restaurant and tour operator rolled into one. These old-style **travellers' cafés** have thus been joined by a dizzying array of dedicated **tour agents**. The situation is further complicated by the tendency for newcomers to adopt the same name as a succesful rival, or something that sounds similar; there's currently a plethora of outfits in the Old Quarter claiming to be affiliated to Ho Chi Minh's Sinh Café. To be on the safe side, it's best to go to one of the longer-established and more reliable agents such as those listed below and on p.405. Always check the details carefully when shopping around, to ensure you're comparing like with like. This applies whether you are arranging an extended tour, for example to the northwest mountains or even down to Ho Chi Minh City, or simply signing up for one of the myriad day-trips on offer (see "Moving on from Hanoi", p.402, for more about organized tours around Hanoi).

Buffalo Tours 11 Hang Muoi ☏04/828 0702, ⓦwww.buffalotours.com. An upscale travel agency offering adventure trips (trekking, kayaking and cycling amongst other activities) and less rugged, "discovery" tours. Prices are on the premium side but trips are well organized and can be individually tailored.

Explore Indochina ⓦwww.exploreindochina.com. Tailor-made, off-the-beaten-track adventure treks on foot or Russian Minsk motorbikes organized by real enthusiasts. Biking trips are best for those with some prior experience as the going can be tough.

Free-Wheelin' Tours (Compagnie Bourlingue) 2f, 51 Cua Dong ☏04/747 0545, ⓦwww.freewheelin-tours.com. Highly rated customized motorbike tours exploring parts of Vietnam foreigners rarely get to. A great way to see the country close up.

Handspan Adventure Travel 80 Ma May & 36 Nguyen Huu Huan ☏04/926 0446, ⓦwww.handspan.com. Adventure-tour specialist offering to show you the "real Vietnam". Options range from sea kayaking in Ha Long Bay to exploring the north by mountain or motorbike. Prices are above average but tours are well organized, with good equipment and back-up, and are restricted to small groups. Handpsan's Ma May booking office is located in their stylish vegetarian restaurant, *Tamarind* (see p.392).

Hanoi Spirit House 50 Hang Be ☏04/826 7356, ⓦwww.azqueencafe.com. Cheap and cheerful mass-market tours, food and accommodation (see p.368), plus Internet access and free film-screenings. Among the cheapest prices in Hanoi but don't expect top-quality service.

Hanoi Toserco 18 Luong Van Can ☏04/828 7552, ⓦwww.tosercohanoi.com. The Hanoi home to Sinh Café's open-tour buses also offers cheap tours aimed at the backpacker market. Their outlet at 33 Luong Van Can has a café and Internet access.

Kangaroo Café 18 Bao Khanh ☏04/828 9931, ⓦwww.kangaroocafe.com. This Australian-run café is recommended for its innovative, well-organized small-group and adventure tours. Helpful staff and a simple restaurant serving good-quality local, Western and vegetarian food round out the picture.

Love Planet Travel 25 Hang Bac ☏04/828 4864, ⓦwww.loveplanettravel.com. A welcoming and reliable tour agent with many years' experience of meeting travellers' needs, Love Planet provides a great all-round service at reasonable prices, including tours (covering some more unusual destinations), tickets and good advice. They also boast Vietnam's biggest collection of secondhand books (6000 and growing, mostly English-language titles) for exchange, rental or sale.

Queen Travel 65 Hang Bac ☏04/826 0860, ⓦwww.queencafe.com.vn. Aims at the middle market with tailor-made and small-group tours, including some interesting adventure options. The new premises will comprise a hotel (due to open in 2004), restaurant and tour agent. Internet access available.

City transport

Getting around **on foot** is the best way to do justice to Hanoi's central district, especially the congested streets of the Old Quarter, taking an occasional **cyclo** or **motorbike** ride to scoot between places. Bear in mind, though, that traffic discipline is an unfamiliar concept in Hanoi: teenagers on their Hondas ride without fear, and everyone drives without signalling or even looking. Despite the chaotic traffic, the **bicycle** is still a good way to get around – for those with strong nerves. If you prefer something solid between you and the maelstrom, and don't mind the expense, there are numerous **taxi** companies operating in Hanoi. Finally, the much improved **city buses** are mainly useful for getting out to the long-distance bus stations.

Cyclo and taxis

Hanoi **cyclo** are wider than the Ho Chi Minh City version and can take two people at a squeeze. An average journey within the city centre should cost around $0.50, but always establish terms before setting off. It's wise to write down the figures, making it clear whether you're negotiating in dollars or dong, for one person or two, a one-way or return journey; having the exact change ready at the end of the journey can also save argument. Hold on tight to your possessions when travelling by cyclo, and if possible avoid taking them at night, particularly women on their own. Cyclo are banned from certain roads in central Hanoi, notably around Hoan Kiem Lake (Dinh Tien Hoang and Le Thai To) and in the Old Quarter, so don't be surprised if you seem to be taking a circuitous route or are dropped off round the corner from your destination.

Motorbike taxis (xe om), which hover at every intersection, compete with cyclo as a cheap means of inner-city transport; prices are slightly lower and they're obviously a lot quicker, but be warned – it's a more hair-raising ride and you're not provided with a helmet. If you come off, the potential for injury is high. In general you should pay slightly under $0.50 for a xe om ride within central Hanoi; a longer journey to the suburbs or out towards West Lake would be slightly more, but rarely more than a dollar.

Regular, metered **taxis** wait outside the more upmarket hotels and at the north end of Hoan Kiem Lake, or you can call one up (see "Listings", p.401). With a short ride averaging under $1 and less than $2 to the suburbs, taxis are definitely worth considering for hopping around the city. Note that prices are metered in dong, though it looks like dollars – for example, 20.00 on the metre means 20,000d, *not* $20.

Bicycle, motorbike and car rental

Though it's no longer as enjoyable as it was just a few of years ago, thanks to chaotic traffic, the **bicycle** is still a cheap and efficient way of getting about the city. If your hotel or guesthouse doesn't rent out bikes, try one of the outlets given on p.401. Prices tend to be lower in the Old Quarter, but are not exorbitant anywhere; expect to pay less than $0.70 per day, and bargain for a longer-term discount. When leaving your bicycle on the street, it's best to fork out the minuscule charge at a supervised bicycle park (*gui xe dap*), rather than run the risk of deflated tyres or a stolen bicycle. Parking is now completely banned along Trang Tien and Hang Khay, while elsewhere in the centre it's allowed only within designated areas – in theory anyway.

Self-drive **motorbikes** are only for the brave in the inner city but are definitely worth considering for exploring sights further afield. You can rent them through guesthouses, tour agencies and specialist outlets (see p.401). A day's rental costs $4–10, including a helmet, depending on the size and make of bike. The same parking recommendations apply as for pedal bicycles; supervised motorbike parks are called *gui xe may*.

Virtually every tour agency will gladly arrange **car rental**, and though the traffic congestion makes this a cumbersome method of sightseeing in the central districts, for day-trips out of Hanoi it offers greater flexibility than tours. Prices average $25 per day for a car with driver, plus an extra $10 for a newer, air-conditioned car; as few drivers speak English, you may also want to hire a guide for another $10–15 a day.

City buses

Hanoi's recently revamped **city bus** service, with newer vehicles, bus lanes, shelters and clearly marked routes, is now much more user-friendly. The network even reaches out to Noi Bai Airport (see p.361), while other useful routes connect the far-flung long-distance bus stations: #3 runs between Gia Lam and Giap Bat with stops on Hang Tre (or Tran Quang Khai, heading south), Phan Chu Trinh, Tran Hung Dao and outside the train station. From the centre of town count on roughly thirty minutes to either Gia Lam or Giap Bat. Route #2 (Tran Quan Du–Ba La) serves the Temple of Literature (10min) and Ha Dong (40min); you'll find stops at the northwest corner of Hoan Kiem Lake and on Trang Thi opposite Vietnam Airlines. Buses on most routes run approximately fifteen to twenty minutes between 5am and 8pm, and are fairly empty except during rush hour (7–9am and after 4pm) when they're hideously overcrowded. The fares are heavily subsidized, with a flat rate of under $0.20 regardless of the distance.

Accommodation

Hanoi's **hotel** scene has changed dramatically over recent years to the extent that there's now an oversupply at all levels. As a host of new luxury hotels came on stream just as the Asian economic crisis hit, prices at the top end have fallen dramatically and there are some excellent bargains to be had – ask about special discounts and promotional rates. Rates have also been dropping – and standards rising – at the budget level, spurred by an explosion of backpacker-oriented places all vying for the tourist dollar, but you'll still find accommodation here more expensive than in Ho Chi Minh. Finding a room shouldn't cause any problems, even during the Tet New Year holiday, when the rest of the city all but shuts down. Be aware that several hotels adopt the same name, for example there are multiple *Classic* and *Prince* hotels, so you'll need an exact address if arriving by either cyclo or taxi.

The city's most sought-after addresses are in the **French Quarter**, headed by the venerable *Metropole* and its newer neighbour, the *Hilton Hanoi Opera*. Here, among the quieter streets and more open spaces, you'll also find a rash of modern business hotels and still a few echoing state-run places, the best now revamped and offering reasonable rates, but very little in the bargain stakes. The best place to look for budget accommodation is amidst the hustle and bustle of Hanoi's **Old Quarter**, and spreading into the area **west of Hoan Kiem Lake**, where the travellers' cafés and dozens of private hotels provide a broad range of reasonable-value rooms, from the most basic dormitories to increasingly ritzy places with air-conditioning and en-suite bathrooms.

The French Quarter

All the following hotels and guesthouses are marked on the map opposite.

Army 33c Pham Ngu Lao ☎04/825 2896, ✉armyhotel@fpt.vn. This mid-range hotel set among trees on a quiet backstreet next to the Ministry of Defence offers reasonable value for such a central location. Well-equipped and spacious rooms, if slightly old-fashioned, occupying two low-rise blocks overlooking a large, salt-water swimming pool ($3.50 to non-guests). ❹

Dan Chu 29 Trang Tien ☎04/825 4937, ⓦwww.danchuhotel.com. This old French hotel is on the expensive side but retains some period flavour in its open corridors, courtyard, wooden floorboards and good-sized bathrooms. Air-con, IDD, satellite TV, and mini-bar come as standard, though cheaper rooms are small and lack windows. ❹

De Syloia 17a Tran Hung Dao ☎04/824 5346, ⓦwww.desyloia.com. A stylish business hotel with just 33 impeccably furnished rooms, some a touch on the small side, behind its mock-colonial facade. Service is good and it also boasts a decent restaurant and a gym. ❹

Guoman 83a Ly Thuong Kiet ☎04/822 2800, ⓦwww.guomanhotels.com. A larger business hotel in neo-colonial style near the train station. It offers high standards of service and tastefully decorated rooms in addition to business and fitness centres as well as a choice of restaurants. ❹

Hilton Hanoi Opera 1 Le Thanh Tong ☎04/933 0500, ⓦwww.hilton.com. Arguably Hanoi's top city-centre address for all-round value, this five-star hotel is carefully designed to blend in with the neighbouring Opera House. Facilities include 269 cheerful and well-proportioned rooms with excellent bathrooms and some local touches in the ceramics and chunky furniture. In-house services include three restaurants, a business centre, tour desk, fitness centre and outdoor swimming pool (summer only). ❺–❻

Lotus 42v, Ly Thuong Kiet ☎04/826 8642, ⓦwww.lotus-guesthouse.com. One of Hanoi's original dorm-style guesthouses, and still popular for its friendly welcome and prime location in the quieter French Quarter. A dorm bed costs $4, while rather cramped en-suite rooms start at $8. Best to book ahead. ❶–❷

Melia 44b Ly Thuong Kiet ☎04/934 3343, ⓦwww.solmelia.com. Hanoi's newest high-rise hotel pitches at the executive traveller. Luxurious rooms have an appealingly funky design, but bathrooms at the cheaper end are small considering the price tag. There's an elevated open-air swimming pool, as well as a gym and business centre and a choice of restaurants. ❻

Nikko 84 Tran Nhan Tong ☎04/822 3535, ⓦwww.hotelnikkohanoi.com.vn. A luxurious hotel on the French Quarter's southern fringes, where well-appointed rooms feature comprehensive five-star facilities. Japanese-owned, it retains a distinctly Japanese, rather minimalist feel and is home to the excellent *Benkay* restaurant and sushi bar. Other facilities include a business centre, health club and outdoor swimming pool. ❻

Saigon 80 Ly Thuong Kiet ☎04/942 4499, ✉saigonhotelhn@fpt.vn. An older government-run hotel facing stiff competition from the slightly superior *Guoman* across the road. Rooms are spacious but somewhat oddly shaped; IDD, bath, satellite TV and air-con are standard. The rooftop bar is open evenings only from April to September. ❺

Sofitel Metropole 15 Ngo Quyen ☎04/826 6919, ⓦwww.accorhotels.com/asia. Despite increasingly fierce competition, the *Metropole* remains one of the most sought-after hotels in Hanoi. Opened in 1901, past guests number Graham Greene, Charlie Chaplin and Jane Fonda. Though rooms in the modern Opera Wing exude international-class luxury, they lack the old-world charm of the original building, with its wooden floorboards, period furniture and bamboo wall coverings. In-house services include a business centre, a small open-air swimming pool, the Clark Hatch Fitness Centre and a range of restaurants, notably *Spices Garden*, serving upmarket Vietnamese fare. ❺–❻

Somerset Grand Hanoi 49 Hai Ba Trung ☎04/934 2342, ✉enquiry.hanoi@the-ascott.com. Billed as "corporate accommodation", these serviced apartments, with up to three bedrooms and fully equipped kitchen, can be rented by the night and make a more homely alternative to an upmarket hotel. They also represent surprisingly good-value, including access to facilities such as an open-air pool, a gym and a children's playroom. ❺

Sunway 19 Pham Dinh Ho ☎04/971 3888, ⓦwww.allsonhotels.com. An award-winning four-star boutique hotel where consistently high standards of service and comfortable rooms make up for a slightly inconvenient location. There's an in-house restaurant and live music nightly in the lobby bar, not to mention the obligatory fitness centre. ❺–❻

Thuy Nga 4 Ba Trieu ☎04/934 1256, ✉thuynga-hotel@hn.vnn.vn. One of the area's few mid-range hotels, the Thuy Nga offers cheerful, well-maintained rooms, though you pay a premium for the location – a stone's throw from Hoan Kiem Lake. ❹

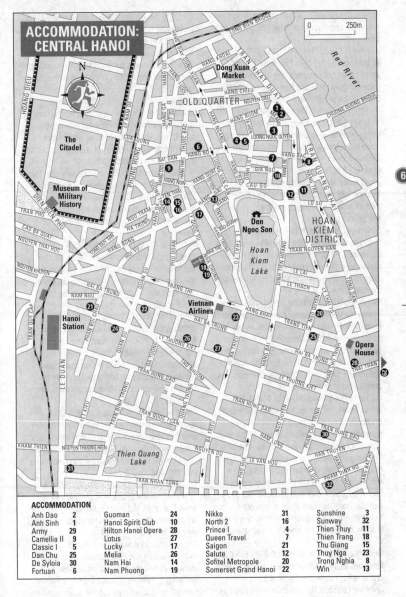

ACCOMMODATION: CENTRAL HANOI

ACCOMMODATION

Anh Dao	2	Guoman	24	Nikko	31	Sunshine	3
Anh Sinh	1	Hanoi Spirit Club	10	North 2	16	Sunway	32
Army	29	Hilton Hanoi Opera	28	Prince I	4	Thien Thuy	11
Camellia II	9	Lotus	27	Queen Travel	7	Thien Trang	18
Classic I	5	Lucky	17	Saigon	21	Thu Giang	15
Dan Chu	25	Melia	26	Salute	12	Thuy Nga	23
De Syloia	30	Nam Hai	14	Sofitel Metropole	20	Trong Nghia	8
Fortuan	6	Nam Phuong	19	Somerset Grand Hanoi	22	Win	13

The Old Quarter and west of Hoan Kiem Lake

All the following hotels and guesthouses are marked on the map above.

Anh Dao 37 Ma May ☎04/826 7151,

Ⓦwww.camellia-hotels.com. Popular, friendly and well-run budget hotel on one of the Old Quarter's liveliest streets. Rooms are all en suite and represent good value for IDD, satellite TV and air-con, while some have balconies and wooden floorboards. ❸

Anh Sinh 7 Dong Thai ☎04/828 2970, ✉anhsinh7@yahoo.com. Functional but fairly well-kept en-suite rooms at the bottom of this price category make this little hotel on a quiet backstreet a popular place to crash. ❷

Camellia II 31 Hang Dieu ☎04/828 5704, ✉camellia2@fpt.vn. Exceptionally friendly staff compensate for the *Camellia*'s increasingly run-down state, though the rooms are clean and comfortable enough for a night or two. ❸

Classic I 22a Ta Hien ☎04/826 6224. A welcome – and welcoming – newcomer boasting forty spotless and well-equipped rooms at reasonable rates. Internet access is available and there's an on-site tour operator. ❸

Fortuan 68 Hang Bo ☎04/828 1324, ✉fortuan@hn.vnn.vn. The communal areas are a bit soulless but cane furniture in the bedrooms makes for a pleasant change. It's worth paying extra for those rooms with balconies and newly fitted bathrooms. ❷

Hanoi Spirit Club 50 Hang Be ☎04/826 7356, ✍www.azqueencafe.com. Large, renovated guest-house popular with backpackers and cyclists for its range of no-frills accommodation, from dorm beds ($2.50) to en-suite rooms with fan (doubles from $7) and air-con (doubles from $9). A tour agency and Internet café, plus bar and restaurant, are situated at ground level. ❶

Lucky 12 Hang Trong ☎04/825 1029, ✉luckyhotel@hn.vnn.vn. A bit faded but best of the bunch along Hang Trong for comfortable accommodation at a range of prices; all the rooms have bathtub, fridge, phone, air-con and satellite TV, plus balconies at higher rates. ❸–❹

Nam Hai 55 Duong Thanh ☎04/928 6630, ✍www.namhaihotel.com. The heavy furniture and wood-panelled or tiled rooms in this glitzy two-star hotel opposite Hang Da market may be too ornate for some. Nevertheless, they are reasonably priced and equipped to a high standard. ❹

Nam Phuong 26 Nha Chung ☎04/824 6894. This little hotel located in the increasingly trendy cathedral area has good-value bright and airy rooms, some with balcony. Has a reputation for being a bit rule-bound. ❶–❷

North 2 5 Tam Thuong ☎04/828 5030, ✉north-hotel@fpt.vn. One of two friendly, family-run hotels located down a quiet alleyway offering basic but perfectly adequate accommodation. Rooms come with private bathroom (some a bit cramped), satellite TV, fridge and phone as standard. The *North 1* at 15 Hang Ga (☎04/826 7242) has similar facilities. ❶–❷

Prince I 51 Luong Ngoc Quyen ☎04/828 0155, ✍www.hanoiprincehotel.com. A smart hotel with huge, spruce rooms and good facilities, including free Internet use, located in the heart of the Old Quarter. ❸

Queen Travel 65 Hang Bac ☎04/826 0860, ✍www.queencafe.com.vn. With its rooftop café, fully equipped rooms and Oriental touches, the new *Queen* hotel promises to be worth a look when it opens in the spring of 2004. ❸

Salute 7 Hang Dau ☎04/825 8003, ✉salutehotelvn@yahoo.com. Relatively smart but good-value hotel located between Hoan Kiem Lake and the Old Quarter. Rooms are comfortable and well equipped with chic marble-effect bathrooms. Top-rated rooms get bathtubs and balconies. ❸

Sunshine 42 Ma May ☎04/926 1559, ✍www.sinhcafetour.com/sunshinehotel01.html. A sparkling new place under the same ownership as the *Classic I* (see above), and offering the same high standards. Bathrooms with coloured tiles make an attractive change. ❸

Thien Thuy 9 Hang Thung ☎04/934 3608, ✉thienthuyhotel@hn.vnn.vn. Well-managed Malay-Viet hotel close to Hoan Kiem Lake offering twenty fully equipped rooms at very reasonable rates. The bathrooms are unusually generous and all fitted with bathtubs. There are plans to open an Indonesian/Malay restaurant downstairs. ❸

Thien Trang 24 Nha Chung ☎04/826 9823, 🖷828 6717. Similar in style to the *Nam Phuong* next door (see above), though slightly smarter and a little more expensive. Rooms are all immaculately kept, while that on the top floor has great views over the town. ❷–❸

Thu Giang 5a Tam Thuong ☎04/828 5734. A family-run hotel with tiny, no-frills rooms for around $6 or $7. Not much in the way of facilities but an interesting location and the hosts make you very welcome. ❶

Trong Nghia 9a Hang Mam ☎04/826 7365, ✉nghiahotel@hn.vnn.vn. Fifteen rooms kitted out with traditional, heavy furniture plus sparkling bathrooms (comprising a tiny shower room at the bottom end) and the usual range of amenities, on the eastern edge of the Old Quarter. ❷

Win 34 Hang Hanh ☎04/288 7371, 🖷824 7448. Well-established and perennially popular hotel on the ultra-cool Hang Hanh café strip. The ten rooms are large, airy and have all mod cons, although rates are on the high side. ❸

The City

Hanoi **city centre** is a compact area neatly bordered by the Red River embankment in the east and by the rail line to the north and west. Its present-day hub and most obvious point of reference is **Hoan Kiem Lake** which lies between the cramped and endlessly diverting **Old Quarter** in the north, and the tree-lined boulevards of the **French Quarter**, arranged in a rough grid system, to the south. West of this central district, across the rail tracks, some of Hanoi's most impressive monuments occupy the wide open spaces of the former **Imperial City**, grouped around Ho Chi Minh's Mausoleum on Ba Dinh Square and extending south to the ancient walled gardens of the Temple of Literature. A vast body of water confusingly called **West Lake** sits north of the city, harbouring a number of interesting temples and pagodas, but the attractive villages that once surrounded West Lake have now largely given way to upmarket residential areas and luxury hotels.

The major tourist sights are nearly all located within the central and western districts; to do both areas justice takes at least two full days. Each district can be covered comfortably on foot, though a bicycle or cyclo helps over longer distances. Seeing the more far-flung sights of West Lake and the outskirts could occupy a further two to three days, depending on how many more pagodas and temples you can take.

Central Hanoi

The commercial core of Hanoi is **Hoan Kiem District**, home to the city's banks, airlines and the GPO, plus most of the hotels, restaurants, shopping streets and markets. But there's a lot more to the area: the **History Museum** boasts some of Vietnam's most valued archeological finds, while the **temples** here date back to the earliest days of the city. Though you'll want to spend time on these individual sights, it's the abundant streetlife and architectural wealth that give the area its special allure.

Hoan Kiem Lake

Early morning sees **Hoan Kiem Lake** at its best, stirring to life as walkers, joggers and *tai chi* enthusiasts limber up in the half-light. Space is at a premium in this crowded city and the lake's strip of park meets multiple needs, at its busiest when lunch-hour hawkers, beggars and shoeshine boys are out in force, and easing down slowly to evenings of old men playing chess and couples seeking twilight privacy on benches half-hidden among the willows. The lake itself is small – you can walk round it in thirty minutes – and not particularly spectacular, but to Hanoians this is the soul of their city.

A squat, three-tiered pavilion known as the **Tortoise Tower** ornaments a tiny island in the middle of Ho Hoan Kiem, "Lake of the Restored Sword". The names refer to a legend of the great Vietnamese hero, Le Loi, who led a successful uprising against the Chinese in the fifteenth century. Tradition has it that Le Loi netted a gleaming sword while out fishing in a sampan and when he returned as King Le Thai To, after ten years of battle, wanted to thank the spirit of the lake. As he prepared the sacrifice there was a timely peal of thunder and the miraculous sword flew out of its scabbard, into the mouth of a golden turtle (turtle and tortoise are the same word in Vietnamese) sent by the gods to reclaim the weapon. At least one hardy giant turtle still lives in the lake, but the one you're most likely to see is a heavily varnished specimen captured in 1968. It's preserved and on view on a second island accessible via the strik-

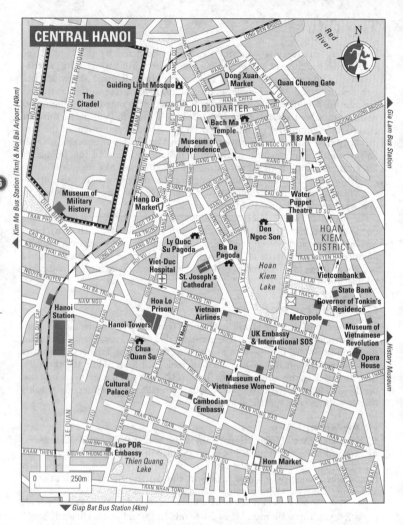

ing **The Huc Bridge**, an arch of red-lacquered wood poetically labelled the "place where morning sunlight rests". Beside the bridge stands a nine-metre-high obelisk, the **Writing Brush Tower**, on which three outsized Chinese characters proclaim "a pen to write on the blue sky".

Crossing over to the island you find the secluded **Den Ngoc Son**, "Temple of the Jade Mound" (daily 8am–6pm), sheltering among ancient trees. This small temple was founded in the fourteenth century and is dedicated to an eclectic group: national hero General Tran Hung Dao, who defeated the Mongols in 1288, sits on the principal altar; Van Xuong, God of Literature; physician La To; and a martial arts practitioner, Quan Vu. The temple buildings date from the 1800s and are typical of the Nguyen dynasty; in the antechamber, look out for the dragon heads, carved with bulbous noses and teeth bared

in manic grins. The giant turtle, over 2m long, resides in a
sanctuary hall, while other buildings house souvenir shops.

Around the lake

A good way to get your bearings in Hanoi is to make a qui
Kiem Lake, a pleasant walk at any time of year and stunnir
trees flower in June and July. In the Sixties these paths, like
city, were studded with hundreds of individual air-raid sh
lined holes big enough for one person, topped with a manh
south from the Writing Brush Tower, you can't miss the stony-faced, grey marble **Hanoi People's Committee** building, about halfway down the lake. Just
to its south lies the green oblong of **Indira Gandhi Park** which marks the
French Quarter's northern extremity, where the cream of colonial society
would gather in the 1890s for weekly concerts held in the bandstand. The next
block is occupied by the **General Post Office**, opposite which stands a small,
brick tower, all that remains of an enormous pagoda complex, Chua Bao An,
after French town planners cleared the site in 1892.

Rounding the lake's southern tip, past the souvenir shops of Hang Khay, and
heading up its west shore, you might want to take a detour to **St Joseph's
Cathedral** at the far end of Nha Tho ("Big Church") Street, passing on the
way the arched entrance to Ba Da Pagoda, which houses an impressive array
of Buddhas. Hanoi's neo-Gothic cathedral was constructed in the early 1880s,
partly financed by two lotteries, and though the exterior is badly weathered
its high-vaulted interior is still imposing. Among the first things you notice
inside are the ornate altar screen and the stained-glass windows, most of
which are French originals. Other points of interest are the votive plaques,
inscribed in Latin, French and Vietnamese, around the Chapel of the Virgin
Mary on the north aisle, and a black marble tomb on the opposite wall where
the previous cardinal of Vietnam was buried in 1990. Over the tomb stands
one of several statues commemorating martyred Vietnamese saints, in this case
André Dung Lac who was executed in 1839 on the orders of the fervently
anti-Christian Emperor Minh Mang. The cathedral's main door is open during services (the celebration of Mass was allowed to resume on Christmas Eve
1990 after a long hiatus); at other times walk round to the small door in the
southwest corner.

Walking north from the cathedral along Ly Quoc Su brings you to **Ly Quoc
Su Pagoda**, at no. 50, a small pagoda with a genuinely interesting collection
of statues. Ly Quoc Su (sometimes also known as Minh Khong) was a Buddhist
teacher, healer and royal advisor who cured the hallucinating King Ly Than
Tong of believing he was a tiger. Quoc Su's image resides between those of the
white-bearded Tu Dao Hanh (see "Thay Pagoda", p.407) and an unidentified
tantric monk on the principal altar of this twelfth-century temple – when it
later became a pagoda they simply added a few Buddhas behind. In front of the
altar, two groups of statues face each other across the prayer floor: four secular,
female figures sit opposite five perfectly inscrutable mandarins of the nineteenth century, clothed in rich red lacquer and bearing symbols of their rank.
Two much older stone figures, perhaps dating from the 1500s, complete the
line up: Tu Dao Hanh's charming mother sits with the women, opposite her
husband, both depicted with unusually distinctive faces.

From Ly Quoc Su retrace your steps to Hoan Kiem Lake and continue
northwards to where *Thuy Ta* café offers respite from the traffic and a particularly fine place to relax; you can down a beer while the sun sets over Den Ngoc
Son on the opposite bank.

Old Quarter

north from Hoan Kiem Lake, across Cau Go, and suddenly you're in the multuous streets of the **Old Quarter**. Hanoi is the only city in Vietnam to retain its ancient, merchants' quarter, a congested square kilometre which was closed behind massive ramparts and heavy, wooden gates until well into the nineteenth century. Apart from one gate, at the east end of Hang Chieu, the walls have been dismantled, but a glance at the map reveals the quarter's jigsaw of narrow streets with evocative names (see box on p.374). There are few individual sights in the quarter; the best approach is simply to dive into the back lanes, fascinating at any time of day but taking on a special atmosphere as the evening traffic dies down, when the stalls blaze with colour and everyone comes out to relax and gossip under dim street lights.

Everything spills out onto pavements which double as workshops for stone-carvers and tinsmiths, and as display space for merchandise ranging from pungent therapeutic herbs and fluttering prayer flags to ranks of Remy Martin and shiny-wrapped chocolates. With so much to attract your attention at ground level it's easy to miss the **architecture**, which reveals fascinating glimpses of the quarter's history, starting with the fifteenth-century merchants' houses otherwise found only in Hoi An (see p.281). Hanoi's aptly named **tube-houses** evolved from market stalls into narrow shops of a single storey, windows no higher than a passing royal palanquin, under gently curving, red-tiled roofs. Some are just 2m wide, the result of taxes levied on street-frontages and of subdivision for inheritance, while behind stretches a succession of storerooms and living quarters up to 60m in length, interspersed with open courtyards to give them light and air; to get a better idea of the layout, pop into the beautifully restored example at **87 Ma May** (daily 9am–5pm). Nowadays, the majority of facades bear distinctly European touches – faded wooden shutters, sagging balconies and rain-streaked moulding – dating from the early 1900s when the streets were widened for pavements. Certain occupants were too wealthy or influential to be shifted and you can find their houses still standing out of line at the west end of Hang Bac and on Ma May. The latter street also retains its own **dinh**, or communal house (at no. 64), which traditionally served as both meeting hall and shrine to the neighbourhood's particular patron spirit, in this case a fourteenth-century mandarin and ambassador to the Chinese court.

Hang Buom and Bach Ma Temple

Walking north along Ma May and onto **Hang Buom**, you pass a wealth of interesting detail typical of the quarter's patchwork architecture: simple one-storey shophouses, some still sporting traditional wood-panel doors (note the particularly attractive row at nos. 10–14); elaborate plaster-work and Art Deco styling from colonial days; and Soviet chic of the 1960s and 1970s – each superimposed on the basic tube-house design. Hang Buom is also home to the quarter's oldest and most revered place of worship, **Bach Ma Temple**. The temple was founded in the ninth century and later dedicated to the White Horse (*Bach Ma*), the guardian spirit of Thang Long who posed as an ethereal site foreman and helped King Ly Thai To overcome a few problems with his citadel's collapsing walls. The present structure dates largely from the eighteenth century and its most unusual features are a pair of charismatic, pot-bellied guardians in front of the altar who flaunt an impressive array of lacquered gold dentures. A festival-float representation of the horse stands to one side, along with an antique palanquin, both used each year to celebrate the temple's foundation on the twelfth day of the second lunar month.

The Guiding Light Mosque

As you explore the quarter you'll come across a great many other sacred sites – temples, pagodas, *dinh* and venerable banyan trees – hidden among the houses. One of the more surprising is the **Guiding Light Mosque** on Hang Luoc, which was built in the 1890s by an Indian Islamic community of traders and civil servants, and now serves Muslims from Hanoi's diplomatic community as the only mosque in northern Vietnam.

Dong Xuan and Long Bien Bridge

East of the mosque, the city's largest covered market, **Dong Xuan**, occupies a whole block behind its original, 1889 facade. Its three storeys are dedicated to clothes and household goods, while foodstuffs are to be found at the rear, spilling out into a bustling street market stacked with multicoloured mounds of fresh vegetables. Head one block east again and you find two ramps taking bicycles and pedestrians up onto **Long Bien Bridge**, a road and rail bridge completed in 1902 and originally named after the then governor-general of Indochina, Paul Doumer. Until Chuong Duong Bridge was built in the 1980s, Long Bien was the Red River's only bridge and therefore of immense strategic significance. During the American War this was one of Vietnam's most heavily defended spots, which American bombs never managed to knock out completely. If you have time, take a bicycle ride across the 1700-metre span of iron lattice-work, but spare a thought for the maintenance staff: in the 1960s, perhaps the last time it was done, it took a hundred workers five years to repaint the bridge.

The Museum of Independence, To Tich and Hang Quat

Cutting back southwards, it was at 48 Hang Ngang that Ho Chi Minh drafted the Declaration of Independence for the Democratic Republic of Vietnam in 1945. The house where he lived for those heady months is now the **Museum of Independence** (Mon–Sat 8am–4.30pm; free). A desultory exhibition downstairs shows yet more photos of Uncle Ho with beaming children, but it's worth taking a look at the two first-floor rooms where he slept, wrote and debated, seemingly surrounded by oversized Western period furniture. From here it's only a couple of minutes' walk down to Hoan Kiem Lake, passing through the traditional street market selling fresh meat, fish and vegetables under an improvised canopy of low-slung sacks that clogs the lanes just behind Cau Go. This southern edge of the Old Quarter, particularly Hang Gai, is where you'll find the biggest concentration of silk and embroidery shops, but before leaving the old streets completely take a quick detour up **To Tich**, a short lane of wood-turners and small restaurants serving fragrant skewers of grilled pork or steaming bowls of *pho*, to walk among **Hang Quat**'s bright-red prayer flags.

The French Quarter

After the hectic streets of the Old Quarter, the grand boulevards and wide pavements of Hanoi's **French Quarter** to the south and east of Hoan Kiem Lake are a welcome relief. Again it's the architecture here that's the highlight, with a few specific attractions spread over a couple of kilometres, so you might want to explore by bicycle or cyclo. The first French concession was granted in 1874, an insalubrious plot of land on the banks of the Red River, southeast of where the Opera House stands today. Once in full possession of Hanoi, after 1882, the

What's in a name

The Old Quarter's **street names** date back five centuries to when the area was divided among 36 artisans' guilds, each gathered around a temple or a *dinh* (communal house) dedicated to the guild's patron spirit. Even today many streets specialize to some degree, and a few are still dedicated to the original craft or its modern equivalent. The most colourful examples are Hang Quat, full of bright-red banners and lacquerware for funerals and festivals, and Hang Ma, where paper products have been made for at least five hundred years. Nowadays gaudy tinsel dances in the breeze above brightly coloured votive objects, which include model TVs, dollars and cars to be offered to the ancestors. A selection of the more interesting streets with an element of specialization is listed below. *Hang* means merchandise.

Street name	Meaning	Modern speciality
Ha Trong	Drum skin	Bag menders, upholsterers
Hang Bo	Bamboo baskets	Haberdashers
Hang Buom	Sails	Imported foods and alcohol, confectionery
Hang Chieu	Sedge mats	Mats, ropes, bamboo blinds
Hang Dau	Oil	Shoes
Hang Dieu	Pipes	Cushions, mattresses
Hang Duong	Sugar	Clothes
Hang Gai	Hemp goods	Silks, tailors, souvenirs
Hang Hom	Wooden chests	Glue, paint, varnish
Hang Ma	Paper votive objects	Paper goods
Hang Quat	Ceremonial fans	Religious accessories
Hang Thiec	Tin goods	Tin goods, mirrors
Hang Vai	Fabrics	Bamboo ladders
Lan Ong	Eighteenth-century scholar-physician	Traditional medicines, towels

French began to create a city appropriate to their new protectorate, starting with the area between the old concession and the train station, 2km to the west. Gradually elegant villas filled plots along the grid of tree-lined avenues, then spread south in the 1930s and 1940s towards what is now Lenin Park.

The Opera House

In the process of building their capital the French destroyed many ancient Vietnamese monuments, including one of Hanoi's oldest pagodas, Bao Thien, which was demolished to make way for the cathedral. They were replaced, however, with some fine, Parisian-style buildings such as the stately **Opera House** (now officially known as the Municipal Theatre), at the eastern end of Trang Tien. Based on the neo-Baroque Paris Opéra, complete with Ionic columns and grey-slate tiles imported from France, the theatre was erected on reclaimed land and finally opened in 1911 after ten years in the making. It was regarded as the jewel in the crown of French Hanoi, the colonial town's physical and cultural focus, until 1945 when the Viet Minh proclaimed the August Revolution from its balcony. After Independence, audiences were treated to a diet of Socialist Realism and revolutionary theatre, but now the building has been restored to its former glory after a massive face-lift. Crystal chandeliers, Parisian mirrors and sweeping staircases of polished marble have all been beautifully preserved, although, unfortunately, there's no access to the public unless you're lucky enough to catch one of the sporadic performances. Instead, feast your eyes on the exterior – particularly stunning under evening floodlights or, better still, the soft glow of a full moon.

The History Museum

One block east of the Opera House is Hanoi's **History Museum**, at 1 Trang Tien (Tues–Sun 8–11.30am & 1.30–4.30pm; $1). Buried among trees and facing the river, the museum isn't immediately obvious, but its architecture is unmissable – a fanciful blend of Vietnamese palace and French villa which came to be called "Neo-Vietnamese" style. The museum was founded in the 1930s by the *Ecole Française d'Extrême Orient*, but after 1954 changed focus to reflect Vietnam's evolution from Paleolithic times to Independence. Exhibits, including many plaster reproductions, are arranged in chronological order on two floors: everything downstairs is pre-1400, while the second floor takes the story up to August 1945.

The ground floor

On the **ground floor**, the museum's prize exhibits are those from the **Dong Son culture**, a sophisticated Bronze Age civilization which flourished in the Red River Delta from 1200 to 200 BC. The display includes a rich variety of implements, from arrowheads to cooking utensils, and a lamp in the form of a graceful figurine, but the finest examples of Dong Son creativity are several huge, ceremonial bronze drums, used to bury the dead, invoke the monsoon or celebrate fertility rites. The remarkably well-preserved **Ngoc Lu Drum** is the highlight, where advanced casting techniques are evident in the delicate figures of deer, birds and boats ornamenting the surface – you can see the detail more clearly in the rubbing displayed nearby. Other notable exhibits on this floor include a willowy Amitabha Buddha of the eleventh century, pale-green celadon ware and amulets from the same period, and a group of wooden stakes from the glorious thirteenth-century battle of the Bach Dang River (see p.486).

The second floor

The museum's **second floor** is dominated by a three-metre-tall stele inscribed with the life story of Le Loi, who spearheaded the resistance against the Chinese occupation in the fifteenth century, but the most interesting exhibits here relate to the nineteenth-century Nguyen dynasty and the period of French rule. A series of ink-washes depicting Hué's imperial court in the 1890s are particularly eye-catching, as are the embroidered silks and inlaid ivory furniture once used by the emperors cloistered in the citadel. But outside the citadel walls the country was again in turmoil, culminating in the struggle for independence led by Ho Chi Minh; the evidence of royal decadence and French brutality gathered here alone explains the strength of popular support for the nationalist cause.

The Museum of Vietnamese Revolution

The story continues at the **Museum of Vietnamese Revolution**, one block north at 216 Tran Quang Khai (Tues–Sun 8–11.30am & 1.30–4pm), housed in a classic colonial building that started life as a customs house. This museum catalogues the "Vietnamese people's patriotic and revolutionary struggle", from the first anti-French movements of the late nineteenth century to post-1975 reconstruction. Much of the tale is told through original documents, including the first clandestine newspapers and revolutionary tracts penned by Ho Chi Minh, and illustrated with portraits of Vietnam's most famous revolutionaries. Things liven up with the War of Independence and the small but well-presented exhibition on the American War, a subject that is treated in greater depth at the Museum of Military History (see p.380).

Residence of the Governor of Tonkin and the Metropole

Back at the Opera House, walking two blocks north on Ly Thai To brings you to the junction with Ngo Quyen, dominated by two very different buildings. The imposing Art Deco structure with a circular portico, once the French Bank of Indochina, now houses the **State Bank** in its lofty halls. Diagonally opposite stands one of Hanoi's most attractive colonial edifices, the immaculately restored **Residence of the Governor of Tonkin**, constructed in 1918; it's now known as the State Guest House and used for visiting VIPs. Unfortunately you can't get inside, but as you peer in take a closer look at the elegant, wrought-iron railings, pitted with bullet-mark souvenirs of the 1945 Revolution. More recently the building's terraces appeared in the film *Indochine* (see p.566).

In comparison, the bright, white Neoclassical facade of the **Metropole** – nowadays *Hotel Sofitel Metropole* – just south at 15 Ngo Quyen, verges on the austere. The then *Grand Metropole Palace* opened in 1901, and soon became one of Southeast Asia's great hotels. Even during the French War, Bernard Fall, a journalist killed by a land mine near Hué in 1967, described the hotel as the "last really fashionable place left in Hanoi", where the barman "could produce a reasonable facsimile of almost any civilized drink except water". After Independence it re-emerged as the *Thong Nhat* or *Reunification Hotel*, but otherwise stayed much the same, including en-suite rats and lethal wiring, until 1990 when Pullman-Sofitel transformed it into Hanoi's first international-class hotel. The *Metropole's* illustrious visitors' book includes Graham Greene, who first came here in 1952, while twenty years later Jane Fonda stayed for two weeks while making her famous broadcast to American troops.

Trang Tien

Trang Tien, the main artery of the French Quarter, is still a busy shopping street where you'll find bookshops and art galleries, as well as the Trang Tien Trade Plaza with its flash boutiques and somewhat incongruous supermarket. South of Trang Tien you enter French Hanoi's principal residential quarter, consisting of a grid of shaded boulevards whose distinguished villas are much sought-after for restoration as embassies or offices or as desirable, expatriate residences. These houses, which like those of the Old Quarter survived largely due to lack of money for redevelopment, run the gamut of early twentieth-century European architecture from elegant Neoclassical through to 1930s Modernism and Art Deco, with an occasional Oriental flourish.

To take a swing through the area, drop down Hang Bai onto Ly Thuong Kiet and start heading west. Just round the corner, the revamped **Museum of Vietnamese Women**, at 36 Ly Thuong Kiet (Tues–Sun 8.30–11.30am & 1.30–4pm), puts a different perspective on national history. Once again, it's the twentieth century that provides the most absorbing material, while the top-floor display of ethnic minority costumes is worth a quick look. Two blocks further west, you arrive at Cho 19–12 (19 December Market), a short covered street of stalls selling mainly vegetables and meat, including the twisted carcasses of roast dog. Beyond, two tower blocks loom over the remnants of French-built **Hoa Lo Prison** at 1 Hoa Lo (Tues–Sun 8–11.30am & 1.30–4.30pm), nicknamed the "Hanoi Hilton" by American PoWs in wry comment on its harsh conditions and often brutal treatment. The jail became famous in the 1960s when American prisoners, mostly pilots and crew members, were shown worldwide in televised propaganda campaigns. The museum, however, mostly deals with the pre-1954 colonial period when the French incarcerated many nationalist leaders here, including no less than five future General Secretaries of the Vietnamese Communist Party. Some of the cells – which were still in use up to 1994 – have been preserved along with rusty shackles and instruments of torture. Other rooms display photos and information on the more famous political prisoners, though unfortunately only the captions are in English.

At the next junction west, turn left down Quan Su to find the arched entrance of **Chua Quan Su**, the Ambassadors' Pagoda, founded in the fifteenth century as part of a guesthouse for ambassadors from neighbouring Buddhist countries, though the current building only dates from 1942. Nowadays Quan Su is one of Hanoi's most active pagodas: on the first and fifteenth days of the lunar month, worshippers and mendicants throng its forecourt, while inside an iron lamp, ornamented with sinuous dragons, hangs over the crowded prayer-floor and ranks of crimson-lacquered Buddhas glow through a pungent haze of burning incense. The compound, shaded by ancient trees, is home to various research institutions and is a centre of Buddhist learning, hence the well-stocked library and classrooms at the rear. Shops roundabout specialize in Buddhist paraphernalia.

Ho Chi Minh's Mausoleum and around

Hanoi's most important cultural and historical monuments are found in the district immediately west of the Old Quarter, where the Ly kings established their Imperial City in the eleventh century. The venerable **Temple of Literature** and the picturesque **One Pillar Pagoda** both date from this time, but nothing else remains of the Ly kings' vermilion palaces, whose last vestiges were cleared in the late nineteenth century to accommodate an expanding French administration. Most impressive of the district's colonial buildings is the dignified Residence of the Governor-General of Indochina, now known as the **Presidential Palace**. After 1954 some of the surrounding gardens gave way in their turn to Ba Dinh parade ground, the National Assembly Hall and two great centres of pilgrimage: **Ho Chi Minh's Mausoleum** and **Museum**. The nearby Botanical Gardens, however, survived to provide a welcome haven from modern Hanoi's hustle and bustle. East of Ba Dinh Square the **citadel** encloses a restricted military area. Its most famous feature is the **Cot Co Flag Tower** which dominates the extreme southwest corner, next to one of Hanoi's most rewarding museums, the **Museum of Military History**. Although there's a lot to see in this area, it's possible to cover everything described below in a single day, with an early start at the mausoleum and surrounding sites, leaving the Museum of Military History and Temple of Literature until later in the day.

Ba Dinh Square and Ho Chi Minh's Mausoleum

The wide, open spaces of **Ba Dinh Square**, 2km west of Hoan Kiem Lake, are the nation's ceremonial epicentre. It was here that Ho Chi Minh read out the Declaration of Independence to half a million people on September 2, 1945, and here that Independence is commemorated each National Day with military parades. The National Assembly Hall, venue for Party congresses, stands on the square's east side, while the west is dominated by the severe, grey bulk of **Ho Chi Minh's Mausoleum** (April–Sept Tues–Thurs 7.30–10.30am, Sat & Sun 7.30–11am; Dec–March Tues–Thurs 8–11am, Sat & Sun 8–11.30am; no charge). In the tradition of great communist leaders, when Ho Chi Minh died in 1969 his body was embalmed, though not put on public view until after 1975. The mausoleum is probably Hanoi's most popular

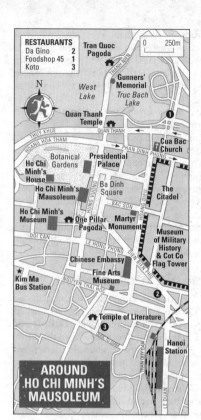

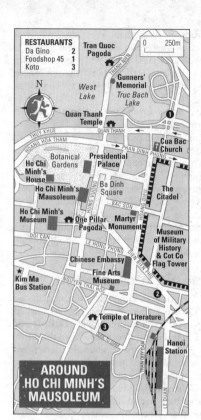

RESTAURANTS
Da Gino — 2
Foodshop 45 — 1
Koto — 3

Tran Quoc Pagoda

West Lake

Gunners' Memorial

Truc Bach Lake

Quan Thanh Temple

Cua Bac Church

Botanical Gardens

Presidential Palace

Ho Chi Minh's House

Ho Chi Minh's Mausoleum

Ba Dinh Square

The Citadel

Ho Chi Minh's Museum

One Pillar Pagoda

Martyr Monument

Museum of Military History & Cot Co Flag Tower

Chinese Embassy

Fine Arts Museum

Kim Ma Bus Station

Temple of Literature

Hanoi Station

AROUND HO CHI MINH'S MAUSOLEUM

sight, attracting crowds of visitors at weekends and on national holidays; from school parties to ageing confederates, all come to pay their respects to "Uncle Ho".

Visitors to the mausoleum must leave bags and cameras at one of the reception centres, the most convenient being that at 8 Hung Vuong, from where you'll be escorted by soldiers in immaculate uniforms. Respectful behaviour is requested, which means **appropriate dress** (no shorts or vests) and removing hats and keeping silence within the sanctum. Note that each year the mausoleum closes for two months (Oct & Nov) while Ho undergoes maintenance.

Inside the building's marble entrance hall Ho Chi Minh's most quoted maxim greets you: "nothing is more important than independence and freedom". Then it's up the stairs and into a cold, dark room where this charismatic hero lies under glass, a small, pale figure glowing in the dim light, his thin hands resting on black covers. Despite the rather macabre overtones, it's hard not to be affected by the solemn atmosphere, though in actual fact Ho's last wish was to be cremated and his ashes divided between the north, centre and south of the country, with each site marked only by a simple shelter. The grandiose building where he now lies seems sadly at odds with this unassuming, egalitarian man.

The Presidential Palace and Ho Chi Minh's house

Follow the crowd on leaving Ho's mausoleum and you enter the grounds of the **Presidential Palace** via the side gate. The palace was built in 1901 as the humble abode of the governor-general of Indochina – all sweeping stairways, louvred shutters and ornate wrought-iron gates of the *belle époque* – and these days is used to receive visiting heads of state. It's closed to the public but you can admire the outside as you walk through the palace gardens to **Ho Chi Minh's house** (Tues–Thurs, Sat & Sun 7.30–11am & 2–4pm). After Independence in 1954 President Ho Chi Minh built a modest dwelling for himself behind the palace, modelling it on an ethnic minority stilthouse, a simple structure with open sides and split-bamboo screens. The ground-level meeting area is equipped with desk, telephones and table used by Ho and the Politburo, while his study and bedroom upstairs are said to be just as he left them, sparsely furnished, unostentatious and very highly polished. Apparently Ho lived here for the last eleven years of his life, even during the American War, tending his garden and fishpond; tradition has it that he died in the small hut next door.

The One Pillar Pagoda

Close by Ho's stilthouse, the **One Pillar Pagoda** rivals the Tortoise Tower as a symbol of Hanoi. It is the most unusual of the hundreds of pagodas sponsored by devoutly Buddhist Ly dynasty kings in the eleventh century, and represents a flowering of Vietnamese art. The tiny wooden sanctuary, dedicated to Quan Am whose statue nestles inside, is only three square metres in size and is supported on a single column rising from the middle of an artificial lake, the whole structure designed to resemble a lotus blossom, the Buddhist symbol of enlightenment. In fact this is by no means the original building – the concrete pillar is a real giveaway – and the last reconstruction took place after departing French troops blew up the pagoda in 1954.

The pagoda's **origins** are uncertain but a popular legend recounts that it was founded in 1049 by King Ly Thai Tong, an ardent Buddhist with no male offspring. The goddess Quan Am appeared before the king in a dream, sitting on her lotus throne and holding out to him an infant boy. Soon after, the king married a village girl who bore him a son and heir, and he erected a pagoda shaped like a lotus blossom in thanks. The fact that King Ly Thai Tong already had a son born in 1022, six years before he came to the throne, gives greater credence to a less romantic version. According to this story, King Ly Thai Tong dreamt that Quan Am invited him to join her on the lotus throne. The king's advisors, deeming this an ill omen, advised him to found a pagoda where they could pray for their sovereign's longevity.

Whatever the truth, most people find the pagoda an anticlimax – partly because of its size and the concrete restoration work, and partly because of the overpowering presence of Ho Chi Minh's Museum. Behind the pagoda grows a **bo tree**, said to be an offshoot of the one under which the Buddha gained enlightenment, which was presented to Ho Chi Minh on a visit to India in 1958. Finally, take a look through the doorway in the southwest corner: inside is a delightfully intimate courtyard full of potted plants and bonsai trees, where a monk occasionally practises acupuncture.

Ho Chi Minh's Museum

The gleaming white building just 200m west of the One Pillar Pagoda is **Ho Chi Minh's Museum** (Tues–Thurs, Sat & Sun 8–11.30am & 2–6pm), built with Soviet aid and inaugurated on May 19, 1990, the hundredth anniversary of Ho's birth. The museum celebrates Ho Chi Minh's life and the pivotal role he played in the nation's history; not surprisingly, this is also a favourite for school outings. Exhibits around the hall's outer wall focus on Ho's life and the "Vietnamese Revolution", in the context of socialism's international development, including documents, photographs, and a smattering of personal possessions, among them a disguise Ho adopted when escaping from Hong Kong (see pp.342-343 for more on Ho's life story). Running parallel on the inner ring are a series of heavily metaphoric "spatial images", six tableaux portraying significant places and events, from Ho's birthplace in Nghe An to Pac Bo cave and ending with a symbolic rendering of Vietnam's reunification. Most exhibits are labelled in English but low lighting and tiny lettering make them hard to read. Go in for the surreal nature of the whole experience, but don't expect to come away having learnt much more about the man.

The Museum of Military History and the Cot Co Flag Tower

From Ho Chi Minh's Museum, head back east past Ba Dinh Square to Dien Bien Phu, a road lined with gnarled trees and former colonial offices interspersed with gingerbread villas. Around 500m from the square, Lenin's statue still stands opposite a white, arcaded building housing the **Museum of Military History** at 28 Dien Bien Phu (Tues–Thurs, Sat & Sun 8–11.30am & 1–4.30pm). While ostensibly tracing the story of the People's Army from its foundation in 1944, in reality the museum chronicles national history from the 1930s to the present day, a period dominated by the French and American wars, though it's noticeably quiet on China and Cambodia.

The museum forecourt is full of weaponry: pride of place goes to a Russian MiG 21 fighter, alongside artillery from the battle of Dien Bien Phu (see box on p.459) and anti-aircraft guns from the American War, while the second courtyard is dominated by the mangled wreckage of assorted American planes piled against a tree. The exhibition proper starts on the arcaded building's second floor and runs chronologically from the 1930 Nghe Tinh Uprising, through the August Revolution to the "People's War" against the French, culminating in the decisive **battle of Dien Bien Phu**. If there's sufficient demand, they'll show an English-language video to accompany the battle's diorama; despite the heavy propaganda overlay, the archive footage is fascinating, including Viet Minh hauling artillery up mountain slopes and clouds of French parachutists. Naturally, General Giap and Ho Chi Minh make star appearances – after the ubiquitous still images, it's a shock to see Ho animated. The American War, covered in a separate hall at the rear, receives similar treatment with film of the relentless drive south to "liberate" Saigon in 1975. The build-up is also well documented, including rare photos of the Ho Chi Minh Trail (see p.336) and the struggle to keep the convoys on the move.

Within the museum compound stands the thirty-metre **Cot Co Flag Tower**, one of the few remnants of Emperor Gia Long's early nineteenth-century citadel, where the national flag now billows in place of the emperor's yellow banner. In 1812, Vietnamese architects added several towers to the otherwise European-designed citadel, and when the French flattened the ramparts in the 1890s they kept Cot Co as a handy lookout post and signalling tower. From the top you can see the metal arches of Long Bien Bridge off to the east, or look down into today's citadel, harbouring the army headquarters and relics of the fifteenth-century Imperial City which are slowly being restored for the city's millennial celebrations in 2010. So far only the citadel's north gate, on Phan Dinh Phung opposite Chau Bac Church, is on view, its brickwork heavily scarred in a French bombardment in 1882.

National Fine Arts Museum

From the Museum of Military History follow Hoang Dieu Avenue south, past the wonderfully flamboyant Chinese Embassy, and turn right on Cau Ba Quat to find a three-storey colonial block with chocolate-brown shutters. The **National Fine Arts Museum** at 66 Nguyen Thai Hoc (Tues–Sun 9.15am–5pm) takes a romp through the main themes of Vietnam's artistic development, kicking off with the inevitable collection of Dong Son drums (see p.375) and a smattering of graceful Cham dancers. Though once again many are reproductions, there are some fine pieces, notably among the seventeenth- and eighteenth-century Buddhist art which spawned such masterpieces as Tay Phuong's superbly lifelike statues of the eighteen arhats (see p.408). Other highlights are the well-displayed collection of folk art and a small but interesting exhibition of twentieth-century artists charting the evolution from a solidly European style through Socialist Realism to the emergence of a distinct, Vietnamese school of art.

Becoming a mandarin

Examinations for admission to the **imperial bureaucracy** were introduced by the Ly kings in the eleventh century as part of a range of reforms which served to underpin the nation's stability for several centuries. Vietnam's exams were based on the Chinese system, though included Buddhist and Taoist texts along with the Confucian classics. It took until the fifteenth century, however, for academic success, rather than noble birth or patronage, to become the primary means of entry to the civil service. By this time the system was open to **all males**, excluding "traitors, rebels, immoral people and actors", but in practice very few candidates outside the scholar-gentry class progressed beyond the lowest rung.

First came **regional exams**, *thi huong*, after which successful students (who could be any age from 16 to 61) would head for Hanoi, equipped with their sleeping mat, ink-stone and writing brush, to take part in the second-level *thi hoi*. These **national exams** might last up to six weeks and were as much an evaluation of poetic style and knowledge of the classic texts as they were of administrative ability; it was even felt necessary to ban the sale of strong liquor to candidates in the 1870s. Those who passed all stages were granted a doctorate, *tien si*, and were eligible for the third and final test, the *thi dinh* or **palace exam**, set by the king himself. Some years as few as three *tien si* would be awarded whereas the total number of candidates could be as high as six thousand, and during nearly three hundred exams held between 1076 and 1779, only 2313 *tien si* were recorded. Afterwards the king would give his new mandarins a cap, gown, parasol and a horse on which to return to their home village in triumphal procession.

The Temple of Literature

Across busy Nguyen Thai Hoc Avenue is Hanoi's most revered temple complex, the **Temple of Literature** or **Van Mieu**, both Vietnam's principal Confucian sanctuary and its historical centre of learning (daily: April–Sept 7.30am–6pm; Oct–March 8am–5pm). The temple is also one of the few remnants of the Ly kings' original city and retains a strong sense of harmony despite reconstruction and embellishment over the nine hundred years since its dedication in 1070.

Entry is through the two-tiered Van Mieu Gate on Quoc Tu Giam. The temple's ground plan, modelled on that of Confucius's birthplace in Qufu, China, consists of a succession of five walled courtyards. The first two are havens of trim lawns and noble trees separated by a simple pavilion; entry to the third is via the imposing Khue Van Cac, a double-roofed gateway built in 1805, its wooden upper storey ornamented with four radiating suns. Central to the third courtyard is the Well of Heavenly Clarity – a walled pond – to either side of which stand the temple's most valuable relics, 82 stone **stelae** mounted on tortoises. Each stele records the results of a state examination held at the National Academy between 1442 and 1779, though the practice only started in 1484, and gives brief biographical details of successful candidates. It's estimated that up to thirty stelae have gone missing or disintegrated over the years, but the two oldest, dating from 1442 and 1448, occupy centre spot on opposite sides of the pond.

Passing through the Gate of Great Success brings you to the fourth courtyard and the main temple buildings. Two pavilions on either side once contained altars dedicated to the 72 disciples of Confucius, but now house administrative offices and souvenir shops. At Tet (Vietnamese New Year) this courtyard is the scene of calligraphy competitions and "human chess games", with people instead of wooden pieces on the square paving stones.

The temple's **ceremonial hall**, a long, low building whose sweeping tiled roof is crowned by two lithe dragons bracketing a full moon, stands on the courtyard's north side. Here the king and his mandarins would make sacrifices before the altar of Confucius, accompanied by booming drums and bronze bells echoing among the magnificent ironwood pillars. Directly behind the ceremonial hall lies the **temple sanctuary**, at one time prohibited even to the king, where Confucius sits with his four principal disciples, resplendent in vivid reds and golds.

The fifth and final courtyard housed the **National Academy**, regarded as Vietnam's first university, which was founded in 1076 to educate princes and high officials in Confucian doctrine. Later the academy held triennial examinations to select the country's senior mandarins (see box on p.381), a practice that continued almost uninterrupted until 1802 when Emperor Gia Long moved the nation's capital to Hué. In 1947 French bombs destroyed the academy buildings but an elegant two-storey pavilion has now been rebuilt to house a small museum and an altar dedicated to three monarchs: King Ly Thanh Tong, the founder of Van Mieu; Ly Than Tong, who added the University; and Le Thanh Tong, instigator of the stelae. The exhibits are mostly post-eighteenth-century, including 1920s photos of the temple and students' textbooks, ink-stones and other accoutrements, such as a wine gourd for the fashion-conscious nineteenth-century scholar. Recitals of traditional music are also held here according to demand.

West Lake

Back in the mists of time, a gifted monk returned from China, bearing quantities of bronze as a reward for curing the emperor's illness. The monk gave most of the metal to the state but from a small lump he fashioned a bell, whose ring was so pure it resonated throughout the land and beyond the mountains. The sound reached the ears of a golden buffalo calf inside the Chinese imperial treasury; the creature followed the bell, mistaking it for the call of its mother. Then the bell fell silent and the calf spun round and round, not knowing which way to go, until it trampled a vast hollow which filled with water and became **West Lake**, *Ho Tay*. Some say that the golden buffalo is still there, at the bottom of the lake, but can only be retrieved by a man assisted by his ten natural sons.

More prosaically, West Lake is a shallow lagoon left behind as the Red River shifted course eastward to leave a narrow strip of land, reinforced over the centuries with massive embankments, separating the lake and river. The lake was traditionally an area for royal recreation or spiritual pursuits, where monarchs erected summer palaces and sponsored religious foundations, among them Hanoi's most ancient pagoda, **Tran Quoc**. In the seventeenth century villagers built a causeway across the lake's southeast corner, creating a small fishing lake now called **Truc Bach** and ringed with little cafés.

In the last decade or so, West Lake has once again become Hanoi's most fashionable address, complete with exclusive residential developments, lakeside clubs and a clutch of five-star international hotels. But for the moment a bicycle ride up the lake's east shore makes a pleasant excursion with one or two sights to aim for, while Hanoi's newest cultural asset, the **Museum of Ethnology**, southwest of the lake, is best tackled by car or bus. Alternatively, the attractions grouped along the causeway, described below, are only about 500m north of the Presidential Palace and can easily be combined with a visit to the monuments around Ba Dinh Square.

The causeway and Truc Bach Lake

The name **Truc Bach** derives from an eighteenth-century summer palace built by the ruling Trinh lords which later became a place of detention for disagreeable concubines and other "errant women", who were put to work weaving fine white silk, *truc bach*. The palace no longer exists but eleventh-century **Quan Thanh Temple** (daily 8am–4.30pm) still stands on the lake's southeast bank, erected by King Ly Thai To and dedicated to the Guardian of the North, Tran Vo, who protects the city from malevolent spirits. Quan Thanh has been rebuilt several times, most recently in 1893, along the way losing nearly all its original features, but it's well worth wandering into the quiet, shady courtyard to see the **statue** of Tran Vo, cast in black bronze in 1677 and seated on the main altar. The statue, nearly 4m high and weighing 4 tonnes, portrays the Taoist god accompanied by his two animal emblems, a serpent and turtle; it was the creation of a craftsman called Trum Trong whose own statue, fashioned in stone and sporting a stylish headscarf, sits off to one side. The shrine room also boasts a valuable collection of seventeenth- and eighteenth-century poems and parallel sentences (boards inscribed with wise maxims and hung in pairs on adjacent columns), some of intricate, mother-of-pearl inlay work.

The gate of Quan Thanh is just a few paces south of the **causeway**, Thanh Nien, an avenue of flame trees that is a popular picnic spot in summer when a cooling breeze comes off the water and hawkers set up shop along the grass verges. Where the road bears gently right, look for a small memorial on the Truc Bach side, which is dedicated to teams of **anti-aircraft gunners** stationed here during the American War. In particular the memorial commemorates the downing of Navy Lieutenant Commander John McCain, who parachuted into Truc Bach Lake in October 1967 and survived more than five years in the "Hanoi Hilton" to become a US Senator and a strong supporter of normalization between America and Vietnam.

Continuing along the causeway you come to Hanoi's oldest religious foundation, **Tran Quoc Pagoda**, occupying a tiny island off Thanh Nien in West Lake (daily 7–11.30am & 1.30–6pm). The pagoda's exact origins are uncertain but it's usually attributed to the sixth-century early Ly dynasty during a brief interlude in ten centuries of Chinese domination. A stone stele of 1639 records that in the early seventeenth century, when Buddhism was enjoying a revival, the pagoda was moved from beside the Red River to its present, less vulnerable location. You can see the stele standing on the pagoda's front porch, but entry is via the back of the building, along a narrow, brick causeway lying just above the water, past a collection of imposing, brick stupas. The sanctuary's restrained interior and general configuration are typical of northern Vietnamese pagodas though there's nothing inside of particular importance. Note that visitors are requested not to wear shorts.

Around West Lake

The east side of West Lake is experiencing rapid urbanization but it does have a sprinkling of mildly interesting far-flung sights that can be reached by bike or car. In contrast, its north side remains largely a region of farmland and villages. It's possible to circumnavigate the lake by bicycle, a total of roughly 13km. To start off, take Yen Phu Avenue, halfway up the Red River embankment from the causeway, rather than compete with the ferocious stream of trucks and buses along the top road, Nghi Tam.

Not far along Yen Phu an arch on the left, inscribed "Lang Yen Phu", marks the entrance to a narrow lane, down which **Yen Phu Temple** is worth a quick detour for its massive entrance hall and a jolly group of statuettes making offerings before the altar. Continuing along the main road, past unusually ostentatious villas – fantasy houses combining a touch of Spanish hacienda with a slice of French château – you get an idea of the pace of development in this district, which for a while outstripped any attempt at planning or design controls. The most notorious example was illegal construction work along Nghi Tam, just east of here, which caused cracks up to 200m long in the city's 1000-year-old flood defences. After a much publicized enquiry, in which a few heads rolled, some offending structures were torn down or simply sliced in half from top to bottom and left gaping by the roadside.

About a kilometre from the causeway are the red-tiled roofs of **Kim Lien Pagoda**, whose best attributes are its elaborate carvings and unplastered brick walls dating from an eighteenth-century rebuild. The surrounding district, **Nghi Tam**, was traditionally a flower-producing area and you'll still find pockets of chrysanthemums, peach or kumquat – depending on the time of year – between the encroaching buildings. If you're an early-riser, it's worth venturing this way at sunrise when Hanoi's flower-sellers gather on a dusty patch of ground to select their choice of blooms at the wholesale **flower market** (see "Shopping and markets", p.398).

The next left turn onto Xuan Dieu, and then left again on Dang Thai Mai, takes you out along the **Ho Tay Peninsula** to a row of popular lakeside restaurants and **Phu Tay Ho**. This temple is dedicated to Thanh Mau, the Mother Goddess, who appeared as a beautiful girl to a famous scholar out boating on the lake in the seventeenth century. She refused to reveal her name, just smiled enigmatically, recited some poetry and disappeared. But when the scholar worked out her identity from the poem, local villagers erected a temple where they still occasionally worship the goddess in trances – as at Hon Chen Temple in Hué (see p.323). Phu Tay Ho attracts few tourists and the petitioners here are mostly young people asking for favours by burning their fake dollars under the banyan trees; according to Chinese belief, the bats depicted on the facades are symbolic of five wishes – for longevity, security, success, happiness and health.

Although the **Museum of Ethnology** (Tues–Sun 8.30am–5.30pm; $2 for an English-speaking guide) is a bit of a trek, out in the suburbs of Hanoi on Nguyen Van Huyen, it more than repays the effort, particularly if you'll be visiting any of the minority areas. Spread across two floors, the displays are well presented and there's a fair amount of information on all the major ethnic groups in Vietnamese, English and French. Musical instruments, games, traditional dress and other items of daily life which fill the showcases are brought to life through musical recordings, photos and plenty of life-size models, as well as captivating videos of festivals and shamanistic rites. This wealth of creativity amply illustrates some of the difficulties ethnologists are up against – the museum also acts as a research institute charged with producing ethnologies for Vietnam's 54 main groups plus their confusion of subgroups (for more on the ethnic minorities, see Contexts, p.521). The grounds contain a growing collection of minority houses as well as a café and a small fair-trade shop selling an array of fabrics, lacquerware and basketry. Once a month (currently the second weekend) the museum organizes events ranging from musical performances and water puppetry to arts and crafts demonstrations. To get there, follow Thuy Khue Avenue along the southern edge of West Lake and then keep heading west to find the museum 6km out of town, signposted left off Hoang Quoc Viet. City bus #14 stops on the main road 500m from the museum, or a cab from the Old Quarter should cost around $4.

The Christmas Bombing

In December 1972 President Nixon ordered intensive bombing raids on Hanoi and Haiphong, targeting transport arteries, power stations, factories and military installations, in the hope of influencing the Paris peace negotiations. This controversial **"Christmas Bombing"** inflicted considerable damage on civilian districts, causing an estimated 1300 deaths in Hanoi, where districts southwest of the train station were the worst-hit. More than two hundred people died in and around Kham Thien Street on December 26, but the most infamous strike was that on Bach Mai hospital in which, miraculously, only eighteen people were killed though seven bombs fell on the cardiology unit alone. At the time the North Vietnamese feared Hanoi would be wiped off the map and even laid out plans for a new capital; in the event, central Hanoi survived relatively unscathed.

On the way back into central Hanoi, you might want to make a brief detour to Ngoc Ha Village, where the mangled undercarriage of an American **B-52 bomber** lies half-submerged in a small lake. The plane was one of 23 shot down in December 1972 and now serves as a memorial to those who died during intensive raids known as the "Christmas Bombing" (see box above). Huu Tiep Lake lies just off Hoang Hoa Tham Avenue towards its eastern end, where a red sign announcing "B-52" points 100m down a narrow lane beside no. 55.

The southern districts

South of the French Quarter colonial villas gradually give way to fairly ordinary urban blocks, while west of Le Duan (Highway 1) the city quickly dissolves into suburban villages. Pockets of high-rise development are beginning to sprout along the major thoroughfares dissecting these **southern districts**, but it's not all city sprawl: remnants of farmland interspersed with a number of lakes relieve the congestion. The area's few attractions are widely scattered and wouldn't appear on anyone's must-see list but, for those with more time, exploring the outskirts adds an insight into everyday life, away from the prime tourist sights.

Between Le Duan and the Red River lies **Hai Ba Trung District**, named after an ancient temple which is also the area's principal tourist sight. **Den Hai Ba Trung** honours two heroic sisters who led the first popular rebellion against Chinese occupation and set up a short-lived independent kingdom in 40 AD (see p.484). When the rebellion collapsed, the Trung sisters threw themselves into a river to escape capture, so that when two stone figures washed up on the banks of the Red River several centuries later they were taken to be the petrified bodies of the two heroines. A shrine was built on the site in 1142 before being moved to its present location in the nineteenth century. Unfortunately, the temple authorities are reluctant to admit visitors, though you might gain entry on the first and fifteenth days of the lunar month, or during the temple festival held in February (on the fifth and sixth days of the second lunar month), when the statues are washed in water brought from the Red River and dressed in new robes.

Chua Lien Phai, "Pagoda of the Lotus Sect", is tucked away in a tangle of narrow alleys a kilometre southwest of Den Hai Ba Trung. The most interesting thing about Lien Phai is the story of its foundation by Lord Trinh Thap who dug up a lotus-root-shaped rock in his back garden. Convinced this was a sign from Buddha, he shaved his head and transformed his palace into the Lotus Pagoda, where his ashes were buried in 1734. Devotees of the Lotus Sect now live in the big, peaceful compound. To reach it, turn down an alley beside

182 Bach Mai and keep heading west until you find the walled compound on your right with a rickety stupa visible through the entrance arch.

North of Lien Phai Pagoda, **Lenin Park** (daily 6am–10pm) has been created out of an expanse of swamp that doubled as Hanoi's rubbish tip prior to 1960. It's green, peaceful and has some wonderful trees, but apart from the annual Tet flower festival it's a bit featureless and appears to be settling slowly back into the marsh, giving the concrete benches a curious incline.

Immediately west of the park, across Le Duan in **Dong Da District**, is an area of tightly packed one- and two-storey houses that suffered particularly badly during the 1972 "Christmas Bombing" (see box above). Vietnamese forces did manage to wreak some revenge, destroying between fifteen and twenty B-52s during the December raids, and you can see one of the planes that brought down an American bomber in the **Air Force Museum**, about a kilometre west of Bach Mai on Truong Chinh (daily 7.30–11am & 1.30–5pm). Since the Vietnamese Air Force was only established in 1959 the museum deals mainly with the American War, plus the odd mention of the anti-Pol Pot campaign and action against China in 1979. Its most interesting exhibits are photos of heroic aircrews and of early efforts to keep airfields open and the force's few planes operational. You can also see Uncle Ho's plush red-velvet flight seat taken from a MiG 4 helicopter, one of several aircraft languishing outside.

Eating

The choice of eating options in Hanoi now rivals Ho Chi Minh City in terms of quality, range and sophistication. You'll find everything from humble **food stalls** and **street kitchens**, the best dishing out top-quality food for next to nothing, to an increasing number of stylish international **restaurants**, mostly found around Hoan Kiem Lake and in the French Quarter; check the English-language listings magazines such as *Vietnam Discovery*, *Time Out* and *The Guide* for the latest newcomers. There's no shortage, either, of **cafés**, whether one-room coffee houses serving thick, strong cups of the local brew, or fancy Western-style places serving cappuccinos and café lattes – for a price. For sugar addicts there are some first-class **patisseries** and even a handful of **ice cream parlours**, catering to all tastes, from green-tea flavour to young rice or rum 'n' raisin.

Even though this is the capital city, you still need to **eat early**: whatever the advertised closing time might be, local places stop serving before 8pm and peak time is 6–7pm, while Western-style restaurants and top hotels tend to allow an extra hour or two.

Food stalls and street kitchens

For sheer value for money and atmosphere your best option is to eat either at the rock-bottom, stove-and-stools **food stalls** or at the slightly more upmarket **street kitchens**. These places usually provide just one type of food, such as basic rice and noodle dishes, including two Hanoi **specialities**: the ubiquitous *pho* noodle soup and *bun cha*, small barbecued pork burgers served with a bowl of rice noodles, which makes a tasty snack. *Bun bo* (noodles with beef) and *bun ga* (noodles with chicken) are also popular, while you might want to nibble at *banh goi*, fried pastries filled with vermicelli, minced pork and mushrooms, and eaten with a thin sweet sauce, parsley and chilli; to sample them, join the crowd at a stall nestling under a giant banyan tree beside the entrance to Ly Quoc Su Pagoda.

You'll find food stalls and street kitchens scattered throughout the city, though for convenience we've concentrated on those in the **Old Quarter** and the streets **west of Hoan Kiem Lake**. While the stalls are, by their nature, itinerant, street kitchens are more permanent operations that tend to cluster together. Often there's no recognizable name and little to choose between individual establishments, but a few that do stand out from the crowd are listed below; alternatively, just head for one of the streets also given below where you'll find a particularly wide choice. All fall within the area covered by the map on p.391, with the exception of Hoa Ma and Nguyen Binh Khiem, both in the southern districts, which appear on the main Hanoi map (pp.358–359).

Individual establishments

Bun Bo Nam Bo 67 Hang Dieu. Hanoi's most famous *bun bo* outlet, at the south end of Hang Dieu, opposite the Old Quarter's Hang Da Market. Tuck into a generous bowlful of lean beef and noodles, topped with a mound of roasted peanuts and garlic.

Com Bia Ma May 72 Ma May. Take your pick from a spread of ready-prepared dishes at this popular and well-priced street kitchen in the Old Quarter. They also serve a decent *bia hoi* (draught beer).

Dac Kim 1 Hang Manh. Sit down to a huge pile of fried spring rolls, *bun cha* and salad greens at the city's most famous *nem* outlet just off Hang Quat in the Old Quarter.

Hoang Lon 70 Hoa Ma. Among a row of unusually large places east of Lenin Park serving *bittet* (steak) and *opla* (omelette) with fries or baguettes to the east of Lenin Park, *Hoang Lon* has a solid reputation.

Huyen Dung 4 Ly Thai To. The sizzling-hot plates of steak, eggs and chips are the closest you'll get to a decent fry-up. Open all day, this Old Quarter outlet is a great place for a filling breakfast or hangover lunch.

Linh Anh 108 Nguyen Huu Huan. Lunch or dinner, tables spill onto the pavement outside this street kitchen, best known for its chicken-rice laced with special herbs, though it's all tasty and freshly prepared (English-language menu available). Located on the Old Quarter's eastern fringes.

Mien Luon 87 Hang Dieu. Feast on spicy noodles with crispy mini-eels, *luon*, opposite Hang Da Market.

Pho Gia Truyen 49 Bat Dan. Reputedly the best *pho bo* in town, said to be made using water purified with a secret concoction of herbs, has them queueing out the door from around 7am. The taste is certainly different, and the meat incredibly succulent – particularly if you opt for *chinh* (well done). Find it on the west side of the Old Quarter.

Pho Lam 7 Nam Ngu. Opposite the *Indochine* restaurant (see p.392), this outlet serves great chicken or beef *pho* all day. To ring the changes, ask them to add a raw egg.

Pho Tu Do 39 Cau Go. Popular morning *pho* joint just north of Hoan Kiem Lake. Get there before 8am.

Thanh Van 14 Hang Ga. A bit out of the way, towards the north of the Old Quarter, but a good place to try *banh cuon*, a sort of fresh spring roll.

Xuan Loc 90 Hang Trong. Excellent *bun cha* served with great mounds of ultra-fresh salad greens, just west of Hoan Kiem Lake.

Streets

Dinh Liet The south end of this Old Quarter street is famous for its *pho* kitchens, while no. 9a also serves a mean *my van than* (wonton soup).

Duong Thanh Opposite Hang Da Market, a clutch of small outlets cater to the shopping crowds: try no. 49 for *chao ca* (thick rice gruel with fish) or no. 41 for *xoi ga* (sticky rice with chicken).

Hang Bac/Hang Mam The alley at the east end of the Old Quarter's Hang Bac, where it becomes Hang Mam, has several popular lunchtime food stalls, serving various noodle and rice dishes in addition to delicacies such as eels, snails and crabs. If none of those appeals, snack on rice noodles served with fried tofu, cucumber and mint.

Le Van Huu On the southern edge of the French Quarter, this street boasts a number of popular outlets, such as *Mai Anh* at no. 32 for *pho ga*. Opposite, *Quan Com Pho* is a slightly more upmarket option (see "Restaurants", p.393).

Nguyen Binh Khiem/Tran Nhan Tong A short walk southwest of Le Van Huu, outlets on these two streets serve lunchtime *com binh dan* ("people's meals"), where you select from a range of ready-prepared dishes; get there before 12.30pm or there won't be anything left. No. 14 Nguyen Binh Khiem has a particularly good reputation.

To Tich The place to go if your looking for a late-night snack. It's located northwest of Hoan Kiem Lake, between Hang Gai and Hang Quat.

Tong Duy Tan In the southwest corner of the Old Quarter, this "food alley" is packed with local eateries, each specializing in a different dish, such as *ga tan*, Chinese-style chicken broth brewed from medicinal herbs, pulses, plums and lotus seed, and *chao* – thick rice soups topped with shredded chicken, fish or lightly cooked beef. Touts can be pushy.

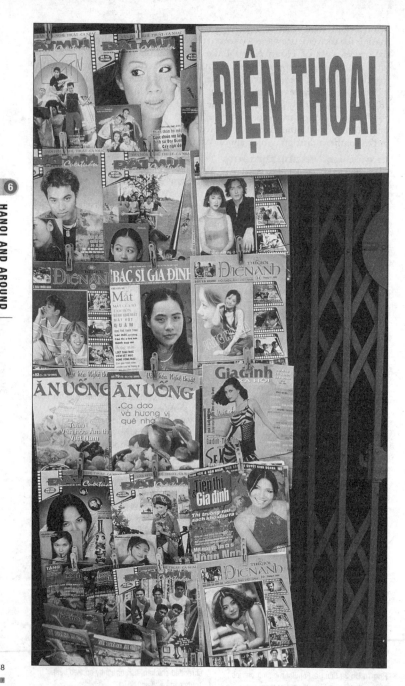

Restaurants

At the inexpensive end of the scale are the excellent-value local **restaurants**, one step up from the street kitchens, where often fine, tasty food makes up for the less than attractive surroundings. Moving up a step you'll find a growing number of moderately priced Western-style establishments which serve a range of cuisine, from classic Vietnamese dishes to salads, pizzas and hamburgers for the homesick. Among these are the stalwart **travellers' cafés**, which double as tour agents and popular, if rather functional, meeting places; though by no means a gourmet dining experience, standards have improved considerably and you can usually eat at any hour of the day. Top-notch restaurants offering Vietnamese or international cuisine in atmospheric surroundings are on the increase, too, as Hanoi challenges Ho Chi Minh's culinary supremacy.

When it comes to number and variety of budget and mid-price eating places, the **Old Quarter** and the streets to the west of Hoan Kiem Lake take some beating, while Hanoi's glitziest dining rooms tend to be located in the **French Quarter**. Here several moderately priced restaurants are charmingly housed in renovated colonial villas; there's also a smattering of less formal, local eating places and cafés to suit more modest budgets. Further out of the centre there are a few places scattered in the outer districts that come in useful for a respite from sightseeing around Ho Chi Minh's Mausoleum and West Lake.

Finally, restaurants tend to be small: in the listings below, we've given phone numbers for places where it's advisable to make **reservations**.

Hanoi's unusual eats

Hanoi has a fantastic selection of **street food**. In additon to the traditional favourites such as *bun cha* and *pho*, goat, dog, rat, snake and porcupine are common treats. Ethically some readers may find this disturbing but the eating of animals is deeply entrenched in Vietnamese culture, and an invitation to share in the feast is to be considered an honour. If you want to sample these dishes yourself we recommend the following. Vegetarians should simply go on to the next section.

If you want to sample **dog meat** (*thit cho*), a northern speciality eaten mostly in winter and never during days one to ten of the lunar calendar month, then head out of Hanoi along the Red River dyke to **Nghi Tam Avenue**. There are dozens of stilt-house restaurants to choose from, though *Tran Muc* is currently regarded as the best; alternatively, just head for the busiest. Traditionally you sit on the floor with a country view. It's believed that dog meat is warming, will bring good luck and is eaten when old friends are reunited. The dog meat comes boiled (*luoc*), grilled (*cha nuong*) and served with green banana and tofu (*rua man*). Even with a few jars of rice wine, prices are still moderate (around $2 per person). Note that you'll be expected to eat with your hands.

Le Mat snake village – 4km over Chuong Duong Bridge in the Gia Lam District – is home to a slew of **snake-meat** restaurants which play to the tourist market with elaborate theatrics, including killing the snake in front of you. It's then served up in every possible form, from soup to snake-belly shavings. The guest of honour gets to eat the still pumping heart – beware, it's alleged to have amphetamine properties. Though not the cheapest of Le Mat's restaurants, *Quoc Trieu* has a reliable reputation; count on up to $10 per head for the full eleven-course meal including drinks. If you'd prefer a more sanitised version, *Highway 4* (see "Restaurants" overleaf) offers a seven-course snake feast without the gory bits; the minimum group size is four people and you must order in advance. Some tourists report being **pickpocketed** while visiting Le Mat, so be wary.

The Old Quarter and west of Hoan Kiem Lake

Bittet 51 Hang Buom. Hidden down a long, dark passage at the back of a tube-house (see p.372), this small and bustling restaurant serves platters of *bittet* – a Vietnamese corruption of French *biftek* – and chips with lashings of garlic, a salad and crusty bread for a mere couple of dollars. There's a seafood option as well. 5–9pm.

Café des Arts 11b Bao Khanh ⊕04/828 7207. A big hit with the Francophile community, this upmarket French café-restaurant has a roof terrace, lots of comfy seating areas and a solid reputation for impressive cuisine with prices to match. A place to splash out and enjoy a good bottle of wine. They also run the cheaper *Stop Café* downstairs. 9.30am–11pm.

Café Puku 2f/60 Hang Trong. With its comfy sofas, great music and homely clutter, *Puku* is a laidback place patronized by Hanoi's merry band of expats plus the odd hardy soul willing to brave the long corridor. House specials include bagels and homemade lasagna, though the menu, which changes daily, has a distinct "Kiwiana" flavour to it. On the social side, it's a good place to keep abreast of what's happening around town. There are plans to open a takeaway branch in the Old Quarter. 7.30am–10pm.

Cha Ca La Vong 14 Cha Ca. Although it's seen better days, this is a local institution. There's only one dish on the menu: *cha ca*, fried fish with fresh dill cooked at your table on a clay brazier, then eaten with cold rice noodles, chilli and peanuts. At nearly $4, prices are moderately expensive for what you get. 10am–10pm.

Dakshin 94 Hang Trong. Just reading the menu is enough to get the taste buds going at this big and deservedly popular Indian vegetarian restaurant. And the generous portions plus authentic flavours will keep you coming back for more. Main dishes are mostly around $2, or you can opt for a thali at just over $3 including a soft drink. 11am–3pm & 6–11pm.

Dong Khinh 73 Cau Go. Cantonese restaurant with views over Hoan Kiem Lake, best for its daily dim sum buffet lunch with a magnificent spread of some forty varieties (11am–2pm; $5). 7am–10pm.

Gekko Bar & Restaurant 14b Bao Khanh ⊕04/928 6125. A former chef of the *Nikko Hotel* has set up in this romantic little restaurant on fashionable Bao Khanh. On offer is gourmet dining, predominantly French-influenced and all excellent, though the seafood is particularly recommended. It's not cheap, of course, but well worth a splurge. 11.30am–10.30pm.

Highway 4 5 Hang Tre. Midway between a restaurant and a bar, *Highway 4* offers moderately priced north Vietnamese foods – steamboats and earthen-pot dishes, as well as more innovative fare such as fish spring rolls – to accompany traditional liquors. These come in over thirty varieties, the medicinal benefits of which are explained in an English-language menu, from a warming combination of mango, ginger and honey to gekko, snake, silkworm and the evidently potent "one night five times" for the more adventurous. A warren of rooms on three floors culminates in a great roof terrace. 9am–2am; food served to 11pm.

Ily Café 97 Ma May. This classy European-style café-restaurant, under a soaring roof-space, is popular for its reasonably priced and wide-ranging all-day menu, covering Vietnamese, Thai, Indian and Western cuisines, with plenty of vegetarian options. There's a pool table and occasional film or music-video screenings. 8am–11pm.

Kangaroo Café 18 Bao Khanh. Quality Australian-run travellers' café (see p.363) serving fresh, wholesome food – including a fine selection of vegetarian fare – prepared as far as possible from organic produce. The all-day breakfasts and bangers-and-mash are recommended. 7.30am–10pm.

La Salsa 25 Nha Tho. Top-notch Spanish and southern French cuisine in the heart of the fashionable cathedral area. Seasonal menu, sangria and authentic tapas plus a good dollop of ambience have made this an expat favourite. 10am–midnight.

Little Hanoi 25 Ta Hien ⊕04/926 0168. Cosy, friendly and great-value restaurant on a bustling sidestreet, serving lip-smacking Vietnamese home cooking among pan pipes and bamboo knick-knacks. Try the fried tuna with sweet and sour sauce or the house special, spicy fried chicken with five tastes. They've just added another premises opposite (no. 14), but even so you might want to book ahead. 7am–11pm.

Little Hanoi 21 Hang Gai. Not to be confused with the above, this intimate café-restaurant on a busy junction just off Hoan Kiem Lake packs them in with its good-value salads, soups, filled baguettes (to eat in or take away) and other light meals, plus an extensive range of bar drinks. 7.30am–11pm.

No Noodles 20 Nha Chung. This excellent sandwich bar has been a Hanoi staple for years thanks to its crusty French baguettes with generous fillings, to eat in or take away. Chicken tandoori hits the button, or you can pig out on a "big filler". 9am–9pm.

Pepperonis I & Pepperonis II 29 Ly Quoc Su &
31 Bao Khanh. With two outlets in the cathedral
area, this lively Western-style pizza chain has
found a winning formula in its all-you-can-eat
pasta and salad lunch buffet (Mon–Fri
11.30am–1.30pm; $1.60) – get there early to grab
a table. Pizzas range from $1.30 to $5 – the

seafood pizza is excellent – and pasta dishes are
under $3, or there are salads, ribs, burgers and
other comfort foods. 8am–11pm.
Quan Bia Minh 7a Dinh Liet. Relaxed terrace
restaurant-bar with an extensive range of cheap
and cheerful Vietnamese and Western foods.
Though it serves everything from breakfast

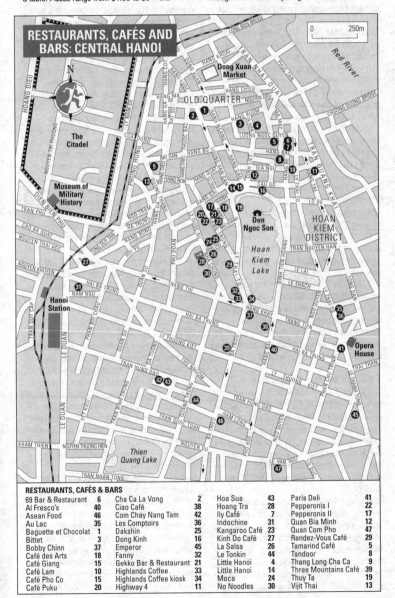

RESTAURANTS, CAFÉS AND BARS: CENTRAL HANOI

RESTAURANTS, CAFÉS & BARS

69 Bar & Restaurant	6	Cha Ca La Vong	2	Hoa Sua	43	Paris Deli	41
Al Fresco's	40	Ciao Café	38	Hoang Tra	28	Pepperonis I	22
Asean Food	46	Com Chay Nang Tam	42	Ily Café	7	Pepperonis II	17
Au Lac	35	Dakshin	25	Indochine	31	Quan Bia Minh	12
Baguette et Chocolat	1	Dong Kinh	16	Kangaroo Café	23	Quan Com Pho	47
Bittet	3	Emperor	45	Kinh Do Café	27	Rendez-Vous Café	29
Bobby Chinn	37	Fanny	32	La Salsa	26	Tamarind Café	5
Café des Arts	18	Gekko Bar & Restaurant	21	Le Tonkin	44	Tandoor	8
Café Giang	15	Highlands Coffee	33	Little Hanoi	4	Thang Long Cha Ca	9
Café Lam	10	Highlands Coffee kiosk	34	Little Hanoi	14	Three Mountains Café	39
Café Pho Co	15	Highway 4	11	Moca	24	Thuy Ta	19
Café Puku	20			No Noodles	30	Vijit Thai	13

onwards, cheap draught beer ensures a good crowd as the sun goes down. 8am–midnight.

69 Bar & Restaurant 69 Ma May. Exposed beams and brickwork give a rustic feel to this traditional house now converted into a lively bar-cum-restaurant. The well-priced menu lists a few unusual choices, among them sticky rice and other northern foods, to accompany a decent selection of rice wines. 8am–late.

Tamarind Café 80 Ma May. A little pricey but worth it for the innovative and beautifully presented contemporary vegetarian food and fresh fruit juices with decor to match: plump sofas and tiled floors, with arty Asian-style seating platforms at the rear. It's also home to the Handspan booking desk (see "Tour agents and travellers' cafés", p.363). 6am–11pm.

Tandoor 24 Hang Be. A perennially popular Indian restaurant under the same ownership as *Dakshin* (see above). Simple decor but cracking curries: fish tikka, tandoori chicken and an extensive range of mouthwatering vegetarian dishes. The thali set lunch offers excellent value at under $4. 11am–2pm & 6–10pm.

Thang Long Cha Ca 31 Duong Thanh. Patronized by locals, this is a newer and less touristy version of *Cha Ca La Vong* (see above). Again, there's only one dish – do-it-yourself fried fish with lashings of fresh dill – for around $4 a head, but portions are generous.

Vijit Thai 16a Duong Thanh ☎04/828 9065. Popular with the local Thai community for its authentic cuisine prepared by a Thai chef; prices are reasonable given the quality of the food. Upstairs is a traditional Thai-style dining space with mats, cushions and low tables, or better still reserve one of the tables in the tiny garden at the rear.

The French Quarter

The following are all marked on the map on p.391.

Al Fresco's 23 Hai Ba Trung ☎04/826 7782. The sister restaurant to *Pepperonis* is a relaxed expat-run place with a pleasant balcony on the first floor. Café, bar and grill in one, the menu includes good-quality American and international fare (including ribs, salads, Australian steaks and a choice of thin- or thick-crust pizzas), all served in hefty portions. 9am–10.30pm.

Asean Food 53 Ba Trieu. Formerly *Mothers Pride*, a no-frills halal restaurant serving tip-top Malay curries, sambal and other specialities. Nasi goreng and ginger chicken are perennial favourites, while Western dishes are also available.

Bobby Chinn 1 Ba Trieu ☎04/934 8577. Hanoi's most decadent dining experience features streamers of silk rosebuds, mood music, contemporary

Vietnamese art and an oh-so-laidback chill-out zone screened by silk-gauze partitions – indulge yourself with an Egyptian water pipe (*shisha*). Nevertheless, the food is not that expensive: tapas are $2 a dish and lunchtime salads start at $3, while in the evening a starter and main course will set you back around $15. The seasonal menu, best described as fusion Asian/Californian, offers such delights as wasabi mash, green-tea smoked duck with black sticky rice and, for afters, grapes coated in goat's cheese and pistachio nuts.

Com Chay Nang Tam 79a Tran Hung Dao. Small, vegetarian restaurant down a quiet alleyway off Tran Hung Dao and named after Vietnamese Cinderella character. Though the decor is decidedly worn, the food's still tasty enough and very affordable. *Goi bo*, a main-course salad of banana flower, star fruit and pineapple, is recommended, or try one of the well-priced set menus all under $3.50. Purists might not like the way the food emulates meat. 11am–1.30pm & 5–10pm.

Emperor 18b Le Thanh Tong ☎04/826 8801. Perhaps the best of Hanoi's upscale Vietnamese restaurants for all-round ambience and quality. The tastes are predominantly from the sweet and spicy south: tiger prawn with tamarind, beef with honey and duck with mandarin sauce, for example. There are set menus at around $15 and $20, or you can eat well from the menu for under $10 a head. If possible, try to get a table in the magnificent traditional stilthouse rather than the newer villa. Reservations recommended for dinner. 11am–2pm & 5.30–10.30pm.

Hoa Sua 28a Xom Ha Hoi ☎04/942 4448. Excellently presented food with a heavy French influence served on the plant-filled patio or in the elegant dining rooms of a colonial villa buried in the backstreets – it's not well signed, but don't give up. *Hoa Sua* is part of a non-profit-making vocational training school giving disadvantaged children a start in the restaurant trade. Try the Vietnamese combo meal ($2), smoked duck salad ($2) or one of the daily specials, but save room for one of the superb desserts. Live music Saturday evenings (7–10pm) and Sunday lunchtime (10am–1pm). 7am–10pm.

Indochine 16 Nam Ngu ☎04/942 4097. Food of consistently high quality at reasonable prices keeps this well-established restaurant up there with its younger rivals. Beautifully presented and original Vietnamese specialities, from seafood spring rolls to steamboats or the famous prawn on sugar cane, served either in the colonial villa or its patio-courtyard. Popular with tour groups, so reservations are recommended. Traditional Vietnamese music Tues, Thurs & Sun (7.30–9.30pm). 11am–2pm &

5.30–10pm.

Le Tonkin 14 Ngo Van So ☎ 04/943 3457. The garden lends more atmosphere to this sister restaurant of *Indochine* (see above), but otherwise it follows the same formula: elegant but not exorbitant dining which makes a great introduction to Vietnamese cuisine. Traditional music on Mon, Wed, Fri & Sun (7.30–9.30pm). 11am–2pm & 5.30–10pm.

Quan Com Pho 29 Le Van Huu. This sanitized version of a street kitchen – and almost as cheap – is a good place to try *pho ga*, *bun cha* and other Hanoi speciality dishes. It's equally popular with locals, expats and tourists. 10.30am–2pm & 4.30–10pm.

Outer districts

The following are all marked on the map on p.000.

Da Gino 11b Dien Bien Phu. The pleasant outdoor seating area well off the street makes this a decent option if you're looking for sustenance out near the Temple of Literature. Pizzas, pasta, salads and a selection of meat dishes are the order of the day, to be followed by the likes of tiramisu and cassata for the sweet-toothed. A pizza plus dessert will cost around $10. 11am–11.30pm.

Foodshop 45, 45 Tran Vu. It's worth going out of your way to eat at this pint-sized Indian restaurant overlooking Truc Bach Lake. It's run by an Indian-trained chef, who magics up a knockout range of dishes from his hole-in-the-wall kitchen. Excellent value for money. 10.30am–2pm & 5–11pm.

Koto 61 Van Mieu. Hugely popular deli-style restaurant staffed by erstwhile street kids under a charity programme to train them in hospitality skills. Start the day with muesli and pancakes, or stop by later for a gourmet sandwich or perhaps grilled tuna marinated in ginger, as long as you leave space for desert – the ginger cake and ice cream is out of this world. Mains are priced at between $3 and $5, with all proceeds being ploughed back into the programmes. 7am–4pm.

Cafés, patisseries and ice-cream parlours

Hanoi's French legacy is particularly apparent in the city's adoption of café culture. The city boasts hundreds of local **cafés**, offering minimum comfort but great coffee – usually small, strong shots of the local brew – although the epicentre of Hanoi's café-bar scene is Bao Khanh/Hang Hanh, a bustling street near Hoan Kiem Lake, where young Vietnamese come to hang out. In addition, there is an ever-increasing number of sophisticated Western-style places, many of which also serve food, and a crop of outlets selling fine pastries, yoghurts and ice cream.

For a more traditional sugar-fix, try **chè**, halfway between a drink and a dessert; there's a clutch of outlets near Hang Da Market, at the south end of Hang Dieu. For a handful of dong you'll get a mug of thick, sweet soup, packed with beans, jelly, coconut and all kinds of seasonal fruits; in winter they also serve it hot, though this brings out the sweetness more.

The following are all marked on the map on p.391.

Au Lac 57 Ly Thai. This popular garden café-bar-restaurant is a pleasant spot to sip your cappuccino or wine while getting a shoeshine and watching the fitness freaks work out in the *Metropole*'s gym opposite. The food also has a strong reputation – try the roast vegetable and goat's cheese pizza.

Baguette et Chocolat 11 Cha Ca. For a calming cuppa in the heart of the Old Quarter, head for this new outlet from the *Hoa Sua* school (see "Restaurants", opposite) comprising a bakery counter on the ground floor and comfy sofas upstairs. They serve everything from coffee, tea, cookies and cakes to open sandwiches and other light meals, both Western and Vietnamese.

Café Giang 7 Hang Gai. A grungy, hole-in-the-wall café famous for its Vietnamese take on a cappuccino, *café trung*, which is delicious and extremely rich coffee frothed up with whipped egg. Alternatively, try *cocao trung* or even *bia trung* for a few thousand dong.

Café Lam 60 Nguyen Huu Huan. This shabby but atmospheric one-room café made its name as a place for artists and young intellectuals to hang out. A few paid their bills with paintings, some of which still adorn the walls, and there's a bohemian vibe.

Café Pho Co 11 Hang Gai. It's easy to miss the entrance to this gem of a café accessed through an art gallery/souvenir stall. You emerge in a courtyard full of plants and birdsong – tempting, but keep going up past the family altar and you eventually reach two roof terraces high above Hoan Kiem Lake. Light meals are also available, but it's a good idea to place your order downstairs first.

Buying your own food: markets, supermarkets and delis

With so much fresh fruit, bread and takeaway food available in the **markets** or hawked on the streets, especially in the Old Quarter, it's easy to prepare excellent do-it-yourself meals, especially as the number of **supermarkets**, gourmet **delicatessens** and **bakeries** has increased dramatically in recent years. You can now buy cold cuts, pâté, milk, yoghurt and cheeses other than the ubiquitous *La Vache Qui Rit* at several outlets, many of which also sell imported canned and dried foodstuffs – as long as you don't mind paying over the odds for a taste of home.

Markets

Cho Dong Xuan Dong Xuan Street. Hanoi's biggest covered market hides its foodstuffs at the rear of the ground floor, from where vegetable stalls spread out towards the river.
Cho Hang Da Hang Da Street. A small covered market with a ground-floor foods section heavy with aromatic mushrooms and the sharp smell of dried fish, while stalls outside sell imported confectionery, wines and spirits. Head upstairs for secondhand and new clothes.
Cho Hom Pho Hué. Large market, with foodstuffs to the rear of the ground floor.
Cho 19–12 Between Hai Ba Trung and Ly Thuong Kiet. A one-street, fresh-food market open until dusk.

Supermarkets

Citimart Hanoi Towers, 49 Hai Ba Trung. Well-stocked mini-market serving the expats in the Towers' offices and apartments, so a little expensive.
Fivimart 210 Tran Quang Khai & 10 Trang Vu. Two big outlets offering a good selection of imported brands and drinks at reasonable prices.
Intimex 22–23 Le Thai To. Decent range of foodstuffs and household goods on two floors, tucked down an alley at the southwest end of Hoan Kiem Lake.
The Trade Centre 7 Dinh Tien Haong. Handy for the Old Quarter, with a modest range of dried or canned foods and toiletries.
Vinaconex 4f, Trang Tien Trade Plaza, Trang Tien. No fresh foods beyond a small cold counter, but a fair selection of imported food and wine in Hanoi's smart new shopping mall.
Western Canned Foods 66a Ba Trieu. Mini-mart boasting the best selection of imported food and wine, albeit at prices slightly above the norm.

Delicatessens and bakeries

Annam 11 Ly Dao Thanh. Expensive European imports from biscuits, chocolates and spices to relishes and even Marmite. They also sell their own range of upscale Vietnamese products.
Au Delice 19 Han Thuyen. Arguably Hanoi's best gourmet deli, with a fine array of charcuterie, pâté, cheese and wine.
B Deli 30b Duong Thanh. Parma ham, mozzarella, Barilla sauces and other goodies at this Italian-run deli, which also serves light meals.
Croissant 35 Quang Trung. The bakery of *Hoa Sua* (see "Restaurants", p.392) turns out excellent breads, cakes and savoury snacks.
Hanoi Gourmet 1b Ham Long. It's worth going out of your way to this little deli with a select choice of cheese, cold cuts and French wines. Salads and sandwiches available to eat in or take away.
Le Beaulieu Gourmand 56 Ly Thai To. The deli of the *Sofitel Metropole* sells a small, select range of imported goods, including goat's cheese, as well as freshly baked breads, cakes and pastries.
The Deli 59a Ly Thai To. On the ground floor of the Press Club, homemade breads, quiches, pies, sandwiches and suchlike to eat in or take away. Also has an extensive wine selection.

Ciao Café 2 Hang Bai. Cheerful Western-style café blending American diner decor with Italian minimalism. The menu covers everything from breakfast to cocktails by way of pizzas, sandwiches and ice cream.

Fanny 48 Le Thai To. French-owned ice-cream parlour serving Hanoi's best ices, ice-cream cakes and sorbets. High prices are offset by good presentation and the most original flavours in town.

Highlands Coffee 6f/38 Le Thai To. It's worth persevering to reach this rooftop café with unbeatable views over Hoan Kiem Lake and the cathedral; to find it walk through the car park to the lift at the rear of the building. Drinks and snack foods available all day both here and at their pretty little kiosk on the lake's southwest shore.

Hoang Tra 2 Nha Chung. There's space for just six people at the counter of this tiny shop selling locally grown teas just down from the cathedral. Flavours range from jasmine, ginger and mountain apple to lotus, a gourmet brew available only in summer.

Kinh Do Café 252 Hang Bong. "Café 252" became famous after Cathérine Deneuve complimented the patron on his yoghurts, which still merit praise, as do the home-baked pastries. The decor's changed little over the years, though they now offer a wider range of foods, including well-prepared Vietnamese dishes, making it popular with locals, tourists and Francophile movie buffs.

Les Comptoirs 59a Ly Thai To. The Press Club's small ground-floor café, which also doubles as a bookshop, serves an extensive range of teas and coffees and you can order food from their deli while you browse.

Moca 14–16 Nha Tho. Located in the hip cathedral area, Moca's huge picture windows are ideal for people-watching over a mug of the creamiest, frothiest café latte in town. In winter hunker by the open fire.

Paris Deli 6 Phan Chu Trinh. Excellent coffee, tea and cakes at this upmarket French-style bakery/café across from the Opera House. They also serve pricey sandwiches, savoury snacks and main meals – good quality but rather meagre portions. Takeaway service available.

Rendez-Vous Café 136 Hang Trong. A bright and airy café/bistro next to the lake. Best at lunch times when they serve a good-value buffet lunch (11am–2pm) for $2 and a Western set menu for $3. Live music nightly. 7am–midnight.

Three Mountains Café 34 Ba Trieu. Laidback café-restaurant in a tastefully decorated French villa with an open fire in winter and a resident piano/violin duo. Offers an extensive list of fresh juices and fruit shakes. Good food, too.

Thuy Ta 1 Le Thai To. A breezy lakeside café that's great for breakfast, an afternoon tea or an evening beer. Also serves pastries, ice creams and a variety of light meals.

Drinking, nightlife and entertainment

For a capital city, Hanoi is pretty sleepy: most **bars** outside the big hotels have swept up by midnight and **nightclubs** don't stay open much later. At the time of writing the authorities are being fairly strict about enforcing a midnight **curfew** on bars and clubs, but one or two places still manage to keep pouring till sunrise or at least till the last customer leaves. The club scene now boasts a couple of quite fancy places with decent music and imported sound-and-light systems. Check the English-language listings magazines (see p.404) for the latest.

Pool and **billiards** are popular with young Vietnamese men, with most bars and cafés having at least one table. Try places along Bao Khanh/Hang Hanh or the *Z Café* at 17 Tong Dan. If **ballroom dancing** is your thing, you can take a turn or two at the Dong Do Dancing Club, 18 Luong Ngoc Quyen (9.30–11.45am, 3.30–5.45pm & 8.30–10.30pm). Even if you're not particularly into Western **classical music**, it's well worth catching a concert or ballet at the Opera House, 1 Trang Tien, for the sumptuous surroundings, all plush red fabrics, mirrors and chandeliers.

As for **traditional entertainment**, a performance of the water puppets, Vietnam's charming contribution to the world of marionettes, should be high on everyone's itinerary. It's also worth catching a performance of *cheo*, a form

Bia hoi bars

Beer drinking tends to be an all-male preserve in Vietnam but don't be put off; **bia hoi** outlets are a fun, friendly and above all cheap way to enjoy a beer and soak up some genuine Vietnamese culture. Many also serve excellent **food**, making them a cheaper option than many restaurants (see "Basics", p.46, for more on *bia hoi*). Though you'll find *bia hoi* bars dotted all over the city, particularly in the French Quarter, below we list a few of the more interesting and accessible places. Note that **last orders** are usually around 9pm.

8 Chan Cam. *Bia hoi* and food on a busy street corner north of the cathedral.

34a Phan Chu Trinh. One of several outlets just up from the junction with Ham Long. This one's recommended for its excellent food served in the streetfront upstairs dining area; look for the "*Bia Suu*" sign, four doors up from the junction.

59 Ly Thuong Kiet. Big, pavement *bia hoi* outlet across from the *Melia Hotel*. Good beer and excellent food.

72 Ma May. Decent *bia hoi* on offer at this well-priced street kitchen (see p.387).

Nguyen Huu Huan/Hang Thung. Take your pick from a number of popular outlets on this junction to the east of the Old Quarter.

Ta Hien/Luong Ngoc Quyen. This crossroads in the heart of the Old Quarter boasts three tiny bars, popular with both backpackers and expats.

Tong Dan. You'll find several good, big *bia hoi* places at the south end of Tong Dan towards the Opera.

---

of traditional theatre, or one of the regular events held at the Museum of Ethnology (see p.384). Otherwise, apart from a few groups playing traditional music at some of Hanoi's main tourist sights, there's little on offer in the cultural sphere that's easily accessible just yet. Very occasionally, events are listed in the English-language press, but are more likely to be announced on street banners or outside the venues themselves, so you'll have to ask around to see if there's anything interesting happening.

Bars, pubs and clubs

Hanoi's bar and club scene can't be described as wild, but the choice of **nightspots** is improving. You're no longer restricted to characterless hotel bars or psuedo-pubs, as the number of dedicated drinking holes, some of them packing a bit of designer flair, gradually increases. A few places now even offer live music. Nevertheless, the busiest venues are without doubt the *bia hoi* outlets selling pitchers of the local brew (see box above), while young Hanoians out on the town tend to prefer intimate cafés, pool halls and karaoke bars.

Apocalypse Now 5c Hoa Ma. Sister establishment to the original bar in Ho Chi Minh City that's seething on Friday and Saturday nights – though don't bother before 11pm. Dark, apocalyptic decor, sleazy reputation and *loud* music. One of Hanoi's top dance spots. 9pm–midnight.

Bamboo Bar 46 Hang Vai. Naff decor and a small drinks list, but this Old Quarter bar is one of the few that consistently stays open late, sometimes even to dawn. 5pm–late.

Funky Monkey 15b Hang Hanh. Though not as popular as it used to be, the vibe's still pretty funky at this jungle-theme bar with its loud music, DJ, pool table and happy-hour beer deals (4–8pm). Closes midnight.

Highway 4 5 Hang Tre. A laidback bar-restaurant (see p.390) where you can sample authentic medicinal liquors. Considering the health benefits, a selection of four shots at under $2 is a steal. 9am–2am.

Jazz Club 31 Luong Van Can. Live jazz every night led by the charismatic – and highly accomplished – Quyen Van Minh, Hanoi's answer to Ronnie Scott. All-day dining as well as drinks. Performances start at 8.30am. 10am–midnight.

Labyrinth 7 Ta Hien. Friendly little bar decked out in cosy reds, with board games and occasional live music. 6pm–2am.

Le Maquis Bar 2a Ta Hien. A few doors up from

Labyrinth, the equally intimate *Le Maquis* goes in for alternative, student grunge. Busiest after midnight when the local expats congregate for beers and snacks. 5pm–2am.

Met Pub *Sofitel Metropole Hotel*, 15 Ngo Quyen. An English-style pub – dark wood, low ceilings, darts – boasting an extensive drinks list and good choice of papers. Other attractions include lunch and dinner buffets ($6–10), and live music (7–10pm). In fine weather, the poolside *Bamboo Bar* has more appeal.

New Century 10 Trang Thi. Hanoi's biggest, brashest nightclub attracts a mixed crowd with its live bands, laser show and great dance music – which compensate for expensive drinks. Entry $2.60 including one drink. 8pm–2am.

Phuc Tan Bar 49 Phuong Phuc Tan. For late-night drinking it's well worth seeking out this pioneering French-owned bar on the "wrong" side of the Red River dyke, where things don't really get going until 2am. 6pm–late.

Polite Pub 5 Bao Khanh. Relaxed spot with a touch more atmosphere than its neighbour, the *GC* (6 Bao Khanh); both are inexpensive places to drink, with some of Hanoi's cheapest happy-hour beers (5–8pm). Full-sized pool table, foozball, music and cocktails. 4pm–2am.

Press Club, 59a Ly Thai To. Hanoi's plush business venue plays the colonial game to the last detail; choose between the old-world elegance of the snug *Library Bar*, or the more casual *Terrace* – weather permitting. Refinement, of course, doesn't come cheap.

Quan Ly 82 Le Van Huu. A small local bar run by local wine connoisseur, Mr Ly, who has personally created over twenty kinds of Vietnamese wine. A quiet spot to sit and dally over a bottle of wine.

And, if you have one too many, Ly's specially blended tea is meant to cure any hangover.

Relax Bar 60 Ly Thuong Kiet. Rustic little bar complete with bamboo arbours, caged birds, a pond and fountain – not to mention a sleazy reputation. 10am–1am.

R&R Tavern 47 Lo Su. Friday night sees them rocking as the White Eagles house band gets on down at Hanoi's very own American-run rock 'n' roll bar. Or, if that sounds way too lively, drop by on a Thursday afternoon to catch a classical string quartet. Strange but true. They also serve decent bar food. 8am–midnight.

Spotted Cow 23c Hai Ba Trung. Loud and beery Australian-run bar with draught beers, darts and seemingly half the expat community rammed into a cramped space on a Sunday afternoon. A real throwback to the 1970s.

Summit Lounge 20f Sofitel Plaza, 2 Yen Phu. Come here during happy hour (4.30–8pm) for what are without doubt the best views in Hanoi. Live music from 8.15pm. 4.30pm–midnight.

The Wave, Sofitel Plaza, 2 Yen Phu. Along with the *New Century* (see above), *The Wave* is Hanoi's hottest nightclub, though in this case far more intimate, like a stylish lounge bar. In addition to the regular DJ, who has an eclectic musical taste, the club occasionally hosts local bands. Other attractions include pool, foozball, darts, all-night happy hour on Friday and Saturday (draught beer and soft drinks only) and, last but not least, no entry charge. 6pm–2am.

Z Café 17 Tong Dan. Regular live music and a pool hall straight out of *The Hustler* make this big, modern café-bar a hit with young Hanoians. 10am–11.30pm.

Traditional entertainment

While in Hanoi most people devote an hour one evening to the **water puppets**, *mua roi nuoc* – literally, puppets that dance on the water – a uniquely Vietnamese art form that originated in the Red River Delta (see p.533 for more background). Traditional performances consist of short scenes depicting rural life or historic events accompanied by mood-setting musical narration. By far the most popular, and most polished, of Hanoi's troupes is the Thang Long Water Puppet Troupe, which presents an updated repertoire and uses modern stage effects to create an engaging spectacle. They give several performances daily at the small, air-conditioned Kim Dong Theatre, 57 Dinh Tien Hoang (T04/824 5117; 5.55pm, 6.30pm, 8pm & 9.15pm, also Sun 9.30am; tickets $2.60 front rows, $1.30 behind, plus extra for camera or video). Though these shows are largely put on for tourists, you can't help but admire the artistry and be charmed by the puppets' antics.

Building on the success of the water puppets, the Hanoi Cheo Theatre group now gives nightly performances in a magical setting outside Den Ngoc Son on Hoan Kiem Lake – weather permitting (8pm; $1.30). **Cheo**, which also has its roots in the Red River Delta (see p.532 for more), is reminiscent of Chinese opera and therefore tolerably easy to get the gist of even if you can't understand the words. If that's whetted your appetite, you might like to check what's on at the Hong Ha Theatre, 15 Duong Thanh, or at the Hanoi Cheo Theatre itself at 15 Nguyen Dinh Chieu.

Apart from the **folk music** groups playing at the Temple of Literature (see p.381) and occasionally at the Museum of Ethnology (see p.384), at present these are the only easily accessible venues showcasing Vietnamese traditional culture in Hanoi. However, the situation is evolving rapidly under the auspices of the Vietnam Arts Resource and Information Centre, 32 Pho Hao Nam (☎04/511 6302, ✉mociford@hn.vnn.vn). Visits to the centre are by appointment only, but you can contact them by phone or email for the latest information.

Shopping and markets

When it comes to shopping for crafts, silk, accessories and souvenirs, Hanoi now offers the best overall in terms of choice, quality and value for money in the country. **Specialities** of the region are embroideries, sandalwood and stone carvings, inlay work and lacquer, and the best areas to browse are the south of the Old Quarter and the streets around St Joseph's Cathedral. Though smarter establishments increasingly have fixed prices, at most shops you'll be expected to **bargain** (see Basics, p.63, for some tips), and the same goes, naturally, for market stalls. Hanoi has over fifty **markets**, selling predominantly foodstuffs (see "Buying your own food", p.394); for a greater variety of wares, **Cho Dong Xuan** sells almost everything or try Cho Hang Da for clothes and brand-name foodstuffs. Cho Hom, on Pho Hué, is surrounded by **specialist shopping streets**: Tran Nhan Tong focuses on shirts and jackets, while Phung Khac Khoan, off Tran Xuan Soan, is a riot of colourful fabrics.

One of Hanoi's more unusual and colourful markets, though you'll have to be up early to catch it, is the **flower market** held each dawn beside Nghi Tam Avenue at its most northerly junction with Yen Phu; action starts around 5am (6am in winter), and lasts roughly an hour. This is primarily a wholesale market catering to the city's army of itinerant flower-sellers, so prices are that bit cheaper than in town and you'll find people peddling wicker baskets, ferns and ribbons besides bundles of fresh-cut blooms.

Fabrics, handicrafts and souvenirs

Compared with Thailand, Vietnamese **silk** is slightly inferior quality but prices are lower and the tailoring is great value, with awesome delivery times. So many silk shops are concentrated on Hang Gai, at the southern edge of the Old Quarter, that it's now referred to as "Silk Street"; competition is fierce, but take care since you'll find a fair amount of tat among the more reputable outlets (see p.399). Classy designer boutiques offering excellent quality at premium prices are also now concentrating around the cathedral. Most bigger places have multilingual staff, accept credit cards and offer more instant souvenirs as well, such as ties, purses, mobile-phone holders – very natty – and sensuous, silk sleeping bags.

Embroideries and drawn threadwork also make eminently packable souvenirs. Standard designs range from traditional Vietnamese to Santa Claus and robins, but you can also take along your own artwork for something different.

Both Tuyet Lan and Tan My (see below) have a reputation for quality and design, while many of the big-name silk and accessories shops also sell embroidered items.

One of the more interesting shops is Craft Link (see overleaf), run by a "not for profit" organization working with ethnic minorities and other small-scale producers of traditional **crafts**. They also organize events in combination with the Museum of Ethnology as well as a charity bazaar each November, which is a great occasion attended by many of the crafts people involved, including representatives from the minority villages.

Most ordinary souvenir shops also stock **ethnic minority crafts**, particularly the Hmong and Dao bags, coats and jewellery that are so popular in Sa Pa. Though it's virtually impossible to tell, in fact the majority of these are now made by factories in Hanoi, partly to meet the huge demand and partly to get a slice of the action. Of course, everyone will insist their goods are genuine, and they are very well made, but it's something to be aware of.

Another eminently portable souvenir is **lacquerware**. Chopsticks, boxes, bowls, vases – the variety of items coated in lacquer is endless. Natural lacquer gives a muted finish, usually in black or rusty reds. However, lacquerware in a rainbow array of colours – made from imported synthetic rather than natural lacquer – is now very popular in Old Quarter souvenir shops.

Other popular mementos are embroidered and printed **T-shirts**: although the selection is limited, you'll find no shortage of places to buy them, notably on Hang Gai and Trang Tien. **Silk lanterns**, **water puppets**, and **silver items** – both plated and solid silver – make manageable souvenirs, as do hand-painted **greetings cards**, usually scenes of rural life or famous beauty spots on paper or silk; the best are unbelievably delicate and sell for next to nothing. It's illegal to export **antiques** from Vietnam, but you'll find plenty of "antique" jewellery or watches on sale, and beautifully crafted copies of ancient religious statues; if you're tempted by anything that might be considered of "cultural or historic significance", even if you know it's a fake, it's best to get an export certificate (see Basics, p.65).

For more unusual mementos, have a look at the traditional Vietnamese **musical instruments** on sale at a clutch of little workshops on Hang Manh and round the corner on Hang Non. Several small shops on Hang Bong supply Communist Party **banners and badges** as well as Vietnamese flags. If you're into **army surplus** gear, hit the stretch of Le Duan south of the train station – for those nifty camouflage boxer shorts.

Clothes and accessories Kana, 41 Hang Trong, stocks fairly traditional Vietnamese designs, while it's all French chic at Song, 5 Nha Tho, and La Boutique, 6 Nha To & 15 Nha Chung. Indigo, 65 Ma May, is a fair-trade outlet selling a limited range of blue-dyed fabrics, clothes and bags. At the other end of the spectrum, Ipa-Nima, 59b Hai Ba Trung (@ipanima@ipanema.com), is famous for its way-out designs. Beautiful handmade silk clothes are available at Co, 18 Nha To (@conhatho@yahoo.com) and Marie-Linh, 1 & 74 Hang Trong (@www .marie-linh.com), while most of the silk shops and some of the embroidery shops listed below also sell ready-made clothes and accessories. If you want an *ao dai* run up, La Hang, 55 Tran Nhan Tong, is perhaps Hanoi's best-known traditional tailor. For hand-made jewellery, Decor, 112 Hang Bong, is worth a look, or you can buy beads, threads and clasps at Shen, 48 Hang Trong (@dexter@hn.vnn.vn), and craft your own.

Embroidery Tan My, 66 Hang Gai, has three floors packed with hand-embroidered bedlinen, table-coths and quilts, as well as ready-made silk items and fabrics; they also do tailoring. Tuyet Lan, 10 Ly Quoc Su (@www.tuyetlanembroidery.com), offers a range of traditional and contemporary designs and also has a lovely line in children's clothes.

Handicrafts Lan Handicrafts, 38 Nha Chung (@www.lan-handicrafts.com), is a not-for-profit outlet featuring goods made by young handicapped and disadvantaged Vietnamese. They specialize in quilts and other items made from silk or cotton patchwork, but also make greetings cards, toys and other imaginatively designed crafts.

Though not so portable, Vietnamese House, 92 Hang Bac (Ⓔvietnamesehouse@hn.vnn.vn), sells stone boxes and vases in attractive modern designs in addition to fine arts and antiques.

Interiors For elegant if pricey home accessories and gifts try L'Image, 34 Nha Chung (Ⓔimage@hn.vnn.vn); Mosaïque, 22 Nha Tho (Ⓔmosaique@fpt.vn); and Song, 7 Nha Tho. La Casa, 12 Nha Tho (Ⓦwww.lacasavietnam.com), sells unusual and upmarket household items from an Italian designer, while Nguyen Frères, 3 Phan Chu Trinh (Ⓔngttuanh@hcm.vnn.vn), specializes in high-end antique and reproduction furniture. For more modest budgets, a young Vietnamese designer showcases his work at 4 Seasons Art, 2a Ngo Bao Khanh (Ⓔcuong227@hotmail.com).

Lacquerware Minh Tam, 2 Hang Bong, use top-quality lacquer for their unusual designs, often incorporting eggshell to give a crazed finish. Another reliable outlet is Anh Duy Lacquer, 25 Hang Trong.

Minority crafts Craft Link, 43 Van Mieu (Ⓔcraftlink@hn.vnn.vn), is another not-for-profit organization working with small-scale producers of traditional crafts, particularly among the ethnic minorities. Other shops worth seeking out include Craft Window, 99 Nguyen Thai Hoc (Ⓦwww.craftwindow.com), and Tribal Pan Flutes, 42a Hang Bac, a real Aladdin's cave.

Musical instruments Browse the shops on Hang Manh, where Thai Khue Music Shop, at no. 1a, is a treasure-trove of inexpensive, unusual instruments.

Shoes To complete your outfit, Pinocchio, 129 Hang Bong, is the place to go for the most gorgeous handmade shoes with lacquered wooden soles and silk or leather uppers. Alternatively, most silk shops sell or will run you up a pair of dainty embroidered slippers.

Silk and tailoring Hanoi's most famous silk shops, Khai Silk, 121 Nguyen Thai Hoc (with branches at 96 Hang Gai and in the *Sofitel Metropole Hotel*; Ⓔkhaisilk@hn.vnn.vn), and Kenly Silk, 108 Hang Gai (Ⓦwww.kenlysilk.com), sell expensive but high-quality Vietnamese silks (raw, taffeta, satin and even knitted) as well as cotton and linen fabrics. They also sell ready-made clothes and have a reputation for reliable tailoring. Other places to try for both fabrics and tailoring include: Cocoon, 30 Nha Chung (Ⓔcocoonvn @hotmail.vn); F-Silk, 82 Hang Gai & 49 Hai Ba Trung; (Ⓔfsilk@hn.vnn.vn); Thanh Ha Silk, 114 Hang Gai & 46 Hang Trong (Ⓔthanhsilk@fpt.vn); and Tien Dung Silk Art, 51 Hang Gai (Ⓔthiendungsilk@fpt.vn).

Art galleries

As Vietnamese art continues to attract international recognition, so ever more **art galleries** appear on the streets of Hanoi. Many of these are no more than souvenir shops selling paintings of variable quality but usually at affordable prices, while many of the big galleries, such as Apricot Gallery, 40b Hang Bong (Ⓦwww.apricot–artvietnam.com), and Red River Gallery on Trang Tien, are essentially commercial concerns. However, there are a number of galleries showcasing more experimental work and promoting promising newcomers.

Art Gallery 2f/43 Trang Tien Ⓦwww .ceae-artgallery.com. Above a bookshop, this government-run gallery combines a small rental space, which may be showing something of interest, with a permanent display of contemporary and traditional art.

Art Vietnam 30 Hang Than Ⓦwww .vietnamesefineart.com. Stunning exhibition space on four floors featuring leading contemporary artists. Gallery owner Suzanne Lecht also organizes cultural events and arranges studio tours on request.

Co Do 46 Hang Bong Ⓦwww.codogallery.com. Relatively flash exhibition space on three floors with a strong showing of lacquer paintings, plus the occasional exhibition.

Duc's House on Stilts Dock 82, Duong Buoi, Ba Dinh District Ⓣ04/762 5452. Nguyen Manh Duc is one of Vietnam's most innovative installation and performance artists. His studio, a Muong stilt-house relocated from Hoa Binh, has become a focus for cutting-edge arts.

Gallery Salon des Beaux Arts 4 Xom Ha Hoi. Atmospheric setting for Vietnamese masters exhibited in an old villa.

Hanoi Studio 13 Trang Tien Ⓔhanoistudio@fpt .vn. Commercial gallery occasionally hosting interesting and well-displayed exhibitions promoting local artists.

Mai Gallery 3b Ngo Phan Huy Chin. Works by Vietnam's most interesting and important contemporary artists hidden away in an old villa in the backstreets.

Nam Son Gallery 41 Trang Tien. Leading contemporary arts gallery showing mainstream works under the auspices of the Ministry of Culture and

Information. Take time to admire the lovely old facade as well.

Salon Natasha 30 Hang Bong ⓦ www.artsalon-natasha.com. Pioneering private gallery, set up in 1990, where Russian-born Natasha and her artist husband Vu Dan Tan live, work and act as an informal meeting place for Hanoi's more experimental artists. Natasha also organizes studio visits on request.

Studio Mai Hien–Anh Khanh 99 Nguyen Thai Hoc. A famous painting couple share wall space in their second-floor gallery, at the back of the courtyard. They also now welcome visitors to their studio in Ngoc Thy Village, Gia Lam District (ⓉTEL04/827 1216); the Muong stilthouse in landscaped gardens makes a wonderful exhibition space and is also a centre for performance and installation art.

Studio Trinh Tuan–Cong Kim Hoa 2f/17 Ly Quoc Su ⓉTEL04/824 597. Vietnam's leading lacquer artists live and work in this small studio-gallery; telephone for an appointment.

Viet Fine Arts Gallery 96 Hang Trong ⓦ www.vietfinearts.com. Flash new gallery on three floors with changing exhibitions of well-known contemporary artists.

Vietnamese Fine Art Exhibition House 16 Ngo Quyen ⓔ huongxuyen@hn.vnn.vn. It's worth popping into this rental space to see what's on offer.

Listings

Airlines Aeroflot, 4 Trang Thi ⓉTEL04/825 6742; Air France, 1 Ba Trieu ⓉTEL04/825 3484; Cathay Pacific, 49 Hai Ba Trung ⓉTEL04/826 7298; China Airlines, 18 Tran Hung Dao ⓉTEL04/824 2688; China Southern Airlines, 360 Kim Ma ⓉTEL04/771 6611; Japan Air Lines, 63 Ly Thai To ⓉTEL04/826 6693; Lao Aviation, 269 Kim Ma ⓉTEL04/846 4573; Malaysia Airlines, 15 Ngo Quyen ⓉTEL04/826 8820; Pacific Airlines, 100 Le Duan ⓉTEL04/518 1503; SAS, 49 Hai Ba Trung ⓉTEL04/934 2626; Singapore Airlines, 17 Ngo Quyen ⓉTEL04/826 8888; Swiss, 44b Ly Thuong Kiet ⓉTEL04/934 4844; Thai International, 44b Ly Thuong Kiet ⓉTEL04/826 6893; Vietnam Airlines, 1 Quang Trung ⓉTEL04/825 0888.

Airport For flight information, call ⓉTEL04/886 6527.

Alliance française 24 Trang Tien (ⓉTEL04/942 2970, ⓦ www.ambafrance-vn.org; Mon–Fri 8am–noon & 2–5pm). Cultural programme of films, concerts and exhibitions, plus library, journals and TV room. Membership $6.50 (two photos and proof of identity required).

Banks and exchange The Vietcombank head office at 198 Tran Quang Khai (foreign exchange counter Mon–Fri 8am–6pm; all other services Mon–Fri 8am–3.30pm, Sat 9am–3pm) handles all services including cash withdrawals on credit cards and telegraphic transfers. Branches at 108 Cau Go, 23 Phan Chu Trinh, 2 Hang Bai and 78 Nguyen Du, amongst other locations, and 24hr ATMs currently at the headquarters, outside the General Post Office and Hanoi Towers, 49 Hai Ba Trung. ANZ Bank, 14 Le Thai To, also has a 24hr ATM for cash withdrawals using Visa and MasterCard, while Citibank, 17 Ngo Quyen, offers an ATM for Citibank card holders only. Sacombank, 87 Hang Bac (Mon–Sat 8am–7pm, Sun 8am–4pm), is not only open outside normal banking hours for foreign exchange, credit card advances and so forth, but also has a 24hr ATM (Visa and MasterCard only). Moneychangers in and around the GPO offer higher rates than banks, but will try to befuddle you with stacks of small denominations – watch out for notes folded to count twice, or better still don't risk it. Apart from the banks, you can change money at certain tour agents and at gold shops – the moneychanger at 31 Hang Trung is reliable and offers reasonable rates. If you have dong left at the end of your stay, you can swop them for dollars at the exchange bureaux in the arrivals hall; you'll need an exchange certificate or ATM receipt to prove you obtained the money legally and there's a $2 commission charge.

Bicycle and motorbike rental There are numerous outlets offering bicycles at well under $1 per day and motorbikes at around $4 or $5 a day along Hang Bac and Ta Hien in the Old Quarter; Cuong's Motorbike Adventure, 40 Luong Ngoc, Quyen; Nguyen Nghia, 26 Hang Bac, and Mr Dao, 42 Hang Bac, are recommended for reliable machines and reasonable rates. In the French Quarter, try Meeting Café, 59b Ba Trieu, or Memory Café, 33b Tran Hung Dao. You will usually be asked to leave your passport or departure card as surety when renting motorbikes; it's perfectly safe to do so.

Bike repair You'll find someone to repair pedal bikes on virtually every street corner. For motorbikes, Cuong at 40 Luong Ngoc Quyen is a biking fanatic who can repair anything, but has a soft spot for Minsks. He also buys, sells and rents bikes. You can pick up spare parts on Phu Doan, just behind the cathedral, and along Thinh Yen at the south end of Pho Hué, in what's known locally as "Thieves' Market".

Books and bookshops By far the best resources are Bookworm, 15a Ngo Van So, with a great selection of new and secondhand English-language books (for sale or exchange), and Love Planet Travel, 25 Hang Bac. The latter stocks over 6000 secondhand books in various languages for sale, exchange, or rent. Both shops also buy used books. Otherwise, there are several state-run bookshops on Trang Tien, of which Savina at no. 44, Hanoi Bookshop at no. 34 and Foreign Language Bookworld round the corner at 32 Hai Ba Trung have the widest choice. Stalls on Trang Tien also sell English-language publications, including pirated guides and phrase books, while

Moving on from Hanoi

For addresses and telephone numbers of airlines and foreign embassies in Hanoi, see "Listings" on pp.401 and 404 respectively.

Planes

The #7 city bus (every 15–20min between 5am and 9pm; 2hr; under $0.20), with stops on Trang Tien and around Hoan Kiem Lake, terminates at the **airport**, or you can take a Noi Bai Minibus (every 30min between 5am and 5.30pm; 45min; $2) from 2 Quang Trung, opposite the Vietnam Airlines office – it's wise to buy your tickets (and check the departure time) in advance. Tour operators and hotels will arrange a car for $8–10. Note that there's an **airport tax** of $14 levied on international departures. The tax on domestic flights is now usually included in the ticket price.

Trains

Tickets and **information** for the Reunification Express are available in the main station building, at 120 Le Duan, at the window marked "Booking Office for Foreigners" (daily 7.30am–12.30pm & 1–10.50pm) located in the hall to the left of the central lobby. It's best to make onward travel arrangements early, especially for sleeping berths to Hué and Ho Chi Minh City, as hard sleepers sell out several days in advance and soft sleepers one or two weeks in advance. There's a separate ticket window (daily 7am–noon & 12.30–7pm) in the right-hand hall for local trains and international services to China (see below for more on travel to China). China-bound trains leave from the main station, but all other services **to the east and north**, including Lao Cai and Haiphong, depart from a back station on Tran Quy Cap. Lao Cai trains are notorious for double-booking, so make sure you get there early to stake your claim. If you're having trouble getting hold of train tickets, it's worth trying the tour agents as they usually get their tickets from intermediaries who buy them in bulk.

Buses

Hanoi has three long-distance bus stations: for points **south**, head for Giap Bat station, 6km south of town on Giai Phong; most northeastern destinations, including **Lang Son** and **Cao Bang**, are served by Gia Lam station, 4km northeast of the centre; and buses to **Son La**, **Dien Bien Phu** and the northwest in general use Kim Ma station, just 2km out at the junction of Giang Vo and Kim Ma. This latter station is also where you'll pick up buses to **Haiphong** and express air-conditioned services to **Ha Long**. It's advisable to check at the station a day or two before you want to travel and to buy your ticket at the station rather than on the bus itself.

The ubiquitous **open-tour buses** make the trek down to **Hué** every night (information and tickets available from Hanoi Toserco and other tour agencies), but it's a long, uncomfortable journey and it's well worth forking out a bit extra for a sleeper on the train.

Travel to China and Laos

Land border crossings are now open between Vietnam and its northern neighbours. Visa regulations and entry formalities change frequently, so check the current situation with the relevant embassy.

most top-class hotels stock a few guides and glossy hardbacks in their souvenir shops. Kids also peddle books, postcards and maps in the Old Quarter and around Hoan Kiem Lake. Bargain hard.

British Council 40 Cat Linh (☎04/843 6780, ⓦ www.britishcouncil.org/vietnam/index.htm;

8.30am–noon & 1.30–5pm). Small selection of British periodicals and an information centre aimed at local Vietnamese learning English.

Business centres All the top hotels provide some facilities; the Press Club, 59a Ly Thai To (☎04/934 0888, ⓦ www.hanoi-pressclub.com) and Regus, 2f/3 Ly Thai To (☎04/934 4300,

The **China** border is currently open to foreigners at Lao Cai, Dong Dang (near Lang Son) and Mong Cai (see p.446, p.476 & p.436 respectively). Direct **train services** between Hanoi and Beijing (50hr) leave Hanoi on Tuesdays and Fridays at around 7pm, and Beijing on Mondays and Fridays; note that only soft-sleeper tickets are available and that it's best to book well in advance. In Vietnam you can board the train only in Hanoi, though you change to the Chinese air-conditioned train in Dong Dang, but across the border it's possible to stop off in Nanning, Guilin and so on. Fares are quoted in Swiss francs, in accordance with international rail agreements, and then converted into dong. You'll need your passport with a valid China visa when you buy the ticket. **Visas** are issued by the Chinese Embassy Consular Section at 46 Hoang Dieu (Mon–Fri 8.30–11am; ☎04/845 3736). A one-month tourist visa takes four working days to process and costs around $30, payable in dollars only. If you're in a hurry there's also a one-day express service available, costing $60.

There are currently two land crossings into **Laos**: via Lao Bao border gate, near Dong Ha (see p.333); and Cau Treo, to the west of Vinh (see p.333). Direct air-conditioned buses travel overnight from Hanoi to Vientiane via Cau Treo (19hr); contact Hanoi tour agents for tickets and further information. **Visas**, which must be arranged in advance for overland travel, can be issued in one day at the Lao Consulate at 22 Tran Binh Trong (Mon–Fri 8–noon & 1–4pm; ☎04/822 9084). Seven-day transit visas cost $30, while a regular one-month visa will set you back $50. Payment must be in dollars. Two-week visas are also available on arrival in **Vientiane airport** for $30.

Organized tours

Tour agencies in Hanoi (see p.363 & p.405) can put together **individual programmes** including vehicle rental, guide and accommodation, or whatever combination you want. This is a useful option to consider for touring the **northern provinces**, where travelling by public transport can be difficult and you'll have more freedom with your own vehicle.

Otherwise, the same agents offer organized **tours** following a **fixed itinerary**, which are often the cheapest and easiest way of exploring further afield. There's an increasingly wide range of options, not only as regards actual destinations, but also details such as the group size and the standard of transport and hotel, with prices that vary accordingly. The most popular of the **day-trips** on offer are the Perfume Pagoda (from $10) and Tam Coc–Bich Dong or Hoa Lu (from $12). **Longer excursions** to Ha Long Bay start at $15 for a two-day tour, rising to $40 plus for three days' cruising round the bay including a night on board plus a visit to Cat Ba National Park. Another tempting option in Sa Pa is **trekking**, since this is more difficult to organize independently. Most agents offer the standard four-day programme including the weekend market at Sa Pa or Bac Ha and walks to a couple of minority villages; prices start at $25 for a basic trip rising to $90 for better transport and accommodation or longer treks overnighting in the villages. Finally, **Mai Chau** trips offer a night in a stilthouse as part of a two-day excursion from $20.

See p.40 of Basics for tips on signing up for a tour in Vietnam.

Ⓦwww.regus.com), offer a range of services at a premium prices.

Car rental Cars with drivers can be arranged through tour and travel agencies (see pp.363 & 405).

Cinema The two main venues for English-language films (including local films subtitled in English) are the multi-screen National Cinema Centre, 87 Lang Ha (☎04/514 1789, or you'll find their programme in the English-language press), and Fansland, 84 Ly Thuong Kiet (☎04/942 4484). Hanoi Spirit Club, 50 Hang Be (☎04/826 7356), shows films on DVD free every night in the bar, and there are screenings of big international movies at the Press Club, 59a Ly Thai To (☎04/934 0888), every other Sunday at 7.30pm ($3.50), while the Alliance française (see above) has a regular programme of French-language films.

Courier services Couriers are mainly found near the GPO. Fedex is at 6 Dinh Le (☎04/824 9054) and DHL has an office at 1 Le Thach (☎08/844 6203).

Dentists The Hanoi Family Dental Clinic at A2 Van Phuc (☎04/823 0281; Mon–Fri 8.30am–12.30pm & 1.30–4.30pm; $35 initial consultation fee) also has a 24hr emergency service (☎0903 446 126). Alternatively, the Hanoi French Hospital and International SOS (see below) also provide dental care.

Embassies and consulates Australia, 8 Dao Tan, Van Phuc ☎04/831 7755; Cambodia, 71 Tran Hung Dao ☎04/942 4788; Canada, 31 Hung Vuong ☎04/823 5500; China, 46 Hoang Dieu ☎04/845 3736; Lao PDR, 22 Tran Binh Trong ☎04/822 9084; Malaysia, Fortuna Hotel, 6b Lang Ha ☎04/831 3400; Myanmar, A3 Van Phuc ☎04/845 3369; New Zealand, 63 Ly Thai To ☎04/824 1481; Singapore, 41–43 Tran Phu ☎04/823 3966; Thailand, 63–65 Hoang Dieu ☎04/823 5092; UK, 4f/31 Hai Ba Trung ☎04/936 0500; US, 7 Lang Ha ☎04/772 1500. For information on visas to China and Laos, see p.402.

Emergencies Dial ☎113 to call the police, ☎114 in case of fire and ☎115 for an ambulance; better still, get a Vietnamese-speaker to call on your behalf.

Export licences for antiques and other items of "cultural or historical significance" are issued by the Ministry of Culture and Information. Apply to 47 Hang Dau.

Goethe Institute 54–56 Hang Duong (☎04/923 0035). Cultural and social activities.

Hospitals and clinics The Hanoi French Hospital, 1 Phuong Mai, offers international-class facilities at prices that aren't too extortionate – at least for the base-level service. As well as an outpatients

clinic (☎04/574 0740; Mon–Fri 8am–4pm, Sat 8–11am; $40–55 consultation), they provide dental and optical care, surgery and a 24hr emergency and ambulance service (☎504/74 1111). Alternatively, the Hanoi Family Practice, Room 109–112, A1 Van Phuc, is well known for its sympathetic pricing: it has an outpatients clinic (☎04/843 0748; Mon–Fri 8.30am–5.30pm, Sat 8.30am–12.30pm; $50 standard consultation fee) and 24hr emergency service (☎0903 401 919). The emergency assistance company, International SOS, at 31 Hai Ba Trung, also provides routine care to members and travellers (☎04/934 0555; Mon–Fri 8am–7pm, Sat 8am–noon; $55–65 consultation fee). Of the local hospitals, best bet is the Viet Duc Hospital at 14 Phu Doan (☎04/825 3531) which has some English-speaking doctors and consultation fees starting at $15.

Immigration department The Hanoi office of the Department of Immigration is at 89 Tran Hung Dao.

Internet access Numerous outlets in the Old Quarter travellers' enclave come and go. Best of the bunch at the time of writing are Amazon Internet Café at 15 Hang Non, Café Kim at 20 Hang Non and, in the French Quarter, Song Pho Internet Café at 60 Tho Nhuom. The going rate is around 3000d per hour.

Language courses The Vietnamese Language Centre of Hanoi Foreign Language College, 1 Pham Ngu Lao (☎04/826 2468), offers practical instruction from $7 per hour. The centre also arranges student exchanges and student visas.

Laundry Most hotels and guesthouses have a laundry service, while top hotels also offer dry cleaning. Alternatively, try one of the low-priced laundries (*giat la*) at 9 Luong Ngoc Quyen, 59 Hang Be, 39 Ma May or along Ta Hien; the standard rate is about $1 per kilo for a one-day service.

Newspapers and magazines A decent selection of foreign-language papers and magazines is on sale at the Hanoi Bookshop (see p.402) and other outlets on Trang Tien, outside the GPO, and in top-class hotels of which the *Nikko* and *Sofitel Metropole* offer the best range, or try the Press Club, 59a Ly Thai To.

Pharmacies The Hanoi Family Practice, Hanoi French Hospital and International SOS (see "Hospitals and clinics", above) all have pharmacies. Of the local retail outlets, those at 3 Trang Thi, 2 Hang Bai and 119 Hang Gai stock a wide selection of imported medicines. Traditional medicines can be bought on Lan Ong, or try the National Institute of Traditional Medicine, 26 Nguyen Binh Khiem (☎04/943 1018), with English-speaking staff.

Photography Print film and developing is readily available around town; the quality is fine for most purposes but keen photographers will probably want to save developing their film until they get home. Slide film is harder to find but Nguyen Long at 17a Ba Trieu is is a reliable source, and also has a good reputation for camera repairs.

Post offices The GPO occupies a whole block at 75 Dinh Tien Hoang (daily 6.30am–9.30pm). The main entrance leads to general mail and telephone services, while international postal services, including parcel dispatch (Mon–Fri 7.30–11.30am & 1–4.30pm), are located in the southernmost hall, with poste restante next door. Useful sub-post offices are at 66 Trang Tien, 66 Luong Van Can, 20 Bat Dan, 38 Quang Trung and on the ground floor of the Hanoi Towers at 49 Hai Ba Trung.

Sports and activities All the five-star hotels have swimming pools and fitness centres which are usually open to non-residents for a daily fee. The *Army Hotel*'s large, open-air salt-water pool ($3.50 to non-guests) is popular in summer, or better still head out to the Sao Mai pool, 10 Dang Thai Mai (June–mid Sept daily 6am–8.30pm; $1), located in the *Ho Tay Peninsula Villa and Serviced Apartments* complex beside West Lake. Hanoi now has a couple of golf driving ranges in the southwestern suburbs: Thang Long Golf, 17 Ngoc Khanh (☎04/846 3095), and Lang Ha Driving Range, 16a Lang Ha (☎04/835 0909). The eighteen-hole King's Island Golf Course, 45km west of Hanoi at Dong Mo in Ha Tay Province (☎034/834666), is open to non-

members on weekdays. Information regarding runs organized by Hanoi Hash House Harriers is available on their web site (🌐 www.hhhh.wso.net) or at the Spotted Cow pub (see p.397). For the less energetic, foot massages are now all the rage. You can treat yourself at Thanh Gia, 2f/38 Le Thai To (☎04/828 8196); an hour's massage costs $5. Finally, the Minsk Club (🌐 www.minskclubvietnam .com) occasionally arranges one-off excursions and other events; contact *Highway 4* restaurant (see p.390) or Cuong's Motorbike Adventure (see p.401) for the latest.

Taxis Reliable, metered taxis wait outside the big hotels, or try calling CP Taxi (☎04/826 2626), Hanoi Taxi (☎04/853 5353) or Noi Bai Taxi (☎04/873 3333). A taxi ride to the airport costs $10.

Tour agents In addition to places listed on p.363, mainstream tour agents with a solid reputation include: Ann Tours, 18 Duong Thanh (☎04/923 1366, ✉ anntours@yahoo.com); Explorer Tours, 75 Hang Bo (☎04/923 0713, 🌐 www.explorevietnam.net); ODC Travel, 43 Hang Bo (☎04/828 8729, ✉ odctravel@hn.vnn.vn); Rainbow Tours, 80 Tran Nhat Duat (☎04/928 3008, 🌐 www.rainbowvietnam.com); and upscale operator Exotissimo, 26 Tran Nhat Duat (☎04/828 2150; 🌐 www.exotissimo.com). Student specialist New Indochina, 4c Dang Thai Than (☎04/933 0599, ✉ new-indochina@fpt.vn), provides services for STA ticket-holders.

Around Hanoi

The **Red River** slides across its delta like a "great warm stream of tomato soup", as the journalist James Cameron put it, along the way feeding brick kilns, rich farmland and the country's most densely populated provinces. Though the northern delta barely makes it above sea level, it's been canalized and cultivated for so many centuries that there's little water in evidence. The landscape is criss-crossed with ancient dykes, averaging a massive 14m high, and is studded with temples, pagodas, churches, family graves, communal houses and all the other leftovers of successive generations.

At least one journey out of Hanoi into delta country is recommended for the experience. There are no absolutely compelling sights, although the cave-shrine of

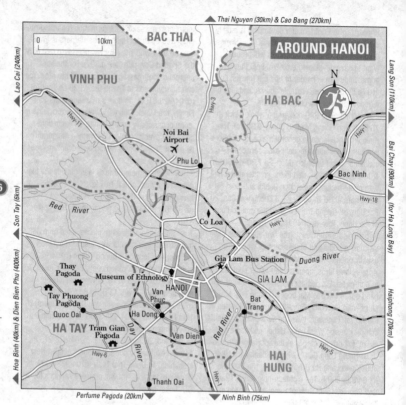

Around Hanoi map showing: Bac Thai, Vinh Phu, Ha Bac, Thai Nguyen (30km) & Cao Bang (270km), Lao Cai (240km), Lang Son (110km), Bai Chay (90km) (for Ha Long Bay), Hwy-11, Hwy-3, Hwy-1, Noi Bai Airport, Phu Lo, Bac Ninh, Hwy-18, Red River, Co Loa, Son Tay (6km), Museum of Ethnology, Gia Lam Bus Station, Duong River, Gia Lam, Haiphong (70km), Thay Pagoda, HANOI, Bat Trang, Tay Phuong Pagoda, Van Phuc, Ha Dong, Quoc Oai, Ha Tay, Tram Gian Pagoda, Hoa Binh (40km) & Dien Bien Phu (400km), Van Dien, Day River, Red River, Hai Hung, Hwy-6, Hwy-5, Thanh Oai, Perfume Pagoda (20km), Ninh Binh (75km)

the **Perfume Pagoda** is one of the country's most sacred locations. It's without doubt the most popular day-trip from Hanoi, though some people may find that the low-key nature of the grotto itself coupled with the long climb and barrage of hawkers en route ultimately make for a bit of a let-down. Of more appeal are the dozens of historic buildings, of which the most strongly atmospheric are the **Thay Pagoda** and **Tay Phuong Pagoda**, buried deep in the delta, both of which are fine examples of traditional Vietnamese architecture. You could spend months exploring the delta's villages – in particular the **craft villages**, which remain more traditional than most you'll find in Vietnam, concentrating on one craft, such as embroidery, conical hats or noodle-making, to the exclusion of all else. These villages are difficult to get to on your own, but **Bat Trang** pottery village is an interesting example within easy striking distance of Hanoi; for the rest you'll really need to take a guide. Finally, **Co Loa**, an ancient citadel just north of the Red River, makes a worthwhile half-day jaunt from Hanoi, mostly on account of its historical significance since there's little to recall its former grandeur.

The Perfume Pagoda

Sixty kilometres southwest of Hanoi the Red River Delta ends abruptly where steep-sided limestone hills rise from the paddy fields. The most easterly of these forested spurs shelters north Vietnam's most famous pilgrimage site, the **Perfume Pagoda**, Chua Huong, hidden in the folds of Ha Tay Province's

Mountain of the Perfumed Traces, and said to be named after spring blossoms that scent the air. The easiest and most popular way to visit the pagoda is on a **day tour** out of Hanoi for $10–30, including lunch and entry fees (see p.403), or with a hired **car** and driver. Alternatively, it's a two- to three-hour **motorbike** ride: follow Highway 6 through Ha Dong as far as the fourteen-kilometre marker where the highway crosses the rail tracks, then turn left on the QL21B heading due south, through Thanh Oai and Van Dinh, to find Duc Khe Village and the Suoi Yen (Yen River) boat station. There's a sightseeing **fee** of $1.60, which includes the return boat trip and entrance to pagodas.

You'll find a few rather overpriced **food stalls** at the boat station and also where the boats drop you at the start of the walk to Chua Thien Chu (see below). At the latter you can expect to pay around $2 for a mediocre meal, but beware the extortionate prices charged for the drinks. A better option is to take your own.

The Perfume Pagoda, one of more than thirty peppering these hills, occupies a spectacular **grotto** over 50m high, the final destination of the hot and not particularly interesting walk up the mountain. The start of the journey is more appealing, a tranquil hour's boat ride up a silent, flooded valley among karst hills where fishermen and farmers work their inundated fields. On the way, it's traditional to offer prayers at Den Trinh, a seventeenth-century temple – last reconstructed in 1951 and renovated in 1997 – erected in honour of the Trinh lords who contributed substantially to developing the main complex. Then, from where the boat finally drops you, a stone-flagged path shaded by gnarled frangipani trees brings you to the seventeenth-century Chua Thien Chu ("Pagoda Leading to Heaven"), in front of which stands a magnificent, triple-roofed bell pavilion. Quan Am, Goddess of Mercy, takes pride of place on the pagoda's main altar; the original bronze effigy was stolen by Tay Son rebels in the 1770s and some say they melted it down for cannonballs (note that respectful attire – long trousers and long-sleeve shirts – is required for entry to Chua Thien Chu). To the right of the pagoda as you face it a **path** leads steeply uphill to the Perfume Pagoda, also dedicated to Quan Am. It's a good idea to bring bottled water for the three-kilometre walk (1–2hr), or put yourself at the mercy of the kids who tag along, lugging cool-boxes of overpriced but very welcome cold cans, though you can also buy refreshing glasses of freshly mangled sugar-cane juice and whole coconuts from stalls along the route. The main grotto reveals itself as a gaping cavern on the side of a deep depression filled with vines and trees reaching for light beneath the inscription "supreme cave under the southern sky". A flight of 120 steps descends into the dragon's-mouth-like entrance where gilded Buddhas emerge from dark recesses wreathed in clouds of incense – a torch comes in handy at this point.

This route is now so well trodden that some people have reported that guides can be rather apathetic about the climb and try to take tourists to smaller pagodas – if you've paid to see the Perfume Pagoda then make sure your guide takes you all the way up there. However, note that the hike is hard going and can be highly treacherous on the descent during wet weather; you'll need good walking shoes and plenty of water, especially in the hot summer months. Other travellers report being hassled aggressively by boat women expecting tips. A tip is discretionary, not mandatory, as the boat trip is included in the ticket price. If you want to give something, just a few thousand dong is sufficient. Finally, it's advisable to steer clear of the Perfume Pagoda during the **festival months** of March and April (from the sixth day of the second lunar month to the end of the third month) when thousands of people flock here to purify themselves at Chua Thien Chu before filing slowly up the mountain, greeting other pilgrims with *Nam mo A Di Da Phat* ("praise to Amitabha Buddha").

Thay Pagoda (the Master's Pagoda)

Thay Pagoda (Chua Thay) or the **Master's Pagoda** – also known as Thien Phuc Tu ("Pagoda of the Heavenly Blessing") – was founded in the reign of King Ly Nhan Tong (1072–1127) and is an unusually large complex fronting onto a picturesque lake in the lee of a limestone crag. Thay Pagoda lies 30km from Hanoi in Sai Son Village, between Ha Dong and Son Tay. As this isn't a popular tour destination, you'll probably need to hire a **car** and driver for the excursion, or rent a **motorbike**. The easiest route is via Highway 6, taking a right turn in front of Ha Dong post office (*buu dien*) onto the TL72/TL80 to Quoc Oai, where the pagoda is signed 4km off to the right. The small entry **fee** includes one of the pagoda's unusually knowledgeable English-speaking guides; note that this is a popular weekend jaunt out of Hanoi, at its busiest on Sundays.

The Master was the ascetic monk and healer **Tu Dao Hanh** (sometimes also known as Minh Khong) who "burned his finger to bring about rain and cured diseases with holy water", in addition to countless other miracles. He was head monk of the pagoda and an accomplished water puppeteer – hence the lake's dainty theatre-pavilion – and, according to legend, was reincarnated first as a Buddha and then as the future King Ly Than Tong in answer to King Ly Nhan Tong's prayers for an heir. To complicate matters further, Ly Than Tong's life was then saved by the monk Tu Dao Hanh. Anyway, the Thay Pagoda is dedicated to the cult of Tu Dao Hanh in his three incarnations as monk (the Master), Buddha, and king.

Despite many restorations over the centuries, the pagoda's dark, subdued interior retains a powerful atmosphere. Nearly a hundred **statues** fill the prayer halls: the oldest dates back to the pagoda's foundation, but the most eye-catching are two seventeenth-century giant **guardians** made of clay and papier-mâché, which weigh a thousand kilos apiece and are said to be the biggest in Vietnam. Beyond, the highest altar holds a Buddha trinity, dating from the 1500s, and a thirteenth-century wooden statue of the Master as a bodhisattva, dressed in yellow garb and perched on a lotus throne. On a separate altar to the left he appears again as King Ly Than Tong, also in yellow, accompanied by two dark-skinned, kneeling figures which are said to be Cambodian slaves, while to the right sits a mysterious, lavishly decorated wooden chamber. The monk's mortal remains and a statue with articulated legs repose in this final, securely locked sanctuary – though a photo on the altar shows the statue's beady eyes staring out of a gaunt, unhappy face – to be revealed only once a year: at 1pm on the fifth day of the third lunar month the village's oldest male bathes Tu Dao Hanh with fragrant water and helps him to his feet. Traditionally, this event was for the monks' eyes only, but nowadays anyone can see, as long as they're prepared to put up with the scrum. The celebrations, attended by thousands, continue for three days and include daily processions as well as a famous **water- puppet festival** held on the lake (fifth to seventh days of the third lunar month).

In front of the pagoda are two attractive, covered bridges with arched roofs built in 1602 and dedicated to the sun and moon: one leads to an islet where spirits of the earth, water and sky are worshipped in a diminutive Taoist temple; the second takes you to a well-worn flight of steps up the limestone hill. When Tu Dao Hanh was near death he followed the same route up to Thanh Hoa cave, now a sacred place hidden behind a screen of aerial banyan roots which lies between a mini-pagoda and a temple dedicated to the monk's parents. Though the sanctuaries themselves are well tended, there's nothing special to see beyond expansive views of a typical delta landscape over the pagoda roofs.

Tay Phuong Pagoda and Tram Gian Pagoda

Only 6km west of the Thay Pagoda (see above), the much smaller "Pagoda of the West", **Tay Phuong Pagoda**, perches atop a fifty-metre-high limestone hillock supposedly shaped like a buffalo. Among the first pagodas built in Vietnam, Tay Phuong's overriding attraction is its invaluable collection of over seventy jackfruit-wood **statues**, some of which are on view at Hanoi's Fine Arts Museum (see p.380). The highlights are eighteen arhats, disturbingly lifelike representations of Buddhist ascetics as imagined by eighteenth-century sculptors, grouped around the main altar; again, a torch would help pick out the finer details. As Tay Phuong is also an important Confucian sanctuary, disciples of the sage are included on the altar, each carrying a gift to their master, some precious object, a book or a symbol of longevity, alongside the expected Buddha effigies. Tay Phuong's most notable **architectural features** are its heavy double roofs, whose graceful curves are decorated with phoenixes and dragons, its unplastered brick walls and an inviting approach via 237 time-worn, red-brick steps. Hawkers from the nearby village peddle the local speciality sweetmeat, *banh che lam*, made of sticky rice pounded together with green bean and sugar.

With time to spare, you could combine a day's outing to the Thay and Tay Phuong pagdoas with a quick detour to the **Tran Gian Pagoda**, roughly 7km south of Quoc Oai Village and 3km from Highway 6; if you're coming from Hanoi, the pagoda's signed to the right of the highway at the kilometre 22 marker. Again, the large, peaceful temple sitting on a wooded hill is best known for its rich array of statuary. Though not as fine as those of Tay Phuong, they number over 150, including more arhats in the side corridors, alongside some toe-curling depictions of the underworld, and an impressive group on the main altar. Among them sits the unmistakable, pot-bellied laughing Maitreya, the carefree Buddha, in stark contrast to the black emaciated figure behind him. According to legend, this is the mumified and lacquered body of Duc Thanh Boi (St Boi), who was born nearby in the thirteenth century. He is credited with numerous miracles, including the ability to fly, and with saving the country from a catastrophic drought by summoning rain, though he had to wait for sainthood until a century after his death when devotees disinterred his body to find it in a perfect state of preservation.

The craft villages

For centuries villages around Vietnam's major towns have specialized in single-commodity production, initially to supply the local market, and sometimes going on to win national fame for the skill of their artisans. A few communities continue to prosper, of which the best-known near Hanoi are **DONG KY** woodcarving village (Ha Bac Province), Bat Trang pottery village and Van Phuc for silk. These are well-run, commercial operations where family units turn out fine, hand-crafted products, and are used to foreigners coming to watch them at work, even setting up salesrooms. Most other villages are far less touristy, and the more isolated tend to treat all visitors with suspicion. Nevertheless, it's worth taking a guide for the day to gain a rare glimpse into a gruelling way of life that continues to follow the ancient rhythms, using craft techniques handed down the generations virtually unchanged.

BAT TRANG, across the Red River in Hanoi's Gia Lam District, is an easy jaunt by road over the Chuong Duong toll bridge, then first right along the levy; note that pedal cyclists have to use Long Bien Bridge, a couple of kilometres further north. After 10km heading generally south, a right turn indicates the village entrance. A return trip by **xe om** should cost under $7 including waiting time.

Bat Trang has been producing **bricks** and **earthenware** since the fifteenth century, and the oldest part of the village beside the river has a medieval aura, with its narrow, high-walled alleys spattered with handmade coal-pats (used as fuel in the kilns) drying in the sun; to reach this area, turn right at the end of the main street and then work your way generally northwest. Through tiny doorways, you catch glimpses of courtyards stacked with moulds and hand-painted pots, while all around rise the squat brick chimneys of the village's eight hundred kilns. Around two thousand families live in Bat Trang, producing traditional, bright cobalt-blue **ceramics** from small workshops as well as mass-produced plant pots and highly glazed banisters for Hanoi's building boom. The village has expanded and there are signs of new wealth everywhere, most notably flashy villas popping up on back alleys, but success has also brought its problems: increasing air pollution and a steady rise in respiratory infections over recent years. Showrooms along the main drag all offer a similar stock and price range and will arrange to export pieces on your behalf. Prices are not necessarily any cheaper than in Hanoi itself, though the choice is superior.

The silk village of **VAN PHUC**, 11km west of Hanoi on Highway 6, is often included as a quick stop on trips to the Perfume Pagoda or can be combined with visits to the Thay and Tay Phuong pagodas (see opposite) – the village is about a kilometre north of Ha Dong post office on the Quoac Hai road. Once through the entrance arch, the clatter of electric looms from the thirty-odd workshops fills the air. You're welcome to wander into any of them, and will be given a brief explanation, but there's nothing much to detain you unless you're shopping for silk. Material is a shade cheaper than in Hanoi, while finished items such as scarves and clothes can be as little as half the price.

Further west, conical hats are the staple product of **CHUONG** Village (also known as Phuong Trung) which lies just off highway 21B a couple of kilometres south of Thanh Oai on the road to the Perfume Pagoda (see p.406). It's best to visit on market days (held six times each lunar month), when hats are piled high in golden pyramids. At other times it's possible to see artisans deftly assembling the dried leaves on a bamboo frame. Traditionally the designs varied according to the different needs: thick and robust for working in the fields, more delicate for outings to the temple and other special occasions, and flat, ornamented hats for fashion-conscious aristocrats. Nowadays the vast majority of families produce the basic conical hat for everyday wear, though two still specialise in the more elaborate designs demanded by theatre and dance troupes.

Most Hanoi tour agents offer organized **day-trips** to a selection of craft villages for around $15 to $25 per person. Note that a few villages levy a small entry fee.

Co Loa Citadel

The earliest independent Vietnamese states grew up in the Red River flood plain, atop low hills or crouched behind sturdy embankments. First to emerge from the mists of legend was Van Lang, presided over by the Hung kings from a knob of high ground, marked today by a few dynastic temples north of Viet Tri (Vinh Phu Province). Then the action moved closer to Hanoi when King An Duong ruled Au Lac (258–207 BC) from an immense citadel at **CO LOA** (Old Snail City), 16km due north of the present capital. These days the once massive earthworks are barely visible and it's really only worth stopping off here in passing, to take a look at a couple of quiet temples with an interesting history.

King An Duong built his citadel inside three concentric ramparts, spiralling like a snail shell, separated by moats large enough for ships to navigate; the outer wall was 8km long, 6 to 8m wide and at least 4m high, topped off with bamboo fencing. After the Chinese invaded in the late second century BC, Co Loa was abandoned until 939 AD, when Ngo Quyen established the next period of independent rule from the same heavily symbolic site. Archeologists have found rich pickings at Co Loa, including 20,000 iron arrowheads, displayed in Hanoi's History Museum (see p.375), which lend credence to at least one of the Au Lac legends. The story goes that the sacred Golden Turtle gave King An Duong a magic crossbow made from a claw that fired thousands of arrows at a time. A deceitful Chinese prince married An Duong's daughter, Princess My Chau, persuaded her to show him the crossbow and then stole the claw before mounting an invasion. King An Duong and his daughter were forced to flee, whereupon My Chau understood her act of betrayal and nobly told her father to kill her. When the king beheaded his daughter and threw her body in a well, she turned into lustrous, pink pearls.

Co Loa's **temple complex** (daily 8am–5pm; $1) is signposted to the right of busy Highway 3, down a tree-lined road running beside what looks just like any other delta embankment though it's said to be a remnant of the fortifications. First thing you come to after a couple of kilometres is an archer's statue; turn left here (west) to find the principal temple, **Den An Duong Vuong**, facing a refurbished lake, with a graceful stele-house to one side. Inside the temple, a sixteenth-century black-bronze statue of the king resides on the main altar, resplendent in his double crown, while a subsidiary altar is dedicated to Kim Quy, the Golden Turtle. More interesting, however, is the second group of buildings, 100m north of the archer, where a large, walled courtyard contains a beautifully simple open-sided hall, furnished with huge, ironwood pillars, and the princess's small temple, **Den My Chau**. Here she is honoured in the surprising form of a dumpy, armchair-shaped stone clothed in embroidered finery and covered in jewels but lacking a head.

Travel details

Trains

Hanoi to: Da Nang (5 daily; 14–20hr); Dong Dang (2 daily; 5hr); Dong Ha (4 daily; 12–16hr); Dong Hoi (5 daily; 9–13hr); Haiphong (3 daily; 2–3hr); Ho Chi Minh City (5 daily; 30–41hr); Hué (5 daily; 11–17hr); Lao Cai (3 daily; 8–9hr); Ninh Binh (2 daily; 2hr 30min); Thanh Hoa (4 daily; 3–4hr); Vinh (4 daily; 5hr 30min–7hr).

Flights

Hanoi to: Da Nang (4 daily; 1hr 15min–1hr 45 min); Dien Bien Phu (1 daily; 1hr); Ho Chi Minh City (10–11 daily; 2hr); Hué (2–3 daily; 1hr 10min–1hr 40min); Nha Trang (1 daily; 2hr).

Buses

It's almost impossible to give the **frequency** with which buses run. Long-distance public buses, though scheduled, won't depart if empty. Moreover, private services, often aged minibuses, ply more popular routes, and depart only when they have enough passengers to make the journey worthwhile. Highway 1 sees a near-constant stream of buses passing through to various destinations, and it's possible to flag something down at virtually any time of the day. Off the highway, to be sure of a bus it's advisable to start your journey early – most long-distance departures are between 5am and 9am, and very few run after midday. **Journey times** can also vary; figures below show the normal length of time you can expect to take by public bus.

Hanoi to: Bai Chay (3hr); Cao Bang (10hr); Haiphong (2hr); Hoa Binh (2hr); Hué (20hr); Lang Son (2–3hr); Mai Chau (3hr 30min); Ninh Binh (2hr); Son La (12hr); Thai Nguyen (3hr); Thanh Hoa (4–5hr).

Ha Long Bay and the northern seaboard

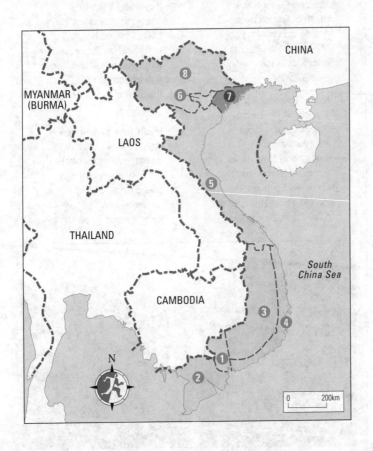

CHAPTER 7

Highlights

* **Haiphong's colonial architecture** Fine examples include the imposing theatre, for which all materials were shipped from France. See p.420

* **Cruising Ha Long Bay** Passing through the maze of limestone pinnacles that punctuate the turquoise water is an unmissable experience. See p.428

* **Hang Thien Cung** The "Grotto of the Heavenly Palace" is the most impressive cave to visit in Ha Long Bay; its liquid contours illuminated by coloured lights make it look like something from a fairy tale. See p.431

* **Cat Ba** With its cluttered harbour, beaches and trekking routes through the nearby national park, this is the best place to base yourself in the region. See p.425

* **Kayaking** Trips to secluded regions of Ha Long Bay are beginning to appear on tour operators' itineraries, allowing you to paddle through the surreal landscape. See p.430

* **Hydrofoils** Linking the region's main coastal towns, hydrofoils offer not only a smooth and speedy ride, but also fabulous views of the karst scenery. See p.435

Ha Long Bay and the northern seaboard

The mystical scenery of **Ha Long Bay** is what draws people to the northeast coast of Vietnam. Thousands of limestone islands jut out of the emerald sea, sculpted into such bizarre shapes as to invite comparisons with anything from chickens and dragons to champagne corks or General de Gaulle's nose. Navigating the silent, secretive channels, past bobbing clusters of fishing boats, and stopping to scramble through caves or swim beneath overhanging cliffs are some of the highlights of a trip to Vietnam. The tourist hordes are easily swallowed up in the bay's generous proportions – though **Bai Chay**, the usual jumping-off point, copes less well and a rapidly spreading zone of mini-hotels detracts from what used to be a pleasantly old-fashioned seaside resort, complete with boulevards, parks and sea-view rooms. Neighbouring **Hong Gai** is a complete contrast: an industrious town with limited tourist facilities, dedicated to fishing, coal and a profitable cross-border trade, though there's still nearly 150km to go, via the grim mining town of **Cam Pha**, to the booming markets of **Mong Cai** and the quiet beach at **Tra Co** near the Chinese border. However, hydrofoil services along the coast now make travel in this region uncharacteristically smooth.

Further back down the coast, **Haiphong** is north Vietnam's second largest city and its only major port. Broach its industrial outskirts and the city reveals a surprisingly agreeable centre with a cluster of nineteenth-century architecture that merits a stopover, and perhaps a visit to **Do Son Beach**. Most travellers, though, are merely passing through on the way to **Cat Ba Island**, lying just off the coast. From **Cat Ba Town**, the southeastern waters of Ha Long Bay are within easy reach and it's worth considering as an alternative base to Bai Chay for touring the bay. The island itself offers some fine scenery as well as being home to **Cat Ba National Park**, a forest and maritime reserve requiring the usual mix of luck and dedication to see anything larger than a mosquito. Hotels are springing up in the town as islanders cotton on to tourism, and it can get very crowded between June and August, but the bustling harbour retains a certain authenticity, and a coracle ride around the bay presents a fascinating glimpse of the waterborne communities.

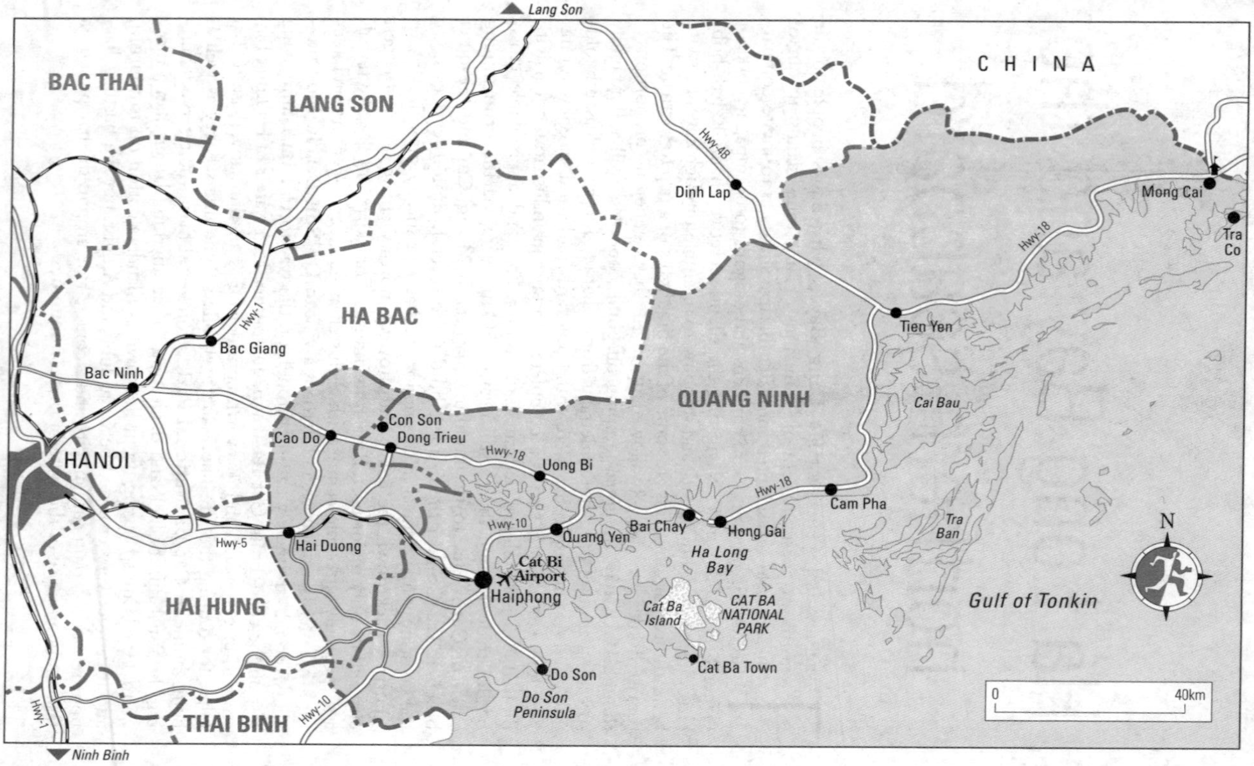
Lang Son
CHINA
BAC THAI
LANG SON
HA BAC
QUANG NINH
HAI HUNG
THAI BINH
HANOI
Bac Ninh
Bac Giang
Hwy-1
Dinh Lap
Hwy-4B
Mong Cai
Tra Co
Hwy-18
Tien Yen
Cai Bau
Tra Ban
Cao Do
Con Son
Dong Trieu
Uong Bi
Cam Pha
Bai Chay
Hong Gai
Quang Yen
Hwy-10
Hai Duong
Hwy-5
Cat Bi Airport
Haiphong
Ha Long Bay
Cat Ba Island
CAT BA NATIONAL PARK
Cat Ba Town
Do Son
Do Son Peninsula
Gulf of Tonkin
N
0
40km
Ninh Binh

Haiphong

Traffic heading out of Hanoi to the northeast coast funnels over the rust-coloured waters of the Red River on Highway 1 and then branches east on Highway 5 across the northern delta's most prolific rice fields. Container trucks pound the highway, squeaking past bicycles and buffalo carts, on the way to **HAIPHONG**, where a vast, smoke-belching cement factory dominates the outskirts. But Haiphong isn't to be written off so easily and it comes as a pleasant surprise to find in the centre of this still moderately small, orderly city an older district with low-key sites and subtle charms, shaded by ranks of flame trees. Broad avenues of well-tended colonial villas add to the impression of quiet prosperity and the city has a cosmopolitan flavour, evident in a profusion of import–export companies and suited businessmen in hotel lobbies talking deals and joint ventures.

Some history

Haiphong lies 100km from Hanoi on the Cua Cam River, one of the main channels of the Red River Estuary. Originally a small **fishing village** and military outpost, its development into a **major port** in the seventeenth century stems more from its proximity to the capital city than from favourable local conditions. In fact it was an astonishingly poor choice for a harbour, 20km from the open sea with shallow, shifting channels, no fresh water and little solid land. The first quay was only built in 1817 and it was not until 1874, when Haiphong was ceded to the French, that a town began to develop. With remarkable determination, the first settlers drained the mosquito-ridden marshes, sinking foundations sometimes as deep as 30m into huge earth platforms that passed for building plots. Doubts about the harbour lingered but then in 1883 the 9000-strong **French Expeditionary Force**, sent to secure Tonkin, established a supply base in Haiphong and its future as the north's principal port was secured.

By 1910 Haiphong, Hanoi and the markets of southern China were connected by rail, and industries began to develop along the Cua Cam River, fed by coal from Cam Pha, but it was not until November 1946 that Haiphong reappeared in the history books. Rising tensions between French troops and soldiers of the newly declared Democratic Republic of Vietnam erupted in a dispute about customs control when shots were exchanged over a Chinese junk suspected of smuggling. The French replied with a **naval bombardment** of Haiphong's Vietnamese quarter, killing hundreds of civilians (estimates range from one to six thousand), and only regained control of the streets after several days of rioting. But the two nations were now set for war – a war that ended, appropriately, with the citizens of Haiphong watching the last colonial troops embark in 1955 after the collapse of French Indochina.

Merely a decade later the city was again under siege, this time by American planes targeting one of the few industrial centres in North Vietnam and a major supply route for Soviet "aid". In May 1972 President Nixon ordered the **mining of Haiphong harbour** in a futile bid to intimidate the North, but less than a year later America was clearing up the mines under the terms of the Paris ceasefire agreement. By late 1973 the harbour was deemed safe once more, in time for the exodus of desperate **boat people** at the end of the decade as hundreds of refugees escaped in overladen fishing boats.

Arrival, information and city transport

Haiphong **train station** is located on the southeast side of town and within easy walking distance of the centre. For once the station provides left-luggage

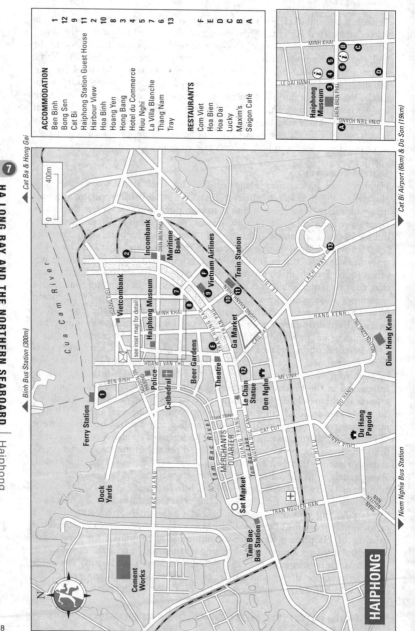

HAIPHONG

▲ Cat Ba & Hong Gai

▲ Binh Bus Station (300m)

◀ Hanoi (100km)

▲ Niem Nghia Bus Station

▶ Cat Bi Airport (6km) & Do Son (19km)

Cua Cam River

Tam Bac River

ACCOMMODATION

Ben Binh	1
Bong Sen	12
Cat Bi	9
Haiphong Station Guest House	11
Harbour View	2
Hoa Binh	10
Hoang Yen	8
Hong Bang	3
Hotel du Commerce	4
Huu Nghi	5
La Villa Blanche	7
Thang Nam	6
Tray	13

RESTAURANTS

Com Viet	F
Hoa Bien	E
Hoa Dai	D
Lucky	C
Maxim's	B
Saigon Café	A

facilities, making it feasible to do a quick tour of Haiphong while passing through; lockers big enough to take rucksacks are in a "reception room" off the main ticket hall, where you can buy ferry tickets for Cat Ba Island. The **ferry station**, serving both Hong Gai and Cat Ba, is on the Cua Cam River about 500m north of the city centre along Ben Binh.

Buses from the south and west usually pitch up at Niem Nghia bus station, out in the southwest suburbs on Tran Nguyen Han, about 3km and twelve minutes by cyclo from the centre. Most Hanoi services drop you closer in at Tam Bac bus station, near the Sat Market and the west end of Tam Bac Lake. Buses from Bai Chay and the northeast come into Binh bus station on the north bank of the Cua Cam River, 300m from the cross-river ferry, but if you're coming from this direction the Hong Gai–Haiphong **ferry** or **hydrofoil** offers a more scenic alternative. There is also a direct, four-hour hydrofoil service to and from Mong Cai. All ferries and hydrofoils arrive at the terminal on Ben Binh (see map opposite), just north of the city centre.

Moving on from Haiphong, Hanoi-bound **buses** leave every few minutes from Tam Bac bus station. Buses to the south and west depart from Niem Nghia bus station.

Haiphong's **Cat Bi Airport** (flights to Ho Chi Minh City and Da Nang only; ☎031/849242) is 7km southeast of the city. A taxi (☎031/841999) to or from the airport should be around $5.

For **information**, you could try the main office of Vietnamtourism in Haiphong at 57 Dien Bien Phu (Mon–Sat 7am–noon & 1.30–5.30pm; ☎031/842432), which can provide guides and car rental, or Haiphong Tourism at 15 Le Dai Hanh (☎031/842989), but don't expect too much of their English skills. City **maps** are on sale at bookstalls on Dien Bien Phu, near the junction with Minh Khai.

There are several **Internet cafés** in town; one of the largest is at 133 Dien Bien Phu.

Cyclos are readily available and a good way of getting around the central district, although it's quite possible to tackle most of it on foot. There's no official bike rental, though you might be able to arrange one through your hotel. For longer distances **car rental** is the only answer: count on $40 per day if renting through Vietnamtourism; and slightly less for unmetered taxis, which can usually be found waiting on Nguyen Duc Canh, just south of Tam Bac Lake.

Accommodation

Haiphong has a fair number of hotels, but prices tend to be high and standards are not great. Budget accommodation is in short supply and tends to fill up early. Most hotels cluster around Dien Bien Phu, the city's main artery, with others near the train and ferry stations.

Ben Binh 6 Ben Binh ☎031/842260, ⓕ842524. An imposing building set in gardens opposite the ferry station. The spacious and high-ceilinged rooms upstairs are more appealing (and more expensive) than the smaller rooms downstairs. Convenient for late arrival or early departure by boat. ❸

Bong Sen 16 Nguyen Duc Canh ☎031/631019, ⓕ855184. Set behind a small restaurant, this place is clean, friendly and comfy. Smallish rooms come with TV, phone, hot water and air-con. ❸

Cat Bi 30 Tran Phu ☎031/921837, ⓕ921181. A two-storey, somewhat run-down place, but with reasonable prices and spacious, comfortably furnished rooms. Handy for the train station. ❸

Haiphong Station Guest House (formerly *Phuong Dong*) 75 Luong Khanh Thien ☎031/855391, ⓕ921347. One of the best deals in town, especially if arriving or departing by train, as it sits in the station courtyard. Large, clean rooms in a generally quiet location. ❷–❸

Harbour View 4 Tran Phu ☎031/827827, ⓕ827828. This internationally run hotel, located on the eastern fringe of town, is as plush as Haiphong gets, with luxurious rooms and impeccable service. Just why anyone would want to gaze over the cranes and rusting hulls in the harbour, however, remains a mystery. ⑤

Hoa Binh 104 Luong Khanh Thien ☏031/859029, ⓕ846907. A popular budget hotel near the station with various-size rooms, but not much character. ③

Hoang Yen 7 Tran Hung Dao ☏031/842383, ⓕ842205. A spruce colonial edifice with shuttered windows in an attractive location with a restaurant downstairs. The rooms themselves aren't oozing with character but they're not bad value, offering all the standard facilities. ③–④

Hong Bang 64 Dien Bien Phu ☏031/842229, ⓕ841044. An aged but friendly, well-run hotel that's popular among business people. Gloomy communal areas but smaller rooms are competitively priced and large rooms include bathtubs. ②–③

Hotel du Commerce 62 Dien Bien Phu ☏031/842706, ⓕ842560. An old colonial-style hotel with a certain period charm and helpful staff. Its big, airy rooms are a bit tatty but have all the basics and offer the cheapest option on the central strip. ②

Huu Nghi 60 Dien Bien Phu ☏031/823310, ⓕ823245. The central strip's glitziest hotel is housed in an unsympathetic eleven-storey block, one of the the tallest buildings in town. A favourite among businessmen and gamblers at nearby Do Son. ③–⑥

La Villa Blanche (also known as the *Navy Guesthouse* or *Nha Khach Hai Quan*) 5 Tran Hung Dao ☏031/842863, ⓕ842278. An impressive, white colonial building opposite the park, plus two smart new villas behind. Upmarket accommodation providing all the trappings, including video – though the already small, cheaper rooms are over-stuffed with ornate dark-wood furnishings. ③–④

Thang Nam 55 Dien Bien Phu ☏031/747216, ⓕ745674. A popular, well-maintained hotel on the central strip run by Vietnamtourism. Choice of small and big rooms, the latter with bathtubs, at reasonable prices. ②–③

Tray 47 Lach Tray ☏031/828555, ⓕ828666. Located a bit far from the action on the south side of town, but offering a wide range of facilities such as swimming pool, fitness centre and Jacuzzis. ⑤–⑥

The city centre

Despite its recent history, old Haiphong is surprisingly well preserved. The crescent-shaped nineteenth-century core, which holds most of interest, lies between the curve of the Tam Bac River and the loop of the train tracks. To the north of the main artery, Dien Bien Phu, you'll find an area of broad, sleepy avenues and Haiphong's most attractive **colonial architecture**. On Dien Bien Phu itself are a number of hotels, an uninspiring selection of shops and the classic wine-red facade of the **Haiphong Museum** (Thurs 2–4pm, Sat & Sun 8–10am & 2–4pm; small admission fee). Even during its advertised opening hours the museum is often closed due to lack of demand, but you're not missing anything. Instead, head south towards the square tower of Haiphong **cathedral**, built in the late nineteenth century and looking very trim after years of neglect, and continue down bustling Hoang Van Thu to the salmon-pink **theatre**. Constructed of materials shipped from France in the early 1900s, the theatre faces onto a wide, open square – a site remembered locally for the deaths of forty revolutionaries during the street battles of November 1946 "after a valiant fight against French invaders".

In earlier times the Bonnal Canal ran past this square, linking the Tam Bac and Cua Cam rivers. For most of its length it's now gardens, cutting a green swathe through the city, but the canal's western section survives as Tam Bac Lake. The wide, shady boulevards bordering the lake and gardens make for a pleasant stroll, and the massive bronze statue of the city's heroine, Le Chan (see opposite), made in the bold style of Soviet social realism, adds to the area's appeal. North of the lake you'll find Haiphong's **merchants' quarter**, these days a dilapidated area of street markets, chandlers and ironmongers between Tran Trinh and Cho Sat. **Sat Market**'s nineteenth-century halls have been replaced by a circular, six-storey block, but there's still plenty of streetlife around. Also of interest in the central district is **Den Nghe**, on Me Linh, an unusually cramped temple, noted for its sculptures. The finest carvings are on the massive stone table in the first courtyard, but make sure you also look above the perfumed haze of incense for some colourful friezes. General Le Chan, who led the Trung Sisters' Rebellion (see p.484), is worshipped at the main altar; on the eighth day of each second lunar month the general receives a birthday treat – platefuls of her favourite food, crab with rice-noodles.

Across the train tracks

There are a couple of sights of passing interest across the train tracks from Haiphong centre, both about 2km to the south. The more rewarding is **Du Hang Pagoda**, located on Chua Hang, an appealing lane of old artisans' dwellings, where you are free to wander around. The pagoda, in its present form dating from the late seventeenth century, is accessed through an imposing triple-roofed bell tower. Interestingly, the architecture here reveals a distinct Khmer influence in the form of vase-shaped pinnacles ornamenting the roof and pillars of the inner courtyard – according to Buddhist legend these contain propitious *cam lo*, or sweet dew. A library to the left of the courtyard holds a valuable collection of Buddhist prayer books, and beyond is a small, walled garden of burial stupas.

It's worth going on to **Dinh Hang Kenh**, a kilometre east on Nguyen Cong Tru, if you haven't yet seen a *dinh*, or communal house. This one is a low, graceful building with a sweeping expanse of tiled roof, facing an ornamental lake: an impressive sight marred by ramshackle gardens and encroaching factories. Thirty-two monumental ironwood columns hold up the roof and populate the long, dark hall which is also noted for its carvings of 308 dragons sculpted in thirty writhing nests – now clothed in the dust of ages.

Eating

Haiphong is well endowed with good **places to eat**, though not so many have English menus. The town's poshest venue is a branch of a Hanoi restaurant, *Com Viet*, at 6 Tran Binh Trong (℡031/859152), serving Vietnamese dishes in a spacious dining room with smartly dressed staff; prices aren't as outrageous as you'd expect, with main dishes costing from $1–3. A small but reliable place is *Lucky* at 22 Minh Khai, with an extensive menu of well-prepared dishes. The vegetable soup and shrimps fried in flour are particularly tasty. Also conveniently situated in the centre is *Maxim's* at 31 Dien Bien Phu, which serves several western dishes. Specializing in seafood, the *Hoa Dai* at 39 Le Dai Anh is a favourite among locals. The *Saigon Café*, located at 107 Dien Bien Phu, offers a limited range of pasta dishes as well as cocktails and live music in the evenings. Several of the big hotels on Dien Bien Phu serve western breakfasts.

A more Vietnamese crowd frequents the strip of **beer gardens** and eateries to the east of the theatre on Tran Hung Dao: most are unnamed but nos. 22, 25 (*Hoa Bien*) and 27 get the majority vote. Alternatively, cruise the **food stalls** near the *Bong Sen Hotel* and in the lanes around Haiphong's largest **market**, Cho Ga, where you can snack on sizzling spring rolls. In the evenings, join the throng trawling Nguyen Duc Canh, to pause at an ice-cream parlour or beneath the flickering lights of sugar-cane and coconut-milk vendors.

The night in Haiphong belongs to the **karaoke bars**, of which there are dozens scattered around town – generally dimly lit, unappealing places. The *Trai Tram* nightclub, on Dinh Tien opposite the theatre, attracts the city's youth looking for a chance to strut their stuff.

Listings

Airlines Vietnam Airlines, 30 Tran Phu (daily 8–11.30am & 1.30–5pm; ☎031/921242), next to the *Cat Bi Hotel*.

Banks and exchange All the following banks change currency and travellers' cheques: Incombank, 36 Dien Bien Phu; Indovina Bank, 30 Tran Phu; Maritime Bank, 25 Dien Bien Phu; Vietcombank, 11 Hoang Dieu.

Hospital Ben Vien Viet–Tiep (Vietnam–Czech Friendship General Hospital), 1 Nha Thuong (☎031/846236).

Post office The GPO is at the junction of Nguyen Tri Phuong and Hoang Van Thu, with a sub-post office at 36 Quang Trung.

Taxi For metered taxis call Haiphong Taxi on ☎031/841999.

Around Haiphong

If Haiphong's subtle vibe lulls you into staying, you might like to make a day-trip to **Do Son**, a peninsula just 20km south of town that boasts not only a beach of sorts but also a big casino, which stays open until the early hours. Big hotels like the *Harbour View* organize expensive bicycle outings to Do Son, but bike rental can probably be organized through other hotels or guesthouses, and a xe om will whisk you there in no time for a small fee. The peninsula is divided into three zones, and the better beaches are in zone 3 down near the southern tip where the casino stands. It's a popular destination for the Vietnamese in summer, but receives few Western visitors. For an overnight stay, the **Van Thong** hotel (☎031/861331; ❷–❸) in zone 2 offers a reasonable choice of accommodation.

Cat Ba Island

Dragon-back mountain ranges mass on the horizon 20km out of Haiphong as you approach **Cat Ba Island**. The island, the largest member of an archipelago sitting on the west of Ha Long Bay, boasts only one settlement of any size, Cat Ba Town, a fishing village now redefining itself as a tourist town. The rest of the island is unspoilt and largely inaccessible, with just one paved road across a landscape of enclosed valleys and shaggily forested limestone peaks, occasionally descending to lush coastal plains. In 1986 almost half the island and adjacent waters were declared a **national park** in an effort to protect its diverse ecosystems, which range from offshore coral reefs and coastal mangrove swamps to vast tracts of tropical evergreen forest. One of the easiest and most rewarding ways to access the park is by boat from Cat Ba Town, passing through the labyrinth of **Lan Ha Bay**, a miniature version of neighbouring Ha Long Bay but one which receives fewer visitors. There are several **pearl farms** in the bay, which some tours include on their itinerary. Other boat trips venture up into Ha Long Bay itself (see p.430), where most sights are within the scope of a day's outing, or to one of the bay's more dramatic caves, **Ho Ba Ham**. A number of islands in the area sport white coral-sand fringes where the water is noticeably cleaner than elsewhere in the bay, and even Cat Ba Town has a few acceptable **beaches** within walking distance.

Archeological evidence shows that humans inhabited Cat Ba's many limestone caves at least 6000 years ago. Centuries later these same caves provided the perfect wartime hideaway – the military presence on Cat Ba has always been strong, for obvious strategic reasons. When trouble with China flared up in 1979, hundreds of ethnic Chinese islanders felt compelled to flee and the exodus continued into the next decade as "boat people" sailed off in search of a better life, depleting the island's population to less than 15,000. Now that prosperity has come in the form of tourism, the population is growing rapidly.

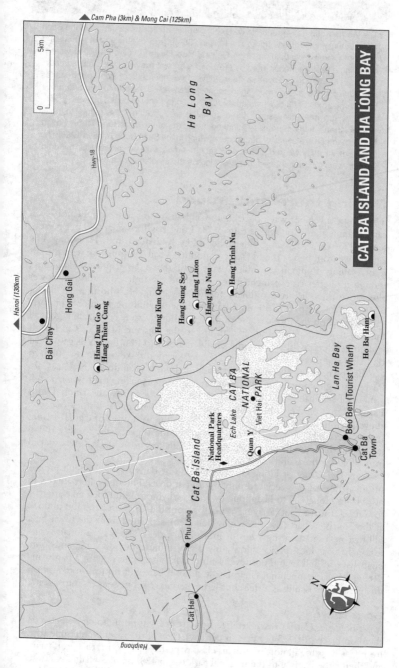

CAT BA ISLAND AND HA LONG BAY

Cam Pha (3km) & Mong Cai (125km)

Hanoi (130km)

Haiphong

5km

Hwy-18

Ha Long Bay

Bai Chay

Hong Gai

Hang Dau Go & Hang Thien Cung

Hang Kim Quy

Hang Sung Sot

Hang Luon

Hang Bo Nau

Hang Trinh Nu

Cat Ba Island

Phu Long

National Park Headquarters

Ech Lake

CAT BA NATIONAL PARK

Quan Y

Viet Hai

Lan Ha Bay

Beo Ben (Tourist Wharf)

Cat Ba Town

Ho Ba Ham

Cat Hai

N

The **Vietnamese navy** fought its two most glorious and decisive battles in the Bach Dang Estuary, east of Haiphong. The first, in 938 AD, marked the end of a thousand years of Chinese occupation when General **Ngo Quyen** led his rebels to victory, defeating a vastly superior force by means of a brilliant ruse. Waiting until high tide, General Ngo lured the **Chinese fleet** upriver over hundreds of iron-tipped stakes embedded in the estuary mud, then counter-attacked as the tide turned and drove the enemy boats back downstream to founder on the now exposed stakes.

History repeated itself some three centuries later during the struggle to repel **Kublai Khan**'s Mongol armies. This time it was the great **Tran Hung Dao** who led the Vietnamese in a series of battles culminating in the Bach Dang River in 1288. The ingenious strategy worked just as well second time round when over four hundred vessels were lost or captured, finally seeing off the ambitious Khan.

Getting there and around

The most convenient way of getting to Cat Ba is with a tour from Hanoi – you can combine the island with a tour of Ha Long Bay for under $30 per person, see p.429 – or, if travelling independently, by **hydrofoil** from Haiphong. The latter leave from beside the old ferry station (6–7 daily; 50min; $6); with the last return sailing at 4pm, it's possible to visit Cat Ba on a day-trip from Haiphong, though it's better to overnight if you can spare the time. As a cheaper, slower alternative there are two ordinary **ferries** departing **Haiphong** each day at 6.30am and 1.30pm (2hr 30min; $4.50). Weather permitting, it's more comfortable to travel on the roof of these overladen antique vessels, but check it goes all the way to Cat Ba Town rather than just to the adjacent island of Cat Hai. If you do get dumped there, take the small ferry over to Phu Long Village on Cat Ba Island and then catch a local bus (1hr; $2) or motorbike for the last 30km to Cat Ba Town. From Haiphong ferries and hydrofoils head down the Cua Cam River through a procession of wallowing coal barges, picking their way through a maze of sandbanks and shifting channels. They then cross the **Bach Dang Estuary**, one of the most famous battle sites in Vietnamese history (see box above), before turning south across open sea to the west coast of Cat Ba Island. It's this second half of the voyage that offers the most spectacular scenery as you sail in the shadow of increasingly dramatic cliffs towards Cat Ba Town, tucked into a fold on the island's southern tip.

From Bai Chay or Hong Gai, getting to Cat Ba is a more difficult proposition, as this route is serviced only by tourist boats. The only alternative is to head from Hong Gai to Haiphong by ferry or hydrofoil, and then take another to Cat Ba. Tourist boats arriving at Cat Ba from Bai Chay are required to dock at the Tourist Wharf (also known as Beo Ben), separated from the town by a hill that necessitates a short bus or motorbike ride. There is occasionally confusion here as local police allow only a few minutes for docking, and some boats have to pull in and out several times while passengers get in a flap wondering what is happening. There is also a hotel here, but no reason to stay on this part of the island, as a free shuttle bus service runs passengers into town.

Boat tours

Most hotels in Cat Ba Town arrange **boat tours**, with little to chose between them on price ($10–15 per person per day). One of the most picturesque trips from Cat Ba is to sail north into Lan Ha Bay, perhaps pay a visit to a pearl farm, and then either walk into the national park (see p.428) or take a half-day cruise around the maze of limestone islands, stopping at one of the pristine coral-sand beaches for a spot of swimming. The going rate for **boat hire** from the local boatmen is between $3 and $7 per hour, depending on the season and your negotiating skills. Lunch on board rates an extra $2 per person. Short trips to nearby islands are also possible and are sometimes included in day-trips.

Alternatively, it's quite feasible to explore **Ha Long Bay** (see p.428) from here, either as a round trip or en route to Bai Chay; count on $50 to hire a boat for a full day, plus a little more if you want to be dropped off in Bai Chay.

Cat Ba Town

Caught between green hills and a horseshoe bay alive with coracles scurrying among multicoloured fishing boats, **CAT BA TOWN**'s west-facing location makes it great for sunsets over outlying islands. A charming, almost European-looking fishing village, it's big on atmosphere but sleepy during siesta time, and retains a calm ambience despite the recent onslaught of tourism which has seen a slew of new hotels and restaurants open along the tree-lined harbour front. It's divided into two sections, separated by a small headland: the tourist facilities are grouped around the new ferry pier; 800m to the west lies the original, workaday fishing village with a bustling market and its accompanying *bia hoi* stalls. Directly behind the pier is a small hill topped by the town's war memorial, erected during Ho Chi Minh's visit to the island in 1953; follow a path up the back to find a quiet, breezy spot from which to contemplate the harbour. If you prefer a close-up view of life afloat, hire one of the **coracles**, essentially water-taxis, that hover round the harbour steps; with hard bargaining an hour should cost $1–2.

A steep road to the east leads to two small, sandy **beaches** (small entrance fee) hiding on the far side of the peninsula which form the harbour's easterly arm. The first you come to is the more popular beach and boasts basic facilities including showers, toilets, a drinks stall and a restaurant. From here, a ten-minute walk further along a cliff-hugging boardwalk leads to a quieter, more secluded beach, where snacks and drinks are also available. A little further east out of town from the first beach road, another road leads to a third beach. Though the sand is quite attractive on all of them, there is little shade on any.

Practicalities

Cat Ba Town has two ferry piers: for most of the year **ferries and hydrofoils** from Haiphong use the new harbour pier in front of the town centre, but between May and August, and whenever strong westerly winds blow, they sail round to the Tourist Wharf on the island's east side (where boats from Bai Chay also arrive). Free shuttle buses wait to take tour groups to the hotel strip along the waterfront (10min), and xe om are always on the prowl. The town's public **bus** stand is in the village centre near the marketplace, from where a few buses a day ply the island's only road to Phu Long Village (1hr; $2.50). However, for serious exploration, your best bet is a **motorbike**: xe om congregate round the marketplace and rental outlets are ubiquitous – expect to pay around $5 per day for a Minsk. Hotels and restaurants will **change money**, but cash only and at poor rates, so it's best to come prepared. International calls can be made from the **post office** (7am–noon & 12.30–9pm), which is located on the opposite corner to the *Van Anh Hotel*.

Most Cat Ba hotels can help arrange boat tours and treks in the national park. The Son Tung Tourism Services Centre on the waterfront offers two typical excursions: a full day-trip with a trek through the national park, lunch in a village, boat trip back to Cat Ba Town via Lan Ha Bay with a swimming stop and a visit to a pearl farm ($10 per person); and a half-day boat trip into Lan Ha with snorkelling, swimming and pearl farm ($8). More reliable, however, are Hanoi's Queen Travel, Red River Tours and Handspan travel companies, who are represented in Cat Ba by an agent at the *Giang Son Hotel* (☎031/888214) and offer trek/boat-trip packages for $15-20.

Some itineraries include kayaking in the calm waters of Lan Ha Bay and camping overnight on deserted beaches. These trips are best suited to those who are keen to explore soft adventure options, and are good swimmers. They provide a great way to see the area at close range while working off that seafood lunch.

Accommodation

Thanks to a building boom, **accommodation** on Cat Ba represents good value: though most of them are basic budget hotels, they're generally clean, comfortable and most have hot water, TV and air-conditioning. Expect to pay a couple of dollars extra for a room with a view, of which there are many facing the bay. Officially all hotels must charge $10 per room (up to three beds) in winter and $15 in the peak summer period of July to September, when the place can get really packed, but off season you'll find the majority are willing to bargain. Most hotels are a stone's throw from the new pier and within earshot of the 6am ferry's claxon, so ignore any touts who accost you at the pier – they have been known to rip tourists off.

Worth a look are the *Hoang Huong* (☎031/888274; ❶) and the large *Gieng Noc* (☎031/888243; ❶), both located at the east end of the bay, or the *Giang Son* (☎031/888214; ❷) at the west end. Just near the pier are the *Van Anh* (☎031/888201; ❷–❸) and the *Noble House* (☎031/888363; ❸), both of which are a bit upmarket, and the *Princes* (☎031/887666; ❷–❸), perhaps the fanciest place in town, is located on the street by the post office. Also on this street are two unappealing but cheap choices – the *Sea River* (☎031/888671; ❶–❷) and the *Pacific* (☎031/888331; ❶), which has expensive Internet access. Two more reasonable alternatives along the front are the *Vien Dong,* also known as *Far Eastern* (☎031/888555; ❸), and the *Huong Cang* (☎031/888399; ❶–❷), with small but clean and cosy rooms.

Eating and nightlife

The number of **restaurants** on Cat Ba is expanding, with most offering good-quality food – especially seafood – at reasonable prices. Most restaurants along the waterfront serve up great dishes like fresh cuttlefish and fried rice with a beer for around $2. For a real seafood challenge, order one of the large, pinkish crabs on display in some restaurants, and crack your way through to its succulent meat. The *Hoang Y* is a good breakfast spot, and the *Huu Dung,* also known as *Coka Cola*, up the road beside the *Hoang Huong Hotel*, is an old favourite for its broad menu of soups and seafood. Finally, the *Flightless Bird Café* further down towards the market is a joint venture between Vietnamese and New Zealand owners, who can help arrange tours and boat trips. If you're tempted to try the floating restaurants in the bay, check prices first, as some hapless travellers have been stung badly here.

In the evening many visitors enjoy a beer or wine sold by vendors along the wide promenade, or take a stroll along to the end of the crescent-shaped bay. The influx of young Westerners has also brought along a disco scene, and two cavernous halls, the *New City* and *Song Xanh*, stand side by side in the street parallel to the front (just beyond the *Princes Hotel*). They get going around 9pm, and just along the same street is a smaller bar, *Blue Note*, which features live music and claims to stay open 24 hours.

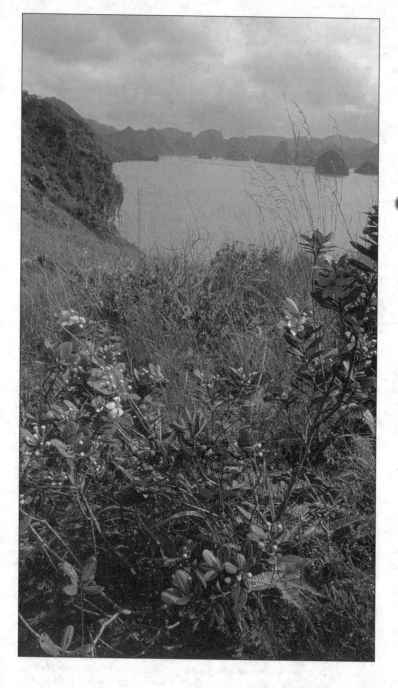

Cat Ba National Park

One of Cat Ba's main draws is its rugged unspoilt scenery. A recommended day's outing is to take a boat ride (best organized by agents in Cat Ba Town or Hanoi) through **Lan Ha Bay** to **Cat Ba National Park** (small entrance fee if not with tour group). The park's most famous inhabitant is a unique subspecies of the endangered golden-headed langur (*vooc* in Vietnamese), a monkey found only in five isolated communities in the limestone forests of Vietnam and southern China. Over seven hundred plant species have been catalogued in the park, including more than one hundred of medicinal value.

After leaving Cat Ba and gliding for an hour or so past karst outcrops and pearl farms in Lan Ha Bay, the boat pulls up to a jetty at the south end of the national park. The route from the jetty follows a leisurely path through a short tunnel and along a sealed road bordered by lush growth for about an hour, to the village of Viet Hai. There are a few restaurants set up for foreign visitors in town, but otherwise it's a sleepy rural village with most homes made of mud and thatch. The fertile valley around the village is rimmed by mountains, and a steep clamber to the top of the eastern ridge leads to one of Ha Long Bay's classic views, over countless islands east of Cat Ba. With luck, on the way you may even see a langur, though they keep mainly to inaccessible cliffs around the shore. Think twice about this walk if the route is wet, as slips can be fatal. Lunch in the village is a welcome break after this strenuous climb, before heading back along the attractive path to the boat and back through Lan Ha Bay to Cat Ba Town.

It's also possible to enter the national park from inland. The road climbs sharply out of Cat Ba Town, giving views over distant islands and glimpses of secluded coves, and then follows a series of high valleys. After 8km look out on the right for the distinctive **Quan Y Cave** (small admission fee), a gaping mouth embellished with concrete, not far from the road. During the American War the cave became an army hospital big enough to treat 150 patients at a time. Another 8km further on are the park gates, where it's wise to pick up a guide (about $10 per day) as people have got seriously lost attempting to follow the unmarked paths. You'll also need good boots, lots of water, potent mosquito repellent, and a compass. The most popular route from the park headquarters is an eight-kilometre walk, two to three hours of hard going, through an area of *kim giao* forest (commonly known as the "chopstick tree" because its wood, said to be sensitive to poisons, was used for the emperors' chopsticks) as far as Ech Lake – most of the frogs (*ech*) after which it's named are presumed to have been eaten.

Ha Long Bay

From Guilin in China to Thailand's Phang Nga Bay, the limestone outcrops which typify the scenery of **Ha Long Bay** are not uncommon, but nowhere else do they feature on such an impressive scale: an estimated 1969 islands at the latest count pepper the 1553 square kilometres of Ha Long Bay itself, with a further two thousand more punctuating the coast towards China. Local legend tells of a celestial dragon and her children, sent by the Jade Emperor to stop an invasion, which spat out great quantities of pearls to form islands and razor-sharp mountain chains in the path of the enemy fleet. After the victory the dragons, enchanted by their creation, decided to stay on, giving rise to the name *Ha Long* ("dragon descending"), and to the inevitable claimed sightings of sea monsters.

In 1469 King Le Thanh Tong paid a visit to Ha Long Bay and was so inspired by the scenery that he wrote a poem, likening the islands to pieces on a chessboard; ever since, visitors have struggled to capture the mystery of this fantasy world. Nineteenth-century Europeans compared the islands to Tuscan cathedrals, while a local brochure opts for meditative "grey-haired fairies", and the bay is frequently referred to as the eighth natural wonder of the world. With so much hyperbole, some find Ha Long disappointing, especially since this stretch of coast is also one of Vietnam's more industrialized regions with a major shipping lane cutting right across the bay to Hong Gai port. The winter weather is also a factor to bear in mind; February and March are the worst months but from November on there can be odd days of cold, drizzly weather when the splendour and romance of the bay is harder to appreciate.

The neighbouring towns of Bai Chay and Hong Gai are officially referred to as Ha Long City, though few locals use this term. The epicentre of tourism in Ha Long Bay is **Bai Chay**, a beach resort on the north shore, which offers an enormous choice of accommodation and restaurants plus hordes of boatmen, all conveniently at hand. For those in search of more local colour, or who are put off by Bai Chay's overwhelming devotion to tourism, there are a couple of attractive alternatives. The first is simply to hop across a narrow channel east of Bai Chay to **Hong Gai**, a town which provides only basic tourist facilities but which has a more bustling, workaday atmosphere. The other option is to tackle the bay from the south and base yourself on Cat Ba Island (see p.422), with the advantages of a scenic ferry ride from Haiphong or Hong Gai and accommodation located on the edge of an attractive fishing village.

Getting there and around

Ha Long Bay is the premier tourist destination in northern Vietnam and the vast majority of visitors come on **organized tours** from Hanoi, travelling by road and staying a night or two in Bai Chay, with one or two boat trips in the package (see "Boat trips", below, for factors to consider). Every Hanoi tour agent offers Ha Long Bay excursions (see p.363 for details). In terms of straight cost, it's hard to beat the tours offered by the travellers' cafés in Hanoi, though there have been complaints of long waits for boats and chaotic organization in Bai Chay. Tour groups from Hanoi usually take a break along the way at **Con Son**, where a small temple marks the land where Nguyen Trai (1380–1442), a poet and warrior, spent many years. The pine-covered hillsides around are very pleasant, but with Ha Long Bay calling, few groups linger long.

Some Hanoi travellers' cafés – notably *Queen Travel* and *Love Planet Café* (see p.363) – are trying to develop alternative destinations among the unexplored islands in Ha Long Bay. One such island is Quan Lan, a remote landmass with a meagre population of 5000 near the Chinese/Vietnamese sea-bound border. Although peaceful with a sandy beach and two untouched grottoes, facilities are basic on Quan Lan. *Love Planet Café* organize three-day trips for $49 each (group of 2–6). Take insect repellent, soap, a towel, loo roll and a good book.

If you'd rather do it yourself, there are frequent **bus** services running out of Hanoi and Haiphong to Bai Chay; these pull in at the Western bus station, at the far end of Ha Long Avenue. Coming from the north, buses terminate at the Eastern bus station; from here, Hong Gai centre is a kilometre back along Le Thanh Tong, or you can cross over to Bai Chay on the passenger ferry (500d) that shuttles between the two bus stations. A slower but far more interesting approach is to take the **train** from Hanoi to Haiphong and then the public **ferry** or **hydrofoil** to Hong Gai (for a total cost of around $10–15). The ferry and hydrofoil pass through some impressive scenery on the bay's northwest fringes – a dawn voyage on the 6am sailing is particularly stunning – and then dock in Hong Gai's eastern harbour. (See "Travel details" on p.438 for outline schedules of all these services.) Ha Long Bay can also be covered by chartered boat from Cat Ba Town (see p.425), allowing easy access to its less visited southern fringes.

Boat trips

It's not difficult to **charter** a boat locally, though it works out more expensive than an organized tour unless you can find people to share costs. The junks with their rust-coloured sails are the most expensive, and though they look elegant and peaceful in the bay, they are engine-powered much of the time. Most hotels and some restaurants in Bai Chay can help with boat hire, as can the Quang Ninh tourist office (see "Listings", p.435). You can negotiate good rates by going direct to the boatmen on the tourist wharves, 2km out of town to the west, or try around the harbour in **Hong Gai**; see p.424 for information on arranging trips **from Cat Ba**. Better still, check prices at the Bai Chay tourist boat station east along Ha Long Avenue from the trio of *Ha Long* hotels, and then enter into negotiations pre-armed with information.

Rates are much the same wherever you base yourself. In the off-season, with some skilled bargaining, you can expect to pay around $5 per hour for a small boat (maximum 10 people), rising to $7 or more in the peak summer season and at holiday weekends. As it takes about an hour to get in among the islands, a **full day**'s boat tour is preferable to two half-days, if it fits your schedule. In a long day (6–8hr) from Bai Chay or Hong Gai, you'll be able to explore a good deal of the western side, visit some of the caves described below and perhaps take a swing through the eastern islands on the way home. An interesting variation is to **overnight on board** (take warm clothes in winter), which means you can also cover the bay's southern reaches, including Cat Ba Island, in one trip.

Meals on board cost an extra $2–4 per person for lunch or dinner, depending on the amount of fresh seafood you devour, and are usually excellent. You also need to add on the costs of entrance fees to caves and pricey drinks on board the boat – it's best to take your own water. Note that you should agree the itinerary in advance and pay at the end of the trip; you may also want to take a look at the boat beforehand, especially if you're going to overnight, checking for rat holes and the like. There have been occasional reports of thefts from these tourist boats, either by crew members or hawkers approaching in coracles; as a precaution, have someone stay on the boat all the time or, if your hotel has a safe, leave valuables there.

More recently there has been talk of developing Ha Long Bay for adventure sports, with **sea-kayaking trips** (see p.363) already up and running, while rafting and climbing trips are under discussion.

The caves and islands

Ha Long Bay is split in two by a wide channel running north–south: the larger, western portion contains the most dramatic scenery and best caves, while to the east lies an attractive area of smaller islands, known as Bai Tu Long or "children of the dragon", though with fewer specific sights apart from **Dao Khi** ("Monkey Island"), with its indigenous monkey population. There are currently fifteen caves open to visitors, with funding from UNESCO going towards providing lighting and building pathways; some of the less frequented caves are still in poor repair.

Most people visit the caves on an organized tour, which includes the $2 ticket that allows entrance to a maximum of five designated caves and includes a coracle to ferry you from your main boat if necessary. If travelling independently, you need to show the pass at each cave, or pay the entrance fee for the smaller caves. Tickets are available at the Bai Chay tourist boat station.

The bay's most famous cave is also the closest to Bai Chay: **Hang Dau Go** ("Grotto of the Wooden Stakes") is where General Tran Hung Dao amassed hundreds of stakes deep inside the cave's third and largest chamber prior to the Bach Dang River battle of 1288 (see p.424). Like many of the older caves, Dau Go is often marred by rubbish and graffiti but is worth a stop because the same island boasts one of the most beautiful caves. A steep climb up 50m to the entrance of **Hang Thien Cung** ("Grotto of the Heavenly Palace") is rewarded by a rectangular chamber 250m long and 20m high with a textbook display of sparkling stalactites and stalagmites – supposedly petrified characters of the Taoist Heavenly Court. This cave was only discovered in 1993 and was further restored in 1998 to make access easier.

Continuing south, past hidden bays, needle-sharp ridges and cliffs of ribbed limestone, you sail into an area particularly rich in caves. This area is home to **Ho Dong Tien** ("Grotto of the Fairy Lake") and the enchanting **Dong Me Cung** ("Grotto of the Labyrinth") where, in 1993, ancient fossilized human remains were found. The yawning mouth of **Hang Bo Nau**, ringed with a flotilla of sampans hawking coral and soft drinks, is of fleeting interest as you move on to **Hang Sung Sot**, with good views from the steps and a scramble up to a high second chamber. Other caves close by, such as **Hang Trong** ("Drum Grotto") and **Hang Trinh Nu** ("Virgin's Grotto"), are of no particular merit and awash with litter; from here it's about ninety minutes' sail back to Bai Chay.

Of the far-flung sights, **Hang Hanh** is one of the more adventurous day-trips from Bai Chay: the tide must be exactly right (at half-tide) to allow a coracle access to the two-kilometre-long tunnel-cave. Note that the hire of a coracle costs an additional $10 and that powerful torches or caving lamps are also useful here. Finally, Dau Bo Island, on the southeastern edge of Ha Long Bay, encloses **Ho Ba Ham** ("Three Tunnel Lake"), a shallow lagoon wrapped round with limestone walls and connected to the sea by three low-ceilinged tunnels that are only navigable by sampan at low tide. This cave is sometimes included in two-day excursions out of Bai Chay but is most easily visited from Cat Ba (see p.424).

Since 1994 fishermen have discovered several **new caves** in Lan Ha Bay, prompted by a local initiative granting them the right to charge a small entry fee for a specified time (usually three to six months) on condition that they install lights, stairways and so forth. For up-to-date information and recommendations, the best people to ask are the boatmen themselves – several of whom speak good English – or the local tourist offices (see "Listings", p.435). A few caverns are still unlit, so take a torch. And if you intend to explore beyond the cave mouths, which usually means scrambling over muddy rocks and through narrow passages, wear shoes with a good grip.

The huge influx of tourism to the area has brought problems, not least the litter and pollution from fume-spluttering boats. Also, it's best not to buy coral from local hawkers, who create these souvenirs by using explosives to break up the remains of the coral reefs.

Bai Chay and Hong Gai

In 1994 Hong Gai, Bai Chay and the surrounding districts were amalgamated to create a new provincial capital called **Ha Long City**, the name now used

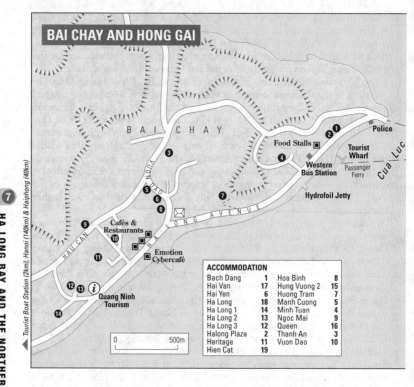

BAI CHAY AND HONG GAI

ACCOMMODATION

Bach Dang	1	Hoa Binh	8
Hai Van	17	Hung Vuong 2	15
Hai Yen	6	Huong Tram	7
Ha Long	18	Manh Cuong	5
Ha Long 1	14	Minh Tuan	4
Ha Long 2	13	Ngoc Mai	9
Ha Long 3	12	Queen	16
Halong Plaza	2	Thanh An	3
Heritage	11	Vuon Dao	10
Hien Cat	19		

on official documents. For the moment, however, locals still stick to the old names – as do ferry services, minibuses and so on – since this is a useful way to distinguish between the two towns of Bai Chay and Hong Gai, lying on either side of the narrow Cua Luc channel, each with its own distinct character and connected by a small ferry.

Neon signs and flashing fairy lights blaze out at night along the **BAI CHAY** waterfront, advertising north Vietnam's most developed resort, with shoulder-to-shoulder hotels and a picturesque backdrop of wooded hills. The town bustles at lunchtime when the tourist buses from Hanoi pull in and the boats return from Ha Long Bay, but by mid-afternoon it can seem rather quiet. Apart from strolling the seafront boulevard and a taking a quick look at its very indifferent beach, Bai Chay has nothing to distract you from the main business of touring the bay. Even the usual *bia hoi* and *com pho* stalls have been replaced by T-shirt hawkers and café owners beckoning tourists with plastic menus. Just out of town, a couple of venues, *Tuan Chau Island Resort* (☎033/842115, ✉eauloco@hn.vnn.vn) and *Royal Amusement Park* (☎033/847209, ✉eroyaljvc@hn.vnn.vn), have multiple entertainments on offer for about $3 a head ($2 for children). The former features dolphin, seal and sea-lion performances in a white-sail-roofed theatre, while the latter has cactus and orchid displays and water puppets.

In contrast to Bai Chay, **HONG GAI** has a compelling, raw vitality plus an attractive harbour to the east, crowded with scurrying coracles. Ignoring the western districts, grey with coal dust from the depots surrounding Hong Gai docks, it's worth spending an hour or so wandering the harbourside paths

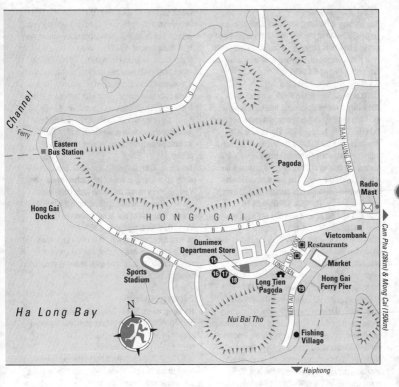

Cam Pha (28km) & Mong Cai (150km)

▼ *Haiphong*

where a picturesque village lies beached under the limestone knuckle of Nui Bai Tho. This mountain is named after a collection of poems (*bai tho*) penned in praise of the beauty of Ha Long Bay; these are carved into the rock, kicking off with King Le Thanh Tong's in 1468. Following the cliffside path clockwise from Long Tien, you pass several of the weathered inscriptions as you walk through the fishing village, though no one seems quite sure which are the royal verses. Also worth a look is the small but colourful **Long Tien Pagoda** on Long Tien. There are frequently ceremonies taking place in its small courtyard, offering fascinating glimpses into local rituals.

Accommodation

Despite a rapid increase in the provision of hotels, there are still temporary **room shortages**, particularly during the Vietnamese summer season (June to early Sept) and holiday weekends. However, during the quieter winter months, when most foreign tourists visit Ha Long Bay, this is less of a problem and room **prices** in the mini-hotels drop (winter rates are given below; mini-hotels may add up to fifty percent during peak periods).

The accommodation in **Hong Gai** may be basic, but the atmosphere of the town has a certain charm and there are a number of acceptable budget places worth a look. **Bai Chay**, on the other hand, has the biggest choice of hotels, most located along the two main drags, Ha Long Avenue and Vuon Dao. The hotels tend to be interchangeable, although it's possible to get real bargains in the off-season, thanks to the building boom that's driving prices down and aesthetics out.

Bai Chay

Bach Dang 2 Ha Long Ave ☎ 033/846330, ℱ 845892. One of the few hotels at the east end of Bai Chay, now rather aged but clean and friendly, if a bit overpriced. Big rooms, all with sea-view balconies, TV and IDD. ④–⑤

Ha Long 1, 2 and 3 Ha Long Ave ☎ 033/846320/1, ℱ 846318/9. A trio of well-established hotels set among trees. *Ha Long 1* (⑤–⑥) offers lavish accommodation in a converted French villa built in 1936. For anyone who wants to take the colonial fantasy to its logical extreme, Cathérine Deneuve stayed in suite 208 during the filming of *Indochine* – it can now be yours for $160 a night. The place has loads of atmosphere but, with only sixteen rooms, a reservation is a must. Both the 1970s-built *Ha Long 2* (④–⑤) and *Ha Long 3* (④–⑤) are popular with tour groups. Rooms are furnished to a reasonable standard – with great views from the higher rooms in no. 3 – but are overpriced.

Hai Yen 57 Vuon Dao ☎ 033/846126, ℮ dhyen.qn@hn.vnn.vn. Friendly mini-hotel with standard rooms and Internet access. ②

Halong Plaza 8 Ha Long Ave ☎ 033/845810, ℱ 846867. This new four-star hotel offers everything you'd expect for this kind of money, including pool, delicatessen and business centre. Rooms range from standard doubles with in-house entertainment and modest views to de luxe suites commanding panoramic sweeps of the bay. ⑥

Heritage 88 Ha Long Ave ☎ 033/846888, ℮ heritagehl.qn@hn.vnn.vn. The *Heritage* group revamped an old hotel to create Bai Chay's first truly de luxe accommodation, although it's now getting a run for its money from other contenders. International ambience doesn't come cheap, though. ⑤–⑥

Hoa Binh 39 Vuon Dao ☎ 033/846009. One of the better mini-hotels on Vuon Dao, this is a clean and welcoming place, with boats for hire. Prices are standard, but the rooms are a cut above the rest with TV, fridge and air-con. ②

Huong Tram Ha Long Ave ☎ 033/846365, ℱ 845930. Signposted up a steep track, about five minutes' walk east of the post office, this is a friendly mini-hotel with good views. It also offers reasonably priced boat hire plus reliable information about the bay. ②

Manh Cuong 79 Vuon Dao ☎ 033/846342. This family-run mini-hotel doesn't have the best views in town but its largish, clean rooms are one of the best deals around. ①–②

Minh Tuan Ho Xuan Huong ☎ 033/846200. The only cheap beds near the bus station, hidden down a sidestreet among attractive old houses. Ten small but clean rooms, each with bathroom and hot water, though some lack windows. ①–②

Ngoc Mai Hau Can ☎ 033/846123. A smart and spacious choice with great views and all facilities, including Internet access, at very reasonable prices. ③

Thanh An Vuon Dao ☎ 033/846959. This competitively priced hotel is one of the highest in Bai Chay. Vast, spotless rooms make the walk uphill worth the effort, as do excellent views from the front balconies. Just don't think about typhoons. ①–②

Vuon Dao Ha Long Ave ☎ 033/846427, ℮ vuondaoht.qn@hn.vnn.vn. A mid-range hotel with a characterless exterior, but the cheaper rooms are quite large and good value. Popular with tour groups. ②–④

Hong Gai

Ha Long 82 Le Thanh Tong ☎ 033/827269. A small guesthouse with helpful staff and the usual amenities like TV and air-con. ②

Hai Van 76 Le Thanh Tong ☎ 033/826279, ℱ 827092. A small, friendly guesthouse. Rooms are nothing to write home about, but they're clean and come with TV and air-con. ②

Hien Cat 252 Ben Tau ☎ 033/827417. Conveniently located right by the ferry pier, this small, family-run guesthouse boasts spectacular panoramic harbour views, with balconies, from the two spacious upper-level rooms. Smallish rooms lower down aren't bad either, with mini-balcony and use of Hong Gai's most scenic bathroom. ①–②

Hung Vuong 2 197 Le Thanh Tong ☎ 033/626767. Not exactly a luxury hotel, but its large, comfy rooms with bathtubs are among the best value to be had in Hong Gai. ③

Queen 70 Le Thanh Tong ☎ 033/826383, ℱ 827268. Supposedly Hong Gai's upmarket accommodation, offering phone, TV, fridge and air-con. The rooms are small though well kept, but it's overpriced. ③

Eating

Fresh **seafood** is the natural speciality of Ha Long Bay, with excellent lobster, crab and freshly caught fish on offer. Restaurants in Bai Chay are accustomed to catering to large coach groups and combine low standards with high prices. In Hong Gai, there are plenty of cheap and cheerful places to choose from in the bustling market, but less English is spoken and there's no concession to Western tastes.

Bai Chay

Despite the onslaught of passing traffic and postcard-sellers at the throbbing epicentre of Ha Long's tourist mecca, the most popular place to eat in Bai Chay remains the strip of **restaurants** on Ha Long Avenue between the post office and the *Heritage Hotel*. There's nothing much to choose between them, but the *Phuong Oanh*, about 100m west of the post office is recommended for good-value meals. Also in this area, the *Binh Minh* and *Phuong Vi* serve decent portions, while cheaper, local eating houses are round the corner on Vuon Dao – the *Anh Tuyet* is clean and friendly. Located just west of the tourist boat station, up a slight slope between shops, the *Nha San Ha Long*, or Ha Long Stilthouse, provides not only an attractive, shady spot to eat, but reasonable food as well. At the east end of Bai Chay, the choice is more limited: cheap *com* and *pho* **stalls** cluster round the bus station. Finally, a branch of Hanoi's *Emotion Cybercafé* is on Ha Long Avenue in the centre of town (☎033/847354, ✉emotion@ftp.vn), offering **snacks**, fast food and drinks as well as **Internet** access.

Hong Gai

The best eating in Hong Gai is at the market **food stalls**, where ingredients come fresh from fishing boats in the harbour next door. Otherwise, try one of the many street kitchens on Long Tien or nearby Le Quy Don. *Banh cuon*, a rice pancake filled with shrimp and vegetables is the local delicacy. Finding an English menu in Hong Gai is no easy task, but the welcoming staff at *Huy Hoang*, on Le Thanh Tong next door to the *Ha Long Hotel*, will do their best to prevent you starving.

Listings

Banks and exchange The larger hotels in Bai Chay change cash, but the only place to handle travellers' cheques is Hong Gai's Vietcombank, at the east end of Le Thanh Tong.
Buses One disincentive to travelling independently by bus in this region is that Westerners are frequently charged double or treble the posted fares. Hanoi and Haiphong services depart from the Western bus station, those for Mong Cai from the Eastern.
Ferries Boats to Haiphong sail four times a day

(6am, 8.30am, 11am, 4pm), and hydrofoils twice (8am and 1pm; 75min) from the Hong Gai pier. Hydrofoils also run to Mong Cai (3hr) at 8am and 1pm daily from a jetty about 100m west of the Western bus station – a comfortable and scenic ride.
Police Located near the Western bus station.
Tourist information Quang Ninh Tourism (☎033/846320), beside the turning for the *Ha Long* hotels in Bai Chay, is the government-run office, while individual hotels and restaurants offer independent advice.

To the Chinese border

Few travellers head on up the coast to Mong Cai, unless they're looking for a back road to Lang Son, a few days' rest on Tra Co Beach, or an adventurous route into China (see p.402 for general information on crossing into China). While Mong Cai itself has few redeeming features, the journey up to it offers great views, and the rural landscapes and windswept coast near the town invite exploration. The alternative routes are by road or sea, with the smooth and speedy approach by **hydrofoil** both the most convenient way to go and an experience to be savoured, especially the succession of karst towers jutting from the water for the first hour or so of the journey. The hydrofoil comes to rest in a protected bay near the northeast border, where smaller craft pull alongside to transfer passengers ashore (in rough weather this can be precarious) and foreigners must then present their passports and customs slip to the police (same procedure on leaving). The final fifteen-kilometre bus ride into town passes duck farms, mangrove swamps and buffaloes ruminating in paddies, before plunging into the dusty streets of Mong Cai, lined with karaoke and massage signs.

The **road** route offers an altogether different experience. The first stretch with views over Ha Long Bay is promising enough, though the road is choked with trucks from the huge open-cast coal mines of **Cam Pha**, where the whole landscape is shrouded in grey dust. You wouldn't want to linger, but the scenes of masked dock-hands ferrying sacks onto blackened barges or grading the coal with hand-held sieves possess a certain post-apocalyptic power. About 20km beyond Cam Pha the scenery gradually revives, as the highway winds through a spur of hills, with signs of shifting agriculture practised by local Thai people, while down below mangroves invade marshy, saltwater lagoons. Then suddenly you're out onto densely populated coastal plains, a fertile landscape painted every conceivable shade of green, where the only town of any size since Cam Pha, **Tien Yen**, marks the turning to Lang Son, a slow 100km away to the west on a rough road. North of Tien Yen, it's all flat rice-growing country until an incongruous clump of high-rise hotels and apartment blocks announces Mong Cai.

Mong Cai and around

Since the border re-opened for trade in 1992, **Mong Cai** has been booming, its markets stuffed with Chinese goods, from apples and beer to TVs and huge pink piles of toilet rolls. An open border has also generated local tourist traffic, mostly curious day-trippers from China who do a quick tour of the markets bunched up behind a flag-toting local guide, bargaining furiously over plastic sandals or packs of noodles. Since few Westerners come here, little English is spoken (in fact Chinese seems to be spoken more than Vietnamese), but the town's compact centre, radiating from a large roundabout, is easy to negotiate and most locals are friendly.

On the southeast corner of the roundabout is the **post office**, immediately south of which is a good **Internet café**. To the northwest of the roundabout a rooftop clock identifies Mong Cai's focal point, the **covered market**, which overflows into the surrounding streets in a frenzy of commerce that continues late into the evening. The town's local bus station is right next to the market, while the main bus station is about 200m along the road running west from the roundabout. The **Chinese border** is just a kilometre away to the north; walk straight up Tran Phu to the junction and turn left to reach the **border gate** (7am–5pm). The **hydrofoil offices**, from where the bus leaves to start the return journey to Bai Chay or Haiphong, are also near the roundabout. Greenlines office is at 43 Tran Phu about 100m north of the roundabout, while the Nosco office is on Hung Vuong just east of the roundabout.

There's not much to choose between Mong Cai's **hotels**, though there are a couple of budget places boasting decent facilities (TV, hot water, air conditioning); the *Bien Hoa* (☎033/882135; ❶), tucked away in a sidestreet northeast of the market, is very reasonable, while the *Thang Loi* (☎033/881002; ❷), on Tran Phu, is also good value. A cluster of more expensive places can be found near the roundabout. Best of the bunch is the

Tuan Thanh (☎033/881481; ❸), to the south of the roundabout. Right opposite is the dingy *Huu Nghi* (☎033/881408; ❸), and round the corner to the east is *Dong A* (☎033/881151; ❸).

Eating is a hit-and-miss affair in Mong Cai, as in many towns unused to foreign visitors. The streets near the covered market turn into open-air **restaurants** in the evening, each stall thronged with customers. One friendly place is the *Hoai Len* at 14 Van Don, just north of the market, where the owner will shepherd you down the side to choose your ingredients.

The windswept countryside around Mong Cai has a timeless feel and is certainly worth exploring by bicycle or motorbike. Xe om can be found all over town, and for a few dollars will run you to places like **Tra Co Beach** – just 9km to the southeast – wait while you look around, then take you back to town. Tra Co is well worth the ride, and might even be considered as a place to rest up from the rigours of the road. Few Westerners make it up here, but it gets its share of Vietnamese and Chinese tourists in summer. Though not of eye-popping beauty, the seventeen-kilometre-long strand is frequently deserted and good for peaceful walks past the curious boats of bamboo and styrofoam lying like beached whales on the hard-packed sand. The town also has an unusual sight in the form of a renovated cathedral, about a kilometre up the town's only road on the left, with colourful statues of saints round the steeple. Basic **accommodation** is provided by several budget hotels, of which the *Gio Bien* (☎033/885802; ❶), just near the beginning of the beach road, is a reliable choice.

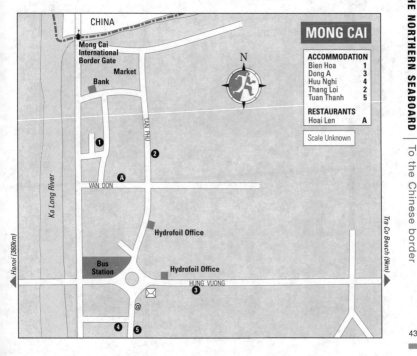

CHINA

Mong Cai International Border Gate

Market

Bank

N

MONG CAI

ACCOMMODATION
Bien Hoa   1
Dong A   3
Huu Nghi   4
Thang Loi   2
Tuan Thanh   5

RESTAURANTS
Hoai Len   A

Scale Unknown

TAN PHU

VAN DON

Ka Long River

Hanoi (360km)

Hydrofoil Office

Bus Station

Hydrofoil Office

HUNG VUONG

Tra Co Beach (9km)

Travel details

Flights

Haiphong to: Da Nang (3 weekly; 1hr 40min); Ho Chi Minh (5 weekly; 2hr).

Trains

Haiphong to: Hanoi (2–3 daily; 2hr–2hr 30min).

Ferries

Cat Ba to: Haiphong (2 daily; 2hr 35min–3hr 15min).
Haiphong to: Cat Ba (1 daily; 4–5hr); Hong Gai (4 daily; 3hr 30min).
Hong Gai to: Haiphong (4 daily; 2hr 30min).

Hydrofoil

Bai Chay to: Mong Cai (2 daily; 3hr).
Cat Ba to: Haiphong (6–7 daily; 50min).
Haiphong to: Cat Ba (6–7 daily; 50min); Hong Gai (2 daily; 1hr 15min); Mong Cai (1 daily; 4hr).
Hong Gai to: Haiphong (2 daily; 1hr 15min).

Mong Cai to: Bai Chay (2 daily; 3hr); Haiphong (1 daily; 4hr).

Buses

It's almost impossible to give the **frequency** with which buses run. Long-distance public buses, though sceduled, won't depart if empty. Moreover, private services, often minibuses or pick-ups, ply more popular routes, and depart only when they have enough passengers to make the journey worthwhile. It's advisable to start your journey early – most long-distance departures are between 5 and 9am, and few run after midday. **Journey times** can also vary; figures below show the normal length of time you can expect the journey to take.

Bai Chay to: Haiphong (3hr); Hanoi (4hr).
Haiphong to: Bai Chay (3hr); Hanoi (2hr); Nam Dinh (4hr); Ninh Binh (5hr).
Hong Gai to: Mong Cai (5hr).
Mong Cai to: Hanoi (9hr); Hong Gai (5hr).

8

The far north

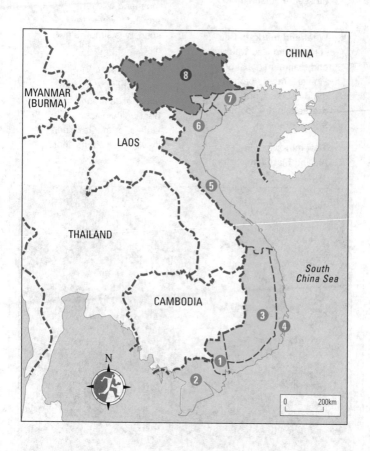

CHAPTER 8

Highlights

✻ **Trekking around Sa Pa**
A hugely popular activity, offering great views of the landscape as well as the chance to spend time with the colourfully dressed *montagnards*. See p.448

✻ **Weekend markets** Bac Ha and Can Cau weekend markets are full of Flower Hmong, perhaps the most dazzling dressers in the country. See p.451

✻ **Thai minority villages**
Around Mai Chau visitors can stay in Thai stilt-houses and see shows of **traditional dancing**. See p.464

✻ **Ha Giang** Gateway to the country's northernmost and wildest province, where the scenery is simply stunning. See p.467

✻ **Ba Be Lake** A laidback spot, where you can either glide around in a boat on its glassy waters, or trek to minority villages near its shore See p.471

8

The far north

s Vietnam fans out above Hanoi towards the Chinese and Laos borders, it attains its maximum width of 600km, the majority of it a mountainous buffer zone wrapped around the Red River Delta. Two arteries carry road and rail links north from the capital towards China and the border crossings of Lao Cai and Dong Dang. The rest of the region is mostly wild and inaccessible, yet contains some of Vietnam's most awe-inspiring scenery, sparsely populated by a fascinating mosaic of ethnic minorities. Most impressive on both counts is the northwest region where the country's highest mountain range and its tallest peak, Fan Si Pan, rise abruptly from the Red River Valley. Within the shadow of Fan Si Pan lies **Sa Pa**, an easily accessible former French hill station, famous for its minority peoples and for its superb scenery with opportunities for trekking out to isolated hamlets. Nearby, **Bac Ha** has one of the most colourful of all minority groups in the form of the Flower Hmong, whose markets are great fun. The attractions of these two towns and the historic battlefield of **Dien Bien Phu**, site of the Viet Minh's decisive victory over French forces in 1954, draw most tourists to the northwest region, while those with enough time are well rewarded if they follow the scenic route back to Hanoi, passing through **Son La**, **Moc Chau** and **Mai Chau**.

The little-travelled provinces east of the Red River Valley also deserve attention, especially the stunning scenery and mountain people in the border area of **Ha Giang** and **Cao Bang provinces**. The northeast region also features **Ba Be National Park**, where Vietnam's largest natural lake hides among forested limestone crags and impenetrable jungle. Not surprisingly, infrastructure throughout the northern mountains is poor: facilities tend to be thin on the ground, and some roads are in terrible condition. However, this area is becoming increasingly popular with tourists as Hanoi's travellers' cafés organize new tours and independent travellers venture into uncharted terrain by jeep or motorbike.

Some recent history

Remote uplands, dense vegetation and rugged terrain suited to guerrilla activities, plus a safe haven across the border, made this region the perfect place from which to orchestrate Vietnam's independence movement. For a short while in 1941, **Ho Chi Minh** hid in the Pac Bo Cave on the Chinese frontier, later moving south to Tuyen Quang Province, from where the Viet Minh launched their August Revolution in 1945. These northern provinces were the first to be **liberated** from French rule, but over in the northwest some minority groups, notably from among the Thai, Hmong and Muong, supported the

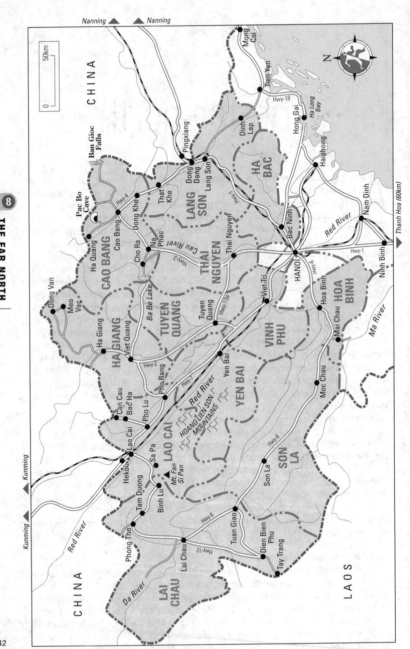

colonial authorities and it took the Viet Minh until 1952 to gain control of the area. Two years later, they staged their great victory over the French at Dien Bien Phu, close to the Lao border. In recognition of these areas' strategic importance and the need to secure their allegiance, soon after Independence Ho Chi Minh created two Autonomous Regions, granting the minorities a degree of **self-government**. In 1975, however, the two regions were broken up and relegated to the status of ordinary provinces. At the same time the government tried to **assimilate** the minorities into Vietnamese life, though with less success here than elsewhere in Vietnam.

During the late 1970s **Sino-Vietnamese** relations became increasingly sour for various reasons, not least Vietnam's invasion of Cambodia. Things came to a head on February 17, 1979 when the Chinese decided to "teach Vietnam a lesson" – in Deng Xiao Ping's famous words – by sending 200,000 troops into northern Vietnam. The Chinese army savaged the border region, destroying most of the border towns as well as bridges, roads and crops, but the battle-hardened Vietnamese army proved they had few lessons to learn, and seventeen days later the invasion force was on its way home, some 20,000 short. Though much of the infrastructural and political damage from the war has been repaired, unmarked minefields along 1000km of frontier pose a more intractable problem. The first phase of mine clearance was completed in 1995 when 2000 hectares were declared safe and 9000 displaced families returned to their land; making safe the whole area could take several more years. The **border war** put a damper on local cross-border trade but it didn't take long before the smugglers were picking their way through anti-tank mines and barbed wire. In 1989, business resumed semi-officially and was fully normalized in 1992: rice, wheat, metals and ready-made clothes are exported to southern China, in exchange for beer, bicycles, and electronic goods – and an increasingly important local tourist industry is developing alongside. Another popular sideline for cross-border traders is the export of endangered animals, many of which end up on dinner tables in southern China. Wildlife organizations in Hanoi are working strenuously to stem the flow.

Vietnam is desperately short of power and these relatively sparsely populated mountain areas offer potential for cheap **hydroelectricity**. The Hoa Binh dam was built to harness this, flooding vast stretches of the Da River Valley in the process, but the project was a disaster for the more than 50,000 Thai and Hmong people who were relocated without adequate compensation or even much consideration as to how they were supposed to earn a living.

Getting around

The mountains of northern Vietnam remain relatively unexplored, largely because of the limited road network and the difficulties of getting around by public transport. Even major highways are little more than single-track, but many roads were under repair at the time of writing and things should gradually improve. Already it is possible to do a complete loop of the north with minimal backtracking, though such a journey requires at least a couple of weeks. One of the most popular routes is the one round the northwest linking Sa Pa, Lai Chau, Dien Bien Phu, Son La and Mai Chau, while a tour of the northeast could take in Ha Giang, Ba Be Lake, Cao Bang and Lang Son. These routes can be combined by cutting across from Sa Pa or Bac Ha to Ha Giang.

Travelling through the northern provinces using local **buses** is possible, though very uncomfortable, and many buses charge Westerners double or treble the regular fare. **Renting a vehicle** gives you more freedom to stop at villages or jaunt off along side tracks. Either a four-wheel-drive jeep or Landcruiser, or a motorbike, is recommended; the cost of hiring a jeep and driver (for three to four passengers) in Hanoi averages around $60 per day, while a motorbike should be between $6 and $12 per day. When **planning your route**, base your itinerary on an average speed of about 30km per hour. Whether you travel by public transport or with your own vehicle, you need to allow around six days' actual **travelling time** to cover the northwestern region; by cutting out side-trips to Dien Bien Phu and Mai Chau you can reduce this to a minimum of four days on the road. Touring the entire north-east requires at least six days including a tour of Ha Giang Province, but more

The ethnic minorities

Around five million minority people (nearly two-thirds of Vietnam's total) live in the northern uplands, mostly in isolated villages. The largest ethnic groups are Thai and Muong in the northwest, Tay and Nung in the northeast, and Hmong and Dao dispersed throughout the region. Historically, all these peoples migrated from southern China at various times throughout history: those who arrived first, notably the Tay and Thai, settled in the fertile valleys where they now lead a relatively prosperous existence, whereas late arrivals, such as the Hmong and Dao, were left to eke out a living on the inhospitable higher slopes (for more on these diverse groups, see Contexts, p.521). Despite government efforts to integrate them into the Vietnamese community, most continue to follow a way of life little changed over the centuries. For an insight into the minorities' traditional cultures and highly varied styles of dress, visit the informative **Museum of the Nationalities of Vietnam** in Thai Nguyen or Hanoi's new **Museum of Ethnology** (see p.470 and p.384 respectively) before setting off into the mountains.

Visiting minority villages

For many people, one of the highlights of travelling in the far north of Vietnam is the experience of visiting minority villages. This is easiest with your own **transport**. If you're reliant on public services, you'll need to allow more time but, basing yourself in the main towns, it's still possible to get out to traditional villages – notably around Sa Pa, Bac Ha, Son La, Mai Chau, Ba Be and Cao Bang – and even to **stay overnight**. Alternatively, a popular, hassle-free option is to join one of the **organized trips** offered by Hanoi tour agencies (see p.363). The usual destinations are Sa Pa and Bac Ha, coinciding with the weekly market, or Mai Chau, and the standard package includes guided visits to at least two different minorities plus, in the case of Mai Chau, a night in a stilthouse. The four-day Sa Pa tour costs around $90 per person according to transport/accommodation arrangements, while two days with one night in Mai Chau is priced at around $25.

If at all possible, it's preferable to visit the minority villages as part of a **small group**, ideally four people or less, as this causes least disruption and allows for greater communication. There's a whole debate about the **ethics** of cultural tourism and its negative impact on traditional ways of life. Most villagers are genuinely welcoming and hospitable to foreigners, appreciating contact with Westerners and the material benefits which they bring; tourism may also help to protect the minorities against enforced Vietnamization, at least in the short term, by encouraging greater respect for cultural diversity.

Village etiquette

Behaviour that we take for granted may cause offence to some ethnic minority people; remember you're a guest. Apart from being sensitive to the situation and keeping an open mind, the following simple rules should be observed when visiting the ethnic minority areas.

• **Dress modestly**, in long trousers or skirt and T-shirt or shirt.

if you want to spend time on Ba Be Lake, or visit Pac Bo Cave or Ban Gioc Waterfall near Cao Bang. Bear in mind that travelling these roads is unpredictable, becoming downright hazardous during the rains (see below), and it's advisable to allow some **flexibility** in your programme.

If you've got only limited time, Sa Pa, Mai Chau and Ba Be National Park make rewarding two- or three-day **excursions out of Hanoi**, either by public transport or hired vehicle. The other alternative is to join an organized tour with one of Hanoi's travellers' cafés (see p.363 for details).

- Be sensitive to people's wishes when taking **photographs**, particularly of older people who are suspicious of the camera; always ask permission first.

- Only go **inside a house** when invited and remove your shoes before entering.

- Small **gifts**, such as fresh fruit from the local market, are always welcome. However, there is a view that even this can foster begging, and that you should only ever give in return for some service or as a sign of appreciation for hospitality. A compromise is to **buy craft work** produced by the villagers – most communities should have some embroidery, textiles or basketry for sale.

- As a mark of respect, learn the local **terms of address**, either in dialect or at least in Vietnamese, such as chao ong, chao ba (see p.571).

- Try to **minimize your impact** on the often fragile local environment; take litter back to the towns and be sensitive to the use of wood and other scarce resources.

- Growing and using **opium** is illegal in Vietnam and is punished with a fine or prison sentence; do not encourage its production by buying or smoking opium.

Trekking practicalities

Foreigners are now permitted to stay in minority villages, which has opened up the possibility of trekking, and created a small industry focused on Sa Pa. **Trekking** packages organized by Hanoi's travellers' cafés (see p.363 for details) normally include two or three days' walking out to minority villages with an overnight in a village or a Sa Pa guesthouse in their standard Sa Pa tour, with an option to continue on to Bac Ha for the Sunday market. In Hanoi you can arrange a tailored individual programme through a **tour agent**; it's important to ask for a guide with a good level of English who is familiar with the villages and the minorities' cultural traditions. In Sa Pa and Bac Ha most **guesthouses** offer trekking opportunities with their own guides and should be able to organize an interesting programme. Note that it's not a good idea to turn up at a minority's village and expect to find accommodation; your hosts may find themselves in trouble with the authorities and there's also a growing problem of petty crime, particularly around Sa Pa. Far better to make arrangements beforehand with someone who knows the current situation. If you go with a local guide, you're also less likely to cause offence and will probably have a more interesting time.

It's important to wear the right **clothing** when walking in these mountains: strong boots with ankle support are the best footwear, though you can get away with training shoes in the dry season. Choose thin, loose clothing – long trousers offer some protection from thorns and leeches; wear a hat and sunblock; take plenty of water; and carry a basic medical kit. If you plan on spending the night in a village you'll need warm clothing as temperatures can drop to around freezing, and you might want to take a sleeping bag, mosquito net and food, though these may be provided on organized tours. Finally, dogs can be a problem when entering minority villages, so it's a good idea to carry a strong stick when trekking, and always be watchful for the poisonous snakes that are common in this area.

Note that once you move north from Hanoi very few places will change **travellers' cheques**, and those that do offer poor rates, so make sure you have all the cash you need – best is a combination of dong and dollars – you need before you leave the capital.

When to go

The **best time** to visit the northern mountains is from September to November or from March to May, when the weather is fairly settled with dry sunny days and clear cold nights. **Winters** can be decidedly chilly, especially in the northeast where night frosts are not uncommon from December to February, but the compensation is daybreak mists and breathtaking sunrise views high above valleys filled with early-morning lakes of cloud. The **rainy season** lasts from May to September, peaking in July and August, when heavy downpours wash out bridges, turn unsealed roads into quagmires and throw in the occasional landslide for good measure. Peak season for foreign tourists is from September to November, while the rainy summer months of July and August are when Hanoians head up to the mountains to escape the stifling heat of the delta.

The northwest

Vietnam's most mountainous provinces lie immediately west of the Red River Valley, dominated by the country's highest range, Hoang Lien Son. Right on the border where the Red River enters Vietnam sits **Lao Cai** Town, a major crossing point into China and gateway to the former hill station of **Sa Pa** and nearby **Bac Ha**, both now firmly on the tourist map for their colourful minority groups and weekly markets. From Sa Pa a road loops west across the immense flank of **Fan Si Pan**, the country's tallest peak, to join the Song Da (Black River) Valley running south, through the old French garrison towns of Lai Chau and Son La, via a series of dramatic passes to the industrial town of Hoa Binh on the edge of the northern delta. The only sight as such is the historic battlefield of **Dien Bien Phu**, close to the Lao border, but it's the scenery that makes the diversion worthwhile. Throughout the region, sweeping views and mountain grandeur contrast with ribbons of intensively cultivated valleys, and here more than anywhere else in Vietnam the **ethnic minorities** have retained their traditional dress, architecture and languages. After Sa Pa, the most popular tourist destination in these mountains is **Mai Chau**, an attractive area inhabited by the White Thai minority, within easy reach of Hanoi.

Lao Cai

Follow the Red River Valley northwest from Hanoi, and after 300km pushing ever deeper into the mountains, you eventually reach the border town of **LAO CAI**, the railhead for Sa Pa and a popular route into China for travellers heading to Kunming. There's little reason to linger in Lao Cai itself but if you need to overnight there are a few reasonably comfortable hotels (see below).

Arrival and transport

Most people arriving from Hanoi will pitch up at Lao Cai **train station**, located next to a **post office** on the east bank of the Red River, nearly 3km due south of the Chinese border.

If you want to head into town, follow the road north from the station towards the border and after 2km you reach Coc Leu Bridge, spanning the river to link up with the bulk of Lao Cai Town over on the opposite bank. Immediately across the bridge, the town's **bus station** and market is on the left. To go to the border, continue north past the bridge for another kilometre. Getting about Lao Cai is most easily done by motorbike; hordes of xe om shuttle between the train station and frontier or across to the bus station.

For those travelling **on to Sa Pa**, a slew of tourist buses ($2) meet the Hanoi train in the early morning for the ninety-minute journey to Sa Pa Town. Local buses (about $1) also run from here and the bus station – and xe om (around $5) are always on the prowl though this is not the best way to tackle the switchback climb if you're a sensitive traveller – grab a seat on the left to enjoy the fantastic view. Note that there have been several thefts on the **night train** between Hanoi and Lao Cai and reports of pickpocketing on Hanoi's station platform. Make sure you keep possessions safe by locking and securely stowing bags in the space under the bottom bunk in the carriage, particularly when you're asleep, and never leave bags unattended while waiting to board the train in Hanoi or Lao Cai. Finally, it's also worth noting that you can take a motorbike onto the train with you for around $6.

The Tulico tourist company (☏020/832788, ✆tulico@hn.vnn.vn) has an office located inside the station complex, which can arrange transport as well as trips to Sa Pa and Bac Ha.

Accommodation and eating

Most of Lao Cai's **hotels** are found on the road running up to the border, Nguyen Hue, though there is also a guesthouse in front of the station. There's not a great choice, and prices are high given the poor quality, yet at weekends rooms still fill up with holidaymakers from both sides of the border. If you do need to stay, the cheapest option is the mock-colonial *Song Hong Guesthouse* (☏020/830004; ❶), just past the border gate and over the rail line on Nguyen Hue. Its fourteen rooms include balconies with views across the river to China. Other possibilities along Nguyen Hue include the *Hanoi* (☏020/832486; ❶), which has basic rooms with few frills, as do the *Binh Minh*

Onward travel to China

The border crossing into China is via the Hekou Bridge **border gate** (7am–5pm), on the east bank of the Red River. When planning cross-border travel, note that China is an hour ahead of Vietnam.

Two trains a week run directly between Hanoi and Kunming in southwestern China (see p.402 for more details), but it's also possible to make your own way to Lao Cai, cross the border on foot, then carry on in China by bus or by rail. Queues are longest in the early morning, when local traders get their day pass over to Hekou. Across on the Chinese side, turn right and Hekou train station is only five minutes' walk away, where a direct train to Kunming departs at 1.30pm every day (Chinese time). At least two regular bus services leave Hekou each day on the twelve-hour journey (520km), but check locally for the latest situation.

Travellers **entering Vietnam** at Lao Cai have occasionally reported problems, usually involving a "fee" of a couple of dollars for paperwork, processing or the like.

(☎020/830085; ●) and the *Huyen Trang* (☎020/832199; ●), all located back towards the train station. The smartest hotel in town is the *Duyen Hai* (☎020/822083, ⨍820177; ❸), a five-storey block on the west bank of the Red River. To find it, turn right immediately after crossing the Coc Leu Bridge, from where it's another 80m. If you're whacked on arrival at the train station, try the *Gia Nga Guest House* (☎020/830459; ●), which is basic but clean.

The road outside the train station is lined with **food stalls**, as good a place as any to eat in Lao Cai, while the market is another obvious hunting ground. The *Thai Du*, located just outside the station, is a decent place to refuel with *bia hoi* and simple dishes before or after the long train journey.

The Town

Lao Cai exudes none of the trading frenzy of other border towns and even its **market**, the only point of interest apart from the border itself, is a small, local affair peddling medicinal leaves, roots and bark from the surrounding forests as well as cheap Chinese imports. Vietnamese traders head over the border to Hekou market, a mass of ramshackle huts clearly visible across the river; coming the other way, but in smaller numbers, are bevies of Chinese tourists having a day out in Vietnam.

Even before the 1979 border war, Lao Cai had seen its fair share of power struggles. The town's most disreputable occupants were the "Black Flags", remnants of the Tai Ping rebel army who fled China to capture Lao Cai in 1868, after a siege lasting almost a year. They were notorious bandits, terrorizing the local population, but, when French incursions along the Red River threatened the status quo, Black Flag mercenaries joined forces with the Vietnamese. Though they killed the first two French commanding officers, Garnier and Rivière, the Black Flags only succeeded in hampering the colonization of northern Vietnam. Lao Cai eventually fell to the French in 1886, though robber bands lived on in the mountains until the end of the nineteenth century.

Sa Pa and around

A metalled road climbs slowly westwards away from Lao Cai along the steep, terraced hillsides of the Hoang Lien Son mountain range. Forty kilometres and ninety minutes later, journey's end is **SA PA**, a rapidly growing town perched dramatically on the western edge of a high plateau, facing the hazy blue peak of **Fan Si Pan**. The refreshing climate and vaguely Alpine landscape struck a nostalgic chord with European visitors, who travelled up from Lao Cai by sedan chair in the early twentieth century, and by 1930 a flourishing hill station had developed, complete with tennis court, church and over two hundred villas. Nowadays only a handful of the old buildings remain, the rest lost to time and the 1979 Chinese invasion, as well as those involved in the current hotel development spree. In fact, there are plans to 'develop' Sa Pa's entertainment and relaxation potential over the next couple of years, which probably means lots of karaoke bars and pony rides, so the town's days as a haven in the hills seem numbered. However, for the moment, what the modern town lacks in character is more than compensated for by its magnificent scenery and walks out to surrounding **minority villages**. The region is home to a mosaic of ethnic groups, principally Hmong, Dao and Giay (see Contexts, p.521, for more on minority peoples). The group most frequently seen in Sa Pa is the Black Hmong, who are not intimidated by the presence of foreigners in their midst. In fact, young Hmong girls can often be seen walking hand in hand with Westerners they have befriended prior to making their sales pitch. By contrast,

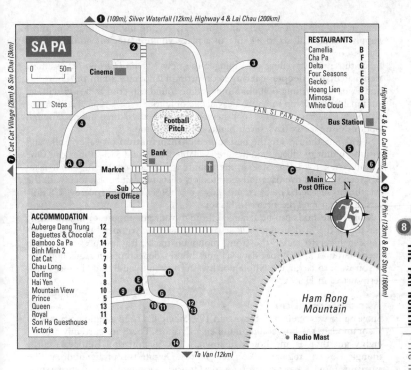

▲ ❶ (100m), Silver Waterfall (12km), Highway 4 & Lai Chau (200km)

SA PA

0   50m

Cinema

TTT Steps

◀ ❼, Cat Cat Village (2km) & Sin Chai (3km)

Highway 4 & Lao Cai (40km) ▶ ❽, Ta Phin (12km) & Bus Stop (1600m)

RESTAURANTS

Camellia	B
Cha Pa	F
Delta	G
Four Seasons	E
Gecko	C
Hoang Lien	B
Mimosa	D
White Cloud	A

Football Pitch

FAN SI PAN RD

Bus Station

❷

❸

❹

Bank

❺

❻

Market

A B

C

Main Post Office

Sub Post Office

N

ACCOMMODATION

Auberge Dang Trung	12
Baguettes & Chocolat	2
Bamboo Sa Pa	14
Binh Minh 2	6
Cat Cat	7
Chau Long	9
Darling	1
Hai Yen	8
Mountain View	10
Prince	5
Queen	13
Royal	11
Son Ha Guesthouse	4
Victoria	3

CAU MAY

D

E F

G

❾

❿ ⓫

⓬ ⓭

⓮

Ham Rong Mountain

Radio Mast

▼ Ta Van (12km)

the Red Dao, another common group here, are very shy and not at all happy to be photographed, despite their eye-catching dress.

Sa Pa's invigorating air is a real tonic after the dusty plains, but cold nights make warm clothes essential throughout the year: the sun sets early behind Fan Si Pan, and temperatures fall rapidly after dark. During the coldest months (Dec–Feb), night temperatures often drop below freezing and most winters bring some snow, so it's worth finding a hotel room with heating. Often a thick fog straight out of a Sherlock Holmes novel can creep over the whole town lending a spooky feel to the market. You'll find the best **weather** from September to November and March to May, though even during these months cold, damp cloud can descend, blotting out the views for several days.

Arrival, information and transport

Though many people visit Sa Pa on an organized **tour** from Hanoi (see p.403), the town is well set up for individual travel. The most popular route is by **train** to Lao Cai, and then the connecting **tourist bus** ($2) up to Sa Pa; while the night train saves on both time and accommodation, a daylight journey is rec-ommended for great views along the Red River Valley. The tourist bus drops you either on Cau May (Sa Pa's main street) or at Sa Pa's **bus station** just round the corner from the main **post office** on the eastern edge of town, from where it's a few minutes' walk into the centre.

Heading back to Lao Cai, **local buses** ($1) leave from various points – Cau May, the church and the bus station. Guesthouse owners can also often arrange a pick-up. Guesthouses will sometimes organize a jeep for a small group back to Lao Cai for $2 a head, and can also book **train tickets**; note that tickets for hard sleepers and soft seats on the night train are in short supply at Lao Cai, so to be sure of a place you're better off booking in Sa Pa.

For those not travelling on a budget, the new *Victoria Hotel Sa Pa* organizes designated **soft sleeper carriages** departing Hanoi at 9.30pm on Thursdays and Fridays, returning 6.30pm Sundays. The round trip costs $90–145 with an optional $12 pick-up in Lao Cai, available only to guests. A typical accommodation package costs $249 per person for two days/three nights, though options of up to six days/seven nights are possible too.

Sa Pa's guesthouses are the best source of **information** on valley walks and visiting minority villages; guides are available for around $15-20 per day. One possible trek is to Fan Si Pan, the country's highest mountain, which takes between three to five days and requires lots of stamina and good luck with the weather to succeed. The bank and most guesthouses **change money** (US dollars only) but rates are better in Hanoi.

Motorbike taxis can be arranged through your guesthouse, or find them by the top of the market steps; self-drive is available but you need to be an experienced biker to tackle the stony, mountain tracks. It's also possible to hire **jeeps** (around $20–30 per day) via guesthouses, depending on availability, but if you want to tackle the whole northwestern circuit you'll find cheaper long-term prices in Hanoi.

Accommodation

Since Sa Pa was opened to tourists in 1993, there has been a building frenzy to accommodate the burgeoning numbers of visitors. There are currently around eighty guesthouses and hotels in town, a few in imitation European villas, though most are regulation concrete blocks. Despite this proliferation, in the **summer** months – peak season for local tourists – rooms can be in **short supply**, pushing up prices by as much as fifty percent. Prices also go up at **weekends** from September to November, when the streets are busy with foreigners, but there are usually enough beds to go round. Come midweek and you'll have your pick of hotels and get a few dollars knocked off the room rate. Needless to say, rooms with an unrestricted view of Mount Fan Si Pan command higher prices.

Foreigners can now stay in **minority villages**; guesthouses in Sa Pa can help with arrangements.

Auberge Dang Trung Cau May ☎020/871243, ⓕ871666. For many years *the* place to stay in Sa Pa, the *Auberge* has been largely robbed of its great views by new construction in front. It's now a steep clamber to the top of their extension to get a glimpse of the mountains. Good restaurant and Internet cafe. ❶–❸

Baguettes & Chocolat Thac Bac ☎020/871766, ⓔehoasuaschoolsp@hn.vnn.vn. Run by the Hoa Sua School for disadvantaged youth, this is a little gem. Only two twins and two doubles, but delightful decor and stylish bathrooms plus a cosy restaurant with inviting goodies downstairs. ❷

Bamboo Sa Pa Cau May ☎020/871075, ⓕ871945. Some of the smartest rooms in town, with excellent views, fake fireplaces and bathtubs. Minority shows in the large restaurant at weekends. ❹

Binh Minh 2 Thi Tran ☎020/871142, ⓕ871141. Boring building in the new part of town, but big rooms with desks and satellite TV at cheap prices. ❶–❷

Cat Cat Cat Cat Road ☎020/871387. One of the town's longest-standing mini-hotels, *Cat Cat* now consists of two buildings, both of which have fantastic panoramic views across to Mount Fan Si Pan from the upper floors. Good restaurant and trekking info, but service is often sloppy. ❶–❸

Chau Long Cau May ☎020/871245, ⓦwww.chaulonghotel.com. Small but smart rooms in this rather attractive edifice. All have bathtubs; some have views. ❸–❹

Darling Thac Bac ☎020/871349. Perched on the valley edge facing Fan Si Pan, this guesthouse has a range of cosy rooms with tasteful furnishings, a swimming pool and an unobstructed view over the

valley and mountain. ❶–❹
Hai Yen Thi Tran ⓣ020/871613, ⓕ871682. Opposite the *Binh Minh 2* and a bit smaller, but its smartly furnished rooms are still good value. ❷
Mountain View Cau May ⓣ020/871334, ⓕ871783. A popular spot with Internet access and tour info, and as the name suggests, the view is good. A few rooms have fireplaces. ❶–❸
Prince ⓣ020/871274. Located opposite the post office, it has only ten rooms but they are bright and airy and well priced. Trekking info, motorbike rental. ❶
Queen Cau May ⓣ020/871301. This budget alternative in the centre is well kept and friendly, and has some of the cheapest rooms with a view in town. ❶
Royal Cau May ⓣ020/871313, ⓔroyalhotel_sapa@yahoo.com. Very good value at this place where prices are the same year-round. Balconies with views, fireplaces, some rooms with bathtubs. Restaurant and tour info. ❷–❸
Son Ha Guesthouse Fan Si Pan ⓣ020/871273. A friendly welcome and useful local information, plus good views from upstairs rooms, which are spacious and have fireplaces. Very competitive rates. Good restaurant, *White Cloud*, downstairs. ❶
Victoria Hoang Dieu ⓣ020/871522, ⓦwww .victoriahotels-asia.com. The *Victoria*'s 77 rooms bring a touch of luxury to Sa Pa and find a regular clientele among expat residents of Hanoi looking for an accessible weekend break. Pool, tennis courts, sauna and Jacuzzi on site. Travel and tours are included in the weekend package for $249 per person (3 nights). ❺–❻

The Town

Sa Pa is now firmly established as the tourist capital of the northern mountains and bearing in mind that at the weekend hotel prices are higher and the place is crawling with Westerners, it's worth considering a midweek visit, when everything's more relaxed. The town itself is ethnically Vietnamese, but its shops and market serve the minority villages for miles around. What initially attracted foreigners was the **weekend market**, which runs from Friday to Sunday. These days the market is housed in a newly constructed concrete eyesore and is a far cry from the original Saturday "love market" where the local ethnic minorities would come to court their sweethearts. The love market has now moved on elsewhere, a result of too many intrusive camera flashes and voyeuristic tourists, though plenty of minority people still turn up to peddle ethnic-style bags and shirts to trekkers. More authentic market fairs can be found on the other side of the Red River at **Can Cau** (Saturday) and **Bac Ha** (Sunday – see section on Bac Ha). The weekends are still bright and lively in Sa Pa, though, with the women coming dressed in their finery – the most eye-catching being Red Dao, wearing scarlet headdresses festooned with woollen tassels and silver trinkets. Hmong are the most numerous group, at over one third of the district's population, and Hmong women are the most commercially minded, peddling their embroidered indigo-blue waistcoats, bags, hats and heavy, silver jewellery at all hours.

Remember always to ask permission before **taking photographs**, especially of older people. Note that Dao and Day in particular believe that being photographed has a detrimental effect on their health; you should ask your guide to seek permission first, or simply respect their wishes. Some minority groups now demand money in return for being photographed, but it's better to offer to buy one of their crafts or items of clothing than just hand out cash for a snapshot.

Eating and drinking

Sa Pa has the widest range of food in the north outside of Hanoi, and one benefit of the building boom is that there are plenty of choices, with new ones opening all the time. Very popular and often crowded is the *Mimosa*, with a wide range of Western and Vietnamese dishes at inexpensive prices. It's located up a small stairway beside the public library off Cau May.

Along this section of Cau May, the town's main street, are several reasonable places, including *Cha Pa*, *Four Seasons* and the Italian *Delta*. The *Auberge* serves a good range of snacks and main dishes, while *Baguettes & Chocolat* offers cakes and pastries, set meals and lunch packs for trekkers. Next to the post office, *Gecko* combines a cosy bar, stylish restaurant and small guesthouse (5 rooms) in one attractive old building. To the west of the market, a small string of restaurants like the *Hoang Lien*, the *White Cloud* and the smarter *Camellia* all offer good food in a clean environment. Several restaurants sell bottles of snake wine, a brew made with a pickled baby cobra, sometimes called Vietnamese Viagra because of its alleged tonic properties. If that sounds a bit too potent for you (it's an acquired taste), try the local mountain apple wine, which is more likely to appeal to Western tastes.

Trips to surrounding villages

There are several Hmong villages within easy walking distance of town, and while directions are given here, it's strongly advisable to go accompanied by a local guide.

One of the most popular walks is to **CAT CAT** Village, directly below Sa Pa in the Muong Hoa Valley, roughly 3km away. To get there, follow the track west from the market square, continue past the steeple-shaped building that is a monitoring centre for the forestry department, and then turn left onto a path that drops steeply beside a line of old electricity pylons down to the river. Cat Cat, a huddle of wooden houses, hides among fruit trees and bamboo, where chickens and pot-bellied pigs scavenge among trailing pumpkin vines. Look out for tubs of indigo dye, used to colour the hemp cloth typical of Hmong dress, and for interlocking bamboo pipes that supply the village with both water and power for de-husking rice. Cat Cat waterfall is just below the village, the site of an old hydroelectric station and now a pleasant place to rest before tackling the homeward journey. For a longer walk, instead of cutting down to Cat Cat Village, continue on the main track turning right at the last bend before a river to follow a footpath up the valley towards Fan Si Pan. After 4km you'll reach **SIN CHAI** Village, a much larger Hmong settlement (nearly a hundred houses) spread out along the path.

You have to venture further afield to reach villages of minorities other than Hmong. One of the most enjoyable treks is to follow the main track from the *Auberge* south down the Muong Hoa Valley for 9km to a wooden suspension bridge and **TA VAN** Village, on the opposite side of the river. Ta Van actually consists of two villages: immediately across the bridge is a Giay community, while further uphill to the left is a Dao village. From here, it's possible to walk back towards Sa Pa on the west side of the river, as far as another Hmong village, **LAO CHAI**, before rejoining the main track. If you don't want to walk all the way back up to Sa Pa, you can pick up a motorbike taxi at one of the huts you'll find every 2 to 3km along the track; expect to pay around $3 one-way (20min). Alternatively, you can take a xe om from Sa Pa for the round trip, but negotiate an acceptable price first.

Following the main road another 3km south from the turn-off to Ta Van, a track leads to the Dao settlement of **GIANG TA CHAI**, or **CHAI MAN**. The path branches off to the right, just after a stream crosses the road and before a small shop. After crossing a suspension bridge, take the left fork, directly across a stream, after which it's a kilometre to the village. Giang Ta Chai can also be reached by footpath from Ta Van, but you need a guide.

From the last turn-off the road deteriorates rapidly for another 6km until it finally dwindles to a footpath just after **SU PAN**, an unprepossessing collection of huts which is home to a number of different minorities. From here, heading 4km straight down into the valley, bearing right at each fork, brings you to the Tay village of **BAN HO**, which straddles the river at a suspension bridge – the settlement comes into view at the bottom of the valley soon after you leave Su Pan. Ban Ho is the staging point for two-, three- and four-day treks in the next valley, best tackled in the company of a guide.

An excursion to **TA PHIN** Village takes you northeast of Sa Pa, along the main Lao Cai road for 6km and then left on a dirt track for the same distance again, past the blackened shell of an old French seminary. Finally a scenic footpath across the paddy leads to a community of Red Dao scattered among a group of low hills; on the way look out for a beautifully engineered rice-husker beside a small stream. The village is known for its handicrafts, but its people are also known for being quite aggressive when it comes to selling their beer. The easiest way to find Ta Phin is to take a xe om from Sa Pa (about $3 each way) and get dropped off at the start of the footpath; as the leg between Sa Pa and the start of this path isn't so attractive, you might also want to keep it for the return journey.

New villages are being explored all the time as more tourists arrive seeking out ever more remote spots. **BANG KHOANG** is a Dao settlement with over a hundred families located 16km north of Sa Pa; look for a right turn after about 10km along the Lai Chau road and follow the road to the village. From here, the road continues to the Hmong settlement **TA GIANG PHINH**, home to 150 families. Both of these villages are best explored by jeep or motorbike in a day-trip from Sa Pa.

All hotels and tour agents in Sa Pa can organize treks to the above villages with the option to overnight in some. Prices start from around $15 a day. The *Auberge, Royal, Prince* and *Son Ha* are all reliable and can arrange excursions to remote markets, a "Conquer Fan Si Pan" trip for around $70, or a Sunday trip to **Muong Hum Market**, 75km from Sa Pa by jeep and a kilometre from the Chinese border, for around $15 per person including jeep and lunch. When booking a guide locally, make sure you get one from Sa Pa and not from Hanoi, as only a local will speak the dialects necessary to communicate within the villages. Always wear strong shoes, carry water, waterproofs and a basic medical kit.

Hoang Lien Son Nature Reserve and Mount Fan Si Pan

The **Hoang Lien Son Nature Reserve** was set up in 1986 to safeguard remnants of natural forest habitat over an area of thirty square kilometres south and west of Sa Pa. Over the years, trees below an altitude of 1500m have largely been cleared for agriculture, building and firewood, but reforestation programmes are under way, adding commercial timbers in an effort to reduce illegal logging. Of the reserve's 56 mammal species, nearly one third are listed as rare or endangered, among them the clouded leopard, tiger and black gibbon. It's easier to spot some of the 150 bird species, a few of which are unique to the mountains of northwest Vietnam.

Vietnam's highest mountain, **Fan Si Pan** (3143m) lies within the reserve boundary, less than 5km as the crow flies from Sa Pa but an arduous three- to five-day round trip on foot. The usual route starts by descending 300m to cross the Muong Hoa River, and then climbs almost 2000m on overgrown paths through pine forest and bamboo thickets, before emerging on the southern ridge. The reward is a panorama encompassing the mountain ranges of northwest Vietnam, south to Son La Province and north to the peaks of Yunnan in China. Although it's a hard climb, the most difficult aspect of Fan Si Pan is its

climate: even in the most favourable months of November and December it's difficult to predict a stretch of settled clear weather and many people are forced back by cloud, rain and cold. A **guide** is essential to trace indistinct paths, hack through bamboo, and locate water sources; Hmong guides are said to know the mountain best. Sa Pa hotels and tour agents can arrange guides and porters as required (about $15 per day for each).

Bac Ha and around

The small town of **BAC HA**, nestling in a high valley 40km northeast of Highway 7, makes a popular day excursion from Sa Pa. There's little to see in the town itself except on Sunday, when villagers of the Tay, Dao, Nung, Giay and above all Flower Hmong ethnic minorities trek in for the lively **market**. At 1200m above sea level compared to Sa Pa's 1600m, Bac Ha is less spectacularly beautiful, although it's still scenic, with cone-shaped mountains bobbing up out of the mist, and it's also much less touristy, giving out a workaday sense of a bustling agricultural community rather than an alpine resort. If you're travelling independently it's worth spending a whole weekend in Bac Ha, in which case you'd also be able to take in the rustic and colourful **market** at Can Cau on Saturday.

Getting to and from Bac Ha

Coming **from Hanoi**, get off the bus or train at Pho Lu, from where there are several buses a day to Bac Ha from the bus station (2hr; $3), which lies on the highway just across from the railway station. Coming **from Lao Cai**, there's only one direct bus a day to Bac Ha, at 1pm (4hr; $4). If this isn't convenient, hop on a bus to Pho Lu and change there. If you're coming **from Sa Pa** on a Sunday, your best bet is to take a tour from one of Sa Pa's guesthouses for about $7, which usually includes spending the morning at the market, a trek in the afternoon and a ride back to Sa Pa, with the option of being dropped off at Lao Cai station. Alternatively, rent a motorbike from your guesthouse in Sa Pa to make the three-hour journey through the mountains. To arrive in time for the market requires an early start and the roads can be bumpy, but views are spectacular and it's a great way to blow away the cobwebs on a Sunday morning. The road that leads in from Pho Lu forms the main street of Bac Ha. Buses stop outside the post office (open 7am–9pm), where a bend in the road marks the centre of town before leading on for another 2km to the local People's Committee headquarters and onwards in the direction of Can Cau. A road branching off to the right immediately beside the post office leads to the market and a couple of guesthouses.

Returning from Bac Ha, buses leave for Lao Cai via Pho Lu at 5am, 7am, 11am and 1pm and direct to Pho Lu at 7am and 11am. A jeep or motorbike can do the journey to Lao Cai in two hours, though there are often road repairs which can cause delays.

It's also possible to go directly from Bac Ha to Ha Giang and continue exploring the little-known northeast, though for this you will need your own transport. Head back down out of the hills towards Lao Cai, but after crossing the bridge over the Chay River, turn left on Highway 70 and follow it about 40km to Pho Rang. This is a good place for a break as there are reasonable food stalls just beyond the bridge on the left and a lively market off to the right a little further down the main street. Turn left just before the bridge and follow Highway 279 to Viet Quang, then left again on Highway 2, which takes you into Ha Giang. The trip takes about six hours, depending on road conditions.

Accommodation and eating

The range of accommodation available in Bac Ha is limited, with few people spending more than one night in town. There are no really fancy places, but most Westerners opt for the *Sao Mai* (☏020/880288; ❸), located down a lane to the west of the town centre. It has big, comfortable rooms and a restaurant, and offers many tours of the local area. Just beyond the *Sao Mai*, the *Toan Thang* (☏020/880444; ❷) is smallish but clean. Back in the middle of town are several reasonably priced places with little to pick between them – the *Hoang Vu* (☏020/880264; ❶–❷), the *Tuan Anh* (☏020/880377; ❶–❷), and the *Dang Khoa* (☏020/880290; ❶–❷). Be warned, though, that in the centre of town, when the government's early morning broadcasts kick in around 5am, you may find yourself getting an unexpected alarm call. Finally there are a couple of options in the street by the post office. The *Tran Sin Guesthouse* (☏020/880240; ❶–❷), is right opposite the market and has clean rooms and a good restaurant. A bit further down the road on the right is the *Anh Duong Guesthouse* (☏020/880329; ❶), where the tiny rooms are the cheapest in town.

Bac Ha's **restaurants** are bursting with tourists on Sundays and practically deserted at all other times. The *Sao Mai* features Western as well as Vietnamese dishes. The *Tran Sin* serves basic meals in decent portions. The *Cong Fu Restaurant*, just off the main road where the first street leads off to the right as you come up the hill from the post office, is another good option. Just beyond this turn-off on the main road, the *Hoa Ngan* also has an English menu and reasonable food, but don't expect to find the culinary choices in Bac Ha that you can get in Sa Pa.

The Town

Bac Ha provides a stark contrast to Sa Pa, with little in the way of tourist facilities beyond a few *pho* and *bia hoi* stalls. The Sunday market, the town's one big attraction, gradually fills up from 8 to 10am and from then till lunchtime it's a jostling mass of colour, mostly provided by the stunningly dressed Flower Hmong girls looking for additional adornments to their costume. The scene is filled out with a sizeable livestock market, meat and vegetable sellers, wine sellers and vendors of farming implements. The town returns to a dusty shadow of its former self by 5pm when the ethnic tribes return to their outlying villages. As Sa Pa becomes saturated with tourists seeking out a more authentic experience, so Bac Ha has attempted to emulate Sa Pa's success by developing its own trekking business focused around the nearby rural markets. For the moment, however, it lacks sufficient infrastructure – which, in many ways, is the key to its charm.

At the northern end of town on the left along the main road, lies the remarkable folly of **Vua Meo**, or Cat King House. Two storeys of pure wedding cake surround a courtyard built in 1924 by the French as a palace for a Hmong leader, Vuong Chiz Sinh, whom they had installed as the local "king" (Meo, or "Cat" in Vietnamese, is a disparaging term formerly applied to the Hmong). The building is now the office of the local People's Committee, but visitors are free to wander through the courtyard.

Trips to surrounding villages

It's only a short stroll to the picturesque Flower Hmong hamlet of **BAN PHO**, 3km from town, but at the time of writing a large highway was being built there which might spoil its traditional atmosphere. To get there head out of town past the *Sao Mai Hotel*, turning left immediately after the next big building, which is the local hospital. The road continues up the hill for a couple of kilometres after the village, and affords good views of the valley. From

Ban Pho, the Tay village of **NA HOI** completes the circuit back to Bac Ha. In the opposite direction, the village of **THAI GIANG PHO**, home to Hmong, Tay and Fula people, is a six-hour round trip by motorbike or jeep from Bac Ha, for which you'll need a guide. Trips can be organized through the *Sao Mai* and other guesthouses in Bac Ha, but be prepared for some rough overland driving.

The village of **CAN CAU**, 18km north of Bac Ha, hosts a market each Saturday, which is every bit as colourful as that in Bac Ha, albeit smaller, and is located in a fairy-tale setting among rolling hills. It consists of a disparate mix of livestock on sale – including horses, ponies, buffalo and cattle – with traders trekking in from as far afield as China in search of bargains, plus many vendors selling bright panels of cloth, which attract the Flower Hmong ladies, already resplendent in their bright outfits. As with Bac Ha, the busy hours are around 10am to lunchtime, and there are some beautiful items of clothing on sale that make great souvenirs. Relatively few visitors get there so the fair retains much of its authenticity, a situation that is likely to change now that there is a reasonably good road. Other than the market there's nothing at all to see in Can Cau, but the ride, across a high, empty range with panoramic views on either side, is glorious. To get there, simply follow the main road north out of town the whole way. You can go there on a tour (about $10 per person in a group of six), but it's not really necessary if you can ride a motorbike (about $5 per day rental), as the market is right by the main road. Another option is a xe om from opposite the post office for $7–8 return. Note that there is a deep ford just outside Bac Ha which becomes impassable after heavy rain.

The *Sao Mai Hotel* in Bac Ha organizes a day-trip to Can Cau, and another to the equally unexplored Tuesday market at Coc Ly. The latter trip includes transport by jeep and a boat trip down the Blue River Valley and costs $15 per person. There are also possibilities of two- and three-day trips costing $20–30 per person, including overnight stays in minority villages.

Further north of Can Cau lie a few other villages – such as the largely Hmong town of Sima Cai – but these are, for the moment, off limits to foreigners due to their proximity to the Chinese border where local conflicts often flare up. Any foreigners who show up are likely to get polite marching orders from the local military.

On to Lai Chau

West of Sa Pa the road climbs over the Hoang Lien Son range and then starts a slow descent along the wall of an immense valley into the least-densely populated region of Vietnam's far north. About two hours' drive (80km) later you come to **TAM DUONG**, which some people use as an alternative stopover to Lai Chau, particularly as **PHONG THO** Village, 30km further west, hosts a Monday **market** of great size and variety. There are only a couple of hotels here, but both of them are cheap, friendly and quite adequate. The *Tam Duong* (T023/875288, F875610; **①–②**), located opposite the market, has large rooms and is a bit cheaper than the *Phuong Thanh* (T023/875235, F875158; **②**), to the east of the market on the main street, though the latter has good views out back. Phong Tho itself also has a basic guesthouse (no phone; **①**). Confusingly, Tam Duong is sometimes referred to as Phong Tho, while Phong Tho is also known as Muong Xo. From here on the route veers south, following the gently attractive Nam Na Valley peopled with Thai villages of impressively solid stilthouses, while higher slopes are farmed by groups of Black Hmong and Dao. For much of this stretch, road and river track a wooded gorge before emerging at the confluence with the Da River near the town of Lai Chau, some 200km (5–6hr) from Sa Pa. The landscape to the north and south of town is some of the most rugged in the northwest, and thus prone to occasional landslides that can delay progress for long periods.

After crossing the Da River the road skirts east of **LAI CHAU**, past a T-junction where the town's one street branches right to the market and an attractive **hotel**, while the **bus station** is located further along on the main highway. Lai Chau is a small sleepy town set among paddy fields on a broad valley floor, with no real centre, just tentacles of buildings stranded above the flood plain. One eerie sight is the shell of the former Cultural Hall that was gutted by a flash flood and now looks like some futuristic sculpture of concrete and weeds. For most travellers this is a one-night stop between Sa Pa and Dien Bien Phu; after a quick walk round the small market, where you can snack on freshly cooked rice cakes, and a wander through the **Black Thai village** on the hillside west of town, there's little else to do – other than enjoy not being on the road. Some years ago Lai Chau lost its status as provincial capital to Dien Bien Phu, since when it's been in slow decline, and may even disappear altogether if plans for a second Da River dam go ahead.

One oddity of this small town is that it boasts what is a rarity in north Vietnam – a hotel with character. The *Lan Anh* (☏ & ⓕ 023/852370; ❷–❸) is set in a leafy compound and consists of over forty rooms housed in a few attractive wooden buildings, all fitted with four-poster beds. Breakfast is included in the price, served in the hotel's restaurant, which also happens to be the best place to eat in town. It's located down a sidestreet to the right beyond the market, just before a bridge over the river. There are a couple of less attractive alternatives on the main highway near the T-junction – the *Song Da* (☏023/852527; ❶) and the *Nam Lay* (☏023/852346; ❶) – that may appeal if budgetary concerns are paramount.

Dien Bien Phu

South of Lai Chau the road splits: Highway 6 takes off southeast to Tuan Giao and is the shortest route to Son La; Highway 12 ploughs on south for more than 100km (about 3–4hr), making slow progress at first but then zipping through the second 50km, to the heart-shaped valley of **DIEN BIEN PHU**, scene of General Giap's triumph in a battle that signalled the end of French Indochina (see box opposite). The isolated valley is roughly 19km by 8km, oriented north–south and edged by low mountains. Though only a trickle of tourists visits Dien Bien Phu, drawn mostly by its historic battlefield, the town is undergoing a construction boom fuelled in part by lucrative smuggling across the border from Laos. The valley's population is predominantly Thai (53 percent), while only one third are Viet in origin and they are concentrated in the urban area. Though there are daily flights from Hanoi, it's a much more interesting journey by road, but this demands a five-day round trip or an overnight stop on the circuit through Vietnam's northwest. For the moment, the **border with Laos**, only 35km away by road to the southwest, remains firmly closed to foreigners. However, there are persistent rumours that it will open soon – check with the embassy in Hanoi (see p.404) for the latest.

The town and the battle sites

Highway 12 enters the valley from the north, skirts the airfield 5km out of town and enters Dien Bien Phu at a T-junction on the western edge of town, where the bus station is located. From here it's a couple of hundred metres, crossing the Nam Rom River, to a dusty roundabout and market which form

The Battle of Dien Bien Phu

In November 1953 General Navarre, Commander-in-Chief in Indochina, ordered the French Expeditionary Force's parachute battalions to establish a base in Dien Bien Phu. Taunted by Viet Minh incursions into Laos, with which France had a mutual defence treaty, Navarre asserted that this would block enemy lines through the mountains, force the Viet Minh into open battle and end the war in Indochina within eighteen months – which it did, but not quite as Navarre intended. His deputy in Dien Bien Phu was **Colonel de Castries**, an aristocratic cavalry officer and dashing hero of World War II, supposedly irresistible to women, although Graham Greene, visiting the base in January 1954, described him as having the "nervy histrionic features of an old-time actor".

Using bulldozers dropped in beneath seven parachutes apiece, the French cleared two airstrips and then set up nine heavily fortified positions on low hills in the valley floor, reputedly named after de Castries' mistresses – Gabrielle, Eliane, Béatrice, and so on. Less than a quarter of the garrison in Dien Bien Phu were mainland French: the rest were either from France's African colonies or the Foreign Legion (a mix of European nationalities), plus local Vietnamese troops including three battalions drawn from the Thai minority. There were also nineteen women in the thick of things (a stranded French nurse, plus eighteen Vietnamese and Algerian women from the Expeditionary Force's mobile brothel).

Meanwhile, **General Giap**, Commander of the People's Army, quietly moved his own forces into the steep hills around the valley, mobilizing an estimated 300,000 porters, road gangs, and auxiliary soldiers in support of up to 50,000 battle troops. Not only did they carry in all food and equipment, often on foot or bicycle over vast distances, but they then hauled even the heaviest guns up the slopes, hacking paths through the dense steamy forest as they went. Ho Chi Minh described the scene to journalist Wilfred Burchett by turning his helmet upside down: "Down here is the valley of Dien Bien Phu. There are the French. They can't get out. It may take a long time, but they can't get out." In early 1954 Giap was ready to edge his troops even closer, using a network of tunnels dug under cover of darkness. By this time the international stakes had been raised: the war in Indochina would be discussed at the Geneva Conference in May, so now both sides needed a major victory to take to the negotiating table.

French commanders continued to believe their position was impregnable until the first shells rained down on March 10. Within five days Béatrice and Gabrielle had fallen, both airstrips were out of action and the siege had begun in earnest; the French artillery commander, declaring himself "completely dishonoured", lay down and took the pin out of a grenade. All French supplies and reinforcements now had to be parachuted in, frequently dropping behind enemy lines, and when de Castries was promoted to general even his stars were delivered by parachute; at the end of the battle, 83,000 parachutes were strewn across the valley floor. The **final assault** began on May 1, by which time the rains had arrived, hindering air support, filling the trenches and spreading disease. Waves of Viet Minh fought for every inch of ground, until their flag flew above de Castries' command bunker on the afternoon of May 7. The following morning, the day talks started in Geneva, the last position **surrendered** and the valley at last fell silent after 59 days. A ceasefire was signed in Geneva on July 21, and ten months later the last French troops left Indochina.

The Vietnamese paid a high price for their victory, with an estimated 20,000 dead and many thousands more wounded. On the French side, out of a total force of 16,500, some 10,000 were captured and marched hundreds of kilometres to camps in Vietnam's northeastern mountains; less than half survived the rigours of the journey, diseases and horrendous prison conditions.

Fifty years on, the Battle of Dien Bien Phu remains one of the most significant military conflicts of the twentieth century, with its importance in Vietnam's struggle for independence commemorated in nearly every town by a street named in honour of that famous victory.

the town centre. To the left the highway leads to Tuan Giao and on to Hanoi or Lai Chau, while heading right you go past the post office to the museum and Viet Minh Cemetery, about 800m to the south.

The town's **museum** (daily 7.30–11am & 2–4pm; small admission fee) is set back slightly from the road on the right-hand side as you head south out of town. There's a display of weaponry including American-made guns of World War II vintage captured from French troops. Alongside them languish Viet Minh guns, also American-made but newer: these were booty from the Korean War which came via China into Vietnam, to be dragged up the battlefield's encircling hills. Familiar photos of the war-torn valley become more interesting in context, as does the scale model where a guide describes the unfolding catastrophe – the message is perfectly clear, even in Vietnamese. Also on display is one of the sturdy bicycles capable of carrying 200-kilo loads along the Viet Minh supply trail, along with plenty more examples of ingenious homemade weapons and equipment.

Directly opposite the museum is the **Viet Minh Cemetery**, where some of the fallen heroes are buried under grey marble headstones marked only with a red and gold star. In 1993 an imposing imperial gateway and white-marble wall of names was added in time for the fortieth anniversary of the battle. The outside of this wall features bas-reliefs in concrete of battle scenes.

A small hill overlooking the cemetery, known as **Hill A1** to the Vietnamese and as Eliane 2 to French defenders, was the scene of particularly bitter fighting before it was eventually overrun towards the end of the battle. You can inspect a reconstructed bunker on the summit and various memorials, including the grave of a Viet Minh hero who gave his life while disabling the French tank standing next to him, and you also get a panorama over the now peaceful, agricultural valley.

There's little to see at the last battle site, a reconstruction of **de Castries' bunker**, but it's a pleasant, twenty-minute walk across the river on a track busy with farm carts. To get there, head back into town from Hill A1 for about 300m before turning left down a road between a small vegetable market and a row of *pho* stalls. Cross a bridge, and turn left when you can see the bunker's low, corrugated roof 100m away, surrounded by barbed wire. Around about are captured tanks, anti-aircraft guns and other weaponry rusting away in the fields. Carrying on straight ahead past the old tank for about 300m you come to a concrete enclosure with a memorial "To those who died here for France".

Accommodation and eating

There's not a great choice of accommodation in Dien Bien Phu, but several new **hotels** were under construction at the time of writing, so things may soon change. For the moment, the most convenient place is the *Muong Thanh* (☎023/810043, ⓕ810713; ❶–❸), which has seventy rooms of varying size and facilities. It's located on Him Lam, about 200m northeast of the town's main roundabout. The hotel also has a large restaurant and small swimming pool, and as with many hotels around the country, a karaoke lounge and massage parlour. It's popular with tour groups, so it may be a good idea to book in advance. On the same road and closer to the roundabout is the *Binh Long* (☎ & ⓕ023/824345; ❶–❷), a small but friendly place. On the road west from the roundabout are a few other possibilities, including the cheap and fairly reasonable rooms at the hotel of Construction Company No.2, or *Cong Ty Xay Dung So 2* (☎023/824386; ❶). Further along the same road the *Airport* (☎023/825052; ❷), occupying the same building as the Vietnam Airlines office, has reasonable rooms, as does the *Phuong Huyen* (☎023/824460; ❸), while the cheaper alternative across the street, the *May Hong* (☎023/826300; ❶), has small and rather dingy rooms. On the road south from the roundabout towards the museum is the *Dien Bien Phu* (☎023/825103; ❶–❷), a classically drab, government-run place with listless staff, though rooms are just about acceptable. Finally, to the east of town near the cemetery is the *Beer Factory Guest House* (☎023/824635; ❶–❷), which is fine for boozers who don't mind basic amenities.

The *Muong Thanh Hotel* has a good **restaurant**, and the *Lien Tuoi* on the street leading to the *Beer Factory Guest House* (between the cemetery and Hill A1) is very popular. A convenient eatery in the town centre is next to the *Airport Hotel*. Locals tend to patronize *com pho* stalls around the roundabout and along the main roads – it's worth wandering around and looking for a big crowd – but they all close by around 7-8pm. The region's speciality food is the Thai minority's black rice (*com gao cam*).

Son La and around

East of Dien Bien Phu the road climbs into steep mountains and passes through constantly changing panoramas before dropping into **TUAN GIAO**, where Highway 6 takes off north to Lai Chau or south to Son La. Tuan Giao is a convenient lunch stop on a day of tough travel, and the obvious place to eat is *Hoang Quang*, where it comes as a surprise to see tablecloths and an English menu. The eponymous owner can also help travellers to find accommodation if necessary. You'll need to be fortified to face the steep and bumpy climb that follows to the Pha Din ("Heaven and Earth") Pass, one of the highest in the north. If you're lucky there are great views from the top, but more often than not it's enveloped in clouds. After a long descent, the road eventually passes through the small town of **THUAN CHAU**, where there's a lively market of predominantly Black Thai people each morning until 9–10am. The last stretch passes through a valley bordered by massive karst pillars before reaching a softer landscape of paddy and banana plantations, where water wheels feed sculpted terraces, to the industrious town of **SON LA**. Son La's welcoming, low-key charm is enhanced by its valley-edge setting, and it merits more than the usual overnight stop. If time allows, there's enough of interest to occupy several days, taking in the old French prison and some nearby caves, as well as making forays to nearby minority villages on foot or by motorbike.

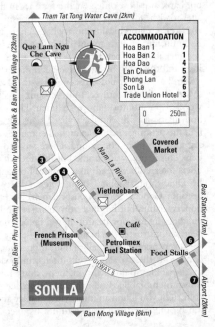

▲ Tham Tat Tong Water Cave (2km)

ACCOMMODATION

Hoa Ban 1	7
Hoa Ban 2	1
Hoa Dao	4
Lan Chung	5
Phong Lan	2
Son La	6
Trade Union Hotel	3

0   250m

SON LA

▼ Ban Mong Village (6km)

Practicalities

There are currently three flights a week (Wed, Fri & Sun) from Hanoi to Son La's Nasan Airport, which lies 20km southeast of town on Highway 6. From there you'll need to take a minibus or xe om into town. Son La **bus station** has moved to about 7km east of town, so it's necessary to take a xe om into the centre. The best place to go for **information** is the helpful *Trade Union Hotel*, where you can also hire transport and English-speaking guides, or arrange to see Thai dancing and sample rice wine. Vietindebank at 30 To Hieu will **exchange** dollars.

When it comes to **accommodation** options, the *Trade Union Hotel* (☏022/852804; ❷–❸) is a welcome exception to the generally gloomy and uninviting government-run places found in many Vietnamese towns. Its range of almost a hundred rooms is the best in town, and it organizes a variety of local trips. You can find more inspiring decor at the *Phong Lan* (☏022/853515; ❸), which has over thirty smart rooms, and the *Lan Chung* mini-hotel (☏022/858088; ❶–❷) is in a convenient location with comfy rooms. Right opposite is the older *Hoa Dao* (☏022/853823; ❷), which has spacious and well-equipped rooms. On the south side of town, the *Hoa Ban 1* (☏022/854600; ❶) is not a bad alternative, but the more central *Son La* (☏022/852702; ❷) is less appealing. There's a *Hoa Ban 2* (☏022/852395, ⓕ852712; ❸) to the north of town, which seems to be often full despite its uninterested staff and inflated prices.

For **food**, the *Trade Union Hotel* has a good restaurant with English menu, but it's open to residents only (closes 10.30pm). If you didn't find black rice (*com gao cam*) in Dien Bien Phu, then try it here in one of the *com pho* stalls near the big junction at the south end of town. For caffeine addicts, there's a combined **café** and dentist on To Hieu, opposite the Petrolimex station.

The Town

The major part of Son La lies off the highway, straggling for little more than a kilometre along the west bank of the Nam La River. There's just one main street, To Hieu, where you'll find all the important municipal buildings, including bank and post office. At the far end, in front of the *Hoa Ban 2 Hotel*, a parallel road heads back south on the opposite side of the river, past the covered **market** – selling local minority handicrafts, including handmade cloth and lively embroideries – to rejoin Highway 6. Between these two roads in the town centre, patches of paddy and vegetable plots are being consumed by new buildings, and two new bridges have been built to ease the constant bustle of traffic.

Son La's principal tourist sight is the **French prison**, Bao Tang Son La (Mon–Sat 7.30–11am & 1.30–4.30pm; small admission fee), which occupies a wooded promontory above To Hieu. The two turn-offs from the highway are both marked with chunky stylized signs suggesting incarceration; walk uphill to find the prison gates and an arched entrance, still announcing "Pénitencier", leading into the main compound. There are also good views down over town from here. This region was a hotbed of anti-French resistance, and a list of political prisoners interred here reads like a roll call of famous revolutionaries – among them Le Duan and Truong Chinh, veteran Party members who both went on to become General Secretary. Local hero To Hieu was also imprisoned for seditionary crimes but he died from malaria while in captivity, in 1944. Most of the buildings lie in ruins, destroyed by a French bombing raid in 1952, but a few have been reconstructed, including the two-storey kitchen block (*bep*), beneath which are seven punishment cells. Political prisoners were often incarcerated in brutal conditions: the two larger cells (then windowless) held up to five people shackled by the ankles. Behind the kitchens, don't miss the well-presented collection of prison memorabilia. Enter the second arched gate and upstairs in the building on your right you'll find an informative display about the dozen or so minorities who inhabit the area, including costumes, handicrafts, jewellery and photos.

Around Son La

There are several **caves** around town that are worth a look, the most convenient being **Que Lam Ngu Che Cave**, which is situated just north of the *Hoa
Ban 2 Hotel* and has a small shrine inside surrounded by strange formations in
the rock. You can go there alone – just look for the sign to the left north of the
hotel, or a guide from the *Trade Union Hotel* will take you for a small fee. **Tham
Tat Tong Water Cave** is located a couple of kilometres further north out of
town, and at the time of writing was closed to visitors, but any excuse to walk
in the countryside around Son La brings rich rewards, such as meetings with
friendly villagers, lush panoramas of karst hills and paddy fields alive with butterflies. Follow the road north from the *Hoa Ban 2 Hotel* for nearly 2km and
turn left just before a concrete bridge onto a footpath tracing the river
upstream to an ancient stone bridge – according to local legend, built by a
Black Thai queen a thousand years ago. Take the first path left on the far side
of the bridge, beside a line of pylons, to reach a barbed-wire enclosure where
the river emerges from the hillside. There's also a second, dry cave directly over-
head – a short scramble up beside the wire – in which, when open, you can
walk the first 50m of a system said to be 7km long. Just beyond the turning for
Tham Tat Tong Cave is one of Son La's nearest, though still rarely visited,
minority villages. Instead of turning left at the concrete bridge continue on
the road towards a cliff-face punched with a round cavern, reputed to contain
gold, about 70m up. Turn left before the cliff and you pitch up in **BAN CO**,
a Black Thai community of about fifty stilthouses constructed of bamboo, and
fenced round with hedges of poinsettia and hibiscus. The dress of the Black
Thai women is particularly striking – especially the brightly embroidered
headscarves that they drape over their long hair piled up in huge buns. Their
tight-fitting blouses with rows of silver buttons, often in the shape of butterflies, are also distinctive. In colder weather, many wear a green, sleeveless
sweater over the blouse, or a modern jacket in pink, blue, green or maroon.

If you've got more time, a popular jaunt takes you out to **BAN MONG**,
another Thai village six scenic kilometres along a luxuriant valley south of Son
La. The houses of this village are solid, wooden structures surrounded by gardens of fruit trees rather than vegetables. A scummy pond at the village edge is
in fact a hot spring that provides water for the bathhouse and laundry at a constant 30°C. To get to Ban Mong, take the turning off Highway 6 opposite the
prison; the valley becomes completely cut off during the rains and at any time
you'll need four-wheel drive, or take a xe om from Son La for the return trip.

It's also possible to take in Ban Mong as part of a longer trek which heads
northwest out of Son La before wheeling south through the villages of several
minorities, eventually linking up with the hot spring. It's about six hours' walking in all, so you'll need a whole day, and take food and plenty of water, as there
are no shops until you get to Ban Mong. As the route's fairly complicated it's best
to drop by the *Trade Union Hotel*, where you can arrange a guide for about $10.

Certain minority villages stage events for tour groups, such as traditional Thai
dancing or supping the local home brew, a sweet wine made of glutinous rice;
it's drunk from a communal earthenware container using bamboo straws, and
hence named *ruou can* or stem alcohol.

Mai Chau and around

Highway 6 climbs east from Son La, passing **YEN CHAU** – a town famous
for its fruit – and some very pretty Black Thai villages on the right after about
80km, particularly **LA KEN**, which can be visited by crossing swaying

suspension bridges over the river. From here the road climbs onto a thousand-metre-high plateau where the cool climate favours tea and coffee cultivation, mulberry to feed the voracious worms of Vietnam's silk industry, and herds of dairy cattle, initially imported from Holland, to quench Hanoi's thirst for milk, yoghurt and ice cream. Just less than 120km out of Son La, the sprawling market town of **MOC CHAU** provides a convenient place for a break. A brief stop at the **milk products** shop, on the right opposite the 126km marker from Son La, is highly recommended. Lovers of thick yoghurt will go gaga over the creamy local stuff, and a glass of fresh hot milk slips down well too. They also sell locally-made milk bars and chocolate, as well as green tea. The rigid lines of tea bushes that border the road round Moc Chau create curious patterns, and though there are few side roads, this is a region in which some might want to linger. Most, however, head on down Highway 6, through valleys where the Hmong live in distinctive houses built on the ground under long, low roofs, and surrounded by fruit orchards, to **MAI CHAU**. The **minority villages** of the Mai Chau Valley, inhabited mainly by White Thai, are close enough to Hanoi (135km) to make this a popular destination, particularly at weekends when it's often swamped with large groups of students. The valley itself, however, is still largely unspoilt, a peaceful scene of pancake-flat rice fields trimmed with jagged mountains.

Arrival and transport

Most people visit Mai Chau on an organized **tour** out of Hanoi (see p.403), which usually includes overnighting in a minority village, or as part of a longer trip into the northwest mountains by jeep or motorbike.

Mai Chau is not the easiest place to get to by **public transport** but it is possible. **From Son La** take any bus heading east to Hoa Binh or Hanoi and ask the driver to let you off at the Mai Chau junction, around 65km after Moc Chau; at the junction pick up one of the waiting xe om for the final 6km up the valley. **From Hanoi**, there's a daily bus (6am) from Kim Ma bus station to Mai Chau. **Leaving Mai Chau**, a local bus departs around 7am bound for Hanoi, arriving at noon; alternatively, take a xe om to the junction with Highway 6 and flag down a bus going in your direction.

Mai Chau Village

Mai Chau is the valley's main settlement, though it's still just a village – a friendly, quiet place which has a bustling morning **market** when minority people trek in to haggle over buffalo meat, star fruit, sacks of tea or ground-nuts. Unlike in Sa Pa, the minorities here have largely forsaken their traditional dress, but there's plenty of colour on the road outside the market where bright hanks of yarn, freshly dyed in primary hues, hang up to dry.

Tour groups tend to stay in the villages of Ban Lac and Pom Coong to the west of Mai Chau and go on organized walks around the valley. If you are one of the rare independent travellers here, a tempting choice is to turn left (east) at the "Guesthouse" sign in the middle of Mai Chau, walk a kilometre across paddy fields and make your base at the stilted *Ban Van Guesthouse* (☎018/ 867182; ❶). Hemmed in by mountains, the village of **Ban Van** has great charm and friendly inhabitants. Alternatively, on the south side of Mai Chau is the *Mai Chau Guesthouse* (☎018/867262; ❶), with fourteen rooms. The larger rooms have a certain funky appeal, but the place is often empty. The *Mai Chau Guesthouse* runs a pretty good **restaurant,** and there are many food stalls clustered around the market back in town, some serving up lip-smacking kebabs. In the mornings you'll find hawkers here selling piping-hot banana fritters and coffee.

The Mai Chau Valley

Just south of the *Mai Chau Guesthouse*, a road to the right (west) leads across a few paddy fields to **BAN LAC**, home to a prosperous community of White Thai, though these days their wealth is derived more from tourist dollars than from farming. This is where most people stay on a two-day tour from Hanoi – it's a settlement of some seventy houses (about four hundred people) where you can buy hand-woven textiles, watch performances of traditional dancing and sleep overnight. Nowadays just about every house in the village doubles as a guesthouse, and many have sit-down toilets fitted below the houses. Some house owners have even changed their roofs from tile back to the original thatch, per-haps to fulfil visitors' expectations. If you turn up without a tour group, just ask around and someone will put you up for about $5 per person for the night, plus $1–2 for a meal depending largely on how much you eat. While too touristy for some, Ban Lac does offer the chance to stay in a genuine stilthouse: an edifying experience, particularly at dawn if your sleeping quarters happen to be above the henhouse. During the day the lanes between houses are draped with scarves, bags and dresses, with local ladies urging passers-by to stop for a quick look. Though it seems a bit commercial, the vendors are not as pushy as their Black Hmong counterparts in Sa Pa, and if it does get tiring then a few minutes walk in any direction from the centre leads out to paddies and a view of the ring of purple mountains which make for some of north Vietnam's most classic scenery. In the evenings, the traditional dance performances shown for tour groups after dinner are also interesting, with coy, long-haired girls acting out agricultural chores in a graceful manner. After the show, the audience are invited to join them in a dance, as well as a sup of local wine from a big bowl through a bamboo tube.

Many houses in Ban Lac rent out **bicycles**, which are an ideal way to explore the valley. One interesting route is to cycle 12km south on Highway 15 to **CO LUONG**, passing timeless rural scenes and reflections of mountains in the pad-dies. At Co Luong, the Ma River joins the road, and huge limestone walls and dense bamboo growth adorn the riverbank. A small **boat hire** shop at the riverside (☎018/867782) can arrange trips for small groups along the river, but there are no other tourist facilities here.

Hoa Binh

There's one final pass to go over before Highway 6 leaves the northwest moun-tains. It's a slow crawl along precipitous hillsides up to a col at 1200m, and then an ear-popping descent through sugar-cane plantations to **HOA BINH**, on the edge of the Red River plain. The town's proximity to Hanoi, 76km on a fast road, plus its hotels and easy access to a variety of minority villages mean that Hoa Binh soaks up a lot of tourist traffic. Unless you need the bus connections, it's preferable to stop over in Mai Chau or push on all the way to Hanoi.

During the French War Hoa Binh was the scene of a disastrous French raid into Viet Minh-held territory, which reads like a dress rehearsal for the epic rout of Dien Bien Phu. In November 1951, French paratroop battalions seized Hoa Binh in a daring attempt to hamper enemy supply routes. They met with little resistance and dug in, only to find themselves marooned as Giap's forces cut both road and river access. In February the following year the French fought their way out towards Hanoi in a battle that came to be known as the "hell of Hoa Binh".

The Town

The main highway thunders straight through the centre of modern Hoa Binh but a hint of quieter days lingers in its shaded main boulevard, Cu Chin Lan. Less than 2km above the city to the northwest, the 620-metre-wide **Hoa Binh**

Dam chokes the Da River to create a lake over 200km long, stretching all the way to Son La. The reservoir is earmarked for tourist development, but its main purpose is to feed Vietnam's largest hydroelectric plant which came on stream in 1994 and has gone some way to solving Vietnam's chronic power shortage. Hoa Binh Tourism (Ⓔehoabinhtourism@fpt.vn, located at the *Hoa Binh Hotel 2*) offers guided tours of the complex, but otherwise you get a worm's-eye view of the dam from the pontoon bridge that links Hoa Binh's main street with industrial suburbs across the Da River. Muong, Thai, Hmong and Dao **minorities** all live in the vicinity, but you'll need to arrange a guide and transport if you want to visit them. Again, Hoa Binh Tourism can help but they're geared primarily to tour groups. Their most popular outing is a day's boat trip on the Da River, visiting Muong and Dao villages ($20 per boat), and they can also arrange a night's accommodation in a showpiece Muong village ($10 per person plus food).

Practicalities

Hoa Binh's main **bus station** lies on its eastern edge, where you'll find the usual gaggle of xe om waiting to take you the kilometre into town. Buses for Hanoi leave regularly, but note that some terminate at Ha Dong, where you have to pick up a Hanoi city bus. Keep an eye on your bags as thefts have been reported on this route.

The most popular **places to stay** for foreigners are the *Hoa Binh 1* and *2* (Ⓣ018/852051 & 852537, Ⓕ854372; ❸–❹), located opposite each other on a hillside 2km west of the town centre along Highway 6. Both have about thirty wood-panelled rooms in long stilthouse, and restaurants. The *Hoa Binh 2* also features folk dancing and music displays and sampling of Thai rice wine from the communal pot. In the same complex, you'll find Hoa Binh Tourism and a shop selling minority crafts, including a tempting selection of traditional clothes and embroidered textiles. If you're just looking for a comfortable bed for the night, the *Thap Vang* (Ⓣ018/852864; ❷), on the main road in the centre of town, is a sound choice, with twenty well-equipped rooms. As well as the restaurants at the *Hoa Binh*s, there's also a group of local **restaurants**, cafés and ice-cream parlours at the west end of Cu Chin Lan, about 50m before the T-junction.

The northeast

The provinces of northeast Vietnam, from Lang Son looping westwards to Ha Giang and Tuyen Quang, lack the grandeur of their counterparts west of the Red River Valley, with the notable exception of the area round Dong Van and Meo Vac. In general the peaks here are lower and the views smaller-scale and of an altogether softer quality. Getting to see everything is not so straightforward as in the northwest either, and you may have to choose between an exploration of the border zone in **Ha Giang Province** or a stay at **Ba Be Lake** along with a visit to attractions near **Cao Bang**. However, with enough time, it's possible to visit all these places without returning to Hanoi.

Highlights of the northeast are its **rural landscapes**, from traditional scenes of green-engulfed villages to dramatic limestone country, typified by pockets of cultivation squeezed among rugged outcrops whose lower slopes are wrinkled with terraces. However, population densities are still low, leaving huge forest reserves and high areas of wild, open land inhabited by **ethnic minorities** practising swidden farming (see p.521). While many have adopted a Vietnamese way of life, in remoter parts the minorities remain culturally distinct – particularly evident when local markets, their dates traditionally set by the lunar calendar, are in full swing. The varied local climate supports a wide range of crops, from anise, peach and pear to tea, rubber and the usual gamut of subtropical and tropical species. In addition, the hills are rich in largely unexploited reserves of gold, copper, zinc, iron ore and other minerals.

Ha Giang and around

HA GIANG is the capital of the north's most remote and least-visited province, where Vietnam's border juts into China and almost reaches the Tropic of Cancer. Until the early 1990s, this region was the scene of fierce fighting between Vietnam and China, and it is still considered a "sensitive area", though its inhabitants nowadays are peaceful and welcoming. The town itself has a few attractions, in the form of a museum, a market and steep, wooded hills that surround it, but the main reason for coming to Ha Giang is to head on to **MEO VAC** and **DONG VAN**, both set in valleys surrounded by forbidding peaks and connected by a hair-raising road with spectacular views. The round trip from Ha Giang is about 300km and takes two full days of driving along narrow, bumpy roads, which may become impassable during the rainy season. This border area is home to several **minority groups**, including the White Hmong and the Lo Lo, the latter having only a few thousand members, and most towns along the route have a **Sunday market** attended by villagers from the surrounding valleys, where you're likely to be the only foreigner.

There are a few practicalities which account for this lack of visitors. Firstly, at present foreigners must obtain a permit to travel for $10 from the police (which can also be arranged by tour agents) in Ha Giang. Secondly, foreigners are required to take a guide (about $15 a day) with them. Thirdly, foreigners are forbidden to climb hills or wander from the road, though in reality there are few officials to check you along the route. Fourthly, there is no road connecting Meo Vac with towns to the south, so it's necessary to return via Ha Giang. And finally, Ha Giang is not yet fully prepared for Western travellers; few people speak English and there are no concessions to Western tastes in the restaurants. All in all, however, these disincentives do not outweigh the rich experience in store.

Arrival and information

Ha Giang lies 290km from Hanoi and buses from the Long Bien terminal take about six hours to reach it via Highway 2, passing through **Vinh Tri** on the banks of the River Lo, and **Viet Quang** (also known as Bac Quang) just 60km before Ha Giang. With a rented vehicle, it's also possible to approach from **Bac Ha** by heading south on Highway 70 to **Pho Rang**, then taking Highway 279 which winds its way eastward to Viet Quang, and finally north to Ha Giang. Either way the journey takes the best part of a day.

The town of Ha Giang straddles the Lo River, with two bridges connecting the older part on the east bank and the newer part on the west bank. The **bus station** is on Nguyen Trai which runs along the west side of the Lo River; the main **post office**, a **bank**, a **museum** and several **hotels**, **guesthouses** and **restaurants** are also along this street. On the east side are more hotels and

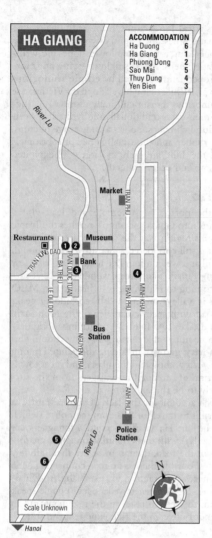

HA GIANG

River Lo

Market

TRAN PHU

Restaurants

Museum

TRAN HUNG DAO

TRAN QUOC TUAN

Bank

BA TRIEU

LE LOI DO

MINH KHAI

TRAN PHU

Bus
Station

NGUYEN TRAI

ANH PHU

Police
Station

N

Scale Unknown

Hanoi

restaurants, as well as many shops. The town's main **tour agent** (Ha Giang Tourist Company) is located on Tran Hung Dao, just west of the northern bridge, while the **police station** is on Anh Phu, just east of the southern bridge. You need to visit one of these to arrange a **permit** for onward travel towards the border.

Accommodation and eating

There are plenty of places to stay in town, and though staff speak very little English this shouldn't be a problem. Arriving from the south along Nguyen Trai, the first place you come to is the *Ha Duong* (☎019/862555; ❷), which has big, smart rooms with good facilities, including a large restaurant and massage rooms. A little further in towards town is the smaller but cosier *Sao Mai* (☎019/863019; ❷). Past the post office on the left and bus station on the right is the government-run *Yen Bien* (☎019/866333; ❶–❷), with forty rooms about the biggest hotel in town. It's a bit run-down, but has large rooms, a café and restaurant, and is conveniently positioned. Just beyond here, opposite the museum, is a cluster of mini-hotels, of which the *Phuong Dong* (☎019/867979; ❶–❷) is a reasonable choice. On Tran Hung Dao, the *Ha Giang* (☎019/864727; ❶) wouldn't win any prizes for its appearance, but its dingy, windowless, dormitory-style rooms are the cheapest in town. Among several options on the east side of the river, the *Thuy Dung* (☎019/862278; ❷–❸) on Minh Khai probably has the nicest rooms.

There are several **restaurants** along Tran Hung Dao, near the northern bridge, and plenty more around the market and streets on the east side of town, though you'll need your phrase book in most places. The *Yen Bien* and *Ha Duong* hotels both have large restaurants, too.

The Town

Ha Giang is a sizeable town, and though its buildings are of no great architectural merit, its setting is very impressive, with the tall Mo Neo and Cam mountains crowding it in. The ochre waters of the Lo River carve southward through the centre of town, and traffic is thick on the bridges that connect the north and south districts. The town's **market** is located in a purpose-built hall just northeast of the northern bridge, and is a frenzy of activity in the early morning when members of **minority groups** can often be seen. If you plan to go to Dong Van, however, you're likely to see more authentic markets along the way. The Ha Giang **museum** (daily 7.30am–noon & 2–4pm, with late opening 7.30–9.30pm on Wed, Sat & Sun; free), is just west of the northern bridge. It's well worth a visit to get a preview of the outfits of the many different minority groups who inhabit the region, as well as to see artefacts such as bronze drums and ancient axe heads that have been unearthed by digs in the region. Archeological evidence shows that there has been a settlement here for tens of thousands of years, and the region seemingly flourished during the Bronze Age judging by the number of beautifully designed drums that have been found.

To Meo Vac and Dong Van

To travel through the north's most isolated region, you must be accompanied by a guide, who can help to arrange a police permit ($10). Highway 4C heads north out of town, at first following the Lo River Valley, then heading east to follow the River Mien. After about 20km the road begins to climb into the hills before crossing Quan Ba Pass ("Heaven's Gate"), where roadside steps lead up to a fine view – when the weather is clear – over **Quan Ba**, 45km from Ha Giang, and the patchwork fields around it. There's a **market** in Quan Ba on Sundays where, apart from the White Hmong, who are the biggest group in this region, you might see Red Dao, Tay, Giay, Co Lao, Pu Peo and Lo Lo people.

After Quan Ba, the road follows a pretty stream for some distance, with steep mountain flanks rising on both sides. After climbing over treeless, terraced hills which serve to increase the feeling of remoteness, it then descends into **Yen Minh**, some 97km from Ha Giang. This makes a good lunch stop and there are a few basic *com pho* stalls near the market on the left in the middle of town. There's also a run-down guesthouse, the *Minh Hai* (☎019/852109; ❶), where it's possible to base yourself, though the government guesthouses in Meo Vac or Dong Van are marginally better.

Just 4km east of Yen Minh, the road splits. The northern fork goes to Dong Van and the southern one to Meo Vac, and this is where the fun really begins. You can follow either road as they join up to form a loop; described below is the route via Meo Vac, which has slightly better accommodation than Dong Van. There's virtually no traffic on the rough road, which passes through rugged limestone landscapes, the scenery gradually getting wilder and more dramatic, and little evidence of settlements at the roadside. For much of the way, the terrain is pocked with blackened knuckles of rock that must make for difficult farming, though small fields of corn are planted here and there, and cone-shaped bundles of corn stalks, used for fodder and fuel, are scattered among the rock-strewn landscape. The locals, for the most part White Hmong, stoop low under heavy burdens of wood, and it's all too evident that around here life is tough.

If you plan to stay in **MEO VAC**, check in at the *People's Committee Guest House* (☎019/871176; ❷), which is behind government buildings next to a playing field in the centre of town, then report your presence to the local police, who may delay you a short time noting down particulars. There's no rush, however, as there's little to see apart from a small statue of Uncle Ho and the town's small market, and it's the town's setting which is most impressive, with a ring of barren mountains forming a bowl around it. Several food stalls can be found in the market, but there aren't too many choices for dinner in this remote place.

The next stage of the journey, covering just 22km on the way to Dong Van, is the most spectacular part of the whole trip. The road climbs up the side of a massive canyon to the Ma Phi Leng Pass at around 1500m, and the views down to the Nho Que River, a ribbon of turquoise far below, are simply dizzying. **DONG VAN** is in a similar setting to Meo Vac, and also has the usual market, police station (where you should also check in) and a *People's Committee Guest House* (☎019/856189; ●), both cheaper and more run-down than the one in Meo Vac. From Dong Van, the road heads back west to the junction outside Yen Minh, and for the first section to **Saiphin**, the scenery is superb – a constant string of cone-shaped peaks standing above fields in the valley below. After 15km from Dong Van, look out on the left for the sturdy building of the People's Committee at Saiphin. If you ask here, they can walk you down to the village to look at the **Vuong Palace**, a large, two-storey residence with three courtyards which was built by the French for the local Hmong king. The thick walls show intricate craftsmanship, and have slits set into them that were used to defend the place with rifles in bygone days. In the shade of pine trees beside the gateway to the palace are several impressive tombs of members of the Vuong family.

West of Saiphin, the constantly changing views continue until finally the road descends from the hills into Yen Minh, and from here you must follow the same route back to Ha Giang.

North through Thai Nguyen

Highway 3 forges due north out of Hanoi across the rice lands of the Red River Delta, gradually leaving behind industrial satellite towns and brickworks for the welcome foothills of the northern massif. Only 16km from Hanoi the highway passes right by **Co Loa**, site of the ancient capital of Vietnam (see p.410), but otherwise there's nothing to stop for until you reach **THAI NGUYEN**, 80km from Hanoi on the edge of the delta. This sprawling steel town makes a surprising home for one of Vietnam's more rewarding museums, the **Museum of the Nationalities of Vietnam**, *Bao Tang Van Hoa Cac Dan Thoc Viet Nam* (Tues, Wed & Sun 8–11am & 2–4pm; small admission fee). Usually staff will show foreign tourists around outside the official opening times, but it's best to make a prior arrangement (☎028/855781). The museum is arranged in five rooms according to language group, Viet–Muong, Tay–Thai, Mon–Khmer and so on, with examples of traditional costume and objects from daily life, as well as plenty of photographs and helpful captions in English. Most impressive is the Mon–Khmer room, refurbished with Swedish assistance, which includes video presentations of festivals and excellent architectural models. The museum, an imposing, puce-coloured building built in 1960, stands on a roundabout in the centre of town – north of the post office radio mast – at 359 Duong Tu Minh. Coming north on Highway 3, turn right (northeast) on Hoang Van Thu, then follow directions for Lang Son to find the museum.

Continuing north from Thai Nguyen on Highway 3, after only a few kilometres Highway 13A turns off left, cutting across country to Tuyen Quang, from where it's possible to join the road to Lao Cai (see p.395). Soon after, the main northbound highway starts to climb gently, following the attractive Cau River through a region inhabited by Nung minorities. **NA PHAC**, a small market town with a well-placed clutch of cafés 200km from Hanoi, marks the turning for Ba Be National Park. If you happen to pass through Na Phac on market day (held at five-day intervals, starting on the first day of the lunar month), you'll be treated to an arresting display of minority dress.

Ba Be National Park

Vietnam's largest natural lake, Ho Ba Be, forms the core of **Ba Be National Park**, which encompasses 23,000 hectares of limestone and tropical semi-evergreen forest. The lake is 7km long, up to 30m deep and up to a kilometre wide. A few islands decorate the surface and the whole lot is enclosed by steep, densely wooded slopes, with some tall and ancient trees, breaking out here and there into white limestone cliffs. Apart from its natural beauty, the park's main attraction is **boat trips** to visit caves, waterfalls and minority villages, with the added bonus of seeing at least a few of the 220 animal, 417 plant and 49 fish species recorded here. Bears, tigers and one of Vietnam's rarest and most endangered primates, the Tonkin snub-nosed monkey (*Rhinopithecus avunculus*), live in a few isolated communities on the fringes of the park, but nearer the lake there's a good chance of spotting the more common macaque monkeys and garrulous, colourful flocks of parrots. Few people are around to disturb the wildlife and outside the months of July and August, when Hanoians take their holidays, you'll usually find only a handful of tourists. What puts some people off Ba Be is difficulty of access by public transport, but if you join a tour from Hanoi or hire your own transport it becomes easier to justify, especially when combined with a visit to a minority market. Even then, though, a two-night stay is sufficient for most people.

Getting there and around

The simplest way of getting to Ba Be National Park is to join a tour or arrange your own transport. Hanoi tour agencies (see p.363) can help with vehicle hire or line up a full programme, either as a three-day excursion or as part of the Cao Bang–Lang Son circuit (4–5 days). Total travelling time from Hanoi to Ba Be is around six hours: from the Na Phac turning on Highway 3 a road threads west across country to Ba Be (47km) via **CHO RA**, another small town that comes to life on market days (every Sunday). If you've got your own vehicle, you can take an interesting alternative route on a back road through stunning rural landscapes: just north of Phu Thong on Highway 3 (near the 174km marker), turn left and after 30km you'll come out beside Cho Ra's *Ba Be Hotel* (see below). **Public transport** to Ba Be is also possible – buses ($3) leave from Gia Lam bus station in Hanoi and pass Thai Nguyen and Bac Can on the way. They pull up in nearby Cho Ra, from where a xe om to Ba Be Lake will cost around $1. If coming from Ha Giang with your own transport, enquire about the condition of Highway 279, which cuts across from Viet Quang to Ba Be. If this road is not passable, you will need to go back down Highway 2 to Tuyen Quang, then head west on Highway 37 to Thai Nguyen, and follow Highway 3 north from there.

On arrival, first stop for independent travellers should be the park headquarters, which is located a couple of kilometres from the boat jetty on the east side of the lake. The entrance fee to the park is less than a dollar, and not always charged. Here you can get **information** about two- to five-day tours run by park guides, costing $25–45 per person, that include **boat trips** to caves and waterfalls and nights spent in minority villages. Most trips are in spacious, covered motorboats, but with a little preparation it's also possible to row (or be rowed) around parts of the lake in a narrow dug-out canoe – a more appropriate way to move about in such a tranquil environment. If you prefer to go it alone at Ba Be, daily rental rates for either type of boat begin at around $20 a day.

Tour groups from Hanoi generally base themselves in the budget hotels in Cho Ra, and the Ba Be itinerary usually begins with a boat trip along the Nang River to **Hang Puong**, where the waters have tunnelled a 300-metre-long, bat-filled cave through a mountain. From here they go on to the **Dau Dang Waterfall**, a stretch of beautiful but treacherous rapids. Take care if you walk on the slippery rocks around the falls as there has been at least one tourist fatality here. Next up is a visit to a **Tay** village on the lakeside, and on longer trips an overnight stay in a stilthouse. A road around the south end of the lake has made **Pac Ngoi** less of an isolated Tay community than it used to be, but several other villages in the area, such as **Buoc Luom**, **Ban Vang** and **Bo Lu**, can accommodate visitors too. Few Tay wear traditional dress these days, and you're most likely to see it at a **minority show** at the *National Park Guest House* (see below).

Accommodation and eating

The most convenient and comfortable **place to stay** is the *National Park Guest House* or *Vuon Quoc Gia Ba Be* (☎0281/894126, ⑤894026; ❸), located next to park headquarters, which offers fifty tastefully arranged rooms, an excellent restaurant, Internet access and occasional minority shows, but is often booked out by party cadres, who find it a good location for meetings, so it's best to reserve ahead. **Cho Ra** is 17km away, and there's little to see or do in this one-street town of huts made of mud and wood, but it does have several mini-hotels, which can also arrange boat trips. The *Ba Be 1* and *2* (☎0281/876115 & 876476; ❷–❸) and *Tuyet Trinh* (☎0281/876117; ❷–❸) have large, clean rooms and expansive views from the back. Tour groups often spend a night in a stilthouse or you can arrange a home stay through the national park. There are also a couple of remote guesthouses on the west side of the lake, one of which (☎0281/894042; ❶) is directly opposite the boat jetty. The owner, Hoang Thi Gam, can usually be found selling refreshments at the jetty.

The speciality in many local **restaurants** is fish from the lake, and the best place to try it is at the *National Park Guest House*, where the set dinners give a good variety of dishes. The guesthouses in Cho Ra also serve food, though the kitchens close early, and there are a few *com pho* stalls around the only road junction in town. Snacks and drinks are available at the boat jetty by Ba Be Lake.

Cao Bang and around

North from Na Phac, Highway 3 climbs up to a high pass (800m), called **Col des Vents** by the French, which marks the watershed between the Red River Valley to the south and China's Pearl River in the north. Over the col lies a region of metamorphic rocks typified by big, rounded hills and denuded summits, known as the **Ngan Son Mountains**. This is the domain of several ethnic minorities, among them the Nung, Dao and San Chay (whose women carry a broad, curved knife tucked in the back of their belts). There are few villages in sight on these wild uplands, just the occasional split-bamboo hut selling wild honey (*mat ong*) beside the road. In fact, apart from **Ngan Son**, lost in a vast, treeless valley, there's no settlement of any size between Na Phac and journey's end, 80km later in **CAO BANG**.

Cao Bang is a likeable place: its centre may be dusty and noisy, but its riverside setting, with dense clumps of bamboo backed by sugar-loaf mountains helps to blur the edges. In winter its climate is fresh, but not downright cold like Sa Pa and Bac Ha, and though the Chinese border is only 30km away, Cao Bang isn't troubled by the frontier atmosphere of Lang Son (see p.475). Few travellers venture this far north, but those who do usually make the pilgrimage out to **Pac Bo Cave**, where Ho Chi Minh lived on his return to Vietnam in

1941, and to **Ban Gioc Falls,** Vietnams highest waterfall, right on the border with China. The province is home to several ethnic minorities, notably the Dao, Nung and Tay who still maintain their traditional way of life in the more remote uplands.

Arrival and information

Cao Bang's **bus station** is on Kim Dong, 400m east along the river from the covered market hall. Immediately east of the bus station is the **immigration office**, where you can obtain a permit to visit Ban Gioc Falls ($10) if going there independently. **Cao Bang Tourism** has an office in the *Phong Lan Hotel*, but it's not exactly a mine of information. The **post office**, on a hill in the centre of town, is recognizable from its radio mast, while the **bank** (exchange facilities for cash only) lies opposite it across a narrow but attractive park.

Accommodation and eating

There are plenty of **places to stay** in and around Cao Bang. The easiest place to find is also the biggest in town – the seventy-room *Bang Giang* (☎026/853431; ❷–❸), right next to the bridge, where the rooms are adequate if not inspiring. Further east on Kim Dong, there are several mini-hotels, of which the *Huang Thom* (☎026/855888; ❷) and *Anh Duong* (☎026/858467; ❶–❷) stand out for their exceptional value; in both places, rooms out back near the top have great views of a wall of limestone peaks. Also on Kim Dong, the government-run *Phong Lan* (☎026/852260; ❶–❷) has around fifty rooms in its two run-down buildings that may be of interest to those on a tight budget. Another government hotel on the hill behind the *Phong Lan*, the *People's Committee Guest House* or *Uy Ban Nhan Dan Tinh Cao Bang* (☎026/852804; ❷–❸), is better cared for, and is also off the busy main road. Finally, just west of the bridge is the *Thanh Loan* (☎026/857026; ❷–❸) with very cosy doubles and singles and breakfast included.

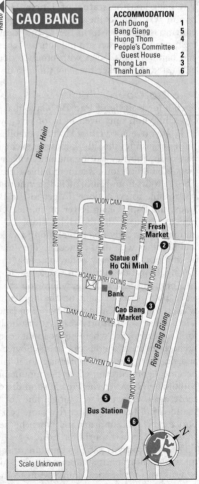

CAO BANG

Hanoi

River Hein

ACCOMMODATION
Anh Duong	1
Bang Giang	5
Huong Thom	4
People's Committee Guest House	2
Phong Lan	3
Thanh Loan	6

VUON CAM

HAN GIANG

LY TU TRONG

HOANG VAN THU

HOANG NHU

HOANG VIET

HONG VIET

Fresh Market

HOANG DINH GIONG

Statue of Ho Chi Minh

KIM DONG

Bank

Cao Bang Market

DAM QUANG TRUNG

PHO CU

River Bang Giang

NGUYEN DU

KIM DONG

Bus Station

Scale Unknown

As for **eating**, several of the above hotels, such as the *Huang Thom*, *Bang Giang* and *Thanh Loan*, also have restaurants, and there are plenty of local eateries in the backstreets near the market, up the road beside the *Phong Lan Hotel* and on Highway 4 near the bridge. First stop on cold mornings should be for a **breakfast soup** ladled from the huge steaming cauldrons in the market. For a great cup of filter coffee, try the café on the left about 50m up past the *Phong Lan Hotel*.

The Town

Cao Bang is built on the southwestern bank of the **Bang Giang River**, on a spur of land formed by the confluence with the Hien River. Highway 3 drops steeply down from the hills and enters town from the west, crossing a bridge onto a tree-lined avenue of self-important edifices, including People's Committee, theatre, bank and post office, before turning right along the river. The narrow, shady park on top of the low hill in the centre of town is worth a wander, and the **statue of Uncle Ho** is a reminder of the fact that this region was vital to the thrust for independence that he led. Held daily, the enormous **markets** form the town's focal points. If possible, try to visit the fresh produce market around sunrise when minority women trek into town and bamboo rafts laden with produce dock beside the bridge. Once you've exhausted the market, the only thing to do is head for the hills north of town.

Pac Bo Cave

Such a lot is made of **Pac Bo Cave** that it comes as a surprise to learn that Ho Chi Minh only lived in it for seven weeks, during February and March 1941. If you're not a fan of Ho memorabilia then neither the cave nor the small museum justifies the fifty-kilometre excursion (2hr each way), though the first part of the journey, passing minority villages moored in rice-paddy seas against craggy blue horizons, is a memorable ride.

Some tours from Hanoi include a visit to the cave on their itineraries, though it's possible to go it alone. To get to Pac Bo from Cao Bang, head northwest across the Bang Giang River on the Ha Quang road until you see a signpost directing you off to the right. From this junction it's another 4km to the entrance (currently no charge), along a valley dotted with memorials to heroes and heroines who died protecting Ho's hideaway. Getting to the cave by public transport is not easy as few buses ply the route between Cao Bang and Ha Quang. If you do take a bus, ask to be dropped off at the turning for Pac Bo, two hours from Cao Bang, where you can pick up a xe om for the last leg.

Pac Bo is situated right on the border with China. When **Ho Chi Minh** walked over from Guangxi Province in January 1941, he took his first steps on Vietnamese soil for thirty years. At first he lived in a Nung village but soon left for the nearby cave where he set about co-ordinating the independence movement, translating the history of the Soviet Communist Party into Vietnamese and, in his spare time, renaming local landmarks: a spring beside the cave became Lenin Stream, while the mountain above he rechristened Karl Marx Mountain. However, the French soon discovered his hideaway and Ho had to move again, this time to a jungle hut not far away where the Viet Minh was founded in May 1941. Later that same year he left for China, to drum up support for his nascent army, and when he next returned to Pac Bo it was after Independence, as a tourist, in 1961.

The **cave** today is a strange mixture of shrine and picnic spot, set in a peaceful wood full of birds and butterflies but marred by rubbish. Guides will offer to walk you up beside Lenin Stream to the cave mouth, pointing out where

Uncle Ho fished, cooked, worked, wrote poetry, even where he sat in 1961. Inside the cave, which it's said Chinese troops vandalized during the border war, you can gaze on a replica wooden bed and a stalagmite bearing an uncanny resemblance to Karl Marx. Unfortunately, exhibits in the small **museum** have no English labels: there's much of interest for the keen student of Vietnamese history, but even an amateur will be able to identify Ho's Hermes Baby typewriter, bamboo suitcase and Mauser pistol.

Over the Ma Phuc Pass

If revolutionary relics aren't your thing, take the road north towards Tra Linh and Quang Uyen and lose yourself among sugar-loaf scenery beyond the **Ma Phuc Pass**. The road from Cao Bang shoots straight up the valleyside and after a disappointing start you're suddenly looking down on a tortured landscape of scarred limestone peaks and streamless valleys typical of karst scenery. The region is inhabited by Nung people who cultivate the valley floors and terraced lower slopes, living in distinctive wooden houses that are built partly on ground level and partly raised on stilts. Even if you don't have time to explore further, views from the top of the pass – a mere 20km (30min) out of Cao Bang – more than repay the effort. Just before the top, the road splits: pick either direction for some great scenery but the right fork takes you to the only specific sight in the area, the **Ban Gioc Falls**, whose location exactly on the frontier with China made them a bone of contention during the border war. Several tour groups include the falls on their itinerary, but if you come here alone, get a permit ($10) from the immigration office in Cao Bang first. At over 90km and over two hours' driving each way, Ban Gioc is really a full day's outing; note that the falls are less than spectacular in the dry season.

Southeast to Lang Son

At Cao Bang you join **Highway 4**, an ambitious road that was originally part of a French military network linking the isolated garrisons right across northern Vietnam's empty mountain country. This road is more subject than many others in the north to falling into disrepair, and the 140km journey to Lang Son takes about four hours, depending on conditions. Beyond **Dong Khe**, a nondescript town roughly 40km out of Cao Bang, the virtually traffic-free road climbs through a gorge of sheer limestone cliffs before cresting the dramatic **Dong Khe Pass**. In 1950 this pass was the scene of a daring ambush in which the Viet Minh gained their first major victory over the French Expeditionary Force. In the ensuing panic, forts all along the border were abandoned, an estimated 6000 French troops were killed or captured, and the Viet Minh netted 950 machine guns, 8000 rifles and a few hundred trucks.

That Khe lies exactly halfway between Cao Bang and Lang Son, and beyond here the road winds through **Na Sam**, an attractive town snuggled beneath a dramatic setting of outcrops. The villages in this area are inhabited by Nung and Tay; their bamboo rafts and huge wooden water wheels, which form part of sophisticated irrigation works, grace the river that weaves along beside the road. Unfortunately this rural idyll comes to an abrupt end, as the speedy Highway 1 from Dong Dang brings you hurtling into Lang Son.

Lang Son

For most people, **LANG SON** is just a meal stop or overnight rest on the journey through the northeast or en route to China, only 18km away to the north. With a fast highway now linking Lang Son to Hanoi, reasons to linger

The majority of people taking this route into China travel **by train**, using one of the two services per week direct from Hanoi to Beijing (see p.402 for details). Make sure to take your passport to the railway station when buying the ticket. Note also that you can only board this train in Hanoi (and not at Dong Dang), though on the Chinese side it's possible to disembark at Pingxiang or Nanning, five hours further up the line.

Alternatively, you can still use the **road crossing** known as the **Huu Nghi** (Friendship) **border gate**, which lies 18km north of Lang Son and 4km from Dong Dang at the end of Highway 1. If you're travelling by **local bus**, your best bet is to overnight in Lang Son (see p.402) and then take a motorbike all the way to the border gate. Otherwise, **minibuses** shuttle between Lang Son's Le Loi Street and Dong Dang Town (look for those marked "Tam Thanh" at the front), but you'll then have to hop on a motorbike for the last leg. **Local trains** from Hanoi (hard seats only) terminate at Dong Dang station, 800m south of the main town, from where you can take a xe om up to the border; station shopkeepers will usually **change money**, but at poor rates.

The Huu Nghi **border gate** is open between 7am and 6pm; it's just a small road checkpoint and has no exchange facilities. There's a walk of less than a kilometre between the two checkpoints. On the Chinese side, take an infrequent minibus to Pingxiang (15km) for the nearest accommodation, or the mid-afternoon train to Nanning. The nearest money exchange across the border is in Pingxiang, so either get some yuan in Lang Son or keep a few small-denomination dollars handy for the minibus fare. Note that China is **one hour ahead** of Vietnam.

Whether you cross the border by train or road, you must have a Chinese **visa**, available from the embassy in Hanoi (see p.323).

are even fewer, though the surrounding countryside does have an endearing quality in the form of endless karst outcrops studding the plain. Having recently acquired the status of a city, Lang Son has a self-important feel, and its booming economy is evident in new construction sites all over town. The few sights worth seeing include the Ky Lua Market, the Den Ky Cung Temple and huge colonial houses in the old town south of the river. At present no nearby tourist attractions are promoted, though the area round Mau Son Mountain, just east of town, is good hiking country. For the intrepid, Lang Son is the start of a little-travelled back road cutting across 100km of empty country to Tien Yen on the east coast, offering a route to (or from) Ha Long Bay.

Arrival and information

Most of Lang Son's facilities are found on the north bank of the river. There is no official tourist office, but the *Bac Son Hotel* on Le Loi may be able to provide a useful map of town for a small fee. The **post office** is also on Le Loi, a little further east. Next door to the post office, at 51 Le Loi, the Vietcombank changes US dollars only. Most hotels **exchange** dollars and yuan, or cross over to the south side of the Ky Cung River to find a couple of banks on the corner of Tran Hung Dao (Highway 1) and Quang Trung. There are also a couple of **Internet cafés** along Le Loi. Ngo Quyen branches off to the right from Le Loi, where about 100m along you'll find the **bus station**, though most long-distance buses will drop you on Le Loi or Tran Dang Ninh, the town's main north–south artery. If you're travelling on to China (see box above), there's no reason to stop in Lang Son, unless you need accommodation (see below).

Accommodation and eating

Market forces have spawned new **hotels** and Lang Son is fairly well provisioned with inexpensive accommodation, although at weekends rooms still fill up with holidaymakers, mostly male, trekking over from China. At the time of writing there were no outstanding places, though several new hotels under construction may change that. A quaint choice at present is the government-run *A1 Guest House* (⑦025/812221; ❸), on the south side of the Ky Lua Bridge in the old part of town. Down Hoa Binh Street, to the northwest of the bridge, are several mini-hotels, of which the *Thanh Tung* (⑦025/875869; ❷) is reliable. More in the centre of things on Le Loi, the *Bac Son* (⑦025/871849; ❸) and *Ngoc Mai* (⑦025/873396; ❸) are both a bit overpriced. Better deals can be found on the main road north, Tran Dang Ninh: the *Hoang Nguyen* (⑦025/874575; ❷–❸) has some reasonably priced rooms, while the *Mao Son* (⑦025/876818; ❶–❸), right opposite the Ky Lua Market, offers probably the best value in town. Its bigger rooms out the back have the bonus of an attractive view over Phai Loan Lake. Almost next door, the *Hoa Binh* (⑦025/870807; ❷–❸) has smaller rooms, but similar views and prices.

There are few fancy **places to eat** in Lang Son, though a large **restaurant** on Phai Loan Lake opposite the Ky Lua Market is well geared up for foreign visitors, and some of the bigger hotels provide food. There are also several street kitchens on Tran Dang Ninh, of which no. 28 is recommended. Near the bus station, the *Binh Dan* at 13 Ngu Quyen serves tasty and cheap rice dishes, while in the evenings, rice and noodle **food stalls** set up on Le Loi near the highway.

The Town

Lang Son started life as a Chinese citadel and has been disputed ever since by Vietnamese, Chinese, French and Japanese armies. The Ky Cung River splits the town in two, leaving the main bulk on the north side of the Ky Lua Bridge and provincial offices to the south. Highway 1 is called Tran Dang Ninh as it passes through town, and it's along here that you'll find the town's main attraction, bustling **Ky Lua Market**. Just east of the highway, this is well worth investigating, especially in the early morning when Tay, Nung and Dao women come to trade. Chinese imports dominate – flowery eiderdowns, fabrics and plastic toys – alongside an amazing array of local produce, from freshwater fish to nuts, vegetables, fruit, and golden bowls of silkworm larvae, according to the season. From the market, walk a kilometre downhill to the river and take a quick look at the small temple, **Den Ky Cung**, tucked under the bridge on the north bank. Founded over 500 years ago, this temple is dedicated to Quan Tuan Tranh, an army officer of the border guard who is reputed to have slain hundreds of Chinese in battle before he himself fell. There's nothing much to see inside apart from a photo of Uncle Ho visiting Lang Son in 1960. Following the road that branches off the highway at Den Ky Cung for about 500m will bring you round a bend in the river to the new, three-storey edifice of **Dong Kinh Market**, a temple to Chinese kitsch, where illuminated Buddhas sit in front of posters of Huangguoshu Falls, China's highest waterfall. The broad boulevards south of the bridge are also worth exploring. The atmosphere is less frenetic than in the centre, and there are some interesting colonial buildings in the tree-lined backstreets. If the weather is good and you have time to spare, take a walk along Da Tuong in the southwest of town, which passes remnants of an ancient wall and heads on into a nearby labyrinth of karst hills.

The region around Lang Son is riddled with caves, and it's likely that soon local or Hanoi tour operators will begin exploring the possibilities for organized tours of the area, so ask in your hotel for the latest information. If you'd like to be a trailblazer, head east of town along Highway 4B and look for a turn after about 14km to Mau Son Mountain. A road leads to the top of the mountain, just over 1000m high, where the *Mau Son Resort* can be found. The hillsides around here are dotted with Dao villages, and orchards of peaches and pears.

Southwest to Hanoi

Highway 1 has recently been widened, creating a road that more resembles a racetrack between Lang Son and Hanoi. Just south of town, the road passes a massive quarry where a couple of huge limestone hills have been reduced to rubble for road and house building, and the air is thick with dust. At times road and rail shadow each other along the 160-kilometre journey, which takes only a couple of hours on the highway, but much longer by train. If you've got used to the slow progress along most roads of the north, the contrast comes as something of a shock. The route passes the **Chi Lang Pass**, scene of yet another of Vietnam's historic victories over the Chinese. On this occasion it was the Ming Chinese who were defeated in 1427, losing thirty thousand men (a third of their force) to the rebel hero Le Loi during an ambush in the pass. The battle is commemorated with a prominent war memorial and two nondescript walls beside the road in a valley roughly 60km out of Lang Son.

A few kilometres further on, the hills begin to fade out on the edge of the Red River Valley as you enter **HA BAC**, a densely populated province famed for its folksy woodblock prints (those from Dong Ho Village are especially prized) and **festivals**. The most endearing festival is held in Lim Village, 20km outside Hanoi near **BAC NINH** Town, on the thirteenth to fifteenth days of each first lunar month, in anticipation of spring. Young men and women compete in *quan ho* or alternate singing, unaccompanied and usually improvised love duets, ranging from the coy to the suggestive, which were traditionally flung back and forth as a prelude to courtship. But the festival at **Den Ba Chua Kho**, a kilometre west of Bac Ninh, is more in keeping with the times: hopefuls flock out of Hanoi on the fourteenth and fifteenth days of the second lunar month to pray for wealth at this temple dedicated to an exemplary business woman of the Ly dynasty. The goddess grants "loans" of paper money or gold leaf which must be repaid, with interest, by the end of the year, either in real money or in reproduction dollar bills. Eleven kilometres outside Hanoi, Highway 1 joins Highway 5 from Haiphong and Ha Long Bay, and the heavy traffic backs up to squeeze over the narrow bridge back into the city.

Travel details

Trains

Dong Dang to: Hanoi (2 daily; 8–10hr).
Lao Cai to: Hanoi (2 daily; 10–11hr).

Flights

Dien Bien Phu to: Hanoi (daily; 1hr).
Son La to: Hanoi (3 weekly – Wed, Fri & Sun; 45min).

Buses

It's almost impossible to give the **frequency** with which buses run. Long-distance public buses, though scheduled, won't depart if empty. Moreover, private services, often minibuses or pick-ups, ply more popular routes, and depart only when they have enough passengers to make the journey worthwhile. It's advisable to start your journey early – most long-distance departures are between 5 and 9am, and few run after midday.

Journey times can also vary; figures below show the approximate length of time you can expect the journey to take.

Cao Bang to: Hanoi (8hr); Lang Son (5hr).

Dien Bien Phu to: Lai Chau (4hr); Son La (8hr).

Hoa Binh to: Hanoi (2hr); Mai Chau (3hr); Son La (6hr).

Lai Chau to: Dien Bien Phu (4hr); Sa Pa (8hr).

Lang Son to: Cao Bang (5hr); Hanoi (3hr).

Lao Cai to: Sa Pa (1hr 30min).

Mai Chau to: Hoa Binh (3hr).

Sa Pa to: Lai Chau (8hr); Lao Cai (1hr 30min).

Son La to: Dien Bien Phu (8hr); Hanoi (12hr); Hoa Binh (10hr), via the Mai Chau junction (8hr).

Contexts

Contexts

Some history

Vietnam as a unified state within its present geographical boundaries has only existed since the early nineteenth century. The national history, however, stretches back thousands of years to a legendary kingdom in the Red River Delta. From there the Viet people pushed relentlessly down the peninsula of Indochina on the "March to the South", Nam Tien. The other compelling force, and a constant theme throughout its history, is Vietnam's ultimately successful resistance to all foreign aggressors.

The beginnings

The earliest evidence of human activity in Vietnam can be traced back to a Paleolithic culture that existed some 500,000 years ago. Over the following centuries these hunter-gatherers slowly developed agricultural techniques, but the most important step came about 4000 years ago when farmers began to cultivate irrigated rice in the Red River Delta. The communal effort required to build and maintain the system of dykes and canals spawned a stable, highly organized society, held to be the original Vietnamese nation. This embryonic kingdom, **Van Lang**, emerged sometime around 2000 BC and was ruled over by the semi-mythological Hung kings from their capital near today's Viet Tri, northwest of Hanoi. Archeological finds indicate that by the first millennium BC these people, the Lac Viet, had evolved into a sophisticated Bronze Age culture whose influence spread as far as Indonesia. Undoubtedly their greatest creations were the ritualistic **bronze drums**, discovered in the 1920s near Dong Son, and revered by the Vietnamese as the first hard evidence of an indigenous, independent culture.

In the mid-third century BC a Chinese warlord conquered Van Lang to create a new kingdom, **Au Lac**, with its capital at Co Loa, near present-day Hanoi. For the first time the lowland Lac Viet and the hill peoples were united. After only fifty years, around 207 BC, Au Lac was itself invaded by a Chinese potentate and became part of **Nam Viet** (Southern Viet), an independent kingdom occupying much of southern China. For a while the Lac Viet were able to maintain their local traditions and an indigenous aristocracy. Then, in 111 BC the Han emperors annexed the whole Red River Delta and so began a thousand years of Chinese domination.

Chinese rule

A millennium under Chinese rule had a profound effect on all aspects of Vietnamese life, notably the social and political spheres. With the introduction of **Confucianism** came the growth of a rigid, feudalistic hierarchy dominated by a mandarin class. This innately conservative elite ensured the long-term stability of an administrative system which continued to dominate Vietnamese society until well into the nineteenth century. The Chinese also introduced technological advances, such as writing, silk production and large-scale hydraulic works, while Mahayana Buddhism first entered Vietnam from China during the second century AD.

At the same time, however, the Viet people were forging their national identity in the continuous struggle to break free from their powerful northern neighbour. The local aristocracy, though they prospered under the Chinese, increasingly resented their vassal status and the heavy taxes demanded in tribute. Much is made of the various insurrections that marked the period, but on at least three occasions the Vietnamese ousted their masters. The first and most celebrated of these short-lived independent kingdoms was established by the **Trung sisters** (Hai Ba Trung) in 40 AD. After the Chinese murdered Trung Trac's husband, she and her sister rallied the local lords and peasant farmers in the first popular insurrection against foreign domination. The Chinese fled, leaving Trung Trac ruler of the territory from Hué to southern China until the Han emperor dispatched 20,000 troops and a fleet of 2000 junks to quell the rebellion three years later. The sisters threw themselves in a river to escape capture, and the Chinese quickly set about removing the local lords. Though subsequent uprisings also failed, the sisters had demonstrated the fallibility of the Chinese and earned their place in Vietnam's pantheon of heroes.

Over the following centuries Vietnam was drawn closer into the political and cultural realm of China. The seventh and eighth centuries were particularly bleak as the powerful Tang dynasty tightened its grip on the province it called **Annam**, or the "Pacified South". As soon as the dynasty collapsed in the early tenth century a series of major rebellions broke out, culminating in the battle of the **Bach Dang River** in 938 AD. In this famous victory, Ngo Quyen, leader of the Vietnamese forces, lured the Chinese navy into the estuary and, as the tide turned, chased them onto stakes embedded in the river mouth (see p.424). Ngo Quyen declared himself ruler of **Nam Viet** and set up court at the historic citadel of Co Loa, heralding what was to be nearly ten centuries of Vietnamese independence.

Funan and Champa

Meanwhile, in the south of Vietnam it was Indian civilization rather than Chinese which dominated, though as a cultural influence rather than as a ruling power. From the first century AD Indian traders sailing east towards China established Hindu enclaves along the southern coast of Indochina. The largest and most important of these city states was **Funan**, based on a port-city called Oc Eo, near present-day Rach Gia in the Mekong Delta (see p.175). By the early third century, Funan had developed into a powerful trading nation with links extending as far as Persia and even Rome. But technological developments in the fifth century enabled larger ships to sail round Indochina without calling at any port, and Funan gradually declined.

At around the same time, another Indianized kingdom was developing along the narrow coastal plains of central Vietnam. Little is known about the origins of **Champa**, but Chinese records indicate the creation of a "barbarian" state in the area towards the end of the second century. Champa's subsequent history is a complicated tale of shifting allegiances between its Chinese, Khmer and, later, Vietnamese neighbours (see box on p.245). For most of its existence, however, Champa was a Hindu kingdom, based on wet-rice farming and maritime trade, ruled over by divine kings who worshipped first Shiva and later embraced Buddhism. Until the late tenth century, Champa extended from the

Hoanh Son Mountains, north of Dong Hoi, down to the Mekong Delta. Their power base was largely the territory around today's Da Nang, and their spiritual heartland the temple complex of My Son. Cham kings sponsored a vast array of sacred buildings, and the red-brick ruins of their towers and temples can be seen all along the coast of south-central Vietnam. While they never attained the magnificence of Angkor, their greatest legacy was a striking architectural style characterized by a wealth of exuberant sculpture.

In general, the Chinese tolerated the relatively weak kingdom on their borders, though they exacted tribute and plundered Champa on several occasions. After the mid-tenth century, however, Vietnamese independence changed the situation dramatically as the Viets, in search of new land, turned their attention southwards. By the end of the eleventh century Champa had lost its territory north of Hué, and four centuries later the whole kingdom became a vassal state under Viet hegemony. For a while Cham princes continued as nominal rulers until the state was finally absorbed into Vietnam in the nineteenth century.

Independent Vietnam

Back in the Red River Delta, the period immediately following independence from Chinese rule in 939 AD was marked by factional infighting. Ngo Quyen died after only five years on the throne and Nam Viet dissolved in anarchy while twelve warlords disputed the succession. In 968 one of the rivals, Dinh Bo Linh, finally united the country and secured its future by paying tribute to the Chinese emperor, a system which continued until the nineteenth century. Dinh Bo Linh, however, took the additional precaution of moving his capital south to the well-defended valley of Hoa Lu, where it remained during the two short-lived Dinh and Early Le dynasties.

These early monarchs laid the framework for a centralized state. They reformed the administration and the army, and instigated a programme of road building. But it was the following **Ly dynasty**, founded by the great **Ly Thai To** in 1009, that consolidated the independence of **Dai Viet** (Great Viet) and guaranteed the nation's stability for the next four hundred years. Ly Thai To and his successors were ardent Buddhists; the ideological basis for their administrative and political reforms, however, was solidly Confucian and borrowed heavily from the Chinese. One of the first actions of the new dynasty was to move the capital back into the northern rice-lands, founding the city of Thang Long, the precursor of modern Hanoi. The construction of more sophisticated irrigation systems in the Red River Delta led to a significant improvement in the national economy. At the same time, reform of both land tenure and the provincial administration created an emerging class of hereditary landowners and provided a stable tax base for the state coffers. In 1076 a Ly king founded Vietnam's first national university in Hanoi's great temple to Confucius, Van Mieu, in order to supply the state with its senior mandarins through competitive examination.

Ly Thai To's successor, Ly Thai Tong (1028–54), carried out a major reorganization of the national army, turning it into a professional fighting force, able to secure the northern borders and also to start expanding southwards. So confident was this new power that in 1076 the army of Dai Viet, under the revered General Ly Thuong Kiet, launched a pre-emptive strike against the Sung Chinese and then held off their counterattack. But this was a mere skirmish compared with what the next dynasty, the Tran, had in store, as Kublai Khan swept his armies down through southern China in the late thirteenth century.

The **Tran dynasty**, which ousted the declining Ly clan in 1225, largely retained the existing administrative system and continued to increase the power of the centralized state. But the Tran's crowning achievements were their spectacular military victories against three successive **Mongol invasions** in the space of thirty years. On the first two occasions, in 1257 and 1284, Mongol forces briefly occupied the capital before having to withdraw, while the last battle, in 1288, is remembered for a rerun of Ngo Quyen's ploy in the Bach Dang River. This time it was the brilliant General Tran Hung Dao, a prince in the royal family, who led Viet forces against the far superior armies of Kublai Khan. While the Mongol navy foundered in the Bach Dang River, its army was also being trounced and the remnants driven back into China; soon after, the Khan died, and with him the Mongol threat.

By the end of the fourteenth century, constant warfare – mostly against Champa – and high taxes had bled the country dry. Famines plagued the northern delta while powerful feudal lords amassed ever-larger land holdings, creating a rebellious population of landless slaves, serfs and peasant farmers. In the confusion that marked the end of the Tran dynasty, an ambitious court minister, Ho Qui Ly, usurped the throne in 1400. Though the **Ho dynasty** lasted only seven years, its two progressive monarchs launched a number of important reforms. They tackled the problem of land shortages by restricting the size of holdings and then rented out the excess to landless peasants, the tax system was revised and paper money replaced coinage, ports were opened to foreign trade, the judiciary was overhauled and public health care introduced. Even the education system came under review and was broadened to include mathematics, agriculture and other practical subjects along with the classic Confucian texts.

Just as the Ho were getting into their stride, so the new Ming dynasty in China were beginning to look south again across the border. Under the pretext of restoring the Tran, Ming armies invaded in 1407 and imposed direct rule a few years later. This time, however, the **Chinese occupation** faced a much tougher problem as the Viet people were now a relatively cohesive force. The Chinese tried to undermine the Viet culture by outlawing local customs and destroying Vietnamese literature, works of art and historical texts. Economic conditions were equally harsh and rebellions erupted throughout the country. Slowly, Vietnamese resistance gravitated towards the mountains of Thanh Hoa, south of Hanoi, where a local landlord and mandarin, **Le Loi**, was preparing for a war of national liberation. For ten years Le Loi's well-disciplined guerrilla force harassed the enemy until he was finally able to defeat the Chinese army in open battle in 1427.

Le Loi, as King Le Thai To, founded the third of the great ruling families, the **Later Le dynasty**, and set in train the reconstruction of Dai Viet, though he died after only five years on the throne. It was the fourth Le monarch, **Le Thanh Tong** (1460–97), who is regarded as the greatest of the Le kings. Under Le Thanh Tong agricultural reforms increased grain production and vast new tracts of land were opened up as the Champa kingdom was pushed south. This new-found prosperity, coupled with a relatively peaceful era, allowed Le Thanh Tong to conduct a national census and a geographical survey of the entire kingdom. He also instigated a new civil and criminal code which formed the basis for Vietnamese law right into the nineteenth century. In other ways, however, Le Thanh Tong was a deeply conservative monarch who promoted Confucian doctrine above all else.

The Vietnamese dynasties			
Ngo	939–965 AD	(Ming Chinese	1407–1428)
Dinh	968–980	Later Le	1428–1789
Early Le	980–1009	Nguyen and Trinh	
Ly	1009–1225	lords	1592–1788
Tran	1225–1400	Tay Son	1788–1802
Ho	1400–1407	Nguyen	1802–1945

The Nguyen and Trinh lords

Initially the Le dynasty reaped the economic rewards of its expanding empire, but eventually their new provinces spawned wealthy semi-autonomous rulers strong enough to challenge the throne. As the Le declined in the sixteenth century, two such powerful clans, the **Nguyen and Trinh**, at first supported the dynasty against rival contenders. Towards the end of the century, however, they became the effective rulers of Vietnam, splitting the country in two. The Trinh lords held sway in Hanoi and the north, while the Nguyen set up court at Hué; the Le, meanwhile, remained monarchs in name only. Sporadic civil war between the two clans lasted until 1674 when they signed a hundred-year truce and formally partitioned the country at the Gianh River, near Dong Hoi.

At around the same time, the Nguyen lords completed their conquest of the Mekong Delta, seizing territory from the fading Khmer empire, and by the mid-eighteenth century Viet people occupied the whole peninsula down to Ca Mau. Nevertheless, severe famines, exacerbated by land shortages in the north and corrupt officials everywhere, plagued Vietnam throughout the eighteenth century. Insurrections rumbled away until the general discontent focused on an uprising at Tay Son in 1771. For a while the rebels held sway, but there was now a new factor in the balance of power.

The arrival of the West

The first Western visitors to the Vietnamese peninsula were probably **traders** from ancient Rome who sailed into the ports of Champa in the second century AD. After the fifth century, however, the main trade routes between East and West bypassed Indochina. Marco Polo sailed up the coast in the thirteenth century on his way to China, but more significant was the arrival of a Portuguese merchant, Antonio Da Faria, at the port of Fai Fo (Hoi An) in 1535. Fai Fo was then one of Southeast Asia's greatest ports, crammed with vessels from China and Japan. The Portuguese established their own trading post at Fai Fo, in the land they called Cochinchina, soon to be followed by other European maritime powers. At this time Vietnam was breaking up into regional factions and the Europeans were quick to exploit growing tensions between the Nguyen and Trinh lords, providing weapons in exchange for trading concessions. However, when the civil war ended in 1674 the merchants lost their advantage. Gradually the English, Dutch and French closed down their trading posts until only the Portuguese remained in Fai Fo.

With the traders came **missionaries**. Portuguese Dominicans had been the first to arrive in the early sixteenth century, but it wasn't until 1615, when Jesuits set up a small mission in Fai Fo, that the Catholic Church gained an established presence in Vietnam. The mission's initial success in the southern, Nguyen territory encouraged the Jesuits to look north. The man they chose for the job was a 28-year-old Frenchman, **Alexandre de Rhodes**, a gifted linguist who, only six months after arriving in Fai Fo, in 1627, was preaching in Vietnamese. His talents soon won over the Trinh lords in Hanoi, where de Rhodes gave six sermons a day and converted nearly 7000 Vietnamese in just two years. During this time de Rhodes was also working on a simple romanized script for the Vietnamese language, which otherwise used a formidable system based on Chinese characters. De Rhodes merely wanted to make evangelizing easier, but his phonetic system eventually came to be adopted as Vietnam's national language, *quoc ngu*.

The missionaries found a ready audience, especially among peasant farmers and others near the bottom of the established Confucian hierarchy. It didn't take long before the ruling elite felt threatened by Christianity's subversive ideas – undermining loyalty to the emperor and denouncing polygamy worried them in particular. Missionary work was banned after the 1630s and many priests were expelled, or even executed. But enforcement was erratic and missionaries came and went according to the political climate. By the end of the seventeenth century the Catholic Church, and particularly the French Society of Foreign Missions, claimed several hundred thousand converts. Then, towards the end of the eighteenth century, the Catholic missions also provided an opening for French merchants wishing to challenge Britain's presence in the Far East. When a large-scale rebellion broke out in Vietnam in the early 1770s, these entrepreneurs saw their chance to establish a firmer footing on the Indochinese peninsula.

The Tay Son rebellion

As the eighteenth century progressed, insurrections flared up throughout the countryside. Most were easily stamped out, but in 1771 three brothers raised their standard in Tay Son Village, west of Qui Nhon, and ended up ruling the whole country. Their **Tay Son rebellion** gained broad support among dispossessed peasants, ethnic minorities, small merchants and townspeople attracted by the brothers' message of equal rights, justice and liberty. As rebellion spread through the south, the Tay Son army rallied even more converts when they seized land from the wealthy and redistributed it to the poor. By the middle of 1786 the rebels had overthrown both the Trinh and Nguyen lords, again leaving the Le dynasty intact. When the Le monarch called on the Chinese in 1788 to help remove the Tay Son usurpers, the Chinese happily obliged by occupying Hanoi. At this the middle brother (Nguyen Hue) declared himself **Emperor Quang Trung** and quick-marched his army 600km from Hué to defeat the Chinese in a glorious battle at Dong Da, on the outskirts of Hanoi. With Hué as his capital, Quang Trung set about implementing his promised reforms, but when he died prematurely in 1792, aged 39, his 10-year-old son was unable to hold on to power.

One of the few Nguyen lords to have survived the Tay Son rebellion in the south was Prince Nguyen Anh. The prince made several unsuccessful attempts to regain the throne in the mid-1780s. After one such failure he fled to Phu

Quoc Island where he met a French bishop, Pigneau de Béhaine. With an eye on future religious and commercial concessions, the bishop offered to make approaches to the French on behalf of the Nguyen. A treaty was eventually signed in 1787, promising military aid in exchange for territorial and trading concessions, though France failed to deliver the assistance due to a financial crisis preceding the French Revolution. The bishop went ahead anyway, raising a motley force of 4000 armed mercenaries and a handful of ships. The expedition was launched in 1789 and Nguyen Anh entered Hanoi in 1802 to claim the throne as **Emperor Gia Long**. Bishop de Béhaine didn't live to see the victory, or to enforce the treaty: he died in 1799 and received a stately funeral.

The Nguyen dynasty

For the first time, **Vietnam**, as the country was now called, fell under a single authority from the northern border all the way down to the point of Ca Mau. In the hope of promoting unity, Gia Long established his capital in the centre, at Hué, where he built a magnificent citadel in imitation of the Chinese emperor's Forbidden City. The choice of architecture was appropriate: Gia Long and the **Nguyen dynasty** he founded were resolutely Confucian. The new emperor immediately abolished the Tay Son reforms, reimposing the old feudal order under a strongly centralized state in which the monarch became increasingly isolated from his subjects. Land confiscated from the rebels was redistributed to loyal mandarins, the bureaucracy was reinstated and the majority of peasants found themselves worse off than before; numerous rebellions were ruthlessly suppressed. Gradually the country was closed to the outside world and to modernizing influences that might have helped it withstand the onslaught of French military intervention in the mid-nineteenth century. On the other hand, Gia Long and his successors did much to improve the infrastructure of Vietnam, developing a road network, extending the irrigation systems and rationalizing the provincial administration. Under the Nguyen, the arts, particularly literature and court music, also flourished.

By refusing to grant any trading concessions, Gia Long disappointed the French adventurers who had helped him to the throne. He did, however, permit a certain amount of religious freedom, though his successors were far more suspicious of the missionaries' intentions. After 1825 several edicts were issued forbidding missionary work, accompanied by sporadic, occasionally brutal, persecutions of Christians, both Vietnamese converts and foreign priests. Ultimately, this provided the French with the excuse they needed to annex the country.

French conquest

French governments grew increasingly imperialistic as the nineteenth century wore on. In the Far East, as Britain threatened to dominate trade with China, France began to see Vietnam as a potential route into the resource-rich provinces of Yunnan and southern China. Not that France had any formal policy to colonize Indochina; rather it came about in a piecemeal fashion, driven as often as not by private adventurers or the unilateral actions of French officials. In 1847 two French naval vessels began the process when they bombarded Da Nang on the pretext of rescuing a French priest. Reports of Catholic persecutions were deliberately exaggerated until Napoleon III was finally persuaded to launch an armada of fourteen ships and 2500 men in 1858. After capturing Da Nang in September, the force moved south to take Saigon, against considerable opposition, and the whole Mekong Delta over the next three years. Faced with serious unrest in the north, Emperor Tu Duc signed a treaty in 1862 granting France the three eastern provinces of the delta plus trading rights in selected ports, and allowing missionaries the freedom to proselytize. Five years later, French forces annexed the remaining southern provinces to create the colony of **Cochinchina**.

France became embroiled in domestic troubles and the French government was divided on whether to continue the enterprise. But their administrators in Cochinchina, backed by the commercial lobby, had their eyes on the north. The first attempt to take Hanoi and open up the Red River into China failed when its leader, the charismatic explorer Francis Garnier, was killed in 1873. In 1882 a larger force was dispatched under the command of Henri Rivière; within a few months, France was in control of Hanoi and the lower reaches of the Red River Delta. Spurred on by this success, the French parliament financed the first contingents of the **French Expeditionary Force** just as the Nguyen were floundering in a succession crisis following the death of Tu Duc. In August 1883, when the French fleet sailed into the mouth of the Perfume River, near Hué, the new emperor was compelled to meet their demands. **Annam** (central Vietnam) and **Tonkin** (the north) became protectorates of France, to be combined with Cochinchina, Cambodia and, later, Laos to form the **Union of Indochina** after 1887. Though the emperor in Hué retained a semblance of power, for the next seventy years Vietnam was once again under foreign occupation.

French rule

Despite much talk of the "civilizing mission" of imperial rule, the French were more interested in the economic potential of their new possession. One of the key architects of colonial policy was Paul Doumer, governor-general from 1897 to 1902. Doumer launched a massive programme of **infrastructural development**, constructing railways, bridges, roads and draining vast areas of the swampy Mekong Delta. These public works were funded by raising punitive taxes, including state monopolies on opium, alcohol and salt, which between them accounted for seventy percent of government revenues. As far as the colonialists were concerned this was a promising start and private capital began to flow into the colony in ever-larger amounts, reaching a peak in the 1920s.

Much of this economic development, however, was built on shaky foundations, and during the Great Depression of the 1930s markets collapsed while commodity prices tumbled. The shift to large-scale rice production for export had not only eroded Vietnam's traditional social systems and undermined the local economy, but also meant that per capita food consumption actually decreased under French rule. Peasants were forced off the land to work as indentured labour in the new rubber, tea and coffee estates or in the mines, often under brutal conditions. Heavy taxes exacerbated **rural poverty** and any commercial or industrial enterprises were kept firmly in French hands, or were controlled by the small minority of Vietnamese and Chinese who actually benefited under the new regime.

On the positive side, mass vaccination and health programmes did bring the frequent epidemics of cholera, smallpox and the plague under control. Education was a thornier issue: overall, education levels deteriorated during French rule, particularly among unskilled labourers, but important reforms saw the introduction of *quoc ngu*, the romanized script of Alexandre de Rhodes. In addition, a small elite from the emerging urban middle class received a broader, French-based education and a few went to universities in Europe. Not that it got them very far: Vietnamese were barred from all but the most menial jobs in the colonial administration. It was this frustrated and alienated group, imbued with the ideas of Western liberals and Chinese reformers, who began to challenge French rule.

The anti-colonial struggle

For a population brought up on legends of heroic victories over superior forces, the ease with which France had occupied Vietnam was a deep psychological blow. The earliest resistance movements naturally focused on the restoration of the monarchy, such as the "Save the King" (*Can Vuong*) movement of the 1890s. But any emperor showing signs of patriotism was swiftly removed by the French administration. Gradually the nationalists saw that a more radical approach was called for. One of the most influential leaders of the early twentieth century was **Phan Boi Chau**, who eventually called for the violent overthrow of the colonial regime. Like many young Asian revolutionaries he was deeply affected by the Japanese defeat of a Russian fleet in 1905, the first Asian victory over a European power. For several years, Phan Boi Chau lived in Japan where he organized the Eastward Movement, providing dissident intellectuals with a political and military education. Later, he moved to south China, where Sun Yat Sen's 1911 revolution was another source of inspiration to many Vietnamese nationalists.

Up until the mid-1920s Vietnam's various anti-colonial movements tended to be fragmented, disorganized and were easily controlled by the *Sûreté*, the formidable French secret police. On the whole the nationalists' aims were political rather than social or economic, and most failed to appeal to the majority of Vietnamese. But in the late 1920s more radical organizations appeared, drawing on the ideas of Phan Boi Chau. The most important of these was the **Vietnam Nationalist Party** (*Viet Nam Quoc Dan Dang*, or VNQDD), established in Hanoi in 1927 and modelled on the Chinese Nationalist Party, the Kuomintang. The new party was pledged to the violent overthrow of the French regime and the establishment of a democratic republic. In February 1930, the VNQDD launched an attack against military outposts in Yen Bai and the north of Vietnam. But the uprising was badly co-ordinated and ended in disaster when it failed to attract widespread support: most of the VNQDD leaders were captured and executed, after which the organization gradually faded from the scene.

Meanwhile, over the border in southern China, a more significant event had occurred a few years earlier, with the foundation of the **Revolutionary Youth League** in 1925. Not only was this Vietnam's first Marxist-Leninist organization, but its founding father was **Ho Chi Minh**. Born in 1890, the son of a patriotic minor official, Ho was already in trouble with the French authorities in his teens. He left Vietnam in 1911, then turned up in Paris after World War I under one of his many pseudonyms, Nguyen Ai Quoc ("Nguyen the Patriot"). In France, Ho became increasingly active among other exiled dissidents exploring ways to bring an end to colonial rule. At this time one of the few political groups actively supporting anti-colonial movements were the communists; in 1920 Ho became a founding member of the French Communist Party and by 1923 he was in Moscow, training as a communist agent. His task was to unite the nascent Vietnamese anti-colonial movements under one organization, the Revolutionary Youth League. Among his many talents, Ho Chi Minh was an intelligent strategist and a great motivator; though he was now committed to Marxist-Leninist ideology, he understood the need to appeal to all nationalists, playing down the controversial goal of social revolution. (See pp.342–343 for more on the chequered life of Ho Chi Minh.)

Although many other subsequently famous revolutionaries worked with Ho, it was largely his fierce dedication, single-mindedness and tremendous charisma that held the nationalist movement together and finally propelled the country to independence. The first real test of Ho's leadership came in 1929 when, in his absence, the League split into three separate communist parties. In Hong Kong a year later, Ho persuaded the rival groups to unite into one **Indochinese Communist Party** whose main goal was an independent Vietnam governed by workers, peasants and soldiers. In preparation for the revolution, cadres were sent into rural areas and among urban workers to set up Party cells. The timing couldn't have been better: unemployment and poverty were on the increase as the Great Depression took hold, while France became less willing to commit resources to its colonies. But perhaps most importantly, Vietnamese workers were themselves becoming politically active, largely under the influence of some of the 100,000 Vietnamese soldiers and auxiliaries returning from World War I with ideas about the power of organized labour.

Throughout the 1930s Vietnam was plagued with strikes and labour unrest, of which the most important was the **Nghe Tinh uprising** in the summer of 1930. The precise role of the Communist Party in the revolt, during which French planes bombed a crowd of 20,000 demonstrators marching on Vinh, has never been made clear. But within days villagers had seized control of much of the surrounding countryside and, in some cases, set up revolutionary councils to evict wealthy landlords and redistribute land to the peasants. Some of these "soviets" held out against the authorities for six months while the movement spread to other districts. The uprising had demonstrated the power of socialist organization but it proved disastrous in the short term. Thousands of peasants were killed or imprisoned, the leaders were executed and the Communist Party structure was badly mauled. Most of the ringleaders ended up in the notorious penal colony of Poulo Condore (Con Dao Island), which came to be known as the "University of the Revolution". It's estimated that the French held some 10,000 Vietnamese communists and other activists in prison by the late 1930s.

World War II

The German occupation of France in 1940 suddenly changed the whole political landscape. Not only did it demonstrate to the Vietnamese the vulnerability of their colonial masters, but it also overturned the established order in Vietnam and ultimately provided Ho Chi Minh with the opportunity he had been waiting for. The immediate repercussion was the **Japanese occupation** of Indochina after Vichy France signed a treaty allowing Japan to station troops in the colony, while leaving the French administration in place. By mid-1941 the region's coal mines, rice fields and military installations were all under Japanese control. Some Vietnamese nationalist groups welcomed this turn of events as the Japanese made encouraging noises about autonomy and "Asia for the Asians". Others, mostly communist groups, declared their opposition to all foreign intervention and continued to operate from secret bases in the mountainous region that flanks the border between China and Vietnam.

By this time, Ho Chi Minh had reappeared in southern China, from where he walked over the border into Vietnam, carrying his rattan trunk and trusty Hermes typewriter. The date was February 1941; Ho had been in exile for thirty years. In **Pac Bo Cave**, near Cao Bang, Ho met up with other resistance leaders, including Vo Nguyen Giap, to start the next phase in the fight for national liberation. The key element was a nationalist coalition, the League for the Independence of Vietnam (*Viet Nam Doc Lap Dong Minh*), better known as the **Viet Minh**, founded in May 1941. The organization was again specifically designed to win broad popular support for independence, followed by moderate social and democratic reforms. The second critical decision reached in Pac Bo was to mobilize mass support with a nationwide propaganda campaign.

Over the next few years Viet Minh recruits received military training in southern China and the first regular armed units were set up, which formed the nucleus of the **Vietnamese Liberation Army** in 1945. Gradually the Viet Minh established liberated zones in the northern mountains to provide bases for future guerrilla operations. Then, as Japanese defeat looked ever more likely, Ho Chi Minh set off once again into China to seek military and financial support from the Chinese and from the Allied forces operating out of Kunming. Ho also made contact with the American Office of Strategic Services (forerunner of the CIA), which promised him limited arms, much to the anger of the Free French who were already planning their return to Indochina. In return for **American aid** the Viet Minh provided information about Japanese forces and rescued Allied pilots shot down over Vietnam. Later, in 1945, an American team arrived in Ho's Cao Bang base where they found him suffering from malaria, dysentery and dengue fever; it's said they saved his life.

Meanwhile, suspecting a belated French counterattack, Japanese forces seized full control of the country in March 1945. They declared a nominally independent state under the leadership of Bao Dai, the last Nguyen emperor, and imprisoned most of the French army. The Viet Minh quickly moved onto the offensive, helped to some extent by a massive famine that ravaged northern Vietnam that summer. Then, in early August, US forces dropped the first atom bomb on Hiroshima, precipitating the **Japanese surrender** on August 14.

The August Revolution

The Japanese surrender left a power vacuum which Ho Chi Minh was quick to exploit. On August 15, Ho called for a national uprising, which later came to be known as the **August Revolution**. Within four days Hanoi was seething with pro-Viet Minh demonstrations and in two weeks most of Vietnam came under their control. Emperor Bao Dai handed over his imperial sword to Ho's provisional government at the end of August and on September 2, 1945 Ho Chi Minh proclaimed the establishment of the **Democratic Republic of Vietnam**, cheered by a massive crowd in Hanoi's Ba Dinh Square. For the first time in eighty years Vietnam was an independent country. Famously, Ho's Declaration of Independence quoted from the American Declaration: "All men are created equal. They are endowed by their Creator with certain inalienable rights, among these are life, liberty and the pursuit of happiness." But this, and subsequent appeals for America's help against the looming threat of recolonization, fell on deaf ears as America became increasingly concerned at communist expansion.

The **Potsdam Agreement**, which marked the end of World War II, failed to recognize the new Republic of Vietnam. Instead, Japanese troops south of the Sixteenth Parallel were to surrender to British authority, while those in the north would defer to the Chinese Kuomintang. Nevertheless, by the time these forces arrived, the Viet Minh were already in control, having relieved the Japanese of most of their weapons. In the **south**, rival nationalist groups were battling it out in Saigon, where French troops had also joined in the fray. The situation was so chaotic that the British commander proclaimed martial law and, amazingly, even deployed Japanese soldiers to help restore calm. Against orders, he also re-armed the 6000 liberated French troops and Saigon was soon back in French hands. A few days later, General Leclerc arrived with the first units of the French Expeditionary Force, charged with reimposing colonial rule in Indochina.

Meanwhile, things were going more smoothly in the north, though 200,000 Chinese soldiers on Vietnamese soil worried the new government. The soldiers acted increasingly like an army of occupation against which the Viet Minh could muster a mere 5000 ill-equipped troops. Forced to choose between the two in order to survive, Ho Chi Minh finally rated French rule the lesser of the two evils and commenced negotiations with the French commissioner. Ho is reputed to have commented, "I prefer to smell French shit for five years, rather than Chinese shit for the rest of my life." In March 1946 Ho's government signed a treaty allowing a limited French force to replace Kuomintang soldiers in the north. In return France recognized the Democratic Republic as a "free state" within the proposed French Union; the terms were left deliberately vague. The treaty also provided for a referendum to determine whether Cochinchina would join the new state or remain separate.

While further negotiations dragged on during the summer of 1946, both sides were busily re-arming as it became apparent that the French were not going to abide by the treaty. By late April the Expeditionary Force had already exceeded agreed levels, and there was no sign of the promised referendum; in September 1946 the talks effectively broke down. Skirmishes between Vietnamese and French troops in the northern delta increased as tensions rose, then boiled over in a dispute over customs control in Haiphong. To quell the rioting, the French navy bombed the town on November 23, killing thousands of civilians. This was followed by the announcement that French troops would assume responsibility for law and order in the north. By way of reply, Viet Minh units attacked French installations in Hanoi on December 19, and then, while resistance forces held the capital for a few days, Ho Chi Minh and the regular army slipped away into the northern mountains.

The French War

For the first years of the **war against the French** (also known as the First Indochina War, or Franco-Viet Minh War) the Viet Minh kept largely to their mountain bases in northern and central Vietnam. While the Viet Minh were building up and training an army, the Expeditionary Force was consolidating its control over the Red River Delta and establishing a string of highly vulnerable outposts around guerrilla-held territory. In October 1947 the French attempted an all-out attack, an ambitious assault against the enemy headquarters. It soon became obvious that they were not fighting a conventional war, but rather a "war without fronts" where Viet Minh troops could simply melt away into the jungle whenever threatened. In addition, the French found they had no secure areas; the enemy taunted them with hit-and-run attacks deep within the delta, protected by a local population who either actively supported or at least tolerated the Viet Minh.

The terrain certainly didn't favour the French, encumbered as they were with tanks and massed battalions, but perhaps most important was the political aspect of the war – as the Americans were to learn twenty years later. As outsiders fighting a war of recolonization, the French were already disadvantaged; they compounded the problem by failing to provide a viable political alternative to the Viet Minh. Non-communist nationalists, particularly in the south, were increasingly disenchanted with the communists, who were not above using terrorist tactics and even murdering their opponents. Attempting to capitalize on this, the French persuaded Bao Dai to return as head of the Associated State of Vietnam in March 1949. Unfortunately, most Vietnamese regarded Bao Dai as a mere puppet of the French and his government won little support. On the other hand the Viet Minh continued to attract new recruits to the **people's war**.

By 1948 a stalemate had been reached, but the communist victory in China in 1949 proved to be a turning point. Almost immediately both China and Russia recognized the Democratic Republic of Vietnam and military aid started to flow across the border. Suddenly Bao Dai's shaky government was seen as the last bastion of the free world and America was drawn into the war, funding the French military to the tune of at least US$3 billion by 1954. As the war entered a new phase, the Viet Minh recorded their first major victory, forcing the French to abandon their outposts along the Chinese border and gaining unhindered access to sanctuary in China. Early in 1951, equipped with Chinese weapons and confident of success, the Viet Minh launched an assault on Hanoi itself. In this first pitched battle of the war, however, the Viet Minh suffered a massive defeat. They lost over 6000 troops in a battle that saw napalm deployed for the first time in Vietnam. But Giap had learnt his lesson, and for the next two years the French sought in vain to repeat their success.

By now France was tiring of the war and in 1953 made contact with Ho Chi Minh to find some way of resolving the conflict. The Americans were growing increasingly impatient with French progress, and at one stage threatened to deploy tactical nuclear weapons against the Viet Minh. The Russians and Chinese were also applying pressure to end the fighting. Eventually, the two sides agreed to discussions at the Geneva Conference, due to take place in May the next year to discuss the Korean peace. Meanwhile in Vietnam, a crucial battle was unfolding in an isolated valley on the Lao border, near the town of **Dien Bien Phu**. Early in 1954 French battalions established a massive camp here, deliberately trying to tempt the Viet Minh into the open. Instead the Viet Minh surrounded the valley, cut off reinforcements and slowly closed in (see p.459 for the full story). After 59 days of bitter fighting the French were forced to surrender on May 7, 1954, the eve of the Geneva Conference. The eight years of war proved costly to both sides: total losses on the French side stood at 93,000, while an estimated 200,000 Viet Minh soldiers had been killed.

The Geneva Conference

On May 8, a day after the French capitulation at Dien Bien Phu, the nine delegations attending the **Geneva Conference** trained their focus upon Indochina. Armed with the knowledge that they now controlled around 65 percent of the country, and with such a decisive win under their belt, the Viet Minh delegation, led by Pham Van Dong, arrived in buoyant mood. But the lasting peace they sought wasn't forthcoming. Hampered by distrust, the conference succeeded only in reaching a stopgap solution, a necessarily ambiguous compromise which, however, allowed the French to withdraw with some honour and recognized Vietnamese sovereignty at least in part. Keen to have a weak and fractured nation on their southern border, the Chinese delegation, headed by Chou En-lai, spurred the Viet Minh into agreeing to a division of the country; reliant upon Chinese arms, the Viet Minh were forced to comply.

Under the terms of July 1954's **Geneva Accords** Vietnam was divided at the Seventeenth Parallel, along the Ben Hai River, pending nationwide free elections to be held by July 1956; a demilitarized buffer zone was established on either side of this military front. France and the Viet Minh, who were still fighting in the central highlands even as delegates machinated, agreed to an immediate ceasefire, and consented to a withdrawal of all troops to their respective territories – communists to the north, non-communists plus supporters of the French to the south. China, USSR, Britain, France and the Viet Minh agreed on the accords, but crucially neither the United States nor Bao Dai's government endorsed them, fearing that they heralded a reunited, communist-ruled Vietnam.

In the long term, the Geneva Accords served to cause a deep polarization within the country and to widen the conflict into an ideological battle between the superpowers, fought out on Vietnamese soil. The immediate consequence, however, was a massive exodus from the north during the stipulated 300-day period of "**free movement**". Almost a million (mostly Catholic) refugees headed south, their flight aided by the US Navy, and to some extent engineered by the CIA, whose distribution of scaremongering, anti-communist leaflets was designed to create a base of support for the puppet government it was concocting in Saigon (see below). Approaching 100,000 **anti-French guerrillas** and sympathizers moved in the opposite direction to regroup, though, as a precautionary measure, between 5000 and 10,000 Viet Minh cadres remained in the south, awaiting orders from Hanoi. These dormant operatives, known to the CIA as "**stay-behinds**" and to the communists as "winter cadres", were joined by spies who infiltrated the Catholic move south.

In line with the terms of the ceasefire, Ho Chi Minh's army marched into Hanoi on October 9, 1954, even as the last French forces were still trooping out.

Diem takes the helm

The Geneva Accords were still being thrashed out as Emperor Bao Dai named himself President and **Ngo Dinh Diem** ("Zee-em") Prime Minister of South Vietnam, on July 7. A Catholic, and vehemently anti-communist, Diem knew that Ho Chi Minh would win the lion's share of votes in the proposed elections, and therefore steadfastly refused to countenance them. His mandate "strengthened" by an October 1955 **referendum** (the prime minister's garnering of 98.2 percent of votes cast was more indicative of the blatancy of his vote-rigging than of any popular support), Diem promptly ousted Bao Dai from the chain of command, declared himself President of the Republic of Vietnam, and knuckled down to consolidating his position.

Diem inherited a political climate that was far from stable, and for a while his heavy-handed approach to government bore fruit. In the countryside, the militias maintained by the **Hoa Hao** and **Cao Dai** religious sects wielded great influence, while a Mafia-like crime syndicate called the **Binh Xuyen** ruled Saigon. By 1956, Diem had emasculated both the Hoa Hao and the Cao Dai, and a few months later the Binh Xuyen were efficiently subdued, though only after pitched battles on the streets of Saigon. Diem was able to turn his attention later the same year to Viet Minh dissidents still in the South, but in this case the iron-fist approach was hopelessly misguided. Although the subsequent **witch-hunt** decimated Viet Minh numbers, the brutal and indiscriminate nature of the operation – all dissenters were targeted (Viet Minh, communist or otherwise), as were those who simply resisted the extortion rackets of Diem's corrupt officials – caused widespread discontent that the president's barefaced **nepotism** and insensitive land reforms did nothing to quell. As the supposed "free world democracy" of the South mutated into a police state, over 50,000 citizens died in Diem's pogrom.

Back in Hanoi...

In Hanoi, meanwhile, Ho Chi Minh's government was finding it had problems of its own as, aided by droves of Chinese advisers, it set about constructing a socialist society. Years of warring with France had profoundly damaged the country's infrastructure, and now it found itself deprived of the South's plentiful rice stocks. Worse still, the **land reforms** of the mid-1950s, vaunted as a Robin Hood-style redistribution of land, saw many thousands (some historians set the number as high as 100,000) of innocents "tried" as landlords by ad hoc **People's Agricultural Reform Tribunals**, tortured, and then executed or set to work in labour camps. "Reactionaries" were also denounced and punished, often for such imperialist "crimes" as possessing works of the great French poets and novelists. The **Rectification of Errors Campaign** of 1956 at least released many victims of the reforms from imprisonment, but as Ho Chi Minh himself said, "one cannot wake the dead".

With Hanoi so preoccupied with getting its own house in order and, at least until 1956, with being seen to be sticking to Geneva's terms, Viet Minh guerrillas south of the Seventeenth Parallel were for several years left to fend for themselves. For the most part, they sat tight in the face of Diem's reprisals, although guerrilla strikes became increasingly common towards the end of the 1950s, often taking the form of assassinations of government officials. Only in 1959 did the erosion of their ranks, witnessed firsthand by Le Duan, prompt Hanoi to shift up a gear and endorse a more overtly military stance. Conscription was introduced in April 1960, cadres and hardware began to creep down the **Ho Chi Minh Trail** (see p.336), and at the end of the year Hanoi orchestrated the creation of the **National Liberation Front** (NLF), which drew together all opposition forces in the South. Diem dubbed its guerrilla fighters **Viet Cong**, or VC (Vietnamese Communists) – a name which stuck, though in reality the NLF represented a united front of Catholic, Buddhist, communist and non-communist nationalists. Numbers were further boosted by erstwhile members of the Binh Xuyen, and the Hoa Hao and Cao Daist militias. Despite its eclectic make-up, the NLF worked in tandem with Hanoi, from where it received its directives.

America enters the fray

American dollars had been supporting the French war effort in Indochina since 1950. In 1954, President Eisenhower wrote of donating an "intelligent program of aid" as a means to "maintaining a strong, viable state", and in early 1955 the White House began to bankroll Diem's government and the training of his army, the **ARVN** (Army of the Republic of Vietnam). Behind these policies lay the fear of the chain reaction that could follow in Southeast Asia, were South Vietnam to be overrun by communism – the so-called **Domino Effect** – and, more cynically, what this would mean for US access to raw materials, trade routes and markets. No change in policy accompanied President John F. Kennedy's short-lived tenure of the White House. Kennedy, who had once described Diem's government as a "finger in the dyke" that held communism at bay, increased the build-up of military advisers and the financial shoring of the Southern regime and, though he balked at the prospect of large-scale American intervention, by the summer of 1962 there were 12,000 American advisers in South Vietnam.

Yet, despite all these injections of money, Diem's incompetent and unpopular government was losing ground to the VC in the battle for the hearts and minds of the population. Particularly damaging to the government was its **Strategic Hamlets Programme**. Formulated in 1962 and based on British methods used during the Malayan Emergency, the programme forcibly relocated entire villages into fortified stockades, with the aim of keeping the VC at bay. Ill-conceived, insensitive and open to exploitation by corrupt officials, the programme in fact had the opposite effect: as Nguyen Van Hieu, a high-ranking member of the Southern resistance, told Western journalist Wilfred Burchett, "Terror and brutal repression are driving everyone into the arms of the resistance." The majority of strategic hamlets were empty within two years, as villagers drifted back to their **ancestral lands**.

Militarily, things were little better. If America needed proof that Diem's government was struggling to subdue the guerrillas, it came in January 1963, at the **Battle of Ap Bac** (see p.307), where incompetent ARVN troops suffered heavy losses against a greatly outnumbered Viet Cong force. Four months later, Buddhists celebrating Buddha's birthday were fired upon by ARVN soldiers in Hué, sparking off riots and demonstrations against religious repression, and provoking **Thich Quang Duc's** infamous self-immolation in Saigon (see p.99). Diem had become a liability. Fearing that the communists would gain further by his unpopularity, America tacitly sanctioned the November 1 **coup** that ousted him; Diem and his brother escaped to Cholon, only to be shot the following day (see p.104).

The escalation of the war

Three weeks later, Kennedy was dead. Whatever private misgivings his successor Lyndon B. Johnson had about **continuing involvement** in what he called "that bitch of a war", he was still determined not to be responsible for America's losing a war to the communists. "Nothing," he said, "would be worse than that." By the end of 1963, America was involved to the tune of US$500 million a year.

The generals who superseded Diem proved no more efficacious, their **factional struggles** through 1964 and into 1965 igniting street demonstrations and riots that crippled Saigon. The capital staggered from coup to coup, but corruption, nepotism and dependence upon American support remained constant. In the countryside, meanwhile, the Viet Cong were forging a solid base of popular support. Observing Southern instability, Hanoi in early 1964 proceeded to send battalions of **NVA** (North Vietnamese Army) infantrymen down the Ho Chi Minh Trail, with 10,000 Northern troops hitting the trail in the first year. For America, unwilling to see the communists granted a say in the running of the South, yet unable to envisage Saigon's generals fending them off, the only option seemed to be to "**Americanize**" the conflict.

In August 1964, a chance came to do just that, when the American destroyer the USS *Maddox* allegedly suffered an unprovoked attack from North Vietnamese craft; two days afterwards, the *Maddox* and another ship, the *C Turner Joy*, reported a second attack. Years later it emerged that the *Maddox* had been taking part in a covert mission to monitor coastal installations, and that the second incident almost certainly never happened. Nevertheless, reprisals followed in the form of 64 **bombing** sorties against Northern coastal bases. And back in Washington, senators voted through the **Tonkin Gulf Resolution**, empowering Johnson to deploy regular American troops in Vietnam, "to prevent further aggression". To Johnson, seeking re-election at the time, this stand against communism was grist to the publicity mill.

Operation Rolling Thunder

An NVA attack upon the highland town of Plei Ku in February 1965 curtailed several months of US procrastination about how best to prosecute the war in Vietnam, and elicited **Operation Flaming Dart**, a concerted bombing raid on NVA camps above the Seventeenth Parallel. Increasingly, the military argument swayed the decision-makers: General Curtis Le May, Commander of the US Air Force, graphically compared previous policy in Vietnam to "swatting flies", when "going after the manure pile" would be more effective. **Operation Rolling Thunder**, a sustained carpet-bombing campaign, kicked in a month later; by the time of its suspension three and a half years later its 350,000 sorties had seen twice the tonnage of bombs dropped (around 800 daily) as had fallen on all World War II's theatres of war. Despite such impressive statistics, Rolling Thunder failed either to break the North's sources and lines of supply, or to coerce Hanoi into a suspension of activities in the South. Bombing served only to strengthen the resilience of the North, whose population was mobilized to rebuild bridges, roads and railways as quickly as they were damaged. Moreover, NVA troops continued to infiltrate the South in increasing numbers, so that by 1967 over 100,000 a year were making the trek south.

As far back as 1954, the American politician William F. Knowland had warned that "using United States ground forces in the Indochina jungle would be like trying to cover an elephant with a handkerchief – you just can't do it". His words fell on deaf ears. The first regular **American troops** from the 3rd US Marine Division landed at Da Nang in March 1965, and their original brief to defend its air base there was soon widened to embrace offensive action in the field. By the end of 1965, 200,000 GIs were in Vietnam – a figure that was to double within a year and approach half a million by the winter of 1967; in addition, there were large numbers of **Free World Military Forces**, comprising substantial contingents of Australians (Australian military advisers had been in South Vietnam since 1962) and South Koreans, plus smaller units of New Zealanders, Thais and Filipinos.

The American mission was largely confined to keeping the NVA at bay in the central highlands – as in the battle for the **Ia Drang Valley** during the autumn of 1965 – and neutralizing the guerrilla threat in the South, particularly the Mekong Delta and the region north of Saigon, the Viet Cong power bases. The war these troops fought was a dirty, dispiriting and frustrating one: for the most part, it was a guerrilla conflict against an invisible enemy able to disappear into the nearest village, leaving them unable to trust even civilians. Missions to flush active Viet Cong soldiers out of villages, which were initiated towards the end of 1965, became known as **Search and Destroy** operations; the most infamous of these resulted in the **My Lai massacre** (see p.266). Other jargon was coined, too, and added to the lexicon of conflict: in the highlands, **fire bases** were established, from where Howitzers could rain fire upon NVA troop movements; elsewhere, **free fire zones** – areas cleared of villagers to enable bombing of their supposed guerrilla occupants – were declared; and **scorched earth**, the policy of denuding and razing vast swathes of land in order to rob the Viet Cong of cover, was introduced. And all the while, generals in the field were quick to establish that most symbolic arbiter in this insane war, the **body count**, according to which missions succeeded or failed.

Hearts and minds

Predictably, it was the **civilians** who suffered most as the conflict in Vietnam rolled on. In the **North**, outrage at the merciless bombing campaign meted out by a remote foreign aggressor engendered a sense of anti-colonial purpose – especially when Hanoi's propaganda machine got into gear. But in the **South**, there was only disorientation. To some, the immensity of the US presence seemed to preclude the possibility of a protracted conflict, and was therefore welcome; to others, it felt so much like an invasion, especially when GIs began to uproot them and destroy their land, that they supported or joined the NLF. The Viet Cong themselves were no angels, though, often imposing a reign of terror, augmented by summary executions of alleged traitors. What's more, successive Saigon governments were corrupt and unpopular, but the alternative was the Northern communists so gruesomely depicted by American propaganda.

To survive, villagers quickly learned to react, and to say the right thing to the right person. The American policy of **pacification**, by which was meant the provision of such commodities as education and healthcare, was introduced to win civilian confidence. But once the Americans had returned to their bases at night, the Viet Cong would commandeer the villages they vacated. Trying to appease the two sets of soldiers they encountered in the space of a day was like treading a tightrope for villagers, creating a climate of hatred and distrust that turned neighbours into informants. Since children were conscripted by whichever side reached them first, brothers and sisters often found themselves fighting on opposing sides.

The Tet Offensive

On January 21, 1968, around 40,000 NVA troops laid siege to a remote American military base at **Khe Sanh**, near the Lao border northwest of Hué. Wary that the confrontation might become an American Dien Bien Phu – an analogy that in reality held no water, given the US's superior air power – America responded, to borrow the military jargon of the day, "with extreme prejudice", notching up a communist body count of over 10,000 in a carpet-bombing campaign graphically labelled "Niagara". However, such losses were seen as a necessary evil by the communists, for whom Khe Sanh was primarily a decoy to steer US troops and attention away from the **Tet Offensive** that exploded a week later. In the early hours of January 31, a combined force of 70,000 communists (most of them VC) violated a New Year truce to launch offensives on over a hundred urban centres across the South. The campaign failed to achieve its objectives of sparking a revolt against the Saigon regime and imposing VC representation in the Southern government as a first step towards reunification. Only in Hué did VC forces manage to hold out for more than a few days; moreover, communist losses were so devastating as to leave the VC permanently lamed.

But success *did* register across the Pacific, where the offensive caused a sea change in popular perceptions of the war. Thus far, Washington's propaganda machine had largely convinced the public that the war in Vietnam was under control; events in 1968 flew in the face of this charade. Around 2000 American GIs had died during the Tet Offensive; but symbolically more damaging was the audacious assault mounted, on the first day of the offensive, by a crack VC commando team on the compound of the **US Embassy in Saigon**. The communists had pierced the underbelly of the American presence in Vietnam: by the time the compound had been secured over six hours later, five Americans had died – and with them the popular conviction that the war was being won.

This shift in attitude was soon reflected in President Johnson's **vetoing** of requests for a massive troop expansion. On March 31, he announced a virtual cessation of bombing; a month later, the first bout of diplomatic sparring that was to grind on for five years was held in Paris; and, before the year was out, a full end to bombing had been declared.

Further proof – if any were needed – of the futility of the American involvement in Vietnam came in the form of the battle for **A Shau Valley**, west of Da Nang in the central highlands, early the next year. One of the exit points for NVA troops labouring down the Ho Chi Minh Trail, the valley had been under communist control for three years. After two abortive attempts to retake the valley, by May 1969 the Americans had finally made some headway, bottling the NVA troops into its western end, where many of them dug in on Hill 937 (Ap Bia Hill). The combined efforts of the American and ARVN troops to take the hill led to the loss of an estimated 700 lives, and earned it the graphically descriptive name of **Hamburger Hill** – because it turned fighting men into hamburger meat. Once defeat became inevitable, NVA forces simply retreated into Laos, and the valley was abandoned by the South.

Nixon's presidency

Richard Nixon's ill-starred term of office commenced in January 1969, on the back of a campaign in which he promised to "end the war and win the peace". His quest for a solution that would facilitate an American pull-out without tarnishing its image led Nixon to pursue the strategy of "**Vietnamization**", a gradual US withdrawal coupled with a stiffening of ARVN forces and hardware. Though the number of US troops in Vietnam reached an all-time peak of 540,000 early on in 1969, 60,000 of these were home for Christmas, and by the end of 1970 only 280,000 remained. Over the same time period, ARVN numbers almost doubled, from 640,000 to well over a million. As part of America's buttressing of the South, Nixon persisted with Johnson's controversial **Phoenix Programme**, which undermined the communist infrastructure in the Mekong Delta by infiltrating Viet Cong cells. Thousands of VC cadres were tortured, imprisoned or killed in the process. Furthermore, the quota system to which agents worked meant that many of the estimated 50,000 people assassinated were in fact innocent.

Nixon didn't limit his attacks to South Vietnam. The NVA had for several years been stockpiling both men and supplies in **Cambodia**, and in March 1969 US covert bombing of these targets commenced. Code-named **Operation Menu**, it lasted for fourteen months, yet elicited no outcry from Hanoi since they had no right to be in neutral Cambodia in the first place. The following spring, an American-backed coup having replaced Prince Sihanouk of Cambodia with Lon Nol and thus eased access for US troops, a **task force** of 20,000 soldiers advanced on communist installations there. The American public was outraged: dismayed that Nixon, far from closing down the war, was in fact widening the conflict, they rallied at massed anti-war demonstrations. At one such demo at **Kent State University**, Ohio, national guardsmen fired shots into the crowd, killing four marchers – an action that spurred 100,000 demonstrators to gather in Washington. As for the forays into Cambodia, they were failures both in terms of their missions, and in the sense that the ineptitude of the ARVN proved beyond doubt that Vietnamization wasn't working – something underlined by an abortive strike on an NVA base in Laos, code-named **Lam Son 719**.

Meanwhile, the stop-start **peace talks** in Paris dragged along, now with Nixon's National Security Adviser Henry Kissinger at the American helm, and Le Duc Tho representing the North (Ho Chi Minh had died on September 2, 1969). Two stumbling blocks hindered any advancement: the North's insistence on a coalition government in the South with no place for the current president, Thieu, and the US insistence that all NVA troops should move north after a ceasefire. Tit-for-tat military offensives launched early in 1972 saw both sides attempting to strengthen their hand at the bargaining table: Hanoi launched its **Easter Offensive** on the upper provinces of the South; while Nixon countered with a resumption of **bombing of the North** – at first targeting routes of strategical importance, but swiftly homing in on Haiphong and Hanoi. Towards the year's end, negotiations recommenced, this time with Hanoi in a mood to compromise – not least because Nixon let rumours spread of his **Madman Theory**, which involved the use of nuclear weaponry. Tragically, the draft agreement produced in October (Nixon was keen to see a resolution before the US elections in November) was delayed by President Thieu in Saigon, and by the time it was finalized in January 1973 Nixon had flexed his military muscles one last time, sanctioning the eleven-day **Christmas Bombing** of Hanoi and Haiphong (see p.385), in which 20,000 tonnes of ordnance was dropped, and 1600 civilians perished.

Under the terms of the **Paris Accords**, signed on January 27 by the United States, the North, the South and the Viet Cong, a ceasefire was established, all remaining American troops were repatriated by April, and Hanoi and Saigon released their PoWs. The Paris talks failed to yield a long-term political settlement, instead providing for the creation of a **Council of National Conciliation**, comprising Saigon's government and the communists, to sort matters out at some future date. The agreements allowed the NVA and ARVN troops to retain whatever positions they held. For this fudged deal, Kissinger and Le Duc Tho were awarded the Nobel Prize for peace, though only Kissinger accepted.

The fall of the South

The Paris Accords accomplished little beyond smoothing the US withdrawal from Vietnam and, with the NVA allowed to remain in the South, it was only a matter of time before **renewed aggression** erupted. Thieu's ARVN, now numbering a million troops and in robust shape thanks to its new US-financed equipment, soon set about retaking territory lost to the North during the Easter Offensive. The communists, on the other hand, were still reeling from losses accrued during that campaign. As for the Viet Cong, Tet had resulted in what Henry Kamm calls "enormous bloodletting" within their ranks – 40,000 deaths is a popular estimate – and the Phoenix Programme resulted in many more; increasingly, the NVA took over the struggle.

By 1974, however, things were beginning to sour for the South. An economy already weakened by heavy **inflation** was further drained by the **unemployment** caused by America's withdrawal; corruption in the military was rife, and unpaid wages led to a burgeoning ARVN desertion rate. By the end of the year, the South was ripe for the taking.

Received wisdom in Hanoi was that a slow build-up of arms in the South, in preparation for a conventional push in 1976, would be the wisest course of action. Then, over the Christmas period of 1974, an **NVA drive** led by General Tran overran the area north of Saigon now called Song Be Province. Duly encouraged, Hanoi went into action, and towns in the South fell like ninepins under the irresistible momentum of the **Ho Chi Minh Campaign**. Within two months, communist troops had occupied Buon Ma Thuot, taking a mere 24 hours to finish a job they'd anticipated would require a week. Hué and Da Nang duly followed, and by April 21 Xuan Loc, the last real line of defence before Saigon, had also fallen. ARVN defiance disintegrated in the face of the North's unerring progress: a famous image from these last days shows a highway scattered with the discarded boots of fleeing Southern soldiers. President Thieu fled by helicopter to Taiwan, and leadership of Saigon's government was assumed by **General Duong Van Minh** ("Big Minh"). Minh held the post for just two days before NVA tanks crashed through the gates of the Presidential Palace and Saigon fell to the North on April 30. Only hours before, the last Americans and other Westerners in the city had been **airlifted out** in the frantic helicopter operation known as "Frequent Wind" (see p.96).

The **toll** of the American War, in human terms, was staggering. Of the 3.3 million Americans who served in Vietnam between 1965 and 1973, over 57,600 died, and more than 150,000 received wounds which required hospitalization. Today, it is estimated that 500,000 veterans suffer from Post Traumatic Stress Disorder and that veteran suicides have now exceeded the total number of US fatalities during the conflict. The ARVN lost 250,000 troops. Hanoi declared that over two million Vietnamese civilians, and one million communist troops, died during the war. Many more on both sides are still listed as "missing in action" (MIA).

Post-reunification Vietnam

For the first time since the French colonization in the 1850s, Vietnam was once again a **unified nation**. So severely had Tet and the Phoenix Programme weakened the NLF that it was effectively a force of wholly Northern soldiers

The "boat people"

In 1979 the attention of the world was caught by images of bedraggled fishing boats packed with Vietnamese **refugees** seeking sanctuary in Hong Kong and other Southeast Asian harbours. An untold number – some say a third – fell victim to typhoons, starvation and disease or pirates, who often sank the boats after seizing the refugees' meagre possessions and raping the women. Others somehow fetched up on the coast of Australia or were picked up by passing freighters. The prime destination, however, was Hong Kong, where 68,000 asylum-seekers arrived in 1979 alone. The exodus was at its peak in 1979, but it had been going on, largely unnoticed, since reunification four years earlier, and continued up to the early 1990s. Over this period an estimated 840,000 boat people arrived safely in "ports of first asylum", of whom more than 750,000 were eventually resettled overseas.

The first refugees were mostly **southerners**, people who felt themselves too closely associated with the old regime or their American allies, and feared communist reprisals. Some were former nationalists and a few were even ex-Viet Cong, disillusioned with the new government's extremism. Then, in early 1978, nationalization of private commerce was instituted in the south, hitting hard at the **Chinese** community, which controlled much southern business and the all-important rice trade. As anti-Chinese sentiment took hold, thousands made their escape in fishing boats, initially from the south but, as relations between China and Vietnam deteriorated in 1979, the panic spread northwards. Large numbers fled across the border on foot, while others paid huge sums – including bribes to local officials – for a passage on the risky voyage to Hong Kong. Though the majority were ethnic Chinese, in the late 1970s more **Vietnamese** began to leave, driven by a series of bad harvests, severe hardship and the prospect of prolonged military service in Cambodia.

By 1979 the situation had become so critical that the international community was forced to act, offering asylum to the more than 200,000 refugees crowding temporary camps around Southeast Asia. Under the auspices of the UN, the **Orderly Departure Programme** (ODP) also enabled legal emigration of political refugees (mainly former American employees, Amerasian children and those seeking to be reunited with their families) to the West, resettling well over 500,000 in more than forty Western countries.

It seemed that the crisis was over, until 1987, when suddenly the South China Sea was once again full of Vietnamese people in overcrowded boats. This **second wave** were mostly northerners – often inflamed by tales of wealth from relatives already overseas – and seemed to be fleeing desperate poverty rather than fear of persecution. Hong Kong again bore the brunt of new arrivals: in 1989, 34,000 boat people entered the camps, bringing the total to 56,000, few of whom had any real chance of resettlement. But governments were less sympathetic this time round and, in an attempt to halt the flow, from early 1989 boat people were denied automatic refugee status. Instead, a screening process was introduced to identify that brought about the fall of Saigon. At first they trod softly, softly in order to impress the international community, but Southerners eyed the future with profound apprehension. Their fears were well founded. Hanoi was in no mood to grant Saigon autonomy: the Council of National Reconciliation, provided for by the Paris Accords, was never established, and the NLF's **Provisional Revolutionary Government** worked beneath the shadow of the Military Management Committee, and therefore Hanoi, until the **Socialist Republic of Vietnam** was officially born, in July 1976. The impression of a conquering army was exacerbated when northern cadres – the *can bo* – swarmed south to take up all official posts. More than one commentator on the war suggested that, in some way, this seizing of the reins of power harked back to earlier centuries and represented the revenge of the Trinh over the Nguyen (see p.487).

"genuine" refugees; the rest, designated "economic migrants", were encouraged to return under the **Voluntary Repatriation Scheme**, which offered concrete assistance with resettlement. Despite numerous complaints about the screening procedures, by 1996 more than 70,000 boat people had returned, keen to leave the prison-like camps and reassured by the changes occurring in Vietnam. In late 1995, in order to encourage voluntary repatriation in a stagnant and increasingly tense environment, the American government proposed a scheme (known as ROVR) under which boat people were invited to register for the opportunity to emigrate to America, but only after they had voluntarily returned to Vietnam.

Then, in early 1996 all parties finally agreed that the only "viable solution" was to send the remaining 40,000 failed asylum-seekers still in Southeast Asian camps back home as quickly as possible; many of these were children born in the camps, who had never set foot in Vietnam. In theory deportations were to take place "without threat or use of force", but clashes with security forces became more violent as the 1997 deadline drew nearer. The situation was worst in Hong Kong, where the government was under pressure to clear the remaining boat people before the handover to China. The first forced repatriations had taken place in Hong Kong in 1989, causing a storm of protest around the world and threats of mass suicide. But in 1996 the rate of repatriation – both voluntary and, increasingly, forced – was stepped up throughout the region and by mid-1997 nearly all the boat people had been either resettled or returned to Vietnam. By the end of 1999 only 1400 refugees remained stuck in limbo in Hong Kong detention centres. No other countries were willing to accept them since many had criminal records or were drug addicts but, as refugees, they could not be sent back to Vietnam. Finally, in February 2000, the Hong Kong government agreed that they could apply for resettlement in the territory.

Up until the end of 1999, returnees were monitored in Vietnam by staff of the UN High Commission for Refugees (UNHCR), who said there was little evidence of persecution or discrimination. Others, however, claimed that the monitoring was inadequate and ineffective, and cited examples of returnees being imprisoned. At the same time, various international bodies, such as the European Union, helped returnees reintegrate into the community through job creation schemes, vocational training programmes and low-interest loans. In 1998 the ROVR scheme (see above) finally got under way and it's estimated that some 16,000 returnees have now been resettled in the United States, mostly southerners who were able to prove some sort of relationship with the Americans during the war.

As the Vietnamese economy improved and as relations between America and Vietnam started to thaw, so the ODP and ROVR programmes were wound up. Their completion marked the end – at least as far as officialdom was concerned – of the whole sorry saga of the boat people.

Monumental **problems** faced the nascent republic. For many years, the two halves of Vietnam had lived according to wildly variant political and economic systems. The North had no industry, its agriculture was based on co-operative farms, and much of its land had been bombed on a massive scale. In stark contrast, American involvement in the South had underwritten what John Pilger describes as "an 'economy' based upon the services of maids, pimps, whores, beggars and black-marketeers", buttressed by American cash that dried up when the last helicopter left the embassy in Saigon.

The slow, cautious merger of economies that the NLF had in mind found no favour in Hanoi, whose top ranks were intent on ushering in a rigid socialist state. At the **Fourth Communist Party Congress** held in December 1976, southern Vietnam was economically restructured in line with the north: privately owned land was confiscated; collectivization of agriculture, based on unwieldy Eastern bloc models, was introduced; and citizens were relocated and gathered into communal farms. The state took control of industry and trade, output dwindled, and some farmers slaughtered cattle rather than rear them only for donation to the cause. Productivity wasn't helped any by the **devastation** wreaked on the nation's forestry and farmland by the lingering effects of chemical warfare waged by the Americans (see "Environmental issues", p.542).

The changes that swept the country weren't limited to economics. Bitterness on Hanoi's part towards its former enemies was inevitable; yet instead of making moves towards national conciliation, and despite the fact that many families had connections in both camps, recriminations drove further wedges between the peoples of north and south. The dissident novelist Duong Thu Huong succinctly states: "Our people are strong in times of war...But to live in a civil society, with a full awareness of individual value, our people are still very young and naive. Notions like democracy, the rights of man, are seen as something very distant, luxuries." Anyone with remote connections with America was interned in a **re-education camp** (in reality, a labour camp), along with Buddhist monks, priests, intellectuals, and anyone else the government wanted to be rid of. Hundreds of thousands of southerners were sent, without trial, to these camps, and some remained for over a decade. Discrimination against those on the "wrong side" in the war continues today, in areas as diverse as healthcare, education and job opportunities – even cemeteries containing southerners' remains have been razed.

Talks aimed at normalizing relations between Vietnam and the United States began in March 1977, but the meetings came to nothing. Instead, 1970's **Trading with the Enemy Act**, which made it a crime for Americans to do business in or with Vietnam, was upheld. In addition, and largely due to American pressure, Vietnam was, until 1993, unable to look to the IMF, World Bank or Asian Development Bank for **development loans**. Soviet aid was all that was available to the country; in 1978, Vietnam joined **Comecon**, the Eastern European economic community.

The quagmire Vietnam found itself in after reunification prompted many of its citizens to flee the country and blunder across the oceans in unseaworthy vessels, hoping to wash up on the shores of a friendly nation (see box above).

A return to war

Three weeks before the fall of Saigon in 1975, **Pol Pot**'s genocidal regime had seized power in Cambodia; within a year his troops were making **cross-border forays** into regions of Vietnam that had once fallen under Khmer sway, around the Mekong Delta and north of Ho Chi Minh City (as Saigon had been renamed). One such venture led to the massacre at **Ba Chuc** (see p.174), in which almost 2000 people died. Reprisals were slow in coming, due to the tacit support Pol Pot enjoyed from the Chinese. Towards the end of the war against America, Hanoi had shifted its allegiances away from Beijing and closer to Moscow; conflict in Cambodia was bound to ruffle feathers in Beijing and so heighten the Sino-Vietnamese tensions that already existed.

However, by 1978, Vietnam could stand back no longer, and on Christmas Day of that year 120,000 **Vietnamese troops invaded Cambodia** and ousted Pol Pot. Whatever the motives for the invasion, and even though it brought an end to Pol Pot's reign of terror, Vietnam was further ostracized by the international community. In February 1979, Beijing's response came in the form of a punitive **Chinese invasion** of Vietnam's northeastern provinces; Chinese losses were heavy, and after sixteen days they retreated. Meanwhile, Pol Pot had withdrawn across the Thai border, from where his army was able to continue attacking the Vietnamese army of occupation. The Vietnamese remained in Cambodia until September 1989, by which time an estimated 50,000 troops had died, the majority of them southern conscripts.

Doi Moi… and the future

A severe famine in 1985 and the 775 percent inflation that crippled the country in 1986 were just two of the many symptoms of the **economic malaise** threatening to tear Vietnam apart during the late 1970s and early 1980s. An experimental hybrid of planned and market economies tried out in 1979 came to nothing, and by the early 1980s the only thing keeping Vietnam afloat was Soviet aid.

The Party's conservative old guard resisted change for as long as it could, but the death of General Secretary Le Duan in 1986 finally cleared the way for more reformist politicians to attempt to reverse the country's fortunes. At the Sixth Party Congress in December, the reformist **Nguyen Van Linh** took over as general secretary, and a raft of market-based economic reforms, known as **doi moi** or "renovation", followed. There were limited moves towards decentralizaton and privatization, collectivized agriculture was abandoned in favour of individual land-holdings and attempts were made to attract foreign capital by liberalizing foreign investment regulations. Political reforms came a poor second, although the congress did instigate purges on corrupt officialdom and gave the press freer rein to criticize. With the **collapse of communism** across Europe in 1989, though, the press was again silenced, and in a keynote speech Nguyen Van Linh rejected the concept of a multi-party state; all economic reforms, however, remained in place. **Soviet aid**, which by the end of the 1980s amounted to US$2 billion a year, continued to provide an important lifeline until it ran dry in 1991. Realizing that Vietnam would henceforth need to stand alone, that year's **Seventh Party Congress** strengthened its commitment to "socialist-oriented" economic reform and set in motion efforts to end Vietnam's isolation.

International rehabilitation, which had already begun with the withdrawal of troops from Cambodia in 1989, gathered momentum in the 1990s, as efforts to aid the US search teams looking for remains of the 2000-plus American soldiers still unaccounted for (MIAs, or Missing in Action) were stepped up. In 1993, a year after the reformist **Vo Van Kiet** became prime minister, the Americans duly lifted their veto on aid, and Western cash began to flow. By the year's end, inflation was down to five percent. The *rapprochement* with the US continued into 1994, as the US trade embargo was lifted by President Clinton, and in February 1995 the two countries opened liaison offices in each other's capitals. Vietnam was admitted into **ASEAN** (the Association of Southeast Asian Nations) in July 1995, and the same month saw full **diplomatic relations restored** with the **US**.

During the next two years foreign investment continued to flood in, pushing economic growth rates close to ten percent per annum. Revenues from oil, manufacturing and tourism took off and everyone was forecasting Vietnam as the next **Asian tiger**. For all the optimism, however, cracks were beginning to appear: the economic upturn was benefiting city-dwellers (particularly in Ho Chi Minh) far more than the rural population; top bureaucrats were openly criticized in **corruption** scandals; and an alarmed government launched a campaign against "**social evils**" – videos, advertising, pornography and other Western imports which were seen to be undermining traditional society.

By 1997 the honeymoon period was definitely over. Economic growth flagged as foreign companies scaled back, or pulled out altogether, frustrated by an overblown bureaucracy, miles of red tape and regulations in a constant state of flux. As the economic crisis in Southeast Asia took hold, Vietnam's mostly inefficient, state-run industries became increasingly uncompetitive, and smuggling grew at an alarming rate. In May 1997, local corruption, growing agricultural unemployment and the ever-widening gulf between urban and rural Vietnam sparked off **demonstrations** by thousands of dissatisfied farmers in Thai Binh Province, part of the traditionally communist north.

National **elections** in July 1997 brought a long-awaited change of government, ushering in a band of younger, more worldly-wise ministers under prime minister **Phan Van Khai**, who was re-elected in 2002. While Khai has continued both the economic reforms and the fight against corruption, behind the scenes power struggles have hampered his ability to force through the necessary, far-reaching structural reforms, and political pluralism is still off the agenda. Under his premiership, however, the dual process of **international reconciliation** and liberalization of trade moved forward apace with the ratification in 2001 of a crucial bilateral trade agreement between Vietnam and America. As a result, exports of certain products subject to low tarrifs (including oil, coffee, fish and textiles) to the US have already doubled, while foreign investment is also on the rise, notably from Singaporean and Hong Kong garment manufacturers in anticipation of continued growth. Whether Vietnam fulfils its part of the bargain by opening its markets to more American goods remains to be seen. Its commitment to structural, political and economic reform will be tested even further as Vietnam pursues its ambition to join the World Trade Organisation by 2005.

There's no doubt, however, that Vietnam has achieved a great deal in a comparatively short time. The **economy** is faring reasonably well in the face of increasingly stiff international competition – not least from China – with annual growth rates holding to around seven percent. The country has also made good progress in reducing population growth and levels of rural poverty, at the same time as pulling in record rice harvests. There have even been a number of high-profile **anti-corruption trials** and in general the authorities appear more tolerant of dissent, although progress on **human rights** is erratic to say the least. Indeed, one of the government's biggest immediate problems is how to reconcile the inherent contradictions between economic liberalization and central political control, while also satisfying the growing aspirations of Vietnamese people. Combine this with the need to speed up the restructuring and privatization of debt-ridden state enterprises without letting unemployment and economic and social inequality spiral out of control, and it's perhaps not surprising that reform is painfully slow.

Religion and beliefs

The moral and religious life of most Vietnamese people is governed by a complex mixture of Confucian, Buddhist and Taoist philosophical teachings interwoven with ancestor worship and ancient, animistic practices. Incompatibilities are reconciled on a practical level into a single, functioning belief system whereby a family may maintain an ancestral altar in their home, consult the village guardian spirit, propitiate the God of the Hearth and take offerings to the Buddhist pagoda.

The primary influence on Vietnam's religious life has been Chinese. But in southern Vietnam, which historically fell within the Indian sphere, small communities of Khmer and Cham still adhere to Hinduism, Islam and Theravada Buddhism brought direct from India. From the fifteenth century on, **Christianity** has also been a feature, represented largely by Roman Catholicism but with a small Protestant following in the south. Vietnam also claims a couple of home-grown religious **sects**, both products of political and social turmoil in the early twentieth century: Cao Dai and Hoa Hao.

The **political dimension** has never been far removed from religious affairs in Vietnam, as the world was made vividly aware by Buddhist opposition to the oppressive regime of President Diem in the 1960s. After 1975, the Marxist-Leninist government of reunified Vietnam declared the state atheist while theoretically allowing people the right to practise their religion under the constitution. In reality, churches and pagodas were closed down, religious leaders sent for re-education, and followers discriminated against if not actively persecuted. Since 1986 the situation has eased, with the right to religious freedom being reaffirmed in the 1992 constitution. A number of high-profile prisoners held on religious grounds have been released, while Party leaders have publicly demonstrated the new freedoms by visiting pagodas and churches. As a result many Vietnamese are once again openly practising their faith. Indeed, as Vietnam faces the onslaught of new ideas and the "social evils" spawned by the breakdown of its moral codes, people are looking to religion both for personal guidance and as a stabilizing force in society. Despite such moves toward greater freedom of worship, however, the government continues to exercise close control on religious groups through such practices as monitoring appointments and publications. It is regularly accused of failing to make real progress on human rights issues and came in for particularly severe criticism for its crackdown on ethnic minority Christians following widespread demonstrations in the central highlands in 2001.

Ancestor worship

One of the oldest cults practised in Vietnam is that of ancestor worship, based on the fundamental principles of filial piety and of obligation to the past, present and future generations. No matter what their religion, virtually every Vietnamese household, even hardline communist, will maintain an **ancestral altar** in the belief that the dead continue to live in another realm. Ancestors can intercede on behalf of their descendants and bring the family good fortune, but in return the living must pay respect, perform prescribed ceremonies and provide for their ancestors' wellbeing. At funerals and subsequent anniversaries, quantities of paper money and other **votive offerings** (these days including television sets and cars) are burnt, and choice morsels of food are regularly placed on the altar. Traditionally this is financed by the income from a designated plot of land, and it is the responsibility of the oldest, usually male, member of the family to organize the rituals, tend the altar and keep the ancestors abreast of all important family events; failure in any of these duties carries the risk of inciting peeved ancestors to make mischief.

The ancestral altar occupies a central position in the home. On it are placed several wooden tablets, one for each ancestor going back five generations. One hundred days after the funeral, the deceased's spirit returns to live in their tablet. People without children to honour them by burning incense at the altar are condemned to wander the world in search of a home. Some childless people make provision by paying a temple or pagoda to observe the rituals, while the spirits of others may eventually take up residence in one of the small shrine houses (*cuong*) you see in fields and at roadsides. Important times for remembering the dead are **Tet**, the lunar new year, and **Thanh Minh** ("Festival of Pure Light"), which falls on the fifth day of the third lunar month.

Spirit worship

Residual animism plus a whole host of spirits borrowed from other religions have given Vietnam a complicated mystical world. The universe is divided into **three realms**: the sky, earth and man, under the overall guardianship of Ong Troi, Lord of Heaven, assisted by spirits of the earth, mountains and water. Within the hierarchy are four **sacred animals** who appear everywhere in Vietnamese architecture: the dragon, representing the king, power and intelligence; the phoenix, embodying the queen, beauty and peace; the turtle, symbol of longevity and protector of the kingdom; and the mythical kylin, usually translated as unicorn, which represents wisdom.

In addition each village or urban quarter will venerate a **guardian spirit** in either a temple (*den*) or communal house (*dinh*). The deity may be legendary, for example the benevolent horse-spirit Bach Ma of Thang Long (modern Hanoi; see p.372), and will often come from the Taoist pantheon. Or the guardian may be a historical figure such as a local or national hero, or a man of great virtue. In either case people will propitiate these tutelary spirits – represented on the altar by a gilded throne – with offerings, and will consult them in times of need. The *dinh* also serves as meeting house and school for the community.

Buddhism

The Buddha was born **Siddhartha Gautama** to a wealthy family sometime during the sixth century BC in present-day Nepal. At an early age he renounced his life of luxury to seek the ultimate deliverance from worldly suffering and strive to reach **nirvana**, an indefinable, blissful state. After several years Siddhartha attained enlightenment while sitting under a bodhi tree, and then devoted the rest of his life to teaching the **Middle Way** that leads to nirvana. The Buddha preached that existence is a cycle of perpetual reincarnation in which actions in one life determine one's position in the next, but that it is

The Buddhist pagoda

The Vietnamese word *chua*, translated as "pagoda", is an exclusively Buddhist term, whereas a temple (*den*) may be Taoist, Confucian or house a guardian spirit. **Pagoda architecture** reached a pinnacle during the Ly and Tran dynasties, but thanks to Chinese invasions and local, anti-Buddhist movements few examples remain. A majority of those still in existence are eighteenth- or nineteenth-century constructions, though many retain features of earlier designs. Generally, pagoda **layout** is either an inverse T or three parallel lines of single-storeyed pavilions. The first hall is reserved for public worship, while those beyond, on slightly raised platforms, contain the prayer table and principal altar. Other typical elements are a **bell tower**, either integral to the building or standing apart, and a **walled courtyard** containing ponds, stone stelae and, particularly in Mahayana pagodas, the white figure of Quan Am symbolizing charity and compassion.

The most interesting feature inside the pagoda is often the **statuary**. Rows of Buddhas sit or stand on the main altar, where the Buddhist trinity occupies the highest level: A Di Da or Amitabha, the Historical Buddha; Thich Ca Mau Ni or Sakyamuni, born Siddhartha Gautama, the Present Buddha; and Di Lac, or Maitreya, the Future Buddha. Lower ranks comprise the same Buddhas in a variety of forms accompanied by bodhisattvas: look out for pot-bellied Maitreya as the laughing carefree Buddha who grants wishes; the omnipotent Avalokitesvara of a "thousand" arms and eyes; and the Nine Dragon Buddha (Tuong Cuu Long). This latter is a small statue, found more often in northern Vietnam, of Sakyamuni encircled by dragons, standing with one hand pointing to the sky and the other to the earth. According to legend, nine dragons descended from the sky to bathe the newborn Buddha, after which he took seven steps forward and proclaimed "on earth and in the sky, I alone am the highest".

Two unmistakable figures residing in all pagodas are the giant **guardians of Buddhist law**: white-faced "Mister Charitable" (Ong Thien), holding a pearl, and red-faced "Mister Wicked" (Ong Ac). Ong Thien sees everything, both the good and the bad, while Ong Ac dispenses justice. From an artistic point of view, some of the most fascinating statues are the lifelike representations of **arhats**, ascetic Buddhist saints; the best examples are found in northern pagodas, where each figure is portrayed in a disturbingly realistic style. Finally, Mahayana pagodas will undoubtedly welcome in a few **Taoist spirits**, the favourites being Thien Hau, the Protectress of Sailors, and Thanh Mau, the Mother Goddess. Somewhere in the pagoda halls will be an altar dedicated to deceased monks or nuns, while larger pagodas usually maintain a garden for their burial stupas. Traditionally Buddhists would bury their dead, but increasingly they practise cremation.

The **best times to visit** a pagoda are the first and fifteenth days of the lunar month (new moon and full moon), when they are at their busiest. Note that it's customary to remove your shoes when stepping on the floor mats and sometimes when entering the main sanctuary – watch what the locals do to be on the safe side.

possible to break free by following certain precepts, central to which are non-violence and compassion. The Buddha's doctrine was based on the **Four Noble Truths**: existence is suffering; suffering is caused by desire; suffering ends with the extinction of desire; the way to end suffering is to follow the eightfold path of right understanding, thought, speech, action, livelihood, effort, mindfulness and concentration.

The history of Buddhism in Vietnam

It's estimated that up to two-thirds of the Vietnamese population consider themselves Buddhist. The vast majority are followers of the Mahayana school which was introduced to northern Vietnam via China in the second century AD. Within this, most Vietnamese Buddhists claim allegiance to the Pure Land sect (*Tinh Do*), which venerates A Di Da or Amitabha Buddha above all others, while the meditational Zen sect (*Thien*) has a moderate following, predominantly in northern Vietnam.

In fact Buddhism first arrived in southern Vietnam nearly one hundred years earlier as **Theravada** or the "Lesser Vehicle", following Indian trade routes through Burma and Thailand. Theravada is an ascetical form of the faith based on the individual pursuit of perfection and enlightenment, which failed to find favour beyond the Khmer communities of the Mekong, where it still claims about 400,000 followers. One of the salient features of **Mahayana** Buddhism, in contrast, is the belief that intermediaries, **bodhisattvas**, have chosen to forgo nirvana to work for the salvation of all humanity, and it was this that enabled Mahayana to adapt to a Vietnamese context by incorporating local gods and spirits into its array of bodhisattvas. The most well-known bodhisattva is Avalokitesvara, usually worshipped in Vietnam as **Quan Am**, the Goddess of Mercy. Mahayana Buddhism spread through northern Vietnam until it became the **official state religion** after the country regained its independence from China in the tenth century. The Ly kings (1009–1225) in particular were devout Buddhists who sponsored hundreds of pagodas, prompting a flowering of the arts, and established a hierarchy of scholar-monks as advisers to the court. Great landowning monasteries came into being and Buddhist doctrine was incorporated into the civil service examinations along with Confucian and Taoist texts as part of the "triple world-view", *Tam Giao*. At the same time it became apparent that Buddhism was unable to provide the unifying ideology required by a highly centralized state constantly fighting for its survival. Consequently, by the mid-fourteenth century Buddhism had lost its political and economic influence, and, when the Later Le dynasty came to power in 1428, Confucianism finally eclipsed it as the dominant national philosophy.

But by then Buddhism was too deeply rooted, particularly in the folk religion of the countryside, to lose its influence completely. Buddhism enjoyed brief periods of **royal patronage**, notably during the seventeenth and eighteenth centuries when new pagodas were built and old ones repaired. To many people it still offered a spiritual element lacking in Confucian doctrine, and during the colonial era Vietnamese intellectuals turned to Buddhism in search of a national identity. Since then the Buddhist community has been a focus of **dissent**, not least in the 1960s when images of self-immolating Buddhist monks focused world attention on the excesses of South Vietnam's Catholic President Diem. At the time, protesting Buddhists were accused of being pro-communist, but their standpoint was essentially neutral. In the event they experienced even greater repression **after reunification** when pagodas were closed, and monks and nuns were sent to re-education camps. Buddhist leaders have persisted in their denunciations of the regime, campaigning for human rights and causing the government acute embarrassment as it seeks international approval. In general, though, the Party has made good its promises of **greater religious freedom** under *doi moi*. In recent years the Buddhist community has been able to resume its social and educational programmes to a certain extent and many pagodas, now bustling with life once again, have been renovated after twenty or more years of neglect.

Confucianism

The teachings of Confucius provide a guiding set of moral and ethical principles, an **ideology** for the state's rulers and subjects onto which ritualistic practices have been grafted.

Confucius is the Latinized name of K'ung-Fu-Tzu (Khong Tu in
Vietnamese), who was born into a minor aristocratic family in China in 551
BC. At this time China was in turmoil as the Zhou dynasty dissolved into rival
feudal states battling for supremacy. Confucius worked for many years as a
court official, where he observed the nature of power and the function of government at close quarters. At the age of 50, he packed it all in and for the next
twenty years wandered the country spreading his ideas on social and political
reform in an effort to persuade states and individuals to live peacefully together for their mutual benefit. His central tenet was the importance of **correct
behaviour** and **loyal service**, reinforced by ceremonial rites whereby the
ruler maintains authority through good example rather than force. Important
qualities to strive for are selflessness, respectfulness, sincerity and non-violence;
the ideal person should be neither heroic nor extrovert, but instead follow a
"golden mean". Confucius remained silent on spiritual matters, though he
placed great emphasis on observing ancient rituals such as making offerings to
heaven and to ancestors.

Confucian **teachings** were handed down in the Analects, but he is also credited with editing the Six Classics, among them the Book of Changes (*I Ching*)
and the Book of Ritual (*Li Chi*). Later these became the basic texts for civil
service examinations, ensuring that all state officials had a deeply ingrained
respect for tradition and social order. Though Confucianism ultimately led to
national inflexibility and the undermining of personal initiative, its positive
legacy has been an emphasis on the value of education and a belief that individual merit is of greater consequence than high birth.

After the death of Confucius in 478 BC the doctrine was developed further
by his **disciples**, the most famous of whom was Mencius (Meng-tzu). By the
first century AD, Confucianism, which slowly absorbed elements of Taoism,
had evolved into a cult and also become the state ideology whereby kings ruled
under the Mandate of Heaven. Social stability was maintained through a fixed
hierarchy of interdependent relationships encapsulated in the notion of filial
piety. Thus children must obey their parents without question, wives their husbands, students their teacher, and subjects their ruler. For their part, the recipient, particularly the king, must earn this obedience; if the rules are broken, the
harmony of society and nature is disturbed and authority loses its legitimacy.
Therefore, by implication, revolution was justified when the king lost his
divine right to rule.

The history of Confucianism in Vietnam

Confucian thinking has pervaded Vietnamese society ever since Chinese
administrators introduced the concepts during the second century BC. Reinforced by a thousand years of Chinese rule, Confucianism (*Nho Giao*) came
to play an essential role in Vietnam's political, social and educational systems.
The philosophy was largely one of an intellectual elite, but Confucian teaching
eventually filtered down to the village level where it had a profound influence
on the Vietnamese family organization.

The ceremonial **cult of Confucius** was formalized in 1070 when King Ly Thanh Tong founded the Temple of Literature in Hanoi. But it wasn't until the foundation of the Later Le dynasty in 1428 that Confucian doctrine gained supremacy over Buddhism in the Vietnamese court. The Le kings viewed Confucian ideology, with its emphasis on social order, duty and respect, as an effective means of consolidating their new regime. In 1442 they overhauled the education system and based it on a curriculum of Confucian texts. They also began recruiting top-level mandarins through doctoral examinations, which eventually gave rise to a scholar-gentry class at the expense of the old landed aristocracy. Confucian influence reached its peak during the reign of King Le Thanh Tong (1460–97), which heralded a golden age of bureaucratic reform when public service on behalf of both community and state became a noble ideal. At the same time, however, a strongly centralized administration, presided over by a divine ruler and a mandarin elite, eventually bred corruption, despotism and an increasingly rigid society. The arrival of Western ideas and French rule in the late nineteenth century finally undermined the political dominance of Confucianism, though it managed to survive as the court ideology until well into the twentieth century. The cult of Confucius continues in a few temples (*Van Mieu*) dedicated to the sage, and he also appears on other altars as an honoured ancestor, an exemplary figure remembered for services to the nation.

Many **Confucian ideals** have been completely assimilated into Vietnamese society. After Independence, the Communist Party struggled against inherent conservatism and the supremacy of the family as a political unit; indeed, leaders can still be heard railing against the entrenched "feudal" nature of rural Vietnam. But the Party was also able to tap into those elements of the Confucian tradition that suited their new classless, socialist society: conformity, duty and the denial of personal interest for the common good. Today, however, Confucian ideals are seriously threatened by the invasion of materialism and individual ambition.

Taoism

Taoism is based on the **Tao-te-Ching**, the "Book of the Way", traditionally attributed to **Lao-tzu** (meaning "Old Master"), who is thought to have lived in China in the sixth century BC. The Tao, the Way, emphasizes effortless action, intuition and spontaneity; the Tao is invisible and impartial; it cannot be taught, nor can it be expressed in words. It is the one reality from which everything is born, universal and eternal. However, by virtuous, compassionate and non-violent behaviour, it is possible to achieve ultimate stillness, through a mystical and personal quest. Taoism thus preached non-intervention, passivity and the futility of academic scholarship; it was viewed by Confucians as suspiciously subversive.

Central to the Tao is the **duality** inherent in nature; the whole universe is in temporary balance, a tension of complementary opposites defined as **yin** and **yang**, the male and female principles. Yang is male, the sun, active and orthodox; yin is female, the earth, flexible, passive and instinctive. Harmony is the balance between the two, and experiencing that harmony is the Tao. Accordingly all natural things can be categorized by their property of yin or yang, and human activity should strive not to disrupt that balance. In its pure form Taoism has no gods, only emanations of the Tao, but in the first century

The **practice of geomancy** is a pseudo-scientific study, much like astrology or reading horoscopes, which was introduced to Vietnam from China. The underlying idea is that every location has harmful or beneficial properties governed by its physical attributes, planetary influences and the flow of magnetic energy through the earth. Geomancy is used mainly in **siting buildings**, particularly tombs, palaces, temples and the like, but also ordinary dwellings.

Geomancers analyse the general **topography** of the site, looking at the location of surrounding hills, as well as rivers, streams and other bodies of water, to find the most auspicious situation and orientation. They may suggest improving the area by adding small hills or lakes and, if a family suffers bad fortune, a geomancer may be called in to divine the cause of the imbalance and restore the natural harmony.

AD it corrupted into an organized religion venerating a deified Lao-tzu. The new cult had popular appeal since it offered the goal of immortality through yogic meditation and good deeds. Eventually the practice of Taoism developed highly complex **rituals**, incorporating magic, mysticism, superstition and the use of geomancy (see box above) to ensure harmony between man and nature, while astrology might be used to determine auspicious dates for weddings, funerals, starting a journey or even launching a new business. Ancient spirit worship, the cult of ancestors and the veneration of legendary or historic figures all fused happily with the Taoist idea of a universal essence.

The vast, eclectic pantheon of Taoist **gods and immortals** is presided over by Ngoc Hoang, the Jade Emperor. He is assisted by three ministers: Nam Tao, the southern star who records all births; Bac Dau, the north star who registers deaths; and Ong Tao, God of the Hearth who reports all happenings in the family household to Ngoc Hoang at the end of the year. Then there is a collection of immortals, genies and guardian deities, including legendary and historic figures. In Vietnam among the most well-known are Tran Vo, God of the North, Bach Ho, the White Tiger of the West, and Tran Hung Dao, who protects the newborn and cures the sick. Confucius is also honoured as a Taoist saint. A distinctive aspect of Taoism is its use of **mediums** to communicate with the gods; the divine message is often in the form of a poem, transmitted by a writing brush onto sand or a bed of rice.

Chinese immigrants brought Taoism (*Dao Giao*) to Vietnam during the long period of Chinese rule (111 BC–939 AD). Between the eleventh and fourteenth centuries the philosophy enjoyed equal status with Buddhism and Confucianism as one of Vietnam's three "religions", but Taoism gradually declined until it eventually became a strand of folk religion. A few Taoist temples (*quan*) exist in Vietnam but on the whole its deities have been absorbed into other cults. The Jade Emperor, for example, frequently finds himself part of the Buddhist pantheon in Vietnamese pagodas.

Christianity

Vietnam's **Catholic community** is the second largest in Southeast Asia after the Philippines. Exact figures are hard to come by but estimates vary between six and eight million (seven to ten percent of the population), of which perhaps two-thirds live in the south. The south is also home to the majority of the 700,000 or so adherents to the **Protestant** faith, known as *Tin Lanh*, or the Good News, which was introduced by American missionaries in the early twentieth century. While the government now officially recognizes the Protestant Evangelical Church of Southern Vietnam, it remains deeply suspicious of another evangelical branch known as "Dega Protestantism" practised mainly by the ethnic minorities of the central highlands. It's not so much the belief system itself that the authorities are concerned about, but rather the movement's potential as a political force and, specifially, its alleged association with demands from certain minority groups for greater autonomy.

The first Christian **missionaries** to reach Vietnam were Portuguese and Spanish Dominicans who landed briefly on the north coast in the sixteenth century. They were followed in 1615 by French and Portuguese Jesuits, dispatched by the pope to establish the first permanent missions. Among the early arrivals was the Frenchman Alexandre de Rhodes, a Jesuit who impressed the northern Trinh lords and won, by his reckoning, nearly 7000 converts. The inevitable **backlash** against Christianity, which opposed ancestor worship and espoused subversive ideas such as equality, was not long in coming. In 1630 the Trinh lords expelled all Christians, including de Rhodes, who returned to France where he helped create the Society of Foreign Missions (*Société des Missions Etrangères*). This society soon became the most active proselytizing body in Indochina; by the end of the eighteenth century it had claimed thousands of converts, particularly in the coastal provinces.

Official attitudes towards the Catholic religion waxed and waned over the centuries, though the Vietnamese kings were generally suspicious of the Church's increasingly political role. The most violent **persecution** of Christians occurred during the reign of Minh Mang (1820–41), an ardent Confucian, and reached a peak after 1832. Churches were destroyed, the faces of converts were branded with the words *ta dao*, meaning "false religion", and many of those refusing to renounce their faith were killed; 117 martyrs, both European and Asian, were later canonized. Such repression, much exaggerated at the time, provided the French with a pretext for greater involvement in Indochina, culminating in full colonial rule at the end of the nineteenth century.

Not surprisingly, Catholicism **prospered** under the French regime. Missions re-opened and hundreds of churches, schools and hospitals were built. Vietnamese Catholics formed an educated elite among a population that counted some two million faithful by the 1950s. When partition came in 1954 many Catholics chose to move south, partly because of their opposition to communism and partly because the new leader of South Vietnam, President Ngo Dinh Diem, was a Catholic. Of the estimated 900,000 Vietnamese who left the North in 1954, it's said that around two-thirds were Catholic; many of these became refugees a second time in the 1970s.

Diem actively discriminated in favour of the Catholic community, which he viewed as a bulwark against communism. As a result he alienated large sections of the population, most importantly Buddhists whose protests eventually contributed to his downfall. Meanwhile in North Vietnam the authorities trod fairly carefully with those Catholics who had chosen to stay, allowing them freedom to practise their religion, but the Church was severely restricted and there were some reports of persecution.

After reunification, churches were permitted to function but still came under strict **surveillance**, with all appointments controlled by the government, and members of the Church hierarchy frequently received heavy jail sentences for opposition to the regime. Since 1986 the Party has been working to reduce the tension by re-opening seminaries, allowing the Church to resume religious educational work and releasing some clergy from prison. Catholics throughout Vietnam now regularly attend Mass, and, when the previous Cardinal of Hanoi died in 1990, thousands attended the funeral in the largest postwar demonstration of Catholic faith. However, the government still insists on vetting all appointments, and it took more than seven years to find a new cardinal acceptable to both Vietnam and the Vatican. Relationships between the two have continued to grow, with the appointment of several new prelates to vacant seats, but it will undoubtedly be several years before the much hoped-for papal visit materializes.

Cao Dai

Social upheaval coupled with an injection of Western thinking in the early twentieth century gave birth to Vietnam's two indigenous religious sects, **Cao Dai** and Hoa Hao. Of the two, Cao Dai claims more adherents, with an estimated following of around two million in south Vietnam, plus a few thousand among overseas Vietnamese in America, Canada and Britain. The sect's headquarters, the **Holy See**, resides in a flamboyant cathedral at Tay Ninh (see p.129), where they also maintain a school, agricultural co-operative and hospital. Vietnam's most northerly Cao Dai congregation worships in Hué.

The religion of Cao Dai (meaning "high place") was revealed by the "Supreme Being" to a middle-aged civil servant working in Phu Quoc, called **Ngo Van Chieu**, during several trances over a period of years from 1919 to 1925. What Chieu preached to his followers was essentially a distillation of Vietnam's religious heritage: elements of Confucian, Taoist and Buddhist thought, intermixed with ancestor worship, Christianity and Islam. According to Cao Dai beliefs, all religions are different manifestations of one **meta-religion**, Cao Dai; in the past, this took on whatever form most suited the prevailing human need, but during the twentieth century could finally be presented in its unity. Thus the **Supreme Being**, who revealed himself in 1925, has had two earlier manifestations, always in human guise: the first in the sixth century BC, appearing as various figures from Buddhism, Taoism and Christianity among many other saints and sages; the second as Sakyamuni, Confucius, Jesus Christ, Mohammed and Lao-tzu. In the third manifestation the Supreme Being has revealed himself through his divine light, symbolized as an all-seeing Eye on a sky-blue, star-spangled globe.

Cao Dai **doctrine** preaches respect for all its constituent religions and holds that individual desires should be subordinate to the common interest. Adherents seek to escape from the cycle of reincarnation by following the five prohibitions: no violence, theft or lying – nor indulgence in alcohol or sexual activity; priests are expected to be completely vegetarian though others need only eschew meat on certain days of the lunar month. The Cao Dai **hierarchy** is modelled on that of the Catholic Church, and divides into nine ranks, of which the pope is the highest. Officials are grouped into three branches, identifiable by the colour of their ceremonial robes: the Confucian branch dresses in red, Buddhist in saffron and Taoist in blue. Otherwise practitioners wear white as a symbol of purity, and because it contains every colour.

The **rituals** of Cao Dai are a complex mixture of Buddhist and Taoist rites, including meditation and seances. Prayers take place four times a day in the temples (6am, noon, 6pm and midnight) though ordinary members are only required to attend on four days per month and otherwise can pray at home. Note that shoes should always be removed when entering a Cao Dai temple or mansion. At the start of the thirty-minute-long ceremony, worshippers file into the temple in three columns, women on the left, men in the middle and on the right; they then kneel and bow three times – to the Supreme Being, to the earth and to mankind. Cao Dai's most important **ceremony**, a sort of feast day for the Supreme Being, takes place on the 9th day of the first lunar month; other special observances are the day of Taoism (15th day of the second month), Buddha's birthday (15th of the fourth lunar month), the day of Confucius (28th of the eighth lunar month) and Christmas Day.

The religion of Cao Dai is further enlivened with a panoply of **saints**, encompassing the great and the good of many countries and cultures: Victor Hugo, Joan of Arc, William Shakespeare, Napoleon Bonaparte, Lenin, Winston Churchill, Louis Pasteur and Sun Yat Sen, alongside home-grown heroes such as Tran Hung Dao and Le Loi. These characters fulfil a variety of roles from prophet to bodhisattva and even spirit medium, through which followers communicate with the Supreme Being. Contact can occur by means of a ouija board, messages left in sealed envelopes or through human mediums – who enter a trance and write using a planchette (a pencil secured to a wooden board on castors, on which the medium rests his hand, sometimes known as a *corbeille à bec*). Apparently Cao Daists once appointed an official to take down the further works of Victor Hugo by dictation from his spirit.

The ideology, which had widespread appeal, attracted **converts** in their hundreds of thousands in the Mekong Delta, but only gained official recognition from the French colonial authorities in 1926. Over the next decade the Holy See developed into a **semi-autonomous state** wielding considerable political power and backed by a paramilitary wing which mustered around 50,000 men in the mid-1950s. Although originally nationalist, Cao Daists clashed with communist troops in a local power struggle, and the sect ended up opposing both the North Vietnamese and President Diem's pro-Catholic regime. Diem moved quickly to dismantle the army when he came to power and exiled its leaders; then after 1975 the communists purged the religious body, closing down Cao Dai temples and schools, and sending priests for re-education. However, Cao Dai survived as a religion and has gained some **new adherents** since 1990 when its temples and mansions, approximately four hundred in all, were allowed to re-open, albeit under strict control.

Hoa Hao

The second of Vietnam's local sects, **Hoa Hao**, meaning "peace and kindness", emerged in the late 1930s near Chau Doc in the Mekong Delta (see p.169). The movement was founded by a young mystic, **Huynh Phu So**, who disliked mechanical ritual and preached a very pure, simple form of Buddhism that required no clergy or other intermediaries, and could be practised at home by means of meditation, fasting and prayer. Gambling, alcohol and opium were prohibited, while filial piety was once more invoked to promote social order.

As a young man Huynh Phu So was cured of a mysterious illness by the monks of Tra Son Pagoda near his home town of Chau Doc. He continued to live at the pagoda, studying under the monk Xom, but returned to his home village after Xom died. During a storm in 1939, So entered a trance from which he emerged to develop his own Buddhist way. The sect quickly gained followers and, like Cao Dai, was soon caught up in **nationalist politics**. To the French, So was a mad but dangerous subversive; they committed him to a psychiatric hospital (where he promptly converted his doctor to Hoa Hao), and then placed him under house arrest. During World War II Hoa Hao followers were armed by the Japanese and later continued to fight against the French while also opposing the communists. At the end of the war Hoa Hao members formed an anti-Marxist political party, prompting the Viet Minh to assassinate So in 1947.

However, the movement continued to grow, its **private army** equalling the Cao Dai's in size, until Diem came to power and effectively crushed the sect's political and military arm. The sect then splintered, with some members turning to the National Liberation Front, while most sided with the Americans. As a result, when the communists took over in 1975 many Hoa Hao leaders were arrested and its priesthood was disbanded. Nevertheless some claim that there are now up to 1.5 million Hoa Hao practising in the Mekong Delta. The government recently recognized the principal Hoa Hao sect, although its more radical offshoots, which are accused of anti-government activities, remain outlawed.

Vietnamese deities

Buddhist deities

A Di Da or **Amitabha** The Historical Buddha, the most revered member of the Buddhist pantheon in Vietnamese pagodas.

Avalokitesvara A bodhisattva often represented with many arms and eyes, being all-powerful, or as Quan Am (see below).

Di Lac or **Maitreya** The Future Buddha, usually depicted as chubby, with a bare chest and a huge grin, sitting on a lotus throne.

Ong Ac or **Trung Ac** One of the two guardians of the Buddhist religion, popularly known as Mister Wicked, who judges all people. He has a fierce red face and a reputation for severity – of which badly behaved children are frequently reminded.

Ong Thien or **Khuyen Thien** The second guardian of Buddhism is Mister Charitable, a white-faced kindly soul who encourages good behaviour.

Quan Am The Goddess of Mercy, adopted from the Chinese goddess, Kuan Yin. Quan Am is a popular incarnation of Avalokitesvara. She is usually represented as a graceful white statue, with her hand raised in blessing.

Thich Ca Mau Ni or **Sakyamuni** The Present Buddha, born Siddhartha Gautama, who founded Buddhism.

Other characters

Ngoc Hoang The Jade Emperor, ruler of the Taoist pantheon who presides over heaven.

Ong Tau God of the Hearth, who keeps watch over every family and reports on the household to the Jade Emperor every New Year.

Quan Cong A Chinese general of the Han dynasty revered for his loyalty, honesty and exemplary behaviour. Usually flanked by his two assistants.

Thanh Mau The Mother Goddess.

Thien Hau Protectress of Sailors.

Tran Vo Properly known as Tran Vo Bac De, Taoist Emperor of the North, who governs storms and generally harmful events.

Hinduism and Islam

Indian merchants carried **Hinduism** to Vietnam in the early years of the first century AD, travelling along the coast of Siam (now Thailand) and down the Mekong to reach the Indianized kingdom of Champa. Cham subjects worshipped the Hindu god Shiva, represented by a lingam, but when Arab traders became paramount during the sixteenth century most Cham converted to **Islam**, though retained certain elements of their Hindu tradition.

Islam currently claims more followers: several thousand Cham and Khmer Moslems live along Vietnam's central coast between Nha Trang and Phan Thiet. There is also a sizeable group in Ho Chi Minh City and a tiny Moslem community in Hanoi. None of these professes a particularly devout form of the religion: prayers are reduced to once on Fridays, Ramadan lasts only three days, no one goes on the Hajj, and there are no restrictions on alcohol – although most do not eat pork; few Vietnamese can read or speak Arabic and little of the Koran has been translated. Both Hindus and Moslems make offerings to Hindu lingams as well as to animist spirits. Ho Chi Minh City has a few Hindu temples which are currently undergoing something of a revival.

Vietnam's ethnic mosaic

The population of Vietnam currently numbers some 80 million people, of whom nearly ninety percent are ethnic Vietnamese (known as Viet or Kinh), while approximately one million are Chinese in origin (Hoa) – see box on p.531. The remaining six to seven million people comprise an estimated 52 ethnic groups divided into dozens of subgroups, some with a mere hundred or so members, giving Vietnam the richest and most complex ethnic make-up in the whole of Southeast Asia.

The vast majority of Vietnam's minorities live in the hilly regions of the **north**, down the Truong Son mountain range, and in the **central highlands** – all areas which saw heavy fighting in recent wars. Several groups straddle today's international boundaries, spreading across the Indochinese peninsula and up into southern China.

Little is known about the origins of many of these people, some of whom already inhabited the area before the ancestors of the **Viet** arrived from southern China around four to five thousand years ago. At some point the Viet emerged as a distinct group from among the various indigenous peoples living around the Red River Delta and then gradually absorbed smaller communities until they became the dominant culture. Other groups continued to interact with the Viet people, but either chose to maintain their independence in the highlands or were forced up into the hills, off the ever-more-crowded coastal plains. Vietnamese legend accounts for this fundamental split between **lowlanders** and **highlanders** as follows: the Dragon King of the south married Au Co, a beautiful northern princess, and at first they lived in the mountains where she gave birth to a hundred strong, handsome boys. After a while, however, the Dragon King missed his watery, lowland home and decamped with half his sons, leaving fifty behind in the mountains – the ancestors of the ethnic minorities.

Vietnam's ethnic groups are normally differentiated according to three main **linguistic families** – Austronesian, Austro-Asian and Sino-Tibetan – which are further subdivided into smaller groups, such as the Viet–Muong and Tay–Thai language groups. Austronesians, related to Indonesians and Pacific Islanders, were probably the earliest inhabitants of the area but are now restricted to the central highlands. Peoples of the two other linguistic families originated in southern China and at different times migrated southwards to settle throughout the Vietnamese uplands.

Despite their different origins, languages, dialects and hugely varied traditional dress, there are a number of similarities among the highland groups that distinguish them from Viet people. Most immediately obvious is the **stilthouse**, which protects against snakes, vermin and larger beasts as well as floods, while also providing safe stabling for domestic animals. The communal imbibing of **rice wine** is popular with most highland groups, as are certain **rituals** such as protecting a child from evil spirits by not naming it until after a certain age. Most highlanders traditionally practise **swidden farming**, clearing patches of forest land, farming the burnt-over fields for a few years and then leaving it fallow for a specified period while it recovers its fertility. Where the soils are particularly poor, a semi-nomadic lifestyle is adopted, shifting the village location at intervals as necessary.

If you're interested in learning more about Vietnam's ethnic diversity, pick up a copy of the slightly dated *Ethnic Minorities in Vietnam* which is on sale in

CONTEXTS | Vietnam's ethnic mosaic

Hanoi and Ho Chi Minh City, or, if you can find it, the newer *Cultural Mosaic of Ethnic Groups in Vietnam*, complete with colour photos. There are also a couple of excellent ethnological museums in Hanoi and Thai Nguyen (see p.384 and p.470 respectively).

Recent history

Traditionally, Viet kings demanded tribute from the often fiercely independent ethnic minorities but otherwise left them to govern their own affairs. This relationship changed with the arrival of Catholic missionaries, who won many converts to Christianity among the peoples of the central highlands – called **montagnards** by the French. Under colonial rule the minorities gained a certain degree of local autonomy in the late nineteenth century, but at the same time the French expropriated their land, exacted forced labour and imposed heavy taxes. As elsewhere in Vietnam, such behaviour sparked off rebellions, notably among the Hmong in the early twentieth century.

The northern mountains

The French were quick to capitalize on ancient antipathies between the highland and lowland peoples. In the northwest mountains, for example, they set up a semi-autonomous Thai federation, complete with armed militias and border guards. When war broke out in 1946, groups of Thai, Hmong and Muong in the northwest sided with the French and against the Vietnamese, even to the extent of providing battalions to fight alongside French troops. But the situation was not clear-cut: some Thai actively supported the Viet Minh, while Ho Chi Minh found a safe base for his guerrilla armies among the Tay and Nung people of the northeast. Recognizing the need to secure the minorities' allegiance, after North Vietnam won independence in 1954 Ho Chi Minh created two **autonomous regions**, allowing limited self-government within a "unified multi-national state".

The central highlands

The minorities of the **central highlands** had also been split between supporting the French and Viet Minh after 1946. In the interests of preserving their independence, the ethnic peoples were often simply anti-Vietnamese, of whatever political persuasion. After partition in 1954, anti-Vietnamese sentiment was exacerbated when President Diem started moving Viet settlers into the region, totally ignoring local land rights. Diem wanted to tie the minorities more closely into the South Vietnamese state; the immediate result, however, was that the Bahnar, Jarai and E De joined forces in an organized opposition movement and called a general strike in 1958. Over the next few years this well-armed coalition developed into the United Front for the Liberation of Oppressed Races, popularly known by its French acronym, **FULRO**. They demanded greater autonomy for the minorities, including elected representation at the National Assembly, more local self-government, school instruction in their own language and access to higher education. While FULRO met with some initial success, the movement was weakened after a number split off to join the Viet Cong. An estimated 10,000 or more remained, fighting first of all against the South Vietnamese and the Americans, and then against the

North Vietnamese Army until 1975. After this, FULRO rebels and other anti-communist minority groups, mainly E De, operated out of bases in Cambodia. The few who survived Pol Pot's killing fields later fled to Thailand and were eventually resettled in America.

During the **American War**, those minorities living around the Seventeenth Parallel soon found themselves on the front line. The worst fighting occurred during the late 1960s and early 1970s, when North Vietnamese troops were based in these remote uplands and American forces sought to rout them. Massive bombing raids were augmented by the use of defoliants and herbicides which, as well as denuding protective forest cover, destroyed crops and animals; this chemical warfare also killed an unknown number of people and caused severe long-term illnesses. In addition, villages were often subject to night raids by Viet Cong and North Vietnamese soldiers keen to "encourage" local support and replenish their food supplies. It's estimated that over 200,000 minority people, both civilian and military, were killed as a result of the American War, out of a total population of around one million. By 1975, 85 percent of villages in the highlands had been either destroyed or abandoned, while nothing was left standing in the region closest to the Demilitarized Zone. At the end of the war thousands of minority people were living in temporary camps, along with Viet refugees, unable to practise their traditional way of life.

Post-reunification

After reunification things didn't really get much better. Promises of greater autonomy came to nothing; even the little self-government the minorities had been granted was removed. Those groups who had opposed the North Vietnamese were kept under close observation and their leaders sent for re-education. The new government pursued a policy of **forced assimilation** of the minorities into the Vietnamese culture and glossed over their previous anti-Viet activities: all education was conducted in the Vietnamese language, traditional customs were discouraged or outlawed, and minority people were moved from their dispersed villages into permanent settlements. At the same time the government created **New Economic Zones** in the central highlands and along the Chinese border, often commandeering the best land to resettle thousands of people from the overcrowded lowlands. According to official records, 250,000 settlers were moved into the New Economic Zones each year during the 1980s. The policy resulted in food shortages among minorities unable to support themselves on the marginal lands, and the widespread degradation of over-farmed upland soils.

Doi moi brought a shift in policy in the early 1990s, marked by the establishment of a central office responsible for the ethnic minorities. Minority languages are now officially recognized and can be taught in schools, scholarships enable minority people to attend institutes of higher education, television programmes are broadcast in a number of minority languages and there is now greater representation of minorities at all levels of government – indeed, the current Secretary General of the Communist Party, Nong Duc Manh, a member of the Tay ethnic group, is the first non-Viet to hold such an elevated position. Cash crops such as timber and fruit are being introduced as an alternative to illegal hunting, logging and opium cultivation. Other income-generating schemes are also being promoted and healthcare programmes upgraded. All this has been accompanied by moves to preserve Vietnam's **cultural diversity**, driven in part by the realization that ethnic differences have greater appeal to tourists. However, in many areas the minorities' traditional lifestyles are fast being eroded and extreme poverty is widespread.

Poverty coupled with grievances over ancestral land-rights and religious freedoms were the issues which sparked widespread **demonstrations** by an estimated 5000 minority people in the central highlands in the spring of 2001. While the prime minister subsequently ordered more favourable land distribution and promised greater socio-economic development for the region, human rights organizations have criticized the authorities for their harsh treatment of demonstrators, some of whom have received jail sentences of up to twelve years.

Minorities in the northern highlands

The mountains of northern Vietnam are home to a large number of ethnic groups, all of them originating from southern China. The dominant minorities are the Tay and Thai, both feudal societies who once held sway over their weaker neighbours. These powerful, well-established groups farm the fertile, valley-bottom land; while Hmong and Dao people, who only arrived in Vietnam at the end of the eighteenth century, occupy the least hospitable land at the highest altitudes. These isolated groups have been better able to lead an independent life and to preserve their traditional customs, though most exist at near-subsistence levels. Local **markets**, usually held at weekly intervals, fulfil an important role in social and economic life in the highlands; the best known is at Sa Pa, though there are others throughout the area (see Chapter Eight, starting on p.439, for details). Most groups maintain a tradition of **alternate singing**, which is performed at ceremonies and festivals.

Tay

The **Tay** are Vietnam's largest minority group living in the highlands, with an estimated population of 1.5 million, concentrated in the northeast, from the Red River Valley east to the coastal plain, where they settled over 2000 years ago. Through centuries of close contact with lowlanders, Tay society has been strongly influenced by Viet culture, sharing many common rituals and Confucian practices. Many Tay have now adopted Viet architecture and dress, but it's still possible to find villages of thatched stilthouses, characterized by a railed balcony around the building. Nowadays it's largely the women who still wear the Tay's traditional long, belted dress of indigo-dyed cloth, with a similarly plain, knotted headscarf peaked at the front and set off with lots of silver jewellery. Tay farmers are famous for their animal husbandry, and they also specialize in fish-farming and growing high-value crops, such as anise, tobacco, soya and cinnamon. The Tay have developed advanced irrigation systems for wet rice cultivation, including the huge water wheels found beside rivers in the northeast. They have had a written language since the fifteenth century, fostering a strong literary tradition; alternate singing is also popular, as are theatrical performances, kite-flying and a whole variety of other games. Some Tay groups in the more remote regions occasionally erect a funeral house, decorated with fluttering slips of white paper, over a new grave.

Thai

The **Thai** minority numbers just over one million, and is the dominant group in the northwest mountains from the Red River south to Nghe An, though most live in Lai Chau and Son La provinces. They are distantly related to the Thai of Thailand and to groups in southern China, their ancestral homeland. However, Thai people have been living in Vietnam for at least 2000 years and show similarities with both Viet and Tay cultures. Traditional Thai society was strongly hierarchical, ruled over by feudal lords who controlled vast land-holdings worked by the villagers. Their written language, which is based on Sanskrit, has furnished a literary legacy dating back five centuries, including epic poems, histories and a wealth of folklore. The Thai are also famous for their unique dance repertoire and finely woven brocades decorated with flowers, birds and dragons, which are on sale in local markets. From their early teens women learn how to weave and embroider, eventually preparing a set of blankets for their dowry. Thai houses are often still constructed on stilts, with wood or bamboo frames, though the architecture varies between regions.

There are two main subgroups: **Black Thai** (around Dien Bien Phu, Tuan Giao and Son La) and **White Thai** (Mai Chau, Lai Chau), whose names are often attributed to the traditional colour of the women's shirts, though this is open to dispute. In fact, the women of both groups tend to wear similar clothes, consisting of long sarong-like skirts, either black or very dark indigo blue, perhaps with a brightly coloured sash or brocade panels. Their close-fitting shirts are fastened with beautiful silver clasps, fashioned in the shape of butterflies or other insects, and on formal occasions they don intricately woven headscarves.

Muong

The lower hills from the Red River Valley south through Yen Bai and Son La down to Thanh Hoa are the domain of the **Muong** ethnic minority, with the majority now living in Hoa Binh Province. Muong people, totalling roughly one million, are believed to share common ancestors with the Viet. It's thought that the two groups split around 2000 years ago, after which the Muong developed relatively independently in the highlands. Society is traditionally dominated by aristocratic families, who distribute communal land to the villagers in return for labour and tax contributions; the symbols of their authority are drums and bronze gongs. Muong stilthouses are similar to those built by the Thai, and the main staple is rice, though fishing, hunting and gathering are all still fairly important. Muong people have a varied cultural tradition, including alternate singing and epic tales, and they are famed for their embroidery, typically creating bold geometric designs in black and white. Older Muong women continue to wear the traditional long black skirt and close-fitting shirt; a broad, heavily embroidered belt is the main accessory, and many women also wear a simple white headscarf.

Nung

Nung people are closely related to the Tay, sharing the same language and often living in the same villages. Their population is estimated at 700,000, mostly in Cao Bang and Lang Son provinces, where they have a long tradition of cultivating wet rice using water wheels for irrigation. Nung farmers terrace the lower slopes to provide extra land, and are noted for the wide variety of crops they grow, including maize, groundnuts and a whole host of vegetables.

In fact, the Nung are reckoned to be the best horticulturalists in Vietnam, while their blacksmiths are almost as renowned. Unusually, the traditional Nung house has clay walls and a tiled roof, and is built either flat on the ground or with only one section raised on stilts.

Most Nung are Buddhist, worshipping Quan Am, though they also honour the spirits and their ancestors. They are particularly adept at alternate singing, relishing the improvised double entendre. Not surprisingly, Nung traditional dress is similar to the Tay, though hemmed with coloured bands. Women often sport a neck scarf with brightly coloured fringes and a shoulder bag embroidered with the sun, stars and flowers, or woven in black and white interspersed with delicately coloured threads.

Hmong

Since the end of the eighteenth century groups of Miao people have been fleeing southern China, heading for Laos, Burma, Thailand and Vietnam. Miao meant "barbarian", whereas their adopted name, **Hmong**, means "free people". In Vietnam the Hmong population now stands at around 600,000, living in the high areas of all the northern provinces down to Nghe An. Poor farming land, geographical isolation and their traditional seclusion from other people have left the Hmong one of the most impoverished groups in Vietnam; standards of health and education are low, while infant mortality is exceptionally high. Hmong farmers grow maize, rice and vegetables on burnt-over land, irrigated fields and terraced hillsides. Traditionally they also grow poppies, though this is now discouraged by the government. Hmong people raise cattle, buffalo and horses, and have recently started growing fruit trees, such as peach, plum and apple. They are also skilled hunters and gather forest products, including honey, medicinal herbs, roots and bark, either for their own consumption or to trade at weekly markets. Hmong houses are built flat on the ground, rather than raised on stilts.

Until recently there was no written Hmong language, but a strong oral tradition of folk songs, riddles and proverbs. Perhaps the Hmong are best known, however, for their handicrafts, particularly weaving hemp and cotton cloth which is then coloured with indigo dyes. To achieve the right intensity of blue, the cloth may be dyed up to thirty times, and then beaten until the surface takes on a lustrous, almost metallic sheen. Many Hmong people still wear traditional indigo apparel: men wear baggy, tubular trousers with a loose shirt, a long waistcoat of burnished cloth and silver or bronze necklaces; female attire is generally a knee-length skirt, an apron, leggings and a waistcoat, plus a collection of chunky silver earrings, bracelets and necklaces. Hmong women often adorn their shirtsleeves with embroidered bands, while the skirts of some groups may also be highly decorated. The main subgroups are **White**, **Red**, **Green**, **Black** and **Flower Hmong**. Though the origin of the names is unknown, there are marked differences in dialect and social customs as well as dress and hairstyle, especially among the women.

Dao

The **Dao** (pronounced "Zao") ethnic minority is incredibly diverse in all aspects of life: social and religious practices, architecture, agriculture and dress. For several centuries, small, localized groups have settled in the northern border region after crossing over from China. Dao people now number approximately 500,000 in Vietnam, with related groups in Laos, Thailand and China.

Long ago the Dao adopted the Chinese writing system and have a substantial literary tradition. One popular legend records the origin of the twelve Dao clans: Ban Ho, a powerful dog of five colours, killed an enemy general and was granted the hand of a princess in marriage, who gave birth to twelve children. Ban Ho is worshipped by the Dao and the five colours of Dao embroidery represent their ancestor. The Dao boast a particularly striking traditional dress, characterized by a rectangular patch of embroidery sewn onto the back of their jackets, and both men and women sport silver or copper jewellery and tasselled shoulder bags. Dao women wear elaborate headgear, usually a triangular-shaped turban, either embroidered or decorated with silver coins, beads and coloured tassels; it's also common for Dao women to shave their eyebrows and sometimes the whole head, coating the skull with wax. Dao people live at all altitudes, their house style and agricultural techniques varying accordingly. While groups living at lower levels are relatively prosperous, growing rice and raising livestock, those in the high, rocky mountains live in considerable poverty.

Giay

The **Giay** (pronounced "Zay") are a relatively small minority group, with a population of around 40,000, living at high altitudes in Lao Cai, Lai Chau and Ha Giang provinces. Traditional Giay society is feudal, with a strict demarcation between the local aristocracy and the peasant classes. All villagers work the communal lands, living in closely knit villages of stilthouses. A few Giay women still wear the traditional style of dress, distinguished by the highly coloured, circular panel sewn around the collar and a shirt-fastening on the right shoulder; the shirt itself is often of bright green, pink or blue. On formal occasions, women may also wear a chequered turban.

Minorities in the central highlands

Nearly all minority groups living in the central highlands are indigenous peoples; most are matrilineal societies with a strong emphasis on community life and with some particularly complex burial rites. Catholic **missionaries** enjoyed considerable success in the central highlands, establishing a mission at Kon Tum in the mid-nineteenth century; then early in the twentieth century Protestantism was also introduced to the region. Most converts came from among the E De and Bahnar, though other groups have also incorporated Christian practices into their traditional belief systems. Likewise, **Vietnamese influence** has been stronger here than in northern Vietnam, while the **American War** caused severe disruption. Nevertheless, their cultures have been sufficiently strong to resist complete assimilation.

Jarai (Gia-rai)

The largest minority group in the central highlands is the **Jarai**, with a population of roughly 250,000. It's thought that Jarai people left the coastal plains around 2000 years ago, settling on the fertile plateau around Plei Ku. Some ethnologists hold that Cham people are in fact a branch of the Jarai, and they certainly share common linguistic traits and a matrilineal social order. Young Jarai women initiate the marriage proposal and afterwards the couple live in the wife's family home, with children taking their mother's name. Houses are traditionally built on stilts, facing north. The focus of village life is the communal house or *rong*, where the council of elders and their elected chief meet. Animist beliefs are still strong and the Jarai world is peopled with spirits, the most famous of which are the kings of Water, Fire and Wind, represented by shamans who are involved in rain-making ceremonies and other rituals. Funeral rites are particularly complex and expensive: after the burial, a funeral house is built over the grave and evocative sculptures of people, birds and objects from everyday life are placed inside. The Jarai also have an extensive musical repertoire, the principal instruments being gongs and the unique *k'long put*, made of bamboo tubes into which the player forces air by clapping their hands.

During the American War the majority of Jarai villagers moved out of their war-torn homeland, many being resettled in Plei Ku; only in recent years are some slowly returning.

E De (Rhadé)

Further south, towards Buon Ma Thuot, around 200,000 people of the **E De** minority live in stilthouses grouped together in a village or *buon*. These long-houses, which can be up to 100m in length, are boat-shaped with hardwood frames, bamboo floors and walls, and topped with a high thatched roof. As many as a hundred family members may live in a single house, under the authority of the oldest or most respected woman, who owns all family property, including the house and domestic animals; wealth is indicated by the number of ceremonial gongs. Other much prized heirlooms are the large earthenware jars used for making the rice wine drunk at festivals. Like the Jarai, E De people worship the kings of Fire and Water among a whole host of animist spirits, and also erect a funeral house on their graves. Both the original long-house and its grave-site replica are often decorated with fine carvings.

The E De homeland lies in a region of red soils on the rolling western plateaux. In the nineteenth and twentieth centuries French settlers introduced coffee and rubber estates to the area, often seizing land from the local people they called Rhadé. Traditional swidden farming has gradually been disappearing, a process accelerated by the American War and the forced relocation of E De into permanent settlements.

Bahnar (Ba-na)

Bahnar people trace their ancestry back many centuries to communities co-existing on the coastal plains with the Cham and Jarai. Now the Bahnar minority, numbering some 150,000, mostly live in the highlands east of Plei Ku and Kon Tum.

The most distinctive aspect of a Bahnar village is its *rong* or communal house, the roof of which may be up to 30m high and slightly curved. This is the centre of village cultural and ceremonial life, and also the home of adolescent boys, who are taught Bahnar history, the skills of hunting and other manly matters. Village houses grouped around the *rong* are typically stilthouses with a thatched or tiled roof, and are often decorated with geometric motifs. For centuries Bahnar people have traded with the Cham and later the Viet people of the lowlands, and as a result have little tradition of handicrafts. However, they are skilled horticulturalists, growing maize, sweet potato or millet, together with indigo, hemp or tobacco as cash crops. Bahnar groups also erect funeral houses decorated with elaborate carvings, although they are less imposing than those of the Jarai. Sometime after the burial, wooden statues, gongs, wine jars and other items of family property are placed in the funeral house.

Sedang (Xo-dang)

According to their oral histories, **Sedang** people once lived further north but are now concentrated in the area between Kon Tum and Quang Ngai and comprise a community of nearly 100,000. The Sedang were traditionally a warlike people whose villages were surrounded with defensive hedges, barbed with spears and stakes, and with only one entrance. Inter-village wars were frequent and the Sedang also carried out raids on the peaceable Bahnar, mainly to seize prisoners rather than territory. In the past, Sedang religious ritual involved human sacrifices to propitiate the spirits – a practice that was later modified into a profitable business, selling slaves to traders from Laos and Thailand. In the 1880s, an eccentric French military adventurer called Marie-David de Mayréna, established a kingdom in Sedang territory by making treaties with the local chiefs (see p.224). A few decades later, the French authorities conscripted Sedang labour to build Highway 14 from Kon Tum to Da Nang; conditions were so harsh that many died, provoking a rebellion in the 1930s. Soon after, the Viet Minh won many recruits among the Sedang in their war against the French. In the American War some Sedang groups fought for the Viet Cong while others were formed into militia units by the American Special Services. But when fighting intensified after 1965, Sedang villagers were forced to flee and many now live in almost destitute conditions, having lost their ancestral lands.

Traditionally, membership of a Sedang village was indicated by the use of a common water source. Each extended family occupies a longhouse, built on stilts and usually facing east; central to village life is the communal house where young men and boys sleep, and where all the major ceremonies take place. Because villages historically had relatively little contact with each other, there are marked variations between the social customs of the subgroups, and so far seventeen Sedang dialects have been identified. Agricultural techniques are more consistent, mainly swidden farming supplemented by horticulture and hunting. Some Sedang farmers employ a "water harp", a combined bird-scarer, musical instrument and appeaser of the spirits. The harp consists of bamboo tubes linked together and placed in a flowing stream to produce an irregular, haunting sound.

Koho (Co-ho) and Lat

The Di Linh plateau at the very southern end of the central highlands is the home of the **Koho** minority. The community of some 100,000 is subdivided into six highly varied subgroups, including the **Lat** people of Da Lat.

The typical Koho house is built on stilts with a thatched roof and bamboo walls and flooring. Despite the fact that many Koho were converted to Christianity in the early twentieth century, spirit worship is widely practised and each family adopts a guardian spirit from the natural world. Catholic missionaries developed a phonetic script for the Koho language but the oral tradition remains strong. Unlike many minorities in this region, the Koho incorporate dance into their religious rites, and it is an important element of them; a variety of musical instruments, such as gongs, bamboo flutes and buffalo horns, are also involved. Subgroups of the Koho minority are famed for their pottery and ironwork, whereas Lat farmers have a reputation for constructing sophisticated irrigation systems.

Mnong

The **Mnong** ethnic minority is probably best known for its skill in hunting elephants and domesticating them for use in war, for transport and for their ivory. Mnong people are also the creators of the lithophone, a kind of stone xylophone thought to be among the world's most ancient musical instruments; an example is on show at the Lam Dong Province Museum in Da Lat (see p.204). The Mnong have lived in the southern central highlands for centuries, and now around 67,000 people are concentrated in the region between Buon Ma Thuot and Da Lat. Mnong houses are usually built flat on the ground and, though the society is generally matrilineal, village affairs are organized by a male chief. Mnong craftsmen are skilled at basketry and printing textiles, while they also make the copper, tin and silver jewellery worn by both sexes. In traditional burial rituals a buffalo-shaped coffin is placed under a funeral house which is peopled with wooden statues and painted with black, red or white designs.

Bru and Ta-oi

Two related minority groups had the extreme misfortune to live on the Seventeenth Parallel, near the border with Laos: the **Bru** (or Bru Van-Kieu), these days numbering around 40,000, and the **Ta-oi**, with a population of only 26,000. Bru people were caught up in the battle of Khe Sanh (see p.337) – both as refugees and as part of an American militia force – while the Ta-oi, among others, helped keep open the Ho Chi Minh Trail for the North Vietnamese Army. During the worst years of fighting, refugees fled south to E De country or crossed over into Laos, and many never returned. Those who did move back found Viet people settled on their best land – the Khe Sanh plateau was declared a New Economic Zone – and were forced into marginal areas.

Of the two groups, Bru people have always had greater contact with the outside world since the ancient Lao Bao trade route passes through their territory to Laos. Bru houses can usually be distinguished by their rounded shape, likened to a tortoise shell, and are occasionally decorated with carved birds or buffalo horns at each end. Both groups are patrilineal, practise swidden farming and worship a huge range of spirits, though ancestor worship is also central to their belief systems.

Minorities in the southern lowlands

As the Viet people pushed down the coastal plain and into the Mekong Delta they displaced two main ethnic groups, the Cham and Khmer. Up until the tenth century powerful **Cham** kings had ruled over most of southern Vietnam (see p.484); nowadays, there are approximately 100,000 Cham people, mostly living on the coast between Phan Rang and Phan Thiet, or on the Cambodian border around Chau Doc, with a small number in Ho Chi Minh City. The coastal communities are still largely Hindu worshippers of Shiva and follow the matrilineal practices of their Cham ancestors; they earn a living from farming, silk weaving and crafting jewellery of gold or silver. Groups along the Cambodian border are Islamic and, in general, patrilineal. They engage in riverfishing, weaving and cross-border trade, with little agricultural activity. On the whole, Cham people have adopted the Vietnamese way of life and dress, though their traditional arts, principally dance and music, have experienced a revival in recent years.

Ethnic **Khmer** are the indigenous people of the Mekong Delta, including Cambodia. Nowadays only about one million remain in the eastern delta under Vietnamese rule, and some of these only arrived in the late 1970s as refugees from Pol Pot's brutal regime in Cambodia. Khmer farmers are noted for their skill at irrigation and wet-rice cultivation; it's said that they farm nearly 150 varieties of rice, each suited to specific local conditions. Traditionally, the Khmer live in villages of stilthouses erected on raised mounds above the flood waters, but these days are more likely to build flat on the earth, along canals and roadways. The pagoda, however, is still a distinctive feature of Khmer villages, its brightly patterned roofs decorated with images of the sacred ancestral dragon, the *neak*. Although ancient beliefs persist, since the late thirteenth century the Khmer have been devout followers of Theravada Buddhism, as practised in Cambodia, Laos and Thailand. Local crafts people produce fine silk and basketry, and the Khmer have retained their tradition of satirical stories, proverbs and folk songs – and still wear their distinctive red–and–white scarves.

Hoa and Viet Kieu

Ethnic Chinese people, known in Vietnamese as **Hoa**, form one of Vietnam's largest minority groups, estimated at around one million. Throughout the country's history Chinese people, mostly from China's southern provinces, have been emigrating to Vietnam, as administrators and merchants or as refugees from persecution. In the mid-seventeenth century the collapse of the Ming dynasty sent a human deluge southwards, and there were other large-scale migrations in the nineteenth century and then the 1940s. Until the early nineteenth century all Hoa, even those of mixed blood, were considered by the Viets to be Chinese. After that date, however, they were admitted to public office and gradually became integrated into Vietnamese society, so that now most have Vietnamese nationality. Nevertheless, the Hoa remain slightly apart, living in close communities according to their ancestral province in China and preserving elements of their own culture, notably their language and traditional lion dances. The Hoa have tended to settle in urban areas, typically becoming successful merchants, artisans and business people, and playing an important role in the economy. Ninety percent of Hoa now live in southern Vietnam, predominantly in Cholon, with small groups scattered through the Mekong Delta and the central highlands.

Viet people have tended to distrust the Hoa, mainly because of their dominant commercial position and their close links with China. After 1975 the Hoa were badly hit when socialist policies were enforced, in what amounted to an anti-Chinese persecution. Tensions rose even further when China invaded Vietnam in 1979 and thousands of Hoa left the country to escape reprisals, forming a large majority of the "boat people" (see box on pp.504–505). It's estimated that up to one third of the Hoa population eventually left Vietnam. Many settled in America, Australia and France, where they joined earlier refugees to become what the Vietnamese call **Viet Kieu**, or overseas Vietnamese, of whom there are perhaps as many as two million worldwide. In recent years the government has gradually made it easier for Viet Kieu not only to return to Vietnam but also to send money back to family members, providing an important source of extra income for individuals and becoming increasingly valuable in the wider economy, especially in the south. Not surprisingly, however, the attitudes of those who stuck it out in Vietnam towards Viet Kieu are ambivalent, and the government itself is unsure about how to handle relations with the Viet Kieu; in general their money and expertise are welcomed but not necessarily their politics, nor their Western ways.

Music and theatre

The binding element to all Vietnam's traditional performing arts is music, and particularly singing (*hat*), which is a natural extension to an already musical language. The origins of Vietnamese music can be traced back as far as the bronze drums and flutes of Dong Son (see p.375), and further again to the lithophone (stone xylophone) called the *dan da*, the world's oldest known instrument. The Chinese influence is evident in operatic theatre and stringed instruments, while India bestowed rhythms, modal improvisations and several types of drum. Much later, especially during the nineteenth century, elements of European theatre and music were co-opted, while during the twentieth century most Vietnamese musicians received a classical, Western training based on the works of Eastern bloc composers such as Prokofiev and Tchaikovsky.

From this multicultural melting pot Vietnamese artists have generated a variety of musical and theatrical forms over the centuries, though, surprisingly, dance is less developed than in neighbouring Thailand, Cambodia and Laos. One of the most famous home-grown performance arts is water puppetry, Vietnam's unique contribution to the world of marionettes, where puppeteers work their magic on a stage of water. The folk tradition is particularly rich, with its improvised courtship songs and the strident, sacred music of trance dances, to which the more than fifty ethnic minorities add their own repertoire of songs and instruments.

Traditionally the professions of artists or performers were hereditary; sadly, the wars and political upheavals of the twentieth century have contributed to the loss of much of this largely oral tradition. Many musicians and actors are now into their eighties and, while certain art forms continue to attract new talent, the younger generation is, on the whole, more interested in higher-paid professions and Vietnamese pop. As revolutionary ("red") music has waned since 1986, so pre-1975 music from the South, previously outlawed as "decadent and reactionary", is back with a vengeance, mixed with a sprinkling of artists from other Asian countries and the West.

The traditional strand

Vietnam's traditional theatre, with its strong Chinese influence, is more akin to opera than pure spoken drama. A musical accompaniment and well-known repertoire of songs form an integral part of the performance, where the plots and characters are equally familiar to the audience. Nowadays, however, the two oldest forms, **Cheo** and **Tuong**, are struggling to survive, while even the more contemporary **Cai Luong** is losing out to television and the video recorder. Other traditional arts have seen something of a revival, though, most notably **water puppetry** and folk-song performances. The stimulus for this came largely from tourism, but renewed interest in the trance music of **Chau Van** and the complexities of **Tai Tu** chamber music has been very much home-grown.

Theatre

Vietnam's oldest surviving stage art, **Hat Cheo**, or "Popular Opera", has its roots in the Red River Delta where it's believed to have existed since at least the eleventh century. Performances consist of popular legends and everyday events, often with a biting satirical edge, accompanied by a selection of tunes drawn as appropriate from a common fund. Though the movements have become highly stylized over the centuries, Cheo's free form allows the actors considerable room for interpretation; the audience demonstrates its approval, or otherwise, by beating a drum. Cheo has the reputation of being anti-establishment, with its buffoon character who comments freely on the action, the audience and current events. So incensed were the kings of the fifteenth-century Later Le dynasty that Cheo was banned from the court, while artists and their descendants were excluded from public office. Nevertheless, Cheo survived and received official recognition in 1964 with the establishment of the Vietnam Cheo Theatre, charged with reviving the ancient art form. It is now promoted as the country's national theatre, with performances held nightly for tourists on Hanoi's Hoan Kiem Lake, although its local popularity continues to decline despite a body of new work dealing with contemporary issues which aims to introduce Cheo to a wider audience.

Hat Tuong (also known as *Hat Boi* or *Hat Bo*), probably introduced from China around the thirteenth century, evolved from classical Chinese opera, and was originally for royal entertainment before being adopted by travelling troupes. Its story lines are mostly historic events and epic tales dealing with such Confucian principles as filial piety and relations between the monarch and his subjects. Tuong, like Cheo, is governed by rigorous rules in which the characters are rendered instantly recognizable by their make-up and costume. Setting and atmosphere are conjured not by props and scenery but through nuances of gesture and musical conventions with which the audience are completely familiar – and which they won't hesitate to criticize if badly executed. Of the clutch of Tuong troupes still in existence, Hanoi's Vietnam Tuong Theatre is one of the most active.

While performances of Tuong are comparatively rare events these days, if you see a large building with peanut and candy sellers outside, the chances are that there's a performance of **Hat Cai Luong**, or "Renovated Theatre", going on inside. Cai Luong originated in southern Vietnam in the early twentieth century, showing a French theatrical influence in its spoken parts, with short scenes and relatively elaborate sets. The action is a tangle of historical drama (such as *The Tale of Kieu*) and racy themes from the street (murder, drug deals, incest, theft and revenge). Its music is a similar hodgepodge: eighteenth-century chamber music played on amplified traditional instruments for the set pieces; electric guitar, keyboards and drums during the scene changes. Cai Luong's use of contemporary vernacular has made it highly adaptable and enabled it to keep pace with Vietnam's social changes.

The origin of **water puppetry**, *mua roi nuoc*, is obscure, beyond that it developed in the flooded rice paddies of the Red River Delta and usually took place in spring when there was less farm work to be done. The earliest record is a stele in Ha Nam Province dated 1121 AD, suggesting that by this date water puppetry was already a regular feature at the royal court.

The art of water puppetry was traditionally a jealously guarded secret handed down from father to son; women were not permitted to learn the techniques in case they revealed them to their husbands' families. This contributed to its decline until the art seemed in danger of dying out altogether. Happily a French organization, *Maison des Cultures du Monde*, intervened and, since 1984, with newly carved puppets, a revamped programme and more elaborate staging, Vietnam's water-puppet troupes have played various international capitals to great acclaim – and can be seen daily in Hanoi (see p.397) and Ho Chi

Minh City (see p.116). Where before gongs and drums alone were used for scene-setting and building atmosphere, today's national troupes often maintain a larger ensemble, similar to Hat Cheo, including zithers and flutes. The songs are also borrowed from the Cheo repertoire, particularly declamatory styles and popular folk tunes, and the show often includes a short recital of traditional music before the puppets emerge to create their own unique illusion.

Music, dance and song

One of Vietnam's oldest song traditions is that of **Quan Ho**, or "alternate singing", a form which thrives in the Red River Delta, particularly Ha Bac Province, and has parallels among the north's ethnic minorities. These unaccompanied songs are usually heard in spring, performed by young men and women bandying improvised lyrics back and forth. Quan Ho traditionally played a part in the courtship ritual and performers are applauded for their skill in complimenting or teasing their partner, earning delighted approval as the exchange becomes increasingly bawdy.

Found in north and central Vietnam, **Hat Chau Van** is a form of ancient, sacred ritual music used to invoke the spirits during trance possession ceremonies. Statues of a pantheon of goddesses are placed in shrines to the Mother Goddess, Thanh Mau, found in both Buddhist pagodas and village temples. Throughout the performance of hypnotically rhythmic music (the performers may be one or many, male or female) a medium enters a trance state and is possessed by a chosen deity. Because of the anti-religious stance of the Vietnamese government until 1986, the style was practised in secret, though some pieces were adapted for inclusion in state-sponsored Cheo theatre. Chau Van is currently being revived by older practitioners in its original religious setting, promoted by a class of nouveaux riches keen for the goddesses to intercede and protect their business interests.

Although the song tradition known as **Ca Tru**, or *Hat A Dao*, dates back centuries, it became all the rage in the fifteenth century when the Vietnamese regained their independence from China. According to legend, a beautiful young songstress, A Dao, charmed the enemy with her songs of the verdant countryside and the way of life in the villages. Fascinated by her voice, the soldiers were encouraged to drink until they became incapacitated and could be pushed into the river and drowned. The lyrics of Ca Tru are often taken from famous poems and are traditionally sung by a woman. The singer also plays a bamboo percussion instrument, and is accompanied by a three-string lute (*dan day*) and drum. She has to master a whole range of singing styles, each differentiated by its particular rhythm, such as *Hat noi* (similar to speech) and *Gui thu* (a more formal style, akin to a written letter). This difficult genre has undergone something of a revival in Hanoi in recent years, while in Hué excerpts from the closely related **Ca Hué** song tradition are performed for tourists on sampans on the Perfume River (see p.319).

The traditional music accompanying Cai Luong theatre originated in eighteenth-century Hué. Played as pure chamber music, without the voice, it is known as **Nhac Tai Tu**, or "skilled chamber music of amateurs". This is one of the most delightful and tricksy of all Vietnamese genres. The players have a great degree of improvisational latitude over a fundamental melodic skeleton; they must think and respond quickly, as in a game, and the resulting independently funky rhythms can be wild. Although modern conservatory training fails to prepare students for this most satisfying of all styles, there is now a resurgence of interest among young players in learning the demands of Tai Tu.

It was also in Hué under the Nguyen emperors that the specialized body of **royal music and dance** reached its peak of sophistication. These solemn ceremonial dances again owed their origins to the Chinese courtly tradition and were categorized into a highly complex system according to the occasion on which they would be performed: ritual dances to be held in temples or pagodas, during feasts or at various civil and military functions, and dances to mark particular anniversaries were just some of the distinctions. As the imperial court fell under European sway in the twentieth century, so the taste – and opportunity – for such music waned, until the late 1980s when it was revived by the provincial authorities with assistance from UNESCO. Hué's former Royal Theatre has now been renovated and is the venue for occasional performances of courtly dance by students of Hué University of Fine Arts.

Traditional instruments

A visiting US general once stepped off a plane with the intention of smoothing relations by attempting a little Vietnamese, a tonal language. Instead of "I am honoured to be here", listeners heard "the sunburnt duck lies sleeping". The voice and its inherent melodic information are behind all Vietnamese music, and most instruments are, to some extent, made to do what voices do: delicate pitch bends, ornaments and subtle slides. According to classical Confucian theory, instruments fall into eight **categories of sound**: silk, stone, skin, clay, metal, air, wood and bamboo. Although few people play by the rules these days, classical theory also relates five occasions when it is forbidden to perform: at sunset, during a storm, when the preparations have not been made seriously, with improper costumes, and when the audience is not paying attention.

Many instruments whose strings are now made of steel, gut or nylon originally had **silk** strings; silk is now out of fashion, more for acoustic than ecological reasons. The most famous of these, and unique to Vietnam, is the monochord **dan bau** (or *dan doc huyen*), an ingenious invention perfectly suited to its job of mimicking vocal inflections. It is made from one string (originally silk obtained by yanking apart the live worm), stretched over a long amplified sounding box, fixed at one end. The other end is attached to a buffalo-horn "whammy bar" stalk which can be flexed to stretch or relax the string's tension. Meanwhile the string is plucked with a plectrum at its harmonic nodes to produce overtones that swoop and glide and quiver over a range of three octaves. Other "silk-stringed" instruments include the *dan nguyet* moon-shaped lute, the *dan tranh* sixteen-string zither, *dan nhi* (two-string fiddle with the bow running between the strings), *dan day* (a three-stringed lute with a long fingerboard used in Ca Tru and also unique to Vietnam), and the *dan luc huyen cam*, a regular guitar with a fingerboard scalloped to allow for wider pitch bends.

The *dan da* **stone** lithophone is the world's oldest instrument, consisting of six or more rocks struck with heavy wooden mallets. Several sets have been found originating from the one slate quarry in the central highlands where the stones sing like nowhere else. The oldest *dan da* is now in Paris, but an identical set exists in Ho Chi Minh City, where it still produces pure ringing tones.

Various kinds of **drums** (*trong*) are used, played with acrobatic use of the sticks in the air and on the sides. Some originated in China, while others were introduced from India via the Cham people, such as the double-headed "rice drum" (*trong com*), which was developed from the Indian *mridangam*; the name derives from thin patches of cooked rice paste stuck on each membrane.

Representing **clay**, four thimble-size teacups are held in the fingers and often played as percussion instruments for Hué chamber music. Representing **metal**, the *sinh tien*, **coin clappers**, are another invention unique to Vietnam, combining in one unit a rasping scraper, wooden clapper and a sistrum rattle made from old coins. Bronze **gongs** are occasionally found in minority music, but Vietnam is the only country in Southeast Asia where tuned gamelan-type gong-chimes are not used.

Air, **wood** and **bamboo** furnish a whole range of wind instruments, such as the many side- and end-blown flutes used for folk songs and to accompany poetry recitals; or the *ken*, a double-reed oboe common across Asia and played, appropriately, in funeral processions and other outdoor ceremonies. Five thin bones often dangle from the *ken* player's mouthpiece to suggest the delicate fingers of a young woman, while disguising the hideous grin necessary to play the instrument. The *song lang* is a slit drum, played by the foot, used to count the measures in *Tai Tu* skilled chamber music, while the *k'long put*, consisting of racks of bamboo pipes, is the only percussion instrument you don't actually touch but clap in front of. Another instrument from the same folk tradition is the *t'rung*, a type of xylophone made of ladders of tuned bamboo.

New folk

Turn on the TV during the Tet Lunar New Year festivities and you can't miss the public face of Vietnamese traditional music: ethnic-costumed dancers, musicians and singers smilingly portraying the happy life of the worker. Fancy arrangements of well-known tunes from all over the country, including some token minorities' music, are spiced up with fancy hats and bamboo pianos. This choreographed entertainment known as **Modernized Folk Music** (*Nhac Dan Toc Cai Bien*) has only been "traditional" since 1956, when the Hanoi Conservatory of Music was founded and the teaching of folk music was deliberately "improved".

For the first time, music was learned from written Western notation (leading to the neglect of improvisational skills while opening the way for huge orchestras), and conductors were employed. Tunings of the traditional eight modes were tempered to accommodate Western-style harmonies, while bizarre new instruments were invented to play bass and to fill out chords in the enlarged bands. Schools, with the mandate of preserving traditional music through "inheritance development", took over from the families and professional apprenticeships which had formerly been passed on via the oral tradition.

Not surprisingly a new creature was born out of all this. Trained conservatoire graduates have spread throughout the country, been promoted through competitions and state-sponsored ensembles on TV, radio, and even in the lobbies of classier hotels. The new corpus of music and song arrangements has become an emblem of national pride and scientific improvement. Folk songs, melodies from the ethnic minorities, Mozart and Chinese tunes are all ripe fodder for the arranger's pen. Much to the chagrin of the few remaining traditional musicians outside this system, this is now the predominant folk-based music generally heard in public. A visitor to the central highlands asked the local tribal musicians how they felt about their music being "improved". At first they replied what an honour it was for their music to be considered by city people, but after the official interview they privately confessed their horror.

Music for new folk is entertaining and accessible, albeit risking tawdriness; at its best, though, it can be an astonishing display of a lively new art form. One family of six brothers (and one sister-in-law), led by Duc Loi, formed a percussion group in Ho Chi Minh City under the name **Phu Dong**, whose members spent time in the highlands learning the instruments of several minorities. Since 1981 they have played together and developed an infectious musical personality. Circular breathing and lightning-speed virtuosity are just some of the dazzling features of a performance, and their collection of instruments is like a zoo of mutant bamboo. Most striking, though, is their use of the lithophone (*dan da*), a replica of the original, 6000-year-old stone marimba. The effect of awakening this ancient voice, whatever changes in performance practice there may have been over the last six millennia, is shattering.

There is no lack of extraordinary recordings of Vietnamese folk music made over the last sixty years; on the contrary, there are over 4000 of them. They are, however, all but totally inaccessible in the guarded bowels of a converted pagoda in Hanoi. The tapes, their rusty dandruff particles floating off with each playing, have lain uncatalogued for the last few decades, although the New York-based Asian Cultural Council is now helping. Now recognized as a national treasure because of the lost traditions they contain, they are being studied on condition that no copies be made; the fears are that someone might make a lot of money out of publishing them abroad, and that their technical quality is embarrassing when compared to modern CDs. The inspired solution is to begin making new field recordings of what's left (which of course does nothing to rescue the lost traditions from their rapidly deteriorating archive).

Vietnamese pop

They pedal from gig to gig, or sit side-saddle on a Honda Dream if they are famous: the **pop** singers of Ho Chi Minh City. Emerging from the traffic, they park their wheels, sit behind a tree near the stage and wait for their turn at the mike, carefully preening their rumpled *ao dai* or suit. If you want to hear the current play-list during the course of one evening, all you have to do is visit one of the many café-bar-hotels where there is a live band. One by one the singers take turns to come on stage, sing a song (two, if they are well known – one slow, one fast) before hopping down the road to repeat the routine.

There is no shortage of pop-star wannabes in Vietnam and the fine line between karaoke hacks on CD and major commercial pop releases can be tough to pinpoint. The vast majority of pop music would be filed under **light pop-rock**, but it is also referred to as "misery pop" or "yellow music". Most composers in the country have tried their hand at writing a pop hit but only about three are acknowledged masters: Van Cao (who also wrote the national anthem), Pham Duy (now in his eighties and writing pointed political songs from the safe distance of California) and Trinh Cong Son (whose life of wine, women and song ended in 2001). Joan Baez was not far off when she dubbed him "the Vietnamese Bob Dylan": the tunes are catchy and the lyrics right-on. His first songs were written while in hiding from the military draft, and in 1969, when his album *Lullaby* sold over two million copies in Japan, Son's works were banned by the South Vietnamese government, which considered the lyrics too demoralizing. Even the new government sent him to work as a peasant in the fields, but after 1979 he lived in Ho Chi Minh City, painting, writing apolitical-but-catchy love songs and celebrating Vietnam's natural wonders, with over six hundred songs to his credit.

There are two main centres for Vietnamese pop-music production: **Ho Chi Minh City** and Southern California. Those in the country have the advantage of being close to the source of folk inspiration (arrangements of traditional Ca Tru and Chau Van songs are currently in vogue), and the young generation has taken singing lessons at the Conservatory (leading to a vast technical improvement of late). Singers of note include: Tran Thu Ha, My Linh, Phuong Thanh, Bang Kieu, Lam Truong, and Thanh Lam. Albums are bootlegged under different titles so just keep an eye out for these names and you'll be fine.

Meanwhile in Orange County, **California**, the scene is busy but somewhat stagnant. The stars of yesterday and today are: Khanh Ha, Don Ho, Lam Nhat Tien, Nhu Quynh, Y Lan, Khanh Ly, Tuan Ngoc, with the young Tran Thai Hoa showing promise. Some of these are the performing children of former superstars, so in many cases the entertainment genes have been passed on despite relocation and social upheaval.

The ubiquitous **pop-rock** band comprises a singer (who may admit of a few modest gyrations), bass guitar and one or two electronic keyboards, hailed throughout the country as the greatest labour-saving device, despite their cheesy sound. Indeed, in rural areas where there is no electricity, these portable keyboards run happily on batteries, and all the rhythm buttons that are so rarely used elsewhere – rumba, tango, bossa nova and surf-rock – are here employed liberally. The slap-echo on the singer's microphone is intentional; without it, they say, it sounds "unprofessional". Each evening, when the traffic noise dies down, you can hear the mournful laments of neighbouring karaoke bars mingling together, the ghostly echoes of lonely pop singers reverberating from another dimension.

Heavy metal and other music that raises the blood pressure have yet to be widely accepted, but the influence from the Asian pop field is strong. It is hard to say whether bands such as Sword of Darkness, symphonic growling Vietnamese black metal from Minnesota, will make it big back home yet. **Group singing** there, however, has taken off since boy band BBMak took the country by storm; there are already equivalent girl groups gyrating agreeably in synch.

Discography

There are now more recordings of traditional music available outside the country than in. But if you find yourself in Hanoi, stop by the Vietnamese Institute of Musicology at 32 Nguyen Thai Hoc (⊛www.vnstyle .vdc.com.vn/vim) and check out their many self-produced historic field recordings.

Traditional

Samplers

Hò! Roady Music from Vietnam
Trikont, Germany. Crass, crazy, funky street music taken from pop cassettes and recorded *in situ* with mopeds and car horns in the soundscape. It opens in cracking style with a plucked *dan bau* doing "Riders in the Sky" with what sounds like fire-

works as well. There's a wild funeral brass band and all sorts of surprises. Highly recommended.

Music from Vietnam Vol 1
Caprice, Sweden. An introduction (in conservatoire style) featuring songs, instrumental tracks and the-

atrical forms. Featured instruments include the *dan bau, dan nguyet* and *k'long put*. Music includes Quan Ho folk songs, Cai Luong and Hat Cheo theatre, Hat Chau Van possession ritual and Nhac Dan Toc Cai Bien new folk.

Stilling Time: Traditional Musics

Theatre

The Art of Kim Sinh King, Japan. Blind singer/guitarist Kim Sinh has something of a cult following and knows how to wrench the emotions from those old Cai Luong opera songs. His venerable musical personality is more affecting than many of the commercial Cai Luong releases available, and one struggles not to make comparisons to the blues. This recording has influenced a whole generation of young California guitarists.

Vietnamese Folk Theatre: Hat Cheo King, Japan. A generous quantity of Cheo theatre, expertly played by the Quy Bon family and record-

of Vietnam Innova, US. A sampler of field recordings from all over Vietnam, including songs and gong music of the ethnic minorities. An introduction to the many surprises in store for the musical traveller. Recorded and compiled by Philip Blackburn.

ed in Hanoi. Features a Chau Van possession ritual and the famous story of the cross-dressing Thi Mau going to a temple. Disappointing liner notes.

Vietnam: Traditions of the South Audivis/UNESCO, France. Southern ritual music from the eclectic Cao Dai, Buddhist and indigenous spirit-possession religions, as well as a good helping of Cai Luong theatre music (the traditional, not the cheesy Western-style band!). The liner notes and recording quality are on the dry side but the music is very lively.

Song and classical music

Anthology of World Music: The Music of Viet Nam Rounder, US. This is the Vietnamese equivalent of the Rosetta Stone, the earliest published recordings of some of the standards of the repertoire, performed by the masters of their day. Music and Theatre of the Court, Ritual Music and Entertainment Music, and the Music of South Vietnam. The presentation may seem a little dusty by modern flashy conservatoire standards but it's still revelatory.

Ca Tru: The Music of North Viet Nam Nimbus, UK. Performed by the Hanoi Ca Tru Thai Ha Ensemble. A tenacious vestige of Vietnam's 500-year tradition of women's "songs for bamboo tokens", Ca Tru (or Hat A Dao) is a private entertainment forced underground until recently. Solo

voice (with "bouncing seeds" vibrato), lute and chopsticks titillate male visitors for hours on end.

Music from Vietnam Vol 2: The City of Hué Caprice, Sweden. Ceremonial music with shawms, drums and a big gong, a military ensemble and a great court orchestra, as well as more intimate chamber groups of singers with *dan bau, dan nguyet, dan nhi* and *dan tranh*. Three local instrumental and vocal groups give the enticing flavour of this city, and the disc features the sprightly aged Nguyen Manh Cam, former drummer to the emperor. Good notes.

Vietnam: Buddhist Music from Hué Inedit, France. An atmospheric recording, full of ceremonial presence. It begins with sonorous drums and bells before two oboes enter for music marking the ascent to the

"Esplanade of Heaven". The complete ceremony of Khai Kinh, "Opening the Sacred Texts", is recorded in one of Hué's best pagodas, the Kim Thien. Not easy listening, but the music is nevertheless impressive. Good notes.

Vietnam: Poésies et Chants
Ocora, France. Master musician Tran Van Khe and friends chant poetry (*ngam tho*) and ravish the *dan tranh* and *dan nguyet* (in the Nhac Tai Tu skilled chamber music repertory). Specialized and intimate performances with excellent notes and translations.

Ethnic minority music

Gongs: Vietnam, Laos Playasound, France. Before there were skipping records or Steve Reich patterns there were these delicious mellifluously clangorous loops filling the jungle nights.

Music from Vietnam Vol 3: Ethnic Minorities Caprice, Sweden. The mosaic of cultures residing in the central and northern mountains have some astonishing musical traditions. This excellent and accessible selection kicks off with a piece from the E De: a beautiful "free-reed" cow-horn solo followed up by clattering polyrhythmic gong patterns. There's also music from the Nung, Muong and Hmong. Wonderful pipes, flutes, mouth organs and songs. Good notes.

Musiques des Montagnards Chant du Monde, France. Two CDs of extraordinary archival and recent recordings (1958–1997) from the central and northern highlands. Fourteen ethnic groups are covered and excellently described in the copious 119-page booklet.

Northern Vietnam: Music and Songs of the Minorities Musique du Monde, France. A selection of recordings from the Giay, Nung, Tay, Dao, Thai and Hmong ethnic groups. A love song, courting melodies, wedding music, funeral music and the extraordinary Hmong *khen*.

New folk

Echoes of Ancestral Voices: Traditional Music of Vietnam Move, Australia. Music performed by husband and wife duo Dang Kim Hien and Le Tuan Hung. No fireworks, just a fragile, uncompromising intensity.

Moonlight in Vietnam Henry Street/Rounder, US. New music expertly played on Vietnam's most extraordinary musical instruments, including the *dan bau*, *k'long put* and a stick-fiddle with a resonating disc held in the player's mouth. The players are a Vancouver-based ensemble led by *dan bau* virtuoso Ho Khac Chi.

The Music of Vietnam Vols 1.1 & 1.2 Celestial Harmonies, US. Accessible, virtuoso and expertly recorded, these discs document an array of Vietnam's best conservatoire-mediated styles. Through a compelling series of pieces, this is an entertaining overview of the full range of Vietnamese instruments. Full documentation.

Pop

Don Ho *Ru Em/Lullaby* Thuy Nga, US. Heart-throb lullabies from one of California's hottest singers.

Khanh Ha *Doi Da Vang/Vacant Rock-strewn Hill* Khanh Ha Productions, US. Bilingual singing legend has been compared (favourably) to Barbra Streisand and Celine Dion.

My Linh *Toc Ngan/Short Hair* My Linh Productions, Vietnam. Hot arrangements of pieces all written for her sultry, crackly voice.

Nguyen Thanh Van *Ho Khoan Le Thuy/River Song* Van Nguyen Productions, US. Passion, pathos and folk references by one of the up-and-coming stars of the Vietnamese pop world, based in San Francisco.

Pham Duy *Voyage Through the Motherland* Co Loa, US. The first Vietnamese CD-ROM, featuring patriotic songs, karaoke options, video and fine photos. A real "coffee table" disc.

Y Lan *Muon Hoi Tai Sao/I Want to Ask Why* Y Lan Productions, US. From a well-known artistic family, she became a café owner before becoming a regular at the *Ritz* and *Paris By Night* circuit.

With contributions by Philip Blackburn (from *The Rough Guide to World Music*)

Environmental issues

Vietnam is endowed with a wide variety of fauna and flora, including an unusually high number of bird species and a rich diversity of primates. Current estimates suggest 12,000 plant species, 280 mammals, 770 birds, 130 reptiles, 80 amphibians and perhaps 2500 species of fish, though remote areas are still being explored. Over the recent years, in the forest reserves bordering Laos, the identification of several species of mammal and bird previously unknown to scientists has caused a sensation in the scientific community.

Such diversity is largely attributable to Vietnam's range of habitats, from the subalpine mountains of the north to the Mekong Delta's mangrove swamps, in a country that is 75 percent mountainous, has 3200km of coastline and extends over 16 degrees of latitude. However, the list of endangered species is also long – 40 mammals and 37 types of bird – as their domains are threatened by population pressure, widespread logging and pollution, particularly of the coastal zone. One of the biggest environmental challenges facing Vietnam is to preserve its rapidly diminishing forest areas by establishing methods of sustainable use. Happily, the government does at least seem to recognize the value of Vietnam's biodiversity and the need to act quickly on such issues.

Ecological warfare

The word "**ecocide**" was coined during the American War, in reference to the quantity of herbicides dropped from the air to deprive the Viet Cong of their safe areas, deep under the triple-canopy forest, and their food crops. The most notorious defoliant used was **Agent Orange**, along with agents Blue and White, all named after the colour of the respective storage containers. Their active ingredient was **dioxin**, a slowly dissolving poison that has a half-life of eight to ten years in the environment – but remains much longer in human tissue. Between 1962 and 1970 it's estimated that over forty million litres of these defoliants were sprayed from American planes criss-crossing the forests and mangrove swamps of South Vietnam and the Demilitarized Zone. Figures vary, but somewhere between twenty and forty percent of the South's land area was sprayed at least once and in some cases more frequently, destroying up to a quarter of the forest cover.

The environmental impact was perhaps greatest on the **mangrove forests**, which are particularly susceptible to defoliants. Mangroves were a valuable resource for the guerrillas, not only for their cover and firewood but also because the young shoots – which remove the salt from sea water – could be chewed to provide a vital supply of fresh water. Spraying destroyed about a half of all Vietnam's mangrove swamps and forests. They don't regenerate naturally, so they're having to be replanted by hand, a slow operation with a low success rate. In other areas vast tracts of forest died, along with the wildlife population, and **crop destruction** left the local people malnourished or starving. Initially, bamboo thickets and "American grass" were the only plants able to tolerate the sun-baked, chemical-soaked soils and only recently have efforts at reforestation been successful. Even now, fires sweep through the dead forests and brittle grasses each dry season, after which monsoon rains wash away the exposed topsoil.

The herbicides also had a severe impact on **soldiers**, both Vietnamese and American, and **villagers** who were caught in the spraying or absorbed dioxins from the food chain and from drinking water. Children and old people were the worst affected: some died immediately from the poisons, while others suffered respiratory diseases, skin rashes and other ailments. Soon it became apparent that the dioxins were also causing abnormally high levels of miscarriage, birth defects, neurological disease and cancers. Surveys suggest that as many as one million Vietnamese may be affected, many of whom now receive a small monthly allowance from the government. For years, doctors in Ho Chi Minh City's Tu Do Hospital, supported by international experts, have been trying to convince the American government of the link between the use of defoliants and these medical conditions, in the hope of claiming **compensation** for the victims. Though so far Hanoi has not officially asked America for compensation, the subject has been raised at various bilateral talks and in 2002 America finally agreed to conduct joint research into the effects of dioxins; critics argue that there is more than enough evidence to establish a link and that the American government is merely dragging its feet for fear of being deluged by lawsuits. For their part, American war veterans who were exposed to dioxins have also been seeking reparations. In 1984, a group of ex-servicemen won a landmark out-of-court settlement from the manufacturers; though the government refused to accept culpability, they were later forced to reimburse the chemical company following legal proceedings.

Apart from using herbicides, American and South Vietnamese troops cut down swathes of forest land with specially adapted bulldozers, called **Rome Ploughs**. These vehicles were capable of slicing through a three-metre-thick tree trunk, and were used to clear roadsides and riverbanks against ambushes, or to remove vestiges of undergrowth and trees left after the spraying. Finally, there were the **bombs** themselves – an estimated 13 million tonnes of explosives were dropped during the course of the war, leaving a staggering 25 million bomb craters, the vast majority in the South. In addition to their general destructive power, explosions compact the soil to the point where nothing will grow, and napalm bombs sparked off forest fires. The worst single incident occurred in 1968 when U Minh forest, at the southern tip of Vietnam, burned for seven weeks; 85 percent of its trees were destroyed.

Since the war, Vietnamese scientists, led by Professor Vo Quy of Hanoi University, have instigated **reforestation programmes**, slowly coaxing life back into even the worst-affected regions. This has involved pioneering work in regenerating tropical forest, planting native species under a protective umbrella of eucalyptus and acacia. In 1987 a record 500 million trees were replanted over 160,000 hectares, and the eventual target is to increase the area under forest by at least three million hectares by 2010. A symbolically significant success of local environmentalists has been the **return of the Sarus crane** to the Plain of Reeds (see p.146), on the Cambodian border. The crane, a stately bird with an elaborate courtship dance, abandoned its nesting grounds when the Americans drained the wetlands, dropped herbicides and then napalm in their attempts to rout Viet Cong soldiers from the marshes. After the war thousands of landless farmers were settled in the area and continued digging canals for rice cultivation and transport. However, the acid soils proved difficult to farm and the provincial governor, Muoi Nhe, succeeded in re-establishing a portion of the wetlands to support commercial crops of melaleucas (tea trees), as well as restoring the natural habitat. The first Sarus cranes reappeared in 1986, after which Tam Nong Bird Sanctuary (see p.146) was set up to protect the crane and other returning species. Though the population remains highly vulnerable, as many as a thousand Sarus cranes now overwinter in the wetlands.

Postwar deforestation

It's estimated that more than 2 million hectares of Vietnam's forest reserves were destroyed during the American War as a result of defoliation, napalm fires and bombing. However, over the last twenty years as much again has been lost to commercial **logging**, agricultural **clearance**, firewood collection – and **population pressure**. Originally, perhaps 75 percent of Vietnam's land area would have been covered by forest: by 1945 this had dwindled to 44 percent and it now stands at less than 20 percent, of which only a tiny amount is natural primary forest. Despite some of the world's most ambitious reforestation programmes, the reserves are still shrinking. Each year somewhere between 100,000 and 200,000 hectares of woodland are felled or burnt, while replanting efforts can cover at most 200,000 hectares annually.

The **worst-affected areas** are Vietnam's northern mountains, the central province of Nghe An, and around Plei Ku in the central highlands. In these areas soil erosion is a major problem, and countrywide floods are getting worse as a result of deforestation along the watersheds. Many rare hardwoods are fast disappearing and the fragile ecosystems are no longer able to support a wildlife population forced into ever-smaller pockets of undisturbed jungle. Much of the blame for this rapid reduction in the forest cover is often laid on the **ethnic minorities** who traditionally clear land for farming and rely on the forests for building timber and firewood. Increased population pressure, exacerbated

Conservation and the national parks

Vietnam recognized the need for conservation relatively early, establishing its first national park in 1962 and adopting a **National Conservation Strategy** in 1985. The more accessible or interesting of Vietnam's ten or so **national parks** are listed below, with page references to the Guide where there's more information about visiting them. Unless you're prepared to spend a lot of time in the parks, it's unlikely that you'll see many animals. Birds, insects and butterflies, however, are more readily visible and often the dense tropical vegetation or mountain scenery are in themselves worth the journey.

Ba Be (see p.471). A park of 8000 hectares (with a proposed expansion to 23,000 hectares), containing Vietnam's largest natural lake – and a few extremely rare Tonkin snub-nosed langur. The park has limited tourist facilities, but boat trips, jungle walks and overnight stays in a minority village are possible.

Bach Ma (see p.303). A small park (22,000 hectares), Bach Ma sits on the climatological divide between the tropical forests of the south and the northern subtropical zone, and contains Vietnam's lushest tropical rainforests. It is also home to a wide variety of bird species, including several rare pheasants, and over 1400 recorded flora species. Bach Ma is well set up for tourism, with a network of marked trails, campsites and guesthouses.

Cat Ba (see p.428). The park covers only 15,000 hectares, but 5000 of these are important marine reserves, including areas of coral reef. The limestone island supports a broad range of habitats, a wealth of medicinal plants, and a highly vulnerable population of Golden-headed langur. The park is accessible to tourists either on foot or by boat from Cat Ba Town.

Cat Tien Dong Nai Province (see p.197). This 74,000-hectare park, together with neighbouring Cat Loc Nature Reserve, is most famous for its small population of Java rhino, the only ones known in mainland Asia. Otherwise the park's wetlands are a haven for water birds, including the white-winged duck and the woolly-necked by lowland Vietnamese settling in the mountains, has meant extending the cultivated area and reducing the fallow period, when natural regeneration would normally have taken place. In response, the government has been trying to encourage forms of sedentary agriculture around permanent village sites. But perhaps a greater threat to the forests is the highly lucrative **timber trade**, both legal and illegal. By **replanting**, it's hoped to create sustainable forests for commercial logging and to protect the remaining areas of primary forests, but **enforcement** is hampered by lack of resources. Recently, the authorities have been experimenting with new ideas of conservation, devolving the management and protection of the forest reserves to local communities, with some success. In 1991, the Vietnamese government announced its intention to establish protection areas covering six million hectares of forest, provide for eleven million hectares of productive woodland, and restore forest reserves over forty percent of Vietnam's land area by the year 2010.

Wildlife

Forest clearance, warfare, pollution and economic necessity have all contributed to the loss of natural habitat and reduced Vietnam's broad species base. In 1994, when Vietnam signed the **Convention on International Trade in Endangered Species** (CITES), which bans the traffic in animals or plants facing

stork, as well as forest birds. Although it's relatively close to Ho Chi Minh City, Cat Tien is not easy to reach by public transport and tourist facilities are fairly limited.

Cuc Phuong (see p.351). Vietnam's first national park, Cuc Phuong was established in 1962 in an area of limestone hills relatively close to Hanoi. The reserve covers 22,000 hectares and contains a number of unique, ancient trees and provides excellent birdwatching, as well as an opportunity to see some of the world's rarest monkeys in its Endangered Primate Rescue Centre. Cuc Phuong is one of the most accessible parks, where it's possible to hike and stay overnight.

Yok Don (see p.215). Lying on the border with Cambodia, Yok Don constitutes a 115,000-hectare reserve carved out of Vietnam's most extensive forests. The area is also one of the most biologically diverse in the whole of Indochina, supporting rare Indochinese tigers and Asian elephants. Visitors can overnight in minority villages or camp; elephant-back rides and boat trips are also on offer.

Note To support **environmental programmes** already taking place in Vietnam, contact the following organizations, some of which also provide opportunities for paying volunteers (see p.66 and p.67).

BirdLife International Wellbrook Court, Girton Rd, Cambridge CB3 0NA, UK (☏01223/277318, ⓦwww.birdlife.net); trip reports are welcomed by their Vietnam office at 11 Lane 167, Tay Son, Dong Da District, Hanoi (ⓦwww.wing-wbsj.or.jp/~vietnam).

Frontier 50–52 Rivington St, London EC2A 3QP, UK (☏020/7613 2422, ⓦwww.frontierprojects.ac.uk); see also p.67 for more on field trips organized by Frontier.

International Crane Foundation E-11376 Shady Lane Rd, PO Box 447, Baraboo, Wisconsin, 53913-0447 USA (☏608/356-9462, ⓦwww.savingcranes.org).

WWF International Avenue du Mont-Blanc, 1196 Gland, Switzerland (☏22/364 9111, ⓦwww.panda.org).

extinction, the species list identified 365 animal species in need of urgent protection. Among these, the Java rhino, the world's rarest large mammal, is reduced to a mere five to eight animals, while no less than five of the world's most endangered primate species, including the Golden-headed (or Cat Ba) langur and the Tonkin snub-nosed langur, survive in small isolated communities in the northern forests. Other severely endangered species include the Indochina tiger and Asian elephant. Vietnam is also home to around 770 species of **birds**, with the highest number of endemic species in the world. Again, many of these are under threat of extinction, including the Vietnamese pheasant, of which only a tiny number survive in the forests of Ha Tinh.

Hunting continues to be a vital source of local income, as a walk round Vietnamese markets soon reveals. Wild animals and birds are sought after for their meat or to satisfy the demand for **medicinal products** and live specimens, an often illegal (but extremely lucrative) business. Since the border with China was re-opened in the early 1990s, smuggling of rare species has increased, among them the Asiatic black bear, whose gall bladder is prized as a cure for fevers and liver problems; relentless hunting has decimated the population to small numbers in the north. Similarly, Vietnam's population of wild Asian elephants is now reduced to less than two hundred individuals, down from two thousand in the 1970s. Not only has their habitat along the Cambodian border declined, but after 1975 poachers began hunting elephants for their tusks. Conservationists hope to maintain two or three viable populations in Dak Lak Province, where domesticated elephants are still used for transport and forestry work.

Nevertheless, quite large areas of the Vietnamese interior remain amazingly untouched, especially the Truong Son Mountains north of the Hai Van Pass, the southern central highlands and lowland forests of the Mekong Delta. These isolated areas are rich in **biodiversity** and have yielded spectacular discoveries in recent years, with much still to be explored. In 1992, Dr John MacKinnon and a team of Vietnamese biologists working in the Vu Quang Nature Reserve, an area of steamy, impenetrable jungle on the Lao border, identified a species of ox new to science, now known as the saola. Two years later the giant muntjac, a previously unknown species of deer, and a new carp were found in the same region, followed in 1997 by a smaller type of muntjac deer and the Grey-shanked douc langur, and in 1999 by a striped rabbit thought to be related to the now extinct Sumatran striped rabbit.

An all-out effort is being made to protect this "biological gold mine" and other similar areas both within Vietnam and over the border in Laos. After the saola was discovered, the reserve was put strictly off limits and the total **protected area** enlarged to almost 160,000 hectares, with buffer zones and corridors linking the reserve to conservation areas in Laos. The task is fraught with difficulties, such as achieving cross-border co-operation and establishing effective policing of the reserve – especially against poaching and illegal logging – with inadequate personnel and financial resources. At the same time, the authorities have been working to find alternative sources of income and food for people living in or near the reserve, and carrying out educational work on the importance of conservation and its relevance to their daily lives. In a related scheme, special protection areas have also been established around Yok Don and Ba Be national parks as part of a five-year project to establish models of stable biodiversity conservation. The government has also been adding to the number of national parks and nature reserves over recent years. Among them, 13,000 hectares of Bai Tu Long, an area of forested limestone islands on the east side of Ha Long Bay, were designated a national park in 2001. As a further boost to conservation efforts, the previous year UNESCO recognized an area of mangrove forest at Can Gio in the Mekong Delta and Cat Tien National Park as Vietnam's first "Man and Biosphere" reserves.

Sustainable tourism

In recent years there's been a growing awareness among tourists and travel companies of the negative impact tourism can have on the environment and local culture – the very things most people come to see. All too often the terms **eco-tourism** and **sustainable tourism** have been reduced to mere marketing gimmicks, but behind them lies a serious desire, albeit ambitious, to find a new model of small-scale tourism which contributes to the long-term development of the local community without destroying its traditional social and economic structures, or the often fragile environment.

Mass tourism didn't really get going in Vietnam until the mid-1990s. From just ten thousand in 1993, the number of foreign visitors (including business trips) rose to over 2.5 million in 2002, while domestic holiday-makers stand at around thirteen million. Not surprisingly, the Vietnamese government is eager to promote tourism as a **key revenue-earner** and is gradually easing visa regulations, among other things, in the hope of pushing foreign arrivals over the three million mark. This sudden influx of sightseers, coupled with a lack of effective planning or control, is putting pressure on some of the country's most famous beauty spots.

In response, the government recently introduced a number of laws and initiatives placing greater emphasis on the conservation of the nation's natural – and cultural – heritage. Local authorities in **Hoi An** (see p.274) have banned cars from the centre and put a block on further hotel construction in addition to introducing restrictive pricing to control the flow of tourists. Some of this revenue is being ploughed back into improving the townscape – for example, renovating the old houses, hiding television aerials and burying cables. In **Ha Long Bay** (see p.428), the problems of notoriously haphazard hotel development are exacerbated by **pollution** from nearby coalfields and the presence of a major port. Concern over the future of this World Heritage Site, however, means that the issues are at least being discussed and alternative strategies are under investigation. The Japanese are funding a comprehensive environmental survey of the bay in order to evaluate various development projects.

Perhaps the key areas, however, are the **uplands** of north and central Vietnam. These are increasingly popular destinations, both for their outstanding natural beauty and their communities of **ethnic minority people**. In the honey-pot market town of **Sa Pa** (see p.448), for example, the number of hotels and guesthouses has mushroomed over the last decade – from none before 1991 to no less than eighty in 2003 – and the famous weekend market attracts more tourists than minority people. Some of these people, disturbed by the unwanted attention and intrusive cameras, now shy away from Sa Pa completely, in favour of more inaccessible markets. Naturally, the tourists have also started to look elsewhere, and the latest "find" is Bac Ha (see p.455). Most of the "minority crafts" on sale are actually shipped up from Hanoi and, though they are the major attraction, the minority people themselves receive very little economic benefit from tourism; the majority goes to Kinh Vietnamese or foreign travel companies. There are even signs of an emerging sex industry in the area and the beginnings of both child prostitution and drug-related crime.

Sa Pa's superb setting and trekking opportunities will continue to make it a popular destination, and it's likely that the surrounding area will be developed further. Several NGOs are now looking at how this can be achieved in a way which contributes to the **long-term development** of the local community while also preserving cultural and biological diversity. The environmental conservation and research organization, Frontier (see p.67), for example, runs projects in ecologically important areas including the Nui Hoang Lien Nature Reserve near Sa Pa and Cat Ba National Park. In Sa Pa, Frontier teams have developed an environmental education programme for local schools, published a guidebook on sensitive tourism and set up income-generating projects for local communities cultivating medicinal plants for sale.

At the **national level**, a World Conservation Union (IUCN) project aims to raise awareness of sustainable tourism issues at all levels, from park rangers to government ministers, as well as among tour operators and tourists themselves, both domestic and international. It also aims to set up a variety of training programmes, and to establish a model of community-based sustainable tourism working with an ethnic minority group.

On a **personal level**, individual action is equally important. Though domestic tourism has the greatest impact through sheer weight of numbers, international travellers can play a positive role by setting examples of **responsible behaviour**. Various NGOs and groups involved in the travel industry (see overleaf) have developed **guidelines** for tourists and travel companies. Some of the most important points are: to avoid buying souvenirs made from endangered species or which damage the environment – notably tortoiseshell, ivory and coral in Vietnam; as far as possible, to eat in local restaurants, buy local produce and stay in locally owned hotels – not only is it usually a lot more fun, but also your money is more likely to benefit smaller communities; to be sensitive to the local culture, including appropriate standards of dress, as well as adopting a responsible attitude towards drugs, alcohol and prostitution.

Books

O f the vast canon of books written on the subject of Vietnam, the overwhelming majority concern themselves, inevitably, with the American War. Indigenous attempts to come to terms with the conflicts that have caused Vietnam such pain are only now beginning to filter through the country's overcautious censorship; the few novels that have reached the West in recent years are reviewed below. French-speakers will have a wider choice of titles.

For a decent copy of a book on Vietnam, your best bet is to scour bookshops before you set off from home – only Hanoi and Ho Chi Minh City have ranges of literature of any breadth, and then often only in photocopied offprint form. The exceptions to this are books produced by local publishers, notably Hanoi's Foreign Languages Publishing House, which you'll have difficulty finding outside Vietnam.

Travellers' accounts

Maria Coffey *Three Moons in Vietnam* Abacus. Delightfully jolly jaunt around Vietnam by boat, bus and bicycle. Coffey conspires to meet more locals in one day than most travellers do in a month, making this a valuable snapshot of modern Vietnam.

Sue Downie *Down Highway One* Allen & Unwin. In 1988 Sue Downie was one of the first Westerners since the American War to travel the length of Highway 1. Returning in the early 1990s, she witnesses the changes – not all good – transforming the country and people's daily lives.

Graham Greene *Ways of Escape* Penguin, UK; Random House, US. Greene's global travels in the 1950s took him to Vietnam for four consecutive winters; the coverage of Vietnam in this slim autobiographical volume is intriguing, but tantalizingly short, its memories of dice-playing with French agents over Vermouths and opium-smoking in Cholon evidently templates for scenes in *The Quiet American*.

Christopher Hunt *Sparring with Charlie* Bantam, UK; Anchor Books, US. Hunt can be a maddening travelling companion, but this account of his jaunt down the Ho Chi Minh Trail on a Russian-made motorbike is undeniably a page-turner.

Norman Lewis *A Dragon Apparent* Eland, UK; Transatlantic Publications, US. When in 1950 Lewis made the journey that would inspire his seminal Indochina travelogue, the Vietnam he saw was still a land of longhouses and imperial hunts, though poised for renewed conflict; the erudite prose of this doyen of travel writers reveals a Vietnam now long gone.

W. Somerset Maugham *The Gentleman in the Parlour* Vintage, UK; Orchid Press, US. The fruit of Maugham's grand tour from Rangoon to Haiphong to recharge his creative batteries, *The Gentleman in the Parlour*, finds him less than enamoured by Vietnam, his last stop. Nevertheless, his accounts of the Hué court teetering on the brink of extinction, and of a run-in with an old acquaintance in a Haiphong café, are vintage Maugham.

Karin Muller *Hitchhiking Vietnam* Globe Pequot Press. A feisty American, Karin Muller went searching for the "real Vietnam", a Vietnam untouched by commercialism and Western culture. On the way she gets deported, is arrested on numerous occasions and meets some motley characters, but eventually finds what she's looking for among the minorities of the northwest mountains. Beautifully told, with great compassion and a never-failing sense of humour.

Andrew X. Pham *Catfish and Mandala* Flamingo, UK; Picador, US. After twenty years in America, Pham takes a gruelling bike ride through Vietnam to rediscover the country, his family and – in the process – himself. A compelling insight into the frustrations and fascinations of Vietnam.

Gontran de Poncins *From a Chinese City* Trackless Sands Press. Believing that "the ancient customs of a national culture endure longer in remote colonies than in the motherland", de Poncins opted for a sojourn in Cholon as a means to a better understanding of the foibles of the Chinese; the resulting document of life in 1955 Cholon is a lively period piece, backed up by fluid illustrations.

Paul Theroux *The Great Railway Bazaar* Penguin. His elaborate circumnavigation of Europe and Asia by train took Theroux, in 1973, to a South Vietnam still bewildered by the recent American withdrawal. In bleak sound-bite accounts of rides from Saigon to Bien Hoa and Hué to Da Nang, he describes the war's awful legacy of poverty, suffering and infrastructural breakdown, but marvels at the country's unbowed, and unexpected, beauty.

Gabrielle M. Vassal *On and Off Duty in Annam* (o/p). An enchanting wander through turn-of-the-century southern Vietnam, penned by the intrepid wife of a French army doctor. A stint in Saigon is followed by a boat trip to Nha Trang (where she was carried ashore "on the backs of natives through the breakers") and a gutsy foray into the central highlands; amazing prints of the Vietnamese and *montagnards* she encountered further enhance the account.

John White *A Voyage to Cochin China* Oxford University Press. Memoirs of a pioneering voyager, who stepped ashore at Saigon several decades before the French took control.

Justin Wintle *Romancing Vietnam* Penguin. Wintle's genial but lightweight yomp upcountry was one of the first of its kind, post-*doi moi*, and remains a pleasing aperitif to travels in Vietnam.

Vietnamese abroad

Donald Anderson (ed.) *Aftermath: An Anthology of Post-Vietnam Fiction* Henry Holt. As the war's tendrils crept across the Pacific to America, they touched not only the people who fought, but also those who stayed at home. In their depictions of Americans, Amerasians and Asians regathering the strands of their lives, these short stories run the gamut of emotions provoked by war.

Le Ly Hayslip *Child of War, Woman of Peace* Pan, UK; Anchor, US. In this follow-up to *When Heaven and Earth Changed Places* (see p.554), Hayslip's narrative shifts to America, where the cultural disorientation of a new arrival is examined.

Robert Olen Butler *A Good Scent from a Strange Mountain* Grove Press. Pulitzer Prize-winning collection of short stories that ponder the struggles of Vietnamese in America to maintain the cultural ley lines linking them with their mother country, and the gulf between them and their Americanized offspring. War veteran Olen Butler's assured prose ensures the voices of his Vietnamese characters find perfect pitch.

Vietnamese literature

John Balaban and Nguyen Qui Duc (eds.) *Vietnam: A Traveller's Literary Companion* Whereabouts Press. The editors of this entertaining volume of short stories, written by Vietnamese writers based both at home and abroad, chose to avoid tales of war and politics during their selection process, though both themes inevitably make their presence felt.

Bao Ninh *The Sorrow of War* Minerva, UK; Riverhead Books, US. This is a ground-breaking novel, largely due to its portrayal of communist soldiers suffering the same traumas, fear and lost innocence as their American counterparts.

Alastair Dingwall (ed.) *Traveller's Literary Companion to South-East Asia* In Print Publishing. Among the bite-sized essays inside this gem of a book is an enlightening thirty-page segment on Vietnam, into which are crammed biopics, a recommended reading list, historical, linguistic and literary backgrounds. Excerpts range from classical literature to the writings of foreign journalists in the 1960s.

Duong Thu Huong *Novel Without a Name* Penguin. A tale of young Vietnamese men seeking glory but finding only loneliness, disillusionment and death, as war abridges youth and curtails loves; a depiction of dwindling idealism, and a radical questioning of the political motives behind the war. Other highly acclaimed works by the same author include *Paradise of the Blind* (HarperColllins) and *Memories of Pure Spring* (Penguin).

Duong Van Mai Elliot *The Sacred Willow* Oxford University Press. Mai Elliot brings Vietnamese history to life in this compelling account of her family through four generations.

Ho Chi Minh *Prison Diary*. Hanoi's Foreign Languages Publishing House also publishes a sawdust-dry, four-volume *Collected Works*, but the touching poems Ho penned while behind bars in 1942, in which he looks to birds' songs and moonlight to ease the loneliness of prison life, are more compelling.

Wayne Karlin, Le Minh Khue and Truong Vu (eds.) *The Other Side of Heaven* Curbstone Press. A unique anthology of postwar fiction by Vietnamese and American authors. Though written by former enemies from all sides of the conflict, these stories echo back and forth the unifying themes of sorrow, pain and survival.

Le Minh Khue *The Stars, The Earth, The River* Curbstone. Fourteen short stories by one of Vietnam's leading contemporary writers, an ex-sapper who gently details the seesaw of "tragedy and hope" which defines her war-torn generation.

Nguyen Du *The Tale of Kieu* Yale University Press. Vietnamese literature reached its zenith with this tale of the ill-starred love between Kieu and Kim.

Nguyen Huy Thiep *The General Retires and Other Stories* Oxford University Press. Perhaps Vietnam's pre-eminent writer, Nguyen Huy Thiep in these short stories articulates the lives of ordinary Vietnamese – instead of following the prevailing trend of re-imagining the lives of past heroes.

Vietnamese Literature Weighty anthology of classic Vietnamese literature available from street sellers in Hanoi and Ho Chi Minh City.

Novels set in Vietnam

Marguerite Duras *The Lover* Flamingo, UK; Pantheon Books, US. A young French girl encounters a wealthy Chinese from Cholon on a Mekong Delta ferry; the ensuing affair initiates her into adulthood, with all its joys and responsibilities. The novel's depiction of a dysfunctional, hard-up French family in Vietnam provides an interesting slant on expat life, showing it wasn't all Vermouths and tennis.

Graham Greene *The Quiet American* Vintage, UK; Penguin, US. Greene's prescient and cautionary tale of the dangers of innocence in uncertain times, which second-guessed America's boorish manhandling of Vietnam's political situation by several years, is still the best single account of wartime Vietnam. Its regular name-drops of familiar locales – Tay Ninh, the *Continental*, Dong Khoi – make it doubly enjoyable.

Anthony Grey *Saigon* Pan, UK; Dell, US. Vietnamese history given the blockbuster touch: a rip-roaring narrative, whose Vietnamese, French and American protagonists conspire to be present at all defining moments in recent Vietnamese history, from French plantation riots to the fall of Saigon.

Kien Nguyen *Tapestries* Abacus. This rich and beautifully woven novel is based on the extraordinary real-life story of the author's grandfather, who eventually became an embroiderer in the royal court of Hué. The context is a country on the cusp of change as French influence gains the upper hand.

Tim O'Brien *Going After Cacciato* Flamingo, UK; Broadway Books, US. A highly acclaimed, lyrical tale of an American soldier who simply walks out of the war and sets off for Paris, pursued by his company on a fantastical mission that takes them across Asia. The savage reality of war stands out vividly against a dream-world of peace and freedom.

Prehistory and history

William J. Duiker *The Communist Road to Power in Vietnam* HarperCollins, UK; Westview Press, US. One of America's leading analysts of the political context in Vietnam takes a long close look at why communist Vietnam won its wars – as opposed to why France and America lost.

William J. Duiker *Ho Chi Minh: A Life* Hyperion. Duiker turns his spotlight on the patriot and revolu-

tionary who led Vietnam to independence. It's a thoroughly researched and exhaustive tome, particularly good on Ho's political evolution, though fails to get under the skin of this enigmatic man.

Bernard Fall *Hell in a Very Small Place* Da Capo Press. The classic account of the siege of Dien Bien Phu, capturing the claustrophobia and the fear, written by a French-born American journalist.

Bernard Fall *Street Without Joy* Stackpole. Another masterpiece by Fall, charting the French debacle in Indochina, which became required reading for American generals and GIs – though it didn't prevent them committing exactly the same mistakes just a few years later.

David Halberstam *Ho* McGraw Hill. Diminutive, sympathetic and highly readable biography of Vietnam's foremost icon, though no attempt is made to apportion blame for the disastrous land reforms of the 1950s.

Charles Higham *The Archaeology of Mainland Southeast Asia* Cambridge University Press. Covering the period from 10,000 BC through to the close of the Angkor Empire, this is an immensely scholarly work that touches on all periods of Vietnam's prehistory and early history, from the hunter-gatherers of the Red River Delta to the empire of Champa.

Stanley Karnow *Vietnam: A History* Penguin. Weighty, august tome that elucidates the entire span of Vietnamese history.

John Keay *Last Post* John Murray, UK; Scribner, US. French colonialism and Vietnam's fight for independence set against the history of Western imperialism in the Far East. Scholarly but highly readable reappraisal of the wider forces at work.

Michael Maclear *Vietnam: The Ten Thousand Day War* Mandarin, UK; Avon, US (o/p). A detailed yet accessible account of the French and American wars, from Ho's alliance with Archimedes Patti, to the fall of Saigon.

David G. Marr *Vietnamese Anti-Colonialism, 1885–1925* University of California Press. Well worth rooting out for its contextualization of Vietnam's struggles against France and America.

Nguyen Khac Vien *Vietnam: A Long History.* Published by Hanoi's Foreign Languages Publishing House, and therefore heavily weighted in favour of the communists, but easier to get hold of in Vietnam than most histories.

Keith Weller Taylor *The Birth of Vietnam* University of California Press. As a GI, Taylor was struck by the "intelligence and resolve" of his enemy. This meticulous account of the dawn of Vietnamese history, trawling the past from the nation's first recorded history up to the tenth century, is the result of his attempt to uncover their roots.

The American War

Mark Baker *Nam* Abacus, UK; Cooper Square Press, US. Unflinching firsthand accounts of the GI's descent from boot camp into the morass of death, paranoia, exhaustion and tedium. Gut-wrenchingly frank at times, the book depicts war as a rite of passage, and moral deterioration as a prerequisite to survival.

Tad Bartimus (ed.) *War Torn: Stories of War from the Women Reporters Who Covered Vietnam* Random House. Nine pioneering women journalists who covered the American War tell their tales, from the struggle to get there in the first place and be recognized in what was then an almost exlusively male profession to their reactions to the war itself and coming to terms with the aftermath.

Michael Bilton and Kevin Sim *Four Hours in My Lai* Penguin. Brutally candid and immaculately researched reconstruction of the events surrounding the My Lai massacre of 1968; as harrowing a portrayal of the depths plumbed in war as you'll ever read.

Philip Caputo *A Rumour of War* Macmillan, UK. One of the classics of the American War, Caputo's straightforward narrative is a powerful account of the numbing daily routine of the ordinary US soldier's life, the strange exhilaration of combat, and the brutalization that accompanies war.

Denise Chong *The Girl in the Picture* Scribner, UK; Penguin, US. Kim Phuc was the little girl running naked away from her napalm-bombed village in what is arguably the most famous – and most harrowing – photo taken during the Vietnam War. Not only did she survive the burns, just, but her resilience and capacity for forgiveness are quite remarkable. Denise Chong tells Kim's story simply, letting the horrific events speak for themselves.

Michael Clodfelter *Mad Minutes and Vietnam Months* McFarland & Co, UK; Pinnacle Books, US. Combat reminiscences from a man who found war's false promise of "courage, sacrifice, glory and adventure" displaced by monotony and, occasionally, atrocity.

Shirley Dicks *From Vietnam to Hell* McFarland & Co. For the subjects of Shirley Dick's 23 case studies, the war has never ended; her interviews with sufferers of Post Traumatic Stress Disorder paint a heartbreaking picture of men and women torn apart by their own memories.

W.D. Ehrhart *Going Back: An Ex-Marine Returns to Vietnam* McFarland & Co. A veteran of the battle for Hué, Ehrhart returned to Vietnam in 1985. *Going Back*, a record of that trip, mixes diary, memory and Ehrhart's own poetry to very readable effect.

Horst Faas and Tim Page (eds.) *Requiem* Jonathan Cape. Turning through this compendium of shots by photographers who subsequently lost their lives in Vietnam, Laos or Cambodia will haunt you for weeks. Never was a book more aptly named.

James Fenton *All the Wrong Places* Grove Press/Atlantic Monthly Press (o/p). In Vietnam at the moment of Saigon's liberation, Fenton somehow managed to hitch a lift on the tank that rammed through the palace gates; his easy prose and poet's eye for detail make his account an engrossing one.

Albert French *Patches of Fire* Vintage, UK; Random House, US. Examining his experiences of the infantryman's life in Vietnam and his attempts to exorcise his war-conjured demons back in the States, French's autobiography is at once moving and engrossing.

Le Ly Hayslip *When Heaven and Earth Changed Places* Pan, UK; Plume, US. For giving a human face to the slopes, dinks and gooks of American writing on Vietnam, this heart-rending tale of villagers trying to survive in a climate of hatred and distrust is perhaps more valuable than any history book.

Michael Herr *Dispatches* Picador, UK; Vintage, US. Infuriatingly narcissistic at times, Herr's spaced-out narrative still conveys the mud, blood and guts of the American war effort in Vietnam. Herr's distinctive tone is also evident in the classic war movie, *Apocalypse Now* (see p.565), for which he wrote the screenplay.

Peter King (ed.) *Australia's Vietnam* (o/p). American troops weren't the only foreigners dragged into the mire of the Vietnam conflict: the Australian role is chronicled in this compendium of essays.

John Laurence *The Cat from Hué* Public Affairs. Highly acclaimed for his coverage of the Vietnam conflict for CBS News from 1965 to 1970,

Laurence has written not only an evocative memoir but also a moving testimony to the courage of the American troops who, like him, came of age in the battlefields of Vietnam.

Tom Mangold and John Penycate *The Tunnels of Cu Chi* Pan, UK; Berkley, US. The most thorough, and the most captivating, account yet written of the guerrilla resistance mounted in the tunnels around Cu Chi.

Robert Mason *Chickenhawk* Corgi, UK; Viking, US. Few people can be better qualified than Mason to deliver an account of the American War: a helicopter pilot with over a thousand missions under his belt, his blood-and-guts, bird's-eye account of the war is harrowing but compelling.

Harold G. Moore and Joseph Galloway *We Were Soldiers Once…and Young* Corgi, UK; Perennial, US. This blow-by-blow account of the ferocious battle of the Ia Drang valley, among the earliest encounters of the American War, makes compelling reading as the authors recapture the chaos and fear alongside moments of incredible courage and the sheer determination to survive.

Tim O'Brien *The Things They Carried* and *If I Die in a Combat Zone* Flamingo, UK; Broadway Books, US. Through a mix of autobiography and fiction O'Brien lays to rest the ghosts of the past in a brutally honest reappraisal of the war, his own actions and the events he witnessed (see also O'Brien's novel *Going After Cacciato*, reviewed on p.552).

Frank Palmos *Ridding the Devils* (o/p). In 1968, Australian correspondent Palmos was the lone survivor of a Viet Cong ambush of a jeep carrying five journalists in Cholon. Twenty years later he returned to Vietnam to seek out the man who had tried to kill him – and allay his nightmares; his story highlights both the mental toll his investigations took, and the plight of Australian veterans.

Barry Petersen *Tiger Men* White Orchid Press. In the run-up to the American War, Australian Barry Petersen was working in the central highlands, forming members of the E De (Rhadé) minority into a crack fighting force, part of a covert CIA programme to deny the Viet Cong control of the villages.

John Pilger *Heroes* Vintage, UK; Southend Press, US. Pilger's systematic dismantling of the myth that America's role was in any way a justifiable "crusade" makes his Vietnam reportage required reading.

William Prochnau *Once Upon a Distant War* Mainstream, UK; Vintage, US. Now that all the journos ever to set foot in Vietnam have published memoirs, Prochnau presents a new twist – the intriguing story of the people (amongst them Neil Sheehan, David Halberstam and Peter Arnett) who wrote the stories of Vietnam.

Jonathan Schell *The Real War* Da Capo Press. Acute and assured reportage, relaying the devastating ferocity of the American war effort in Vietnam – first the onslaught on the village of Ben Suc (in the Iron Triangle), then the laying waste of Quang Ngai Province.

Neil Sheehan *A Bright Shining Lie* Pimlico, UK; Vintage, US. This monumental and fluently rendered account of the war, hung around the life of the soldier John Paul Vann, won the Pulitzer Prize for Sheehan; one of the true classics of Vietnam-inspired literature.

Justin Wintle *The Vietnam War* (o/p). Written in reaction to the shelves of long-winded texts available on the subject, Wintle's succinct overview manages to condense this mad war into less than two hundred pages.

Tobias Wolff *In Pharaoh's Army* Random House, UK; Vintage US. A former adviser based in My Tho, Wolff's honest, gentle autobiographical tale takes a wry look at life away from the "front line".

Postwar Vietnam

Bui Tin *Following Ho Chi Minh* University of Hawaii Press. An erstwhile colonel in the North Vietnamese Army, Bui Tin effectively defected to the West in 1990, since when he has been an outspoken critic of Vietnam's state apparatus. These memoirs don't flinch from addressing the underside – corruption, prejudice, naivety and insensitivity – of the Party.

Adam Fforde and Stefan de Vylder *From Plan to Market* Westview Press. Highbrow, laudably researched book plotting the route Vietnam has taken from Stalinist central planning to market economy: Fforde and de Vylder hold the fabric of *doi moi* up to the light for examination.

Gabriel Kolko *Vietnam: Anatomy of a Peace* Routledge. No other recent account of contemporary Vietnam has done a better job of describing the social, political and economic upheavals that Vietnam has suffered over the past decade.

David Lamb *Vietnam, Now: A Reporter Returns* Public Affairs. After covering the American War for UPI in the late 1960s, journalist David Lamb returned in 1997 for a four-year stint as the *Los Angeles Times'* bureau chief in Hanoi, the erstwhile "enemy capital". Lamb's earlier experiences provide a depth of perspective to his analysis, but this is primarily a commentary on contemporary Vietnam and its prospects for the future. He is ultimately optimistic, though his criticisms of the government – in particular its failure to reconcile the still deep divisions between north and south – were sufficient to get the book banned.

Tim Page *Derailed in Uncle Ho's Victory Garden* Scribner, UK; Simon & Schuster, US. The war photographer with a legendary ability to defy death, returns to Vietnam; buried among the flashbacks and meandering discourse, Page's eye for detail and his delight in the bizarre gives a flavour of modern Vietnam.

Neil Sheehan *Two Cities: Hanoi and Saigon* Picador. Sheehan returned to Vietnam in 1989 to witness firsthand the legacy of the war. Down south, the memories really begin to flow as encounters and travels trigger wartime flashbacks, interspersed with commentary on re-education camps and other deprivations of the dark, pre-*doi moi* years.

Robert Templer *Shadows and Wind* Penguin. This hard-hitting book casts a critical eye over Vietnam's decades of reform, from corruption and censorship to the emergence of a consumer-oriented youth culture.

Gavin Young *A Wavering Grace* Penguin. The poignant tale of a Vietnamese family torn apart by the war and its aftermath, as witnessed by this veteran adventurer, and a testament to the author's long, resilient love affair with the country.

Culture and society

Lou Dematteis *A Portrait of Viet Nam* W.W. Norton. A stunning photographic record of daily life in Vietnam.

Annabel Doling *Vietnam on a Plate* Roundhouse (o/p). Fascinating culinary journey through Vietnam, peppered with snippets of history and cultural insights, as well as a practical guide to the best of Vietnamese cuisine.

Claire Ellis *Culture Shock! Vietnam* Kuperard, UK; Graphic Arts Center, US. A cultural bible detailing how to avoid such faux pas as sticking your chopsticks into your food, pointing the sole of your foot at somebody and arranging a business meeting for an inauspicious day of the month...Invaluable if you're doing business in Vietnam, interesting even if you aren't.

Gabriel Gobron *History and Philosophy of Cao Daism*. Standard text on Cao Daist history and beliefs, readily available from street sellers in Ho Chi Minh City.

Gerald Cannon Hickey *Shattered World* University of Pennsylvania Press. Detailed but readable account of ethnic minorities living in Vietnam's central highlands by one of the region's leading ethnologists. A fascinating analysis of the minorities' tragic struggle to survive both war and peace.

Pierre Huard and Maurice Durand *Vietnam: Civilization and Culture* (o/p). Sections on topics as diverse as teeth-blackening, ear-cleaning, literature, fishing and astrology make this a cornucopia of trivial info and hard fact. Chunks are now out of date, but in areas such as social relations, festivities and rice cultivation there's still much of value.

Henry Kamm *Dragon Ascending* Arcade Publishing. Rather than relying upon the endless self-aggrandizing anecdotes favoured by many reporters, Pulitzer Prize-winning correspondent Kamm prefers to let the Vietnamese – art dealers, ex-colonels, academics, doctors, authors – speak for themselves. This they do eloquently, resulting in a convincing portrait of contemporary Vietnam.

Norma J. Livo and Dia Cha *Folk Stories of the Hmong* Greenwood Press, UK; Libraries Unlimited, US. The Hmong's fading oral tradition is captured in this unique collection, gleaned from US immigrants, while its scene-setting introduction offers a valuable overview of Hmong culture, accompanied by illustrations of traditional costume and embroidered "storycloths".

William S. Logan *Hanoi: Biography of a City* New South Wales University Press. A heritage adviser, Logan peels back the layers of history revealed in Hanoi's architecture and streetscapes to provide an academic but engaging account of the city over the last thousand years. In doing so, he also examines the challenges facing Hanoi as it strives to preserve its unique heritage while also meeting the needs of its citizens.

Nguyen Van Huy *Cultural Mosaic of Ethnic Groups in Vietnam*. Comprehensive, if a little dry, round-up of Vietnam's minorities; available from street sellers in Hanoi and Ho Chi Minh City.

Christina Noble *Bridge Across My Sorrows* Corgi. Life-affirming autobiography by a Dublin woman spurred by a dream to channel her considerable strengths into helping Ho Chi Minh City's *bui doi*, or street children. In her sequel, *Mama Tina* (John Murray, UK), Noble continues the story of her work in Vietnam, and describes her more recent campaign for children's rights in Mongolia.

Philip Rawson *The Art of Southeast Asia* Thames & Hudson. In this attractive glossy volume, crammed with colour plates, Vietnam is represented by chapters on Indochina and Champa.

Vietnam on film

Gilbert Adair *Hollywood's Vietnam: From the Green Berets to Full Metal Jacket* (o/p). Adair's excitable prose guides you past the fire-fights, f-words and R&R hijinks, to a real appreciation of how Hollywood reflected shifting American attitudes to the war.

Jeremy Devine *Vietnam at 24 Frames a Second* University of Texas Press. The most wide-ranging analysis of Vietnam movies, covering more than 400 films.

Linda Dittmar and Gene Michaud (eds.) *From Hanoi to Hollywood* Rutgers University Press. Collected essays on the way the American War encroached on Hollywood.

Natural history and ecology

Elizabeth Kemf *Month of Pure Light* The Women's Press. One of very few accounts looking at the long-term environmental impact of the American War and the subsequent "re-greening" of Vietnam. Written as a travelogue rather than a scientific survey, with an optimistic message of rebirth underscored by a personal story of renewal.

Craig Robson *A Field Guide to Birds of South East Asia* New Holland Publishers. Seminal study of the region's ornithological diversity.

Vietnam in the movies

The embroilment of France and the US in Vietnam and its conflicts has spawned hundreds of movies, ranging from fond soft-focused colonial reminiscences, to blood-and-guts depictions of the horrors of war. As a means of brushing up on your Indochinese history, their value is questionable: for the most part, they're hardly objective. Yet, through the reflections they cast of the climates in which they were created, these films amplify the West's efforts to come to terms with what went on there, and for this reason they demand attention.

Early depictions

Hollywood was setting movies in Indochina long before the first American troops splashed ashore at Da Nang. As early as 1932, Jean Harlow played a sassy Saigon prostitute to smouldering Clark Gable's rubber-plantation manager, in the steamy pot-boiler, **Red Dust**. At this early stage, however, Vietnam was no more than an exotic backdrop.

Even by the mid-1950s, as the modest beginnings of American involvement elicited from Hollywood its first real moves to acquaint itself with Vietnam, the country was often treated less as a nation with its own discernible identity and unique set of political issues, and more as a generic Asian theatre of war, in which the righteous **battle against communism** could be played out. In its portrayal of noble and libertarian French forces, aided by American military specialists, confronting the evil of communism, **China Gate** (1957) is an early example of this trend. Dedicated to the French *colons* who "advanced this backward society to its place as the rice bowl of Asia", its laboured plot, concerning an attempt to destroy a Viet Minh arms cache, is of much less interest than its heavy-handed politics.

Vietnam provided Hollywood with a golden opportunity to project its militaristic fantasies, and a chance to tap into the prejudices brought to the surface by more than a decade of anti-Japanese World War II movies – prejudices that painted American involvement as a reprise of past battles with the inscrutable **Asian hordes**. Rather more depth of thought went into the making of **The Quiet American** (1958), in which Michael Redgrave played the British journalist and cynic, Fowler, while Audie Murphy (America's most decorated soldier in World War II) played Pyle, the eponymous "hero" of Graham Greene's novel. To Greene's chagrin, Pyle was depicted not as a representative of the American government, but of a private aid organization – something which the author felt blunted his anti-American message; nevertheless, the movie retained its source's sense of the futility of attempting to make sense of Vietnam's political quagmire.

Gung ho!

The military mandarins who led America into war failed to get the message, though: with American troops duly deployed in a far-flung corner of the globe by 1965, it was only a matter of time before **John Wayne** produced a patriotic movie to match. This came in the form of the monumentally bad **The Green Berets** (1968), in which a paunchy Wayne starred as "Big" Bill Kirby, a lovable colonel leading an adoring team of American soldiers into the central highlands. That Wayne, while on a promotional trip out to Vietnam, handed out cigarette cases inscribed with his signature and the message "Fuck communism", speaks volumes about the film's subtlety. Kicking off with a stirring marching song ("Fighting soldiers from the sky, Fearless men who jump and die..."), the movie depicts American soldiers in spotless uniforms and perma-grins fighting against no less a threat than total "Communist domination of the world", yet still abiding, as the critic Gilbert Adair has it, "by Queensberry rules". In stark contrast to the squeaky-clean GIs are the barbaric Viet Cong, depicted as child-abusing rapists who whoop and holler like madmen as they overrun a US camp, all to the strains of suitably eerie Oriental music.

Sweeping Vietnam under the carpet

The war in Vietnam was a much dirtier affair than *The Green Berets* made it seem, its politics far less cut and dry. As the struggle turned into tragedy and popular support for it soured, movie moguls sensed that the war had become **taboo**. "Vietnam is awkward," said the journalist, Michael Herr, "...and if people don't even want to hear about it, you know they're not going to pay money to sit there in the dark and have it brought up." It was to be a full decade before another major combat movie was released. Instead, film-makers trained their gaze upon returning Vietnam veterans' doomed attempts to ease back into society. The resulting pictures were low in compassion: America's national pride had been collectively compromised by the failure to bring home a victory, and sympathy and forgiveness were at a premium.

A raft of **exploitation movies** was churned out, boasting names such as *Born Losers* (1967), *Angels from Hell* (1968) and *The Ravager* (1970), in which the mental scars of Vietnam provided topical window-dressing to improbable tales of martial arts, motorbikes and mayhem. At best, vets were treated as dysfunctional vigilantes acting beyond the pale of society – most famously in **Taxi Driver** (1976), which has Robert De Niro's disturbed insomniac returnee, Travis Bickle, embarking on a one-man moral crusade to purge the streets of a hellish New York. At worst, they were wacko misfits posing a threat to small-town America. With veterans being portrayed as anything but heroes, it was left to the stars of the **campus riot movies**, and films lionizing **draft-dodgers**, to provide role models.

Coming to terms with the war

Only in **1978** did Hollywood finally pluck up courage enough to confront the war head-on, and so aid the nation's healing process – **movies-as-therapy**. In the years since John Wayne's *Green Berets* had battened down the hatches against communism, America had first lost sight of justification for the war, and then effectively lost the war itself. Movies no longer sought to make sense of past events, but to highlight their futility; for the generation of young Americans unfortunate enough to live through Vietnam, mere survival was seen as triumph enough. As audiences were exposed to their first dramatized glimpses of the war's unpalatable realities, they were confronted by disaffected troops seeking comfort in prostitution and drug abuse, along with far more shocking examples of soldiers' fraying moral fibre.

Such themes were woven through the first of the four movies of note released in 1978, **The Boys in Company C**, which follows a band of young draftees through their basic training stateside, and then into action. In one particularly telling scene, American lives are lost transporting what turns out to be whisky and cigarettes to the front. A similar futility underpins **Go Tell the Spartans**, in which Burt Lancaster's drug- and alcohol-hazed troops take, and then abandon, a camp – an idea reused nine years later in *Hamburger Hill*.

Coming Home (1978), which cast Jane Fonda as a military career-man's wife who falls in love with a wheelchair-bound veteran (Jon Voight), was significant for its sensitive consideration of the emotional and physical tolls exacted by the war, and initiated the trend for more measured and intelligent vet movies.

Similarly concerned with the ramifications of the war, both home and away, was **The Deer Hunter**, in which the conscription of three friends fractures their Russian orthodox community in Pennsylvania. The friends' "one-shot" code of honour, espoused on a last pre-Vietnam hunting trip, contrasts wildly with the moral vacuum of the war, whose random brutality is embodied in the movie's central scenes of Russian roulette. The picture's ending, with its melancholy rendition of *God Bless America* by the central characters, is only semi-ironic, and alludes to the country's regenerative process. For all its power, *The Deer Hunter* is marred by overt racist stereotyping of the Vietnamese who, according to John Pilger, are dismissed as "sub-human Oriental barbarians and idiots". The Vietnamese we see are grotesque caricatures interested only in getting their kicks from gambling and death, and there's a strong sense that American youths ought never to have been exposed to such primordial evil as existed across the Pacific.

Francis Ford Coppola's hugely indulgent but visually magnificent **Apocalypse Now** (1979) rounded off the vanguard of postwar Vietnam combat movies. Described by one critic as "Film as opera … it turns Vietnam into a vast trip, into a War of the Imagination", the picture's Dantean snapshots of the war rob Vietnam of all identity other than as a "heart of darkness". Fuelled by his desire to convey the "horror, the madness, the sensuousness, and the moral dilemma of the Vietnam war", Coppola totally mythologizes the conflict, rendering it not so much futile as insane. The usual elements of needless death, casual atrocity, moral decline and spaced-out soldiers leaning heavily on substance abuse are all here, played out against a raunchy soundtrack. However, with its stylized representation of *montagnards* as generic savages deifying Westerners, and its depiction of the Viet Cong as butchers who happily lop the arms off children who have had "American" inoculations, *Apocalypse Now* is little more enlightened than *The Deer Hunter*. Coppola subsequently compared the creation of the film itself to a war: "We were in the jungle, there were too many of us. We had access to too much money and too much equipment and little by little we went insane" – a process graphically depicted in **Hearts of Darkness: A Filmmaker's Apocalypse** (1991).

Returning home

The precedent set by *Coming Home* of sympathetic consideration for **returning veterans'** mindsets spurred many movies along similar lines in subsequent years. These focused on the disillusionment and disorientation felt by soldiers coming back, not to heroes' welcomes, but to indifference and even disdain.

One of the first of these movies was **First Blood** (1982), which introduced audiences to Sly Stallone's muscle-bound super-vet, John Rambo. As we witness Rambo's torment in small-town America, the picture is more "shoot 'em up" than cerebral. Yet its climax, in which Rambo's former colonel becomes a surrogate father figure to him, underscores the tender ages of the troops who fought the war. Other movies of the genre – among them Alan Parker's **Birdy** (1984) and Oliver Stone's **Born on the 4th of July** (1989) – reiterated the message of stolen youth and innocence by screening idyllic, elegiac scenes of childhood. Stone has his hero (played by Tom Cruise) swallowing the anti-communist line, and returning to an indifference symbolized by the squalor of the army hospital in which he recuperates and by the breakdown of his relationship with his mother. In *Birdy*, doctors at a loss as to how to treat a catatonic patient turn to a fellow vet for help – this sense of America's inability to relate to returnees subsequently resurfaces in **Jacknife** (1989).

Rewriting history

Not content with squaring up to the war in Vietnam, Hollywood during the 1980s attempted, bizarrely, to rewrite its script, in a series of **revisionist movies**. Richard Gere had made the armed forces hip again in 1982's weepie **An Officer and a Gentleman**; and a year later the first of an intriguing sub-genre of films hit cinemas, in which Americans returned to Vietnam, invariably to rescue MIAs, and "won". Given a righteous cause (and what could be more righteous than rescuing fellow soldiers), and freed from the chains of moral degradation that had shackled him in previous movies, the US soldier could now show his true mettle. In stark contrast to the comic-book superhuman Americans of these pictures, are the brainless **Vietnamese**, who appear only as cannon fodder.

Uncommon Valor (1983), a rather silly piece about an MIA rescue starring Gene Hackman, kicked things off, closely followed by **Missing in Action** (1983), in which Chuck Norris, the poor man's Stallone, karate-kicks his way towards the same resolution with sufficient panache to justify a speedy follow-up. The mother of them all, though, was **Rambo: First Blood, Part II** (1985), in which the hero of *First Blood* gets to settle some old scores. "Do we get to win this time?" asks Rambo, at the top of the movie. As he riots through the Vietnamese countryside in order to extricate a band of American PoWs, he answers his own question by slaying Vietnamese foes at an approximate rate of one every two minutes.

"It don't mean nothing"

The backlash to the patent nonsense of the revisionist films came in the form of a series of shockingly realistic movies which attempted, in the words of the director Oliver Stone, to "peel the onion" and reveal the **real Vietnam**, routine atrocities, indiscipline and all. There are no heroes in these GI's-view movies, only fragile, confused-looking young men in fatigues, emphasizing that this was a war that affected a whole generation – not just its most photogenic individuals.

In **Platoon** (1986), Oliver Stone, himself a foot soldier in Vietnam, created the most realistic cinematographic interpretation of the American involvement yet. Filmed on location in the Philippines, this movie reminded audiences that killing gooks wasn't as straightforward as Rambo made it seem. As well as portraying the depths to which humankind can sink, Stone shows the circumstances under which it was feasible for young American boys to become murderers of civilians. Its oppressive sensory overload powerfully conjures the paranoiac near-hysteria spawned by fear, confusion, loss of motivation and inability to discriminate between friend and foe. Inherent in its shadowy, half-seen portrayal of the enemy is a grudging respect for their expertise in jungle warfare.

If *Platoon* portrays a dirty war, in **Hamburger Hill** (1987), which dramatizes the taking of Ap Bia hill during May 1969's battle for the A Shau Valley, it has degenerated into a positive mud bath. As troops slither and slide on the flanks of the hill in the highland mists, they become indistinguishable, and the image of an entire generation stumbling towards the maws of death is strengthened by the fact that the cast includes no big-name actors – the men who fall on the hill are neighbours, sons or brothers, not film stars. American losses are taken in order to secure a useless hill, a potent symbol of the futility of America's involvement in the war; as one soldier says, time after time, in a weary mantra, "it don't mean nothing, not a thing". Stanley Kubrick's **Full Metal Jacket** (1987) picks up *Hamburger Hill's* theme of the war's theft of American youth in its opening scene, as the camp barber strips conscripts of their hair and, by implication, their individuality. A brutal drill-sergeant completes the alienation process by replacing the soldiers' names with nicknames of his choosing, and then sets about expunging their humanity – on the grounds that it will only hamper them when they experience firsthand the insanity of the war. However, as US troops plod wearily through a smouldering Hué in the movie's final scene, the usual macho marching tunes are replaced with a plaintive echo of youth: "Who's the leader of the club that's made for you and me, M-I-C, K-E-Y, M-O-U-S-E".

A different perspective

French cinema only began to tackle the subject of Vietnam in the 1990s. If in **Dien Bien Phu** (1992) it confronted its own ghosts, on the whole its output has been limited to visually captivating colonial whimsies, to which the Vietnamese setting merely adds an exotic tang. For example, **The Lover** (1992) works not because it does justice to Marguerite Duras's poignant rites-of-passage novella, but because its extended interludes of heaving flesh are cloaked with a veneer of Oriental mystique created by location filming in Ho Chi Minh City and Sa Dec. **Indochine** (1993) starts off in similarly rose-tinted fashion amid the seductively rarefied atmosphere of a French colonial rubber plantation, and from there it veers off to take full advantage of the romantic possibilities of Ha Long Bay.

Even **The Scent of Green Papaya** (1993), filmed entirely in Paris by French-Vietnamese director Tran Anh Hung, is a fondly nostalgic period piece in which the East's languorous elegance and beauty are shown, minus its squalor, and nothing of import is said about the war experience. Tran Anh Hung's second film, *Cyclo* (1996), is an altogether different matter, a grimy tale of murder and prostitution set in a bleak rendition of Ho Chi Minh City – so bleak that the film is banned in Vietnam. Nevertheless, Tran Anh Hung obtained permission to shoot his latest offering, **At the Height of Summer** (2000), on location in Hanoi. It's a gentler film with the same languid, dreamlike quality of *Cyclo*, in which three sisters prepare to commemorate their parents' deaths. As they do so, the dark secrets lying beneath the mask of middle-class respectability are gradually revealed. The censors lightened up a little more in allowing Vietnamese director Dang Nhat Minh to make his groundbreaking **The Season of Guavas** (2001), which deals with the extremely sensitive issue of 1950s communist land reforms – the film, however, has yet to be released in Vietnam. Other **Vietnamese directors** beginning to attract an international audience include Tran Van Thuy (*Sand Life*, 2000), Bui Thac Chuyen (*Course de Nuit*, 2000), and Le Hoang (*The Long Journey*, 1996; *Bar Girls*, 2003).

In Hollywood's output, Vietnamese people have mostly been noticeable by their absence, or through the filter of blatant stereotyping … only Americans suffered during the struggle. **Heaven and Earth** (1993), the final part of Oliver Stone's Vietnam trilogy, went some way towards rectifying this imbalance. Its depiction of a Vietnamese girl's odyssey (based on the life of Le Ly Hayslip; see p.550 and p.554), from idyllic early childhood to the traumas of life as a wife in San Diego, symbolizes the trials and tribulations of the country as a whole, and acts as a timely reminder that not only Americans suffered during the struggle. Almost a decade later, Randall Wallace brings a certain impartiality to **We Were Soldiers** (2002), his adaptation of Lt Col Hall Moore and Joe Galloway's blow-by-blow account of the catastrophic battle of Ia Drang (see p.555) with Mel Gibson as the caring commander. Not that it met with Vietnamese approval: the government banned the film, saying it distorted Vietnamese history, and branded actor Don Duong a "traitor" for his portrayal of the NVA leader pitting his wits – and his men – against the Americans.

Only in the late 1990s were American movie-makers allowed to shoot on location in Vietnam again. Filmed in Ho Chi Minh City, **Three Seasons** (1999) was directed by Vietnamese-Californian Tony Bui, and features Harvey Keitel at the head of a predominantly local cast. It provides a lyrical and graceful portrayal of a city trying to come terms with the return of the West – personified by an ex-marine (Keitel) looking for the Amerasian daughter he abandoned decades before. The film doesn't dwell upon the war – the state censors on set during filming made sure of that. Nevertheless, by focusing upon the disenfranchised prostitutes, cyclo drivers and street children of the city, it ensures that the conflict's ravages are implicit.

However, it took until the new millennium for a big-budget Hollywood movie to be filmed almost entirely in Vietnam. Philip Noyce's atmospheric remake of **The Quiet American** (2002) sticks much closer to Graham Greene's novel in its indictment of American involvement in Vietnam. This, coupled with its portrayal of the Vietnamese struggle as a patriotic fight against colonial oppression, earned the film official approval, allowing it to be screened widely within Vietnam – a first for a major Hollywood production.

Some to look out for...

Apocalypse Now 1979. Vietnam becomes one long trip in this all-powerful picture in which Martin Sheen is dispatched upriver towards the Cambodian border to assassinate Kurtz (played by Marlon Brando), an American colonel who, destabilized by the horrors of the war, has set himself up as leader of a tribe of *montagnards*. In *Apocalypse Now Redux* (2000) director Francis Ford Coppola reinstated nearly one hour of footage – fascinating for film buffs, though the original remains the better film.

Birdy 1984. When post-traumatic stress leads Birdy (Matthew Modine) to believe he's one of the birds of which he was so fond as a child, his buddy Al (Nicolas Cage) is called in to try to snap him out of his spell and coax him back into the real world.

Born on the 4th of July 1989. Having skipped off to war head-full of anti-communist ideals, Ron Kovic (Tom Cruise) returns home having lost the use of his legs, and taken the life of a fellow American in a friendly-fire incident. Oliver Stone's rendering of his tortuous passage through guilt, confession, redemption and finally regeneration is harrowing and affecting.

Coming Home 1978. A career soldier's departure for Vietnam leaves his wife with time on her hands to help out at a local hospital. There she meets a paraplegic veteran played by Jon Voight, and commences a love affair that wildly alters life for all three of them.

Cyclo 1996. An impoverished cyclo driver working Ho Chi Minh City's mean streets takes to a life of crime to supplement his income. Made by the same director as *The Scent of Green Papaya*, though a world away from it in style and content.

Dear America: Letters Home from America 1987. Enormously moving documentary in which readings from soldiers' correspondence home are intercut with contemporary footage of the war.

The Deer Hunter 1978. Three friends from the same steel town in Pennsylvania are captured by Viet Cong and forced to play Russian roulette. One is terribly wounded in the ensuing escape and returns home in a wheelchair; another (played by Christopher Walken) continues to dice with death in Saigon; and the third, played by Robert De Niro, returns to rescue him.

Dien Bien Phu 1992. Tens of thousands of Vietnamese extras see to it that this epic reconstruction of France's darkest Indochinese hour impresses. Director Pierre Schoendoerffer, himself a veteran of Dien Bien Phu, intercuts the battle scenes with depictions of the last days of colonial Hanoi.

First Blood 1982. Ignoring a small-town sheriff's order to leave ironically named Hope lands Vietnam vet John Rambo in prison; there, ill-treatment induces a Vietnam flashback, a jailbreak and a gripping manhunt in which Rambo's jungle-warfare training pays dividends.

Full Metal Jacket 1987. A film of two halves, and gripping from start to finish. The first half showcases the brutality of an American army boot camp and its tragic effect on an overweight conscript; the second focuses on an in-country unit's attempts to neutralize a sniper.

Good Morning Vietnam 1987. Robin Williams shines as a military DJ who ruffles feathers by trying to enliven broadcasts and so heighten morale; the movie is little more than a vehicle for his hilarious monologues – pleasing, but ultimately lightweight.

Hamburger Hill 1987. Powerful, unremittingly depressing dramatization of the taking of Ap Bia hill in the A Shau Valley (see p.501).

Heaven and Earth 1993. By following a young Vietnamese girl on her personal odyssey from childhood in a village near Da Nang, through prostitution, to married life in America, this film concerns itself with the war's rending of the physical, social and spiritual fabric of Vietnamese family life.

Indochine 1993. Cathérine Deneuve as a plantation owner whose lover (a naval officer) falls for her adopted Vietnamese daughter. With the lover's posting in Tonkin and the daughter's flight after him, the movie shifts to Ha Long Bay. Visually sumptuous.

Jacknife 1989. Robert De Niro again, this time turning in a typically fine performance as Vietnam veteran Megs, whose blossoming relationship with the sister of wartime buddy Dave sprouts tensions that say much about the loneliness of veterans.

The Lover 1992. Steamy interpretation of Marguerite Duras's novella, in which a young French girl living in the Mekong Delta enters into a passionate affair with a wealthy Chinese from Cholon. The story of her sexual awakening and its repercussions is told through the melancholy narrative of the girl herself, now grown up.

Platoon 1986. Life on patrol as described in the letters home of wide-eyed new boy, Chris (Charlie Sheen), whose platoon is torn in two by its divided allegiance to sergeants Barnes (Tom Berenger) and Elias (Willem Dafoe), symbolizing the dark and light, the animal and human, sides of American involvement in Vietnam.

The Quiet American 1958. During the final days of colonial Saigon, a young American's naive vision of ending the war by arming a "third force" has disastrous results. Graham Greene disapproved of this version of his famed Vietnam novel, but it's lent a wonderful glaze of authenticity by the location shooting in Saigon.

The Quiet American 2002. Philip Noyce gives a more faithful rendering of Greene's book in this beautifully crafted remake starring Michael Caine as the world-weary British journalist who learns that it's impossible to stand on the sidelines, and Brendan Fraser as the meddling CIA agent. Noyce captures vividly the decadence and desperation of the last days of French rule.

Rambo: First Blood, Part II 1985. *First Blood*'s John Rambo again, this time single-handedly hauling a band of MIAs out of their jungle captivity and to safety – and blowing away a staggering number of Vietnamese in the process.

The Scent of Green Papaya 1993. A country girl called Mui is sent to work as servant to a Saigon family, and soon develops an unspoken love for the son of the house; years later, she keeps house for him. A dignified and nostalgic glance back at a Saigon before the Americans.

Taxi Driver 1976. Hollywood's most famous veteran (barring John Rambo), insomniac cabbie and angst-ridden social misfit Travis Bickle (Robert De Niro) turns moral crusader, with a mission to "wash all the scum off the streets".

Three Seasons 1999. A beautiful snapshot of contemporary Ho Chi Minh City, *Three Seasons* tells the interweaving stories of an ex-marine, a street kid, a cyclo driver, a prostitute and a flower-seller.

Language

Language

Language

L inguists are uncertain as to the exact roots of Vietnamese, though the language betrays Thai, Khmer and Chinese influences. A tonal language, it's extremely tricky for Westerners to master, though the phrases below should help you get by. English superseded Russian as *the* language to learn following the sweeping changes of *doi moi*, and you'll generally find that Vietnamese isn't called for. Then again, nothing will endear you to locals as much as showing conversational willingness.

Vietnamese was set down using Chinese characters until the fourteenth century, when an indigenous **script** called *chu nom* was created. This, in turn, was dropped in favour of *quoc ngu*, a Romanized script developed by a French missionary in the seventeenth century, and it's this form that's universally used today – though you'll still occasionally spot lavish *chu nom* characters daubed on the walls of more venerable pagodas and temples.

Three main **dialects** – northern, central and southern – are used in Vietnam today, and although for the most part they are pretty similar, pronunciation can be so wildly variant that some locals have trouble understanding each other; in the words and phrases listed below, we indicate important differences between variants used in the north and south. Bear in mind, too, that Vietnam's minority peoples have their own languages, and may look blankly at you as you gamely try out your Vietnamese on them.

If you want more scope than the expressions below allow, invest in a **phrasebook**. *Vietnamese: A Rough Guide Phrasebook* is the last word in user-friendly phrasebooks, combining everyday phrases and expressions with a dictionary section and menu reader, all with phonetic transliterations. Otherwise, you should have no trouble picking up a copy of the Hanoi Foreign Languages Publishing House's *Speak Vietnamese* in either Hanoi or Ho Chi Minh City. The same applies to the *Tu Dien Anh–Viet* or *English–Vietnamese Dictionary*, though if you can find it go for the excellent **dictionary** compiled by Nguyen Dinh Hoa. If you're determined to master the basics of spoken Vietnamese, there are a number of **self-teaching packs** on the market, such as *Language '30* produced by Audio-Forum (⊛www.microworld.ndirect.co.uk).

Pronunciation

The Vietnamese language is a **tonal** one, that is, one in which a word's meaning is determined by the pitch at which you deliver it. Six tones are used – the mid-level tone (syllables with no marker), the low falling tone (syllables marked à), the low rising tone (syllables marked ả), the high broken tone (syllables marked ã), the high rising tone (syllables marked á) and the low broken tone (syllables marked ạ) – though you'll probably remain in the dark until you ask a Vietnamese person to give you spoken examples of each of them. Depending upon its tone, the word *ba*, for instance, can mean three, grandmother, poisoned food, waste, aunt or any – leaving ample scope for misunderstandings and diplomatic faux pas.

With tones accomplished, or at least comprehended, there are the many vowel and consonant sounds to take on board. These we've listed below, along with phonetic renderings of how they should be pronounced.

Vowels

a	'a' as in father	o	'o' as in hot
ă	'u' as in hut (slight 'u' as in unstressed English 'a')	ô	'aw' as in awe
â	'uh' sound as above only longer	ơ	'ur' as in fur
e	'e' as in bed	u	'oo' as in boo
ê	'ay' as in pay	ư	'oo' closest to French 'u'
i	'i' as in -ing	y	'i' as in -ing

Vowel combinations

ai	'ai' as in Thai	oe	'weh'
ao	'ao' as in Mao	ôi	'oy'
au	'a-oo'	ơi	'uh-i'
âu	'oh' as in oh!	ua	'waw'
ay	'ay' as in hay	uê	'weh'
ây	'ay-i' (as in 'ay' above but longer)	uô	'waw'
eo	'eh-ao'	uy	'wee'
êu	'ay-oo'	ưa	'oo-a'
iu	'ew' as in few	ưu	'er-oo'
iêu	'i-yoh'	ươi	'oo-uh-i'
oa	'wa'		

Consonants

c	'g'	ng/ngh	'ng' as in sing
ch	'j' as in jar	nh	'n-y' as in canyon
d	'y' as in young	ph	'f'
d-	'd' as in day	q	'g' as in goat
g	'g' as in goat	t	'd' as in day
gh	'g' as in goat	th	't'
gi	'y' as in young	tr	'j' as in jar
k	'g' as in goat	x	's'
kh	'k' as in keep		

Useful words and phrases

How you greet and then speak to somebody in Vietnam depends very much on their sex, and on their age and social standing, relative to your own. As a general rule of thumb, if you address a man as *ông*, and a woman as *bà*, you can be sure you aren't being impolite. If you find yourself in conversation, either formally or informally, with someone of your approximate age, you can use *anh* (for a man) and *chi* (for a woman). You can also use the same formula to address someone when you know their name. Vietnamese names are traditionally written with the family name first (Nguyen, Tran, Le and Pham are among the most common) and the given name last and between them a qualifying name, which often indicates a person's sex or the particular branch of the family to which they belong. People are usually referred to by their given name so, for example, you would address an older man called Nguyen Van Hai as Ong Hai.

Greetings and small talk

Hello	chào ông/bà	My name is...	tên tôi là...
How are you?	ông/bà có khỏe không?	Where do you come from?	ông/bà ở đâu đến?
Fine, thanks	tôi khỏe cám ơn	I come from…	tôi ở…
Pleased to meet you	hân hạnh gặp ông/bà	…England	…nước Anh
		…America	…nước Mỹ
Goodbye	chào, tạm biệt	…Australia	…nước Úc
Good night	chúc ngủ ngon	What do you do?	ông/bà làm gì?
Excuse me (to say sorry)	xin lỗi	Do you speak English?	ông/bà biết nói tiếng Anh không?
Excuse me (to get past)	xin ông/bà thứ lỗi		
Please	làm ơn	I don't understand	tôi không hiểu
Thank you	cám ơn ông/bà	Could you repeat that?	xin ông/bà lập lại?
Thank you very much	cám ơn nhiều	Yes	vâng (north); dạ (south)
Don't mention it	không có chi		
What's your name?	ông/bà tên gì?	No	không

Emergencies

Can you help me?	ông/bà có thể giúp tôi không?	Please call a doctor	làm ơn gọi bác sĩ
		hospital	bệnh viện
There's been an accident	có một vụ tai nạn	police station	đon cong an

Getting around

Where is the...?	ở đâu…?	ticket	vé
How many kilometres is it to…?	bao nhiêu cây số thì để…?	aeroplane	máy bay
		airport	sân bay
How do I get to…?	tôi phải đi…bằng cách nào?	boat	tàu bè
		bus	xe buýt
We'd like to go to...	chúng tôi muốn đi…	bus station	bến xe buýt
To the airport, please	làm ơn đưa tôi đi sân bay	train station	bến xe lửa
		taxi	tắc xi
Can you take me to the...?	ông/bà có thể đưa tôi đi…?	car	xe hơi
		filling station	trạm xăng
Where do we catch the bus to…?	ở đâu đón xe đi…?	bicycle	xe đạp
		baggage	hành lý
When does the bus for Hoi An leave?	khi nào xe Hội An chạy?	bank	nhà băng
		post office	sổ bưu điện
Can I book a seat?	tôi có thể đặt ghế trước không?	passport	hộ chiếu
How long does it take?	phải tốn bao lâu?	hotel	khách sạn

restaurant	nhà hàng	north	phía bắc
Please stop here	xin dừng lại đây	south	phía nam
over there	bên kia	east	phía đông
here	đây	west	phía tây
left/right	bên trái/bên phải		

Accommodation and shopping

Do you have any rooms?	ông/bà có phòng không?	room with a private bathroom	một phòng tắm riêng
How much is it per night?	mỗi đêm bao nhiêu?	cheap/expensive	rẻ/đắt
How much is it?	bao nhiêu tiền?	single room	phòng một người
How much does it cost?	cái này giá bao nhiêu?	double room	phòng hai người
		single bed	giường một người
Can I have a look?	xem có được không?	double bed	giường đôi
Do you have...?	ông/bà có không...?	air-conditioner	máy lạnh
I want a...	tôi muốn một...	fan (electric)	quạt máy
I'd like...	cho tôi xin một...	mosquito net	cái màn
How much is this?	cái này bao nhiêu?	toilet paper	giấy vệ sinh
That's too expensive	đắt quá	telephone	điện thoại
Do you have anything cheaper?	ông/bà còn gì rẻ hơn không?	laundry	quần áo dơ
		blanket	chăn (north); mền (south)
Could I have the bill please?	làm ơn tính tiền?	open/closed	mở cửa/đóng cửa
room with a balcony	một phòng có bao lơn		

Time

What's the time?	mấy giờ rồi?	tomorrow	mai
noon	buổi trưa	yesterday	hôm qua
midnight	nửa đêm	now	bây giờ
minute	phút	next week	tuần tới
hour	giờ	last week	tuần vừa qua
day	ngày	morning	buổi sáng
week	tuần	afternoon	buổi chiều
month	tháng	evening	buổi tối
year	năm	night	ban đêm
today	hôm nay		

Numbers

Note that for numbers ending in 5, from 15 onwards, *lăm* is used in northern Vietnam and *nhăm* in the south, rather than the written form of *năm*. Also, bear in mind that an alternative for numbers that are multiples of ten is *chục* – so, for example ten would be *một chục*, twenty would be *hai chục*, etc.

zero	không	four	bốn
one	một	five	năm
two	hai	six	sáu
three	ba	seven	bảy

eight	tám	nineteen	mười chín
nine	chín	twenty	hai mười
ten	mười	twenty-one	hai mười một
eleven	mười một	twenty-two	hai mười hai
twelve	mười hai	thirty	ba mười
thirteen	mười ba	forty	bốn mười
fourteen	mười bốn	fifty	năm mười
fifteen	mười lăm /nhăm	one hundred	một trăm
sixteen	mười sáu	two hundred	hai trăm
seventeen	mười bảy	one thousand	một ngàn
eighteen	mười tám	ten thousand	mười ngàn

Eating and drinking

Useful phrases

bat (north); chen (south)	bowl	dua	chopsticks
bao nhieu tien?	how much is it?	it duong	a little sugar
can chen (north); can ly (south)	cheers!	lanh	cold
		nguoi an chay	vegetarian
chuc suc khoe	to your good health	toi khong an thit	I don't eat meat or fish
cop	cup		
da	ice	nong	hot
dung bo da cam on	no ice, thanks	rat ngon	delicious

Rice and noodles

bun	round rice noodles	com trang	steamed or boiled rice
bun bo	beef with bun noodles	chao or xhao	rice porridge
bun bo gio heo	chicken, beef and pork with bun noodles	mi xao	fried noodles
		pho	flat rice noodles, usually in soup
bun ga	chicken with bun noodles	pho bo tai	noodle soup with rare beef
com	cooked rice		
com rang (north); com chien (south)	fried rice	pho bo chin	with medium-done beef
		pho co trung	with eggs

Fish, meat and vegetables

ca	fish	thit	meat
ca ran (north); ca chien (south)	fried fish	bit tet	beefsteak
		bo	beef
cua	crab	ga	chicken
luon	eel	lon (north); heo (south)	pork
muc	squid	vit	duck
tom	shrimp or prawn	rau co or rau cac loai	vegetables
tom hum	lobster	cai bap	cabbage

ca chua	tomato	mang	bamboo shoots
ca tim	aubergine	ngo (north); bap (south)	sweetcorn
dau	beans	rau xao cac loai	stir-fried vegetables
gia	bean sprouts	sa lat	salad
khoai tay	potato	sa lat ca chua	tomato salad
khoai lang	sweet potato	sa lat rau xanh cac loai	green salad

Desserts and fruit

banh ngot	cakes and pastries	dua hau	watermelon
duong	sugar	du du	papaya
kem	ice cream or cream	khe	star fruit
mat ong	honey	mang cau (north); qua na (south)	custard apple
sua chua	yoghurt	mang cut	mangosteen
trai cay	fruit	mit	jackfruit
buoi	pomelo/grapefruit	nhan	longan
cam	orange	qua bo	avocado
chanh	lemon/lime	sau rieng	durian
chom chom	rambutan	soai	mango
chuoi	banana	tao tay	apple
dau tay	strawberry	thang long	dragon fruit
dua	coconut	vai	lychee
dua (north); thom (south)	pineapple		

Miscellaneous

banh	cake (sweet or savoury)	mut	jam
banh mi	bread	ot	chilli
bo	butter	tao pho (north); dau hu (south)	tofu
pho mat, fo mat or fromage	cheese	tieu	pepper
lac (north); dau phong (south)	peanuts (groundnuts)	trung	egg
		trung om let or op lep	omelette
muoi	salt	trung ran or trung op la	fried eggs

Drinks

bia	beer	ca phé sua	coffee with milk
ca phé	coffee	ca phé sua nong	hot milk coffee
ca phé da	iced coffee	tra	tea
ca phé den	black coffee	tra voi chanh	tea with lemon
ca phé den khong duong	black coffee without sugar	tra sua	tea with milk
ca phé nong	hot coffee	khong da	no ice
		nuoc	water

nuoc khoang	mineral water
nuoc so da	soda water
nuoc cam	orange juice
nuoc chanh	lime juice
nuoc dua	coconut milk
ruou ran	snake wine

ruou trang or choum	rice alcohol
so da cam	orange soda
so da chanh	lime soda
sua	milk
sua tuoi	fresh milk
sua ong tho	long-life milk

Glossaries

Words and abbreviations

Agent Orange Defoliant herbicide used by the Americans during the American War to deprive guerrillas of forest cover.

Annam ("Pacified South") A term coined by the Chinese to refer to their protectorate in northern Vietnam before 939 AD; the French later applied the name to the middle reaches of their protectorate, from the southern central highlands to the edge of the Red River Delta.

ao dai Traditional Vietnamese dress for women, comprising baggy pants and a long, slit tunic.

arhats Ascetic Buddhist saints, whose statues are found in northern pagodas.

ARVN (Army of the Republic of Vietnam) The army of South Vietnam.

ben xe Bus station.

Bo doi Northern soldiers.

boat people Ethnic Chinese who fled Vietnam by boat in the late 1970s to escape persecution at the hands of the communists.

bodhisattva An intermediary who has chosen to forgo Buddhist nirvana to work for the salvation of all humanity.

body count Term coined by the Americans to measure the success of a military operation, determined by the number of dead bodies after a battle.

bonze Buddhist monk.

buu dien Post office.

Cao Daism Indigenous religion, essentially a hybrid of Buddhism, Taoism and Confucianism, but hinged around an attempt at unification of all earthly codes of belief (see p.130).

Champa Indianized Hindu empire that held sway in much of the southern half of Vietnam until the late seventeenth century (see p.245).

cho Market.

chu nom Classic Vietnamese script, based upon Chinese.

chua Pagoda (Buddhist place of worship).

Cochinchina A Portuguese term adopted by the French colonial government for their southern administrative region.

colon French colonial expatriate.

cyclo Three-wheeled bicycle with a carriage on the front.

dao Island.

den Temple (Taoist or other non-Buddhist place of worship).

dinh Communal meeting hall.

DMZ ("dee-em-zee") The Demilitarized Zone along the Seventeenth Parallel, marking the border between North and South Vietnam.

doi moi Vietnam's economic restructuring.

DRV (Democratic Republic of Vietnam) The North Vietnamese state established by Ho Chi Minh following the August Revolution in 1945.

duong Avenue.

FULRO (United Front for the Liberation of Oppressed Races) An opposition movement formed by the ethnic minorities of the central highlands, demanding greater autonomy.

Funan Indianized empire, a forerunner of the great Khmer empires.

GI (General Infantryman) Soldier in the US Army.

gopuram Bank of sculpted deities over the entrance to a Hindu temple.

"grunt" American infantryman.

gui xe Bicycle compound.

hang Cave.

ho Lake.

Ho Chi Minh Trail Trail used first by the Viet Minh and later by the North Vietnamese Army to transport supplies to the South, via Laos and Cambodia.

Hoa Ethnic Chinese people living in Vietnam.

Honda om Literally "Honda embrace" – a motorbike taxi.

"Huey" Nickname given to American helicopter, the HU-1.

Indochina The region of Asia comprising Vietnam, Laos and Cambodia.

kalan Sanctuary in a Cham tower.

khach san Hotel.

Khmer Ethnic Cambodian.

kylin Mythical, dew-drinking animal (often translated as unicorn); a harbinger of peace.

Lien Xo Translating as "Soviet Union", this is used as a term of abuse – and may very occasionally be hurled at foreigners in more remote regions.

lingam A phallic statue representing Shiva, often seen in Cham towers.

mandapa Meditation hall in Cham temple complex.

MIAs (Missing in Action) Soldiers who fought – on both sides – in the American War, but have still not been accounted for.

montagnards French term for Vietnam's ethnic minority peoples.

mua roi nuoc Water-puppet show.

mui Cape.

mukha lingam Lingam fashioned into the likeness of a deity.

napalm Jellied fuel dropped by US forces during the American War, and capable of causing terrible burns.

ngo Alley.

nha hang Restaurant.

nha khach Hotel or guesthouse.

nha nghi Guesthouse.

nha tro Basic dormitory accommodation, usually found near stations.

NLF (National Liberation Front) Popular movement formed in South Vietnam in 1960 by opponents to the American-backed Southern regime.

nui Mountain.

nuoc mam Fish sauce.

NVA (North Vietnamese Army) The army of the Democratic Republic of Vietnam.

Oc Eo Ancient seaport of the Funan Empire, east of modern-day Rach Gia in the Mekong Delta.

ODP (Orderly Departure Programme) A United Nations-backed scheme enabling legal emigration of Vietnamese refugees.

paddy Unharvested rice.

PoW Prisoner of war.

quan District.

R&R ("Rest and Recreation") Term coined during the American War to describe a soldier's temporary leave of duty.

roi nuoc *see* mua roi nuoc.

rong Communal house of ethnic minorities in the central highlands.

RVN (Republic of Vietnam) The official name for South Vietnam from 1954 to 1976.

sampan Small, flat-bottomed boat.

song River.

SRVN (Socialist Republic of Vietnam) The post-liberation amalgamation of the DRV and RVN, and the official name of modern Vietnam.

tai chi Chinese martial art, commonly performed as early-morning exercise.

Tet Vietnam's Lunar New Year.

thung chai Coracles.

Tonkin The third administrative region of French colonial Vietnam, from Ninh Binh northwards.

tunnel rats American soldiers trained for warfare in tunnels such as those at Cu Chi.

VC (Viet Cong) Literally "Vietnamese communists"; used to describe the guerrilla forces of the NLF.

Viet Kieu Overseas Vietnamese.

Viet Minh Shortened version of **Viet Nam Doc Lap Dong Minh**, the League for the Independence of Vietnam, established by Ho Chi Minh in 1941.

VNQDD Abbreviation for **Viet Nam Quoc Dan Dang**, the Vietnam Nationalist Party, founded in 1927.

xe lam Motorized three-wheeler buggy carrying numerous passengers.

xe om Northern equivalent of the Honda om, a motorbike taxi.

Street names

In travelling around Vietnam, it doesn't take long before you can recite the **street names**, a litany of the principal characters in Vietnamese history. Just a few from this cast list of famous revolutionaries, Party leaders, legendary kings and peasant heroes are given below. Other favoured names commemorate the glorious victories of Bach Dang and Dien Bien Phu, and the momentous date when Saigon was "liberated" in 1975: 30 Thang 4 (30 April).

Hai Ba Trung The two Trung sisters led a popular uprising against the Chinese occupying army in 40 AD and established a short-lived kingdom (see p.483).

Hoang Hoa Tham (or De Tham) Famous pirate with a Robin Hood reputation and anti-French tendencies, assassinated in 1913.

Hung Vuong The semi-mythological Hung kings ruled an embryonic kingdom, Van Lang, around 2000 BC.

Le Duan General Secretary of the Communist Party, 1960–86.

Le Hong Phong Leading communist and patriot who died from torture in Poulo Condore prison (Con Son Island) in 1942.

Le Loi One of the most revered Vietnamese heroes, Le Loi defeated the Ming Chinese in 1427, and then ruled as King Le Thai To.

Ngo Quyen First ruler of an independent Vietnam following his defeat of the Chinese armies in 938 AD (see p.485).

Nguyen Hue Middle member of the three Nguyen brothers who led the Tay Son rebellion in the 1770s (see p.488), and then ruled briefly as Emperor Quang Trung.

Nguyen Thai Hoc Founding member of the Vietnam Nationalist Party (VNQDD), executed in 1930 following the disastrous Yen Bai uprising (see p.491).

Nguyen Thi Minh Khai Prominent anti-colonialist revolutionary of the 1930s, the wife of Le Hong Phong (see above) and sister-in-law of General Giap.

Nguyen Trai Brilliant strategist who helped mastermind Le Loi's victories over the Chinese. His ideas on the popular struggle ("it is better to conquer hearts than citadels") were used to good effect by Northern leaders in the French and American wars.

Pham Ngu Lao General in the army of Tran Hung Dao (see below).

Phan Boi Chau Influential leader of the anti-colonial movement in the early twentieth century (see p.491).

Tran Hung Dao Thirteenth-century general who beat the Mongols twice in the space of four years, and reached the ripe old age of 87.

Tran Phu Founding member and first General Secretary of the Indochinese Communist Party (see p.491), he died in prison in 1931 at the age of 27.

Index

and small print

Index

Map entries are in colour

A Rough Guide to Rough Guides

In the summer of 1981, Mark Ellingham, a recent graduate from Bristol University, was travelling round Greece and couldn't find a guidebook that really met his needs. On the one hand there were the student guides, insistent on saving every last cent, and on the other the heavyweight cultural tomes whose authors seemed to have spent more time in a research library than lounging away the afternoon at a taverna or on the beach.

In a bid to avoid getting a job, Mark and a small group of writers set about creating their own guidebook. It was a guide to Greece that aimed to combine a journalistic approach to description with a thoroughly practical approach to travellers' needs – a guide that would incorporate culture, history and contemporary insights with a critical edge, together with up-to-date, value-for-money listings. Back in London, Mark and the team finished their Rough Guide, as they called it, and talked Routledge into publishing the book.

That first *Rough Guide to Greece*, published in 1982, was a student scheme that became a publishing phenomenon. The immediate success of the book – with numerous reprints and a Thomas Cook prize shortlisting – spawned a series that rapidly covered dozens of destinations. Rough Guides had a ready market among low-budget backpackers, but soon also acquired a much broader and older readership that relished Rough Guides' wit and inquisitiveness as much as their enthusiastic, critical approach. Everyone wants value for money, but not at any price.

Rough Guides soon began supplementing the "rougher" information about hostels and low-budget listings with the kind of detail on restaurants and quality hotels that independent-minded visitors on any budget might expect, whether on business in New York or trekking in Thailand.

These days the guides – distributed worldwide by the Penguin group – offer recommendations from shoestring to luxury and cover more than 200 destinations around the globe, including almost every country in the Americas and Europe, more than half of Africa and most of Asia and Australasia. Our ever-growing team of authors and photographers is spread all over the world, particularly in Europe, the USA and Australia.

In 1994, we published the *Rough Guide to World Music* and *Rough Guide to Classical Music*; and a year later the *Rough Guide to the Internet*. All three books have become benchmark titles in their fields – which encouraged us to expand into other areas of publishing, mainly around popular culture. Rough Guides now publish:

- Travel guides to more than 200 worldwide destinations
- Dictionary phrasebooks to 22 major languages
- History guides ranging from Ireland to Islam
- Maps printed on rip-proof and waterproof Polyart™ paper
- Music guides running the gamut from Opera to Elvis
- Restaurant guides to London, New York and San Francisco
- Reference books on topics as diverse as the Weather and Shakespeare
- Sports guides from Formula 1 to Man Utd
- Pop culture books from *Lord of the Rings* to Cult TV
- World Music CDs in association with World Music Network

Visit **www.roughguides.com** to see our latest publications.

SMALL PRINT

Rough Guide Credits

Text editor: Clifton Wilkinson, Geoff Hpward
Managing Director: Kevin Fitzgerald
Series editor: Mark Ellingham
Editorial: Martin Dunford, Jonathan Buckley, Kate Berens, Ann-Marie Shaw, Helena Smith, Olivia Swift, Ruth Blackmore, Geoff Howard, Claire Saunders, Gavin Thomas, Alexander Mark Rogers, Polly Thomas, Joe Staines, Richard Lim, Duncan Clark, Peter Buckley, Lucy Ratcliffe, Clifton Wilkinson, Alison Murchie, Matthew Teller, Andrew Dickson, Fran Sandham, Sally Schafer, Matthew Milton, Karoline Densley (UK); Andrew Rosenberg, Yuki Takagaki, Richard Koss, Hunter Slaton (US)
Design & Layout: Link Hall, Helen Prior, Julia Bovis, Katie Pringle, Rachel Holmes, Andy Turner, Dan May, Tanya Hall, John McKay, Sophie Hewat (UK); Madhulita Mohapatra,
Umesh Aggarwal, Sunil Sharma (India)
Cartography: Maxine Repath, Ed Wright, Katie Lloyd-Jones (UK); Manish Chandra, Rajesh Chhibber, Jai Prakesh Mishra (India)
Cover art direction: Louise Boulton
Picture research: Sharon Martins, Mark Thomas
Online: Kelly Martinez, Anja Mutic-Blessing, Jennifer Gold, Audra Epstein, Suzanne Welles, Cree Lawson (US); Manik Chauhan, Amarjyoti Dutta, Narender Kumar (India)
Finance: Gary Singh
Marketing & Publicity: Richard Trillo, Niki Smith, David Wearn, Chloë Roberts, Demelza Dallow, Claire Southern (UK); Geoff Colquitt, David Wechsler, Megan Kennedy (US)
Administration: Julie Sanderson
RG India: Punita Singh

Publishing Information

This 4th edition published November 2003 by
Rough Guides Ltd,
80 Strand, London WC2R 0RL.
345 Hudson St, 4th Floor,
New York, NY 10014, USA.
Distributed by the Penguin Group
Penguin Books Ltd,
80 Strand, London WC2R 0RL
Penguin Putnam, Inc.,
375 Hudson Street, NY 10014, USA
Penguin Books Australia Ltd,
487 Maroondah Highway, PO Box 257,
Ringwood, Victoria 3134, Australia
Penguin Books Canada Ltd,
10 Alcorn Avenue, Toronto, Ontario,
Canada M4V 1E4
Penguin Books (NZ) Ltd,
182–190 Wairau Road, Auckland 10,
New Zealand
Typeset in Bembo and Helvetica to an original design by Henry Iles.
Printed in Italy by LegoPrint S.p.A

632pp includes index
A catalogue record for this book is available from the British Library

ISBN 1-84353-095-3

The publishers and authors have done their best to ensure the accuracy and currency of all the information in **The Rough Guide to Vietnam** however, they can accept no responsibility for any loss, injury, or inconvenience sustained by any traveller as a result of information or advice contained in the guide.

1 3 5 7 9 8 6 4 2

Help us update

We've gone to a lot of effort to ensure that the 4th edition of **The Rough Guide to Vietnam** is accurate and up to date. However, things change – places get "discovered", opening hours are notoriously fickle, restaurants and rooms raise prices or lower standards. If you feel we've got it wrong or left something out, we'd like to know, and if you can remember the address, the price, the time, the phone number, so much the better.

We'll credit all contributions, and send a copy of the next edition (or any other Rough Guide if you prefer) for the best letters. Everyone who writes to us and isn't already a subscriber will receive a copy of our full-colour thrice-yearly newsletter. Please mark letters: **"Rough Guide Vietnam Update"** and send to: Rough Guides, 80 Strand, London WC2R 0RL, or Rough Guides, 4th Floor, 345 Hudson St, New York, NY 10014. Or send an email to **mail@roughguides.com**

Have your questions answered and tell others about your trip at
www.roughguides.atinfopop.com

SMALL PRINT

Acknowledgements

Thanks are due to Geoff Howard and, especially, Clifton Wilkinson for the editorial side of things; to Miles Irving, Ed Wright and Maxine Repath for the cartography; to Veneta Bullen for the picture research; to Louise Boulton for the cover; to Dan May for the typesetting; to Derek Wilde for the proof reading; and to Karoline Densley for the index.

Jan I'm indebted to the indefatigable Sammy Coomber and to Ron Emmons for all their hard work. Real troopers, both of them. A big thank you is also due to Brett Moore, Max & Hue, Thuc & Duong, Tim Doling, Digby, Dan & Markus (cheers, guys), Marie Ryan, Elliot, Natasha, Thuan Anh, Freddo, Mike Small, Mike Seiburg and Ms Do Nhu Quynh in Hanoi; Troels & Thao Knudsen and Jaime Cusco in Hoi An; Dieter Bischoff and Le Than Vu in Da Nang; Nguyen Hong Quan in Vinh; Mr & Mrs De, Xuan and Tuc in Ninh Binh; Jarrod Dellamarta (keep pedalling), Victor Borg, Doug Reese and Paul Harris; and, last but not least, heartfelt thanks to my very good friends Tuyet in Hué and Liem and Phuong in Hanoi for all their kindness over the years.

Mark Love and thanks, as ever, to my wife and family.

Ron First and foremost I'd like to thank Dang Duc Thuc in Hanoi and Le Van Sinh in HCMC, whose tireless efforts have contributed greatly to this edition.Others who opened new insights on the country or just pointed me in the right direction are as follows: in HCMC – Tony Nong, Luong Gia, Phuoc Long, Lawson Johnston and Tom McDonough; in My Tho – Nguyen Viet Tho; in Vinh Long – Tran Thi Yen Xuan; in Long Xuyen – Ngyuyen Thanh Cuong; in Ca Mau – Lam Thanh Sy; in Rach Gia – Ngo Van Trieu; in Phu Quoc – Huynh Van Anh; in Da Lat – Pham Thi My Linh; in Buon Ma Thuot – Dang Thi Hong, Le Van Duc and Keith Mundy; in Plei Ku – Siu Cham; in Kon Tum – Nguyen Do Huynh; in Vung Tao – Tran Van Dung; in Nha Trang – Nguyen Anh Thai; in Qui Nhon – Barbara Dawson; in Mong Cai – Hoang Ninh; in Son La – Tran Van Long; in Sa Pa – Ha Duc Thanh; and in Bac Ha – Dang Trung Hoang. Thank you all.

Readers' letters

Thanks to all the readers who have taken the time and trouble to write in with comments and suggestions. Listed below are those who were especially helpful: apologies for any errors, ommissions or misspellings.

Xavier Alcober, Amber, Andy Brouwer, Richard Brown, Carlos, Christine & Malcolm Clark, Mark Colegrave, Ursula Cook, Oliver Craig, Ruth Crampton, Mark Danter, Dave, Des, Don Ecclestone, Mike Ellis, Ed Elsey, David Fay, Lisa Ferguson, Jonathan Fine, Scotty Flower, Gabriel, Brian Goldstein, Gerd Heineke, Tanya Hines, Claire Hoffman, John, Paul John, Kaisa, Kim, Jelle Kobessen, Martin, Judy McInerney, Michael, Sebastian Millies, Miranda, Angela & Keith Morris, Steve Moulding, Leo Muraro, Thomas N., Henning Petersen, Hans Petro, Laura Porter, Elaine Proudley, Edward T Rebholz Jr, Richard, Elizabeth Rowin, RTJ, Sonia, Rick Schumacher, Tara Shioya, Simon, David Taillandier & Tran Dieu Loc, David Tran, XQ, Matthias Zehner.

Photo Credits

Cover credits

Main front, Vung Tau
Small front top picture Vietnamese flag, J. Marshall
Small front lower picture Incense sticks, J. Marshall
Back top picture, J. Marshall
Back lower picture Cham tower, J. Marshall

Introduction

Incense © Ron Emmons
Cyclists, Hanoi © T. Bognar/TRIP
Sa Pa © J. Sweeney/TRIP
Fisherman, China Beach © Steve Raymer/CORBIS
Workers in rice paddy © P. Syder/TRIP
Hoi An © Simon Cooper/Impact
Drying rice, Bat Temple, Soc Trang © Steve Raymer/CORBIS
Water puppet show, Ho Chi Minh City © Wolfgang Kaehler/CORBIS
Mao women, Muong So © G. Stokoe/TRIP
Pho, Cholon Market © Tim Hall/AXIOM
Fishing junks, Ha Long Bay © © Catherine Karnow/CORBIS
Woman © Ron Emmons

Things not to miss

Binh Tay Market, Cholon © T. Lester/TRIP
Traditional musicians, Tay Ninh Temple © J. Sweeney/TRIP
Northern highlands © R. Squires/TRIP
Silks © Ron Emmons
Nha Trang © J. Sweeney/TRIP
Mekong Delta © K. Mclaren/TRIP
Sacred Eye, Cai Dai church © Ron Emmons
Dak Lake © Ron Emmons
Rice fields, Son La province © G. Stokoe/TRIP
Honour guard, Khai Dinh Mausoleum © G. Stokoe/TRIP
Snake wine © Charles Coates/IMPACT
Hon Chong peninsula © Ron Emmons
Cyclo, Hue © T. O'Brien/TRIP
Hue railway station, © Mark Henley/IMPACT
Street café in Cholon © Owen Franken/CORBIS

Phu Quoc © Ron Emmons
Rug shop, Hanoi © T. Bognar/TRIP
Hmong women © G. Stokoe/TRIP
Cu Chi tunnels © Ron Emmons
Canoes on Whale Beach Island © Ron Emmons
Bao Loc Falls © T. Bognar/TRIP
Cham Temples, My Son © Doug McKinlay/AXIOM
Ha Long Bay © Mark Crator/IMPACT
Hanoi Opera House © Brent Madison
Bia hoi © Brent Madison
Water puppets © Dallas and John Heaton/CORBIS
Coffee © Macduff Everton/CORBIS
Tortoise Pagoda, Hanoi © T. Bognar/TRIP
Japanese covered bridge, Hoi An © T. Bognar/TRIP
Rong © Ron Emmons
Ha Gang Province © Ron Emmons
Tet, Ho Chi Minh City © Chris Lisle/CORBIS

Black and whites

Hanoi cityscape © Ron Emmons (p.74)
Notre Dame Cathedral, Ho Chi Minh © A. Tovy/TRIP (p.118)
Floating market on the Mekong Delta © T. Bognar/TRIP (p.134)
Boys playing on a boat © A. Tovy/TRIP (p.153)
Dambri Falls © Ron Emmons (p.192)
Sculpture © Ron Emmons (p.217)
Surf at Nha Trang © Axiom/Jim Holmes (p.228)
Cham tower © Ron Emmons (p.254)
My Son Cham © T. Bognar/TRIP (p.270)
Praying, Vietnam © Nigel Amies /IMPACT PHOTOS (p.312)
Religious festival procession © Jim Holmes/AXIOM (p.356)
Magazine stand © Ron Emmons (p.388)
Paddy field © Ron Emmons (p.414)
Ha Long Bay © Rick Squires/TRIP (p.427)
Stilt bamboo house, Kho Mu © G. Stokoe/TRIP (p.440)
Man in doorway © Ron Emmons (p.454)

TRAVEL • MUSIC • REFERENCE • PHRASEBOOKS

Key   🌐 map   🖹 phrasebook   ⊙ cd

Rough Guides publishes new books every month

Rough Guides music & reference

check www.roughguides.com for the latest news

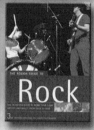

Notes

Adopt-A-Minefield raises awareness and funds to clear landmines and help the survivors of mine explosions. We work through the United Nations to support projects that save lives in nine countries. One of these is Vietnam. Vietnam has one of the most serious landmine problems in the world - the legacy of the Vietnam War.

www.landmines.org.uk

"Every 27 minutes, somewhere in the world, a landmine claims another victim. The need for a continued, concerted drive to rid the world of landmines is as great now as it ever was."
Heather Mills McCartney and Paul McCartney, Patrons of Adopt-A-Minefield.

Landmines don't recognise ceasefires and peace treaties. They don't distinguish between a soldier and a child. Millions of these weapons remain in the ground in more than 90 countries. They kill and maim innocent people long after wars have ended.

Mine clearance and survivor support save lives. They are also crucial to sustainable development.

The presence of mines affects human rights, disarmament, reconstruction and political reconciliation. They stop refugees from returning home. Landmine survivors endure a lifetime of physical and psychological hardship.

The Adopt-A-Minefield guide to staying safe...

Adopt-A-Minefield funds mine clearance and survivor projects in Vietnam. Our partners on the ground are Mines Advisory Group, Clear Path International, and Vietnam Veterans Memorial Fund. 100% of donations received by us are sent to our partners.

There is a landmine and unexploded ordnance problem across Vietnam. The most dangerous areas are to be found in the middle of the country on both sides of the old Demilitarised Zone (DMZ), and around the Ho Chi Minh Trail.

WHEREVER YOU ARE TRAVELLING:

Stick to well trodden paths and roads and pay attention to signs.

Listen to local people. If you are uncertain - ask a local person whether a route is safe.

Look out for areas which have seen military activity. Indicators include: abandoned military and civilian vehicles; animal skeletons; craters; old barbed wire and fencing.

Many minefields are not marked with the familiar skull and cross bone signs. Look out for signs made by local people. These may include: deliberately piled stones; crossed stakes in the ground; gashes or paint on trees; other unusual features.

IF YOU FIND YOURSELF IN AN AREA YOU THINK MAY BE DANGEROUS:

Stay still. Try and attract attention from where you are.
If you expect to be travelling in dangerous places, carry a flare.

Together we can stop landmines from blowing holes in people's lives.

For information on landmines and ethical tourism visit
www.landmines.org.uk/254
To help solve the landmine crisis visit www.landmines.org.uk

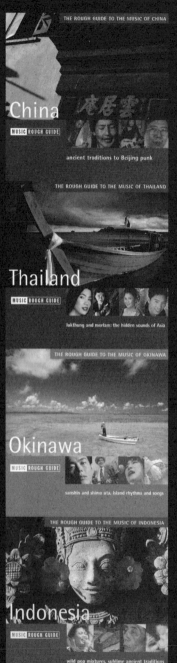

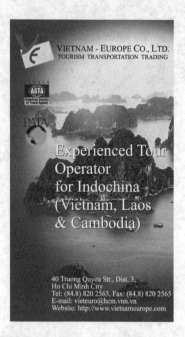

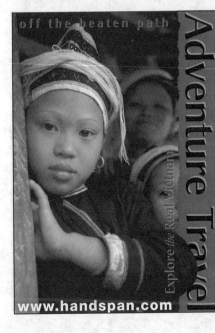

ANN TOURS

www.anntours.com   Info@anntours.com

COME WITH US
AND DISCOVER VIETNAM

SERVICES

PACKAGE TOURS THROUGHOUT VIETNAM, LAOS, AND CAMBODIA GROUP &
PRIVATE TOURS, SPECIAL HOTEL DISCOUNTS, AIR TICKETS, CAR RENTALS,
GUIDES AND VISA PROCESSING, LEISURE AND CORPORATE TRAVEL.

HEAD OFFICE
58 TON THAT TUNG, BEN THANH, DISTRICT 1,
HO CHI MINH CITY, VIETNAM
TEL: 84-8-833-4356 / 2564 **FAX:** 84-8-832-3866
HANOI OFFICE
18 DUONG THANH ST., HOAN KIEM DISTRICT, HANOI, VIETNAM
TEL: 84-4-923-1366 **FAX:** 84-8-835-9458

ANN'S TOURIST & TRADING CO., LTD. (ANN TOURS)